International Law and the Global South

Perspectives from the Rest of the World

This book series aims to promote a complex vision of contemporary legal developments from the perspective of emerging or developing countries and/or authors integrating these elements into their approach. While focusing on today's law and international economic law in particular, it brings together contributions from, or influenced by, other social sciences disciplines. Written in both technical and non-technical language and addressing topics of contemporary importance to a general audience, the series will be of interest to legal researchers as well as non-lawyers. In referring to the "rest of the world", the book series puts forward new and alternative visions of today's law not only from emerging and developing countries, but also from authors who deliberately integrate this perspective into their thinking. The series approach is not only comparative, post-colonial or critical, but also truly universal in the sense that it places a plurality of well-informed visions at its center.

The Series

- Provides a truly global coverage of the world in reflecting cutting-edge developments and thinking in law and international law
- Focuses on the transformations of international and comparative law with an emphasis on international economic law (investment, trade and development)
- Welcomes contributions on comparative and/or domestic legal evolutions

More information about this series at https://link.springer.com/bookseries/13447

Julien Chaisse · Jędrzej Górski · Dini Sejko
Editors

Regulation of State-Controlled Enterprises

An Interdisciplinary and Comparative Examination

Springer

Editors
Julien Chaisse
School of Law
City University of Hong Kong
Kowloon, Hong Kong, China

Jędrzej Górski
Department of Asian and International Studies
City University of Hong Kong
Kowloon, Hong Kong, China

Dini Sejko
Faculty of Law
Chinese University of Hong Kong
Shatin, NT, Hong Kong SAR, China

ISSN 2510-1420 ISSN 2510-1439 (electronic)
International Law and the Global South
ISBN 978-981-19-1367-9 ISBN 978-981-19-1368-6 (eBook)
https://doi.org/10.1007/978-981-19-1368-6

This Springer imprint is published by the registered company Springer Nature Singapore Pte Ltd.
The registered company address is: 152 Beach Road, #21-01/04 Gateway East, Singapore 189721, Singapore

The original version of the book was revised: The missed out corrections has been updated for the chapters 3, 12, 17 and 20. The correction to the book is available at https://doi.org/10.1007/978-981-19-1368-6_31

Acknowledgements

This thirty-chapter book, exploring issues in law, economics and politics of the return to state capitalism and the growing presence of state-controlled enterprises (SCE) in the global economy, comprises the introduction and twenty-two original chapters. The seeds for this book were planted over three years ago in summer 2018 when we offered to work on an edited-journal-issue project tentatively titled '*The Changing Paradigm of State-controlled Entities Regulation: Laws, Contracts and Disputes*' to the Transnational Dispute Management journal (TDM) published by Maris B.V.[1] The call for papers was released in August 2018, and the TDM issue was published in October 2020 as the sixth issue of 2021 [(2020) 17(6) TDM]. We had invited Christophe Bondy, Helena Chen and Romesh Weeramantry to the editorial board of that TDM special issue. We are very grateful to the co-editors for their cooperation, efficient review of several articles and invaluable comments made during that process. We also thank TDM editor-in-chief Mark Kantor for accepting our initial proposal.

While working on the journal project, we also invited a substantial number of original papers, not only in the field of law but also economics, politics and international relations, to add to the selection of legal TDM articles and combine such multi-disciplinary perspectives in this book. We are very grateful to Maris B.V. for agreeing to the use of that TDM special issue's content, Maris' editorial team for

[1] TDM articles republished in this book or chapters of this book significantly drawing upon TDM articles include Chap. 3 by Górski, Chap. 5 by Sabatino, Chap. 6 by Chan, Chap. 7 by Slawotzky, Chap. 13 by Sabatino, Chap. 19 by Garzón, Chap. 22 by Svoboda, Chap. 27 by Yin and Zhang, and Chap. 29 by Li.

coordinating their efforts with the contributors and with the acquisition editors at Springer Nature, and Leïla Choukroune, the editor of Springer's *International Law and the Global South* series, for invaluable comments on this book's composition and help on reaching an agreement between Maris B.V. and Springer Nature.

Hong Kong
August 2021

Julien Chaisse
Jędrzej Górski
Dini Sejko

Contents

Editors and Contributors

About the Editors

Julien Chaisse Ph.D. (2007), is Professor of Law at City University of Hong Kong (CityU HK) and Advisory Board Member, Asian Academy of International Law (AAIL). His publications include *China's International Investment Strategy* (2019), *The Regulation of Global Water Services* (2017) and *International Economic Law and Governance* (2016); and Springer published volumes—*Paradigm Shift in International Economic Law Rule-Making*, and *Asia's Changing International Investment Regime* (both co-edited and published in 2017)'. Professor Chaisse is also a co-editor in chief of a Springer Living Reference—*Handbook of International Investment Law and Policy.*

Jędrzej Górski Ph.D. (2016) is a research fellow at the City University of Hong Kong. Formerly research associate at UCL Australia (2017), Endeavour Research Fellow at MLS (2014) and associate at CMS (2010-2012). His publications include *The Belt and Road Initiative, Law, Economics, and Politics* (Nijhoff 2018, eds with J. Chaisse), *The Law and Policy of New Eurasian Regionalization: Economic Integration, Trade, and Investment in the Post-Soviet and Greater Eurasian Space* (Nijhoff 2021, eds with A. Aseeva) and *Palgrave Handbook of Social License to Operate and Energy Transitions* (2023, eds with G. Wood and G. Mete).

Dini Sejko Ph.D. (2019) is a research associate at the Centre for Comparative and Transnational Law at the Chinese University of Hong Kong, Faculty of Law, a research affiliate at The Fletcher Network for Sovereign Wealth and Global Capital, Tufts University, and a mediator (MCIArb). Dr Sejko's research focuses on international economic law and the governance of state-owned enterprises and sovereign wealth funds (SWFs). For his research on the impact of UN sanctions on the governance of the Libyan SWF, Dr Sejko received the Society of International Economic Law PEPA Best Paper Award 2018. He is the author of several articles, book chapters, and a series of policy reports on the “Belt and Road in Southeast Asia” (IEMS-UOB 2020).

List of Contributors

Andrés Eduardo Alvarado Garzón Saarland University, Saarbrücken, Germany

Larry Catá Backer Pennsylvania State University, State College, USA

Julien Chaisse City University of Hong Kong (CityU HK), Kowloon Tong, Hong Kong

Kai-chieh Chan International University of Rabat, Rabat, Morocco

Usman W. Chohan Director, Economic Affairs & National Development, Centre for Aerospace and Security Studies (CASS), Islamabad, Pakistan

Peter Enderwick Department of International Business, Strategy and Entrepreneurship, Auckland University of Technology, Auckland, New Zealand

Vasilii Erokhin School of Economics and Management, Harbin Engineering University, Harbin, China

Jorge Arturo González Utrecht University, Utrecht, Netherlands

Matthew Gouett International Institute for Sustainable Development (IISD), Winnipeg, Canada

Jędrzej Górski Department of Asian and International Studies (AIS), City University of Hong Kong, Kowloon, Hong Kong, China

Geoffrey Hale Political Science at the University of Lethbridge, Lethbridge, AB, Canada

Viet Hoang Ho Chi Minh City University of Law, Thành phố Hồ Chí Minh, Vietnam

Shixue Hu Faculty of Law, The Chinese University of Hong Kong, Sha Tin, NT, Hong Kong SAR

Ji Ma Research Associate, The University of Oxford “China, Law and Development” Project, Shenzhen, China

Thomas Papadopoulos Department of Law, University of Cyprus, Nicosia, Cyprus

Gianmatteo Sabatino Zhongnan University of Economics and Law, Wuhan, China

Flora Sapio University of Naples “L’Orientale”, Naples, Italy

Patrick J. Schena Tufts University, Medford, USA

Gianni Lo Schiavo European Central Bank, Frankfurt, Germany

Dini Sejko Faculty of Law, Chinese University of Hong Kong, Shatin, Hong Kong SAR

Dingsha Shi Research Center of General Administration of Customs of China, Beijing, China

Joel Slawotsky IDC Law and Business Schools, Reichman University, Herzliya, Israel

Alessandro Spano Faculty of Laws, University College London (UCL), London, England

Gao Tianming School of Economics and Management, Harbin Engineering University, Harbin, China

Xinquan Tu China Institute for WTO Studies, University of International Business and Economics, Beijing, China

Yingying Wu China University of Political Science and Law, Beijing, China

Wei Yin School of International Law, Southwest University of Political Science and Law and Research Fellow, China-ASEAN Legal Research Centre, Chongqing, China

Anran Zhang Erasmus School of Law, Erasmus University Rotterdam, Rotterdam, Netherlands

Chunlin Zhang World Bank, Washington D.C., USA

Abbreviations

ADB	Asian Development Bank
AfCFTA	African Continental Free Trade Area
AfDB	African Development Bank
AI	Artificial intelligence
AIIB	Asian Infrastructure Investment Bank
AML	Anti-Monopoly Law
AoA	Articles of Association
AREFA	Act on Acquiring Real Easter by Foreigners of 1920 (Poland)
ASEAN	Association of Southeast Asian Nations
AWG	Foreign Trade and Payments Act (Germany)
AWV	Foreign Trade and Payments Ordinance (Germany)
BIT	Bilateral investment treaty
BLT	Build–lease–transfer
BOO	Build–own–operate
BOOT	Build–own–operate–transfer
BOT	Build–operate–transfer
BRI	Belt and Road Initiative
CAAC	General Administration of Civil Aviation (China)
CAITEC	Chinese Academy of International Trade and Economic Cooperation
CCCC	China Construction Communications Co.
CCIA	COMESA Common Investment Area
CCP	China Communist Party
CEE	Central and Eastern Europe
CFIUS	Committee on Foreign Investment in the United States
CFLP	China Federation of Logistics and Purchasing
CIA	Critical Infrastructure Act of 2010 (Poland)
CIC	China Investment Corporation
CIT	Corporate Income Tax
CJEU	Court of Justice of the EU
CNCP	China National Petroleum Corporation
CNMC	Chinese National Minerals Corporation

COMESA	Common Market for Eastern and Southern Africa
CPC	Central Product Classification
CPTPP	Comprehensive and Progressive Agreement for Trans-Pacific Partnership
CRBC	China Road and Bridge Corporation
CSR	Corporate social responsibility
CTBA	China Tendering and Bidding Association
DBFO	Design–build–finance–operate
DBOT	Design–build–operate–transfer
DCMF	Design–construct–manage–finance
DFIs	Development finance institutions
DPS	Dividends per share
EAEU	Eurasian Economic Union
EBRD	European Bank for Reconstruction and Development
ECOWAS	Economic Community of West African States
EEA	European Economic Area
EIB	European Investment Bank
EPS	Earnings per share
ETF	Exchange-Traded Funds
EU	European Union
EUA	European Units of Account
FDI	Foreign direct investment
FFRDC	Federally funded research and development centre
FIEs	Foreign-invested enterprises
FIRRMA	Foreign Investment Risk Review Modernization Act of 2018 (USA)
FOCAC	Forum for China-African Cooperation
FSB	Financial Stability Board
FTZs	Free trade zones
GATS	General Agreement on Trade in Services
GCC	Gulf Cooperation Council
GFC	Global Financial Crisis
GPA	Government Procurement Agreement
GPL	Government Procurement Law (China)
GSA	Golden Share Act of 2005 (Poland)
IADB	Inter-American Development Bank
ICA	Investment Canada ACT
ICSID	International Centre for Investment Dispute Settlement
IFC	International Finance Corporation
IFIs	International financial institutions
IFSWF	International Forum for Sovereign Wealth Funds
IIA	International investment agreement
IMF	International Monetary Fund
IPAs	Investment promotion agencies
ISDS	Investor-state dispute settlement
ISM	Investment Screening Mechanism

JVs	Joint venture(s)
LNG	Liquefied natural gas
M&A	Merger(s) and acquisition(s)
MAOIE	Measures for the Administration of Overseas Investment of Enterprises (China)
MDA	Macdonald Dettwiler Associates
MDB	Multilateral development bank
MFN	Most-favoured-nation clause
MIGA	Multilateral Investment Guarantee Agency
MNCs	Multinational Corporations
MOFCOM	Ministry of Commerce of China
MOFTEC	Ministry of Foreign Trade and Economic Cooperation (China)
MOHURD	Ministry of Housing and Urban-Rural Development (China)
MWR	Ministry of Water Resources
NASA	National Aeronautics and Space Administration
NDRC	National Development and Reform Commission
NHS	National Health Service
NIGP	National Institute of Governmental Purchasing
OECD	Organisation for Economic Co-operation and Development
OEEC	Organisation for European Economic Co-operation
P3	Public–private partnership
PIT	Personal Income Tax
POE	Privately owned enterprises
PPP	Public–private partnership
PSA	Production sharing agreement
PSD2	Payment services Directive (EU) 2015/2366
PVT	Public value theory
R&D	Research and development
ROE	Return on equity
ROFIEG	Expert Group on Regulatory Obstacles to Financial Innovation
ROI	Return on investment
RTA	Regional trade agreement
SADC	Southern African Development Community
SAFE	State Administration of Foreign Exchange (China)
SASAC	State-owned Assets Supervision and Administration Commission
SCA	Strong customer authentication
SCE	State-controlled enterprises; state-controlled entities
SDG	Sustainable Development Goals
SEZs	Special Economic Zones
SINOPEC	China Petroleum and Chemical Corporation
SMEs	Small and medium enterprises
SODIGA	Spanish regional development agency
SOEMNE	State-owned multinational enterprise
SOEs	State-owned enterprises
SPV	Special purpose vehicle

SRPBs	Sales revenue of principal businesses
SWF	Sovereign Wealth Funds
SWFI	Sovereign Wealth Fund Institute
TFEU	Treaty of the Functioning of the European Union
TL	Tendering Law (China)
TPA	Trade Promotion Authority
TRIMS	Agreement on Trade-Related Investment Measures
TTIP	Transatlantic Trade and Investment Partnership
UNCITRAL	United Nations Commission on International Trade Law
UNCLOS	United Nations Convention on the Law of the Sea
USMCA	United States–Mexico–Canada Agreement
VCLT	Vienna Convention on the Law of Treaties
WTO	World Trade Organization

List of Figures

The Expansion of China's State-Owned Enterprise Sector Since the Global Financial Crisis: What Insights Do Official Statistics Afford?

How to Handle State-Owned Enterprises in EU-China Investment Talks

State-Owned and Influenced Enterprises and the Evolution of Canada's Foreign Direct Investment Regime

List of Tables

The Expansion of China's State-Owned Enterprise Sector Since the Global Financial Crisis: What Insights Do Official Statistics Afford?

Sovereign Wealth Funds and Public Value Theory

Investment Screening Mechanism (ISM) in Central and Eastern Europe (CEE): Case Study of Poland

Political Support, Competitive Advantage, and the Regulation of State-Owned Enterprises (SOEs)

Vietnam's Reform of State-Owned Entities: Domestic and External Drivers

How to Handle State-Owned Enterprises in EU-China Investment Talks

Confronting the Challenges of State Capitalism: Trends, Rules, and Debates

Julien Chaisse, Jędrzej Górski, and Dini Sejko

1 From Neoliberalism to State Capitalism

The worldwide emancipation of private enterprise from state actors has significantly lost the momentum to revive governmental economic activity controls over the last decade or two. The global drivers for the detachment of private capital from national allegiances have been significantly exhausted. In the past, the end of ideological struggle between two competing economic blocks previously divided by the iron curtain had gone in tandem with the outcomes of the General Agreement on Tariffs and Trade's (GATT) Uruguay Round. The *realpolitik* of the unipolar moment with globalisation processes enhancing the United States' (US) combined with the establishment of the World Trade Organisation (WTO) fuelled liberation of strategic flows goods, services, and investment over expanding geographical area devoid of prohibitive barriers to multi-jurisdiction economic enterprises. The boundaries between domestic and foreign capital had been blurred quickly. With that came massive privatisation programmes all across the former Eastern block and the institution of state-owned enterprises (SOEs), or otherwise state-controlled enterprises (SCEs) was in decline. Centrally planned or heavily statists economic systems throughout the post-Soviet and non-aligned worlds collapsed one after another, like the house of cards remaining non-capitalist in name only.[1]

[1] Ian Bremmer, 'State Capitalism Comes of Age - The End of the Free Market' (2009) 88 Foreign Aff 40, 41.

J. Chaisse (✉)
City University of Hong Kong (CityU HK), Kowloon Tong, Hong Kong
e-mail: julien.chaisse@cityu.edu.hk

J. Górski
The Department of Asian and International Studies (AIS) CityU HK, Kowloon Tong, Hong Kong

D. Sejko
Faculty of Law, Chinese University of Hong Kong (CUHK), Shatin (NT), Hong Kong

J. Chaisse et al. (eds.), *Regulation of State-Controlled Enterprises*, International Law and the Global South, https://doi.org/10.1007/978-981-19-1368-6_1

The liberalisation of trade and investment might have been nonlinear in that significant hidden non-tariff barriers to trade might have persisted all across Asia, including South Korea and Japan, while North America and Europe (so-called collective West) opened their markets genuinely. Foreign investors' exclusive ownership of local establishment might have been restricted significantly in most significant emerging markets like the People's Republic of China's (PRC), India, Vietnam, or Indonesia. The resentment against foreign capital across the post-colonial societies might have also persisted. However, the trend towards complete privatisation and limiting governments' functions in cross-border economic activity seemed unstoppable. Top-down, cross-border economic activity had been taken over by multinational companies (MNC) capable of circumventing and navigating local obstacles mentioned above, overpowering governments of emerging economies if need be. Bottom-up, the success of domestic grassroots small and medium enterprises (SMEs) sprouting in newly freed economies had incentivised its replication elsewhere and the marketisation of large inefficient SOEs and sectors previously subjected to comprehensive government control. The remnants of centrally directed SOEs previously enjoying monopolies and lacking the price-discovery mechanisms shifted towards state-capitalism[2] paradigm combining governmental influence over the enterprise with market forces shaping SOE's behaviours. Strategic companies in sectors like energy, mining utilities, health care, airlines, etc., had been partially privatised worldwide, mainly via public offerings to small and/or passive investors, still allowing government control despite state treasuries' share in such companies' equity falling below fifty per cent. However, the end of privatisation processes had been nowhere in sight. Ergo, state capitalism could seem vestigial and transitional.

In the present, the tide has turned considerably as, to quote Chaisse, 'the role of the state has arguably grown in importance in the sphere of national and transnational business activities'.[3] Many point to the global financial crisis of 2007–2008 (GFC) at the tipping point of *laissez-fairism* and the rebirth of interventionism in the West. Nevertheless, Bremmer observed interestingly in 2009 that the predominantly Western interventionists' reaction to the GFC constituted merely the *fourth wave* of state-capitalism novel. Its participating governments included not only the governments of the merging markets but also the Western ones.[4] Three preceding waves originated in the emerging markets and did not spill over to the West. On Bremmer's timeline, first was the Organisation of the Petroleum Exporting Countries (OPEC) creation. A concerted effort by mostly Gulf-based oil SCE allowed them to improve their margins in the global market and eventually overshadow their Western counterparts, ending a post-colonial exchange of undervalued commodities

[2] "The term 'state capitalism' means an economic system in which the state controls a substantial part of, or even all of capital, industry, and business". *See* See Julien Chaisse, 'Untangling the Triangle: Issues for State-controlled Entities in Trade, Investment, and Competition Law' in Julien Chaisse and Tsai-yu Lin (eds), *International Economic Law and Governance: Essays in Honour of Mitsuo Matsushita* (OUP 2016) 233, 238.

[3] *See* generally, Chaisse (n 2).

[4] Bremmer (n 1) 49.

in return for overvalued Western-manufactured merchandise[5] (from a perspective of oil-exporting economies and their consumers). Second, came the brisk industrialisation and growth in the club combing post-communists and previously heavily statist economies since the 1990s, among which Bremmer counter in Brazil, China, India, Mexico, Russia, and Turkey.[6] Finally, in Bremmer's view, the third wave of state capitalism came about upon sovereign wealth funds (SWF) leap to prominence since the mid-2010s.[7] Ergo, enterprises with close ties to their government gradually gained equal footing with their Western countries counterparts, first in oil production, and by extension, other commodities extraction, second in manufacturing, and third in cross-border financial flows and investment.

The *second wave* went initially unnoticed because of the Western delusion about the vestigial and transitional nature of state participation in emerging economies mentioned above. However, it was most conducive to the present prominence of state-capitalism models. It laid the foundations for bridging the technological gap between the emerging and most developed economies thanks to growing industrial bases generating homemade innovation. In contrast, the first oil-related wave had merely allowed high living standards thanks to imports in return for natural resources, whereas the third SWF-related wave has been merely a function of financial surpluses generated in the first and the second wave. In retrospect, the partial liberalisation and privatisation of markets proved to be a goal in itself rather than a means of embracing liberal Western separation of state and enterprise fully. Initially, to quote Bremmer, '[r]ich-world governments once took little notice of them, since these countries had little or no influence in international markets'.[8] Now, though, to quote Bower, Leonard and Paine, 'in the 21st century, some developing nations are giants, [and, t] o the extent that Russia, China, and India play by their own rules, they have the potential to disrupt market capitalism[9] as it is practised in the developed world'.[10] Ergo, the current prominence of statist attitudes is a product of anti-liberal views on private enterprises hold is some portion of the world economy multiplied by the economic success of economies whose decision-makers hold on to such anti-liberal views.[11]

---

[5] ibid 46.

[6] ibid.

[7] ibid 48–49.

[8] Bremmer (n 1) 48.

[9] One might disagree with the use of term 'market capitalism' in this context because 'state capitalism' of also mostly based price-discovery and other market mechanism.

[10] Joseph L Bower, Herman B Leonard and Lynn S Paine, 'Global Capitalism at Risk. What are You Doing about It?' (2011) 89(9) Harv Bus Rev 104.

[11] Such a bold observation follows from above cited pieces by Bremmer and Bower, in which (1) Bower noticed that 'For centuries, developing nations have adopted variations of mercantilist policies to accelerate economic growth'. [Bower, Leonard and Paine (n 10)] meaning the size and economic success matters for the survival of market capitalism].

Table 1 Classification of state-owned enterprises (SCEs)

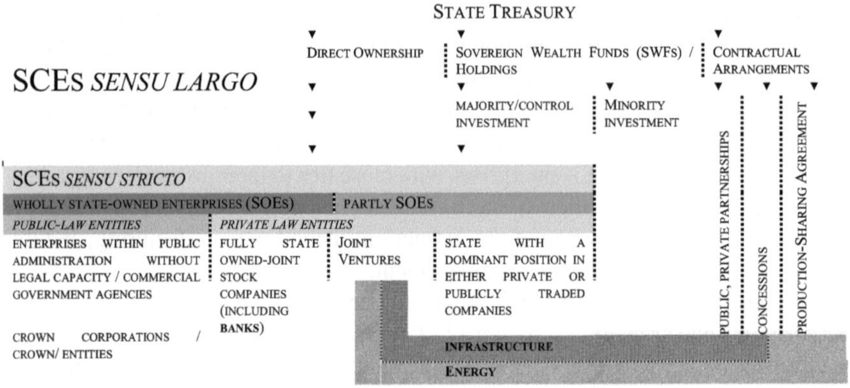

See Jędrzej Górski, 'Global Liberalisation of Public-Private Partnerships (PPPs) as Form of State-Controlled Enterprises (SCEs)' (online 22 June 2020) Transnational Dispute Management 1–73, Table 1 in Sect. 22.

2 Landscape of the State-Controlled Entities

The state-capitalism paradigm materialises through state-controlled enterprises (SCEs), which include a broad panoply of entities that have various structures with different degrees of control by governments at the central or sub-central level (Table 1).[12] The most obvious incarnation of SCEs is state-owned enterprises (SOEs). Decision-makers within governments like high-profile politicians and top civil servants can foremost exercise control over enterprises through treasuries' formalised ownership, allowing people in political or administrative power to exercise voting rights and appoint the directors plus executives. For the most part, SOEs are ordinary private-law companies wholly or partly owned by state treasuries, local governments or other state agencies.

However, SOEs can also be structured as entities without separate legal capacity, such as units of public administration carrying out economic activities. Moreover, they can be structured as legal entities of public law such as or 'crown corporations' in Anglo-Saxon jurisdictions or 'state unitary enterprises' (государственные унитарные предприятия), in the post-Soviet space and former satellite countries.[13] Finally, functional SWFs usually characterised by diversified portfolios of passive

[12] This classification of SCE draws upon the editorial of the special issues of Transnational Dispute Management (TDM) deveted to which SCE, from which this book project originates. *See* Jędrzej Górski, 'The Changing Paradigm of State-controlled Entities Regulation: Laws, Contracts and Disputes: Introduction' (2020) 17(6) 1–10.

[13] Interestingly, 'государственные унитарные предприятия' in Russian-speaking post-Soviet countries or 'przedsiębiorstwa państowe' in Poland being by far the largest former satellite country had a separate legal capacity but did not own their assets which all belonged to the treasuries because under the principle of uniform state ownership being one of the cornerstones of socialist property law.

investments in non-majority equity holdings can also be structured under tailor-made public-law legislation or private laws vehicles such as investment funds or holding companies.

However, the notion of control is much broader than ownership and can be detached from it, which is why we distinguish SCE as a broader category and SOEs as a narrower. Legally well-defined non-equity-based control mechanisms are prominent in *strategic industries*, such as utilities, infrastructure, and natural resources. In the case of long-established flagship enterprises, varying special-voting-rights, golden shares, government-appointed representatives on companies' boards, government-approved companies' liaison officers, or similar instruments can be placed anywhere on the spectrum ranging from preferred stocks structured within the framework of purely private company-law to purely public-law administrative powers to interfere with enterprises' affairs regardless of equity levels held by treasuries. Likewise, in the case of investments in new ventures, public-private partnerships (PPPs) in the field of infrastructure and joint-operating-agreements/production sharing agreements (JOAs/PSAs) in the extractive industries can be structured as purely contractual relations between wholly privately owned enterprises with governments without having to establish joint ventures (JVs) with treasuries' equity participation.

We might also look at informal or semi-formal linkages between governments and seemingly independent private enterprises in a more grey control zone. The reliance on highly discretionary government licencing in heavily regulated industries such as telecommunications, media, or transportation on top of already mentioned energy, infrastructure, and natural resources perforce necessitates some degree of politicians' and civil servants' favour. The same could for long be sensed about highly discretionary merger-control procedures in which, in high-profile cases, the market analysis could not be detached from implied geopolitical considerations, at least in public perception. That is before the gradual worldwide ascendancy of investment screening mechanisms (ISMs) since the late 2000s, allowing governmental interference with private transactions and cross-border capital flaws based on even more discretionary or expressly geopolitical considerations embodied in state and public security notions and interest.

Next comes heavy reliance on government financing in the forms of grants, soft loans, export guarantees, commercial loans extended by commercial state-own banks, or venture capital flowing from SWFs whereby government has the upper hand in relations with their borrowers.[14] Finally, some dysfunctional kleptocratic political systems might necessitate informal ties and patronage between government officials and private entrepreneurs to run any large-scale economic activity.[15]

The SCE's landscape overview would not be complete without an insight into government control over partially SOEs and how various ownership distributions might affect it. We could discern two significantly different model situations in this regard. The first model situation covers newly established partially SOEs with

[14] Chaisse, (n 2) 237.

[15] Bremmer, (n 1) 44–45.

Table 2 Minority shareholders in SCEs (Scenario 1)

		PPP				
Government (Host State) ►	Government al/ public/region al municipal agency ►	▲ Public partner	▲ Private Partner	◄ SCE (controlled by a foreign state)	◄ Foreign government **OR** ◄Foreign SWF **AND** ◄ Other private stakeholders	◄ Foreign government

See Jędrzej Górski, 'Global Liberalisation of Public-Private Partnerships (PPPs) as Form of State Controlled Enterprises (SCEs)' (online 22 June 2020) Transnational Dispute Management 1–73, Table 2 in Sect. 22

usually well-defined power-sharing arrangements. These include JVs between private investors and the state treasuries, typically indirectly via state-owned holding/parent companies or SWFs, and PPPs/JOAs/PSAs being a kind of JVs between private partners and government agencies directly. A minimal number of partners (a government plus one or a few private enterprises), the absence of minor diluted shareholders, and contractual shareholders' agreements effective *inter partes* supplementing provisions of company law and JVs' articles of association (AoA) promise precise allocation or right and responsibilities among the partners. The same applies to purely contractual PPPs/JOAs/PSAs. Although one could find it challenging to determine which partner has a dominant position in the sense of company law in such entities, precise public-law semi-administrative contracts and conditions of concessions are likely to warrant the same level of certainty concerning power-sharing as in the case PPPs/JOAs/PSAs established as companies with treasuries' equity participation (*see* Table 2).

The second scenario covers the long-established national champions, which used to be wholly SOEs, but they were partially privatised (see Table 3). Under this scenario, ownership of privatised SOEs is split into state treasuries with the most significant portion of equity on the one hand and an unlimited number of minor investors in the stock markets on the other hand.[16] The latter include various minor individual investors, or SOEs employees allocated minor share packages for free irrelevant for the decisions made at shareholders' annual general meetings (AGMs) or passive institutional investors like pensions funds that will not exercise their voting right. Therefore, the apparent rationale behind the privatisation via public offerings instead of selling stakes to one or a few strategic investors is to maintain effective governmental control over partially SOEs even with state-owned equity falling below fifty per cent significantly. However, such control strategies are neither perpetual nor immune to aggressive takeover or unexpected fluctuations in the stock markets.

As we can see in both Tables 2 and 3, the analysis of governmental control over SOEs and power-sharing with private investors gets more complicated when 'private' investors are essentially foreign SCEs, whether partially or wholly SOEs or otherwise

[16] Notably, as shown in Table 3, such a long-established formerly wholly SOE and presently partly SOE can also itself be a private partner in PPPs/JOAs/PSAs, in which case private minority investors in such an enterprise might have indirect stake in PPSs with minimal or no control over such public-private JVs' their operations.

Table 3 Minority shareholders in SCEs (Scenario 2)

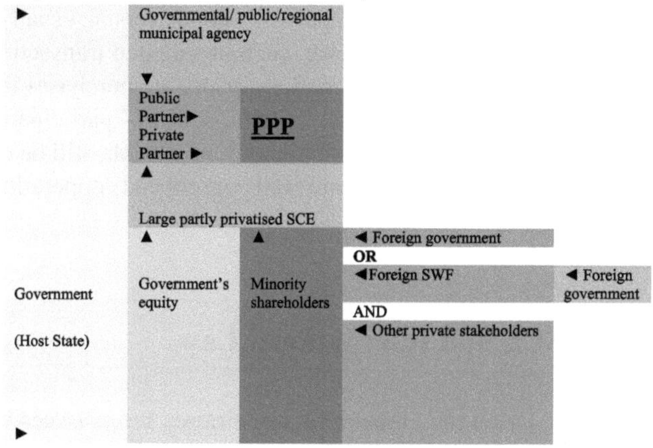

See Jędrzej Górski, 'Global Liberalisation of Public-Private Partnerships (PPPs) as Form of State Controlled Enterprises (SCEs)' (online 22 June 2020) Transnational Dispute Management 1-73, Table 3 in Sect. 22

controlled by foreign governments. The acquisitions by foreign SCEs are arguably the most internationally contentious element of globalised state capitalism and gave rise to the mentioned emergence or expansion of ISM in numerous jurisdictions across the West. Indeed, as mapped by Chaisse, the potential market distortions unwelcome in the host states might include[17]:

- Foreign SOEs or SWFs acquiring critical assets to advance foreign policy goals endangers national security;
- Threat to national identity posed by an enterprise in which a foreign sovereign owns assets closely associated with national heritage;
- Whether the SOE would be capable of 'picking favourites' when allocating scarce resources (such as energy) within a country;
- Concerns about any privileged access to scarce resources (such as land, water, and energy) for the benefit of SWFs/SOEs: resource hoarding in violation of commercial norms;
- If SOE obtains credit at a lower rate than a non-state-owned enterprise in comparable circumstances, the SOE may benefit both at home and abroad from an implicit subsidy;
- The laws and tax requirements that the new SOE could be exempt from;
- Strategic investments by SOE/SWF to assist national champions or others;
- Whether SOE enjoy preferential access to public procurement market;
- Concern when state-owned enterprises are compared to other enterprises for determining national treatment (NT) under an investment treaty.

---

[17] Chaisse, (n 2) 239–240.

However, the unsolicited (by host states) acquisitions by foreign SCEs in the domestic partially SOEs markets are exceptionally controversial, usually of strategic sectors and critical infrastructure. However, such unsolicited transactions can only be attempted via tender offers on stock markets or private purchases from existing significant private minority shareholders. In foreign SCEs' participation in PPPs, JOAs/PSAs as private partners, such economic presence might still be controversial in public perception. Nonetheless, it requires full consent and cooperation of the host states.

3 The Rise of SCE and International Law

The emergence of SCEs on the global FDI scene raises broad issues in regulatory fields as diverse as company law, trade law, investment law, competition law, or international taxation. Recently, the most contentious appear to be the laws on ISM or outright economic sanctions newly adopted or amended in many jurisdictions in reply to the challenges identified above. The question of governmental control over multinational companies potentially clashing with host states' (i.e. other governments') regulatory autonomy or national interest will increasingly lead to many normative controversies in academia and complex transnational disputes in real life. The contention closing the preceding sections that the elements of state control might be identified to various degrees on both ends of cross-border direct investment implies that one could map specific legal controversies stemming from state control from two distinct perspectives. The *investment-in-SCEs* perspective revolves around legal controversies arising in SCEs without full ownership like partially SOEs about the relations with minority shareholders according to the scenarios illustrated in Tables 2 and 3. Furthermore, the *investment-by-SCEs* perspective revolves around legal controversies arising in SCEs expanding and investing globally in addition to political controversies mentioned in the previous section *in fine*. The analyses from both perspectives reveal controversies within purely domestic or at least partly international regulatory domains whereby the *investment-in-SCEs* outlook seems slightly more entangled with domestic-law and post-establishment controversies. At the same time, the *investment-by-SCEs* appears somewhat more interwoven with international law and pre-establishment issues.

The *investment-in-SCEs* controversies are indeed unlikely to arise in the pre-establishment phase, whether that be the lack of access for foreign investors under the General Agreement on Trade in Services's (GATS) Mode 3,[18] various international investment agreements (IIAs),[19] obstacles to the establishment as merger controls, ISM, or other domestic law. The access to minority-stake investments in

[18] I.e. trade in services 'by a service supplier of one Member, through commercial presence in the territory of any other Member'. *See* GATS Art I.2.c.

[19] Like Bilateral Investment Treaties (BITs) and Preferential Trade and Investment Agreements (PTIAs).

large, partially privatised, and partially SOEs is often unilaterally liberalised regardless of jurisdiction-specific international liberalising commitments. An intention to make such a minority-stake investment in an SCE could trigger ISM procedure or a denial-of-admission under the admission-clause-model over a certain equity threshold. However, such an intention would highly unlikely trigger a national security exception under GATS or IIAs on the part of a host stake, let alone a mergers block on the grounds of completion law, seeing that control over an enterprise cannot be gained by acquiring a minority stake. In turn, the access to public-private JVs like PPPs, JOAs/PSAs rests on individual understanding between a specific investor (private partner) and a host state (public partner) entirely, even if it involves performance or technology-transfer requirements. Ergo, it falls more within the ambit of the host state's commercial activities *de iure gestionis* rather than access-regulating activity *de iure imperi.*[20]

In contrast, the post-establishment phase of *investment-in-SCEs* might turn out contentious given the conflicting interest of minority shareholders seeking a decent return on their investment in line with the wealth-maximisation paradigm and host states seeking to advance their non-commercial goals via SCE despite their partial privatisation. Mismanagement *de iure gestionis* in partially SOEs of any kind as perceived by their minority shareholders, profit-diminishing price-controls imposed *de iure imperi* on utility companies, adverse changes to the fiscal environment, or performance requirements altering the profitability of special rights under PPPs/JOAs/PSAs long could all lead to investment claims.[21]

The *investment-by-SCEs* controversies in the pre-establishment phase are, in turn, plentiful as all fears about penetration by the foreign state capital incentivise host-state creativity as regards the means of scrutinising, and if need be, blocking such investment. Prevention (blocking investment) might simply appear better than cure (tempering foreign SOEs in the post-establishment phase), especially when available therapies are few and far between. For example, the legitimate fears of host states in the field of potential domestic market distortions, among others, include governmental supports of expanding SOEs/SCEs, such as subsidised/soft loans, equity injections, debt write-offs, export credits,[22] direct governmental grants, preference treatment in terms of access to the production factors (commodities and raw materials, utilities, land, etc.) government procurement, or other forms of subsidies.

---

[20] Subject to that the selection of private partners in PPPs, JOAs/PSAs are increasingly subjected to the international government procurement rules under complex high-standard regional trade agreements with procurement chapters whereby PPPs are classified as the most sophisticated form of government contracts. *See* chapter of this book drawing upon: Jędrzej Górski, 'Global Liberalisation of Public-Private Partnerships (PPPs) as Form of State-Controlled Enterprises (SCEs)' (2020) 17(6) Transnational Dispute Management 1–73.

[21] Pretty obviously, in the case of host-state action breeching regulatory or fiscal stability clauses, or actions amounting to indirect expropriations, private partners in PPPs/JOAs/PSAs are infinitely much more likely to file investment claims compare with minority-stake shareholders for whom transactions costs relative to their investment might be too high.

[22] E.g. in violation of the OECD Arrangement on Export Credits.

Blocking investments of foreign SCEs by host states could arguably be the only risk-eliminating solution in the lack of more fitting and honest internationally accepted measures remedying such other governments' distortive supports akin to countervailing measures under the Agreement on Subsidies and Countervailing Measures ('SCM Agreement').[23] Moreover, the same logic could apply to the fears about national security, especially in the case of foreign SCEs' local subsidiaries engaged in telecommunications, networks, data flows and storage and other utilities. Host states catching locally established foreign SCE red-handed with smoking guns once investments are made and fully operative—whether that be mere domestic market distortions due to subsidisation or more nefarious behaviour—would highly likely lead to more economical, political and diplomatic tensions with locally established SCE's controlling governments that had such investments been opposed in the first place by host states.

Hence, the enormous rise of the ISM laws all across the West under the assumption that risks associated with foreign state control could be identified and mitigated upfront, among other issues considered in the course of ISM. Precisely, the OECD mapped in 2018 that the inward FDI share subjected to cross-sector security-related ISM across fifty-eight countries participating in the 'OECD-hosted dialogue on international investment policies', increased from about twenty per cent in the early 2000s to about fifty per cent in the late 2010s.[24] For example, Germany set this trend in 2009, introducing a cross-sector ISM to its Foreign Trade and Payments Ordinance (*Außenwirtschaftsverordnung*—AWV),[25] which supplements subsequent versions of the Foreign Trade and Payments Act (*Außenwirtschaftsgesetz*—AWG),[26] both consolidated in 2013.[27] The cross-sector ISM evolved into a two-tier system in July 2017 with different rules for security-related and ordinary sectors and different

---

[23] The rationale of the SCM Agreement is to remedy to the distortions of international trade flows as a result of either prohibited subsidies (SCM art 3) or actionable subsidies (SCM art 5) benefitting operations physically situated in other countries. It is not to cure domestic market distortions even if cause by such 'cross-border subsidies'. Also, the countervailing measures provided for the SCM Agreement are meant to counter trade imbalances caused by subsidised imports and by no means suited to address such cross-border subsidies to locally stablished foreign SCE.

[24] OECD, 'Current trends in investment policies related to national security and public order (OECD, November 2018). <https://www.oecd.org/daf/inv/investment-policy/Current-trends-in-OECD-NatSec-policies.pdf>, 2nd table at p 3. *See* also generally, CD, 'Acquisition and ownership-related policies to safeguard essential security interests: New policies to manage new threats: Research note on current and emerging trends' (OECD, 12 March 2019). <https://www.oecd.org/investment/Current-and-emerging-trends-2019.pdf>.

[25] Foreign Trade and Payments of 2 August 2013 (Federal Law Gazette I S. 2865), as last amended by art 7 seco 19 of the Act of 12 May 2021 (Federal Law Gazette I S. 990) (*Außenwirtschaftsverordnung* – AWV).

[26] Foreign Trade and Payments Act of 6 June 2013 (Federal Law Gazette I, p. 1482), as last amended by art 4 of the Act of 20 July 2017 (Federal Law Gazette I, p. 2789) (*Außenwirtschaftsgesetz* - AWG).

[27] As a matter of fact, the original AWG entered into force in 1961 and the AWV in 1987, and mostly regulated arms and other sensitive technology exports controls. *See* Tamotsu Aoi, 'Historical Background of Export Control Development in Selected Countries and Regions' (Mitsui & Co Ltd, April 2016). <https://www.cistec.or.jp/english/service/report/1605historical_background_export_control_development.pdf>.

application thresholds since April 2019. with the ISM triggering in equity investment over twenty-five per cent in less sensitive sectors and over ten per cent in more sensitive sectors.[28] In Austria, the original application threshold of twenty-five per cent of target enterprises' equity adopted in the 2011 Foreign Trade Act (*Außenwirtschaftsgesetz*)[29] was proposed to be reduced to ten per cent in May 2019.[30] Italy detached its controls mechanism from ownership in 2012 by replacing treasury's golden share rights adopted in 1994 and questioned under the EU law[31] with two' golden powers' mechanisms differentiating between national security-related and other strategic sectors.[32] Portugal introduced controls of specific critical infrastructure assets' purchases in 2014.[33] Norway adopted its modern ISM only in January 2019 to kick in the purported acquisition of control or more than one-third of equity in enterprises operating in specific sectors or possessing specific strategic infrastructure assets.[34]

France has had a limited ISM covering several sectors since 1966, which had to be modified many times in the wake of particular controversial takeovers revealing its shortcoming.[35] The direction of changes has been to protect more sectors and lower equity thresholds.[36] Hungary introduced its first cross-sector ISM in January 2019, differentiating between sectors subjected to scrutiny above ten or twenty-five per cent equity acquisitions.[37] Latvia introduced its ISM in March 2017, limiting it to a positive list of enterprises in critical sectors.[38] Romania adopted its ISM-like instrument initially in 2011 by authorising national-defence-related agencies to intervene in merger controls and only supplemented it with a self-standing ISM in strategic sectors in February 2020.[39] The ISM design has also been a work in progress

---

[28] OECD (n 24) paras 439-445 at 127-129.

[29] Außenwirtschaftsgesetz 2011 (AußWG 2011) StF: BGBl. I Nr. 26/2011 DAF/INV/RD(2013)3. See DAF/INV/RD(2012)6 for the notification of the initial legislation. For the unofficial translation of the AußWG 2011, *see* OECD, 'Investment Measure Relating to National Security: Notification by Austria' (3 October 2013) DAF/INV/RD(2013)3. *See* also, Frédéric Wehrlé, Joachim Pohl, 'Investment Policies Relatedto National Security: A Survey of Country Practices' (OECD 2016) Working Papers on International Investment 2016/02. <https://dx.doi.org/10.1787/5jlwrrf038nx-en>, 46.

[30] OECD (n 24) paras 393-396 at 115-116.

[31] Case C-326/07, *Commission of the European Communities v Italian Republic* (26 March 2009, Judgment of the Court, Third Chamber: Failure of a Member State to fulfil obligations - Articles 43 EC and 56 EC - Articles of association of privatised undertakings - Criteria for the exercise of certain special powers held by the State) [2009] ECR I-02291.

[32] *Decreto-Legge 15 marzo 2012, n. 21: Norme in materia di poteri speciali sugli assetti societari nei settori della difesa e della sicurezza nazionale, nonche' per le attivita' di rilevanza strategica nei settori dell'energia, dei trasporti e delle comunicazioni.* (12G0040); OECD (n 24) paras 458-463 at 133-135.

[33] OECD (n 24) paras 506-508 at 145-146.

[34] ibid paras 495-496 at 143.

[35] *See* further sec 5.1.4 on France's problems with the EU-law compliance of some of such measures.

[36] ibid paras 435-438 at 126-128.

[37] ibid paras 447-448 at 130.

[38] ibid paras 472-473 at 139-139.

[39] ibid paras 509-512 at 145.

in several jurisdictions, including Sweden since October 2020[40] and Ireland since December 2019.[41]

The independent and unilateral EU Member States' initiative led eventually to the adoption of the Regulation 2019/452 establishing a framework for the screening of foreign direct investments into the Union,[42] recognising that '[i]t should be possible for Member States to assess risks to security or public order arising from significant changes to the ownership structure or key characteristics of a foreign Investor',[43] COVID only reinforced the rationales behind the adoption of Regulation 2019/452 as the need to repel easy takeovers in the moment of economic turmoil seemed to require coordinating measures exceeding what Regulation 2019/452 originally required.[44] Indeed, provisions of Regulation 2019/452 are somewhat superfluous except for the new coordination procedures.[45] Crucially, Regulation 2019/452 did not require ISM in any situations and left greenlighting specific transactions within Member States' discretion. However, in the wake of the COVID outbreak, the European Commission supplemented Regulation 2019/452 with guidelines, calling the Member States to make full use of their existing ISMs or pass necessary legislation as soon as possible.[46]

The compatibility of such domestic investment laws and their contestability under GATS and IIAs has been a genuine riddle, especially regarding more stringer treatment of foreign SCEs than private inward FDI.[47]

Concerning international compatibility, on the one hand, the lack of a clear international national security definition has weakened the global push for investment liberalisation significantly and decentralised the liberalisation process by shifting from a purported international consensus on permissible exceptions to free trade and investment to differing self-judging assessments made at the national level. On the other hand, however, globalist and sovereigntist tendencies have had to be balanced as, to quote Chaisse, '[i]t seems from WTO case law that trade liberalisation and international regulation do not prevail over Members' vital interests in maintaining the core of sovereignty and they cannot restrain Members' freedom to preserve and defend their very existence'.[48] Ergo, while several WTO members, like at least the

[40] ibid paras 536-539 at 152.

[41] ibid paras 536-539 at 152.

[42] Regulation (EU) 2019/452 of the European Parliament and of the Council of 19 March 2019 establishing a framework for the screening of foreign direct investments into the Union PE/72/2018/REV/1 (21 March 2019). OJ L 79I, pp 1–14 ('Regulation 2019/452').

[43] ibid preamble, point 11.

[44] See generally, OECD, 'Inventory of investment measures taken between 16 September 2019 and 15 October 2020' (OECD, December 2020). <https://www.oecd.org/daf/inv/investment-policy/FOI-investment-measure-monitoring-October-2020.pdf>.

[45] Regulation 2019/452 (n 42) Art 4.2.

[46] European Commission, 'Guidance to the Member States concerning foreign direct investment and free movement of capital from third countries, and the protection of Europe's strategic assets, ahead of the application of Regulation (EU) 2019/452 (FDI Screening Regulation)' (25 March 2020) C(2020) 1981 final, at 2.

[47] Chaisse, (n 2) 249.

[48] ibid 249–250.

US and Canada, made reservations in their GATS Mode 3 commitment schedules about certain foreign-controlled investments, one could wonder whether making such reservations in GATS's or IIA's schedules is not superfluous in the light of the lax approach to national security exceptions across the board in the international trading system?

Concerning international contestability of domestic investment laws, it is true that enforcement of market access commitments is usually confined to the state-to-state dispute settlement without access to compensation.[49] However, what business organisation facing obstacles in potential host states, if not SCE, is more likely to convince their home governments to intervene?

The global divergencies and irregularities in the understanding of national security extend to the concept of 'essential security' the *investment-by-SOE* post-establishment phase, where akin to the pre-establishment market access issue, to quote Chaisse, 'BITs and FTAs have a role to play, but they probably favour governments and not investors'.[50] Moreover, one could wonder if the locally established foreign SCEs could be deprived of protections against discriminatory treatment just because of foreign state control, placing such SCEs not 'in like circumstances' compared with private enterprises similar in all other respects? Moreover, how to apply such a proposition to the discrimination against locally established foreign SCEs competing with domestic SCEs?[51] Furthermore, how to employ international law measures, if any, once the investment has not been blocked in the pre-establishment phase, and domestic market distortions emerge due to mentioned foreign governments' supports of their expanding SCEs, cheap credit, equity injections, debt forgiveness, or other preferences? We have already noticed that the SCM Agreement, in principle, could not apply to such situations as its rationale has been to remedy international trade flows distortions and not to domestic ones.[52] However, what if a host state attempted to prove the occurrence of actionable subsidies by claiming that subsidies benefitting locally established foreign SCEs affected adversely the host state's enterprises' ability to compete in the exports markets?[53] Or, what if a host state attempted to prove the occurrence of prohibited subsidies, claiming that subsidies benefitting locally established foreign SCEs were conditional upon preferring inputs imported from their home states to the host state's domestic

---

[49] ibid 249.

[50] ibid 251.

[51] ibid 250.

[52] *See* n 23.

[53] Actionable subsidies (SCM Art 5) are not prohibited per se. The need to adversely affect WTO Member's interests like by (1) 'injury to the domestic industry of another Member' (SCM Art 5.a) (2) 'nullification or impairment of benefits accruing directly or indirectly to other Members under GATT 1994 in particular the benefits of concessions bound under Article II of GATT 199412' (SCM Art 5.b), or (3) 'serious prejudice to the interests of another Member' (SCM Art 5.c). Therefore, very theoretically, one of the conditions to established 'serious prejudice' which is that the effect of the subsidy is to displace or impede the exports of a like product of another Member from a third country market" (SCM Art 6.3.b).

inputs, being a kind of inverted local content subsidies?[54] There are more questions than answers.

Naturally, the distinction between measures and legal institutions is problematic from either *investment-in-SCEs* or *investment-by-SCEs* perspective is not always clear-cut. For instance, we presented the rise of ISM laws as an *investment-by-SCEs* problem. However, it could also appear in the *investment-in-SCEs* context—despite our observation earlier in this section that minority-stake are usually not contentious—seeing the discussed global trend to lower the ISM application threshold to a mere 10% of equity in specific sectors. Likewise, we mentioned the concerns about control over teleconnections networks or data services in the *investment-by-SCEs* context, with large expanding foreign telecommunications SCE in mind. However, even a minority-stake investment by private foreign enterprises in partially privatised telecom SCE might alert the host state, etc., which the global expansion of ISMs' application has meant to address.

4 Overview of the Book

Part I of the book on The Regulatory Framework of State Capitalism: Laws, Treaties, and Contracts opens with Chap. 2 titled 'The Latest Regulatory Regime of SOEs under International Trade Treaties', where **WU Yingying** addresses how to regulate SOEs in the international trade and investment regime. The author submits that the latest bilateral treaties and multilateral agreements in trade and investment have paid extensive attention to SOEs, whether during the negotiation or the outcome of the final texts. The rules relating to SOEs tend to imitate one another. The author aims to find the nature and essence of these rules relating to SOEs by looking at the rules specified in the draft Trans-Pacific Partnership Agreement (TPP), Comprehensive Progressive Trans-Pacific Partnership (CPTPP), the Transatlantic Trade and Investment Partnership (TTIP), etc. These rules, in general, regulate SOEs in terms of their advantages received from governments, their activities in the market, their monopolistic status in the market, their relationship with governments, etc. By comparison with rules speculated in the General Agreement of Tariffs and Trade (GATT), World Trade Organisation (WTO), and other bilateral trade and investment agreements decades ago, the author observes that new developments in international law have taken place following the role of SOEs played in international trade and investment areas. The author analyses the evolution of these rules relating to SOEs and the direction they will go forward in the coming days.

In Chap. 3 titled, 'Global Liberalisation of Public-Private Partnerships (PPPs) as Form of State-Controlled Enterprises (SCEs)', **Jędrzej Górski** observes that public projects in the field of public infrastructure, energy, utilities, or any significant public

[54] Local content subsidies are one of the two categories of prohibited subsidies and are defined as 'subsidies contingent, whether solely or as one of several other conditions, upon the use of domestic over imported goods' (SCM Art 3.1.b).

projects are increasingly outsourced via PPPs and lure multinational enterprises spanning their operations across multiple jurisdictions with varying market entry barriers for foreign investors. The incentives and hindrances to participation in PPPs by such foreign investors could be tied to the level of international liberalisation, primarily of government procurement markets, and secondarily of investment and provision of services in heavily regulated sectors, like utilities. These also rest on proper protection of investment by foreign persons, along with the position of such persons in resolving controversies that might arise between a public and a private partner. The opening of PPP markets is increasingly addressed in procurement chapters of high-standard regional trade agreements (RTAs) like the CPTPP. This follows the developments in the WTO Government Procurement Agreement (GPA) and EU procurement directives. Expressly, PPPs have been gradually incorporated into coverage of the WTO GPA by the back door, i.e. party-specific schedule of commitments. Furthermore, the EU's public-procurement-derived procedural framework has been gradually perfectioned to reflect the complexity of PPPs. The instruments like the GATS and the Agreement on Trade-Related Investment Measures (TRIMs) are relevant for the liberalisation of PPPs to the extent that general-commerce freedom of the provision of services and investment by foreign persons in most cases is a prerequisite for access to PPP markets. The related dispute settlement issues can be differentiated into disputes emerging before and after the conclusion of PPP contractors. Market-access procurement-derived instruments set a framework for resolving disputes between potential private partners competing for PPP contracts on the one side with contracting authorities (public partners) on the other side. Such instruments also essentially secure the stability of PPPs agreement, adding to the investment protection environment. In turn, the bilateral investment agreements (BITs) and investment chapters of RTAs in principle cover PPPs classifiable as a foreign investment despite excluding public procurement from their scope of application expressly.

In Chap. 4 titled, Ways of 'Control': Changes and Implications from China's Reform of State-Owned Enterprises', **Hu Shixue** aims to provide the necessary knowledge of China's current regulation and basic facts about Chinese SOEs/SCEs as the basis for further discussion. The author primarily focuses on China's methods of controlling its SOEs after the 2015 reform. The party-state has different control purposes for SOEs, sets up different controlling administrations and levels, encourages control through ownership between private and public sectors, and increases the party's political control to achieve efficiency and political priorities better. The author offers a more nuanced understanding of 'control' not only for a clearer picture of Chinese SOEs but also for the discussions about SCEs transnational and international governance.

In Chap. 5 titled 'The Legal Issues of "Going Global" and the Trans-Nationalisation of the Chinese Public-Private Partnership Model', **Gianmatteo Sabatino** looks into how the People's Republic of China's (PRC) international cooperation policy deals with the challenges represented both by the underdevelopment issues still affecting Chinese economic law and by the necessity to interact with the different legal system in order to carry out cooperation projects? The PPP model might represent one of the answers. As its diffusion and success within the border of the PRC gradually advances, the Chinese PPP model has also been experiencing increasing success concerning international cooperation projects, especially within the framework of the Belt & Road initiative (BRI). Though still in its early developing stages, the transnational Chinese PPP already faces several issues concerning shaping a complex and mature legal environment able to support the spread of such a model. The solution to such issues is ultimately aimed at facilitating the 'going global' of the Chinese enterprises, in first place SOEs. However, it must necessarily stem from the construction of a comprehensive Chinese domestic legal model of PPP to approach, in second place, the challenge of developing a transnational PPP model. The author intends to sketch an overview of the issues mentioned above and layout some possible solutions.

In Chap. 6 titled 'Elephant in the Room: On the Notions of SCEs in International Investment Law and International Economic Law', **CHAN Kai-Chieh** submits that, with the rise of state capitalism, SCEs) have been evolving, and their activities are becoming more complex, both in terms of ownership, control and their business development strategies. Against this background, the author first argues that international investment law, as it stands now, is insufficiently equipped to deal with the level of structural and managerial flexibility that some SCEs have attained today. While early tribunals have tried to create some bright-line rules regarding the notions relating to SCEs, their efforts eventually prove futile. Given various ambiguities in relevant customary rules, tribunals today seem to rely on an eclectic, highly fact-sensitive approach, leading to many legal uncertainties and scholarly criticisms. The author proposes two extra-legal tools that can guide future tribunals in determining the legal status of SCEs. Firstly, the author submits that they can invoke relevant rules in international trade law, such as the law of the WTO and other new trade deals applicable between the parties. On the one hand, judicial bodies of the WTO have produced abundant case law concerning the notions of SCE. On the other hand, unlike most early investment treaties, some recent trade deals have addressed the current State of SCEs. They can be invoked based on Art. 31(3) and Art. 32 of the Vienna Convention on the law of treaties. Secondly, the author submits that they may refer to national competition rules. These rules can offer more insight into how the entities are treated in their domestic legal systems. By paying due respect to domestic legal regimes, tribunals can alleviate the concern that international law is unfairly biased against developing States.

In Chap. 7 titled 'Regulating Sovereign Shareholders: The Role of Securities Disclosures', **Joel Slawotsky** submits that while the US–China hegemonic rivalry has proximately caused a global tightening of national security review of investments, overlooked is the incipient rise of economic nationalism and a potential trend of incorporating tenets of state capitalism. The willingness of market capitalism practising nations to consider entering capital markets and engaging in cross-border investment is an essential and transformative dynamic with immense implications. At a minimum, dominant or controlling owners can influence a business to favour the owner's interests. For private owners, this is acknowledged as focusing on private economic motivations. Sovereign owners may also have other motives aside from profit, such as advancing national objectives. Sovereigns as shareholders are empowered to vote for directors and control corporations, thus potentially substantially influencing and/or controlling another sovereign's political governance, industrial strength and economic future. Share purchases potentially enable control of the 'economic/technological high ground' and are effectuated through a method that is generally below the radar without attracting the regulatory attention associated with large transactions or takeovers. Share acquisition can form a stealth stratagem to impact an adversary or obtain valuable information. Therefore, the author suggests that nations should update securities disclosure laws to reflect the transformational developments in emerging technology, directly and indirectly, implicate national security concerns. Foreign governmental entities purchasing shares should be strictly monitored to protect core economic sectors and emergent technology. The trigger percentage should be lowered for governmental buyers. Legitimate governmental investors should not object to heightened disclosure and reporting requirements.

In Chap. 8, 'EU Merger Control and China's State-owned Enterprises: Is Ownership Separate from Control?', **Alessandro Spano** submits that in recent years, the investment activities of Chinese SOEs in the European Union (EU) have been subject to greater scrutiny to assess their effect on market competition, social stability and national security. The debate has been sparked in two main areas: investment arbitration and merger regulation. This chapter discusses the approach taken by the EU Commission in the application of the EU Merger Regulation to recent transactions of Chinese SOEs in the EU. The analysis aims to demonstrate that mere economic analysis fails to capture the nature of the operations of Chinese SOEs. Instead, these should be read into the broader context of China's system of governance, which recognises a special status and role to Chinese SOEs. This situation calls for a more holistic approach in competition law enforcement by implementing complementary normative instruments at the EU level. The EU should seek a higher level of legal harmonisation and more coordination between national and supranational institutional actors. The implementation of standard normative instruments in investment protection, for example, represents an important step to complement the existing competition law regime and, perhaps, to lead to more political and economic cohesion in the EU.

Part II of the book on Economic and Institutional Expansion of State Capitalism opens with Chap. 9 titled 'The Public Value Creation of State-owned Enterprises', in which **Usman W Chohan** aims to examine the value contribution of SOEs through the prism of public value theory to (1) situate SOEs more sturdily within the public administration literature and (2) to advance public value theory by addressing an institutional form that melds elements of both the state and the market. The author considers various important rationales for SOE proliferation and highlights their growing international importance. The author then emphasises the need to go beyond the state versus market dichotomy and applies public value's strategic triangle to identify aspects of SOE legitimacy, recognition of value, and operational resources. The author concludes that SOEs offer an innovative public value lens for several reasons and that public value helps explain essential elements of SOE performance.

In Chap. 10 titled 'Privatisations of State-owned Companies and Justifications for Restrictions on EU Fundamental Freedoms: Past, Present and Future Perspectives', **Thomas Papadopoulos** reviews and critically evaluates privatisations of state-owned companies and justifications for restrictions on EU fundamental freedoms. Past, present, and future perspectives are considered. First, the author analyses past perspectives on justifications for restrictions on EU fundamental freedoms in the context of CJEU's golden shares case law. According to CJEU's golden shares case law, special rights in privatised companies restrict EU fundamental freedoms. The CJEU examined the possibility of justifications for such restrictions on public interest considerations. The author scrutinises the evolution of justifications for such restrictions, focuses on legitimate justifications and explores under which conditions the EU Member States could continue to have special prerogatives in privatised companies based on public interest considerations. The author emphasises the conditions established by *Commission v. Belgium*, the only golden shares case, where the restrictions were found justified. Secondly, regarding current perspectives on available justifications, the author discusses justifications for restrictions on freedom of establishment in the recent case *Associação Peço a Palavra*, where the conditions of a privatisation process were scrutinised. This latter case scrutinised the justification for restrictions resulting from tender specifications governing the conditions to which a privatisation process of a state-owned company was subject. The importance of *Associação Peço a Palavra* is analysed. Thirdly, the author considers future perspectives on privatisations and available justifications for restrictions on EU fundamental freedoms in the light of corporate social responsibility (CSR). Overall, the author examines whether CSR goals in privatised companies could be underpinned by justifications for restrictions on EU fundamental freedoms; looking into previous case law provides valuable guidance on how CSR could be integrated into privatised companies through tender specifications or golden shares.

In Chap. 11 titled 'The Expansion of China's State-Owned Enterprise Sector Since the Global Financial Crisis: What Insights Do Official Statistics Afford?', **ZHANG Chunlin** analyses the expansion of China's SOE sector in the decade following the global financial crisis in 2008 using statistics for non-financial SOEs regularly published by the Ministry of Finance of China in its *Financial Yearbook of China* and statistics from other official sources. After characterising the observed expansion, the author addresses three questions within the limit of data availability: How large is China's SOE sector in terms of its share in the gross domestic product (GDP) before and after the expansion? What are the objectives that the observed SOE sector expansion appears to have served? How was the expansion of the SOE sector financed? Where data constraints do not allow an adequate answer to a question, the author attempts to draw practical observations as much as possible and raise questions for further work.

In Chap. 12, 'Re-imaging Development Finance: Sustainability, *Catalytic* Capital, and the Role of Sovereign Wealth Funds', **Patric J Schena** and **Matthew Gouett** submit that the COVID crisis has vividly highlighted persistent gaps in global investment, particularly in key sustainable development sectors. The eventual transition to a full post-COVID recovery will further accentuate these imbalances. As states compete for scarce resources, domestic investment institutions with robust governance and strong operational capacity can enhance the ability of governments to catalyse inward foreign investment. The authors argue that SWFs are suited to occupy this critical middle ground, not solely or even principally as funding sources, but, to greater effect, as domestic investment partners with local experience and expertise, operational capacity, and professional legitimacy authors refer to as operational alpha. Moreover, an SWF's professional standing may not only assuage concerns about transactional governance but also strengthen social licence while mitigating operational and political shortcomings that often accompany institutional gaps.

In Chap. 13 titled 'Going "Beside" and "Beyond" the State: Corporations' and Sovereign wealth funds' Planning Strategies', **Gianmatteo Sabatino** submits that the role of multinational corporations as market regulators, although commonly accepted among scholars, has rarely been assessed from a structural point of view. Corporations, as legal entities, exercise prerogatives within the global market that closely resembles, to some extent, those of states. Indeed, their legitimacy and inner hierarchy are founded over the same anthropological and sociological justifications that ensure the functioning of sovereign entities. One of these justifications is undoubtedly the functional approach to economic planning. Economic operators in the corporate form widely employ forms of long-term planning through mechanisms and decision-making processes directly relatable to provisions developed by the most advanced countries in terms of planning law, such as the PRC. On account of such structural analogy, when corporations and economic entities are state-controlled—more or less directly—a peculiar phenomenon may occur: the state may pursue long-term development strategies through formally private economic operators. To do so, it exploits the inner management structures of the corporation and lays out regulatory frameworks that often are meant to promote corporations' investments. The author aims to briefly sketch some of this global phenomenon's main features and issues from a legal perspective. In the first place, the topic will be discussed from the general point of view of legal anthropology, by defining the role of States and Corporations in the market, to be regarded as a society where the 'power' may be either centralised or diffused according to the dynamics in place. In the 'society of market', States and corporations interact with each other also through long-term planning strategies. Therefore, in the second part of the analysis, the author assesses planning strategies and rules for corporations and state-controlled entities (such as sovereign wealth funds). In particular, the author points out that such rules are elaborated, implemented, and enforced similarly to state plans. In the third, the author discusses legal interaction between States and corporations by pointing out how States may use legal instruments to influence corporations and pursue specific objectives. The author concludes with some remarks regarding the influence of such a phenomenon on the very notion of State and State power in the modern global market.

In Chap. 14 titled, 'Sovereign Wealth Funds and Public Value Theory', **Usman W Chohan** situates SWFs in the context of public value theory (PVT). The author explores five PVT aspects: measurement, collaboration, value arbitration, imagination, and short-termism. This demonstrates the balance that SWFs must strike in creating value for the public while reconciling the realities and impositions of private interest. The author also informs a subjacent question in public administration about how public managers can co-create value through novel arrangements that are reconcilable with the logic of the market. The author's findings suggest that SWFs represent a unique co-mingling of public trust and private interest. Their peculiar traits offer a dual value proposition to society since they strike a complex balance between public stewardship and enterprise dynamism.

Part III of the book on The Accountability of State Capitalism: Exploring the Forms of Liabilities opens with Chap. 15 titled '*Un Somaro Piumato*'—Rethinking the Scope and Nature of State Liability for Acts of their Commercial Instrumentalities: State-Owned Enterprises and State-Owner Liability in the Post-Global", in which **Larry Catá Backer** asks under what circumstances a state might be subject to liability for the conduct of its SOEs? That question, always controversial but settled by the end of the last century, has once again become necessary as the old conceptual categories for liability have become unsettled. It is now no longer clear that states may authoritatively claim immunity for themselves and the SOEs' non-commercial activities. The author examines the effect of substantial transformations in the legal environment of enterprise operation on the conceptual framework within which principles of immunity (and its waiver) was grounded. The legalisation of responsible business conduct through disclosure, supply chain due diligence legislation and the rise of human rights business torts based on production chain responsible governance responsibility have upended the traditional conceptual framework of immunity and the separation of the state from its economic organs. The governmentalisation of economic activities and the extension of regulatory responsibilities of apex economic enterprises across their supply chains have produced a context in which private enterprises now assert sovereign authority even as states exercise private market power through their management and control of autonomous economic actors in markets. In this context, in Part 2, the author considers the challenge to the standard model of state owner liability for the conduct or activities of SOEs in the form of the new supply chain due diligence laws and the Modern Slavery reporting provisions being enacted in Europe and Australia. In Part 3, the author then considers the challenge to traditional human rights tort law development models. The author argues that the resulting context provides a basis for either for extending sovereign immunity to those regulatory responsibilities of all economic actors (irrespective of their public or private ownership) or of the reconception of sovereign regulation through legal compliance obligations as inherently commercial and thus not protected principles of sovereign immunity when undertaken by SOEs. Further, the author suggests that this emerging conception of the role of economic actors produces a context in which the state can become its own legal subject, the state can simultaneously serve as the apex body corporate subject to regulatory obligations within its production chain and liable therefore and at the same time the sovereign authority to enforces those obligations.

In Chap. 16 titled 'Corporate Social Responsibility with 'Chinese Characteristics' An Overview of the Obligations of Chinese State-owned Enterprises', **Flora Sapio** sheds new light on the mechanisms used to monitor Chinese multinational corporations' (MNCs) compliance with their CSR obligations. China's state-owned

MNCs play a pivotal role in implementing the Belt and Road Initiative and continue to account for roughly 30 per cent of domestic GDP. SOEs' position within China's governance system and the ideological features of China's governance model makes CSR obligations a binding regulatory duty of state-owned MNCs and their domestic and foreign subsidiaries. In Western legal systems, CSR and its more recent business and human rights evolution are understood as a form of regulation that public and private enterprises may adopt entirely voluntarily and integrate within their business model. China's case is different. In the first part of the chapter, the author places the notion of CSR (*gongsi shehui zeren*) against the backdrop of non-state-based compliance and monitoring mechanisms specific to state-owned MNCs. Next, the author describes the central CSR norms and mechanisms grounded within the system of regulations of the Chinese Communist Party. In the concluding section, the author presents some reflections on the main features of CSR in China and their relevance to the Belt and Road Initiative.

In Chap. 17 titled 'National Security Review for Foreign Investment in China: A Transnational Evolution', **MA Ji** submits that the national security review mechanisms for foreign investments in China are influenced strongly by cross-border factors. Since China's reform and opening, the national security review mechanisms for foreign investment have gone through four phases. Facing peculiar economic and political situations in different phases, China adopted special security review measures for foreign investments. The beginning phase is from 1979 to 1994, focusing on administrative licencing procedures of establishing enterprises; the second phase is from 1995 to 2002, strengthening the approvals of foreign companies' access to specific industries or sectors; the third phase is from 2003 to 2014, emphasising to establish a national security review mechanism for foreign mergers and acquisitions; and the fourth phase is from 2014 to the present, striving to build a uniform national security review mechanism for foreign investments.

Along with these transformations, China has gradually unified the approach to the governance of foreign investments by enacting the Foreign Investment Law, which will be effective from the beginning of 2020. At the same time, China has created a uniform national security regime by enacting National Security Law and related security regulations. Following the gradually clear national security framework and the unified approach to foreign investments, the next step would be to establish a uniform and consistent mechanism of national security review for foreign investments. While transnational communities and regimes help shape domestic regulations, many domestic institutions, including state-owned enterprises, play critical roles in these transformations. The author shows how critical events in these four periods led to these transitions by examining the transitions of Chinese national security review mechanisms for foreign investment. The author argues that the development of the national security review mechanisms for foreign investments in China is a transnational approach: the communications between international communities and China government have contributed significantly to the transformations of Chinese security review mechanisms for foreign investments; in return, China will share her unique approach to the national security review mechanisms for foreign investments. The author emphasises that, in finding its path towards establishing the mechanisms of national security review for foreign investments, China can both learn from and teach other countries.

In Chap. 18 titled 'Dispute Settlement Mechanisms in Foreign Investment Contracts with Central American State-Owned Enterprises', **Jorge Arturo González** submits that foreign investment contracts entered between foreign investors (or their local subsidiaries) and SOEs are susceptible to unique risks. This author aims to explore different possible dispute settlement mechanisms to be used in the context of this type of contract in Central America. The author proposes that opting for domestic arbitration in the host State as a dispute settlement forum may be undesirable and expose the foreign investor to some risks that arbitration is supposed to avoid. This leaves international arbitration in a third neutral country and/or amicable dispute settlement mechanisms as more reliable avenues for foreign investors.

In Chap. 19 titled 'From State-Controlled Enterprises to Investment Screening: Paving the Way for Stricter Rules on Foreign Investment', **Andrés Eduardo Alvarado Garzón** submits that SCEs, either as SWFs or SOEs, are a rising cause of concern among states receiving their investments. The possibility of creating market distortion and the ties of SCEs with their home state governments arouse distrust in several host states. Although international instruments have been developed to address most of the criticisms of investments made by SCEs, states prefer to rely on domestic regulations. In this context, investment screening laws are becoming more popular in recent years. States use concepts such as 'national security' or 'essential security' to preserve maximum autonomy and discretion in designing those laws. Nevertheless, investment screening could go beyond legitimate concerns towards investments of SCEs, leading to undercover economic protectionism.

In Chap. 20 titled 'Investment Screening Mechanism (ISM) in Central and Eastern Europe (CEE): Case study of Poland', **Jędrzej Górski** submits that Poland, like many other countries of the Central and Eastern Europe (CEE) region, has undergone a sinusoidal evolution of its investment screening mechanism (ISM) in the course of a turbulent transition from planned to a market economy. Initial strict inward foreign direct investment (FDI) controls of the late eighties and early nineties, similar to current solutions in more assertive emerging markets, were soon dismantled under the pressures of European integration. Government control of the strategic enterprises was for long achieved via equity stakes across the region. As treasuries' capital participation in such companies faded due to gradual privatisation, the European institutions have often questioned solutions like golden shares leaving strategic enterprises exposed to a hostile takeover. However, as the priorities of the Western European economies channelled by the European Institutions shifted from securing a free rein in CEE to shielding bloc's enterprises from takeovers by East Asian competitors; also the CEE countries were allowed to follow suit. Poland's ISM-related developments have been consistent with those trends, though it accumulated a uniquely complicated mosaic of sector-specific ISMs. Throughout the transformation, Poland has kept uninterruptedly olden restrictions on the real estate purchases by foreigners, investment controls in special economic zones (SEZs) and ISM-elements in heavily regulated sectors like aviation, banking, insurance and financial services. On top of that, it (1) replaced golden shares challenged by the European Commission with strict controls of enterprises possessing critical infrastructure assets listed secretly in 2010, (2) built sector-specific ISM into hydrocarbon mining permitting in 2014, (3) subjected several designated enterprises operating in the energy and telecommunications sectors to ISM handled by the treasury in 2015, and (4) introduced a temporary cross-sector ISM covering nearly whole economy in the wake of COVID's outbreak in 2020.

In Chap. 21 titled 'Political Support, Competitive Advantage, and the Regulation of State-Owned Enterprises (SOEs)', **Peter Enderwick** submits that SOEs' internationalisation can impose competitive distortions on host country economies because of structural and behavioural differences. The recent growth of SOEs from emerging markets adds new dimensions to these distortions where the state influences both competitive learning and upgrading and accelerated internationalisation. In addition, the economic transition of emerging markets and associated changes in the ownership structure of SOEs alter the economic incentives faced by cross-border SOEs. These considerations reinforce the case for subjective evaluation of SOE investment, the separation of national security from net economic benefit tests, and the need for consistency in decision-making.

In Chap. 22 titled, 'The End of European Naivety: Difficult Times Ahead for SCEs/SOEs Investing in the European Union', **Ondřej Svoboda** submits that while being open to foreign investment, the European Union has witnessed some new investment trends which have recently raised essential concerns and attracted political and public attention. In particular, the influx of Chinese foreign direct investment by SCEs and SOEs in the EU has triggered a strong call for a screening mechanism in the still decentralised and fragmented EU environment. In response to this changing economic reality, the EU adopted in March 2019 a new regulation, which has entered into force in April 2019. The regulation should answer the increasing role of non-traditional sources of FDI and safeguard European strategic assets. This change in EU investment policies is motivated by national security concerns, but there is always a risk that it could be used as a protectionist tool in the future. It is to be seen whether the EU can protect its vital security interests as well. This author explores the recent development of screening regulations in the EU, its ramifications for SOEs, and the broader policy context.

Part IV of the book on regional and country perspectives opens with Chap. 23 titled 'Vietnam's Reform of State-owned Entities: Domestic and External Drivers', in which **Dini Sejko** and **Viet Hoang** examine the reform of SCEs in Vietnam. Since Vietnam joined the World Trade Organisation, it has pursued an active trade and investment policy and negotiated bilateral and multilateral agreements deepening its integration in the global value chains and investment flows. Concurrently, Vietnam has implemented reforms of the state-controlled economic structure leading to the equitisation of Vietnamese state-controlled entities (SCE) to improve their management and governance. Recently, Vietnam ratified the Comprehensive and Progressive Agreement for Trans-Pacific Partnership (CPTPP) and the European Union-Vietnam Free Trade Agreement (EVFTA). The chapter examines the innovative EVFTA and CPTPP provisions that directly regulate state-controlled entities and provides an overview of other treaty obligations that indirectly affect SCEs. The chapter sustains that the treaty obligations contain norms on SCEs that stimulate the domestic SCEs' reform even though several carve outs and treaty exceptions ensure special treatment for some of the most important SCEs.

In Chap. 24 titled 'How to Handle State-owned Enterprises in EU-China Investment Talks', **Alicia García-Herrero** and **XU Jianwei** submit that Chinese SOEs are among the main obstacles preventing China and the European Union from agreeing on a BIT. Given the benefits that both China and the EU could obtain from a BIT, the question of SOEs should be addressed most effectively. The authors examine the main differences between Chinese and European SOEs regarding their sectoral coverage and, most importantly, their corporate governance. The authors argue that preferential market access for Chinese SOEs in China is the key to their undue competitive advantage globally and why global consumers might not necessarily benefit from Chinese SOEs in terms of welfare gain. Preferential market access in China, rather than ownership of SOEs, should be critical when evaluating the undue advantage of Chinese corporates because private companies with ties to the Chinese government might also benefit from preferential market access. The authors also offer a checklist of issues for EU–China investment talks concerning Chinese SOEs. First, creating barriers to prevent Chinese companies from acquiring European assets will not solve the problem. Instead, equal market access in China is a much better goal to pursue to reduce the seemingly unlimited resources that Chinese SOEs seem to have to compete overseas. Second, bringing Chinese corporate governance closer to global market principles is also essential to ensure European and Chinese corporates operate on an equal footing in their cross-border investment decisions.

In Chap. 25 titled 'State-Owned and Influenced Enterprises and the Evolution of Canada's Foreign Direct Investment Regime', **Geoffrey Hale** submits that Canada liberalised its foreign investment regime significantly during the 1980s, intending to open all but a handful of strategic sectors to FDI, leading to further institutionalisation through a series of bilateral, regional and multilateral trade agreements. However, the growing global profile of state-owned and influenced enterprises has led to regulatory and legislative changes since 2009, increasing the opacity and unpredictability of such processes, mainly by national security factors. The author explores the evolution of Canadian foreign investment review policies with particular attention to state-owned and influenced enterprises and distinguishes between market-based and politically influenced governance models in both inward and outward foreign investment. The author notes the persistence of the 'net benefit' test in screening FDI under the Investment Canada Act (ICA), along with principles that have come to shape their application to investment and takeover proposals by state-controlled and influenced enterprises. The author also notes the evolving design and implementation of national security provisions to proposed transactions since policy and legislative changes were introduced in 2013, changes in concepts of 'strategic' or 'critical' sectors, and their application to several contested transactions in recent years.

In Chap. 26 titled 'FinTech Regulation and its Impact on State-owned Companies in Europe', **Gianni Lo Schiavo** submits that FinTech can be described as the innovative use of technology in providing financial services through digital technologies and IT systems. FinTech services' evolution requires a degree of critical examination to avoid either an excessive degree of regulation, which could hamper new technologies or too loose regulation that risks negatively affecting markets and consumers. In this context, particular attention should be paid to the impact of FinTech on SOEs. The public nature of these companies risks being jeopardised if there is uncontrolled and unsystematic use of FinTech services. The author intends to look at the FinTech (r)evolution in Europe and critically examine the challenges and risks connected with FinTech services used by SOEs. While it would be excessive to argue for specific European rules on FinTech services for SOEs, the author submits that the new FinTech regulatory dimension needs to be considered, especially given the increasing attention of EU regulators on the matter.

In Chap. 27 titled 'Chinese State-Owned Enterprises in Africa: Always a Black-and-White Role?', **YIN Wei** and **ZHANG Anran** analyse the role of Chinese SOEs and their investment in Africa. The authors aim to help understand the complexity of issues concerning Chinese SOEs and clarify the misconceptions about them. The authors discuss Chinese investment in Africa in general and Chinese SOEs in particular. The concerns and benefits of investment by Chinese SOEs and the impacts of their practice are assessed. The authors explore the regulatory challenges for both China (as the home State of investors) and African countries (as host States of foreign investment). Further action of the Chinese side is examined with a discussion on China's domestic reform and the implication of the BRI. The authors argue that the enhanced Sino-African cooperation and the corresponding regulation of Chinese overseas investment are necessary for both sides' sustainable development and interests.

In Chap. 28 titled 'Policy Framework on Procurement of SOEs in China', **TU Xinquan** and **SHI Dingsha** submit that SOEs are an essential pillar of the Chinese economy, accounting for almost half of the total output of China. The internal procurement management level of SOEs has a decisive influence on their competitiveness and development. Procurement activities of SOEs are characterised by numerous projects, large scale of funds, and broad influence. They have a leading and exemplary role in strengthening macro-control, cultivating a fair competition market system and promoting the standardisation of markets. With China's economic system development and improvement, SOEs have accelerated operating mechanisms and development approaches. They innovate procurement models, improve internal control systems and actively explore to promote the specialisation, informatisation and centralisation of bidding and procurement, which have achieved apparent achievements. However, some problems are also exposed. The authors review and comb the development of SOE-procurement. The authors summarise the laws, regulations, and industry standards related to procurement. The authors also analyse the current problems and prospects of state-owned enterprise procurement in the background of the supply side structural reforms and the further expansion of opening up.

In Chap. 29 titled 'Port and Rail Investments: Reform of Chinese Regulations, Paradigm Shift of Chinese State-Controlled Entities and Global Freedom of Investments', **Carlos K. L. Li** aims to fill in the gaps in previous legal research conducted with Prof. Chaisse in 2017. These gaps include the reform on Chinese inbound foreign investment regimes for reciprocal market access of other jurisdictions, the latest corporate practices of SCEs regarding enhancing transparency and accountability and the US and EU's compliance with WTO's GATS Mode 3 and various OECD guidelines. In the context of outbound FDIs in port and rail infrastructures, this research focuses on how Chinese SCEs interact with foreign jurisdictions regarding freedom of investments and national security. Recently, many host states such as the US and EU adhere to protectionism to counteract Chinese FDIs for national security or public interest. This act is entirely contrary to freedom of investments conventionally upheld by the global community. In response to this new phenomenon, China has carried out a series of reforms on its regulations to create a more favourable environment for its port and rail FDIs. Further, the paradigm of SCEs has started to move towards higher transparency and greater accountability by complying with specific international rules such as IMF's Santiago Principles and OECD Guidelines on Corporate Governance of State-owned Enterprises and some private practices. With these paradigm shifts of regulations and SCEs, host states adopt different approaches to Chinese port and rail FDIs. In the context of port and rail FDIs, the author provides an insight into (1) reform of Chinese regulations, (2) paradigm shift of SCEs, and (3) global freedom of investments.

In Chap. 30 titled 'Chinese Enterprises and Investments in the Arctic: Implications for the Development of the Polar Silk Road', **Vasily Erokhin** and **GAO Tianming** submit that China has identified the Arctic as a region of growing scientific, economic, and political concern In the past years. China is a non-Arctic state and still has considerable national interests in the Arctic, specifically in resources, shipping, research, and international collaboration. The Arctic policy approved in 2018 demonstrates that new China's initiative of the Polar Silk Road is aimed at the exploration of the possibilities of opening the Arctic passages as alternative routes for the BRI, involvement in the infrastructure construction in the High North, and expansion of 'win-win' polar partnerships with Arctic states, primarily, Russia and Nordic countries. Chinese enterprises are encouraged to participate in joint investment projects in the Arctic, extraction of hydrocarbons and minerals, and infrastructure development. China invests in developing oil, gas, mineral resources and other non-fossil energies, fishing and tourism, and other projects in the region. In this study, the authors overview Chinese foreign direct investments across various sectors in Nordic countries and Russia, analyse the existing challenges and problems for China and recipient economies and attempt to develop the solutions for the effective China-Russia and China-Nordic investment collaboration in the light of existing regulatory frameworks and widespread economic, social, and political perceptions surrounding China's emerging role in the Arctic.

The Regulatory Framework of State Capitalism: Laws, Treaties, and Contracts

The Latest Regulatory Regime of SOEs Under International Trade Treaties

Yingying Wu

1 Introduction

State-/government-controlled commercial enterprises (SOEs) that produce goods or services are in an extent number globally. Looking at the data of SOEs' number, value, size, sector and country distribution, it can be found that SOEs are pervasive globally.[1] SOEs' presence in global markets nowadays is expanding by trade and investment.[2] Concerns arise accordingly relating to SOEs' existence, SOEs' behaviour, SOEs' receiving non-commercial assistance and SOEs' transparency. This essay will examine how SOEs are treated in past decades and how regulations on SOEs evolve in recent years.

[1] *See* Grzegorz Kwiatkowski & Pawel Augustynowicz, "State-owned Enterprises in the Global Economy-Analysis Based on Fortune Global 500 List" (Conference "Managing Intellectual Capital and Innovation for Sustainable and Inclusive Society", Bari, 27–29 May 2015 <http://www.toknowpress.net/ISBN/978-961-6914-13-0/papers/ML15-353.pdf>.

[2] Max Büge, Matias Egeland, Przemyslaw Kowalski, Monika Sztajerowska, "State-owned Enterprises in the Global Economy: Reason for Concern?" (*VOX: CEPR's Policy Portal*, 2 May, 2013) <https://voxeu.org/article/state-owned-enterprises-global-economy-reason-concern>.

Y. Wu (✉)
China University of Political Science and Law, Beijing, China
e-mail: wyyfada@163.com

J. Chaisse et al. (eds.), *Regulation of State-Controlled Enterprises*, International Law and the Global South, https://doi.org/10.1007/978-981-19-1368-6_2

2 Traditional Regulations

2.1 *Global Regulations: GATT and WTO*

There are no explicit rules governing SOEs in the early GATT nor WTO. Some rules may be found relevant relating to SOEs, such as rules on state trading and subsidies. However, they do not directly address the issue of SOEs and their behaviour. Although non-commercial assistance granted to SOEs could be partially caught by rules on subsidies in GATT and WTO, subsidies are regulated to the extent that they undermine negotiated tariff commitments under the GATT, and these rules do not distinguish SOEs from privately owned/controlled enterprises (POEs).[3] The GATT/WTO assumes that private firms are primary players in international trade, rather than state enterprises.[4] Hence, special rules are levied on state trading.

2.1.1 Subsidies Rules

Beginning in 1943, delegations had started negotiations on subsidies. Throughout the first preparatory meeting held in London in 1946,[5] the 1947 Geneva Conference, the Geneva draft GATT Article XVI, the 1954–55 review session, the Subsidies Code generated by the Tokyo Round negotiation (1973–9)[6] and in the end, the Agreement on the Subsidies and Countervailing Measures (the "SCM Agreement") came into being.

The following rules partially catch non-commercial assistance granted to SOEs in the WTO. In the area of trade in goods, Article III (8) (b) of GATT provides that subsidies are an exception to the national treatment obligation. The WTO sets a special rule on subsidies provided in the SCM Agreement as well as Article XVI of GATT, Note to Article XVI in the Annexes,[7] and Article VI about countervailing duties. The SCM Agreement is a *lex specialis* in relation to GATT Articles VI and XVI.[8]

Upon the SCM Agreement, subsidies are defined as a "financial contribution by a government or a public body that confers a benefit and is specific", or "there is any

---

[3] Douglas Irwin, Petros Mavroidis & Alan Sykes, *The Genesis of the GATT* (CUP 2008), 157–161.

[4] Andreas F. Lowenfeld, *International Economic Law* (2nd edn OUP 2008), 24–5.

[5] It was held by the UN Preparatory Committee for the International Conference on Trade and Employment. The documentation for the conference was published by the Economic and Social Council of the United Nations document series E/PC/T, there are several committees, and one committee was for GATT <https://www.wto.org/gatt_docs/1946_50.htm>.

[6] Agreement on Interpretation and Application of Articles VI, XVI and XXIII of the General Agreement on Tariffs and Trade (the Subsidies Code) (5 April 1979) MTN/NTM/W/236 <https://www.wto.org/gatt_docs/English/SULPDF/91990092.pdf>.

[7] Annex I, Ad Art. XVI of GATT.

[8] John H. Jackson, *The World Trading System: Law and Policy of International Economic Relations* (2nd edn, MIT Press 1997), 290.

form of income or price support in the sense of Article XVI of GATT 1994".[9] The provisions are all applicable to subsidies granted to any recipient including SOEs given that it does not distinguish SOEs from POEs among recipients.

However, the SCM Agreement is not applicable to trade in services,[10] in which Article XV of GATS prescribes negotiation obligations for Members to develop multilateral disciplines to avoid trade-distortive effects of subsidies. Members have the obligation to exchange information on all subsidies to their domestic service suppliers related to trade in services and also have the consultation obligations. To date, there are no new rules on subsidies in the areas of trade in service.[11] To that end, there are no rules relating to non-commercial assistance granted to SOEs that are services suppliers.

As for trade-related investment, the TRIMs Agreement, which is the WTO agreement regarding investment measures related to trade in goods, does not have rules on subsidies.[12] The TRIMS Agreement is essentially about the national treatment obligation and general elimination of quantitative restrictions.[13] Hence, non-commercial assistance granted SOEs who compete with foreign investments related to trade in goods are subject to rules that are similar to those applicable to trade in goods. In contrast, non-commercial assistance granted to SOEs, who compete with foreign investments related to trade in services, may fall out of disciplines of the WTO.[14]

In addition to that, it is yet under discussion on whether "public body" in the provision relating to the subject of subsidies or the givers of subsidies confronts with SOEs. However, cases in the Dispute Settlement Mechanism of the WTO has addressed this issue to some extent. One view is that a SOE could be deemed as a public body as the latter is defined "any entity that is controlled by the government". On the contrary, the Appellant Body rejected this view. It held that a public body is an entity that has been invested with governmental authority, and SOEs are not per se public bodies depending on a case-by-case analysis of the nature and behaviour of SOEs in question. Hence, SOEs as givers of non-commercial assistance to other SOEs are largely out of the hoop of the WTO.

---

[9] Art. 1.1(a)(2) of the SCM Agreement.

[10] Art. 1 of the SCM Agreement expressly refers to purchases of goods but omits any reference to purchases of services, *see* Panel Report, US — Large Civil Aircraft (2nd Complaint), para. 7.968.

[11] Alan O. Sykes, "The Limited Economic Case for Subsidies Regulation" (2015) E15 Initiative, International Centre for Trade and Sustainable Development (ICTSD) and World Economic Forum <http://e15initiative.org/wp-content/uploads/2015/09/E15-Subsidies-Sykes-FINAL.pdf>.

[12] The Agreement on Trade-Related Investment Measures (the "TRIMs Agreement").

[13] Art. 2 of the TRIMs Agreement.

[14] Yingying Wu, *Reforming WTO Rules on State-Owned Enterprises—In the Context of SOEs Receiving Various Advantages* (Springer 2019), 159.

2.1.2 Rules Regarding State Trading

GATT negotiators initially focused on cartels and restrictive business practices.[15] In the London Conference, Article 32 of the London Draft dealt with state monopolies of individual products and Article 33 dealt with the extraordinary case of complete state monopolies of import trade.[16] The New York Conference added a provision proposed by the US providing that "The charging by a state enterprise of different prices for its sales of a product in different markets, domestic or foreign, is not precluded by the provision of the Article, provided that such different prices are charged for commercial reasons".[17] It remains in Article XVII of the GATT.[18] Overall, the GATT rules were fairly limited in their effect on STEs.[19]

SOEs that are granted exclusive trading rights or a monopoly of trading with respect to goods are subject to GATT Article XVII, which provides that "Each contracting party undertakes that if it establishes or maintains a State enterprise, wherever located, or grants to any enterprise, formally or in effect, exclusive or special privileges…". Hence, Article XVII of GATT 1994 allows the existence of monopolies and grants of exclusive rights in respect of exportation and importation. Nevertheless, Article XVII:3 provides a negotiation obligation to reduce such obstacles caused by state trading, as it recognizes that enterprises granted exclusive rights or monopolies might be operated to create severe obstacles to trade. Under Article XVII:1(a) and (b), Members are required to undertake that their STEs shall "act in a manner consistent with general principles of non-discriminatory treatment prescribed in this Agreement…" and undertake that STEs shall "make purchases or sales solely in accordance with commercial considerations". GATT Article II:4 further provides that a Member that has an import monopoly "shall ensure that its tariff concessions are not violated via import monopoly power".[20] In addition, Article XVII:4 imposes the transparency obligation for Members about the existence of STEs and relevant products subject to them.[21] The WTO Understanding on the Interpretation of Article

---

[15] Douglas Irwin, Petros Mavroidis and Alan Sykes, *The Genesis of the GATT* (CUP 2008), 60.

[16] 'Report of the First Session of the London Preparatory Committee of the United Nations Conference on Trade and Employment' (London Draft, October 1946) UN Document E/PC/T/33.

[17] In the footnote, paragraph 1 (e), Art. 31, Report of the Drafting Committee of the Preparatory Committee of the UN Conference on Trade and Employment, UN Document E/PC/T/34 (Lake Success, NY, 5 Mar. 1947) (New York Draft) <https://www.wto.org/gatt_docs/1946_50.htm>, <https://www.wto.org/gatt_docs/English/SULPDF/92290038.pdf>.

[18] The Interpretative Note Ad Art. XVII of GATT.

[19] Yingying Wu (n 14), 47–48.

[20] Kyle Bagwell and Robert W. Staiger, *The Economics of the World Trading System* (MIT 2002), 149.

[21] In the case of an import monopoly of a product, which is not the subject to a concession under Art. II, Art. XVII (4)(b) provides a notification obligation of the import mark-up or the resale price, on the request of another Member.

XVII of the GATT 1994 provides mechanism for notification, including that notification of any support or benefits provided to STEs that can influence the level of imports or exports.[22]

In the area of trade in service, GATS allows the grants of service monopolies and exclusive rights for service areas without a market-access commitment. In services areas with a market-access commitment, XVI:2 (a) of GATS prohibits limitations on the number of service suppliers, whether in the form of numerical quotas, monopolies, or exclusive service suppliers in sectors where market-access commitments are undertaken.[23] However, this is about limitations on foreign service suppliers, rather than prohibiting granting domestic monopolies and exclusive rights to domestic SOEs. To that end, foreign service suppliers may confront with SOEs who are granted domestic monopolies or exclusive rights.[24]

SOEs that have been granted monopolies or exclusive service rights are partially subject to Article VIII of GATS.[25] Specifically, Article VIII (1) of GATS provides that "a monopoly supplier or exclusive service supplier may not act in a manner inconsistent with a member's MFN obligations and specific commitments regarding market access and national treatment".[26] As for the obligation of specific commitments on NT and market access that shall be observed by the monopoly supplier or exclusive service suppliers, the rules only concern service sectors where specific commitments are undertaken. However, the number of service sectors subject to commitments is limited for many WTO Members.

To the extent that Article VIII (1) of GATS only concerns "supply of the monopoly service", a monopoly's behaviour in its input market is not disciplined.[27] Taking the production and distribution of energy and communications services as examples, the monopoly or exclusive service suppliers might be the only consumer exclusively of some inputs. Lacking in competition in the inputs market, monopoly or exclusive suppliers may utilize their bargaining power to purchase inputs at prices lower than normal prices, thereby getting a cost advantage in their primary market.[28]

---

[22] The Working Party is set up on behalf of the Council for Trade in Goods to review notifications and counter-notifications through questionnaires. Membership of the Working Party shall be open to all Members indicating their wish to serve on it. *See* paragraph 5 of the Understanding on the Interpretation of Art. XVII of the GATT 1994; The Working Party reviews the questionnaires associated with the notifications. The questionnaire requires that all exclusive or special rights or privileges granted to the STE, as well as any other support or assistance provided by the government, are to be specified. *See* WTO "Technical Information on State Trading Enterprises" <https://www.wto.org/english/tratop_e/statra_e/statra_info_e.htm>.

[23] Para 2 of Art. XVI of GATS.

[24] Yingying Wu (n 14), 160–61.

[25] Arts. XXVIII (h) and VIII:5 of GATS.

[26] Art. VIII of GATS.

[27] Aaditya Mattoo, "Dealing with Monopolies and State Enterprises: WTO rules for Goods and Services", in Thomas Cottier and Petros C. Mavroidis (eds) *State Trading in the Twenty-First Century* (University of Michigan Press 1998), 37–70, 39.

[28] ibid. 37–38.

In addition, Article VIII (2) of GATS disciplines the field where the entity in question competes with other service suppliers outside the field of its monopoly, provided that the field of service outside the monopoly service is subject to specific commitments in its schedule.[29] It prohibits cross-subsidization for monopoly service suppliers, i.e. transferring advantages of the monopoly in the reserved sector to services outside the scope of its monopoly rights.[30]

2.2 *Regional Regulations: The European Community Rules*

In terms of the existence of SOEs, Article 345 of TFEU stipulates the neutrality of property ownership.[31] To that end, the existence of SOEs is permitted. In integrating markets in the European countries, SOEs and grants of various advantages came to be partially caught by the competition rules on state aid and public undertakings with exclusive rights.[32]

2.2.1 State Aids Rules

As for non-commercial assistance granted to SOEs, state aid is prohibited unless authorized.[33] Article 107 (1) regulates "any provision of state resources in any form whatsoever which distorts or threatens to distort competition by favouring certain undertakings or the production of certain goods".[34] Article 107 (2) provides exceptions for automatically allowing three types of state aids.[35] Article 107 (3) is about situations under which state aid may be authorized.[36] As for the remedy, the illegal aid must be withdrawn from the recipient with potential exceptions.[37] Hence, rules on state aid are applicable to non-commercial assistance granted to SOEs, regardless of their ownership or controllers.[38]

---

[29] Jacques H. J. Bourgeois, "EC Rules on State Monopolies and Public Undertakings: Any Relevance for the WTO?" in Thomas Cottier and Petros C. Mavroidis (eds) *State Trading in the Twenty-First Century* (University of Michigan Press, 1998) 161–180, 173–174.

[30] Yingying Wu (n 14), 163.

[31] Art. 345 of TFEU (Art. 222 of ECT).

[32] For a brief introduction of rules of EU, *see* OECD, "State Owned Enterprises and the Principle of Competitive Neutrality, Policy Roundtables", DAF/COMP(2009)37, (2009), 51–52.

[33] Arts. 107 and 108 of TFEU.

[34] Art. 107.1 of TFEU.

[35] Art. 107. 2 of TFEU.

[36] Art. 107.3 of TFEU.

[37] *See* George Bermann, Roger Goebel, William Davey and Eleanor Fox, *Cases and Materials on European Union Law* (3rd edn, West Academic Publishing 2010), 1085; Bourgeois (n 29), 165.

[38] Yingying Wu (n 14), 50–51.

2.2.2 Public Undertakings Rules

Concerning monopolies or exclusive rights granted to SOEs, Article 106 on public undertakings granted special or exclusive rights and Article 37 on state monopolies of a commercial character are relevant.[39] The first issue is applicability. Article 106 provides broad definition of public undertakings, i.e. "any entity that carries out economic activities, where the state exercises some degree of control through holding the majority of the share capital or the votes or having the right to appoint the majority of the seats in the executive organ of the entity",[40] which can capture SOEs to some extent. Even if SOEs fall outside the scope of public undertakings, SOEs with special or exclusive rights can be subject to Article 106. Article 37 can reach out to grants of monopolies to SOEs as long as the SOEs are of a commercial character.[41]

Second, grants of monopolies or exclusive rights to SOEs are allowed according to Article 37 and Article 106 of the TFEU pertaining trade in goods. It might be inferred that the grants of monopolies to SOEs are allowed given that the obligation of "adjustment" in Article 37 is only limited to non-discrimination.[42] Nevertheless, those provisions have been interpreted by case law more widely beyond prohibiting discrimination.[43] Meanwhile, the grants of monopolies or exclusive rights may be incompatible with Article 106 if Article 106 (1) is taken together with other provisions in the Treaty, given that Article 106 (1) refers to "other provisions in the Treaty". Hence, combining Article 106 (1) with other provisions like competition rules, such as Article 102 of TFEU on the prohibition on abuses of dominant position by an undertaking or undertakings, it was held that the grants of exclusive rights or monopolies were incompatible with Article 106 if such grants can inevitably induce the undertaking to abuse its dominant position, even in the absence of actual abusive behaviour.[44] Combining Article 106 (1) with Articles 34 and 35 on the free movement of goods, the grants of monopolies or exclusive rights of importation or exportation may constitute a restriction of trade in goods with effects equivalent to

---

[39] Art. 106 of TFEU (ex. Art. 86 TEC, ex. Article 90 Treaty of Rome).

[40] The ECJ confirmed the Commission's decision that any undertaking over which the public authorities directly or indirectly exercise a dominant influence is a public undertaking. *See France, Italy and United Kingdom v. Commission*, joint cases 188 to 190/88, ECR 1982 p. 2545, ECLI:EU:C:1982:257, Judgement of 6 July 1982, 26; Commission Directive 80/723 O.J. 1980 L 197/35; Bourgeois (n 29) 164.

[41] Yingying Wu (n 14), 51.

[42] Art. 37 of TFEU (ex. Art. 31 TEC).

[43] For instance, it has been seen how import monopolies are contrary to Art. 37. *See* Bourgeois (n 29) 169.

[44] Art. 102 of TFEU (ex. Art. 82 TEC); United Brads Company en United Brands Continentaal BV tegen Commissie van de Europese Gemeenschappen. European Court Reports 1978-00207, (United Brands [1978] ECR 207), ECLI identifier: ECLI:EU:C:1978:22 (2 Feb 1978) <http://eur-lex.europa.eu/legal-content/NL/ALL/?uri=CELEX:61976CJ0027>; Petros C. Mavroidis and Patrick A. Messerlin, "Has Article 90 ECT Prejudged the Status of Property Ownership?" in Thomas Cottier and Petros C. Mavroidis (eds) *State Trading in the Twenty-First Century* (University of Michigan Press 1998), 345–360, 351; Bourgeois (n 29), 171.

those of quantitative restrictions, and hence violate Article 106 (1).[45] Similarly for trade in services, Article 106 allows grants of monopolies or exclusive rights to SOEs in services while such grants may be challenged if Article 106 are applied together with Article 56 on the free movement of services to the extent that a restriction on trade in services is found.[46]

Third, SOEs with monopolies or exclusive rights are subject to competition rules, non-discrimination rules and free movement rules.[47] What's more, states that give monopolies or exclusive rights to SOEs should not violate their obligations under free movement rules, competition rules and non-discrimination rules through such grants.[48] Article 106 (2) provides an exception where the performance of the special task assigned to the undertaking will be obstructed. Nevertheless, this exception is strictly restricted by the ECJ.[49] Looking at the jurisprudence, the derogation under Article 106 (2) is not available in cases where grants of monopolies or exclusive rights are found to be in violation of rules on free movement. In contrast, the derogation under Article 106 (2) is available in cases where such grants are in violation of Article 37.[50] It could be found that rules on free movement is the cornerstone that is hard to derogate.

2.3 Commonalities

In summary, first, early GATT, WTO and EU rules do not directly confront with the issue of SOEs. The definition of SOEs is not given within the abovementioned rules. To that end, SOEs per se are not to be regulated. In other words, the existence of SOEs is allowed as along with POEs. SOEs are not treated differently from POEs. Second, non-commercial assistance, either reframed as subsides within the WTO framework or as state aids within the EU framework, are regulated to some extent as non-commercial assistance undermines states commitment to tariff concession as well as non-commercial assistance creates unfair competition. However, the rules regarding

---

[45] Art. 34 (ex. Art. 28 TEC); Art. 35 (ex. Art. 29 TEC). Andre Sapir, "The Role of Articles 37 and 90 ECT in the Integration of EC Markets: The Case of Utilities", in Thomas Cottier and Petros C. Mavroidis (eds) *State Trading in the Twenty-First Centur* (University of Michigan Press 1998), 231–244, 237; Bourgeois (n 29), 169.

[46] Art. 56 of TFEU, ex. Article 49 of TEC; Elliniki Radiophonia Tileorassi [1991] ECR I-2925; M. Kerf, "The Impact of EC Law on Public Service Concessions", (1995) 18 (85) World Competition 101.

[47] ibid. 167.

[48] Sapir (n 45), 237.

[49] The principle of proportionality would be applied to such exemption that the task granted would be impossible to carry out if the Treaty is applied, not merely more difficult to carry out. *See* Bourgeois (n 29), 165–166.

[50] Judgement of the Court of 10 July 1984, Campus Oil Limited and others v. Minister for Industry and Energy and others, Campus Oil [1984] ECR 2742, at 19, Case 72/83. *European Court Reports 1984-02727*, ECLI identifier: ECLI:EU:C:1984:256, <http://eur-lex.europa.eu/legal-content/EN/TXT/?uri=CELEX%3A61983CJ0072>; Bourgeois (n 29) at 169–70.

subsidies and state aids do not distinguish SOEs from POEs when they are receivers. Neither the emphasis was made regarding whether it is to be disciplined that SOEs as givers of non-commercial assistance to other SOEs, in the replacement of governments as givers. In fact, the situation where SOEs give non-commercial assistance to other entities, especially other SOEs, although it has generated great controversy and discussion, rules within the GATT, WTO and EU do not lay disciplines in this regard.

Third, with respect to monopolies or exclusive rights granted to SOEs, GATT rules regarding STEs disciplined them to some extent over time all the way to the WTO. However, it only concerns importation and exportation by focusing on any entity with a monopoly or exclusive rights on importation or exportation. SOEs with monopoly or exclusive right of production or distribution are out of regulatory coverage. In addition, when it comes to the behaviour of SOEs, SOEs are treated the same as POEs. POEs and SOEs are free to carry out any conduct subject to certain behaviour regulations (such as acting solely according to commercial consideration) if they qualify as state trading within the WTU rules or public undertakings within the EU rules. For instance, the EU targets the behaviour issue in the competition law framework without picking up SOEs in particular.

3 New Regulations in Recent Years

Recent free trade agreements (FTAs), particularly those concluded by the US, go in the direction that is much different from the paths taken by the GATT, WTO and EU, in terms of rules relating to SOEs. An earlier version of this new trend or direction can be traced back to the US–Singapore FTA, which was concluded in 2003. Later on, regional FATs negotiations initiated by the US and EU, like the Trans-Pacific Partnership (TPP) negotiation, renegotiation of NAFTA, US–Euro negotiation, EU–Vietnam FTA, US–Japan negotiation, largely modelled the US–Singapore FTA with further development in terms of rules regarding SOEs.

3.1 US–Singapore FTA

The US–Singapore FTA was one of the earlier versions that the US is pursuing for its future FTAs. It has a chapter on anticompetitive business conduct, designated monopolies and government enterprises. Rules related to anticompetitive business conduct are actually competition rules, which will not be elaborated here since competition rules apply to all enterprises regardless of enterprises' ownership or controllers. Rules related to designated monopolies and government enterprises are relevant here, given that they do have a connection with SOEs.

In respect of government enterprises, the US–Singapore FTA defines government enterprise, while the definitions are different for the two sides. For the US, a government enterprise means an enterprise owned or controlled through ownership interests by that Party. For Singapore, a government enterprise means an enterprise in which that Party has effective influence. As for what constitutes an effective influence, it also gives a Chart illustrating an entity in which the government or government entity collectively own more than 20% shares will be presumed to be a government enterprise. It better explains the definition of "effective influence", which exists where the government and its government enterprises, alone or in combination: (a) own more than 50% of the voting rights of an entity; or (b) can exercise substantial influence over the composition of the board of directors or any other managing body of an entity, to determine the outcome of decisions on the strategic, financial, or operating policies or plans of an entity, or otherwise to exercise substantial influence over the management or operation of an entity. Where the government and its government enterprises, alone or in combination, own 50% or less, but more than 20%, of the voting securities of the entity and own the largest block of voting rights of such entity, there is a rebuttable presumption that effective influence exists. Annex 12A illustrates how the analysis of effective influence should proceed.

To that end, a government enterprise on the Singapore side covers all SOEs in question here. The existence of SOEs is under attack. The US–Singapore FTA prescribes that Singapore shall continue reducing, to eliminate substantially its aggregate ownership and other interests that confer effective influence in entities organized under the laws of Singapore, take into account, in the timing of individual divestments, the state of relevant capital markets. In summary, Singapore is under obligation to gradually reduce the presence of SOEs.

The US–Singapore FTA also imposes behaviour obligations on government enterprises. On the US side, it assumes the obligation to ensure that any government enterprise accords non-discriminatory treatment in the sale of its goods or services to covered investment. On the Singapore side, it assumes the obligation to ensure that any government enterprise acts sole in accordance with commercial considerations in its purchase or sale of goods or services, does not, either directly or indirectly, including through its dealings with its parent, subsidiaries, or other enterprises with common ownership: (A) enter into agreements among competitors that restrain competition on price or output or allocate customers for which there is no plausible efficiency justification, or (B) engage in exclusionary practices that substantially lessen competition in a market in Singapore to the detriment of consumers. In addition, it imposes the "non-interference from government" obligation by providing that Singapore shall take no action or attempt in any way, directly or indirectly, to influence or direct decisions of its government enterprises, including through the exercise of any rights or interests conferring effective influence over such enterprises, except in a manner consistent with this Agreement. However, Singapore may exercise its voting rights in government enterprises in a manner that is not inconsistent with this Agreement.

Concerning monopolies, first, it allows a monopoly's existence by prescribing that "nothing in this chapter shall be construed to prevent a Party from designating a monopoly".[51] Hence, a monopoly may be privately owned or a government monopoly. The FTA also defines government monopoly by providing that a government monopoly means a monopoly that is owned or controlled through ownership interests, by the national government of a Party or by another such monopoly. It imposes on monopolies regardless of privately owned monopoly or government monopoly the obligation to act solely in accordance with commercial considerations in its purchase or sale of the monopoly good or service in the relevant market, the obligation to provides non-discriminatory treatment to covered investments, to goods of the other Party, and to service suppliers of the other Party in its purchase or sale of the monopoly good or service in the relevant market, and the obligation not to use its monopoly position to engage, either directly or indirectly, including through its dealings with its parent, subsidiaries, or other enterprises with common ownership, in anticompetitive practices in a non-monopolized market in its territory that adversely affect covered investments.[52]

Last, the transparency obligation in the US–Singapore FTA is outstanding. It is provided that Singapore shall: (i) at least annually, make public a consolidated report that details for each covered entity: (A) the percentage of shares and the percentage of voting rights that Singapore and its government enterprises cumulatively own; (B) a description of any special shares or special voting or other rights that Singapore or its government enterprises hold, to the extent different from the rights attached to the general common shares of such entity; (C) the name and government title(s) of any government official serving as an officer or member of the board of directors; and (D) its annual revenue or total assets, or both, depending on the basis on which the enterprise qualifies as a covered entity. (ii) on receipt from the US of a request regarding a specific enterprise. Furthermore, at the other Party's request, each Party shall make available public information concerning government enterprises and designated monopolies, public or private. Requests for such information shall indicate the entities involved, specify the particular products and markets concerned and include some indicia that these entities may be engaging in practices that may hinder trade or investment between the Parties.[53]

In summary, Singapore is under obligation to gradually reduce the presence of SOEs. While Monopolies are allowed to be granted, it does not distinguish between trade in goods and trade in services in terms of obligations imposed on monopoly or government enterprises, departing from the path the WTO takes for extensive rules for trade in goods while less burdensome on trade in services. Except for the obligation to act solely in accordance with commercial considerations and to provide non-discriminatory treatment, the US–Singapore FTA expands the behaviour obligation for monopolies, such as no abuse of monopoly, i.e. the obligation not to use its monopoly position to engage in anticompetitive practices in a non-monopolized

[51] Art. 12.3 of US–Singapore FTA.

[52] Art. 12.3 of US–Singapore FTA.

[53] Art. 12.5 of US–Singapore FTA.

market in its territory that adversely affects covered investments. Furthermore, it lists detailed obligations for each party's government enterprises, i.e. the US assumes the obligation to ensure government enterprises accord non-discriminatory treatment, and Singapore assumes the obligation to ensure its government enterprises act solely in accordance with commercial considerations and does not restrain competition by cartel agreement or exclusionary practices.

Additionally, it imposes the "non-interference from government" obligation by providing that Singapore shall take no action or attempt in any way, directly or indirectly, to influence or direct decisions of its government enterprises. It is unique in that different definitions apply to respective parties, i.e. the definition of government enterprises for the US is a little bit different from that for Singapore. It is also unique that parties assume different obligations. Given that the US–Singapore FTA is a bilateral treaty, it is not abnormal that special attention was paid to government enterprises and monopolies in Singapore at that time of 2003. The US-Singapore FTA constitutes a model for future US FTAs.

3.2 TPP and CPTPP

In the past decades, in the light of Chinese SOEs being actively engaging in regional and international markets, concerns arise in regional rules negotiations, particularly the US, which pushed hard on rules on SOEs on the Trans-Pacific Partnership (TPP) negotiations.[54] In the TPP negotiations, there were proposals from its members about disciplines on SOEs.[55] Ultimately, the TPP was concluded with a chapter on SOEs, i.e. Chap. 17 titled State-owned Enterprises and Designated Monopolies.[56] This chapter has provisions regarding non-commercial assistance to SOEs or given by

[54] The US industry wants rules in a TPP agreement to ensure that SOEs do not "nullify or impair" market access in the party's home market, the markets of other TPP countries, or in third-country markets. *See* Ian F. Fergusson, Mark A. McMinimy and Brock R. Williams, "The Trans-Pacific Partnership (TPP) Negotiations and Issues for Congress", Congressional Research Service, 7-5700 www.crs.gov R42694 (20 March 2015) <https://www.fas.org/sgp/crs/row/R42694.pdf>; William Krist, edited with an introduction by Kent HugHes, "Negotiations for a Trans-Pacific Partnership Agreement", Program on America and the Global Economy Woodrow Wilson International Center for Scholars, ISBN: 978-1-938027-08-6 <https://www.wilsoncenter.org/sites/default/files/PAGE_TPP_REPORT.pdf>.

[55] The US's proposals and position can be found in Office of the US Trade Representative, "State-Owned Enterprises and Competition Policy: SOEs: Leveling the Playing field for American Workers through Fair Competition", <https://ustr.gov/trade-agreements/free-trade-agreements/trans-pacific-partnership/tpp-chapter-chapter-negotiating-7>; For a general discussion about SOEs in the context of TPP Agreement Negotiations, *see* Tsuyoshi Kawase, "Trans-Pacific Partnership Negotiations and Rulemaking to Regulate State-Owned Enterprises". (29 July 2014) <http://voxeu.org/article/trans-pacific-partnership-negotiations-and-rulemaking-regulate-state-owned-enterprises>.

[56] Chapter 17 of the TPP Agreement.

SOEs; obligations imposed on SOEs' behaviour, such as non-discriminatory treatment and the requirement to act in the light of commercial considerations; transparency of SOEs; designated monopolies, particularly state monopolies; and various exceptions and long transitional periods. These rules were drafted with an eye on Chinese SOEs, although China was not a party to the TPP negotiations.[57]

TPP draft allows the existence of SOEs and monopolies without imposing obligations on parties to reduce the presence of SOEs nor eliminating shares hold by the government in an SOE, by providing that "Nothing in this Chapter shall be construed to prevent a Party from: (a) establishing or maintaining a state enterprise or a state-owned enterprise, or (b) designating a monopoly".[58] Chapter 17 of the TPP draft defines state-owned enterprises and monopolies, including government monopolies. As for SOEs, it defines that an SOE means an enterprise that is principally engaged in commercial activities in which a Party: (a) directly owns more than 50% of the share capital; (b) controls, through ownership interests, the exercise of more than 50% of the voting rights; or (c) holds power to appoint a majority of members of the board of directors or any other equivalent management body.[59] TPP draft uses the phrase "SOEs" rather than "government enterprises". This definition is narrower than the "effective influence" standard adopted by the US–Singapore FTA for the Singapore side's government enterprise and broader than the scope for the US side's government enterprise in that FTA. It could be found that the US would like to capture more SOEs by referring to them as SOEs with broader coverage rather than government enterprises.

Concerning behaviour regulation, Article 17.4 prescribes non-discriminatory treatment and commercial considerations. It obligates each party to ensure that each of its SOEs, when engaging in commercial activities, acts according to commercial considerations in its purchase or sale of a good or service, except to fulfil any terms of its public service mandate. It also obligates each party shall ensure that each of its SOEs, when engaging in commercial activities, accords non-discriminatory treatment in its purchase and sale of a good or service. As for monopolies, the TPP draft obligates that each party shall ensure that each of its designated monopolies acts in accordance with commercial considerations in its purchase or sale of the monopoly good or service in the relevant market and accords non-discriminatory treatment in its purchase and sale of the monopoly good or service. In addition, each party shall ensure that each of its designated monopolies does not use its monopoly position to engage in, either directly or indirectly, including through its dealings with its parent, subsidiaries or other entities the Party or the designated monopoly owns, anticompetitive practices in a non-monopolized market in its territory that negatively affect

[57] Keith Bradsher, "International Business: Trans-Pacific Partnership's Potential Impact Weighed in Asia and US' *New York Times* (8 July 2015) <http://www.nytimes.com/2015/07/09/business/international/trans-pacific-partnerships-potential-impact-weighed-in-asia-and-us.html?_r=0>; Tuong Lai, 'What Vietnam Must Now Do' *New York Times* (The Opinion Pages), translated by Nguyen Trung Truc from the Vietnamese (6 April 2015) <http://www.nytimes.com/2015/04/07/opinion/what-vietnam-must-now-do.html>.

[58] 17.2.9 of TPP draft.

[59] 17.1 of TPP draft.

trade or investment between the Parties. SOEs and monopolies are allowed to accord differential treatment or refusal of purchase or sale in accordance with commercial considerations.[60]

With respect to non-commercial assistance, provisions in Article 17.6 of the TPP about non-commercial assistance prohibit SOEs from giving non-commercial assistance if it causes adverse effects to the interest of another party, as well as prohibit SOEs from receiving non-commercial assistance from SOEs, state enterprises and states if it causes adverse effects to the interests of another Party, by providing that "No Party shall cause adverse effects to the interests of another Party through the use of non-commercial assistance that it provides, either directly or indirectly, to any of its state-owned enterprises", and "Each Party shall ensure that its state enterprises and state-owned enterprises do not cause adverse effects to the interests of another Party through the use of non-commercial assistance that the state enterprise or state-owned enterprise provides to any of its state-owned enterprises". To that end, it regulates situations of SOEs as givers of non-commercial assistance and SOEs as receivers of non-commercial assistance. In addition, it also extends to SOEs that is a covered investment in the territory of that other Party. It excludes[61] the initial capitalisation of a state-owned enterprise, or the acquisition by a Party of a controlling interest in an enterprise, that is principally engaged in the supply of services within the territory of the Party, as non-commercial assistance by providing that these situations shall be deemed not to cause adverse effects.

However, specific exceptions are permitted by specifying party-specific annexes in Article 17.9 with a list of SOEs or designated monopolies that are not subject to provisions regarding non-discriminatory treatment obligation and commercial consideration as well as non-commercial assistance and transparency requirements. For instance, sub-central SOEs are subject to less regulation.

Apart from that, the TPP draft also provides that SOEs could be sued in domestic courts for civil claims, and administrative bodies shall impartially exercise regulatory discretion regardless of an enterprise being an SOE or a POE.[62] Transparency requirements are also provided in terms of a list of SOEs and designated monopolies, as well as detailed information on request.[63] TPP draft also establishes a committee on SOEs and designated monopolies composed of government representatives of each Party, to function as reviewing and considering the operation and implementation of this chapter regarding SOEs and designated monopolies, consulting, developing cooperative efforts, to promote the principles underlying the disciplines contained in this chapter in the free trade area and to contribute to the development of similar disciplines in other regional and multilateral institutions in which two or more Parties participant.[64] The ambition could be found in this provision that rules regarding SOEs

[60] 17.4 of TPP draft.

[61] 17.7 of TPP draft.

[62] 17.5 of TPP draft.

[63] 17.10 of TPP draft.

[64] Art. 17.12 of TPP draft.

and designated monopolies are intended to be widely adopted by other FTAs and institutions.

The TPP draft is more advanced than the US–Singapore FTA in that it has a more systematic and comprehensive set of rules regulating SOEs and monopolies. The TPP draft was actually stalled after the US exited. Instead, the Comprehensive and Progressive Agreement for Trans-Pacific Partnership (CPTPP) was signed by 11 states and came into effect in 2018. Some provisions in TPP are suspended when it is incorporated into CPTPP. Rules regarding SOEs and designated monopolies remain exactly the same.[65]

3.3 NAFTA and USMCA

The US commenced bilateral trade negotiations with Canada more than 30 years ago, resulting in the US–Canada Free Trade Agreement, which entered into force on 1 January 1989. In 1991, bilateral talks began between US and Mexico, which Canada joined. The NAFTA followed, entering into force on 1 January 1994. Tariffs were eliminated progressively, and all duties and quantitative restrictions, with the exception of those on a limited number of agricultural products traded with Canada, were eliminated by 2008.

NAFTA also includes chapters covering rules of origin, customs procedures, agriculture and sanitary and phytosanitary measures, government procurement, investment, trade in services, protection of intellectual property rights and dispute settlement procedures. The rules of NAFTA have a chapter on monopolies and state enterprises in its Chapter. 15 title "Competition Policy, Monopolies and State Enterprises". Rules are more like a framework without many details, and imposed obligations are much fewer than what has been provided by later FTAs.

Monopolies, either government monopoly or privately owned monopoly designated, are allowed to be in existence under NAFTA. However, written notification is required and endeavour to introduce such conditions on the operation of the monopoly as will minimize or eliminate any nullification or impairment of benefits if the monopoly may affect the interest of persons of another party. Concerning behaviour obligation, NAFTA obligates that each party shall ensure that any monopoly provides non-discriminatory treatment to investments of investors, to goods and service providers of another party in its purchase or sale of the monopoly good or service in the relevant market, and does not use its monopoly position to engage, either directly or indirectly, including through its dealings with its parent, its subsidiary or another enterprise with common ownership, in anticompetitive practices in a non-monopolized market in its territory that adversely affect the investment of an investor of another Party, including through the discriminatory provision of the monopoly good or service, cross-subsidization or predatory conduct. However, no commercial consideration obligation is required.[66]

[65] *See* Annex II-List of Suspended Provisions of the CPTPP.

[66] Art. 1502 of NAFTA.

State enterprises are also allowed to be in existence. NAFTA defines a state enterprise as an enterprise owned or controlled through ownership by a party. NAFTA also gives country-specific definitions of state enterprises, (a) concerning Canada, means a Crown corporation within the meaning of the *Financial Administration Act* (Canada), a Crown corporation within the meaning of any comparable provincial law or equivalent entity that is incorporated under other applicable provincial law; and (b) concerning Mexico, does not include, the Compañía Nacional de Subsistencias Populares (National Company for Basic Commodities) and its existing affiliates, or any successor enterprise or its affiliates, for purposes of sales of maize, beans and powdered milk. It actually provides some exceptions.[67]

Concerning behaviour obligation, NAFTA requires that each party shall ensure that any state enterprise that it maintains or establishes accords non-discriminatory treatment in the sale of its goods or services to investments in the Party's territory of investors of another Party. However, state enterprises are not under the obligation of acting solely in accordance with commercial considerations.[68]

In 2017, US Trade Representative Robert Lighthizer informed Congress that the President intends to commence negotiations with Canada and Mexico concerning NAFTA.[69] The US wanted to incorporate detailed SOEs rules in updated FTAs. The US has pushed to include detailed rules on SOEs found in the TPP to be also in the planned NAFTA renegotiations. The US announced its intent to renegotiate NAFTA and listed objectives for this renegotiation.[70] Among many things, one objective in the list concerns state-owned and controlled enterprises, including the definition of SOEs, ensuring the behaviour of SOEs accords with non-discriminatory treatment and with the requirement to make decisions based on commercial considerations, ensuring additional subsidy disciplines on SOEs, transparency requirements, overcoming evidentiary problems associated with litigation on SOEs, etc.[71] These objectives in the NAFTA renegotiation are similar to the objectives and provisions in the TPP draft. Hence, it was foreseeable that provisions and rules on SOEs in the TPP draft and the US's other FTAs will be largely incorporated in the updated NAFTA. The new US–Mexico–Canada Agreement (USMCA) was signed in November 2018, and NAFTA currently remains in effect. The USMCA can come into effect following the

[67] Annex 1505 of NAFTA.

[68] Art. 1503 of NAFTA.

[69] <https://ustr.gov/trade-agreements/free-trade-agreements/north-american-free-trade-agreement-nafta>.

[70] *See* Office of the US Trade Representative, "USTR: Trump Administration Announces Intent to Renegotiate the North American Free Trade Agreement" (*USTR Press Release*, May 2017) <https://ustr.gov/about-us/policy-offices/press-office/press-releases/2017/may/ustr-trump-administration-announces>.

[71] *See* USTR, "Summary of Objective for the NAFTA Renegotiation", (17 July, 2017), p. 11, <https://ustr.gov/sites/default/files/files/Press/Releases/NAFTAObjectives.pdf>; although Art. 1503 of NAFTA touches SOEs, it leaves much to the hand of the WTO rules. The TPP Agreement may divert some attention from the WTO to elsewhere.

completion of TPA procedures, including a Congressional vote on an implementing bill.[72]

USMCA has a chapter on state-owned enterprises and designated monopolies. Designated monopoly includes privately owned monopoly designated and government monopoly. It also defines a government monopoly, which means to be a monopoly owned or controlled through ownership interests, by a party or by another government monopoly. A state-owned enterprise means an enterprise that is principally engaged in commercial activities, and in which a Party: (a) directly or indirectly owns more than 50% of the share capital, (b) controls, through direct or indirect ownership interests, the exercise of more than 50% of the voting rights, (c) holds power to control the enterprise through any other ownership interest, including indirect or minority ownership, or (d) holds power to appoint a majority of members of the board of directors or any other equivalent management body.[73]

Concerning behaviour obligation, Article 22.4 about non-discriminatory treatment and commercial considerations provides that each party shall ensure that each of its state-owned enterprises when engaging in commercial activities, acts in accordance with commercial considerations and accords non-discriminatory obligations in its purchase or sale of a good or service. These two obligations also apply to monopolies. Each party also assumes the obligation to ensure that each monopoly does not use its monopoly position to engage in either directly or indirectly, including through its dealings with its parent, subsidiaries, or other entities the Party or the designated monopoly owns, anticompetitive practices in a non-monopolized market in its territory that negatively affect trade or investment between the Parties.

Concerning non-commercial assistance, it is slightly different from the TPP draft. USMCA divided non-commercial assistance as a prohibited type, as opposed to adverse effects caused thereof. In the TPP draft, it only concerns non-commercial assistance that causes adverse effects, which means that adverse effects must be proved. USMCA provides that "The following forms of non-commercial assistance, if provided to a state-owned enterprise primarily engaged in the production or sale of goods other than electricity, are prohibited: (a) loans or loan guarantees provided by a state enterprise or state-owned enterprise of a Party to an uncreditworthy state-owned enterprise of that Party; (b) non-commercial assistance provided by a Party or a state enterprise or state-owned enterprise of a Party to a state-owned enterprise of that Party, in circumstances where the recipient is insolvent or on the brink of insolvency, without a credible restructuring plan designed to return the state-owned enterprise within a reasonable period of time to long-term viability; or (c) conversion by a Party or a state enterprise or state-owned enterprise of a Party of the outstanding debt of a state-owned enterprise of that Party to equity, in circumstances where this would be inconsistent with the usual investment practice of a private investor". Rules on the rest type of non-commercial assistance given by SOEs or given to SOEs are similar

---

[72] US-Mexico-Canada Agreement, Office of the US Trade Representative <https://ustr.gov/trade-agreements/free-trade-agreements/united-states-mexico-canada-agreement>.

[73] Art. 22.1 of USMCA.

to that of the TPP draft. In other words, rules regarding non-commercial assistance in USMCA is more stringent than those in TPP/CPTPP.

The party-specific annexes provide exceptions for lists of SOEs or monopolies from certain obligations, such as non-discriminatory treatment obligation, commercial consideration obligation, non-commercial assistance as well as transparency obligations. It is much like provisions in TPP or CPTPP. USMCA also provides jurisdiction to courts over the commercial activities of foreign SOEs.

3.4 Transatlantic Trade and Investment Partnership and EU's FTAs

The Transatlantic Trade and Investment Partnership (T-TIP) is an ambitious, comprehensive, and high-standard trade and investment agreement being negotiated between the US and the European Union (EU). On 25 July 2018, President Trump and European Commission President Juncker issued a joint statement in Washington announcing the formation of an Executive Working Group that will seek to reduce transatlantic barriers to trade, including by working to eliminate non-auto industrial tariffs and non-tariff barriers. On 16 October 2018, US Trade Representative Robert Lighthizer officially notified Congress that the Trump Administration intended to start negotiations following the completion of necessary domestic procedures. This began a congressionally mandated 90-day consultation period under Trade Promotion Authority prior to the launch of negotiations. There have been negotiating objectives and proposals made so far as follows.[74]

The framework regarding State-Owned and Controlled Enterprises (SOEs) is laid out as follows.

(1) Define SOEs based on government ownership or government control through ownership interests, including situations of control through minority shareholding. (2) Retain the ability to support SOEs engaged in providing domestic public services. (3) Ensure that SOEs accord non-discriminatory treatment concerning the purchase and sale of goods and services. (4) Ensure that SOEs act in accordance with commercial considerations concerning the purchase and sale of goods and services. (5) Ensure strong subsidy disciplines applicable to SOEs, beyond the disciplines, set out in the WTO Agreement on Subsidies and Countervailing Measures (SCM Agreement). (6) Require that SOEs not cause harm to the US through the provision of subsidies. (7) Require that SOEs not cause harm to the domestic industry of the US via subsidized SOE investment. (8) Ensure impartial regulation of SOEs, designated monopolies and private companies. (9) Provide jurisdiction to courts over the commercial activities of foreign SOEs. (10) Allow Parties to request information related to the level of government ownership and control of a given enterprise and the extent of government support. (11) Develop a fact-finding mechanism to help overcome the evidentiary

[74] US-EU Trade Agreement Negotiations, USTR US-European Union Negotiations, "Summary of Specific Negotiating Objectives'" (January 2010) <https://ustr.gov/sites/default/files/01.11.2019_Summary_of_U.S.-EU_Negotiating_Objectives.pdf>.

problems associated with litigation on SOEs.[75] This framework is much like that in the TPP.

One of the FTAs entered by the EU that can be a good illustration is the EU–Vietnam Free Trade Agreement. "Vietnam has become the EU's second-biggest trading partner in the Association of Southeast Asian Nations after Singapore and ahead of Malaysia".[76] The EU–Vietnam Free Trade Agreement was signed in 2018.[77] There is a chapter called "State-Owned Enterprises, Enterprises Granted Special Rights, or Privileges and Monopolies" in the draft of the EU–Vietnam FTA. It basically requires SOEs to behave according to the non-discrimination principle and based on commercial considerations. The subsidies rules are embedded in the Chapter of "Competition Policy", which provides the exception of "public policy objective" for providing subsidies. However, it does not have provisions specifically regarding SOEs giving or receiving non-commercial advantages. The wording of subsidies rules and SOE rules in the EU–Vietnam FTA is similar to that in the TPP except that the EU–Vietnam FTA has more exceptions.[78] The EU–Vietnam FTA includes provisions guaranteeing protection of EU exports from counterfeit goods, fair competition between foreign companies and subsidized Vietnamese state-owned enterprises.[79]

3.5 *Commonalities*

In general, rules in the US FTAs, such as US–Singapore FTA, TPP draft, NAFTA, USMCA, T-TIP, have much more regulations on SOEs with an independent chapter on SOEs and designated monopolies with specific exceptions available for this independent chapter. That is the mode on which basis further development are made. The extent of regulating SOEs has become much more durable as compared to GATT, WTO and NAFTA, as well as FTAs concluded decades ago.

The regulatory mode in detail is explained further here. First, the existence of SOEs, as well as the designation of monopolies, is allowed, although transparency is required. One exception is the US–Singapore FTA, while Singapore must reduce shares or effective influence in SOEs. It is largely because Singapore is a developed country, and the obstacle to reducing the presence of SOEs is much less than that in other developing countries, like China, Vietnam, Malaysia, etc. Second, definitions for SOEs and government monopolies are all provided in these FTAs, although definitions vary from one FTA to another. It is more likely that definitions may even be party specific, i.e. definitions of SOEs are different among states at the earlier FTAs,

---

[75] US-European Union Negotiations, 'Summary of Specific Negotiating Objectives' (January 2010) <https://ustr.gov/sites/default/files/01.11.2019_Summary_of_U.S.-EU_Negotiating_Objectives.pdf>.

[76] European Commission, "EU and Vietnam Finalize Trade and Investment Discussion," (26 June 2018) <http://trade.ec.europa.eu/doclib/press/index.cfm?id=1875>.

[77] ibid.

[78] EU–Vietnam Trade and Investment Agreements, Annex 10-a.

[79] Briefing International Agreements in Progress (February 2018) <https://www.europarl.europa.eu/RegData/etudes/BRIE/2018/614702/EPRS_BRI(2018)614702_EN.pdf>.

such as US–Singapore FTA as well as NAFTA. With the passage of time, universal definitions typically apply to all contracting parties. Despite that, one compromise could be found that there is usually a schedule of a party-specific annexe listing SOEs. In other words, each party could propose its particular SOEs or designated monopoly by putting forward a list of names of enterprises. The list of SOEs or designated monopolies is put forward to be subject to obligations prescribed in the FTA or to be exempted from obligations prescribed in the FTA. Gradually, it also could be figured out that the definition of SOEs switch from focusing on ownership to other controller methods, i.e. not only ownership but also voting power and influence in the management board.

The obligations imposed relating to these SOEs and monopolies are that each contracting party shall ensure that each of its SOEs or monopolies to act solely based on commercial considerations and accord non-discriminatory treatment. In addition, as for designated monopolies, the party shall ensure that each of its monopolies does not abuse monopoly and do not engage in anticompetitive practices in a non-monopolized market. The exempted obligations for these particular SOEs or designated monopolies are normally non-discriminatory treatment, commercial considerations and non-commercial assistance. Occasionally, the obligation of transparency is also exempted. There might be exceptions for SOEs owned or controlled by a sub-central level of government or for a designated monopoly designated by a sub-central level of government in some FTAs. Furthermore, the distinctions made between trade in goods and trade in services in terms of regulations on SOEs are fading.

4 Implications and Conclusions

The vast differences or changes could be observed by examining traditional regulations all the way to FTAs nowadays. In general, Rules in the US FTAs, such as US–Singapore FTA, TPP draft, NAFTA, USMCA, T-TIP, have much more regulation on SOEs than traditional FTAs, such as early GATT, WTO and EU. There is no distinction between SOEs and POEs in the WTO or EU rules. The rules in the earlier GATT and WTO do not focus on SOEs in particular. Rules regarding subsidies apply both to private entities that receive subsidies and to SOEs that receive subsidies. However, a FTA has a separate chapter on SOEs and government monopolies nowadays. It seems that FTAs nowadays are going forward in the direction of a universal mode with a slight difference. The standing out of SOEs to be subject to a separate set of rules are more likely to take place in future FTAs in a sense that the existence of SOEs and designated government monopolies are not to be condemned while their behaviour is subject to regulations.

Yingying Wu LLB (CUPL), LLM (UIUC), LLM (NYU) JSD (UIUC).

Global Liberalisation of Public–Private Partnerships (PPPs) as Form of State-Controlled Enterprises (SCEs)

Jędrzej Górski

1 Introduction

Participation in projects related to public infrastructure, energy, other utilities, or any significant public projects carried out by governments and their agencies worldwide is a lucrative business for multinational enterprises spanning their operations across multiple jurisdictions with varying market entry barriers for foreign investors. The incentives and hindrances to participation in such projects by foreign persons could be tied foremost to the level of international liberalisation of government procurement markets. They could well be associated with the level of liberalisation of investment and provision of services in heavily regulated monopolistic or oligopolistic sectors, like utilities. The scale of foreign investment in such sectors also rests on proper protection of investment by foreign persons, along with the position of such persons in the resolution of controversies that might arise between a public and a private partner.

From the international law perspective, the favourable investment climate for public–private partnerships (PPPs) depends on a specific jurisdiction's network of trade-and-investment-related commitments. From the domestic law perspective,

This chapter draws upon the author's original publication also available at https://www.transnational-dispute-management.com/journal-advance-publication-article.asp?key=1836. Reprinted by permission from Maris BV: Maris BV, *Transnational Dispute Management* (TDM, ISSN 1875-4120), "Global Liberalisation of Public-Private Partnerships (PPPs) as Form of State Controlled Enterprises (SCEs)", Jędrzej Górski, Copyright (2000). Please cite accordingly.

The original version of chapter was inadvertently published prematurely, before incorporation of the final corrections, which has now been updated. The correction to this chapter can be found at https://doi.org/10.1007/978-981-19-1368-6_31

J. Górski (✉)
The Department of Asian and International Studies (AIS), City University of Hong Kong, Kowloon Tong, Hong Kong
e-mail: sclavius@gmail.com

J. Chaisse et al. (eds.), *Regulation of State-Controlled Enterprises*, International Law and the Global South, https://doi.org/10.1007/978-981-19-1368-6_3

which shall not be entirely disregarded, this climate hinges on a set of jurisdiction-specific public-law norms. The public-law norms, which regulate the details of the selection process of private partners, are most often interwoven or nested in domestic public procurement laws. Such norms are also perforce convergent across different jurisdictions, complying with the framework imposed by the World Trade Organization's (WTO) Government Procurement Agreement (GPA), and following best procurement and PPP-related practices delineated in the regional procurement models such as the European Union's (EU) directives or the procurement chapter of the Comprehensive and Progressive Agreement for Trans-Pacific Partnership (CPTPP). Less coherent and convergent across various jurisdictions are public-law norms, which modify private-law norms in the fields of contracts and business organisation to reflect the specificity of contractual arrangements or joint ventures (JVs) between private and public partners.

PPPs can take variously structured forms when the participation of private enterprises in government-run projects goes beyond a pure supply of goods and services or the performance of construction works without subsequent management of the completed project. In other words, PPPs come into existence when the participation in government-run projects goes beyond conservatively and narrowly comprehended 'government procurement' (in the WTO's parlance), 'public procurement' (in the EU's parlance), or 'government contracts' (a term used state-side). PPPs can be structured as merely contractual arrangements similar to non-registered partnerships in private law, somewhat blurring the lines with government procurement sensu stricto. However, more often, PPPs are formed as registered special-purpose vehicles (SPVs) established based on jurisdiction-specific company laws, whether modified by public-law norms or not. Public and private partners join forces to carry out various scenarios of cooperation such as 'build–operate–transfer' (BOT), 'build–own–operate–transfer' (BOOT), 'build–own–operate' (BOO), 'build–lease–transfer' (BLT), 'design–build–finance–operate' (DBFO), 'design–build–operate–transfer' (DBOT), or 'design–construct–manage–finance' (DCMF). PPPs might also take sector-specific forms, such as production sharing agreements (PSAs). As such, PPPs fall within the concept of state-controlled enterprises. Namely, governments, in one subtle way or another, have the upper hand over their private partners regardless of simple indicators of control such as a share in the equity of PPP-SPVs.

PPPs involving on the private-side foreign persons are found in a rather peculiar international law situation. Such a legal environment can be characterised as anything from a grey zone to a conflict between the regime of global regulation and liberalisation of government procurement on the one side and the regime of investment protection on the other side. One could actually analyse two phases of foreign participation in PPP projects. The first phase covers the period of the competition for being selected as a private partner. This phase also potentially includes challenge-procedures related to the selection process. The second phase covers the relations between the public partner (in essence, the state) and the private partner once the PPP has been established. Depending on the coverage of bilateral investment treaties (BITs) or investment chapters of regional trade agreements (RTAs), PPPs could indeed fall under the radar of investment-protection regimes, including the investor-state-dispute-settlement (ISDS) mechanism. The thing is that, on the one hand, the first phase is increasingly subjected to the rules governing international liberalisation of government procurement markets under which PPPs are classified as a specific and sophisticated form of government procurement. On the other, BITs or FTA investment chapters often expressly exclude government procurement. In such cases, foreign investors in PPP JVs might enjoy less legal protection than different types of foreign investment, and their means of appeal in the second phase could be confined to domestic courts of the host states.

In other words, the opening of PPP markets is increasingly addressed in procurement chapters of high-standard RTAs rather than in other parts of such RTAs. As a matter of fact, PPPs could alternatively be addressed in provisions on the liberalisation of services, investment by foreign economic operators in specific sectors, or some provisions on the operation of foreign-owned subsidiaries. Applying public-procurement-specific provisions, with all their complexity and precision, to PPPs is arguably the most efficient way of securing international liberalisation of the PPPs' market. For example, public-procurement-specific provisions of RTAs typically include a mechanism of resolving disputes between bidders (potential suppliers, contracts, or private partners in PPPs) and contracting authorities granting government contracts, which allow foreign bidders to challenge various decisions of contracting authorities in the course of the procurement process before domestic courts. However, such public-procurement provisions do not further address the resolution of disputes arising after selecting a private partner, typically leaving such disputes exclusively for domestic contract law, domestic company law, and local courts. Foreign investors in PPP project prima facie could not benefit from ISDS should domestic measures in the combined case of (1) PPP projects being classified under some RTAs as a sophisticated form of public procurement and (2) the express exclusion of government procurement from the coverage of a specific BIT or FTA investment chapter.

The game is on here not for solving some doctrinal issues arising under hypothetical scenarios but rather for addressing future real-life problems in the markets worth billions. For example, drawing upon the data from the Private Participation-in-Infrastructure (PPI) base,[1] a World Bank study from 2016[2] revealed that the investment in PPP projects in the Emerging Market and Developing Economies (EMDEs)

---

[1] World Bank, 'Private Infrastructure Projects Database' <https://ppi.worldbank.org/about-us/about-ppi> accessed 17 June 2019.

[2] "The PPI Database gathers data on investment commitments in infrastructure projects with private sector participation, including different contractual agreements3. It does not distinguish pubic from private investments. Therefore, the analysis that follows includes PPP arrangements only, and excludes divestitures and merchant projects. This report covers the energy, transport, and water and sanitation sectors, and excludes the telecom sector. All monetary values are expressed in U.S. dollars at 2015 prices (adjusted by the U.S. Consumer Price Index). Hereafter, this series is denominated as 'PPP investments.'" *See* World Bank, 'The State of PPPs Infrastructure Public–Private Partnerships in Emerging Markets & Developing Economies 1991–2015 ' (June 2016) Public–Private Infrastructure Advisory Facility (PPIAF), 7.

grew steadily since 1991 over a long period. However, this growth was also susceptible to global crises in the wake of which such investment experienced medium-term downward trends. Namely:

> PPPs grew steadily from $7 billion in 1991 to $91 billion in 1997 when governments felt the repercussions of the Asian financial crisis (1997-1998). After that, there was a period of contraction until investments in PPPs reached a minimum of $21.9 billion in 2002. When the global economy picked up steam in the mid-2000s, a second growth phase culminated in record investment of $158 billion in 2012. This second growth phase was unaffected by the global financial crisis of 2008 because many countries increased the public share in the financing of infrastructure projects to help boost investment. A significant decline of about 40% occurred in 2013. Since then, however, investment commitments in PPPs have grown, albeit slowly, reflecting the overall slowdown in key emerging markets, particularly Brazil and India.[3]

This study also pointed to the concentration of PPP markets in the EMBE in just five countries, including Brazil, China, India, Mexico, and Turkey.[4]

As it is further discussed below, a somewhat subliminal premise of any discussion about participation of entrepreneurs of public projects in cooperation with governments and their agencies along with the very language of the PPP (public–private partnership with an emphasis on 'private') is that it literally is a 'private' sector/private entrepreneurs that cooperate with governments. However, this would not always be the case. Pretty obviously, many significant enterprises active in PPP-able sectors (chiefly utility and energy might be separate for-profit entities established and operating under private business/company law and have foreign governments or their sovereign wealth funds (SWFs) as their major shareholders at the same time.

This chapter is structured as follows. Sect. 2 offers the necessary conceptual framework, including discussing the notion of PPP (Sect. 2.1) and the relations between the notion of PPP and SCEs (Sect. 2.1). Section 3 broadly addresses opening PPPs to international markets, including instruments or platforms of liberalisation such as the WTO GPA (Sect. 3.1), the GATS and the TRIMS (Sect. 3.2), the past EU procurement directives (Sect. 3.3), and the current fifth-generation procurement directive (Sect. 3.4). Section 4 brambly addresses dispute-resolution issues related to PPPs, including pre-contractual dispute settlement most often concerning market

[3] World Bank (n 2) 2. As far as the share of such PPP projects in the GDP of the EMDEs is concerned, this study stated that: "Investments in PPP projects as a percentage of GDP have remained flat in the last decade, without recovering the levels achieved prior to the Asian financial crisis. The trend in infrastructure investments for PPPs as a share of GDP grew solidly all through the 1990s—from 0.1% in 1991 to over 1.1% in 1997. Post-Asian crisis, however, this figure declined steadily over the next seven years. Although slight growth occurred, it never fully recovered from the Asian crisis. Total global investment in PPPs experienced a second wave of expansion (2005–2012) in absolute terms with levels of investments much higher than the previous growth phase. During the same period, infrastructure investments as a percent of GDP remained relatively low between 0.2% and 0.6% and these investments did not surpass the previous record of 1.1% in 1997." *See* ibid.

[4] "The top five's share of total investment has been trending up from 40% in the early 1990s to a peak of 81% in 2009. Since then total investment has decreased to 63% (2014). The top five economies have contributed to the global PPP investment total in numbers that are out of proportion to their share of GDP among emerging markets and developing economies, or EMDEs (52%). In 2015, the top five's share of total investment declined to 54%, a level not seen since 2001." *See* ibid.

access (Sect. 4.1) and post-contractual dispute settlement (Sect. 4.2), differentiating between dispute settlement regulated under market-access instruments (Sect. 4.2.1) and investment-protection instruments (Sect. 4.2.2). Sect. 5 offers conclusions.

2 Conceptual Framework

2.1 The Notion of PPP

PPP is a rather complicated and multi-dimensional yet well-defined concept. This is chiefly because lawmakers in various jurisdictions have had rather precisely to determine what PPP stands for. The subject was not entirely left to academic scholarship in the field of law, public administration, management, or economics. Depending on jurisdiction or geographical region, alternative terms are also frequently used in place of PPP to chiefly denominate the same phenomenon. As listed by Yescombe, PPI is used mainly in the context of development and Multilateral Development Banks (MDBs). Private-sector participation (PSP) overlaps with the notion of PPPs, and similar to the PPI, it is also used in the MDB-related context. P3 is preferred in North America. Privately financed projects (PFP) is preferred in Australia. Private finance initiative (PFI) originates in Britain and also caught on in Japan and Malaysia.[5] To start with think-tanks offering the most general and flexible definitions, Brookings Institution, in its documents, defines PPP:

- in the context of US road infrastructure as: "a contractual agreement between a public agency and a private sector entity resulting in greater private sector participation in the delivery and/or financing of infrastructure projects,"[6]
- in the context of foreign development aid granted by (USAID) as a "project or initiative which engages the private sector (including global and local businesses, foundations, industry associations, and others) as a core re-source partner. This definition of PPPs differs from other ways of engaging the private sector, such as contracting a for-profit implementer, in that this definition of PPPs requires private sec-tor actors to be co-investing skills, technologies, other core business

[5] Yescombe, E. R., 'What are Public–private Partnerships?' in Yescombe, E. R. (ed), *Public–Private Partnerships for Infrastructure: Principles of Policy and Finance* (Butterworth-Heinemann, 2007), 4.

[6] Emilia Istrate and Robert Puentes, 'Moving Forward on Public Private Partnerships: U.S. and International Experience with PPP Units' Brookings (December 2011) Brookings-Rockefeller Project on State and Metropolitan Innovation <https://www.brookings.edu/wp-content/uploads/2016/06/1208_transportation_istrate_puentes.pdf> [*citing* U.S. Department of Transportation, "Status of the Nation's Highways, Bridges, and Transit: Conditions and Performance Report to Congress," (2009)].

capabilities, or financial resources to the project or activity to achieve development outcomes."[7]

In turn, the PPP-related 'Reference Guide' coreleased by the World Bank, the Asian Development (ADB) and the Inter-American Development Bank (IADB)[8] generally defined PPP as "[a] long-term contract between a private party and a government entity, for providing a public asset or service, in which the private party bears significant risk and management responsibility, and remuneration is linked to performance."[9] For comparison, the National Institute of Governmental Purchasing (NIGP) based in the USA defines PPPs alternatively as:

- in the 2016 P3 best-practice guide: "A public–private partnership (P3) is a broad term used to describe public facility and infrastructure contracts that minimally include components of design and build (e.g., construction, renovation, rehabilitation) in a single contract. Components of financing, operations, maintenance, or management may be included within this single contract. A P3 contract allocates risks to the party (the government or the contractor) best able to manage the risks and may assign a higher level of responsibility for means and methods to the private partner,"[10] or
- in the 2015 research report authored by Roman: "A PPP conceptualised as a contractual agreement between one or more governments/public agencies and one or more private sector or nonprofit partners for the purpose of supporting the delivery of public services or financing, designing, building, operating and/or maintaining a certain project."[11]

The long-awaited 2020 UNCITRAL (United Nations Commission on International Trade Law) Model Legislative Provisions on Public–Private Partnerships

---

[7] George M. Ingram, Anne E. Johnson and Helen Moser, 'USAID's PublIc–Private Partnerships: A data picture and review of business engagement' Brookings (February 2016) Global Economy and Development Working Paper No. 94, 14 (*citing* USAID, 'Public-Private Partnerships Historical Dataset Background," background paper that accompanies the USAID PPP data set').

[8] World Bank, Asian Development Bank, Inter-American Development Bank, 'Reference Guide Public-Private Partnerships Version 2.0' () 90384.

<http://documents.worldbank.org/curated/en/600511468336720455/pdf/903840PPP0Refe0 Box385311B000PUBLIC0.pdf>.

[9] World Bank (n 8), 14.

[10] NIGP, 'Public Procurement Practice PUBLIC-PRIVATE PARTNERSHIP (P3): Facilities and Infrastructure' (2016) NIGP Principles and Practices of Public Procurement <https://www.nigp.org/docs/default-source/new-site/global-best-practices/public-private-partnership-(p3)-facilities-and-infrastructure.pdf?sfvrsn=355d907a_0> accessed 2 May 2020, 1.

[11] Alexandru V. Roman, 'A Guide to Public-PrivatePartnerships1 (PPPs): What Public Procurement Specialists Need to Know' (2015) NIGP Research Report <https://www.nigp.org/docs/default-source/New-Site/research-reports/guidetopublic-privatepartnerships(ppps)-whatpublicprocurementspecialistsneednowfinal.pdf?sfvrsn=af15ed40_4> accessed 2 May 2020, 1.

('2020 Model Provisions')[12] eventually expanded and replaced the 2004 UNCITRAL Model Legislative Provisions on Privately Financed Infrastructure Projects[13] and earlier 2001 UNCITRAL Legislative Guide on Privately Financed Infrastructure Projects.[14] While the previous documents evaded defining PPP, the 2020 Model Provisions now clearly sets forth that:

> Public-private partnership (PPP)" means an agreement between a contracting authority and a private entity for the implementation of a project, against payments by the contracting authority or the users of the facility, including both those projects that entail a transfer of the demand risk to the private partner ("concession PPPs") and those other types of PPPs that do not entail such risk transfer ("non-concession PPPs").[15]

As far as academic definitions of PPP are concerned, those have been comprehensively compiled, e.g. in Roman's NIGP Research Report. For the sake of argument, it suffices to say here that, for example, Yescombe defines PPP as:

- a long-term contract (a 'PPP Contract') between a public-sector party and a private-sector party;
- for the design, construction, financing, and operation of public infrastructure (the 'Facility') by the private-sector party;
- with payments over the life of the PPP Contract to the private-sector party for the use of the Facility, made either by the public-sector party or by the general public as users of the Facility; and
- with the Facility remaining in public-sector ownership, or reverting to public-sector ownership at the end of the PPP Contract.[16]

Importantly for the further discussion about the inclusion of PPPs in RTAs' procurement chapters, Yescombe generally explains the relation between public procurement and PPPs in the way that, unlike in public procurement, "[i]n a PPP (…) the Public Authority specifies its requirements in terms of 'outputs," which set out the public services which the Facility is intended to provide, but which do not specify how these are to be provided,"[17] and "[i]t is then left to the private sector to design, finance, build and operate the Facility to meet these long-term output specifications."[18] Thus, as summarised by Yescombe, many risks normally encumbering governmental agencies are transferred to private partners, such as uncertainty as to the

---

[12] UNCITRAL, 'Model Legislative Provisions on Public–Private Partnerships' (adopted during UNCITRAL's fifty-second session held in Vienna, 8–19 July 2019, published January 2020) ISBN 978-92-1-130,401-5 ('2020 Model Provisions').

[13] UNCITRAL, 'Model Legislative Provisions on Privately Financed Infrastructure Projects' (adopted during UNCITRAL's thirty-sixth session, held in Vienna from 30 June to 11 July 2003, published 2004) ISBN 92-1-133583-3 ('2004 Model Provisions').

[14] UNCITRAL, 'UNCITRAL Legislative Guide on Privately Financed Infrastructure Projects' (adopted during UNCITRAL's thirty-third session held in New York from 12 June to 7 July 2000, published 2001). A/CN.9/SER.B/4 ISBN 92-1-133632-5. ('2001 Legislative Guide').

[15] 2020 Model Provisions (n 12) Model Provision 2.a.

[16] Yescombe (n 5) 3.

[17] ibid 4.

[18] ibid.

cost of the design and construction of the infrastructure, actual income generated by the infrastructure, which is to be determined by market conditions or the maintenance of the infrastructure developed within the framework of a particular PPP.[19] Moreover, to quote Roman's NIGP report, PPPs "are usually developed with the implicit and explicit objectives of leveraging additional financing resources and expertise, which otherwise might not have been available for public purposes through traditional procurement practices."[20] In other words, the use of the PPP model relieves a public authority from having to operate and expend on the completed procured infrastructure.

On the other hand, however, the process of selecting a public partner, instead of a general contractor of construction works, must perforce turn more complicated, burdensome, and time consuming compared with ordinary public procurement. Indeed, the NIGP 2016 P3 best-practice guide states that, in the case of PPP, "[p]rocurement must use an increased degree of diligence and expertise to find a way to market the opportunity, seek full and open competition, and balance all the risks and responsibilities associated with the project."[21]

2.2 PPP as a State-Controlled Enterprise (SCE)

PPPs perforce fall under the broad umbrella of state-controlled enterprises (SCE). This is even though the notion of control by the state might not be as straightforward as in the case of fully or partially state-owned enterprises (SOEs), in which case the control by the state is easily measured with stakes in enterprises. In fact, SCEs include a much broader panoply of entities than SOEs (see Table 1). SCEs can sprout in numerous ways and with a differing degree of control exercised by states at a central or regional level. Of course, states can control enterprises through ownership of equity, along with all derivate shareholders' rights. However, a right to appoint management or approve as well as to block strategic decisions can be divorced from the ownership of equity and granted to states by public-law special-voting rights.

Moreover, SCEs can be established as entities without separate legal capacity, such as units of public administration which carry out some economic activities and at least partially rely on commercial or quasi-commercial revenue. This category is embodied by the institutions that provide quasi-public goods like public healthcare systems, leisure facilities, or cultural institutions that do not require private partners' involvement. Such a category of SCEs is naturally furthermost from the interest of this paper as the lack of private partners implies that the problems of the liberalisation of foreign investment are non-existent. The same applies to SCEs formed as separate legal entities yet under provisions of national public law like 'crown corporations' instead of private company law. In such cases, private investors, let alone foreign

[19] ibid.

[20] Roman (n 11) 1.

[21] NIGP (n 10) element 4 at 3.

Table 1 Classification of state-owned enterprises (SCEs)

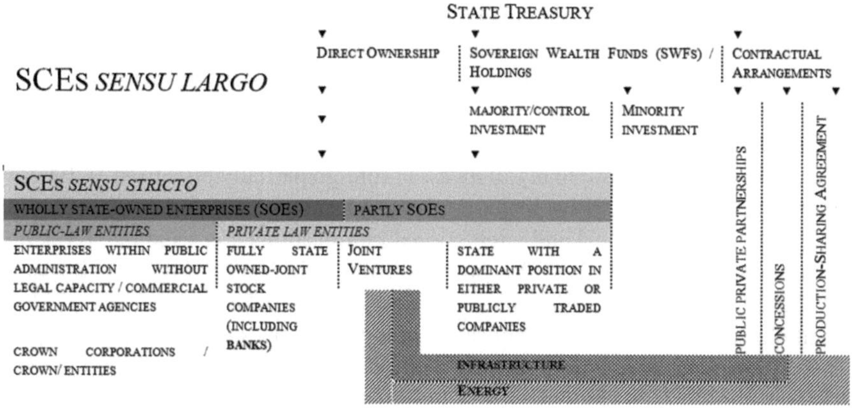

private investors, cannot acquire stakes in such SCEs as minority stakeholders either. Nonetheless, for example, the hysteria over British National Health Service (NHS) in the context of the negotiations on the EU–EU Transatlantic Trade and Investment Partnership (TTIP) and subsequently a purported post-Brexit bilateral US-UK trade deal[22] best illustrates that the question of the participation by foreign investors in the provision of public services is dormant in the case of potentially commercially viable sectors. Moreover, whenever full or partial privatisation of public-sector bodies is lobbied for, or even only hypothetically considered, the question of the eligibility of foreign investors to participate in privatisation comes to the fore.

[22] *See, e.g.*, Mike Lean, Graham Watt, Hugh Bishop, Anne Mullin and Kenneth Barker on behalf of 51 signatories, 'Privatisation of the Scottish NHS: TTIP and independence' (13–19 September 2014) 384(9947) Lancet e38; Holly Jarman, Martin McKee and Tamara K Hervey, 'Health, transatlantic trade, and President Trump's populism: what American Patients First has to do with Brexit and the NHS' (4–10 August 2018) 392(10145) Lancet 447–450; Joan Costa-Font, 'The National Health Service at a Critical Moment: When Brexit Means Hectic' (2017) 46(4) Journal of Social Policy 783; Nick Fahy, Tamara Hervey, Scott Greer, Holly Jarman, David Stuckler, Mike Galsworthy and Martin McKee 'How will Brexit affect health and health services in the UK? Evaluating three possible scenarios' (4–10 November 2017) 390(10107) 2110–2118; BeckyMcCall, 'Brexit, health care, and life sciences: plan for the worst (29 September–5 October 2018) 392(10153) Lancet 1101–1102; Nick Fahy, Tamara Hervey, Scott Greer, Holly Jarman, David Stuckler, Mike Galsworthy, Martin McKee, 'How will Brexit affect health services in the UK? An updated evaluation' (2–8 March 2019) 393(10174) Lancet 949–958.

Next come sovereign wealth funds (SWFs),[23] which are quasi holding-companies entirely owned by states that actively themselves manage diversified portfolios of investment in various classes of assets such as equity, debt real estate, row material and hydrocarbon futures, precious metals, or outsource active portfolio management in various investment, private-equity or hedge funds by buying stakes in such entities. The SFWs *per se* would, in principle, also fall outside the interest of this paper. However, SWFs are likely to invest in foreign partially privatised SCEs or in private-side interests in PPPs, including critical foreign utilities and infrastructure. This has profound political and international ramifications. For example, Dyck and Morse found in 2011 that the SFWs are on average rather inclined to invest in 'transportation, energy and telecommunication,' second only to the financial sector.[24] It is, nonetheless, true that SWFs typically are minor passive investors implying that SWFs cannot exercise any meaningful control over enterprises in which SWFs hold stakes. However, the 2008 Sovereign Wealth Funds: Generally Accepted Principles and Practices (GAPP or 'Santiago Principles')[25] specify concerning active investment that:

- "If an SWF chooses to exercise its ownership rights, it should do so in a manner that is consistent with its investment policy and protects the financial value of its investments. The SWF should publicly disclose its general approach to voting securities of listed entities, including the key factors guiding its exercise of ownership rights."[26]
- "SWFs' demonstrated ability to contribute to the stability of global financial markets results in part from their ability to invest on a long-term, patient basis. The exercise of voting rights is seen to be important by some SWFs for their capacity to hold assets and preserve value rather than becoming a forced seller and, by definition, a shorter-term investor. The exercise of ownership rights is also seen

[23] The Sovereign Wealth Funds: Generally Accepted Principles and Practices (GAPP or 'Santiago Principles') published by the International Working Group of Sovereign Wealth Funds" (IWG-SWF) define SWFs as: "special-purpose investment funds or arrangements that are owned by the general government.5,6Created by the general government for macro-economic purposes, SWFs hold, manage, or administer assets to achieve financial objectives, and employ a set of investment strategies that include investing in foreign financial assets.7 SWFs have diverse legal, institutional, and governance structures. They are a heterogeneous group, comprising fiscal stabilization funds, savings funds, reserve investment corporations, development funds, and pension reserve funds without explicit pension liabilities." *See* IWG-SWF, 'The Sovereign Wealth Funds: Generally Accepted Principles and Practices' (October 2008) <https://www.ifswf.org/sites/default/files/santiagoprinciples_0_0.pdf> accessed 6 May 2020, 3.

[24] "Perhaps most importantly, we find a distinct industry tilt. SWFs allocate 21% of the portfolios (in both private and public equity) to the finance industry and they own nearly 5% of the public equity capitalization in finance. Other than finance, the industries favored by SWFs include a 15% allocation to energy, 9% to transportation, and 7% to telecommunications." *See* Alexander Dyck and Adair Morse, 'Sovereign Wealth Fund Portfolios' (February 2011) Chicago Booth Business School Working Paper No. 11–15 SSRN ID 1792850, 6.

[25] Santiago Principles (n 24).

[26] GAPP (n 24) Principle 21.

> by some SWFs as a mechanism for keeping the company's management accountable to the shareholders, thus contributing to good corporate governance and a sound allocation of resources. To dispel concerns about potential noneconomic or nonfinancial objectives, SWFs should disclose ex ante whether and how they exercise their voting rights. This could include, for example, a public statement that their voting is guided by the objective to protect the financial interests of the SWF. In addition, SWFs should disclose their general approach to board representation. When SWFs have board representation, their directors will perform the applicable fiduciary duties of directors, including representing the collective interest of all shareholders. To demonstrate that their voting decisions continue to be based on economic and financial criteria, SWFs could also make appropriate ex post disclosures."[27]

Moreover, Dyck and More found "a surprising level of active ownership,"[28] which supports the proposition that SWFs and SCEs are intersecting sets. However, at the same time, Dyck and Morse found a strong bias towards investing in "home-regions" in the field of "finance, transportation and telecommunications"[29] arguably because of the above-discussed widespread negative sentiment towards foreign' government's investment.Such finding, in turn, implies that, while enterprises invested in the SWFs might be classified as SCEs in the case of SWFs' active ownership and possession of a controlling stake, SWFs are not inclined to heavily invest in highly regulated sectors outside of domestic and neighbouring markets. Ergo the scale of tensions generated by active sovereign investment in foreign strategic industries, including in the form of PPPs, is arguably much smaller than it would otherwise be if SWFs were much more inclined to invest in such sectors in distant, non-regional jurisdictions with a low level of mutual investment liberalisation between the SFW's country and the host country.

Next, we might look at the landscape of minority stakes in SCE, among which one could find foreign private and sovereign investors. In this regard, we might consider two model scenarios. The first scenario characterises relatively and small undertakings. Namely, the number of minority shareholders in SOEs might be small: one or a few, in case of joint-ventures between states and private investors. In the case of some PPPs, being a kind of joint ventures between governments and private partners, the determination of which partner is dominant might actually prove difficult unless stakes of governments and public partners are determined by shares in PPPs' equity (see Table 2).

The second scenario characterises the largest long-lived SCEs, which used to be wholly SOEs yet have been partly privatised. In such a situation, ownership of privatised equity is most often dispersed and free-floating on stock exchanges due to a privatisation strategy via public offerings on capital markets rather than finding one or a few strategic investors. The idea behind diluted private ownership is to

[27] GAPP (n 24) Explanation and commentary to Principle 21.

[28] ibid 3.

[29] ibid 6.

Table 2 Minority shareholders in SCEs (scenario 1)

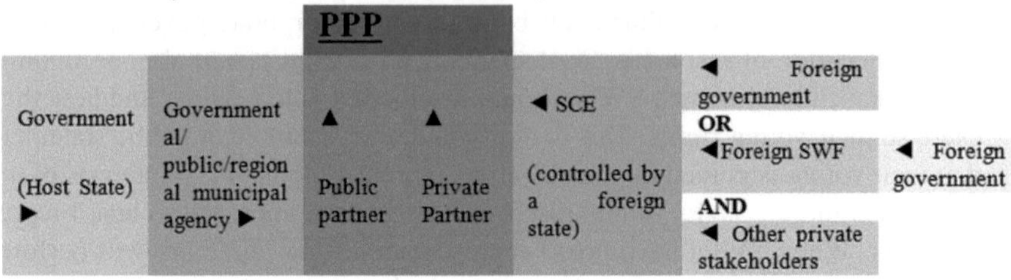

Table 3 Minority shareholders in SCEs (scenario 2)

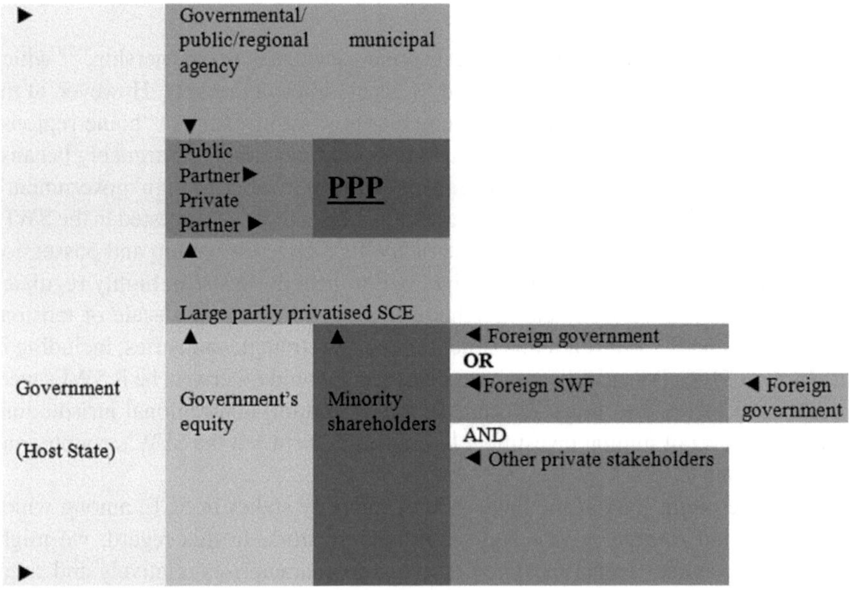

allow the government to still effectively exercise control over SCEs even despite the government's stakes falling below 50% of equity (Table 3).

3 Opening PPPs to International Markets

Any attempt to review the current state of the global liberalisation of the investment in PPPs by foreign investors faces an obstacle that it is not always clear in which field of international economic law PPPs actually belong. Ought PPPs be classified as the most sophisticated form of government procurement of services or construction works and, therefore, fall within the scope of the WTO, public-procurement-related chapters of RTAs, EU's procurement directives? Alternatively, ought PPPs be classified as provision of services and, therefore, fall under the umbrella of the WTO General Agreement on Trade in Services (GATS)[30] and services-related chapters of RTAs? Could PPPs benefit from both regimes? Moreover, could PPPs be covered by sector-specific chapters of modern high-standard RTAs which open, e.g. energy and utility sectors to foreign investment, also apply to PPPs?

To further complicate the matter, we might also look at the dispute-settlement mechanism available for private partners against host states to more precisely assess the level of PPPs' liberalisation (see further Sect. 4). Specifically, a formal abstract ability to compete and be granted PPP contracts would barely be conducive to actual foreign investment in PPPs in the case of unstable legal environments. From a perspective of a prospective private partner, firstly, why bother at all to expend on the tendering process in the case of vague rules on the selection of private partners and in the lack of judicial review (see further Sect. 4.1)? Secondly, why bother to risk entering into a PPP contract without sufficient guarantees against expropriation of private partners, like the investor-state-dispute-settlement (ISDS) mechanism (see further Sect. 4.2)? Let us now scrutinise all such elements that determent levels of PPP's international liberalisation one by one.

3.1 WTO GPA

The global liberalisation of public procurement markets is secured by several international instruments, some of which expressly address opening PPP to international competition. To start with WTO GPA, this agreement last amended in 2012 (GPA12[31]) does not expressly refer to PPPs as a specific form of government procurement covered by the GPA (so-called 'covered procurement,' i.e. subjected to the rules of international liberalisation) which, otherwise, is defined by the GPA as the procurement:

- "of goods, services, or any combination thereof (i) as specified in each Party's Annexes to Appendix I; and (ii) not procured with a view to commercial sale or resale, or for use in the production or supply of goods or services for commercial sale or resale,"[32]
- "by any contractual means, including purchase; lease; and rental or hire purchase, with or without an option to buy,"[33]

---

[30] GATT, 'General Agreement on Trade in services' (Final Act Embodying the Results of the Uruguay Round of Multilateral Trade Negotiations, Marrakesh, 15 April 1994) Annex I.B (GATS).

[31] WTO, 'Decision on the Outcomes of the Negotiations under Article XXIV:7 of the Agreement on Government Procurement' (2 April. 2012) GPA/113 (GPA12).

[32] GPA12 (n 32) art II.2.a.

[33] ibid art II.2.b.

- "for which the value, as estimated in accordance with paragraphs 6 through 8, equals or exceeds the relevant threshold specified in a Party's annexes to Appendix I, at the time of publication of a notice in accordance with Article VII,"[34]
- "by a procuring entity,"[35] and "that is not otherwise excluded from coverage in paragraph 3 or a Party's annexes to Appendix I."[36]

Moreover, the procuring entity is defined as "an entity covered under a Party's Annex 1, 2 or 3 to Appendix I."[37] However, tenebrous these provisions might look, in simple terms, procurement coverage includes three dimensions: (1) subjective coverage, (2) objective coverage, and 3) value thresholds.[38] The notion of 'subjective coverage' means that only some procuring bodies covered, which are typically listed in GPA Appendix 1, including (1) covered central-government-entities in Annex 1, (2) covered subcentral-government-entities in Annex 2, and (3) all other entities[39] in Annex 3. The notion of 'objective coverage' means that only some goods and services are covered, which are typically listed in GPA Appendix 1, including (1) covered goods in Annex 4, (2) covered services in Annex 5, and (3) covered construction services in Annex 6. Finally, the notion of value thresholds means that only contracts above a particular value are subject to liberalisation rules. Ergo, in practice, we always have to look at the party-specific annexes to the GPA to determine to which arrangements the GPA does or does not apply.

A partial shift in the determination of coverage from the use of positive lists (only listed goods, services or construction services are covered) to negative lists (all listed goods, services or construction services are covered unless expressly excluded) has undoubtedly improved the general level of government procurement liberalisation. However, this shift has also somewhat blurred the readability of annexes and the actual scope of the party-specific commitments. Let us confine the analysis of the annexes to the objective coverage and look only at the coverage of services, construction services and general notes while omitting the coverage of goods. The shift to negative lists has much more concerned construction services than services. Coverage of construction services is determined with negative lists by Australia, Armenia, Canada, the EU, Hong Kong, Iceland, Japan, Korea, Moldova, Montenegro, Netherlands-Aruba, New Zealand, Norway, Taiwan, Ukraine, and USA, whereas

---

[34] ibid art II.2.c.

[35] ibid art II.2.d.

[36] ibid art II.2.e.

[37] ibid art I.o.

[38] *See* Jędrzej Górski, 'Public Procurement in 21st Century: Balancing Liberalisation, Social Values and Protectionism' (PhD in Laws Thesis, CUHK 2016) proquest ID10307336, 58.

[39] It is possible that some of 'all other entities' might actually be classified as PPPs. However, the role of PPPs is the context of subjective coverage (covered procuring entities) fundamentally differs to the role of PPPs in the context of objective coverage (covered procured goods and services). In the case PPPs looked at as covered entities, the liberalization of the procurement of goods and services is at stake, ergo ordinary government procurement although by some SCEs instead of non-commercial governmental agencies. Not the selection of the private partners and participation of foreign investors in such a process, which is at stake in the case of PPPs looked at as very complex covered entities.

negative lists for construction services are still used by Israel, Liechtenstein, and Singapore. On the country, the coverage of services is still mainly determined with positive lists, including Canada, the EU, Hong Kong, Iceland, Israel, Japan, Korea, Liechtenstein, Moldova, Montenegro, Netherlands-Aruba, Norway, Singapore, and Taiwan, whereas Australia, Armenia New Zealand, Ukraine and the USA have moved to determine their coverage of services with negative lists.

Positive lists benefit this analysis in that perusal of these lists allows to smoothly identify services which are (1) potentially PPP-related and (2) commonly covered by the vast majority of the GPA Parties in line with the United Nations Provisional Central Product Classification (CPC).[40] Regarding construction services, most often, all such services are covered (entire CPC class 51). Construction services are a core component of any BOT, BOO, BLT, DBFO or DCMF arrangement, each of which includes a common denominator of B for 'build' or C for 'construct.' As far as other services are concerned, typically positively listed are several construction-related services, including architectural services (CPC 8671), engineering services (CPC 8672), integrated engineering services (CPC 8673), urban planning and landscape (CPC 8674), management consulting service (CPC 865), general construction work for buildings (CPC 512), general construction work for civil engineering (CPC 513). As far as other services are concerned, worth mentioning seem to be, e.g. hospital services (CPC 9311), other human health services (CPC 9319), social services (CPC 933), libraries, archives, museums and other cultural services (CPC 963), or sporting and other recreational services (CPC 964. What better way to stimulate private participation in the provision of healthcare, leisure, and cultural infrastructure, while still keeping private business under control than establishing a long-term PPP under the BOT or other scenarios?

However, there are strong arguments against the proposition that PPPs fall under the GPA regime. Firstly, one might see it as blatant overinterpretation that the GPA impliedly covers PPPs, at least in the case of the GPA parties, which separately cover bands of services and construction services that altogether could make for PPPs when combined.[41] After all, a number of GPA parties reserve for the sake of clarity that the GPA does not apply to procurement which such parties did not expressly covered in their respective appendices. Secondly, a proposition that PPPs fall under the GPA regime begs the question of how to apply GPA's procedural framework to the selection of private partners in the lack of PPP-tailored provisions? For example, the GPA's requirements about the valuation of contracts, which serve to "ascertain[…] whether it is a covered procurement"[42] and prevent so-called splitting

[40] "The secretariat indicated in its informal note containing the draft classification list (24 May 1991) that it would prepare a revised version based on comments from participants. The attached list incorporates, to the extent possible, such comments. It could, of course, be subject to further modification in the light of developments in the services. negotiations and ongoing work elsewhere." *See* WTO, 'Services Sectoral Classification List Note by the Secretariat'. (Multilateral Trade Negotiations the Uruguay Round, Group of Negotiations on Services, 10 July 1991) MTN.GNS/W/120.

[41] Even in the case of negative lists, in no point does the CPC list BOTs or similar formulas. *See* ibid.

[42] GPA12 (n 32) art II.6 in initio.

of contracts,[43] cannot be used to determining the value of BOT or similar contracts by any means. Likewise, the entire structure of 'time-periods' designed to apply to the default non-negotiated open tendering procedures[44] is not good for selecting private partners. This process perforce must involve lengthy negotiations, which, though allowed under the GPA,[45] have always been a rather undesirable exception to simple open tendering. For the same reason, the electronic auctions added to and promoted by the GPA12, particularly those involving "automatic evaluation methods,"[46] are out of the question in the case of PPPs. Finally, the domestic review procedures,[47] mandated by the GPA as this agreement's core enforcement mechanism, could not secure PPPs market liberalisation to the same extent as they can in the case of simple procurement of goods, services and construction services through open tendering. Among these, most prominent in practice are "rapid interim measures to preserve the supplier's opportunity to participate in the procurement," which, again, are meant to streamline open tendering procedures with fixed timelines rather than lengthy negotiated procedures.

It is thus beyond astonishing that, notwithstanding all of the above considerations, several GPA parties have indeed expressly covered arrangements close to PPPs in their appendices despite the lack of a proper procedural framework. To start with the EU, the EU listed 'works concessions' (see further Sects. 3.3–3.4) yet only towards a limited collection of GPA parties comprising members of the European Economic Area (EEA), plus some countries aspiring to EU membership as well as special-status territories:

> Works concessions contracts, when awarded by Annex 1 and 2 entities, are included under the national treatment regime for the construction service providers of Iceland, Liechtenstein, Norway, the Netherlands on behalf of Aruba, Switzerland and Montenegro, provided their

---

[43] "[A] a procuring entity shall [...] neither divide a procurement into separate procurements nor select or use a particular valuation method for estimating the value of a procurement with the intention of totally or partially excluding it from the application of this Agreement." GPA12 (n 32), art II.6 in initio.

[44] GPA12 (n 32) art XI.

[45] "1. A Party may provide for entities to conduct negotiations: (a) in the context of procurements in which they have indicated such intent, namely in the notice referred to in paragraph 2 of Article IX (the invitation to suppliers to participate in the procedure for the proposed procurement); or (b) when it appears from evaluation that no one tender is obviously the most advantageous in terms of the specific evaluation criteria set forth in the notices or tender documentation." GPA12 (n 32) art XV.

[46] "[E]lectronic auction means an iterative process that involves the use of electronic means for the presentation by suppliers of either new prices, or new values for quantifiable non-price elements of the tender related to the evaluation criteria, or both." GPA12 (n 32) art I.f. resulting in a ranking or re-ranking of tenders;

[47] "1. Each Party shall provide a timely, effective, transparent and non-discriminatory administrative or judicial review procedure through which a supplier may challenge: (a) a breach of the Agreement; or (b) where the supplier does not have a right to challenge directly a breach of the Agreement under the domestic law of a Party, a failure to comply with a Party's measures implementing this Agreement." *See* GPA12 (n 32) XVIII.

> value equals or exceeds 5,000,000 SDR and for the construction service providers of Korea; provided their value equals or exceeds 15,000,000 SDR.[48]

Japan referred to its domestic PPP-related legislation by stipulating in its Annex 6 that the "[p]rocurement with regard to a construction project within the scope of the Act on Promotion of Private Finance Initiative as of 30 November 2011 is covered."[49] Korea, in turn, covered PPPs in rather an elaborate manner, listing:

> A build-operate-transfer contract is any contractual arrangement the primary purpose of which is to provide for the construction or rehabilitation of physical infrastructures, plants, buildings, facilities, or other government-owned works and under which, as consideration for a supplier's execution of a contractual arrangement, a procuring entity grants to the supplier, for a specified period of time, temporary ownership or a right to control and operate, and demand payment for the use of such works for the duration of the contract.[50]

Next comes Montenegro as an example of a country aspiring to EU membership, which stated in its Annex 6 that:

> Works concessions contracts, when awarded by Annex 1 and 2 entities, are included under the national treatment regime for the construction service providers of the EU, Iceland, Liechtenstein, Norway, the Netherlands on behalf of Aruba and Switzerland, provided their value equals or exceeds SDR 5,000,000 and for the construction service providers of Korea; provided their value equals or exceeds SDR 15,000,000.[51]

It is all the more astonishing that several GPA parties included PPPs in their schedules seeing that several other GPA parties did not, begging many questions related to the reciprocity of commitments under the GPA or the sense of the most-favoured-nation clause (MFN) under this agreement.[52] Most importantly, the USA expressly excluded items such as:

- "[a]ll transportation services, including Launching Services (CPC Prov. 71, 72, 73, 74, 8859, 8868),"[53]

---

[48] WT/Let/977, annex 6.

[49] WT/Let/952, annex 6. However, Japan's Annex 7 might indicate some PPP-relevant reservations: "3. Architectural, engineering and other technical services related to construction services, with the exception of the following services when procured independently, are covered: a. Final design services of CPC 86712 Architectural design services; b. CPC 86713 Contract administration services; c. Design services consisting of one or a combination of final plans, specifications and cost estimates of either CPC 86722 Engineering design services for the construction of foundations and building structures, or CPC 86723 Engineering design services for mechanical and electrical installations for buildings, or CPC 86724 Engineering design services for the construction of civil engineering works; and." *See* WT/Let/952, annex 7.

[50] WT/Let/1162, annex 6.

[51] WT/Let/1120, annex 6.

[52] "With respect to any measure regarding covered procurement, each Party, including its procuring entities, shall accord immediately and unconditionally to the goods and services of any other Party and to the suppliers of any other Party offering the goods or services of any Party, treatment no less favourable than the treatment the Party, including its procuring entities, accords to: (a) domestic goods, services and suppliers [National Treatment Clause]; and (b) goods, services and suppliers of any other Party [MFN Clause]." *See* GPA12 (n 32) art IV.1.

[53] WT/Let/950, annex 5, point 2.a.

- "[s]ervices associated with the management and operation of government facilities, or privately owned facilities used for governmental purposes, including federally funded research and development centres (FFRDCs),"[54]
- "public utilities services, including Telecommunications and ADP-related [[55]] telecommunications services except enhanced (i.e., value-added) telecommunications services,"[56]
- "Research and Development services."[57]

A very explicit exclusion of 'launching services' in the US schedules must draw our particular attention. Such exclusion clearly alludes to the partnership between the US National Aeronautics and Space Administration (NASA) and Elon Musk's SpaceX. It illustrates that subjecting the selection of private partners to any rigid rules of international competition is hardly possible in the case of great powers and the context of hegemonic rivalry. Express exclusions by other GPA parties are, of course, less spectacular. Canada, for example, excluded (1) "services for the management and operation of government facilities or privately owned facilities used for government purposes, including federally-funded research and development," (2) public utilities, and (3)"architectural and engineering services related to airfield, communications and missile facilities."[58] Iceland excluded "contracts awarded to an entity which is itself a contracting authority within the meaning of the Public Procurement Act: "Lög um opinber innkaup" (84/2007) on the basis of an exclusive right which it enjoys pursuant to a published law, regulation or administrative provision."[59] Israel excluded "procurement for the purchase of water and for the supply of energy and of fuels for the production of energy."[60] New Zealand excluded (1) procurement of public health services,[61] (2) procurement of education services,[62] (3) procurement of welfare services."[63] Finally, Taiwan excluded (1) "any form of government assistance, including, but not limited to, cooperative agreements (...),"[64] and (2) "procurements in respect of national security exceptions including procurements made in support of safeguarding nuclear materials, radwaste management, or technology."[65]

[54] ibid annex 5, point 2.b.
[55] ADP stands for Automated Data Processing.
[56] WT/Let/950, annex 5, point 2.c.
[57] ibid annex 5, point 2d b.
[58] WT/Let/954, annex 5, point 3.
[59] WT/Let/985, annex 7.
[60] WT/Let/947, annex 7, point 2.
[61] CPC Prov. 931, including 9311, 9312 and 9319 *See* WT/Let/1085, annex 5 point 2.a.
[62] CPC Prov. 921, 922, 923, 924, and 929 *See* WT/Let/1085, annex 5 point 2.b.
[63] CPC Prov. 933 and 913. *See* WT/Let/1085, annex 5 point 2.c.
[64] WT/Let/978, annex 7 point 7.
[65] WT/Let/978, annex 7 point 9.

The above-listed exclusions make a very small share of all exclusions, reservations, etc., made by the GPA parties throughout annexes, whether that be services-specific, construction-specific or general exclusions, or whether that be third-party-specific exclusions or exclusions applicable to all other GPA parties. Only a case-by-case analysis of a particular PPP scenario juxtaposed against the exclusions applicable to specific bilateral commitments under the GPA could reveal which reservations could apply to such a scenario. Moreover, some PPP-relevant exclusions applicable to the GPA might also be found in GATS (see further Section 3.1). GPA annexes are primarily aligned with GATS annexes, and several GPA parties reserved in the GPA that GATS exclusions shall accordingly apply to their GPA commitments, including Canada,[66] Israel,[67] Moldova,[68] Singapore,[69] and Ukraine.[70]

Notwithstanding all the limits of the GPA's application to PPPs, one could argue that the GPA's general principles could still be applied while selecting private partners.[71] The principle of non-discrimination against domestic tenders (national treatment clause)[72] and the tenderers based in other GPA parties (MFN)[73] could be easily applied to the selection of private partners. The same goes for (1) the ban on the discrimination of locally established yet foreignly owned tenderers,[74] (2) non-discriminative use of electronic means,[75] (3) the prohibition of the use of different rules of origin compared with general commerce in the course of procurement,[76] (4)

66 WT/Let/954, annex 5 point 1.

67 WT/Let/947, note to annex 5.

68 WT/Let/1169, notes annex 6.

69 WT/Let/951/Corr.1, note to annex 5; note to annex 6;

70 WT/Let/1150, annex 7.

71 "Security and General Exceptions" 1. Nothing in this Agreement shall be construed to prevent any Party from taking any action or not disclosing any information that it considers necessary for the protection of its essential security interests relating to the procurement of arms, ammunition or war materials, or to procurement indispensable for national security or for national defence purposes. 2. Subject to the requirement that such measures are not applied in a manner that would constitute a means of arbitrary or unjustifiable discrimination between Parties where the same conditions prevail or a disguised restriction on international trade, nothing in this Agreement shall be construed to prevent any Party from imposing or enforcing measures." *See* GPA12 (n 32) art III.

72 *See* n 53.

73 ibid.

74 "With respect to any measure regarding covered procurement, a Party, including its procuring.

entities, shall not: (a) treat a locally established supplier less favourably than another locally established supplier on the basis of the degree of foreign affiliation or ownership; or (b) discriminate against a locally established supplier on the basis that the goods or services offered by that supplier for a particular procurement are goods or services of any other Party." *See* GPA12 (n 32) art IV.2.

75 *See* GPA12 (n 32) art IV.3.

76 "For purposes of covered procurement, a Party shall not apply rules of origin to goods or services imported from or supplied from another Party that are different from the rules of origin the Party applies at the same time in the normal course of trade to imports or supplies of the same goods or services from the same Party." *See* GPA12 (n 32) art IV.5.

the ban of offsets,[77] (5) requirements as to information about procurement systems[78] as well as notices of planned and intended procurement,[79] (6) the prohibition on conditions of participation in tendering which is not directly relevant for a specific procurement process,[80] (7) drafting technical specifications in a non-discriminative manner,[81] (8) transparency of procurement process and disclosure of information,[82] or (9) the general exceptions about security and general exceptions to the GPA.[83]

3.2 *GATS and TRIMS*

The participation of foreign investors in PPPs also needs to be looked at in the broader context of liberalisation of the provision of services in general commerce (as opposed to purchases subjected to government procurement rules) under the GATS or the TRIMS.[84] Much more realistic are scenarios under which foreign investors with long-lasting commercial establishments in host jurisdictions enter into cooperation with host governments than complete novices in such markets. Novices, perhaps, could merely rely on the PPP-related liberalisation instruments or even one-off project-specific investment agreements determining the details of particular PPP arrangements, dispute resolution included. For the most part, however, foreign investors, that seek to become private partners of host governments, would have already been present in host markets and relied upon a combination of general-commerce and public-procurement instruments of liberalisation by the time such investors are in a position to compete for been awarded PPP contracts (see Table 4).

Let us consider the example of the telecommunications industry and robust champions of this sector expanding in foreign markets, like proverbial Huawei. The enterprises like Huawei would typically first enter foreign markets by selling domestically

[77] GPA12 (n 32) art IV.6.

[78] ibid. art VI.

[79] ibid. art VII.

[80] "A procuring entity shall limit any conditions for participation in a procurement to those that are essential to ensure that a supplier has the legal and financial capacities and the commercial and technical abilities to undertake the relevant procurement." *See* GPA12 (n 32) art VIII.1.

[81] GPA12 (n 32) art X.

[82] ibid. arts XVI-XVII.

[83] "Security and General Exceptions 1. Nothing in this Agreement shall be construed to prevent any Party from taking any action or not disclosing any information that it considers necessary for the protection of its essential security interests relating to the procurement of arms, ammunition or war materials, or to procurement indispensable for national security or for national defence purposes. 2. Subject to the requirement that such measures are not applied in a manner that would constitute a means of arbitrary or unjustifiable discrimination between Parties where the same conditions prevail or a disguised restriction on international trade, nothing in this Agreement shall be construed to prevent any Party from imposing or enforcing measures." *See* GPA12 (n 32) art III.

[84] GATT, 'Agreement on Trade-Related Investment Measures' (Final Act Embodying the Results of the Uruguay Round of Multilateral Trade Negotiations, Marrakesh, 15 April 1994) Annex I.A p 139 (TRIMS).

Table 4 General-commerce versus public procurement-specific liberalisation instruments

	Foreign investor's portfolio in the host market	*General – commerce liberalisation instruments*	*PPP-specific liberalisation instruments*		*Type of client/procurer / public partner*	
Foreign Investor / tenderer /private partner ►	Novice, OR selling to the government only ►	SKIPPED ►	GPA, procurement chapters of RTAs ►	Public procurement including PPPs	Government	Host country
	Long-standing presence and diversified portfolio ►	GATS, TRIMS, services- and investment-related chapters of RTAs, BITS or bilateral agreement on cross-border data flows►			Private business subjected to public procurement regulations	
			SKIPPED ►	Private B2B procurement, or joint ventures between private partners	private business	

made goods to such markets, including a whole host of products like cell phones or tablets mainly targeting consumers or network hardware (switches, routers, WLAN, storage, etc.) targeting telecommunications operators in the host markets. To that point, such an enterprise would have relied on the WTO/GATT MFN clause and applicable trade-in-goods-related chapters of RTAs, before it moves onto providing services.

Next, such an enterprise would establish a local presence in host markets to offer services to both private and public clients. In the case of Huawei in mid-2020, in the lack of a more illustrative example, services targeting governments would include 'eGovernment Cloud,' 'eGovernment Network Platform,' 'Intelligent Smart City' targeting public authorities,' 'Smart Education,' 'Safe City,' 'Safe City Extra.'[85] Services targeting commercial yet most likely government-owned clients would, for example, include (1) 'eHospital,' 'Regional Health,' and 'Multi-Channel HD Telemedicine' in the healthcare sector,[86] and (2) 'Digital Railway' and 'Digital Urban Rail' in the transportation industry.[87] Finally, service targeting predominantly private enterprises would include (1) 'Intelligent Bank Branch,' 'Converged Financial Data Lake,' 'All-Flash Storage for Finance,' 'Financial Big Data,' 'Financial Cloud,' and 'Intent-Driven Network for Finance' in the financial sector,[88] (2) 'Over The Top/Multi-Tenant Data Center (OTT/MTDC),' 'Internet Exchange Point (IXP),' 'Internet Access Provider (IAP),' in the internet-service-provider (ISP) industry,[89] (3) 'Design & Simulation,' 'Planning & Analytics,' and 'Digital Production' in the

[85] <https://e.huawei.com/en/solutions/industries/government> ; <https://e.huawei.com/en/solutions/industries/smart-city>; <https://e.huawei.com/en/solutions/industries/education>; <https://e.huawei.com/en/solutions/industries/public-safety> .

[86] <https://e.huawei.com/en/solutions/industries/healthcare> .

[87] <https://e.huawei.com/en/solutions/industries/transportation> .

[88] <https://e.huawei.com/en/solutions/industries/smart-finance>.

[89] < https://e.huawei.com/en/solutions/industries/isp>.

manufacturing sector,[90] (4) 'Oil & Gas IoT [internet of things],' 'Digital pipeline,' and 'HPC [high-performance computing] & Operations Management,' in the oil-and-gas-industry,[91] or (5) 'Smart Store,' and 'Retail Cloud Platform' in the retail sector.[92] To provide such a host of services, an enterprise like Huawei would have relied on general-commerce instruments like GATS, TRIMs, services- and investment-related chapters of RTAs, BITS, or bilateral agreement on cross-border data flows before it moves onto providing services to clients subjected to public-procurement rules in host markets.

It follows that a foreign investor interested in PPP arrangements in host markets had ideally be better covered by some combination of general-commerce and public-procurement-specific liberalisation instruments. While mutually exclusive, both regimes of liberalisation, to some extent, offer a similar solution to opening markets (private or public) to international competition. These regimes are separate in that, like the GATT, the GATS expressly excludes government procurement, including PPPs, to the extent that PPPs can be classified as government procurement (see Sect. 3.1.). Specifically, just like the GATT47,[93] the GATS stipulates that "[a]rticles II [MFN], XVI [market access] and XVII [national treatment] shall not apply to laws, regulations or requirements governing the procurement by governmental agencies of services purchased for governmental purposes and not with a view to commercial resale or with a view to using in the supply of services for commercial sale."[94] The uncertainty as to whether PPPs are nothing but a sophisticated form of government procurement or not puts PPPs in a grey zone in the entire WTO framework. On the one side, a conviction that PPPs are a form of government procurement implies that PPPs fall within the scope of the GATS' exclusion of government procurement. On the other hand, *a fortiori*, a conviction to the contrary (i.e. that PPP are not any form of government procurement) does not imply by any means that PPPs do not fall within the scope of the GPA and fall under the GATS rules. *A minore ad maius*, if the GATS does not cover simple government procurement (less), the participation in PPPs (more) is not covered by the GATS either. The same uncertainties apply to TRIMs which incorporates GATT's exclusions by reference.[95]

The relevance of GATS' and TRIMs' general-commerce and public-procurement-non-related provisions starts with that GATS applies not only to the supply of services

---

90 <https://e.huawei.com/en/solutions/industries/manufacturing>.

91 <https://e.huawei.com/en/solutions/industries/oil-gas>.

92 <https://e.huawei.com/en/solutions/industries/retail>.

93 "The provisions of this Article [National Treatment on Internal Taxation and Regulation] shall not apply to laws, regulations or requirements governing the procurement by governmental agencies of products purchased for governmental purposes and not with a view to commercial resale or with a view to use in the production of goods for commercial sale." *See* GATT, 'The General Agreement on Tariffs and Trade (GATT 1947)' (Geneva, 13 October 1947) republished in GATT, 'Text of the General Agreement' (Geneva, July 1986) <https://www.wto.org/english/docs_e/legal_e/gatt47_e.pdf> (GATT47), art III.8.a.

94 GATS (n 31) art XIII.1.

95 "All exceptions under GATT 1994 shall apply, as appropriate, to the provisions of this Agreement." *See* TRIMS (n 85) art 3.

"from the territory of one Member into the territory of any other Member"[96] or "in the territory of one Member to the service consumer of any other Member"[97] but also "by a service supplier of one Member, through commercial presence in the territory of any other Member."[98] As discussed above in this section, among all three modes of services' supply, the provision of services through commercial presence appears to be the most reliable basis for entering into PPP arrangements with hosts governments. Once foreign investors establish a commercial presence, the host state ought to refrain from maintaining or adopting several discriminatory measures, including (1) "limitations on the number of service suppliers whether in the form of numerical quotas, monopolies, exclusive service suppliers or the requirements of an economic needs test,"[99] (2) "limitations on the total value of service transactions or assets in the form of numerical quotas or the requirement of an economic needs test,"[100] and (3) "limitations on the total number of service operations or on the total quantity of service output expressed in terms of designated numerical units in the form of quotas or the requirement of an economic needs test."[101]

This constraint imposed on the host state is complemented by restrictions imposed by the TRIMs, which bans host states from applying "any TRIM that is inconsistent with the provisions of Article III [National Treatment on Internal Taxation and Regulation] or Article XI [General Elimination of Quantitative Restrictions] of GATT 1994."[102] The exemplificatory TRIMs included in an annex to the TRIMs are not unlike the above-discussed GPA's ban on discriminating against a locally established supplier on the basis that the goods or services offered by that supplier for a particular procurement are goods or services of any other party[103] (see Sect. 3.1.), except for that TRIMS does not cover services leaving it to the GATS.[104] Such exemplificatory banned measures, among others, include requirements (1) of "the purchase or use by an enterprise of products of domestic origin or from any domestic source, whether specified in terms of particular products, in terms of volume or value of products, or terms of a proportion of volume or value of its local production,"[105] and (2) "that an enterprise's purchases or use of imported products be limited to an amount related to the volume or value of local products that it exports."[106] In addition, telecommunication-specific measures can also be found in an annex to the TRIMS.

---

[96] GATS (n 31) art I.2.a.

[97] ibid art I.2.b.

[98] ibid art I.2.c.

[99] ibid art XVI.2.a.

[100] ibid art XVI.2.b.

[101] ibid art XVI.2.c.

[102] TRIMS (n 85) art 2.1.

[103] *See* n 75.

[104] "This Agreement applies to investment measures related to trade in goods only (referred to in this Agreement as "TRIMs")." *See* TRIMS (n 85) art 1.

[105] TRIMS (n 85) Annex, point 1.1.

[106] ibid Annex, point 1.2.

A comprehensive perusal of GATS schedules for PPP-relevant times is a highly arduous exercise. The number of schedules of commitments under the multilateral GATS with WTO 164 members as of mid-2020, to analyse, is incomparably larger than mere 47 members[107] of the plurilateral GPA. Nonetheless, some highlights are worth noting.

Going from the most recently updated schedules to older ones, the EU, for example, reserved that "[a]ll EC [European Community] Member States: services considered as public utilities at a national or local level may be subject to public monopolies or to exclusive rights granted to private operators1."[108] As far as Member-State-specific provisions of the EU's schedules are concerned, Hungary, for example, expressly noted in the field of rail transport services and pipeline transport, that "[s]ervices may be provided through a Contract of Concession granted by the state or the local authority."[109] Sweden, in the field of maintenance and repair of rail transport equipment, reserved that while "[o]perators [are]allowed to establish and maintain their own terminal infrastructure facilities, subject to space and capacity constraints,"[110] "[p]ublic utility concession or licensing procedures may apply in case of occupation of the public domain."[111]

Laos, in the field of environmental services, reserved that "[s]ervices considered as public utilities at a national or local level may be subject to public monopolies or to exclusive rights granted to private operators."[112] The Russian Federation, for public utilities in all sectors, reserved that "services considered as public utilities as of the date of accession at a national or local level may be subject to public monopolies or to exclusive rights granted to private operators."[113] Montenegro replicated the EU's reservations about public utilities and concessions.[114] Ukraine, in the field of storage

[107] The WTO website mentions 48 Members, whereby 48 includes the EU in addition to all Member State.

[108] GATS/SC/157 (7 May 2019), 3. According to the explanatory note: "Public utilities exist in sectors such as related scientific and technical consulting services, R&D services on social sciences and humanities, technical testing and analysis services, environmental services, health services, transport services and services auxiliary to all modes of transport. Exclusive rights on such services are often granted to private operators, for instance operators with concessions from public authorities, subject to specific service obligations. Given that public utilities often also exist at the sub-central level, detailed and exhaustive sector-specific scheduling is not practical. This limitation does not apply to telecommunications and to computer and related services." *See* ibid.

[109] GATS/SC/157 (7 May 2019), 181–182, 196.

[110] ibid 182.

[111] ibid fn 60 at 182.

[112] GATS/SC/150 (22 April 2013), 11.

[113] GATS/SC/149 (5 November 2012), 4. According to the explanatory note: "Exclusive rights on such services may be granted to private operators, for instance operators with concessions from organs of state power and local self-governmental organs, subject to specific services obligations. Given that public utilities often also exist at the level of the subjects of the Russian Federation and at the level of local self-government, detailed and exhaustive sector-specific scheduling is not practical." *See* ibid fn 4 at 4.

[114] GATS/SC/146 (5 June 2012), 2, footnote 1 at 2. See also GATS/SC/157 (n 109) ibid.

and warehousing services, reserved that "[p]ublic utility concession or licensing procedures may apply in case of occupation of the public domain."[115]

Next comes Vietnam, which in the field of container handling services (under a wider category of maritime auxiliary services) reserved that "[p]ublic utility concession or licensing procedures may apply in case of occupation of the public domain."[116] Cambodia, in the field of pipeline transport services, reserved that "[s]ervices must be provided through a contract of concession granted by the state on a case-by-case basis."[117] Jordan, for all sectors, reserved that "[a]ll investments in public utilities are generally subject to concession. In sectors where service provision is granted by concession, commercial establishment must be in the form of [p]ublic [s]hareholding [C]ompanies."[118] Albania, in the field of storage and warehousing services, reserved that "[p]ublic utility concessions or licensing procedures may apply in case of occupation of the public domain."[119]

The express references to public concessions in the GATS schedules, which by design have not been made to address PPPs as a sophisticated form of government procurement, corroborates the proposition put forth above in this subsection that the liberalisation of the provision of services through commercial presence is often inseparable from the regulation of PPPs, particularly in highly regulated utility sectors. For the multinational enterprises deeply invested in utility services, any public-procurement-specific and PPP-specific measures are akin to general-commerce restrictions for multinational enterprises primarily invested in private markets. Indeed, heavy regulatory (*de iure imperii*) and commercial (*de iure gestionis*) involvement in public utilities of host governments does, after all, affect the entirety of the former's business. Though perhaps superfluous, the express reservations about public concessions are nothing but a memento towards other GATS parties that the domestic PPP-related requirements supersede any conflicting liberalisation measures under the GATS.

3.3 *Past EU Directives*

3.3.1 First-Generation Directives

The express and systematic integration of PPP-specific rules into public procurement regimes has been by far the most advanced in the EU. Concessions were first mentioned in the first-generation public-procurement directives[120] as early as 1971.

---

[115] GATS/SC/144 (10 March 2008), 31.

[116] GATS/SC/142 (19 March 2007) fn 29 at 52.

[117] GATS/SC/140 (25 October 2005), 22.

[118] GATS/SC/128 (15 December 2000), 2.

[119] GATS/SC/131(22 November 2000) fn ** at 45.

[120] First-generation directive include: Commission Directive 70/32/EEC of 17 December 1969 on the provision of goods to the State, to local authorities and other official bodies [1970] OJ L 13

On the one hand, concessions were excluded from the rules on public procurement generally applicable to the selections of the providers of construction works. Specifically, Directive 71/305 concerning the coordination of procedures for the award of public works contracts' stipulated that:

> In the event of the authorities awarding contracts concluding a contract of the same type as that indicated in Article1(a) [i.e. public works contracts] except for the fact that the consideration for the works to be carried out consists either solely in the right to exploit the construction or in this right together with payment, the provisions of this Directive shall not apply to this so-called 'concession' contract [...].[121]

On the other hand, however, a separate simultaneous directive of the first generated hinted that the discriminatory measures against potential foreign private partners should be eliminated from the single market. Namely, the preamble of the Directive 71/304 'concerning the abolition of restrictions on freedom to provide services in respect of public works contracts and on the award of public works contracts to contractors acting through agencies of branches' stipulated that:

> Whereas works contracts coming within ISIC Major Group 40 [[122]] may be awarded to or performed by bodies holding concessions granted by the State, by regional or local authorities or by other legal persons governed by public law; whereas this Directive must, therefore, include such contracts in its scope which represent a considerable number of works; whereas otherwise its scope would be substantially reduced.[123]

Concessions were also subsequently regulated in the Council Directive 72/277/EEC on the publications of notices primarily drafted for the procurement of public works[124] (which, technically, amended the Directive 71/305). The Directive 72/277 provided that:

---

p. 1–3; Council Directive 71/304/EEC of 26 July 1971 concerning the abolition of restrictions on freedom to provide services in respect of public works contracts and on the award of public works contracts to contractors acting through agencies or branches [1971] OJ L 185, p 1–4 (English special edition: Series I Chapter 1971(II), p 0678; Council Directive 71/305/EEC of 26 July 1971 concerning the co-ordination of procedures for the award of public works contracts [1971] OJ L 185, p 5–14 (English special edition: Series I Chapter 1971(II), p 682).

[121] Directive 71/305/EEC (n 121) art 3.1.

[122] The ISIC stands for United Nation's International Standard Industrial Classification and the 'Major Group 40' generally referred back then to 'constriction,' including 1) 'construction (non-specialised, demolition' (class 400), 2) 'construction of buildings (dwellings or other)' (class 401), 3) 'civil engineering; building of roads, bridges, railways, etc.' (class 402), 4) 'installation work' (class 403), 5) 'decorating and finishing' (class 404). At present, ISIC's 'Major Group 40,' is replaced with ISIC's 'section F construction.' *See* UN (Department of Economic and Social Affairs, Statistics Division), 'International Standard Industrial Classification of All Economic Activities Revision 4' (2008) ST/ESA/STAT/SER.M/4/Rev.4 ISBN: 978-92-1-161518-0, 52.

[123] Directive 71/304/EEC (n 121) Preamble.

[124] Council Directive 72/277/EEC of 26 July 1972 concerning the details of publication of notices of public works contracts and concessions in the 'Official Journal of the European Communities' 1972[] OJ L 176 p 12–16. Similar to the Directive 71/305 (n 121) it defines 'public works concession' as "a contract of the same type as that indicated in (a) except for the fact that the consideration for the works to be carried out consists either solely in the right to exploit the construction or in this right together with payment" (Directive 72/277 art 1.d).

- "[w]hereas, in view of the increasing importance of concession contracts in the public works area and of their specific nature, the rules concerning advertising should be brought,"[125]
- "Notices of public works contracts to be published in the Official Journal of the European Communities in conformity with articles 12 and 19 of Directive no 71/305/EEC shall not be longer than one page of that Journal, namely about six hundred and fifty words,"[126]
- "Article 1 [cited in the preceding para] shall apply to notices relating to works concessions and subcontracts provided for under titles I and II of the Declaration of 26 July 1971."[127]
- "[t]he contract notices referred to in Article 2 [cited in the preceding para] and provided for under Title II of the Declaration of 26 July 1971 shall be drawn upon the basis of the headings set out in the model in Annex II."[128]

What draws immediate interest is the reference to the Declaration of 26 July 1971.[129] That Declaration somewhat cured the above-cited exemption of concessions (by way of reminder, in essence, contracts for public works "except for the fact that the consideration for the works to be carried out consists either solely in the right to exploit the construction or in this right together with payment"[130]) from the Directive 71/305. Specifically, the declaration required that, should the contracting authorities want to award public works contracts in the form of concession above value the threshold of 1 million of European Units of Account (EUAs),[131] they ought to prepare notices covering (1) the subject of concession allowing prospective concessionaires to evaluate the call for tenders,[132] (2) personal, technical and financial conditions that ought to be satisfied by the prospective concessionaires,[133] and (3) core criteria that

[125] Directive 72/277 (n 125) Preamble.

[126] ibid art 1.

[127] ibid art 2.

[128] ibid art 3 para 2.

[129] Council [Conseil], 'The Declaration of 26 July 1971 of representatives of the governments of the Member States Meeting within the Council concerning procedures to be followed in the field of public works concession' [Déclaration des représentants des gouvernements des États membres, réunis au sein du Conseil, sur les procédures à suivre en matière de concessions de travaux] (16 August 1971) OJ C82 p 13.

[130] Directive 71/305/EEC (n 121) art 3.1.

[131] "Les États membres conviennent que le pouvoir adjudicateur désireux d'avoir recours à la concession dans les conditions prévues à l'article 3 paragraphe 1 de la directive du Conseil, du 26 juillet 1971, portant coordination des procédures de passation des marchés publics de travaux (1), lorsque le montant global des travaux prévu dépasse un million d'unités de compte, fait connaître son intention au moyen d'un avis." *See* Council (n 130) sec I.

[132] "Cet avis décrit l'objet de la concession de façon suffisamment précise pour permettre une appréciation valable de la part des entrepreneurs intéressés." *See* Council (n 130) sec I.

[133] "Il précise les conditions personnelles, techniques et financières qui devront être remplies par le candidat." *See* Council (n 130) sec I.

will be applied while granting the concession,[134] and (4) allowing at least thirty-five days for submitting tenders.[135]

The Declaration also imposed rather a peculiar requirement on concessionaires concerning subcontracting. Namely, the contracting authorities were obliged to either (1) require the concessionaires to subcontract at least 30% of the total value of public works covered by the concession contract while allowing concessionaires to subcontract a higher share of the concession contract,[136] or (2) invite prospective concessionaires to declare in their bids what percentage of the concession contract they would subcontract to third parties.[137]

Regarding first-generation directives, it is also noteworthy that Directive 71/305 extended the rules of public procurement to concessionaires themselves acting as contracting authorities, by stipulating that "[w]hen the concessionaire is himself one of the authorities awarding contracts, he must apply the national procedures for the award of public works contracts adapted to the provisions of this Directive for works to be carried out by third parties."[138] This move initiated the trend of subjecting various categories of private business to public procurement rules in subsequent generations' directives, including utilities or beneficiaries of public aid, which all are verging on the concept of PPP.

Finally, the framework of Directive 71/305, from which PPPs had been exempted, combined with the Directive 72/277, was not unlike the above-discussed framework of the GPA (see Sect. 3.1). In fact, the perusal of primary sources from preparatory works carried out by several researchers reveals that the works on the first-generation directive substantially overlapped, in terms of involved governments and negotiators as well as discussed problems, with the works at the OEEC's/OECD's (Organisation for European Economic Cooperation/Organisation for Economic Cooperation and Development) 'Machinery Committee,' the results of which were later conveyed to GATT's Tokyo Round.[139]

---

[134] "Il mentionne les principaux critères qui seront retenus pour attribuer le marché..." *See* Council (n 130) sec I.

[135] " et il accorde un délai qui ne peut être inférieur à trente-cinq jours pour la présentation des candidatures." *See* Council (n 130) sec I.

[136] "... soit d'imposer au concessionnaire de confier à des tiers des marchés représentant un pourcentage minimum de 30% (indiqué dans le contrat de concession) de la valeur globale des travaux faisant l'objet de la concession, tout en prévoyant la faculté pour les candidats de majorer ce pourcentage." *See* Council (n 130) sec II.1.a.

[137] "...soit d'inviter les candidats concessionnaires à indiquer eux-mêmes dans leurs offres le pourcentage minimum de la valeur globale des travaux faisant l'objet de la concession, qu'ils comptent confier à des tiers." *See* Council (n 130) sec II.1.b.

[138] Directive 71/305/EEC (n 121) art 3.1. art 3.2.

[139] *See* Górski (n 39) 68–70. *See also* Harvey Gordon, Shane Rimmer and Sue Arrowsmith. 'The Economic Impact of the European Union Regime on Public Procurement: Lessons for the WTO' (1998) 21(2) World Econ 159, 160, 163; Annet Blank and Gabrielle Marceau. 'History of the government procurement negotiations since 1945' (1996) 4 Pub Proc L Rev 77, 88–90. While this is not very relevant for PPPs, it must be noted that the supplies of good were not immediately subjected to the full procedural framework unlike PPP-relevant services which were subjected to some procedural requirement under the Directive 71/305 (n 121). The first-generation goods-related

3.3.2 Second-Generation Directives

Core second-generation directives (Council Directive 88/295/EEC on the supply of goods and Council Directive 89/440/EEC on public works), technically, were brief amendments to the first-generation directives on supplies of goods and provision of public-works-contracts.[140] They were also accompanied by two new directives. Specifically, the Council Directive 89/665/EEC covered the review and appeal procedures against contracting authorities,[141] whereas the Council Directive 90/531/EEC covered procurement by utility companies.[142] The Directive's 89/440 preamble foretold ordering the regulation of concessions for public works by prescribing that "in view of the increasing importance of concession contracts in the public works area and of their specific nature, the rules concerning advertising should be brought within Directive 71/305/EEC."[143] Indeed, the above-cited exemption of concessions from the Directive 71/305 was repealed.[144] Moreover, the definition of 'public-works-concession' mirroring the scope of the repealed exemption was integrated into the amended Directive 71/305/EEC to read follows:

> is a contract of the same type as that indicated in (a) except for the fact that the consideration for the works to be carried out consists either solely in the right to exploit the construction or in this right together with payment.[145]

Likewise, Directive 72/277 was repealed to integrate rules on notices with the amended Directive 71/305,[146] implying that the Declaration of 26 July 1971 became defunct. Apart from such a legislative fine-tuning, it is worth noting that the amended Directive 71/305 prescribed a minimum period of fifty-two days from the date of the notice, in which to submit tenders.[147]

Directive 70/32 (n 121) was akin to the above-discussed Directive 71/304/EEC (n 121) in that both merely generally required Member States to remove discriminatory measures and listed examples of such measures. The procedural framework for the supply of goods was provided a few years later in the Council Directive 77/62/EEC of 21 December 1976 coordinating procedures for the award of public supply contracts [1977] OJ L 013 p 1–14.

[140] Council Directive 88/295/EEC of 22 March 1988 amending Directive 77/62/EEC relating to the coordination of procedures on the award of public supply contracts and repealing certain provisions of Directive 80/767/EEC, OJ [1988] L 127 p 1–14; Council Directive 89/440/EEC of 18 July 1989 amending Directive 71/305/EEC concerning coordination of procedures for the award of public works contracts, [1989] OJ L 210 p 1–21.

[141] Council Directive 89/665/EEC of 21 December 1989 on the coordination of the laws, regulations and administrative provisions relating to the application of review procedures with the award of public supply and public works contracts [2000] OJ L 395 p 33–35.

[142] Council Directive 90/531/EEC of 17 September 1990 on the procurement procedures of entities operating in the water, energy, transport and telecommunications sector [1990] OJ L 297 p -48.

[143] Directive 89/440 (n 141) Preamble.

[144] "Article 3(1), (2) and (3) is hereby repealed…" *See* Directive 89/440 (n 141) art 1.4.

[145] Directive 89/440 (n 141) art 1.1; Directive 71/305/EEC (n 121) as amended by the Directive 89/440 (n 141) art 1.d.

[146] "Directive 77/277/EEC of 26 July 1972 is hereby repealed." Directive 89/440 (n 141) art 2.

[147] Directive 71/305/EEC (n 121) as amended by the Directive 89/440 (n 141) art 15.a.

3.3.3 Third-Generation Directives,

The significant change in the coverage of the EU's procurement regimes in the third-generation directives[148] consisted in adding ordinary services on top of previously covered supplies of goods and the provision of 'public works' (i.e. construction works) along with works concessions. The EU's procurement regime had to be aligned with the developments at the GATT/WTO, including the adoption of the GATS and adding services to the coverage of the GPA. Concessions remained regulated only in the context of public works. The Directive 93/37, repealing the Directive 71/305/EEC as amended by the Directive 89/440, updated the threshold of the application of rules on notices for concessions to EUR5m.[149]

While the Directive 71/305/EEC (both original and the version amended by the Directive 89/440) clearly listed the instances when contracting authorities are allowed to resort to 'direct sourcing' (negotiated procedure without prior notice) for awarding public works, only the Directive 93/37 clarified that such exceptions also ought to apply to public works concessions.[150] These exceptions included:

- "the absence of tenders or of appropriate tenders in response to an open or restricted procedure insofar as the original terms of the contract are not substantially altered and provided that a report is communicated to the Commission at its request,"[151]
- "when, for technical or artistic reasons or for reasons connected with the protection of exclusive rights, the works may only be carried out by a particular contractor,[152]
- "insofar as is strictly necessary when, for reasons of extreme urgency brought about by events unforeseen by the contracting authorities in question, the time limit laid down for the open, restricted or negotiated procedures referred to in paragraph 2 cannot be kept. The circumstances invoked to justify extreme urgency must not, in any event, be attributable to the contracting authorities,"[153]
- "for additional works not included in the project initially considered or in the contract first concluded but which have, through unforeseen circumstances,

[148] Council Directive 93/36/EEC of 14 June 1993 coordinating procedures for the award of public supply contracts [1993] OJ L199 p 1–53; Council Directive 93/37/EEC of 14 June 1993 concerning the coordination of procedures for the award of public works contracts [1993] OJ L 199 p 54–83; Council Directive 92/50/EEC of 18 June 1992 relating to the coordination of procedures for the award of public service contracts [1992] OJ L 209 p 1–24; Council Directive 93/38/EEC of 14 June 1993 coordinating the procurement procedures of entities operating in the water, energy, transport and telecommunications sectors [1993] OJ L 199, p 84–138; Council Directive 92/13/EEC of 25 February 1992 coordinating the laws, regulations, and administrative provisions relating to the application of Community rules on the procurement procedures of entities operating in the water, energy, transport, and telecommunications sectors [1992] OJ L 76 p 14–20.

[149] Directive 93/37 (n 149) art 3.

[150] "An advertisement is not, however, required where works contracts meet the conditions laid down in Article 7 (3)." *See* Directive 93/37 (n 149) art 3.4 first para *in fine.*

[151] Directive 93/37 (n 149) art 7.3.a.

[152] ibid art 7.3.b.

[153] ibid art 7.3.c.

become necessary for the carrying out of the work described therein, on condition that the award is made to the contractor carrying out such work:

- when such works cannot be technically or economically separated from the main contract without great inconvenience to the contracting authorities, or
- when such works, although separable from the execution of the original contract, are strictly necessary to its later stages."

Directive 93/37 also straightened the issue of subcontracting. Namely, unlike the Declaration of 26 July 1971, which mandated such a solution, Directive 93/37 allowed contracting authorities, at their discretion, to require that at least 30% of the concession contract value shall be subcontracted to third parties or not.[154] Moreover, the dichotomy between subcontracting-share discretionally imposed by the contracting authorities or freely declared by prospective concessionaires[155] was cured by the requirement that a minimum subcontracting-share fixed by the contracting authorities shall come along with "the option for candidates to increase this percentage."[156] Worth mentioning from a perspective of foreign investors interested in PPPs are exemptions from subcontracting requirements granted to for (1) consortia ("[u]ndertakings which have formed a group to obtain the concession contract"[157]), and 'affiliated entities defined as:

> any undertaking over which the concessionaire may exercise, directly or indirectly, a dominant influence or which may exercise a dominant influence over the concessionaire or which, in common with the concessionaire, is subject to the dominant influence of another undertaking by virtue of ownership, financial participation or the rules which govern it. A dominant influence on the part of an undertaking shall be presumed when, directly or indirectly in relation to another undertaking, it: - holds the major part of the undertaking's subscribed capital, or - controls the majority of the votes attaching to shares issued by the undertakings, or - can appoint more than half of the members of the undertaking's administrative, managerial or supervisory body.[158]

The Commissions' interpretative communication from April 2000[159] on the application of the Directive 93/37 elucidated black-letter-law on concessions in several respects. Foremost, the Communication clarified that all the rules of the single markets apply to all possible forms of PPPs that go much beyond the concept of public-works-concessions, by noting that the fact that:

> other forms of concessions do not fall within the scope of the directives on public contracts (…) does not mean that concessions are not subject to the rules and principles of the Treaty. Indeed, insofar as these concessions result from acts of State, the purpose of which is to

[154] "The contracting authority may:…" *See* Directive 93/37 (n 149) art 3.2.

[155] *See* Council (n 130) sec I (cited in n 137).

[156] Directive 93/37 (n 149) art 3.2. second *tiret*.

[157] ibid art 3.4s para.

[158] ibid art 3.4 third para.

[159] Commission, 'Commission interpretative communication on concessions under Community law' (29 April 2000) vol 43OJ C 121 p 2.

> provide economic activities or the supply of goods, they are subject to the relevant provisions of the Treaty and to the principles which derive from the Court Case law.[160]

Among other issues, the Communication addressed the problem of 'service concessions' unregulated in the second generation's directive devoted to services,[161] to which at least the general antidiscriminatory rules of the single market would apply.[162] The Communications noted that (1) "[w]orks concessions are assumed to serve a different purpose from service concessions [which] may lead to possible differences in terms of investment and duration between the two types of concessions,"[163] and (2) "it is worth determining exactly what this type of concession is, especially if it is a mixed contract which also includes a service element [which] is virtually always the case in practice, since public works concessionaires often provide services to users on the basis of the structure they have built."[164]

The latter issue had been settled in *Gestión Hotelera* in a way that "where the works [...] are merely incidental to the main object of the award, the award, taken in its entirety, cannot be characterised as a public works contract."[165] However, in *Data Processing*, the ECJ found that "[t]he purchase of the equipment required for the establishment of a data-processing system can be separated from the activities involved in its design and operation. The Italian Government could have approached companies specialising in software development for the design of the data-processing systems in question and, in compliance with the directive, could have purchased hardware meeting the technical specifications laid down by such companies"[166]—meaning, as summarised by the Communication, that "when a contract includes two elements which may be separated (e.g. supplies and services), the rules which apply to each should be applied separately."[167]

The Communication also addressed the problem of concessions in the utility sectors, differentiating between three scenarios (Table 5):

- "In the first case, the State or other public authority not operating specifically in one of the four sectors governed by the utilities Directive awards a concession involving an economic activity in one of these four sectors. The rules and principles of the Treaty described above apply to this award, as does the works Directive if it is a works concession."[168]

---

[160] Commission (n 160) point 2 at p 2–3.

[161] Directive 92/50 (n 149).

[162] *See eg* Judgment of the Court of 26 April 1994. - Commission of the European Communities v Italian Republic. - Concession for the lottery computerization system. - Case C-272/91 (*1*994) ECR p I-01409 (*Lottomatica*).

[163] Commission (n 160) point 2.2. sixth para at p 4.

[164] ibid. point 2.2. sixth para at p 4.

[165] Judgment of the Court (Sixth Chamber) of 19 April 1994. Case C-331/92, ECR (1994) I-1329 (*Gestión Hotelera*), para 26.

[166] Judgment of the Court of 5 December 1989. Case C-3/88 (1989) ECR p 4035. (*Data Processing*), para 19.

[167] Commission (n 160) point 2.3 s para at p 4.

[168] ibid point 3.3 third para at p 10.

Table 5 Utility concessions in the third-generation classical directive

Concession grantor	Sectors	Application of the treaties	Application of the directive 93/37
Public authority	Not listed in Directive 93/38	Yes	Yes
	listed in Directive 93/38 (water, energy, transport and telecommunications	Yes	No
Private entity	All	No	No

- "In the second case, a public authority operating specifically in one of the four sectors governed by the utilities Directive decides to grant a concession. The rules and principles of the Treaty are therefore applicable insofar as the grantor is a public entity. Even in the case of a works concession, only the rules and principles of the Treaty are applicable, since the works Directive does not cover concessions granted by an entity operating specifically in one of the four sectors governed by Directive 93/38/EEC."[169]
- "Lastly, if the grantor is a private entity, it is not subject to either the rules or the principles described above."[170]

3.3.4 Fourth-Generation Directives

Codification

So-called codification was the highlight of the fourth generation.[171] Previously separate directives for the supply of goods, provisions of public works, and provisions of services were merged into one Directive 2004/18, often referred to as the 'Classical Directive.'[172] In contrast, procurement by utilities and review procedures remained regulated in separate directives, respectively 2004/17[173] and 2007/66.[174]

[169] ibid point 3.3 fourth para at p 10.

[170] ibid point 3.3 fifth para at p 10.

[171] Directive 2004/18/EC of the European Parliament and of the Council of 31 March 2004 on the coordination of procedures for the award of public works contracts, public supply contracts and public service contracts [2004] OJ L 134 p 114–240; Directive 2004/17/EC of the European Parliament and of the Council of 31 March 2004 coordinating the procurement procedures of entities operating in the water, energy, transport and postal services sectors, [2004] OJ L 134 p 1–113; Directive 2007/66/EC of the European Parliament and of the Council of 11 December 2007 amending Council Directives 89/665/EEC and 92/13/EEC with regard to improving the effectiveness of review procedures concerning the award of public contracts [2007] OJ L 335 p 31–46.

[172] Directive 2004/18 (n 172).

[173] Directive 2004/17 (n 172).

[174] Directive 2007/66 (n 172).

Concessions Under Classical Directive

On top of public-works-concessions defined as before,[175] the Classical Directive eventually introduced a legal concept of 'service concession' defined as "a contract of the same type as a public service contract except for the fact that the consideration for the provision of services consists either solely in the right to exploit the service or in this right together with payment."[176] However, the Classical Directive also peculiarly excluded such service concessions subject to a somewhat opaque reservation that such exemptions shall be without prejudice to the directive's requirements concerning granting special or exclusive rights.[177] Those requirements read as follows:

> Where a contracting authority grants special or exclusive rights to carry out a public service activity to an entity other than such a contracting authority, the act by which that right is granted shall provide that, in respect of the supply contracts which it awards to third parties as part of its activities, the entity concerned must comply with the principle of non-discrimination on the basis of nationality.[178]

It follows that, unlike public-works-concessions, services concessions were not subjected to any particular procedural rules (Table 6). However, similar to the Commission Communication from 2003 (see Sect. 3.3.3 *in fine*) the Classical Directive reminded contracting authorities that the general rules of non-discrimination in the single European markets enshrined in the EU Treaties still apply to all public services contracts. In the case of public-works-concessions, the rules remained pretty much unaltered, including publication of notices,[179] time limits,[180] or requirements concerning the scope of subcontracting.[181] The Classical Directive updated the threshold to EUR624,200,[182] and also differentiated thresholds for contracts further subcontracted by concessionaires to third parties depending on whether a concessionaire is a contracting authority sensu stricto[183] or a private entity subjected to public

[175] Directive 2004/18 (n 172) art 1.3.

[176] ibid art 1.4.

[177] Directive 2004/18 (n 172) art 17. The directive also exempted 'Service contracts awarded on the basis of an exclusive right': "This Directive shall not apply to public service contracts awarded by a contracting authority to another contracting authority or to an association of contracting authorities on the basis of an exclusive right which they enjoy pursuant to a published law, regulation or administrative provision which is compatible with the Treaty." *See* Directive 2004/18 (n 172) art 18.

[178] Directive 2004/18 (n 172) art 3.

[179] ibid art 58.

[180] ibid art 59.

[181] ibid art 60.

[182] ibid art 56.1.

[183] For clarity, the Directive 2004/18 (n 172) replicated the definition of 'contracting authorities' from the second-generation directive Directive 89/440 (n 141) whereas the second-generation Directive 71/305/EEC (n 121) had been much more laconic to merely specify that: "[t]he State, Regional or Local Authorities and the Legal Persons Governed by Public Law Specified in Annex I Shall Be Regarded as " Authorities Awarding Contracts" (art 1.B). The Directive 2004/18 (n 172) is much more elaborate to specify that contracting authorities' "means the State, regional or local authorities,

procurement rules. Contracting authority sensu stricto, i.e. chiefly government agencies,[184] that can be awarded concessions based on special or exclusive rights without having to apply the rules of the Directive 2044/18,[185] had to apply standard thresholds (EUR162,000 or EUR249,000 for public supply and service contracts depending on circumstances, and EUR 6,242,000 for public works contracts[186]).[187] In contrast, private concessionaires that are not contracting authorities sensu stricto could apply the threshold of EUR6,242,000 across the board, below which advertising on subcontracts was not mandatory regardless of whether concessionaires subcontracted supply of goods, provision of services, or performance of public works (Table 7).[188]

Concessions Under Utilities Directive

Depending on the interpretation, the selection of concessionaires in the utility sectors (water, energy, transport and postal services sectors) was found either a regulatory vacuum or remained regulated under the Classical Directive rather than the Utilities Directive. This issue had previously been clearly settled in second-generation neither

---

bodies governed by public law, associations formed by one or several of such authorities or one or several of such bodies governed by public law" (art 1.9 *in initio*) including anybody 1) "established for the specific purpose of meeting needs in the general interest, not having an industrial or commercial character" (art 1.9.A), 2) "having legal personality" (art 1.9.B), and 3) "financed, for the most part, by the State, regional or local authorities, or other bodies governed by public law; or subject to management supervision by those bodies; or having an administrative, managerial or supervisory board, more than half of whose members are appointed by the State, regional or local authorities, or by other bodies governed by public law" (art 1.9.C),

[184] For clarity, the Directive 2004/18 (n 172) replicated the definition of 'contracting authorities' from the second-generation directive Directive 89/440 (n 141) whereas the second-generation Directive 71/305/EEC (n 121) had been much more laconic to merely specify that: "[t]he State, Regional or Local Authorities and the Legal Persons Governed by Public Law Specified in Annex I Shall Be Regarded as " Authorities Awarding Contracts" (art 1.B). The Directive 2004/18 (n 172) is much more elaborate to specify that contracting authorities' "means the State, regional or local authorities, bodies governed by public law, associations formed by one or several of such authorities or one or several of such bodies governed by public law" (art 1.9 *in initio*) including anybody 1) "established for the specific purpose of meeting needs in the general interest, not having an industrial or commercial character" (art 1.9.A), 2) "having legal personality" (art 1.9.B), and 3) "financed, for the most part, by the State, regional or local authorities, or other bodies governed by public law; or subject to management supervision by those bodies; or having an administrative, managerial or supervisory board, more than half of whose members are appointed by the State, regional or local authorities, or by other bodies governed by public law" (art 1.9.C),

[185] Directive 2004/18 (n 172) art 18 cited in n 178.

[186] Directive 2004/18 (n 172) art 7.

[187] ibid art 62.

[188] ibid art 63.

Table 6 Service and works concessions plus subcontracting under the fourth-generation classical directive

Selection of concessionaire			Subcontracting		
Concession type	Application of the treaties	Application of the directive 2004/18	Type of concessionaire	Application of the treaties	Application of the directive 2004/18
Works concession	YES	YES	Public authority	Yes	Full application
			Private	Yes	Limited application
Service concession	Yes	No, subject to special and exclusive right	Public authority	Yes	No
			private	Unclear	No

Table 7 Utility concessions in the fourth generation

Sector	Concession type	Application of the treaties	Application of the directive 2004/18	Application of the directive 2004/17
Not listed in arts 3–7 of the Directive 2004/17	Works concession	Yes	Yes	No
	service concessions	Yes	No, subject to special and exclusive right	No
Listed in arts 3–7 of the Directive 2004/17	Works concession	Yes	No, only postal services	No (exclusion under art 18)
	service concessions	Yes	Unclear, if 'yes', then limited to special and exclusive rights	

in the Directive 89/440 on public works nor in the Directive 90/531 on procurement by utility companies.[189] The third-generation directives did not address it either.[190]

[189] This lacuna in the second generation consisted in that, on the one hand, the Directive 71/305/EEC (n 121) as amended by the Directive 89/440 (n 141) excluded "works contracts awarded by contracting authorities, in so far as those contracts concern the production, transport and distribution of drinking water, or those contracting authorities whose principal activity lies in the production and distribution of energy" (art 1b.4.b.). On the other hand however, the provisions of the Directive 90/531 (n 143) concerning 'concessions' were rather perfunctory and used the term of 'concessions' in an inconsistent manner. In the main text, Directive 90/531 (n 143) only once referred to 'concessions or authorizations' in context of interim measures in the field of exploration or Extracting of oil, gas, coal or other solid fuels (art 3.3.).

[190] This lacuna in the second generation consisted in that, on the one hand, the Directive 93/37 (n 149) stated in its preamble that "this Directive does not apply to certain works contracts which are awarded in the water, energy, transport and telecommunication sectors covered by Directive

In the fourth generation, though, the critical provision, to dwell on, is that "this Directive shall not apply to works and service concessions which are awarded by contracting entities carrying out one or more of the activities referred to in Articles 3–7 [chiefly utilities], where those concessions are awarded for carrying out those activities."[191] This begs the question of how, if at all, the selection of concessionaires in the utility sectors was regulated in the fourth generation?

For starters, the activities allotted for being regulated the Utilities Directive, similar to the second-generation Directive 90/531,[192] included all possible fields in which to form PPPs such as (1) gas sector, including "the provision or operation of fixed networks intended to provide a service to the public in connection with the production, transport or distribution of gas or heat, or […] the supply of gas or heat to such networks,"[193] (2) electricity sector including "the provision or operation of fixed networks intended to provide a service to the public in connection with the production, transport or distribution of electricity, or[…] the supply of electricity to such networks,"[194] (3) water sector including "the provision or operation of fixed networks intended to provide a service to the public in connection with the production, transport or distribution of drinking water, or […] the supply of drinking water to such networks,"[195] (4) transport sector including the "provision or operation of networks providing a service to the public in the field of transport by railway, automated systems, tramway, trolley bus, bus or cable,"[196] 5) postal sector including "sorting, routing and delivery of postal items,"[197] (6) exploration and extraction of "oil, gas, coal or other solid fuels,"[198] and finally (7) "the provision of airports and maritime or inland ports or other terminal facilities to carriers by air, sea or inland waterway."[199] Compared with the second and third generations, the Utilities Directive ceased to subjecting telecommunications companies to public procurement rules.[200]

Secondly, similar to the second-generation Directive 90/531 and third-generation Directive 93/38 on utilities, the fourth-generation Utilities Directive differentiated

---

90/531/EEC." On the other hand, the main text of the Directive 93/38 (n 149) which replaced the Directive 90/531(n 143) did not mention 'concessions at all.'.

[191] Directive 2004/17 (n 172) art 18.

[192] Directive 90/531 (n 143) art 2.

[193] Directive 2004/17 (n 172) art 3.1.

[194] ibid art 3.3.

[195] ibid art 4.1.

[196] ibid art 5.1.

[197] ibid art 6.2.b.

[198] ibid art 7.a.

[199] ibid art 7.b.

[200] "(…)A legislative framework, as mentioned in the Fourth report on the implementation of the telecommunications regulations of 25 November 1998, has been adopted to open this sector. One of its consequences has been the introduction of effective competition, both de jure and de facto, in this sector. (…) It is therefore no longer appropriate to maintain the Advisory Committee on Telecommunications Procurement set up by Council Directive 90/531/EEC of 17 September 1990 on the procurement procedures of entities operating in the water, energy transport and telecommunications sectors(9). *See* Directive 2004/17 (n 172) Preamble, points 5 and 6.

between three categories of 'contracting entities,' including (1) contracting authorities sensu stricto defined as in the Classical Directive,[201] (2) 'public undertakings' defined as "any undertaking over which the contracting authorities may exercise directly or indirectly a dominant influence by virtue of their ownership of it, their financial participation therein, or the rules which govern it,"[202] and (3) private entities to the extent that these "have as one of their activities any of the activities referred to in Articles 3–7 [utility sectors[203]], or any combination thereof and operate on the basis of special or exclusive rights granted by a competent authority of a Member State. 'Special or exclusive right' were defined as "rights granted by a competent authority of a Member State by way of any legislative, regulatory or administrative provision the effect of which is to limit the exercise of activities defined in Articles 3–7 to one or more entities, and which substantially affects the ability of other entities to carry out such activity."[204]

It follows from these provisions that the Utilities Directive was designed to merely regulate procurement by the utility companies, which, in a sense, is a systematic equivalent of subcontracting by concessionaires. Indeed, in a conceptual rather than strictly legal sense, both utility companies with special or exclusive rights and concessionaires are a kind of governments' private partners which further subcontract simple contracts for the supply of goods, provision of services of performance of construction works to third parties (Table 8). Before such private partners subcontract a part of their operation to third parties, they need to be selected by governments as governments' private partners, whether that be a grant or special and exclusive rights, an award of the concession contract, or a combination thereof.

Nonetheless, at the same time, the Utilities Directive was not designed to regulate the selection of concessionaires in the utility sectors (Table 7, this subsection *in initio*). As mentioned above in this subsection, the Utilities Directive excluded awarding concessions for carrying out activities in the sectors such as gas, electricity, water, transport, postal services, airports, ports, and other transportation terminals.[205] Logically then, awards of such concession should have been regulated in the Classical Directive if not for the fact that the Classical Directive did not apply to such sectors at all.[206] If the Utilities Directive did not apply to simple "contracts in the water, energy, transport and postal services sectors,"[207] it all the more did not apply to

[201] Directive 2004/17 (n 172) arts 2.1 and 2.2.a; the Directive 2004/18 (n 172) art 1.9 cited in note 184; Directive 90/531 (n 143) art 2.1.a.

[202] Directive 2004/17 (n 172) arts 2.1.b and 2.2.a; Directive 90/531 (n 143) art 2.1.a.

[203] *See* ns 194–200.

[204] Directive 2004/17 (n 172) art 2.3.

[205] Directive 2004/17 (n 172) art 18.

[206] "This Directive shall not apply to public contracts which, under Directive 2004/17/EC, are awarded by contracting authorities exercising one or more of the activities referred to in Articles 3 to 7 of that Directive and are awarded for the pursuit of those activities, or to public contracts excluded from the scope of that Directive under Article 5(2) and Articles 19, 26 and 30 thereof." *See* Directive 2004/18 (n 172) art 12 first para.

[207] Directive 2004/18 (n 172) art 12 heading.

Table 8 Special and exclusive rights versus concessions

Selection of the private partner				Subcontracting by the private partner	
Arrangement with the government	Application of the treaties	Application of the directive 2004/18	Type of private partner	Application of the treaties	Applicable directive
Special and exclusive right	Yes	NO, except for postal services	Utility Company With Special and exclusive rights	Yes	2004/17
Works concession contract	Yes	Yes	public authority		
			private	Yes	Full application
Service concession contract	Yes	No, subject to special and exclusive right	public authority	Yes	Limited application
			private	Yes	No

concessions in such sectors, with the surprising exception of postal services. Namely, the Classical Directive provided that:

> However, this Directive shall continue to apply to public works concessions awarded by contracting authorities carrying out one or more of the activities referred to in Article 6 of Directive 2004/17/EC and awarded for those activities, insofar as the Member State concerned takes advantage of the option referred to in the second subparagraph of Article 71 thereof to defer its application.[208]

3.4 *Fifth-Generation Directives (Current)*

3.4.1 Scope of Application

Most of the previous legislative shortcomings discussed above were remedied in the fifth generation.[209] Concessions lived to eventually see a separate Directive 2014/23[210] devoted to such a complex form of public procurement. The references

---

[208] ibid art 12s para.

[209] Directive 2014/24/EU of the European Parliament and of the Council of 26 February 2014 on public procurement and repealing Directive 2004/18/EC (2014) OJ L 94, p. 65–242; Directive 2014/25/EU of the European Parliament and of the Council of 26 February 2014 on procurement by entities operating in the water, energy, transport, and postal services sectors, and repealing Directive 2004/17/EC (2014) OJ L 94, p. 243–374; Directive 2014/23/EU of the European Parliament and of the Council of 26 February 2014 on the award of concession contracts (2014) OJ L 94, p. 1–64.

[210] Directive 2014/23 (n 210).

to concessions in the New Classical Directive[211] and the New Utilities Directive[212] are limited to the provisions on "mixed contracts containing elements of supply, works and service contracts and of concessions," which settle which directive ought to be applied in a particular case depending on the share and value of each element in a particular mixed contract.[213] Likewise, the Concession directive differentiated between mixed contracts, which are objectively separable into different parts, and those mixed contracts which are not[214] (Table 9). In the case of inseparable contracts, the choice between the Concessions Directive, the New Classical Directives and the New Utilities Directive depends on the primary subject matter of the mixed contract.[215] In the case of separable contracts, a contracting authority might either decide to split the mixed contract or not do so. In the case of split contracts, pretty obviously, "the decision as to which legal regime applies to anyone of such separate contracts shall be taken on the basis of the characteristics of the separate part concerned."[216] In the case of contracts that have not been split despite being separable, the Concession Directive could only be applied to the entire mixed contract only on the condition that the mixed contract does not contain elements covered by the New Classical and Utilities Directives. In such a case, either the New Classical Directive or the New Utilities Directive shall apply to the entire mixed contract.[217]

The improvements on the fourth generation commenced with a much more elaborate definition of concessions, to read as follows:

> 'concessions' means works or services concessions, as defined in points (a) and (b):
>
> (a) 'works concession' means a contract for pecuniary interest concluded in writing by means of which one or more contracting authorities or contracting entities entrust the execution of works to one or more economic operators the consideration for which consists either solely in the right to exploit the works that are the subject of the contract or in that right together with payment;
>
> (b) 'services concession' means a contract for pecuniary interest concluded in writing by means of which one or more contracting authorities or contracting entities entrust the provision and the management of services other than the execution of works referred to in point (a) to one or more economic operators, the consideration of which consists

---

[211] Directive 2014/24/EU (n 210).

[212] Directive 2014/25/EU (n 210).

[213] *See* Directive 2014/24/EU (n 210) art 3.4 third para; Directive 2014/25/EU (n 210) art 5.3 third para.

[214] Directive 2014/23 (n 210) art 20.2.

[215] "In the event such contracts involve both elements of a services concession and of a supply contract, the main subject-matter shall be determined according to which of the estimated values of the respective services or supplies is the higher." *See* Directive 2014/23 (n 210) art 20.5.

[216] Directive 2014/23 (n 210) art 20.5 first para.

[217] ibid art 20.4. There are also separate 'conflict-of0laws' rules regarding mixed contracts which contain elements covered by the 'Defence Directive,' the discussion of which would, however, go beyond the scope of this paper. *See* ibid art 20. *See also* Directive 2009/81/EC of the European Parliament and of the Council of 13 July 2009 on the coordination of procedures for the award of certain works contracts, supply contracts and service contracts by contracting authorities or entities in the fields of defence and security, and amending Directives 2004/17/EC and 2004/18/EC (2019) OJ L216 p 76–136.

Table 9 Mixed contracts in fifth generation

Type of a mixed contract	The decision of the contracting authority	Application of the Directive 2014/23	Application of the Directive 2014/24 or 2014/2015 -
Inseparable contract	No choice	Yes, if it applies to the main subject matter of the contract	Yes if it applies to the main subject matter of the contract
Separable contract	The contract is not split nonetheless	Yes, to the whole contract **unless** it contains elements covered by 2014/24 or 2014/25	Yes, to the whole contract **if** it contains elements covered by 2014/24 or 2014/25
	The contract is not split	Yes, if it applies to any of the separated parts	Yes if it applies to any of the separated parts

either solely in the right to exploit the services that are the subject of the contract or in that right together with payment.[218]

The Concessions Directive filled in the *lacuna* concerning awarding concession contracts in utility sectors. This directive provided that it shall apply the award of works or services concessions by both 'contracting authorities' and 'contracting entities,' the latter of which to the extent that the works or services covered by the concession contract are intended for the pursuit of one of the activities in utility sectors.[219] The new list of utility sectors subjected to the rules on awarding concessions was in principle aligned with the scope of application of the New Utilities Directive.[220] The list has included (1) in the sector of gas and heat, "the provision or operation of fixed networks intended to provide a service to the public in connection with the production, transport or distribution of gas or heat,"[221] along with the supply of gas or heat to such fixed networks,"[222] (2) in the sector of electricity, "the provision or operation of fixed networks intended to provide a service to the public

[218] Directive 2014/23 (n 210) art 2.1. This same art *in fine* continued to further clarify that: "The award of a works or services concession shall involve the transfer to the concessionaire of an operating risk in exploiting those works or services encompassing demand or supply risk or both. The concessionaire shall be deemed to assume operating risk where, under normal operating conditions, it is not guaranteed to recoup the investments made or the costs incurred in operating the works or the services which are the subject-matter of the concession. The part of the risk transferred to the concessionaire shall involve real exposure to the vagaries of the market, such that any potential estimated loss incurred by the concessionaire shall not be merely nominal or negligible."

[219] Directive 2014/23 (n 210) art 1.1. However, [n]on-economic services of general interest shall fall outside the scope of this Directive." *See* ibid art 1.2.

[220] Directive 2014/25/EU (n 210) art 8 (gas and heat), art 9 (electricity), article 10 (water), art 11 (transport services), art 12 (ports and airports), art 13 (postal services), art 14 (extraction of oil and gas and exploration for, or extraction of, coal or other solid fuels).

[221] Directive 2014/23 (n 210) annex II point 1.a.

[222] ibid annex II point 1.b.

in connection with the production, transport or distribution of electricity,"[223] along with "the supply of electricity to such fixed networks,"[224] (3) in the "transport by railway, automated systems, tramway, trolley bus, bus or cable,"[225] (4) in the sector of "airports and maritime or inland ports or other terminal facilities to carriers by air, sea or inland waterway,"[226] (5) in the sector of postal services,[227] (6) in the sectors of oil or gas extraction[228] plus exploration and extraction of coal or other solid fuels.[229] However, neither the Concession Directive nor the New Utilities Directive shall apply to so-called 'exempt markets,' i.e. markets exposed to sufficient competition based on the assessment by the Commission.[230]

The distinction between 'contracting authorities' and 'contracting entities' is rather unfortunate because, etymologically, it alludes to the subjective coverage of the Concession Directive, i.e. who the public partner is. In contrast, this distinction de facto merely differentiates between the objective coverage of the Concession Directive, i.e. what the subject matter of the partnership is (*see* Table 10). If this distinction was to determine Concession's Directive subjective coverage, then it is not a proper taxonomy. Namely, 'contracting authorities,' are defined as "State, regional [[231]] or local authorities [[232]], bodies governed by public law [[233]] or associations formed by one or more such authorities or one or more such bodies governed by public law

[223] ibid annex II point 2.a.

[224] ibid annex II point 2.b.

[225] ibid annex II point 3.

[226] ibid annex II point 4.

[227] ibid annex II point 5.

[228] ibid annex II point 6.a.

[229] ibid annex II point 6.b.

[230] ibid art 16. *See also* Commission Implementing Decision (EU) 2016/1804 of 10 October 2016 on the detailed rules for the application of Articles 34 and 35 of Directive 2014/25/EU of the European Parliament and of the Council on procurement by entities operating in the water, energy, transport and postal services sectors (notified under document C(2016) 6351) OJ L275 p 39–53.

[231] "'Regional authorities' includes all authorities of the administrative units listed non-exhaustively in NUTS 1 and 2, as referred to in Regulation (EC) No 1059/2003 of the European Parliament and of the Council." *See* Directive 2014/23 (n 210).

[232] "'Local authorities' includes all authorities of the administrative units falling under NUTS 3 and smaller administrative units, as referred to in Regulation (EC) No 1059/2003." *See* Directive 2014/23 (n 210).

[233] "Bodies governed by public law' means bodies that have all of the following characteristics: (a) they are established for the specific purpose of meeting needs in the general interest, not having an industrial or commercial character; (b) they have legal personality; and (c) they are financed, for the most part, by the State, regional or local authorities, or by other bodies governed by public law; or are subject to management supervision by those bodies or authorities; or have an administrative, managerial or supervisory board, more than half of whose members are appointed by the State, regional or local authorities, or by other bodies governed by public law." *See* Directive 2014/23 (n 210).

Table 10 Contracting authorities and contracting entities in fifth generation

<table>
<tr><th>Subjective Coverage</th><th>Objective coverage</th><th>Need special or exclusive rights to be covered?</th></tr>
<tr><td rowspan="2">State, regional or local authorities bodies governed by public law</td><td>‘Contracting authorities, i.e. activities other than Annex II</td><td rowspan="3">No</td></tr>
<tr><td rowspan="3">Contracting entities, i.e. activities listed Annex II</td></tr>
<tr><td>Public undertaking</td></tr>
<tr><td>Private enterprise</td><td>Yes</td></tr>
</table>

other than those authorities, bodies or associations which pursue one of the activities referred to in Annex II and award a concession for the pursuit of one of those activities.”[234]

For comparison ‘contracting entities’ are defined as (1) “State, regional or local authorities, bodies governed by public law or associations formed by one or more such authorities or one or more such bodies governed by public law,”[235] (2) public undertakings,[236] (3) other entities “which operate on the basis of special or exclusive rights, granted for the exercise of one of the activities referred to in Annex II.”[237] It follows that ‘State, regional or local authorities, bodies governed by public law’ can fall under a different concept under the same legislative act, depending on the nature of their activities in a specific context. This per se would be an example of a poor legislative technique. However, this terminological chaos merely reflects that the procurers subjected to the New Classical Directive are referred to as ‘contracting authorities’ while the procurers subjected to the New Utilities Directive are referred to as ‘contracting entities.’[238]

The terminological and sematic issues aside, the inclusion of ‘other’ entities (i.e. private commercial enterprises) along with contracting authorities[239] and public

[234] Directive 2014/23 (n 210) art 6.1.

[235] Directive 2014/23 (n 210) art 7.1.a.

[236] ibid art 7.1.b. ‘Public undertaking’ is defined as “any undertaking over which the contracting authorities may exercise, directly or indirectly, a dominant influence by virtue of their ownership thereof, their financial participation therein, or the rules which govern it” whereby “[a] dominant influence on the part of the contracting authorities shall be presumed in any of the following cases, in which those authorities, directly or indirectly: (a) hold the majority of the undertaking’s subscribed capital; (b) control the majority of the votes attaching to shares issued by the undertaking; (c) can appoint more than half of the undertaking’s administrative, management or supervisory body. *See* Directive 2014/23 (n 210) art 7.4.

[237] Directive 2014/23 (n 210) art 7.1.c.

[238] Funnily enough, unlike the Concessions Directive which repeats the same phrases, the New Utilities Directive defines ‘contracting entities’ by referring to ‘contracting authorities,’ stating that “[f]or the purpose of this Directive contracting entities are entities, which [...] are contracting authorities or public undertakings and which pursue one of the activities referred to in Articles 8 to 14.” *See* Directive 2014/23 (n 210) art 4.1.a.

[239] *See* n 236.

undertakings[240] in the concept of 'contracting entities' is a huge novelty. This provision implies that the detailed rules boosting competition now also apply to private enterprises that choose their private partners in the capacity of public partners.[241] In other words, just like in the case of simple supply, works, and service contracts under the New Utilities Directive and previous utility-sectors-related provisions, the rules of competition apply to concession contracts if private enterprises (which act in the capacity of public partners and are seeking private partners) operate in the utility sectors based on special or exclusive rights. In line with the developments in the New Utilities Directive, the definitions of such rights have also been updated to read as follows:

- 'exclusive right' "means a right granted by a competent authority of a Member State by means of any law, regulation or published administrative provision which is compatible with the Treaties the effect of which is to limit the exercise of an activity to a single economic operator and which substantially affects the ability of other economic operators to carry out such an activity,"[242]
- 'special right' "means a right granted by a competent authority of a Member State by means of any law, regulation or published administrative provision which is compatible with the Treaties the effect of which is to limit the exercise of an activity to two or more economic operators and which substantially affects the ability of other economic operators to carry out such an activity."[243]

There are dozens of instances in which the Concession Directive would not apply to a specific scenario despite *prima facie* fitting the most general concepts of concessions, Annex II activities, contracting authorities, contracting entities, public undertakings or special and exclusive rights. The institution of exempt markets covered by Annex II yet exposed to sufficient competition has already been mentioned above.[244] Noteworthy also are instances where other entities *prima facie* have rights in principle classifiable as special or exclusive, yet such rights ought not to be so classified. This is the case of special or exclusive rights granted "by means of a procedure in which adequate publicity has been ensured and where the granting of those rights was based on objective criteria,"[245] including rights being granted under (1) procurement procedures involving a prior call for competition in conformity with the New Classical Directive, New Utilities Directive or the Defence Directive,[246]

---

[240] *See* n 237.

[241] It is a completely distinct issue from, whether private partners, under such scenario, would have to apply public procurement rules further down the line while awarding simple supply, works and service contracts. They would if private partners themselves, under whatever specific facts, fall under the definition of either the 'contracting authorities' in the New Classical Directive or 'contracting entities' in the New Utilities Directive.

[242] Directive 2014/23 (n 210) art 5.10.

[243] ibid art 5.11.

[244] See n 231.

[245] Directive 2014/23 (n 210) art 7.2.

[246] ibid art 7.2.a.

and (2) procedures "ensuring adequate prior transparency for granting authorisations on the basis of objective criteria" listed in Annex III to the Concession Directive."[247] These procedures include (1) "[g]ranting authorisation to operate natural gas installations in accordance with the procedures laid down in Article 4 of Directive 2009/73/EC,"[248] (2) "[a]uthorisation or an invitation to tender for the construction of new electricity production installations in accordance with Directive 2009/72/EC,"[249] (3) "[t]he granting in accordance with the procedures laid down in Article 9 of Directive 97/67/EC of authorisations in relation to a postal service which is not or shall not be reserved,"[250] (4) "[a] procedure for granting an authorisation to carry on an activity involving the exploitation of hydrocarbons in accordance with Directive 94/22/EC,"[251]and (5) "[p]ublic service contracts within the meaning of Regulation (EC) No 1370/2007 for the provision of public passenger transport services by bus, tramway, rail or metro, which have been awarded on the basis of a competitive tendering procedure in accordance with its Article 5(3), provided that its length is in conformity with Article 4(3) or (4) of that Regulation."[252]

3.4.2 Rules Applicable to Covered Concessions

The procedural rules under the Concession Directive, which aim to open the concessions market to international competition,[253] became very complex in the fifth generation. At the same time, these rules became very orderly compared to the pretty chaotic situation before. To start with concessions' valuation, the threshold did not change subject to inflation indexation, was set up at EUR 5186 000 upon Concession Directive's entry into force.[254] While calculating concession's value for determining whether Concession Directive applies, several factors ought to be taken into consideration including (1) "the value of any form of option and any extension of the duration of the concession,"[255] (2) "revenue from the payment of fees and fines by the users of the works or services other than those collected on behalf of the contracting authority or contracting entity,"[256] (3) "payments or any financial advantage in any form whatsoever made by the contracting authority or contracting entity or any other public

---

247 ibid art 7.2.b.

248 ibid Annex III point 1.

249 ibid Annex III point 2.

250 ibid Annex III point 3.

251 ibid Annex III point 4.

252 ibid Annex III point 5.

253 Of course, primarily in the European regional context. However, opening procurement markets to rules of competition and to supplies, services providers, works contractors, or concessionaires regardless of their original have proven to de facto open those markets not only to persons originating from other Member states but also third countries.

254 Directive 2014/23 (n 210) art 8.1.

255 ibid art 8.3.a.

256 ibid art 8.3.b.

authority to the concessionaire, including compensation for compliance with a public service obligation and public investment subsidies,"[257] (4) "the value of grants or any other financial advantages, in any form, from third parties for the performance of the concession,"[258] (5) "revenue from sales of any assets which are part of the concession,"[259] (6) "the value of all the supplies and services that are made available to the concessionaire by the contracting authorities or contracting entities, provided that they are necessary for executing the works or providing the services,"[260] 7) "any prizes or payments to candidates or tenderers."[261]

The most general rule of awarding concessions is that, while contracting authorities or contracting entities "shall have the freedom to organise the procedure leading to the choice of concessionaire,"[262] they have to adhere to the principles of equal treatment, non-discrimination and transparency.[263] Foremost, they shall particularly avoid "provid[ing] information in a discriminatory manner which may give some candidates or tenderers an advantage over others."[264] The concession-notice[265] ought to delineate a period for the receipt of tenders not shorter than thirty days from the notice[266] or twenty-two days for the initial tenders in case of multi-stage selection procedures.[267] On the one hand, such time limits can be shortened by five days each in case the contracting authorities or entities accept tenders submitted via electronic means.[268] On the other hand, such time limits shall be extended by as much as objectively necessary if projects require visits to the site or on-the-spot inspection by the prospective private partners.[269] Once a private partner is selected, the concession-award-notice ought to be published within forty-eight days.[270]

This is where all the requirements end for the 'concessions for social and other specific services,'[271] which among others include (1) health, social, and related services, (2) administrative, social, educational, healthcare, and cultural services, (3) compulsory social security services, (4) 'benefit services,' (5) "other community, social and personal services including services furnished by trade unions, political organisations, youth associations and other membership organisation services," (6) religious services, (7) hotel and restaurant services, (8) "provision of services to the

[257] ibid art 8.3.c.

[258] ibid art 8.3.d.

[259] ibid art 8.3.e.

[260] ibid art 8.3.f.

[261] ibid art 8.3.g.

[262] ibid art 31.1.

[263] ibid art 41.2 first sentence.

[264] ibid art 41.2s sentence.

[265] For the general requirement as to concession notices see Directive 2014/23 (n 210) art 31.

[266] Directive 2014/23 (n 210) art 39.2.

[267] ibid art 39.3.

[268] ibid art 39.4.

[269] ibid art 39.2.

[270] ibid art 32.

[271] ibid art 19.

community," or (9) investigation and security services.[272] The Concessions Directive is simply aligned in this regard with public-services-related directives, which ever since the Directive 92/50, differentiated between so-called 'priority services' and 'non-priority services.'[273] The priority services, also then known as 'Annex I.A,' are the typical commercially viable competitive services falling within the interest of international business, to which the entire procedural framework shall apply. In contrast, the non-priority services, also known as 'Annex I.B' services because of their nature, are way less lucrative and/or competitive, to which only minimal rules shall apply. This distinction continues in the fifth generation both in the New Classical Directive[274] and the New Utilities Directive.[275] Hence, also for concessions confined to such non-priority services, a relaxed regime *perforce* needs to exist.

Leaving such 'non-priority concessions aside,' the entire framework applicable to typical concessions covering priority services is not as complex, precise and inflexible as under the New Classical and New Utilities Directives. Foremost, unlike those directives, the Concession Directive does not differentiate at all between open and restricted procedures for the selection of private partners—a distinction which is at the core of simple procurement regulation under the GPA, procurement chapters of the FTA or EU procurement directives. Instead, the concession directive always allows contracting authorities or contracting entities to "limit the number of candidates or tenderers to an appropriate level, on condition that this is done in a transparent manner and on the basis of objective criteria" so long as "[t]he number of candidates or tenderers invited shall be sufficient to ensure genuine competition."[276] It follows that the gap between the complexity of requirements applicable to priority concessions against non-priority concessions is much narrower than the analogical gap between the complexity of the regime applicable to priority services and non-priority services.

3.4.3 Assess by Business from Third Countries

The Concessions Directive remains confusing as to the position of the EU lawmakers concerning opening concessions markets to international competition. This is not surprising because the GPA is very confusing in this regard, too, as discussed above (see Sect. 3.1). Specifically, the Concession Directive merely brushers over its relationship with the WTO GPA and procurement-relevant RTA in its preamble. Firstly, the preamble recognises that international trade is governed by reciprocity whereby the directive's framework "would also afford greater legal certainty to economic operators and could be a basis for and means of further opening up international

---

[272] ibid Annex IV.

[273] *See* Directive 92/50 (n 149) art 9. which states that "contracts which have as their object services listed in Annex I B shall be awarded in accordance" only the 'common rules in the technical field; and some of the 'common advertising rules.'.

[274] *See* Directive 2014/24 (n 210) arts 74–77 and Annex XIV.

[275] *See* Directive 2014/24 (n 210) arts 91–94 and Annex XVII.

[276] Directive 2014/23 (n 210) art 37.3.

public procurement markets and boosting world trade [and] [p]articular importance should be given to improving the access opportunities of SMEs throughout the Union concession markets."[277]

Secondly, similar to the preambles of the New Classical Directive and the new Utilities Directive, the Concessions Directive's preamble reminds that the contracting authorities and contracting entities shall not apply this directive "in a way that discriminates directly or indirectly against economic operators from the other Member States or from third countries parties to the World Trade Organisation Agreement on Government Procurement [...] or to Free Trade Agreements to which the Union is party."[278] The thing is, as discussed above (see Sect. 3.1) that the GPA's text itself remains tacit regarding PPP with only minimal traces of PPPs-related items in party-specific appendixes. The same can be observed about RTAs concluded by the EU with third countries. The procurement chapters of such RTA typically incorporate GPA's framework by reference,[279] implying that such chapters do not regulate PPPs clearly either. If so, one could wonder, from which international agreements concluded by the EU the quoted obligation not to discriminate business competing for concessions from third countries actually stems.

3.5 RTAs

Pretty obviously, the regional model of liberalisation and regulation of government procurements in the EU, PPPs included, cannot be easily replicated in other regional trading blocks. The level of the interference in the domestic regulation of Member States by the EU's supranational lawmaker would not be commensurate with the level of economic integration between parties to ordinary RTAs. A meticulous perusal of all trade agreements as to whether their procurement chapters refer to 'concessions,' 'PPPs' or similar concepts would go way beyond the scope of this paper, let alone a perusal of all the coverage lists attached to such agreements. Nonetheless, it is safe to say that the only significant RTA which refers to PPPs is the CPTPP.[280]

The framework of the CPTPP's procurement chap15 very ambitiously covers all build-operate-transfer contracts and public works concession contracts by default,

[277] ibid Preamble para 1.

[278] ibid Preamble para 65.

[279] For example: "The Parties reaffirm their rights and obligations under the Agreement on Government Procurement contained in Annex 4 to the WTO Agreement (hereinafter referred to as the 'GPA 1994') and their interest in further expanding bilateral trading opportunities in each Party's government procurement market." *See* Free Trade Agreement between the European Union and its Member States, of the one part, and the Republic of Korea, of the other party (done at Brussels on the sixth day of October in the year two thousand and ten) OJ [2011] L 127/6, art 9.1.1.

[280] Comprehensive and Progressive Agreement for Trans-Pacific Partnership (Santiago, 18 March 2018) accessed 25 April 2018 <https://www.mfat.govt.nz/assets/CPTPP/Comprehensive-and-Progressive-Agreement-for-Trans-Pacific-Partnership-CPTPP-English.pdf> accessed 25 April 2018 (CPTPP).

using two definitions. Firstly, the CPTPP defines 'covered procurement' as "government procurement: (a) of a good, service or any combination thereof as specified in each Party's Schedule to Annex 15-A; (b) by any contractual means, including purchase; rental or lease, with or without an option to buy; build-operate-transfer contracts and public works concessions contracts."[281] Secondly, the CPTPP defines build-operate-transfer contracts and public works concessions contracts as:

> contractual arrangement the primary purpose of which is to provide for the construction or rehabilitation of physical infrastructure, plants, buildings, facilities or other government-owned works and under which, as consideration for a supplier's execution of a contractual arrangement, a procuring entity grants to the supplier, for a specified period of time, temporary ownership or a right to control and operate, and demand payment for the use of those works for the duration of the contract.

Of course, the devil lies in the schedules. The express exclusions of concessions and BOTs by several CPTPP parties hints that the common understating among the parties leans towards accepting that PPPs are in principle covered in the absence of reservations to the contrary. Malaysia, in general notes, excluded "any Public–Private Partnership (PPP) contractual arrangements including build-operate-transfer (BOT) and public work concessions."[282] Mexico, in general notes, excluded "build-operate-transfer contracts and public works concessions contracts."[283] In addition, in services-specific notes, Mexico also excluded "the operation of government facilities under concessions."[284] Vietnam, in general notes, excluded "build-operate-transfer contract and public works concession contract."[285] The only express indication as to concessions is found in the schedule of Peru, informing that "[a] information on government procurement is published on the following websites: […] Procuring opportunities on BOT contracts and public works concessions contracts: www.proinversion.gob.pe."[286]

One might, therefore, accept that the framework provided in CPTPPchap15 by default applies to works concessions and BOTs. However, the questions persist, like in the case of the GPA, how to apply this framework to much more complex contracts than ones for which this framework is designed.

4 Dispute Resolution

The scope of PPPs' international liberalisation in a specific jurisdiction depends not only on the market-access provisions discussed in the previous section but also on safety valves related to dispute resolution. As far as dispute settlement in

[281] CPTPP (n 281) art 15.2.2.b.

[282] ibid chap15 Annex for Malaysia, sec G point 1.c at p 15.

[283] ibid chap15 Annex for Mexico, sec G point 9 at p 18.

[284] ibid chap15 Annex for Mexico, Notes to sec E point 1 at p 15.

[285] ibid chap15 Annex for Viet Nam, sec G point 1a at p 34.

[286] ibid chap15 Annex for Peru, Notes to sec A point 2 at p 2.

the context of government procurement is concerned, government procurement is rather pretty unique. On the one side of the dispute-resolution spectrum, there is general-commerce cross-border supplies of goods subjected to the GATT and cross-border provisions of services subjected to the GATS. On this side of the spectrum, economic operators have virtually no recourse to any review or appeal procedures instated by international instruments if denied market access. Those disputes are left to government-to-government interactions, including diplomacy, consultations or formal trade disputes like under the WTO Dispute Settlement Understanding (DSU).[287]

On the other side of the spectrum are foreign investors with establishments in the host countries who seek to protect their investment, defined for example by the CPTPPchap9 on investment as "every asset that an investor owns or controls, directly or indirectly, that has the characteristics of an investment, including such characteristics as the commitment of capital or other resources, the expectation of gain or profit, or the assumption of risk."[288] Depending on a specific BIT or investment chapter of an RTA, the investors could have recourse to ISDS in case of expropriation without proper compensation.

The field of government procurement, PPPs included, is found somewhere in the middle of the spectrum, in that it combines the availability of measures against (1) the denial of market access provided in the government-procurement-specific instruments (see Sect. 4.1), and (2) the measures against expropriation without proper compensation provided in investment-specific instruments to the extent that such instruments can be applied to government procurement (see Sect. 4.2).

---

[287] GATT, 'Understanding on Rules and Procedures Governing the Settlement of Disputes' (Final Act Embodying the Results of the Uruguay Round of Multilateral Trade Negotiations, Marrakesh, 15 April 1994) Annex II (DSU).

[288] CPTPP (n 281) art 9.1. This article further clarifies that 1) "[f]orms that an investment may take include: (a) an enterprise; (b) shares, stock and other forms of equity participation in an enterprise; (c) bonds, debentures, other debt instruments and loans; (d) futures, options and other derivatives; (e) turnkey, construction, management, production, concession, revenue-sharing and other similar contracts; (f) intellectual property rights; (g) licences, authorisations, permits and similar rights conferred pursuant to the Party's law; and (h) other tangible or intangible, movable or immovable property, and related property rights, such as leases, mortgages, liens and pledges" (art 9.1.), 2) "[s]ome forms of debt, such as bonds, debentures, and long-term notes, are more likely to have the characteristics of an investment, while other forms of debt, such as claims to payment that are immediately due and result from the sale of goods or services, are less likely to have such characteristics" (fn 2 to art 9.1), 2) "[a] loan issued by one Party to another Party is not an investment" (fn 3 to art 9.1), 3) "[w]hether a particular type of licence, authorisation, permit or similar instrument (including a concession to the extent that it has the nature of such an instrument) has the characteristics of an investment depends on such factors as the nature and extent of the rights that the holder has under the Party's law. Among such instruments that do not have the characteristics of an investment are those that do not create any rights protected under the Party's law. For greater certainty, the foregoing is without prejudice to whether any asset associated with such instruments has the characteristics of an investment" (fn 4 to art 9.1).

4.1 Pre-contract Dispute Settlement (Market Access)

The measures against the denial of market access in the field of government procurement available to individual enterprises are known as 'domestic review procedures' under the GPA. The GPA12 requires that "[e]ach Party shall provide a timely, effective, transparent and non-discriminatory administrative or judicial review procedure through which a supplier may challenge: [...] a breach of the Agreement; or [...] where the supplier does not have a right to challenge directly a breach of the Agreement under the domestic law of a Party, a failure to comply with a Party's measures implementing this Agreement, arising in the context of covered procurement, in which the supplier has, or has had, an interest [...]."[289]

Unsurprisingly, the GPA12 encourages amicable resolution of disputes between contracting authorities on the one side and prospective supplies, contractors, or private partners/concessionaires on the other side. It suggests that (1) "the Party of the procuring entity conducting the procurement shall encourage the entity and the supplier to seek resolution of the complaint through consultations,"[290] and (2) "[t]he entity shall accord impartial and timely consideration to any such complaint in a manner that is not prejudicial to the supplier's participation in ongoing or future procurement or its right to seek corrective measures under the administrative or judicial review procedure."[291]

In the event where a formalised dispute cannot be avoided, the GPA12 prescribes that bidders shall have the right to apply to an impartial body and seek either 'interim measures' in the course of the procurement process or 'corrective measures,' compensation included in case of proved breaches of the GPA. Specifically, the purpose of the 'rapid interim measures' is to "to preserve the supplier's opportunity to participate in the procurement [which] may result in the suspension of the procurement process."[292] Timewise, "[e]ach supplier shall be allowed a sufficient period of time to prepare and submit a challenge, which in no case shall be less than 10 days from the time when the basis of the challenge became known or reasonably should have become known to the supplier."[293] In turn, in the case of proven breaches "corrective action or compensation for the loss or damages suffered, which may be limited to either the costs for the preparation of the tender or the costs relating to the challenge or both."[294] It implies that that the GPA12 does not go as far as to require invalidation of procurement or concession contracts in case of proven breaches of this agreement.

---

[289] GPA12 (n 32) art XVIII.1.

[290] ibid art XVIII.3.

[291] ibid.

[292] ibid art XVIII.7.a. *in initio*. The same art clarifies "The procedures may provide that overriding adverse consequences for the interests concerned, including the public interest, may be taken into account when deciding whether such measures should be applied. Just cause for not acting shall be provided in writing." *See* ibid art XVIII.7.a *in fine*.

[293] GPA12 (n 32) art XVIII.3.

[294] ibid art XVIII.7.b.

Another flaw of the 'domestic review procedures,' from a perspective of international investors interested in PPPs, consists in that these are, indeed, domestic, without any recourse to international arbitration, which is the case with the ISDS. Specifically, the GPA12 merely requires that (1) "[e]ach Party shall establish or designate at least one impartial administrative or judicial authority that is independent of its procuring entities to receive and review a challenge by a supplier arising in the context of covered procurement,"[295] (2) "[w]here a body other than an authority referred to in paragraph 4 initially reviews a challenge, the Party shall ensure that the supplier may appeal the initial decision to an impartial administrative or judicial authority that is independent of the procuring entity whose procurement is the subject of the challenge,"[296]and (3) "[e]ach Party shall ensure that a review body that is not a court shall have its decision subject to judicial review."[297]

RTAs' procurement chapters replicate this model. The CPTPPchap15, for example, requires that "[e]ach Party shall maintain, establish or designate at least one impartial administrative or judicial authority (review authority) that is independent of its procuring entities to review, in a non-discriminatory, timely, transparent and effective manner, a challenge or complaint (complaint) by a supplier that there has been: [...] a breach of this Chapter; or [...] if the supplier does not have a right to directly challenge a breach of this Chapter under the law of a Party, a failure of a procuring entity to comply with the Party's measures implementing this Chapter, arising in the context of covered procurement, in which the supplier has, or had an interest. The procedural rules for all complaints shall be in writing and made generally available."[298]

Analogical to the GPA12 are CPTPPchap15's provisions on (1) the amicable dispute resolution,[299] establishment of impartial bodies,[300] (2) the limitation of the "compensation for the loss or damages suffered to either the costs reasonably incurred in the preparation of the tender or in bringing the complaint, or both,"[301] (3) the

[295] ibid art XVIII.4.

[296] ibid art XVIII.5.

[297] ibid art XVIII.6. The same art offers an alternative to judicial review in the form of procedures "that provide that: a) the procuring entity shall respond in writing to the challenge and disclose all relevant documents to the review body; b) the participants to the proceedings (hereinafter referred to as "participants") shall have the right to be heard prior to a decision of the review body being made on the challenge; c) the participants shall have the right to be represented and accompanied; d) the participants shall have access to all proceedings; e) the participants shall have the right to request that the proceedings take place in public and that witnesses may be presented; and f) the review body shall make its decisions or recommendations in a timely fashion, in writing, and shall include an explanation of the basis for each decision or recommendation." *See* ibid.

[298] CPTPP (n 281) art 15.19.1.

[299] ibid art 15.19.2.

[300] ibid art 15.19.3.

[301] ibid art 15.19.4.

differentiation between interim and corrective measures,[302] and (4) ten days' period for filing for interim measures.[303]

Much more complex and elaborate domestic review requirements are offered by the amended by the Council Directive 89/665/EEC on the coordination of the laws, regulations and administrative provisions relating to the application of review procedures to the award of public supply and public works contracts,[304] which now also applies to the Concession Directive.[305] Under the amended Directive 89/665, the bidders can request review bodies to:

- "take, at the earliest opportunity and by way of interlocutory procedures, interim measures with the aim of correcting the alleged infringement or preventing further damage to the interests concerned, including measures to suspend or to ensure the suspension of the procedure for the award of a public contract or the implementation of any decision taken by the contracting authority,"[306]
- "either set aside or ensure the setting aside of decisions taken unlawfully, including the removal of discriminatory technical, economic or financial specifications in the invitation to tender, the contract documents or in any other document relating to the contract award procedure"[307]
- "award damages to persons harmed by an infringement."[308]

As far as the requirements concerning domestic review bodies are concerned, the amended Directive 89/665 focuses on the required characteristics of bodies which "are not judicial in character."[309] This is arguably because the notion of Member States' courts is very well developed in the community statutory and case law. Obviously, similar to the GPA, the amended Directive 89/665 requires that the decision made by the bodies, which are not judicial in nature, shall "be the subject of judicial review or review by another body which is a court or tribunal within the meaning of Article 234 of the Treaty and independent of both the contracting authority and the review body."[310] Nonetheless, the amended Directive 89/665 still mandates that

---

[302] ibid art 15.19.6.

[303] ibid art 15.19.5.

[304] For the original text, *see* Directive 89/665 (n 142). For the consolidate version *see* Commission, 'Consolidated text: Council Directive of 21 December 1989 on the coordination of the laws, regulations and administrative provisions relating to the application of review procedures to the award of public supply and public works contracts (89/665/EEC)' (17 April 2014) 1989L0665-EN-003.001.

[305] "This Directive also applies to concessions awarded by contracting authorities, referred to in Directive 2014/23/EU of the European Parliament and of the Council (9) unless such concessions are excluded in accordance with Articles 10, 11, 12, 17 and 25 of that Directive. Contracts within the meaning of this Directive include public contracts, framework agreements, works and services concessions and dynamic purchasing systems." *See* Directive 89/665 as amended (n 305) art 1 paras 2 and 3.

[306] Directive 89/665 as amended (n 305) art 2.1.a.

[307] ibid art 2.1.b.

[308] ibid art 2.1.c.

[309] ibid art 2.9.

[310] ibid first para.

non-judicial bodies, unlike courts/judicial bodies, ought always to deliver "written reasons for their decisions."[311] Moreover, in the case of non-judicial bodies:

> The members of such an independent body shall be appointed and leave office under the same conditions as members of the judiciary as regards the authority responsible for their appointment, their period of office, and their removal. At least the President of this independent body shall have the same legal and professional qualifications as members of the judiciary. The independent body shall take its decisions following a procedure in which both sides are heard, and these decisions shall, by means determined by each Member State, be legally binding.[312]

Time limits for applying for review measures are longer under the amended Directive 89/665 than under the GPA in that 10-days limits only applies in the case when electronic communication is allowed. Otherwise, the limit stands at 15 days.[313] These limits are aligned with the analogical standstill period, before the expiry of which the contracting authority cannot finalise a contract/concession conclusion.[314]

Crucial for the market access is the amended Directive's 89/665 provisions on the invalidation of concluded contracts, referred to under this act as 'ineffectiveness.' Contracts ought to be invalided, among others (1) "if the contracting authority has awarded a contract without prior publication of a contract notice,"[315] (2) in the breach of the duty to allow a bidder to "first seek review with the contracting authority" under art 1(5),[316] (3) in the breach of the duty not to conclude "the contract before the review body has made a decision on the application either for interim measures or for review"[317] under art 2(3), and (4) in the deprivation of bidders of "sufficient time for effective review of the contract award decisions taken by contracting authorities."[318]

4.2 *Post-contract Dispute Settlement*

4.2.1 Market-Access Instruments

Post-contract dispute settlement between public and private partners chiefly falls within the ambit of domestic contract and company law as well as international investment law. However, some minimal provisions concerning public contracts past their conclusion can also be found in some procurement-related market-access international instruments discussed above. Specifically, similar to simple government contracts, the Concessions Directive substantially curbs the ability of public and

[311] ibid.

[312] ibid second para.

[313] ibid art 2c.

[314] ibid art 2a.2.

[315] ibid art 2d.1.a.

[316] ibid art 2d.1.b.

[317] ibid.

[318] ibid.

private partners to modify contracts during their term, to prevent collusion between and circumvention of procurement rules between them. True that these rules in principle aim at preventing public partners from offering better deal terms to private partners, implying that the latter would have no economic interest in litigating against their public partners. However, one could reasonably argue that the curbs imposed on the modification of concession contracts, out of momentum, also prevent modifications to the detriment of private partners. Hence, such curbs add to the regulatory stability in host counties and improve conditions for foreign enterprises invested in PPPs. In detail, the Concession Directive only allows the modification of the concession contract in the following situations:

- "when the modifications, irrespective of their monetary value, have been provided for in the initial concession documents in clear, precise and unequivocal review clauses, which may include value revision clauses or options,"[319]
- "for additional works or services by the original concessionaire that have become necessary and that were not included in the initial concession."[320] with a cap of the increase set up at fifty per cent of the original concession's value,[321]
- where "the need for modification has been brought about by circumstances which a diligent contracting authority or contracting entity could not foresee,"[322] so long as "the modification does not alter the overall nature of the concession,"[323]also with a cap of fifty per cent,[324]
- "where a new concessionaire replaces the one to which the contracting authority or the contracting entity had initially awarded the concession as a consequence of either […] an unequivocal review clause or option […] [or] universal or partial succession into the position of the initial concessionaire, or […] "in the event that

[319] Directive 2014/23 (n 210) art 43.1a. The same article further clarifies that "[s]uch clauses shall state the scope and nature of possible modifications or options as well as the conditions under which they may be used. They shall not provide for modifications or options that would alter the overall nature of the concession." *See* ibid second sentence.

[320] Directive 2014/23 (n 210) art 43.1b. The same art further clarifies that that the modification in this instance is only allowed when the change of concessionaire 1) "cannot be made for economic or technical reasons such as requirements of interchangeability or interoperability with existing equipment, services or installations procured under the initial concession," (art 43.1.b.i) and 2) "would cause significant inconvenience or substantial duplication of costs for the contracting authority or contracting entity" (art 43.1.b.ii).

[321] The cap does not apply to private contracting entities with special or exclusive rights. *See* Directive 2014/23 (n 210) art 43.b last para first sentence. The same art further clarified that "Where several successive modifications are made, that limitation shall apply to the value of each modification. Such consecutive modifications shall not be aimed at circumventing this Directive." *See* ibid second sentence.

[322] Directive 2014/23 (n 210) art 43.1.c.i.

[323] ibid art 43.1.c.ii.

[324] ibid art 43.1.c.iii.

the contracting authority or contracting entity itself assumes the main concessionaire's obligations towards its subcontractors where this possibility is provided for under national legislation."[325]

- "where the modifications, irrespective of their value, are not substantial,"[326]
- where the value of the modifications is below both the threshold of the application of the Concessions Directive[327] and ten per cent of the value of the concession.[328]

More conducive to international investment disputes are the procurement-related provisions which force contracting authorities to terminate concession contracts because of the violations of public procurement rules. Namely, the Concession Directive requires termination of a concessions contract if (1) the concession was modified beyond the allowed boundaries listed above,[329] (2) the concessionaire should have been excluded from bidding because of a previous criminal conviction in several categories of illicit activities,[330] and (3) "the Court of Justice of the European Union finds [...] that a Member State has failed to fulfil its obligations under the Treaties by the fact that a contracting authority or contracting entity belonging to that Member State has awarded the concession in question without complying with its obligations under the Treaties and this Directive."[331]

However, such rigid rules on the termination of concessions under the Concession Directive are somewhat mitigated by the amended Directive 89/665, again adding to the regulatory stability favouring foreign investors. Specifically, the amended Directive 89/665 allows Member States not to terminate public procurement contracts, concessions contracts included, "even though [they] ha[ve] been awarded illegally [...] if the review body finds, after having examined all relevant aspects, that overriding reasons relating to a general interest require that the effects of the contract should be maintained."[332] However, if such a safety valve is used to keep a concession contract, so-called 'alternative penalties' should be applied, such as fines on

---

[325] ibid art 43.1.d.

[326] ibid art 43.1.e. The same art further clarifies that "[a] modification of a concession during its term shall be considered to be substantial [...], where it renders the concession materially different in character from the one initially concluded. In any event, without prejudice to paragraphs 1 and 2, a modification shall be considered to be substantial where one or more of the following conditions is met: (a) the modification introduces conditions which, had they been part of the initial concession award procedure, would have allowed for the admission of applicants other than those initially selected or for the acceptance of a tender other than that originally accepted or would have attracted additional participants in the concession award procedure; (b) the modification changes the economic balance of the concession in favour of the concessionaire in a manner which was not provided for in the initial concession; (c) the modification extends the scope of the concession considerably; (d) where a new concessionaire replaces the one to which the contracting authority or contracting entity had initially awarded the concession [...]." *See* ibid art 43.3.

[327] Directive 2014/23 (n 210) art 43.1.e.i.

[328] ibid art 43.1.e.ii.

[329] ibid art 44.a.

[330] ibid art 44.b. Those illicit activities are listed in art 38.4.

[331] ibid art 44.c.

[332] Directive 89/665 as amended (n 305) art 2d.3 first para first sentence.

the contracting authority or shortening the concession's duration.[333] Interestingly from the perspective of international investment law, the amended Directive 89/665 clarifies that (1) "[e]conomic interests in the effectiveness of the contract may only be considered as overriding reasons if in exceptional circumstances ineffectiveness would lead to disproportionate consequences,"[334] however, (2) "economic interests directly linked to the contract concerned shall not constitute overriding reasons relating to a general interest."[335]

The elements addressing civil-law consequences of disputes between public and private partners are perforce fragmentary, if not non-existent, in public-law market-access legal instruments such the GPA, procurement-related chapters of RTAs (or EU procurement directives which are the most sophisticated instruments of regional liberalisation of procurement markets). PPP contracts are almost always governed by domestic laws of host states, which do substantially vary from one jurisdiction to another. Nonetheless, some common-sense solution has been gathered in the 2020 Model Provisions.[336] Instead of setting up some rigid rules, the 2020 Model Provisions emphasise that the questions of compensation and termination of concessions had better be clearly regulated contractually. As far as compensation for changes in legislation is concerned, the 2020 Model Provisions suggest that:

> The PPP contract shall set forth the extent to which the private partner is entitled to compensation in the event that the cost of the private partner's performance of the PPP contract has substantially increased or that the value that the private partner receives for such performance has substantially diminished, as compared with the costs and the value of performance originally foreseen, as a result of changes in legislation or regulations specifically applicable to the infrastructure facility or the services it provides.[337]

As far as the termination of PPPs is concerned, the 2020 Model Provisions are more elaborate. While drafting contractual provisions on the compensation in the case of terminations, public and private partners are advised to regulate "compensation for the fair value of works performed under the PPP contract, costs incurred or losses sustained by either party, including, as appropriate, lost profits."[338] Moreover, the contractual provisions on 'wind-up and transfer measures' ought to cover (1) "[m]echanisms and procedures for the transfer of assets to the contracting authority,"[339] (2) "[t]he compensation to which the private partner may be entitled in respect of assets transferred to the contracting authority or to a new private

[333] ibid arts 2d.3 first para second sentence and 2e.2.

[334] ibid art 2d.3s para.

[335] ibid art 2d.3 third para. The same art further clarifies that "[e]conomic interests directly linked to the contract include, inter alia, the costs resulting from the delay in the execution of the contract, the costs resulting from the launching of a new procurement procedure, the costs resulting from the change of the economic operator performing the contract and the costs of legal obligations resulting from the ineffectiveness." *See* ibid art 2d.3 fourth para.

[336] 2020 Model Provisions (n 12).

[337] ibid, Model Provision 44.

[338] ibid, Model Provision 53.

[339] ibid, Model Provision 54 point a.

partner or purchased by the contracting authority,"[340] (3) "[t]he transfer of technology required for the operation of the facility,"[341] (4) "[t]he training of the contracting authority's personnel or of a successor private partner in the operation and maintenance of the facility,"[342] (5) "[t]he provision, by the private partner, of continuing support services and resources, including the supply of spare parts, if required, for a reasonable period after the transfer of the facility to the contracting authority or to a successor private partner,"[343] (6) "[m]echanisms and procedures for the decommissioning of the infrastructure, including the preparation of a decommissioning plan and the parties' respective obligations for carrying it out and their financial obligations in that respect."[344]

4.2.2 Investment-Protection Instruments

Disputes arising from PPP contracts are covered by the applicable BITs or RTAs' investment chapters so long as such disputes fall under the definition of investment under the particular agreement. This is irrespective of whether such investment-related agreements expressly cover such contracts or not. Some do, like the agreements concluded based on the 2004 US Model BIT,[345] which exemplifies 'investment' among others with "turnkey, construction, management, production, concession, revenue-sharing, and other similar contracts"[346] or "licenses, authorizations, permits, and similar rights conferred pursuant to domestic law."[347] In a footnote to this list, the 2004 US Model BIT further clarifies that:

> Whether a particular type of license, authorization, permit, or similar instrument (including a concession, to the extent that it has the nature of such an instrument) has the characteristics of an investment depends on such factors as the nature and extent of the rights that the holder has under the law of the Party. Among the licenses, authorizations, permits, and similar instruments that do not have the characteristics of an investment are those that do not create any rights protected under domestic law. For greater certainty, the foregoing is without prejudice to whether any asset associated with the license, authorization, permit, or similar instrument has the characteristics of an investment.[348]

Thus, how can one square the observation that PPP fall under BITs or RTAs' investment chapters with the observation that such investment-protection instruments

[340] ibid, Model Provision 54 point b.

[341] ibid, Model Provision 54 point c.

[342] ibid, Model Provision 54 point d.

[343] ibid, Model Provision 54 point e.

[344] ibid, Model Provision 54 point f.

[345] The Office of the United States Trade Representative (USTR), 'U.S. Model Bilateral Investment Treaty (BIT)' (*USTR.gov*) <https://ustr.gov/archive/Trade_Sectors/Investment/Model_BIT/Section_Index.html> (2004 US Model BIT).

[346] 2004 US Model BIT (n 346) art 1 item 'investment' point e.

[347] ibid art 1 item 'investment' point g.

[348] ibid fn 2 to art 1 item 'investment' point g.

at the same time very often expressly excluded government procurement, which after all embraces PPPs? The only way to rationally construe all those procurement-excluding clauses is that 'procurement' in such clause merely refers to market-access measures, the regulation of which is left to procurement-specific measures (GPA, RTAs procurement chapters or EU procurement directives). *A contrario*, 'procurement' in this context, does cover foreign investors stakes in governments contracts after their conclusion, PPPs included. Only the most modern and complex RTAs address this distinction.

For example, the CPTPPchap9 on investment precisely determines which investment-related rules do not apply to the government otherwise regulated in chap15. Foremost non-applicable to government procurement are chap's 9 provisions on national treatment, MFN clause, and on senior management and board of directors.[349] Neither does apply to government procurement the duty of refrain from imposing some of the 'performance requirements' disallowed by chap9, including requirements (1) "to achieve a given level or percentage of domestic content,"[350] (2) "relat[ing] in any way the volume or value of imports to the volume or value of exports or to the amount of foreign exchange inflows associated with the investment,[351] (3) to transfer a particular technology, a production process or other proprietary knowledge to a person in its territory,[352] (4) "to supply exclusively from the territory of the Party the goods that the investment produces or the services that it supplies to a specific regional market or to the world market."[353] In the procurement context, such market-access-related issues are separately regulated in CPTPPchap15.

5 Conclusions

This chapter aimed to set a broad stage for further research on more specific issues in the international liberalisation of PPP markets. The goal has been to grasp the most general image of this problem and to capture a somewhat vague position of instruments regulating PPPs in the ambit of international economic law. Section 1, apart from introductory remarks, explained the increasing intersections between traditionally domestic PPP markets and FDI, driven by multinational companies' interest in lucrative utility and infrastructure sectors in as many jurisdictions as possible. The aim of Sect. 2 on the relevant conceptual framework has been to present the various dimensions of the PPP concept in a structured and orderly manner. Sect. 2.1 presented PPPs, from a normative perspective, as the most sophisticated form of

[349] CPTPP (n 281) art 9.12.6.a. The same selection of chap's 9 provisions shall not apply to "subsidies or grants provided by a Party, including government-supported loans, guarantees and insurance." *See* ibid art 9.12.6.b.

[350] CPTPP (n 281) arts 9.10.2.f and 9.10.1.b.

[351] ibid arts 9.10.2.f and 9.10.1.c.

[352] ibid arts 9.10.2.f and 9.10.1.f.

[353] ibid arts 9.10.2.f and 9.10.1.g.

government procurement to explain the link between PPPs and public-procurement instruments such as the WTO GPA, EU procurement directives, or procurement chapters of various trade agreements. Sect. 2.2 presented PPPs, from a more theoretical perspective as a specific form of SCEs, to explain the link between PPPs and a broader discussion on foreign investment screening mechanisms aiming to prevent foreign interferences with strategic domestic sectors. Sect. 3, broadly covering access to PPP markets by foreign investors, explained how the selection of private partners has gradually been falling under the umbrella of government procurement regulation. Sect. 3.1 demonstrated how despite no mentioning in the main text of the WTO GPA, PPPs have been gradually incorporated into coverage of the WTO GPA by the back door, i.e. party-specific schedule of commitments. Sect. 3.2 pondered on the extent to which access to PPP markets is also affected by the GATS and TRIMS, concluding that general-commerce freedom of the provision of services and investment by foreign persons in most cases is a prerequisite for access to PPP markets. Sects. 3.3 and 3.4 demonstrated how the public-procurement-derived procedural framework has been gradually perfectioned to reflect the complexity of PPPs. Sect. 3.5 demonstrated how the combination of the developments in the WTO GPA and EU procurement directives spilt over the landscape of RTAs with an emphasis on the CPTPP, which fully and expressly embraced PPPs as a form of public procurement. Sect. 4 broadly covering PPP-related dispute-settlement issues differentiated between disputes emerging before and after the conclusion of PPP contractors. Sect. 4.1 offered an overview of the procurement-derived measures setting a framework for resolving disputes between potential private partners competing for PPP contracts on the side with contracting authorities (public partners) on the other side. As far as post-contractual disputes are concerned, Sect. 4.2.1 demonstrated how procurement-derived market-access measures largely secure the stability of PPPs agreement, adding to the investment-protection environment. In turn, Sect. 4.2.2 demonstrated that BITs and investment chapters of RTAs in principle cover PPPs classifiable as foreign investment and explained how to square it with the parallel observation that hat BITs and investment chapters of RTAs also happen to exclude public procurement from their scope of application expressly.

Ways of "Control": Changes and Implications from China's Reform of State-Owned Enterprises

Shixue Hu

1 Introduction

What is the meaning of "control" in state-controlled enterprises (SCEs)? By popular assumption, enterprises with 51% of public ownership would be considered state-controlled. It becomes a legally contentious question for enterprises with fewer public shares and, too often, a political one. In China's party-lead-all context, it is hard, if ever possible, to draw a clear line between public and private enterprise if we take a loose definition of "control."[1] The state's influence can be felt through public ownership, managerial appointments, and policy impact on decision-making in any type of firm. It is neither necessary nor realistic to consider every firm under some form of aforementioned state influence an SCE. China's legislation and policies explicitly refute such an approach. In fact, Chinese policy-makers have been progressively clarifying the boundary of "control" since China opened up to the global economy. This article will focus on the ways of "control" in our discussion of SCEs, basing on the recent changes in the domestic SOE regulations in China.

In the second part, the article will illustrate the major shifts in control methods by the party-state. The 2015 Guidelines issued by the Central Committee of the China Communist Party (CCP) and the State Council symbolized a policy transition to reform Chinese SOEs. After reviewing this landmark policy document, the article will analyze the details of the new regulatory framework that concern four aspects of "control": purposes of control, the controlling administration, ownership control, and the party's political control. Based on the interpretation of the policy and the

[1] Black's Law Dictionary: "control n. (16c) The direct or indirect power to govern the management and policies of a person or entity, whether through ownership of voting securities, by contract, or otherwise; the power or authority to manage, direct, or oversee."

S. Hu (✉)
Faculty of Law, The Chinese University of Hong Kong, Sha Tin, NT, Hong Kong SAR
e-mail: shixue.hu@cuhk.edu.hk

J. Chaisse et al. (eds.), *Regulation of State-Controlled Enterprises*, International Law and the Global South, https://doi.org/10.1007/978-981-19-1368-6_4

legislation that followed, the third part of this article will further discuss the implications of the current domestic reform in China for transnational and international policy-makers.

2 China's Reform of "Control": A Mixed-Approach of State-Firm Relationship

The new nationwide reform, the so-called 2015 Guiding Opinions of Deepening SOE Reform, was initiated by the CCP in response to acute problems the SOEs faced under the "Going-Global Strategy" in the previous decade.[2] Following the party's policy, a series of new legislations have been published since 2015 by the State Council and the State-owned Assets Supervision and Administration Commission (SASAC). This part will first summarize the party's 2015 policy guidelines and then illustrate the related legislative changes concerning the state's governance and control of its SOEs.

2.1 The 2015 Guidelines and the Policies of SOE Reform

The CCP has set up various policy goals in the current SOE reform for the SOEs' corporate governance, state assets' management and supervision, the state-owned economy, and the party's political leadership within the SOEs.[3] The Guidelines then list seven major measures to achieve these goals.[4]

Corporate governance. The Guidelines reemphasize the importance of corporate governance and propose a flexible reform schedule for different types of SOEs. According to the plan, SOEs will be categorized into commercial SOEs, commercial SOEs with strategic importance, and public service SOEs. Each category of SOEs and their managers will then be supervised and evaluated by different metrics so that commercial SOEs can focus on improving efficiency while public service SOEs can better fulfil their social responsibilities. The 2015 Guidelines also require SOEs with overseas plans to limit the scope of investment projects to their core business. Overseas investment should be within or highly related to SOE's industry in the domestic market. Accordingly, the state will have separate investment policies for each SOE

---

[2] The official publication admitted the problems occurred during the "Going-Global" period. *See* Guiding Opinions of the CCP Central Committee and the State Council on Deepening the Reform of State-owned Enterprises [herein after "The 2015 Guidelines"], introduction (2015), Zhonggong Zhongyang Guowuyuan Guanyu Shenhua Guoyou Qiye Gaige de Zhidao Yijian.

[3] The 2015 Guidelines, Section 1. (3)

[4] The 2015 Guidelines, Section 2–8. The policies and measures are translated and summarized by the author.

category. The reform also aims at improving corporate structures by enforcing the supervision power of the board of directors, the supervisors, and the labor union.

State Asset. The Guidelines plan to set up a state capital operating and investing company and a non-governmental enterprise to replace SASAC's direct participation in SOEs' daily operations. SASAC, currently a governmental agency, will shift its regulatory focus from SOEs' business operations to asset management. The reform also suggests new evaluation metrics for SOEs, incentivizing productivity and efficiency of capital utilization.

State-owned economy. The Guidelines encourage mixed-ownership partnerships between public and private capital so that individual SOEs can form powerful alliances either with other SOEs or enterprises of different ownership types and vice versa. Ultimately, the policy aims at accelerating the development of a larger number of world-class multinational companies. At the same time, the reform demands more transparency and efficient regulations and more explicit liability rules to prevent the loss of state assets in this mixed-partnership reform.

Party's political leadership in SOEs. The Guidelines not only deal with reforms of SOEs but also redefine the relationship between the SOEs and the CCP. The party will strengthen its political leadership and primary-level organizations in these entities. It also plans to specify its criteria and procedures for board personnel changes, relying on the board to select managers and encourage competition among them. Additionally, the reform asks both the party's branches and governmental agencies to upgrade the legal and policy environment for SOEs' development, shifting the social functions of some SOEs to governmental or social agencies.

After the 2015 policy guidelines, a series of legislations have been published.[5] The reform will be progressively carried out before the end of 2020.

Corporate Governance: differentiating the purposes of control.

The new legislation that followed the 2015 Guidelines categorize SOEs into three groups. Each group will pursue different goals, and their corporate governance structure will be regulated separately according to these goals.

The first category of SOEs has the nature of public welfare. These SOEs are primarily required to ensure the supply of public goods and services for the domestic. They can introduce a market-oriented mechanism to increase their efficiency and profitability, but the fundamental purpose of the firms is to focus on public service and social responsibilities. The state sets a lower priority on the return of capital and overseas expansion but emphasizes their social responsibilities in the local community.[6] The total salary of employees will mainly be linked to indicators such as cost control, quality of product or service, operating efficiency and security. The evaluation also considers the goal of efficiency and appreciation of state assets. Salary levels of employees will be reasonably determined based on the quality of public goods

---

[5] *See infra Annex.* The list summarizes the major rules that cover SOEs' corporate governance and overseas investment.

[6] The 2015 Guidelines, Section (6).

produced and the economic performances of the enterprise, taking into account the income distribution and average wage within the industry.[7]

The second group of SOEs includes "commercial SOEs whose core business belongs to industries of competition." As designed by the reform, SOEs of this category should seek efficiency and profitability for state assets.[8] Their pecuniary-oriented purposes thus distinguish them from the first group. The state refrains itself from taking a controlling position in these entities to ensure the independence of management. Managers of this group will be evaluated on capital gains and competitiveness in the market.[9] The state can be either a controlling shareholder or a passive shareholder. The reform policy also invites mixed-ownership to attract other types of capital for these SOEs' international development.[10] SASAC will link the SOEs' total salary budget to indicators such as total corporate profit, net profit, economic value-added and net asset growth rate, and the return on net assets reflect economic benefits, the preservation and appreciation of state capital, and market competitiveness.[11] It will also regulate the SOEs' overseas investment projects through capital management, which includes directing investment flows, optimizing investment portfolio and structure, supervising decision-making procedures and capital transactions, focusing on capital returns, and ensuring the safety of the state asset in overseas projects.[12] The reform thus pushes the second group of SOEs toward further market liberalization for profitability.

As for the third type of SOEs, they are also "commercial SOEs," yet their core business belongs to industries concerning national security or are assigned "special tasks" that are usually not wholly commercial.[13] The function of this group of SOEs is twofold: on the one hand, they are profitable SOEs that emphasize value appreciation of public assets; on the other hand, they will be evaluated on their efforts to serve the public interest, including national security, national strategies, or completion of particular tasks.[14] Not surprisingly, managers of these SOEs will be evaluated mainly on whether they have successfully carried out their tasks and national strategies. However, they should also aim to retain the value of state assets in cross-border businesses.[15] The state will maintain its controlling shareholder position in these SOEs,[16] and SASAC supervises their ODI to ensure consistency with the national

[7] Measures for the Administration of Total Salary of Central SOEs, art.13 (2019), *Zhongyang Qiye Gongzi Zong'e Guanli Banfa.*

[8] The 2015 Guidelines, Section (5), para.2.

[9] The 2015 Guidelines, Section (5), para.1, 2.

[10] The 2015 Guidelines, Section (5), para.2.

[11] Measures for the Administration of Total Salary of Central SOEs, art.11 (2019), *Zhongyang Qiye Gongzi Zong'e Guanli Banfa.*

[12] Measures for the Supervision and Administration of Overseas Investments by Central SOEs, art.3, 4 (2017), *Zhongyang Qiye Jingwai Touzi Jiandu Guanli Banfa.*

[13] The 2015 Guidelines, Section (5), para.3.

[14] ibid.

[15] The method for Evaluating the performance of the Senior Managers of Central SOEs, (2019), *Zhongyang Qiye Fuzeren Jingying Yeji Kaohe Banfa.*

[16] The 2015 Guidelines, Section (5), para.1, para.3

strategies.[17] While the total salary of employees is mainly linked to indicators of economic profits and appreciation of state capital, it can reflect interests of national security, contributions for the macroeconomy and strategic industries, and implementation of particular tasks. The salary level of employees will mainly depend on the economic performances of the enterprise, combined with other factors such as the average salary level of employees in the industry.[18] In short, the purposes of control in this group include both profitability and non-commercial state interests.

Since the 2015 SOE Reform, the evaluation metrics of SOE performances have also been changed. Before the reform, SOEs were evaluated under a comparatively unified framework that includes indicators such as total profit, economic value-added, the value of the state asset, and completion of strategic objectives.[19] After the reform, the evaluation emphasizes the efficiency of capital utilization, risk prevention, overcapacity cuts, innovation ability, international influence and environmental protection, etc., differentiating indicators among different SOEs.[20]

By adopting a more flexible evaluation, the government can achieve separate policy goals through different types of SOEs. Most explicitly, the state can continue to serve many non-monetary public interests through SOEs that have been playing a critical role in achieving these interests in a system with a long history of the planned economy. These interests include but are not limited to national security, consistent supply of public utilities, environmental protection, and stable employment.

More importantly, the efficiency of SOEs has been an important policy priority for Beijing. The government needs profit generated by state assets to supplement fiscal revenue. The tax cuts in 2018–19 have caused a noticeable slowdown in tax revenue, which means that the government has to rely more on dividends from SOEs. Accordingly, all central-level SOEs must transfer 10% of their equity to the social security funds by the end of 2020 to make up the funds' shortfalls. SOEs also need to increase their productivity and efficiency for the sake of their sky-shooting corporate loans and bonds.[21] Efficiency is not only the primary determinant for the survival of SOEs but also benefits the national treasury and the long-term development of the Chinese economy.

---

[17] Measures for the Supervision and Administration of Overseas Investments by Central SOEs, ch.1 (2017), *Zhongyang Qiye Jingwai Touzi Jiandu Guanli Banfa.*

[18] Measures for the Administration of Total Salary of Central SOEs, art.12 (2019), *Zhongyang Qiye Gongzi Zong'e Guanli Banfa.*

[19] Interim Measures for the Administration of Total Salary of Central SOEs, (2010), Zhongyang Qiye Gongzi Zong'e Yusuan Guanli Zanxing Banfa. The Interim Measures for Evaluating the performance of the Senior Managers of Central SOEs, (2012), *Zhongyang Qiye Fuzeren Jingying Yeji Kaohe Zanxing Banfa.*

[20] The method for Evaluating the performance of the Senior Managers of Central SOEs, (2019), Zhongyang Qiye Fuzeren Jingying Yeji Kaohe Banfa. See also the summary of SASAC, <http://www.sasac.gov.cn/n2588030/n2588954/c10650828/content.html> accessed 31 January 2020.

[21] W Raphael Lam and others (eds), *Modernizing China: Investing in Soft Infrastructure* (International Monetary Fund 2017) ch 11.

2.2 *State Asset and Supervision: Various Institutions and Different Levels of Control*

SOEs' assets account for a significant portion of the Chinese economy. At the end of 2018, non-financial SOEs had a total asset of RMB 210 trillion and total liabilities of RMB 135 trillion, equivalent to 230% and 148% of China's GDP, respectively.[22] Chinese SOEs are under different supervision entities and are subject to varying levels of governance, a practice that is often overlooked.

The local governments manage several thousand SOEs, each of which then controls several subsidiaries. As recorded in the yearbook of the State Council, local governments controlled RMB 129.6 trillion at the end of 2018, accounting for more than 60% of the total state-corporate assets.[23] Although large in numbers, they only make up a minority of China's total SOE overseas investment in the last decade, as the majority comes from SOEs controlled by the central government.[24]

The central government only directly controls 128 SOE groups, each of which controls dozens of subsidiaries, but they account for 40% of the total state-corporate assets. They are smaller in numbers, but larger in size and are often regarded as the "national champions" of China's capitalism.

Among these 128 SOE groups, 96 are non-financial groups that are commonly referred to as "central SOEs" and supervised by SASAC. Half of them are "core SOEs" for their strategic function in China's economy and their critical role in national security. The leaders of the core SOEs are appointed by the CCP's personnel branch, the Central Organization Department (COD). SASAC appoints the leaders of the other 47 central SOEs.[25]

There are 27 financial SOE groups that are under the supervision of the Ministry of Finance, not SASAC. Fourteen of them have leaders appointed by the COD and 12 with leaders appointed by financial regulators. An exception is China Investment Corporation. Its chairman is nominated directly by the State Council, which exercises shareholder's rights on behalf of the state.[26]

Additionally, there are 5 SOE groups with regulatory functions in culture, railway, tobacco, and post. They are under the control of relevant ministries, respectively, and the COD, not SASAC, appoints their leaders.

---

[22] SASAC, <http://www.sasac.gov.cn/n2588025/n2588119/c12390466/content.html> accessed 31 January 2020.

[23] SASAC, <http://www.sasac.gov.cn/n2588025/n2588119/c12390466/content.html> accessed 31 January 2020.

[24] Calculated by the author, basing on the database of China Global Investment Tracker, American Enterprise Institute and The Heritage Foundation.

[25] SASAC, <http://www.sasac.gov.cn/n2588035/n2641579/n2641645/index.html> accessed 31 January 2020.

[26] CIC, <http://www.china-inv.cn/chinainven/Governance/Organizational_Structure.shtml> accessed 31 January 2020.

2.3 *Public and Private Ownership: Control Transfers Both Ways*

Although the mixed-ownership reform is still ongoing, it seems so far the policy is allowing ownership control transfers in both directions.

On the private capital front, SASAC launched a "double-hundred campaign" in August 2018 and asked 444 central and local SOEs to attract private capital and reform their corporate governance structure within two years. One year later, 228 of these SOEs (57.87%) have attracted private capital totalling RMB 538.4 billion. 302 of them (76.65%) have established a board of directors, and 620 professional managers were recruited from the private sector.The broader access to SOEs also increased the influence of private firms, which reported a continuous growth rate of the asset since August 2018 and reached 13% in August 2019.[27] Such progress has brought a significant change of control in many firms.

In the other direction, SOEs are buying into private firms. Many private enterprises sought assistance from SOEs when under financial distress. SOEs also have strong incentives to acquire private firms with better performance so that they can improve overall efficiency after the merger. Since November 2018, there are 178 A-share listed companies that have reported changes in the actual controller. 40 of them (22.5%) were transferred from private owners to local governments and 10 of them (5.6%) from private owners to the central government. Both numbers almost doubled from a year ago.[28]

2.4 *The Party's Political Control*

The blurred boundary between the government and the SOEs is largely path-dependent. Many central SOEs were successors of governmental ministries dissolved in the 1980s and 90s. As a result, managers of these ministry-turned-SOEs still had strong influences on shaping new industrial policies. Their close relationship with the regulators changed the power dynamics in the SOEs' corporate governance and decision-making process. An SOE's chairman also had a high chance of returning to the government, usually working in a ministry that regulates that SOE.

This revolving door was ultimately supervised by the CCP's Central Committee and its personnel branch, the organizing department. Before and even after the SASAC was established, the chairman and senior managers of SOE groups were assessed by the party's COD annually.[29] The COD's review on SOE managers included multiple non-commercial elements such as "accomplishment of special

---

[27] SASAC, <http://www.sasac.gov.cn/n2588020/n2877938/n2879597/n2879599/c11884990/content.html> accessed 31 January 2020.

[28] Data collected and summarized by Plenum China, basing on China A-Share Database.

[29] Ministry of Finance on the issue of enterprise performance evaluation, para.2 (1999), *Caizhengbu Guanyu Qiye Xiaoji Pingjia Gongzuozhong Youguan Wenti Jieda.*

tasks concerning national strategy," "contribution to the society," "labor union and ideology works," "contribution to maintain the social stability," which in total weighed about a-third when evaluating and ranking the SOEs' senior managers and directors who are party members.[30] The scoring and ranking system served as a necessary reference for the CCP to find capable party members to nominate for more prominent governmental positions and positions in other institutions of the party-lead meritocracy.[31]

Another way for the Party to supervise the SOEs is through anti-corruption campaigns. All central SOEs have been inspected at least once in the past seven years by the "central inspection tour," an integral part of China's anti-corruption supervision system. Just in a short period of two years, there have already been several inspection tours at the central SOEs, and hundreds of SOE managers were removed from their positions.[32]

The third way of control is through the Party's primary-level organizations in the SOEs. At the end of 2019, following the 2015 Guidelines, the COD issued a new policy document to regulate better party cells within SOEs that are wholly owned by the state or where the state has a majority shareholding position. The new document requires these SOEs to ensure the CCP's political leadership in the firm's charter and specify the party cell's duty and power in corporate governance. It encourages the SOE party committee members to sit on the boards or become managers and the directors and senior managers to enter the SOE party committee. It also explicitly demands that certain critical issues be discussed by the party cells before the board and managers make final decisions. It requires SOEs to appoint a full-time deputy party secretary to oversee the firm's party building. This secretary will also sit on the board of directors but would not take business responsibilities as a manager.[33]

Clearly, the CCP's political control over SOEs is increasing, not decreasing, but this does not necessarily mean that all decisions and transactions made by the SOEs are entirely political. The tightened political control aims at achieving two goals. First, it aims at increasing the supervision of the leaders and managers of SOEs to avoid agency problems. Second, by emphasizing the party's political leadership, it

---

[30] *See generally* THE 5TH Bureau of Organization Department of the CCP, Study on the Term of Office and Evaluation Index of Leaders of Central SOEs (Dangjian Duwu Chubanshe 2003). *See also* Provisional Measures Concerning the Integrated Evaluation of the Top Management Teams and Managers of the Central Enterprises, (2009), Zhongyang Qiye Lingdao Banzi he Lingdao Renyuan Zonghe Kaohe Pingjie Banfa (Shixing). Noted that this party law was only provisional and its proposed market-oriented policies were criticized of been not effective. *See also* Jiang Xingwang, Research on Leadership Institution of State-Owned Enterprises (Dongbei University of Finance and Economics Press 2011) ch.2.

[31] Li-Wen Lin, 'State Ownership and Corporate Governance in China: An Executive Career Approach' [2013] Columbia Business Law Review 743.

[32] CPC Central Committee for Discipline Inspection and China National Supervisory Committee, 'Reports of Central Inspection Works' <http://www.ccdi.gov.cn/special/zyxszt/index.html> accessed 31 January 2020.

[33] Provisional Regulation of the Communist Party of China on the Work of Primary Organizations in State-owned Enterprises, (2019), Zhongguo Gongchandang Guoyou Qiye Jiceng Zuzhi Gongzuo Tiaoli (Shixing).

also empowers the party's grassroots organizations that represent workers' interests and protect their labor rights. As mentioned earlier in this paper, the purposes of control are designed distinctively among SOEs. Because the party has separate policy preferences for these groups, its increasing political control will lead to different policy results. For commercial SOEs, the Party's priority is efficiency. The policy to encourage mix-ownership, the hard look on corruption, and further separating SOEs managers in the political system could eventually accelerate market-oriented reforms in these SOEs and transform them into more competitive firms in the market. For non-commercial SOEs, the policy priority is stability. The party's control further ensures the supply of public goods in the domestic market and increases public supervision. For sure, these SOEs have more non-commercial considerations and bear more social responsibilities. However, the business and operation of these SOEs focus on the domestic market not an international one.

3 Implications for Better Governance of SCEs

This study focuses on China's methods of state control in its SOEs. It debunks the assumption that all Chinese SOEs are public bodies of the government or controlled similarly by the party-state.[34] Although Chinese SOEs have the same parent, they are not equal brothers, but different in their relationship with the government, their relationship with the CCP, and their ultimate business goals. This reality is grossly misunderstood or politically ignored in many contexts, even after China's thirty-year development.[35] China's 2015 SOE reform is not only a reform of corporates but also one that includes changes of "control." Although the reform is still ongoing, it has implications for future policy-makers.

3.1 For China's Reformers: A Bumpy Road of De-control

Chinese SOEs have been reformed several times since China opened up to the world in the late 70s, adapting to evolving political and economic environments. Much influenced by the global norm of "good corporate governance," Chinese SOEs have been trying to establish legal structures of "modern corporates" under the party's leadership. Changing the relationship between the state and the firms has been a long and bumpy road.

[34] 'U.S. and China Clash at WTO over Ideology, State's Role' *Reuters* (26 July 2018) <https://www.reuters.com/article/us-usa-trade-wto/u-s-and-china-clash-at-wto-over-ideology-states-role-idUSKBN1KG22G> accessed 31January 2020. *See also* The world trading system is under attack, The Economist, July 21-27, 2018, at 15–17.

[35] Ming Du, 'The Regulation of Chinese State-Owned Enterprises in National Foreign Investment Laws: A Comparative Analysis' (2016) 5 Global J. Comp. L. 118.

Before China's open-up, the notion of "private property rights" was against orthodox Marxist ideas,[36] and China's economy had been primarily controlled and conducted by thousands of publicly owned state-operating enterprises.[37] These companies were not independent legal persons but were regarded and operated as governmental agencies.[38] The government used to control all SOEs, which in turn controlled the economy. The SOEs were public agencies, and their managers were civil servants.

Today's SOEs are no longer their ancestors. After the SOE reforms in the 80s and 90s, they have evolved from being parts of government administrations to legally independent enterprises with a modern corporate structure.[39] They are empowered to make their own managerial, operational and production decisions.[40] The state also progressively changed its ways of control. It slowly retreated from directing SOE daily operations, instead established independent and professional institutions to represent state-owned shares and modified rules continuously to push SOEs toward better corporate governance.[41]

---

[36] Zhang Xiaoyang, 'Protecting Private Property in China - Whose Property' (2013) 25 Denning Law Journal 19.

[37] The state-operating enterprises are not only owned by the State, but also operated directly by the government agencies. In other words, the separation of ownership and control in state-operating enterprises is less and weaker than that in state-owned enterprises.

[38] *See* Constitution of the People's Republic of China, (1954), Zhonghua Renmin Gongheguo Xianfa. *See also* Barry Naughton, 'China's Experience with Guidance Planning' (1990) 14 Journal of Comparative Economics 743.

[39] China's first SOE legislation in 1988 differentiated the management of SOEs from administrative directives of governments and ensured certain independence of SOEs' managers. It marked a formal separation between SOEs as independent actors in law and State as their dominant shareholder. China's Company Law of 1993 set up a new relationship between SOEs and the State. Since then, SOEs were independent legal personae under the law and grouped either as limited liability companies or shareholding companies.

[40] Du (n 35).

[41] The first step was in the 1999 amendment of the corporate law, which established a two-board structure in SOEs, one board of directors, and one board of supervisors. Following that, a 2001 administrative regulation made by China Securities Regulatory Commission suggested all listed companies, including SOEs, should include independent directors to sit on their board of directors. In 2003, the State Council established a specialized agency, State-owned Assets Supervision and Administration Commission (SASAC), to regulate and represent the state assets in SOEs. *See also* Li-Wen Lin and Curtis J Milhaupt, 'We Are the (National) Champions: Understanding the Mechanisms of State Capitalism in China' (2013) 65 Stanford Law Review 697.

Unlike previous SOE reforms that adopted a somewhat unified approach and applied one model to all SOEs, the 2015 reform took a more diversified approach, differentiating SOEs' corporate governance and changing the old way of state control over these entities. It sets up state-owned holding companies to represent the state as shareholders and distances SASAC from direct involvement in SOEs businesses, orientating the control method toward Singapore's Temasek model.[42]

It is not surprising that Temasek has been the role model for Chinese reformers for a long time, given the policy, cultural, and political similarities between the two. However, the success of this world-known SCE is not only supported by a good corporate structure but also largely based on "the respect, tolerance, and self-restraint of the government,"[43] which are not easily replicated in another jurisdiction with a weaker rule of law but a stronger hand of the party.

Suppose Chinese policy-makers are heading toward Temasek's path. In that case, they need to deepen reforms in more areas than the SOEs themselves, dedicating attention to a more transparent relationship between CCP's political leadership in the SOEs, more robust public governance, the role of foreign activities and market forces in the economy, and the government's desire to behave as a market player.[44] These changes are not easy but necessary to overcome the pediments along the bumpy road.

3.2 *For Transnational Regulators*

Chinese SCEs are not unique. As of 2010, worldwide SOEs accounted for about one-fifth of global market capitalization.[45] In 2012, SOEs' average size of mergers and acquisitions was four times larger than private firms'.[46] By 2016, worldwide data showed that SOEs accounted for 20–30% of economic activities in relatively advanced emerging economies, and this number was even higher in smaller developing economies.[47] In 2018, among the top 100 multinational enterprises SOEs, 16

---

[42] Li-Wen Lin, 'A Network Anatomy of Chinese State-Owned Enterprises' (2017) 16 World Trade Rev. 583.

[43] Christopher Chen, 'Solving the Puzzle of Corporate Governance of State-Owned Enterprises: The Path of the Temasek Model in Singapore and Lessons for China' (2016) 36 Nw. J. Int'l L. & Bus. 303.

[44] ibid.

[45] 'China Buys up the World' *The Economist* <https://www.economist.com/leaders/2010/11/11/china-buys-up-the-world> accessed 2 February 2020.

[46] OECD, 'International Investment by SOEs' 195, 200.

[47] OECD, 'State-Owned Enterprises as Global Competitors: A Challenge or an Opportunity?' <https://www.oecd-ilibrary.org/finance-and-investment/state-owned-enterprises-as-global-competitors_9789264262096-en> accessed 2 February 2020.

are state-owned, and the new entrants are SOEs from major emerging markets.[48] SOEs contribute to global development, and it is not a unique phenomenon.[49]

While SOEs, especially SOEs from emerging markets, have been active in international markets and development in the last five years, many host countries have started to have similar concerns regarding foreign SOEs that seek to invest in their jurisdiction.[50] Such concerns include but are not limited to preferential treatment from SOEs' home country, national security, transparency, and their influence on competition.[51] The U.S., for example, amended its investment law in 2018 and significantly enlarged the jurisdiction of CFIUS, the agency in charge of national security reviews of foreign investment into the USA. Now, the agency would examine any transaction involving governmental interest, especially firms with state ownership.[52] Not only did the U.S. amend the rules, but other countries have also adopted similar changes as new policies.[53] The transnational regulators have tremendously expanded their power and scrutiny to cover investment from SOEs and even private firms without state ownership.

Although the new laws aim at protecting the safety, fair competition, and the public interest of the host countries, the crude application of these rules is not without criticism. The vague definition of control, unclear interpretation of the standard, close-door reviewing process, and unlimited reviewing power without checks have been criticized for being tools of economic protectionism and causing unnecessary waste of public resources rather than really addressing regulatory concerns.[54] In this

---

[48] UNCTAD, *World Investment Report* (United Nations 2019) 24.

[49] ibid.

[50] UNCTAD (n 48) 26.

[51] Sara Sultan Balbuena, *Concerns Related to the Internationalisation of State-Owned Enterprises: Perspectives from Regulators, Government Owners and the Broader Business Community* (OECD Publishing 2016).(conducting surveys in 17 OECD members and summarizing policy concerns from local regulators and business group) Curtis J Milhaupt and Mariana Pargendler, 'Governance Challenges of Listed State-Owned Enterprises around the World: National Experiences and a Framework for Reform' (2017) 50 Cornell International Law Journal 473.

[52] *See* Foreign Investment Risk Review Modernization Act of 2018, SEC.1703 Definitions. (5) "Covered Transaction" and (7) "foreign government-controlled transaction". SEC.1706 Declarations Relating to Certain Covered Transactions.

[53] Du (n 35).

[54] ibid. *See also* Yiheng Feng, 'We Wouldn't Transfer Title to the Devil: Consequences of the Congressional Politicization of Foreign Direct Investment on National Security Grounds' (2009) 42 New York University Journal of International Law and Politics 253; Stanley Lubman, 'China's State Capitalism: The Real World Implications', The Wall Street Journal, (March 1, 2012); Paul Rose, 'Sovereigns as Shareholders' (2008) 87 North Carolina Law Review 102; Henry J. Graham, 'Foreign Investment Laws of China and the United States: A Comparative Study' (1996) 5Journal of Transnational Law and Policy 253.

respect, better understandings of the differences among foreign SCEs and the various methods of state control could significantly improve the host countries' regulatory efficiency. More nuanced rules that address differences among SCEs can balance policy needs to safeguard domestic safety and attract foreign resources to prosper the domestic economy. More transparent reviewing procedures involving foreign SCEs will increase the regulators' legitimacy in host countries and force multinational SCEs to be more transparent in the global market. For transnational regulators, the very first step to achieve these desirable goals is to know the details of control with local contexts.

At the international level, international organizations such as OECD and the World Bank have been paying close attention to SOEs and created a list of whole-packaging policy prescriptions for the best SOE corporate governance practices.[55] The international soft law has a real influence on state practices; however, it has also been criticized for being too general and treating SCEs without enough granularity, as if they should all be transformed into private enterprises.[56]

This study provides a China case that shows the possibility as well as the diversity of controls in state enterprises. It further raises the challenges of a unified soft-law regulatory framework at the international level. It calls for more nuanced policies within the international law regime to guide local practices. Hopefully, more cooperative regulations and comparative studies would generate more knowledge in this area (Table 1).

[55] *See* Alexandre Arrobbio and others, 'Corporate Governance of State-Owned Enterprises : A Toolkit' (The World Bank 2014) 91347 <http://documents.worldbank.org/curated/en/228331468169750340/Corporate-governance-of-state-owned-enterprises-a-toolkit> accessed 2 February 2020; See also 'OECD Guidelines on Corporate Governance of State-Owned Enterprises - OECD' <https://www.oecd.org/corporate/guidelines-corporate-governance-soes.htm> accessed 2 February 2020.

[56] Milhaupt and Pargendler (n 51).

Table 1 Summary of China's 2015 SOE reform regulations

Date	Title	Type	Summary
12-07-2015	Guiding opinions classification of SOEs basing on functions	Department regulation/SASAC	Commercial SOEs shall increase efficiency and competitiveness to compete in the international market. SOEs with strategic importance or special projects shall determine their scope of business, increase the State ownership depending on the characteristics of industries, and play an even bigger role in serving national macroeconomic control, safeguarding national security and national economic operation, accomplishing special tasks
06-30-2016	Report of the State Council on the state-owned assets management and system reform	State Council regulation	Continue to promote international operations, actively participate in the "Belt and Road" construction and international capacity cooperation, and expand the scale of overseas operations and business
08-02-2016	Opinions on establishing an accountability system for business operations and investment in violation of regulations by SOEs	State Council regulation	It is the first regulation that specifically addresses the accountability for business operations and investment in violation of the regulations by state-owned and state-controlled enterprises. The articles include the scope, determination, and implementation of accountability, etc.
01-07-2017	Measures for the supervision and administration of ODI by central SOEs	Department regulation/SASAC	It supersedes the previous 2012 Interim Measures and creates more structured regulation for SOEs ODI. It includes rules governing the ODI regulatory system, regulations ex ante ODI, management of ODI, ex post ODI, risk management and accountability
04-24-2017	Guiding opinions on further improving the corporate governance structure of SOEs	State Council regulation	It reemphasizes and detailed the policies concerning the corporate structure in the 2015 Guidelines

(continued)

Table 1 (continued)

Date	Title	Type	Summary
4-27-2017	Guidelines of functional transformation of SASAC	State Council regulation	Emphasizes the separation between the government and SOEs, between ownership and management. Clarify that the role of SASAC is to manage state assets as a shareholder, not to exercise administrative functions, not to interfere with the independence of SOEs SASAC shall create a negative list of ODI investments, strengthen the guidance for the international operation of central enterprises, strengthen the construction of an overseas investment supervision system, increase the intensity of auditing and control, and strictly control investment risks SASAC shall set up the insurance fund and investment guidance fund to promote innovation and development of central SOEs
07-18-2017	Implementing plan of the corporate-style restructuring of central SOEs	State Council regulation	Continue to finish the corporatization of all central-level SOEs. It requires all SOEs to adopt modern enterprise structures and improve operation under the rule of the market. efforts should also be made to prevent the loss of state assets and strengthen the Party's political leadership in SOEs
07-14-2018	Implementation opinions of the State Council on advancing the pilot program of the reform of state capital investment and operation companies	State Council regulation	State capital investment companies shall use the financial instruments to guide investment, promote industry clustering, resolute overcapacity, develop core competitiveness and innovative capabilities, vigorously participate in international competition, and pay particular attention to improving the control and influence of state capital

(continued)

Table 1 (continued)

Date	Title	Type	Summary
08-24-2018	Implementation plan for assessment of central SOEs according to their classifications	Department regulation/SASAC	Set up different evaluation standards according to SOEs' categorization: For commercial SOEs-efficiency, competitiveness, profitability; for strategic SOEs-national security, serve national strategy, perform special tasks; for public welfare SOEs-ensure public service, social responsibility Going-Global projects with strategic importance will be evaluated separately
12-27-2018	Measures for the administration of total salary of central SOEs	Department regulation/SASAC	Reemphasize the fundamental role of the market in salary evaluation, link the salary to the net profit of SOEs and labor productivity, set up different metrics according to SOEs' categorization
03-01-2019	Method for evaluating the performance of the senior managers of central SOEs	Department regulation/SASAC	Set up different evaluation standards according to SOEs' categorization. Specifically taking SOEs' participation in Belt-Road Initiative into consideration. Also, for SOEs under reforms, the evaluations on managers are assessed individually

The Legal Issues of "Going Global" and the Trans-nationalization of the Chinese Public-Private Partnership Model

Gianmatteo Sabatino

1 Introductive Remarks: Legal Issues of "Going Global"

As suggested by its 13th Five-Year Plan for National Economic and Social Development,[1] the PRC has entered a new stage of its "Reform and Opening Up" (改革开放). The interest toward foreign investment which once was a feature of Chinese socialism has now turned into a bidirectional approach. In other words, the integration between China and foreign and international markets is expressed on one hand by the flow of foreign capitals and on the other by the Foreign Direct Investments (FDI) carried out by Chinese enterprises toward overseas markets.[2] This development path implies the occurrence of regulatory necessities, for two essential and closely linked reasons:

[1] '13th Five-Year Plan for National Economic and Social Development (2016–2020)' <http://en.ndrc.gov.cn/policyrelease/201612/P020161207645766966662.pdf> accessed March 2, 2019, Part XI.

[2] Xiaowei Ding, Huizhen Li, "On the Role of Industry Associations in Assisting Enterprises to Manage Overseas Investment Risks under the Background of the Belt and Road Initiative" ("一带一路" 背景下中国企业海外投资风险的管控) (2015) 32(5) Journal of Political Science and Law 123.

This chapter draws upon the author's original publication also available at https://www.transnational-dispute-management.com/journal-advance-publication-article.asp?key=1836. Reprinted by permission from Maris BV: Maris BV, *Transnational Dispute Management* (TDM, ISSN 1875-4120), "The Legal Issues of "Going Global" and the Trans-Nationalisation of the Chinese Public-Private Partnership Model", Gianmatteo Sabatino, Copyright (2000). Please cite accordingly.

G. Sabatino (✉)
Zhongnan University of Economics and Law, Wuhan, China
e-mail: sabatinogianmatteo@gmail.com

J. Chaisse et al. (eds.), *Regulation of State-Controlled Enterprises*, International Law and the Global South, https://doi.org/10.1007/978-981-19-1368-6_5

- An objective reason, i.e., the rationalization of the allocation of resources through investment regulation, in order to ensure protection of national interest,
- A subjective reason, i.e., the circumstance that an important part of Chinese FDI is carried out by state-controlled enterprises[3] (SCEs), so that strategies of economic development may be pursued by public authorities through such economic operators.

In the new era of socialism with Chinese characteristics, the achievement of optimal market regulation and coordination relies on the development of a clear legal framework where strategic goals, legal instruments to pursue and monitoring structures are defined and put in the proper hierarchy. The law becomes, at the same time, a guarantee for the exercise of rights and prerogatives by economic operators and a tool to ensure the harmonization of economic strategies under the principles of socialist market economy set out by the Communist Party of China. Given these premises, the "going global" of Chinese enterprises—especially state-controlled ones—undoubtedly implies legal issues, both at the domestic and at the international level. In first place, the regulation of the outward expansion of Chinese investments requires a legal definition of their scope and limits. In second place, it requires the elaboration of efficient legal instruments and structures for outward-investing SCCs to operate.

While these represent just two of the many issues related to the topic, they become much more significant when assessed within the framework of wide-scope international cooperation initiatives, such as the Belt and Road initiative (BRI), originally *Yīdài yīlù* (一带一路).[4] In this context, the definition of a legal regime for FDIs as well as of proper legal structures for them to operate in concrete may function as the core of a new transnational legal order, an order which develops around the contractual relation between domestic enterprises and foreign governments, concerning international cooperation projects. The challenge becomes, therefore, to adopt effective legal mechanisms to avoid, as much as possible, legal conflicts over the path of international cooperation.

---

[3] With the expression "State-Controlled Enterprises," I refer to all those enterprises whose capital is wholly or partially owned by public bodies such as governments, ministries, administrative authorities. Obviously, where such public bodies own just a part of the capital, such part must be relevant enough for the public shareholder to exercise an effective control over the enterprise. Indirectly, even an enterprise controlled by a SCE may be regarded as a SCE.

[4] Angang Hu, "The Belt and Road: Revolution of Economic Geography and the Era of Win-Winism" in Liu Wei (ed), *China's Belt and Road Initiatives* (Springer and Shanghai Jiaotong University Press 2018) 15–32.

2 The Overseas Dimension of Chinese Enterprises and its Regulatory Framework

The outward expansion of Chinese economy relies on the establishment of a mature phase of socialist market economy. The *guo jin min tui* policy era,[5] embodied in the Hu Jintao leadership, had paved the way for the development of a threefold economic law, aimed at ensuring macroeconomic regulation, harmonization and control. In parallel, the gradual reform of SOEs had endured an acceleration with the creation of the State-Owned Assets Supervision and Administration Commission (SASAC),[6] which represented, formally, the full shifting from the soviet-fashioned model of bureaucratic SOE toward that of SCEs. Chinese public enterprises are therefore, in great majority, not collocated within an administrative structure headed by an economic ministry. They function instead in corporate form, while their capital is controlled by one or several state departments.[7]

This is the model of SCEs which carries the flag of the "going global" policy. In addition, the establishment of the China Investments Corporation[8] in 2007—i.e., the Chinese sovereign wealth fund—reassessed the idea of a comprehensive state capitalism which clearly looked abroad. In the near future, the model of the SCEs could further evolve into that of mixed-ownership enterprise,[9] combining public and private capital toward foreign investments. However, in line with the evolution of the Chinese legal system, such process needed its proper legal discipline.

The most relevant documents, over the years, have been those regarding the administration of foreign investment of enterprises, the most recent being the Measures for the Administration of Overseas Investment of Enterprises (hereinafter also MAOIE)[10] of 2017. The first element that must be noted is that the MAOIE (Art. 2) clearly define the notion of "overseas investments" (境外投资) as "*investment activities where an enterprise in the territory of the People's Republic of China (…), directly or through an overseas enterprise controlled by it, acquires overseas any ownership, right of control, right of business management, or other relevant rights and interests, by contributing assets or rights and interests, providing financing or*

---

[5] Gianmatteo Sabatino, "Legal Features of Chinese Economic Planning" in Ignazio Castellucci (ed), *Saggi di Diritto Economico e Commerciale Cinese* (Editoriale Scientifica 2019) 73–74.

[6] *guowuyuanguoyouzichangjianduguanliweiyuanhui* 国务院国有资产监督管理委员会 , established in 2003.

[7] Feng Deng, "Indigenous Evolution of SOE Regulation" in Benjamin L. Liebman and Curtis J. Milhaupt (eds), *Regulating the Visible Hand?: The Institutional Implications of Chinese State Capitalism* (Oxford 2015).

[8] Jing Li, "State as an Entrepreneur: A Study of the Investment Contractual Terms and Level of Control of China's Sovereign Wealth Fund in its Portfolio Firms" (2015) 3(1) Peking University Transnational Law Review 1.

[9] Dahong Liu, Honglei Duan, "Mixed Ownership, Public-private Partnership and the Reform of Market Access Law" (混合所有制、公私合作制及市场准入法 的改革论纲) (2017) 19(5) Journal of Shanghai University of Finance and Economics 91.

[10] *qiyejingwaitouziguanlibanfa*(企业境外投资管理办法).

security, or any other means." Incidentally, it must be noted that the MAOIE introduces an element of uncertainty in transnational perspective, since the notion of investment they embrace is different from the notion defined in each one of the bilateral investment treaties between China and foreign partners (for example that of the BRI), which vary from treaty to treaty.[11]

The MAOIE, with regard to sensitive projects, design a mechanism of prior approval for project investment managed by the National Development and Reform Commission[12] and based on four main criteria (Art. 26): (1) compliance with Chinese laws and regulations, (2) compliance with development plans and macroeconomic policies, (3) compliance with international treaties and agreements, (4) compliance with national interest and security.

In transnational perspective, the compliance with international agreements entered in by China has to take into account the aforementioned divergence between the regulatory frameworks set out in the different treaties. In particular, the BITs regulating FDIs between China and its BRI partners differ not only in the definition of "investment," but also in the stipulation of reciprocal obligations, dispute resolution mechanisms, etc.[13] This aspect, coupled with the variety of political, social and economic landscapes to be found along the BRI, renders FDIs a risky business for Chinese enterprises.[14] Therefore, how to harmonize the national and transnational regulatory frameworks and reduce the risks for Chinese companies?

Given the absence of a clear transnational legal regime for FDIs along the BRI, the focus of the regulation of international cooperation projects shifts toward the private law instruments involved in the process. In particular, the PPP model is being increasingly regarded as an efficient instrument of economic cooperation even in transnational perspective and in particular with regard to the economic initiatives promoted along the "一带一路".

In his speech at the 31st group study session of the Political Bureau of the 18th CPC Central Committee, chairman Xi Jinping stated that "*to promote the initiative* (i.e., the "Belt and Road" initiative) *we must give play to both the role the government and that of the market. The government must play a leading role in promotion, coordination and building mechanisms. At the same time, it is important to put in place a market-based regional economic cooperation mechanism for enterprises. The government should encourage enterprises and other social forces to participate in the initiative.*"

Following such broad and comprehensive approach, in January 2017 the National Development and Reform Commission established a "working mechanism" regarding PPP projects with other 13 State Council departments and commenced on

[11] Tingting Deng, Meiyu Zhang, 'The treaty protection of Chinese overseas investment under "the Belt and Road Initiative"' ("一带一路"倡议下中国海外投资的条约保护) (2016) 22(6) *Zhongnandaxuexuebao* (中南大学学报) 37.

[12] If the investor is a local enterprise and the amount of investment is under USD 300 million, the recordation authority is instead the local development and reform commission of the province where the investor is registered.

[13] ibid.

[14] Ding and Li (n 2).

strengthening the cooperation with foreign countries along the BRI with the purpose of developing infrastructure projects involving PPP.

The classic scheme involves a Chinese enterprise negotiating with a foreign government a partnership contract concerning the realization of infrastructure projects. The partnership enables the public actor to retain both ownership of the facilities employed in the project as well as of the project's outcome—especially in case of infrastructure works—and supervisory powers over the private actor which, in turn, manages, from the operational perspective, the project, bears its risks and, at least for an initial period of time, gains profit from the management of the service connected to the project.[15]

Therefore, the real issue is twofold. On the one hand, within China, there is the need for a comprehensive regulation of PPPs harmonized with the provisions about FDIs. On the other hand, the Chinese PPP model may become, once fully developed, a model for transnational partnership contracts along the BRI. This second occurrence implies the consideration for the profound economic, political and cultural differences between the various countries involved. In order to assess the feasibility of such transnational partnership model contract, the analysis must first focus on the state of development of Chinese PPP legislation.

3 The PPP Legal Model in the People's Republic of China

The PPP model in the PRC reflects a development pattern in the evolution of the legal mechanisms of macroeconomic coordination and control.[16] The development of a sound socialist market economy implies a broad and dynamic approach to the relationship between the state and the economy. Given that, as also sanctioned by the constitution, the state-controlled economy must play a guiding role (art 7), the introduction of market oriented mechanisms leads—or at least should lead—to a shift from direct public intervention into the economy to indirect intervention. In other words, the state appears to be advocating for a coordinating, supervising and regulatory role rather than an operative one.

The PPP model developed in the PRC right after the opening up and reform, as an instrument to attract foreign capitals into the PRC.[17] It was only in 2002 that Chinese local governments as well were encouraged to engage in public-private cooperation projects.[18] In 2003, with the establishment of the SASAC, the majority of former

[15] Cheng Zhang, "Analysis of legal relationships of PPP agreement (PPP" 协议的法律关系分析) (2017) 16(6) Journal of Taiyuan Normal University (Social Science edition) 32.

[16] Gianmatteo Sabatino, "Linee Evolutive del Partenariato Pubblico-Privato (PPP) nell'ordinamento giuridico della Repubblica Popolare Cinese" (2018/2019) 4 Rivista Trimestrale degli Appalti 1309.

[17] Beijing Mingshu Data Technology Co., Ltd. Southeast University PPP International Research Center, "Policy Analysis of PPP development in China (1984–2017)" (2017); Zhiyong Liu e Yamamoto, "Public-Private Partnerships (PPPs) in China: Present Conditions, Trends, and Future Challenges," (2009) 15(2) Information Sciences 223.

[18] ibid.

SOEs were subjected to the Company Law, enabling them to act as private market operators, albeit under the direction and control of the state.

The evolution of a Chinese model of cooperation between public and private capital was further accelerated by the consolidation of a Bidding Law (1999) and a Procurement Law (2002). The intervention of the governments in 2002 opted for the concession agreement to be the main instrument to realize public-private cooperation. Since then, the PPP model has been experiencing a steady increase in its frequency and success over China. Its regulatory provisions are, up to today, mostly contained in administrative regulations and policy documents.[19]

The two most important national legal sources regarding the Chinese PPP are the Contract Guidelines for Public and Private Capital Cooperation Projects (政府和社会资本合作项目通用合同指南) of the National Development and Reform Commission (NDRC) and the PPP Project Contract Guide (PPP项目合同指南) of the Ministry of Commerce. From the analysis of these sources, it may be argued that the Chinese PPP is a contract whose object is the realization of a project by a private (or a state-controlled) economic operator under the direction, coordination and monitoring of a public actor. So far, most of Chinese PPPs involve a local government or a local administrative department as public actor. Indeed, the introduction of partnerships was also advocated in order to tackle the issue of local governments' public debt.[20]

One of the main foundations of the PPP model lies in the sharing of benefits between the public and the private actor, which, nevertheless, it is not the same as common interests. In other words, the interests of the public and the private actors are, more often than not, divergent, since the first pursues public interests and the second economic interests.[21] As a consequence, the proper functioning of the agreement relies on the adequate coordination between conflicting interests. In the Chinese context, the concrete experience of the application of PPP models has, so far, displayed several issues related to the public-private relation, often related to the exercise, by the public actor, of excessive discretionary powers in violation of the contractual equilibrium.[22]

Actually, as mentioned by some researches, a relevant percentage of PPP initiatives involve SCEs as "private" partners. This circumstance implies the presence of a private partner managed through criteria of profitability but ultimately subjected to policy directives issued by the controlling body. From the perspective of the

[19] Wengguang Yu, "Research on the legislative issues of PPP regulation" (PPP规制中的立法问题研究) (2016) 2 *dangdaifaxue* (当代法学) 77.

[20] Yafang Zheng, "The Distinguishment of Public-Private Legal Relations in PPP Agreements" (论我国PPP协议中 公私法律关系的界分), *xingzhengfaxueyanjiu* (行政法学研究) (2017) 6, 35.

[21] Gairong Hu, "Conflict and Coordination of Public and Private Interests in the PPP Model" (PPP 模 式 中 公私利 益 的 冲 突 与协调) (2015) 11 *zhuantiyanjiu* (专题研究(法学)) 30.

[22] Youyong Zhou and Dong Zhai, "The Legal Construction of PPP Model in Urban Transit" (城市交通PPP模式的利益失衡及其法治构建) (2017) 25(10) *henanshehuikexue* (河南社会科学) 89; Shaocheng Yin, "The challenge faced by government supervision over public welfare industries under PPP pattern and its countermeasures" (PPP模式下公用事业政府监管的挑战及应对) (2017) 6 *xingzhengfaxueyanjiu* (行政法学研究) 114.

market, the problem becomes instead the efficiency and transparency of the tendering procedures.[23]

The above-mentioned critical points hold even more significance when referred to a transnational context such as the BRI one.[24] Indeed, given the range of different legal systems involved in the BRI, the development of a clear contractual framework may be the best instrument to prevent interests' imbalance, underperformance and excessive costs.

Public actors involved in PPP contracts, in China, may be bound by a series of long-term development programs, such as the Five-Year Plan for Economic and Social development.[25] These plans define in first place the projects holding priority; in second place, they may also lay out some of the concrete instruments and modalities to carry out such projects. Plan indications, therefore, function as the most immediate interpretative criterion of the PPP contract.

Furthermore, the PPP, as a contract, is subjected to general provisions of contract law, in first place Article 6, laying out the principles of honesty and credit. These principles have been often associated with the concept of good faith[26] which, in light of Chinese legal tradition, may serve the purpose of ensuring the survival of the long-term partnership relation, even through the adjustment, overtime, of certain clauses.[27] Incidentally, it may be highlighted, as it will be also reminded later, that the same principles of good faith as well as of equity may very well function as interpretative criteria for BRI BITs, in order to ensure the smooth realization of transnational PPP projects.

The establishment of a mutually beneficial cooperation based on market mechanisms—as mentioned in the 2014 Guidelines for government and social capital cooperation projects[28]—is the ultimate goal of the PPP. In order to achieve it, the Chinese legal system seems to have embraced a notion of partnerships built upon a notion of contract with organizational purposes instead of exchange purposes.[29] In other words, the object of the contract is in first place the plan/project and in second

[23] It must be pointed out that, on the one hand, the PRC Public Procurement Law leaves quite wide discretionary for the choice of the selection procedures; on the other hand, the Bidding Law does not clearly explain the criteria to determine the winner of the bid and refers to the definition of such criteria in the bid-invitation (art 41).

[24] Gang Xing, 'Research on the Legal issue of government unilateral contract amendments in PPP projects under the background of the "Belt and Road" construction' ("一带一路"建设背景下PPP项目中政府单方变更合同法律问题研究) (2017) 6, *dongfangfaxue*(东方法学).

[25] Contract Guidelines for Public and Private Capital Cooperation Projects, Ch 3, § 1.

[26] Zhang Mo, *Chinese Contract Law* (Martinus Nijhoff) 2006, 74.

[27] Ignazio Castellucci, "Rule of Law and Legal Complexity in the People's Republic of China" (2012) Università degli Studi di Trento, Dipartimento di Scienze Giuridiche, Quaderni del Dipartimento no. 103, 122–126.

[28] Contract Guidelines, Ch 1 § 1.

[29] On the notion of organizational contract, *see* Stefan Grundmann, Fabrizio Cafaggi, Giuseppe Vettori, "The organizational contract: from exchange to long-term network cooperation in European contract law" (Ashgate 2013).

place the definition of the obligations of the parties from the perspective of the realization of such project, thus from a long-term perspective. The PPP Project Contract Guide mentions, indeed, that "*A series of contracts will be established around the PPP project.*" Therefore, the agreements itself functions as a framework for several contracts which will, presumably, regulate each operative issue over the course of the project realization timeframe.

Moreover, the rights and reciprocal obligations of the parties constitute the core of the PPP contractual system (as laid out in the Project Contract Guide). The socio-economic function of the PPP contract, therefore, appears to lie in the coordination of the private and public role for the purpose of reaching the common aim. This particular feature, which makes the PPP contract resemble a plan,[30] at least in some aspects, leads to some significant assumptions:

- in the first place, the PPP agreement can serve as a contractual instrument—thus, not a purely administrative one—to govern long-term relationships with regard to complex projects or performances.[31] The PPP develops, in essence, as a cycle, where the general agreement serves as the main and fundamental source of obligations and the successive contracts define and adjust such obligations according to the circumstances,
- in second place, the PPP easily links with policy directives and plans since it basically replicates their structure by building up an "organizational contract". From this perspective, it is worth mentioning that the PPP could be regarded as a mean to carry out and implement plan directives and indicators, especially with regard to policy fields such as infrastructures, transports, social services, etc.

As far as the SOEs and the SCEs are concerned, regarding the PPP as an organizational contract fits into a comprehensive legal framework which subjects those economic entities to economic and strategic plans given the state-owned nature of their assets. In transnational perspective, the PPP contract is a particularly dynamic instrument, which enables enterprises to "go abroad" and be involved in transnational projects. For a country, a PPP initiative may indeed represent a way to attract foreign capital and accelerating the development of certain infrastructure or projects when, for instance, the government lacks the resources to do so. Given its long-term and broad perspective, the PPP contract can easily function as the framework of a cooperation initiative between a certain enterprise and a foreign country's government. The subsequent practical and operative aspects of the relationship stemming

---

[30] In this context, the notion of "plan" (规划 or *guihua*) refers to a legal act incorporating a long-term vision of the future development of a socio-economical field. The most relevant example of such category is undoubtedly the Five-Year Plan for the National Economic and Social Development. However, for the purpose of this analysis it is the concepts that counts, not its several implementations.

[31] The nature of the PPP contract is debated. While Chinese courts follow two main positions—i.e., public nature and private nature—in my opinion it could be associated with the concept of "administrative contract" (行政合同). On the issue, *see* Guodong Cheng, "The Administrative Contract as a mean of public resources allocation" (作为公共资源配置方式的行政合同) (2018) 30(3), Peking University Law Journal, 821.

from such initiative have to be covered by successive contracts negotiated between the parties but always in light and according to the purposes, main obligations and conditions laid out in the general agreement. From this point of view, contract is an instrument fit to manage overseas investment way better than the BIT.

4 PPPs and FDIs: Harmonizing Legal Frameworks

The existing legal provisions concerning PPPs and FDIs are very different. However, they have a fundamental common element: both of them focus on the concept of "project."

The PPP contract, as already pointed out above, is essentially a project contract. The definition of the project justifies the mutual obligations of the parties. On the other hand, the MAOIE also tie the investment to a project that must be evaluated by the competent authorities. Furthermore, two elements must be highlighted. In the first place, as it has been noted, projects for overseas investment must not violate international treaties and/or agreements. In the second place, the MAOIE take into account the manifold risks that Chinese enterprises investing overseas may encounter. In particular, Article 43 states that "*Where any major casualty involving personnel sent overseas, major loss of overseas assets, damage to the diplomatic relations between China and relevant country, or other major adverse condition occurs in the process of overseas investment, the investor shall, within five working days of the occurrence of the relevant condition, submit a major adverse condition reporting form through the network system.*" The NDRC—or the other competent department—may also issue risk alerts concerning the status of the economy and society at home and abroad (Article 47).

The dimension of risk is particularly relevant also with regard to the development of PPP projects.[32] Chinese enterprises are well aware of the differences between the legal systems they invest in. From this perspective, the PPP agreement also serves the purpose of ensuring the proper coordination between the Chinese enterprise and the foreign government. In other words, the partnership contracts aims at avoiding defaults coming from the public partner.[33] To this end, the PPP is complementary to the international investment treaties (IIT), in the sense that while the IITs lay out the general conditions for investments in a specific country, the PPP contract operates in concrete, transposing those conditions into a project and defining the obligations of both parties. From the available data, it may be argued that several transnational PPP projects are already in place. Some of them led to project agreements which defined the work to be carried out, its modality and the duration of the contractual relationship. The economic sectors involved span from infrastructures to energy.

---

[32] Nansheng Sun, "Risk Response Mechanisms of Foreign Investments PPP Projects under the Background of Belt & Road" ("一带一路"背景下对外投资PPP项目的风险应对机制) (2018) 3, *fazhixiandaihuayanjiu* (法治现代化研究), 32.

[33] ibid.

Chinese scholars point out how political turmoil and government's overturn may lead to abrupt termination in PPP contracts or, as noted before, unilateral changes. Furthermore, given the absence of transnational provisions, the regime of the PPP may be subject to changes depending on the domestic law of the host country regarding franchising, outsourcing and even the very nature of the PPP agreement, which may be deemed as public—thus governed by administrative law, private—thus governed by contract and civil law—or mixed. In order to tackle some of these issues, the "working mechanism" established by the NDRC is in charge of analyzing the political, diplomatic and financial environment of the different transnational projects, thus providing enterprises involved in riskier projects with specific measures to minimize risks. Beyond that, the most effective and reasonable mean to avoid negative externalities still is the partnership contract, which should clearly define the rights and obligations of the private party and provide compensatory measures in case of nationalization, unilateral changes, etc.

A further element of contact and interchange between the FDIs and PPPs legal frameworks is the reference to economic and social development plans as guiding criteria to assess the legitimacy and scope of both instruments. In general, it could be argued that both transnational PPPs and FDIs are incorporated in the relevant planning documents. The state-controlled economic operators investing overseas act as private actors before the foreign government but, indeed, implement national development strategies. This does not mean that the economic operators have no degree of autonomy in the management of the partnership relation. On the contrary, the detailed content of the contractual relation as well as the day-by-day realization of the project is arguably left to the negotiation between the parties. However, such autonomy is functional to the achievement of common objectives. Chinese SCEs are subjected, in their overseas investment activities, to a series of legal provisions aimed at pursuing public interests.

Such occurrence is also reflected in the coordination of different strategies concerning the "going global." Transnational PPPs sustained by FDIs fit into a precise framework of manifold activities, which often constitute the real benefit or "counter-performance" required to the foreign government in order to guarantee the functioning of the partnership relation. Chinese SCEs are often granted, through contract, franchise rights over the infrastructures realized or other infrastructures and/or resources. In some cases, the all-encompassing aim of the cooperation is clearer. For instance, the evolution of the international cooperation between China and Pakistan concerning the port of Gwadar saw the construction of the port itself by Chinese companies and the subsequent lease to the China Overseas Port Holding Company. Furthermore, Chinese activities in Pakistan include today the construction of several infrastructure projects regarding, for instance, energy power plants.[34] The public relevance of such PPPs is also reassessed by the fact that Xi Jinping himself referred to the National People's Congress about their implementation state.

The proper functioning of the model is ensured through the integration of public international law—i.e., BITs—and contract law. From the Chinese perspective, the

---

[34] *See* <http://www.sohu.com/a/162754450_498881> accessed September 30, 2018.

legal provisions regulating, to different extents, the activities of enterprises investing overseas all reflect a common development logic. Such logic is not directly reflected in the BITs but reemerges in the specific partnership contracts stipulated between Chinese enterprises and foreign governments, on account—among other aspects—of the economic and political influence exercised by China over its international partners.

Therefore, the Chinese model of PPP—though not thoroughly developed—becomes the trace, the leading path for the construction of the transnational PPP along the BRI. The PPP is then complementary to the FDI, in the sense that it carries out the same policy direction at a lower level.

Moreover, if at the domestic level the involvement of SCEs in PPPs may lead to some malfunctioning given the inherent public scope of the SCEs and the subsequent mingling of political relationships,[35] at the international level the situation is different. Indeed, the SCEs, especially those involved in infrastructure projects, appear to be better equipped to negotiate with foreign governments, for several reasons. In first place, they may better represent the development strategy which justifies the transnational partnership they want to partake in. In second place, they have higher chances of obtaining proper credit from state-controlled financial institutions and at better rates or conditions. In other words, transnational PPPs involving SCEs better respond to a circular logic of cooperation and outward expansion of Chinese economy.

The legal framework regulating FDIs is, at least today, more developed than the one regulating PPPs. Apart from the nation-wide measures, some local governments, such as the Municipality of Beijing, issued their own for the administration of overseas investment.

How may such documents be coordinated with the existing provisions concerning PPPs and SCEs in order to promote the "going global" of Chinese enterprises? With regard to enterprises, the now in force legislation does not seem to raise fundamental issues. As it has been noted, the majority of SCEs operates according to the Company Law, as implicitly reaffirmed by the State-Owned Assets Law[36] too. Furthermore, the State-Owned Assets Law ensures that the economic fields where SCEs operate are in line with the priorities of national development. Today, the harmonization between SCEs' industrial strategies and national socio-economic programs may be furtherly ensured by the Supervision Law,[37] whose subjective scope includes "managers of State-Owned enterprises" (Article 15).

When Chinese enterprises invest overseas and establish partnerships with foreign government, they, indeed, operate following the few legal instruments that Chinese law designs in order to regulate and define the PPP contract. They are projects

[35] Daxue Fu, Fangzhu Lin, "On the scope of "private" in Public-Private Partnerships" (论公私合作伙伴关系 (PPP) 中"私"的范围) (2015) 5, *jianghuailuntan* (江淮论坛), 109.

[36] Law of the People's Republic of China on the State-Owned Assets of Enterprises (中华人民共和国企业国有资产法) (2008).

[37] Supervision Law of the People's Republic of China (中华人民共和国监察法) (2018).

contracts, with a strong emphasis on the organizational scope and are aimed at commencing a cooperation rather than at defining its details and possible evolutions.

Franchising is a legal form which is often used partly because it is the only one which, in Chinese law, enjoys a sufficiently complex elaboration. BITs, as already noted, do not contain uniform and precise definitions, nor are interested in building up contractual framework for cooperation initiatives.

Up to today, therefore, the "project" dynamic laid out in the MAOIE represent the major and most important reference for the promotion of a transnational model of PPP. The domestic model of partnership is likely to become, in the near future, the model employed along the BRI in the majority of cooperation initiatives involving Chinese enterprises. This may occur in account of basic reasons of political and economic influence.

The future developments of the transnational PPP require a prior evolution of the Chinese domestic PPP model, although with certain remarks. For instance, if internally the establishment of the PPP as an administrative law contract (行政合同)[38] may, to some extent, imply a transparent and coordinated application of the provisions concerning procurement, bidding and budget, in transnational perspective Chinese enterprises may have interest in negotiating the main points of the partnership relation *vis-à-vis* the foreign government. The focus of the negotiation procedures should be, once again, the project, already approved by the Chinese authorities but once again object of a pre-contractual phase affected by the public interests in the international cooperation between the States, without activating specific procurement procedures etc.

In last place, the question must be assessed from another perspective, that of international economic law. As already pointed out, the MAOIE include international treaties among the relevant sources to assess the legitimacy of a FDI. Now, it is important to highlight how the PRC[39] is today an observant member of the Government Procurement Agreement (GPA), but negotiating the adhesion. Indeed, most of the central Asian countries involved in the BRI are today either observant members[40] or not members with regard to the GPA.

The GPA does not explicitly mention PPPs but, as it has been noted,[41] its influence over the development of Chinese PPPs legal model may be exerted through the adjustment of public procurement provisions. In particular, pursuant to the non-discrimination clause of Article IV of the GPA, the Chinese procurement market should open up to foreign enterprises, that today represent just a small part of such market. Two instruments appear to be particularly fit to serve such purpose: on the one hand the clause of Article 24 of the Government Procurement Law, pursuant to which "*Two or more natural persons, legal persons or other organizations may form*

[38] Guodong Chen (n 31) 821.

[39] The Special Administrative Region of Hong Kong is instead already part of the GPA.

[40] Among them, Tajikistan and Kyrgyzstan are the only ones negotiating the adhesion.

[41] Dingsha Shi, Research on the employment of foreign capital in Chinese PPP Projects under the background of the WTO "Government Procurement Agreement" negotiation, (2017) 3, *hongguanjingjiyanjiu* (宏观经济研究), 48.

a complex so as to participate in government procurements as a provider." On the other hand, the transformation of previously wholly state-owned economic operators into mixed ownership enterprises could leave space for foreign investments.[42]

This possible pattern of evolution, nevertheless, so far has only been associated with foreign investment into China and not with Chinese FDI. In other words, Chinese enterprises, when going global, still prefer to negotiate *vis-à-vis* the foreign partner, without being bound by specific procurement procedures. Furthermore, BRI's PPPs could not even be formally subjected to the GPA, since the countries involved are not full members of the agreement.

5 The PPP as the Core of a "BRI Legal Order"

The regulation of overseas investment and the definition of a transnational approach to overseas activities carried out by Chinese enterprises functions differently depending on the perspective employed. With regard to the domestic legal system of the PRC, the FDI law serves the purpose of ensuring control and coordination over the investment policy of the enterprises. On the other hand, as far as transnational cooperation is concerned, a further scope arises, that of ensuring the functioning and benefits of cooperation itself. As a consequence, the legal models which govern the activities funded by those investments—such as the PPP—must have features fit to pursue a win-win cooperation logic.

However, when such initiatives operate within the context of a wider project, concerning the establishment of a space for collaboration and cooperation between sovereign states, the issues grow even more complex. It is necessary, in other words, to wonder whether or not, in light of investment policies and legal instruments described, such space may assume a defined legal nature.

Thinking of the BRI as a legal concept is a perilous operation but, at the same time, fascinating. If the BRI was regarded as a supranational legal order, we would assist to a new and original creation. Those who studied the BRI from a normative perspective[43] in first place highlighted how such initiative represents, at the global level, the transposing of a development and cooperation path within the international community, advocated by China and based on an active role of the Chinese development model in the construction of the world socio-economic order. During this construction process, China would dialectically interact with other development models without disrupting nor denying each other legitimacy.

Such vision represents the "constitutional" foundation of the BRI. According to such premises, it may be argued that the first step toward the legalization of such transnational order is the enactment, within China, of a promotional legislation for the

---

[42] ibid.

[43] Anastas Vangeli, "The Normative Foundations of the Belt and Road Initiative," in Wenhua Shan, Kimmo Nuotio, Kangle Zhang (ed), *Normative Readings of the Belt and Road Initiative*, (Springer 2018), 59–80.

initiative. Such legislation should define the organizational structures to govern the cooperation initiative as well as adopt the relevant support and incentives measures.[44]

Furthermore, it has been highlighted that the construction of a BRI legal order is founded on two different levels of cooperation, one international and one domestic.[45] If on the international level the goal is to coordinate and harmonize economic policies, on the domestic level the creation of the BRI means an integrated regional development strategy with regard to those areas, within the border of one country, at particular disadvantage. These two levels of cooperation reciprocally imply.

Given such context and the interests at play, the PPP model may realize the primary stage of cooperation needed both on the domestic and on the international level. Especially as far as infrastructures and transport are concerned, the establishment of efficient PPPs enables local authorities to implement development strategies for disadvantaged areas in terms of infrastructures and facilities construction. Then, the same pattern may be employed when dealing with transnational projects, thus involving national governments as well as local governments of different countries.

In second place, a PPP legislation—i.e., a domestic legislation but also serving the purpose of "going global"—should start from a conception of PPP as an organizational contract.

The legislation should, as clearly as possible, define the partnership agreement as a framework, where the private party and the public party agree on a project, share the risks connected to it and determine each party's rights and obligations. The object of the agreement should be in line with the strategic priorities set in the relevant development plans and/or documents. If the partnership is transnational such documents could be bilateral and multilateral agreements as well as joint declarations and statements by country's heads of state and/or heads of government.

Reference to development strategies should serve an interpretative key in order to detect the relevant public interests and the foreseeability of their evolution, so to render it possible to assess the legitimacy of the behavior of the parties in light of the agreement's object. Furthermore, the agreement, as already specified in the General Guidelines of 2014, should define the financing instruments related to the project.

In transnational perspective, it could prove useful to define the conditions and the procedure following which project bonds can be issued, in order to finance the project itself. With regard to such topic, the National Development and Reform Commission issued, in 2017, the "Guideline for Issuance of the Special Bonds of Public-Private Partnership (PPP) Projects." On the basis of the framework contract, then, the public and private actors—i.e., within the Belt and Road context, a country's government and a foreign enterprise—may agree on the specific instruments to be employed in order to carry out the partnership, e.g., the creation of a special purpose vehicle or a franchise contract.

---

44 Pi-liang Shangguan, "Constitutional Issues on the Belt and Road Initiative' ("一带一路"建设中的宪法问题) (2017) 3, *suzhoudaxuexuebao* (苏州大学学报) 36.

45 Gang Wang, 'On the Legal Issues and the Establishment of Legal Mechanism in the "Belt and Road" Construction' ("一带一路"建设中的法律问题 及法治机制构建) (2017) 2 *faxuezazhi* (法学杂志), 30.

Chinese scholars, not only legal scholars, have already regarded the PPP as a precious instrument for the internationalization of Chinese enterprises.[46] The reasons for such argument are quite clear: the PPP fits fairly well into the win-win cooperation scheme. In first place, it ensures the inflow of capital for the construction of infrastructures and facilities in areas whose governments often do not have sufficient financial resources. In second place, the PPP contract revolves around the double relation public actor/private actor and supervision/enactment. The partnership agreements often provide for the facility constructed to belong to the public actor, i.e., the foreign government. On the other hand, the private actor, i.e., the Chinese enterprise, may be granted franchise and management rights. While the authority of the foreign government is fully respected, Chinese enterprises may effectively widen not only their commercial scope but also their bargaining power in future cooperation initiatives with the same government.

As far as this last observation is concerned, it must be pointed out that there may be no structural difference in the investments carried out by SCEs or by Chinese private enterprises. Indeed, the regulatory framework for overseas investments, as we have seen, is clearly aimed at subordinating such investments to a precise national economic policy, a state interest in the economic field involved. Therefore, when investing overseas, it could be argued that Chinese enterprises act as SCEs even when they are not formally public. Once again, it is the project which ensures that such coordination may occur.

The several and deep differences between the legal systems involved in the Belt and Road initiative may not be questioned. As a consequence, the risk of conflicts in the choice and application of relevant legal provisions is particularly high. So far, the functioning of the cooperation mechanisms has relied heavily on China's political capacity to attract foreign governments toward Chinese enterprises' overseas investments. This does not mean that issues may not occur or have not occurred.[47] However, as it has been pointed out, although such conflicts are to some extent unavoidable, effective mechanisms may be adopted to reduce or minimize their impact.[48]

There are several possible solutions: The simplest is to prioritize international law.[49] Such view, however, displays some critical points. In particular, as we have already pointed out, Bilateral Investment Treaties do not provide for the necessary details to regulate the disputes arising from transnational PPP contracts.

---

[46] Jia Xu, "The use of the PPP model within the context of the Belt & Road strategy" ("一带一路"战略下的PPP模式运用) (2015) 30, *kejizixun* (科技资讯), 190; Jin Lin Nan, "Risks and coping strategies for overseas PPP projects" (2015) 9, *guojirongzi* (国际融资), 45.

[47] Xiangyang Li, The prominent problems in the Belt & Road Initiative and their solutions ("一带一路" 面临的突出问题和出路) (2017) 4, *guojimaoyi* (国际贸易) 4; Nansheng Sun (n 32), 31.

[48] Gang Wang (n 45), 30.

[49] ibid.

On the other hand, there are proposals for the establishment of a Belt and Road dispute resolution mechanisms or several mechanisms specialized in different matters.[50]

From the perspective of this paper, it is indeed interesting to point out how the PPP contract itself may function as an effective dispute resolution prevention mechanism. The key to prevent conflicts lies, in first place, on the very nature of the framework agreement, which sets general principles and could/should refer to development plans and common statements of the parties. In second place, the contract might also refer to some general principles, such as good faith and equity, and reassess the priority of international law. The PPP contract does not need to define all the relevant clauses and details of the partnership agreement; it may very well be readjusted over the course of a long-term project realization. However, it needs to clarify the intentions of the parties, the exchange of mutual benefits and the scope of the activity to be realized. From this perspective, the PPP may be regarded as a sort of middle ground between the international cooperation treaties and the private law instruments that my serve the purpose of realizing the project. It is, indeed, a contract which is also a plan, and a plan which is also a contract.

The topics above discussed are under constant evolution, and therefore, many conclusions or statements try to formulate hypotheses on the basis of the current legal framework regarding PPPs. The main point that the paper wants to raise is that the development of a "Belt and Road Public Private Partnership" model might pave the way for the establishment of a unique and transnational legal order which now is still not detectable.

Within this context, Chinese law serves as the engine and the model for the creation and development of supranational rules. This occurs in first place on account of the fact that Chinese enterprises are so far the best equipped to "go global" and conclude partnerships agreement with foreign governments. In second place, China is undoubtedly the main sponsor and advocator of the whole initiative as well as the most resourceful country in terms of capital, organizational means, labor force and prestige.

In third place, the Chinese model of PPP has so far displayed characteristics which render it able to adapt to different legal contexts: its mixed nature, its organizational purpose and its dynamic approach in terms of relationship between private and public actors appear to be shaping the main features of a new and original legal instrument of public economic management and coordination on a transnational level.

Future comparative analysis will probably be able to assess whether or not, following such pattern of cooperation, BRI countries will amend their legislation or issue new legislation about PPPs or FDIs following the Chinese model.

The Chinese transnational PPP model represents, within the global context, something new. It draws from the main features of domestic PPPs but, at the same time, reflects the win-win logic which advocates. It is based on a delicate balance of law and policy. It refers to three major sources:

[50] Xiaojun Zhang, Wei Chen, "Construction of a Belt & Road regional investment dispute settlement mechanism" (2017) 3, *xueshuluntan* (学术论坛), 50.

- International Cooperation Agreements such as IITs and BITs. However, as already mentioned, such sources generally do not address PPPs. As a consequence, they often lay out, with regard to such projects, just the general purposes of the cooperation, reassessing the intention to welcome investments according to domestic and international laws and regulations. As far as disputes are concerned, such treaties usually lay out a two-step approach: in first place the resolution of disputes through diplomatic negotiation and consultation; in second place the referral of the dispute to an *ad hoc* arbitral tribunal[51];
- Long-term development plans and programs,[52] providing for policy and investment directives concerning strategic economic fields;
- Project contracts, through which Chinese domestic solutions are transposed on to the transnational level and whose features, have been already discussed.

On the basis of the interaction of these elements, the "going global" of Chinese enterprises functions according to an original set of rules. Such rules shape a model of partnership different from the one upheld by other important legal sources. Moreover, it appears that FDI of Chinese enterprises follow a different policy pattern than investment of foreign enterprises into China.

This double regime is so far sustaining the development of original solutions. It is nevertheless likely that it will be affected by the influence, over Chinese law, of international economic law such as in the case of GPA. The real question is: to what extent? The transversal position of the BRI with regard to other international and supranational organizations may justify the peculiarity of its PPP system. Indeed, as already noted, most of the BRI countries are not even part of the GPA.

The real core issue may therefore arise from another aspect, i.e., a change in the attitude of BRI countries toward the very concept of cooperation promoted by the Beijing government. Apart from the differences in economic, social, legal and cultural contexts, another risk faced by the BRI is the possible distrust of foreign governments toward great investment from Chinese enterprises.

So far, the BRI initiative is still in its embryonal phase. It certainly relies on a strong commitment from the Chinese government and on successful cooperation initiatives. It still lacks a proper legal framework as well as a legal "dignity" in terms of supranational legal order. Its functioning is driven by Chinese FDIs and the legal issues it faces stem from the concrete use of such investments.

Nevertheless, the BRI prompted the development—still ongoing and far from finished—of a transnational model of partnership agreement which, in my opinion, may be regarded as the common core of a "BRI legal order." It is a model shaped according to the Chinese PPPs which has yet to reach a proper formalization. It is, however, an original model which displays both public and private features and is,

---

[51] For instance, *see* art 8 of the Agreement between the government of the People's Republic of China and the government of the Union of Myanmar of the promotion and protection of investments; art 9 of the Agreement between the Government of the People's Republic of China and the government of the Islamic Republic of Pakistan on the reciprocal encouragement and protection of investments.

[52] *See* Part XI of the 13th PRC Five-Year Economic and Social Development Plan.

ideally, in dialogue with both international cooperation agreements and contracts stipulated regionally in the relevant areas of the BRI.

Gianmatteo Sabatino, Ph.D. (Trento), is Research Fellow in Comparative and European Law at the Sino-Italian Institute of the Zhongnan University of Economics and Law.

Elephant in the Room: On the Notions of SCEs in International Investment Law and International Economic Law

Kai-chieh Chan

1 Introduction

Scholars and practitioners have produced voluminous works on the legal personality and attribution of acts of state-controlled enterprises ('SCEs'). Indeed, SCEs, as 'hybrids' of private and public characteristics, can hardly be reconciled by the traditional schism between a subject (States) and non-subject in international law.[1] Despite its difficulty, the problem of the legal personality of SCEs is central to international economic law, as it is well established that treaty provisions would lose their *effet utile* if contracting States could avoid their treaty obligations by simply delegating their power to a private organisation with separate legal personality. This rule applies equally to international investment law and the law of the World Trade Organization ('WTO law'): as cautioned by Prof. Thomas Wälde, '*Authoritarian states will try to disguise an abuse of State power under a cloak of legal correctness in formal terms. What they appear to do formally and publicly will often not be the*

[1] Mikko Rajavuori, 'Making International Legal Persons in Investment Treaty Arbitration: State-owned Enterprises along the Person/Thing Distinction' (2017) 18 (5) GLJ 1183, 1194-6.

[2] Thomas Wälde, '"Equality of Arms" in Investment Arbitration: Procedural Challenges' in Katia Yannaca-Small (ed) *Arbitration Under International Investment Agreements: A Guide to the Key Issues* (OUP 2010) 176.

This chapter draws upon the author's original publication also available at https://www.transnational-dispute-management.com/journal-advance-publication-article.asp?key=1836. Reprinted by permission from Maris BV: Maris BV, *Transnational Dispute Management* (TDM, ISSN 1875-4120), "Elephant in the Room: On the Notions of SCEs in International Investment Law and International Economic Law", Kai-chieh Chan, Copyright (2000). Please cite accordingly.

K. Chan (✉)
International University of Rabat, Rabat, Morocco
e-mail: kaichieh.chan@sciencespo.fr

J. Chaisse et al. (eds.), *Regulation of State-Controlled Enterprises*, International Law and the Global South, https://doi.org/10.1007/978-981-19-1368-6_6

same as what occurs through secret and informal channels. ... [T]he proper approach to use is to 'lift the veil' from what happens in closed or clandestine channels.'[2]

Notwithstanding the disagreement on various points, scholars generally agree that the idea of SCEs, as well as the attribution of their acts to the State, are undergoing drastic challenges. On the one hand, SCEs nowadays have increasingly varying operation objectives, ownership structures, and levels of state control.[3] On the other hand, with the rise of state capitalism and non-market economies, one can expect SCEs to be more present in the arena of international economic law. As will be detailed in the following sections, SCEs have acted as claimant and respondent (by means of attribution) in recent investment disputes.

It is perhaps appropriate to illustrate the difficulty of defining State public bodies with the recent Judgement of the International Court of Justice ('the Court') in the *Certain Iranian Assets* case (*Iran v United States*).[4] In its Judgement on the preliminary objections, the Court had to rule on whether Bank Markazi, the central bank of Iran, is a 'company' under the 1955 Treaty of Amity, Economic Relations and Consular Rights ('Treaty of Amity') between Iran and the US. According to the Treaty, only companies and nationals of the contracting States are entitled to freedom of access to the courts of justice and administrative agencies (Art. III, para. 2) and the right to fair and equitable treatment (Art. IV, para.1).

The Treaty of Amity itself provides a definition of 'company' that is relatively broad: Art. III, para. 1 provides that: '*As used in the present Treaty, "companies" means corporations, partnerships, companies and other associations, whether or not with limited liability and whether or not for pecuniary profit.*' Since this definition does not contain the nature of activities as a criterion, Iran argues that the activities carried out by Bank Markazi are immaterial to its status as a company.[5] The Court nevertheless rejected this argument because such an interpretation would fail to take into account the context of Article III, para. 1 as well as the object and purpose of the entire Treaty. For the Court, the Treaty '*is aimed at guaranteeing rights and affording protections to natural and legal persons engaging in activities of a commercial nature, even if this latter term is to be understood in a broad sense. [...] an indication of which can also be found in the title of the Treaty (Treaty of Amity, Economic Relations, and Consular Rights).*'[6] As such, for the majority of the Court, companies that do not engage in any 'activities of a commercial nature' would fall outside the scope of the Treaty even in the absence of explicit treaty language.[7] However, on whether Bank

---

[3] Yueh-Ping Yang and Pin-Hsien Lee, 'State Capitalism, State-Owned Banks, and WTO's Subsidy Regime: Proposing an Institution Theory' (2018) 54 (2) Stan J Intl L 117, 123–8.

[4] *Certain Iranian Assets* (*Iran v. United States*), Preliminary Objections, Judgment of 13 February 2019 [2019].

[5] ibid para 83 (arguing that "*the definition of "companies" given in Article III, paragraph 1, is deliberately broad*").

[6] ibid para 91.

[7] ibid (stating that "*an entity carrying out exclusively sovereign activities, linked to the sovereign functions of the State, cannot be characterized as a "company" within the meaning of the Treaty*").

Markazi engages in 'activities of a commercial nature', the majority of the Court considers that it does not have before it all the facts necessary to rule on the issue. The question is therefore left to the merit stage.[8] This decision has notably divided members of the Court.

In their joint separate opinion, Judge Peter Tomka and Judge James Crawford objected to the majority's approach of adding 'activities of a commercial nature' to the definition of the term 'company'.[9] Other judges also seem to contest against adding such a condition. For instance, in his separate opinion, Judge Patrick Robinson suggests that the activities *de jure imperii* of Bank Markazi should be protected by the Treaty as long as these activities 'have a sufficient relationship' with other acts of a commercial nature. In this case, even though the Bank's role in regulating the transfer of payments and in providing currency exchange services may not be qualified as *de jure gestionis*, the Bank should still be protected under the Treaty since these acts are 'vital for the achievement of the Treaty's object and purpose', which is the encouragement of commerce between the two States.[10]

Nevertheless, the opinions mentioned above do not touch upon whether Bank Markazi actually engages in activities of a commercial nature. The problem was dealt with by Judge *ad hoc* Charles Brower, who is also a prominent arbitrator in investment law. In his separate opinion, he considers the acts of Bank Markazi to be exclusively *jure imperii.* Therefore, he is of the opinion that the Bank would not constitute a 'company' for the purposes of the Treaty.[11] In essence, Judge *ad hoc* Brower adopted a structural-control test and stated that under the Iranian Monetary and Banking Act, the Bank '*acts exclusively as the Central Bank of Iran, and is at all times subject to the control of Iran's Government*'.[12] As the evidence of control, he stressed that '*Bank Markazi's General Meeting is composed of Cabinet-level*

Note that the word 'exclusively' is significant as the majority of the Court readily admits the possibility that a single public entity can engage both in activities of a commercial nature and in sovereign activities (*see* para 92).

[8] ibid para 97. The reason behind this decision seems to be that the Court considers the parties have not sufficiently discussed the Monetary and Banking Act of Iran, which contains the statutes of Bank Markazi (*see* para 95).

[9] *Certain Iranian Assets* (*Iran v. United States*), Joint separate opinion of Judges Tomka and Crawford, at p. 4, para. 10 (stating that '*the definition of the term "companies", in Article III, paragraph 1, of the Treaty of Amity does not refer to "activities" as a criterion for determining whether an entity is a company for the purposes of the Treaty.*').

[10] *Certain Iranian Assets* (*Iran v. United States*), Separate opinion of Judge Patrick Robinson, at p. 4, paras. 11-12. For a similar reasoning, *see* Separate opinion of Judge *ad hoc* Momtaz, at p. 5, para. 12 and Separate opinion of Judge Kirill Gevorgian, at p. 2, para. 4 (stating that '*Bank Markazi plays a crucial role in the conclusion of commercial transactions by Iranian companies in the US, to the point that the attachment of its assets may have rendered such transactions impossible*').

[11] *Certain Iranian Assets* (*Iran v. United States*), Separate opinion of Judge *ad hoc* Charles N. Brower, at p. 12, para. 32.

[12] ibid para 26.

ministers, and the President of Iran appoints the Bank's Governor.'[13] On Iran's argument that Bank Markazi can enter into purchase or sale contracts and are capable of buying and selling securities in the open market, he considers that since these acts are '*essential to the support and maintenance of any institution*', they are '*not an indication of a central bank engaging in "commercial activities" whatsoever as that term is understood in the law of sovereign immunity.*'[14]

The position of Judge *ad hoc* Brower can be contrasted with that of Judge Giorgio Gaja, who in turn emphasises the part of the Iranian Monetary and Banking Act that grants Bank Markazi separate legal personality.[15] In the same vein, he considers '*the fact that Bank Markazi exercises sovereign functions does not exclude that it also operates as a commercial bank ... [the] sale of securities is not different from that executed by any commercial bank and should enjoy the same protection under the Treaty.*'[16]

Three observations can be made on the *Certain Iranian Assets* case for the purpose of the discussion on SCEs below. Firstly, the status of SCEs can raise difficult questions that divide various members of the eminent Court. It is perhaps precisely due to this difficulty that the majority of the Court considers itself under-prepared to rule on the issue at the jurisdictional stage. Secondly, from the disagreement between Judge *ad hoc* Brower and Judge Gaja, one can argue that the line drawn by jurists between *jure imperii* and *jure gestionis* is not sufficiently clear. While considering the nature of Bank Markazi's 'commercial activities,' for instance, neither of the Judges invoke any legal basis or specific standard applicable to the instant case.[17] Faced with the same Statute of the Bank and the same Banking Act, they could not follow a set of methodology in reaching their respective conclusions. Thirdly, from the members' disagreement on the meaning of the broad term 'company', one can argue that the term's ordinary meaning does not shed sufficient light on the notion of SCEs; neither would invoking the object and purpose offer much assistance. For the majority of the Court, the object and purpose of treaties would exclude companies that perform solely acts *jure imperii*. On the other hand, the minority of the Court considers that the object and purpose would go against such interpretation. It is evident that the conundrums faced by the Court in the *Certain Iranian Assets* case are reminiscent to the ones that investment tribunals encounter on a constant basis when dealing with SCEs.

---

[13] ibid.

[14] ibid para 28.

[15] *Certain Iranian Assets* (*Iran v. United States*), Separate opinion of Judge Giorgio Gaja, at p 1 para 2.

[16] ibid para. 3.

[17] While Judge *ad hoc* Brower invokes briefly that the activities of the Bank would not qualify as 'commercial' under the 'law of sovereign immunity' (para 28), he did not elaborate on the authority or content of such law. Similarly, although Judge Gaja cited the *United Nations Convention on Jurisdictional Immunities of States and Their Property* at one point, he later doubted the relevance of it (para 3).

These observations reveal the chaos and uncertainty of the interpretation of the concepts involving SCEs. In light of this, the present chapter aspires to explore, as *lex ferenda*, the potential means that are consistent with the rule and practice of international law that may assist the court or the tribunal by enhancing the reasoning of their interpretation. To do so, this chapter proposes that, while dealing with the terms' companies' and 'enterprises' without specific qualification in the treaty, reference could be made to neighbouring notions in other fields of international economic law. For the purpose of this chapter, international economic law consists of international investment law, WTO law and competition law.[18] Section 2 outlines the major difficulties and criticisms that international investment law have to deal in regard to identifying the acts of SCEs. It is submitted that tribunals and the Court alike are not sufficiently equipped with the legal tools to deal with the issue. Section 3 explores whether and how the neighbouring notions in other international economic law, namely international trade law (including WTO law) and competition law may help investment law tribunals with their interpretation of these notions. Section 4 concludes the chief proposals.

2 State Instrumentality and Attribution in International Investment Law: A Dismal Science

'Every opinion tends to become a law.'
—Oliver Wendell Holmes[19]

The section explores some critical issues that investment tribunals have to deal with while deciding if a SCE constitutes State instrumentality and whether the acts are attributable to the State. Although the doctrine of attribution plays a pre-eminent role in international law,[20] one can be startled while comparing the awards and the doctrinal works on these issues. In practice, tribunals' reasonings on the standing or the attribution of acts and omissions of SCEs are usually succinct. In *Československá obchodní banka v Slovak Republic*, the leading case concerning the issue, the tribunal held that '*the focus must be on the nature of [the Claimant's] activities and not their purpose*' without citing any authority.[21] It was speculated that the lack of reasoning

---

[18] For a similar definition of international economic law *see* Marion Jansen, Joost Pauwelyn, and Theresa Carpenter 'Introduction' in Marion Jansen, Joost Pauwelyn, and Theresa Carpenter (eds) *The Use of Economics in International Trade and Investment Disputes* (CUP 2017).

[19] Dissenting in *Lochner v New York*, 198 U.S. 45 (1905).

[20] Simon Olleson, 'Attribution in Investment Treaty Arbitration' (2016) 31:2 ICSID Rev. 457.

[21] *Československá obchodní banka v Slovak Republic*, ICSID Case No. ARB(AF)/97/4, Decision of the Tribunal on Objections to Jurisdiction, 24 May 1999 [*ČSOB*], para. 20. Although the award acknowledges the Broches test as applicable at para. 17, it does not elaborate the relation between the test and its determination at para. 20. On this point, Blyschak observes that: "*Whereas contemporary decisions on jurisdiction in investment disputes consistently result in lengthy awards numbering hundreds of pages and citing large numbers of authorities and legal instruments, the ČSOB decision on this point produced only twelve paragraphs and referenced only a single source.*" Paul Blyschak,

may be answered by the fact that the case was decided prior to the recent increase in the size, number and influence of SCEs and sovereign wealth funds.[22] However, a review of more recent cases reveals that tribunals nowadays cannot be said to have adopted a more sophisticated approach. For example, in *Masdar Solar & Wind Cooperatief U.A. v Spain*, without dwelling on the notion of control or examining the Broches test (which the tribunal acknowledged as relevant), the Respondent's objection was rejected simply on the basis of insufficient proof.[23] Commenting on a similar case, an author found these reasoning to be 'unconvincing [and] entirely naïf.'[24]

The alleged lack of rigour in practice stands in sharp contrast with the generally vehement scholarly criticisms directed towards different tribunals. Scholars have notably held the tribunals accountable for their insufficient legal reasoning,[25] for allowing the circumvention of State responsibility,[26] and for '*rendering Third World sovereignty vulnerable and dependent*' by imposing '*standards of (Western) liberal law*'.[27] Before addressing how these difficulties and criticisms can be dealt with, this section classifies them in three broad categories: the first concerns the controversies in structural and functional tests (2.1); the second relates to the *lex specialis* (2.2), and the third pertains to the extra-judicial concerns of attribution (2.3). The last sub-section summarises the difficulties (2.4).

'State-Owned Enterprises and International Investment Treaties: When are State-Owned Entities and their Investments Protected?' (2011) 6:2 JILIR 1, 32.

[22] Blyschak (n 21), ibid.

[23] *Masdar Solar & Wind Cooperatief U.A. v. Kingdom of Spain*, ICSID Case No. ARB/14/1, Award, 16 May 2018 [*Masdar Solar*], paras. 170-171.

[24] Albert Badia, 'Attribution of Conducts of State-Owned Enterprises Based on Control by the State' in Crina Baltag (eds) ICSID Convention after 50 Years: Unsettled Issues (Kluwer 2016) 189, 208 (concluding that "*When it comes to evidential matters, the test of the ILC Article 8 has proved to be a hard nut to crack…We all know that, generally, it is an upriver task to prove that a State is behind a particular act of another entity. So it is fair, at least, to have an open mind.*").

[25] Mark Feldman, 'State-Owned Enterprises as Claimants in International Investment Arbitration' (2016) 31:1 ICSID Rev. 24, 33–34 (commenting on the *ČSOB* case); Blyschak (n 21), 32; Walid Ben Hamida, 'Sovereign FDI and International Investment Agreements: Questions Relating to the Qualification of Sovereign Entities and the Admission of their Investments under Investment Agreements' (2010) 9 LPICT 17, 29 (stating that "*The [ČSOB] Tribunal did not identify a clear methodology that permits to determine if the entity is public or private. It did not examine with precision the activities carried out by CSOB to identify if there were public or private in nature.*").

[26] According to Carlo de Stefano, this was done by incorrectly ignoring the customary rules of attribution as codified by the ILC; *see* Carlo de Stefano, 'Attributing to Sovereigns the Conduct of State-Owned Enterprises: Towards Circumvention of the Accountability of States under International Investment Law' (2017) 32:2 ICSID Rev. 267, 273–274.

[27] Rajavuori (n 1), 1183, 1218, 1223-4.

2.1 Structural Test and Functional Test

The most discussed topic relating to SCEs in investment law is their standing to bring a claim. This problem is particularly pertinent in the context of International Centre for Settlement of Investment Disputes ('ICSID') arbitrations: the first sentence of the Preamble of the ICSID Convention mentions 'the role of *private* international investment' (emphasis added). Authors generally acknowledge that the *travaux préparatoires* of the ICSID Convention it silent on the issue of jurisdiction *ratione personae* over SCEs.[28] One exception is Moshe Hirsh, who suggests in an early work that in borderline cases, the tribunal should adopt a narrow interpretation and reject claims brought by bodies that 'cooperate with states' and cases in which States played an 'important role'.[29]

In the absence of indication within the Convention, the best guideline is the one formulated by Aron Broches, who is known as one of the main architects of the ICSID Convention. In his Course at the Hague in 1972, he states that '*a mixed economy company or government-owned corporation should not be disqualified as a "national of another Contracting State" unless it is acting as an agent for the government or is discharging an essentially governmental function.*' This is nowadays known as the Broches test. He believes '*it is safe to say that there was a consensus on this point among those participating in the preparation of the Convention*'.[30] Broches himself had not provide concrete examples or further clarifications on the test, stating that it would be a 'difficult task'.[31] The use of the term 'or' implies that satisfying either of the two conditions would disqualify a SCE from brining a claim under the ICSID Convention. However, the interpretation of both conditions has produced much uncertainty in practice.

Firstly, certain controversies arise from the definition of 'an agent for the government'. This criterion was examined by the tribunal in *Maffezini v Spain*, in which it had to determine whether a Spanish regional development agency ('SODIGA') had acted as an agent of the State. In the absence of specific treaty language, the tribunal decided to look into '*various factors, such as ownership, control, the nature, purposes and objectives of the entity whose actions are under scrutiny*'.[32] More

---

[28] Christoph H. Schreuer, Loretta Malintoppi, August Reinisch, and Anthony Sinclair, '*The ICSID Convention: A Commentary* (2nd edn, CUP 2009) 161; Claudia Annacker, 'Protection and Admission of Sovereign Investment under Investment Treaties' (2011) 10 Chinese J Intl L 531, 554–555.

[29] Moshe Hirsh, *The Arbitration Mechanism of the International Centre for the Settlement of Investment Disputes* (Martinus Nijhoff 1993), 55–56 (cited in Walid Ben Hamida, *supra* note 25, 25-26.)

[30] Aron Broches, *The Convention on the Settlement of Investment Disputes between States and Nationals of Other States* (Collected Courses of The Hague Academy of International Law, 1972), 355.

[31] *See* Reza Mohtashami and Farouk El-Hosseny, 'State-Owned Enterprises as Claimants before ICSID' (2016) 3 (2) BCDR Intl Arb Rev 371, 376–377.

[32] *Emilio Agustín Maffezini v The Kingdom of Spain*, ICSID Case No. ARB/97/7, Decision of the Tribunal on Objections to Jurisdiction, 25 January 2000 [*Maffezini*], para. 76.

importantly, it held that: '*a finding that the entity is owned by the State, directly or indirectly, gives rise to a rebuttable presumption that it is a State entity. The same result will obtain if an entity is controlled by the State, directly or indirectly.*'[33] The tribunal also acknowledged the relevance of the Broches test.[34] Upon examining, *inter alia*, the ownership structure of the SODIGA (which at one point was held 88% by the Spanish government), it held SODIGA to be a State entity acting on behalf of the Kingdom of Spain.[35] The 'structural test' developed by *Maffezini* was cited with approval by the tribunal in *Salini v Morocco*, who went on to examine the ownership structure of the State-owned entity in that case.[36] An author argues that the methodology developed by *Maffezini* had laid the foundations of attribution in investment law.[37]

However, the significance of ownership structure have been challenged by other tribunals and scholars.[38] In *Tulip v Turkey*, the tribunal explicitly criticised the approach taken by *Maffezini* and *Salini*, stating that '*there is no basis under international law to conclude that ownership of a corporate entity by the State triggers the presumption of statehood.*'[39] For it, ownership is just another factor to be taken into account.[40] Another criticism is that, instead of examining the general structure of the entity, emphasis should be put on its conduct 'in the fact-specific context' of the dispute.[41] The majority of the Court in *Certain Iranian Assets* case seems to have embraced the same position.[42] In the same vein, scholars have downplayed the importance of ownership by suggesting that: '[t]he *concept of "agency" should be read not in structural terms but functionally. This means that whether the "agency" is a corporation, whether and to what extent it is government-owned and whether it*

[33] ibid para 77.

[34] ibid para 79 (emphasis added).

[35] ibid paras 83-86.

[36] *Salini Costruttori S.p.A. and Italstrade S.p.A. v Kingdom of Morocco*, ICSID Case No. ARB/00/4, Decision on Jurisdiction, 31 July 2001 [*Salini*], paras 31-32.

[37] Csaba Kovács, *Attribution in International Investment Law* (Kluwer 2018) 145.

[38] Badia, *supra* note 24, 194-196 (considering that the tests employed in *Maffezini* and *Salini* '*have fallen in disuse*').

[39] *Tulip Real Estate v Republic of Turkey*, ICSID Case No. ARB/11/28, Award, 10 March 2014 [*Tulip*], para. 289.

[40] Some have also disagreed with the tribunals in *Maffezini* and *Salini* regarding their attribution analysis at the jurisdiction stage. For them, it is more appropriate to treat issues of ownership and attribution with the merits. *See* Annacker, *supra* note 28, 558–559; Olleson (n 20) 469.

[41] *Beijing Urban Construction Group Co. Ltd. v Republic of Yemen*, ICSID Case No. ARB/14/30, Decision on Jurisdiction, 31 May 2017 [*Beijing Urban Construction*], paras 38-39 (rejecting the Respondent's reliance on *Maffezini*); *see* also, Olleson (n 20) 468 (commenting that the issue "*cannot be resolved by a global analysis of the status and powers of the relevant State-owned entity, without reference to the specific conduct which is relied upon as constituting a breach of the treaty.*")

[42] *Certain Iranian Assets* (*Iran v. United States*), Judgment of 13 February 2019, para 97 (finding that it is necessary "*to determine whether Bank Markazi was carrying out, at the relevant time, activities of the nature of those which permit characterization as a "company" within the meaning of the Treaty*"). However, the opposing opinion of Judge Tomka and Judge Crawford cannot be ignored; *see* Joint separate opinion of Judges Tomka and Crawford, at p 4, para. 10.

has separate legal personality are of secondary importance. What matters is that it performs public functions'.[43]

However, when it comes to the function test, the applicable criteria for governmental function is equally ambiguous. One may recall the disagreement between Judge *ad hoc* Brower and Judge Gaja on the activities of Bank Markazi in the *Certain Iranian Assets* case mentioned in the previous section. This limb of the Broches test was arguably neglected in *ČSOB*, the landmark case on the issues concerning SCEs.[44] Admittedly, it is generally '*impossible to delineate the public and private sectors solely on functional grounds, since nearly all functions undertaken by government are also performed by the private sector*'.[45] Customary rules offer little help to define the idea of function, as the ILC has consistently refrained from providing any guidance on the notion of 'governmental authority' ('*puissance publique*').[46]

The difficulty is most apparent with regards to the determination of the public character of the act. The termination of a commercial contract to which a party is an SCE, for instance, is commercial in *nature*, even though it may well have been motivated by political *purposes*.[47] Nevertheless, such an over-emphasis on the nature of the act would overlook the range of *acta jure imperii* that may be accomplished by commercial means. In *Crystallex v Venezuela*, for instance, a Venezuelan SCE (*Corporación Venezuelana de Guyana, CVG*) unilaterally terminated the contract (Mining Operation Contract, 'MOC') with the claimant. Even though the Respondent argued that the termination of the contract was '*an act of contractual nature performed by the President of the CVG in the exercise of his powers and arising from the prior breach of contract by the Claimant*',[48] the tribunal ultimately found that even though the nature of the termination is allegedly contractual, its purpose is '*to give effect to the Respondent's unconcealed political agenda*'.[49]

From the above, it is submitted that the nature/purpose distinction is inadequate and, as such, other grounds or interpretive tools need to be found to delineate the public from the private.

---

[43] Schreuer, Malintoppi, Reinisch, and Sinclair (note 28) 153, 243 (emphasis added).

[44] Feldman (n 25) 628; Blyschak (n 21) 33-34 (describing the "*deficiencies of the ČSOB Tribunals ruling on the essentially governmental function limb of the Broches test*".)

[45] Ian Lienert, 'Where Does the Public Sector End and the Private Sector Begin' (2009) IMF Working Paper, WP/09/122, 7.

[46] *F-W Oil Interests, Inc. v The Republic of Trinidad and Tobago*, ICSID Case No. ARB/01/14, Award, 3 March 2006, para. 203. Kovács, *supra* note 37, 185-186 (stating that '*There is no consensus as to the scope of governmental authority and, in light of the many ways that States can organise their governmental activities, the ILC did not attempt to identify the scope of the notion of governmental authority.*')

[47] *ČSOB*, Decision of the Tribunal on Objections to Jurisdiction, para 20 (stating that "*in discharging these functions, exercised governmental functions, the focus must be on the nature of these activities and not their purpose*"); *see* also, *Beijing Urban Construction*, paras 40, 42-43.

[48] *Crystallex International Corporation v Venezuela*, ICSID Case No. ARB(AF)/11/2, Award, 4 April 2016 [*Crystallex*], para 408.

[49] ibid para 705.

2.2 On Lex Specialis

Lex specialis derogat legi generali is a general principle of law. Indeed, as the Court has admitted in the *Diallo* case, '*international agreements, such as agreements for the promotion and protection of foreign investments and the Washington Convention, have established special legal regimes governing investment protection*'.[50] As a principle dealing with conflict of norms, two conditions need to be met for the principle to be applicable: first, for a true conflict to exist, the norms must deal with the same subject matter; second, one norm needs to be more general than the other *in concreto*.[51]

An immediate illustration is the treatment of the Broches test as a *lex specialis* for ICSID arbitrations. Some authors have thus argued that the Broches test does not apply for non-ICSID cases since there would be no legitimate basis to distinguish between SCEs and non-SCEs in the absence of specific treaty language.[52] Put otherwise, these authors contend that '*State entities generally should be able to qualify as "investors" even when acting in a governmental capacity.*'[53] This approach has been endorsed by the recent case *Beijing Shougang and others v Mongolia*, in which the tribunal, operating under UNCITRAL rules, refused to examine the ownership structure, business purpose and control of the claimants (Chinese SCEs) in the absence of '*indication that the Treaty drafters intended to assign any special meaning to the term "economic entities"*'.[54] Interestingly, this conclusion can be compared with that of the Court in the *Certain Iranian Assets* case, in which it held that the broad term 'company', if read in conjunction with the object and purpose of the treaty, would exclude the companies that do not carry out activities of a commercial nature.[55] If

[50] *Ahmadou Sadio Diallo* (*Republic of Guinea v Democratic Republic of the Congo*), Preliminary Objections, Judgment of 24 May 2007, *ICJ Reports* 2007, 615, 89-90. Despite some scholarly criticisms, the Court's position remains unchanged, *see Obligation to Negotiate Access to the Pacific Ocean* (*Bolivia v. Chile*), Judgment of 1 October 2018, 162. (stating that the principle of legitimate expectations only constitutes a *lex specialis* in investment law.)

[51] Dirk Pulkowski, '*Lex Specialis Derogat Legi Generali/Generalia Specialibus Non Derogant*' in Joseph Klingler, Yuri Parkhomenko et al (eds) *Between the Lines of the Vienna Convention? Canons and Other Principles of Interpretation in Public International Law* (Kluwer 2018) 169-171; Kovács (n 37) 52-3: stating that ("*In order to confirm the existence of* lex specialis *on attribution, it should be considered not only whether the same subject matter is dealt with by two provisions, but also whether there is some inconsistency between the general and special rules.*")

[52] Kovács (n 37) 287 (concluding that "*In the absence of a treaty limitation or exclusion with respect to State Enterprises, no issue of attribution arises under the particular IIA, whose protection thus extends to State Enterprises even assuming that they act in a governmental capacity*").

[53] Feldman (n 25) 629; Annacker (n 28) 551-552 (stating that 'sovereign claimants' are not uncommon in investment disputes.)

[54] *Beijing Shougang and others v Mongolia*, UNCITRAL, PCA Case No 2010-20, Award, 30 June 2017 [*Beijing Shougang*], para 408.

[55] *Certain Iranian Assets* (*Iran v. United States*), Preliminary Objections, Judgment of 13 February 2019, para 91.

one accepts the position taken by the majority of the Court, there is perhaps room to argue for the application of the Broches test in non-ICSID cases.[56]

Another controversy arises with the exclusion of the customary rules of attribution as codified by the *Draft articles on Responsibility of States for Internationally Wrongful Acts* ('ARSIWA') of the ILC. The most relevant attribution rules in the ARSIWA are Art. 4 '*Conduct of organs of a State*', Art. 5 '*Conduct of persons or entities exercising elements of governmental authority,*' and Art. 8 '*Conduct directed or controlled by a State*'. The most contentious yet relevant rule is that of Art. 8, which, when applied to our case, suggests that States are responsible for actions and omissions of SCEs when the latter are '*in fact acting on the instructions of, or under the direction or control of, that State*'.[57] Concerning SCEs, the ILC's Commentary of ARSIWA notes that '*international law acknowledges the general separateness of corporate entities at the national level, except in those cases where the corporate veil is a mere device or a vehicle for fraud or evasion…where there was evidence that the corporation was exercising public powers, or that the State was using its ownership interest in or control of a corporation specifically in order to achieve a particular result, the conduct in question has been attributed to the State*'.[58] One can readily observe that, for the ILC, attribution of the act of the actions of SCEs is exceptional.[59]

Indeed, the Commentaries of ARSIWA envisage the possibility for parties to derogate from customary international law regarding attribution.[60] While tribunals frequently apply these customary rules, some have found *lex specialis* in the treaty and have thus excluded the application of ARSIWA. The findings of tribunals, however, have created some confusion and uncertainty. For example, the tribunal in *Mesa Power v Canada* held that Art. 1503(2) of North American Free Trade Agreement ('NAFTA') constitute *lex specialis* of the rules codified in ARSIWA.[61] However, dealing with the same Article in a similar factual context, the tribunal in *Windstream v Canada* found no conflict between Art. 1503(2) and ARSIWA.[62]

The impact of this challenging intellectual exercise may be significant as the *lex specialis* argument could be used to exclude the broad terms of attribution in

---

[56] There is equally room to argue that the opinion of the Court is not unanimous, as evidenced from the Separate Opinion of Judges Tomka and Crawford, at p 4 para 10.

[57] Emphasis added.

[58] ILC, 'Commentary to the Articles on the Responsibility of States for Internationally Wrongful Acts', (2001) II/1 ILC YB 48, para 6 (emphases added).

[59] *EDF (Services) Limited v. Romania*, ICSID Case No. ARB/05/13, Award, 8 October 2009 [*EDF*], para 200.

[60] ILC, 'Commentary to the Articles on the Responsibility of States for Internationally Wrongful Acts', (2001) II/1 ILC YB 140, para 3.

[61] *Mesa Power Group v Canada*, UNCITRAL, PCA Case No 2012-17, Award, 24 March 2016, para 362. The article states that Contracting States will only be responsible for the acts of their State Enterprises if they "*exercises regulatory, administrative or other governmental authority delegated to it by that NAFTA Party*".

[62] *Windstream Energy v Canada*, UNCITRAL, PCA Case No 2013-22, Award, 27 September 2016, para 233.

ARSIWA. In *Al Tamimi v Oman*, the dispute concerned the Oman Mining Company ('OMCO'), a limited liability company established by a 1981 Royal Decree. On the facts, 99 per cent of OMCO's shares were owned by the Omani Ministry of Oil and Minerals. The government appointed its directors, and its board of directors included current and former ministers.[63] The tribunal, however, refused to examine the 'instructions, or direction or control' test set out in Art. 8 of ARSIWA, as it was considered to be replaced by the *lex specialis* within the treaty. For the tribunal, the requirement set out in Art. 10.1.2 of the US-Oman FTA limits Oman's responsibility for the acts of a state enterprise to the extent that: (a) the state enterprise must act in the exercise of 'regulatory, administrative or *governmental authority*,' and (b) that authority must have been *delegated* to it by the State.[64] As there is nothing in the 1981 Royal Decree that expressly delegates regulatory, administrative or governmental powers to OMCO, the tribunal ultimately held that the acts of OMCO were not attributable to the State.[65] It suggested, nevertheless, that the acts of OMCO would have been attributable to the Respondent if the standards in ARSIWA had been applicable.[66]

The complete exclusion of customary law in *Al Tamimi v Oman* was criticised on the basis that Art. 10.1.2 of the US-Oman FTA does not deviate from the basic content of the rules in ARSIWA. In order words, the second condition described above, namely 'one norm needs to be more general than the other *in concreto*,' was not met. Accordingly, '*the* lex specialis *at issue does not restrict the scope of attribution of conduct of parastatal entities provided by the* lex generalis.'[67] At the present stage, there seems to be no solution to the interpretive conundrum on *lex specialis*.

2.3 Extra-judicial Concerns of Attribution

The traditional international law approach is known to draw rigid boundaries between the 'legal' and the 'non-legal'.[68] While doing so may preserve some autonomy of the doctrine by hardening an 'internal point of view' amongst members of the legal community, there is also no reason to ignore the social and political ramifications that the legal rules at hand would generate.[69]

---

[63] *Adel A Hamadi Al Tamimi v Sultanate of Oman*, ICSID Case No. ARB/11/33, Award, 3 November 2015 [*Al Tamimi*], paras 52, 317.

[64] ibid para. 322 (emphasis added).

[65] ibid para. 326.

[66] ibid para 337.

[67] Carlo de Stefano (n 26), 273.

[68] Andrea Bianchi, *International Law Theories* (OUP 2016) 26-28.

[69] It is sometime referred to as 'effect- or impact-based international law ascertainment': Jean d'Aspremont, *Formalism and the Sources of International Law* (OUP 2011) 122-126.

On the international law governing SCEs, some authors have criticised the arbitrators' unfounded piercing of the corporate veil, and some have accused them of discriminating against the global south. Julian Arato, for one, argues that the patterns of treaty interpretation in investment arbitration '*are distorting foundational principles of national private law*' and have thus '*created far-reaching swathes of international private law*'.[70] For him, while municipal laws everywhere provide at least minimal rules on separate legal personality, tribunals have constantly ignored them.[71] This situation is exacerbated by the recalcitrant attitude of the tribunals towards inquiring into the applicable law or standard (both municipal and international) before piercing the corporate veil.[72] What is done is then '*impressionistic balancing*'.[73] All this, he concludes, has led to investment law's failure to create a '*crystalline rules-based*' methodology of treating separate legal entities and have thereby produced '*substantial uncertainty over who speaks for the firm in a cross-border context.*'[74]

Arato's criticisms above can be applied to the attribution of the acts of SCEs. It is true that part of the comments is irrelevant: as Arato himself briefly points out, tribunals tend to take municipal laws into account in this context.[75] Upon extensive survey of relevant jurisprudence, Csaba Kovács concludes that the '*separate legal personality of a public sector entity establishes a strong presumption that the entity is not a State organ as a matter of international law.*' '*To overturn the same presumption,*' he adds, '*tribunals have relied on internal law provisions concerning the function or role performed by the entity, including the character or the objectives of the functions performed, or relating to the entity's institutional dependence on the State.*'[76]

However, Arato's comment is highly pertinent to SCEs in the sense that investment tribunals seem to have failed to create a 'crystalline rules-based' methodology concerning the status of SCEs. On this, Kovács confirms that '*tribunals have placed different weight on the same internal law factor, such as the appointment or dismissal of the management.*'[77] In the same vein, Rajavuori contends that by playing with the '*malleability of attribution doctrines*', the '*imagination of practitioners*' has unjustifiably imposed the '*standards of (Western) liberal law*' to SCEs of developing countries.[78] The author thereby accuses that '*assigning Third World societies with legal personality emerges as an effort to render them visible in international law only for a*

[70] Julian Arato, 'The Private Law Critique of International Investment Law' (2019) 113 AJIL 1-2.

[71] ibid 40.

[72] ibid 42.

[73] ibid.

[74] ibid 50.

[75] It shall be noted that although Arato does mention the attribution of 'acts of a state-owned corporation to the host state' (at p 43), he does not deal with the problem *per se* in detail.

[76] ibid.

[77] ibid. However, it is noteworthy that for him, the failure to apply an uniform approach was inevitable as '*the multitude and diversity of public sector entities and related internal law regulations … mean that there will be inevitably a myriad of paths to take*' (ibid).

[78] Rajavuori (n 1), 1217-1218.

moment and only for the purposes of appropriation and subjugation.'[79] Rajavuori's article ends with the figurative suggestion of '*reconfiguring SOEs' international legal personality in their own terms and not that of a slave*'.[80]

2.4 Concluding Remarks

The survey above demonstrates that tribunals have used various methodologies when deciding on defining the SCEs and attributing their acts to States. Approaches adopted in early landmark cases such as *ČSOB* (the nature test) and *Maffezini* (the presumption of statehood by ownership structure) are not obsolete, regardless of the amount of criticisms they receive. Recent awards are less inclined to set out crystalline rules: the legal test of attribution now revolves around several fundamental notions, such as ownership, *de jure* structure, *de facto* control, nature, public function and purpose. The definition, as well as the weight to be accorded to each notion, remains, again, undetermined.

The same can be said on the operation of the general principle of *lex specialis*. In the overwhelming majority of investment treaties do not contain any provisions governing SCEs, the customary international rules (as codified by the ILC in ARSIWA) of attribution apply.[81] However, as the rules in ARSIWA are deliberately formulated broadly, some tribunals have preferred to rely on equally ambiguous terms in the treaty as *lex specialis*.

Although it might not be necessary (or even possible) to develop a bright-line rule,[82] it would be desirable for international lawyers to have recourse to new interpretive means as a first step to achieving greater clarity. Keeping in line with the extra-judicial considerations above, this process would likely be done by emphasising the municipal law of the host state.

---

[79] ibid 1220.

[80] ibid 1227.

[81] Carlo de Stefano (n 26), 272.

[82] *See* also, Blyschak (n 21) 48 (arguing against developing a crystalline rule: "*No rigid formula for determining control should be mapped and each case should be viewed in the totality of its particular circumstances.*").

3 Interactions of the Notions of Public Body and Attribution in Economic Law

The current paradigm of treating SCEs, either developed in the framework of the ICSID Convention in the 1970s or in the framework of general international law,[83] is no longer sufficient to deal with the challenge of modern state capitalism.[84] On the one hand, as evidenced by the section above, it might be desirable to draw attention from the notion of SCEs that are outside the traditional boundaries of ARSIWA. In this regard, this section envisages the possibility of drawing inspiration from international trade law (3.1). On the other hand, while scholars have advocated for more attention on the status of SCEs in their own legal systems, they have not further articulated how this could be done. This section ventures the idea that the competition law of the state might be taken into account (3.2).

3.1 Neighbouring Ideas in International Trade Law

Within the matrix of international law, authors have suggested that international trade law may provide a robust background against which the broader operation of investment law is read.[85] On a macro level, international trade and investment laws share the common object and purpose of providing predictability to economic actors and increasing prosperity by reducing barriers to goods, services, and investment flows.[86] Both WTO law and investment law grapple with the core issue of designing standards that eliminate adverse treatment against foreigners without encroaching too far upon domestic regulatory sovereignty.[87] The central ideas shared between investment and trade law include nondiscrimination, necessity and likeness (in an inquiry of national treatment).

---

[83] For example in *Bayindir v Pakistan*, ICSID Case No. ARB/03/29, Award, 27 August 2009, para 130, the tribunal stated that: "*the approach developed in such areas of international law [*ARSIWA*] is not always adapted to the realities of international economic law*".

[84] *See* generally the analysis on Chinese state capitalism by Ji Li, 'State-Owned Enterprises in the Current Regime of Investor-State Arbitration' in Shaheeza Lalani and Rodrigo Polanco (eds), *The Role of the State in Investor-State Arbitration* (Brill 2014) 402-404 (describing how modern SCEs multitask and asserting that "*in countries characterized by State capitalism, it is difficult to delineate the boundaries of the State*").

[85] Ahmad Ghouri, *Interaction and Conflict of Treaties in Investment Arbitration* (Kluwer 2015) 140 (arguing that "*When interpreting similar exceptional provisions of investment treaties, investor-State arbitral tribunals can benefit from the AB's interpretive approach for Article XX.... such objects and purposes reflect the common will of international society based on collective values, and/or have transformed into the principles of international public policy reflected in other treaties.*")

[86] Valentina Vadi, *Analogies in International Investment Law and Arbitration* (CUP 2016) 209-211.

[87] Nicholas DiMascio and Joost Pauwelyn, 'Nondiscrimination in Trade and Investment Treaties: Worlds Apart or Two Sides of the Same Coin?' (2008) 102 AJIL 89 (discussing the similarities of the two regimes in national treatment standards).

On a micro level, some investment tribunals have cited jurisprudence in WTO law to reinforce the persuasiveness of their general legal argument.[88] The tribunal in *Continental Casualty v Argentina* ventured further by interpreting the term 'measures *necessary* for the maintenance of public order' in the US-Argentina BIT in line with WTO case law, according to which 'necessary' is not synonymous with 'indispensable'.[89] The tribunal based its decision on the origin of the treaty term and on the observation that the notion of necessity has constantly been dealt with in the jurisprudence of GATT and WTO.[90]

In this respect, one may envisage borrowing the notions relating to SCEs developed in WTO jurisprudence to investment law. Firstly, like that of necessity, the judicial bodies of WTO are not unfamiliar with the notion of SCEs. The 1994 General Agreement on Tariffs and Trade ('GATT') refers to 'governmental agencies' (Art. III:8) and 'state trading enterprises' (Art. XVII:1). The Agreement on Subsidies and Countervailing Measures ('SCM Agreement') mentions 'public bodies' (Art. 1.1(a)(1)). Secondly, suppose one accepts the contention that 'there is no major lex specialis on attribution in international trade law'. In that case, it can be argued that the rules of attribution applied by WTO bodies are nothing else than customary law.[91] As warranted by the Appellate Body ('AB') in *US - Anti-Dumping and Countervailing Duties*, '*despite certain differences between the attribution rules of the ILC Articles and those of the SCM Agreement, our above interpretation of the term "public body" coincides with the essence of Article 5* [OF ARSIWA]'.[92]

A recent WTO case law survey reveals the AB's effort to provide a multi-factor test to determine whether an entity constituted a 'public body', thereby rejecting state ownership to be a dispositive factor. Before 2011, the leading case concerning the public body was the Panel Report in *Korea - Vessel*, which concerned the Export-Import Bank of Korea ('KEXIM'). In determining whether KEXIM constituted a public body within the definition of the SCM Agreement, the Panel rejected Korea's

---

[88] For example, the tribunal in *Confor v US* cited the GATT Panel in *Canada - Import Restrictions on Ice Cream and Yoghurt* to reinforce the argument that exceptions were to be interpreted narrowly. *Confor v US*, UNCITRAL, Decision on Preliminary Question, 6 June 2006, para. 187. Similarly *see Phoenix Action v Czech Republic*, ICSID Case No. ARB/06/5, Award, 15 April 2009, para. 77 (citing WTO jurisprudence to support the position that special branches of international law should be interpreted with due regard to general principles of law).

[89] *Continental Casualty Company v The Argentine Republic*, ICSID Case No. ARB/03/9, Award, 5 September 2008, para. 292.

[90] Indeed, while some praised the award for its effort to fight fragmentation, others have criticised it for apply the wrong law. *See* Vadi (n 87) 214-216.

[91] Santiago Villalpando, 'Attribution of Conduct to the State: How the Rules of State Responsibility May be Applied within the WTO Dispute Settlement System' (2002) 5 Journal of International Economic Law 395.

[92] Appellate Body Report, *United States - Definitive Anti-Dumping and Countervailing Duties on Certain Products from China*, WT/DS379/AB/R, 11 March 2011, para. 310. However *contra.* Mitsuo Matsushita, Thomas J. Schoenbaum, Petros C. Mavroidis, and Michael Hahn, *The World Trade Organization: Law, Practice, and Policy* (3rd edn OUP 2015) 314 (stating that "*[t]he drafters of the SCM did not want to draw on that insight and the well-established pertinent jurisprudence; rather, they included their own* lex specialis".)

argument that a state-owned bank is not a public body if its general practice of lending is on a commercial basis.[93] The Panel, much like the tribunal in *Maffezini*, adopted an ownership test by stating that '*an entity will constitute a "public body" if the government controls it*.'[94] After finding that, *among other things*, KEXIM was wholly owned by the Korean government and that the Korean Minister of Finance and Economy also appointed and dismissed KEXIM's deputy president and executive directors, the Panel found KEXIM to be a 'public body.'[95] In 2011, however, the AB in the *US - Anti-Dumping and Countervailing Duties* overturned the theory established by the *Korea - Vessel* Panel. Here the AB refused to uphold the Panel's interpretation that the term '*public body*' meant '*any entity controlled by a government.*' It also rejected the United States' argument that a majority state ownership of an SCE would demonstrate *per se* that the enterprise was indeed a public body.[96] Instead, the AB considered that it is necessary to examine whether the entity '*possess[ed], exercise[ed], or [was] vested with governmental authority.*'[97] This approach was affirmed by the AB in the *US - Carbon Steel* case, in which it ruled that the Indian government's 98 per cent ownership would not necessarily qualify the company as a public body. Relying on *US - Anti-Dumping and Countervailing Duties*, it stressed that determining whether particular conduct is that of a public body must be made by focusing on whether the entity has indeed exercised governmental authority.[98] By virtue of this trend, there is room to argue (but not without some controversy) against the presumption of statehood by majority state shareholding in *Maffezini*. Investment tribunals may also refer to a wealth of different approaches of the AB's to the notions of '*vested government authority*', '*government agency*' and '*government control*'.[99]

Beyond the case law of WTO judicial bodies, inspiration may also be drawn from multilateral and bilateral trade deals. Regarding the political atmosphere today and the existential crisis of the AB, people are already talking about life without the WTO. However, life without the WTO does not mean life without international trade law; on the contrary, the downfall of WTO may create more room for regional or bilateral trade deals.[100]

---

[93] Panel Report, *Korea - Measures Affecting Trade in Commercial Vessels*, WT/DS273/R, 7 March 2005, para 7.46.

[94] ibid para 7.50.

[95] ibid. For a similar analysis, *see* the Panel Report, *EC and Certain Member States - Large Civil Aircraft*, WT/DS/316/R, 30 June 2010, para 7.1359 (finding the Crédit Lyonnais to constitute a 'public body' as it was controlled by the French government.)

[96] Appellate Body Report, *United States - Definitive Anti-Dumping and Countervailing Duties on Certain Products from China*, *supra* note 90, paras. 318-322.

[97] ibid para. 317.

[98] Appellate Body Report, *US - Carbon Steel*, WT/DS436/AB/R, 8 December 2014, para 4.52.

[99] The AB's approaches to these ideas have been succinctly reviewed in Yingying Wu, Reforming WTO Rules on State-Owned Enterprises (Springer 2019) 139-144.

[100] Michael Fakhri, 'Life Without the WTO – Part II: Looking to the Everyday' (*EJIL: Talk!*, 26 April 2019) <https://www.ejiltalk.org/life-without-the-wto-part-ii-looking-to-the-everyday/> accessed 28 April 2019.

The new trade deals may be invoked by parties to an investment dispute based on Art. 31, paragraph 3 and Art. 32 of the Vienna Convention on the Law of Treaties ('VCLT'). Firstly, Art. 31, paragraph 3, provides, *among other things*, that there *shall* be taken into account, together with the context, (a) any *subsequent agreement* between the parties regarding the interpretation of the treaty or the application of its provisions; (b) any *subsequent practise* in the application of the treaty which establishes the agreement of the parties regarding its interpretation; and (c) '*any relevant rules of international law applicable in the relations between the parties*'. Secondly, arbitral tribunals can look into subsequent practice in applying the treaty as a supplementary means of interpretation under Art. 32 of the VCLT. Investment tribunals, as well as the ILC's recent Commentaries on the *Draft conclusions on subsequent agreements and subsequent practice in relation to the interpretation of treaties* (2018), have agreed that subsequent agreement and practice can take various forms.[101] The practical implications on investment arbitration of the ILC's *Draft conclusions* remain to be seen.[102]

The possibility of invoking subsequent treaty practice to the notion of SCEs was mentioned in the *Beijing Shougang* case, in which the Respondent invoked special provisions in other Chinese treaties on state-owned entities.[103] The tribunal, however, did not consider China's treaty practise to be relevant to the interpretation of the term 'economic entities' in the China-Mongolia BIT. First, it pointed out that the Respondent has only cited two treaties that China has signed with other countries.[104] Second, the Respondent has provided no support that the practice is shared by or common to Mongolia's treaty practice.[105] From this award, one can reason *a contrario* that subsequent practices may have more impact on the notions of SCEs if they are shared by parties to the treaty and are sufficiently indicative of the parties' intentions.[106]

---

[101] ILC, 'Draft conclusions on subsequent agreements and subsequent practice in relation to the interpretation of treaties with commentaries' (2018) A/73/10, para 35 at p 36; Tarcisio Gazzini, *Interpretation of International Investment Treaties* (Hart 2016) 192-194.

[102] However, the broad definitions of 'subsequent practice' in the Commentaries of the Draft conclusions have already been cited in *Clayton & Bilcon v Canada*, PCA Case No. 2009-04, Award on Damages, 10 January 2019, para 378.

[103] *Beijing Shougang*, para 408.

[104] ibid fn 790 at p 138.

[105] ibid para. 414. The tribunal apparently did not consider art. 32 of the VCLT. In this respect, the ILC is clear that the distinction between subsequent practice under art 31, para 3 (b), as an authentic means of interpretation, and other subsequent practice (which does not require practice from all parties to a treaty) under art 32, simply implies that a greater interpretative value should be attributed to the former (ILC, 'Draft conclusions on subsequent agreements', *see* ILC (n 102) para. 33).

[106] This is important as neither relevant rules of international law nor subsequent practice can defy treaty parties' express intentions. This is why in the NAFTA context, where the treaty parties have carefully distinguished between organs of State and different forms SCEs, tribunals have declined to referred to definitions of 'public body' made by the AB. *See United Parcel Service of America, Inc. v. Government of Canada*, UNCITRAL, Award on the Merits, 24 May 2007, para 61; *Mesa Powers*

In any event, when drawing from external sources of interpretation, tribunals enjoy broad discretion in terms of the weight to be given to other rules of international law.[107]

An example would be the Trans-Pacific Partnership ('TPP'), partly entered into force on 30 December 2018 under the Comprehensive and Progressive Agreement on TPP. The guidelines contained in TPP could be relevant if the host State and the investor's home State have both participated in it. In particular, it defines 'commercial activities' as '*(1) the activities must be carried out for profit-making, not on a cost-recovery or not-for-profit basis; (2) the activities must result in production of a good or supply of a service that will be sold to a consumer in the relevant market in quantities; and (3) the enterprise must be able to determine the price on its own.*'[108] Art. 17.1 of the TPP provides definitions of SCEs based on state ownership, voting rights, and power to appoint board members. Art. 17.2.3 includes a substantial list of entities that would be excluded from SCE related regulations, including, *inter alia*, a central bank or monetary authority performing regulatory or supervisory activities or conducting monetary and related credit policy.[109]

Admittedly, interpreting investment treaties with neighbouring concepts in trade law or with Art. 31, paragraph 3 of the VCLT entails a particular risk of 'boundary crossing'.[110] After all, these techniques involve a level of analogy or cross regime macro-comparison: unrelated concepts cannot be thereby imported to rewrite the ordinary meaning of treaty terms or the parties' intentions at will. However, as recently states by the ILC in the context of subsequent agreements and practices, although conclusions reached using these techniques are not '*legally binding*' unless the parties agreed otherwise, they nevertheless possess '*a specific authority regarding*

(n 61) para 346. More recently, in *B-Mex, LLC and Others v United Mexican States*, it was claimed that the word 'ownership' in NAFTA should be interpreted in accordance with that contained in General Agreement on Trade in Services (GATS). The argument was rejected as the tribunal found that the treaty parties deliberately chose the broader term to avoid such an interpretation. *B-Mex, LLC and Others v United Mexican States*, ICSID Case No. ARB(AF)/16/3, Partial Award, 19 July 2019, para 204.

[107] This is the conclusion of Rumiana Yotova's recent study on art. 31(3)(c) of the VCLT. *See* Rumiana Yotova, 'Systemic Integration: An Instrument for Reasserting the State's Control in Investment Arbitration?' (2017) Legal Studies Research Paper Series of the University of Cambridge, 26.

[108] *See* generally, Minwoo Kim, 'Regulating the Visible Hands' (2017) 58 Harv Intl L J 242.

[109] ibid.

[110] Jose E. Alvarez, 'Beware: Boundary Crossings - A Critical Appraisal of Public Law Approaches to International Investment Law' (2016) 17 JWIT 171; Jean Salmon, 'Le raisonnement par analogie en droit international public' in *Mélanges offerts à Charles Chaumont: Le droit des peuples à disposer d'eux-mêmes* (Pedone 1984) 495, 524 (stating that '*la préoccupation d'appliquer à des cas analogues des solutions identiques n'est rien d'autre qu'un acte créateur et, en fin de compte, politique, substituant la volonté de l'interprète à celle des sujets de droit intéressés. Ceci ne veut pas dire que tout recours à l'analogie et tout construction ou systématisation soient, en elles-mêmes, critiquables, mais bien que, pour être légitimes elles doivent s'appuyer sur la volonté des Etats en cause dûment constatée.*').

the identification of the meaning of the treaty' that *shall* (in the case of Art. 31 of the VCLT) or *may* (in the case of Art. 32 of the VCLT) be taken into account.[111]

As the ILC points out, the real problem is not about whether to blindly follow the conclusions reached employing these techniques; the adjudicators should care about the weight to be assigned to them. Put otherwise, the choice is not a binary one: the weight of these techniques depends, *among other things*, on consistency and breadth. The more consistency and breadth a practice has, the more weight it possesses. The element of consistency relates to whether and how far conduct deviates from an otherwise established pattern—the element of breadth. The element of breadth concerns the number of parties that engage in it.[112]

In the example of SCEs, if a country (or many countries) repeatedly signs trade treaties containing particular definitions of SCEs, depending on the circumstances, there may be little reason not to consider them when interpreting an investment treaty signed by that country. Similarly, suppose a country (or many countries) consistently defines SCEs based on a series of criteria in trade treaties. In that case, there might be less reason to abide by the structural test defined in Maffezini strictly. In this sense, one can link the definition of 'commercial activities' in trade treaties and the 'essentially governmental function' limb in the Broches test for the purpose of jurisdiction *ratione personae* of a SCEs. To take the example of the TPP, one may argue, depending on the circumstances, that if an SCE was able to determine the price on its own for the goal of making a profit and produces a good or supplies a service that will be sold to a consumer in the relevant market, it is likely that the parties to the investment intended for it to have standing under the treaty.

3.2 *Neighbouring Ideas in Competition Law*

The idea of looking at SCEs with the eyes of national competition rules may seem far-fetched. Indeed, objection to this approach may be found on Art. 27 of the VCLT, which forbids States of invoking '*the provisions of its internal law as justification for its failure to perform a treaty.*' However, as the ILC points out, the 'enactment of domestic legislation' also qualifies as a subsequent practice within the meaning of Art. 31 of the VCLT[113]: '*[w]hereas article 27 of the 1969 Vienna Convention is certainly valid and important, this rule does not signify that national legislation may not be taken into account'* for the purpose of treaty interpretation.[114] Furthermore, since it is common practice for tribunals and judges to scrutinise municipal

[111] ILC, 'Draft conclusions on subsequent agreements and subsequent practice in relation to the interpretation of treaties with commentaries' (2018) A/73/10, para 35 at p 24.

[112] ibid para 12 at p 74.

[113] ILC, 'Draft conclusions on subsequent agreements and subsequent practice in relation to the interpretation of treaties with commentaries' (2018) A/73/10, para 35 at p 24. This paragraph of the Commentary has been cited with approval by the tribunal in *Clayton & Bilcon v Canada*, PCA Case No. 2009-04, Award on Damages, 10 January 2019, para 378.

[114] ibid para 19 at p. 32.

regulations establishing or concerning the SCE, such objection cannot stand.[115] If one wants to emphasise national rules (as suggested by Arato and Rajavuori), it is submitted that it may be appropriate to consider the relevant national competition rules concerning the specific SCE(s) at hand.

The most compelling reason for doing so is that the treatments of SCEs in investment law and competition law apply the same set of rules regarding sovereign immunities. There is broad consensus amongst scholars that the 'government function' or 'state instrumentality' criteria in investment law '*is rooted in the notion of* acta jure imperii *vis-à-vis* acta jure gestionis, *which entails the application to the activity at issue of a nature test in substance imported from the law of State immunity.*'[116] They agree that the distinction can be reflected in national legislation and case law concerning sovereign immunity.[117] In this respect, national competition laws integrate the similar concern of the non-justiciability of the acts of State.[118]

In the US, for instance, the 'State Action' doctrine provides that US state or local government enterprises may enjoy exemption from antitrust enforcement if the challenged conduct is a foreseeable result of a '*clearly articulated and affirmatively expressed state policy*' and that it is '*actively supervised*' by the state.[119] Subject to some disagreement amongst lower courts, the doctrine is generally applicable if the challenged conduct is attributable to a foreign State.[120] Similarly, in Singapore, section 33(4) of the *Competition Act* of Singapore explicitly excludes any activity carried on by any agreement entered into, or any conduct by the Government, any statutory body, or any person acting on behalf of the Government or that statutory body. Importantly, the Competition and Consumer Commission of Singapore has clarified that exclusion only applies when the Government and/or statutory body participates in any market directly in such capacity, and not when government-linked companies ('GLCs') or private companies which the Singapore Government or its statutory boards own or are shareholders or engage in commercial or economic activities in any market.[121] In Korea, for another example, the definition of state owned entity for the purpose of competition regulation is given by Articles 4 and

---

[115] For example, in the *Certain Iranian Assets* case, the Court had to examine the Monetary and Banking Act of Iran to determine the status of Bank Markazi.

[116] Carlo de Stefano (n 26) 271; *see* also, Feldman (n 25) 30; Blyschak (n 21) 30; *Certain Iranian Assets* (*Iran v. United States*), Separate opinion of Judge *ad hoc* Charles N. Brower, para. 28.

[117] Annacker (n 28) 556; Blyschak (n 21) 31.

[118] Marek Martyniszyn, 'Foreign State's Entanglement in Anticompetitive Conduct' (2017) 40 World Competition 303.

[119] US Supreme Court, *California Retail Liquor Dealers Association v Midcal Aluminum Co.*, 445 U.S. 97, 105 (1980).

[120] *See* eg, *Sea Breeze Salt v. Mitsubishi Corp.*, 899 F.3d 1064 (9th Cir. 2018) in which the 9th circuit held that the doctrine precluded liability for a Mexican corporation in an antitrust case, relying only on the fact that he Mexican government owns 51 percent of the corporation and appoints a majority of its board of directors and its Director General. But *contra* cf. the cases discussed in Martyniszyn (n 119).

[121] Competition and Consumer Commission of Singapore, 'Frequently Asked Questions' <https://www.cccs.gov.sg/faq/competition-act-and-government-agencies> accessed 30 April 2019.

5 of the *Act on the Management of Public Institutions.*[122] These provisions provide some bright-line criteria, including the share of self-generated revenue, government ownership and power to appoint executive officers.

This chapter does not purport to provide an exhaustive review of municipal competition regulations of SCEs. Instead, it wishes to point out that, firstly, in terms of attribution of the acts of SCEs, municipal competition laws apply similar criteria as international tribunals do investment law, such as the appointment of officers, ownership, commercial activities, *etc*. Invoking them would, therefore, not drastically overwrite established rules of attribution in international law. Secondly, in comparison with international rules, municipal competition laws offer more precise and sophisticated standards that can help differentiate between the public and the private in SCEs.

By means of judicial interpretation in their respective national legal systems, these laws might also provide a more coherent view on how SCEs are treated in their own legal order. This could be important as competition rules can offer a different perspective other than municipal statutes concerning SCEs, since the latter often put emphasis solely on their separate legal personality.[123] In this context, as Julien Chaisse aptly points out, the regulations of SCEs under competition law instruct us to look at several criteria, including (1) whether the SCE would manipulate prices and (2) whether direct or indirect subsidies give the SCE an unfair advantage.[124] Therefore, if a company is repeatedly and definitely determined, for the purpose of domestic competition law, to have these anti-competitive characteristics, there might be more room to argue that it performs an 'essentially governmental function' for the purpose of the Broches test. Similarly, suppose an SCE's actions are exempted from domestic competition law review due to its public character. In that case, there might be more chance that its actions and omissions are attributable to the State. Again, as discussed above, according to the ILC's Commentaries on subsequent practices, the presence of such elements does not per se determine jurisdiction ratione personae and attribution issues. They are evidence that carries a certain weight that shall or may be taken into account by the tribunal depending on the circumstances of the case.

---

[122] Statute of the Republic of Korea, 'Act on the Management of Public Institutions' <https://elaw.klri.re.kr/eng_service/lawView.do?hseq=41210&lang=ENG> accessed 30 April 2019.

[123] As seen in the disagreement between Judge *ad hoc* Brower and Judge Gaja in the *Certain Iranian Assets* case, municipal laws on the legal status of SCEs (such as the Iranian Monetary and Banking Act) may not yield coherent results.

[124] Julien Chaisse, 'Untangling the Triangle - Issues for State-Controlled Entities in Trade, Investment and Competition Law' in Julien Chaisse and Tsai-yu Lin (eds) *International Economic law and Governance - Essays in the Honour of Mitsuo Matsushita* (OUP 2016) 246.

4 Conclusion

As opposed to many doctrinal works on attribution and SCEs, this chapter aspires to present the current landscape of the field as one that contains substantial conflicts both in practice and in doctrinal works. The aim is to justify a new paradigm that deals with the notion of SCEs.

With the rise of state capitalism, SCEs have been evolving and their activities are becoming more complex, both in terms of ownership, control and their business development strategies. Early efforts by tribunals to develop bright-line rules to treat the idea of SCE have proven to be futile. In the absence of guidance from the treaty, the vast majority of the tribunals have to resort to the customary rules of attribution, as codified by the ILC in ARSIWA. However, as these customary rules are deliberately formulated broadly, they end up considering and balancing a plethora of elements, from ownership to control, from the municipal law to the company's articles of incorporation, from nature to the purpose of its activities. This approach, highly fact-sensitive, has been heavily criticised for generating uncertainty and discriminating against the Global South. In the hope of achieving greater clarity, other tribunals have tried to focus on specific wording in the treaty at hand, such as 'delegation' or 'governmental authority.'[125] By holding these equally vague terms as *lex specialis*, they were able to exclude the application of ARSIWA. But authors and tribunals have doubted whether such treaty language is really more specific than those found in ARSIWA.

Against this background, the chapter suggests that future tribunals look into other fields in international economic law for inspiration. These fields, namely international trade law and municipal competition laws, can offer more precise and sophisticated guidelines than customary law. On the one hand, WTO jurisprudence on the attribution of the acts SCEs is also based on customary international law. On the other hand, national competition laws on state actions integrate the same distinction of *acta jure imperii* vis-à-vis *acta jure gestionis* as investment tribunals do. There is thus no reason why the tribunal should not look at these instruments if they turn out to be helpful. Furthermore, if international trade law and competition laws are taken into account, they are likely to be characterised as primary or supplementary means of interpretation and not as formal sources of law. The difficult problem of *lex specialis*, therefore, does not arise.

As such, the chapter first submits that future tribunals can invoke relevant rules in international trade law, such as the law of the WTO or other trade deals applicable between the parties. On the one hand, judicial bodies of the WTO have produced abundant case law concerning the terms 'public body' and 'government authority' and 'governmental control'. Investment tribunals in the past have already borrowed the notions of exception and necessity developed in WTO law; there is no reason why they cannot do the same with SCEs. On the other hand, unlike most early

[125] *Mesa Powers*, (n 61) para 362; *Al Tamimi*, (n 63) para 322.

investment treaties, some recent trade deals have paid more attention to the current state of SCEs. They can be invoked based on Art. 31(3) and Art. 32 of the VCLT. The ILC's Commentaries on a subsequent agreement and subsequent practice have defined subsequent practice broadly. What matters is then the interpretive weight to be accorded to such practice, left to the tribunal's discretion. Secondly, the chapter submits that tribunal may refer to national competition rules. These rules can offer more insight into how the entities are treated in their own legal systems. By paying due respect to domestic legal regimes, tribunals may alleviate the concern that international law is unfairly biased against developing States.

These proposals are, for the moment, *lex ferenda*. As Hersch Lauterpacht famously pointed out, although these proposals may end up to be misleading, '*they are never dangerous*': they are only wrong in assuming, rather prematurely, '*the existence of a legal regulation where, in fact, no such regulation yet exists*'. This, as he put it, is a fault which is '*less heinous than that of not knowing that there is a necessary law at all.*'[126]

Acknowledgements The author wishes to thank Dr. Dini Sejko for his helpful suggestions and review of this article.

Kai-chieh Chan Ph.D. Candidate at Université Paris 2 Panthéon-Assas. B.A., National Taiwan University; M. A., Institut d'études politiques de Paris (*cum laude*); M.A., Université Paris 2 Panthéon-Assas.

---

[126] Hersch Lauterpacht, *Private Law Sources and Analogies of International Law* (Longmans, Green & Co. Ltd. 1927) 86.

Regulating Sovereign Shareholders: The Role of Securities Disclosures

Joel Slawotsky

1 Introduction

Several transformational developments in the global political economy are simultaneously increasing the long-term prospect of sovereign ownership of publicly traded corporations. One, the United States and China are vying for dominance, particularly in emerging technology in which corporations play a leading role in developing. Two, the ostensible success of China's economy may serve as a lure and/or competitive driver to incorporate aspects of state-centric governance in market-capitalism nations. Three, discontent in Western nations over perceived corporate power abuses and wealth gaps have led to both a rise in economic nationalism and calls for state intervention—as exemplified in trends towards populism, economic nationalism and socialism. All of these developments incentivise Western sovereigns to acquire shares, and sovereign share ownership is, therefore, likely to increase going forward. Even the leader of market capitalism, the United States, has considered acquiring shares in foreign corporations as a hedge against Chinese dominance in 5G.[1] Foreign State ownership of shares presents a dilemma; attracting capital is

[1] New York Times, 'Really? Is the White House Proposing to Buy Ericsson or Nokia?' (7 Feb 2020) <https://www.nytimes.com/2020/02/07/business/dealbook/bill-barr-huawei-nokia-ericsson.html> ("President Trump has made it very clear that he is worried about Huawei's leading role in 5G wireless technology. Now his attorney general, Bill Barr, has offered a radical solution: having the U.S. invest in the Chinese company's European counterparts.").

J. Slawotsky (✉)
IDC Law and Business Schools, Reichman University, Herzliya, Israel
e-mail: jslawotsky@idc.ac.il

J. Chaisse et al. (eds.), *Regulation of State-Controlled Enterprises*, International Law and the Global South, https://doi.org/10.1007/978-981-19-1368-6_7

important, yet allowing a foreign sovereign to dominate or control an important business poses risks that the shareholder will elect directors and influence the corporation to make business decisions favouring the foreign owner. Updating disclosure requirements to lower reporting thresholds might constitute an essential measure taken to defend economic and technological interests. However, balance is crucial. Heightened regulation must endeavour to avoid protectionism and thwarting FDI. This chapter will focus on securities regulation—specifically disclosures of share purchases and will make several suggestions on updating the existing disclosure architecture.

1.1 State-Centric Capitalism

China today is essentially a capitalist nation, and its governing authority—the Chinese Communist Party—is communist in name only.[2] China's economic governance model embraces state-centric capitalism as illustrated by industrial policies, extensive state ownership of strategic economic sectors and promotion of national strategic objectives.[3] State-centric capitalism has no single definitive definition but can be conceptualised as government direction of economic and corporate governance. Such direction would include governmental share ownership of publicly traded corporations, setting industrial policies, promotion of economic nationalism, protection of national champions and selecting sectors or individual businesses for preferential treatment.[4] State-centric capitalism cuts against the US-led Western market-capitalism model where economic governance interference is discouraged, and private market decisions are based on economic motivations instead of political or strategic factors.[5]

---

[2] China's governing leadership, the CCP, transformed its economy under Premier Deng Xiaoping from a failed Soviet inspired communist command control model to state-capitalism. *See* Deng Xiaoping (*quotepark.com*) <https://quotepark.com/quotes/1749304-deng-xiaoping-we-mustnt-fear-to-adopt-the-advanced-management-m/> ("We mustn't fear to adopt the advanced management methods applied in capitalist countries (…) The very essence of socialism is the liberation and development of the productive systems (…) Socialism and market economy are not incompatible (…) We should be concerned about right-wing deviations, but most of all, we must be concerned about left-wing deviations.").

[3] *See* Ji Li, 'I Came, I Saw, I… Adapted: An Empirical Study of Chinese Business Expansion in the United States and its Legal and Policy Implications' (2016) 36 Nw. J. Int'l L. & Bus. 143, 157 (State capitalism is the "unique Chinese model of state-business relationships has been labeled state capitalism.").

[4] *See* Chuin-Wei Yap, 'State Support Helped Fuel Huawei's Global Rise' (*Wall Street Journal*, 25 Dec 2019) <https://www.wsj.com/articles/state-support-helped-fuel-huaweis-global-rise-11577280736> ("Tens of billions of dollars in financial assistance from the Chinese government helped fuel Huawei Technologies Co.'s rise to the top of global telecommunications, a scale of support that in key measures dwarfed what its closest tech rivals got from their governments.").

[5] Whether the profit motive is the sole driver such as shareholder-value based governance in Delaware or whether an EU stakeholder model is the model, economic profit and less government involvement has been the mantra in recent decades.

At its core, China's state-centric capitalism is a model of political-economic partnership; the sovereign sets forth national objectives and assists businesses to promote those goals.[6] "The way that the Chinese government exercises 'state capitalism' is that it directly or indirectly controls a large number of powerful SOEs, especially in the strategic and critical sectors."[7]

The economic system of China is dominated by governmental political, and industrial policies rather than free-market principles.[8] Indeed, Chinese SOEs are commonly understood as advancing state objectives in addition to being motivated by profit.[9] In contrast, the United States market-capitalism endeavours to limit state involvement and encourages businesses to engage solely in profit-generating objectives. Thus, the United States and Chinese models are inherently conflicting political-economic governance models. It could be argued that the trade conflict was not merely a tool to diminish the trade deficit but reflects American objection to China's economic model as *producing an unfair competitive advantage to China Inc.,* which ultimately, if unchecked, would lead to China eventually surpassing the US as an economic power. The question of whether the US-initiated trade war against China is a legitimate invocation of national security and the role of the two fundamentally incompatible political-economic models in international trade is a fascinating separate legal issue.[10]

1.2 The Hegemonic Rivalry

Given the strategic rivalry, the impact of national security considerations on corporate and economic governance are likely to increase and become more extensive.[11] For

---

[6] *See* Joel Slawotsky, The Impact of Geo-economic Rivalry on U.S. Economic Governance (2022) 16 Virginia Law and Business Review 559.

[7] Julien Chaisse, 'Demystifying Public Security Exception and Limitations on Capital Movement' (2015) 37 U Penn J Intl L 583, 589.

[8] Thomas J. Schoenbaum & Daniel C.K. Chow, The Perils of Economic Nationalism and a Proposed Pathway to Trade Harmony, (2019) 30 Stanford Law & Policy Review 115, 185.

[9] Perceptions of unfairness also fuels resentment against foreign investment. *See* Locknie Hsu, 'The Role and Future of Sovereign Wealth Funds: A Trade and Investment Perspective' (2017) 52 Wake Forest L Rev 837 ("Nationalist sentiments can also play a role in recipient countries, contributing to public outcry at particular investments.").

[10] Ru Ding, 'Interface 2.0 in Rules on State-Owned Enterprises: A Comparative Institutional Approach' (2020) 23 JIEL 637, 638 ('[the] 'trade war' between the USA and China is not a temporary economic incident, but 'rather an outgrowth of a long-brewing tension in the multilateral trade system,' which is essentially a problem of the interface between China's economic model and the US economic model.').

[11] Alexandra Alper, David Lawder, 'Trump considers delisting Chinese firms from U.S. markets', (Reuters 27 Sept 2019) <https://www.reuters.com/article/us-usa-trade-china-limits/trump-considers-delisting-chinese-firms-from-u-s-markets-sources-idUSKBN1WC1VP> (U.S. considering measures including de-listing Chinese shares).

example, in 2017, China's Ant Financial sought to take over a United States financial services corporation, MoneyGram, outbidding a competing offer by a significant margin—providing a boon to shareholders. The transaction was cancelled due to national security grounded US regulatory objection[12] over the possibility that a foreign buyer would manage the business in favour of the home jurisdiction,[13] which trumped shareholder value in the home of shareholder-value governance.[14] The rejection of Ant's offer constituted a quintessential exemplar of the hegemonic rivalry's impact on financial markets and economic governance.[15]

The failed bid of Ant Financial was proximately caused by the contentious relationship between the current dominant global power,[16] the United States, and its ascendant challenger, China.[17] The United States is the current Chief Architect[18]

---

[12] National security concerns are not solely related to finance. *See* e.g. Jonathan Soble, 'Why the US Fears a Chinese Bid for Westinghouse Electric' (*New York Times* 7 April 2017) <https://www.nytimes.com/2017/04/07/business/us-china-toshiba-westinghouse.html?_r=0> accessed 31 August 2018 (describing claims that Westinghouse technology is the target of Chinese espionage causing national security concerns within the USA). *See* also Dini Sejko, 'The Transnational Law of Sovereign Wealth Funds: Governing State Capitalism at the Time of Protectionism', Edward Elgar Publishing (forthcoming 2022) Chapter 6 (discussing the heightened U.S. investment review mechanisms, CFIUS and FIRRMA).

[13] Peter Rudegeair and Kate O'Keeffe, 'US Bars Merger of MoneyGram, China's Ant Financial' (*Wall Street Journal*, 3 Jan 2018) <https://www.wsj.com/articles/moneygram-and-ant-financial-halt-merger-deal-1514931496> (noting that CFIUS had concerns over national security).

[14] The function of the US publicly-traded corporation – and the guiding principle of U.S. corporate law is - to advance the wealth of its shareholders. For example, Delaware directors are charged with the fiduciary duty to make business decisions and manage the corporation in furtherance of the goal of shareholder value maximization. *See* David Gelles and David Yaffe-Bellany, 'Shareholder Value Is No Longer Everything, Top CEOs Say' (*New York Times*, 19 August 2019) <https://www.nytimes.com/2019/08/19/business/business-roundtable-ceos-corporations.html> (CEOs of large corporations claiming shareholder value governance is no longer the objective). Interestingly, some pushback against this mantra of corporate purpose has been voiced. *See* e.g. Letter of Corporate CEOs NY Times arguing that the purpose of a corporation should not be solely focused on shareholder-value).

[15] The world's largest hedge fund manager believes that capital markets will inevitably find themselves in the cross-hairs of geo-politically driven economic combat. *See* Thomas Franck, 'Ray Dalio says 'capital wars' will be the next front in the US-China economic conflict' (15 Nov 2019) <https://www.cnbc.com/2019/11/15/ray-dalio-says-us-china-capital-wars-could-be-next-stage-of-feud.html>.

[16] The United States has referred to itself as the indispensable nation. *See* Obama (n 23).

[17] China's perspective is markedly different; viewing its rise as a restoration of China's historical status. *See* Joel Slawotsky, 'China's Long-March' (2 June 2019). <http://lcbackerblog.blogspot.com/2019/06/joel-slawotsky-on-chinas-long-march.html> ("China may in fact view the West's domination of the global economy and governance architecture as an aberration which is naturally correcting to the mean. From this historical perspective, the United States – a relatively "new power" was "in the right place at the right time" and is in fact the "revisionist" - an upstart nation of not even 250 years as compared to China's thousands of years of civilization. Pursuant to this narrative, the United States will need to embrace the developing Chinese order – a nation with thousands of years of history wielding an Empire long before the United States Constitution even existed.").

[18] *See* Joel Slawotsky, 'The Clash of Architects: Impending Developments and Transformations in International Law' (2017) 3(2) The Chinese Journal of Global Governance 83–159 <https://doi.org/10.1163/23525207-12340025> (discussing the effects of China's ascendancy and how this will affect international law and global governance as well as potentially impacting domestic governance of sovereigns militating towards a Chinese governance model.

of the global governance architecture, wielding dominant positions in the triad of hegemonic power levers.[19] However, an ambitious China seeks to restore itself and replace the US[20] as the world's major economic, political and military power.[21] President Xi acknowledges that China has global leadership ambitions in the geostrategic context, conceding that China's rise has immense global implications,[22] "[b]eing a big

---

[19] *See* Joel Slawotsky, 'The National Security Exception in US-China FDI and Trade: Lessons from Delaware Corporate Law' (2018) 6(2) The Chinese Journal of Comparative Law <https://doi.org/10.1093/cjcl/cxy012> pp 241–245 (noting economic, technological and military power as the triad of hegemonic status).

[20] The prospect of hegemonic defeat was considered by U.S. elites unthinkable just a few years ago. *See* Barack Obama, 'Remarks by the President at the United States Military Academy Commencement Ceremony' (28 May 2014) <https://www.whitehouse.gov/the-pressoffice/2014/05/28/remarks-president-united-states-military-academy-commencementceremony> ("In fact, by most measures, America has rarely been stronger relative to the rest of the world…. Our military has no peer…. Meanwhile, our economy remains the most dynamic on Earth; our businesses the most innovative. Each year, we grow more energy independent. From Europe to Asia, we are the hub of alliances unrivaled in the history of nations. America continues to attract striving immigrants…. So[,] *the United States is and remains the one indispensable nation. That has been true for the century passed and it will be and true for the century to come.*") (emphasis added).

[21] Perception is key – China does not view its rise as dethroning the United States but restoring its rightful status. From the historical perspective, the Chinese perceive the United States as the "revisionist" - an upstart nation of not even 250 years as compared to China's thousands of years of civilization. *See* Daniel Blumenthal, The Unpredictable Rise of China (*The Atlantic*, 3 February 2019) <https://www.theatlantic.com/ideas/archive/2019/02/how-americans-misunderstand-chinas-ambitions/581869/> ("In 2012, soon after he became secretary general of the CCP and president of the People's Republic of China, he delivered the rejuvenation speech at a historical exhibition within China's National Museum, in Beijing….Xi reminded his audience that the CCP had long struggled to restore China to its historic centrality in international affairs. 'Ours is a great nation,' he said, that has 'endured untold hardships and sufferings.' But the Communist Party, he said, had forged ahead, 'thus opening a completely new horizon for the great renewal of the Chinese nation.'"). China's ambition is to *reclaim* its former hegemonic status. *See* Robert L Kuhn, 'Xi Jinping's Chinese Dream' (*New York Times*, 4 June 2013) <https://www.nytimes.com/2013/06/05/opinion/global/xi-jinpings-chinese-dream.html> (China seeks to restore its former status as global economic leader). In contrast, the US views China as an "upstart" and a "challenger". *See* Panos Mourdoukoutas, 'America Begins to See The Consequences of The Past Policy Errors that Helped China's Rise' (Forbes, 25 May 2019)< https://www.forbes.com/sites/panosmourdoukoutas/2019/05/25/america-begins-to-see-the-consequences-of-the-past-policy-errors-that-helped-chinas-rise/#21a98cec7981> citing: Robert D Blackwill, 'Trump's Foreign Policies Are Better Than They Seem' Council on Foreign Relations (April 2019) Council Special Report No. 84 <https://www.cfr.org/report/trumps-foreign-policies-are-better-they-seem> ("From the South China Sea to the Indian Ocean and the African Continent, China is rising fast, *challenging America's long dominance.*") (emphasis added); 'The Joint Force in a Contested and Disordered World', <https://www.airuniversity.af.edu/Portals/10/CMSA/documents/Required_Reading/Joint%20Operating%20Environment%202035%20The%20Joint%20Force%20in%20a%20Contested%20and%20Disordered%20World.pd> (2016) at page 29 ("Russia, China, and other *revisionist states* may also increasingly partner and coordinate with each other or with smaller, but militarily-active partners such as Pakistan or North Korea.") (emphasis added).

[22] *See* Zheping Huang, 'Chinese president Xi Jinping has vowed to lead the "new world order"' (*Yahoo Finance*, 22 February 2017) <http://finance.yahoo.com/news/chinese-president-xi-jinping-vowed-084654413.htm> ("China should take the lead in shaping the 'new world order' and safeguarding international security.").

country means shouldering greater responsibilities for regional and world peace and development."[23] China—recognising the importance of alliances—has endeavoured to engage US allies, bringing them within China's orbit of influence.[24]

The link between conflicting economic models and the hegemonic rivalry brings corporate power into the equation. By successfully integrating state control and the private sector, China has achieved national goals through commercial activities[25] transforming China into a near-peer US rival forecasted by some to be on track to overtake the US economy by 2028.[26] Significantly, China has engineered a narrowing of the technology gap with the United States achieving impressive successes in emergent technologies which will form the basis of future economic power and

---

[23] Michael Schuman, 'Whose Money Will the World Follow?' (*Bloomberg*, 15 may 2015) <https://www.bloomberg.com/news/articles/2015-05-14/u-s-china-rivalry-whose-money-will-the-world-follow> Unsurprisingly, China envisages an increasing military role to protect Chinese national interests overseas and is rapidly developing a powerful military. *See* Anthony H Cordesman, 'China's New 2019 Defense White Paper: An Open Strategic Challenge to the United States, But One Which Does Not Have to Lead to Conflict' CSIS (24 July 2019) <https://www.csis.org/analysis/chinas-new-2019-defense-white-paper> ("The PLA actively promotes international security and military cooperation and refines relevant mechanisms for protecting China's overseas interests. To address deficiencies in overseas operations and support, it builds far seas forces, develops overseas logistical facilities, and enhances capabilities in accomplishing diversified military tasks.").

[24] *See* <http://www.xinhuanet.com/english/2019-12/10/c_138620210.htm> (China-Israel cooperation); <https://www.cnbc.com/2019/03/27/italys-joins-chinas-belt-and-road-initiative.html> (Italy joins BRI).

[25] Ted C. Fishman, China, Inc.: How the Rise of the Next Superpower Challenges America and the World (2006); Mark Wu, 'The 'China, Inc.' Challenge to Global Trade Governance' 57 (2016) Harvard International Law Journal 1001, 1063.

[26] Lizzy Burden, 'U.S. economy to drop to No. 2 earlier due to pandemic' (Fortune, 26 Dec 2020) <https://fortune.com/2020/12/26/u-s-china-economy-rankings-pandemic/> (CEBR forecasts China overtaking U.S. in 2028).

global leadership: blockchain[27]; space exploration[28]; nuclear fusion[29]; AI[30]; and quantum computing[31] and empowering China's military power.[32]

China has also adroitly initiated policies and programs to increase Chinese structural power over global governance. International financial institutions such as the AIIB and NDB, the massive BRI and efforts at internationalising the Yuan all signal an ambitious China. "No country presents a broader, more severe threat to our ideas, our innovation, and our economic security than China."[33] In response, the US has attempted to contain China more vigorously and has dramatically expanded

[27] *See* Joel Slawotsky, 'US Financial Hegemony: The Digital Yuan and Risks of Dollar De-Weaponization' (2020) 44 Fordham Int'l LJ 39 (China likely to be the first sovereign to introduce a CBDC).

[28] Matthew S Schwartz, 'China Becomes First Country, To Land On Far Side Of Moon, State Media Announce' (*NPR*, 3 January 2019) <https://www.npr.org/2019/01/03/681825762/china-becomes-first-country-to-land-on-far-side-of-moon-state-media-announces> (China fist to land on Far Side of the moon).

[29] William Zheng, 'China turns on its 'artificial sun' in quest for nuclear fusion energy' (*SCMP*, 5 December 2020) <https://www.scmp.com/news/china/science/article/3112684/china-turns-its-artificial-sun-quest-nuclear-fusion-energy> (China progressing in its quest to harness fusion).

[30] Fabian Westerheide, 'China – The First Artificial Intelligence Superpower' (*Forbes*, 14 January 2020) <https://www.forbes.com/sites/cognitiveworld/2020/01/14/china-artificial-intelligence-superpower/?sh=206b71982f05> (China leading in AI).

[31] Fred Guterl, 'As China Leads Quantum Computing Race, U.S. Spies Plan for a World with Fewer Secrets' (Newsweek, 14 Dec 2020) <https://www.newsweek.com/2020/12/25/china-leads-quantum-computing-race-us-spies-plan-world-fewer-secrets-1554439.html> (China the global leader in quantum computing).

[32] DoD (US), 'Military and Security Developments Involving the People's Republic of China 2020' <https://media.defense.gov/2020/sep/01/2002488689/-1/-1/1/2020-dod-china-military-power-report-final.pdf>, Executive summary at vii ("China has already achieved parity with—or even exceeded—the United States in several military modernization areas, including: – Shipbuilding: The PRC has the largest navy in the world, with an overall battle force of approximately 350 ships and submarines including over 130 major surface combatants. In comparison, the U.S. Navy's battle force is approximately 293 ships as of early 2020. China is the top ship-producing nation in the world by tonnage and is increasing its shipbuilding capacity and capability for all naval classes.").

[33] *See* DoJ (US), 'Attorney General Jeff Session's China Initiative Fact Sheet' (1 November 2018) <https://www.justice.gov/opa/speech/file/1107256/download> (American officials believe that "[n]o country presents a broader, more severe threat to our ideas, our innovation, and our economic security than China."). *See* also Pence (n 41) on the Administration's Policy Toward China ("China's aggression was on display this week, when a Chinese naval vessel came within 45 yards of the USS Decatur as it conducted freedom-of-navigation operations in the South China Sea, forcing our ship to quickly maneuver to avoid collision. Despite such reckless harassment, *the United States Navy will continue to fly, sail, and operate wherever international law allows and our national interests demand. We will not be intimidated and we will not stand down*….[O]ur message to China's rulers is this: *This President will not back down.*") (emphasis added). In contrast, just a few years ago, the United States perceived itself as "the exceptional nation".

the concept of national security to encompass economic, technological and ideological interests.[34] For example, the US has endeavoured to convince allies not to allow Huawei 5G[35] and to reduce economic integration with China.[36] Therefore, the power contest between the United States and China will likely increase inevitably influencing capital markets.[37]

2 State Ownership of Corporations: National Security and Corporate Governance Implications

In the context of the hegemonic rivalry, economic dominance translates into influence and profits and is therefore critical. Leveraging economic engagement to shape global governance and acquire allies is thus fundamental to the strategic objectives of both China and the United States.

> In a move certain to cause consternation among American officials and leaders of the European Union, Italy appears poised to help China extend its vast global infrastructure push deeper into Western Europe, part of Beijing's sweeping plan to advance its economic interests and influence around the world.[38]

In the past, concerns about obtaining leverage over another sovereign's economic and technological power via controlling corporate assets would be relatively modest to non-existent since virtually all economic players and investors were private actors. Governments, by and large, were involved in public actor functions while private actors pursued business objectives based upon the profit motive divorced from any ideological interests or political agenda. However, states now are involved in the

---

[34] *See* Joel Slawotsky, 'The Fusion of Ideology, Technology and Economic Power: Implications of the Emerging New United States National Security Conceptualization' (2021) 20 Chinese Journal of International Law 3.

[35] Christopher Bing, Jack Stubbs, 'U.S. to press allies to keep Huawei out of 5G in Prague meeting: sources' (16 April 2019) <https://www.reuters.com/article/us-usa-cyber-huawei-tech/u-s-to-press-allies-to-keep-huawei-out-of-5g-in-prague-meeting-sources-idUSKCN1RR24Y> (U.S. pressuring allies to ban Huawei 5G). *See also* Michael Schuman, 'The U.S. Can't Make Allies Take Sides Over China' (*The Atlantic*, 25 April 2019) <https://www.theatlantic.com/international/archive/2019/04/us-allies-washington-china-belt-road/587902/>.

[36] Ivan Levingston, 'Caught in Trump's Trade Crossfire, Israel Chases China Deal' (23 December 2019) <https://www.bloomberg.com/news/articles/2019-12-23/caught-in-trump-s-trade-crossfire-israel-chases-deal-with-china> (U.S. pressuring Israel to reduce economic cooperation with China).

[37] Illustrative of the potential impact on financial markets: the United States is considering the unprecedented de-listing of Chinese ADRs traded on U.S. capital markets and the possible de-listing of Chinese companies. *See* Alexandra Alper, David Lawder, 'Trump considers delisting Chinese firms from U.S. markets' (*Reuters*, 27 Sept2019) <https://www.reuters.com/article/us-usa-trade-china-limits/trump-considers-delisting-chinese-firms-from-u-s-markets-sources-iduskbn1wc1vp> (U.S. considering measures including de-listing Chinese shares).

[38] Jason Horowitz and Jack Ewing, 'Italy May Split with Allies and Open Its Ports to China's Building Push' (*New York Times*, 6 March 2019) <https://www.nytimes.com/2019/03/06/world/europe/italy-ports-china.html> (noting allies such as Italy may be tempted to partner with China.).

private sector economy resulting in a risk that governments will invest and make business decisions for reasons not necessarily solely for profit. Generally speaking, there are two primary risks proximately caused by governmental involvement in private markets: (1) national security and (2) corporate governance. Although discussed separately, in fact, corporate governance and national security are inter-connected since national economic security and financial stability is an essential pillar of security.

2.1 National Security Concerns

Government-owned or controlled businesses generate concerns over motivations linked to governmental objectives.[39] "SOE [state owned enterprises] objectives often go beyond mere profit maximisation and include societal objectives."[40] Indeed, security concerns are inherently raised when foreign States acquire shares overseas, even among allies.[41]

> [H]ost countries cannot summarily assume that [SOE] investments will never be guided by political objectives or that the management of [SOEs] will never be motivated by 'nationalistic considerations' deviating from conventional wealth maximisation…[42]

Foreign government shareholders may wish to promote the government's strategic agenda.[43] At a minimum, large corporations can be influential and implicitly promote a state's interest and international agenda.[44]

---

[39] Jonathan Soble, 'Why the U.S. Fears a Chinese Bid for Westinghouse Electric' (*New York Times*, 7 April 2017) <https://www.nytimes.com/2017/04/07/business/us-china-toshiba-westinghouse.html?_r=0> ("Westinghouse is believed to have been targeted by Chinese spies. If a Chinese entity were to buy the company, China could obtain secrets without the cloak and dagger").

[40] European Commission, 'State-Owned Enterprises in the EU: Lessons Learnt and Ways Forward in a Post-Crisis Context' (July 2016) Institutional Paper 031, <https://ec.europa.eu/info/sites/info/files/file_import/ip031_en_2.pdf>, 1.

[41] Toby Sterling, Tim Hepher and Sudip Kar-Gupta, 'Air France-KLM shares slump on surprise Dutch Stake Buy' (*Reuters*, 27 February 2019) <https://www.reuters.com/article/us-netherlands-air-france-klm/air-france-klm-shares-slump-on-surprise-dutch-stak> e-buy-idUSKCN1QG0XM ("Shares in Air France-KLM fell sharply as the Dutch government amassed a 14 percent stake in the airline to counter French influence, in a surprise move highlighting tensions over the company's strategic direction.").

[42] Chaisse (n 7) 594–5.

[43] Larry Cata Backer, 'The Emerging Normative Structures of Transnational Law: Non-State Enterprises in Polycentric Asymmetric Global Orders' (2016) 31 (1) BYU J Pub. L 1 (corporations can be deployed to advance state goals).

[44] Rachel Brewster and Philip J. Stern, 'Introduction to the Proceedings of the seminar on Corporations and International Law' (2018) 28 Duke Journal Comparative and International Law 413, 415 ("[L]arge multinational corporations may have greater expertise in understanding international law, particularly as compared to developing states, and use this expertise as a means of resisting and reshaping global regulatory development.").

Promoting the Chinese government's goals (even economic objectives) amplifies the perceived customary "state ownership" concerns because China is ruled by one political party (i.e. one ultimate shareholder). The ruling party's domination of Chinese SOEs is of critical importance since the *raison d'être* of the Chinese SOE is the advancement of governmental objectives. Moreover, in most, if not all Chinese SOEs, party members are embedded in the management of the business, and this may be true of large strategic private businesses as well.[45]

Illustrating this concern was Canada's blocking of a Chinese investment based upon this factor.

> Intelligence agencies in both Canada and the USA have warned that *companies owned or partly owned by the Chinese government are not merely profit-seeking operations*; *they are also prone to passing on information or technology to Beijing* and *making business decisions that could conflict with Canadian interests but serve the agenda of the authoritarian Communist Party of China*.[46]

China also is concerned about potential national security risks associated with foreign investors, although ostensibly, such concerns should be limited since American companies are not controlled by governmental entities[47] (unless extraordinary circumstances require such intervention).[48] Yet revelations of United States governmental access via "partnerships" at large US companies clearly would be of national security concern to China's government.[49]

> Yahoo, Microsoft and Google deny they co-operate voluntarily with the intelligence agencies, and say they hand over data only after being forced to do so when served with warrants. The NSA told the Guardian that the companies' co-operation was "legally compelled".[50]

Recent revelations that the United States CIA and NSA intelligence agencies were the true owners of a private business named "Crypto" that monitored communications globally on both allies and adversaries on behalf of the United States and Germany would corroborate that both the US and China (and others) if empowered, will utilise

---

[45] *But see* infra Huawei where even an ostensibly private business may in fact be controlled by the Chinese government.

[46] Robert Fife and Steven Chase, 'Trudeau Cabinet Blocks Chinese Takeover of Aecon over National Security Concerns' (*The Globe and Mail*, 23 May 2018) <https://www.theglobeandmail.com/politics/article-ottawa-blocks-chinese-takeover-of-aecon-over-national-security/> (emphasis added).

[47] *See* Amanda Lee, 'China tightens 'national security' review for foreign investments, sparking fears of trade war retaliation' (*SCMP* 13 May 2019) <https://www.scmp.com/economy/global-economy/article/3010002/china-tightens-national-security-review-foreign-investments> (China tightening national security reviews similar to the intensified Western screening).

[48] US Department of the Treasury, 'Investment in American International Group (AIG)'. <https://www.treasury.gov/initiatives/financial-stability/TARP-Programs/aig/Pages/default.aspx>.

[49] *See* Ewen MacAskill and Dominic Rushe, 'Snowden document reveals key role of companies in NSA data collection' (*Guardian*, 1 November 2013) <https://www.theguardian.com/world/2013/nov/01/nsa-data-collection-tech-firms> (U.S. NSA obtaining information and intelligence through corporate allies and partners).

[50] ibid.

the private sector to promote governmental objectives and profit.[51] Crypto was a private company, and the CIA bought out the minority stake of the German BND in the early 1990s in a business transaction.[52] Not surprisingly, China and Russia were not customers of this ostensibly private business concerned over ties to Western nations.[53]

Thus, national-security-related concerns with respect to the coupling of state-corporate interests exist and will likely increase if trends continue. As corporations increasingly invest overseas, host States will need to monitor foreign sovereign investments more intensively and evaluate the national security risks.

2.1.1 Corporate Governance Concerns

Classic corporate governance concerns are also raised when States become shareholders, particularly as controllers.

> Russia and China are regularly singled out as countries with major strategic and political interests shown in their [sovereign wealth fund] SWF usage. These countries also have strategies to control critical assets, such as infrastructure, *and this raises issues of market integrity* as well as concerns over national security.[54]

Moreover, corporate governance concerns are not limited to China or Russia as sovereign shareholders. Governance concerns are applicable anytime sovereigns become shareholders, and it is widely understood that government-owned and controlled businesses are more prone to corruption, inefficiencies, and a lack of

[51] *See* Greg Miller, 'The intelligence coup of the century' (*Washington Post*, 11 Feb 2020) <https://www.washingtonpost.com/graphics/2020/world/national-security/cia-crypto-encryption-machines-espionage/> ("At times, including in the 1980s, Crypto accounted for roughly 40 percent of the diplomatic cables and other transmissions by foreign governments that cryptanalysts at the NSA decoded and mined for intelligence, according to the documents. All the while, Crypto generated millions of dollars in profits that the CIA and BND split and plowed into other operations.").

[52] ibid.

[53] ibid. ("The program had limits. America's main adversaries, including the Soviet Union and China, were never Crypto customers. Their well-founded suspicions of the company's ties to the West shielded them from exposure, although the CIA history suggests that U.S. spies learned a great deal by monitoring other countries' interactions with Moscow and Beijing.").

[54] Chaisse (n 7) 594–5 (emphasis added). *See also* State-Owned Enterprises in the EU (n 38) ("Competition may be distorted, should SOEs be able to enjoy a soft budget constraint or any other form of advantage over the rest of the market participants. At the same time if inefficient practices of SOEs are not sanctioned, they may result in rent extractions and higher prices for consumers.").

productivity.[55] Endemic corruption problems in Brazilian SOEs exemplify the risk of governmental involvement in private corporations.[56]

SOEs located in the EU are also known to be inefficient, distort the economic performance and create financial instability risks. The need to reform EU SOEs to address governance problems is widely agreed.

> Recent experience has shown that State-Owned Enterprises (SOEs) can be an important source of concerns in at least three areas: market functioning, public finances and financial stability.[57]

China has also acknowledged the crucial need to reform its inefficient SOEs.[58] Major reform of Chinese SOEs is always a possibility but absent a real decoupling of the government from large economic actors, the concern over Chinese SOEs governance remains. Indeed, the risk to financial stability is starkly exemplified by a 'mountain of bad loans' China's state-owned banks caused by China's state-capitalism corporate governance.[59] In addition, some nations' official disclosures may be subject to nuanced 'massaging' for either domestic or global consumption.

> China's banks may have a flood of bad loans waiting in the wings. Not that you'd know it from looking at *official levels* for 2018, which suggest the problem was broadly contained. The reality is that newly soured debt was coming through the front door as fast as banks could shovel it out the back.[60]

State-owned banks in China for example, may be subject to pressure to provide liquidity to important or State-linked businesses even if the bank would ordinarily not lend additional capital to that business. Losses might build when lenders are encouraged by governmental directives.

---

[55] *See* OECD, 'State-Owned Enterprises and Corruption: What Are the Risks and What Can Be Done?' (OECD Publishing 2018).
<https://www.oecd-ilibrary.org/executive-summary_5j8mrpgm7s8n.pdf?itemId=%2Fcontent%2Fcomponent%2F9789264303058-3-en&mimeType=pdf> (extensive corruption problems at SOEs globally).

[56] Lie Uema do Carmo, Maria Lima and Paulo Clarindo Goldschmidt, 'Corruption and Brazilian Crisis: the Case of Petrobras' in Maria Lima and José Ghirardi (eds) *Global Law: Legal Answers for Concrete Challenges* (Juruá Editora 2018) 109 (Petrobras as an exemplar of corruption issues in SOEs) at 122"[S]upplier firms and operators in the Petrobras drilling process 'coincidentally' have as shareholders some of the same construction and contractor enterprises.".

[57] State-Owned Enterprises in the EU (n 38) 5.

[58] Wendy Leutert, 'China's Reform of State-Owned Enterprises' (2016) 21 Asia Policy 83, 86. <https://www.brookings.edu/wp-content/uploads/2016/07/Wendy-Leutert-Challenges-ahead-in-Chinas-reform-ofstateowned-enterprises.pdf>.

[59] Christopher Balding, 'China's banks have a hidden wave of bad debt' (*Straits Times*, 18 March 2019) <https://www.straitstimes.com/business/banking/chinas-banks-have-a-hidden-wave-of-bad-debt> ("These issues may require backstopping by the People's Bank of China to succeed. The central bank last month swapped 1.5 billion yuan of its one-year bills for perpetual bonds, the first use of a new tool aimed at increasing market acceptance of the securities and encouraging commercial lenders to sell more.").

[60] ibid. (emphasis added).

> Chinese lenders are sitting on more than 2 trillion yuan ($295 billion) of soured loans after flooding the financial system with cheap credit for years to prop up economic growth. […] Bad loans may keep piling up as the government pushes banks to lend more to risky small and private businesses to reinvigorate the economy.[61]

Thus, allowing a foreign State to become shareholders in the financial services sector creates risk that lenders will be willing to sustain losses as a result of unwise lending practices encouraged by a foreign government.

> [E]arly last year, […] all lenders were forced to reclassify loans overdue for more than 90 days as non-performing. The move soon led to a record quarterly surge in soured debt and wiped-out capital at some small lenders.[62]

Accordingly, large foreign governmental investment creates not just national security concerns; classic controlling/dominant shareholder conflicts arise, which may intersect with national security. Even without national security concerns, bad governance in the financial services sector elevates risks of moral hazard and instability.

2.2 *The Dynamic of Government Investment in Stock Markets*

Sovereigns, with rare exceptions, have not been active capital market participants. Private entities were the driving force of investment and shareholding. However, this strict dichotomy has markedly changed, and governments are increasingly involved in private capital markets and economic activity.[63] Sovereign activity in capital markets and engaging in cross-border investment is a significant potential dynamic. Governmental share acquisition has critical implications. States are increasingly willing to project economic power in their own jurisdictions to protect domestic economic sectors and *project power abroad.* Moreover, governmental buyers are not ordinary institutional investors—sovereign share buyers wield tremendous financial resources.

---

[61] Bloomberg News, 'China to Impose Stricter Policy on Bad-Loan Recognition' (*Bloomberg*, 6 May 2019) <https://www.bloomberg.com/news/articles/2019-05-06/china-is-said-to-impose-stricter-policy-on-bad-loan-recognition>.

[62] ibid.

[63] The traditional sharp lines of distinction between states and corporations have become increasingly blurred; states are becoming investors in private-markets and in parallel, private corporations are now involved in historically public-functions. *See* Joel Slawotsky, 'The Global Corporation as International Law Actor' (2012) 52 Va J Int'l L Dig 79, 84; Ru Ding, 'Public Body or Not: Chinese State-Owned Enterprise' (2014) 48 Journal of World Trade 167 (SOEs may contain both public and private characteristics). *But see* Joel Slawotsky, 'Corporate Liability for Violating International Law Under the Alien Tort Statute: The Corporation Through the Lens of Globalization and Privatization,' (2013) (6) International Review of Law 1–24, 17 ("To be sure, there have been prior examples of corporations wielding state like power over private citizens. For example, the British East Indies Company […] was a state-controlled company that was enormously influential over India and wielded both private and public actor power.").

Sovereign share purchasing exercised extraterritorially trumps the traditional power of the sovereign, allowing the nation to punch far above its weight measured in traditional indicia of power.

> What distinguishes this sovereign activity from its mid-20th Century form is the willingness of states not only to limit their control of internal economies, but also to invest their financial wealth outside their national borders. *In this respect, states assume the very role of the private economic actors that they once feared so much. The 21st Century is witnessing a dramatic rise in the willingness of states to project economic power both at home and in host states through the same economic vehicles that threatened the states' power in the 20th Century….* Consequently, some states seem to have become, to some extent, pools of national economic wealth, *the power of which matches or exceeds their traditional sovereign power.*[64]

Projecting sovereign power overseas is a critical factor in the context of the United States-China hegemonic rivalry not merely for the two contestants but for other nations seeking to protect their own interests. Sovereign share ownership empowers States to exert substantial influence over core economic sectors. For example, sovereign wealth funds are major stock market investors, which depending upon the level of investment, can impact large swaths of economic activity. Foreign government-controlled SWFs are already buying shares in publicly traded companies.

> CIC invests in a wide range of financial products globally, including public equity, fixed income, alternative assets and cash and others. Public equity refers to equity investment in listed companies.[65]

State-owned banks may expand overseas by investing in other financial institutions.

> Chinese banks established themselves in the country or acquired shares of Brazilian or international banks already operating in Brazil.[66]

Foreign sovereign control over important businesses by electing directors and engaging in shareholder activism can substantially impact the host nation.[67]

> States and corporations are now capable of deploying forces in the field—sometimes states hire corporations that serve as mercenary armies that protect its own operations as well as those of the institutions of the state from sub-national and supra-state threats.[68]

[64] Larry Cata Backer, 'Sovereign Investing in Times of Crisis: Global Regulation of Sovereign Wealth Funds, State-Owned Enterprises, and the Chinese Experience' (2010) 19 Transnatl J Contemp Probs 3, 10–11 (emphasis added).

[65] China Investment Corporation (CIC), 'Investment Portfolio'. <http://www.china-inv.cn/chinainven/Investments/Portfolio_Management.shtml>.

[66] China-Brazil Business Council, 'Chinese Investments in Brazil' (2016) <https://www.cebc.org.br/sites/default/files/investimentoschinesesnobrasil2016_en.pdf>, 8.

[67] Larry Backer, Sovereign Investing and Markets-Based Transnational Rule of Law Building: The Norwegian Sovereign Wealth Fund in Global Markets (2013) 29 American University International Law Review 1, 92–94; Joel Slawotsky, 'Sovereign Wealth Funds as Emerging Superpowers: How U.S. Regulators Should Respond' (2009) 40 Geo J Int'l L 1239, 1255.

[68] Cata Backer (n 43) 50.

Share ownership of critical corporations by foreign governments enables foreign governments to potentially exercise influence and possible control over another state or, alternatively at a minimum, become embedded in vital economic sectors. Deployment of corporate power is a potential security threat in as much as domestic financial stability, technological prowess, and critical industries can be threatened. Therefore, corporate share ownership and national security are now inextricably linked.

Foreign governmental acquisition of shares on the open market is often 'quieter' than announcements of a joint venture, private investment or takeover offer. For example, China's Ant Financial endeavoured to purchase MoneyGram,[69] but CFIUS blocked the deal on national security concerns. But Ant Financial has purchased small stakes in global companies which severally may result in significant foreign influence in a sovereign's financial services sector.[70] In contrast to large deals or ventures which might invite scrutiny, acquiring shares below the disclosure trigger may constitute an attractive option for States.

Control and ownership of essential corporations can also be used defensively. Purchasing shares by a state can be a measure employed to thwart losing industrial and technological superiority or defend economic strength.[71] In one example, the Finish Government, through a sovereign investment fund, acquired a stake in Finnish national champion Nokia.[72]

Further demonstrating the allure of sovereign ownership, Germany has contemplated acquiring stakes in national industrial champions.

> Germany could take stakes in companies to prevent foreign takeovers in some key technology areas, Economy Minister Peter Altmaier said on Tuesday, presenting a new industrial strategy he said was necessary for the country's cohesion. The pivot to a more defensive industrial policy is driven by German concerns about foreign — particularly Chinese — companies acquiring German know-how and eroding the manufacturing base on which much of Germany's prosperity is built.[73]

---

[69] Greg Roumeliotis, 'U.S. blocks MoneyGram sale to China's Ant Financial on national security concerns' (*Reuters*, 2 January 2018) <https://www.reuters.com/article/us-moneygram-intl-m-a-ant-financial/u-s-blocks-moneygram-sale-to-chinas-ant-financial-on-national-security-concerns-idUSKBN1ER1R7> ("The MoneyGram deal is the latest in a string of Chinese acquisitions of U.S. companies that have failed to clear CFIUS.").

[70] John Jannarone, 'China's Ant Financial to Buy $100 million of Brazil's Stone Shares after IPO' (*Yahoo Finance*, 22 October 2018) <https://finance.yahoo.com/news/china-ant-financial-buy-100-203140637.html> ("Chinese fintech firm Ant Financial has agreed to buy $100 million of shares in Brazilian digital-payments company StoneCo (ticker: STNE), adding to a list of high-profile buyers that have taken interest in the IPO slated to price this week at a valuation of up to $6.2 billion.").

[71] Michelle Martin, Paul Carrel and Reinhard Becker, 'Germany ready to buy stakes in automakers, other companies to protect them' (*Autoblog*, 5 February 2019) <https://www.autoblog.com/2019/02/05/germany-buy-stakes-automakers-protection/> (state acquiring shares to prevent a foreign government from controlling corporation).

[72] Nick Fildes, 'Finnish government buys stake in Nokia' (13 March 2018) <https://www.ft.com/content/8a6741b8-26a9-11e8-b27e-cc62a39d57a0>.

[73] Martin and others (n 71).

Governments are incentivised to increase holdings of important corporations both as an 'offensive' tactic as well as a 'defensive' tool as the hegemonic contest becomes increasingly linked to economic and technological supremacy.

2.3 *The Dynamic of National Security as Technological and Economic Dominance*

The failed bid by Ant Financial, the discussion of the US buying a foreign corporation and other markers of economic nationalism are proximately caused by the transformative era of hegemonic rivalry between the current dominant global power,[74] the United States, and its ascendant challenger, China.[75] The contest has fundamentally shifted the strategic narrative and a more or less open political-economic-technological confrontation shapes US-China relations.[76]

The capital markets and corporations are now inextricably intertwined with the hegemonic rivalry. While historically, national security had little or no connection to corporate shares trading on capital markets and focused on classic military attack and conquest, pure military power is no longer the sole factor with respect to national security threats. Pure military capability has been trumped by the importance of emergent technologies such as AI, 5G, robots, space exploration as well as an economic power.[77] Dominance in emerging technologies is critical to both the US and China for two reasons: One, emerging technologies such as AI can be wielded *even in the non-military context*—and are potentially devastating. Such power includes an array of possibilities such as hacking elections, interfering with capital markets and degrading an adversary.[78] In addition, superiority in emerging technologies can greatly aid military efforts and include communications interference, overriding defence systems, robot combatants and hypersonic missiles.

---

[74] The United States has referred to itself as the indispensable nation. *See* Obama (n 23).

[75] China likely views its rise as a restoration of its historical status. *See* Slawotsky (n 20) ("China may in fact view the West's domination of the global economy and governance architecture as an aberration which is naturally correcting to the mean. From this historical perspective, the United States – a relatively "new power" was "in the right place at the right time" and is in fact the "revisionist" - an upstart nation of not even 250 years as compared to China's thousands of years of civilization. Pursuant to this narrative, the United States will need to embrace the developing Chinese order – a nation with thousands of years of history wielding an Empire long before the United States Constitution even existed.").

[76] *See* Corinne Ramey and Kate O'Keefe, 'China's Huawei Charged With Racketeering, Stealing Trade Secrets' (*Wall Street Journal*, 13 Feb 2019) <https://www.wsj.com/articles/chinas-huawei-charged-with-racketeering-11581618336> ("Huawei Technologies Co. and two of its U.S. subsidiaries were charged with racketeering conspiracy and conspiracy to steal trade secrets in a federal indictment unsealed Thursday, opening another front in the Trump administration's battle against the Chinese telecommunications firm.").

[77] Joel Slawotsky (n 19) 228–264.

[78] Defensive capabilities will become increasingly crucial as well.

Two, leadership in emergent technologies will result in new economic sectors enriching the States that can commercialise new technologies.[79] Central Bank Digital Currencies and the digitalisation of finance is another economically significant emerging technology.

National corporate champions, strategic industrial assets and critical economic sectors are intertwined with national security.

> Strategic' industries […] include armaments, power generation and distribution, oil and petrochemicals, telecommunications, coal, aerospace, and airfreight. 'Pillar' industries […] include[e] equipment manufacturing, automobiles, electronic communications, architecture, steel, nonferrous metals, chemicals, surveying and science and technology.[80]

Ownership of these businesses, via share acquisition, is available on capital markets. Moreover, dominating the economic high ground as well as innovating (or extracting) emerging technology can thus be achieved by share ownership which empowers the holder to exercise voting power and elect corporate directors.[81]

2.4 *Increased Sovereign Involvement in Capital Markets*

What might drive market-capitalism nations to consider increasing share acquisition? The potential to utilise corporate power to advance state goals is a strong motivator. Projecting sovereign power is critical, and foreign States may opt to gain a foothold in critical corporations and/or sectors, thus providing extraordinary leverage and potential influence in another economy. Share ownership of critical corporations by foreign governments enables foreign governments to exercise influence and possible control over another state as the potential exists that the corporation will be more

---

[79] Ross Chainey, 'The global economy will be $16 trillion bigger by 2030 thanks to AI' (*WEF*, 27 January 2017) <https://www.weforum.org/agenda/2017/06/the-global-economy-will-be-14-bigger-in-2030-because-of-ai/>.

[80] 2006 Guiding Opinion on Promoting the Adjustment of State-Owned Capital and the Reconstruction of State Owned Enterprises cited in Ru Ding, 'Public Body or Not: Chinese State-Owned Enterprise' (n 63) 187 ("Chinese policy is for sole ownership and absolute state control over strategic sectors such as weapons, energy, power generation and communications and aims to have majority state ownership of "pillar" industries such as steel, chemicals, technology, manufacturing, autos and equipment manufacturing.").

[81] *See* Andrew Verstein, 'The Corporate Governance of National Security' (2018) 95 Wash U L Rev 775, 786 ("Whether a sovereign wealth fund, a state-owned enterprise, or just a wealthy resident of another foreign jurisdiction, foreign investors may have geopolitical interests they hope to advance through their investments. Unauthorized disclosure of a secret plan or proprietary technology may directly benefit the investors' home nation….For foreign groups and nations, investment can be an effective supplement to other strategies of espionage. For example, "foreign contingents" are known to visit facilities and attempt "to gain access to and collect protected information that goes beyond that permitted and intended for sharing." This is clearly easier if foreigners own the enterprise and can claim commercial motives for a visit.").

loyal to the home nation of its shareholders.[82] Expanding a sovereign's economic, military and strategic influence globally may be a contributing, let alone proximate cause of financial investment.[83] A significant outcome of the hegemonic rivalry is the likely increase in state ownership of publicly traded shares. The acquisition of shares is an attractive option to sovereigns—the ability to both profit from and influence a sovereign simultaneously.

Financial services businesses such as banks are attractive targets for foreign adversaries.[84] As an alternative to cyber-attack, foreign States may opt to gain a foothold in the banking sector, thus providing extraordinary leverage and potential influence in another economy. State-owned foreign banks have already expanded overseas by investing in financial institutions located in other jurisdictions.[85]

By controlling financial services companies as shareholders, states can direct lending activities towards specific sectors and influence significant capital sums. Major shareholders are empowered to elect directors who, in turn, hire the officers. It would be sensible to presume that as implementation policy is set from the top, enforcement against nations which are large shareholders may be lacklustre at best and at worst stonewalled. Doing so would constitute a routine corporate governance conflict of interest. One need not only examine the repeated serial misconduct of significant financial institutions that have engaged repeatedly in sanctions evasion and money laundering to appreciate that doing so at the behest of important shareholders is not an unreasonable presumption.[86]

---

[82] Mariana Pargendler, 'The Grip of Nationalism on Corporate Law' (January 2019) ECGI Law Working Paper N° 437/2019 <https://ecgi.global/sites/default/files/working_papers/documents/finalpargendler1.pdf> at p 6 ("The central idea motivating the inquiry into corporate control is that the nationality of the individuals who control the firm determines their loyalty to the nation.").

[83] *See* Cata Backer (n 43) (corporations can be deployed to advance state goals).

[84] *See* Erica Borghard, 'Protecting Financial Institutions Against Cyber Threats: A National Security Issue' (24 September 2018) <https://carnegieendowment.org/2018/09/24/protecting-financial-institutions-against-cyber-threats-national-security-issue-pub-77324> ("Nation states, either directly or working through proxy actors, have already demonstrated a willingness and capability to target global financial services infrastructure. North Korean cyber attacks against the financial sector, for instance, are highly connected to the U.S. sanctions regime; Pyongyang has circumvented sanctions and funded its nuclear program through, among other things, a series of heists using SWIFT, a global messaging system, against the Bank of Bangladesh in 2016 and Taiwan's Far Eastern Bank in 2017. The Iranian DDoS attacks against the U.S. financial sector between 2011 and 2013 and the North Korean attack against South Korean banks in 2013 are other notable examples. Beyond criminal entities, the actors targeting financial institutions are highly capable states, such as Russia, China, Iran, and North Korea, or proxy actors enabled by these governments").

[85] Santiago Bustelo, Tulio Cariello, Gabriel Fragoso, 'Chinese Investments in Brazil 2016' (May 2017) <https://www.cebc.org.br/sites/default/files/investimentoschinesesnobrasil2016_en.pdf> at page 8 ("Chinese banks established themselves in the country or acquired shares of Brazilian or international banks already operating in Brazil").

[86] *See* Joel Slawotsky, 'Reining in Recidivist Financial Institutions' (2015) 40 Delaware Journal of Corporate Law 280, 316 ("The criminal behavior of the financial services industry is not limited to a specific area of misconduct. To the contrary, corrupt behavior is widespread and envelops a wide array of conduct. Iconic financial institutions involved in serious wrongdoing include: JPMorgan ($13 billion); BNP ($10 billion); Citigroup ($7 billion); HSBC ($1.9 billion); Standard Chartered

3 The State as Controlling Shareholder

As discussed above, the likelihood of increasing sovereign shareholding is likely. Sovereigns as major shareholders is a new dynamic, fundamentally different from private controllers.

3.1 *Sovereign Controlling Shareholders—Fundamentally Different*

For purely profit-seeking private investors, controlling shareholders are incentivised to prioritise their own economic interests over minority shareholders and other stakeholders. Controlling shareholders may engage in control-agency conflicts and reap *financially motivated* secondary awards.[87] The extraction of secondary benefits materially advantageous to the controlling owner includes close communications with senior executives and directors, visits to a corporation, and product demonstrations and conduits to extracting proprietary and possibly insider information.[88]

For private actors, both primary and secondary benefits are linked to monetary gain.[89] But controlling sovereign shareholders may be interested in prioritising the state's geopolitical strategic interests.[90] Control or influence over national champions and/or crucial economic sectors may potentially be government-controlled buyers' objective.[91] The ability to elect directors and direct corporate affairs, and to extract proprietary information can also be used to further a foreign government's insights and technically sensitive information, which can serve the state's interests.

To a degree, the governance problems induced by governmental control is similar regardless of whether the controlling shareholder is a private actor or a state: the leverage to extract benefits to the controlling shareholder at the expense of the

($667 million); ING ($619 million); Credit Suisse ($536 million); Lloyds TSB Group ($350 million); and Barclays ($298 million).").

87 The primary benefit is the ability to elect directors and direct corporate affairs.

88 *See* Zohar Goshen and Assaf Hamdani, 'Majority Control and Minority Protection' in Wolf-Georg Ringe and Jeffrey N Gordon (eds) *The Oxford Handbook of Corporate Law and Governance* (OUP 2018) 450 (numerous benefits accrue to important shareholders).

89 Corporate policy such as dividend issuance can be "controlled" by electing "friendly" directors who are beholden to the controlling shareholder. Secondarily, close communications with corporate insiders can provide an unmatched understanding of future corporate developments as well as serve as a pathway of imparting, informally, the desires of the controlling shareholder. Directors.

90 European Commission (n 40) 1 ("SOE objectives often go beyond mere profit maximization and include societal objectives.").

91 *See* Alan P Larson and David M Marchick, *Foreign Direct Investment and National Security: Getting the Balance Right* (Council on Foreign Relations Press 2006) 21 ("In certain cases, government ownership and control can create national security issues, particularly when the foreign company's decisions become an extension of the government's policy decisions rather than the company's commercial interests.").

minority shareholders and/or other stakeholders. Yet, governmental ownership is also fundamentally different from being controlled by private economic actors. Businesses will naturally seek to favour a powerful entity that wields the power to prosecute, grant waivers, lobby other nations and obtain subsidies. The unique governance problem applies to both domestic states as investors inasmuch as that corporation is subject to that government's rules. Regulations and judicial system. Moreover, it is also relevant because many corporations do business globally and may, in fact, be conducting (or wish to conduct) business in the jurisdiction of that foreign governmental shareholder.

Naturally, corporations will seek to curry favour with a sovereign whose power to regulate the business is a serious business risk and can either "make or break" the corporation. "[E]xtensive state intervention in the economy, weak formal institutions to check state power, and the pervasive influence of the Communist Party—encourages all firms to seek rents from the state by cultivating ties to party and government organs *and by aligning their business models with the policy objectives of the Party-state.*"[92]

Thus, there is a real risk that a corporation may seek an advantage by advancing the state's interest. However, endeavouring to win favour with a dominant state shareholder can be costly and take time away from running the business.[93] In addition, prioritising the state usually does not lead to superior financial results.[94] From a corporate governance perspective, lacklustre oversight and/or purposeful abuse of the corporate assets will adversely impact the economic vitality of the domestic economy.

Accordingly, obtaining economic leverage and technological prowess over an adversary through share accumulation and share voting provides a compelling, attractive alternative (with a potential benefit of profiting from such leverage/supremacy) to open military confrontation and the costs and risks of loss.

---

[92] Li-Wen Lin and Curtis J Milhaupt, 'Bonded to the State: A Network Perspective on China's Corporate Debt Market' (March 2017) 3(1) Journal of Financial Regulation 1–39 <https://doi.org/10.1093/jfr/fjw016> (emphasis added).

[93] Jeffrey Sparshott and Erik Holm, 'End of a Bailout: U.S. Sells Last AIG Shares' (Wall Street Journal, *11 Dec 2012*) <https://www.wsj.com/articles/SB10001424127887323339704578172960483282372> ("Following the government's selling the last of its AIG stake, "AIG's management "can now devote 100% of its attention to driving returns and improved financial performance.").

[94] Lin and Milhaupt (n 92) ("The state capitalist approach has fostered tremendous growth in the issuance of corporate debt instruments, but it is not obvious that the consequences are favourable for China. The very entities that are underserved by the banking system and equity markets—POEs and SMEs—have benefitted the least from development of the corporate bond market. Instead, benefits have disproportionately flowed to the state sector: in fact, the principal role of the corporate bond market has been to *supplement* the loan market as a privileged financing channel for SOEs. It has played this role by providing even lower cost financing to SOEs than is available in the loan market and by creating a means of circumventing bank lending limits to favoured SOE borrowers. Meanwhile, the rapidly developing shadow banking system (discussed below), illustrates the limitations of the corporate debt market as a financing channel for SMEs. In short, instead of developing a competitive bond market with diverse products serving multiple classes of credit-worthy issuers, the Chinese government's approach has been to prioritize SOE interests in a tightly managed market that is simultaneously massive in scale and seriously underdeveloped institutionally.").

Economic superiority is a critical factor in the contest between China and the US, and extensive holdings by state-owned shareholders of domestic concerns might result in adverse financial results or instability. As noted above, foreign government shareholders may be interested in prioritising the state's interests and objectives. Extraction of corporate knowledge and injecting those interests into a decision may impinge national security. The next sub-section describes the corporate governance issues relating to market stability, economic efficiencies and increased moral hazards.

3.2 Increasing Risks of Instability, Inefficiencies, Moral Hazards and Corruption

The importance of capital market stability cannot be under-appreciated; financial stability is a crucial component of domestic stability. Even assuming arguendo that foreign government shareholders will not leverage their holdings to transfer technology to their home governments, poor corporate governance by itself risks financial stability and constitutes a threat to economic stability.[95]

Illustrative is the fact that excessive state intervention can lead to moral hazards in the context of state support and guarantees—all risks to financial stability.[96] The "implicit guarantee" to protect state-owned corporate champions may simply lead to throwing good money after bad. The risk to financial stability is starkly exemplified by a "mountain of bad loans" China's state-owned banks proximately caused by China's state-capitalism corporate governance.[97] Critics have opined that official disclosures may be subject to nuanced "massaging" and that despite denials, a large debt problem looms for Chinese banks.[98] Estimates of the potentially hidden problem

---

[95] *See* Paul Tucker, 'Securities regulators have to be actively involved in preserving financial stability, Fundamental Challenges for Securities Regulation: A Political Economy Crisis in the Making?' in Pablo Gasós, Ernest Gnan and Morten Balling (eds), *Fundamental Challenges for Securities Regulation* ("With the financial sector evolving at an increasingly rapid pace, jurisdictions need to closely monitor and adapt their governance frameworks to ensure that they continue to facilitate an environment of trust, transparency and accountability. Such an environment contributes to financial stability and stronger economic growth") at page 13.

[96] *See* Jeromin Zettelmeyer, 'The Troubling Rise of Economic Nationalism in the European Union' (PIIE, 29 March 2019) <https://www.piie.com/blogs/realtime-economic-issues-watch/troubling-rise-economic-nationalism-european-union> ("It is also well established that political backing for national champions creates risks for consumers and taxpayers, through implicit guarantees and by raising the risk of regulatory capture.").

[97] *See* Christopher Balding, 'China's banks have a hidden wave of bad debt' (*Strait Times*, 18 March 2019) <https://www.straitstimes.com/business/banking/chinas-banks-have-a-hidden-wave-of-bad-debt> ("These issues may require backstopping by the People's Bank of China to succeed. The central bank last month swapped 1.5 billion yuan of its one-year bills for perpetual bonds, the first use of a new tool aimed at increasing market acceptance of the securities and encouraging commercial lenders to sell more.").

[98] ibid. ("China's banks may have a flood of bad loans waiting in the wings. Not that you'd know it from looking at *official levels* for 2018, which suggest the problem was broadly contained. The

are staggering—according to the PBOC, roughly 10% of China's banks may have problems.[99]

Even though China's regulators recognise the moral hazards of state capitalism,[100] the Chinese government is reluctant—for a good reason—to allow market forces to cause severe damage to financial stability.[101]

By no means is the example of Chinese banks a unique criticism of China—Western nations are also grappling with "moral-hazard" questions. For example, US financial institutions have been incentivised to repeatedly lend recklessly, engage in high-risk financial engineering and evade US laws.[102] As a result, even in the quintessential shareholder-model and private market jurisdiction—the United States—the state stepped in to rescue large corporations at risk of collapse a decade ago to prevent a contagion of financial instability caused by the sub-prime crisis. Similar to China's interests in avoiding a financial collapse, Western government shareholders are incentivised to influence financial institutions to make business decisions that may present a substantial risk to financial stability.

Government shareholdings of financial services corporations may lead to increased moral risk. The moral hazards of misconduct are also exemplified by recidivist American financial institutions which have systemically engaged in criminal misconduct with little concern for punishment. Both the United States and other

---

reality is that newly soured debt was coming through the front door as fast as banks could shovel it out the back.") (emphasis added).

[99] Washington Post, 'No More Bailouts? China's New Approach to Bank Stress' (9 Aug 2019) <https://www.washingtonpost.com/business/no-more-bailouts-chinas-new-approach-to-bank-stress/2019/08/09/08170e20-ba5d-11e9-8e83-4e6687e99814_story.html> ("China's central bank, concluding its *first review into industry risks, said in November that about one in 10 of the nation's 4,000 banks received a "fail" rating....* Jason Bedford, a UBS Group AG analyst who had flagged the problems at Baoshang and Jinzhou, says China's smaller banks face a potential capital shortfall of 2.4 trillion yuan ($340 billion). He estimates the size of assets "in distress" held by a broader universe of Chinese lenders at 9.2 trillion yuan – about 4% of the commercial banking system *and nearly 10% of gross domestic product.*") (emphasis added).

[100] *See* Shuli Ren,' Why China Has Chickened Out of Another Bank Seizure' (Bloomberg, 29 July 2019) <https://Www.Bloomberg.Com/Opinion/Articles/2019-07-29/Why-China-Has-Chickened-Out-Of-Another-Bank-Rescue> ("The PBOC tried to do the right thing with the Baoshang takeover. But now, fearful of market jitters, the central bank is chickening out. Instead, China has resorted to the old trick of a national team rescue, which does little to break the implicit guarantee of state support. ...To calm things down, the central bank not only injected massive amounts of cash into the banking system but also walked back its initial tough stance. A central bank-affiliated newspaper reported that 99.98% of Baoshang's corporate creditors were being fully repaid.").

[101] See Nathaniel Taplin, Another Month, Another Chinese Bank Bailout, (*Wall Street Journal*, 26 July 2019) <https://www.wsj.com/articles/another-month-another-chinese-bank-bailout-11564142953> ("Beijing dislikes bailing out state companies—particularly banks—but can't seem to kick the habit.").

[102] *See* Slawotsky (n 86) (numerous examples of repeated financial institutional misconduct).

Western nations have not vigorously prosecuted "TBTF"[103] or "TBTJ"[104] financial institutions despite these institutions engaging serially in corrupt conduct.[105]

Furthermore, corruption at government-owned and controlled entities is known to lead to inefficiencies and a lack of productivity. Government-owned corporations are known to be inefficient, distort the economic performance and create financial instability risks.

Recent experience has shown that State-Owned Enterprises (SOEs) can be an essential source of concerns in at least three areas: market functioning, public finances and financial stability.[106] Generally, corruption at government-owned and controlled entities leads to inefficiencies, lack of productivity and endemic corruption problems. For example, persistent corruption issues in EU[107] and Brazilian SOEs highlight the risk of governmental involvement in private corporations.[108] There is widespread agreement that SOEs must be reformed to address general governance problems, market inefficiencies and risks to economic stability.[109]

Thus, the potential problems when the state is a large investor is not just national security; there are traditional corporate governance conflicts of interest as in any corporation with a dominant or controlling shareholder.

4 Updating Existing Securities Regulation

In light of the hegemonic rivalry and burgeoning national security concerns, updating regulations may develop into an essential potential regulatory measure

[103] *See* Eric Dash, 'If It's Too Big to Fail, Is It Too Big to Exist?' (*New York Times*, 20 June 2009) <https://www.nytimes.com/2009/06/21/weekinreview/21dash.html?partner=rss&emc=rss> (discussing the background of the phrase).

[104] *See* Ted Kaufman, 'Why DOJ Deemed Bank Execs To Big to Jail' (*Forbes*, 29 July 2013) <https://www.forbes.com/sites/tedkaufman/2013/07/29/why-doj-deemed-bank-execs-too-big-to-jail/#22ba3a9a3703> ("[T]he argument seems to be that, if the president of a major bank were to be indicted for criminal behavior, his prosecution would endanger the bank itself and the jobs of all of its employees.").

[105] *See* Joel Slawotsky, Reining in Recidivist Financial Institutions, 40 Delaware Journal of Corporate Law 280 (2015) (discussing reasons such as the revolving door, little risk of prison and profits dwarfing the fines imposed as encouraging repeated misconduct).

[106] European Commission (n 40) 5.

[107] *See* OECD (n 55) (extensive corruption problems at SOEs globally).

[108] *See* Maria Lima and Jose Garcez Ghirardi (eds), *Global Law: Legal Answers for Concrete Challenges* (Jurua 2018) (Petrobras as an exemplar of corruption issues in SOEs) at 122 "[S]upplier firms and operators in the Petrobras drilling process 'coincidentally' have as shareholders some of the same construction and contractor enterprises.").

[109] *See* Leutert (n 58). *See also* OECD (n 55) (urgent reform of SOEs needed).

to thwart losing industrial and technological superiority.[110] As governments increasingly recognise the importance of technological, industrial and financial services sectors, governments will probably seek more corporate investments, which may manifest in protectionist self-buying of corporate shares of economic champions as well as strategic investing in foreign stock markets. Interestingly, the present extent of foreign government ownership of publicly traded shares may be vastly under-estimated—many shareholdings might be unknown and/or undisclosed.

> Importantly, the available figures underestimate the true size and scope of China's ambitions in Europe…*[N]ot included: greenfield developments or stock-market operations totaling at least $40 billion.*[111]

Updating existing securities laws is an important tool to defend core domestic interests. Given the importance of share ownership to national security, the likelihood is that governments will need to re-examine and update regulatory mechanisms focusing on foreign government purchases in domestic stock markets. One method of potentially monitoring foreign governmental ownership is the regulatory disclosure process. For example, in numerous jurisdictions, a party is obligated to report ownership upon acquiring a triggering percentage—often 5%—of the shares of a public company.[112]

The problem of multiple parties acquiring less than a trigger percentage, but the joint holding is in excess of filing would, for example, under US law be considered jointly if the parties holding the shares constitute "a group". Creative lawyering and avoiding the strictures of "a group" is a hallmark of hedge funds and other activist investors in a stratagem known as wolf-pack investing.[113] The successful tactic occurs when multiple buyers do not conspire but simply buy shares during the same general time frame in order to extract benefits for themselves. Foreign governmental investors might engage in this conduct as well. To avoid disclosure and the ensuing scrutiny, foreign governmental entities could potentially buy small stakes under the trigger percentage in companies, essentially flying under the radar. Modest share purchases among several like-minded foreign governmental entities such as SOEs/SWFs could, when combined, present an intriguing method of acquiring influence/control over a publicly traded company. Wolf-pack investing has been critiqued as short-term profit by investors seeking at the expense of the long-term profitability of the corporation

---

[110] Sterling, Hepher and Kar-Gupta (n 41) ("Shares in Air France-KLM fell sharply as the Dutch government amassed a 14 percent stake in the airline to counter French influence, in a surprise move highlighting tensions over the company's strategic direction.").

[111] Andre Tartar, Mira Rojanasakul and Jeremy Scott Diamond, 'How China Is Buying Its Way Into Europe' (*Bloomberg*, 23 April 2018) <https://www.bloomberg.com/graphics/2018-china-business-in-europe/> 8 (emphasis added).

[112] *See* 15 U.S.C. § 78 m(d) (requiring public disclosure upon ownership of 5% of a public company's shares); OECD, 'Disclosure of Beneficial Ownership and Control in Listed Companies in Asia' (OECD Publishing 2016) <https://www.oecd.org/daf/ca/Disclosure-Beneficial-Ownership.pdf> (China trigger 5%).

[113] Joel Slawotsky, 'Hedge Fund Activism in an Age of Global Collaboration and Financial Innovation: The Need for a Regulatory Update of United States Disclosure Rules' (2015) 35 Rev. Banking Fin L. 275, 279 (describing hedge fund activism via wolf-pack investing).

but could be employed by foreign State investors for strategic motivations as well (i.e. diminishing the relative strength of a rival's industrial or technological sector). While wolf-pack investing is permissible under existing securities regulation, the injection of national security is a factor that may alter the regulation/legality of multiple government investors so acting.[114] Securities regulators will need to address this potential wolf-pack stratagem potentially employed by foreign governments.

4.1 Defining Foreign Governmental Investors

A crucial preliminary issue is defining a State buyer. Under what circumstances should a foreign government-linked entity be conceptualised as a governmental buyer? The question is further complicated given jurisdictions' fundamental differences. As an example, in China, "the majority share of the state is not a determinative factor as to the 'meaningful control' of the government and much less to the requirement of 'governmental authority.'"[115] Some Chinese entities might very well be considered "private" and, in good faith, believe that for purposes of US reporting requirements, the trigger percentage is the same as for similar private buyers—5%. There may also be a lack of transparency in home nations, thus obscuring the actual structure, ownership and ultimate parent of an entity. Alternatively, deliberate obfuscation might be a tactic to avoid disclosure requirements. Significantly, ostensibly private corporations may, in fact, be "fully private" yet under the ultimate influence/direction of a foreign government.

Illustrative of the problematic nature of understanding the ownership structure of foreign corporations is Huawei whose shares are not publicly traded and therefore is ostensibly a private market actor. Huawei states:

> *Huawei is an independent private company wholly owned by its employees.* Huawei's capital structure and shareholder composition have been filed with China's assets supervision and administration authorities and comply with applicable Chinese laws and regulations.
>
> *The Chinese government has no ownership stake in or control of the company.* Huawei conducts normal business activities in more than 170 countries and regions. All of our decisions are based on business needs. Our operations and management comply with all applicable laws and regulations as well as the company's regulations and processes.[116]

Yet Huawei's connections to the Chinese Government are not contestable.[117] Whether the relationship constitutes governmental control is unknown at the time

[114] Shareholder activism has strong arguments in its favor as well but even proponents will admit risks exist. Id. Such risks are magnified in the context of national security.

[115] Ru Ding (n 63) 179.

[116] <https://www.huawei.eu/does-huawei-receive-support-chinese-government> (emphasis added).

[117] Raymond Zhong, 'Who Owns Huawei? The Company Tried to Explain. It Got Complicated.' (*New York Times*, 25 April 2019) <https://www.nytimes.com/2019/04/25/technology/who-owns-huawei.html>.

of this writing. Huawei's corporate shares are evidently 100% owned by a holding company. The holding company is 99% owned by a trade union committee which some allege is a government organ.

> Given the public nature of trade unions in China, if the ownership stake of the trade union committee is genuine, and if the trade union and its committee function as trade unions generally function in China, then Huawei may be deemed effectively state-owned.[118]

Thus, defining foreign government control over a share buyer may be substantially more difficult than examining whether a foreign government owns 51% or more of the shares of the buyer or directly exercises control in a recognisable fashion. A narrow set of specific benchmarks to identify whether a foreign government is the buyer might prove ineffective. Regulators will need to update reporting requirements with the above-referenced complexities in mind.

4.2 Suggested Modifications for Updated Regulation

Updating regulations, of course, leads to questions such as to what extent sovereigns should restrict or limit foreign governmental investment in domestic stock markets and which lower disclosure threshold can effectively identify such investments. In addition, enhancing reporting triggers needs to be balanced so as to avoid protectionism and unduly blocking legitimate foreign investment. While addressing all of the issues and the balancing needed is beyond the scope and word limit of this chapter, several suggestions will now be articulated with respect to core updating issues. While attracting investors is vital to economic health, it would constitute naïve policy to underestimate the potentially disastrous damage of allowing adversaries to influence corporate decision-making and access to strategic knowledge.

(1) In determining whether a buyer is a foreign government entity, control must be conceptualised broadly to encompass the ability to direct the buyer either through voting or via another means. To direct a company is being empowered to exert director/officer control over lawful business decisions and business strategy implementation or to override such policy and strategy by other means. If, for example, the entity's directors or officers are elected by private shareholders but need to be 'approved' by a governmental entity or organ, governmental control may exist even without significant shareholdings.

> Foreign government-owned or controlled or linked entities should be defined broadly and include any entity with *any* of the following attributes: the extent of direct or indirect sovereign share ownership; veto power over transactions; ability to appoint, approve or vote for directors, executives, managers of the entity; indicia proving the reasonable likelihood *of State influence to direct the entity.*

[118] Christopher Balding and Donald C. Clarke, Who Owns Huawei? (April 17, 2019) <https://papers.ssrn.com/sol3/papers.cfm?abstract_id=3372669>.

(2) Regulators should lower triggering reporting percentages for foreign government-owned or controlled, or linked entities buyers. Such entities should report share purchases of 1% or more of any domestic publicly traded company listed on any capital market. The disclosure should be made immediately or within one day of acquisition. The stricter reporting threshold will alert regulators and policy-makers, including national security monitors a foreign State has invested in the business. The disclosure should at a minimum:

- identify the name, address and citizenship, place of organisation of the buyer and relationship to the foreign State as well as any other governmental ties,
- the total number of shares of the securities beneficially owned and total beneficial ownership percentage,
- the source of funding, amount of funds provided or any other consideration financial or otherwise used to purchase the shares, disclosure of any other party with an interest in the transaction governmental or private, whether voting rights are held solely by the reporting persons or shared with any other party and identify same.

Further disclosure should be mandatory if any material change ensues to the filed report, including additional purchases of 0.5% of the company's shares.

(3) States should establish a list of industries or economic sectors or specific companies for which foreign government ownership is indeed capped at a specific percentage or alternatively completely banned from investing in. Nations may also consider limiting overall foreign ownership in particular sectors to reduce national security risks. Such limitations might be beneficial to avoid multiple States acting as a wolf-pack.

(4) A (sometimes) rebuttable presumption should exist that multiple foreign sovereign buyers from the same nation are acting as a group. This is sensible inasmuch as the ultimate parent is the same foreign government. A question arises as to whether the presumption should be rebuttable and, if so, under what circumstances. For particularly sensitive core interest sectors, a prudent approach might be to have the presumption irrefutable. At the same time, other sectors may be "open" to having different governmental agency shareholders from the same nation prove that the buyers are independent of each other and do not share the same objectives. A related question arises with respect to multiple States and the prospect that these owners might potentially be informally acting as a group. Again, limiting overall foreign State ownership might be beneficial in avoiding this problem

(5) Regulators should consider a rule compelling foreign State-linked entities who own shares to formally disclose all public-shareholdings on a quarterly basis even if the triggering percentages are less than 1%. Such disclosure would serve to alert regulators and national security agencies of patterns of ownership in particular companies and/or economic sectors.

5 Conclusion

Large corporations are powerful global actors embedded in all facets of critical infrastructure and are at the vanguard of emerging technologies and revolutionary financial services destined to revolutionise finance. Extensive shareholdings can empower shareholders to leverage their share ownership to influence and/or control business decisions. While private shareowners are motivated by profit, State owners (and controlling owners in particular) are empowered to influence the decision-making to further the owner's objectives—which could be a foreign sovereign.[119] Therefore, the linkage between national security and global capital markets is manifestly clear. Indeed vanquishing an adversary, once understood as a traditional military-based attack involving human soldiers, fighter jets and tanks, is now achievable through dominating economic sectors and/or extracting strategic information from portfolio companies. Therefore, securities regulation should be updated, and heightened reporting is required for State-linked buyers. To defend national security, foreign governmental buyers should be strictly monitored to ensure core economic sectors and emergent technology are protected. Legitimate foreign States should not object to heightened disclosure and reporting requirements.

Joel Slawotsky Former Law Clerk to the Hon. Charles H. Tenney, U.S.D.J., S.D.N.Y. and AV-rated litigator at Dentons.

[119] Alan P. Larson and David M. Marchick, *Foreign Direct Investment and National Security: Getting the Balance Right* (Council on Foreign Relations Press 2006) 21 ("In certain cases, government ownership and control can create national security issues, particularly when the foreign company's decisions become an extension of the government's policy decisions rather than the company's commercial interests.").

EU Merger Control and China's State-Owned Enterprises: Is Ownership Really Separate from Control?

Alessandro Spano

1 Introduction—China's Socialist Market Economy: A *Sui Generis* System of Governance

The Fourteenth Committee of the Chinese Communist Party represented a watershed in China's economic reform process and opening up to the outside world. Following the incontestable success of Deng Xiaoping's policies, under Jiang Zemin's leadership, the theory of "socialism with Chinese characteristics' became the cornerstone of the revised Party Constitution".[1] The foundation of this political and economic programme was the establishment of the "socialist market economy" (*shehui zhuyi shichang jingji*), a *sui generis* system of governance and economic model where adherence to the competitive process would coexist, with no apparent contradiction, with "adherence to public ownership, with the state economy playing the leading role in the national economy; and adherence to socialist direction, especially to state macro-control over the economy".[2] Hence, China's traditional approach, in which the market was merely supplementary to central planning, was progressively abandoned. Market mechanisms started to be recognised as an alternative and possibly much better tool to address the country's future economic challenges.[3] Subsequently, China's accession to the World Trade Organisation (WTO) in 2001 represented another milestone in Chinese history, particularly for accelerating the implementation of liberation policies (*da gaige kaifang*) and integrating the Chinese

[1] Tony Saich, The Fourteenth Party Congress: A Programme for Authoritarian Rule*.

[2] Jijian Yang, *Market Power in China: Manifestations, Effects and Legislation,* Review of Industrial Organization, Vol. 21, (2002) 167–183, at 168.

[3] Kjeld Erik Brødsgaard and Koen Rutten, 'The Emergence and Development of the Socialist Market Economy (1992–2003)' in Kjeld Erik Brødsgaard and Koen Rutten, *From Accelerated Accumulation to Socialist Market Economy in China* (China Studies vol 38, Brill 2017) 94–127.

A. Spano (✉)
Faculty of Laws, University College London (UCL), London, England
e-mail: a.spano@ucl.ac.uk

J. Chaisse et al. (eds.), *Regulation of State-Controlled Enterprises*, International Law and the Global South, https://doi.org/10.1007/978-981-19-1368-6_8

economy into the globalisation process. Since then, China's economic landscape has underpinned epochal changes. While commentators may debate the success of some of the country's economic reforms, China today indisputably possesses a (more) market-oriented economy.

However, industrial policies have continued to play a prominent role also under China's socialist market economy. For instance, over the years, the Chinese government has implemented a series of policies to stimulate the development of national companies and, in particular, state-owned enterprises with the goal, *inter alia*, of establishing national champions to compete globally. Indeed, the "going out policy" is the most famous example. Launched in 1999, the proposed goal of this policy has been to provide financial support to Chinese SOEs to promote their growth and their possibility to conduct investment activities abroad. Additionally, a national normative framework aimed to shield SOEs from the competition of foreign investors in the domestic market has helped Chinese SOEs enhance their international competitiveness and, ultimately, that of the Chinese economy as a whole.[4] Hence, although China's attitude towards the principles of a market economy has undergone a definite reversal, steps in this direction have been instrumental in achieving the economic objectives pursued by the Chinese government at a particular time. Within this context, also the investment activities of Chinese SOEs do not enjoy an entirely autonomous status. These have been closely connected to those governmental policies strategic for developing China's socialist market economy. Hence, under China's system of governance, the investment activities of Chinese SOEs assume a symbolic role as they reflect the close correlation between China's political and economic processes. In conclusion, from this point of view, SOEs have actively contributed to the advancement of China's socialist market economy.

2 China's State-Owned Enterprises and the EU Merger Control Regime

These preliminary considerations may help shed some light on the concerns that have gradually started to emerge in the EU Member States in relation to the possible implications of the investment activities of Chinese SOEs in their national economies. In recent years, the investment activities of Chinese SOEs in the EU have been subject to greater scrutiny from the Member States to assess their effect not only on market competition but also on social stability and national security. One of the envisaged risks is that domestic technology, resources, and jobs may move from Europe to

[4] See for discussion, *inter alia*, Hongying Wang, *A deeper look at China's "going out" policy*, CIGI Commentary, (March 2016); Yongjin Zhang, *China Goes Global*, Foreign Policy Centre – Working Paper, (2005), 1–32; Peter Nolan, *China and the Global Economy: National Champions, Industrial Policy and the Big Business Revolution*, Palgrave Macmillan, (2001).

China and, consequently, undermine the development of national companies and local communities.[5]

The debate has been sparked in two main areas: investment arbitration and merger regulation. In the area of investment arbitration, the focus has been on using ISDS mechanisms within the context of the EU-China Bilateral Comprehensive Agreement on Investment (CAI).[6]

In the area of merger regulation, the discussion focused on two recent decisions of the European Commission regarding the investment activities of China's SOEs in the EU. On 27 May 2015, the European Commission received notification of a proposed concentration under Article 4 of the Merger Regulation by which the China National Tyre & Rubber Co. Ltd (CNRC, China), wholly owned by the China National Chemical Corporation ("ChemChina"), would acquire control of the whole of Pirelli & C S.p.A. (Pirelli, Italy).

The European Commission noted that to assess the impact on competition of the proposed operation, it was necessary to consider whether ChemChina was an independent economic unit or part of a more comprehensive economic structure, including all the Chinese SOEs. The European Commission had previously assessed several transactions involving SOEs.[7] When assessing the degree of economic independence of SOEs, factors once taken into consideration included "the degree of interlocking directorships or the existence of adequate safeguards ensuring that commercially sensitive information is not shared between such undertakings".[8] When assessing the chain of control of SOEs, the European Commission noted that the first step consisted of identifying whether or not the SOEs have independent decision-making power and, in the case of CNRC/Pirelli, the decision-making power could belong either to ChemChina itself or to the Chinese government through the Central SASAC.[9]

---

[5] Wang (n 4) 4.

[6] At the 16th EU-China Summit held on 21 November 2013, the launch of negotiations of a comprehensive EU-China Investment Agreement was announced. The first round of negotiations was held in Beijing on 21–23 January 2014. On 30 December 2020, the EU and China concluded in principle the negotiations for the CAI. The agreement aims at the progressive liberalisation of investment and the elimination of restrictions for investors in both the EU and China. For discussion, see European Commission (2013). For discussion on the issue of investment arbitration within the context of the EU-China CAI, *see* Alessandro Spano, "The EU-China Bilateral Comprehensive Agreement on Investment (CAI) and the EU Principle of Effective Judicial Protection: Challenges Ahead" (October 2020); Alessandro Spano, "The status of state-owned enterprises in ISDS from a European perspective" in Yuwen Li, Tong Qi, Cheng Bian (eds), *China, the EU and International Investment Law Reforming Investor-State Dispute Settlement* (Taylor & Francis 2019).

[7] *See*, for example, M.5508 Soffin/Hypo Real Estate; M.5861 Republic of Austria / HYPO GROUP ALPE ADRIA; M.931 Nestle/IVO.

[8] Para. 9 of the Decision. See also Case COMP/M.6082 China National Bluestar-Elkem, 31 March 2011.

[9] Para. 10 of the Decision.

In the end, however, the European Commission failed to address the matter. Under the EU Merger Regulation, the initial step is to assess whether the European Commission has jurisdiction to review a proposed transaction. And, this depends, among other factors, on the relevant turnover in the EU of each party to a proposed operation.

If the parties to a proposed transaction possess a combined global turnover of over EUR 5 billion, each party must have over EUR250 million turnover in the EU to trigger a filing procedure. Alternatively, in case the combined global turnover of the parties is at least EUR2,5 billion, each party must then possess at least EUR100 million turnover in the EU (and the parties must have a combined turnover of over EUR100 million in at least three Member States (where they also individually possess a turnover over EUR25 million).[10]

In CNRC/Pirelli., it was found that the Chinese SOE possessed a sufficient turnover in the EU by itself. Hence, in reviewing the operation, the EU Commission noted in this decision that: "For the purposes of establishing jurisdiction, there is no need to conclude on whether the turnover of other companies owned by the Chinese State and under the supervision of the Central SASAC should be taken into account, since the turnover thresholds are met based on ChemChina's and Pirelli's turnovers alone".[11] Therefore, there was no need for the Commission to provide a clear decision on the matter of the autonomy of the decision-making power of the Chinese SOEs.[12]

However, the matter re-emerged in the EDF/ CGN/ NNB Group of companies' case one year later. In this case, the CGN did not possess sufficient turnover in the EU by itself. Thus, the European Commission had to consider whether the SOE in question enjoyed adequate autonomy from the Chinese State.

The Commission's Jurisdictional Notice on merger control[13] specifies that Article 5(4) of the Merger Regulation should be read in conjunction with recital 22 of the Regulation declaring that, in order to avoid discrimination between the public and private sectors, "in the public sector, calculation of the turnover of an undertaking concerned in a concentration needs, therefore, to take account of undertakings making up an economic unit with an independent power of decision, irrespective of how their capital is held or of the rules of administrative supervision applicable to them".[14]

Thus, Member States (or other public bodies) are not "undertakings" for the purposes of calculating aggregate turnover simply because they possess interests in other undertakings satisfying the conditions listed in Article 5(4). Instead, calculating the turnover of state-owned undertakings should be based on assessing whether these

---

[10] *See* Article 1(2) of the EU Merger Regulation.

[11] Para 7.

[12] On 2 July 2015, the European Commission announced that it decided under Article 6(1)(b) of the EU Merger Regulation to approve the acquisition of Pirelli by CNRC.

[13] Commission Consolidated Jurisdictional Notice under Council Regulation (EC) No 139/2004 on the control of concentrations between undertakings (2008/C 95/01).

[14] Para 192 of the Notice. On this point, see also Case IV/M.216 — CEA Industrie/France Telecom/Finmeccanica/SGS-Thomson, of 22 February 1993.

undertakings belong to the same economic unit, having the same independent power of decision.[15]

It follows that where an SOE is not subject to any coordination with other SOEs, it should be considered independent of calculating its turnover. The turnover of other SOEs should be ignored. However, several SOEs fall under the same independent centre of commercial decision-making. If so, then their turnover should be viewed as part of the group of the undertaking concerned for the purposes of turnover calculation under the Merger Regulation. The parties submitted to the Commission that the CGN was independent of Central SASAC. The proposed operation did not require notification under the Merger Regulation as CGN's turnover in the EEA did not meet the required threshold.[16]

In referring to Article 6 of the Law of the People's Republic of China on the State-Owned Assets of Enterprises of 2008 (PRC law on SOEs), they noted that the Chinese government would perform the contributor's function "based on the principles of separation of government bodies and enterprises, separation of the administrative functions of public affairs and the functions of the state-owned assets contributor, and non-intervention in the legitimate and independent business operations of enterprises".[17]

Additionally, they submitted that Central SASAC would not be able to influence the company's strategic business conduct and/or to remove the company's directors unless they acted improperly or in violation of the laws and/or CGN Articles.[18] Finally, it was submitted that CGN would not have any interlocking directorships with Central SASAC. An internal confidentiality policy would be in place to preclude any exchange of confidential information with any other SOE.[19]

The European Commission, however, disagreed with the parties' view. The Commission first noted that the wording of Article 6 of PRC law on SOEs was extremely broad in relation to the general principle of separation of government bodies and enterprises and non-intervention in business operations.[20] Furthermore, it noted that several provisions in the PRC law on SOEs and the Interim Measures for the Supervision and Administration of the Investments by Central Enterprises released in May 2003 (Interim Measures on Supervision) supported the fact that Central SASAC had an actual influence on CGN's major decision-making and, thus, that the company was not autonomous from the state authorities in deciding matters such as strategy, business plan or budget.[21]

In its analysis, the Commission found that Central SASAC could interfere with CGN's strategic investment decisions and intervene either to force or facilitate coordination, if not between CGN and any Chinese SOEs, at least concerning SOEs

[15] Para 193 of the Notice.

[16] Para 33 of the Decision.

[17] Para 34.

[18] Para 35.

[19] Para 36.

[20] Para 37.

[21] Para 38.

operating in the energy sector. Thus, the Commission concluded that since CGN and other Chinese SOEs in the relevant industry did not enjoy sufficient independent decisional power from Central SASAC, it decided to aggregate the turnover of all companies operating in the energy industry that this state agency controlled.[22]

However, it is worth noting that the Commission's decision did not fully address whether Local SASACs (such as Local Guangdong SASAC) also had to be considered as forming a had to be considered as constituting a single entity with the CGN. On this point, the Commission concluded that there was no need to address the matter as the turnovers of Chinese SOEs controlled by Central SASAC already met the thresholds of the Merger Regulation.[23]

3 Principles of Legislative Drafting in China

The remarks of the European Commission on the broad wording of Article 6 of PRC law on SOEs should not come as a surprise to those familiar with the principles of legislative drafting in China. Most Chinese laws are drafted in general or abstract form.[24] This situation reflects a specific vision about the role of law within the Chinese legal system. One of the main features of legislative drafting in China is that laws should be both "general" (*yuanzexing*) and "flexible" (*linghuoxing).*[25] These are intrinsic characteristics of Chinese lawmaking and have been referred to as the policy of "preferring the coarse to the fine" (*yicu bu yixi*).[26]

The underlying philosophy behind this approach is that in this manner, the law can be more easily implemented and, when necessary, better adapted to local circumstances.[27] As Perry Keller noted: "The principle of generality and flexibility captures the essential concept of Chinese lawmaking that legislation must reflect the unitary nature of the state while satisfying the needs of regional diversity".[28] Furthermore, "It also accords the principles of legislative stability (*wendingxing*), as it permits the effective amendment of the law through changes in interpretation rather than through alterations of the actual text".[29]

Considering that, in China, the policy of the CCP is the foundation of law and contains most of its guiding principles, Chinese legislation often formalises the

---

[22] Para 49.

[23] Para 50.

[24] For a discussion on law drafting in China, *see* Perry Keller, 'Legislation in the People's Republic of China' (1988–1989) 23 University of British Columbia Law Review 653–688.

[25] Perry Keller, 'Sources of Order in Chinese Law,' (1994) 42 American Journal of Comparative Law 711–759, 750. It was noted that the origin of this vision dates back to Chairman Mao who praised the Chinese Constitution of 1954 for its generality and flexibility. *See* ibid.

[26] ibid.

[27] ibid.

[28] ibid 751.

[29] ibid.

Party's approach in a more specific manner as it is considered as a complementary tool to exert economic and social control of China's socialist market economy. For instance, the resemblance between the wording of legislative provisions and the content of policy statements of CCP's leaders supports the view of the instrumental nature of Chinese legislation. Thus, to better understand the role of economic laws in China, it is necessary to read them through the lens of existing governmental policies.

In China, the primary source of law remains "actuality" (*shiji*) as determined by the Communist Party.[30] The idea that "actuality" produces law comes from the traditional Marxist doctrine, which emphasises the necessity for the state to pursue continual legal reform. The enactment of ad hoc legislation should accompany each phase of China's social development. Law should adapt to the development and change of the political, economic and social context.

Only by doing this "there be harmony and consistency between the different laws and regulations and society. When changes arise in society, the law should change to re-harmonise the internal relations within society".[31] Through "actuality", the CCP inextricably links law to its policy.[32] The shift from the idea of law as an instrument of class struggle to the idea of law as an instrument of economic development exemplifies this link. The Party first determines what "actuality" is. Then by means of policy, issues appropriate legislation.[33] Although in recent years, also as a result of more openness to Western legal theory and external pressure from international institutions, notably the WTO, requiring more transparency and commitment to the rule of law on behalf of Chinese institutions, the debate in academic and government circles in China about the proper relationship between law and Party policy has been reopened and the most conservative views have partly been softened, the dominant position still holds that the CCP policy is the foundation of law and it contains its guiding principles.[34]

In conclusion, *"actuality"* as determined by the CCP favours an instrumental, pragmatic and, often, experimental interpretation and enforcement of Chinese laws.

---

[30] For discussion, *see* Yu Xingzhong, 'Legal Pragmatism in the People's Republic of China' (1985) 3 Journal of Chinese Law 29–51, 42. *See* also, J. Chen, *Chinese Law: Towards an Understanding of Chinese Law, Its Nature and Development* (The London-Leiden Series on Law, Administration and Development, Kluwer Law International 1999).

[31] Xingzhong (n 30) 43.

[32] ibid at 47.

[33] ibid.

[34] For further discussion, *see* Pitman B. Potter, 'Legal Reform in China: Institutions, Culture and Selective Adaptation' (April 2004) 29(2) Law & Social Enquiry 465–495.

4 The Role and Status of Chinese SOEs Under China's Socialist Market Economy

These considerations on China's legal system help to better understand that mere economic analysis may not suffice to capture the nature of the investment activities of Chinese SOEs globally. Instead, these should read into the broader context of China's system of governance, which recognises a special status and role to Chinese SOEs.

In China, the public sector is often referred, in official statements, to as "backbone enterprise" (*gugan qiye*), "pillar industry" (*zhizhu chanye*), "central enterprise" (*zhongyang qiye*), and "key industry" (*zhongdian hangye*).[35] Nonetheless, these expressions belong more to the language of politics than to that of law. Compared to previous stages of China's economic reform, where the emphasis was on privatisation, the current trend is to maintain ownership (and control) over SOEs to pursue specific economic and social goals.

In China, macroeconomic policy tools remain the preferred instruments to intervene in the market. Indeed, the Chinese government moved away from directly planning to implementing specific industrial policies to redistribute economic resources into the national economy.[36] Nowadays, the Chinese government is much "more flexible, entrepreneurial, legalistic and technocratic",[37] and it does not monopolise economic development as in the past. However, it still intervenes in the economy through macroeconomic policies.[38] Far from repudiating the state's role in the economy, this approach privileges a more detached and indirect control of economic development through the implementation of policies and legislation. In reality, Chinese leaders seem to exclude the possibility of sacrificing China's cultural and ideological purity to pursue temporary economic growth.[39]

Thus, the state's role within this socialist framework is the component that differentiates China's economy from Western market economies. In conclusion, under China's system of governance, the relationship between the Chinese government and Chinese SOEs has particular implications also for the investments activities of Chinese SOEs abroad.

---

[35] Mikael Mattlin, 'Chinese strategic state-owned enterprises and ownership control' Institute of Contemporary China Studies (2007) 4(6) BICCS Asia Paper 1–28, 12.

[36] For discussion, *see* Jude Howell, 'The Impact of the Open Door Policy on the Chinese State' in Gordon White (ed) *The Chinese State in the Era of Economic Reform* (Studies on the Chinese Economy, Palgrave Macmillan 1991). *See* also, Jude Howell, *China Opens its Doors: The Politics of economic Transition* (Lynne Rienne Publishers 1993).

[37] Yehua Dennis Wei, *Regional Development in China- States, Globalization, and Inequality*, (Routledge 2002), 24.

[38] ibid.

[39] For discussion, *see* Carlos Wing-Hung Lo, 'Socialist Legal Theory in Deng Xiaoping's China' (1998) 11 Columbia Journal of Asian Law 469–486.

5 Chinese SOEs and Investment Arbitration

The matter, however, is not confined to the area of merger regulation. For instance, in the area of investment arbitration, the particular market status and role of Chinese SOEs within the context of China's socialist market economy have started to generate imbalances and asymmetries in the application of ISDS globally. This was evident, for example, in two recent cases where arbitration tribunals had to decide the standing of Chinese SOEs as claimants under investor-state dispute settlement mechanisms (ISDS).[40]

In the ICSID arbitration case Beijing Urban Construction Group Co. Ltd. V. Republic of Yemen (BUCG v. Yemen)[41] based on China-Yemen BIT, the Yemeni government sustained that the tribunal did not have jurisdiction *ratione personae* over the dispute because BUCG (a Chinese provincial SOEs responsible for building an airport terminal) could not qualify as "a national of another contracting state" under the ICSID Convention Article 25(1). By taking into account the "Broches test", the Yemeni government noted that Chinese SOE's BUCG was at the same time operating as an agent of the Chinese government "and exercised governmental functions even in its ostensible commercial undertakings".[42] The Yemeni government considered several official publications and directives of Chinese authorities to prove the role of BUCG in promoting China's national interest.[43] It was further noted that "[…] the Communist Party committees in State-owned enterprises such as BUCG are required to focus not only on supervising human resources, finance and materials but are as well responsible for "monitoring the implementation of the scientific concepts of development and national policies, to promote enterprises to play a leading role in carrying out political and social responsibility".[44] However, the Tribunal recognised that despite the specificities of the Chinese economy, in the specific case, BUCG could act as a claimant, and the tribunal had jurisdiction.[45]

A similar situation emerged within the context of China-Mongolia BIT in the case of China Heilongjiang International Economic & Technical Cooperative Corp., Beijing Shougang Mining Investment Company Ltd., and Qinhuangdaoshi Qinlong International Industrial Co. Ltd. V. Mongolia (Heilongjiang v. Mongolia).[46] In this case, the Mongolian government pointed out that the two Chinese companies, Beijing

---

[40] For discussion, *see* Spano, 'The status of state-owned (n 6).

[41] Beijing Urban Construction Group Co. Ltd. v. Republic of Yemen, ICSID Case No. ARB/14/30, Decision on Jurisdiction, 31 May 2017.

[42] Para 29 of the Decision.

[43] Para 37–38 of the Decision.

[44] ibid. *See* also, para. 47 of the Decision. The Yemeni government expressly addressed the issue of China's constitutional system and system of governance by referring to the concept of "democratic centralism" in Article 3 of China's Constitution.

[45] Bryan Mercurio and Dini Sejko, Holes in the Silk: Investor Protection under China's Belt and Road Initiative, (2019) 14(5) Global Trade and Customs Journal.

[46] China Heilongjiang International Economic & Technical Cooperative Corp., Beijing Shougang Mining Investment Company Ltd., and Qinhuangdaoshi Qinlong International Industrial Co. Ltd. v. Mongolia, UNCITRAL, PCA Case No.2010–20, Award, 30 June 2017.

Shougang and China Heilongjiang, could not be considered investors since they operated as "quasi-instrumentalities of the Chinese government".[47]

In fact, this phenomenon is quite common in China, and it is referred to with the concept of "sectoral monopolies". This occurs when Chinses SOEs integrating both administrative and business functions also enjoy regulatory powers in a specific sector of the Chinese economy. These SOEs are often affiliated with state departments which, in turn, may grant them a special status when they operate on the market.[48]

The political and financial support of the Chinese government has allowed Chinese SOEs to expand and compete globally. At the same time, in China, state assets are managed by state authorities that explicitly profess their intention to retain control over strategic industries. It is arduous to assess the level of independence Chinese SOEs enjoy from the state authorities within the context. Accordingly, significant concerns will continue to arise regarding the potential effect of the investment activities of Chinese SOEs. Furthermore, mechanisms of corporate governance and the internal organisational structure of Chinese SOEs remain opaque.

From a legal point of view, establishing evidence of actual control or, at least substantial coordination, of Chinese SOES by state authorities is not an easy task. For instance, direct communication between state bodies and the company's management is not indispensable for coordination.[49]

6 The EU Foreign Investment Screening Mechanism: A New Complementary Tool to the EU Competition Law Regime?

Back to the discussion on competition law enforcement in the EU, the European Commission seems to have adopted a "worse-case scenario" approach in reviewing merger transactions involving Chinese SOEs.[50] As seen, the Commission tried to assess the anti-competitive effect of proposed operations by assuming that all Chinese SOEs operating in the industry should be treated as a single entity. On this point, Angela Zhang noted: "Paradoxically, addressing both the over-inclusion and under-inclusion problems that Chinese SOEs have posed to the existing legal framework

---

47 Para. 271 of the decision.

48 For discussion, *see* Chaowu Jin and Wei Luo, *Competition Law in China* (Chinese Law Series, William S Hein & Co Inc (2002),. 82–83. In general, for a discussion on this issue see, *inter alia*, Alwyn Young, 'The Razor's Edge: Distortions and Incremental Reform in the People's Republic of China' (2000) 115(4) Quarterly Journal of Economics 1091–1135; Andrew Hall Wedeman, *From Mao to market: rent seeking, local protectionism, and marketization in China* (CUP 2003); Belton M Fleisher, Nicholas C Hope, Anita Alves Pena and Dennis Tao Yang, *Policy reform and Chinese markets: progress and challenges*, Edward Elgar Pub, (2008).

49 For discussion, *see* Angela Huyue Zhang, 'The anti-competitive effects of state ownership' (*CPI*, March 2017) <https://www.competitionpolicyinternational.com/the-anti-competitive-effects-of-state-ownership/> .

50 ibid. 4.

would require the Commission to simultaneously narrow and expand the concept of control, a mission impossible to achieve within the EUMR".[51]

Within this context, the challenges posed by the investment activities of Chinese SOEs in the EU have highlighted the shortfalls of the existing EU competition law regime. This situation should call for a more holistic approach in the areas of competition law enforcement through the implementation of complementary normative instruments at the EU level.

In recent years, EU authorities have started considering national security review mechanisms complementing the existing legislative framework. In this regard, it was noted that that competition law and national security law "share an overlapping interest in preventing a foreign state from accumulating a significant market position in a strategic domestic product market, but national security review provides more flexibility and room for regulators to deal with such competition concerns harmonisingy. More fundamentally, the basis for the optimal regulatory response to the acquisitions by SOEs hinges not only on economics but also, perhaps more importantly, on politics".[52]

In this regard, an EU framework would operate as a complementary tool to the EU competition law regime and would serve the purpose to address in a more coherent and systemic manner the challenges associated with the status of Chinese SOEs within the context of China's socialist market economy.

In March 2019, the European Union adopted the FDI screening regulation, which established an EU-wide framework to coordinate the actions of the European Commission and the Member States on foreign investments. After it entered into force in April 2019, the European Commission and the Member States have been working together to put in place the necessary requirements for the application of the Regulation, which became operational on 11 October 2020. This process has included:

> the notification by EU Member States of their existing national investment screening mechanisms to the Commission.
>
> The establishment of formal contact points and secure channels in each Member State and within the Commission for the exchange of information and analysis developing procedures for Member States and the Commission to quickly react to FDI concerns and to issue opinions updating the list of projects and programmes of Union interest annexed to the Regulation.[53]

The Regulation established an ad hoc framework for the screening by the Member States of foreign direct investments into the EU on the grounds of security or public order and for a mechanism for cooperation between the Member States, and between the Member States and the Commission, in relation to foreign direct investments which is likely to affect security or public order. Furthermore, it introduces the possibility for the Commission and the Member States to issue opinions and express comments on specific operations.[54]

---

[51] ibid at 8.

[52] Zhang (n49) 8.

[53] <https://ec.europa.eu/commission/presscorner/detail/en/ip_20_1867> .

[54] *See* Article 1.

Within this context, following a series of recommendations by the European Commission in its March 2020 guidance,[55] Member States have also expressed their consent to informal cooperation on FDI screening if a foreign investment could impact the internal market of the EU. The framework has a far-reaching goal. It targets a broad range of investment activities that establish or maintain lasting and direct links between investors from third countries, including State entities and undertakings conducting business operations in the Member States.[56]

Member States and the Commission would be able to consider all relevant factors, including the effects on critical infrastructure, technologies (including key enabling technologies) and inputs essential for security or the maintenance of public order, the disruption, failure, loss or destruction of which would have a significant impact in a Member State or the Union. Additionally, the Regulation expressly indicates that the Member States and the Commission should be able "to take into account the context and circumstances of a direct investment and, in particular, whether a foreign investor is controlled directly or indirectly, for example through significant funding, including subsidies, by the government of a third country or is pursuing State-led outward projects or programmes".[57]

Greater coordination and information sharing between the EU Commission and the Member States is welcome. However, the road is still long. The EU mechanism only set minimum requirements for national mechanism, but it falls short of fully harmonising existing laws. Currently, 14 Member States have implemented their own national screening legislation. However, these norms still differ substantively.

7 Concluding Remarks

In conclusion, the challenges posed by the investment activities of Chinese SOEs' in strategic industries of the EU Member States assume significance not only for the future of EU-China relations but also for the EU system of governance. The EU should seek a higher level of legal harmonisation and more coordination between national and supranational institutional actors. The implementation of common normative instruments in the area of investment protection, for example, represents an important step to complement the existing competition law regime and, perhaps, to lead to more political and economic cohesion in the EU. However, following this path calls for a model of governance transferring more prerogatives to EU institutions to give full effect to these instruments. The failure to move in this direction carries the risk of adverse consequences on the ongoing market integration process and the realisation of a more unified polity in the EU.

---

[55] <https://trade.ec.europa.eu/doclib/docs/2020/march/tradoc_158676.pdf> .

[56] *See* recital 9 of the Regulation.

[57] Recital 13.

Economic and Institutional Expansion of State Capitalism

The Public Value Creation of State-Owned Enterprises

Usman W. Chohan

1 Introduction

This chapter aims to examine the value contribution of State-Owned Enterprises (SOEs) through the prism of *public value theory*,[1] which represents a leading discourse in the discipline of public administration.[2] Whereas public administration scholarship has long demonstrated a keen interest in SOEs,[3] the theoretical elements of public value have not been sufficiently deployed in assessing SOE value contribution heretofore in the literature.[4] This theorisation is valuable for two reasons: (1) it helps to situate SOEs more sturdily within the public administration literature; and (2) it helps to advance public value theory by addressing an institutional form that melds elements of both the *state* and the *market*. That reciprocal benefit justifies the enquiry of this chapter, and it is thereby structured as follows.

First, this introductory section proceeds to highlight the importance of SOEs in the world economy. After that, definitional issues pertaining to SOEs, along with essential rationales for their function, are enumerated with a particular focus on their concordance with public value's precepts. The following section examines the forced

[1] Another chapter in this volume on the public value of sovereign wealth funds (SWFs), which may be treated a special form of SOEs, discusses various salient aspects of public value as well.

[2] A comprehensive review of public value's precepts can be found in Usman W Chohan, *Public Value and Budgeting: International Perspectives*. (Routledge 2019).

[3] A useful review is presented in Talis Putniņš 'Economics of state-owned enterprises' (2015) 38(11) International Journal of Public Administration, 815–832.

[4] However, practitioner expositions of SOEs' public value have received some important attention, see for example Price Waterhouse Coopers '*State-Owned Enterprises: Catalysts for public value creation?*' (2015) PWC Reports.

U. W. Chohan (✉)
Director, Economic Affairs & National Development, Centre for Aerospace and Security Studies (CASS), Islamabad, Pakistan
e-mail: cass.thinkers@gmail.com

J. Chaisse et al. (eds.), *Regulation of State-Controlled Enterprises*, International Law and the Global South, https://doi.org/10.1007/978-981-19-1368-6_9

historical dichotomy between state and market that lays the backdrop for the more nuanced meld of SOEs, with an added focus on how SOEs do not just participate in markets but also shape them. This also includes considerations for structuring SOEs so as to produce public value more optimally without negating markets themselves. A well-regarded public value framework, the *strategic triangle,* is then applied to assess the modes of SOE value contribution.[5] Finally, a consideration of the continued pertinence of the SOE model to diverse economies is reiterated.

To begin, for the purposes of this chapter, any corporate entity recognised by national law as an enterprise with at least partial state ownership will be deemed an SOE.[6] So this list is quite extensive in global terms.[7] The foundation of that ownership may be through shareholding or exercise of a similar degree of control. Such a broad brushstroke is applied to facilitate the theorisation of subsequent sections of the chapter.

SOEs represent an increasingly powerful cohort of international players. Nearly a decade ago, it was observed that, although SOEs represented less than 1% of total firms, they accounted for more than 10% of global foreign direct investment (FDI) flows; and the numbers have only increased since.[8] In OECD ("developed") countries, SOEs account for 15% of GDP, while, in transition and developing economies, they can reach up to 20–30% of GDP.[9] An emphasis on the developing world's SOEs is essential, since they comprise more than half of the largest companies in China, UAE, Russia, Indonesia, Malaysia, Saudi Arabia, India, and Brazil.[10] For more specific examples, the OECD estimated in 2011 that SOEs account for 30% of Chinese GDP, 38% of Vietnamese GDP, and 25% of Indian GDP.[11]

This has been true for nearly a decade, as a snapshot in 2012 indicated that SOEs dominate various subsectors of the MSCI emerging market index, representing two-thirds of the energy subsector, more than half of the utilities subsector, nearly one-third of the telecom services subsector and one-third of the financial services sector.[12] Their size in the global economy is now difficult to dispute: the World Bank estimates

---

[5] A review and critique of the strategic triangle is presented in John Alford and Janine O'Flynn, 'Making sense of public value: Concepts, critiques and emergent meanings' (2009) 32(3/4) *International Journal of Public Administration*, 171–191.

[6] Other chapters in this volume discuss more nuanced attributes of what would qualify more technically as an SOE.

[7] Some definitional ambiguities are addressed in Price Waterhouse Coopers (n 4) at 8.

[8] OECD, 'State-owned enterprise governance reform: An inventory of recent change' (2011) OECD Working Papers.

[9] OECD, 'State-owned enterprise governance reform: An inventory of recent change' (2011) OECD Working Papers.

[10] Przemyslaw Kowalski; Max Büge; Monika Sztajerowska; and Matias Egeland, 'State-Owned Enterprises: Trade Effects and Policy Implications' (2013) OECD Trade Policy Paper, No. 147.

[11] ibid.

[12] The Economist., 'Share of national/state-controlled companies to MSCI emerging market index' (2012) Economist. The Visible Hand., 4.

that SOEs account globally for 20% of investment and 5% of global employment.[13] To put it in absolute terms, a recent estimate placed SOE global revenues at $8 trillion, almost equivalent to the combined GDPs of Germany, France, and the UK.[14]

Many SOEs figure among the world's largest companies, representing more than 10% of the world's 2000 largest companies and similarly more than 10% share of sales value.[15] They have continued to rise up the world rankings of firms by capitalisation since the 2008 Global Financial Crisis (GFC), which decimated many private-sector market giants.[16] Chinese SOEs, in particular, have spearheaded this rise of SOEs among Fortune 500 company rankings, from their 9% in 2005 to 23% by 2014.[17] SOEs are also an essential driver of international commerce since the eight countries with the highest SOE shares in their economy[18] have together represented more than 20% of world trade, with China alone accounting for more than 10% of the world's merchandise exports as far back as 2010.

As such, SOEs are found throughout the world and fulfil countless roles in the economy, including industrial policy, regional development, the supply of public goods, the prioritisation of specific national objectives, the financing of projects that would not be received by market appetite, as well as the fulfilment of *natural monopolies* where competitive markets would not be feasible, among still others. This makes their enquiry, particularly from a public value perspective, necessary for a meaningful understanding of contemporary global economics.

2 SOEs: Rationales and Public Value

In looking for a synergistic understanding between public value theoretically and the practitioner experience of SOEs, it is first useful to consider the genesis of public value and the SOE model. Above all, both were influenced by the ideological movement of *neoliberalism*. Public value was a response to the neoliberal movement in that it sought to re-legitimise the role of the public manager. As one scholar has put it, the public value was "developed initially in the USA in the early to mid-1990s, at the height of the dominance of the neoliberal ideology which privileged models based on individual consumers within a private competitive market over communal citizens

---

[13] World Bank. 'World Bank Group Support for the Reform of State-Owned Enterprises, 2007–2018' An IEG Evaluation (World Bank Publications 2018).

[14] ibid.

[15] ibid.

[16] This is particularly true of the financial services sector, where many large-scale insolvencies and acquisitions in the banking sector, along with declines in capitalization, led to a decline in the ranking or even removal of many private financial giants in both North America and Europe.

[17] Price Waterhouse Coopers (n 4).

[18] These are China, United Arab Emirates, Russia, Indonesia, Malaysia, Saudi Arabia, India and Brazil.

Table 1 Public value and SOE rationales/criteria

Theme	SOE Rationale/Criteria	Public value
Value	Maximising value for society	Maximising value for the public
Roles	Clear delineation of SOEs' roles	Clear delineation of public manager roles
Accountability	Political accountability is important for oversight of SOEs	Public value creation requires mechanisms of accountability
Relationship	The state should have a clear-set relationship with each SOE	Every public manager institution should be situated within the larger public value creation effort of the state

Source OECD; Author's Research

within a public democratic state".[19] Meanwhile, SOEs too are an embodiment of a counter-narrative to neoliberalism's insistence on privatising the resources of society. As the World Bank observes, "despite a phase of rapid privatisation in the 1990s, the public ownership of assets and economic activity via SOEs has persisted and in some economies has even grown".[20] Their role as counter-narratives to the now waning neoliberal movement is a noteworthy element in the message that both public value theory and SOE models transmit. Beyond this, several rationales speak both to the practitioner experience of SOEs and to public value theory, and they are presented in the following Table 1.

Foremost among the areas of concordance between public value theory and the rationales/criteria for SOEs is the objective of *maximising value* created for the public (society). Public value is a discourse that seeks to underscore the need for maximising the value that public managers can create for society despite the various difficulties of measurement. SOEs constitute a class of public manager institutions, given their ownership by the state or state-related entities, and they participate in economic activity in specific ways that have a broader agenda for society in mind, whether it be through addressing market failure, serving as a natural monopoly, or addressing particular national objectives, among others. Already then, it is evident that SOEs offer an interesting lens for public value considerations due to the agreement between their fundamental objective and the precepts of public value.

The second area of concordance lies in the emphasis on achieving clarity of *roles performed* by institutions. Given the diversity of this class of institutions, it is somewhat challenging to make generalisations about the roles that an SOE can fulfil since they can be created for a multiplicity of aims. Public value mirrors this concern by emphasising delineating clear roles for public managers whenever possible. In fact, recent research has shown that public value offers useful approaches for identifying roles for public manager institutions,such as in the *advisory-costings framework* that

[19] John Benington, 'Creating the public in order to create public value?' (2009) 32(3/4) International Journal of Public Administration, 232.

[20] World Bank (n 13) (2018), 4.

has been designed to assign to distinct roles for an institution known as a legislative budget office.[21]

For SOEs, the roles and responsibilities for which they are put in charge require careful delimitation, and it is through clarity of purpose that SOEs are made capable of pursuing value maximisation strategies effectively. Their scope and mandate can help to facilitate significantly the field of economic activity wherein they must operate. Conversely, an ambiguity in their roles is likely to cause various sorts of frictions, including an underutilisation of resources, overlap with other institutions, overextension, and conflicts with other state institutions or market participants.[22] To avoid such stumbling blocks, SOEs require support from a broader base of stakeholders: the state, private interest, politicians, and civil society. This speaks to public value's concept of *value co-creation*,[23] wherein SOEs act as but one group of agents within a multi-stakeholder framework that works synergistically towards the production of value for society.

The third area of concordance between public value and SOEs lies in the realm of *accountability*. Public value stresses the need for structures of accountability to oversee and direct the value creation efforts of public managers[24] and lays particular importance on the exercise of accountability by political institutions (e.g. the legislature). In fact, politicians are described as the "final arbiters of value",[25] although this notion is being increasingly contested within the literature.[26] SOEs must be situated within an architecture of accountability that involves both political structures as well as public managerial institutions. As the OECD puts it, SOEs must "be subject to appropriate procedures of political accountability and disclosed to the general public".[27]

This claim also draws in the notion of transparency, as separate from but related to the notion of accountability. From a public value perspective, this is essential because transparency is considered to be a "precondition" for effective value creation.[28] On that point, "high standards of transparency and accountability are needed to allow the public to assure itself that the state exercises its powers in accordance with the public's

---

[21] The pioneering work on advisory-costings framework can be found in Usman Chohan and Kerry Jacobs, 'Public value in politics: A legislative budget office approach' (2017) 40(12) International Journal of Public Administration, 1063–1073.

[22] Some of these issues are discussed at length in World Bank (n 13).

[23] Discussions of value co-creation are given considerable treatment in Mark Moore and John Donahue, *Ports in a Storm: Public Management in a Turbulent World* (Brookings 2012).

[24] Joe Wallis and Robert Gregory, 'Leadership, accountability and public value: Resolving a problem in "new governance"?' (2009) 32(3–4) International Journal of Public Administration, 250–273.

[25] *See* Mark Moore, *Creating Public Value: Strategic Management in Government* (Harvard University Press 1995), 22.

[26] Chohan (n 2).

[27] *See* OECD, *OECD Guidelines on Corporate Governance of State-Owned Enterprises*, (2015 edn, OECD Publishing 2015), 17.

[28] Scott Douglas and Albert Meijer, /Transparency and public value: Analyzing the transparency practices and value creation of public utilities' (2016) 39(12) International Journal of Public Administration, 940–951.

best interest".[29] The World Bank has observed that "SOEs frequently lack adequate governance and oversight arrangements, regulation, and levels of transparency and disclosure, which can foster mismanagement, corruption and underperformance".[30] It may thus be surmised that appropriate mechanisms for accountability and transparency are likely to strengthen the functioning abilities of SOEs, and that is a point that resonates strongly with the public value discourse.

The fourth area of concordance lies in the *nature of the relationship* between SOEs and centralised public administration.[31] Governments usually create SOEs to fulfil specific objectives, and so the relationship between each SOE and centralised administration takes on increased importance in light of their strategic mandates. To see the parallel with public value theory, it must be noted that, more than anything, public value encourages a sense of cooperation among public managerial institutions.[32] It argues that value creation processes are most optimal when agents in society work towards co-creating value. This co-creative approach is premised on solid relationships between administrative and political institutions and a repudiation to the long-standing *politics-administration dichotomy*.[33] Yet relationships may not necessarily construe a loss of authority, and it has been argued that "governments should allow SOEs full operational autonomy to achieve their defined objectives and refrain from intervening in SOE management" while also ensuring that "the state should let SOE boards exercise their responsibilities and should respect their independence" as a best practice.[34] Public value asserts that public managers must negotiate their "right to operate" in an "authorising environment",[35] and SOEs exemplify this whenever they pursue value creation while engaging with centralised public administration.

As can be gleaned from the discussion above, this section, in identifying areas of concordance between public value's claims and SOEs' expectations, asserts that there is a possibility of mutual reinforcement through enquiry. On the one hand, it suggests that public value is apt to explain features of SOE structures, orders, and roles. On the other, it suggests that SOEs can act as a useful lens in public value research going forward. However, understanding the degree to which SOEs negotiate the market logic is a precondition for understanding how much value they can create, which is why the next section broaches this question more directly.

---

[29] *See* OECD (n 29), 31.

[30] World Bank (n 13).

[31] By "central," it is not necessarily meant here that it is the federal centralized bureaucracy that is in charge. In fact, many subnational, regional, and local municipal entities also create and manage SOEs. *See* Price Waterhouse Coopers (n 4), 11.

[32] Moore and Donahue (n 25).

[33] *See* Usman W. Chohan, 'Independent Budget Offices and the Politics–Administration Dichotomy' (2018) 41(12) International Journal of Public Administration, 1009–1017.

[34] *See* OECD (n 29), 20.

[35] *See* Moore (n 27). 114.

3 SOEs and the State-Market Dichotomy

An ideological battle erupted in the nineteentn century and fomented during the twentieth century between "the state and the market".[36] On either side, the more hard-line proponents treated the problem of resource allocation in the economy as if it were a dichotomy of state vs market that would remain irreconcilable.[37] The insistence upon this dichotomy permeated many disciplines in the social sciences, including economics, political science, and public administration. The extreme advocates of the market reigned supreme on one side of the twentieth century's iron curtain, arguing that the market was somehow always the best solution for resource allocation in any situation.

By contrast, the extreme advocates of the state reigned supreme on the other side of the curtain and insisted on the state's dominion over the allocation of all material resources.[38] Post-communist societies were born in the wake of the USSR's dissolution in the early 1990s and had to reset their social bargain from an entirely state-oriented approach towards a market one,[39] which seemed to herald what was grandiosely called the "end of history" and a repudiation of the communist state-driven model.[40] However, consistent *market failures* taught the less partisan social scientists that total dependence on market solutions would not just be foolhardy but dangerous for society.

Furthermore, the problem created by forcing a dichotomy into the sub-disciplines of the social sciences, when none was required, meant that theorisations of a more nuanced character could not emerge. For example, in the public administration literature, the emphasis on "state vs market" meant that an understanding of other social agents, including civil society, was left gravely wanting.[41] The extreme proponents of either camp notwithstanding, both the theory and praxis of economic development, have led to a nuanced category of firms known as SOEs, which eponymously act in an entrepreneurial (market) capacity but have a shareholder base that is in whole or in part state-owned.

As with another chapter in this volume regarding sovereign wealth funds (SWFs), this chapter also examines a type of institution that negotiates both the state and the market while also acting as a trustee in the public interest.[42] For SOEs, the negotiation

[36] *See* Benington (n 19), 240.

[37] Chohan (n 2), 98.

[38] Donna Bahry, 'Measuring communist priorities: Budgets, investments, and the problem of equivalence' (1980) 13(3) Comparative Political Studies, 267–292.

[39] *See* post-communist public value in Chohan (n 2), 62–77.

[40] *See* Fukuyama's assertion about the "end of history in" Francis Fukuyama, 'The end of history?' 1989) The National Interest 16, 3–18.

[41] This has been discussed in John Benington (2009). Creating the public in order to create public value? *International Journal of Public Administration*, 32(3/4), p.232–249.

[42] SWFs may in fact be described as a "special kind of SOE," see Price Waterhouse Coopers (n 4), 12.

of their authorising environment entails engagement with the market logic as well,[43] but with the additional note that they might exercise greater power over the market than the market might exercise over them. The remainder of this section considers market-related considerations for SOEs as agents for public value creation.

If market mechanisms exist for value creation, and it is determined that they should be preserved or strengthened, then SOEs must create value for the public in a manner that recognises the market's role as well. For the state, then, it must be able to separate its function as the owner of SOEs from other functions it serves, such as a market regulator. Various conflicts of interest are bound to arise if such a disaggregation does not occur. At the crux of the SOE's role in the market, the environment is the need for careful management of the degree to which it is exempt from applying the state's rules, including from legal, regulatory, financing, procurement, input-cost, and tax perspectives.[44] To protect creditors, consumers, competitors, and investors, the state must ensure that proper and timely redress is made available through impartial institutions, including the courts and arbitration mechanisms. International bodies tend to argue that "as a guiding principle, SOEs undertaking economic activities should not be exempt from the application of general laws, tax codes, and regulations", and that "laws and regulations should not unduly discriminate between SOEs and their market competitors".[45]

At the same time, SOEs should adhere to high levels of transparency in their financial statements so as to give a more accurate picture of their revenue and cost structures. This will also help to reduce the conflicts of interest between the state's SOE activities and its market regulation role. It has been remarked that "whatever the motivation, the future SOE will need to be much more actively owned and managed if it is to deliver real public value, and avoid competing unfairly in markets where private and third sector enterprises can deliver more efficiently and effectively the goods and services that citizens need and want".[46]

An equally pressing concern arises from the question of access to credit. SOEs in practice can receive market-inconsistent (preferential) conditions when applying for debt and equity finance. For example, the country with the most prevalent and robust SOE culture, the People's Republic of China, faces a growing concern about its SOEs primarily due to the market-inconsistent nature of their balance sheets.[47] For China, general government debt amounted to roughly 60% of GDP in 2015, but the debt amassed by SOEs as of that year was another 110% of GDP.[48] The debt-at-risk

---

[43] It is certainly true that some SOEs do not engage with the market logic, but the degree to which they can withdraw from this raises questions about whether they can really be called 'enterprises' in that case.

[44] Some of these perspectives receive detailed treatment in other chapters of this book.

[45] See OECD (n 29), 31.

[46] Price Waterhouse Coopers (n 4).

[47] For a discussion of market inconsistencies as reflected in Chinese SOE balance sheets, *see* Benno Ferrarini and Marthe Hinojales, 'State-Owned Enterprises Leverage as a Contingency in Public Debt Sustainability Analysis: The Case of the People's Republic of China' (2018) Asian Development Bank Economics Working Papers N0. 534.

[48] ibid.

for China's SOEs varies by sector, with steel, aluminium, and coal SOEs having the highest, while electronics and utilities and electronics holding negligible debt-at-risk proportions.[49]

Other preferential items which confer SOEs with an advantage over private competitors might include preferential financing, tax arrears or preferential trade credits from other SOEs. A common allowance for SOEs, and a significant one at that, is in the reduced input costs such as energy, water, or land. Furthermore, the procurement process for SOEs, whether as a bidder for a contract or procurer issuing one, may not always be market-competitive, thereby creating a disadvantageous situation for private market participants. Appropriate levels of transparency in the procurement process can help to alleviate this risk.

One aspect where SOEs and SWFs differ is the return rate that they are expected to attain. For SWFs, the benchmarking is typically done versus an index,[50] but for SOEs, the rates of return may or may not be gauged against returns earned by private players of a similar size. It has been observed that at least some SOEs "display low productivity and efficiency levels with a detrimental impact on growth" and that "their sometimes poor financial performance and practices can generate substantial fiscal losses (or contingent liabilities) for governments.[51] On this point, an IMF study of Eastern Europe's SOEs finds that "profitability and efficiency of resource allocation of SOEs lag those of private firms in most sectors, with substantial cross-country variation".[52]

In commenting on the market-comparable performance of SOEs, it is essential not to make generalisations, as successful SOEs are found throughout the world, and variation between countries can also be a significant explanatory factor. Nevertheless, the risks of SOE underperformance can be listed as follows: (1) balance sheet problems can impact public finances (as mentioned above); (2) financial stability can be at risk, particularly for state ownership of bank and non-bank financial companies; and (3) negative productivity impacts can extend outwards from large SOEs into the larger economy.[53]

Furthermore, aside from the value creation that SOEs may undertake independently, there is another formulation of SOE engagement that relies on a sense of partnership with the private sector. This hybrid model of project execution is known as a public-private partnership (PPP).[54] The arrangements of PPPs can be quite diverse, but it is appropriate to infer that they represent an accommodative space

---

[49] ibid.

[50] *See* another chapter in this volume for an extensive discussion of the measurement of value by SWFs.

[51] World Bank (n 13).

[52] Uwe Bower, 'State-Owned Enterprises in Emerging Europe: The Good, the Bad, and the Ugly' (2017) IMF Working Papers. Paper 17/221.

[53] ibid.

[54] It may be observed that the PPP model also challenges the old dichotomy between the state and the market.

between public institutions and private players to work towards economic development in specific cases for mutual benefit, where the "benefit" accrues both to private interests as well as the wider society.[55] There is a great deal of research potential in examining this grey zone of PPPs that straddles both the state and market, and public value scholars have begun to critique its forms and implementation quite proactively.[56]

As such, that the interplay between state and market that serves as the backdrop to SOEs' public value creation comprises both risks and responsibilities. Adherence to market-consistent factors is essential insofar as the state accords due consideration to the market's integrity. SOEs can act as large, if not the largest, players in many industries, and therefore do not just engage with the market but can actively shape it. This, in turn, behoves the overall regulatory architecture to demand accountability and transparency mechanisms that direct SOE activity towards value creation. For public value theory, this sets an example of how to incorporate private interest into the discourse and of how public managers can influence and even shape private interest as a corollary to their value creation efforts.

4 The Strategic Triangle

To examine SOEs more specifically through the prism of public value, it may help to situate them within the "central symbol" of public value,[57] known otherwise as the *strategic triangle.*[58]As a framework for evaluating the public value creation of institutions, the strategic triangle has gained increasing importance, both due to its applicability and its simplicity.[59] It posits that three key ingredients inform an institution's value proposition for the public: its *legitimacy*, a *recognition* of its value contribution, and the *operational resources* conferred upon it. Rather than examining a specific SOE case study, it is more appropriate for this chapter to consider each node of the triangle conceptually concerning the SOE context. This section applies the strategic triangle's perspectives to state-owned enterprises, as follows.

First, the *legitimacy* of a public institution is a significant determinant of its value-creating potential. The conferral of legitimacy here refers to that which is given by the three primary agents of public value: politicians, citizens, and other bureaucratic institutions. When an SOE is devoid of sufficient legitimacy, it risks being sidelined,

---

[55] Stephen Osborne, *Public-private partnerships: Theory and practice in international perspective* (Routledge 2000).

[56] *See* for example Sami Ullah Bajwa, Naveda Kitchlew, Khuram Shahzad, and Khaliq Ur Rehman, 'Public–Private Partnership (PPP) as an interdependent form (I-Form) organization' (2018) 41(11) International Journal of Public Administration, 859–867.

[57] The characterization of the strategic triangle as central symbol is attributable to Alford and O'Flynn (n 5), 173.

[58] *See* Moore (n 27), 22.

[59] *See* Usman Chohan, 'Public value and bureaucratic rhetoric' in Ali Farazmand (ed) *Global Encyclopedia of Public Administration, Public Policy, and Governance* (Springer 2017).

mismanaged, or dissolved. Exogenous pressures, particularly those from foreign governments or multilateral institutions, can also impact the legitimacy of SOEs. A salient example of this is in the World Bank's neoliberal efforts to force privatisation movements around the world after the 1990s, which came to pressurise governments in developing countries to sell off strategic industries and SOEs to private interests as part of what it termed "liberalisation efforts".[60] Aside from outside pressures, legitimacy in the domestic environment plays an important role in situating SOEs within the economic architecture. For example, citizens may hold a positive view of SOEs if their key concern is in employment generation, since SOEs generally tend to be more accommodative of employment growth than solely profit-driven private interests are, particularly when this is an enshrined objective.[61]

Other public managerial institutions may hold a diverse set of views about SOEs, whether due to a market regulatory perspective, a financial stability perspective, or a strategic resource perspective.[62] Politicians may hold divergent views based on their party's ideological affiliation, and at the risk of generalisation, it may be loosely construed that left-leaning parties advocate for a greater role of the state and SOEs, while right-leaning parties advocate for a stronger market presence, deregulation, and private enterprise.[63] That being a generalisation, it should be noted that attitudes towards SOEs differ within the respective cohorts of OECD and developing countries, often as part of a historical process and political evolution.[64]

The country with the highest number of major SOEs is China, which has forged a model that is sometimes termed as a form of *State Capitalism*.[65] The Chinese government has been a staunch advocate of weighty but dynamic SOEs as drivers of economic growth[66] and so has conferred a significant degree of legitimacy on its SOEs, even after specific market liberalisation measures were taken. In Russia, by contrast, the dissolution of the USSR's SOEs was met with a chaotic period and momentous upheavals that led to conflicting views about the legitimacy of the oligarchic market players that emerged in their wake.[67]

In the USA, where the market has been ideologically upheld, SOEs are at best considered a necessary evil,[68] and preference is given to private corporatism in value

---

[60] World Bank (n 13).

[61] *See* Ferrarini and Hinojales (n 49).

[62] These perspectives have been alluded to in earlier sections of this chapter.

[63] *See* Graeme Hodge, *Privatization: An international review of performance* (Routledge 2018).

[64] A recent analysis which considers this factor is in Ezra Suleiman, and John Waterbury, *The political economy of public sector reform and privatization* (Routledge 2019).

[65] James Rickards, *Currency Wars: The Making of the Next Global Crisis* (Portfolio 2011).

[66] Chong-En Bai, Lu Jiangyong and Zhigang Tao, 'The multitask theory of state enterprise reform: empirical evidence from China' (2006) 96(2) *American Economic Review*, 353–357.

[67] The history of the tumultuous Russian transition to privatization is well explained in Michael McFaul, 'State power, institutional change, and the politics of privatization in Russia' (1995) 47(2) *World Politics*,, 210–243.

[68] This discussion is presented in a nuanced manner by Andrei Shleifer, 'State versus private ownership' (1998) 12(4) *Journal of economic perspectives*, 133–150.

creation, even though there are various manifestations of state presence in commercial, industrial, and financial markets in the USA.[69] In times of crisis, for example, the US government has taken a more than 50% stake in institutions that were "too big to fail", such as when it took over Fannie Mae and Freddie Mac after the Global Financial Crisis (GFC) of 2008.

Nevertheless, as statistics cited in the introductory portion of this chapter reveal, SOEs are still growing in popularity around the world, and particularly in the developing world (despite the pressures of multilateral neoliberal institutions), as a means to protect strategic resources or industries. That interest is unlikely to wane, particularly in the wake of the 2008 GFC.[70] For this reason, it may be inferred that the legitimacy of SOEs in many jurisdictions is likely to remain quite elevated, if not to increase, in the coming years.

Second, although closely tied to the notion of legitimacy, a *recognition* of SOE public value is a more nuanced concept because it requires both tacit and overt channels of signalling an acceptance of the potential for SOEs to contribute value. In addition to legal mechanisms and formal enshrinement in law, politicians can use parliamentary forums, public speeches, and voting behaviour to signal recognition. Meanwhile, citizens can do so through indirect and direct engagement with political vehicles such as the legislature, citizen activism, civil society, and academia, among other options. Meanwhile, other public managerial institutions can do so through direct engagement with SOEs.

That said, what is equally important to note in expressing formalised recognition of the public value contribution of SOEs is that they may be extensively privileged vis-à-vis market participants. In other words, a recognition of their value may translate into preferential agreements and conditions which can disadvantage private interests in the same domain. As discussed in the previous section, insofar as a role for the market is also recognised, the state must then strike a balance between according recognition to SOEs and other enterprises.

Third, the strategic triangle considers the *operational resources* of public institutions. Although this is a broad categorisation, it may be seen to encompass the various forms of capital: infrastructure, technologies, mandates, leadership, and labour that could translate into value creation. Irrespective of the size of an SOE, its operational resources must be commensurate with the aims stipulated in its function. The leadership of SOEs must be adept at translating their proscribed mandates into results, but without veering towards overstepping those mandates. Skilled and unskilled labour, as well as requisite technologies and infrastructure, must be accorded to SOEs in line with their goals. Capital must similarly be allocated based on the SOE's requirements, but with the proviso of an earlier section about preferential access to financing, procurement, and technology.

At the same time, the provision of operational resources to SOEs must be judicious, not simply because of a desire for market integrity but also because there are concerns

[69] Rickards (n 67).

[70] The World Bank has expressed its cognizance of this sustained interest in SOEs, *see* some of these issues are discussed at length in World Bank (n 13).

about many SOEs generating low returns on capital. To provide a *carte blanche* to SOEs in operational resources may also prove to be a risk in the efficiency of their operations. Therefore, in this aspect of the strategic triangle, the state must strike a balance between allocating adequate operational resources and maintaining some degree of efficient outputs from that allocation.

It should be gleaned from the preceding discussion that the strategic triangle continues to serve as a useful public value lens for state institutions, including those engaged in some form of enterprise. Conferring a degree of legitimacy, recognising the value of SOEs at various levels, and provisioning adequate levels of operational resources together illustrate in unambiguous terms how SOEs can be made to serve a wider value creation effort. What is unique in the instance of SOEs is that a balance must be struck, particularly in terms of recognition (preferential terms) and operational resources (preferential endowments), between under-provision and excessive transfers.

5 Conclusion

This chapter aimed to discuss the value contribution of SOEs through the prism of public value theory, particularly since public value's theoretical (as opposed to practitioner) elements had not been deployed to help contextualise SOEs' value contribution. As such, it was argued that this theorisation is valuable for two reasons: (1) it would help to situate SOEs more sturdily within the public administration literature; and (2) it would help to advance public value theory by addressing an institutional form that melds elements of both the *state* and the *market*. In transposing SOEs into public value frameworks, several findings have emerged. First, there is a natural concordance between the rationales/criteria for SOEs establishment and the public value discourse, in terms of the emphasis on the maximisation of value; the need for a clear delineation of the state's and the SOEs' roles; the need for an architecture of accountability; and the need for a clear-set relationship between the SOE and the larger bureaucratic structure of the state. With this in mind, it was appreciable that a base footing for transposing SOEs into public value could occur.

After that, it was essential to recognise that SOEs are a melding of two realms that have been dichotomised in the social sciences (including in the public administration literature): the *state* and the *market*. SOEs are founded on full or partial state ownership or state control, and yet they operate in an entrepreneurial capacity with market dynamics. As such, they exemplify the need for the literature to move beyond the imposition of dichotomies where they are not necessitated. Yet equally importantly, SOEs do not just absorb the underlying dynamics of markets; they actively shape them. SOEs can and do wield significant size and influence, and they can therefore shape the market in which they participate. This nuance contributed to the public value discourse in that it stressed how public institutions could wrest with private interest, but that too with the power to reshape the field. This, in turn, brings with it considerable responsibility. Hence, the need for accountability systems for the oversight of SOEs and the need for transparency to inform the public about their conduct.

Finally, public value's central symbol of the strategic triangle was employed to situate the importance of legitimacy, recognition of value creation, and operational resources in assuring the success of SOEs in terms of their public value creation effort. Reciprocally, SOEs also informed the strategic triangle model in two ways: (1) they reinforced the assertions of Moore's original thinking on public value,[71] and (2) they added the nuance that SOEs must receive an adequate but not excessive amount of operational resources and recognition of their public value. On this second point, the emphasis in this chapter was on the need to strike a balance between strengthening the value creation potential of SOEs and avoiding the excess of endowments such that they would risk causing market disruption, or even public value destruction.

In addition to this theoretical exploration of SOEs as value-creating institutions, there is also a practitioner consideration of SOE growth internationally that makes them very pertinent in international research. As noted earlier, in OECD countries, they account for 15% of GDP, but in emerging markets their contribution is much more significant, particularly in the Chinese state capitalist model where SOEs have served as a centrepiece of their public value effort. The sheer size of many SOEs also bolsters their influence, particularly in terms of global investment flows, employment generation, and international commercial activity. Although ample warnings of SOE mismanagement abound globally, there is some motivation to consider them an essential option in the broader value creation effort.

It has been remarked that "the motivations for state ownership can wax and wane over time, but state-owned enterprises (SOEs) appear to be an enduring feature of the economic landscape and will remain an influential force globally for some years to come".[72] Given the value-creating opportunity that they provide and the unique space between the state and market they bestride, further research into the effective deployment of SOEs in terms of roles, resources, aims, and mandates, can be expected to continue at the currently observable brisk pace well into the future.

[71] Moore (n 27), 22.

[72] Price Waterhouse Coopers (n 4).

Privatizations of State-Owned Companies and Justifications for Restrictions on EU Fundamental Freedoms: Past, Present and Future Perspectives

Thomas Papadopoulos

1 Introduction

Privatizations of State-owned companies and justifications for restrictions on EU fundamental freedoms is an evolving topic, which is developing significantly and presents important past, present and future perspectives. Justifications for restrictions on EU fundamental freedoms were scrutinized extensively by the Court of Justice of the EU's (CJEU) golden shares case law.[1] However, the issue of justifications

[1] For analysis of the golden shares case law, *see* S. Grundmann and F. Moslein,'Golden Shares-State Control in Privatised Companies: Comparative Law, European Law and Policy Aspects' (2004) EBFLJ (Euredia) 623; M. Andenas and F. Wooldridge, *European Comparative Company Law* (CUP 2010), 14–20; N. De Luca, *European Company Law* (CUP (2017), 352–364. J. Adolff, 'Turn of the Tide?: The "Golden Share" Judgments of the European Court of Justice and the Liberalization of the European Capital Markets' (2002) 3 German LJ 1–14; V. Kronenberger, 'The rise of the 'golden' age of free movement of capital: A comment on the golden shares judgments of the Court of Justice of the European Communities' (2003) 4 EBOR 115–135; C. O'Grady Putek,'Limited but not lost: A comment on the ECJ's Golden Share Decisions' (2004) 72 Fordham L Rev:2219–2285; A, Looijestijn-Clearie, 'All That Glitters Is Not Gold: European Court of Justice Strikes Down Golden Shares in Two Dutch Companies' (2007) 8 EBOR 429–453; S. Rammeloo, 'Past, Present (and Future?) of the German Volkswagengesetz under the EC Treaty' (2007) 4 ECL 118–121; J. Van Bekkum, J. Kloosterman, and J. Winter (2008) Golden Shares and European Company Law: the Implications of Volkswagen' (2008) 5 ECL 6–12. U. Ehricke, 'Case Note-Case C-174/04 Commission v Italy' (2006) 43 CMLRev 1457–1467; A. Artés, 'Advancing Harmonization: Should the ECJ Apply Golden Shares' Standards to National Company Law?' (2009) 20 EBLR: 457–482; N, Gaydarska and S. Rammeloo, 'The Legality of the 'Golden Share' under EC Law. Maastricht Faculty of Law' (2009) 5 (9) Maastricht Faculty of Law Working Paper 1–27; S. Soltysiński, 'Golden Shares: Recent Developments in ECJ Jurisprudence and Member States Legislation' in: S. Grundmann and others (eds), F*estschrift Für Klaus J. Hopt Zum 70. Geburtstag Am 24. August 2010: Unternehmen, Markt Und Verantwortung* (De Gruyter 2010)) 2571–2595.

T. Papadopoulos (✉)
Department of Law, University of Cyprus, Nicosia, Cyprus
e-mail: papadopoulos.thomas@ucy.ac.cy

J. Chaisse et al. (eds.), *Regulation of State-Controlled Enterprises*, International Law and the Global South, https://doi.org/10.1007/978-981-19-1368-6_10

for restrictions[2] on EU fundamental freedoms is not only a topic concerning old privatizations cases regarding golden shares. Justifications for restrictions on EU fundamental freedoms are also relevant to current cases of privatizations, such as *Associação Peço a Palavra*. Moreover, justifications for restrictions could also face future challenges on privatizations, such as the growing significance of corporate social responsibility (CSR). Lessons learned from previous golden shares case law and from the recent case of *Associação Peço a Palavra* could provide useful guidance to the integration of CSR into the privatization process.

This chapter seeks to explore under which conditions EU Member States could continue to have special prerogatives in privatized companies on the basis of public interest considerations. Member States often invoke public interest considerations in order to justify their privileges and control over privatized companies. This chapter discusses the justifications that Member States are invoking to justify golden shares infringing EU fundamental freedoms. *Commission v Belgium*[3] is the only case where the CJEU accepted the justifications invoked by the Belgian government. The specific conditions for the acceptance by the CJEU of justifications for restrictions were specified in this latter case. In the context of *Associação Peço a Palavra*, this chapter also examines the justification for restrictions deriving from tender specifications governing the conditions to which a privatization process of a State-owned company is subject. According to this latter case, Member States wishing to continue to exercise control on the basis of public interest over a privatized company could choose to adopt tender specifications governing the conditions to which a privatization process of a State-owned company is subject. Moreover, this chapter considers some future perspectives and explains how the discussion about privatizations and justified restrictions on EU fundamental freedoms could contribute to the integration of CSR into the privatization process. This chapter reaches some useful conclusions on how Member States could preserve special privileges and control over privatized companies in order to promote public interest considerations.

[2] This chapter does not scrutinize extensively the issue of restrictions on EU fundamental freedoms, but only the issue of justifications for restrictions. Restrictions on EU fundamental freedoms are discussed only as a prerequisite of the analysis of the justifications for restrictions on EU fundamental freedoms. This chapter does not discuss which fundamental freedom applies primarily to national privatization schemes. It does not discuss whether free movement of capital or freedom of establishment or both freedoms apply to such national golden shares schemes. Hence, this chapter does not discuss the evolution of case law with regard to the applicable freedom to golden shares and to privatization schemes.

[3] Case C-503/99 *Commission v Belgium* ECLI:EU:C:2002:328.

2 Lessons from the Past: Golden Shares of Privatized Companies and Justified Restrictions on EU Fundamental Freedoms

2.1 The European Commission's Strategy Towards Golden Shares

In the 1990s, the European Commission started scrutinizing the privatization programmes of many EU Member States. The European Commission was particularly concerned with many special rights retained by Member States in privatized undertakings, which were thought to infringe free movement of capital (Art. 63 TFEU) and freedom of establishment (Art. 49 TFEU).[4] These special rights were introduced by golden shares in the capital of privatized companies. "Golden shares" are defined as special rights that States retain in certain privatized companies, which do not often correspond to the State's shareholding in the company. Hence, with regard to golden shares, there is no proportionality between capital and control. The adoption of these special rights is based usually on public interest considerations. These special rights constitute frequently veto rights over certain corporate decisions, the direct appointment of board members and powers to inhibit certain acquisitions of shares or voting rights above a certain percentage in the privatized company.[5] Golden shares are mechanisms of exerting State control over privatized companies. Member States deciding to privatize certain State-owned companies are unwilling to give up completely their previous control over these companies, which were offering quite often services general interest. Finally, the European Commission decided to initiate infringement proceedings against Member States holding golden shares. These infringement proceedings before the CJEU resulted in the golden shares case law, a series of cases scrutinizing the compatibility of these golden shares with fundamental freedoms.

In its 1997 Communication,[6] with regard to justifications for restrictions on freedom of establishment (Art. 49 TFEU), the European Commission referred to the possibility of justification for restrictions on the basis of activities connected with the exercise of official authority (Art. 51 TFEU[7]) and on the grounds of public

[4] E. Szyszczak, 'Golden Shares and Market Governance' (2002) 29 LIEI 255–284; C. Barnard,'The Substantive Law of the EU-The Four Freedoms' (5th edn, OUP 2016) 535–536. For a detailed analysis of the relationship between free movement of capital and company law, *see* M, Andenas, G. Tilmann and M. Pannier, 'Free Movement of Capital and National Company Law' (2005) 16 EBLR 757–786.

[5] Van Bekkum, Kloosterman and Winter (n 1) 6.

[6] Communication of the Commission on certain legal aspects concerning intra-EU investment [1997] OJ C 220/15.

[7] Art. 51 TFEU (ex Art. 45 TEC) "*The provisions of this Chapter shall not apply, so far as any given Member State is concerned, to activities which in that State are connected, even occasionally, with the exercise of official authority. The European Parliament and the Council, acting in accordance*

policy, public security or public health (Art. 52 TFEU[8]). With regard to justifications for restrictions on the free movement of capital (Art. 63 TFEU), the European Commission referred to Art. 65(1)(a)(b)TFEU.[9,10] The European Commission stressed that compliance with the principle of proportionality was essential, according to the relevant CJEU's case law: "*[t]he proportionality test means that the restriction in question constitutes a necessary measure to assure the protection of the grounds mentioned above (i.e. public policy, public security,* etc.*) and, at the same time, there is (are) no other measure(s) which, while achieving the same results, is (are) less restrictive for the freedom concerned*".[11] Regarding the free movement of capital, the similarities and overlaps between the derogations of Art. 65 TFEU and the derogations of other Treaty articles make the CJEU refer to its case law on other EU fundament freedoms when it construes the derogations of Art. 65 TFEU.[12] Moreover, with regard to justification for restrictions on freedom of establishment and on the free movement of capital, the European Commission mentioned the possibility of justification under the judicially introduced and construed imperative requirements in the general interest and pointed out to the well-known *Gebhard* test.[13] Hence,

---

with the ordinary legislative procedure, may rule that the provisions of this Chapter shall not apply to certain activities.".

[8] Art. 52 (ex Art. 46 TEC) "*1. The provisions of this Chapter and measures taken in pursuance thereof shall not prejudice the applicability of provisions laid down by law, regulation or administrative action providing for special treatment for foreign nationals on grounds of public policy, public security or public health. 2. The European Parliament and the Council shall, acting in accordance with the ordinary legislative procedure, issue directives for the coordination of the abovementioned provisions.*".

[9] Art. 65 (ex Art. 58 TEC): "*1. The provisions of Article 63 shall be without prejudice to the right of Member States: (a) to apply the relevant provisions of their tax law which distinguish between taxpayers who are not in the same situation with regard to their place of residence or with regard to the place where their capital is invested;*

(b) to take all requisite measures to prevent infringements of national law and regulations, in particular in the field of taxation and the prudential supervision of financial institutions, or to lay down procedures for the declaration of capital movements for purposes of administrative or statistical information, or to take measures which are justified on grounds of public policy or public security.".

[10] Communication of the Commission on certain legal aspects concerning intra-EU investment [1997] OJ C 220/15, para 5. For a comprehensive analysis of Art. 65 (1)(a)(b)TFEU, *see* S. Hindelang, *The Free Movement of Capital and Foreign Direct Investment: The Scope of Protection in EU Law.* (OUP 2009) 214–247.

[11] Communication of the Commission on certain legal aspects concerning intra-EU investment [1997] OJ C 220/15, para 5.

[12] Barnard (n 4) 546.

[13] The European Commission referred to the four conditions of the *Gebhard* test: "*the case law of the Court of Justice has recently confirmed that 'national measures liable to hinder or make less attractive the exercise of fundamental freedoms guaranteed by the Treaty must fulfil four conditions: they must be applied in a non-discriminatory manner; they must be justified by imperative requirements in the general interest; they must be suitable for securing the attainment of the objective that they pursue; and they must not go beyond what is necessary in order to attain it'*". Case C-148 /91 *Veronica* ECLI:EU:C:1993:45 para 9. Case 19/92 *Kraus* ECLI:EU:C:1993:125 para 32. Case 55/94 *Gebhard* ECLI:EU:C:1995:411, para 37. Case 415/93 *Bosman*, ECLI:EU:C:1995:463 para

restrictions on freedom of establishment and free movement of capital could be justified by express derogations laid down by TFEU provisions (for the justification for directly discriminatory national measures) or by mandatory requirements in the general interest developed by the CJEU (for the justification for indirectly discriminatory national measures, non-discriminatory national measures and national measures which prevent or impede market access).[14] Nevertheless, irrespective of whether freedom of establishment or free movement of capital applies, the available justifications are construed quite narrowly, limiting Member States' possibility of introducing golden shares.[15]

The European Commission categorized the privileges granted to Member States in the capital of privatized companies into the following categories: (1) discriminatory prohibition on investors from another EU Member State acquiring more than a limited amount of voting shares in domestic privatized companies and/or having to get authorization for the acquisition of shares above a certain threshold,[16] (2) non-discriminatory general authorization measures, e.g. both EU and national investors wanting to acquire a stake in a domestic privatized company beyond a certain threshold, (3) the rights given to governments, in derogation of company law, to veto and, as a result, to block certain major decisions to be taken by the domestic privatized company, as well as the imposition of a requirement for the appointment of some directors as a means of exercising the right of veto, etc.[17] The first category could be justified only according to the express derogations of public policy, public security and public health of Arts. 51 and 65 TFEU. In addition to the express derogations of Arts. 51 and 65 TFEU, the second and third category of non-discriminatory

---

104. Communication of the Commission on certain legal aspects concerning intra-EU investment [1997] OJ C 220/15, para 5. For a comprehensive analysis of imperative or mandatory requirements in the general interest with regard to justification for restrictions on free movement of capital, *see* Hindelang (n 10) 255–274.

[14] Barnard (n 4) 449–450. Adolff (n 1) 3–4. *See also* C. Barnard, 'Derogations, justifications and the four freedoms: Is state interest really protected?' in C. Barnard and O. Odudu (eds) *The outer limits of European Union Law* (Hart 2009) 273–306; V. Hatzopoulos, 'Justifications for Restrictions to Free Movement: Towards a Single Normative Framework?' in: Andenas M, Bekkedal T, Pantaleo L (eds) The Reach of Free Movement. T.M.C. (Asser Press 2017) 131–156. Moreover, there is an interesting debate about the scope of discretion enjoyed by Member States in the structuring of their public interest considerations capable of justifying restrictions on EU fundamental freedoms. It was argued that the CJEU should not interfere to a significant degree with non-economic domestic policy choices in areas not caught by EU harmonization where the EU fundamental freedoms continue to apply, because Member States could exercise their residual competence, according to EU constitutional law. *See* D. Thym, 'The Constitutional Dimension of Public Policy Justifications' in P. Koutrakos, N.N. Shuibhne and P. Syrpis (eds.) *Exceptions from EU Free Movement Law* (Hart 2016) 170–189, 185–188.

[15] T. Szabados,'Recent Golden Share Cases in the Jurisprudence of the Court of Justice of the European Union' (2015) 16 German LJ, 1099–1130. *See also* European Commission, 'Commission Staff Working Document, Special rights in privatized companies in the enlarged Union – a decade full of developments' (2005), 27.

[16] European Commission, 'Communication of the Commission on certain legal aspects concerning intra-EU investment' [1997] OJ C220/15, para 7.

[17] C220/15 (n 16) para 8.

restrictions "*can be justified by imperative requirements in the general interest and are based on a set of objective criteria, stable over time and made public (in the sense of reducing to a minimum the discretion of national authorities), without which they could be implemented in such a way that control of the firm in question remains in the hands of national operators*".[18] The prerogatives retained by the Member States in the capital of privatized companies are based on their public interest considerations (i.e. "national interest" considerations).[19] An important deficit of many of these public interest considerations is that they are not sufficiently transparent and could result in discrimination against foreign investors and legal uncertainty. These public interest considerations[20] embrace both economic and non-economic grounds exceeding the derogations of Arts. 51 and 65 TFEU and the mandatory requirements in the general interest, which were interpreted strictly by the CJEU. The European Commission doubted and expressed its concerns whether these public interest considerations could be used as a legal cover for State prerogatives in privatized companies.[21]

It is interesting to discuss the justifications for restrictions invoked by Member States in the golden shares case law. This will assist us in understanding the approach followed and the criteria identified by the CJEU regarding these justifications. This examination of national efforts to justify restrictions in the CJEU's golden shares case law provides the essential background for analysing the distinction between lawful and unlawful justifications. Hence, it is necessary to acquaint the reader with the CJEU's approach regarding justifications for restrictions in the golden shares cases. The justifications for restrictions are examined in the following golden shares cases: *Commission v France*,[22] *Commission v Portugal (first Portuguese golden shares case)*,[23] *Commission v Belgium*,[24] *Commission v Spain*,[25] *Commission v Italy (second Italian golden shares case)*,[26] *Commission v Netherlands*,[27] *Commission v*

[18] ibid. paras 7–8.

[19] For a general analysis of public interest considerations/national interest considerations in the context of internal market, *see* M. Papp,'Member State Interests and EU Internal Market Law' in M. Varju (ed) *Between Compliance and Particularism* (Springer 2019) 103–127.

[20] The main public interest considerations invoked by Member States for retaining a degree of disproportionate corporate control over a privatized company were: (1) protection against hostile takeovers by unwelcome bidders; (2) to ensure that the company has its previous corporate objective and jurisdiction of incorporation; (3) to prevent the sale of strategic and key company assets while retaining the current corporate structure, purpose and form of the undertaking; (4) to ensure that the new owners of privatized enterprises comply with certain commitments included in the sales agreement; (5) to guarantee the provision of services of general interest in sensitive sectors of the economy; (6) to safeguard public security, public health and national defence. *See* European Commission (n 15) 6.

[21] C220/15 (n 16), para 8.

[22] Case C-483/99 *Commission v France* ECLI:EU:C:2002:327.

[23] Case C-367/98 *Commission v Portugal* ECLI:EU:C:2002:326.

[24] Case C-503/99 *Commission v Belgium* ECLI:EU:C:2002:328.

[25] Case C-463/00 *Commission v Spain* ECLI:EU:C:2003:272.

[26] Case C-174/04 *Commission v Italy* ECLI:EU:C:2005:350.

[27] Joined Cases C-282 and C-283/04 *Commission v Netherlands* ECLI:EU:C:2006:608.

Germany,[28] *Commission v Italy (fourth Italian golden shares case)*,[29] *Commission v Portugal (second Portuguese golden shares case)*,[30] *Commission v Portugal (third Portuguese golden shares case)*,[31] *Commission v Portugal (fourth Portuguese golden shares case)*[32] *and Commission v Greece*.[33] Nevertheless, the following golden shares cases are not examined, because they do not present an interest for the topic of justifications for restrictions on EU fundamental freedoms: *Commission v Italy (first Italian golden shares case)*,[34] *Commission v UK*[35] *and Federconsumatori (third Italian golden shares case)*.[36]

---

[28] Case C-112/05 *Commission v Germany* ECLI:EU:C:2007:623.

[29] Case C-326/07 *Commission v Italy*, ECLI:EU:C:2009:193.

[30] Case C-171/08 *Commission v Portugal* ECLI:EU:C:2010:412.

[31] Case C-543/08 *Commission v Portugal* ECLI:EU:C:2010:669.

[32] Case C-212/09 *Commission v Portugal* ECLI:EU:C:2011:717.

[33] Case C-244/11 *Commission v Greece* ECLI:EU:C:2012:694.

[34] The first Italian golden shares case is Case C-58/99 *Commission v Italy* ECLI:EU:C:2000:280, but it is not discussed in this chapter. This case does not present an interest for the topic of justifications for restrictions on EU fundamental freedoms, because Italy conceded the case and the CJEU held that the Italian measures were infringing the freedom of establishment and the free movement of capital without discussing the issue of justifications. *See* A. Dashwood, D. Wyatt and others, *Wyatt and Dashwood's European Union Law* (Hart 2011), 665.

[35] Case 98/01 *Commission v UK* ECLI:EU:C:2003:273. In *Commission v UK*, the CJEU examined the golden shares held by UK in the privatized British Airports Authority (BAA) owning and operating seven international airports in the United Kingdom. The CJEU found that the UK government infringed free movement of capital by maintaining in force the provisions limiting the possibility of acquiring voting shares in BAA as well as the procedure requiring consent to the disposal of the company's assets, to control of its subsidiaries and to winding-up. In that case, the CJEU did not examine any justifications for these restrictions on free movement of capital, because the UK government expressly stated that it did not wish to rely on any justification based on possible overriding requirements relating to the general interest. The UK Government did not invoke any public interest in order to justify this restriction on free movement of capital. Case 98/01 *Commission v UK* ECLI:EU:C:2003:273, para 13, 50, 49, 22. The UK government tried to defend unsuccessfully its golden shares through other grounds (application of *Keck and Mithouard* doctrine, private company law mechanisms, normal operation of company law). Case 98/01 *Commission v UK* ECLI:EU:C:2003:273, paras 45–48; I. Antonaki,'Keck in Capital? Redefining 'Restrictions' in the 'Golden Shares' Case Law' (2016) 4 Erasmus LR, 177–188.

[36] Joined cases C-463/04 and C-464/04 *Federconsumatori* ECLI:EU:C:2007:752. In *Federconsumatori (third Italian golden shares case)*, the CJEU did not proceed to an in-depth analysis of justifications for restrictions on EU fundamental freedoms. This case concerned "*a national provision under which the articles of association of a company limited by shares may confer on the State or a public body with a shareholding in that company the power to appoint directly one or more directors which, on its own or in conjunction with a provision which grants that State or public body the right to participate in the election on the basis of lists of the directors it has not appointed directly*", which granted to that State or public body corporate control over this company violating the principle of proportionality between capital and control. These prerogatives were liable to discourage investors from other Member States from investing in the company's capital and, as a result, constituted restriction on free movement of capital. Joined cases C-463/04 and C-464/04 *Federconsumatori* ECLI:EU:C:2007:752, para 18, 29. With regard to justifications for such restriction, the CJEU referred to the 1997 European Commission's Communication and to previous case law. The CJEU accepted the possibility that some public policy considerations could justify the

2.2 *Efforts to Justify Restrictions on EU Fundamental Freedoms in the CJEU's Golden Shares Case Law*

2.2.1 *Commission v France*[37]

In *Commission v France*, the CJEU examined "*the rules vesting in the French Republic a golden share in Société Nationale Elf- Aquitaine, whereby any holding of shares or voting rights which exceeds certain ceilings must be authorized in advance by that Member State and a decision to transfer or use as security the majority of the capital of four subsidiaries of that company may be opposed.*"[38] The CJEU held that these prerogatives of the French government were infringing free movement of capital. The French legislation was aiming at ensuring the security of petroleum supplies in the event of a crisis.[39] Energy security was a public security ground invoked by the French government.[40]

After finding that the French rules in question were infringing free movement of capital,[41] the CJEU examined the possibility of justifications. Free movement of capital could be justified either by the express derogations of Art. 65 TFEU or by overriding requirements of the general interest developed by the CJEU. The

---

preservation by Member States of a degree of control over undertakings that were initially public and subsequently privatized, where those undertakings were active in fields involving the provision of public interest or strategic services. Communication of the Commission on certain legal aspects concerning intra-EU investment [1997] OJ C 220/15. Joined cases C-463/04 and C-464/04 *Federconsumatori* ECLI:EU:C:2007:752, para 41. Nevertheless, a justification on public interest grounds was not available for Italian legislation, because Italian rules did not subject such prerogatives to any condition. The CJEU held: "*However, as noted by the national court, Article 2449 of the Civil Code clearly does not make inclusion in the articles of association of a company limited by shares of a right for the State or a public body holding shares in that company to appoint directly one or more directors subject to any condition, so that such a provision cannot be considered to be justified.*" Joined cases C-463/04 and C-464/04 *Federconsumatori* ECLI:EU:C:2007:752, para 42. Italian law did not declare any public interest concern as a rationale for its adoption and, as a matter of fact, justification for this infringement of free movement of capital was not possible.

[37] Case C-483/99 *Commission v France* ECLI:EU:C:2002:327.

[38] Case C-483/99 *Commission v France* ECLI:EU:C:2002:327, para 20.

[39] Case C-483/99 *Commission v France* ECLI:EU:C:2002:327, para 26.

[40] The CJEU stated that: "*The French Government argues, first, that the availability of supplies of petroleum products in the event of a crisis, guaranteed, first, by the right to requisition the crude oil reserves of Société Nationale Elf-Aquitaine located abroad and, second, by the authorization procedures designed to ensure that the central decision-making body of that company remains in France, are matters of public security.*" Case C-483/99 *Commission v France* ECLI:EU:C:2002:327, para 28.

[41] Case C-483/99 *Commission v France* ECLI:EU:C:2002:327, paras 40–42. For detailed comments on this case, *see*: P. Câmara,'The End of the "Golden" Age of Privatisations? - The Recent ECJ Decisions on Golden Shares' (2002) 3 EBOR 503–513.; Kronenberger (n 1)115–135; H. Fleischer, 'Case Note- Case C-367/98,Commission of the European Communities v. Portuguese Republic (Golden shares); C-483/99,Commission of the European Communities v. French Republic (Golden shares); and C-503/99,Commission of the European Communities v. Kingdom of Belgium (Golden shares). Judgments of the Full Court of 4 June 2002' (2003) 40 CMLRev 493–501.

CJEU stressed that an accepted justification on these grounds must also comply with the principle of proportionality.[42] With regard to compliance with the principle of proportionality, the CJEU referred to previous case law on the free movement of capital.[43] The CJEU accepted that the objective pursued by the French legislation, which was the safeguarding of supplies of petroleum products in the event of a crisis, fell undoubtedly within the scope of the notion of public interest.[44] The same reasoning, which was adopted by *Campus Oil*[45] in the context of free movement of goods, also applied to free movement of capital, which included public security as a justifying ground in Art. 65 TFEU.[46] The notion of public security was a strictly interpreted autonomous EU legal concept and, according to previous case law, could be invoked only if there was a genuine and sufficiently serious threat to a fundamental interest of society.[47] The broad discretionary power enjoyed by the French Minister in the context of the special rights granted to him by French legislation was against the principle of legal certainty, because these special rights were not exercised under precise and objective criteria.[48] As a result, these special rights did not comply with the principle of proportionality, because they went "*beyond what is necessary in order to attain the objective pleaded by the French Government, namely the prevention of any disruption of a minimum supply of petroleum products in the event of a real threat.*"[49] Hence, the justification invoked by France was not accepted by the CJEU due to non-compliance with the proportionality principle, and, as a matter of fact, French legislation was found to infringe the free movement of capital.

2.2.2 *Commission v Portugal (First Portuguese Golden Shares Case)*[50]

In *Commission v Portugal (first Portuguese golden shares case)*, the CJEU examined Portuguese rules precluding investors from another Member State from acquiring more than a given number of shares in certain Portuguese undertakings and the requirement that prior authorization must be obtained for the acquisition of an

[42] The CJEU held that: "*…in order to be so justified, the national legislation must be suitable for securing the objective which it pursues and must not go beyond what is necessary in order to attain it…*" Case C-483/99 *Commission v France* ECLI:EU:C:2002:327, para 45.

[43] Joined Cases C-163/94, C-165/94 and C-250/94 *Sanz de Lera and Others* ECLI:EU:C:1995:451, para 23. Case C-54/99 *Église de Scientologie* ECLI:EU:T:2002:20, para 18. Case C-483/99 *Commission v France* ECLI:EU:C:2002:327, para 45.

[44] Case C-483/99 *Commission v France* ECLI:EU:C:2002:327, para 47.

[45] Case 72/83 *Campus Oil* ECLI:EU:C:1984:256, paras 34 and 35.

[46] Case C-483/99 *Commission v France* ECLI:EU:C:2002:327, para 47.

[47] Case C-54/99 *Église de Scientologie* ECLI:EU:T:2002:20, para 17. Case C-483/99 *Commission v France* ECLI:EU:C:2002:327 para 48; P. Koutrakos,'Public Security Exceptions and EU Free Movement Law' in P. Koutrakos, N. N. Shuibhne, P. Syrpis (eds) *Exceptions from EU Free Movement Law* (Hart 2016) 190–217.

[48] Case C-483/99 *Commission v France* ECLI:EU:C:2002:327, paras 49–53. Barnard (n 4) 552.

[49] Case C-483/99 *Commission v France* ECLI:EU:C:2002:327, para 51.

[50] Case C-367/98 *Commission v Portugal* ECLI:EU:C:2002:326.

interest in a Portuguese undertaking above a certain level.[51] The CJEU found that this Portuguese privatization scheme was infringing free movement of capital.

The CJEU accepted the possibility of justification for golden shares.[52] The justifying grounds for the adoption of these prerogatives in privatized Portuguese companies, which were invoked by the Portuguese State, were the following:

(a) to modernise economic entities and make them more competitive, and to contribute to strategies for restructuring the sector or undertaking concerned;
(b) to strengthen national business capacity;
(c) to help reduce the role played by the State in the economy;
(d) to contribute to the development of the capital market;
(e) to permit widespread participation by Portuguese citizens in the share capital of undertakings, by means of an adequate capital spread, with particular attention being paid to workers in the undertakings concerned and small scale shareholders;
(f) to preserve the property interests of the State and to develop other national interests;
(g) to help reduce the burden of public debt in the economy.[53]

The Portuguese government argued that overriding requirements of the general interest justified the Portuguese privatization scheme. The Portuguese government ensured that, with regard to the protection of public interest, the economic policy objectives pursued by the privatization process were capable of justifying restrictions. It is evident that the invoked justifications of the Portuguese government were based on the financial interests of the Portuguese Republic.[54]

The CJEU examined whether the justifying grounds invoked by the Portuguese government constituted overriding requirements of the general interest and whether they complied with the principle of proportionality. In this case, the CJEU applied the well-known *Gebhard* test.[55] With regard to the financial interests of the Portuguese

---

[51] Case C-367/98 *Commission v Portugal* ECLI:EU:C:2002:326, paras 24–25. For detailed comments on this case, *see* Câmara (n 41) 503–513, Kronenberger (n 1) 115–135, Fleischer (n 41) 493–501.

[52] The CJEU stated that "*As is also apparent from the 1997 Communication, it is undeniable that, depending on the circumstances, certain concerns may justify the retention by Member States of a degree of influence within undertakings that were initially public and subsequently privatized, where those undertakings are active in fields involving the provision of services in the public interest or strategic services (see today's judgments in Case C-483/99 Commission v France, not yet published in the European Court Reports, paragraph 43, and Case C-503/99 Commission v Belgium, not yet published in the European Court Reports, paragraph 43).*" Case C-367/98 *Commission v Portugal* ECLI:EU:C:2002:326, para 47. Barnard (n 4) 544.

[53] Case C-367/98 *Commission v Portugal* ECLI:EU:C:2002:326, para 10.

[54] The Portuguese government alleged that these economic policy objectives could include the choice of a strategic partner where the undertaking tries to internationalize its activities or enhancing the competitive structure of the market concerned or restructuring and making stronger the efficiency of means of production. Case C-367/98 *Commission v Portugal* ECLI:EU:C:2002:326, para 31. Moreover, the Portuguese Government argued that a Member State should be allowed to protect its financial interests in the course of a privatization and concluded that financial interests constitute overriding requirements of the general interest. Case C-367/98 *Commission v Portugal* ECLI:EU:C:2002:326, para 32.

[55] Barnard (n 4) 541.

Republic, the CJEU repeated its well-established case law: "*the general financial interests of a Member State cannot constitute adequate justification. It is settled case-law that economic grounds can never serve as justification for obstacles prohibited by the Treaty.*"[56] The CJEU applied this reasoning to the economic policy objectives of Portuguese legislation ("*namely choosing a strategic partner, strengthening the competitive structure of the market concerned or modernizing and increasing the efficiency of means of production*") and found that these economic objectives could not be accepted as a valid justification for restrictions on the free movement of capital.[57] Hence, according to the CJEU's approach, the economic policy objectives of Portuguese legislation constituted general financial interests of Member States and, as a result, they could not be accepted as legitimate justifying grounds for restrictions on the free movement of capital. The CJEU did not discuss the proportionality principle, because the Portuguese government failed to submit a legitimate justifying ground.

2.2.3 *Commission v Belgium*[58]

Commission *v Belgium* is probably the most important of the golden shares cases, because it is the only case where the CJEU accepted that the restrictions on EU fundamental freedoms were justified. It is the only case where the CJEU accepted the justifications invoked by a Member State. This case constitutes a guide for the rest of the Member States planning to privatize State-owned companies and to introduce golden shares in their capital. In this case, the CJEU examined the Belgian rules introducing golden shares into the capital of two Belgian privatized energy companies (SNTC and Distrigaz). It is important to present the Belgian rules on the basis of which these golden shares were introduced to these privatized undertakings.

Belgian law conferred on the Belgian government a golden share in the capital of these two privatized companies granting the following special rights. First, advance notice of any transfer, use as security or change in the intended destination of the strategic assets must be given to the relevant Minister, who has the right to oppose such operations if he considers that they adversely affect the national interest in the energy sector. Prior notice of such operation must be given to the Minister, who may adopt detailed rules concerning the form and contents of such notice and who may exercise his right of opposition within 21 days after receiving such notice of an operation.[59] Secondly, the relevant Minister can appoint two representatives of the Belgian government to the board of directors of the company, who could

[56] In the context of free movement of goods, *see* Case C-265/95 *Commission v France* ECLI:EU:C:1997:595, para 62. In the context of freedom to provide services *see* Case C-398/95 *SETTG* ECLI:EU:C:1997:282, para 23. Case C-367/98 *Commission v Portugal* ECLI:EU:C:2002:326, para 52.

[57] Case C-367/98 *Commission v Portugal* ECLI:EU:C:2002:326, para 52. Barnard (n 4) 541.

[58] Case C-503/99 *Commission v Belgium* ECLI:EU:C:2002:328.

[59] Case C-503/99 *Commission v Belgium* ECLI:EU:C:2002:328, paras 1, 9.

apply/propose, within four working days, to the Minister the annulment of any decision of the board of directors, which they regard as contrary to the guidelines for the country's energy policy, including the Belgian government's objectives concerning the country's energy supply. This special right is exercised according to a specific procedure, "*that time limit of four working days shall run from the date of the meeting at which the decision in question was adopted, if the representatives of the Government were duly invited to attend that meeting, or, if they were not, from the date on which the representatives of the Government or any one of them became aware of the decision. The application to the Minister shall have suspensory effect. If the Minister does not annul the decision in question within eight working days from the date of that application, the decision shall become final.*"[60]

The CJEU found that the Belgian rules in question constituted a restriction on the free movement of capital and proceeded to examine its proposed justification.[61] The CJEU referred to the 1997 European Commission's Communication on certain aspects of intra-EU investment and reaffirmed that "*certain concerns may justify the retention by Member States of a degree of influence within undertakings that were initially public and subsequently privatized, where those undertakings are active in fields involving the provision of services in the public interest or strategic services*".[62] Restrictions on the free movement of capital could be justified by derogations of Art. 65(1) TFEU or by overriding requirements of the general interest. Moreover, such justification must be in accordance with the principle of proportionality.[63] The CJEU accepted that the goal pursued by the Belgian golden shares, which was the safeguarding of energy supplies in the event of a crisis, constituted a legitimate public interest consideration. More specifically, energy security falls within the scope of public security of Art. 65 (1) TFEU.[64] However, the CJEU stressed that public security as an exception to an EU fundamental freedom must be interpreted strictly and not unilaterally by each Member State, but according to common standards: "*public security may be relied on only if there is a genuine and sufficiently serious threat to a fundamental interest of society.*"[65]

After finding that Belgian golden shares serve a legitimate public interest ground, the CJEU started examining its compliance with the principle of proportionality. First, the CJEU held that the Belgian golden shares introduced an opposition regime,

---

[60] Case C-503/99 *Commission v Belgium* ECLI:EU:C:2002:328, paras 1, 9.

[61] Case C-503/99 *Commission v Belgium* ECLI:EU:C:2002:328, paras 39–42. For detailed comments on this case, *see* Câmara (n 41) 503–513, Kronenberger (n 1) 115–135, Fleischer (n 41) 493–501.

[62] Case C-503/99 *Commission v Belgium* ECLI:EU:C:2002:328, para 43.

[63] Case C-503/99 *Commission v Belgium* ECLI:EU:C:2002:328, para 45.

[64] The ground of public security regarding safeguarding energy supplies in the event of a crisis, which is prescribed by the free movement of capital derogations of Art. 65 TFEU, follows the similar interpretation of derogation to free movement goods as it was analyzed by *Campus Oil*. Case 72/83 *Campus Oil and Others* [1984] ECR 2727. Barnard (n 4) 551–552. Case C-503/99 *Commission v Belgium* ECLI:EU:C:2002:328, para 46.

[65] Case C-54/99 *Église de Scientologie* ECLI:EU:T:2002:20, para 17, Case C-503/99 *Commission v Belgium* ECLI:EU:C:2002:328, para 47. Koutrakos (n 47) 192–197.

a regime of ex post facto control. According to this opposition regime, the exercise of control by the relevant Minister demanded an initiative on the part of Belgian authorities, which was a completely different process than a system of prior approval; this opposition regime respected the decision-making autonomy of the privatized company and required the Belgian authorities to comply with strict time limits.[66] Secondly, these special rights are restricted "*to certain decisions concerning the strategic assets of the companies in question, including in particular the energy supply networks, and to such specific management decisions relating to those assets as may be called in question in any given case.*"[67] Thirdly, the ministerial intervention provided by the Belgian golden shares was exercised only where the energy policy goals were endangered, must be formally justified and could be challenged before national courts.[68]

The CJEU held that the Belgian golden shares served a legitimate public interest consideration in compliance with the principle of proportionality: "*The scheme therefore makes it possible to guarantee, on the basis of objective criteria which are subject to judicial review, the effective availability of the lines and conduits providing the main infrastructures for the domestic conveyance of energy products, as well as other infrastructures for the domestic conveyance and storage of gas, including unloading and cross-border facilities. Thus, it enables the Member State concerned to intervene with a view to ensuring, in a given situation, compliance with the public service obligations incumbent on SNTC and Distrigaz, whilst at the same time observing the requirements of legal certainty*".[69] Although the Belgian rules were restricting the free movement of capital, the CJEU concluded that these restrictions were justified on the basis of energy security in the event of a crisis.[70] The CJEU did not proceed to a thorough examination of any restrictions on freedom of establishment, because even if Belgian rules constituted restrictions on freedom of establishment, such restrictions would be justified on the basis of public security provided by Art. 52 TFEU following the same approach as that adopted in this case for the justification for restrictions on the free movement of capital on the basis of public security.[71]

2.2.4 *Commission v Spain*[72]

In *Commission v Spain*, the CJEU scrutinized the system of prior administrative approval in the Spanish privatization scheme of certain enterprises. The CJEU held that Spanish rules implementing a system of prior administrative approval constituted a restriction on the free movement of capital, because these indistinctly applicable

66 Case C-503/99 *Commission v Belgium* ECLI:EU:C:2002:328, para 49.

67 Case C-503/99 *Commission v Belgium* ECLI:EU:C:2002:328, para 50.

68 Case C-503/99 *Commission v Belgium* ECLI:EU:C:2002:328, para 51.

69 Case C-503/99 *Commission v Belgium* ECLI:EU:C:2002:328, para 52.

70 Case C-503/99 *Commission v Belgium* ECLI:EU:C:2002:328, para 55.

71 Case C-503/99 *Commission v Belgium* ECLI:EU:C:2002:328, para 59. Koutrakos (n 47) 192–197.

72 Case C-463/00 *Commission v Spain* ECLI:EU:C:2003:272.

restrictions on investment operations could discourage investors from other Member States from making such investments and, consequently, affect market access.[73] After identifying this restriction on the EU free movement of capital, the CJEU proceeded to examine the available justifications.[74] Public interest considerations could constitute the basis of justification for restrictions on the free movement of capital.

The CJEU followed its usual approach. It stated that the free movement of capital, as an EU fundamental freedom, could be restricted only by national rules justified by Art. 65 (1) TFEU or by overriding requirements of the general interest and which must comply with the proportionality principle.[75] The CJEU examined the argument of the Spanish government that the prior administrative approval regime was justified by overriding requirements of the general interest linked to strategic imperatives and the need to ensure continuity in public services. The CJEU found that two Spanish companies under privatization, which were active in regular commercial activities, did not perform any public services. More specifically, the following two Spanish companies were not offering any public services: Tabacalera SA producing tobacco products and Corporación Bancaria de España SA (Argentaria), constituting a group of commercial banks that operated in the traditional banking sector and which were not performing any of the functions of a central bank or similar public body.[76] Hence, the prerogatives of the Spanish State in these two companies performing solely normal business operations without any element of public service could not be justified on the basis of public interest considerations.

While State privileges in a privatized tobacco industry and a bank could not be justified on the basis of public interest, other undertakings active in the petroleum, telecommunications and electricity sectors were deemed to serve public interest considerations and, more specifically, public security.[77] It is easily understood that a Member State could not invoke public interest considerations to justify its special rights in privatized companies, which did not offer public interest or strategic services and which were simply offering regular commercial services as any other similar

---

[73] Case C-463/00 *Commission v Spain* ECLI:EU:C:2003:272, paras 61–62.

[74] The CJEU accepted without any hesitation that, as in previous golden shares cases, "*depending on the circumstances, certain concerns may justify the retention by Member States of a degree of influence within undertakings that were initially public and subsequently privatized, where those undertakings are active in fields involving the provision of services in the public interest or strategic services*". Case C-367/98 *Commission v Portugal* ECLI:EU:C:2002:326, para 47. Case C-483/99 *Commission v France* ECLI:EU:C:2002:327, para 43. Case C-503/99 *Commission v Belgium* ECLI:EU:C:2002:328, para 43. Case C-463/00 *Commission v Spain* ECLI:EU:C:2003:272, para 66.

[75] The CJEU stated: "*Furthermore, in order to be so justified, the national legislation must be suitable for securing the objective which it pursues and must not go beyond what is necessary in order to attain it, so as to accord with the principle of proportionality.*" Case C-463/00 *Commission v Spain* ECLI:EU:C:2003:272, para 68.

[76] Case C-463/00 *Commission v Spain* ECLI:EU:C:2003:272, para 70.

[77] The CJEU held that "*it is undeniable that the objective of safeguarding supplies of such products or the provision of such services within the Member State concerned in the event of a crisis may constitute a public-security reason*". Case C-463/00 *Commission v Spain* ECLI:EU:C:2003:272, para 71.

privately-held company. The CJEU submitted the derogations of public security to its well-established test of strict interpretation, according to which public security is an autonomous EU legal concept not determined separately by each Member States and could be invoked "*only if there is a genuine and sufficiently serious threat to a fundamental interest of society*".[78] This meant that the Spanish rules in question concerning these three Spanish undertakings under privatization must secure that, in the event of a genuine and serious threat, a minimum supply of petroleum products and electricity and a minimum level of telecommunications services could be maintained and, at the same time, must comply with the proportionality principle.[79]

These Spanish rules failed to comply with the proportionality principle due to the lack of legal certainty. This lack of legal certainty derived from the broad discretion enjoyed by the State. In the context of this wide discretion, the special rights of the State were not subject to any conditions and the investors were not given any information on the specific and objective circumstances under which prior approval would be granted or withheld.[80]

The Spanish golden shares system of prior administrative approval was compared with the Belgian golden shares, which passed the CJEU's justification test and, as a result, were accepted.[81] The CJEU summarized the criteria of *Commission v Belgium* that a golden share must fulfil in order to be accepted as justified.[82] The Spanish rules did not satisfy the criteria adopted by *Commission v Belgium*. The CJEU examined the various characteristics of the Spanish legislation in the light of the criteria introduced by *Commission v Belgium*: (1) not all the assets or shareholdings seeking to achieve the objective of the enterprise under privatization were specified in legislation, (2) the decisions for the voluntary winding-up, demerger or merger of the enterprise under privatization or a change in its object were decisions of paramount importance for the structure and operation of that enterprise and not, like in *Commission v Belgium*, decisions about very specific and predetermined management issues, (3) the State

[78] Case C-463/00 *Commission v Spain* ECLI:EU:C:2003:272, para 72. Koutrakos n (47) 192–197.

[79] Case C-463/00 *Commission v Spain* ECLI:EU:C:2003:272, para 73.

[80] Case C-463/00 *Commission v Spain* ECLI:EU:C:2003:272, paras 74, 76. Hence, investors could not be notified about the scope of their rights and obligations on the basis of exercising free movement capital due to this lack of precision of conditions and of information, which results in an encroachment of the principle of legal certainty. Case C-463/00 *Commission v Spain* ECLI:EU:C:2003:272, para 75.

[81] The Spanish golden shares system concerned a "*prior administrative approval of decisions on the winding-up, demerger or merger of the undertaking, on the disposal or charging of the assets or shareholdings necessary for the attainment of the undertakings' objects and on any change in the undertakings' objects*". Case C-463/00 *Commission v Spain* ECLI:EU:C:2003:272, para 77.

[82] These criteria were: (1) the Belgian golden share was one of ex post facto opposition, which is less restrictive than a system of prior approval such as that in the present case; (2) the Belgian rules listed specifically the strategic assets concerned and the management decisions which could be challenged in any given case; (3) any intervention by the administrative authorities to exercise veto and to block certain corporate decisions was strictly limited to cases in which the objectives of the energy policy were endangered; (4) any decision taken in that context had to be supported by a formal statement of reasons (formal justification of an administrative act) and was subject to an effective judicial review by the Belgian courts. Case C-463/00 *Commission v Spain* ECLI:EU:C:2003:272, para 77.

intervention and exercise of special rights in the privatized enterprise were not subject to any condition restricting the discretion of the State, like in *Commission v Belgium*, (4) The possibility of judicial review before national courts did not mitigate this wide discretion enjoyed by the State, because national courts did not have sufficiently precise and specific criteria to give them the possibility to review how the State exercised its discretion.[83] This lack of legal certainty, which was due to the lack of any objective and precise criteria in Spanish rules, resulted in a breach of the proportionality principle.[84] These Spanish rules could not be justified and were found to infringe the free movement of capital.

2.2.5 *Commission v Italy (Second Italian Golden Shares Case)*[85]

In *Commission v Italy (second Italian golden shares case)*,[86] the CJEU examined Italian privatization rules in the energy sector. The CJEU found that Italian law providing for the automatic suspension of voting rights attaching to holdings in excess of 2% of the capital of undertakings operating in the electricity and gas sectors, where those holdings were acquired by public undertakings not quoted on regulated financial markets and enjoying a dominant position in their own domestic markets, infringed free movement of capital.[87]

The Italian government argued that Italian law was seeking to secure sound and fair conditions of competition in the energy markets of Italy, which were opened up to competition.[88] The rationale of Italian law could not constitute a valid justifying ground, according to CJEU's previous case law: an interest in generally enhancing the competitive structure of the specific market did not constitute valid justification for restrictions on the free movement of capital.[89]

---

[83] Case C-463/00 *Commission v Spain* ECLI:EU:C:2003:272, para 79.

[84] Case C-463/00 *Commission v Spain* ECLI:EU:C:2003:272, para 80.

[85] Case C-174/04 *Commission v Italy* ECLI:EU:C:2005:350.

[86] The first Italian golden shares case is Case C-58/99 *Commission v Italy* ECLI:EU:C:2000:280, but it is not discussed in this chapter. This case does not present an interest for the topic of justifications for restrictions on EU fundamental freedoms, because Italy conceded the case and the CJEU held that the Italian measures were infringing the freedom of establishment and the free movement of capital without discussing the issue of justifications. *See* Dashwood, Wyatt et. al (n 34) 665.

[87] Case C-174/04 *Commission v Italy* ECLI:EU:C:2005:350, para 42. For detailed comments on this case, *see* Ehricke (n 1) 1457–1467.

[88] Italian law makes sure "*that, pending effective liberalization of the energy sector in Europe, the Italian market is not subjected to anticompetitive attacks by public undertakings operating in the same sector in other Member States that have been placed at an advantage by domestic legislation which has kept them in a privileged position. If control of undertakings operating in the Italian electricity and gas markets were acquired by public undertakings of that kind, the efforts of the Italian authorities to open up the energy sector to competition might be negated*". Case C-174/04 *Commission v Italy* ECLI:EU:C:2005:350, para 36.

[89] Case C-367/98 *Commission v Portugal* ECLI:EU:C:2002:326, para 52. Case C-174/04 *Commission v Italy* ECLI:EU:C:2005:350, para 37. At that point, the CJEU stressed the importance of Merger Regulation in order to prove how redundant and irrelevant the Italian law was. Merger

The Italian government also invoked as a possible justification the need to safeguard the supply of energy within Italian territory.[90] While energy security could, under specific conditions, justify restrictions on the free movement of capital, the Italian government could not stipulate how a limitation of voting rights affecting only one specific category of public undertakings was essential to achieve that goal.[91] Hence, the Italian government could not demonstrate that Italian law's rationale was necessary to safeguard the energy supplies in Italy.[92]

2.2.6 *Commission v Netherlands*[93]

In *Commission v Netherlands*, the CJEU scrutinized Dutch golden shares in privatized companies offering telecommunication and postal services (KPN and TPG). The CJEU found that "*by maintaining in the memorandum and articles of association of KPN and TPG certain provisions, providing that the capital of those companies is to include a special share held by the Netherlands State, which confers on the latter special rights to approve certain management decisions of the organs of those companies, which are not limited to cases where the intervention of that State is necessary for overriding reasons in the general interest recognized by the Court and, in the case of TPG in particular for ensuring the maintenance of universal postal service, Netherlands infringed free movement of capital.*"[94] After stating that restrictions on the free movement of capital could be justified by Art. 65 TFEU or by overriding reasons in the general interest, the discretion of Member States regarding the structuring and promotion of these public interest considerations was stressed. Member States could determine the level of protection they would give to such public interest considerations and how this protection would be attained. These public interest considerations must follow the interpretation provided by CJEU's case law and must comply with the proportionality principle.[95] With regard to justification on the basis of public interest considerations, the Dutch government invoked the

---

Regulation could prohibit concentrations with a Union dimension which would significantly impede effective competition in the common market or a substantial part thereof. Regulation 139/2004 on the control of concentrations between undertakings (Merger Regulation) [2004] OJ L24/1. Case C-174/04 *Commission v Italy* ECLI:EU:C:2005:350, para 38.

[90] Case C-174/04 *Commission v Italy* ECLI:EU:C:2005:350, para 39.

[91] The CJEU held: "*In particular, it has not explained why it is necessary for the shares of undertakings operating in the energy sector in Italy to be held by private shareholders or by public shareholders quoted on regulated financial markets for the undertakings concerned to be able to guarantee sufficient and uninterrupted supplies of electricity and gas in the Italian market.*" Case 72/83 *Campus Oil* ECLI:EU:C:1984:256, paras 34 and 35. Case C-503/99 *Commission v Belgium* ECLI:EU:C:2002:328, para 46. Case C-174/04 *Commission v Italy* ECLI:EU:C:2005:350, para 40.

[92] Case C-174/04 *Commission v Italy* ECLI:EU:C:2005:350, para 41.

[93] Joined Cases C-282 and C-283/04 *Commission v Netherlands* ECLI:EU:C:2006:608.

[94] Joined Cases C-282 and C-283/04 *Commission v Netherlands* ECLI:EU:C:2006:608, para 44. For detailed comments on this case, see: Looijestijn-Clearie (2007), pp. 429–453.

[95] Joined Cases C-282 and C-283/04 *Commission v Netherlands* ECLI:EU:C:2006:608, paras 32–33.

"*universal postal service and, more particularly, in order to protect the solvency and continuity of TPG, which is the only undertaking currently capable in the Netherlands of providing that universal service at the level required by statute.*"[96]

The CJEU, according to its previous case law, accepted that the guarantee of a service of general interest, such as universal postal service, might constitute an overriding reason in the general interest capable of justifying an obstacle to the free movement of capital.[97] Nevertheless, the Dutch rules were not complying with the principle of proportionality. The Dutch golden shares went beyond the goal to safeguard the solvency and continuity of the provider of the universal postal service, because these golden shares were not restrained only to that company's activities as a provider of universal postal service, but they also expanded to other corporate activities. The exercise of these golden shares was not based on any specific and detailed conditions and was not required to be justified by specific reasons, which could be subject to judicial review by national courts.[98] It is evident that the Dutch golden shares did not follow the criteria prescribed by *Commission v Belgium.*

2.2.7 *Commission v Germany*[99]

In *Commission v Germany*, VW law introducing certain State prerogatives into Volkswagen, the German automaker, was scrutinized. German legislation "*which, in derogation from ordinary company law, combines a limitation of the voting rights of every shareholder in a given company to 20% of that company's share capital with the requirement of a majority of over 80% of the company's capital for the adoption of certain decisions by the general assembly, and which, in derogation from the general law, allows a Member State and a territorial entity of that State each to appoint two representatives to the company's supervisory board*" constituted a restriction on the free movement of capital.[100] The German government was seeking to justify this restriction on the basis of overriding reasons in the general interest. It argued that these provisions were aiming at the protection of Volkswagen's employees and

[96] Joined Cases C-282 and C-283/04 *Commission v Netherlands* ECLI:EU:C:2006:608, paras 32–33.

[97] Joined Cases C-388/00 and C-429/00 *Radiosistemi* [2002] ECR I-5845, para 44. Joined Cases C-282 and C-283/04 *Commission v Netherlands* ECLI:EU:C:2006:608, para 38.

[98] AG Maduro has rightly pointed out in paras 38 and 39 of his Opinion. Opinion of Mr Advocate General Poiares Maduro, Joined Cases C-282 and C-283/04 *Commission v Netherlands* ECLI:EU:C:2006:234. Joined Cases C-282 and C-283/04 *Commission v Netherlands,* ECLI:EU:C:2006:608, paras 39–40. Barnard (n 4) 545; J. Rickford,'Protectionism, Capital Freedom, and the Internal Market' in U. Bernitz, W-G Ringe (eds) *Company Law and Economic Protectionism* (Oxford University Press 2010) 54–94, 64–65.

[99] Case C-112/05 *Commission v Germany* ECLI:EU:C:2007:623.

[100] Case C-112/05 *Commission v Germany* ECLI:EU:C:2007:623, Summary, para 1.

minority shareholders.[101] The CJEU rejected both grounds, and VW law was found to infringe free movement of capital.[102]

The CJEU was reluctant to accept the broad social policy justifications submitted by the German government.[103] Regarding the protection of employees, the German government did not explain why the German law was essential for the German authorities to retain a strong and entrenched position in the capital of Volkswagen to protect the interest of employees.[104] The CJEU rejected the power of German authorities to appoint representatives to the supervisory board, because German law required already a representation of employees in that body.[105] Hence, the protection of employees as a justifying ground was accepted by the CJEU, but the German government failed to explain how the German golden shares could achieve this objective. Germany did not explain how the national measures in question could maintain jobs in VW. However, it referred only to a general risk of shareholders prioritizing their personal interests against the interests of employees.[106] This approach revealed the rigorous way under which the CJEU examined requirements other than those relating to authorization in the light of the principle of proportionality.[107]

The CJEU followed the same approach with regard to the protection of minority shareholders, which was the other justifying ground invoked by the German government. While the protection of minority shareholders could constitute an overriding reason in the general interest, the German government did not prove why it was essential for the German authorities to retain the power to exercise a greater level of control than would normally be linked to their investment in order to protect the

[101] Case C-112/05 *Commission v Germany* ECLI:EU:C:2007:623, para 70.

[102] For detailed comments on this case, *see* Rammeloo (n 1) 118–12. G-J. Vossestein,'Volkswagen: the State of Affairs of Golden Shares, General Company Law and European Free Movement of Capital – A discussion of Case C-112/05 Commission v Germany of 23.10.2007' (2008) 5 ECFR 115–133; W-G. Ringe, 'Case Note-Case C–112/05, Commission v. Germany ("VW Law")' (2008) 45 CMLRev 537–544; W. Ringe, 'Company law and free movement of capital' (2010) 69 Cambridge LJ 378–409. F. Sanders,'Case C-112/05, European Commission v. Federal Republic of Germany: The Volkswagen Case and Art. 56 EC - A Proper Result, Yet Also a Missed Opportunity?' (2008) 14 Columbia J Eur L 359–369; C. Gerner-Beuerle,'Shareholders between the market and the State. The VW law and other interventions in the market economy' (2012) 49 CMLRev 97–143; Van Bekkum, Kloosterman and Winter (n 1) 6–12; P. Zumbansen, D. Saam,'The ECJ, Volkswagen and European Corporate Law: Reshaping the European Varieties of Capitalism' (2007) 8 German LJ 1027–1051; V. Cherevach and B. Megens,'Commission of the European Communities v Federal Republic of Germany, Case C-112/05, The VW Law Case; Some Critical Comments. (2009) 16 MaastrichtJEurCompL 370–376; E. Werlauff,'Safeguards against Takeover after Volkswagen – On the Lawfulness of such Safeguards under Company Law after the European Court's Decision in "Volkswagen"' (2009) 20 EBLR 101–117.

[103] Rickford (n 98) 75–76.

[104] Case C-112/05 *Commission v Germany* ECLI:EU:C:2007:623, para 74.

[105] Case C-112/05 *Commission v Germany* ECLI:EU:C:2007:623, para 75.

[106] Case C-112/05 *Commission v Germany* ECLI:EU:C:2007:623, para 80.

[107] Barnard (n 4) 544.

general interests of minority shareholders.[108] It was not made clear how VW law would achieve the objective of the protection of minority shareholders.[109]

2.2.8 *Commission v Italy (Fourth Italian Golden Shares Case)*[110]

In *Commission v Italy (fourth Italian golden shares case),* the criteria applicable to the exercise of the powers of opposition to the acquisitions of shareholdings or the conclusion of contracts by shareholders representing at least 5% of voting rights were found to be incompatible with free movement of capital.[111] The Italian legislation was based on certain "*common interests*" (public interests), which encompassed "*the minimum supply of energy resources and goods essential to the public as a whole, the continuity of public service, national defense, the protection of public policy and public security and health emergencies*".[112] These public interest grounds were accepted by the CJEU as valid justifications on the free movement of capital, as long as they complied with the principle of proportionality.[113]

The simple acquisition of a holding of more than 10% of the capital of a company belonging in the energy sector or any other acquisition of shares granting important influence on such a company's management could not constitute a real and serious threat to energy security.[114] The fact that these criteria were structured in a general and imprecise manner, along with the fact that there was no link between these criteria and the special powers to which they relate, increased legal uncertainty characterizing the exercise of these powers and granted wide discretion to the relevant national authorities, which encroached the principle of proportionality.[115] Hence, these powers of opposition were found to infringe the free movement of capital.[116]

---

[108] Case C-112/05 *Commission v Germany* ECLI:EU:C:2007:623, paras 77–78.

[109] Moreover, the CJEU stressed the danger the German authorities to promote public interests to the detriment of economic interests of Volkswagen and, as a result, also of the interests of the rest of the shareholders. Case C-112/05 *Commission v Germany* ECLI:EU:C:2007:623, para 79.

[110] Case C-326/07 *Commission v Italy*, ECLI:EU:C:2009:193.

[111] Case C-326/07 *Commission v Italy*, ECLI:EU:C:2009:193, paras 44, 55. For detailed comments on this case, *see* J. Van Bekkum,'Golden Shares: A New Approach' (2010) 7 ECL 13–19; M. O'Brien,'Case Note-Case C-326/07, Commission of the European Communities v. Italian Republic, Judgment of the Court of Justice (Third Chamber) of 26 March 2009' (2010) 47 CMLRev 245–261.

[112] Case C-326/07 *Commission v Italy*, ECLI:EU:C:2009:193, para 45. Barnard (n 4) 542.

[113] Case C-326/07 *Commission v Italy*, ECLI:EU:C:2009:193, para 46. The criteria related to the exercise of the powers of opposition were not complying with the principle of proportionality, because there was no link between the criteria and the power. Case C-326/07 *Commission v Italy*, ECLI:EU:C:2009:193, para 47.

[114] Case C-274/06 *Commission v Spain* ECLI:EU:C:2008:86, paras 38, 51. Case C-326/07 *Commission v Italy*, ECLI:EU:C:2009:193, para 48.

[115] Case C-326/07 *Commission v Italy*, ECLI:EU:C:2009:193, para 52. Szabados T (n 15) 1126.

[116] Case C-326/07 *Commission v Italy*, ECLI:EU:C:2009:193, para 55.

The CJEU also examined the criteria set out in Italian law relating to the exercise of the power of veto against corporate resolutions.[117] The public interest underpinning this veto power was founded on the fact that such resolutions affect the existence of these companies and, as a result, could endanger the continuity of the public service or on the maintenance of a minimum national supply of goods essential to the public as a whole.[118] The previous thought proves the connection between the special power of veto and the criteria fixed in Italian law for the exercise of such veto.[119] In this case, the circumstances of the criteria for the exercise of the power of veto were not clear and contained no details: "*in consequence, it must be considered, as the Commission argues, that the situations allowing the exercise of the power of veto are potentially numerous, undetermined and undeterminable, and that they leave the Italian authorities broad discretion.*"[120] Hence, Italian rules were found to infringe freedom of establishment.[121]

2.2.9 *Commission v Portugal (Second Portuguese Golden Shares Case)*[122]

In *Commission v Portugal (second Portuguese golden shares case)*, the Portuguese golden shares in privatized Portugal Telecom SGPS SA ('PT') were scrutinized by the CJEU. The Portuguese golden shares granted special rights to the Portuguese government with regard to the election of directors, the election of members of the executive committee, the election of a director to deal specifically with certain management questions and the adoption of specific decisions of the general meeting.[123] These golden shares conferring on the Portuguese government special rights disproportionate to its shareholding in PT could discourage investors from other Member

[117] This power of veto is exercised against "*resolutions for the dissolution of the company, transfer of the undertaking, merger, demerger, transfer abroad of the company headquarters, alteration of the company's objects and amendment of the articles of association removing or modifying the special powers relate to important aspects of the management of those companies*" Case C-326/07 *Commission v Italy*, ECLI:EU:C:2009:193, para 60.

[118] Case C-326/07 *Commission v Italy*, ECLI:EU:C:2009:193, para 61.

[119] Case C-326/07 *Commission v Italy*, ECLI:EU:C:2009:193, para 62.

[120] Case C-326/07 *Commission v Italy*, ECLI:EU:C:2009:193, paras 63, 66.

[121] Case C-326/07 *Commission v Italy*, ECLI:EU:C:2009:193, para 74.

[122] Case C-171/08 *Commission v Portugal* ECLI:EU:C:2010:412.

[123] The CJEU referred to "*....alterations to the articles of association and increases in share capital, any limit on or abolition of priority rights, [...] relocation of its registered office anywhere within the national territory, approval of the acquisition of ordinary shares exceeding 10% of the share capital by shareholders engaged in an activity which competes with those carried on by companies controlled by PT (...) decisions approving the general objectives and fundamental principles of PT's policies or defining the general principles of its policy in respect of the acquisition and disposal of shareholdings in companies or groups, when the general meeting's prior authorization is required*" Case C-171/08 *Commission v Portugal* ECLI:EU:C:2010:412, para 6.

States from making direct or portfolio investments into the capital of PT and, as a result, constituted an infringement of free movement of capital.[124]

Regarding the justifications based on overriding requirements in the public interest, which Portugal invoked, the CJEU rejected two of these justifying grounds at the outset. First, it did not accept that securing the conditions of competition on a particular market constituted a valid justifying ground capable of justifying a restriction on the free movement of capital.[125] Secondly, the justifying ground of preventing a possible disruption of the capital market was an economic ground, which could not be accepted as an overriding requirement in the public interest capable of justifying a restriction on the free movement of capital, as it was also stated by previous case law.[126]

With regard to justifications on the basis of Art. 65 TFEU, the CJEU accepted that the rationale of Portuguese law seeking to ensure the security of the availability of the telecommunications network in case of crisis, war or terrorism may constitute a ground of public security, which may justify a restriction on the free movement of capital.[127] Nevertheless, this justifying ground was rejected for two reasons. First, the Portuguese government did not submit any evidence of why these golden shares could prevent such a genuine and sufficiently serious threat to a fundamental interest of society.[128] Secondly, the Portuguese golden shares did not comply with the principle of proportionality. The exercise of these golden shares on behalf of the Portuguese government was not subject to any specific and objective condition or circumstances and was characterized by a discretionary latitude, which could not be considered proportionate to the objectives pursued.[129]

2.2.10 *Commission v Portugal (Third Portuguese Golden Shares Case)*[130]

In *Commission v Portugal (third Portuguese golden shares case)*, the golden shares in the electricity company, Energias de Portugal (EDP), held by the Portuguese State, were scrutinized by the CJEU in the light of the free movement of capital and freedom of establishment. These golden shares granting disproportionate special rights to the

---

[124] Case C-112/05 *Commission v Germany* ECLI:EU:C:2007:623, paras 50–52. Joined Cases C-282 and C-283/04 *Commission v Netherlands* ECLI:EU:C:2006:608, para 27. Case C-171/08 *Commission v Portugal* ECLI:EU:C:2010:412, paras 60–61.

[125] Case C-174/04 *Commission v Italy* ECLI:EU:C:2005:350, paras 36–37. Case C-274/06 *Commission v Spain* ECLI:EU:C:2008:86, para 44. Case C-171/08 *Commission v Portugal* ECLI:EU:C:2010:412, para 70.

[126] Case C-367/98 *Commission v Portugal* ECLI:EU:C:2002:326, para 52. Case C-171/08 *Commission v Portugal* ECLI:EU:C:2010:412, para 71.

[127] The CJEU drew an analogy with energy supply. Case C-274/06 *Commission v Spain* ECLI:EU:C:2008:86, para 38. Case C-171/08 *Commission v Portugal* ECLI:EU:C:2010:412, para 72.

[128] Case C-171/08 *Commission v Portugal* ECLI:EU:C:2010:412, paras 73–74.

[129] Case C-171/08 *Commission v Portugal* ECLI:EU:C:2010:412, paras 75–77.

[130] Case C-543/08 *Commission v Portugal* ECLI:EU:C:2010:669.

Portuguese State, which did not correspond to its shareholding in that company, were restrictions on the acquisition of holdings and participation in the management of the privatized company and, as a result, were found to infringe free movement of capital and freedom of establishment. These special rights were the right of veto over certain resolutions of EDP's general assembly, the exemption enjoyed by the Portuguese State from the 5% voting ceiling applying to the votes of other shareholders and the right to appoint a director, in the event that the State has voted against the nominees successfully elected as directors of that company. The CJEU found that these special rights constituted restrictions on the free movement of capital due to their deterrent effect on direct or portfolio investments.[131] Restrictions of freedom of establishment were a direct consequence of restrictions of free movement of capital, and the CJEU did not proceed to a separate examination of restrictions and their justification in the context of freedom of establishment.[132]

With regard to justification, the CJEU reiterated its well-established case law that restrictions on the free movement of capital could be justified on the grounds of Art. 65 TFEU or by overriding requirements in the public interest in compliance with the principle of proportionality. According to the CJEU, the goal of the Portuguese golden shares, which was to ensure secure energy supply in that Member State in case of a crisis, war or terrorism, could constitute a legitimate ground of public security capable of justifying a restriction on the free movement of capital.[133] Although the CJEU accepted energy security as a legitimate justifying ground, it subjected this ground to certain conditions. Public security, including energy security, must be interpreted strictly and must be invoked "*only if there is a genuine and sufficiently serious threat to a fundamental interest of society.*"[134] Even though the CJEU seemed to understand and respect the Portuguese government's argument that the threat to energy security should not be immediate or imminent,[135] it did not accept a justification on public security in such a case. This is because the Portuguese government did not provide with clarity and precision why it considered that these special rights would manage to impede a severe possible frustration of energy security as a fundamental interest of society.[136] Additionally, these special rights did not comply with the principle

[131] Case C-543/08 *Commission v Portugal* ECLI:EU:C:2010:669, Summary and para 64.

[132] Case C-543/08 *Commission v Portugal* ECLI:EU:C:2010:669, Summary and paras 98–99.

[133] Case C-543/08 *Commission v Portugal* ECLI:EU:C:2010:669, para 84.

[134] Case C-543/08 *Commission v Portugal* ECLI:EU:C:2010:669, para 85. Koutrakos (n 47) 192–197.

[135] The CJEU held that "*[g]iven that each Member State is obliged to guarantee the security of a regular and uninterrupted supply of electricity and natural gas, the Portuguese Republic can legitimately equip itself with the means required to guarantee the fundamental interest of security of supply even if there is no imminent threat. In that regard, since the risk of serious threats to the security of energy supply cannot be excluded and since such threats are by definition sudden and, in the majority of cases, unforeseeable, it is the duty of the Member State concerned to ensure that adequate mechanisms are put in place to enable it to react rapidly and effectively to guarantee that the security of that supply is not interrupted*" Case C-543/08 *Commission v Portugal* ECLI:EU:C:2010:669, para 86.

[136] Case C-543/08 *Commission v Portugal* ECLI:EU:C:2010:669, para 87.

of proportionality, because the exercise of such rights by the Portuguese State was not subject to any specific and objective condition.[137] This uncertainty regarding the exercise of special rights gave a wide discretionary power to the Portuguese State, which did not comply with the principle of proportionality.[138]

The Portuguese State invoked as a justifying ground Art. 106(2) TFEU on undertakings entrusted with the operation of services of general economic interest. The CJEU held that Art. 106(2) did not apply to that case and, as a result, could not be accepted as a justification for restrictions on EU fundamental freedoms.[139] The CJEU adopted this non-applicability of Art. 106 (2) TFEU, because this case was not about the granting of special or exclusive rights to EDP or with the classification of EDP's activities as services of general economic interest, but about the compatibility with EU fundamental freedoms of the special rights enjoyed by the Portuguese State as a shareholder owning golden shares in the capital of EDP.[140]

2.2.11 *Commission v Portugal (Fourth Portuguese Golden Shares Case)*[141]

In *Commission v Portugal (fourth Portuguese golden shares case)*, the CJEU examined the compatibility of golden shares held by the Portuguese State in GALP Energia SGPS SA (GALP). The privileges introduced by these golden shares held by the Portuguese State included: "*the election of the chairman of the Board of Directors and conferring on it a right of veto with regard to the appointment of a number of directors not exceeding one third of the total, and for resolutions amending the company's articles of association, those authorising the conclusion of certain contracts concerning the structure and control of groups of companies and those that might in any way jeopardise the country's supply of oil or gas, or of products derived therefrom.*"[142] Following its previous approach, the CJEU found that these Portuguese golden shares infringed free movement of capital due to their deterrent effect.[143] With regard to the justification for such restrictions on the free movement

[137] Case C-543/08 *Commission v Portugal* ECLI:EU:C:2010:669, paras 90–91.

[138] Case C-543/08 *Commission v Portugal* ECLI:EU:C:2010:669, para 92.

[139] With regard to Art. 106(2) TFEU on services of general economic interest, this approach has important repercussions on the possibility of Member States to justify golden shares in privatized companies offering services of general economic interest. Many State-owned companies offering services of general economic interest were privatized, while Member States retained golden shares in their capital. According to this CJEU's approach, Art. 106(2) TFEU is not applicable to such golden shares and could not justify the special rights enjoyed by Member States after the privatization of these companies offering services of general economic interest. Case C-543/08 *Commission v Portugal* ECLI:EU:C:2010:669, para 96.

[140] Case C-543/08 *Commission v Portugal* ECLI:EU:C:2010:669, para 95. Szabados (n 15) 1127.

[141] Case C-212/09 *Commission v Portugal* ECLI:EU:C:2011:717.

[142] Case C-212/09 *Commission v Portugal* ECLI:EU:C:2011:717, Summary and paras 2–13.

[143] Case C-212/09 *Commission v Portugal* ECLI:EU:C:2011:717, paras 46–69.

of capital, the CJEU followed the same approach as in *Commission v Portugal (third Portuguese golden shares case)*.[144]

The CJEU accepted that energy security invoked by the Portuguese government was a legitimate public security ground.[145] As in *Commission v Portugal (third Portuguese golden shares case)*, the CJEU embraced the same approach regarding the strict interpretation of the requirements of public security,[146] the lack of exact reasons why these special rights would defend public security[147] and the lack of specific and objective conditions or circumstances for the exercise of these special rights,[148] which resulted in an uncertainty violating the principle of proportionality.[149] A new element illustrating dangers of the modern international economic environment that the CJEU took into account in this case during the examination of energy security as a public security consideration was that "*at the present time concerns exist about certain investments made particularly by sovereign wealth funds, or investments that might be linked to terrorist organizations, in undertakings in strategic sectors, which constitute a threat of that nature in relation to energy supply.*"[150] Moreover, the CJEU followed the same interpretation of Art. 106(2) with *Commission v Portugal (third Portuguese golden shares case)* and found that provision inapplicable and not capable of being accepted as a valid justification for restrictions.[151]

2.2.12 *Commission v Greece*[152]

In *Commission v Greece*, the CJEU scrutinized the Greek prior authorization scheme and the arrangements for ex-post control in Greek strategic companies partially privatized and traded on the stock exchange and found that they constituted restrictions

[144] Case C-543/08 *Commission v Portugal* ECLI:EU:C:2010:669, para 84.

[145] The CJEU stated: "*…safeguarding a secure energy supply in that Member State in case of crisis, war or terrorism may constitute a ground of public security*". Case C-212/09 *Commission v Portugal* ECLI:EU:C:2011:717, para 82. Koutrakos (n 47) 192–197.

[146] Case C-212/09 *Commission v Portugal* ECLI:EU:C:2011:717, para 83.

[147] Case C-212/09 *Commission v Portugal* ECLI:EU:C:2011:717, para 85.

[148] Case C-212/09 *Commission v Portugal* ECLI:EU:C:2011:717, para 88.

[149] Case C-212/09 *Commission v Portugal* ECLI:EU:C:2011:717, paras 89–90. Koutrakos (n 47) 192–197.

[150] Case C-212/09 *Commission v Portugal* ECLI:EU:C:2011:717, para 84.

[151] Case C-212/09 *Commission v Portugal* ECLI:EU:C:2011:717, paras 91–96. Szabados (n 15) 1127. Similarly with *Commission v Portugal (third Portuguese golden shares case)*, restrictions of freedom of establishment was a direct consequence of restrictions of free movement of capital and the CJEU did not proceed to a separate examination of restrictions and their justification in the context of freedom of establishment. Case C-212/09 *Commission v Portugal* ECLI:EU:C:2011:717, para 98.

[152] Case C-244/11 *Commission v Greece* ECLI:EU:C:2012:694.

of freedom of establishment.[153] With regard to the justification for these restrictions, the Greek government argued that the aim of the Greek legislation was "*to guarantee the continuity of basic services and the operation of networks considered to be necessary to the economic and social life of a country, in particular that country's necessary energy and water supply and the provision of telecommunications services.*"[154] According to Art. 51 TFEU as interpreted by CJEU's case law, the Greek government insisted that the Greek legislation was seeking to serve the public interest and, more specifically, public policy, public security and public health, which could justify restrictions on freedom of establishment, in the context of the security of supply in the petroleum, telecommunications and energy sectors.[155]

The CJEU accepted that "*in the case of undertakings carrying out activities and supplying public services in the petroleum, telecommunications and energy sectors, the Court has held that the objective of guaranteeing the security of supply of such products or the supply of such services in the event of a crisis, on the territory of the Member State at issue, may constitute a public security reason and, therefore, possibly justify an obstacle to the free movement of capital.*"[156] Additionally, the CJEU confirmed that the protection of public interest concerning public policy, public security and public health could justify restrictions on freedom of establishment of companies, in accordance with Art. 51 TFEU.[157]

The CJEU held that the Greek prior authorization scheme was not suitable and proportionate for securing the objective of energy security.[158] The simple acquisition of a shareholding of more than 10% of a company's capital could not constitute a genuine and sufficiently serious threat to energy security.[159] A non-exhaustive enumeration of the criteria of the prior authorization scheme granted the relevant national authorities wide discretion, which suffered from legal uncertainty and was very difficult to review by national courts.[160] This wide discretion was against the principle of proportionality.[161] The terms and circumstances for the exercise of the power to oppose the acquisition of shareholdings in the strategic companies

---

153 Case C-244/11 *Commission v Greece* ECLI:EU:C:2012:694, para 7–8. For an analysis of this case, *see* T. Papadopoulos, 'Privatized Companies, Golden Shares and Property Ownership in the Euro Crisis Era: A Discussion after Commission v. Greece' (2015) 12 ECFR 1–18.

154 Case C-244/11 *Commission v Greece* ECLI:EU:C:2012:694, para 38.

155 Case C-326/07 *Commission v Italy*, ECLI:EU:C:2009:193, para 69. Case C-244/11 *Commission v Greece* ECLI:EU:C:2012:694, para 39.

156 Case C-463/00 *Commission v Spain* ECLI:EU:C:2003:272, para 71. Case C-244/11 *Commission v Greece* ECLI:EU:C:2012:694, para 65. Koutrakos (n 47) 192–197.

157 Case C-244/11 *Commission v Greece* ECLI:EU:C:2012:694, para 66. With regard to the legislative goal of security of energy supply, the CJEU repeated its previous case law that energy security could be invoked only if there is a genuine and sufficiently serious threat to a fundamental interest of society. Case C-207/07 *Commission v Spain* ECLI:EU:C:2008:428, para 47. Case C-244/11 *Commission v Greece* ECLI:EU:C:2012:694, para 66.

158 Case C-244/11 *Commission v Greece* ECLI:EU:C:2012:694, para 68.

159 Case C-244/11 *Commission v Greece* ECLI:EU:C:2012:694, para 69.

160 Case C-244/11 *Commission v Greece* ECLI:EU:C:2012:694, paras 74–75, 79.

161 Case C-244/11 *Commission v Greece* ECLI:EU:C:2012:694, para 75.

were general and imprecise, which did not permit the investors to understand with certainty the conditions under which an authorization could be refused.[162] Hence, the justification for restricting freedom of establishment deriving from the Greek prior authorization scheme was not accepted by the CJEU.

Regarding the arrangements for ex-post control of certain decisions taken by the strategic public limited companies at issue, the CJEU examined the compatibility of the Greek rules with the criteria about the accepted justifications adopted by *Commission v Belgium.*[163] Although this Greek scheme of control was one of ex-post nature, the CJEU did not accept the compatibility of such a Greek scheme with the criteria of *Commission v Belgium.*[164] This approach of the CJEU towards the Greek scheme for ex-post control over certain corporate decisions was based on the following grounds: (1) the decisions listed in Greek provisions were not specific management decisions but decisions fundamental to the life of an undertaking,[165] (2) there was no specific list of the strategic assets concerned,[166] (3) although the right to object certain decisions aimed at guaranteeing public interest considerations (the continuity of services supplied and the operation of networks), there were no details and further information of the actual circumstances and conditions under which the right to object may be exercised and, as a result, the investors were not able to know when it may be applicable.[167] Hence, the justification for the restrictions on freedom of establishment deriving from the Greek scheme for ex-post control of certain decisions taken by strategic companies was not accepted by the CJEU.

2.3 *Scrutinizing Justifications for Restrictions on EU Fundamental Freedoms in the CJEU's Golden Shares Case Law*

Commission v Belgium is a unique case. It is the only golden shares case, where the CJEU held that Belgian golden shares constituted justified restrictions of EU fundamental freedoms. The Belgian rules passed the CJEU's test with regard to justification for restrictions on EU fundamental freedoms. The Belgian government managed to convince the CJEU about the suitability of Belgian rules to achieve their public interest consideration in compliance with the principle of proportionality.[168]

---

[162] Case C-244/11 *Commission v Greece* ECLI:EU:C:2012:694, paras 77–78.

[163] Case C-244/11 *Commission v Greece* ECLI:EU:C:2012:694, para 80.

[164] Case C-244/11 *Commission v Greece* ECLI:EU:C:2012:694, para 82.

[165] Case C-463/00 *Commission v Spain* ECLI:EU:C:2003:272, para 79. Case C-244/11 *Commission v Greece* ECLI:EU:C:2012:694, para 83.

[166] Case C-244/11 *Commission v Greece* ECLI:EU:C:2012:694, para 84.

[167] Case C-244/11 *Commission v Greece* ECLI:EU:C:2012:694, para 84.

[168] For a general analysis of the principle of proportionality in EU law, *see* P. Craig, *EU Administrative Law* (OUP 2012) 590–640; T. Tridimas, *The General Principles of EU Law* (2nd edn, OUP 2006) 136–241. T-I Harbo,'The Function of the Proportionality Principle in EU Law' (2010) 16

It is the first and only case where the CJEU accepted as legitimate the justification invoked by a Member State enjoying special privileges in the capital of a privatized company.[169] This uniqueness increases the significance of this case. This case is particularly important, because it offers guidance to other Member States planning to privatize certain State-owned companies and to continue to exert influence through golden shares over such privatized companies. The approach of the CJEU in *Commission v Belgium* constitutes a compass[170] for Member States planning to introduce golden shares in their State-owned companies under privatization.

In golden shares case law, the CJEU accepts very often the public interest considerations proposed by Member States either on derogations of Art. 65 TFEU or on the mandatory requirements of public interest. Member States are, in most cases, successful in convincing the CJEU about the public interest considerations pursued by their national golden shares schemes. The point where almost all Member States fail, except for Belgium, is compliance with the principle of proportionality.[171] While the CJEU accepts the public interest considerations pursued by national golden shares schemes, the special rights introduced by national golden shares schemes fail to comply with the principle of proportionality.[172] It should be stressed that, with regard to justifications on public security, the CJEU is proceeding to a very intensive and detailed examination of proportionality.[173] This demonstrates the emphasis given by the CJEU on the justification for restrictions deriving from golden shares. In many golden shares cases, like in *Commission v Belgium*, Member States were seeking to justify their golden shares schemes on the grounds of public security, which requires a thorough examination of proportionality.

In addition to serving an accepted public security ground (energy security), the Belgian rules managed to comply with the principle of proportionality. This is exactly the major difference between *Commission v Belgium* and the rest of the golden shares cases. The Belgian golden shares managed to pass the CJEU's proportionality test, while the rest of the golden shares cases failed to fulfil the conditions of the principle of proportionality. While most of the Member States managed to convince the CJEU about the validity of certain public interest considerations, only *Commission v Belgium* also complied with the principle of proportionality and the rest of the golden shares cases breached that principle. In *Commission v Belgium*, the CJEU

Eur LJ 158–185; W. Sauter, 'Proportionality in EU Law: A Balancing Act?' (2013) 15 Cambridge Yearbook of European Legal Studies 439–466. A.L. Young and G. de Búrca,'Proportionality' in S, Vogenauer and S. Weatherill (eds) General Principles of Law-European and Comparative Perspectives, (Hart 2017) 133–143; J. Kokott, C. Sobotta,'The Evolution of the Principle of Proportionality in EU Law-Towards an Anticipative Understanding?' in S. Vogenauer and S. Weatherill (eds) General Principles of Law-European and Comparative Perspectives, (Hart 2017) 167–177.

[169] European Commission (n 15) 11.

[170] Szabados (n 15) 1125.

[171] For a discussion of the proportionality test applied by the CJEU with regard to derogations of Art. 65 (1)(b)TFEU, *see* Hindelang (n 10) 228–234.

[172] Szabados (n 15) 1125.

[173] Koutrakos (n 47) 193–194.

provided specific directions on what could constitute a proportionate justification for restricting the free movement of capital by means of golden shares.[174]

The characteristics, which differentiate Belgian golden shares from the rest of the golden shares scrutinized by the CJEU, were the specific, detailed, clear and comprehensive procedural safeguards of the Belgian golden shares scheme stipulating exactly when and how the special rights in the privatized companies could be exercised. A basic difference of Belgian golden shares was that it was an opposition regime introducing an ex post facto control and not a system of prior notification, like other golden shares. Moreover, the Belgian right of veto was not about decisions relating to the ownership of shares or capital of the privatized companies (like in Commission *v Spain, Commission v France and Commission Portugal (first Portuguese golden shares case))*, but it concerned the use of means and installations with a view to securing compliance with the public service obligations fulfilled by the specific privatized companies, namely energy security.[175] Generally, a system of prior authorization imposed by a golden share breaches the principle of proportionality.[176] In addition to the existence of an opposition regime imposing ex post facto control, the requirements adopted by *Commission v Belgium* demanded the special rights to protect a legitimate general interest (e.g. energy security), to be subjected to specific time limits and to be restricted to specific and predetermined strategic assets and specific and predetermined management decisions. Explanation of the grounds and full justification for the administrative decision on the basis of which these special rights in privatized companies were exercised were also required. Moreover, such decisions triggering the special rights in privatized companies must be open to judicial review by the competent national court.[177]

All these requirements for golden shares adopted by *Commission v Belgium* could curb the wide discretion enjoyed by Member States holding golden shares in the capital of privatized companies. A system of ex post facto control respects the decision-making independence of the privatized company, because State intervention is limited only to very specific situations.[178] Additionally, all these requirements could contribute to legal certainty, which is necessary for investors from other Member States planning to invest and acquire privatized companies' shares. The

---

[174] European Commission (n 15) 29.

[175] ibid. 11–12.

[176] Barnard (n 4) 543. The CJEU has not excluded the possibility a system of prior authorization to be compatible with EU fundamental freedoms. Nevertheless, the threshold of the proportionality test as structured by the CJEU is so high that it is very difficult for a national system of prior authorization to pass it. This argument is underpinned by Case C-244/11 *Commission v Greece* ECLI:EU:C:2012:694, para 73 and Case C-274/06 *Commission v Spain* ECLI:EU:C:2008:86, para 47. A. De Luca,'The EU and Member States: FDI, Portfolio Investments, Golden Powers and SWFs' in F. Bassan (ed) *Research Handbook on Sovereign Wealth Funds and International Investment Law* (Elgar 2015) 178–205, 193–195.

[177] European Commission (n 15) 30. For a critique of judicial review as a requirement of the principle of proportionality, *see* S. Prechal,'Free Movement and Procedural Requirements: Proportionality Reconsidered' (2008) 35 LIEI 201–216, 206–207, 210–213.

[178] Barnard (n 4) 552.

criteria adopted by *Commission v Belgium* give comfort to potential investors against the risk of abuse and prevent golden shares to have a de facto discouraging effect on potential investors from other Member States.[179] It is evident that, in *Commission v Belgium*, the CJEU reconciled the overarching aim of market integration with the requirement to protect the national interests of a Member State.[180] However, the mere existence of an ex-post control scheme introduced by golden shares does not secure compatibility with EU fundamental freedoms. This argument is underpinned by *Commission v Greece*, where the CJEU held that the Greek golden shares scheme for ex-post control of certain decisions taken by strategic companies did not fulfil the rest of the criteria of *Commission v Belgium* and was found to infringe EU fundamental freedoms.[181]

While the requirement of prior authorization is deemed to infringe free movement of capital, a requirement of prior declaration/notification might be compatible with the free movement of capital. The declaration/notification requirement was examined in the free movement of capital case law concerning immovable property[182] and currency exports.[183] In *Bordessa*, the CJEU compared prior authorization with prior declaration/notification in the context of currency exports. While prior authorization made the exercise of free movement of capital illusory and infringed free movement of capital, declaration/notification might be more proportionate to the realization of public interest considerations and, as a result, lawful.[184] The CJEU did not have the chance to examine a golden shares scheme requiring prior declaration/notification of the acquisition of shares in a privatized company. Considering the CJEU's previous case law on immovable property and currency exports, a similar approach might be followed for golden shares. Hence, it is possible that a golden shares scheme demanding prior declaration/notification might be compatible with free movement of capital as a less interfering and less intensive measure than prior authorization. Nevertheless, a system of prior declaration/notification might be proved to be insufficient

---

179 Rickford (n 98) 75.

180 Barnard (n 4) 492.

181 Case C-244/11 *Commission v Greece* ECLI:EU:C:2012:694, paras 80–84. Greek provisions did not prescribe specifically the corporate decisions and the strategic assets subjected to this ex post facto control, did not require formal justification for the relevant decision and did not provide the possibility of judicial review. Szabados (n 15), 1126.

182 Case C-302/97 *Klaus Konle v Republik Österreich* ECLI:EU:C:1999:271 paras 44–48, Joined cases C-515/99, C-519/99 to C-524/99 and C-526/99 to C-540/99 *Hans Reisch and Others* ECLI:EU:C:2002:135 para 36. Barnard (n 4) 543.

183 Joined cases C-358/93 and C-416/93 *Criminal proceedings against Aldo Bordessa and others* ECLI:EU:C:1995:54 paras 24–27. Barnard (n 4) 543–544.

184 The CJEU stated that: "*a prior declaration, on the other hand, may be one of the requisite measures which Member States are permitted to take since, unlike prior authorization, it does not entail suspension of the transaction in question but does still allow the national authorities to exercise effective supervision in order to prevent infringements of their laws and regulations*" Joined cases C-358/93 and C-416/93 *Criminal proceedings against Aldo Bordessa and others* ECLI:EU:C:1995:54 paras 24–27. Barnard (n 4) 544.

to deal with a specific threat to public policy or public security, which could affect the possible use of prior declaration/notification in a golden shares mechanism.[185]

Apart from express derogations of Arts. 52(1) and 65(1) TFEU, the CJEU has applied, by reference to case law from other EU fundamental freedoms, mandatory requirements in the public interest allowing Member States to justify restrictions on EU fundamental freedoms. In *Gebhard*,[186] the CJEU specified the conditions of the available justifications on mandatory requirements in the public interest. According to the so-called *Gebhard* Test, national measures liable to hinder or make less attractive the exercise of fundamental freedoms guaranteed by the Treaty must fulfil four conditions: (1) they must be applied in a non-discriminatory manner, (2) they must be justified by imperative requirements in the general interest, (3) they must be suitable for securing the attainment of the objective which they pursue, and (4) they must not go beyond what is necessary to attain it.[187] A fairly intensive review of the principle of proportionality could be involved in the application of these conditions. The CJEU did not doubt that the public interest considerations invoked by Member States in principle could justify national measures but rejected the arguments made on proportionality grounds.[188] This is exactly the CJEU's approach in the golden shares case law. The principle of proportionality raises two questions: first, whether the national rules are suitable for securing the attainment of the objective and, secondly, whether they go beyond what is necessary to attain it.[189] On the one hand, it has been argued that the first question only requires a marginal control of the aptitude or suitability of the national legislation to obtain the aim pursued. On the other hand, the second question demands courts to identify whether the public interest pursued cannot be served by other, less restrictive means.[190]

The CJEU accepted the majority of public interest considerations invoked by Member States as express derogations provided by TFEU or as mandatory requirements in the general interest capable of justifying restrictions on EU fundamental freedoms. Regarding the definitions of public policy or public security grounds of Art. 65(1) TFEU, the CJEU referred to its case law from other EU fundamental freedoms. The notion of public policy or public security, as derogations to free movement of capital (Art. 65(1) TFEU), is explained by *Association Eglise de Scientology*, which

---

[185] In *Association Eglise de scientology*, the CJEU stated that: "*In the case of direct foreign investments, the difficulty in identifying and blocking capital once it has entered a Member State may make it necessary to prevent, at the outset, transactions which would adversely affect public policy or public security. It follows that, in the case of direct foreign investments which constitute a genuine and sufficiently serious threat to public policy and public security, a system of prior declaration may prove to be inadequate to counter such a threat.*" Case C-54/99 *Association Eglise de scientologie* ECLI:EU:C:2000:124 para 20. Barnard (n 4) 551. *See also* Dashwood, Wyatt et. al (n 34) 664.

[186] Case 55/94 *Gebhard* ECLI:EU:C:1995:411. See also: Rickford (n 98) 74–75.

[187] Case 55/94 *Gebhard* ECLI:EU:C:1995:411, para 37; European Commission (n 15) 12.

[188] Dashwood, Wyatt et. al (n 34) 575.

[189] Case C-67/98, *Zenatti* ECLI:EU:C:1999:514 para 29. Barnard (n 4) 489.

[190] G. Straetmans, 'Case Note-Case C-124/97, Lärä, Judgment of the Court of 21 September 1999 and Case C-67/98, Zenatti, Judgment of the Court of 21 October 1999' (2000) 37 CMLRev 991–1005. 1002. Barnard (n 4) 489.

was referred subsequently by several golden shares cases. This notion of public policy or public security of Art. 65(1) TFEU is based on the notion of public policy or public security of the free movement of persons case law (*Rutili, Calfa, Unectef v Heylens and Others*[191]).[192] The notion of public policy or public security must be interpreted strictly.[193] A few examples of public policy or public security grounds of Art. 65(1) TFEU accepted by the CJEU are energy security/safeguarding of energy supply in the event of a crisis,[194] safeguarding the provision of telecommunications services in case of a crisis, war, terrorism, natural disasters and other types of threat,[195] the protection of the interests of workers and minority shareholders and the fact that a big size company could affect the general interest[196] and the minimum supply of energy resources and goods essential to the public as a whole, the continuity of public service, national defence, the protection of public policy and public security and health emergencies.[197] In recent golden shares case law, the CJEU considered current perspectives regarding the content of justifying grounds. The CJEU incorporated current developments and modern challenges into the content of justifying grounds, e.g. the dangers of terrorism were considered for the derogation of public security.[198] However, the problem occurs with regard to compliance

[191] Case 36/75 *Rutili* ECLI:EU:C:1975:137, paras 26–28, Case C-348/96 *Calfa* ECLI:EU:C:1999:6, para 21, Case 222/86 *Unectef v Heylens and Others* ECLI:EU:C:1987:442, paras 14 and 15.

[192] The CJEU held: "*It should be observed, first, that while Member States are still, in principle, free to determine the requirements of public policy and public security in the light of their national needs, those grounds must, in the Community context and, in particular, as derogations from the fundamental principle of free movement of capital, be interpreted strictly, so that their scope cannot be determined unilaterally by each Member State without any control by the Community institutions (see, to this effect, Case 36/75 Rutili v Minister for the Interior [1975] ECR 1219, paragraphs 26 and 27). Thus, public policy and public security may be relied on only if there is a genuine and sufficiently serious threat to a fundamental interest of society (see, to this effect, Rutili, cited above, paragraph 28, and Case C-348/96 Calfa [1999] ECR I-11, paragraph 21). Moreover, those derogations must not be misapplied so as, in fact, to serve purely economic ends (to this effect, see Rutili, paragraph 30). Further, any person affected by a restrictive measure based on such a derogation must have access to legal redress*". Case 222/86 *Unectef v Heylens and Others* ECLI:EU:C:1987:442, paras 14 and 15. Case C-54/99 *Association Eglise de scientologie* ECLI:EU:C:2000:124 para 17. Barnard (n 4) 550–551. For an analysis of Art. 65 TFEU in the light of justifications for restrictions on free movement of goods, *see* J. Usher, *The Law of Money and Financial Services in the European Community* (2nd edn, OUP 2000) 34–38.

[193] European Commission (n 15) 29.

[194] Case C-483/99 *Commission v France* ECLI:EU:C:2002:327.

[195] Case C-171/08 *Commission v Portugal* ECLI:EU:C:2010:412. E. Paliou,'Article 65 TFEU' in V. Christianos (ed) *Commentary on TEU and TFEU* (Nomiki Viliothiki publications 2012, in Greek). 408.

[196] Case C-112/05 *Commission v Germany* ECLI:EU:C:2007:623. Rickford (n 98) 75–76.

[197] Case C-326/07 *Commission v Italy*, ECLI:EU:C:2009:193, para 45. *See also* C. Esplugues, *Foreign Investment, Strategic Assets and National Security* (Intersentia 2018) 395–398.; Hindelang (n 10) 225–228.

[198] A new element illustrating dangers of the modern international economic environment that the CJEU considered during the examination of energy security as a public security consideration was that "*at the present time concerns exist about certain investments made particularly by sovereign wealth funds, or investments that might be linked to terrorist organizations, in undertakings in*

with the principle of proportionality.[199] Almost all justifying grounds invoked by Member States fail to comply with the principle of proportionality. Even if the CJEU accepts the justifying ground, the measures adopted to achieve the specific objective are disproportionate.[200] While the CJEU accepts grounds invoked by Member States as express derogations provided by Treaty articles or as mandatory requirements in the public interest, these grounds in all cases, apart from *Commission v Belgium*, do not comply with the principle of proportionality and, as a matter of fact, do not constitute legitimate justifications for restrictions on EU fundamental freedoms.

The analysis of the derogation of public security embraces, first, the clearly narrow terms in which the notion of public security was defined by case law and, secondly, the detailed analysis and strict application of the principle of proportionality.[201] In golden shares case law, the CJEU follows its usual approach with regard to the examination of justifications for restrictions on fundamental freedoms. In the context of this examination, the CJEU examines first the content and the validity of such grounds invoked by Member States. More specifically, the CJEU examines whether the content of these grounds invoked by Member States falls within the scope of express derogations provided by TFEU or mandatory requirements in the public interest. After the CJEU accepts these grounds as legitimate public interest considerations on the basis of express derogations provided by TFEU or of mandatory requirements in the public interest, it proceeds to examine their compliance with the principle of proportionality.

According to the golden shares case law discussed above, compliance with the principle of proportionality requires specific and detailed provisions for the exercise of special rights deriving from golden shares. The golden shares provisions must prescribe in detail how a Member State could exercise these special rights in the share capital of a privatized company in order to comply with the principle of proportionality. While national golden shares schemes state that the exercise of special rights could take place on the basis of public interest, the main problem is that they do not explain in detail what public interest exactly means.[202] Lack of transparency on the conditions under which special rights in privatized companies could be exercised results in infringement of free movement of capital.[203] The Belgian legislation examined in *Commission v Belgium* described comprehensively the powers of the Belgian government to exercise the special rights granted by golden shares and restricted the discretion enjoyed by the Belgian government for the exercise of these special

---

strategic sectors, which constitute a threat of that nature in relation to energy supply." Case C-212/09 *Commission v Portugal* ECLI:EU:C:2011:717, para 84.

[199] For an analysis of the principle of proportionality and other grounds limiting the possibility of justification for restrictions on EU fundamental freedoms, see Barnard (n 14) 273–306.

[200] Barnard (n 4) 492.

[201] Koutrakos (n 47) 195.

[202] Szabados (n 15) 1125.

[203] A. Biondi, 'When the State is the Owner—Some Further Comments on the Court of Justice 'Golden Shares' Strategy' in U. Bernitz, W-G. Ringe (eds) *Company Law and Economic Protectionism* (OUP 2010) 95–102, 99. For a critique of the requirements of procedural guarantees for the criteria applying to administrative procedures related to granting or rejecting an authorization, which constitute part of the principle of proportionality, *see* Prechal (n 177) 202–210.

rights. Hence, compliance with the principle of proportionality was secured due to this detailed and specific legal framework.[204] The CJEU stresses that national law must distinguish the public interest consideration at stake and structure specifically and comprehensively the connection between the criteria and the specific powers to which they relate.[205] It is easily understood that the need for details, specification and clarity is of utmost importance for the legal framework for the exercise of golden shares. The Member States should explain how these special rights would contribute to the protection of public interest considerations promoted by the derogations of Art. 65 TFEU or by the mandatory requirements of the public interest. The link between the exercise of special rights and the promotion of public interest must be described precisely, clearly and exhaustively in order to contribute to legal certainty and, as a result, to compliance with the principle of proportionality. Obviously, without a clear and sufficient explanation of the link between the exercise of special rights and the promotion of public interest, the national measures introducing these special rights are lacking legal certainty and do not comply with proportionality. It is deduced that the level, quality, quantity and specification of information provided by the legal framework adopting such special rights in the capital of privatized companies are crucial for compliance with the principle of proportionality and, obviously, for the successful justification for the relevant restrictions.

In the golden shares case law, the emphasis is also given on compliance with the principle of legal certainty. Although legal certainty is a general principle of EU law, only in the area of free movement of capital, the application of this general principle is so clearly mentioned.[206] National rules constituting restrictions on EU fundamental freedoms must be consistent with the objective pursued, transparent and sufficiently legally certain. It is deduced that these national rules constituting restrictions must be clear, precise and predictable regarding their legal effects. If such national rules do not have the above characteristics, they are not proportionate to their objective.[207]

---

[204] J. van Bekkum criticizes the CJEU's approach regarding the rejection of justification for the Italian golden shares in *Commission v Italy (fourth Italian golden shares case).* He argues that, in comparison with *Commission v Belgium*, it is unclear and unconvincing why the CJEU rejected the justification for restrictions on fundamental freedoms deriving from the Italian golden shares. He believes that "*the Belgian criteria seem to be more vague that the Italian ones*". He also comments on the need for specific, clear and detailed criteria for the exercise of golden shares as being too excessive for Member States: "*In any event, the main lesson to be learned from Commission v. Italy 2009 [fourth Italian golden shares case] is that such legislation needs to define the circumstances in which golden shares will be used very precisely, perhaps too precisely from a Member State's point of view*". Van Bekkum (n 111) 15.

[205] This was revealed by *Cibrian Fernandez.* Case C-35/08 *Grundstücksgemeinschaft Busley and Cibrian Fernandez v Finanzamt Stuttgart-Körperschaften* ECLI:EU:C:2009:625 para 32. Barnard (n 4) 545.

[206] Barnard (n 4) 546–547. For a discussion of the principle of legal certainty and other grounds limiting the possibility of justification for restrictions on EU fundamental freedoms, *see* Barnard (n 14) 289.

[207] Case C-275/12 *Elrick* EU:C:2013: 684, para 33. Joined Cases C-25 and 26/14 *UNIS* EU:C:2015:821, para 38. Case C-318/10 *SIAT* EU:C:2012:415, paras 58–59. Case C-342/14 *X-Steuerberatungsgesellschaft* ECLI:EU:C:2015:827, para 59. Barnard (n 4) 491.

National rules specifying the exercise of golden shares in privatized companies, which are clear, precise and predictable, diminish the wide discretion enjoyed by Member States. Thus, legal certainty is achieved by limiting the wide discretion enjoyed by Member States holding golden shares.[208] In the golden shares case law, it is interesting that the principle of proportionality was linked to the principle of legal certainty. Special rights described by precision and comprehensiveness could be proportionate to the achievement of their proclaimed objective and, as a result, could be characterized by legal certainty. The examination of the compatibility of special rights with the principle of proportionality also requires a parallel examination of their compliance with the principle of legal certainty. Compliance with legal certainty contributes to compliance with proportionality. These two principles are interconnected. A specific, clear and detailed legal framework for golden shares contributes to legal certainty and is proportionate to the public interest objective. The principle of proportionality in its examination at golden shares case law is not expressed in terms of balancing interests but by using some objective benchmarks, like transparency and legal certainty.[209] The CJEU should examine compatibility with the principles of proportionality and legal certainty when it scrutinizes the justification for restrictions deriving from special rights in privatized companies. Hence, Member States should ensure compliance with both the principle of proportionality and with the principle of legal certainty when they structure their golden shares introducing special rights to privatized companies. When Member States are drafting the legal framework of golden shares in their privatized companies, they should use as a guide the Belgian legislation of golden shares and should provide an extensively detailed, clear and specific description of how these golden shares could be exercised. This detailed, clear and specific description contributes to legal certainty, which, as a matter of fact, secures compliance with the principle of proportionality.

The CJEU did not accept certain grounds invoked by Member States as legitimate public interest considerations capable of justifying restrictions on EU fundamental freedoms. Regarding the financial interests of the State holding shares in privatized companies, the CJEU examined whether they could fall within the scope of Art. 65(1)(b) TFEU. The CJEU followed its established case law stating that economic and financial grounds can never justify infringements prohibited by the Treaty.[210] In *Commission v. Portugal*, the CJEU stated that this reasoning was equally applicable to the economic policy objectives illustrated by the objectives referred by the Portuguese Government, namely choosing a strategic partner, strengthening the competitive structure of the market concerned or modernizing and increasing the efficiency of means of production. Such interests could not constitute a legitimate

[208] Dashwood, Wyatt et. al (n 34) 664.

[209] Biondi (n 203) 98.

[210] For the debate around economic grounds as justifications for restrictions on EU fundamental freedoms, *see* J. Snell, 'Economic Justifications and the Role of the State' in P. Koutrakos, N.N. Shuibhne, P. Syrpis (eds), *Exceptions from EU Free Movement Law* (Hart 2016) 12–31; S. Arrowsmith,'Rethinking the Approach to Economic Justifications under the EU's Free Movement Rules' (2015) 68 Current Legal Problems 307–365.

justification for restrictions on EU fundamental freedoms.[211] Hence, economic and financial grounds cannot constitute acceptable public interest considerations when the State holds golden shares in a privatized company.[212] Categories of mandatory requirements in the public interest, which the CJEU does not accept as valid public interest considerations, are pure financial considerations. These financial considerations appear in profit-making privatized companies engaged with various commercial activities. It is evident that the public interest is missing from these commercial transactions.[213]

From all these golden shares cases through these years, it seems that Member States face significant difficulties with making their golden shares schemes compatible with the principle of proportionality. These difficulties are pretty surprising, taking into account that *Commission v Belgium* was decided in 2002. Member States should have followed the paradigm of Belgian law and the criteria endorsed by the CJEU in *Commission v Belgium.*[214] Although the clear conditions for the justifications for restrictions on EU fundamental freedoms introduced by golden shares were already known to Member States since 2002, Member States did not follow them and continued to adopt their own standards, which were found to infringe the principle of proportionality in subsequent golden shares cases decided by the CJEU.[215] It is

[211] Case C-367/98 *Commission v Portugal* ECLI:EU:C:2002:326, para 52. *See also* Case C-319/02 *Manninen* ECLI:EU:C:2004:484 para 49, Case C-35/98 *Verkooijen* ECLI:EU:C:2000:294 paras 47–48. Barnard (n 4) 541, 547.

[212] Regarding a justification based on the safeguard of State's own financial interests, see also *Sint Servatius*: requirements related to public housing policy in a Member State and to the financing of that policy can constitute overriding reasons in the public interest and therefore justify a restriction on free movement of capital. Case C-567/07 *Sint Servatius* [2009] ECR I-9021, para 30; F. Benyon, *Direct Investment, National Champions and EU Treaty Freedoms* (Hart 2010) 33–34.

[213] In *Commission v. Spain*, the CJEU found that considerations of a purely economic or administrative nature could not in any event constitute a mandatory requirement in the public interest. The CJEU focused on specific companies active in certain commercial activities without public service objectives and stated that State privileges in the tobacco manufacturer, Tabacalera SA, and in the banking association, Corporación Bancaria de España SA (Argentaria), could not, *prima facie*, be justified on the basis of mandatory requirements in the public interest. Barnard (n 4) 544. Case C-463/00 *Commission v Spain* ECLI:EU:C:2003:272, paras 35 and 70. In *Commission v. Germany*, the CJEU did not consider that the public interest was invoked in the framework of a particular manufacturing company, Volkswagen. Rickford (n 98) 74.

[214] For a discussion about the proposal introducing golden shares to influence the remuneration policy of banks in the Netherlands and the effects of *Commission v Belgium, see* (15 November 2018) J. Nijland, 'Polishing golden shares' (*leidenlawblog*) <https://leidenlawblog.nl/articles/polishing-golden-shares> accessed 15 March 2022. Additionally, golden shares case law has significant impact on the privatizations taking place at EU candidate countries, such as Montenegro: V. Savkovic, 'The Alleged Case of Golden Shares in Montenegro: A Candidate Country's Experience as an Incentive for Including Acta Jure Gestionis within the Range of Restrictions on Free Movement of Capital' (2016) 41 Review of Central and East European Law 117–156.

[215] It is interesting to mention that the European Commission examined the compatibility of the new Polish law giving certain special rights to Polish government in specific Polish companies of special importance, found it compatible with EU fundamental freedoms and characterized it as "a model solution", "a model piece of legislation" for the rest of the Member States, which should follow it in their national golden shares schemes. *See* F. Grzegorczyk,'The New Polish Law on the

difficult to explain the reason behind this persistence of several different Member States not to apply the conditions for the justification for restrictions stipulated by *Commission v Belgium.* Perhaps, Member States might be hoping that the CJEU would overturn its previous case law in *Commission v Belgium* and accept their less detailed, clear and specific criteria for the justification for restrictions. Maybe, political reasons would push national governments to defend their golden shares schemes at all costs. Hence, governments might think of the CJEU as a last resort in defending their golden shares schemes.[216] Governments would probably like to show to the public that they did not abolish their national golden shares schemes without fighting hard to preserve them. A case brought before the CJEU is the best proof that national governments did their best to defend their national golden shares schemes. Another reason behind this inconsistent behaviour might be that Member States would like to keep their influence on privatized companies for as long as possible and wait until a decision is issued by the CJEU.

3 Recent Case Law on Privatizations and Justifications for Restrictions on EU Fundamental Freedoms: *Associação Peço a Palavra*

3.1 Introductory Comments on Associação Peço a Palavra

The current jurisprudential perspectives on privatizations and justifications for restrictions on EU fundamental freedoms present a great interest. In the recent case *Associação Peço a Palavra*, the CJEU had the chance to examine the justification for restrictions resulting from certain conditions imposed by the Member State on an investor during a (re)privatization process.[217] The CJEU examined the compatibility with freedom of establishment of tender specifications governing the conditions under which a (re)privatization process of an air carrier company (TAP) would occur.[218] These conditions obliged the new purchaser of shares/investor in the privatized company to respect certain predetermined requirements. More specifically, the CJEU scrutinized in the light of freedom of establishment certain "conditions" prescribed by the tender specifications for choosing the purchaser to acquire shares representing up to 61% of the share capital of a privatized air carrier company, which

'Golden Veto': A Model Act for Member States of the European Union?' (2012)9 ECL 21–25, 21–22.

[216] For an analysis of the standard that Member States must satisfy to prove their public interest claims successfully, *see* N.N. Shuibhne and M. Maci,'Proving public interest: The growing impact of evidence in free movement case law' (2013) 50 CMLRev 965–1005.

[217] Case C-563/17 *Associação Peço a Palavra* ECLI:EU:C:2019:144.

[218] This case concerned a "reprivatization". However, this chapter would refer to this process as "privatization" in order to secure simplification and consistency with the rest of the chapter referring to "privatization".

include requirements relating, first, to the public service obligations imposed on that company, secondly, to keeping the headquarters and effective management of the group to which those companies belong in Portugal, and, thirdly, to maintaining and developing the existing national hub.[219]

3.2 *The Relationship Between Golden Shares and Tender Specifications Governing the Conditions to Which a Privatization Process of a State-Owned Company is Subject*

Although these conditions do not constitute *stricto* sensu golden shares, like those discussed in the previous case law, they could be assimilated with golden shares and have a similar effect as golden shares. The similar effect between golden shares and tender specifications of the conditions under which privatization would take place concerns the limitation of the decision-making power of the privatized company. The conditions of the Portuguese privatization process result in restrictions on the decision-making powers normally available to the bodies of the company of a purchaser of shares representing up to 61% of TAP's share capital, which are comparable to those restrictions deriving from the exercise by a Member State of

[219] Case C-563/17 *Associação Peço a Palavra* ECLI:EU:C:2019:144, para 34. The conditions for choosing the purchaser to acquire shares of the privatized company were described by Art. 5 of Portuguese Council of Ministers' Decision No 4-A/2015:

"'Selection criteria':

'The criteria to be used for selecting one or more entities which will purchase the shares identified in Article 1(2) are as follows:

(a) The contribution to strengthening the economic and financial capacity of [TAP SGPS], [TAP] and of their capital structure, ... in such a way as to contribute to the sustainability and enhancement of the companies, and to the growth of their business, and to preserve the relative weight and value of the remaining capital held by the State and the value of the put option;...

(c) The submission of, and performance guarantee for, an adequate and coherent strategic plan with a view to preserving and promoting the growth of [TAP] whilst achieving the objectives defined by the government for the reprivatisation process; promoting the enhancement of its competitive position as a global air carrier operator in its current markets and in new markets; maintaining the integrity, corporate identity and independence of the TAP Group, in particular preserving the TAP trade mark and its association with Portugal and ensuring that the headquarters and effective management of the TAP Group remain in Portugal; contributing to preserving and developing the operational and commercial qualities of the TAP Group, and enhancing and developing its human resources;

(d) The capacity to ensure proper compliance, in good time, with the public service obligations of [TAP], including the flight connections between the main national airports and the airports of the autonomous regions, where applicable, and the continuation and further development of the routes serving the autonomous regions, the diaspora and Portuguese-speaking countries and communities;

(e) The contribution to the growth of the national economy, including maintaining and developing the current national hub as a platform of vital strategic importance in relations between Europe, Africa and Latin America;" Case C-563/17 *Associação Peço a Palavra* ECLI:EU:C:2019:144, para 19.

the powers of golden shares granting to it special rights intended to protect general interests.[220]

The common denominator between golden shares and tender specifications of the conditions for privatization is that certain decisions promoting the economic interests of the privatized company could be blocked on the basis of public interest considerations. Special rights deriving from golden shares could block on the basis of the protection of public interest specific decisions taken by the organs of the privatized company as being in the economic interests of the latter.[221] While a decision taken by the privatized company is in favour of its economic interests, that decision might be against public interest and could be blocked through the special rights of golden shares. The same pattern applies to tender specifications governing the conditions of privatization, which are pursuing the public interest. These public interest conditions applying to the new investor, who purchased the shares of the privatized company and who is exercising decisive control over it, would stop him from taking certain decisions promoting the economic interests of the privatized company. The new controlling shareholder of the privatized company sometimes cannot make financially beneficial decisions for his company, because he is bound by certain conditions included in the tender specifications.

3.3 Justification for Restrictions Resulting from Tender Specifications Governing the Conditions to Which a Privatization Process of a State-Owned Company is Subject

The CJEU found that these tender specifications, governing the conditions to which a privatization process is subject, constitute restrictions on the EU fundamental freedom of establishment. The CJEU held that the tender specifications for the purchaser of shares subject to this privatization process, which require from this purchaser of shares to preserve the headquarters and effective management of this air carrier company in Portugal and to maintain and develop the existing national hub, constitute restrictions on the freedom of establishment, because they prohibit, impede or render less attractive the exercise of that freedom.[222] As usual, the CJEU proceeded to an examination of possible justifications for such restrictions.

For these justifications for restrictions, the CJEU examined the various overriding reasons in the public interest, which must comply with the principle of proportionality.[223] Art. 5(c) and (e) of Portuguese Council of Ministers' Decision No 4-A/2015 invoked as justifications for the adopted tender specifications the following grounds:

[220] Case C-563/17 *Associação Peço a Palavra* ECLI:EU:C:2019:144, para 57.

[221] Joined Cases C-282 and C-283/04 *Commission v Netherlands* ECLI:EU:C:2006:608, para 30. Case C-563/17 *Associação Peço a Palavra* ECLI:EU:C:2019:144, para 57.

[222] Case C-563/17 *Associação Peço a Palavra* ECLI:EU:C:2019:144, paras 53–55.

[223] ibid. para 63.

"*preserving and promoting the growth of TAP, reinforcing the economic strength of that company, contributing to preserving and developing the operational and commercial qualities of the TAP Group and contributing to the growth of the national economy*"; these considerations constitute purely economic grounds (e.g. in particular, promotion of the national economy or its proper functioning) and, according to settled case law, cannot be used as valid justifications for restrictions on EU fundamental freedoms.[224]

The next public interest consideration invoked for the justification for restrictions on freedom of establishment, in the context of overriding reasons in the public interest, was "*safeguard[ing] the continuation and further development of TAP's air routes which serve third countries with particular historical, cultural and social ties to the Portuguese Republic in which Portuguese is the official language or one of the official languages, such as the Republic of Angola, the Republic of Mozambique or the Federative Republic of Brazil*".[225] Taking into account the above rationale of Portuguese tender specifications, the CJEU examined whether the ground of "*safeguarding the public interest service aimed at ensuring that there are sufficient scheduled air services to and from Portuguese-speaking third countries with which Portugal has particular historical, cultural and social ties*" constituted a valid public interest consideration.[226] This latter ground proclaimed by Portuguese legislation constituted guarantee of a service of general interest, which the CJEU accepted as an overriding reason in the public interest capable of justifying a restriction on EU fundamental freedoms.[227]

The justification for restrictions resulting from tender specifications related to maintaining TAP's headquarters and effective management in Portugal was scrutinized by the CJEU. In the context of justification for such tender specifications constituting restrictions on freedom of establishment, the CJEU accepted as a valid justifying ground "*the overriding reason in the public interest of ensuring that there are sufficient scheduled air routes to and from the Portuguese-speaking third countries concerned with which Portugal has particular historical, cultural and social ties*" and examined whether it complied with the principle of proportionality.[228] The bilateral agreements between Portugal and Portuguese-speaking third countries with particular historical, cultural, and social ties to Portugal were subjecting TAP's traffic

---

[224] ibid. para 70.

[225] ibid. para 71. It could be argued that this public interest consideration falls within the scope of cultural policy justifications. B. de Witte, 'Cultural Policy Justifications' in P. Koutrakos, N.N. Shuibhne and P. Syrpis (eds.) Exceptions from EU Free Movement Law (Hart 2016) 131–142. With regard to cultural policy as a justifying ground, see the following case law of the CJEU: Case C-288/89 *Gouda* ECLI:EU:C:1991:323, Case C-353/89 *Commission v Netherlands* ECLI:EU:C:1991:325, Case C-23/93 *TV10 SA* ECLI:EU:C:1994:362, Barnard (n 4) 484.

[226] Case C-563/17 *Associação Peço a Palavra* ECLI:EU:C:2019:144, para 73.

[227] This justifying ground was also accepted by the CJEU in the golden shares case *Commission v Netherlands*. Joined Cases C-282 and C-283/04 *Commission v Netherlands* ECLI:EU:C:2006:608, para 38. Case C-563/17 *Associação Peço a Palavra* ECLI:EU:C:2019:144, para 71.

[228] Case C-563/17 *Associação Peço a Palavra* ECLI:EU:C:2019:144, para 76.

rights for air routes with those countries to maintain TAP's principal place of business in Portugal.[229] According to these bilateral agreements, TAP would lose its traffic rights on routes to or from those third countries if it ever decided to transfer its principal place of business outside of Portugal. The provision of traffic rights on routes to or from those third countries only as long as TAP has its principal place of business in Portugal made this tender specification proportionate to this specific public interest consideration. This particular implication of losing traffic rights made the tender specification that TAP's principal place of business must be maintained in Portugal to be proportionate to the fulfilment of the accepted public interest objective of sufficient scheduled air routes.[230] Additionally, the fact that the tender specifications related to maintaining TAP's headquarters and effective management in Portugal allowed TAP to set up secondary establishments, according to Arts. 49 and 54 TFEU, contributed to compliance with the principle of proportionality, because it did not restrict excessively TAP from exercising and enjoying the fundamental freedom of establishment.[231]

The justification for restrictions deriving from tender specifications related to maintaining and developing the existing national hub was analysed by the CJEU. The CJEU examined whether the Portuguese tender specifications were proportionate to "*the objective of safeguarding the public interest service of ensuring that there are sufficient scheduled air route services to and from the Portuguese-speaking third countries concerned with which Portugal has particular historical, cultural and social ties*."[232] It was found that the tender specification imposing such conditions was not proportionate to the proclaimed public interest ground. Non-compliance with the principle of proportionality was based on two pillars. First, it was not explained how the maintenance of this specific current organizational model of the air connection services of the existing national hub was essential for attaining the invoked public interest ground. A different organizational model could possibly attain this public

[229] ibid. para 75.

[230] This public interest objective mentioned above is "*the overriding reason in the public interest of ensuring that there are sufficient scheduled air routes to and from the Portuguese-speaking third countries concerned with which Portugal has particular historical, cultural and social ties*". Case C-563/17 *Associação Peço a Palavra* ECLI:EU:C:2019:144, para 76. Moreover, according to Art. 8(1) of Regulation 1008/2008, losing the validity of the operating licence and of "air operator certificate (AOC)" after a transfer of TAP's headquarters and effective management outside Portugal was a very serious consequence, which could be avoided only by a prohibition of such transfer. Maintaining TAP's headquarters and effective management in Portugal was a proportionate measure to secure that there were sufficient scheduled air routes to and from the Portuguese-speaking third countries concerned with which Portugal has particular historical, cultural and social ties. Otherwise, after a revocation of operating licence and of "air operator certificate (AOC)" due to such transfer of its headquarters and effective management outside Portugal, TAP cannot serve this public interest consideration. Regulation 1008/2008 on common rules for the operation of air services in the Community [2008] OJ L 293/3–20. Case C-563/17 *Associação Peço a Palavra* ECLI:EU:C:2019:144, para 77.

[231] Case C-563/17 *Associação Peço a Palavra* ECLI:EU:C:2019:144, para 78.

[232] ibid. para 79.

interest ground.[233] Secondly, the current organizational model of the air connection services of the existing national hub applied to all air routes and not only to those to and from the Portuguese-speaking third countries concerned.[234] The fact that the specific current organizational model of the existing national hub also covered other air routes, which were not related to this public interest objective of securing sufficient scheduled air route services to and from the Portuguese-speaking third countries concerned, went beyond what was necessary to attain the intended objective of ties with those Portuguese-speaking third countries concerned and, as a result, was disproportionate.[235]

3.4 The Importance of Associação Peço a Palavra

Two out of three tender specifications (the requirement to fulfil public service obligations and the requirement to maintain air carrier company's headquarters and effective management in Portugal) governing the conditions to which a privatization process of an air carrier company was subject were found to be compatible with freedom of establishment. The requirement to maintain air carrier company's headquarters and effective management in Portugal was found to be a justified restriction on freedom of establishment of companies, because it served proportionately "*the overriding reason in the public interest of ensuring that there are sufficient scheduled air routes to and from the Portuguese-speaking third countries concerned with which Portugal has particular historical, cultural and social ties.*"[236] However, the third category of tender specifications, which introduced a requirement that the purchaser of shares ensured that the existing national hub was maintained and developed, went beyond what was necessary to achieve this latter public interest ground and, as a result, was an unlawful restriction on freedom of establishment.[237]

The importance of this case is that certain conditions related to the privatization process were found to be justified restrictions on EU fundamental freedoms. In this case, the CJEU accepted the justifying grounds invoked by Member States, as well as their compliance with the principle of proportionality. This is the second case, after *Commission v Belgium*, where the CJEU found that the national measures were justified restrictions. In both cases, the national measures were found to pursue the public interest objectives invoked by Member States and to be proportionate to such objectives. In addition to *Commission v Belgium*, *Associação Peço a Palavra* constitutes a second unique case, where national measures restricting the powers of a controlling shareholder over the privatized company in favour of the protection of public interest are accepted as justified restrictions.

---

[233] ibid. para 80.

[234] ibid. para 81.

[235] ibid. para 82.

[236] ibid. para 82.

[237] ibid. para 82.

Associação Peço a Palavra provides an alternative choice for Member States. Instead of introducing golden shares giving special rights, Member States wishing to continue to exercise control on the basis of public interest over a privatized company could choose to adopt tender specifications governing the conditions to which a privatization process of a State-owned company is subject. Member States aiming to protect public interest do not have only the choice of golden shares when they want to continue to enjoy a certain degree of influence after the privatization. Member States could subject the purchaser of shares of the privatized company to certain conditions to secure pursuing public interest after the privatization. Hence, pursuing public interest could not be achieved only through golden shares following the criteria adopted by *Commission v Belgium*, but it could also be achieved through the tender specifications governing the conditions to which a privatization is subject, according to *Associação Peço a Palavra*.

However, a difference between golden shares and tender specifications introducing certain conditions for privatizations is that golden shares result in direct control through special rights over the privatized company. In contrast, tender specifications result in indirect control through the imposition of certain conditions, which the privatized company is obliged to respect. Golden shares give a more decisive influence over the privatized company than tender specifications, because there is a difference regarding the flexibility and the timing of this influence. On the one hand, in the case of golden shares, after the completion of the privatization process, the State continues to participate in the capital of the privatized company and to enjoy stronger power regarding certain special prerogatives exercised through special rights, according to evolving public interest objectives complying with EU law. On the other hand, tender specifications imposing certain conditions have a fixed content, which is predetermined before the initiation of the privatization process, and, usually, it is not possible to change or even adjust it after the completion of the privatization process. Hence, the justification of lawful golden shares, in accordance with *Commission v Belgium*, could take into account the evolving notion of public interest. In contrast, the justification of tender specifications would follow a more static notion of public interest.

Taking into account the similarity between the golden shares and tender specifications governing the conditions to which a privatization process is subject, it is interesting to comment on the justifications for restrictions on EU fundamental freedoms. The fact that the CJEU accepted specific tender specifications governing the conditions to which a privatization process of a State-owned company is subject to be justified restrictions brings new possibilities to Member States planning to exert a certain degree of influence on privatized companies. Member States planning to privatize certain State-owned companies could adopt tender specifications imposing certain conditions according to the directions provided by *Associação Peço a Palavra*. According to the findings of *Associação Peço a Palavra*, Member States could follow the example of the Portuguese legislation inserting certain conditions through tender specifications, which the privatized company must respect. As it became clear from the discussion of the CJEU's decision above, Member States planning to adopt similar conditions through tender specifications of their privatization process must consider compliance with the principle of proportionality very carefully. Member States should pay special attention to the requirements of the principle of proportionality. The meticulous approach of the CJEU towards proportionality was revealed by the fact that the third category of tender specifications requiring that the existing national hub was maintained and developed was found to infringe the principle of proportionality and was not accepted as a justified restriction. Hence, compliance with the principle of proportionality must be a priority for Member States wishing to impose certain public interest considerations on the privatized company through tender specifications governing the conditions to which a privatization process is subject.[238]

4 Future Perspectives on the Privatizations of State-Owned Companies and Justified Restrictions on EU Fundamental Freedoms: Integrating Corporate Social Responsibility (CSR) into the Privatization Process

Considering the great emphasis given on CSR at the EU level,[239] it would be interesting to see how CSR could be integrated into privatizations through justification for

[238] This additional choice to impose certain public interest considerations after the end of the privatization might be particularly important for Member States currently running large privatization programmes, such Greece and Cyprus. As part of obligations of their bailout agreements due to the Eurocrisis, these two Member States were bound by their MoUs with their international creditors to implement intensive privatization programmes. It seems that these privatizations would take place without the introduction of golden shares. Hence, these Member States could use tender specifications governing the conditions to which a privatization process of a State-owned company is subject in order to serve lawfully certain public interest considerations.

[239] For an overview of the EU approach towards CSR, see the following website: <https://ec.europa.eu/growth/industry/sustainability/corporate-social-responsibility_en> accessed 15 March 2022.

restrictions on EU fundamental freedoms.[240] It is essential that CSR[241] should exist as an integral component within the process of privatization. During the divestment of its shareholding, the State could pursue CSR. The purchasers of State shares, the new shareholders of the privatized company, should be obliged to achieve CSR goals. Several recommendations could be introduced to ensure that new shareholders pursue efforts of CSR. CSR goals could be pursued during the selection of the new shareholders and share transfer to the new shareholder. First, the State should impose certain CSR standards, which the private investor planning to submit a bid to the tender process of privatization and to acquire the shareholding of the State should comply with. Only investors who fulfil these CSR standards might be able to participate in the tender process and acquire part or all the shareholding of the State. Any investors who fail to comply would be excluded from the tender process and the acquisitions of shares in the privatized company. Secondly, the State could introduce CSR requirements at the time of transfer of shares by compelling the new shareholders purchasing these shares from the State to consent to certain CSR requirements within the share purchase agreement. Hence, this agreement could contain certain clauses, which require the new investors to comply with certain CSR requirements and to participate in sustainability efforts following the transfer of the shares, and as a matter of fact, the transfer of the corporate control. Subsequently, there will be an enhancement in compliance with CSR goals by the new shareholders through requirements set out by the share purchase agreement.

At this point, useful guidance could be provided by *Associação Peço a Palavra*. The fact that in this case the CJEU held that certain tender specifications governing the conditions to which a privatization process of a State-owned company is subject were justified restrictions on freedom of establishment provides valuable directions to

---

[240] The European Commission provided the following definition for CSR: "*"the responsibility of enterprises for their impacts on society". Respect for applicable legislation, and for collective agreements between social partners, is a prerequisite for meeting that responsibility. To fully meet their corporate social responsibility, enterprises should have in place a process to integrate social, environmental, ethical, human rights and consumer concerns into their business operations and core strategy in close collaboration with their stakeholders, with the aim of:*

– maximising the creation of shared value for their owners/shareholders and for their other stakeholders and society at large;

– identifying, preventing and mitigating their possible adverse impacts. […].

To maximise the creation of shared value, enterprises are encouraged to adopt a long-term, strategic approach to CSR, and to explore the opportunities for developing innovative products, services and business models that contribute to societal wellbeing and lead to higher quality and more productive jobs." *See* European Commission, 'Communication from the Commission to the European Parliament, the Council, the European Economic and Social Committee and the Committee of the Regions. A renewed EU strategy 2011–14 for Corporate Social Responsibility' (25 October 2011) COM/2011/0681 final, 6. Moreover, the European Commission stresses the role of public authorities in the promotion of CSR. Public authorities could support the efforts of enterprises towards the realization of CSR goals through an efficient combination of voluntary policy measures and complementary regulation, in order, for example, to make companies to pursue responsible business conduct. *See* ibid at 7.

[241] U. Beyerlin, 'Sustainable Development' in R. Wolfrum (ed) *Max Planck Encyclopedia of Public International Law*. (OUP 2014).

Member States interested in inserting such CSR requirements to the share purchase agreements during the tender process of privatization of a State-owned company. Member States could structure their tender specifications on the basis of CSR requirements, according to the CJEU's approach to this case. The CJEU's analysis of the justifying grounds and of compliance with the principle of proportionality with regard to conditions introduced by tender specifications of privatization could assist Member States in drafting their national rules carefully in order to avoid infringing EU fundamental freedoms.

Moreover, the realization of CSR could be achieved through golden shares. Governments can retain some influence over privatized enterprises to pursue CSR goals and golden shares facilitate this. States might exercise their special rights deriving from golden shares in privatized companies, according to CSR goals. The State, which remains a minority shareholder in a privatized company, could seek to achieve through golden shares certain CSR goals, such as environmental protection, better working conditions for employees, gender equality, human rights protection, consumer protection, support of local communities, etc. The exercise of golden shares in favour of CSR is often compatible with the objectives of certain privatized companies, which are offering public services (transports, telecommunications, energy, etc.). These prerogatives, which the State continues to enjoy in privatized companies through golden shares, could be exercised to support CSR objectives. If private investors did not have any interest in CSR goals, the government would have the capacity to assert its rights through golden shares in pursuance of any CSR-related targets to offset their disinterest.[242] For instance, endeavours, which promote environmental protection, advance the utilization of clean energy, bolster social equality within board membership, contribute to consumer protection, provide donations and other methods of support to local communities,[243] amount to CSR goals, which the government could support through the exercise of special rights granted through golden shares. Furthermore, a State-owned company's articles of association could be amended before privatization, in which provisions could be instituted promoting CSR requirements and making bypassing these requirements more difficult, with time limits and with increased quorum and supermajority.[244] Nevertheless, the possibility

[242] There is very often a divergence of interests between the State and the new purchaser of shares of the privatized company. It was argued that, in such cases, an oversight is required, which would secure that the State's interests continue to be served by the privatized companies responsible for specific activities. Without an oversight, privatized companies controlled by the new shareholders would direct their business conduct towards new shareholders' interests, which sometimes conflict with State interests. Regarding our discussion, golden shares could constitute such an oversight mechanism capable of promoting CSR goals supported by Member States. *See*. M. Strauss, *Hostile Business and the Sovereign State* (Routledge 2019), 82.

[243] *See* Sustainable Development Goals (SDGs) of United Nations, 'Transforming Our World: The 2030 Agenda for Sustainable Development' (2015) A/RES/70/1.

[244] For an interesting discussion about the possibility of adapting the objective of public limited liability companies in their articles of association to better accommodate the promotion of public interests, in the context of government undertakings, *see*: J. Nijland,'Governance of Government Undertakings. Ensuring Public Interests in the Netherlands, Germany and France' (2014) 11 ECL 281–289.

of a State to preserve golden shares in privatized companies falls within the scope of internal market law and must comply with its requirements and especially with the findings of golden shares case law.

Member States may maintain some control over privatized enterprises through golden shares, while also remaining compliant with the CJEU's golden shares case law. This control can be implemented in pursuit of CSR goals. The content of various individual CSR goals is also the same as the content of many justifying grounds provided by express derogations of TFEU or by mandatory requirements in the general interest. It could be argued that the legitimate justifying grounds for golden shares could be equated with various goals of CSR, such as environmental protection and climate action, human rights protection, employment protection, protection of public health, consumer protection, clean energy, reduced inequalities, gender equality, regional policy, protection of local communities, etc.[245] Hence, individual CSR goals could also constitute legitimate public interest justifying grounds capable of justifying restrictions on EU fundamental freedoms resulting from golden shares. These justifying grounds constitute lawful derogations to EU fundamental freedoms only if they adhere to the golden shares case law and, in particular, to the standards and principles adopted by *Commission v Belgium*. These justifying grounds are public interest considerations, which also constitute CSR goals and which the State as a shareholder could pursue through golden shares in State-owned companies. Once an enterprise has been privatized, thereby no longer controlled and managed by the State and instead privately controlled and managed, the government would still be able to address these public interest considerations related to CSR by way of golden shares.

It should be mentioned that such integration of CSR into the privatization process through golden shares or tender specifications governing the conditions of the privatization process has not yet taken place. However, considering the emphasis given by EU and Member States on CSR, it is quite possible to see CSR being a part of the privatization process in the near future. CSR might play an important role in privatized companies, especially in those privatized companies offering public services. Member States would be looking for available and convenient tools for introducing CSR into the privatization process. It remains to see in future whether golden shares or tender specifications would be used as tools for the incorporation of CSR into the privatization process.

5 Conclusion

This chapter examined past, present and future perspectives on privatizations of State-owned companies and justifications for restrictions on EU fundamental freedoms. This approach provided an overarching analysis of the issue of justifications, which

[245] See Sustainable Development Goals (SDGs) of United Nations, *Transforming Our World: The 2030 Agenda for Sustainable Development* (2015) A/RES/70/1.

allowed a better understanding of the evolution of this topic. First, this chapter scrutinized justifications for restrictions on EU fundamental freedoms in the CJEU's golden shares case law. It analysed the justifications that the Member States were invoking to justify golden shares infringing free movement of capital and freedom of establishment. This chapter explored how the Member States could justify golden shares based on public interest considerations to preserve some special rights after privatization. *Commission v Belgium* is a unique case. It is the only golden shares case where the CJEU held that national golden shares constituted justified restrictions on EU fundamental freedoms. Member States are successful in convincing the CJEU about the public interest considerations pursued by their national golden shares schemes. The point where all Member States, except for Belgium, fail is compliance with the principle of proportionality. Compliance with the principle of proportionality requires specific, clear and detailed provisions for the exercise of special rights deriving from golden shares. In the golden shares case law, the emphasis is also given on compliance with the principle of legal certainty. The CJEU's approach towards justifications for restrictions in *Commission v Belgium* constitutes a guide for Member States planning to introduce golden shares in their State-owned companies under privatization. Secondly, the recent case *Associação Peço a Palavra* was also analysed in the light of privatizations and justifications for restrictions on EU fundamental freedoms. Regarding this recent case, this chapter examined justification for restrictions resulting from tender specifications governing the conditions to which a privatization process of a State-owned company is subject. Thirdly, future perspectives were also considered in the light of past and current experiences. This chapter explored the integration of CSR into the privatization process through golden shares or tender specifications governing the conditions of the privatization process.

This analysis of privatizations and justifications for restrictions on EU fundamental freedoms is very useful for Member States, because it presents important practical implications for them. Member States could learn a lot from this analysis. This knowledge could be useful for their current and future privatizations projects. The evolution of justifications for restrictions could affect the privatization policies of Member States and could provide uniform conditions, which Member States must follow in the politically sensitive sector of privatizations. Member States are allowed to retain special privileges and to exercise a certain degree of influence over privatized companies in order to satisfy certain public interest considerations, as long as they follow the useful directions provided by CJEU's case law. This case law could assist Member States in making their privatization projects compatible with internal market law. At the same time, they keep a certain level of control over the privatized companies on the basis of public interest considerations. Past experiences from golden shares and current experiences from tender specifications governing the conditions to which a privatization process is subject provide invaluable guidance to Member States facing future challenges to privatizations, such as incorporating CSR into the privatization process.

The Expansion of China's State-Owned Enterprise Sector Since the Global Financial Crisis: What Insights Do Official Statistics Afford?

Chunlin Zhang

1 Introduction

The expansion of the state-owned enterprise (SOE) sector has been a subject of discussion in China for more than a decade. More recently, the issue has received growing international attention as the debate over China's state-led development model intensified.[1] This chapter attempts to improve the understanding of some basic facts regarding the expansion of China's SOE sector in the decade following the global financial crisis in 2008 by studying the official statistics for non-financial SOEs in the *Finance Yearbook of China* (FYC) published by an agency affiliated with the Chinese Ministry of Finance[2] (FYC Editorial Committee, Various years), as well as related statistics from the National Bureau of Statistics (NBS)[3] (National

[1] For example, *see* N R Lardy, *The State Strikes Back: The End of Economic Reform in China* (PIIE 2019).

[2] Unless indicated otherwise, all data used in this chapter are from the FYC. *See* FYC Editorial Committee.. *Finance Yearbook of China (中国财政年鉴)* (China Fiscal and Economic Publishing House / 中国财政经济出版社, Various years).

[3] National Bureau of Statistics, *China Statistical Yearbook (中国统计年鉴* (China Statistical Publishing House/中国统计出版社, various years). Also available at <http://www.stats.gov.cn/tjsj/ndsj/> .

This chapter draws upon and is an updated version of the author's World Bank Working Paper—Zhang, Chunlin. 2019. How Much Do State-Owned Enterprises Contribute to China's GDP and Employment?. World Bank, Washington, DC. © World Bank. https://openknowledge.worldbank.org/handle/10986/32306 License: CC BY 3.0 IGO.

C. Zhang (✉)
Former Lead Private Sector Development Specialist, World Bank, Washington D.C., USA
e-mail: zhangchunlin19@outlook.com

J. Chaisse et al. (eds.), *Regulation of State-Controlled Enterprises*, International Law and the Global South, https://doi.org/10.1007/978-981-19-1368-6_11

Bureau of Statistics, Various Years) and the State Council State Assets Supervision and Administration Commission (SASAC).[4]

The FYC data are aggregations of financial statements submitted to the Ministry of Finance by SOEs. Despite various limitations, some of which are highlighted in this chapter, they remain the only regular and comprehensive official data for Chinese SOEs. The SASAC dataset is also about SOEs, but it covers only those in the portfolio of State Council SASAC and 37 subnational SASACs, and available only for 2004–2016 at the time of this study, while FYC data cover all non-financial SOEs and available from the early 1990s up to 2017. The SASAC dataset also appears not coordinated with the FYC one (see Sect. 4 for details). The NBS releases the most regular and detailed data for industrial enterprises, including SOEs, that are above a "cutoff scale".[5] They are consistent with the FYC data, but NBS data for non-industrial SOEs are relatively scarce. Both FYC and NBS report data about SOE employment, but they do not seem to be consistent.

This chapter is organised as follows. Section 2 looks at the growth of the SOE sector in the past two decades and characterises its expansion since the global financial crisis. Sections. 3–5 address three questions:

- How large is China's SOE sector in terms of its share in the gross domestic product (GDP) before and after the expansion?
- What are the objectives that the observed SOE sector expansion appears to have served?
- How was the expansion of the SOE sector financed?

Data constraints do not always allow firm and precise answers to these questions. Wherever this is the case, attempts are made to draw practical observations as much as possible and raise questions for further work. Key findings are summarised in Sect. 6.

2 Was There an Expansion of the SOE Sector?

China has a large SOE sector. The FYC reports 187,000 SOEs operating in the non-financial sectors in 2017,[6] while state-owned financial institutions dominated

[4] State Council SASAC, *China's State-Owned Assets Supervision and Administration Yearbook (中国国有资产监督管理年鉴)* (China Economic Publishing House/ 中国经济出版社 2016).

[5] Industrial enterprises that had a sales revenue of RMB20 million or higher. Note that the cutoff scale was modified several times since the 1990s. The enterprises that are above the cutoff and therefore covered by the NBS data can vary across years as some join and others drop out.

[6] This chapter assumes that the FYC have either covered all non-financial SOEs or otherwise been consistent in its coverage, but this will need to be confirmed. Starting from 2010, the NBS reports the number of state-controlled enterprises (<http://data.stats.gov.cn/easyquery.htm?cn=C01 >, Overview Chapter). However, this set of data is inconsistent with both the FYC and the NBS' own data of the 3rd Economic Census, possibly due to difference in definition (<http://www.stats.gov.cn/tjsj/pcsj/jjpc/3jp/indexch.htm >).

the financial sector. As an overarching indicator of the public resources devoted to SOEs, the State Council reported to the National People's Congress in 2018[7] that the value of state-owned equity in business enterprises at the end of 2017 stood at RMB66.5 trillion (USD10.2 trillion), including RMB50.3 trillion (USD7.7 trillion) in non-financial SOEs and RMB16.2 trillion (USD2.5 trillion) in state-owned financial institutions.

Among the 187,000 non-financial SOEs, 58,000 are supervised by the national (central) government and 129,000 by subnational (local) governments. Most of them have the State Assets Supervision and Administration Commissions (SASACs) at the central, provincial and municipal levels acting as their state shareholder. Still, many of them are outside the portfolio of SASACs and supervised by other government departments,[8] which are covered by the FYC dataset but not the SASAC one.

As the economy grows, SOEs tend to grow as well. So, was there an expansion of the SOE sector? If yes, in what sense?

FYC data for 1998–2017 suggest that there was indeed an expansion of the SOE sector since the global financial crisis. As shown in Fig. 1a, the growth of the SOE sector after 2007–2008 differs significantly from before. It has since then experienced an expansion in two senses. First, the declining trend of the number of non-financial SOEs reported by the FYC since the 1990s stopped in 2008 and has been reserved since then. By 2017, it had recovered to the level of 2000. Second, in line with the increasing trend of the number of enterprises, there has been an acceleration of the growth of their total assets since 2007, an indicator of the amount of resources under their control. From 1998 to 2007, total assets of non-financial SOEs grew by 1.6 times. In comparison, the decade of 2007–2017 witnessed a much more aggressive surge of 4.3 times. In 1999–2006, the annual increase of total assets of non-financial SOEs was in the range of RMB1-3 trillion before climbing to RMB7 trillion in 2007–2008. It jumped further to over RMB10 trillion in 2010 and over RMB20 trillion in 2015. One significant result of the expansion is that in terms of the size of the balance sheet, about 80% of the SOE sector that existed in 2017 was created after 2007.

The growth of fixed assets and sales revenue of non-financial SOEs has been broadly in line with that of total assets, although fixed assets have grown slower than total assets, the reason for which is unclear. However, the recent decade has seen little growth of their total employment (Fig. 1b) if the FYC data of SOE employment

---

[7] *See* <http://www.npc.gov.cn/npc/xinwen/2018-10/25/content_2063928.htm > . On October 24, 2019, the State Council reported to the National People's Congress the following numbers as of end of 2018: value of state-owned equity in business enterprises: RMB75.9 trillion; those in non-financial SOEs: RMB58.7 trillion; (USD7.7 trillion) in non-financial SOEs; those in state-owned financial institutions: RMB17.2 trillion.

See <http://www.mof.gov.cn/zhengwuxinxi/caizhengxinwen/201910/t20191024_3408398.htm> .

[8] According to FYC, 42,718 of the 58,000 central SOEs are "central government supervised" and 15,626 are "central department supervised. FYC does not explain the distinction between the two. Most likely, the former refers to those in the portfolio of State Council SASAC. However, this cannot be confirmed. The latest data provided by State Council SASAC about the number of SOEs supervised by all SASACs is for 2015 (State Council SASAC, 2016) (State Council SASAC n 4), and they contradict the FYC data.

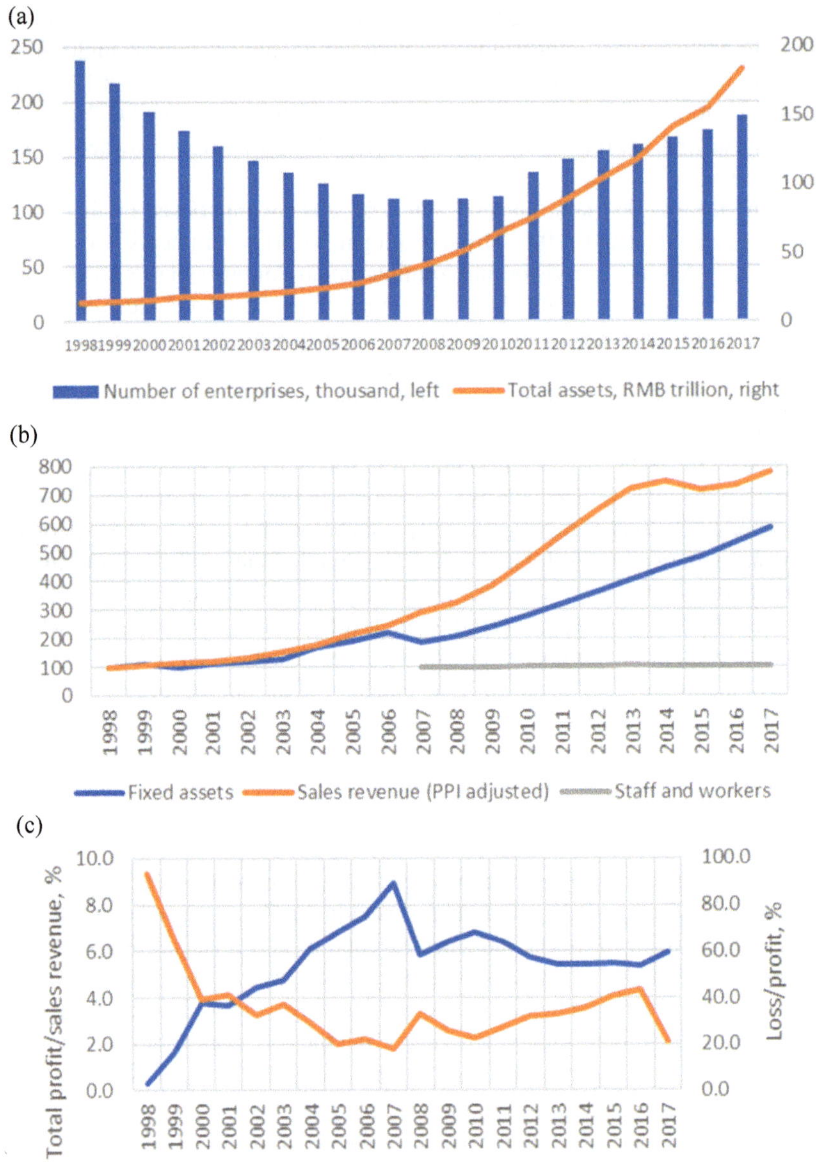

Fig. 1 China's SOE sector expansion in the recent decade. **a** Number of non-financial enterprises and their total assets, 1998-2017, **b** index of fixed assets, sales revenue (1998=100) and employment (2007=100) of non-financial SOEs. *Note* Data for staff and workers are not available before 2007. Sales revenue is adjusted using Producer Price Index for Industrial Products (工业生产者出厂价格指数, PPI) released by the NBS at <http://data.stats.gov.cn/english/easyquery.htm?cn=C01> . **c** Total profit (net of loss) as a percentage of sales revenue and loss as a percentage of the profit of non-financial SOEs, 1998-2017

is accepted (see Sect. 3 for more discussion). On the other hand, the year 2008 was also a turning point in SOE profitability, as reported by FYC (Fig. 1c). The year 1998 was one of the worst of Chinese SOE performance since the reform started when loss-making SOEs lost RMB307 billion, or 93% of the RMB328 billion profit made by profit-making ones. Total profit (net of loss) was only 0.3% of sales revenue. Thanks to the radical reform and restructuring in the late 1990s, the following decade witnessed a steady improvement of SOE performance. By 2007, total profit as a percentage of sales revenue reached 9%, and loss as a percentage of profit dropped to 18%. This trend was reversed in the next decade. Total profit as a percentage of sales revenue declined in 2008 and had never gone above 7% by 2017. Loss as a percentage of profit bounced back and reached 43% in 2016 before a sharp drop, but it was still 20% in 2017.

3 How Large is the SOE Sector Before and After the Expansion?[9]

Has the expansion of the SOE sector resulted in an increase in its share in the Chinese economy? How much does it account for China's GDP before and after the expansion?

China's official statistics, which the NBS releases on its website[10] and the *China Statistical Yearbook,*[11] (Natioal Bureau of Statistics) do not break down GDP by ownership. Various efforts have been made to estimate the ownership structure of the economy in terms of contributions to GDP. For example, in 2000, when China's domestic private sector started to boom, a study of the International Finance Corporation of the World Bank Group[12] (International Finance Corporation, 2000) broke down China's 1998 GDP into three segments: 37% from the state sector, 12% from the collective sector and 45% from the private sector including rural households. Nicholas Lardy, in examining the role of the private sector in the Chinese economy in the early 2010s, conducted a detailed analysis of the relevant Chinese data sector by sector.[13] More recently, in 2018, Carsten Holz (Holz, 2018) estimated SOE shares in sectorial value added (VA) and added them up to conclude that SOEs contributed

[9] Part of this section was published earlier as a separate note. *See* C Zhang, 'How Much Do State-Owned Enterprises Contribute to China's GDP and Employment?' (World Bank 2019) <https://elibrary.worldbank.org/doi/pdf/10.1596/32306> .

[10] <http://data.stats.gov.cn/easyquery.htm?cn=C01> . Unless otherwise specified, all NBS data used in this note are from its website as well as the *China Statistical Yearbook* (National Bureau of Statistics, Various Years) which is also available electronically in its website.

[11] National Bureau of Statistics (n 3).

[12] International Finance Corporation, 'China's emerging private enterprises: prospects for the new century' (September 2000) <http://documents.worldbank.org/curated/en/923231468744007740/pdf/multi-page.pdf> .

[13] N Lardy, *Markets over Mao: The Rise of Private Business in China* (PIIE 2014) <https://piie.com/bookstore/markets-over-mao-rise-private-business-china> , chap 3.

39% of GDP in 2015.[14] In October–November 2018, senior Chinese government leaders made multiple speeches about domestic privately owned enterprises (POEs), in which they stated that POEs contribute "more than 60% of GDP".[15]

Building on the author's previous work,[16] this section estimates SOE shares in GDP and employment in 2017 and 2007 using official statistics from FYC, NBS and other official sources.

3.1 SOE Share in GDP: 2017[17]

NBS breaks down China's 2017 GDP into VA of nine sectors, including one of "others". Estimation of SOE share in GDP involves estimating their share in each of the nine sectors. However, there is no VA data at the sectoral level for SOEs. One of the closest proxies for VA is "sales revenue of principal businesses" (SRPBs), which is reported for non-financial SOEs at the sectoral level by the FYC, as well as by NBS for all enterprises in some sectors. However, the FYC uses its own sectorial classification that does not entirely match the standard one used by NBS—a challenge that has to be dealt with. In what follows, SOE share in SRPBs is used as a proxy for their share in VA wherever feasible. Otherwise, employment or other data are used to fill the gap. The estimates and methodologies are described below with regard to the nine sectors. Adding them up, the share of SOEs in China's 2017 GDP should be 27.5%.

(1) *Farming, foresty, animal husbandry and fishing: 4.6%.* The starting point is the share of primary industry (farming, foresty, animal husbandry and fishery) in GDP, which, according to NBS, was 7.6% in 2017. The primary sectors are dominated by private households but participated by state-owned farms as well as other kinds of enterprises. NBS data show that in 2017, the contribution of state-owned farms includes 6.6% of the gross value of farming output; 3.1% of the number of large livestock and 2.9% of the total output of pork, beef and lamb; 2.5% of the total output of seafood. This allows an estimation as in Table 1. Assuming that state-owned farms account for 4.6% of the primary industry GDP, which was 7.6% of total GDP, their contribution to total GDP should be 0.35% in 2017.

---

[14] C A Holz, 'The Unfinished Business of State-owned Enterprise Reform in the People's Republic of China' (December 2018) SSRN no 3392986 or <http://dx.doi.org/10.2139/ssrn.3392986> .

[15] *See* Vice Premier Liu He's interview on October 19, 2018 at <http://www.gov.cn/guowuyuan/2018-10/19/content_5332515.htm> ; and President Xi Jinping's speech on November 1, 2018 at <http://www.xinhuanet.com/politics/2018-11/01/c_1123649488.htm > . According to them, POEs also account for more than 80% of urban employment.

[16] C Zhang, 'How Much Do State-Owned Enterprises Contribute to China's GDP and Employment?' (World Bank 2019) <https://elibrary.worldbank.org/doi/pdf/10.1596/32306> .

[17] This subsection draws on C Zhang, 'How Much Do State-Owned Enterprises Contribute to China's GDP and Employment?' (World Bank 2019) <https://elibrary.worldbank.org/doi/pdf/10.1596/32306> .

Table 1 Share of state-owned farms in agricultural outputs (%), 2017

Sector	Sector's share in total gross value of the output of the four primary sectors	Assumed share of state farms in the sector's output	Estimated share of state farms in total gross value of the output of the four primary sectors
Farming	53.10	6.6	3.51
Forest	4.56	n/a	n/a
Animal husbandry	26.86	3	0.83
Fishing	10.59	2.5	0.26
Total	100		4.60

Note n/a = no data available
Source NBS. See C Zhang, "How Much Do State-Owned Enterprises Contribute to China's GDP and Employment?" (World Bank 2019) <https://elibrary.worldbank.org/doi/pdf/10.1596/32306>

(2) *Industry: 21.1%.* NBS publishes data for all above-scale industrial enterprises as well as SOEs (state-owned and state-controlled). To account for the output of below cutoff scale enterprises, it is assumed that they contributed 10% of the total output. As such, 2017 SRPBs of all industrial enterprises amount to RMB125.9 trillion (RMB113.3 trillion × (10/9)), while that of SOEs, which are assumed to be all above-scale, is RMB26.5 trillion, resulting in a share of 21.1%.

(3) *Construction: 38.5%.* This is the share of construction sector SOEs' 2017 SRPBs (FYC data) in that of the whole sector (NBS data). SOEs in the construction sector are often more capital intensive than others, implying that its share in sales revenue can be higher than in VA. However, their share in employment (4.9% using the same data) would be an under-estimation.

(4) *Wholesale and Retail: 36.9%.* The estimation for this sector is derived by addressing two sources of complications.

- First, NBS data cover only trading enterprises above cutoff scale as in the case of industry, and there is a considerable number of below cutoff scale trading enterprises. Comparison of NBS' 2013 data with Table A1-09 of the Third Economic Census shows that 94% of the wholesale and retail sector legal-person entities are below cutoff scale enterprises, which is mainly an issue of the private sector because SOEs are typically much larger.[18] The same issue exists in the case of industry, but the number of enterprises left out in 2013, using the same date, was 85%. It is, therefore, assumed that below cutoff scale, wholesale and retail enterprises contribute 20% of the sector's SRPBs, making its total RMB61.4 trillion.
- Second, FYC's classification clusters wholesale and retail with catering and stopped providing breakdown after 2013. In 2013, catering accounted for

[18] National Bureau of Statistics, *China Economic Census Yearbook 2013 (中国经济普查年鉴)* (China Statistical Publishing House / 中国统计出版社 (2013). Also available at <http://www.stats.gov.cn/tjsj/pcsj/jjpc/3jp/indexch.htm> .

3.7% of the sectorial total, which is assumed still the case in 2017. As such, SRPBs of SOEs in the wholesale and retail sector were estimated at RMB22.6 trillion, or 36.9% of the national total.

(5) *Transport, Storage and Post: 77.3%.* No SRPBs or other output data are available for this sector. Employment is used as a proxy. FYC provides SOE employment data after 2007 for two sectors: "transport and storage" and "post and communications". However, NBS employment data after 2011 have two subsectors missing: urban transport and communication. The 2011 data of total sectorial employment (7,795,215) and SOE employment (6,023,000) are used as a proxy, leading to an SOE share of 77.3%. It is worth noting that employment is an imperfect substitute for output indicators, particularly for this sector. First, the use of 2011 data, the latest year when complete data are available, may overstate the share of the SOEs to the extent that private sector participation (e.g. in express delivery) has increased since 2011; second, it may in the meantime understate the share of SOEs due to a general trend of increased capital intensity. FYC data show that staff and workers of transport, storage, post and communications combined increased only 11.2% from 2007–2017 when their sales revenue did 1.7 times and assets 4.6 times. However, there seems no better data to use for adjustment, as no indicator reported by NBS for these two sectors is broken down by ownership.

(6) *Hotel and catering: 8.8%.* NBS data indicate a total SRPBs in hotel and catering in 2017, which is RMB873.6 billion. However, there is no FYC data for this sector due to its unique classification. The NBS does report SRPBs for this sector but only by "registration type", which leaves some SOEs mixed up with non-SOEs in categories such as "limited liability companies" and "joint stock companies".[19] This is fixed in the following way:

- In 2011, FYC data for sales revenue of principal business of catering SOEs were 0.353 times larger than the sum of "state-owned enterprises" and "wholly state-owned companies" reported by NBS data due to the presence of SOEs in other categories of NBS data.
- Assuming this is still the case in 2017, the sum of SRPBs of two categories, "state-owned enterprises" and "wholly state-owned companies", is scaled up by a factor of 1.353, resulting in a proxy for SOE SRPBs in hotel and catering, which is RMB77.23 billion, or 8.8% of the national total.

(7) *Finance: 88%.* FYC reports data only for non-financial SOEs. NBS website and *China Statistical Yearbook* do not have output or assets data broken down by ownership. Data from two other sources are used, and the share of state-owned financial institutions in total assets of the financial sector is taken as their share in financial sector VA:

[19] For a detailed discussion on this issue, see Lardy (n 13) (Lardy N., 2014).

- In its *China Financial Stability Report 2018*,[20] the People's Bank of China states that total assets of the financial sector, excluding the central bank, was RMB273.8 trillion at the end of 2017.
- In a report to the National People's Congress, the State Council states that the total assets of state-owned financial institutions at the end of 2017 was RMB241 trillion, which is 88% of the total as reported by the People's Bank of China.

(8) *Real estate: 24.6%.* NBS reports in *China Statistical Yearbook* 2018 that SRPBs of all enterprises in the real estate sector was RMB9.6 trillion in 2017, while that of SOEs was RMB2.4 trillion, or 24.6%, according to FYC.

(9) *Others: 7.7%.* NBS leaves nine economic sectors in the residual category of "others" regarding sectorial VA.

- Six of them have five roughly comparable counterparts in the FYC classification. They are (i) information transmission, computer services and software (NBS)—information technology services (FYC), (ii) health, social security and social welfare (NBS)—health, sports and welfare (FYC), (iii) education as well as culture, sports and entertainment, two sectors (NBS)—education, culture and broadcast (FYC), (iv) scientific research, technical services and geological survey (NBS)—scientific research and technical services (FYC), (v) public administrations and social organisations (NBS)—administrations, organisations and others (FYC). NBS data suggest 53.22 million of total employment of these five sectors in 2017, while according to FYC, SOE employment in these sectors was 2.21 million in 2017 or 4.2% of the total.
- Three other sectors do not have a counterpart in the FYC classification: leasing and business services; irrigation, environment and public facilities management; services to residents and other services. Their total employment in 2017 was 8.69 million. On the other hand, two sectors of the FYC classification are not matched by NBS data: geological survey and irrigation, social services, with total employment of 2.54 million. Assuming that NBS and FYC data are comparable for this leftover group of sectors, the share of SOEs is 29.2%. This is mainly driven by the FYC category of "social services", which has proliferated over the past decade, but its definition is unclear (see Sect. 4).
- Taking a weighted average of the above, the share of SOEs in the employment of the nine "other" sectors left out by the NBS data is estimated as 7.7%, and this is used as a proxy for their share in VA.

[20] <http://www.gov.cn/xinwen/2018-11/04/5337137/files/48b31c0c3cec41ac977b18a2b6b9590a.pdf> , p 175.

3.2 SOE Share in GDP: 2007

What happened to the SOE share in GDP in 2007–2017 when the SOE sector experienced an expansion? The SOE share in GDP in 2007 can be estimated using the same approach, as the same methodology and data from the same sources as in the previous sub-section are feasible, with finance being the only exception.

The critical challenge regarding the financial sector is that there is no 2007 data for total assets of state-owned financial institutions comparable with the data released by the State Council for 2017. The issue is further complicated by a structural change of China's financial sector in recent years when a rapidly growing share of financial sector assets is found in asset management businesses. According to the World Bank's Financial Sector Assessment (World Bank, 2017), asset management businesses, whose ownership structure is more challenging to determine than traditional businesses, accounted for 24.9% of total assets of the financial system in 2016, up from only 2.7% in 2010.[21] Nonetheless, the following are known:

- The total assets of "large commercial banks", "policy banks" and the China Development Bank, the largest state-owned financial institutions, as a share of total assets of banking institutions declined from 62.5% in 2007 to 47.2% in 2016, suggesting increased private sector participation in the banking sector, which accounted for a lion share of the financial system (World Bank, 2011) (World Bank, 2017).[22]
- The share of state-owned financial institutions in total assets of the financial system was 88% in 2017, suggesting that it may well be above 90% in 2007 but should undoubtedly be below 100%.
- NBS data suggest that the finance sector accounts for only 5.6% of the GDP in 2007, implying that any over-or under-estimate of the share of state-owned financial institutions can hardly significantly impact the total share of SOEs in GDP. One percentage point of over-or under-estimation results in a difference of 0.04% points in the total share of SOEs in GDP.

Considering the above, it is assumed that the share of state-owned financial institutions in total assets of the financial system in 2007 is 95%. As such, the total share of SOEs in 2007 GDP is 29.1%.

Table 2 summarises the estimates for both 2017 and 2017. As shown there, the SOE sector expansion did not result in a larger share of SOEs in China's GDP. This was mainly driven by the rapid growth of the private sector, particularly in industry, which accounted for 41.4% of GDP in 2007.

---

[21] World Bank, 'China - Financial Sector Assessment' (November 2017) Finance & Markets Global Practice EAST Asia and the Pacific Regional vice Presidency <http://documents.worldbank.org/curated/en/361891512597572360/China-Financial-sector-assessment> .

[22] World Bank, China: Financial Sector Assessment (November 2019). SecM2011-0492 <https://www.worldbank.org/content/dam/Worldbank/document/WB-Chinas-Financial-Sector-Assessment-Report.pdf> ; World Bank (n 24).

Table 2 Estimating the share of SOEs in China's GDP in 2017 and 2007[23]

Sector	Value added (RMB 100 million)		Assumed share of SOEs in sectorial value added (%)		Estimated value added of SOEs (RMB 100 million)		Estimated share of SOEs in total value added (%)	
	2017	2007	2017	2007	2017	2007	2017	2007
Farming, foresty, animal husbandry, fishery	64,660	28,484	4.60	4.00	2974	1139	0.362	0.422
Industry	278,328	111,694	21.10	27.60	58,727	30,828	7.155	11.41
Construction	55,314	15,348	38.50	31.00	21,296	4758	2.595	1.762
Wholesale and retail	77,658	20,938	36.85	38.70	28,619	8103	3.487	3.000
Transport, storage, post	37,173	14,605	77.27	93.50	28,722	13,656	3.499	5.056
Hotel and catering	14,690	5548	8.84	20.30	1299	1126	0.158	0.417
Finance	65,395	15,174	88.00	95.00	57,548	14,415	7.012	5.337
Real estate	53,965	13,810	24.60	14.90	13,275	2058	1.617	0.762
Others	173,571	44,492	7.67	5.76	13,308	2565	1.621	0.950
Total	820,754	270,092			225,768	78,647	27.51	29.12

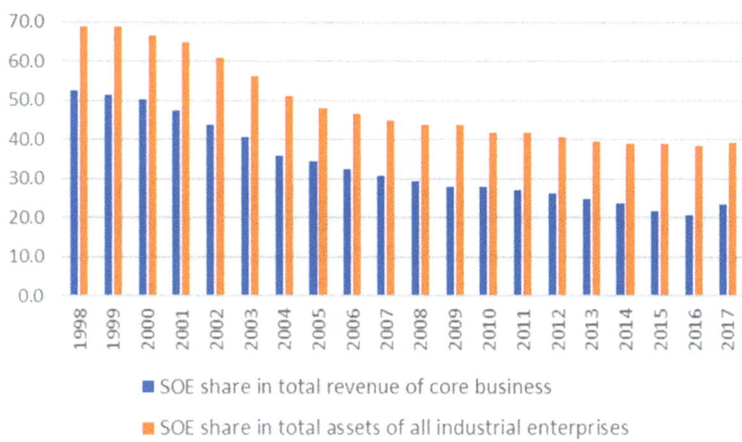

Fig. 2 SOE share (%) in total assets and revenue of all industrial enterprises (above cutoff scale)

However, it is worth noting that the trend has moderated in recent years, as shown in Fig. 2. The shares of SOEs in SRPBs and total assets of above-scale industrial

[23] This table draws on C Zhang, 'How Much Do State-Owned Enterprises Contribute to China's GDP and Employment?' (World Bank 2019) <https://elibrary.worldbank.org/doi/pdf/10.1596/32306> .

enterprises all stopped declining in 2017. More latest data are needed to see whether this is a trend change. However, sector-wise, SOEs did increase their shares in a few sectors, most notably in real estate (from 14.9 to 24.6%), but also in construction and "others". Section 4 will further analyse the sectoral distribution of SOE assets.

3.3 SOE Share in Employment

In addition to GDP, SOE share in employment can be another indicator of its prominence in the economy. This can be estimated for both 2017 and 2007, but data issues limit their usefulness.

Since the FYC reports the total number of "staff and workers" in non-financial SOEs after 2007 and the NBS reports total employment every year, the estimation appears straightforward. The gap of SOE employment in the financial sector can be filled with NBS data for "state-owned unit" employment in the financial sector. It is true that "state-owned units" include both SOEs and other non-SOE public institutions such as public service units (PSUs, *shiye danwei*), of which data availability does not allow a separation, but state-owned units in the financial sector are dominated by state-owned banks and other financial institutions, which are all SOEs. Non-SOE public employment in the financial sector should be minimal.

The result obtained this way is that SOEs account for 4.5% of total employment in 2017 and 4.9% in 2007 (Table 3). The problem with this result is that it appears to be significantly inconsistent with other NBS employment data when an effort is made to account for non-SOE employment (Zhang 2019). In 2017, the residual unaccounted for amounts to 11.8% of total employment (91.3 million), while in 2007, this is as high as 18.5% (139.4 million). The NBS does not report employment for non-financial SOEs. Instead, it uses "state-owned unit" as the key concept. Its 2017 data put state-owned unit employment at 60.6 million, of which 46 million is found in the sector of "public management and social organisation" as well as five other sectors which are dominated by PSUs, leaving only 13.4 million for SOEs, even lower than the 34.7 million reported by FYC for non-financial SOEs.

It is quite possible that the FYC data understate SOE employment. SOEs may not have reported migrant workers and other temporary workers as their "staff and workers[24]" in the FYC data, while they are captured in NBS' total employment numbers. Indeed, NBS released a number for employment of "state-owned and controlled enterprises" in 2016, which was 45.87 million,[25] or 9.67 million larger than the FYC number. However, this is still too small to explain the discrepancy of 91.3 million. There are PSUs in sectors other than the five covered in Table 3,

[24] Staff and workers of an SOE are defined as open-ended employees or employees holding a labor contract, who are found in the SOE's HR system and receive wages from the SOE. *See* Ministry of Finance. *Summary of Enterprise Financial Reports Nationwide (企业财务会计报告数据摘要)* (China Finance and Economic Publishing House / 中国财政经济出版社 2012, 392.

[25] China Labor Statistics Yearbook 2017, Tables 4 and 5.

Table 3 Breakdown of China's employment by ownership type of employer, 2017 and 2007[26]

Employers by ownership type	Employment (million)		As % of total		Basis of estimation
	2017	2007	2017	2007	
Total employment	776.40	753.21	100	100	NBS data
POEs and business individuals	341.07	127.49	43.9	16.9	NBS data
Rural households	237.46	394.19	30.6	52.3	Rural employment minus rural POE employment and business individuals (*getihu*), all NBS data
Government and PSUs	46.07	39.46	5.9	5.2	Sum of government and PSU employment
Government	17.1	12.85	2.2	1.7	NBS data, state unit employment in the sector of "public management and social organisation"
PSUs	28.97	26.61	3.7	3.5	NBS data, state unit employment in five sectors where most PSUs operate: agriculture, science and technology, education, health and culture
FIEs	25.81	15.83	3.3	2.1	NBS data
SOEs	34.69	36.83	4.5	4.9	Sum of non-financial SOE employment and financial SOEs employment
Non-financial SOEs	33.26	35.22	4.3	4.7	FYC data
Financial SOEs	1.43	1.61	0.2	0.2	State unit employment in the sector of finance. Assuming it is equal to SOE employment in finance
Residual	91.3	139.4	11.8	18.5	Total minus all above

but again, the omission is unlikely very significant compared with the size of the residual.

Nonetheless, it is clear that the SOE expansion in 2007–2017 has not resulted in a larger share of SOEs in total employment. Even if all the unexplained residuals are added to SOE employment, the SOE share would still have dropped from 23.4% to 16.3%. The single most important driving force of the evolution of the structure of China's employment is that the share of POEs jumped from 16.9% in 2007 to 43.9% in 2017.

[26] This table draws on C Zhang, 'How Much Do State-Owned Enterprises Contribute to China's GDP and Employment?' (World Bank 2019) <https://elibrary.worldbank.org/doi/pdf/10.1596/32306> .

4 What Appear to be the Objectives of the SOE Sector Expansion?

A common perception about China's state-led development model is that it involves identifying "strategic sectors" by the government and providing support for them with state capital through SOEs. Indeed, the Chinese government's own reform objective calls for a greater concentration of state capital in strategic sectors. It is, therefore, highly likely that the observed expansion of the SOE sector took place to serve the government's strategic priorities.

If this is what happened, the acquisition of assets and equity stakes in non-financial SOEs should have been guided by a list of strategically prioritised sectors, whatever they are, and the observed SOE sector expansion should exhibit such a sectorial structure accordingly. Available data allow two ways to investigate whether this is the case.

- One is to look at the sectoral structure of the SOE sector after the expansion (around 2017) to see in what sectors SOE dominance is the most prominent. This can be seen from two different angles: either from the sectorial distribution of resources controlled by the SOE sector or the SOE share in output and employment of each sector.
- Another is to look at how the increased assets and equity in 2007–2017 (the "flow") were distributed among sectors and compare it with the sectorial distribution of the SOE assets and equity in 2007 (the "stock"). Suppose a sector was treated as a higher priority (lower priority) in the expansion in 2007–2017, it should account for a larger (smaller) share of the flow, and its share in the flow should be larger (smaller) than its share in the 2007 stock, indicating a rising (declining) concentration of state capital in that sector.

However, there is one data issue: FYC's sector-level data in 2017 do not add up to the national total it released, indicating quality problems. Data for 2016 are used here instead.[27] And as mentioned earlier, FYC uses its own sectorial classification, which does not match the standard one defined by NBS.

4.1 *Sectorial Structure of the SOE Sector Around 2017*

Table 4 looks at the sectorial structure of key aggregate indicators of non-financial SOEs in 2016 as reported by the FYC. A few observations can be made:

- *One-third of the SOE sector is about infrastructure.* In terms of total assets, infrastructure accounts for 30% of non-financial SOEs in 2016, including 14% for

[27] The discrepancy between the published national aggregate number and the sum of sectorial level numbers for owners' equity is only 0.7% in 2016.

Table 4 Sectorial distribution of China's non-financial SOEs (% of total), 2016

Sector and subsector	Total assets	Owners' equity	Sales revenue	Profit	Staff and workers
Infrastructure	30.0	35.3	25.4	27.5	39.6
Coal, oil and petrochemical	5.4	7.7	6.0	0.5	12.7
Electricity	6.7	6.7	8.0	10.6	5.8
Urban utilities	1.5	1.8	1.3	1.5	2.3
Transport	14.0	15.0	6.5	7.9	13.7
Communication	2.4	4.2	3.6	7.0	5.2
Farming, forest, animal husbandry and fishing	0.8	0.8	0.6	0.2	6.8
Manufacturing	12.0	13.4	20.3	17.6	25.4
Construction	7.6	6.3	11.7	6.7	7.5
Wholesale, retail and catering	4.5	4.0	34.1	13.4	5.9
Real estate	10.5	8.7	4.0	10.1	2.4
Education, health, culture, sports	0.7	1.1	0.7	1.2	1.6
Scientific research, technical services and IT services	1.9	2.7	2.1	3.6	3.3
Social services	17.6	23.8	0.2	10.4	6.2
Administration, organisation and others	14.4	3.8	1.0	9.3	1.3

Note "Manufacturing" is the sum of sectors under "Industry", excluding coal, oil and petrochemical, electricity and urban utilities

transport, 12.1% for energy (coal, oil and petrochemical,[28] electricity), 2.4% for communication and 1.5% for urban utilities. The pattern is similar in terms of owners' equity, which is closer to be a proxy for state equity capital invested in SOEs.

- *In contrast, manufacturing does not appear to be as important.* Manufacturing sectors[29], as defined by FYC, jointly account for only 12% of total assets and 13% of equity in non-financial SOEs, although with a twice larger share in total employment (25.4%).
- *Three sectors dominate the tertiary industry:* Real estate, social services and administrations, organisation and others. Jointly they account for 42.5% of total assets and 36.3% of equity of non-financial SOEs, although their shares in sales

[28] The FYC data do allow a separation between oil extraction and processing.

[29] "Industry" net of coal, oil and petrochemical, electricity and urban utilities.

Table 5 SOE shares (%) in sales revenue of principal businesses of industrial subsector, 2017

Subsector	SOE share in the subsector	Subsector's share in total
Mining	57.3	4.2
Manufacturing	17.7	90.0
Utilities	86.7	5.8
Subsectors with 50% or higher SOE shares		
Tobacco	99.3	0.8
Electricity	91.5	5.1
Mining support	83.9	0.1
Oil and gas extraction	84.3	0.7
Water	69.0	0.2
Coal	64.1	2.2
Petrochemical	56.2	3.6
Gas supply	49.8	0.6
Some other sectors		
Automobiles	43.8	7.5
Railway, vessel, aerospace and other transport equipment	41.8	1.5
Chemical	18.0	7.2
Special purpose machinery	12.5	3.2
General-purpose machinery	9.8	4.0
Electronics	9.1	9.4
Pharmaceuticals	8.7	2.4

Source NBS data at http://data.stats.gov.cn/easyquery.htm?cn=C01

revenue and employment are disproportionately smaller (see further discussion below).

While Table 4 reflects the sectoral distribution of resources under state ownership, in what sectors do SOEs dominate?

As already seen in Table 2, finance and transport are the top two sectors where SOE dominance is the most prominent, which are followed by construction, trade and real estate, where SOEs account for one quarter to one-third of sectoral outputs. On the other hand, SOE share in industrial output is much lower.

However, "industry" is large and has the highest SOE contribution to GDP. It is, therefore, necessary to look further into the distribution of SOEs among industrial subsectors using NBS data.[30] As shown in Table 5, SOEs dominate utilities and, to a lesser extent, mining, but in manufacturing, which accounts for 90% of the industrial output, SOE share was only 18% on average in 2017. Looking further into the 40 subsectors classified by the NBS (excluding the subsector of "mining of other ores",

30 <http://data.stats.gov.cn/easyquery.htm?cn=C01> .

which is negligible), there are eight in which SOEs had a share of 50% or higher. Apart from tobacco, which the government monopolises by law, and "mining support", which is tiny and negligible, the other six are either energy or utilities. In seven other subsectors that are likely to be "strategic", SOEs appear to dominate automobiles and other transport equipment manufacturing but not others. In subsectors commonly seen as innovation-intensive, such as electronics and pharmaceuticals, their shares are below 10%.

4.2 *Sectorial Structures of the Flow Compared with that of the Stock*

Table 6 presents results obtained following the second approach. Precisely, the following are calculated:

- Share in stock: a sector's share in total number and assets of all non-financial SOEs in 2007.
- Share in flow: a sector's share in the total increases of number and assets of all non-financial SOEs in 2007–2016.
- Difference (D value): residual after deducting the share in stock from the share in flow.

As mentioned earlier, if a sector was treated as a higher (lower) priority in the expansion, it should account for a larger (smaller) share in the flow, and its share in the flow should be larger (smaller) than its share in the stock, resulting in a positive (negative) D value. Looking at the picture in terms of total assets, the following stand out as the top five "winners":

(1) **Social services**: Out of the RMB120 trillion total increase of assets in non-financial SOEs in 2007–2016, 20.5% was added to the sector of "social services". The percentage was 29.4% in terms of owners' equity. This represents the most radical adjustment compared with the sector's shares in 2007, a D value of 12.6 percentage points in terms of total assets and 20.6 in terms of equity, as if the state had decided to give top priority to this sector.

(2) **Administrations, organisations and others**. In the same sense, the sector of "administrations, organisations and others" was the second biggest "winner", with a D value of 12% points in terms of total assets and 2.7 in terms of equity. It accounts for 17.1% of the RMB120 trillion assets added to the SOE sector in 2007–2016.

(3) **Real estate**. The real estate sector follows with a D value of 5.3 percentage points in terms of total assets. It received 11.7% of the assets increase (10.4% of the equity) in 2007–2016.

(4) **Construction**. Its share in the flow was 3 percentage points larger than in the 2007 stock in terms of total assets (4.9 in terms of owners' equity). It captured about 8% of the assets added to the SOE sector in 2007–2016.

Table 6 Sectoral structure of the expansion of non-financial SOEs in 2007–2016 (%)

Sector	Subsector	No. of enterprises			Assets		
		Share in stock	Share in flow	Difference (ppt)	Share in stock	Share in flow	Difference (ppt)
Agriculture, forest, animal husbandry, Fishery		6.2	0.0	−6.2	1.1	0.7	−0.4
Industry		26.4	22.3	−4.1	47	19.4	−27.6
	Coal	1.4	1.1	−0.4	3.6	2.1	−1.5
	Oil and petrochemical	0.5	0.4	0.0	7.9	1.6	−6.3
	Metallurgy	1.6	1.3	−0.3	6.7	2	−4.7
	Construction materials	1.4	2.5	1.2	0.8	0.6	−0.2
	Chemicals	2.2	0.8	−1.4	2.3	1.1	−1.2
	Timber processing	0.2	−0.1	−0.3	0	0	0
	Food processing	2.0	−0.5	−2.5	0.4	0.2	−0.2
	Tabaco	0.1	0.1	0.1	1.5	0.3	−1.2
	Textile	1.0	−1.0	−1.9	0.4	0	−0.4
	Pharmaceutical	0.6	0.3	−0.3	0.4	0.2	−0.2
	Machinery	5.5	2.3	−3.2	5	2.8	−2.2
	Electronics	1.1	0.9	−0.2	1.1	0.6	−0.5
	Electricity	3.0	6.9	3.9	12.2	5	−7.2
	Public utilities	2.2	5.5	3.3	1.3	1.6	0.3
	Other industries	3.7	1.6	-2.1	3.3	1.2	−2.1
Construction		5.2	8.4	3.1	5.3	8.3	3
Geological exploration and irrigation		1.0	1.1	0.1	0.4	0.7	0.3
Transport, storage and communication		14.1	2.3	−11.9	13.8	14	0.2
	Rail transport	0.3	1.5	1.2	4.1	5.2	1.1
	Road transport	1.5	4.6	3.1	3.3	5.7	2.4
	Waterway transport	0.7	1.2	0.5	1.4	0.6	−0.8
	Aviation	0.3	0.5	0.2	1.5	0.7	−0.8
	Storage	9.8	−6.1	−15.9	1.6	1.5	−0.1
	Post and communications	0.4	1.7	1.4	9	0.5	−8.5
Wholesale, retail trade and catering		19.8	5.6	−14.3	6.6	3.9	−2.7
Real estate		5.5	17.9	12.4	6.4	11.7	5.3

(continued)

Table 6 (continued)

Sector	Subsector	No. of enterprises			Assets		
		Share in stock	Share in flow	Difference (ppt)	Share in stock	Share in flow	Difference (ppt)
Information technology services		0.8	2.4	1.6	0.4	0.3	−0.1
Social services		12.6	22.5	10.0	7.9	20.5	12.6
Health, sport and welfare		0.3	1.0	0.7	0	0.2	0.2
Education, culture and broadcast		3.4	4.3	0.9	0.6	0.5	−0.1
Scientific research and technical services		2.9	8.9	6.0	0.6	1.1	0.5
Administrations, organisations and others		1.4	1.7	0.2	5.1	17.1	12

(5) **Road transport**. Similarly, the share of this sector in the flow was 2.4 percentage points larger than in the 2007 stock in terms of total assets (4 percentage points in terms of owners' equity). It received 6% of the assets added to the SOE sector in 2007–2016.

Together, the five sectors account for around 60% of the assets and equity increases of non-financial SOEs in 2007–2016, while their collective share in 2007 was less than 30%.

What sectors are the "losers" then? It turns out that the industry is the biggest loser. While it accounted for around 50% of the total assets and owners' equity of non-financial SOEs in 2007, it only captured around 20% of the assets and equity added to them in 2007–2016. At the subsector level, electricity, oil and petrochemical, metallurgy, machinery appear to be the big losers. Going beyond industry, the post and communication sector also saw its share in the flow significantly lower than in the 2007 stock.

In between are some sectors that gained or lost only in a marginal sense, including scientific research and technical services, geological survey and irrigation, storage, public utilities, health and sports, construction materials, and agriculture.

The results presented in Table 6 are broadly consistent with those in Table 2, where SOE shares in sectorial output are calculated using NBS VA data as the denominator.

The picture is similar in terms of the number of enterprises. About 40% of the increase in the number of non-financial SOEs in 2007–2016 was found in two sectors: social services and real estate. They had their share in the total number of non-financial SOEs increased by more than 10% points from 2007 to 2016. Three other sectors account for 21%: scientific research and technical services, electricity and public utilities. Given the significant size difference of enterprises across sectors, the assets data serve better the purpose of the investigation in this section.

4.3 A Closer Look at the Two Top "Winners"

The FYC does not provide a clear definition for the sectors of "social services" and "administrations, organisation and others". NBS standard classification does not have one of "social services". Instead, it puts "business services" and "consumer services and other services" into two different sectors. The FYC sector of "social services" might have covered SOEs in both business services, consumer services and other services, but this requires official confirmation. On the other hand, the NBS classification does have a sector of "public management and social organisations", which presumably is the same as "administrations, organisations and others". However, neither government departments nor social organisations affiliated with them are SOEs by definition. It is, therefore, still unclear what kind of SOEs are included in this sector in the FYC. A view from experts suggests that it might be those SOEs that are neither found in the portfolios of SASACs nor supervised directly by ministry and departments of finance that are temporally parked here until further classification into the relevant sectors. However, this will need to be confirmed by the authorities. Nonetheless, given the critical role of the two sectors, it is necessary to look further into other available FYC data about them, as in Table 7.

The key observation that can be drawn from Table 7 is that both sectors experienced "balance sheet expansion" in 2007–2016: the growth of their total assets and total liabilities has been much more aggressive than other indicators. In both cases, the size of the balance sheet increased by around ten times, funded by a similar surge of liabilities and a slightly less dramatic one of equity. In the meantime, the number of enterprises increased by less than one time, employment by less than two times, profit by less than four times.

What kind of SOEs could they be? The profile, as highlighted by Table 7, may suggest some sort of investment vehicle. They could be local government financing platforms, government guidance funds, or investment vehicles, including securities trading firms created by SOE conglomerates. However, it is unclear whether they are classified as "financial" or "non-financial" SOEs. Obviously, more data and research are required to have a clearer idea. However, in any case, it would be surprising if they turn out to be some SOEs of "strategic sectors" in any sense.

4.4 Other Possible Objectives

Putting together the insights gained from the above analysis, the most outstanding fact the data reveal seems that the observed SOE sector expansion does not appear to have been guided by a list of national strategic priorities. While some sectors that appear to have received priority can be "strategic", such as road transport, others such as real estate are certainly not. Indeed, real estate was a sector from which the State

Table 7 Index of some key indicators of the sectors of "social services" and "administrations, organisation and others" in 2007–2016 (2007 = 100)

Year	Number of enterprises	Total assets	Total liabilities	Owners' equity	Profit	Staff and workers
Social services						
2007	100	100	100	100	100	100
2008	104	133	137	128	91	109
2009	112	199	210	187	127	118
2010	118	245	256	232	160	119
2011	153	365	379	349	242	130
2012	171	468	479	455	262	143
2013	167	568	574	561	267	145
2014	172	700	701	698	316	140
2015	186	862	850	876	422	144
2016	199	997	997	996	379	164
Administrations, organisations and others						
2007	100	100	100	100	100	100
2008	111	147	126	260	49	197
2009	106	184	165	286	111	110
2010	112	411	416	381	153	159
2011	92	412	457	164	174	158
2012	95	498	551	205	229	167
2013	105	589	651	244	233	172
2014	117	716	788	316	364	190
2015	138	1198	1313	562	587	220
2016	165	1257	1347	758	498	263

Council has explicitly required central SOEs to withdraw.[31] On the other hand, some sectors that are often seen as strategically or socially important, such as electronics, information technology, pharmaceutical, machinery and public utilities, did not stand out as priorities. The data would provide much better support to a proposition that the SOE sector expansion in 2007–2016 was not driven by a clear list of national strategic priorities. So, what other objectives might it have served?

The first possibility is that the observed expansion was simply a response to the global financial crisis. It is fair to say that the expansion was at least triggered by

[31] On March 18, 2010, State Council SASAC announced that 16 central SOEs (with 373 legally independent subsidiaries) are approved as having real estate as their "core business" and 78 others (with 227 legal independent subsidiaries) were required to withdraw from the sector. *See* <http://news.xinhuanet.com/fortune/2010-03/18/content_13194385.htm>. Media report later suggests that implementation of the decision was a challenge. By end of 2012, only 20 of the 78 had done what they were required to do. *See* <http://news.sina.com.cn/c/nd/2017-02-07/doc-ifyafcyw0466223.shtml>
.

the global financial crisis as well as China's response to it, including the stimulus package rolled out in 2008. However, the fact that it has lasted since then without any sign of scaling back defies a characterisation of it as only a crisis response.

The second possibility is that the SOE sector expanded to preserve and create jobs. It is common for SOEs in the world to pursue employment policy objectives, but this does not seem the case in China in the past decade, which was preceded by a massive wave of SOE restructuring in the late 1990s that downsized the SOE labour force by about a half. And it certainly has no support from the aggregate data of FYC. "Staff and workers", or formal employees, of non-financial SOEs stayed in the range of 35–37 million in 2007–2017 with little growth. As discussed above, the FYC data likely understate the size of SOE employment because an acceptance of the FYC data would make it difficult to account for as large as 12% of total employment in 2017 and even a larger fraction in 2007. However, if there is any under-reporting, it should be about other employees who do not hold the status of "staff and workers", such as migrant workers. Systematic under-reporting of "staff and workers" for a period of ten years is highly unlikely. However, there is an essential difference between the two kinds of employees when it comes to incentives: SOEs management and their supervising authorities have strong incentives to preserve jobs for their existing staff and workers, but it is hard to believe they are motivated to raise capital and acquire new assets to create jobs for migrant workers and others in the labour market.

The third possibility is that the SOE sector expansion resulted from the pursuit of financial returns by SOEs. After creating SASACs in 2003, the government reinforced its insistence on return on state capital ("state assets value preservation and appreciation") in SOE governance and SOEs, in general, became more commercially oriented than before. It is, therefore, possible that the observed expansion of the SOE sector was driven by investments made by SOEs and their shareholder entities in a decentralised manner in pursuit of financial return.

However, a hypothesis like this receives little support from the aggregate data as reported by the FYC. As Fig. 3 suggests, at the aggregate level, the state appears to have doubled down its acquisition of equity in non-financial SOEs at a time when their average return on equity (ROE) was declining, from 12.4% in 2006 to 4.6% in 2017.

A closer look at the top five sectors that seem to have received priority in the SOE sector expansion in 2007–2016 results in a similar conclusion. While it is widely believed that central SOEs expanded into sectors such as real estate to chase easy profit, this is not broadly supported by FYC data as in Fig. 4, where ROE of SOEs operating in the real estate sector hardly outperforms national and industrial sector averages; and that of three others, construction, road transport and social services, are outperformed by national and industrial sector averages. Only the sector of "administration, organisation and others" is different.

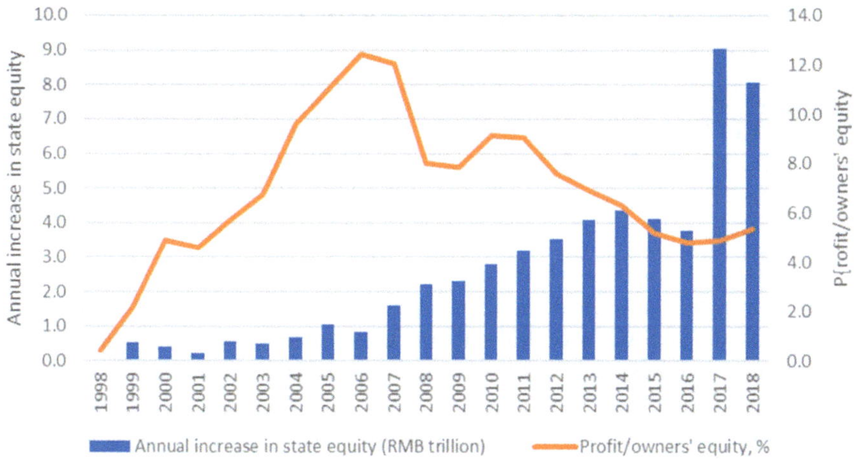

Fig. 3 Annual increase in state equity in non-financial SOEs and their average return on equity, 1998–2018

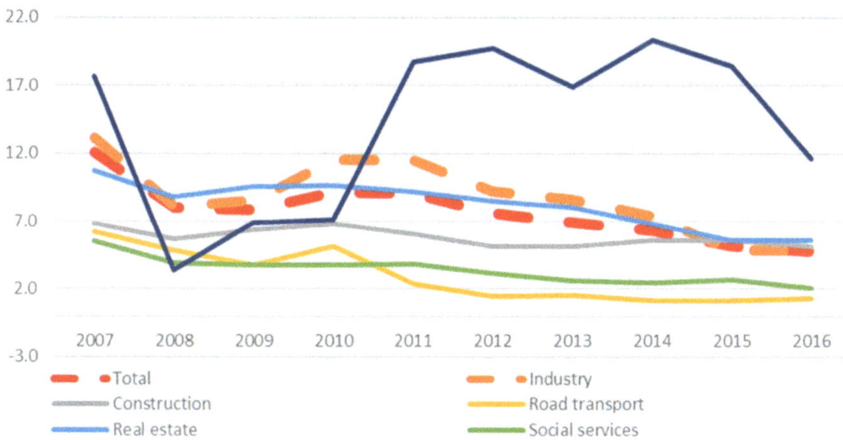

Fig. 4 Average return on equity (%) of non-financial SOEs in selected sectors, 2007–2016

5 How Was the SOE Sector Expansion Financed?

If the SOE sector expansion was not driven by national strategic priorities and financial return, and very likely not that of employment either, how could it be financed? What are the sources of funding for investment? Again, FYC data do not allow a clear and comprehensive answer, but some valuable observations can still be made, together with questions for further research.

5.1 The Institutional Framework of SOE Finance

Before addressing the question of financing, it is helpful to highlight the institutional framework of SOE financing in China because investments that generate the SOE sector expansion can be made in different ways by different entities.

In terms of funding sources, investment can be made by three kinds of entities (Fig. 5):

- *Non-SOE public entities*. These are not SOEs themselves. They are public entities that have state-owned capital to invest. They include ministry and finance departments, SASACs at central and local levels, other government ministries and departments, PSUs, and social organisations attached to government ministries and departments.
- *State capital management entities*. They are SOEs with one or more non-SOE public entities as their state shareholders, operating as the intermediate tier between the government and other SOEs. They invest with resources on their own balance sheets. These kinds of entities include parent companies of SOE groups (e.g., the 100 under State Council SASAC) as well as various kinds of state capital investment vehicles such as investment companies and funds.
- *Subsidiary SOEs*. They are either subsidiaries of SOE groups or otherwise held by state capital investment companies, state investment funds or simply other SOEs. They also invest with resources on their balance sheets, but their state shareholders are other SOEs instead of non-SOE public entities.

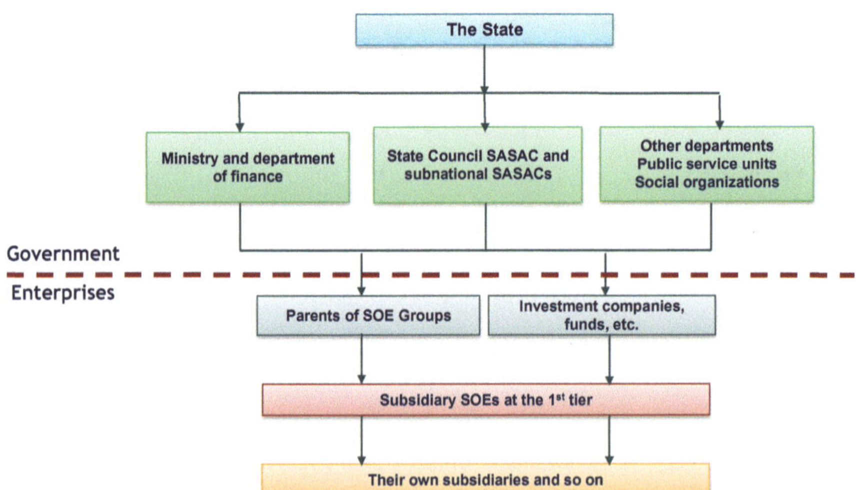

Fig. 5 Multiple-tier shareholding structure of non-financial SOEs in China. *Source* author's elaboration

Due to the large and increasing number of SOEs, almost all China's SOEs are organised in a pyramid shareholding structure, often known as "enterprise groups", in which one parent company or other kinds of state capital management entity that is 100% state-owned holds shares in its first-tier subsidiaries, which in turn do the same in the second-tier subsidiaries, and so on. The number of tiers can be as many as nine. A few years ago, around one-third of the SOE groups supervised by the State Council SASAC had five tiers.[32] As a result, most SOEs are "subsidiary SOEs" in the sense that another SOE holds them on behalf of the state.

Under such a structure, there are many different ways in which the entities can invest on behalf of the state, which are likely to be reflected in the FYC data differently. For example, they could invest to increase the assets of existing SOEs or to create new SOEs, as well as to acquire controlling or non-controlling stakes in POEs[33] or companies of other countries.

What are their possible funding sources of investment in SOEs? While the reality is complicated at a greater level of detail, it is helpful to highlight four key funding sources available to the three kinds of entities.

The first and the most conventional is, of course, the government budget. China has four budgets: The General Public Budget, the Government Funds Budget, the State Capital Management Budget (SCMB) and the Social Insurance Funds Budget. Among them, only the SCMB has an explicit line of expenditure for SOE equity capital injection. Of course, funding from other budgets can end up in SOEs as equity or debt, but there is no other explicit line of expenditure devoted to SOE equity capital injection.

However, there is a significant omission. Profit of SOEs attributable to the state owner is still off-budget except that the SCMB encompasses a small fraction of the SOE profit on its revenue side, i.e., SOE dividend submitted to the government budget. This is despite that the Chinese Budget Law requires "all government incomes" to be entered into the state budget.[34]

The second is borrowing from commercial banks, which are primarily state-controlled. Bank loans are often found accounting for two-thirds of liabilities of balance sheets of Chinese SOEs. In the pre-reform system where both SOEs and state banks had little financial independence from the state budget, the entire state

---

[32] *Premier Li Keqiang Set Timetable for Central SOEs to "Get Slimmer and Fitter"*. Retrieved from http://www.gov.cn/xinwen/2016-05/19/content_5074853.htm.

[33] A state ownership stake of 51% or higher is the usual criterion for an enterprise to be seen as state-controlled, but the NBS has a broader definition that encompasses other enterprises in which the state has control without owning an absolute majority of its shares. According to the Ministry of Finance (Ministry of Finance, 2012), in 2011, the latest year with data available, state-controlled enterprises accounted for 54% of owners' equity of all non-financial SOEs, a share that might have become higher in 2017. The current FYC statistics do not capture non-controlling minority stakes held by the state in enterprises that are not state-controlled, except that the State Capital Management Budget has covered dividend incomes from non-controlling state ownership stakes.

[34] Budget Law of the People's Republic of China <http://www.npc.gov.cn/wxzl/gongbao/2014-11/02/content_1892137.htm> , art 4.

sector was run like one company in which state banks acted as its financing department that borrowed from the household sector to finance investment and operation of SOEs. After four decades of economic reform, China has, of course, left this model far behind and become much closer to a market-oriented model in which both SOEs and state banks are financially independent, with the state acting only as a shareholder with limited liabilities. Nonetheless, to the extent that the state owner has ultimate control over both SOEs and state banks and takes final responsibilities for their financial results, it is still analytically useful to think about the state sector as one giant conglomerate with non-financial and financial SOEs as its subsidiaries.

However, the analogy must be limited. One key difference between the state sector today and that of four decades ago is that SOEs now have the autonomy to raise capital directly from the private sector without going through government budget and state banks. As such, there is a third source of funding for SOE investment, namely private sector equity capital. The stock markets, both domestic and overseas, are the primary source for SOEs to raise equity capital from the private sector directly, but there are many other ways. Private enterprises and individuals, including SOE managers and employees, can invest in SOEs without going through the stock markets. An SOE may acquire a controlling stake of a private enterprise and turns it into a state-controlled enterprise, which the FYC data should capture and treat it as an SOE. Similarly, SOEs can also borrow directly in the corporate bonds market, which provides the fourth possible funding source for their investment.

Since funds from various sources can already be mixed up before they reach an SOE to finance an investment, there is a limitation to the extent to which the various funding sources of the observed SOE sector expansion can be distinguished. In particular, there is an essential distinction between financial transactions between the state sector and the private sector and those that are essentially internal flows within the state sector. For example, one SOE could borrow from a state bank and invest in equity of its wholly owned subsidiary, which in turn uses it to finance arrears owed by other SOEs. This brings up a critical data issue, the difference between consolidated and non-consolidated balance sheets.

5.2 Are the FYC Balance Sheet Data Consolidated?

This question concerns a technical complication associated with the pyramid shareholding structure, as seen in Fig. 5. Under such a structure, aggregate data generated by summing up balance sheet data of individual SOEs contain double counting (Lardy N. R. 2019, p. 137).[35] For example, when an SOE invests 100 to acquire equity stakes in its subsidiary, which in turn spends the 100 on machinery. The 100 appears twice as assets in their balance sheets: first as a long-term investment (or another item on the assets side) in the SOE's balance sheet, second as fixed assets in its subsidiary's

[35] Lardy (n 1) 137.

balance sheet. When their balance sheets are simply added up, the state equity investment of 100 generates an increase of 200 in terms of their total equity as well as total assets. Elimination of the double counting requires a consolidated financial statement that covers all the non-financial SOEs.

Fortunately, the State Council SASAC has made a valuable effort towards this direction by reporting both "consolidated" (*he bing*) and "summed-up" (*he ji*) amounts of the value of state equity holding concerning two coverages of SOEs: those in the portfolios of SASACs, including State Council SASAC and 37 subnational SASACs, and all SOEs (presumably non-financial only) including those that are not in the portfolio of any SASAC.[36] For SOEs in the portfolio of SASACs, total assets in consolidated terms were also reported. In 2015, the latest year for which such data are available, the consolidated value of state equity holding in the 124,966 SOEs in the portfolio of SASACs was RMB27.8 trillion, while the unconsolidated or summed-up amount was RMB64.3 trillion. In other words, the difference was 1.3 times.

However, the State Council SASAC does not provide data for non-financial SOEs that are as detailed and regular as the FYC data. Can the FYC data be taken as consolidated in the same sense as defined by the State Council SASAC? The FYC itself does not provide a relevant definition. Lardy (Lardy N. R. 2019, p. 137) believes they are, but he does not elaborate on why.[37] Comparing the FYC numbers with the consolidated numbers reported by State Council SASAC shows significant discrepancies between data from the two sources, suggesting that they are not coordinated. However, the discrepancies appear to be too small to support a hypothesis that the FYC data are not consolidated.

At the national level, State Council SASAC reports 113,771 SOEs with 31 million staff and workers and RMB24.3 trillion state assets in them in 2015 in consolidated terms (State Council SASAC 2016, p. 689).[38] In comparison, the corresponding FYC numbers are all larger, by 46.8% in terms of the number of SOEs, 17.7% in terms of staff and workers, and 55.6% in terms of state assets in them. Since the number of firms and their employment should not have been affected by consolidation, the discrepancy in terms of state assets may have at least partially reflected a discrepancy of coverage between the two datasets.[39] If the discrepancy in state assets data results from the difference between consolidated and non-consolidated numbers, it should have been much larger than 55.6%.

Since the SASAC data also include consolidated numbers of total assets and state assets at the provincial level, a comparison with FYC data by province is possible. As shown in Fig. 6, which is drawn from the 2015 data of both datasets, the FYC data cover more SOEs than the SASAC data regarding most provinces. This is associated

[36] State Council SASAC (n 4) 689.

[37] Lardy (n 1) 137.

[38] State Council SASAC (n 4) 689.

[39] As mentioned above, State Council SASAC also reports the consolidated totals of SOEs that are in the portfolios of State Council SASAC and 37 SASACs at the subnational levels, which are larger than the national totals: 10% in number and 14% in terms of state assets, perhaps due to

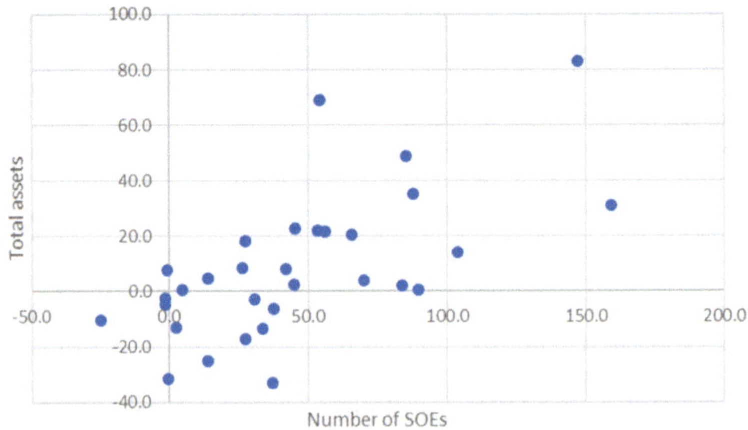

Fig. 6 Discrepancy (%) between the FYC data and SASAC data in terms of number of SOEs and total assets in them, 2015. *Note* The value of each dot is the percentage by which the FYC data value is larger than the SASAC data value concerning a province. For example, the dot at the most upper right corner means the FYC data value is 147% larger than the SASAC data value in terms of the number of SOEs and 83% larger in terms of total assets

with larger amounts of total assets in most cases, but also smaller ones in a few others. However, with three exceptions, the discrepancy in terms of total assets is within the range of 40%, which appears, again, too small to support a hypothesis that the FYC data are not consolidated. It seems, therefore, reasonable to take the FYC as consolidated in the same sense as the SASAC data until the authorities further clarify the issue. Some experts share this view. Double counting is not entirely eliminated, of course, when a consolidated financial statement is produced only for SOE enterprise groups, not for the entire SOE sector.

5.3 *Was the SOE Sector Expansion Financed by Debt or Equity?*

Bearing in mind the institutional framework and data issues described above, what can be said concerning the combination of debt and equity finance of non-financial SOEs?

Many may expect the expansion of the SOE sector to be predominantly debt-financed when China experienced credit expansion after the global financial crisis. This is true in that total liabilities have grown as aggressively as total assets in 2007–2017, by 4.9 times. However, the average debt-to-equity ratio of non-financial SOEs has managed to stay relatively stable, in the range of 1.5–2, as depicted in Fig. 7a.

double counting being cancelled off when consolidating with SOEs that are not in the portfolios of SASACs.

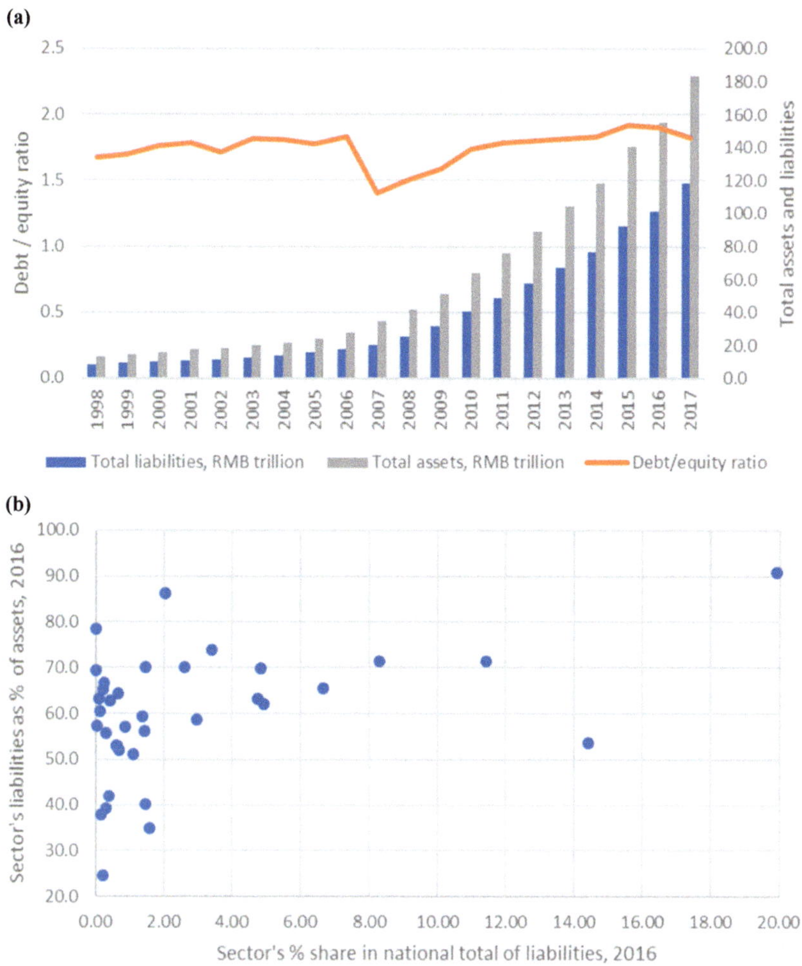

Fig. 7 Indebtedness of non-financial SOEs in China

This was due to almost equally strong growth of owners' equity, by 3.2 times in the same period. In the shareholding structure, as shown in Fig. 5, an SOE can borrow a loan to finance an equity investment in its subsidiary. As a result, at least part of the equity growth could be driven by debt growth, but no data are available to allow any further insight into this issue.

Of course, the debt-to-equity ratio is a firm-level concept by definition. National level average may mask variations among SOEs. While firm-level data are not available, sector-level data reported by FYC suggest does suggest some variation across sectors (Fig. 7b), but most sectors appear to have 50–70% of their assets in 2016 financed by debt when the national average is 65.5%. The most striking outliner is the sector of administration and organisations, with 90.8% of its assets financed by debt. Other outliners on the high end include storage (86.3%), timber processing (78.5%), metallurgy (73.9), construction and real estate (71.4% for both), as well as tobacco (24.6%), oil and petrochemical (34.9%), pharmaceutical (37.7%), and education and culture (39.3%) at the low end.

What are then the sources of funding that financed the growth of debts and equities?

In terms of debt, the FYC data do not provide further information other than that total liabilities of non-financial SOEs increased by RMB98 trillion. Suppose this is a consolidated number that has cancelled off debts owed by non-financial SOEs among each other. In that case, it should include increases in bank loans, payables to private enterprises, debts to other financial institutions and outstanding bonds, among others. However, attributing it to various sources would require better data and a separate study.

In terms of equity, owners' equity of non-financial SOEs increased by RMB50.6 trillion in 2007–2017 and state owner's equity by RMB39.4 trillion, implying that RMB11.2 trillion or 22% was from private sources. With data of listed SOEs, it should be possible to identify further the amount raised from domestic and overseas stock markets, but this will, again, take a separate investigation.

Data from FYC and other sources of the Ministry of Finance allow a bit further analysis on the sources of the RMB39.4 trillion state equity increase. First of all, explicit budget allocation does not appear to be significant. As stated earlier, China's four government budgets have only one explicit expenditure line for equity injection into SOEs, namely "paid-in capital injection" of the SCMB. In 2016–2018, for which nationwide data are available, the amount of injection was below RMB 0.1 trillion every year, too little to explain the increase of state-owned equity as reported by FYC, which amounts to RMB 3.8 trillion in 2016 and RMB 9 trillion in 2017.

The most likely funding source is SOEs' profit, which was primarily retained in the SOE sector. In 2007–2017, the total profit of non-financial SOEs amounted to RMB25.1 trillion. The government started collecting dividends from SOEs on a pilot basis in 2007–2008 with a small amount of RMB58 billion (Zhang 2009).[40] During 2012–2017,[41] the government at both central and local levels collected RMB1.1 trillion from non-financial SOEs. More than RMB23 trillion of SOE profit should be retained by SOEs and added to state equity.[42] To the extent that the FYC numbers are consolidated, it is likely that the observed increase of state-owned equity, which helped to stabilise the debt-to-equity ratio when SOEs borrowed aggressively, was predominantly funded by retained profit.

[40] C Zhang. 'Effective Discipline with Adequate Autonomy: the Direction for Further Reform of China's SOE Dividend Policy' (Zhang 2009) <http://documents.worldbank.org/curated/en/963631468011136270/Effective-discipline-with-adequate-autonomy-the-direction-for-further-reform-of-Chinas-SOE-dividend-policy> .

[41] Nationwide data are not available before 2012.

[42] See statements of the Ministry of Finance on "financial accounts of national state capital management budget", (various years) at <http://yss.mof.gov.cn/qgczjs/201807/t20180712_2959952.html> .

However, the observed expansion of equity base of non-financial SOEs could also be financed by debt, as mentioned earlier. One SOE could borrow from the financial sector and invest in its subsidiary as equity capital injection. This could happen particularly in local government financing platforms, which borrowed from banks as well as in the bond market. More data are needed to have a firm view on this possibility. In addition, appreciation of assets value through re-evaluation can also appear to be an increase of equity. However, information is too little to allow any further assessment of this possibility.

FYC does provide a breakdown of owners' equity by its four components: paid-in capital, capital reserves, surplus reserves and undistributed profit, which should have been a source of insights. However, the data are plagued with a severe problem starting in 2007: the sum of the four components falls short of the reported total by more than 20% every year. This appears to be related to the enactment of a new accounting standard in 2007, but little can be drawn from the data until the nature of the shortfall is understood.

5.4 Was the SOE Sector Expansion Central or Local?

China's fiscal system means relatively straightforward lines between coffers of the national government and every subnational one when it comes to financing SOEs. Did the observed SOE sector expansion take place mainly in central or local SOEs?

From 2008 to 2017, the total number of non-financial SOEs increased by 77,000, of which 46.8% was central, and 53.2% was local. In terms of total assets, central SOEs accounted for 38% of the total increase from 2008 to 2017, and local SOEs accounted for 62%. And local SOEs do not appear to be more dependent on debt finance: they are responsible for only 58.5% of the increase in total liabilities of all non-financial SOEs, with the rest 41.5% being accounted for by central SOEs. Figure 8 further confirms that central and local SOEs expanded roughly simultaneously, although central SOEs grew a bit faster than local ones in number.

Did the SOE sector expansion concentrate in some provinces? Table 8 presents the provincial breakdown of the data for local non-financial SOEs for 2007–2016. As shown there, the total number of local non-financial SOEs increased by 26,100 and their assets by RMB66.9 trillion in this period. All provinces saw their local SOE assets increased, but 58% of the increase took place in 10 provinces. They are Jiangsu (9.3%), Beijing (6.4%), Guangdong (6.3%), Shandong (5.7%), Shanghai (5.5%), Zhejiang (5.4%), Chongqing (5.3%), Sichuan (5.2%), Tianjin (5.0%) and Guizhou (4.1%). In terms of the number of SOEs, six provinces account for 64% of the increase: Beijing (16.6%), Zhejiang (10.9%), Guangdong (10.1%), Shandong (9.8%), Fujian (8.4%) and Jiangsu (8%).

When it comes to the share in total number and assets of all local non-financial SOEs, provinces differ. They can be put in four groups.

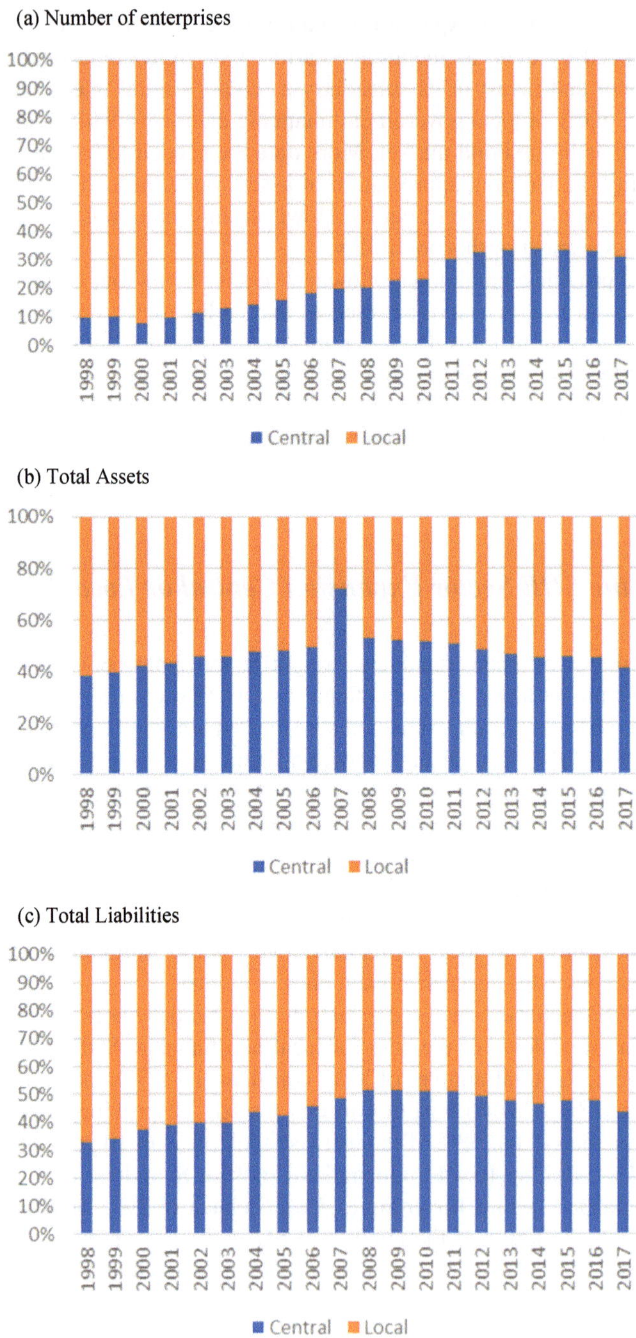

Fig. 8 SOE sector expansion broken down by central and local (% of total non-financial SOEs)

Table 8 Expansion of local non-financial SOEs in 2007–2016 by province (%)

	No. of enterprises (thousand)			Assets (RMB trillion)		
	Stock in 2007	Flow in 2007–2016		Stock in 2007	Flow in 2007–2016	
Total amounts	90.4	26.1		17.4	66.9	
Shares of provinces (%)						
Province	Share in stock	Share in flow	Difference (flow-stock, percentage point)	Share in stock	Share in flow	Difference (flow-stock, percentage point)
Group 1						
Jiangsu	3.8	8.0	4.2	6.1	9.3	3.1
Chongqing	2.3	5.8	3.5	3.4	5.3	1.9
Sichuan	3.1	7.0	3.9	3.5	5.2	1.7
Hubei	2.3	2.5	0.2	1.8	3.0	1.2
Yunnan	2.4	6.3	3.9	2.8	3.7	1.0
Inner Mongolia	1.0	1.7	0.7	1.3	2.1	0.9
Gansu	1.3	2.7	1.4	1.0	1.7	0.7
Fujian	3.9	8.4	4.5	3.0	3.5	0.5
Anhui	2.7	2.7	0.0	3.5	3.8	0.3
Hainan	0.7	0.8	0.1	0.3	0.6	0.2
Qinghai	0.5	0.6	0.1	0.5	0.7	0.2
Group 2						
Guizhou	2.6	0.1	-2.4	1.6	4.1	2.5
Guangxi	4.3	0.4	-3.8	1.8	3.2	1.4
Shaanxi	3.5	3.3	-0.1	2.3	3.7	1.3
Xinjiang	1.4	1.3	-0.2	0.6	1.3	0.7
Jiangxi	2.4	0.4	-2.0	1.5	2.0	0.5
Hunan	2.3	1.4	-0.9	1.9	2.0	0.1
Tibet	0.5	0.3	-0.2	0.2	0.2	0.0
Ningxia	0.5	0.1	-0.4	0.3	0.2	0.0
Group 3						
Shandong	4.5	9.8	5.3	6.2	5.7	−0.5
Beijing	5.0	16.6	11.6	7.1	6.4	−0.7
Zhejiang	4.7	10.9	6.1	6.1	5.4	−0.7
Guangdong	8.2	10.1	1.9	9.1	6.3	−2.8
Group 4						
Tianjin	4.1	1.7	−2.4	5.1	5.0	−0.1

(continued)

Table 8 (continued)

	No. of enterprises (thousand)			Assets (RMB trillion)		
	Stock in 2007	Flow in 2007–2016		Stock in 2007	Flow in 2007–2016	
Heilongjiang	3.4	−0.7	−4.1	1.3	1.2	−0.1
Jilin	1.7	−2.5	−4.1	1.1	0.3	−0.8
Hebei	3.4	−2.6	−6.0	2.7	1.9	−0.8
Shanxi	4.8	3.7	−1.2	3.8	2.8	−1.0
Henan	4.3	0.2	−4.1	3.4	2.1	−1.3
Liaoning	3.5	1.0	−2.5	3.4	1.9	−1.5
Shanghai	11.1	−2.1	−13.2	13.3	5.5	−7.9

- *Group 1: 11 provinces such as Jiangsu.* They increased their shares in terms of both number and assets. Six of them are located in China's western region and two in the central region.
- *Groups 2: 8 provinces such as Guizhou.* Their shares in terms of assets increased, but not in terms of number, suggesting that they added assets either to existing SOEs or to larger new ones. They include six western provinces and two central ones.
- *Group 3: 4 provinces, including Beijing, Guangdong, Zhejiang and Shandong.* Their shares decreased in terms of assets but increased, quite sharply in the case of Beijing, in terms of number, suggesting that they added smaller SOEs. Four of them all belong to the eastern region.
- *Group 4: 8 provinces such as Shanghai.* They saw their shares in terms of both assets and number declined. This is particularly dramatic in the case of Shanghai, whose shares in local non-financial SOEs declined by 13.2% points in terms of number and 7.9% points in terms of assets. Notably, all the three northeastern provinces, which have suffered from slow growth in the recent decade, are found in this group, as well as Shanxi, Hebei, Henan and Tianjin.

Except for Jiangsu and Fujian, a rough pattern appears that the regional distribution of local SOE assets in 2016 was tilted towards less developed regions than that of 2007, even though some more developed provinces such as Beijing created more SOEs in number.

6 Summary of Findings

The study of official statistics in this chapter points to an expansion of China's SOE sector after the global financial crisis in two senses: the reversal of the declining trend of the number of non-financial SOEs and the acceleration of the growth of their assets. The number of non-financial SOEs declined from 238,000 to 110,000 in 1998–2008 and has bounced back to 187,000 in 2017. Their total assets increased by 4.3 times in 2007–2017 compared with 1.6 times in 1998–2007. The growth of fixed assets and sales revenue of non-financial SOEs has been broadly in line with that of total assets. The improving trend of SOE profitability in 1998–2007 has also been reversed since 2008.

Despite the recent expansion, the share of SOEs in China's GDP has declined from 2007 to 2017, thanks to the solid growth of the private sector. SOEs account for 27.5% of China's GDP in 2017, compared with about 29.1% in 2007. This was mainly driven by greater private sector participation in the manufacturing sectors. SOE dominance in 2017 is found mainly in finance and infrastructure while manufacturing sectors as a whole is no longer an area of SOE dominance. However, there remain substantial SOE presence on average and dominance in some subsectors, and the declining trend of SOE shares in industrial assets and output has moderated in recent years and stopped in 2017. SOE expansion in 2007–2017 appears to have taken place mostly in real estate, construction and some other services sectors, including two sectors whose definitions are unclear, "social services" and "administrations, organisations and others", which appear to have been top priorities of the SOE sector expansion since 2007.

The data do not support a hypothesis that the SOE sector expansion took place to serve some national strategic priorities, nor an objective of financial return. Employment objective is unlikely to be the driving force as well. The overall allocation of state capital across economic sectors does not seem to be under the complete control of one central authority. For example, SOE share in the real estate sector rose from 15% in 2007 to 25% in 2017 despite a policy directive from the State Council to limit the involvement of large central SOEs in the sector. On the other hand, some sectors that are often seen as strategically or socially important, such as electronics, information technology, pharmaceutical, machinery and public utilities, did not stand out as priorities in the SOE sector expansion. The observed expansion is likely an outcome of uncoordinated investment actions of many state sector entities with varying motives.

Concerning the funding sources of the observed SOE sector expansion, the data analysis raised more questions than answered. In terms of the national total, the assets growth of the non-financial SOEs was accompanied by equally strong growth of debt and slightly less strong growth of equity, leaving a debt-to-equity ratio in the range of 1.5–2. Sectorial variation notwithstanding, the overall expansion of the SOE sector was not predominantly debt-financed. Retained profit of SOEs themselves appears to be the primary source of funding for the growth of equity capital base. At the same time, no data suggests any significant contribution from other parts of the government budget. However, a complete account is not possible until more data are available.

SOEs at both the central and local levels seem to have expanded at a similar pace. At the local level, larger and more developed provinces contributed more to the growth. However, this was mainly because they were significant. The regional distribution of local SOE assets in 2016 was tilted towards less developed regions compared with that of 2007.

Acknowledgements This research benefited from helpful comments and inputs from Luan Zhao, Economist of the World Bank, as well as guidance from Martin Raiser, Country Director for China, the World Bank. The author wishes to thank the Caixin Media of China for an opportunity to present findings of this chapter in a workshop it organised in Beijing on 8 November 2019, in which Zhang Guochun (Director General of Assets Management Department, Ministry of Finance), Lu Lei (Deputy Director General of the State Administration of Foreign Exchange), Xu Xianchun (Proferssor of the School of Economics and Management, Tsinghua University), Wang Xiaolu (Deputy Director General, National Economic Research Institute), Zhang Wenkui (Deputy Director General, Enterprise Research Institute of the Development Research Centre of the State Council), Zhou Fangsheng (Deputy Director General, China Enterprise Reform and Development Society) and Li Peng (Deputy Director, State Capital and Enterprise Research Centre, Deloitte) offered invaluable comments and suggestions, for which the author is grateful.

Re-imaging Development Finance: Sustainability, *Catalytic* Capital, and the Role of Sovereign Wealth Funds

Patrick J. Schena and Matthew Gouett

1 Introduction

In 2014, UNCTAD's *World Investment Report* estimated that developing countries face a $2.5 trillion annual investment gap in key sustainable development sectors.[1] World Bank Group President Jim Yong Kim noted that the billions spent annually on official development assistance would not be enough to fill this gap, requiring trillions in private investment.[2] In the intervening years, neither the gap nor the requirement for private capital has waned. Rather the need for effective partnering has become more acute and, indeed, further exacerbated by the COVID-19 crisis.

In both academic and practitioner discourse on the development finance gap, there has been a considerable focus on prospective global funding sources of sufficient scale to reduce shortfalls. In this regard, the respective roles of the multilateral development banks (MDBs), regional development banks (RDBs), development

[1] United Nations Conference on Trade and Development (UNCTAD), 'World Investment Report 2014: Investing in the SDGs: An Action Plan' (UNCTAD 2014) <https://unctad.org/en/PublicationsLibrary/wir2014_en.pdf>. accessed 29 March 2021.

[2] Jim Yong Kim, 'Billions tTo Trillions: Ideas to Actions' (Addis Ababa, 13 July 2015) <https://www.worldbank.org/en/news/speech/2015/07/13/billions-trillions-ideas-action-event>.

The original version of chapter was inadvertently published prematurely, before incorporation of the final corrections, which has now been updated. The correction to this chapter can be found at https://doi.org/10.1007/978-981-19-1368-6_31

P. J. Schena (✉)
Tufts University, Medford, USA
e-mail: Patrick.Schena@tufts.edu

M. Gouett
International Institute for Sustainable Development (IISD), Winnipeg, Canada

J. Chaisse et al. (eds.), *Regulation of State-Controlled Enterprises*, International Law and the Global South, https://doi.org/10.1007/978-981-19-1368-6_12

finance institutions (DFIs), and sovereign wealth funds[3] (SWFs) have all been evaluated. However, comparatively fewer studies focus discretely on the domestic financial capacity and institutional strength of recipient countries.[4] Traditional funding models, largely credit based, consisting of loans and guarantees, sometimes concessionary, continue to dominate. Domestically, the role of national development banks—where they exist—garner critical attention, even while governments explore complementary institutional structures—e.g. bilateral investment treaties (BIT) or international investment agreements (IIA)—to reduce market frictions to increase capital flows.

While the Global Financial Crisis (GFC) certainly exacerbated an already deteriorating funding situation, in important respects, it also served as a reckoning, turning the search for innovative solutions inward. In the intervening period, we have seen a rapid increase in the launch of special-purpose government-linked investment funds, deemed development or strategic investment funds, that are explicitly tasked with mobilising foreign capital to support domestic economic development objectives. In this chapter, we consider the funding gap through the lens of these institutions, examining their organisational structures, evaluating their governance frameworks, and identifying key features that contribute directly to their operational relevance to foreign co-investors and so to their ability to catalyse inward direct investment.

The remainder of this chapter is organised as follows. We begin with a reconsideration of the development conundrum concerning capital mobilisation and then position development finance institutions in this context. We next introduce sovereign wealth funds as one such institutional type, then discuss the evolution of SWF mandates with domestic objectives to effectively identify the key operating features of associated funds. Here we focus our analysis on uses of organisational design, governance, and capitalisation. However, our central thesis is that while these are essential to enhance institutional quality, together, they are not sufficient to mobilise foreign capital effectively. Apropos to sustainable development, we argue that they must be augmented by operational experience and expertise. In an investment context we view this as a form of alpha or the capacity of national funds, investing domestically, to drive financial and socio-economic returns to co-investors through their operational awareness, their access to resources and people, their local market expertise, and their ability to strengthen the social licence between foreign investors and domestic stakeholders to reduce market frictions.

---

[3] *See* Santiso (n 30) and more recently, Marco Kamiya, and Winston Ma, "Sovereign Investment Funds Could Be the Answer to the SDGs", World Economic Forum, December 2019, <https://www.weforum.org/agenda/2019/12/sovereign-wealth-funds-sdgs/> accessed 29 March 2021.

[4] Nancy Lee, 'More Mobilizing, Less Lending: A Pragmatic Proposal for MDBs' (Center for Global Development 2018) CGD Brief; Nancy Lee, 'Trillions for the SDGs? Time for a Rethink' (Center For Global Development, 22 January 2019) <https://www.cgdev.org/blog/trillions-sdgs-time-rethink> accessed 1 October 2020; Samantha Attridge and Lars Engen, 'Blended Finance in the Poorest Countries: The Need for a Better Approach' (Overseas Development Institute 2019) <https://www.odi.org/sites/odi.org.uk/files/resource-documents/12666.pdf>. accessed 29 March 2021.

2 Mobilising Capital for Development: Puzzles and Paradoxes

Since the publication of the 2014 UNCTAD *World Investment Report*, foreign direct investment (FDI) into developing countries has grown by 0.2% annually; conversely, inflows to developed economies have increased by 3.6% annually. This growth is in addition to total developed market FDI stocks that were already 106% higher than those in developing economies in 2014. This dichotomy is important to highlight because developing countries represented the thirty fastest-growing economies in 2019.[5] Certainly, attempts to explain "puzzles" in capital flows between developed and developing economies have burdened researchers for many years. Lucas, in his seminal article on this question,[6] argued that differences in human capital and the existence of capital market imperfections—what he referred to as political risks arising from threats of expropriation or the non-enforceability of investment or credit agreements—limit capital inflows and inhibit the equalisation of factor prices across markets.[7]

Following Lucas, multiple studies have attempted to explain his "paradox". One stream of work has focused on what we would refer to as hard barriers to FDI flows: specifically, host and home countries' tax policies and the capital controls imposed by host countries. In both cases, the literature is clear that capital controls and tax rates are negatively correlated with FDI flows from developed to developing countries.[8] Notwithstanding, recipient governments can change these policies readily through legislation. Less easily mitigated are reputational concerns among foreign investors resulting from weak institutional quality.

The second stream of work has examined the role of corruption and its impact on the quality of the domestic institutions concerning FDI flows.[9] Corruption and weak institutions lead to elevated levels of investment risk due to expropriation, legal and

---

[5] United Nations Conference on Trade and Development (UNCTAD), 'Foreign Direct Investment: Inward and Outward Flows and Stock, Annual' (UNCTAD 2020) <https://unctadstat.unctad.org/wds/TableViewer/tableView.aspx>; International Monetary Fund, 'World Economic Outlook, April 2020: The Great Lockdown' (IMF 2020) <https://www.imf.org/en/Publications/WEO/Issues/2020/04/14/weo-april-2020> accessed 1 October 2020.

[6] Robert Lucas, 'Why Doesn't Capital Flow from Rich to Poor Countries?' (1990) 80 American Economic Review 92.

[7] Patrick J Schena, 'When States Invest at Home' (2017) 52 (4) Wake Forest Law Review, 917.

[8] Victor M Gastanaga, Jeffrey B Nugent and Bistra Pashamova, 'Host Country Reforms and FDI Inflows: How Much Difference Do They Make?' (1998) 26 World Development 1299; Christian Bellak and Markus Leibrecht, 'Do Low Corporate Income Tax Rates Attract FDI? – Evidence from Central- and East European Countries' (2009) 41 Applied Economics 2691; Elizabeth Asiedu and Donald Lien, 'Capital Controls and Foreign Direct Investment' (2004) 32 World Development 479.

[9] Shang-Jin Wei, 'How Taxing Is Corruption on International Investors?' (2000) 82 The Review of Economics and Statistics 1; Peter J Montiel, 'Obstacles to Investment in Africa: Explaining the Lucas Paradox' (International Monetary Fund 2006) <https://www.imf.org/external/np/seminars/eng/2006/rppia/pdf/montie.pdf> accessed 29 March 2021; see also Christian Daude and Ernesto Stein, 'The Quality of Institutions and Foreign Direct Investment' (2007) 19 Economics & Politics 317; Laura Alfaro, Sebnem Kalemli-Ozcan and Vadym Volosovych, 'Why Doesn't Capital Flow

regulatory barriers, a physical risk to investor assets, as well as investor reputational risk. From an investor perspective, these are beyond the bounds of operational risks to projects that might be expected to arise in markets with sufficiently robust institutions. These "auxiliary" exposures can materially impact project returns by increasing costs or reducing, delaying, or even eliminating cash flows to make the investments untenable.

To mitigate risks associated with such barriers, states have innovated institutional arrangements to reduce market frictions to attract foreign capital. These include the creation of foreign direct investment promotion boards and agencies (IPAs), the establishment of special economic zones (SEZs), and the adoption of bilateral and multilateral investment treaties and international investment agreements (BITs and IIAs) all to "bond" to higher levels of institutional governance.

Concerning promotion agencies, Morisset and Andrews-Johnson find that their effectiveness is dependent on the investment environment in a country.[10] They conclude that countries with poor investment climates or low per capita income should remediate these issues before committing scarce capital investment promotion. On the relationship between IPAs and SEZs, a survey for UNCTAD's 2019 *World Investment Report* indicates that only 35% of national IPAs reported that their SEZs were sufficiently or fully utilised, and also that 22% reported that their SEZs were largely vacant. Such findings do little to resolve the Lucas paradox but rather highlight investors' sensitivity to soft barriers even in cases that offer suitable returns but potentially increase operational exposures, particularly arising from environmental or social factors.

The third type of institutional structure—bilateral investment treaties and international investment agreements—has actually been growing in adoption. While these take on various forms, they are essentially designed to protect investor rights by establishing fair treatment for cross-border investors in signatory countries. Evidence from the multitude of these agreements yields mixed results on the matter of increased FDI from developed to developing countries. Bhagwat et al. find that the impacts of BITs and IIAs are not uniform across countries; they have significant effects in countries with medium levels of political risk but not in countries with very low or high levels of political risk.[11] They argue that investors in low-risk countries do not need substitutions to protect their investor rights and that investors in high-risk countries believe BITs and IIAs to lack credibility because they can be subject to withdrawal. This corroborates Tobin and Rose-Ackerman's earlier work that BITs cannot entirely substitute for a weak investment environment and that these arrangements only have

from Rich to Poor Countries? An Empirical Investigation' (2008) 90 The Review of Economics and Statistics 347.

[10] Jacques Morisset and Kelly Andrews-Johnson, 'The Effectiveness of Promotion Agencies at Attracting Foreign Direct Investment' (World Bank 2004) FIAS Occasional Paper 16 <https://openknowledge.worldbank.org/bitstream/handle/10986/15073/271500PAPER0Ef1f0promotion0agencies.pdf?sequence=1&isAllowed=y> accessed 29 March 2021.

[11] Vineet Bhagwat, Jonathan Brogaard and Brandon Julio, 'A Bit Goes a Long Way: Bilateral Investment Treaties and Cross-Border Mergers' <http://www.ssrn.com/abstract=2872989> accessed 29 March 2021.

credibility if investors agree that host governments have the necessary institutions to execute under such agreements.[12] Another issue with BITs regards the evolution of the state's approach towards FDI and the difficulty of modifying treaties that were suitable to signal an initial reform and market access but are then insufficient to effectively protect investors' interest when facing issues with the FDI recipient country.[13]

The studies cited above highlight persistent challenges posed to host countries arising from investment risk exposures. While such institutions can help lower FDI barriers and enhance capital mobilisation, we suggest that they are not in and of themselves sufficient to drive inward capital flows at scale effectively. This may be due in part to residual institutional barriers that these institutions are not capable of bridging. However, we suggest that it is also due to the persistence of frictions in the market for development capital that arise from operational barriers across the investment process from deal sourcing and origination to implementation and monitoring.

3 DFI: Catalysing Inward Capital Flows

Development finance institutions (DFIs) are critical players in discussions of the Lucas puzzle. National (or bilateral) and multilateral DFIs are specialised development banks or subsidiaries set up to support private sector development in developing countries. Bilateral DFIs, such as the United States Development Finance Corporation (US DFC), United Kingdom's CDC Group, and Netherlands Development Finance Company (FMO), are usually majority owned by national governments and source their capital from national or international development funds or benefit from government guarantees. Multilateral DFIs are the private sector arms of international financial institutions (IFIs) that have been established by more than one country. Their shareholders are generally national governments but could also occasionally include other international or private institutions. The most prominent multilateral DFIs are the International Finance Corporation (IFC), Multilateral Investment Guarantee Agency (MIGA), European Bank for Reconstruction and Development (EBRD), and European Investment Bank (EIB).[14]

DFIs differ in their approach to development when compared to international assistance agencies. International assistance usually takes the form of grant capital

[12] Jennifer L Tobin and Susan Rose-Ackerman, 'When BITs Have Some Bite: The Political-Economic Environment for Bilateral Investment Treaties' (2010) 6 The Review of International Organizations 1.

[13] See Bryan Mercurio and Dini Sejko, Holes in the Silk: Investor Protection under China's Belt and Road Initiative, (2019) 14 5 Global Trade and Customs Journal, 251, remarking the limited protection that older Chinese BITs offer to Chinese investors, in particular SOEs and SWFs.

[14] Organisation for Economic Co-operation and Development, 'Development Finance Institutions and Private Sector Development' (2020) <https://www.oecd.org/development/development-finance-institutions-private-sector-development.htm> accessed 29 March 2021.

or loans with concessionary interest rates. While this assistance is allocated among many sectors in developing countries, it is rarely viewed as mobilising private investment. International assistance, in this regard, has a longer-term time horizon and, through a variety of interventions, works to create conditions that support economic growth and enhanced human welfare. Conversely, DFIs make investments in businesses, projects, and fund structures, by employing loans, equity, lines of credit, risk management instruments, and guarantees. While DFIs pursue the similar goal of supporting economic growth and enhancing human welfare, they pursue these goals by making investments in the private sector of developing countries, i.e. investments in which the host government is largely absent.

To maximise the impact of their investments, DFIs have the secondary goal of using the concessionary capital they have received directly from their government or through government guarantees to invest in such a way as to catalyse private sector investment. This catalytic role sometimes means that the DFI will accept disproportionate risk and/or concessionary returns relative to a conventional investment in order to generate positive impact and enable third-party investment that otherwise would not be possible.[15]

The efficacy of a DFI's catalytic role is linked to its risk appetite and specifically the instruments it uses and the position in which it invests in a project or investment's capital structure. The most common instruments employed by DFIs are loans and equity investments. DFIs have traditionally favoured loans as they tend to be less risky, simpler and allow DFIs to recycle capital.[16] Loans also allow DFIs who borrow to fund their lending to match their repayment schedules. For most DFIs, equity remains a limited share of their portfolios and, when employed, is usually channelled through fund of funds and private equity structures.[17] Because equity investments are riskier than loans, have longer payback periods, and, especially in the case of direct investing, require significant due diligence, only the largest and most experienced DFIs have significant equity exposure on their balance sheets.

The Global Future Council on Development Finance of the World Economic Forum writing in 2019[18] describes a paradigm shift in development finance from a "funding" model to a "financing" model. In this regard, it recognises as an essential function of many DFIs to provide access to capital across the development finance "stack" while also exploiting "their 'non-financial tools' to help investors overcome risks (both real and perceived) and other barriers to investment, across various stages

[15] MacArthur Foundation, 'Catalytic Capital at Work' (12 March 2019) <https://www.macfound.org/press/article/catalytic-capital-work/>. accessed 29 March 2021.

[16] Chris Humphrey and Annalisa Prizzon, 'Guarantees for Development: A Review of Multilateral Development Bank Operations' (Overseas Development Institute 2014) ODI Report <https://www.odi.org/publications/9130-guarantees-development-review-multilateral-development-bank-operations> accessed 29 March 2021.

[17] Attridge and Engen (n 4).

[18] World Economic Forum, 'From Funding to Financing: Transforming SDG Finance for Country Success' (April 2019) <http://www3.weforum.org/docs/WEF_From_Funding_to_Financing.pdf> accessed 29 March 2021.

of a project's maturity".[19] Thus, DFIs' participation in a project's financing can provide validation to co-investors, particularly concerning the level and quality of due diligence and screening protocols related to environmental, social, and governance (ESG) standards. For example, the IFC's Performance Standards on Environmental and Social Sustainability are the leading set of standards followed by most DFIs and are among the most rigorous among all investors. Moreover, because the reputational risk of not meeting such standards is arguably higher for DFIs than for private investors, DFIs extend conventional risk sharing to those related environmental, social, and governance exposures, including their operational dimensions.[20] These higher standards extend to performance disclosures as DFIs report impacts beyond standard economic metrics, such as jobs created, to environmental and social metrics, such as greenhouse gas emissions avoided, and finally to more bespoke metrics tied directly to performance against specific UN Sustainable Development Goals (SDG).

As catalytic investors, DFIs can help bridge institutional shortfalls and extend the benefits of risk sharing to include those central to advancing sustainability objectives. They can offer counterparties access to expertise and global experience in deal sourcing, due diligence, financial structuring, and asset management. In that capacity, they can provide a market "bridge" for other institutional investors, including sovereign wealth funds, *when investing internationally.*

4 Sovereign Wealth Funds and Their Mandates

Since Andrew Rozanov coined the term "sovereign wealth fund" in 2005, SWFs have attracted considerable analytic scrutiny from a wide variety of investigators, from academic researchers to policy analysts and journalists.[21] Frequently, commentary focuses on SWFs' behaviour, motives, and investment activities and somewhat less frequently on their policy roles. It is crucial to establish that SWFs are fiscal policy institutions with domestic-facing objectives that inform their outward-facing policies and actions, particularly concerning investment.

In their most basic form, SWFs are institutionalised pools of government savings. Rozanov noted that these pools might be created to help monetary authorities sterilise unwanted liquidity, to build up savings for future generations, or to mobilise capital for economic and social development. Given such objectives, an SWF can have profound effects on many dimensions of domestic economic performance, including aggregate demand, monetary and exchange rate stability, fiscal strength, and sector growth and development. In the particular case of resource economies, SWF design has been informed by discrete macroeconomic effects that foster real exchange rate

---

[19] ibid.

[20] For a detailed analysis of the role of DFI in mitigating social risks in institutional infrastructure projects, *see* the broader study on this topic by Patrick J Schena and Eliot Kalter, 'Social Risks and the Practice of Direct Infrastructure Investment' (2020) <https://sites.tufts.edu/sovereignet/new-research-social-impacts-and-the-practice-of-direct-infrastructure-investment/> accessed 29 March 2021.

[21] Andrew Rozanov, 'Who Holds the Wealth of Nations?' (2005) 15 Central Banking 52.

volatility in order to counter Dutch Disease[22] and so to avoid the sectoral displacement of workers.[23]

In fact, the mandates of SWFs span several key policy objectives, including stabilisation, reserve management, long-term pension reserve accumulation, intergenerational savings, *and development*.[24] Importantly, as we show below, mandates are not static but evolve based on both local fiscal requirements and constraints, as well as the scale of an asset—i.e. *wealth*—accumulation. Moreover, although much commentary on SWFs elicits visions of massive asset pools (e.g. Abu Dhabi Investment Authority, China Investment Corporation, and Norway's Government Pension Fund-Global), the vast majority of SWFs hold less than $50 billion in assets under management.[25]

Acknowledged in the IMF's definition of a sovereign fund are so-called development mandates. However, these are frequently overlooked when considering the investment activities of sovereign funds. In 2008, Santiso[26] described the development role of SWF in two dimensions. The first of these, and more immediately the focus of his paper, suggests that SWFs could serve a development finance role by investing in emerging markets that potentially offered solid returns. The second of these referenced a domestic role for SWFs investing in economic transformation *in their own economies*. The latter point was not lost on capital-constrained emerging market countries that struggled to justify investing large volumes of reserve capital in foreign markets. At the same time, both physical and commercial infrastructure gaps impeded their domestic economic development. They were, in fact, contributing to the very circumstances that gave rise to Lucas' paradox!

[22] Dutch Disease, as defined by Corden and Neary, "is the phenomenon whereby a boom in one traded goods sector squeezes profitability in other traded goods sectors, both by directly bidding resources away from the and by placing upward pressure on the exchange rate."

[23] W Max Corden and J Peter Neary, 'Booming Sector and De-Industrialisation in a Small Open Economy' (1982) 92 The Economic Journal 825; Ashby Monk, 'Avoiding the Resource Curse' (*Oxford SWF Project*, 23 March 2010) <http://oxfordswfproject.com/2010/03/23/avoiding-the-resource-curse/> accessed 29 March 2021; Dramane Coulibaly, Luc Desire Omgba and Helene Raymond, 'Exchange Rate Misalignments in Energy-Exporting Countries: Do Sovereign Wealth Funds Matter?', *32èmes Journées Internationales Monnaie Banque Finance* (2015) <http://gdrenice2015.sciencesconf.org/56579/document> accessed 29 March 2021.

[24] For further details, *see* the IMF's original definition at <https://www.imf.org/external/np/pp/eng/2008/022908.pdf> accessed 29 March 2021.

[25] Global SWF, 'Top 100' (October 2020) <https://globalswf.com/top-100> accessed 29 March 2021.

[26] Javier Santiso, 'Sovereign Development Funds: Key Financial Actord in the Shifting Wealth of Nations' (OECD, October 2008) <https://www.oecd.org/dev/41944381.pdf> accessed 29 March 2021. Santiso's case is that sovereign wealth funds can be important complements to financing development in emerging economies, both in their own countries and as investors in other emerging market countries.

5 Sovereign Funds and Domestic Investment

When initially introduced by Rozanov, the idea of the "sovereign wealth fund" emerged from the realm of the "official institution". In a financial or monetary context, these include central banks and finance ministries, as well as state funds of various types, such as natural resource-based sovereign wealth funds. The latter began to take on more prominence in the 1980s and 1990s[27] as governments sought to effectively manage revenue volatility emanating from swings in commodity prices, particularly oil. As fiscal and foreign reserve balances increased during high commodity prices, the management challenge shifted to balancing near-term expenditures with long-term savings to promote sustainable economic development while maintaining fiscal integrity.[28]

Integral to the design of most resource funds is the "permanent income hypothesis", which implies linking constant government consumption of commodity resources to income streams from the accumulation of resource wealth.[29] Fundamental to their operational design, most funds have maintained an exclusively international mandate to stabilise domestic economies with constrained absorptive capacity from any ill effects of proportionately large-scale capital inflows. As noted above, these include specifically those posed by Dutch Disease. With time, countries with well-integrated fiscal institutions, such as Norway, grew fund assets under management dramatically to eventually outstrip the capital required for stabilisation. As a result, investment strategies of many resource-based funds evolved to support long-term savings objectives while still mainly investing in a globally diversified portfolio.

Notwithstanding, the prescriptive advice of multilateral institutions against domestic investment persisted. In addition to traditional—and very legitimate—concerns of macroeconomic disruption, arguments centred on the risks posed by divergence from overall fiscal policy considerations, opportunities for rent seeking and other forms of corruption or abuse, and challenges in assessing the impact

[27] For a partial list of resource funds that includes their origination dates, see Natural Resource Funds <https://resourcegovernance.org/resource-governance-index/report/natural-resource-funds> accessed 29 March 2021.

[28] ibid.

[29] *See* Alonso Segura, 'Management of Oil Wealth Under the Permanent Income Hypothesis: The Case of Sao Tome and Prencipe' IMF (July 2006) WP/06/183, p 8, <https://www.imf.org/external/pubs/ft/wp/2006/wp06183.pdf> accessed 29 March 2021.

of domestically deployed capital on aggregate demand and competitiveness if off-budget.[30] These concerns were amplified by the extra-budgetary nature of fund investments and resulting opacity, which undermine budgetary control and lead to unequal treatment of different types of spending.[31]

Andrew Bauer's argument serves to summarise this thesis. Bauer defines an SWF as an extra-budgetary fund, i.e. operating outside of a government's budget process. This characterisation is essential to underline his core critique: investments by the fund can undermine public financial management, leading to sub-optimal investment decisions and facilitating corruption.[32] Fundamentally, Bauer argues against creating "parallel budgets" with distinct appraisal, procurement, and monitoring systems. His guidance is to implement discreet fiscal rules to determine the amount of resource revenue to be saved or spent, advising that all spending be channelled through national or subnational budget processes or state-owned entities, such as development banks, operating at arm's length from the government. Notably, he reiterates that all savings be invested through an SWF *in offshore markets* with the goal of generating financial returns.[33]

Notwithstanding the persistence of similar arguments against SWF domestic investment, sovereign funds with strategic development objectives have emerged. Their pace of expansion has accelerated sometimes in direct response to the economic or financial crisis (e.g. the Ireland Strategic Investment Fund) or gaps in capital availability to build out critical local infrastructure (e.g. the Nigeria Sovereign Investment Authority). These are not novel; funds with domestic holdings had actually existed for many years. Among the most noted is Temasek, which was established in 1974. The earliest of these were capitalised by the intergovernmental transfer of shares of state-owned enterprises and tasked with the efficient management of these operating companies. However, in the wake of the 2008–09 financial crisis, these institutions' scale and scope increased progressively. Notably, this occurred in parallel with a reconsideration of the traditional risks—and arguments—against domestic investment.

In 2016, the World Bank undertook a detailed evaluation of these trends in sovereign capital deployment and acknowledged in many such mandates a scope of engagement that went beyond capital allocation to include attracting private capital, deepening domestic capital markets, and building out the capacity of governments to

---

[30] Rolando Ossowski, Steven Barnett, James Daniel, and Jeffrey Davis, "Stabilization and Savings Funds for Nonrenewable Resources, International Monetary Fund", April 2001, https://www.elibrary.imf.org/view/IMF084/06475-9781589060197/06475-9781589060197/ch04.xml?redirect=true accessed 29 March 2021.

[31] Udaibir Das, et al., 'Setting up a Sovereign Wealth Fund: Some Policy and Operational Considerations' IMF (August 2009) WP/09/179 <https://www.imf.org/external/pubs/ft/wp/2009/wp09179.pdf> accessed 29 March 2021.

[32] Andrew Bauer, 'Why Sovereign Wealth Funds Should Not Invest at Home' IMF (IMF *Public Financial Management Blog*, 9 April 2015) <https://blog-pfm.imf.org/pfmblog/2015/04/why-sovereign-wealth-funds-should-not-invest-at-home-.html> accessed 29 March 2021.

[33] ibid.

serve as effective long-term professional investors.[34] From this analysis, the World Bank defined a new type of sovereign fund, referred to as a strategic investment fund or SIF, that exhibited six discrete characteristics. These included sponsorships and, at least, partial capitalisation by a single government, several governments, or multilateral or regional financial institutions. Strategic investment funds were to have mandates that included a "double bottom line" seeking both financial and economic returns. Consistent with this mandate, SIFs were to crowd in actively, catalysing private capital at either the fund or the project level. The foundation of a SIF's capital commitment was to be long term, primarily through equity. Perhaps most importantly, according to the World Bank's definition, a SIF would serve as a professional co-investor with foreign and private domestic counterparties on behalf of its sponsors.[35]

While not all development and strategic funds necessarily share a SIF's double bottom line purpose, as a cohort, they remain similar in the directionality of capital deployment and the importance of professional capacity to the effective execution of their mandates. Over the past ten years, the rate of introduction of development and strategic funds has increased further. The World Bank reports 18 such funds having been established since 2010.[36] At least thirteen of these since 2013 have become new members of the International Forum of Sovereign Wealth Funds (IFSWF), such that by 2019 over 40% of the IFSWF members had domestic mandates.[37] A sampling includes the Nigerian Sovereign Investment Authority, FONSIS, which is the sovereign fund of Senegal, the National Development Fund of Iran, the Russia Direct Investment Fund, the Ireland Strategic Investment Fund, the Turkey Wealth Fund, the National Infrastructure Investment Fund of India, and the Sovereign Fund of Egypt. These joined several other funds investing domestically and established earlier: Temasek, Khazanah, the sovereign fund of Malaysia, Mubadala, which is one of the sovereign funds of the United Arab Emirates, the Palestine Investment Fund, and others in Vietnam, Bahrain, Angola, and Kazakhstan.

Extensive empirical analysis on the introduction of strategic development and investment funds is lacking. However, based on our critical review, we suggest that explanations for the progressive introduction of such funds might reasonably be attributable to four factors. First among these is undoubtedly the persistence of market and institutional gaps that have stifled the flow of inward investment. Second, and we believe consistent with the first, is a material reduction in investment in emerging markets in the wake of the GFC and its later extension to the

[34] Havard Halland, Michel Noel, Silvana Tordo, and Jacob J. Kloper-Owens, 'Strategic Investment Funds: Opportunities and Chellenges' World Bank Group (October 2016) WPS7851, <http://documents1.worldbank.org/curated/en/235311475681523659/pdf/WPS7851.pdf> accessed 29 March 2021.

[35] ibid.

[36] *See* Shanthi Divakaran, 'Strategic Investment Funds,' (IFSWF Annual Meeting, Juneau Alaska, September 11, 2019) unpublished, (in copy with the authors).

[37] ibid.

Eurozone.[38] The third is the availability of resources for enhanced training and skills development from the World Bank and others to strengthen the capacity of governments and ministries to design and manage developed-oriented funds. Lastly, we also believe pertinent is an argument proposed initially by Jeffrey Chwieroth regarding SWF creation generally: when countries create funds to manage policy uncertainty related to discrete economic conditions, other countries with similar challenges—in this instance, economic development—follow the lead of peers to create like institutions.[39] Thus, we argue that *group emulation* has also contributed to the expansion of development and strategic funds in the wake of the GFC.

6 Strategic Development Mandates and Institutional Governance

Though sovereign development and strategic investment funds share the pursuit of domestic mandates, diversity detracts from this characteristic serving as the common denominator of a distinct investor class. Operating objectives differ widely, from promoting direct foreign investment as a stable, long-term source of capital to facilitating strategic restructuring in the buildout for national competitiveness; gapping infrastructure capital investment requirements; funding strategic economic development projects; and financing small and medium-size enterprise growth.[40] In addition, some funds also include in their objectives developing and extending local capital markets, particularly private markets for equity capital.

When surveying the development and strategic fund landscape, we identify at least six operating models that characterise development and strategic funds. These include (1) the domestic holding company model, under which a fund is responsible for managing a government's holdings in the state-owned enterprises and other state operating assets, (2) the internationally diversified holding company model—e.g. Temasek—combines SOE holdings with an internationally diversified portfolio of strategic investments, (3) the multi-fund model that includes at least one development mandate under a hybrid fund structure, (4) a single-sector model that mobilises capital to gap a strategic need, such as infrastructure, (5) a strategic investment fund model that invests nearly exclusively in the domestic economy consistent with a national

[38] According to World Bank economists, investment growth and emerging market economies slowed significantly from 10% per year in 2010 to less than 3.5% in 2016. They find that this investment slowdown is broad based and accentuated by both financial market end policy uncertainty. *See* M Ayan Kose, Franziska Ohnsorge, and Lei Sandy Ye, 'Capital Slowdown' (June 2017) 54(2) Finance and Development <https://www.imf.org/external/pubs/ft/fandd/2017/06/kose.htm> accessed 29 March 2021.

[39] Jeffrey W. Chwieroth, 'Fashions and Fads in Finance: The Political Foundations of Sovereign Wealth Fund Creation' (December 2014) 58(4) International Studies Quarterly.

[40] With respect to "financialisation", *see* Peter B Clarke and Ashby HB Monk, 'Sovereign Development Funds: Designing High Performance, Strategic Investment Institutions' (September 2015) <https://papers.ssrn.com/sol3/papers.cfm?abstract_id=2667974> accessed 29 March 2021.

economic plan or agenda (e.g. Ireland Strategic Investment Fund),[41] and (6) strategic investment funds that invest in whole or in part *internationally* to help diversify and transform the domestic economic base.

The sovereign wealth fund of Egypt, for example, was established in 2018 to attract private investments to Egypt to promote co-investment in state-owned assets to maximise their value and efficiency in the Egyptian economy.[42] The Palestine Investment Fund describes itself as a *sovereign development fund*, but with a double bottom line objective to invest for *impac*t in key sectors of the local economy, targeting sustainable returns.[43] The Ghana Infrastructure Investment Fund's mandate is "to mobilise, manage, coordinate and provide financial resources for investment in a diversified portfolio of infrastructure projects in Ghana for national development".[44] Finally and perhaps most discretely articulated, the mission of FONSIS, Senegal's sovereign fund for strategic investment, is to promote the role of the Senegalese state "as an investor, partner and complement of the private sector, with the aim of supporting direct investments in order to accelerate the economic and social development of the country".[45]

In addition to mandate, development and strategic funds can also differ widely based on the integrated configuration of their organisational design, the scope and structure of their governance, and their capitalisation. Concerning organisational design, two forms dominate. These are the holding company model, often organised under local corporate or company law, and the fund model usually organised under a securities law regime. Funds organised as corporations can hold state-owned operating assets of the government, usually in the form of state-owned enterprises. Examples of these types of entities include Temasek, Khazanah, Mumtalakat of Bahrain, and Samruk Kazyna of Kazakhstan. Notably, many such funds have access to international capital markets and are capable of raising (or guaranteeing issuances of) external capital for liquidity, investment, or providing financing to subsidiary holdings through a form of an internal capital market.[46] Often overlooked, this sovereign credit channel can be a key source of capital for funds that benefit from embedded

[41] The ISIF emerged from Ireland's Pension Reserve Fund which was used to recapitalise the country's two largest banks. The remainder of a 23 billion euro fund, approximately 8 billion euro, took on a mandate to invest domestically to strengthen the foundations of Ireland's economy.

[42] *See* The Sovereign Fund of Egypt, <https://tsfe.com> accessed 29 March 2021.

[43] *See* Palestine Investment Fund, <http://www.pif.ps/home/> accessed 29 March 2021.

[44] *See* Ghana Infrastructure Investment Fund <https://siga.gov.gh/sector/ghana-infrastructure-investment-fund/ accessed 29 March 2021.

[45] *See* Fonds Souverain d'Investissements Stratégiques <https://www.fonsis.org/en/who-we-are/mission> accessed 29 March 2021.

[46] *See*, for example, recent filings by Temasek (Singapore) <https://www.temasek.com.sg/content/dam/temasek-corporate/our-financials/temasek-bonds/MTN/2019-oc/Temasek_Financial_(I)_Limited_US$20billion_GMTN_Programme_OC_dated_15July2019.pdf> accessed 29 March 2021; Khazanah (Malaysia) <https://links.sgx.com/FileOpen/Offering%20Circular%20(Final).ashx?App=Prospectus&FileID=39492> accessed 29 March 2021; and Mumtalakat (Bahrain) <https://www.ise.ie/debt_documents/Base%20Prospectus_7deba74c-11a6-4cbc-950a-ed12c5778785.PDF> accessed 29 March 2021.

governance structures under the bond indentures that promote transparency and managerial discipline.[47]

Funds organised under securities law are structured more along the lines of a mutual fund or limited partnership. An example of such a structure is the National Infrastructure Fund of India. The NIIF is set up as a fund of funds registered with the Securities in Exchange Board of India (SEBI) as in Alternative Investment Fund (AIF). Under this structure, the Government of India's total commitment to the Fund cannot exceed 49%. Thus, while the National Infrastructure and Investment Fund Trustee is a government-linked company, the fund itself will have 51% private shareholding.[48] The strategic objective of the NIIF is to aggregate commitments from SWFs, other long-term foreign investors, and government-linked institutions both within and outside of India as permitted under the AIF's regulations. The fund's goal is to make direct investments into the infrastructure sector in India by being catalytic in crowding in international capital.[49]

Organisational design and capitalisation are inextricably linked to investment efficiency and governance. Strong governance is essential to building institutional quality and overcoming the genuine challenges to the objective evaluation of domestic projects posed by parochial political interests. First, basic governing principles should clearly establish the independence of the fund's decision-making in the context of a well-articulated investment objective, investment strategy, and operating model. These should include defining the specific role and responsibilities of the fund's government sponsor or "owner", as well as those of designated managers. Next, the objectives of the fund concerning risk and return should be clearly stated. For example, will the fund seek competitive financial returns? Will it pursue a "double bottom line" strategy that also targets measurable development impacts? Also, the operating boundaries of the fund should be established vis-à-vis other government fiscal and economic institutions.[50] For example, will projects with concessionary return structures be referred to the central budget for consideration?

The case of the Ireland Strategic Fund serves to illustrate. The ISIF was established in 2014 in the wake of the Irish banking crisis. The fund's owner is the Minister for Finance of the Republic of Ireland. Management responsibility is designated to the National Treasury Management Agency. The fund's mandate is clearly defined as holding and investing state assets on a commercial basis to support economic

---

[47] Note here the counter argument exemplified by 1MDB.

[48] Nishith Desai Associates, 'NIIF – India's Mega Find Initiaitve toward Infrastructure Development' (5 February 2016) <http://www.nishithdesai.com/information/navigation/navigation2/deal-corner/deal-corners/article/niif-indias-mega-fund-initiative-toward-infrastructure-development.html> accessed 29 March 2021.

[49] ibid. *See* also 'The NIIF Wants to Be Investor' Gateway to India' (*Infrastructure Investor*, 7 June 2019) <https://www.infrastructureinvestor.com/gateway-to-india/> accessed 29 March 2021.

[50] Establishing boundaries for the execution of a fund's strategy provides clarity related to the operational role of the fund as a local financial institution. For a critical view of the potential challenges posed by any measure of operational ambiguity, see "NIIF and Infrastructure Finance – What is the Additionality", <https://gulzar05.blogspot.com/2019/12/niif-and-infrastructure-finance-what-is.html> accessed 29 March 2021.

activity and employment in the country. Its investment performance is measured on both investment returns and economic impact, with an investment performance goal to exceed the average cost of general government debt in any year. Essential to the ISIF's operating model is its definition of economic impact, defined by three discrete criteria: additionality, displacement, and deadweight. Together these serve as a governance framework to ensure that fund investments contribute materially to Ireland's economic growth while not marginalising private sector investment. The fund refers to additionality as the additional economic benefits to gross value added and gross domestic product, which will arise from the target investment beyond those that would have otherwise occurred. Displacement refers to cases where the additionally created growth by investment is offset by a reduction in benefits elsewhere in the local economy. Finally, deadweight occurs when benefits arising from a project would have otherwise been achieved even in the absence of the investment.[51]

As highlighted in several of the examples above, a critical function of many development and strategic funds is to *crowd in* direct investment, i.e. to co-invest with both public and private investors to fund local projects. Partnering contributes to the capacity development of the local fund by permitting management and staff to both access and leverage external expertise, including that related to deal structuring and pricing. A structural feature of fund governance is sometimes operationalised by limiting the extent to which the local fund can hold a majority position in invested companies or projects (note our earlier reference to the NIIF). This is achieved by constraining fund ownership in any specific investment to minority interest to ensure a voice for external investors in price determination, as well as deal-level monitoring and governance.[52] In this way, a domestic-oriented fund can multiply the impact of its own capital while at the same time leveraging the governance and investment monitoring expertise of outside investors. The ISIF generally holds minority equity stakes. It describes its investment strategy as long term to be a source of patient capital, investing on equal terms with private investors to "generate a multiplier effect" while balancing its compliance with European Union rules against providing unfair financial support to private sector enterprises.[53]

Returning lastly to capitalisation, we observe that development and strategic funds generally tend to operate on a more limited capital footing when compared to sovereign wealth funds.[54] In fact, whereas the legacy of sovereign wealth funds derives from large holdings of fiscal and foreign exchange reserves and the goal to

[51] A very useful primary source of data on the operating and governance structures of development and strategic funds can be found in the self-assessments of funds who are members of the IFSWF, <https://www.ifswf.org/assessments> accessed 29 March 2021. The ISIF's 2019 self-assessment was accessed at https://www.ifswf.org/assessment/ireland-strategic-investment-fund.

[52] See for example the Russia Direct Investment Fund's investment limitations which cannot exceed 50% of the share capital of an investment <https://rdif.ru/Eng_Investment/> accessed 29 March 2021: and also CDP-Equity's (Italy) operating model <https://en.cdpequity.it/what-we-do/investment-criteria.kl> accessed 29 March 2021.

[53] ISIF Self-assessment (n 51).

[54] *See* Patrick J Schena, Juergen Braunstein, and Asim Ali, "The Case for Economic Development Through Sovereign Investment: A Paradox of Scarcity", (2018) 9(3) Global Policy 365.

manage wealth, development and strategic funds seek to *create wealth* when they "multiply" their capital by catalysing investment.[55] Sources of capitalisation have included budgetary transfers, allocations from reserve assets, and/or the transfer of equity interests in operating assets, as noted in the case of Temasek. Innovation in this regard involves monetising *illiquid assets* via the securitisation of future flows. Future flow securitisations, particularly in developing economies, have existed for many years. They permit the monetisation of assets, such as receivables from the licensing and sale of commodities, remittances, airline tickets, and even tax revenues.[56,57] Finally, strategic funds can be capitalised through offerings of shareholding or partnership interests. Such structures include joint venture and co-investment platforms with embedded governance features to reduce foreign investors' risks further. The Russia Direct Investment Fund, for example, has mobilised approximately $40B through a series of co-investment funds with a variety of sovereign and other institutional investors.[58] Conversely, the NIIF functions as an investor-owned manager and solicits equity participation from both domestic and foreign strategic institutional anchor investors through three fund structures: a master fund, a fund of funds, and a strategic investments fund. As noted earlier, the government of India's participation in this platform cannot exceed 49%.[59]

Thus, as we have attempted to illustrate, a comprehensive strategic investment programme that exhibits strong governance and professionalism, independent management, effective monitoring and audit, and operational transparency can reduce market frictions that inhibit FDI and mobilise foreign capital for inward investment.[60] But are these features sufficient? We now turn to this question in the context of sovereign investment in sustainable development.

---

[55] Clarke and Monk (n 40).

[56] Suhas Ketkar and Dilip Ratha, 'Future Flow Securitiation for Development Finance' in Innovative Financing for Development (The World Bank, 2009), 26.

[57] Ghana, the world's seventh-largest producer of gold at over 142 metric tons, has announced plans to securitise gold royalities. Ghana intends to sell equity interests in a government-owned gold royalty company to finance new mining projects. The structure—Agyapa Mineral Royalty Limited–mobilises capital through the monetisation of future revenue streams once the mine begins production. Agyapa's majority shareholder is Ghana's Minerals Income Investment Fund, established in 2018 to manage the equity interests of the country's in mining companies. *See* Agyapa Royalties, <https://www.mofep.gov.gh/sites/default/files/news/Agyapa_Info_Graphs_v2.pdf> accessed 29 March 2021. For a more critically analytic assessment, *see* 'Risk and Reward in Ghana's Agyapa Gold Royalties Deal: Eight Points for Consideration' National Resource Governance Institute (1 October 2020), <https://resourcegovernance.org/blog/risk-reward-ghana-agyapa-gold-royalties-deal> accessed 29 March 2021. For more details on the MIIF, see Minerals Income Investment Fund Act, 2018 (ACT 978), <https://www.bcp.gov.gh/acc/registry/docs/MINERALS%20INCOME%20INVESTMENT%20FUND%20ACT,%202018%20(ACT%20978).pdf> accessed 29 March 2021.

[58] *See* RDIF Partnerships, <https://rdif.ru/Eng_Partnership/> accessed 29 March 2021.

[59] 'Guidance Note on National Infrastructure Banks and Similar Financing Facilities' (*Global Infrastructure Hub*, June 2019 <https://cdn.gihub.org/umbraco/media/2621/gih-national_infrastructure_banks_-full_report-web.pdf> accessed 29 March 2021.

[60] Halland et al. (n 34).

7 Leveraging Strategic Funds for Sustainable Development

As suggested originally by Santiso (2008) and echoed today, much of the global narrative related to sovereign wealth funds and sustainable development centres on them as sources of development capital. The World Economic Forum analysis cited above frames a path for development finance "from funding to financing"[61] and portrays sovereign wealth funds as one of several international public sources of funding for the SDGs that include DFIs and bilateral donors.[62] In making its case, the WEF emphasises the importance of *investible governance* at the country level, i.e. the capacity of policy-makers to attract both international and domestic capital by building investor confidence, including undertaking non-investment activities that improve governance, such as building strong legal and regulatory structures that promote private finance.[63]

The WEF study did not identify—but neither did it preclude—sovereign wealth funds as endowed with this institution-building mandate. Certainly, others have made similar arguments concerning the role of SWFs serving as professional co-investors on behalf of their governments.[64] Our thesis is somewhat more concrete: while institutional features, such as organisational design and capitalisation, can promote governance and so enhance the professional legitimacy of a sovereign fund as a credible domestic partner, we argue that these are not sufficient in themselves to mobilise capital flows. Integral to our argument is that the operational capacity and professionalism of the institution—elements of *alpha*—are essential to effective execution.[65]

The NIIF, for example, sees as its most important role to be catalytic in crowding in international capital. The fund has an extensive professional staff with deep experience in local markets, headed by Sujoy Bose, who joined the NIIF in 2016 after having spent 25 years at the International Finance Corporation, including as Global

---

61 'From Funding to Financing' (n 18). *See* also, Seedwell Hove, 'Sovereign Wealth Funds and Infrastructure Development in Africa' (2016) Proceedings of the Economics and Finance Conferences, International Institute of Social and Economic Sciences, <https://ideas.repec.org/p/sek/iefpro/4206708.html> accessed 29 March 2021, and finally, *see* Kamiya and Ma (n 3).

62 In practical terms, the vast majority of sovereign wealth funds do not actively undertake direct investments in international markets. Moreover, developed markets continue to attract the majority of direct equity investments by sovereign wealth funds. This includes most specifically the USA. *See* selected editions of the Sovereign Wealth Lab at IE University Annual Report on Sovereign Wealth Funds, <https://sites.tufts.edu/sovereignet/tag/ie-sovereign-wealth-labs/> accessed 29 March 2021.

63 'From Funding to Financing' (n 18).

64 By way of example, for a well-research article on SWFs and the financing of the UN Sustainable Development Goals in Africa, *see* Julia Chen, 'Financing the Sustainable Development Goals: The Role of African Sovereign Wealth Funds' (July 2019) 51(4) International Law and Politics <https://nyujilp.org/wp-content/uploads/2019/09/NYI405.pdf> accessed 29 March 2021.

65 In an investment context, alpha refers to sources of excess return. Clarke and Monk (n 40), refer to "structural alpha", as a source of superior performance of sovereign funds, attributable in part to local market knowledge and internal control over the investment process. We use the term here to highlight key operational features of SWFs that we argue are necessary to drive both financial and socio-economic returns to stakeholders.

Co-head and Director for Infrastructure and Natural Resources. The NIIF's strategy is to create investment partnerships that link assets with expertise through effective governance and long-term capital commitments. In this respect, the fund deliberately seeks out investors who can take long-term exposures. It serves as an effective counterparty with unique professional investment capacity in the market for Indian infrastructure.[66]

The Ghana Infrastructure Investment Fund professes a similar commitment. The GIIF has project funding experience in the domestic market, as well as a strong operational presence, which it views as a competitive benefit to international partners when structuring financing and building out projects. Its role as a credible local co-investor intends to ensure foreign capital that a state investment partner is taking the same commercial risks and sharing similar financial and operational commitments.[67] This role as a catalytic "bridge" investor might be illustrated by the case of Terminal 3 of the Kotoka International Airport (KIA), for which GIIF's financing enabled the DFI tranche, which included the African Development Bank and the Development Bank of Southern Africa.[68]

Concerning sustainability, the GIIF introduced the Social and Environmental Management System (SEMS) to proactively identify and assess social and environmental risks before funding decisions and monitor social and environmental performance post-investment. From an operational perspective, these risk assessment procedures are integrated into the GIIF's due diligence and investment risk management frameworks, under which the fund screens for excluded activities, as well as social and environmental risks.[69]

Also in West Africa, FONSIS, the sovereign fund of Senegal, functions as an investment holding company, i.e. as a private equity investor, on behalf of the government. It invests primarily, though not exclusively, on commercial terms and maintains a hurdle rate of about 12%. Its objective is to deliver value in both financial and as social and economic terms. In 2016, Amadou Hott, then CEO of the fund, commented to the World Bank that the only way to achieve the sustainable development goals is to use more public capital strategically for unlocking private investment, particularly in infrastructure.[70] The fund sees this as a key investment objective. It has functioned as the government's lead investor in sustainable projects, such as a solar energy power plant, for which its role was to structure financial terms, finalise

---

[66] Infrastructure Investor (n 49).

[67] Solomon Asamoah, CEO, Ghana Infrastructure Investment Fund (GIIF): Interview, Oxford Business Group, <https://oxfordbusinessgroup.com/interview/financing-solutions-solomon-asamoah-ceo-ghana-infrastructure-investment-fund-giif-strategies> accessed 29 March 2021.

[68] 'GIIF Prioritises Financing Environmentally Friendly Projects' (*GhanaWeb*, 1 March 2020) <https://www.ghanaweb.com/GhanaHomePage/business/GIIF-prioritizes-financing-environmentally-friendly-projects-881929> accessed 29 March 2021.

[69] ibid.

[70] Havard Halland and Michel Noel, 'Development Finance Frontline: Senegal's Strategic Investments Fund' (*World Bank Blogs*, 22 April 2016) <https://blogs.worldbank.org/psd/development-finance-frontline-senegal-s-strategic-investments-fund> accessed 29 March 2021.

purchase power agreements with off-takers, identify potential investors, and negotiate that debt and equity stacks. FONSIS views its operational capacity as embedded in its professional staff with experience across international financial centres and in multinationals in core sectors of the Senegalese economy. This has afforded the fund access to a global network of private investors.[71] Hott argues that the strength of this professional cohort further enhances the credibility of the state among international investors by contributing global experience in deal structuring and deal negotiation.[72]

The Palestine Investment Fund,[73] established in 2003 as a public shareholding company registered with the Ministry of National Economy, operates in an especially challenging and isolated domestic market. Its role is to invest in strategic sectors such as energy, agriculture, health, infrastructure, real estate, and entrepreneurship in Palestine. The fund maintains a double bottom line investment objective investing in strategic projects in Palestine's key sectors while achieving sustainable returns. The PIF monitors its performance across several key economic indicators: job opportunities created, size of investment in strategically important zones, such as Jerusalem, contribution to the GDP, contribution to decreasing the trade deficit, number of projects, and small enterprises benefitting from PIF programmes and investments. The PIF's attention to sustainability informs its requirement for additionality, i.e. contributing materially to project development when market gaps exist. It monitors and measures performance based on discrete project level KPIs. The effectiveness of its domestic role is enhanced by its size as a local investor, its track record, which drives confidence in its ability to function effectively as a credible domestic investor, and the strength of its external relationships (including with DFIs). These, combined with its professional experience, enhance its operational capacity to add value and reduce the operational risks of projects in which it invests.

A recent OECD study on the relationship between SWFs and strategic funds in sustainable finance examined potential channels of cooperation and investment partnering and identified several operational "value-adds" that strategic funds offer to sovereign and other institutional investors: (1) project monitoring and surveillance, (2) screened local market deal flow, (3) investment/transaction cost sharing, (4) enhanced governance rights and greater direct control over investments, and (5) mitigation of operational and political risks.[74] We see these discretely operational contributions as essential to defining the critical role of SWFs, particularly in sustainable development, i.e. not (only) as funding sources, but rather as *domestic* development partners that offer foreign investors a professional counterparty, with operational capacity and expertise—*alpha*—to not only enforce transactional governance in the local market but also to strengthen social licence, while mitigating operational and political exposures that emanate from persistent institutional gaps.

---

[71] ibid.

[72] ibid.

[73] For details, *see* Palestine Investment Fund at <http://www.pif.ps/home/> accessed 29 March 2021.

[74] 'The Role of Sovereign and Strategic Investment Funds in the Low Carbon Transition' OECD, (25 June 2020) <https://www.oecd.org/development/the-role-of-sovereign-and-strategic-investment-funds-in-the-low-carbon-transition-ddfd6a9f-en.htm> accessed 29 March 2021.

8 A Concluding Postscript

As we begin to emerge from the COVID-19 crisis, it has become apparent that the development financing gaps that have plagued emerging economies for decades are being significantly extended by the effects of the pandemic. More troubling, the debt burden of many developing economies has worsened since the onset of the crisis, with increasing signs of stress in markets for emerging sovereign debt.[75] For their part, many sovereign funds have been mobilised in COVID-19 relief efforts to address revenue gaps; reported withdrawals are estimated to be about $100 billion.[76] For perspective, that scale of withdrawals is approximately 1.25% of the assets of the 90 largest SWFs or approximately 25% of projected annual earnings on an aggregate asset base of $8T.[77] Moreover, such policy actions are consistent with the current—and former—stabilisation mandates of many funds. Critically relevant, however, is that the real impacts of such withdrawals are most consequential—and threatening—to those funds least resilient to large capital outflows.

In addition to withdrawals directed at fiscal shortfalls, funds have launched discrete initiatives—rent supplement programmes, SME credit facilities, etc.—to provide relief to, especially vulnerable populations. For the Ireland Strategic Investment Fund, the response has been structural: the reallocation of 2 billion euro in assets to a sub-portfolio—the Pandemic Stabilisation and Recovery Fund—to finance medium to large enterprises in Ireland.[78] As the post-COVID-19 transition takes hold, full recovery will require mobilising vast amounts of capital globally. Governments will compete for scarce resources; institutions with robust governance and strong operational capacity will enhance the ability of governments to catalyse inward flows and contribute immeasurably to national initiatives to "build back better".

Patrick J. Schena PhD, BLR Professor of Practice, Department of Economics, Tufts University; Adjunct Professor of International Business at The Fletcher School, Tufts University.

Matthew Gouett BBA (WLU), MA (McMaster) Ph.D (Carleton), Sustainable Finance Analyst at the International Institute for Sustainable Development (IISD).

---

[75] Jonathan Wheatley, 'Borrow to Fight Economic Impact of Pandemic, Says World Bank's Chief Economist' Financial Times (London, 8 October 2020) <https://www.ft.com/content/0582e495-765a-46a1-98f9-ac48e80a139c> accessed 16 October 2020.

[76] *See* for example, Tom Arnold, 'Sovereigns Raid Rainy Day Funds for $100 Billion after Covid-19 Storm' (14 September 2020) <https://in.reuters.com/article/uk-swf-assets-analysis/sovereigns-raid-rainy-day-funds-for-100-billion-after-covid-19-storm-idUKKBN2650RY> accessed 29 March 2021.

[77] Based on an expected annual return of 5%.

[78] Investments under the fund will be considered only for domestic companies that were financially viable prior to the COVID-19 crisis and that can demonstrate their ability to return to viability post the pandemic. *See* Pandemic Stabilisation and Recovery Fund, <https://isif.ie/pandemic-stabilisation-and-recovery-fund> accessed 29 March 2021.

Planning "Beside" and "Beyond" the State: Multinational Corporations as Anthropological Institutions of Global Economic Law

Gianmatteo Sabatino

1 Introduction

The role of multinational corporations (MNCs) as market regulators, although commonly accepted among scholars, has rarely been assessed from a structural point of view. MNCs, as legal entities, exercise prerogatives, within the global market, that closely resemble, to some extent, those of states. Their legitimacy and inner hierarchy are founded over the same anthropological and sociological justifications that ensure the functioning of sovereign entities. One of these justifications is undoubtedly the functional approach to economic planning. Economic operators in corporate form widely employ forms of long-term planning through mechanisms and decision-making processes directly relatable to provisions developed by the most advanced countries in terms of planning law.

The purpose of the paper is to briefly sketch some of the main features and issues, from a legal perspective, of this global phenomenon. In the first place, the topic will be discussed from the general point of view of legal anthropology, by defining the role of states and MNCs in the market, to be regarded as a society where the "power" may be either centralized or diffused according to the dynamics in place. In the "society of market", states and MNCs interact with each other also through long-term planning strategies. Therefore, the second part of the analysis is focused

This chapter draws upon the author's original publication also available at https://www.transnational-dispute-management.com/journal-advance-publication-article.asp?key=1836. Reprinted by permission from Maris BV: Maris BV, T*ransnational Dispute Management* (TDM, ISSN 1875-4120), ""Planning "beside" and "beyond" the State: Multinational Corporations as Anthropological Institutions of Global Economic Law", Gianmatteo Sabatino, Copyright (2000). Please cite accordingly.

G. Sabatino (✉)
Zhongnan University of Economics and Law, Wuhan, China
e-mail: sabatinogianmatteo@gmail.com

J. Chaisse et al. (eds.), *Regulation of State-Controlled Enterprises*, International Law and the Global South, https://doi.org/10.1007/978-981-19-1368-6_13

on the assessment of MNCs planning strategies and rules. On the third part of the analysis, I will outline some legal interactions between the states and MNCs.

2 MNCs as Anthropological Institutions of Economic Law

Over the course of the history of economic law, many institutions (e.g. households, guilds, cities, etc.) have functioned as anthropological and legal institutions of development planning.[1] MNCs represent, to some extent, the most advanced expression, other than the state, of these institutions. The idea of MNCs as semi-autonomous legal system[2] is reinforced by the presence of two elements highlighted by legal anthropologists: hierarchy and fidelity.[3] Each MNC has a hierarchical structure which may be expressed through different schemes. If we consider a single economic entity, its inner hierarchy is implemented by defining subordination links between departments, offices, etc., so that, as it is obvious, each functional cell refers to a higher one. If we instead consider a so-called actor-based multinational corporation,[4] whose global structure relies on subsidiaries, affiliates and local branches, the subordination is, in concrete, realized through the ownership of the subsidiaries' capital. Where subsidiaries are owned and operated by an independent dealer, a hierarchy may still be established through the employment of specific contracts such as franchising. Similarly, the contract shapes the hierarchical connections in network-based economic environments.[5] So are defined the situations where the leading MNC relies on an extensive network of suppliers which produce and/or assemble parts or components of a product. Here, the hierarchical nature is embedded in the economic asymmetry connoting the contract.[6]

As far as fidelity is concerned, the inner order of each MNC requires the maintenance of a mutual trust between the different units and the different people forming the MNC. In network-based contexts, it is once again the contract which, defining the reciprocal obligations of the parties on the basis of their, at least in theory, common

[1] R. Sacco, Antropologia Giuridica (il Mulino, Bologna, 2007); T. Ruskola, 'Conceptualizing Corporations and Kinship: Comparative Law and Development Theory in a Chinese Perspective' (2000) 52(6), Stanford Law Review, 1599–1729; S. Ogilvie, "Whatever Is, Is Right'? Economic Institutions in Pre-Industrial Europe' (2007) 60(4), The Economic History Review, 649–684; S. Epstein, Craft Guilds, Apprenticeship, and Technological Change in Preindustrial Europe (1998) 58(3), The Journal of Economic History, 684–713; S. Williston, History of the Law of Business Corporations before 1800. I (1888) 2(3), Harvard Law Review, 105–124.

[2] S. Falk Moore, 'Law and Social Change: The Semi-Autonomous Social Field as an Appropriate Subject of Study' (1973) 7(4), Law & Society Review, 719–746.

[3] R. Sacco (n 1), 155–167.

[4] J. Ruggie, 'Multinationals as global institution: Power, authority and relative autonomy' (2017), in Regulation & Governance, John Wiley & Sons Australia.

[5] ibid.

[6] T. Tajti, 'Franchise and Contract Asymmetry: A Common Trans-Atlantic Agenda?' (2016) 37, Loy LA Int'l & Comp Rev, 245–273.

interests, pursues the establishment of such trust. Within each unit, instead, it is the work relation, as laid out in the employment contract, to ensure fidelity, for example by providing for non-disclosure clauses, non-competition clauses, etc., or, simply, by opting for a subordinate employment contract.[7]

Most of the legal systems recognize both of these two elements. Corporation law defines the inner structure of companies emphasizing their hierarchy, e.g. by holding the chief corporation liable for certain conducts of its subsidiaries.[8] On the other hand, labour law not only allows but often requires the respect of fiduciary duties such as non-disclosure and non-competition, as well as the respect of the directive powers of hierarchical superiors. With regard to directors and executives, it is corporate law which lays out a series of corporate fiduciary duties.[9]

In my opinion, these occurrences simply give state sanction to a social dynamic which is inherent in the anthropological constitution of the MNC. It has been pointed out how, in the American corporate environment, both the duty of loyalty and the duty of care are rarely enforced through external sanctions.[10] Moreover, many MNCs autonomously codify their inner structure in their codes of conducts,[11] laying out an ethical framework binding on each employee. The Code of Conduct of BNP Paribas, for instance, regulates the prohibition of use of inside information in personal transaction and the avoidance of conflicts of interests (§ 4). Codes of Conduct is usually signed by each employee[12] and incorporated into the obligations arising from the employment contract.

Regardless of formal regulatory structures, the institutional autonomy of MNCs is often expressed through the enforcement of conciliatory procedures of "dispute resolution". For instance,[13] among the inner structures of BNP Paribas are two hierarchically shaped channels, i.e. the commercial one and the credit supervision one. Credit supervisors, pursuant to inner regulations, exercise their tasks without any influence from the commercial units. Their evaluation of ongoing practices cannot be overruled by the correspondent commercial unit. In order to carry out an operation which has received a negative opinion from the supervisor, the commercial unit may, however, activate a sort of "appeal" procedure, referring the issue to the hierarchically superior commercial department.

According to a hierarchic logic, the chief department is able to review the issue already evaluated by the supervisor and give consent to the operation, at the same time taking full responsibility for it. In practice, however, such "appeal procedure" is almost never activated, due to inner self-restraint from competent units and to an

---

[7] R. Sacco (n 1), 160–161.

[8] Art 2497 of the Italian Civil Code.

[9] C. Milhaupt (ed.), *Global Markets, Domestic Institutions* (Columbia University Press, 2003), 49.

[10] ibid.

[11] S. Murphy, 'Taking Multinational Corporate Codes of Conduct to the Next Level' (2005) 43, Colum. Transnat'l L.

[12] As referred during an interview with an employee in charge of the monitoring sector of an Italian regional branch of a financial institution.

[13] ibid.

inherent despise, from chief departments, towards such procedure. The basic idea is that divergences of opinion must be, as much as possible, composed informally, so that supervisors (especially chief ones) may be encouraged to exert moral suasion or to directly examine the most important operations.

The institutional nature of MNCs qualifies them as legal systems operating in the global society. The fluid and polycentric character of modern global law[14] would imply, at least to some extent, a detachment from territorialisation,[15] or, even better, the embracement of a transversal geographical dimension of law. Such process has often relied, overtime, on a wide interpretation of the concept of contractual freedom, which empowered parties of business contracts to derogate, for instance, to national legal rules about jurisdiction, eliminating the requirement for a geographic nexus to the chosen state.[16]

MNCs exercise their governance power over a more or less structured community of both individuals (e.g. employees) and other corporations (e.g. subsidiaries or ancillary economic operators) all over the world.

Soft law instruments issued by international organizations and especially addressed to MNCs uphold a functional concept of such economic entities, whose purpose goes well beyond profit-seeking and involves contributing "*to economic, environmental and social progress with a view to achieving sustainable development*".[17] This role gives rise to a dialectical relationship between MNCs, national governments and international organizations, where sometimes MNCs are held responsible for violations of fundamental rights when pursuing independent economic policies,[18] but sometimes they establish pre-emptive monitoring mechanisms to verify the compliance of their actions with fundamental rights, common development policies and progress.[19] In other cases, MNCs cooperate with national governments in deploying law enforcement personnel ensuring the smooth functioning of the activity carried out.[20]

---

[14] L. Backer, 'The structure of global law, fracture, fluidity, permeability and polycentricity' (2012), CPE Working Papers, No. 2012-7/1, 102–122.

[15] ibid.

[16] S. Potts, Reterritorializing economic governance: Contracts, space, and law in trans-border economic geographies (2016) 48(3), in Environment and Planning, 523–539.

[17] OECD Guidelines for Multinational Enterprises, Chapter II (General Policies).

[18] F. Wettstein, Multinational Corporations and Global Justice (Stanford University Press 2009).

[19] § 7 of the BNP Code of Conduct, which requires employees to always consider the direct and indirect impacts of their activities on Human Rights and environmental protection around the world.

[20] C. Riziki Majinge, 'Can Multinational Corporations Help Secure Human Rights and the Rule of Law? The Case of Sudan' (2011) 44(1), in Verfassung und Recht in Übersee/Law and Politics in Africa, Asia and Latin America, 7–31.

2.1 MNCs and the Market Society

There is an ongoing debate over the role of MNCs in the international legal order.[21] According to traditional view, public international law is a law of states, intended as organizations exercising effective powers over space and subjects.[22] Therefore, individuals and entities formally subjected to state sovereignty could not be international legal subjects. The idea of a state-based international law[23] relies on the assumption that since "*individuals are always in a territorial space, their interests and needs are best represented and served by the sovereign state on whose territory they find themselves*".[24] Other theories deny the international legal subjectivity to MNCs on the basis of their (in)capacity to: (i) make claims for breach of international law; (ii) enter into valid international agreements; (iii) enjoy privileges and immunities from national jurisdiction.[25] Therefore, MNCs could not be subjected to international human rights and environmental protection provisions.[26]

Indeed, the debate, as noted by recent academic works, holds a mainly theoretical value. What is most important, in concrete, is not assessing the subjectivity or limited international legal personality of MNCs, but rather determining obligations and rights concerning MNCs arising from international law.[27]

Furthermore, in anthropological perspective, by looking at the incidence of inner hierarchical structures of MNCs over their functioning on a global scale, we could argue that MNCs are indeed part of another society that of the global market.

According to Backer,[28] in global law "*governance (...) is dependent not on meeting the requirements for legitimacy (...) under international law, but rather of a self-constituting character marked by boundaries functionally differentiated from those of other groups*".

Within the modern global market, the self-constituting character of the MNCs' legal order is exercised on the outside through the contractual freedom enjoyed by economic entities at the international level.[29] MNCs may stipulate bilateral and multilateral economic contracts between each other and are free to decide the national

---

[21] E. Oshionebo, *Regulating Transnational Corporations in Domestic and International Regimes* (University of Toronto Press 2009); C. Ryngaert, 'Non-State Actors in International Law: A Rejoinder to Professor Thirlway' (2017) 64, in Neth. Int. Law Rev., 155–162; M. Karavias, 'Shared Responsibility and Multinational Enterprises' (2015) 62, in Neth. Int. Law Rev., 91–117.

[22] B. Conforti, *Diritto Internazionale* (Editoriale Scientifica, Napoli, 2014), 11 ff.; N. Ronzitti, *Introduzione al Diritto Internazionale* (Giappichelli 2013) 19–20.

[23] H. Thirlway, 'The Role of Non-State Actors: A Response to Professor Ryngaert' (2017) 64, Neth. Int. Law Rev., 141–153.

[24] Ryngaert (n 21).

[25] Oshionebo (n 21).

[26] ibid.

[27] J. Wouters and A. Chané, 'Multinational Corporations in International Law' (2013), Leuven Centre for Global Governance Studies, Working Paper no. 129.

[28] Backer (n 14), 111.

[29] F. Cafaggi, 'Regulation through contracts: supply-chain contracting and sustainability standards' (2016), in ERCL, 12(3), 218–258.

jurisdiction competent to hear eventual disputes. Such occurrence, however, leads to what has been defined as a process of "legal commodification". In other words, "*if economic entities may now effectively choose among legal regimes (...) the legal maturity of a political state will have a significant regulatory effect. Where states have a less developed legal system (...)multinational corporations may be able to assert more effective control over their operations in that state*".[30]

The globalization of the market, in principle, is independent from the globalization of regulatory frameworks.[31] The second globalization (i.e. of regulatory frameworks) has evolved trying to address the issue of commercial barriers between the states and the regulation of governments' intervention in the economy.[32] International legal sources addressing MNCs have dealt with the respect of human rights,[33] while "*many powerful states continue to oppose the idea of a direct relationship between international law and economic collectives*".[34] Taking advantage of regulatory vacuum, MNCs have gradually established autonomous regulatory frameworks not relying on the three traditional elements of state, state law and territory.[35]

In the definition of the content of MNCs' contracts, they follow centrally drafted development strategies where national legal systems may become functional elements to be taken advantage of or ignored depending on the strategic priorities set by the MNC. In the market society, MNCs dialogue with states. States may choose, where they have such capacity, to attract MNCs' investment or to regulate/limit them. Conversely, MNCs decide whether or not to align their development strategies to objectives pursued by certain states.

Sometimes, this whole system is incorporated into legal provisions, such as, typically, antitrust law. Many modern antitrust legal regimes explicitly allow exemptions, by allowing anticompetitive agreements which contribute to improvement in production and distribution systems or, more in general, to socio-economic development.[36] In practice, competition authorities carry out investigations assessing the scopes of the agreements under scrutiny.[37] In the investigation process, which involves not

---

[30] L. Backer, 'Multinational Corporations as Objects and Sources of Transnational Regulation' (2008) 14(2), ILSA Journal of International & Comparative Law, 1–26.

[31] P. Drahos, *Regulatory Theory* (2017), ANU Press, 249 ff.

[32] We may think about the World Trade Organization (WTO) as the main example of such evolutionary pattern. *See* ibid.

[33] Backer (n 30); J. Campagna, 'United Nations Norms On The Responsibilities Of Transnational Corporations and Other Business Enterprises With Regard To Human Rights: The International Community Asserts Binding Law On The Global Rule Maker's (2004) 37(4) J. Marshall L Rev, 1205 ff.; D. Weissbrodt, M. Kruger, 'Norms on the Responsibilities of Transnational Corporations and Other Business Enterprises With Regard to Human Rights' (2003) 97(4), J. Int'L L., 901 ff.

[34] Backer (n 30).

[35] Backer (n 30).

[36] *See* for instance, art. 101 § 3 of the Treaty on the Functioning of the European Union, art. 6 of the East African Community Competition act, art. 15 of the Anti-Monopoly Law of the People's Republic of China.

[37] *See* for instance, Council Regulation (EC) No 1/2003 of 16 December 2002 on the implementation of the rules on competition laid down in Articles 81 and 82 of the Treaty (now Articles 101 and 102 of the TFEU).

only anticompetitive agreements but also mergers, the economic entities involved may carry out lobbying,[38] not only to promote their own interest but also to undermine the interests of competitors, for instance by promoting grievances against other MNCs.[39]

The instrumental power exercised through lobbying often relies, as it could be obvious, on a structural power determined by the economic "size" of the operator or, in other words, by its ability to "*affect outcomes in its favor*".[40] Where such structural power is particularly high, MNCs may restrain from using instrumental powers such as lobbying, being able to rely on their sole economic relevance. Lobbying's influence power is inherently linked to the decrease or absence of publicly-owned economic operators. However, this does not necessarily mean that lobbying is an epiphany of the regulatory state.

The evidence shows that the most transparent and standardized decision-making procedures (e.g. tendering procedures for public administrations' purchases) are of little interest to interest groups. On the other hand, highly discretional decision-making procedures are where the big guns come out.[41] In most cases, lobbying revolves around an issue of informational asymmetry. Where public powers are in need of information in order to issue coherent and effective decisions, interest groups related to MNCs offer such information in exchange for favourable regulatory frameworks.[42] This explains why antitrust law represents one of the regulatory fields where lobbying is more prominent.

In legal systems where the integration between state powers and economic operators is particularly high, such as the People's Republic of China, lobbying also becomes a tool to enforce a principle of inclusiveness in the elaboration and implementation of state planning strategies.[43] In the market, states and MNCs shape a precise hierarchy. MNCs holding relevant structural power determine the development priorities of the market, and other economic entities often follow suit. Sometimes bigger MNCs bind smaller ones through supply chain contracts. MNCs, in exercising power over their own structures and operating network, may appear to

---

[38] Ruggie (n 4), 5–7.

[39] Ruggie (n 4), 6 reminds how "*Microsoft reportedly spends more money on lobbying in Brussels, the EU's capital, than any European company – although apparently primarily to promote grievances against its competitor, Google, on anti-trust grounds rather than to undermine specific public interests*".

[40] Ruggie (n 4), 7–9.

[41] A. Bitonti, P. Harris (eds), *Lobbying in Europe*, (Palgrave Macmillan 2017) 4–13.

[42] S. Koehler, Lobbying, Political Uncertainty and Policy Outcomes, (Palgrave Macmillan, Cham, 2019) 9 ff.

[43] S. Kennedy, The Business of Lobbying in China, (Harvard University Press, Cambridge, 2005). On the inclusiveness of Chinese economic planning see G. Sabatino, Legal Features of Chinese Economic Planning, in I. Castellucci (eds), Saggi di Diritto Economico e Commerciale Cinese, (Editoriale Scientifica, Napoli, 2019) 33–78.

satisfy the requirements of effectiveness and independence upheld by some international legal scholars as the fundamental elements of international legal subjectivity of states.[44]

On the other hand, states (and supranational legal orders such as the European Union) try to tackle the market distortions produced by certain MNCs' economic behaviour and lay out antitrust legal frameworks as well as rules regarding, for instance, employment contracts, environmental standards, etc. Lobbying becomes, somewhat, the dimension through which the *vis-à-vis* dialogue between these different actors occurs. If the parties do not reach an agreement and states apply their relevant laws to constrain MNCs' conducts or sanction them, MNCs may issue unilateral acts such as de-localizations, resembling the international law of concept of "retaliation".[45] These acts, indeed, display the inherent weakness of state regulatory powers.

If we think about market as a society where different legal systems interact, we should consider it a society whose power is both centralized and diffused, depending on the legal systems involved.[46] MNCs are able to establish *vis-à-vis* relations between each other and with states, relying on the fundamental principles of private property and freedom of contract.[47] Soft hierarchies may be established due to force relations as well as political and ethical prestige. Similarly, international organizations may issue soft law sources, such as OECD Guidelines. In its structural foundations, however, this layer of the market remains acephalous, exactly like the international legal order composed by states.[48]

Things change, however, if we consider the connection between big multinational enterprises and small and medium locally based enterprises. Here the wide difference in instrumental and structural power leads to the centralization of power. A power is in first place economic, concerning the object and the means of economic production and distribution. Small enterprises, especially the ones located in less-developed countries, do not hold the same technical knowledge, prestige and wealth of MNCs. Their value is retained, essentially, in the low costs of production they offer, due to the poor standards of their work environment and methods.[49] Consequently, they are subjected to the constraints imposed by more powerful MNCs, easily enforceable through the termination of the contractual relationships.

---

[44] B. Conforti (n 22).

[45] B. Conforti (n 22), 408 ff.

[46] On the distinction between centralized-power societies and diffused-power societies, see M. Fortes, E. Evans Pritchard, African Political Systems, (Oxford University Press, Oxford, 1940); R. Sacco (n 1).

[47] J. Ruggie (n 4), 10–11.

[48] R. Sacco (n 1), 109–113.

[49] S. Nanda, R. Warms, Culture Counts: a concise introduction to cultural anthropology, (Wadsworth, Belmont, 2012) 311–312.

3 Corporate Planning

The polycentric nature of the market society implies that MNCs, when acting as global regulators, do interact with several other actors apart from states.[50]

In order to sustain the consequent dialectic process, they need an inner structure able to define strategic, management, operative and monitoring competences. In other words, they need planning. Through planning MNCs: (i) define their inner organization and hierarchical links; (ii) set out objectives and development strategies valid not only for the parent company but, obviously, for the subsidiaries as well; (iii) define the standards to be incorporated in the supply contracts stipulated with several other economic entities.[51] In order to reach such ambitious goals, they widely employ numerical indicators, directives and criteria for performance evaluation.

The first two decades of the twentieth century represented a turning point for the whole idea of development planning. While, on the "public front", World War One and, subsequently, the Bolshevik Revolution laid the basis of the war collectivism[52] that was to shape modern planning,[53] on the "private front" an organizational revolution took place. Already since the Second Industrial Revolution, the geographical expansion of the markets imposed a shift from the concept of owner–manager to that of salaried professional manager still dominant today.[54] However, the progressive increase in product diversification and market expansion forced a reconsideration of the whole organizational model of big corporations. The multifunctional system which concentrated on the top management of all the decision-making procedures suffered from overload.[55] It was therefore, gradually, replaced by the so-called M-form model, i.e. multidivisional system.[56] Two main consequences arose from such evolution: in first place, the establishment of separate functional divisions with decision-making powers raised the problem of coordination, monitoring and supervision.[57] In the second place, "*with the operational top management overload reduced by the M-form structure, senior management was freed, in principle, to think more strategically. Senior management was encouraged to adopt strategies aimed*

---

[50] L Backer, 'Economic Globalization and the Rise of Efficient Systems of Global Private Lawmaking: Wal-Mart as Global Legislator' (2007) 39(4), Connecticut Law Review, 1–46, 13.

[51] ibid.

[52] The term was employed, although in a negative perspective, in M. Rothbard, 'War Collectivism in World War One', in Radosh and Rothbard, *A New History of Leviathan* (E.P. Dutton & Co. New York, 1972).

[53] S. Malle, The Economic Organization of War Communism, (Cambridge University Press 1985); Wang Shaoguang (王绍光) and Yan Yilong (鄢一龙), 'A Democratic Way of Decision-Making: Five Year Plan Process in China' (中国民主决策模式, 以五年规划制定为例), (Library of Marxism Studies 1, 2016), 13–14.

[54] S. Johnston, Headquarters and Subsidiaries in Multinational Corporations, (Palgrave Macmillan 2005) 17–19.

[55] ibid.

[56] ibid.

[57] ibid.

at further long-term growth via *diversification*".[58] The logic outcome of the new development was, therefore, the birth of a modern concept of corporate planning.

Emphasizing the functional distinction between objective, means, implementation and organizational structures,[59] it was possible to comprehend the fluid and dynamic nature of corporate development, opposed to the limited dimension of national sovereignty.[60] It was therefore argued that MNCs contributed to the diffusion of global standards of civilization.[61]

3.1 Planning Hierarchy and Categories

MNCs' planning concerns, firstly, a relation between objectives and means.[62] As already noted, objectives do not necessarily deal with profit, although most of them actually do it. They may also concern improvements in coordination mechanisms, respect of environmental standards or other fundamental rights, etc.

The organizational principle of MNCs' planning is the hierarchy among plans. Each functional unit develops a plan. Within a single entity, the various departments or the local offices issue their strategic plans. Similarly, each subsidiary issues its own plan in addition to the one of the parent companies. In network-based MNCs, the plans issued by various entities are even formally independent, since there, the leading MNC does not exercise formal capital control over the other enterprises. In these cases, the planning efficiency is ensured through the definition of the contractual agreements.[63]

The plans issued at the higher level must be respected by the plans issued at the lower level. This rule may be tempered by the involvement of the different levels in the planning process, in particular widely scoped consultations carried out between employees,[64] or with social bodies like trade unions. The degree of strictness of planning hierarchy, however, varies depending on the economic objective pursued. It has been noted[65] that when a firm investing in a country holds a competence and expertise which the host country competitors lack, corporate headquarters tend to employ tight planning systems over marketing and product strategies concerning the host market, retaining knowledge and critical functions at the central level. Where,

---

[58] ibid.

[59] K. Hayashi, 'Corporate Planning Practices in Japanese Multinational' (1978) 21(2), Academy of Management Journal, 21(2).

[60] J. Weinstein, J. McIntyre, 'Multinational Corporations and the Diffusion of World Standards: A Theoretical Exploration' (1986), Studies in Comparative International Development, 51–84.

[61] ibid.

[62] Hayashi (n 59).

[63] Backer (n 50).

[64] From an interview realized with an employee in charge of the monitoring sector of an Italian regional branch of a financial institution.

[65] Johnston (n 54), 34–35.

instead, local competition responsiveness is particularly high, the production and marketing strategies are elaborated and implemented locally, in order to better fit the demands of the specific markets involved. Headquarters and parent companies, however, always retain control over key financial indicators[66] and strategies. So, for instance, if the headquarter of parent company decides to expand on the African market, all the subsidiaries and local units must take into account such priority.[67] Again, if a financial institution decides to prioritize the real estate market, this directive will mean, in concrete, that each functional unit will have to support the access to credit to individuals and enterprises interested in investing on the real estate market.

MNCs also establish an implementing structure where different departments or different subsidiaries are in charge of managing specific economic activities. BNP Paribas, for instance, holds control over a subsidiary (Arval) specialized in full service vehicle leasing. BNP is also controller of BNL (i.e. "Banca Nazionale del Lavoro), the sixth-largest bank in the Italian market.[68] The dynamics of corporate structure are continuously evolving and depend by commercial choices taken each day. What, instead, does not change is the pattern of corporate planning, following the two principles of decentralization and differentiation. BNL is in charge of implementing BNP general strategies with regard to the Italian market. On the other hand, Arval is in charge of a specific economic field. Subsidiary tasks widely differ and may concern production and distribution along the supply chain.[69] They may also concern independent economic activities.

Vancil and Lorange, in 1975, distinguished three main categories of corporate planning[70]:

1. In the first place, there is proper corporate planning, dealing with the definition of company objectives and goals, with the acquisition of "*the resources needed to attain those objectives*"[71] and with the allocation of resources among business lines (e.g. real estate market, financial market, etc.),
2. In the second place, business planning concerns the determination of the "*the scope of a division's activities that will satisfy a broad consumer need, of deciding on the division's objectives in its defined area of operations, and of establishing the policies adopted to attain those objectives*".[72] Business planning is carried out not at the highest level of a corporation but at the level of each business unit, for instance a subsidiary in charge of distribution,

---

66 ibid.

67 From an interview realized with an employee in charge of the monitoring sector of an Italian regional branch of a financial institution.

68 BNP Registration Document and Annual Financial Report of 2017.

69 S. Johnston (n 54), 66 ff.

70 R. Vancil, P. Lorange, 'Strategic Planning in Diversified Companies' (1975) January-February, Harvard Business Review.

71 ibid.

72 ibid.

3. In the third place, functional planning is carried out by departments, divisions and functional units within the business entity in order to elaborate coordinate action programmes to attain the objectives laid out.

In capitalist societies, resource allocation usually functions according to market dynamics, whereas in traditional planned economies, resources are centrally allocated by state authorities. However, within each MNC, market dynamics usually do not operate. Departments and offices are given a budget determined according to the objectives to be reached. In liberal-democratic legal orders, the principle of private economic initiative is also expressed through freedom of economic organization and management. Then, MNCs, as economic entities, spontaneously organize themselves according to strictly hierarchical principles.

Through planning, MNCs express their relative independence, as legal orders, from national systems. At the very same time, MNCs, as legal orders, are exposed to legal pluralism derived from several dynamics which can occur within their planning structure.[73] MNCs' management holds, in concrete, a monopoly over decision-making and that implies an unequal distribution of resources or opportunities.[74] MNCs' interns may develop relationship networks deriving from familial ties, political lobbying, friendship or personal interests which directly affect their strategic choices in the elaboration but, more significantly, in the implementation of planning.[75]

3.2 *Plans' Structure and Content*

In terms of structure and content, MNCs' plans are similar to their state counterparts. In fact, they have a general part, where the plans describe the macroeconomic environment as well as the development results achieved in the past years.[76] In the second part of each plan, different objectives are laid out. The nature and quality of the instruments employed depend on the sectors involved. Commercial sectors, in charge of retail activities, may be subjected to numerical indicators regarding business volumes to be reached.[77] The achievement of these goals is sometimes ensured through incentive systems for employees and offices' directors, whereas, in case

[73] V. Shlapentokh, J. Woods, *Feudal America* (Penn State University Press 2011), 32 ff.

[74] ibid.

[75] This is what, in the Chinese context, is commonly referred to as *guanxi* (关系), which still today plays an important role in the functioning and development of Chinese firms, with both positive and negative outcomes. *See* on the topic, U. Braendle, T. Gasser, J. Noll, 'Corporate Governance in China - is Economic Growth Potential Hindered by *guanxi*?' (2005), available at SSRN: https://ssrn.com/abstract=710203 or http://dx.doi.org/10.2139/ssrn.710203; Y. Mao, K. Peng, C. Wong, 'Indigenous research on Asia: In search of the emic components of *guanxi*' (2012) 29(4), Asia Pac J Manag, 1143–1168.

[76] Information obtained through an interview realized with an employee in charge of the monitoring sector of an Italian regional branch of a financial institution.

[77] ibid.

of severe under-achievements, the same employees or directors may be transferred to other offices.[78] Sometimes, the incentives mechanisms are automatic, meaning that employees working in a department which reaches outstanding results will obtain rewards without a prior assessment of individual performances. In general, employees and/or directors efficiently fulfilling plans and objectives are more likely to get promoted.[79]

Other sectors, not directly related to "countable" or "quantitative" activities, are governed through directives. These are brief descriptions of the *way* that a certain activity should be carried out. For instance, departments in charge of monitoring financial stability of the customers within a bank may be required to focus on certain criteria or certain aspects of each customer's profile.[80] Given the nature of the activity, it would be impossible to lay out specific numerical indicators, but it may nevertheless happen that directors, in agreement with higher managers, define, for instance, the number of files that have to be processed each day and communicate such decision to each employee.[81]

As previously mentioned, another relevant feature of corporate planning is organizational provisions. Taking the "Carrefour 2022" transformation plan as the example, we may argue that such organizational rules regard: (i) cost reductions and rationalization, to be achieved through reorganization of offices, personnel reduction as well as targeted investment into new technologies or saving costs procedures, (ii) investments, concerning, for instance, opening of new offices or improvement in existing functional structures and (iii) personnel management.

3.3 MNCs, Planning and Contract

Transnational supply networks rely on chains of contracts between enterprises located in different areas of the globe, operating according to a defined purpose, that is the realization of a final product or of a certain activity, e.g. the distribution/retail under the brand of a MNC pursuant to a franchising contract.

Contracts governing a transnational supply chain are usually medium to long-term contracts. As such, they reflect not only the "static" economic asymmetry between two operators but also the "dynamic" one, interpreted in the light of the evolution of the relevant market. Furthermore, long-term contracts tend to develop an organizational nature[82] as well, since they regulate, in concrete, a series of performances

---

[78] ibid.

[79] ibid.

[80] Information obtained through an interview realized with an employee in charge of the monitoring sector of an Italian regional branch of a financial institution.

[81] ibid.

[82] On the notion of organizational contract, *see* S. Grundmann, F. Cafaggi, G. Vettori, The organizational contract: from exchange to long-term network cooperation in European contract law, (Ashgate, 2013).

in several aspects, e.g. object and modality of productions, quality standards, prices, work conditions, etc.

In economical perspective, what happens within such production chains is that the lead corporation is the most significant, if not the only one, contractual counterpart of the smaller enterprises.[83] A MNC is able to exercise a significant contractual influence towards several small enterprises competing to enter into the supply chain. Such influence might concern the definition of the price of the performances involved[84] or the choice of a certain national jurisdiction to hear disputes. It might also concern the incorporation, in the final contract, of standards of production, work organization and ethics determined by the leading MNC through its codes of conducts and plans.[85]

Contractual freedom, as principle accepted in the international economic order, comes to be an instrument in the hands of the leading MNCs to implement their plans and limit, in turn, the freedom of the suppliers.

Asymmetry does not necessarily have a negative impact. There are examples of MNCs either implementing systems of shared responsibility with suppliers[86] or transposing ethical and labour standards in legal relationships with suppliers and, in general, with enterprises involved in the production chain.[87] In doing so, the MNC imposes standards even exceeding the requirements of the applicable law, as mentioned by the Amazon Supply Chain Standards.

However, this is not always the case. In fact, MNCs, exercising through contracts their self-regulating autonomy,[88] would also be able to decide to invest in national contexts, where regulatory frameworks are weaker and/or international labour standards are weakly enforced.

4 Legal Interactions Between States and MNCs

In the market society, states and MNCs often interact on an equal footing. In this context, the relation between common interests and economic freedoms becomes critical.

International soft law instruments such as the OECD Guidelines for Multinational Enterprises try to strike a balance between the private autonomy of such economic

---

[83] M. Anner, 'Multinational Corporations and Economic Inequality in the Global South: Causes, Consequences, and Countermeasures' (2014), Paper Prepared for the 9th Global Labour University Conference "Inequality within and among Nations: Causes, Effects, and Responses", Berlin.

[84] ibid.

[85] Backer (n 50).

[86] Wettstein (n 18), 291–293.

[87] Backer (n 50), 14–18.

[88] L. Backer, 'Private Actors and Public Governance Beyond the State: The Multinational Corporation, the Financial Stability Board, and the Global Governance Order' (2011) 18(2), Indiana Journal of Global Legal Studies, 751–802.

operators and the social dimension they should operate it. In fact, the OECD Guidelines make several references to the applicable international standards,[89] aiming at taking multination enterprises under the shield of international law treaties and convention. Civil society organizations and media as well play an important role[90]: the first ones elaborating standards or upholding existing international standards; the second ones serving "*as a critical factor in the effectiveness of private monitoring*"[91] and advocating patterns of development for corporate planning.

However, as noted by those who deny international subjectivity to MNCs, rights and obligations under international law, even if addressing MNCs, formally bind states, since only states are accountable before international courts and tribunals (save for the International Criminal Court). Therefore, regulation of MNCs' conduct arises mainly from two sets of legal rules: on the one hand, soft law international instruments and on the other hand national or macro-regional regulatory frameworks, such as EU law. It is impossible to thoroughly address each of the many and diverse legal instruments employed by states in order to interact with MNCs, but certain general features are worth pointing out.

4.1 The Ethical Corporation: Corporate Social Responsibility and Enforcement of Ethical Standards

Ethics, as a regulatory force over business activities, arose from the withdrawal of public powers from regulatory efforts.[92]

The development of ethical and productive standards from MNCs addressed two major issues: on one hand ensuring the diffusion of "standards of civilization" on the basis of instances brought on by aware consumers and social bodies in the Western countries; on the other hand, the (re)affirmation of chief corporations' control over supply chains, i.e. the implementation of private governance mechanisms.[93]

The main outcome of such peculiar integration of social awareness and control need has been the rise of the Code of Conduct as a regulatory cornerstone of international business.[94]

---

[89] *See* for instance, Sections IV and V of the OECD Guidelines.

[90] Backer (n 50), 18–21.

[91] ibid.

[92] G. Le Baron, J. Lister, P. Dauvergne, 'Governing Global Supply Chain Sustainability through the Ethical Audit Regime' (2017) 14(6), Globalizations, 958–975, 959–961; G. Conte, 'Vincoli Giuridici, Principi Economici e Valori Etici nello Svolgimento dell'Attività d'Impresa' (2009) 3, Contratto e Impresa, 679 ff.

[93] G. Le Baron, J. Lister, P. Dauvergne (n 92).

[94] G. Conte, 'Codici Etici e Attività d'Impresa nel Nuovo Spazio Globale di Mercato' (2006) 1, Contratto e Impresa, 108 ff.

The Code of Conduct signed by the employees of a corporation or by several corporation along a supply chain is, by all regards, a model of regulatory, organizational contract.[95] Through a common agreement, it seeks to regulate, in its evolution, a contractual relationship. In practice, its binding force relies on the asymmetry between the parties and extends the effects of a legal system (that of the MNC) well beyond national borders and national standards.

This explains why public powers have gradually sought to encourage the adoption and implementation of such codes. A wide range of soft law sources addresses the issue. Among them, the Global Compact was launched by former UN Secretary Kofi Annan in 1999 and operative since 2000 and based on nine universal principles to involve enterprises and economic operators in a form of universal cooperation to promote work security, human rights and environment protection.[96] More recently, the UN 2030 Agenda for Sustainable Development reaffirms a social dimension of global business.

The seventeen development goals laid out by the Agenda have been formally incorporated as the new development strategy of the European Union. Therefore, EU development strategies and investment and structural funds in their next cycle (2021–2027) will be targeted upon such broad goals and will displace funds according to the priorities set by the Agenda.

The logic is undoubtedly promotional and founded over a soft enforcement and positive incentives. The main regulatory effort, however, is left to the economic operators themselves.[97] Indeed, many MNCs today implement quite complex supervisory systems concerning supply and production chains. One of the most appreciated supervisory instruments is the "Ethical Audit Regime", where audit based on socio-ethical criteria is carried out by the MNCs towards their subsidiaries and affiliated smaller companies.[98]

However such supervisory systems gained worldwide recognition and praise, some authors (and civil society organizations) expressed doubts concerning their ability to carry out independent assessments. Case studies confirmed that audits are a "weak management mechanism for detecting and addressing non-compliance".[99] Most of such weakness is due to the "disproportionate power and control that companies yield over the pathway, timing and implementation of audits".[100] In other words, MNCs audit systems clearly suffer from a problem of conflict of interests between, once again, their corporate social responsibility settings and their development planning strategies.

The practice seems to indicate that the enforcement of MNCs ethics must necessarily rely on positive legal rules. The issue is therefore how to do it, given the inherent

---

[95] G. Gitti, Contratti Regolamentari e Normativi (Cedam, Padova, 1994).

[96] G. Conte (n 94).

[97] G. Conte (n 92).

[98] G. Le Baron, J. Lister, P. Dauvergne (n 92).

[99] ibid.

[100] ibid.

weakness of traditional civil and administrative law instruments to deal with MNCs planning strategies.

The possible answer varies depending on the nature of the economic relations corporations are engaged in. In an administrative contract, i.e. a contract stipulated by a private party and a public party (e.g. a public administration) for the execution of a public interest performance, the control of the corporation's socio-ethical standards often occurs through the regulation of tendering procedures.

EU law on public procurement now explicitly favours the introduction of environmental and social considerations among the criteria to evaluate the most economically advantageous offer in tendering procedures.[101] On such basis, national legal orders developed instruments to empower public administration to take into account the aforementioned instances. In Italy, public administrations, when setting the evaluation criteria for tendering procedures for public infrastructure projects, may introduce the so-called Minimum Environmental Criteria (*Criteri Ambientali Minimi*—CAM), according to which participants in the procedure are also evaluated on the basis of the compliance of their working techniques and instruments with environmental standards.[102]

The CAM are not binding for public administrations. However, when they choose not to include them among the criteria, they are required to offer explanations.[103] Recent studies have demonstrated that, although the number of tendering procedures including CAM is not particularly high, their presence is constant.[104]

In Italy, public administration often evaluate offers on the basis of CSR standards as well, granting additional points to operators holding CSR official certifications. The actual legal value of such certifications is debated. In 2013, a decision of the Italian Council of State (the highest administrative court)[105] ruled that, in the first place, enterprises operating in Italy are subjected per se to Italian legal standards concerning workers' rights, so to render independent certifications void of legal significance; in the second place, it held that the issuance of a Code of Conduct, in its form of regulatory contract binding each employee, proves the adoption of adequate CSR standards, without the need for any additional certification.

More recently, a decision of the Administrative Regional Tribunal of Campania[106] recognized the proving value of CSR certifications and denied that an equivalent effect could be exerted by other documents attesting the respect of CSR standards.

Regardless of the legal value of CAM and CSR certifications, they may play their full role just in public–private legal relations. Their relevance, from a contractual

---

[101] Art. 67 of EU Dir. 24/2014.

[102] S. Colombari, Le considerazioni ambientali nell'aggiudicazione delle concessioni e degli appalti pubblici (2019) 1, Urbanistica e appalti, 5.

[103] *See* the Decree of the Ministry of Environment and of Protection of the Territory and the Sea, 11 October 2017.

[104] M. Cozzio, L. Gili (eds), 'Osservatorio di diritto comunitario e nazionale sugli appalti pubblici' Newsletter of November 2018.

[105] Decision n. 5375/2013 of the Italian Council of State (5th Chamber).

[106] Decision n. 1295/2016 of the Regional Administrative Tribunal of Campania (Salerno).

perspective, is closely linked to the administrative contract concluded at the end of the tendering procedure. They are not enforceable by judicial authorities if a MNC carries out large-scale operations on the market which do not involve relations with a public party but are, as usually happens, addressed to other operators and consumers.

In such cases, the most effective answer to the need for regulation for MNCs activities comes from consumer law and from the extension of the notion of unfair commercial practices.

Indeed, a Code of Conduct and Ethical Standards may take the form of a fully binding contract for the MNCs employees, but to consumers they are, by all effects, a representation of a particular development philosophy embraced by the corporation. They are therefore criteria able to affect the choices of the consumers and, if deceitful, they distort the consumers' economic behaviour, thus falling under to notion of unfair practices, as elaborated by EU law.[107]

This consideration puts Code of Conducts under the "umbrella" of European legal principles, in first place the principles of effectiveness and effective judicial protection (art 47 of the Charter of Fundamental Rights of the EU). Therefore, national judges are empowered to determine remedies according to the logic of a "horizontal application" of the notion of effective protection.[108]

This process led to a debate, fuelled by judicial decisions, about the proper remedy to address unfair practices, given the silence of statutory law. In particular, it is disputed whether or not, in addition to the compensatory remedies (deriving from pre-contractual liability), the consumer may also ask for the nullity of the contract stipulated also on the basis of an unfair practice.[109]

From this perspective, the combination of rules of validity and of responsibility becomes a way to enforce Code of Conducts by looking at their reflection upon the market choices of the final consumers.

However, such developments touch MNCs planning strategies only by reflection or indirectly. The attention of the legislature and the courts is, here, directed at consumer protection, not at public policy purposes. On that regard, the most common legislative instrument to regulate MNCs is still that of laying out duties of disclosure regarding social or non-financial information concerning the business strategies and methods of MNCs, as for instance the EU Dir. N. 95/2014.

---

[107] C. Magli, Pratiche Commerciali Scorrette e Rimedi Civilistici nel Contesto della Responsabilità Sociale d'Impresa (2019) 2, Contratto e Impresa, 716 ff.

[108] E. Navarretta, *Costituzione Europa e Diritto Privato. Effettività e «drittwirkung» ripensando la complessità giuridica* (Giappichelli, Torino, 2017).

[109] A. Seminara, 'La tutela civilistica del consumatore di fronte alle pratiche commerciali scorrette' (2018) 6, Contratti, 689 ff..; A. Verdesca, 'Pratiche commerciali scorrette e tutela dei consumatori: tra conformazione del contratto e poteri delle authorities' (2019) 7, Corriere Giur., 934 ff.

4.2 Antitrust Law and "Dynamic Efficiencies"

Over the past decades, antitrust law has gradually become almost a synonym for public economic management. Its ability to affect development strategies of MNCs lies in the "openness" and "dynamicity" of its rules. It is not just a matter of lobbying. Antitrust regulation, structurally, leaves some spaces for exemptions, exceptions and discretional assessments. In moving around these spaces, authorities pursue their own economic policies, inspired by more liberal or more regulatory theoretical stances.

In recent years, the evolutionary pattern of antitrust law dealing with MNCs has been expressed mainly by merger cases. Discretional powers, in merger regulation, take the form of "efficiencies" that may be taken into account in order to justify a merger which objectively creates concerns in terms of competition. Positive European law, so far, only takes into account the externalities that are able to produce, in short-term perspective, benefits for consumer or contribute to technical and economic progress as long as such progress favours the consumers.[110] This is what, in economic perspective, may be defined as "static efficiency" and usually reflects a liberal-democratic socio-economic thought.

On a comparative level, however, several legal systems gradually shaped antitrust rules which focus on "dynamic efficiencies"[111] as well, i.e. those efficiencies pertaining to long-term effects of market conducts over the national economy, the development of jobs market, the advancement of technical knowledge, not so much to bring benefits to consumer but rather to foster national socio-economic progress. In concrete, such efficiencies are transposed into prospective evaluations carried out by antitrust authorities and justified by legal provisions. In some cases (e.g. Jordan, South Africa), antitrust legislation explicitly mentions that the development and protection of the national economy are an element to be considered when assessing the legitimacy of a merger. In other cases, authorities use the discretional powers granted by legal provisions and interpreted in the light of the principles of national antitrust law, as in China.

In some cases, the integration between antitrust and national development policies is carried out in the evaluation of the legitimacy of the merger. This happened when the Chinese Ministry of Commerce (MOFCOM) prohibited the merger between Coca-Cola and Huiyuan on account of its prospective impact over the development of the national market of beverages and domestic small and medium enterprises.[112]

In other cases, the integration is transposed into conditionalities or "remedies", to which the approval of the merger is subordinated. Antitrust authorities, all around the world, have shaped such conditionalities with different degrees of intensity and incidence over private economic operators' business strategies. The use of remedies

[110] Art. 2 § 1(b) of Reg. 139/2004.

[111] G. Gundlach, D. Moss, 'The Role of Efficiencies in Antitrust Law: Introduction and Overview' (2015) 60(2), The Antitrust Bulletin, 91–102 ff.

[112] MOFCOM Decision of 18 March 2009.

is well known in "coordinative" antitrust legal regimes such as the Chinese one.[113] However, they have recently gained importance in other contexts.

In 2016, the South African Competition Commission evaluated a proposed merger between Coca-Cola Beverages Africa Limited and series of other enterprises operating in the field of beverages bottling.[114] In approving the merger, the Commission laid out several conditionalities concerning, among the others, (i) the guarantee that a certain percentage of raw goods supplies would be purchased from domestic operators; (ii) the maintenance of several productive chains in South Africa; (iii) the investment of a certain amount of capital in R&D projects in South Africa and concerning South African black personnel.

In this way, in concrete, antitrust authorities interact with corporations at the level of business strategies and seek to influence, on the basis of public interest considerations, the future development of corporate plans.

The whole concept of "efficiency" of market regulation is updated and comes to comprise several elements regarding socio-economic development, sustainability, etc. On the other hand, this approach to antitrust regulation undoubtedly opens new spaces for lobbying and reinforces the idea of antitrust law as a "sponge",[115] an inherently open and porous system, easily influenced by non-purely market-driven instances and, on top of all, strongly coordinative in its nature.

4.3 Investment Regulation

In December 2018, Indian Foreign Investment Law saw the introduction of a rule which raised the attention of many observers around the world. The rule prohibits FDIs in the so-called "inventory model" of e-commerce, that is the model "where inventory of goods and services is owned by ecommerce entity and is sold to the consumers directly".[116] In other words, such provision wants foreign e-commerce operators (e.g. Amazon, Flipkart) to rely on domestic sellers and act as a mere intermediary or facilitator between the consumer and the producer/retailer.

The real impact of such rule on the Indian digital market is still uncertain and up to debate. The regulatory intervention, however, proves that Investment Law is a globally recognized tool to harmonize MNCs' planning strategies and public economic interests.

[113] J. Clarke, 'Current Issues in Merger Law' in J. Duns, A. Duke, B. Sweeney (eds), *Comparative Competition Law* (Edward Elgar 2015), 189–190.

[114] The decision was first issued by the Competition Commission and later confirmed by the Competition Tribunal with decision n. LM243Mar15.

[115] A. Ezrachi, 'Sponge' (2017) 5, Journal of Antitrust Enforcement, 49–75.

[116] *See* Indian Ministry of Commerce & Industry, Review of policy on Foreign Direct Investment (FDI) in e-commerce, 26 December 2018.

The critical role of Investment Law in the balance between state policies and public interest is well attested among scholars.[117] From this perspective, Asia offers interesting examples of how international investment legal regimes empower states to coordinate their development policies with those of MNCs. For instance, the Indian reform fits into an evolutionary pattern which already produced, in 2016, a new model of Bilateral Investment Treaty (BIT) whose attention to public policy has been emphasized by scholars.[118]

The model BIT shapes, in the first place, a notion of investment which requires a significance for the development of the country where the investment is made. In practice, such clause widens the interpretative discretion enjoyed by arbitral tribunals in investment disputes. Furthermore, the model BIT seems to aim at protecting the discretion of public powers in regulation the investment regime. Arbitrariness as a ground to challenge the behaviour of the host state is notably absent from the model.[119] On the other hand, the non-precluded measures clause lists a wide array of occurrences.[120]

In such regulatory framework, as in antitrust law, the integration among different instances is mainly carried out through definition of discretionary powers of wide clauses. A clearer functionalization of investments to public policies is instead shaped, on a legislative level, by the Chinese legal order.[121] The Measures for the Administration of Overseas Investment of Enterprises (MAOIE) of 2017 design a mechanism of prior approval for project investment managed by the National Development and Reform Commission and based on four main criteria (art 26): (1) compliance with Chinese laws and regulations, (2) compliance with development plans and macroeconomic policies, (3) compliance with international treaties and agreements and (4) compliance with national interest and security. Correspondingly, the Foreign Investment Law provides (art 14) for the state to "encourage and direct foreign investors to invest in particular industries, fields and regions" on the basis of the needs of "national economic and social development".

The coordinative effort here operates both inward and outward. Chinese enterprises investing abroad are required to act according to projects evaluated on the basis of national economic policies. On the other hand, foreign enterprises investing in China are encouraged to select particular fields of action. In practice, this means that in those fields, approval procedure may be smoother and evaluations less strict.

Investment Law is an increasingly relevant instrument of macroeconomic regulation and an essential feature of every coherent industrial policy. The incidence

---

[117] J. Chaisse, T. Ishikawa, S. Jusoh (eds), *Asia's Changing International Investment Regime* (Springer 2017) 13–21.

[118] P. Ranjan, 'Investment Protection and Host State's Right to Regulate in the Indian Model Bilateral Investment Treaty: Lessons for Asian Countries', in Chaisse, Ishikawa, Jusoh (n 117), 52.

[119] Ranjan (n 118), 56–58.

[120] Ranjan (n 118), 59–61.

[121] On the Chinese legal model for investments, *see* L. Trakman, 'China's Regulation of Foreign Direct Investment', in J. Chaisse, T. Ishikawa, S. Jusoh (n 117), 67 ff.; G. Sabatino, 'The Legal Issues of "Going Global" and the Trans-Nationalisation of the Chinese Public-Private Partnership Model' (2019), Transnational Dispute Management, Advance Publication on May 2019.

that Chinese law exerts over private operators' business strategies is a quite unique example so far; however, the need to tighten control over investing foreign corporations, especially when mixed with geopolitical considerations, is a constant source of inspiration for evolving regulatory contexts. The most recent of them is the European one.

With Reg. n. 452/2019, the EU legislature established a general common framework for foreign investment screening, following the USA and China which already have such an instrument. As noted by scholars, the regulation reflected regulatory concerns of EU institutions for strategic financial operations carried out by foreign enterprises (especially Chinese state-owned enterprises or "SOEs") in relevant economic fields such as high-tech.[122] The regulation, indeed, does not establish a common mechanism. It just demands that MSs introduce one, striving towards a cooperation between the MSs and the Commission of the basis of the Common Commercial Policy (art 207 TFEU). The grounds for the screening mainly concern public security and public order. Art 4 of the regulation lists factors that may be considered when evaluating such broad criteria. Among them are the potential effect of the foreign investments over "critical infrastructure, whether physical or virtual, including (…) media, data processing or storage (…) critical technologies (…) access to sensitive information, including personal data, or the ability to control such information". Furthermore, MSs and the Commission may also consider, among others, whether the foreign investor is directly or indirectly controlled by the government.

It has been suggested that the new EU regulatory framework is not actually inspired by protectionist instances. It is, on the other hand, aimed at strengthening the bargaining power of the EU institutions in transnational trade relationships with other countries. The dynamic application of screening standards could, in other words, promote the establishment of comprehensive trade agreements, at the same time upholding European standards of evaluation.[123]

Within this framework, where do MNCs fit? Once again, their role is to take advantage of the discretional spaces left open by formal law. When controlled by public powers, MNCs (e.g. SOEs) effectively act as vehicles for public policies and, as such, must deal with the inevitable concerns transposed into the screening standards. They may, however, act as powerful intermediate bodies between governments, to direct the interpretation of positive rules as well as the drafting of new ones, in exchange for softer approaches towards their own strategies. The same role is played by privately owned MNCs, which, in these new rules, see other relevant spaces opened up for inter-institutional bargaining and lobbying to take place.

[122] W. Zwartkruis, B. De Jong, 'The EU Regulation on Screening of Foreign Direct Investment: A Game Changer?' (2019), European Business Law Review, forthcoming.

[123] S. Schill, 'The European Union's Foreign Direct Investment Screening Paradox: Tightening Inward Investment Control to Further External Investment Liberalization' (2019) 46(2), Legal Issues of Economic Integration, 105–128.

5 The Sovereign Wealth Funds: The State as a Global Entrepreneur

One phenomenon represents the attempt, from national states, to play their role in the market society by employing some of the typical structures of transnational global law. I am referring to the Sovereign Wealth Funds (SWFs).[124] Although these funds are becoming "*increasingly important players in the current international monetary and financial system*",[125] their proper definition is still debated. Functionally, they are "*special-purpose vehicles that invest sovereign assets in private financial markets*".[126] Their overseas focus has also justified their conceptual distinction from traditional SOEs.[127] Indeed, SWFs are not bound by the choice of the enterprise form. They may also function under special provisions of public law (i.e. as public economic entities) or as assets portfolios.[128] So far, most SWFs employ models of Western corporate governance,[129] but hold special organizational features. The first and probably most significant one is the absence of significant liabilities. SWFs are responsible only towards the government that owns them, so their liabilities may only be "intra-governmental".[130] They are indeed set up for the purpose of serving national development, although they may also be established for specific scopes, such as the Norwegian SWF.[131] When diversifying the investments, they therefore follow strategies indicated by the government. Such strategies always comprise a significant business dimension, at is obvious, but may also, exactly like private corporations, pursue other interests, such as the diffusion of standards of respect of human rights.[132]

Which planning strategies do SWFs develop? There are different categories. I have just mentioned one of them: a social enhancement planning strategy, linked to

---

[124] G. Clark, A. Dixon, A. Monk, *Sovereign Wealth Funds* (Princeton University Press 2013); Li Jing, 'State as an Entrepreneur: A Study of the Investment Contractual Terms and Level of Control of China's Sovereign Wealth Fund in its Portfolio Firms' (2015) 1, Peking University Transnational Law Review, 1 ff.; L. Backer, 'Sovereign Wealth Funds as Regulatory Chameleons: The Norwegian Sovereign Wealth Funds and Public Global Governance Through Private Global Investment' (2009) 41(2), Law Journal, 101–192; L. Backer, 'Sovereign Investing in Times of Crisis: Global Regulation of Sovereign Wealth Funds, State Owned Enterprises and the Chinese Experience' (2008) 19(1), Transnational Law & Contemporary Problems, 101–294; Mou Yinzhi (繆因知), 'Legal Regulation of Sovereign Wealth Funds from the perspective of State Owned Enterprises' (国有企业视野下的主权财富基金法律规制) (2014) 14, 经济法研究 (*jingjifayanjiu*), 267–279.

[125] Li Jing (n 127).

[126] G. Clark, A. Dixon, A. Monk (n 127).

[127] Mou Yinzhi (n 127).

[128] ibid.

[129] G. Clark, A. Dixon, A. Monk (n 127), 8.

[130] G. Clark, A. Dixon, A. Monk (n 127), 16.

[131] The scope of the Norway SWF is to support long-term management of oil revenues and facilitate savings to meet future pensions expenditures. Therefore, it has a specific social security scope.

[132] Mou (n 127); Backer (n 127, 2009).

stability of social security schemes as well as overseas promotion of ethical corporate standards. Furthermore, SWFs certainly pursue business goals and develop business plans. These may be mainly addressed to investments "*markets where value is captured*".[133] On the other hand, they may also support development of domestic firms, for example by ensuring domestic economies access to strategic resources.[134] Focusing on the national market, SWFs may also support domestic firms, for instance by granting them access to credit. In this case, the SWF functions as a sort of public development fund or a structural investment fund.[135]

Where a national legal system already employs a complex model of development planning, the SWF will tend to function as an implementing instrument of national plans. This is the case with the China Investment Corporation (CIC), the Chinese SWF. Directly controlled by the State Council, the CIC plays an essential role in the implementation of the "Going Global" strategy.[136]

SWFs are, in most cases, corporations. Their main scope is however to invest sovereign assets. Therefore, their influence over the global market takes the form of corporate investments in projects and other corporations. SWFs are thus able to exercise voting rights, as shareholders, in the corporations they participate in. In other words, through the exercise of voting rights, SWFs are able to introduce the instances of state development *in* private corporations. Being a particularly sensible issue, in some cases SWFs refrain from acquiring controlling stakes in corporations. Furthermore, they may renounce to exercise voting rights, as it happened when the CIC gave up the right to vote in the shareholders' assemblies of Blackstone, Morgan Stanley, Chesapeake Energy, Northstar Tambang Persada Ltd., EIG Global Energy Partners, and Cheniere Energy.[137]

So far the SWFs have been, in my opinion, the most effective legal instrument enacted by states in order to coordinate corporate planning, due to its structural nature. Focusing on the institutional aspects, SWFs are able to act as market players, taking advantage of market dynamics while pursuing public interests.

6 Conclusion

The fragmentation of global economic law is reconstructed in the shaping of institutional relations between economic actors. Among them, MNCs, in the past decades, acquired a capital role which has hardly been reflected by legislative developments. MNCs are not only formal legal entities established within the border of a state, but also semi-autonomous social orders, capable of establishing hierarchical structures and planning their own development. In the interaction between corporations and

---

133 G. Clark, A. Dixon, A. Monk (n 127), 40.

134 G. Clark, A. Dixon, A. Monk (n 127).

135 *See* for instance, the French "*Fonds Stratégique d'Investissement*", as assessed in ibid.

136 Backer (n 127, 2008).

137 Li Jing (n 127).

states, formal legal rules do not always prevail while corporations' "inner law" may exercise great influence over public institutions.

A comparative analysis of the instruments that different states have developed in order to interact, in the market, with corporations, shows, in my opinion, that a general reconsideration of economic law is slowly taking place. Highly discretional rules, with mixed results, are increasingly being favoured by public powers which, at the same time, openly engage in corporate activities through special legal forms.

Traditional instruments of international economic law appear unable to address these new interactions. On the other hand, relevant pieces of international soft law shaped an active role for MNCs in the pursuit of sustainable development strategies, a role that national legal orders are gradually incorporating into positive rules. What responsibility regimes cannot achieve, however, is a coordination, at the level of business strategies, among the different actors involved. From this perspective, foreign investment and market competition control make full use of their inherent "variable geometries" to build interactive frameworks between public and private powers of the global economy.

Gianmatteo Sabatino PhD (Trento), Research Fellow in Comparative and European Law at the Sino-Italian Institute of the Zhongnan University of Economics and Law.

Sovereign Wealth Funds and Public Value Theory

Usman W. Chohan

1 Introduction

Sovereign wealth funds (SWFs) have emerged as a promising model for the public management of strategic resources in a globalised financial system with its concomitant market-based logic. In other words, SWFs are structured as state-owned institutions that hold the proceeds of key resources in trust for the furtherance of the public good but operate via the deployment of a capital endowment towards market-oriented activities and asset classes. As such, SWFs represent a co-mingling of public trust and private interest, and this generates a set of unique traits in their value proposition to society. This chapter aims to delve into the nature of those traits using the lens of *public value theory*,[1] which represents an important discourse in the domain of public administration.[2] Such a line of enquiry contributes to the literature in two reciprocal ways. First, it helps to underscore the balance that SWFs must strike in creating value for the public while reconciling the realities and impositions of private interest in the realm of the market. Second, it informs a subjacent question in the public administration literature about how public managers can co-create value through interesting and novel arrangements, wherein SWFs are a particularly intriguing and hitherto unexplored case study.

To that end, it is important to provide a glimpse of public value's premises as they pertain to this chapter's discourse.[3] Public value describes the purpose of public

[1] *See* the founder Mark Moore's introductory work to public value in Mark Moore, *Creating Public Value: Strategic Management in Government* (Harvard University Press 1995), 22.

[2] For a fuller review and more rigorous treatment of public value theory, see various chapters in Usman Chohan. *Public Value and Budgeting: International Perspectives* (Routledge 2019).

[3] ibid.

U. W. Chohan (✉)
Director, Economic Affairs & National Development, Centre for Aerospace and Security Studies (CASS), Islamabad, Pakistan
e-mail: cass.thinkers@gmail.com

J. Chaisse et al. (eds.), *Regulation of State-Controlled Enterprises*, International Law and the Global South, https://doi.org/10.1007/978-981-19-1368-6_14

Table 1 Some precepts of public value

Public value precept	Explanation
Measurement	Public value begins by noting that the performance or contribution of the public sector cannot be measured as neatly as that of the private sector. The art is nevertheless to decipher "what" value is being created by the public sector
Collaboration	Public value stipulates that politicians, as democratically elected representatives of the people, should be the "final arbiters" of value; and public managers should take note of the democratic element that drives the articulation of society's values
Value arbitration	Public value stresses the need for public managers to "co-create" value with other stakeholders in society, rather than compete with them or operate alone
Imagination	Public managers are thought to wield a "value-seeking imagination" and sense of enterprise that propels them to create value for the public
Short-termism	Public value asserts that public managers have a duty to look beyond the neoliberal ethos of short-term results (such as quarterly reporting) and seek to create lasting value in a dynamic environment

Source Author's Research

administrative institutions, as well as their primary agent: the "public manager", as being one of co-creating value with other agents in society—notably politicians and citizens. Public managers are therefore to work in concert with other agents to (1) create value for the public and (2) translate the values that are articulated by the public.[4] Five precepts of public value theory shall be considered in this chapter: measurement, collaboration, value arbitration, imagination, and short-termism. These can be expressed in Table 1. Each of these precepts will be systematically examined to illustrate how public value theory's assumptions can be fruitfully re-contextualised through sovereign wealth funds. But to proceed along that line of enquiry, some definitional work is required.

For this chapter, SWFs include those state-owned investment management entities worldwide that have a mandate to manage a capital endowment in the public trust through investments in asset classes that increase the returns to the pooled endowment for future generations. The International Monetary Fund (IMF) divides SWFs into five categories according to the Santiago principles[5]: stabilisation funds, savings funds, pensions reserve funds, and reserve investment funds, and reserve investment corporations. SWFs now constitute a significant presence in the global investment

[4] *See* John Benington, 'Creating the public in order to create public value?' (2009) 32(3/4) International Journal of Public Administration, 40.

[5] The Santiago Principles are generally accepted principles and practices that reflect SWF structures and operations, *see* Abdullah Al-Hassan, Michael Papaioannou, Martin Skancke, and Cheng Chih Sung, 'Sovereign wealth funds: Aspects of governance structures and investment management' (International Monetary Fund 2013) No. 13–23), 4–5.

space. According to the Sovereign Wealth Fund Institute (SWFI), they accounted for $7.4 trillion in assets in 2017, representing a more than doubling of the $3.4 trillion that they held a decade prior.[6] Out of this, $4.2 trillion in assets were held by extractive industry funds, indicating the overarching consideration among these funds to preserve and grow capital for future generations from extractive activity.[7] Some of the most well-known among these include the SWFs of Norway, Kuwait, and Saudi Arabia. However, the SWF of China, known in English as the *China Investment Corporation* (CIC), has roughly $1 trillion in assets under management and has not depended on an extractive resource endowment. This speaks to the diversity of the SWF cohort internationally.

According to survey data from the International Forum for Sovereign Wealth Funds (IFSWF), SWFs tend to allocate 70% of their funds to foreign markets rather than their domestic capital markets, and their bias tends to be towards developed capital markets (rather than emerging ones) since more than 90% of their allocations go to asset classes in developed countries.[8] In addition, 70% of their assets are on listed exchanges, with only 30% falling in the category of off-index illiquid assets. In my judgement, this indicates a preference for (1) stability, (2) diversification, and (3) liquidity in their endowments and speaks to the adherence to a public commitment for value creation. Yet the degree to which active portfolio management is undertaken is not definitive, according to the IFSWF data, since only 55% of global SWF fund allocation is done actively, with the remainder put into passive management.[9]

Nevertheless, while there is considerable diversity among the global cohort of SWFs, they can nonetheless be characterised by certain shared traits. The first is that they recognise the role for state-owned (public) administration of strategic resources in the public interest. The second is that they delve into the market's logic of growing an endowment through re-investment in assets that are tradeable in markets. The third is that they are given a degree of leeway to exercise judgement in managing their portfolios. The fourth is that they show a recognition of the need to have sustainable intergenerational fiscal outcomes. These common threads connecting their functional logic make them pertinent to explorations within the discourse of public value. Furthermore, it is how SWFs successfully transcend the dichotomy between state and market that enables them to advance the public value literature, since it has been

---

[6] *See* Sovereign Wealth Fund Institute, 'Sovereign Wealth Research and Statistics' (2017) <https://www.swfinstitute.org/research>.

[7] Extractive industries include the oil and natural gas sectors, along with other non-renewable sectors.

[8] International Forum of Sovereign Wealth Funds (IFSWF). 'New challenges, private markets: Sovereign wealth funds' changing investment strategies. Subcommittee 2: Investment & Risk Management' (November 2016).

[9] ibid.

noted that this dichotomy has held back theorisations within public value,[10] notable vis-à-vis agents such as civil society.[11]

With that in mind, the structure of the remainder of this chapter adheres to the following general outline: each of the assumptions mentioned above about public managers in public value theory is reconsidered using the lens of SWFs. These include measurement, collaboration, value arbitration, imagination, and short-termism. After that, a concluding section examines how public value theory itself can be pushed forward through novel lenses such as SWFs, so as to advance the public administration literature.

2 One: Measurement

Public value theory begins with a consideration of the inherent difficulty in measuring the quantity/quality of value that is created by the public sector.[12] As opposed to private agents, who have metrics such as return on investment (ROI), dividends per share (DPS), or earnings per share (EPS), the public sector does not and cannot have an identical set of rubrics.[13] As Chohan notes:

> Part of [public value's founder, Mark] Moore's impetus was in fact to juxtapose public management with private sector performance so as to find metrics that did justice to the contribution of public managers to society. Indeed, the argument went both ways: the private sector could also learn from the value creation by governments. It is easy to measure private sector value creation through the bottom-line metric of profit. By contrast, the public sector's value creation cannot be measured through any "profit" form of bottom line, and in fact part of their value creation might be in undertaking loss-making activities, negative in "profit" terms, for the public good. But public managers do provide *some* form of good [emphasis in the original], and public value is in essence a debate around what this value is, how it can be measured, and how it can be enhanced.[14]

Along these lines, it has also been remarked that public value was constructed as a public service "parallel to a corporate bottom line or a stock price" but by contrast "described benefits that applied to all of society".[15] Similarly, public value would extend beyond "narrow monetary outcomes to include that which benefits and is

---

[10] This argument was put forth in John Benington (2009, n 4), 40.

[11] Recent work has sought to address this gap in the public value literature, such as civil society explorations in Chohan (n 2), 21–40.

[12] *See* John Alford, and Janine O'Flynn, 'Making sense of public value: Concepts, critiques and emergent meanings' (2009) 32(3/4) International Journal of Public Administration, 171–191.

[13] That said, much effort has been made as part of a neoliberal wave in the public administration of the Anglosphere countries to mirror public sector performance along private sector rubrics. This movement is generally termed *New Public Management* (NPM).

[14] *See* Usman Chohan (n 2), 2.

[15] *See* Mark Prebble. 'Is "we" singular? The nature of public value' (2016) 48(2) *American Review of Public Administration*, 114.

valued by the citizenry more generally".[16] Therefore, public value has sought to identify the modes by which the public sector creates value. Invariably, this effort has faced immense limitations and left public value bereft of empirical rigour.[17] It is an important aspect of this chapter to highlight that sovereign wealth funds offer an interesting case where a public managerial organisation *does* inherently measure its value creation through private sector rubrics. This is attributable to their participation in a market-based logic, whereby they must grow and preserve the capital in their endowments through strategic investments that earn measurable returns over a long-term horizon.

The most salient metrics used for measuring the value created by SWFs are those that pertain to the realm of investment management.[18] Investment management firms may have their returns gauged on an absolute or relative basis in the private sector.[19] For absolute returns, the net positive/negative change in the fund value matters, which is why it is commonly used by many (but not all) SWFs. The contrasting relative return basis measures the performance of a fund in comparison to a benchmark index. For example, an SWF measuring the returns of its global equities portfolio may use an index such as the MSCI World index and compare its portfolio's performance over periodic intervals relative to the index. Relative performance reflects an active portfolio management approach, but survey data indicates that nearly half (45%) of SWFs use a passive investing approach.[20] In passive approaches, a portfolio consists of instruments that directly track the movements of an index (or multiple indices), thereby reproducing very closely (if not identically)[21] the returns that would be earned by simply investing in the index itself. The most common method of directing a passive approach is to invest in exchange-traded funds (ETFs), and since the global financial crisis (GFC) of 2008, ETFs have gained increasing popularity at the expense of actively managed portfolios.[22]

Considering the current international financial landscape (as of this writing), SWFs are facing difficulties in creating value due to their overinvestment in developed markets, because of which they face "a low-growth, low-yield environment" where there are "greater challenges to make high enough returns to meet their mandates".[23] The present juncture in capital markets is characterised by "bond yields at near-record lows, over $13 trillion of fixed-income securities commanding negative interest rates, and global stock markets looking increasingly volatile or overvalued", which exacts

---

[16] *See* Iestyn Williams and Heather Shearer, 'Appraising public value: Past, present and futures' (2011) 89(4) *Public Administration*, 1367.

[17] ibid.

[18] *See* Shai Bernstein, Josh Lerner, Antoinette Schoar, 'The investment strategies of sovereign wealth funds' (2013) 27(2) *Journal of Economic Perspectives*, 219–38.

[19] *See* Amnon Schreiber, 'Economic indices of absolute and relative riskiness' (2014) 56(2) *Economic Theory*, 309–331.

[20] IFSWF (n 8).

[21] Mitch Kosev and Thomas Williams, 'Exchange-traded funds' (March 2011) RBA Bulletin, 51–59.

[22] *See* discussion in Joanne M. Hill, Dave Nadig, and Matt Hougan, 'A comprehensive guide to exchange-traded funds (ETFs)' (2015) CFA Institute Research Foundation.

[23] IFSWF (n 8).

pressures on SWFs to earn returns on their endowment. At the same time, international headwinds such as US-China tensions hatch the sort of uncertainty which long-run investors such as SWFs seek to avoid.[24,25] To put it another way, market trends present challenges for the value creation of SWFs, even as it may be more measurable than that of public managers traditionally studied in public value theory.

3 Two: Collaboration

There are three ways in which collaboration can be situated within the case context of SWFs: traditional public value collaboration, market-based collaboration, and collaboration through distributed dividends to the public. To take the first form, it is worth noting that traditional forms of collaborative value creation in public value theory involve the nexus of interactions between public managers and other social agents, particularly civil society and politicians. In the context of SWFs, the relationship between SWF public managers and political structures can hold significant importance. In parliamentary systems, SWFs are generally established under the auspices of parliament, which can then be seen as "owners" of SWFs.[26] Then there is a degree of interaction between SWFs and other bureaucratic structures. As an alternative to parliamentary control, Ministries of Finance can also be designated as "owners" of SWFs. In addition, the auditor-general plays a bureaucratic accountability role vis-à-vis SWFs in many countries.[27] These are some of the traditionally understood forms of interaction that can lead to public value co-creation. As the IMF notes, "close coordination with macroeconomic policies and the management of other assets and liabilities in the public sector is essential",[28] which is to say that coordinated public manager collaboration is necessary to achieve a greater magnitude of value creation.

The second form of collaboration is of the sort that pertains to SWFs' challenge to competition within financial markets. The tone prevalent in contemporary microeconomic theory suggests that economic growth is bolstered by a degree of competition[29] so long as it does not turn firms into extractive monopolies.[30] This notion was perhaps best encapsulated by the Schumpeterian notion of *creative destruction*, whereby the ceaseless competition among many private agents would ultimately lead

---

[24] The issue of their long-term orientation is discussed in a subsequent section.

[25] However, depending on the root of their endowment, SWFs may gain disproportionately from specific forms of market moves such as spikes in commodity prices.

[26] Al-Hassan, Papaioannou and others (n 5), 12.

[27] ibid.

[28] Al-Hassan, Papaioannou and others (n 5), 3.

[29] *See* Torsten Persson, and Guido Tabellini, *Political economics* (MIT Press 2016).

[30] This discourse has a long history in the economics discipline, *see* George Stigler, 'The economists and the problem of monopoly' (1982) Occasional Papers L. Sch. U. Chi., 19, 1.

to more creative outbursts of energy and economic growth.[31] Yet this sense of competition was deliberately challenged in the public administration literature, historically because of its emphasis on developing sound regulations and administrative exercise over society,[32] but more recently in public value theory due to its sentiment of greater value achieved through collaborative approaches.[33] As mentioned earlier, public value theory asserts that public managers must co-create value through engagement with other stakeholders in society.[34] The logic of competition does not sit well with the spirit of public value and nor does it cohere with the praxis of sovereign wealth funds.

SWFs are significant players in global markets, given the trillions of dollars under their management. As such, any moves that would even be considered "moderate" at their scale could risk causing upheaval in financial markets. This has colloquially been termed the *whale effect* in niche financial spaces such as cryptocurrencies,[35] where particularly large players can move the markets suddenly and dramatically for personal gain. It is a general trait of SWFs that they do not make significant market moves due to the disruptions that this would entail.[36] As the speed of trading in technologically overburdened financial markets approaches the scale of milliseconds, any sudden moves would risk creating a cascade effect at the onset of market panic.

In such circumstances, the public managerial ethos of SWFs, as one of preserving a capital endowment through careful long-term investing,[37] acts as a counterweight to the competitive psyche of private players in financial markets. SWFs thus act as public managers ensuring greater stability in markets.[38] This is all the more evident due to their preference for assets in developed markets, their penchant for liquid investments, and their propensity towards passive investing. This approach should be drawn into the public value sensibility towards collaboration rather than competition. Most SWFs measure capital preservation and growth on an absolute basis,[39] with long-term investments that sidestep the zero-sum approach of many large financial institutions of private interest.

---

[31] An illustrative economic model includes Philippe Aghion and Peter Howitt, 'A model of growth through creative destruction' (1990) National Bureau of Economic Research No. w3223.

[32] Murray Horn. *The political economy of public administration: Institutional choice in the public sector* (CUP 1995).

[33] Much of the original work on collaborative public value came from the founder Mark Moore himself, *see* Mark Moore and John Donahue, *Ports in a Storm: Public Management in a Turbulent World* (Brookings 2012).

[34] I believe the absence of private interest as an agent of value co-creation is a significant omission which public value theory must begin to confront.

[35] Usman W. Chohan, 'Cryptocurrencies and Inequality' (2019) Notes on the 21st Century (CBRI).

[36] Bernstein, Lerner and Schoar (n 18), 219–38.

[37] Raphael Lam, and Marco Rossi, 'Sovereign wealth funds–investment strategies and financial distress' (2010) 15(4) Journal of Derivatives & Hedge Funds, 304–322.

[38] *See* their role in stability promotion in Al-Hassan, Papaioannou and others (n 5).

[39] IFSWF (n 8).

The third form of collaboration that applies to SWFs is in the distribution of dividends to a broader public. It has been argued, above all by adherents of the monetarist school in economics,[40] that typical private institutional players in financial markets have first and foremost a responsibility to maximise shareholder value,[41] after that proceeding to other considerations including corporate social responsibility (which is itself contentious both in theory and praxis).[42] Companies that follow this premise centre their concerns on their shareholder base, and their earnings are distributed via dividends to this comparatively narrow group of equity-holders. For sovereign wealth funds, by contrast, the dividends and capital appreciation that they realise flows out to a larger base of citizens. In other words, the proceeds of SWFs are distributable to all members of a sovereign entity, and by this account, SWFs create value in a collaborative sense for a wider public. This broader stakeholder base of citizens explains why the value contribution of SWFs through financial investments is greater than that of private financial institutions, and SWFs, therefore, represent a useful value-creation model for a more expansively constructed public.

4 Three: Short-Termism

Public value is an outcomes-based approach that evaluates meaningfully over the long run,[43] and public institutions, therefore, require approaches that encapsulate a more extended horizon in their value creation efforts. However, financial markets are characterised by an in-built short-termism attributable to the need for the regular reporting of performance, often quarterly.[44] Due to the pressures of reporting periodic performance, there is a distortionary decision-making calculus in the executive circles of listed companies that have to report their successes or failures to shareholders at the risk of adjustments to the price of their stocks.[45] This short-termism detracts from the ability to make decisions that, while perhaps challenging in the immediate term, tend to confer longer-term benefits to organisations. This also reflects why, in contrast to the generally long careers for senior public managers within traditionally understood bureaucracies, CEO tenure rates at "blue-chip" companies are comparatively low,

[40] *See* review in George Tavlas, 'Was the Monetarist Tradition Invented?' (1998) 12(4) *Journal of Economic Perspectives*, 211–222.

[41] *See* the Miltonian argument as weighed in H. Jeff Smith, 'The Shareholders vs. Stakeholders Debate' (2003) 44(4) *MIT Sloan Management Review.*

[42] *See* a critique in Denni Arli, Patrick van Esch, Gavin Northey, Michael S. Lee and Radu. Dimitriu, 'Hypocrisy, skepticism, and reputation: the mediating role of corporate social responsibility' (forthcoming) *Marketing Intelligence & Planning.*

[43] Benington (n 4), 40.

[44] *See* critique in John R. Graham, Campbell R. Harvey, Shiva Rajgopal, 'Value destruction and financial reporting decisions' (2006) 62(6) Financial Analysts Journal, 27–39.

[45] *See* early work in Robert G. May, 'The influence of quarterly earnings announcements on investor decisions as reflected in common stock price changes' (1971) *Journal of Accounting Research*, 119–163.

since shareholders can switch between owning the stock of one company and another in deep capital markets rather quickly and can punish a company's stock value through share sell-offs when presented with unfavourable periodic reports.[46]

Sovereign wealth funds, by contrast, follow a pattern of long-term holdings in reputable assets to realise capital appreciation over a longer timeframe.[47] Their buy-and-hold strategies are geared towards maintaining capital values through conservative and patient investment.[48] SWFs would be loath to engage in market sell-offs or trigger market panic, as mentioned earlier, despite their capability of doing so given their large asset holdings. Indeed, the "benchmark of legitimacy ensures that the capital of the SWF is not immediately spent and instead is gradually disbursed across the present and future generations".[49] Furthermore, "the long-term horizon requires an SWF to consider the long-run equilibrium benchmark of the markets in which the SWF invests and the long-term externalities affecting the SWF".[50] This sense of awareness about the externalities of investments characterises the public value creation of SWFs as one of stable investments made in public trust for future generations. This, however, may come with trade-offs in terms of returns. Certain studies indicate that SWFs may not provide the sorts of risk-adjusted long-term returns that other institutional investors may provide.[51] However, further research on the broader sample of international SWFs, over a fuller time horizon, is necessary for this to be conclusively determined. Nevertheless, the IMF notes that "SWFs that were heavily invested in equities [did] experience large losses from sharp declines in equity markets [during the financial crisis of 2008–09], but they recovered most of the losses in the subsequent years by demonstrating their willingness to be long-term investors and riding out the financial turmoil".[52]

---

[46] *See* analysis by Dan Marcec, 'CEO Tenure Rates' (2018) *Harvard Law School Forum*. Available at: <https://corpgov.law.harvard.edu/2018/02/12/ceo-tenure-rates/>.

[47] An exception to this long-term orientation of SWFs is the subcategory of 'stabilisation funds', which are more short-term in their investment horizon and tend to remain confined to highly liquid assets as emergency-response instruments.

[48] This is particularly true for pension funds & savings funds/.

[49] *See* Andrew Ang, 'The four benchmarks of sovereign wealth funds' (2010) *Corporate Finance: Governance, Corporate Control & Organization eJournal* SSRN: 1680485.

[50] ibid.

[51] *See* Bernardo Bortolotti, Veljko Fotak, and William L. Megginson, 'The sovereign wealth fund discount: Evidence from public equity investments' (2015) 28(11) *The Review of Financial Studies*, 2993–3035.

[52] Al-Hassan, Papaioannou and others (n 5), 3.

5 Four: Imagination

The founder of public value, Mark Moore, emphasised the need for public managers to deploy a "value-seeking imagination",[53] whereby they would draw upon a sense of enterprise in pursuing their value-creation efforts.[54] This would entail a degree of creativity and "judgmental latitude",[55] along with recognising the responsibilities and risks that important decisions involve. SWFs represent an interesting and somewhat more evident example of Moore's value-seeking imagination because the public managers of SWFs are afforded an opportunity to deploy capital and engage in portfolio management with a considerable degree of judgemental latitude, including decisions on various portfolio parameters such as asset selection and allocation.

However, they are still bound by the contours of their official mandate, and they are also accountable for significant portfolio-related decisions that they take, whether by a parliament, finance ministry, or auditor-general. To exceed the confines of their mandate might constitute a breach of public trust. But it should be remembered that such mandates are not just the exclusive purview of SWFs and apply more generally to any institutional investors that must act with fiduciary duty. Similarly, exceeding the risk-bearing capacity (risk tolerance) stipulated for the SWF would also act as a violation of trust. For this reason, many SWFs, such as those of Chile, New Zealand, and Singapore, have explicit stipulations for their risk tolerance.[56] In that sense, private institutional investors and SWFs are not dissimilar in their adherence to various investment mandates and guidelines.[57]

That said, the value-seeking imagination of public managers at SWFs may not always be sought upon, since roughly 45% of SWFs do not pursue active management strategies but instead rely on passive investing approaches. Passive investing requires far less judgemental latitude and cannot, therefore, be thought of as an avenue of imaginative value creation per se. There is a parallel to be drawn here between the degrees of public manager value creation through active vs passive investing and the work on advisory vs costings roles that have been developed in the public value literature.[58] According to this framework, which draws upon Legislative Budget Offices (LBOs) as its lens, the value-seeking imagination behind advisory work creates a higher degree of public value, but it also turns into a more politically contentious risk for the public managers. By contrast, the mechanistic costings work of public managers creates a lesser (albeit still important) degree of public value,

[53] *See* foundational work in Moore (n 1), 22.

[54] The degree to which public managers have channelled such an imagination is considered in various case studies within Chohan (n 2).

[55] ibid, 68.

[56] A useful analysis can be found at the International Monetary Fund, *see* Al-Hassan Papaioannou and others (n 5).

[57] ibid.

[58] The pioneering work on advisory-costings framework can be found in Usman W. Chohan, Kerry Jacobs (2017) 40(12) Public value in politics: A legislative budget office approach. *International Journal of Public Administration,* 1063–1073.

but it tends to be less politically contentious.[59] Similarly, the active management of funds involves using a greater value-seeking imagination for fund managers, but it also entails greater risks in the case of relative or absolute asset value decline. By contrast, passive management involves lesser judgemental latitude but also entails lesser risk for SWF public managers. SWFs have been designed to reflect these trade-offs differently across countries, and this is expressed in their differing mandates for active or passive management.

6 Five: Value Arbitration

Public value proposes that, as part of a democratic dispensation, public managers should recognise politicians as the "final arbiters of value".[60] The premise of conferring such powers to politicians over public managers represents one response to a long tussle in the discipline of public administration known as the *politics-administration dichotomy*.[61] A growing body of research argues that in fact public manager deference to politicians, as argued initially in public value, faces severe limitations, whether due to political interference, anti-expertise sentiment, and a veering towards illiberal democracies, among a host of other problems.[62] It remains a point of heated contention in public value (not to mention public administration more broadly) whether the dichotomy should really be resolved on the terms of politicians.

Yet, in the case of SWFs, the dichotomy requires more nuance. On the one hand, SWF public managers enjoy a mandate to pursue value creation without *direct* political meddling (in general). Yet, they are still bound by rules and structures of accountability to politicians. For example, the IMF observes the following:

> The owner of the SWF is typically the central government. The parliament approves the laws that establish the legal structure of the SWF and, thus, the legal basis for its operations. Depending on the general division of authority between the parliament and the executive branch of government, parliament may also have a role in determining the appropriate aggregate risk level of the SWF.

At the same time, there is a considerable difference between the countries that have established SWFs for any generalisations about their political architectures to be made effectively, and public value theory must begin to encapsulate this heterogeneity. Consider countries as diverse as Norway, Saudi Arabia, China, the UAE, Canada, Singapore, and Chile. The diversity in their political arrangements creates a wide array of outcomes for public managers within SWFs. Nevertheless, despite their heterogeneity, the inference from various studies is that the aim of SWFs is economic

---

59 ibid.

60 *See* Moore (n 1), 22.

61 *See* Usman W. Chohan, 'Independent Budget Offices and the Politics–Administration Dichotomy. International' (2018) 41(12) *Journal of Public Administration*, 1009–1017.

62 Each of these limitations is discussed in Chohan (n 2).

and not political.[63] In fact, it is now being forcefully argued that the various concerns that were largely held in the 2000s about the influence of sovereign wealth funds in politics have largely been dispelled by observations of their praxis.[64] Politics, of course, is not just internal or domestic when it comes to SWFs. International politics also risks being affected by the influence of SWFs on financial markets, not to mention risks relating to espionage, market manipulation, and internal security challenges. Further research is required in this regard, but the current appreciation of this issue seems to be that the fears of SWF interference in these domains have remained largely unfounded.[65]

Irrespective of the political arrangements by which they are bound, the literature expresses a consensus on the idea that governance structures play an important role in the successful oversight and function of SWFs.[66] As authors at the IMF explain:

> The governance structure must ensure a clear division of roles and responsibilities between the various governing bodies, as well as operational independence for the manager and a supervisory system with appropriate checks and balances. This is necessary in order to build legitimacy for sovereign investment, reduce risk of fraud and mismanagement, and build a competent investment organisation.[67]

Given that the legitimacy of public managerial institutions is an important consideration in public value creation,[68] SWFs must ensure that their investment mandate is fulfilled in a responsible manner. The sense of legitimacy that SWFs may enjoy depends ineluctably on their successful performance as fund managers, but so too does it depend on their relationships with other bureaucratic and political structures, such as the auditor-general, Ministry of Finance, and/or parliament, among others. Do these institutions act as "arbiters" of an SWF's value creation? To a significant degree, it can be said that they do, but as discussed in an earlier section on the measurement of value, what sets SWFs apart from other public managerial institutions is that their value creation can and does follow a market-based logic and therefore market-based performance metrics such as return on investment (ROI) and fund outperformance. Therefore, the market is another agent, heretofore seldom considered in the public value literature, which must also be considered an arbiter of value.

---

[63] *See* Bader Alhashel, 'Sovereign Wealth Funds: a literature review' (2015) 78 *Journal of Economics and Business*, 1–13.

[64] *See* Christopher Balding, 'A portfolio analysis of sovereign wealth funds' in *Sovereign Wealth: The Role of State Capital in the New Financial Order* (2011), 43–70.

[65] ibid.

[66] *See* analysis in Al-Hassan, Papaioannou, and others (n 5).

[67] ibid, 3.

[68] *See* legitimacy in the strategic triangle of public value in Chohan and Jacobs (n 58), 1063–1073.

7 The Public Value of SWFs

Since its inception nearly three decades ago, public value has become a mainstay in public administration scholarship due to its emphasis on the contribution of public managers to society as co-creators of value. Yet much of the scholarship on public value has found itself relegated to traditional forms of public administrative institutions. As a result, its examinations have yet not sufficiently pierced the veil that enshrouds longstanding questions in public administration, including the measurement of value, the arbitration of value in the politics-administration dichotomy, the long-term approach to value creation, and the purpose of a value-seeking imagination. This chapter has sought to demonstrate that applying new lenses to the extant public value discourse can help push the dialogue forward, specifically through the examination of novel types of public manager institutions. In that context, sovereign wealth funds have demonstrated their utility as a lens in revisiting old questions.

The nature of enquiry in this chapter is reciprocal since public value helps to theorise on the value creation of SWFs as well, particularly in light of their co-mingling of public trust and private interest that generates a set of unique traits. First, SWF creates value through a collaborative process in three ways: distributing the dividends of their fund endowments to a broader public. They collaborate with other public institutions. And they maintain a long-term presence in financial markets that, in turn, improves market integrity and stability. Second, they offer an example of how precisely the value contribution of a public managerial institution can be measured, using the logic of market-based portfolio returns. Third, they allow for an evaluation of value over the longer-run, since they overcome the short-termism that too often characterises private interest in financial markets. Fourth, SWFs permit the deployment of a value-seeking imagination when they are premised on active portfolio management strategies requiring fund managers' inputs and judgments. Fifth, they present a nuanced example of value arbitration since, while they act in an independent expert capacity, they are nevertheless tied into the accountability architecture that might include parliaments, auditors-general, and finance ministries.

As such, SWFs can be more deeply conceptualised by regarding them as a case in the realm of public administration, but a unique one in that they strike a balance in creating value for the public while reconciling the realities and impositions of private interest through the market. In other words, SWFs have emerged as a promising model for the public management of strategic resources in a globalised financial system with its concomitant market-based logic since they have successfully transcended the dichotomy between state and market. Further research must delve into such examples of unique public managerial institutions to enrich the scholarly study of value creation by public institutions.

7 The Public Value of SWFs

The Accountability of State Capitalism: Exploring the Forms of Liabilities

'*Un Somaro Piumato*' ('A Befeathered Ass')—Rethinking the Scope and Nature of State Liability for Acts of Their Commercial Instrumentalities: State-Owned Enterprises and State Owner Liability in the Post-global

Larry Catá Backer

1 Introduction

> The development of the productive forces is also a kind of revolution — a very important one. It is the most fundamental revolution from the viewpoint of historical development.[1]
>
> *Un somaro, ma solenne. Quando a un tratto, ho che portento! Su le spalle a cento a cento Gli spuntavano le penne Ed in alto, fsct, volò! Ed in cima a un campanile Come in trono si fermò.* [A ass, but solemn. When all of a sudden, oh what a wonder! Up on his back in the

[1] Deng Xiaoping, "To Build Socialism We Must First Develop the Productive Forces" (Marxists.org, 5 May 1980) <https://www.marxists.org/reference/archive/deng-xiaoping/1980/101.htm accessed 22 June 2021>. The reference here is to the Chinese Marxist Leninist notion of economic capacity comprehensively understood. ibid. The idea was to shift the focus from the strict division of public and private of political-regulatory spheres and economic-productive spheres, in the interlinking of economic activity (in whatever form organised) and the political-regulatory authority (and objectives) of the state. At its base, it is grounded in the assumption that governmental interventions in markets must necessarily serve the interests of the state and augment, supplement or constitute an alternative form of objectives based regulatory and administrative authority. This forms a core premise of Chinese Marxist–Leninism enshrined in the Constitution of the Communist Party of China 24 October 2017 <http://www.xinhuanet.com//english/download/Constitution_of_the_Communist_Party_of_China.pdf> ("In building socialism in China, the basic tasks are to further release and develop the productive forces and gradually achieve socialist modernization and, to this end, reform those elements and areas within the relations of production and the superstructure that are unsuited to the development of the productive forces." ibid., General Program).

[2] Giacomo Rossini, *La Cenerentola* (Jacopo Ferretti (Librettist) premiered Teatro Valle, Rome, 26 January 1817), Act I, Scene 2, 'Miei rampolli femminini'. The reference is to an interrupted dream related by Don Magnifico to his two daughters about his triumph through their (marriage) activities. Don Magnifico and his daughters provide a buffo metaphor for the state and its enterprises in a larger context in which superior forces may yet constrain their ambitions.

L. C. Backer (✉)
Pennsylvania State University, State College, USA
e-mail: lcb911@me.com

J. Chaisse et al. (eds.), *Regulation of State-Controlled Enterprises*, International Law and the Global South, https://doi.org/10.1007/978-981-19-1368-6_15

> hundreds Feathers were poking out And into the air, fact, he flew! And to the top of a bell tower To perch as if on a throne.][2]

This contribution starts with two odd and oddly juxtaposed quotations. The first sets the stage for the arguments that follow. More specifically, it is a reminder that the orthodox structures for allocating liability within and among enterprises and between enterprises and their owners are only as powerful as the core organising principles on which they are based. In this case, those principles—grounded in a consequential division between public and private functions, between autonomous institutions and divisible functions within such organisations, and between regulation and management—may be losing their coherence in the face of new regulatory structures centred on production chains and national development models. The second, and more ironic, suggests the nature of transition and the risks of presumptions that seem perfectly reasonable to one actor (from the inside) appears ridiculous to everyone else (when viewed from the outside). In this case, of course, the inside speaks to traditional allocations of legal risks to states engage in economic activity.

From these kernels of insight, the analysis focuses on the arc of development of state liability for their economic activities. More specifically, it aims to examine the challenges to the current state of law and practice respecting governments' liability for the obligations of their state-owned enterprises (SOEs).[3] That object, once legal marginalia or the creature of 'socialist' law studies, has become an increasingly important element in the battles for the control and rationalisation of global production chains and with that control and rationalisation authority over the machinery of meaning-making in the fields of law, politics and economic organisation.

> State-owned enterprises (SOEs) are an important element of most economies, including many more advanced economies. SOEs are most prevalent in strategic sectors such as energy, minerals, infrastructure, other utilities and, in some countries, financial services. The presence of SOEs in the global economy has grown strongly in recent years. Today they account for over a fifth of the world's largest enterprises as opposed to ten years ago where only one or two SOEs could be found at the top of the league table. This means that high standards of corporate governance of SOEs are critical to ensure financial stability and sustain global growth.[4]

[3] Like most terms with legal consequences, there is no consensus on the meaning of the term 'state-owned enterprise' (SOE) or its application to the increasing variety of state interventions in markets and engagement in economic activity. Most definitions converge around a core of meaning that posits an entity of some sort, separable from other aspects of organisational structures, over which the state exercises significant, and perhaps decisive, control. *See,* e.g. PwC, Report: State Owned Enterprises: Catalysts for Public Value Creation? (PwC, April 2015) <https://www.pwc.com/gr/en/publications/assets/state-owned-enterprises-catalysts-for-public-value-creation.pdf> This essay will argue that such definitions that focus on the twin attributes of entity and control may fail to include significant emerging forms of SOE forms.

[4] Organization of Economic Cooperation and Development, *Ownership and Governance of State-Owned Enterprises: A Compendium of National Practices* (OECD, 2018), Foreword, p 4.

Much excellent academic[5] and policy[6] work continues at the margins of this area. That is, there is a concentration on reform that does not suggest a challenge to the structure on which the current premises of the rules of (and risk allocations to) states engaging in economic activity now rest.[7]

Nonetheless, the return of state capitalism, now within the structures and operating under the premises of post-1945 global economic order, may well augur a transformation of state free-riding (with respect to liability at least) as states seek to project their economic activity globally.[8] What once, not so long ago, had been well settled, even if controversial, may now be challenged from two distinct sources, both products of a mature post-1945 system of globalisation. The first emerges from the development of a transnational private law of human rights torts that European and possibly Canadian courts increasingly recognise.[9] The second is a consequence of the governmentalisation of the economic sphere and the resulting administrative functions of such organs. This development directly challenges the conceptual basis on which state sovereign immunity rules were created a generation or more ago.[10] Hanging over these developments are the trajectories of internationalisation that produced first the authority of soft law principles and then the convergence of those norms with hardening through the traditional forms of international law and practice.[11] The contribution's thesis is this: the increasing willingness to impose responsibilities and liability on upstream owners of operating companies challenges the viability of the current rules that shield states from both responsibility and liability for the acts of their SOEs, including their operations in global production chains. Convergence appears to be moving towards a greater difficulty in sustaining the authority of a theoretical

---

[5] W Mark C Weidemairer, 'Piercing the (Sovereign) Veil: The Role of Limited Liability in State Owned Enterprises' [2021] 46(3) BYU Law Review 795; Garry D. Bruton, Mike W. Peng, David Ahlstrom, Ciprian Stan, and Kehan Xu, 'State-owned Enterprises Around the WORLD as Hybrid Organizations' [2014] 29(1) Academy of Management Perspectives; H Chen, J Z Chen, G J Lobo, Y Wang 'Association Between Borrower and Lender State Ownership and Accounting Conservatism' (2010) 48(5) Journal of Accounting Research, 973–1014.

[6] Przemyslaw Kowalski, Max Büge, Monika Sztajerowska, and Matias Egeland 'State-Owned Enterprises Trade Effects and Policy Implications' (2013) OECD Trade Policy Papers No. 147 (OECD Publishing, Paris) <https://doi.org/10.1787/5k4869ckqk7l-en>.

[7] For a discussion at the very start of the construction of the current system with respect to sovereign immunity, see, Arthur K. Kuhn 'The Extension of Sovereign Immunity to Government Owned Commercial Corporations' [1945] The American Journal of International Law 772–775.

[8] Aldo Musacchio, and Francisco Flores-Macias 'The Return of State-Owned Enterprises: Should We Be Afraid?' [4 April 2009] Harvard International Review (website) <http://hir.harvard.edu/2009/04/the-return-of-state-owned-enterprises/> accessed 26 June 2021.

[9] *See,* e.g. *Okpabi v Royal Dutch Shell Plc* [2021] UKSC 3; *Vedanta Resources PLC & Another v Lungowe & Others* [2019] UKSC 20; *Nevsun Resources Ltd. v. Araya*, 2020 SCC 5 (CanLII), <https://canlii.ca/t/j5k5j>, retrieved on 2021-06-27.

[10] The current approach was codified in the Foreign Sovereign Immunities Act (FSIA) of 1976 28 U.S.C. §§ 1330, 1332, 1391(f), 1441(d), and 1602–1611. See also, e.g. Republic of Argentina v. Weltover, 504 U.S. 607 (1992); OBB Personenverkehr AG v. Sachs, 577 U.S. – (2015), 136 S.Ct. 390 (2015) and generally American Law Institute, Restatement 4th Foreign Relations Law of the United States paras 453–454 (American Law Institute 2017).

[11] *See* Surya Deva *Regulating Corporate Human Rights Violations* (Routledge 2012).

model that would shield states from the responsibility and liability already emerging from private apex entities in global production chains managed through chains of operating companies.

Part 2 considers the challenge to the standard model of state owner liability for the conduct or activities of SOEs in the form of the new supply chain due diligence laws and the Modern Slavery reporting provisions being enacted in Europe and Australia. It starts from the baseline of contemporary premises about ideal participants in ideal markets and the expectations of state behaviour when it organises sub-national entities to participate in this idealised (or ideologised) space. It then suggests the way that current developments—effectively governmentalising aspects of economic activity and extending the authority of enterprises along vertically arranged structures of production—now challenge the logic and viability of the 'deal' that the contemporary premises reflect.[12] In the process, it suggests that at least concerning sustainability and human rights responsibilities, SOEs and private forms are converging as simultaneously sovereign and economic entities. But it does more than that; it suggests a reconstitution of the state as the apex body corporate of SOE systems onto which responsibility (and liability) is also imposed. Here one deals with the transformation of attribution rules that either strip the state of immunity or extend sovereign immunity to the governmentalised functions of private enterprises.[13]

Part 3 then considers the challenge to traditional models that may emerge from the development of human rights tort law, especially in common law states and the Netherlands,[14] and the effects of emerging soft law responsibility regimes on the authority of the traditional narrative of state immunity from the consequences of the economic activities it controls or directs. Both challenges then suggest the context in which state and private enterprise control of economic activity within global production chains merge. In both cases, the merger ought to affect the application of agency, veil piercing and sovereign immunity rules to states respecting their SOEs.[15] But here, the rise of human rights torts also suggests the rise of a private duty

[12] Insightfully considered recently in Judith Schönsteiner, 'Attribution of State Responsibility for Actions or Omissions of State-Owned Enterprises in Human Rights Matters' (2019) 40(4) U. Pa. J. Int'l L. 896.

[13] This effectively flips the logic of the traditional debate that produced, in its time, the contemporary approach to immunity grounded in waivers for commercial activity. *See,* e.g. Arthur K. Kuhn 'The Extension of Sovereign Immunity to Government Owned Commercial Corporations' [1945] The American Journal of International Law 772–775. Yet the issue has long been attached to the challenge of privatisation of governmental services. For a useful discussion in the US context, see, Lauren Villa, 'Public Service, Private Entity: Should the Nature of the Service or Entity be Controlling on Issues of Sovereign Immunity' (2004) 78 St. John's Law Review 1257.

[14] *See,* e.g. *The State of the Netherlands v. Urgenda*, No. 19/00135 ECLI:NL:HR:2019:2007 (20 December 2019) <http://climatecasechart.com/climate-change-litigation/wp-content/uploads/sites/16/non-us-case-documents/2020/20200113_2015-HAZA-C0900456689_judgment.pdf>; *Vereniging Milieudefensie* et al. *v Royal Dutch Shell PLC* No C/09/571932/HA ZA 19-379 ECLI:NL:RBDHA:2021:5339 (26 May 2021) <http://climatecasechart.com/climate-change-litigation/wp-content/uploads/sites/16/non-us-case-documents/2021/20210526_8918_judgment-2.pdf>.

[15] Recently considered in its connection to sovereign immunity in Weidemairer (n 5).

of state owners to ensure that their downstream enterprises comply with their human rights and sustainability duties. Passive ownership is, in this case, a potential trigger for liability for failure to undertake duties of reasonable oversight, and reasonable oversight may, in turn, produce the sort of connection between the state and its SOEs to support a veil piercing or agency relationship.

2 The Conceptual Challenge to the Traditional Arrangement

The traditional 'deal' that shapes the current set of expectations touching on the role of states and the apportioning of liability to government for the conduct of SOEs is a composite of two distinct components. One is grounded in the soft law normative consensus expectations developed by the globe's most developed states through the Organization for Economic Cooperation and Development (OECD), respecting the ideal relationship between a state and the deployment of its productive forces.[16] The other is grounded in the domestic and international legal regimes of sovereign immunity.[17] Sovereign immunity can be understood in the context of this contribution as operating on several overlapping levels. Two are related to the forms of operation, distinguishing between government apparatus generally and entities or other forms through which commercial (economic) activity is undertaken. In that case, the issue that is the subject of interest is the liability of the owning or controlling body corporate (the state) for the delicts of its operating entity.

In that context, one encounters the issue of immunity attaching first to the operating entity itself and second to the state that owns or controls the entity. Another set of issues distinguish between the operation of SOEs in their home states from their operation (directly or indirectly) in host states. Here one also encounters the issue of immunity for either or both bodies corporate by or through foreign sovereigns on the territories (broadly construed at times in the form of effects tests[18]) over which they claim sovereignty. States are free to grant or limit immunity to their economic vessels as they like (and according to their legal traditions) when these operate in their home territories. Where SOE activities are projected abroad, international law principles and trade realities are the only factors that constrain a host state in assigning liability to either the SOE or its 'state' owner. It is especially in this context that the general acceptance of soft law normative consensus plays a decisive role in protecting states against liabilities of the SOEs operating abroad.

16 OECD (n 4).

17 *See* citations in n 5.

18 On the extraterritorial reach of 'effects' tests, see, Austen Parrish, 'The Effects Test: Extraterritoriality's Fifth Business' (2008) 61 Vand. L. Rev. 1455.

This section first critically examines the structure of the ideal set of relationships and operational modalities between a state—here understood as a model apex political body corporate[19] with its own obligations to its shareholders (the general public)[20]—and then the way that fundamental human rights and sustainably initiatives are undermining the integrity of the model in ways that may open the door to the erosion of state immunity from liability for the delicts of its operating entities.

2.1 *The 'Deal'*

The contemporary, traditional model, then, operates straightforwardly. In return for conformity to a set of normative soft law expectations, the state may more or less insulate itself from liability for the actions (and their consequences) of their economic enterprises engaging in commercial activities. The 'deal' thus has two parts. The first is structural—conformity to a specific ideal of how states must organise and operate their projections of resources and activities in the economic sphere. The second is consequential—the development of exceptional rules of veil piercing (complete waivers of liability) and agency (context-specific waivers) in the form of the contemporary approaches of restrictive sovereign immunity and its commercial activities and tort exceptions.

The 'deal' is not unique to SOEs. A variation was also crafted in the wake of the global financial crisis of 2006–2008 to apply to (and protect) states operating sovereign wealth funds (SWFs).[21]

> What was then required was a simple and straightforward application of well-worn hard and soft law regimes to tame the SWF, or at least to create a more or less fungible investment vehicle that could be regulated and evaluated much like any other private investment fund. All of this was nicely framed within the general principles developed at the height of (…) the Great Recession, when the lust of western states for investment inflows into their capital markets exceeded their fear of rapidly developing and cash-flush states now seeking to project their financial power into the capital markets abroad. This was undertaken by a collective allegiance to the [Santiago] principle that such states would forego the use of their financial

[19] There is an ancient tradition to that effect in English constitutional-political theory, though hardly applied in the manner suggested here. *See*, e.g. FW Maitland 'The Crown as Corporation' (1901) 17 LQ Rev. 131.And yet its essence, that the state is a body corporate in the sense that like private companies it is autonomous of its government though incarnated through its apparatus, and itself property in the hands of the ultimate sovereigns (share/stake) holders is quite susceptible to plausible transposition to the context of states as they contrive complex interlocking structures of autonomous bodies (within itself) or that they control, that operate in private markets engaged in activities opened to non-governmental actors.

[20] OECD (n 4), Annotations to Chapter 1 ("The members of the public whose government exercises the ownership rights are the ultimate owners of SOEs. This implies that those who exercise ownership rights over SOEs owe duties toward the public that are not unlike the fiduciary duties of a board toward the shareholders, and should act as trustees of the public interest" ibid p 29).

[21] Larry Catá Backer 'Sovereign Wealth Funds, Capacity Building, Development, and Governance' (2017) 52 Wake Forest Law Review 735.

power for political ends by projecting investment as an enhanced weapon of international relations.[22]

This 'deal' provides not merely the ideal but also the master narrative through which legal frameworks based on the ideal could be authenticated and legitimated.[23] Lamentably, both parts of the 'deal' were developed at the end of an era of globalisation in which the legalisation of human rights and sustainability (including climate change) responsibilities had not yet appeared in their current forms. The 'deal' was also crafted before the current forms of governmentalisation of enterprises began to collapse liability rules or, better, enlarge the scope of legal risk across production chains.[24] Nonetheless, that deal framework remains the most authoritative formal expression of legal–political aspiration, and for that reason alone, worth a brief but careful review.[25]

At the heart of the traditional approach are two key elements. The first touches on the definition of SOEs. The object is to distinguish among different forms of public intervention in economic activity.[26] The second is concerned with the scope of conduct of the SOE within which protection can be built, which is the sort of economic activity that falls within the boundaries of market-based economic activity rather than political activity to be exercised by the SOE instrumentality of state sovereignty. Both are nicely developed in the OECD's Principles of SOE Governance.[27] At the

---

[22] ibid. (emerging realities of SWFs as means of projecting state policy through its investment decisions and as an active shareholder, SWFs as development funds, SWF joint venturing in projects with other SWFs, SWFs as owners or controlling shareholders of SOEs and SWFs as a means for strengthening governance in weak governance zones). For the Santiago Principles themselves, *see* International Forum of Sovereign Wealth Funds, *Sovereign Wealth Funds: Generally Accepted Principles and Practices "Santiago Principles"* (IWG 2008).

[23] A master narrative is a theory of postmodernism that posits that a societies' storytelling in a historical sense centres or focuses on that societies' particular point of view. *See,* e.g. Jean-Francois Lyotard, *The Postmodern Condition: A Report On Knowledge* (Manchester University Press 1984). For a discussion of the SWF master narrative, *see* Larry Catá Backer, 'SWFs in Five Continents and Three Narratives: Similarities and Differences' in Fabio Bassan (ed.), *Research Handbook on Sovereign Wealth Funds and International Investment Law* 57–98 (Edward Elgar 2015).

[24] Larry Catá Backer 'The Human Rights Obligations of State-Owned Enterprises: Emerging Conceptual Structures and Principles in National and International Law and Policy' (2017) 50 Vand. J. Transnat'l L. 827.

[25] Larry Catá Backer, 'Sovereign Wealth Funds, Capacity Building,' supra (Among its more important uses has been as a global centring element around which rational discussion could be organized. It produced an ideology of sorts. The ideology was framed around a core set of principles).

[26] On the critical importance of meaning making for the language and rationalisation of law, see, Jan Broekman *Meaning, Narrativity, and the Real* (Springer 2016). It is in that context that Lacan's master narrative evidences itself in a semiotic guise. Broekman perceptively notes: "There is first of all the *horizontal* dimension of text. Texts do intertwine continuously and that intertwining creates legal meanings that words pretend to indicate. And there is furthermore the *vertical* dimension of texts (and languages in general) showing us a surface, which belongs to our daily life-the surface of the sign pool-and often precariously concealed deep structure in which vales, norms, habits and related social powers are influential, even before they are properly articulated." (ibid., pp. 142–143.

[27] Organization for Economic Cooperation and Development *OECD Guidelines on Corporate Governance of State Owned Enterprises* (OECD, 2015) (hereafter *OECD SOE Governance*).

heart of the OECD's normative model is the objective of preserving the efficient functioning of global markets and, with it, the integrity of post-1945 globalisation principles.[28] "The Guidelines aim to: (i) professionalise the state as an owner; (ii) make SOEs operate with similar efficiency, transparency and accountability as good practice private enterprises; and (iii) ensure that competition between SOEs and private enterprises, where such occurs, is conducted on a level playing field."[29] More importantly, the objectives of the OECD SOE Governance are to ensure that public and private enterprises operate on a level playing field in terms of their access and relation to the market.[30] That requires both an autonomous economic enterprise and the embrace of the ideologies of private economic institutionalisation memorialised in the expectations of the operations of private economic entities.

These objectives, then, require that the SOE be understood in quite narrow terms. The object is to construct a form of state structure for the participation in economic activity, which in virtually all respects mimics the private corporation (or similar form) against which SOEs would compete. That mimicry is essential to the core premise to be protected the integrity of global markets, the essence of which is open, robust and unsubsidised competition among economic actors. It follows then that the only form in which state-based economic activity[31] can be recognised as such is through separate entities organised in forms recognisable for their similarity to private analogues.

> For the purpose of the Guidelines, any corporate entity recognised by national law as an enterprise, and in which the state exercises ownership, should be considered as an SOE. This includes joint stock companies, limited liability companies and partnerships limited by shares. Moreover statutory corporations, with their legal personality established through specific legislation, should be considered as SOEs if their purpose and activities, or parts of their activities, are of a largely economic nature.[32]

State ownership or controls based on notions of the state as ultimate beneficiary, or the state as majority shareholder, or equivalent means of control.[33] "The Guidelines

[28] Angel Gurría, Preface, in *OECD SOE Governance* (n 27) ("Good governance of state-owned enterprises (SOEs) is essential for efficient and open markets at both the domestic and international level." p 7). The text of the *OECD SOE Governance* makes this objective explicit: "Consequently, good governance of SOEs is critical to ensure their positive contribution to economic efficiency and competitiveness. Experience shows that market-led development is the most effective model for efficient allocation of resources." ibid p 11.

[29] OECD SOE Governance (n 27) p 11.

[30] ibid., Annotations to Chapter III: State Owned Enterprises in the Marketplace (pp 45–50).

[31] OECD SOE Governance (n 27) also defines economic activity in ways that align with the commercial activities exception to sovereign immunity. "For the purpose of these Guidelines, an economic activity is one that involves offering goods or services on a given market and which could, at least in principle, be carried out by a private operator in order to make profits." ibid 15. Market structure is essentially irrelevant. ibid. But the context in which such activity occurs is important. "Economic activities mostly take place in markets where competition with other enterprises already occurs or where competition given existent laws and regulations could occur." ibid.

[32] ibid 14.

[33] ibid (minority shareholding is sometimes sufficient if as a result of that holding the state effectively exercises control over the entity. ibid).

are generally not intended to apply to entities or activities whose primary purpose is to carry out a public policy function, even if the entities concerned have the legal form of an enterprise."[34] How these distinctions are made and the extent to which they might now become difficult to discern are explored below. The normatively ideal SOE is one developed for a limited set of purposes and following an idealised structure. Its ultimate purpose is a modified form of profit maximising societal (the ultimate shareholders of the state as the apex body corporate of the productive forces of politics) value,[35] but in a functionally differentiated[36] manner through "efficient allocation of resources."[37] The ideal SOE is transparent with respect to its ownership structure, its purposes and the role of corporate ownership by the state.[38] Indeed, under this ideal model, the state itself is understood as a public purpose corporation which is itself both an autonomous set of institutions and property in the hands of its 'shareholder' (the 'general public'). Thus, measures of accountability that mimic those available to shareholders in private enterprises are part of its constitution.[39] Lastly, the public policy objectives of the SOE must be "clearly mandated" and "disclosed."[40]

Like the ideal SWF,[41] the normative construction of the state's role as owner is developed to create that soft conceptual wall of separation that mimics the rules of autonomy between shareholders and corporations in the private sector. The object is the same—the transposition of a public version of private asset partitioning.[42] That requires, in turn, both the institutional autonomy of the economic abstraction—SOE—into structures within which that manifestation can be incarnated. The

[34] ibid., p. 16.

[35] ibid., para I(A). *See* also ibid., Annotations to Chapter 1 p. 29 ("good practice calls for governments to consider and articulate how any given enterprise shall be adding value to the members of the public that are its ultimate owners, through an efficient allocation of resources." ibid., p 29 §A).

[36] *See* Philip G Cerny, 'Functional Differentiation, Globalization and the New Transnational Neopluralism' in Mathias Albert, Barry Buzan, and Michael Zürn (eds) *Bringing Sociology to International Relations* (Cambridge 2013), p 205.

[37] OECD SOE Governance (n 27) para I(A).

[38] ibid. para I(B).

[39] ibid. para I(C) ("The ownership policy should be subject to appropriate procedures of political accountability and disclosed to the general public. The government should review at regular intervals its ownership policy.").

[40] ibid., para I(D).

[41] *See* Larry Catá Backer, 'Sovereign Investing and Markets-Based Transnational Rule of Law Building: The Norwegian Sovereign Wealth Fund in Global Markets' (2014) 29 Am U Int'l L. Rev. 1.

[42] Discussed in its contemporary framework in Larry Catá Backer 'The Autonomous Global Corporation: On the Role of Organizational Law beyond Asset Partitioning and Legal Personality' (2005) Tulsa L Rev 541; criticised in Henry Hansmann and Richard Squire, External and Internal Asset Partitioning: Corporations and Their Subsidiaries, in Jeffrey N Gordon and Wolf-Georg Ringe (eds.) The Oxford Handbook of Corporate Law and Governance (OUP 2018); David Milton, 'Piercing the Corporate Veil, Financial Responsibility, and the Limits of Limited Liability' (2007) Emory LJ 1305; Stephen M. Bainbridge, 'Abolishing Veil Piercing (2001) 26J. Corp. L. 479.

parallels to national corporate law are made explicit.[43] If the operating company has "full operational autonomy,"[44] then the role of the state must resemble that of a corporate parent, "as an informed and active owner and should exercise its ownership rights according to the legal structure of each enterprise."[45] Norway's Pension Fund Global also has applied a principle of active ownership with respect to the (minority share) holdings of the SWF.[46]

This functionally differentiated division of authority within the state then permits the state to retain its immunity (to the extent it desires) concerning its regulatory, public policy, or sovereign activities (i.e. those activities which are not traditionally accounted for as having commercial or economic value in the classical sense) while creating a rationalised and relatively easy to delineate space where it can operate like other private actors (and be subject to liability for those activities) in common with non-state actors engaging in the same functionally differentiated sphere.[47] The construction of states of equivalence between SOEs and private enterprises carries over to disclosure and transparency obligations.[48] This applies with particular force to financial accounting,[49] operating results, governance structures, the usual information about board members, risk factors and state aids.[50] In this context, the state as regulator assumes the obligation to create legal structures that promote parity within its domestic legal order. Included are assumptions for the functioning of an independent board.[51] The state owner, in turn, is responsible for the establishment of its own oversight organ, and responsible as well to the elected bodies representing

[43] OECD SOE Governance (n 27) para II(A).

[44] ibid. para II(B).

[45] ibid., para II(F). The object is to ensure separation of the managerial from the regulatory functions of the state. And to that end, of course, to ensure that the state restricts itself to actions in its sovereign capacity—which are protected by sovereign immunity principles—even as its operating entities may be liable under the commercial activities exception to sovereign immunity. But more importantly, autonomy ensures the separation of the two spheres in the way that the liabilities of the enterprise are partitioned from the responsibility of shareholders. The meeting point of management and state policy comes in attenuated and formally transparent forms, for example "maintaining continuous dialogue with external auditors and specific state control organs." ibid. para II(F)(6).

[46] *See,* e.g. Salar Ghahramani, 'Governments, Financial Markets and International Human Rights: The State's Role as Shareholder' (2011) Yale J. Int'l Aff. 85.

[47] This is nicely elaborated, for example, in ibid., para III (state-owned enterprises in the marketplace) (e.g. "SOEs' economic activities should face market consistent conditions regarding access to debt and equity finance." ibid., para III(F). It is also elaborated in the norms respecting treatment of non-state minority shareholders. ibid., para IV (Equitable Treatment of Shareholders and Other Investors).

[48] ibid para VI ("State-owned enterprises should observe high standards of transparency and be subject to the same high quality accounting, disclosure, compliance and auditing standards as listed companies.").

[49] Included as well are responsibilities for independent external audits, ibid., para VI(B).

[50] ibid VI(A).

[51] ibid para VIII.

the general public.[52] But here, the state as an owner must walk a fine line. On the one hand, the state is expected to exercise its ownership rights actively but in accordance with law and in a way that mimics active ownership by private parties.[53] On the other hand, the state is cautioned against political interference or neglect.

The difficulty, unresolved, centres on the realities of the dual nature of the state as owner and regulatory—and the flimsiness of the barriers that keep those functions separated as states go about the business of managing those activities under their charge. "There is less consensus about how a level playing field is to be obtained in practice—particularly where SOEs combine their economic activities with non-trivial public policy objectives."[54] The OECD has suggested a set of best practices that minimise but do not eliminate the challenge.[55] The challenge is not trivial. This is the traditional context in which state ownership moves from autonomy to control and where the enterprise is transformed from primarily an economic actor to a political instrumentality of the state exercising politics through interventions in the market. This marks a political control that augments the usual issue-effective operational control of the enterprise of the sort that tends to serve as a basis for veil piercing.[56]

And from this conceptual framework, it is relatively simple to legalise the 'deal'. [57] First, constructing an autonomous vessel through which economic activity is conducted creates a presumption of a legal distinction between the entity and the state owner.[58] In the public domain, this reproduces the basic presumption of asset partitioning at the heart of the corporate veil piercing doctrine. Second, that separation of juridical existence is then the basis for constructing the rules of sovereign immunity (of the state and its instrumentalities) and its (for our purposes) principal exception for commercial activities.[59] But it also shields the state from liability when the liability arises from the state's use of its sovereign and regulatory authority, even in the context of commercial activity.[60] Only concerning commercial activities, and only in the context of such property, may the state, when it transgresses the usual rules

---

[52] ibid Annotations to Chapter II §E ("The ownership entity should be held clearly accountable for the way it carries out state ownership. Its accountability should be, directly or indirectly, to bodies representing the interests of the general public, such as the legislature" ibid p 37).

[53] ibid Annotations to Chapter II §F (outlining the broad scope of shareholder rights to be exercised by the state in a way that preserves SOE autonomy, ibid pp 38–43).

[54] ibid Annotations to Chapter III: State Owned Enterprises un the Marketplace p 45.

[55] Organization for Economic Cooperation and Development, *Competitive Neutrality: Maintaining a Level Playing Field Between Public and Private Business* (OECD, 2012).

[56] Discussed in Weidemaier (n 5) 821–36.

[57] *First Nat. City Bank v. Banco Para el Comercio Exterior de Cuba ("Bancec")*, 462 U.S. 611 (1983).

[58] *Bancec,* 462 U.S. at 626–27 ("government instrumentalities established as juridical entities distinct and independent from their sovereign should normally be treated as such"); ibid. at 627 (discussing the "presumption of independent status").

[59] *See* discussion in *Rubin v Islamic Republic of Iran*, 583 U.S. ___,138 S. Ct. 816 (2018).

[60] *Bridas S.A.P.I.C. v. Gov't of Turkm.*, 447 F.3d 411, 416–20 (5th Cir. 2006) (misuse of corporate form, traditional grounds for veil piercing, not the exercise of sovereign powers resulting in a wrong to the plaintiff).

protecting asset partitioning, may be held liable and (some) of its property subject to levy to satisfy a judgement.[61] There is another consequence—where the SOE is "entitled to perform and are actually performing acts in the exercise of sovereign authority of the State"[62]—its actions may effectively evidence its control by the state (and the loss of its autonomy) to the extent that state and SOE merge. But as a consequence, and concerning those activities, both state and SOE are protected by sovereign immunity from either jurisdiction or liability.

Here one can visualise the beplumed donkey atop the tower as if on a throne.[63] The transformation of the state to a donkey in this sense is a product of its own making and one that touches on another contradiction—the consequences of the governmentalisation of the private sphere.[64] In that project, it becomes much more difficult for state owners to avoid the sort of control necessary to meet their statutory responsibilities (or otherwise maintain a level playing field) concerning human rights and sustainability.[65] Just as "Business actors also increasingly audit their own suppliers regarding human rights standards, acting with quasi-regulatory authority in their own right,"[66] so might the state audit that of its SOEs. In both cases, that connection may weaken—substantially—the principle of the autonomy of SOE from their state owners in ways that substantially undermine both the ideal of states as regulators detached from and SOEs as economic actors in markets. As that separation is eroded, so too might the insulation of states from liability for the actions of their economic instrumentalities might also be reduced.

2.2 *Challenging the 'Deal'*

Both elements on which the 'deal' is fashioned are now challenged (from the legal flanks[67]). The first is by the increasing convergence of regulatory and entity models in state control of economic activity, making the traditional soft law categorical structures and ideal operations harder to maintain. The second is by changes in the

---

[61] Critically examined to good effect in Weidemairer (n 5).

[62] UN Convention on Jurisdictional Immunities of States and Their Property, Arts. 2 and 10(3), U.N. Doc. A/59/508, (2 Dec 2004), <https://treaties.un.org/doc/source/recenttexts/english_3_13.pdf[https://perma.cc/HN5B-82UY]> Art. 2.1b.iii. The definitions of commercial activities with respect to which limited waiver of immunity is created is set out ibid., Art.2.1c.

[63] *See*, n 2 supra.

[64] Larry Catá Backer, 'Human Rights Responsibilities of State Owned Enterprises' in Surya Deva and David Birchall (eds) Research Handbook on Human Rights and Business (E Elgar, 2020).

[65] David McGrogan, 'The population and the individual: The human rights audit as the governmentalisation of global human rights governance' (2018) 16(4) ICON 1073-1100 (the human rights audit as a modality of control).

[66] ibid., 1079.

[67] "The main feature of an offensive battle is the out-flanking or bypassing of the defender." US Army 'Field Manual FM 100-5 Operations' (Headquarters US Army; Washington DC June 1993), p 7-1.

domestic law of asset partitioning as applied to private forms and their shareholders[68] now transposed to public sector ownership/control relations. Again, the focus here is not on the transformation of the SOE and SOE responsibility in tandem with changes in responsible business conduct of private entities, but rather the way that those changes may impact the ability of the state to insulate itself, under the traditional consensus idealised structures of SOE structure and sovereign immunity, from direct liability for actions undertaken through their SOEs.

The opening for this transformation is itself now built into the OECD ideal. Part V of the *OECD SOE Governance* itself opens the door innocuously enough by proving parity between SOE and private enterprises concerning responsible business conduct.[69] The recognition of responsible business conduct obligations is conservatively expressed. It is limited to those established by law or mutual agreement.[70] It covers traditional areas of stakeholder relations, including labour, creditors, and affected communities.[71] Expectations are to be established by the state and disclosed.[72] Responsible business conduct responsibilities focus on accountability and compliance through internal controls.[73] But these are to be "based on country norms, in conformity with international commitments and apply to the SOE and its subsidiaries."[74] And they touch on fiduciary duty (of officials controlling the apparatus of state).[75]

As Judith Schönsteiner nicely suggests in her recent work, the challenge comes when the traditional system and its immunities are upended. This occurs in a most pronounced way in the context of the governmentalisation of the private enterprise, especially concerning human rights and sustainability-based regulatory obligations.

> Not because the SOE is governed or administered as a public organ; rather, because the SOEs private body is closely linked to the State-by control or by function. To use an image, this research looks at making sense of the fact that SOEs continue to be linked to the State through complex but not less evident, umbilical cords.[76]

Where private enterprises, as well as SOEs both "perform and are actually performing acts in the exercise of sovereign authority,"[77] then either a case can

---

[68] *See,* e.g. Henry Hansmann and Richard Squire, External and Internal Asset Partitioning: Corporations and Their Subsidiaries, in Jeffrey N. Gordon & Wolf-Georg Ringe (eds) The *Oxford Handbook of Corporate Law and Governance* (OUP 2018).

[69] Its chapeau provision declares: "The state ownership policy should fully recognise SOEs' responsibilities towards stakeholders and request that SOEs report on their relations with stakeholders. It should make clear any expectations the state has in respect of responsible business conduct by SOEs" OECD SOE Governance (n 27) para V.

[70] ibid para V(A).

[71] ibid para V(B).

[72] ibid para V(D).

[73] ibid para V(C).

[74] ibid.

[75] ibid para V(E).

[76] ibid 914.

[77] UN Convention on Jurisdictional Immunities of States and Their Property, supra, Art. 2.1biii.

be made for the extension of sovereign immunity to all enterprises now obligated to undertake quasi governance and regulatory administrative responsibilities under emerging legal structures such as the German Supply Chain Due Diligence Law[78] or the Australian Modern Slavery Act,[79] or the obligation might be attributed to the state, and with it, a remedial responsibility-if only after all remedies are exhausted against the SOE. The issue, then, is not merely one of immunity, but of the nature of attribution when the state, through the legal delegation of responsibility for certain human rights and sustainability objectives, overseen by the state, effectively transforms (again, at least with respect to the spheres of delegation) SOEs in particular, but all firms in general, into something like a privatised administrative organ of the state. Now the issue becomes acute. Where such attribution might under classical approaches then support immunity[80] under regimes of human rights and sustainability rules, the opposite may be true.[81]

The reason is straightforward. The privatisation of sovereign functions to be undertaken within a commercial context necessarily changes the character of that function from sovereign to commercial. That is, the sovereign function is subsumed within the function whose realisation it serves.[82] But in the case of everything from codes of conduct conforming to the corporate responsibility to respect human rights of the *UN Guiding Principles for Business and Human Rights*[83] to the reporting and assessment requirements of the Modern Slavery and Supply Chain Due Diligence laws, the reverse appears to be the case. The sovereign act of delegating these responsibilities down and into the heart of the economic function of these enterprises (public or private) changes its character from sovereign to private. And it imposes further a duty of the superior owner (in the case of the SOE its sovereign owner) a duty (remediable) to ensure compliance.

One gets a better sense of this transformation, its challenge to the old premises about the SOE-state nexus, and the rules for allocating immunity, by considering the German 'Act on Corporate Due Diligence in Supply Chains' enacted 11 June 2021.[84] The GSCDDL enters into law in 2023 and applies to the largest companies

---

[78] Entwurf eines Gesetzes über die unternehmerischen Sorgfaltspflichten in Lieferketten Drucksache 19/28649 <https://dserver.bundestag.de/btd/19/286/1928649.pdf>.

[79] Australia Modern Slavery Act 2018 (no 153, 2018) (An Act to require some entities to report on the risks of modern slavery in their operations and supply chains and actions to address those risks, and for related purposes) <https://www.legislation.gov.au/Details/C2018A00153>.

[80] Schönsteiner (n 12) pp 914–915.

[81] For a useful summary in English, though one with a specific political view, along with an unofficial translation of the GSCDDL, see Initiative Lieferketten Gesetz, de 'What the New Supply Chan Act Delivers-and What it Doesn't (June 2021) <https://lieferkettengesetz.de/wp-content/uploads/2021/06/Initiative-Lieferkettengesetz_Analysis_What-the-new-supply-chain-act-delivers.pdf>.

[82] That itself is a reversal of the traditional hierarchy that assumes a superior role for the sovereign function and its effect to transform commercial and private to sovereign and public.

[83] UN Guiding Principles for Business and Human Rights (UN 2011), at Pillar 2 corporate responsibility to respect human rights.

[84] Entwurf eines Gesetzes über die unternehmerischen Sorgfaltspflichten in Lieferketten Drucksache 19/28649 <https://dserver.bundestag.de/btd/19/286/1928649.pdf>.

(companies with 3,000 employees in 2023 and 1,000 employees from 2024). The GSCDDL requires companies subject to its provisions to identify risks of human rights violations and environmental degradation that may arise in the company's operation and its direct suppliers[85] and, in some cases, indirect suppliers,[86] wherever located. The GSCDDL incorporates the spirit of the UN Guiding Principles for Business and Human Rights.[87] That, in turn, includes both notions of the positive duty of state oversight and corporate responsibility respecting—for corporations, at least these include not just the normative principles of domestic law but also the International Bill of Human Rights.[88] Once actionable risk is identified, covered companies must then take and document action to avoid, mitigate or remedy these violations. To that end, companies must report to the Federal Office for Economic Affairs and Export Control (BAFA). For the purposes of this contribution, most telling is the consensus view that the GSCDDL creates a strong regulatory oversight of enterprise activity—and that it delegates the primary operational responsibility on which oversight is exercised to the apex owner in supply chains.[89] It vests the general public with the right to demand that public oversight authorities take action in support of enterprise obligations under GSCDDL and cover both environmental and human rights obligations.

More generally, and with respect to its implications for core movements in fundamental premises about governance, the GSCDDL appears to deepen a number of important trends.

First, it adds another element in the general trend within liberal democratic political orders to deepen the scope of the governmentalisation of the private transnational sphere through multinational enterprises. This trend appears to be the answer to the initial challenge posed by John Ruggie as he sought to produce a framework for business and human rights—the core problem of governance gaps in a world legal

---

[85] With respect to direct suppliers, the obligation is proactive and ongoing.

[86] The obligation with respect to indirect suppliers is triggered where the company obtains 'substantial knowledge' of potential violation.

[87] There is much literature on this framework. See, e.g. Larry Catá Backer, 'Moving Forward the UN Guiding Principles for Business and Human Rights: Between Enterprise Social Norm, State Domestic Legal Orders, and the Treaty Law that Might Bind Them All' (2015) 38 Fordham Int'l LJ 457; Larry Catá Backer 'Governance Polycentrism or Regulated Self-Regulation — Rule Systems for Human Rights Impacts of Economic Activity Where National, Private and International Regimes Collide' in Kerstin Blome, Hannah Franzki, Andreas Fischer-Lescano, Nora Markard and Stefan Oeter (eds.) *Contested Collisions: Interdisciplinary Inquiries into Norm Fragmentation in World Society* (Cambridge, 2015); Michael Addo 'The Reality of the United Nations Guiding Principles on Business and Human Rights' (2014) 14(1) Human Rights Law Review 133–147; Jonathan Bonnitcha, Robert McCorquodale 'The Concept of 'Due Diligence' in the UN Guiding Principles on Business and Human Rights' (2017) 28(3) European Journal of International Law 899–919.

[88] John Ruggie 'The Social Construction of the UN Guiding Principles on Business and Human Rights' in Surya Deva and David Bilchall (eds) Research Handbook on Human Rights and Business (E Elgar 2020) pp 66–83.

[89] Consider Claire Bright, Axel Marx, Nina Pineau and Jan Wouters 'Toward a Corporate Duty for Lead Companies to Respect Human Rights in Their Global Value Chains?' [2020] 22(4) Business and Politics 667–697.

order in which national law tends to be constrained by the territorial character of sovereign authority. Professor Ruggie proposed a markets-driven answer in the form of the corporate responsibility to respect human rights operating in tandem with the formal and legal realm of state duty to protect human rights.[90] States have found it easier to constitute the multinational enterprise as an extension of national territory—including because of control relations, all of those foreign legal persons resident or operating abroad.[91]

Second, this process of governmentalisation—of transforming the multinational enterprise from an economic organ to an organ through which state power may be applied directly[92]—has several collateral effects. One of the most interesting is the acceleration in the transformation of the character of corporate or enterprise governance. Increasingly governmentalisation, within a framework of risk version incentives wrapped around concepts like prevent-mitigate-remedy, appears to be changing the working style of multinational enterprises so that they increasingly adopt the sensibilities and operating style of administrative agencies. MNEs increasingly might be understood by state actors to conveniently serve them as global administrative agencies (with functionally differentiated jurisdiction based on their supply chains) with human rights regulatory authority. That regulatory authority may not be identical to the authority that public regulatory bodies might exercise, but the operation of the MNE as an administrative agency remains the same, and in that sense, extends and internationalises the reach of host state administrative organs. In the process, the static understanding of what it means to be either an SOE or the scope of the activities conceived of as private and not sovereign becomes contested. The 'deal' framework elaborated above has yet to confront the implications—for purposes of both attributing markets-based actions to the state and the legal effects of the characterisation of those activities as sovereign or commercial for purposes of sovereign immunity.[93]

Third, these private economic actors now play a double role—they are the instruments of economic activity representing large amounts of aggregated productive forces—and at the same time, they serve as the private sector administrative organ of the state that assumes oversight of the enterprise and can hold them accountable (through public elected and administrative bodies). What this bodes for the future of administrative law remains only at the periphery of investigation for the moment,

[90] Protect, Respect and Remedy: A Framework for Business and Human Rights, A/HRC/8/5 (April 7, 2008 <http://www.reports-and-materials.org/Ruggie-report-7-Apr-2008.pdf>. For a useful commentary, see Christina Ochoa 'The 2008 Ruggie Report: A Framework for Business and Human Rights' (2008) 12(12) ASIL Insights <https://www.asil.org/insights/volume/12/issue/12/2008-ruggie-report-framework-business-and-human-rights>.

[91] Discussed in Larry Catá Backer, 'Moving Forward the UN Guiding Principles for Business and Human Rights' supra.

[92] *See* essays in Jean-Philippe Robé, Antoine Lyon-Caen, and Stéphane Vernac *Multinationals and the Constitutionalization of the World Power System* (Routledge 2016).

[93] There has been a continued focus on privatisation, but always consonant with the traditional premises. See, e.g. Organization for Economic Cooperation and Development, *Privatization in the 21st Century: Summary of Recent Experience* (OECD, 2010).

but these trajectories of legalisation demand greater attention.[94] It is worth underlining in this context that the GSCDDL does not permit private actions but instead creates an administrative mechanism through which the regulatory elements of the state organs could oversee and discipline the responsibilities (now positive) of corporations—including it might seem, both SOEs and the state ownership agencies. The MNE then serves as the administrative regulator of a double delegation. The first is a delegation of regulatory responsibility for the state; the second is the normative regulatory objectives represented by international norms (that might or might not be incorporated into the domestic legal orders of the states asserting oversight power). The MNE is expected to use its private lawmaking authority (through the contract and internal governance mechanisms) to harden internal norms, the success of which is to be a matter of accountability to a national organ asserting a domestic agenda through law.

Fourth, the consequences are already appearing. The first is regulatory and administrative competition. For every assertion of national legislative power, there is the possibility of blocking legislation. These block then reproduce the sort of governance gaps which efforts like GSCDDL are meant to overcome. The second comes in the form of inconsistent or extreme incompatible administrative delegations. Germany, for example, is not the only state with ambitions in this regulatory arena, even within Europe. It is not clear, as well, how the German measure will align with those of France and its Supply Chain Due Diligence Law,[95] or for that matter, the UK's Modern Slavery Act.[96] Reaching farther out along complex and interlinked supply chains, the laws of other jurisdictions will also become a factor.[97] Third, these inconsistencies add not merely to the regulatory burdens of MNEs (and strategic responses) but also enhance the sort of regulatory incoherence that was also one of the significant challenges to be overcome through the vision represented by the UNGPs. Enterprises will be required not merely to internalise the regulatory burden of compliance (i.e. hardly new or unexpected), but also the positive obligations respecting the hardening

[94] *See,* e.g. Sabino Cassese 'New Paths for Administrative Law: A Manifesto' (2012) 10(3) International Journal of Constitutional Law 603–613. There are intersections here-with implications for responsibility, attribution, immunity, and control, within emerging structures of public-private partnerships (of which this may appear to be an abstract form). See California Debt and Investment Advisory Commission, Issue Brief: Privatization Vs. Public-Private Partnerships: A Comparative Analysis (CDIAC #07-04) August 2007). All of this, in turn, is interlinked with the developing field of global administrative law, see Benedict Kingsbury and Megan Donaldson 'Global Administrative Law' Oxford Public International Law (OUP 2015).

[95] *See* Devoir de vigilance des sociétés mères et des entreprises donneuses d'ordre Loi n° 2017-399 du 27 mars 2017 (Due diligence of corporations and main contractors) (applies to French companies with more than 5,000 employees or any other enterprise with no less than 10,000 employees who are required to publish and implement a surveillance plan (plan de vigilance) to prevent serious violations of human rights the breach of which could result in administrative civil fines).

[96] *See*, UK Modern Slavery Act 2015 (2015 c. 30) <https://www.legislation.gov.uk/ukpga/2015/30/contents/enacted>.

[97] *See* e.g. Australia's Modern Slavery Act 2018 (no 153, 2018) (An Act to require some entities to report on the risks of modern slavery in their operations and supply chains and actions to address those risks, and for related purposes) <https://www.legislation.gov.au/Details/C2018A00153>.

of soft international law and its administration is now required. The result, of course, is to augment the incentives towards not just governmentalisation but also towards the adoption of the institutional style and practices of an administrative agency in the enterprise's relationship to its economic activity. Certainly, proponents of a thousand legislative flowers blooming take comfort in the expectation that variations will be minor and eventually there will be convergence. But these are the same hopes built on, for example, a studied ignoring of the muscular development of Marxist Leninist approaches to human rights-based economic activity or the approach to developing states' human rights. Not everyone shares the same world view, expectations and experiences of those brought up among the best that Berlin, Paris or New York can offer those with means enough to enjoy them.

Fifth, it is worth considering the extent to which normative obsolescence is built into projects like the GSCDDL. It is no longer possible to continue to ignore, or worse, to silo human rights as something not also profoundly integrated with sustainability and climate change issues. Accountability for human rights, unconnected to the reciprocal relationships between human rights, sustainability and climate change, can contribute to a distortion of the comprehensive interconnection between these aspects of responsible business conduct.[98]

Sixth, the focus on triggering events and the need to consume and analyse vast amounts of data (the substantiated information requirements and its likely imposition of positive obligations to develop and manage global accountability systems) across states and regions will prove to be somewhat challenging in at least two respect. The first touches on the ability to use data in the face of national restrictions. Foremost among these restrictions are emerging tendencies to prevent the storage or transport of data across borders. Recent Chinese data protection legislation might, in that case, be extended to more aggressively prevent the inclusion of data from Chinese operations to facilitate the requirements of German law.[99] Other states may produce similar restrictions. The second touches on developing objective standards and coordinated analytics that make it possible to utilise the data analytics on which compliance is essential in ways that may be used to compare enterprises with each other and against any emerging legal standard. The legal standard against which liability is to be assessed also leaves something to be desired. The effect of the legislation, then, on better developing mechanisms of enterprise and governance trust (and to create a

[98] *See,* e.g. Framework Principles on Human Rights and the Environment (24 January 2018) (A/HRC/37/59) <https://undocs.org/A/HRC/37/59> (16 principles related to human rights and the environment that are based on existing work of the human rights system).

[99] Yan Luo, Zhijing Yu and Vicky Liu 'China Enacts Data Security Law' Inside Privacy (11 June 2021) <https://www.insideprivacy.com/cybersecurity-2/china-enacts-data-security-law/>; Helen Hwang and Eric Carlson 'China's proposed data security and personal information protection laws will impact investigations' The FCPA Blog (18 May 2021) <https://fcpablog.com/2021/05/18/chinas-proposed-data-security-and-personal-information-protection-laws-will-impact-investigations/> ("Article 41 of the PIPL includes a nearly identical prohibition on transferring personal information stored in China to a judicial or enforcement agency outside of China without prior approval").

legal basis for presuming the human rights trustworthiness of complying enterprises) remains at best a work in progress, one that might still not be realised.

Lastly, the collateral effects of compliance with German law might also produce some interesting extraterritorial effects. This might be particularly the case concerning human rights tort law development in the UK and Canada.[100] It might also contribute to transforming the agency standards in those states that might make it easier to extend liability through a supply chain while avoiding (and ultimately making less relevant to jurisprudence) the traditional law of veil piercing. They remain to be seen, but a litigator in those jurisdictions might well be tempted to use the disclosures and presumptions of the German (and the French) Acts to advantage.

The general challenge thus described can be understood as grounded in two core conditions: first is the legal attribution of responsibility for delegated sovereign objectives to the highest level of ownership in a production chain (in the case of the SOE, the state itself). Second, the transformation of the character of the responsibility imposed form a sovereign public objective to a private objective that is inherently commercial in nature as a necessary attribute of the conditions and practices of commercial activity now imposed through law. While the state engaged in the sovereign act of enacting such measures, it acts solely in its private character as a controlling entity, which itself is subject to the law and rules of its own making. That, ironically enough, then preserves the deal that is at the heart of the normative standards expressed through the *OECD SOE Governance* principles. Conceptually, at least, one here goes beyond veil piercing or balancing of attributes. And it might as well limit the immunity preclusive effects of attribution to avoid the line drawing (increasingly incoherent) between sovereign and commercial activities of enterprises (including the that of the state itself) and between sovereign and commercial control activities of states themselves.

To get a flavour of these distinctions, one might reconsider that ancient though even for the somewhat remarkable case of *Baccus SRL v. Servicio Nacional de Trigo*.[101] The case involved a commercial agreement between a private Italian company and a Spanish entity, established as a state-owned corporation, to sell tens of thousands of tons of rye. The case, ultimately heard by the courts in England (as stipulated in the parties' contract), was dismissed on the grounds of sovereign immunity at the request of the Spanish Ambassador on behalf of the Spanish state. The rationale was that the Spanish company was performing sovereign actions in transnational agricultural markets so that the character of the transactions, though they appeared at first glance to mimic commercial transactions, was instead better signified as sovereign. According to the Spanish litigants, that signification was reinforced by the company's control exercised by the Ministry of Agriculture, whose directives the company was bound to follow. Here one can apply traditional veil piercing rules,

---

[100] Briefly discussed in Section 3.

[101] *Baccus SRL v Servicio Nacional de Trigo* [1956] 3 WLR 948; discussed in PJ Kincaid, 'Sovereign Immunity of Foreign State Owned Corporations' (1976) 10J World Trade L 110.

which result in the effective merger of the company with the state[102]—but as a result, *the company* enjoys the state's sovereign immunity. Alternatively, one can reject veil piercing and instead rely on the sovereign character of the specific transaction in this case. And again, *the transaction* at least is protected by principles of sovereign immunity. In either case, the premise of attribution is reinforced.

Yet it is also possible, applying the premises underlying contemporary governmentalisation of human rights and sustainability duties throughout a production chain that the same facts could be signified in very different ways. Here the attribution is required—in whatever form is contextually legally plausible within a domestic legal order—but which then produces the opposite effect on sovereign immunity.[103] It is possible to break the Spanish state into two distinct functional categories (the way one traditionally broke apart the SOE). The first is the state as sovereign; the second is the state as a market participant. The possibility, then, exists for the state (as it often does through its own internal regulations) to create legal conditions (including consequential conditions like the waiver of sovereign immunity) under which its 'sovereign self' can regulate its 'commercial' self as if it were an ordinary enterprise. That, of course, is the implicit premise of governmentalising delegations of regulatory power to the private firms—the idea that such firms can exercise both commercial and sovereign roles directly in the market. In either case, there would be no expectation of sovereign immunity. At the heart of the OECD narrative, the parity principle would then work to transpose that premise not just to the SOE but to that functionally distinct portion of the state apparatus that itself exercises ownership power.[104]

Now the vectors of immunity are reversed. If, indeed, the Spanish Ministry of Agriculture controls the SOE, then the Spanish State itself (in its operational form as the apex authority for corporate commercial conduct) on principles of veil piercing. But because the acts complained of are now understood as primarily commercial (because they are effectuated in and through markets), then the entity does collapse back into the state, but the state now bears liability for breach of commercial contract. Likewise, under an attribution regime, it may be conceded that the transaction at the heart of the contract breach was controlled by and attributed to the state. But here again, the actions of the enterprise were in furtherance of directives of the state which, if it had been issued under the law to private companies, would have produced

[102] It is important to note that the levels of control between the state ownership entity (as the OECD describes that functionally distinct state operation) and the SOE can vary as widely as between operating companies and apex corporations in the private sector. There is never an identity between the state owner and the SOE as a matter of theory. Cf. Garry D. Bruton, Mike W. Peng, David Ahlstrom, Ciprian Stan And Kehan Xu 'State Owned Enterprises Around the World as Hybrid Organizations' (2015) 29(1) Academy of Management Perspectives 92–114. To that end the developing cases applying vel piercing and agency in distinctly new ways in the emerging area of human rights torts are worth considering, and will likely be applicable. *See* Section 3.

[103] This is in essence the key and valuable insight (at least for me) of Schönsteiner (n 12).

[104] Recall here OECD SOE Governance premises respecting the constitution of a body within the state charged with exercising ownership authority. OECD SOE Governance (n 27) p16 ('Ownership entity' can be understood to mean either a single state ownership agency, a co-ordinating agency or a government ministry responsible for exercising state ownership ibid.).

no immunity. In both cases, the reason is simple—the state organ responsible for the action was not engaged in sovereign acts—it was merely complying with legal requirements. The state directed these requirements in its sovereign capacity. Thus, the state could both order itself to control the operations of its SOEs in ways that collapse autonomy, or could direct the SOE, through the state controlling organ, to breach a contract—in both cases, the state organ to which that action is attributable would not be the state apparatus operating in its sovereign capacity. The state, then, would be liable and a functionally differentiated amalgam of authority operating under the law.

This conceptual form may be especially useful in the context of Socialist (especially Chinese) SOEs.[105] The application is made more relevant by the move among Chinese SOEs and their state oversight organs to adopt and implement corporate social responsibility codes.[106] And, indeed, one of the most interesting areas of convergence (structured under ether veil piercing—agency or attribution analysis) turns on the decisions about outward investment strategies of SOEs as well as the valuing and risk mapping of critical decisions or outcomes.[107] These strategic decisions are inevitably made, but it is understood as an aspect of strategic planning in the context of private multinational production chains. In the context of SOE activity, any such guidance necessarily includes at least a modicum (perhaps otherwise sufficient for immunity) of a sovereign character. But that sovereign character is then potentially decisive for attributing the conduct to the state or building a successful veil piercing case or agency. The relevance is enhanced even as Chinese authorities have sought to better conform the management of their SOEs to the core premises of the 'deal' described above, but with quite pronounced Socialist characteristics.[108]

3 The Rise of Human Rights Torts

The challenges to the traditional structures of presumptions that effectively insulated states from liability for the conduct—even the commercial conduct—of their SOEs are contested not merely conceptually but also in the development (again

[105] *See,* e.g. Lee Jones and Yizheng Zou 'Rethinking the Role of State-Owned Enterprises in China's Rise (2017) 22(6) New Political Economy 743–760. More particularly, the attribution rules with respect to such SOEs when they project power out through their supply chains would be relevant and complex. *See,* e.g. Klaus E Meyer, Yuan Ding, Jing Li and Hua Zhang 'Overcoming distrust: How state-owned enterprises adapt their foreign entries to institutional pressures abroad' (2014) 45(8) Journal of International Business Studies 1005–1028.

[106] Qinghua Zhu, Junjun Liu and Kee-hungLai 'Corporate social responsibility practices and performance improvement among Chinese national state-owned enterprises' (2016) 171 International Journal of Production Economics 417–426.

[107] Ming Hua Li, Lin Cui and Jiangyong Lu 'Varieties in state capitalism: Outward FDI strategies of central and local state-owned enterprises from emerging economy countries' (2004) 45(8) Journal of International Business Studies 980.

[108] *See,* e.g. Li-Wen Li 'Reforming China's State Owned Enterprises: From Structure to People (2017) 229 China Quarterly 107–129.

from the flanks) of what appears to be an international common law of human rights torts. The cases arise from corporate action grounded broadly in the UNGP's second pillar, corporate responsibility to respect human rights and the elaboration of codes of conduct as quasi-regulatory frameworks applicable to the production chains over which the 'legislating' enterprise presides.[109] The emerging jurisprudence also suggests that their principles apply not just to private apex corporations under agency principles but also the state as the apex body corporate of SOEs. This is especially potent for state-based responsivities such as supply chain due diligence and the accountability for applying the domestic legal order throughout the SOEs chain of influence or control. A sense of the emerging jurisprudence suggests the trajectory of not merely the substantive standards for human rights torts in business conduct, but also the scope of liability, one that seeks to push liability up the production chain to its highest point without otherwise disturbing settled principles of veil piercing or agency law.

Let us start with the structural implications of climate change litigation.

> Climate change litigation is increasingly viewed as a tool to influence policy outcomes and corporate behaviour. Strategic cases are designed to press national governments to be more ambitious on climate or to enforce existing legislation, while cases against major emitters seek compensation for loss and damage. Routine planning and regulatory cases are increasingly including climate change arguments, exposing courts to climate science and climate-related arguments even where incidental to the main claim.[110]

In the USA, climate change followed a two-prong strategy before 2021. The first was to develop a positive constitutional right to protection against climate change.[111] The second focused on expanding enforcement of current law or efforts to block the abandonment of climate-positive legislation. Public and private actors sought to use either the law of nuisance or tort against fossil fuel enterprises.[112] Though mostly unsuccessful, these sought to create a set of positive obligations that would have two distinct effects. The first was to impose on states a regulatory obligation that requires sovereign action. The second was to impose on states and other actors a delegable responsibility for administering the operationalisation of this sovereign obligation.

---

[109] For excellent grounding in the conceptualisation of this development, see, e.g. Anna Beckers *Taking Corporate Codes Seriously: Towards Private Law Enforcement of Voluntary Corporate Social Responsibility Codes* (2014); Birgit Spiesshofer, *Responsible Enterprise* (CH Beck, Hart, Nomos 2018); Jennifer A. Zerk, *Multinationals and Corporate Social Responsibility, Limitations and Opportunities in International Law* (CUP 2006); Penelope A. Bergkamp 'Models of Corporate Supply Chain Liability' (2018) 2 Jura Falconis Jg. 55.

[110] Joanna Seltzer and Rebecca Byrnes 'Global Trends in Climate Change Litigation: 2019 Snapshot' Centre for Climate Change Economics and Policy (July 2019) <https://www.lse.ac.uk/GranthamInstitute/wp-content/uploads/2019/07/GRI_Global-trends-in-climate-change-litigation-2019-snapshot-2.pdf>.

[111] Juliana v. US No. 18-36082 (9th Cir. 2020).

[112] *See,* e.g. *Rhode Island v,. Chevron Corp* No. 19-1818 (1st Cir 2020); Pacific Coast Federation of Fishermen's Associations v. Chevron 3:18-cv-07477 (ND CA).

As a result, cases like *State of the Netherlands v Urgenda*[113] are significant not merely because of their narrow holding—in that case that the Dutch government has a positive obligation to take measures to prevent climate change in general and to reduce its greenhouse emissions by 25% in particular. For the exposure to liability of states for the actions of their SOEs, the case becomes more interesting for the consequential effects of that ruling. In particular, the development of a legal basis for transposing the sovereign duty into the administrative and regulatory responsibility of all actors may contribute to the effort. In this case, that suggests that the Dutch government may have a sovereign legal obligation to exercise its sovereign authority, and that obligation may not be subject to immunity when it derives from a higher legal source. In this case, the Netherland's own constitutional order precluded either waiver of duty or avoidance of judgement. At the same time, the remedy was administrative in nature—in the form of a compulsory order to comply with the requirements of law.[114] The extension in Milieudefensie et al. v. Royal Dutch Shell plc. suggests the trajectory.[115] In that case, the argument was made that the state's positive obligation translated into (or were devolved into a direct responsibility) a corresponding responsibility of Royal Dutch Shell as the parent company of the Shell group[116] and the policy setting apex entity of the Shell group.[117] The more interesting question would have been, had the Dutch state been liable for its failure to compel Royal Dutch Shell to comply with the legal mandates already binding in the state in its sovereign capacity. In each case, the court's notion of partial responsibility produces partial obligation—liability would apply in equal measure.

The principle of upstream liability based on attribution or control (the key concepts around which theories of state liability for SOE activities are formed) has been developed to better effect in the human rights tort cases.[118] One example will suffice here—*Okpabi v. Royal Dutch Shell.*[119] The claimants, Nigerian nationals, asserted that oil spills from pipelines had caused them damage and that the spills were caused by the negligence of a Nigerian subsidiary Shell Petroleum Development Company

---

[113] State of the Netherlands v. Urgenda, ECLI:NL:HR:2019:2006 <https://uitspraken.rechtspraak.nl/inziendocument?id=ECLI:NL:HR:2019:2006>.

[114] Relying in part on the rule in *Demir and Baykara v. Turkey* (Application no. 34503/97) (Grand Chamber 12 November 2008) <https://hudoc.echr.coe.int/eng#{%22itemid%22:[%22001-89558%22]}>.

[115] *Milieudefensie et al. v. Royal Dutch Shell* C/09/571932 / HA ZA 19-379 ECLI:NL:RBDHA:2021:5339.

[116] ibid., para 3.

[117] ibid., para 4.4(1) (unwritten standard of care applicable under written Dutch law).

[118] The first and germinal case Chandler v Cape plc[2012] 1 WLR 3111 remains influential. *See* also, Lungowe v Vedanta Resources plc (2019) UKSC 20; (2020) AC 1045. UK cases have been influential elsewhere. *See,* e.g. *Garcia v. Tahoe Resources Inc.*, 2017 BCCA 39 –CanLII (where a claim against a Canadian parent company is going ahead on similar grounds to this litigation); *Yaiguaje v. Chevron Corporation*, 2015 SCC 42, (2015) 3 S.C.R. 69; *Friday Alfred Akpan* et al. *v. Shell*, Court of Appeal The Hague 17 December 2015. e.

[119] Okpabi v Royal Dutch Shell (12 February 2021) <https://www.supremecourt.uk/cases/docs/uksc-2018-0068-judgment.pdf>.

of Nigeria Ltd. (SPDC) of Royal Dutch Shell a UK domiciled company.[120] SPDC operated the pipelines for an unincorporated joint venture between a Nigerian SOE and the local subsidiaries of other global enterprises.[121] The plaintiffs claimed that the parent Royal Dutch Shell owed them a common law duty because

> it exercised significant control over material aspects of SPDC's operations and/or assumed responsibility for SPDC's operations, including by the promulgation and imposition of mandatory health, safety and environmental policies, standards and manuals which allegedly failed to protect the appellants against the risk of foreseeable harm arising from SPDC's operations.[122]

The case was decided on the jurisdictional issue (as are many cases of this type)—whether there is a triable issue against the defendant.[123] Then, the extent of potential liability was not based on veil piercing or agency but a form of attribution based on control short of either agency or disregard of corporate autonomy. Relying on Lungowe,[124] the court explained:

> The appellants' legal argument has accordingly been recast in the light of Vedanta. It is now contended that a duty of care arises by what they describe as Vedanta routes (1) to (4), namely: (1) RDS taking over the management or joint management of the relevant activity of SPDC; (2) RDS providing defective advice and/or promulgating defective group-wide safety/environmental policies which were implemented as of course by SPDC; (3) RDS promulgating group-wide safety/environmental policies and taking active steps to ensure their implementation by SPDC, and (4) RDS holding out that it exercises a particular degree of supervision and control of SPDC.[125]

The plaintiffs based their claims on the control by the parent of health and safety policy, parent monitoring (a necessary responsibility under principles of human rights due diligence according to soft law frameworks like the UN Guiding Principles for Business and Human Rights), the establishment of a CSR Committee at the parent level, the actual monitoring undertaken by the parent and the establishment by the parent of facilities and infrastructure standards.[126] The Court rejected a rule that would have provided that the promulgation by a parent company of group-wide policies can never in itself give rise to a duty of care (and thus to liability for its breach).[127] They rejected the standard of control as dispositive.

> In a sense, all parents control their subsidiaries. That control gives the parent the opportunity to get involved in management. But control of a company and de facto management of part of its activities are two different things. A subsidiary may maintain de jure control of its

---

[120] ibid paras 3–6.

[121] ibid para 5.

[122] ibid para 7.

[123] ibid para 20.

[124] *Lungowe v Vedanta Resources plc* [2019] UKSC 20; [2020] AC 1045 which represented the synthesis of the case law standard developed to date.

[125] Okpabi v Royal Dutch Shell (n 119) para 26.

[126] ibid 29. These connections were then elaborated at length in the opinion. ibid. paras 30–70.

[127] ibid para 143.

activities, but nonetheless delegate de facto management of part of them to emissaries of its parent.[128]

The court determined that the allegations put forward raised triable management and control issues sufficient to trigger liability.[129]

Two points here are worth underlining with relevance to the liability of state owners of SOEs. The first is that issues of control are grounded in regulatory aspects of inter-corporate relations. That is, they were based on the application of rule systems meant to rationalise the operation of the enterprise throughout its production chain. The control did not arise from economic activities, rather economic activities were in part a function of the operation of the regulatory environment. The second point worth noting is that the de facto rather than the de jure relationship among entities was decisive for determining responsibility. That suggests that purely production-oriented controls are not necessarily the limiting category for the determination of liability, nor is it necessary either to find an agency relationship. Attribution of control over management grounded in legal or normative compliance is sufficient. For state owners of SOEs that might appear to broaden the scope within which they might—in their private capacity as owner entity—be liable where the operating SOE fails to prevent actionable harm. Alternatively, taking insight from the climate cases might suggest that such findings of control may then open the door not to direct liability to harmed individuals but to administrative measures against the state by the state itself. That is, the state as a sovereign might then hold accountable the state as the apex body corporate of the economic unit, the operational entity of which is the SOE.

The logic of the old categories and premises applied in these emerging contexts suggests that the delegation itself creates in the state a commercial organ whose implementation of sovereign objectives is a necessary component of commercial (economic) activity, the control of which is vested in the apex owner (the state) by the terms of the delegation of such authority itself. In this case, the very act of legislating a delegation of sovereign authority and sovereign (administrative) responsibility through the economic sector, to be applied in markets and market centred activities, bifurcates both the state and the private sector enterprises operating in and through markets. On the one hand, they each engage in economic activity to which the ordinary rules of veil piercing apply to allocate risk based on core principle of asset partitioning (based on control relationships—either by way of ownership or contract). On the other hand, they each engage in sovereign activities for which the traditional state protective attribution rules apply. In one case, no sovereign immunity principles apply either to private entities or SOEs. In the other, sovereign immunity ought to apply to the sovereign activities of an enterprise, either private or SOE. In

[128] ibid para 147 (quoting Lord Briggs in Vedanta: "the parent may incur the relevant responsibility to third parties if, in published materials, it holds itself out as exercising that degree of supervision and control of its subsidiaries, even if it does not in fact do so.").

[129] ibid. paras 156–159.

both cases, the state is understood to have 'two bodies.'[130] As the apex body corporate,[131] the state itself is the subject of this delegation—in this case, to itself in its manifestation as the corporate owner of the operating enterprises through which the state engages in commercial activities. In that manifestation, the state itself is subject to the ordinary obligations of corporate ownership in vertical chains of authority and to the disregard of the autonomy of its operating enterprises under theories of agency and veil piercing. *The state, in this sense, becomes its own legal subject*[132]—and when it operates as the apex entity owner of SOEs, the bearer of rights and duties pari passu with those of other (private) entities in the same position.

This conceptual position of legal subjectivity is made stronger in the context where it is a host state that seeks to hold a home state liable for the failings of its SOE operating in host state territory. In that context, the host state can well treat the home state simultaneously as (1) the apex enterprise overseeing the operations of the SOE concerning both the SOEs commercial and regulatory responsibilities and (2) the sovereign entity exercising sovereign regulatory over itself and its enterprises. This conceptualisation requires a transformation already well demonstrated in the context of human rights and sustainability legislation: the privatisation of governance and its delegation to private sector economic activities undertaken in enterprise form, compliance with which remains a sovereign prerogative. That, in turn, effectively changes the character of delegated (privatised) regulatory administration within a production chain, the ultimate responsibility of which is vested in the apex governing body corporate (in the case of SOEs under the OECD normative framework that would be the sovereign itself through its ownership entity). The state, in this context, can be both sovereign (and immune) and corporate (waiving immunity pari passu with such waivers accorded to private enterprises in the same circumstances). Alternatively, the logic of the model and its development through governmentalisation and delegation of sovereign regulatory authority generally to market forces operating in enterprise form is to extend sovereign immunity to all economic actors engaging in sovereign actions or as agents (here a distinctive application of traditional attribution rules) of the state in its sovereign capacity. The result is to substantially narrow the ability of individuals to assert actions where they have suffered damage—but an increase in the state's regulatory authority and convergence of administrative and economic institutional models.

---

[130] Ernst Kantorowicz, *The King's Two Bodies (subtitled, A Study in Mediaeval Political Theology* (Princeton 1957) (the physical body of the state in the contemporary form of the apparatus of government joined in and the incarnation of the body politic, but at the same time physically distinct and autonomous).

[131] In that context see a useful discussion in Walter D. Love 'Edmund Burke's Idea of the Body Corporate: A Study in Imagery' (2009) 27(2) Review of Politics 184–197. As Rayman-Bacchus noted: "Governments have been relinquishing control of state enterprises to the body corporate. There is a sense in which the body corporate has become a Hobbesian leviathan." Les Raymond-Bacchus 'Reflecting on Corporate Legitimacy' (2006) 17(2–3) Critical Perspectives in Accounting 323–335.

[132] Drawing on, e.g. John Dewey 'The Historic Background of Corporate Legal Personality' [1926] 35(6) Yale Law Journal 655–673.

That choice has yet to be made. The legislative approaches favour a model of convergence of economic and administrative institutional models and the limiting of enforcement authority to the state. The judicial approaches favour a responsibility-based model driven by individual claimants asserting claims for damage caused by a breach of a legal duty. It is a private law model in contrast to the administrative and public law model of statutory approaches. In either case, there is no conceptual basis for treating the state corporate owner any differently from any other enterprise in markets. That is the 'deal' now transformed by the augmentation of the regulatory responsibilities of enterprises in markets driven by human rights and sustainability-based reforms to conceptions of what it means to operate in the market.

Taken together, this development of the expectations for the global development of productive forces produces the contradiction around which academics, policy-makers and others seek to bend the logic and premises of the traditional framework for the allocation of liability and the characterisation of state activity (especially when projected abroad) to new realities. Traditional rules of attribution, agency and veil piercing all lend themselves either to odd results or to calls for substantial development. Yet those efforts do not necessarily satisfactorily confront the contradiction—not of the governmentalisation of the economic sector, but rather of the allocation of liability for, and expectations of duties within, that sector by the state as a participant. To that end, the notions of sovereign categorisation must be abandoned or refashioned (the word choice suggests political rather than operational consideration). And it leaves those who shape narrative—and the legal structures that are its incarnation, with choices—likely unpalatable: (1) develop a new theory of enterprise immunity (that includes private entities and SOEs) respecting the sovereign functions and activities which have been delegated to them, (2) attribute such delegation to the state which, at least as the apex body corporate of its sovereign commercial activities, opens the state to liability (broadening the human rights tort model) or (3) develop, on the German Supply Chain Due Diligence model, an immunity to liability to individuals but to vest the state (in its sovereign capacity) the power to impose civil and administrative measures against the entity (and the state in its role as the apex owner) where the responsibility for operational level misconduct is vested in the highest level corporate organ.

4 Conclusion

There are no easy answers to the questions posed in this contribution. There are effectively only political choices, and as John Dewey noted almost a century ago, legal significs are grounded in the calculus of politics, society and culture.[133] The essay thus concludes where it started—with revolution and a feathered donkey perched

[133] John Dewey 'The Historic Background of Corporate Legal Personality', supra (as a thing that "signifies what the law makes it signify... [but where such signification] depended upon a mass of non-legal considerations" ibid p 655).

atop a tower as if it were a throne. One returns, then, to that marvellous aria in Act 1 Scene 2 of Giacomo Rossini's *La Cenerentola* that nicely frames the framework and analysis of this essay on what may be the emerging scope of the liability of state owners of economic instrumentalities organised as state-owned enterprises or otherwise. Act I, Scene Two opens immediately after the two naughty step sisters are informed, along with Cinderella, of the desire of the prince to find a wife. At that moment, their father, Don Magnifico, emerges in a fog to relate a most strange dream, one that had been interrupted by the cacophony of the princely invitation. He dreams that he has been symbolically transformed into an ass with feathers that has taken flight to perch on a bell tower as if on a throne. Don Magnifico divines: he himself is the ass, his daughters his feathers, and the fight is towards a significant rise in rank through the reproductive capabilities of his children, each of whom is a little ass, and all to the greater glory of the principal ass-Don Magnifico himself.[134] Of course, Don Magnifico is made an ass by his stepdaughter and the prince who marries her.

This essay considered the risk—liability consequences of a framework in which the state assumes the role of a Don Magnifico—an ass with feathers (its economic enterprises) whose dream, though interrupted, still appears to portend sitting atop a tower as his progeny reproduces themselves as little kingdoms all for the greater glory of the state; a state that remains a beplumed ass untouched perched atop a throne like a tower. More specifically, as forms and functions of states and other entities converge within the economic sphere, it becomes harder to maintain the complex systems of legal liability allocations and of systems of legal risk, developed for a time in which the ideal state-regulated and the ideal private body corporate engaged in economic

[134] Giacomo Rossini, La Cenerentola (Jacopo Ferretti (Librettist) premiered Teatro Valle, Rome, 26 January 1817), Act I, Scene 2. The libretto of Don Magnifico's aria,: Miei rampolli femminini follows in the original and in an English translation: *Don Magnifico: Miei rampolli femminini, Vi ripudio; mi vergogno! Un magnifico mio sogno, Mi veniste a sconcertar. Come son mortificate! Degne figlie d'un Barone!* Via*: silenzio ed attenzione. State il sogno a meditar. Mi sognai fra il fosco e il chiaro Un bellissimo somaro. Un somaro, ma solenne. Quando a un tratto, ho che portento! Su le spalle a cento a cento Gli spuntavano le penne Ed in alto, fsct, volò! Ed in cima a un campanile Come in trono si fermò. Si sentiano per di sotto Le campane sdindonar. Col cì cì, ciù ciù di botto Mi faceste risvegliar. Ma d'un sogno sì intralciato Ecco il simbolo spiegato. La campana suona a festa? Allegrezza in casa è questa. Quelle penne? Siete voi. Quel gran volo? Plebe addio. Resta l'asino di poi? Ma quell'asino son io. Chi vi guarda vede chiaro Che il somaro è il genitor. Fertilissima Regina L'una e l'altra diverrà; Ed il nonno una dozzina Di nepoti abbraccierà. Un Re piccolo di qua. Un Re bambolo di là. E la gloria mia sarà.*" [trans. Don Magnifico: My female offspring, I repudiate you; I'm ashamed! A wonderful dream of mine You managed to interrupt. How embarrassing they are! Worthy daughters of a Baron! Shoo!: silence and attention. While I ponder the dream. I dreamed half clearly, half hazily, of A beautiful donkey. A ass, but solemn. When all of a sudden, oh what a wonder! Up on his back in the hundreds Feathers were poking out And into the air, fsct, he flew! And to the top of a bell tower To perch as if on a throne. But then I heard as if from below The bells clanging. Col cì cì, ciù ciù di botto You made me wake up. But even from a disrupted dream Its meaning can be derived. Does the bell ring in celebration? This means there is joy in the house. Those feathers? They are you. That great flight? Farewell plebs. Does the donkey then remain? But that donkey is me. Whoever looks at you sees clearly That the ass is the parent. Queen of fertility From one the others will emerge; And the grandfather of a dozen Nephews will embrace them all. A little King over here. A baby King there. And the glory will all be mine.].

activity. The regulation of the development of productive forces and its actualisation were considered distinct provinces of law and spheres of legal liability. Globalisation has produced a convergence in which the logic of the old framework becomes less coherent. This essay has sought to examine that incoherence and point the way to what appears as the emerging approach to allocating legal risk and liability.

When the state engages in economic activity, it occupies a space at the meeting place of several increasingly important legal developments that are likely to change the nature and character of the relationship between the state, its economic instrumentalities, its exposure to liability, and the scope of its responsibilities as a shareholder of productive forces[135] engaged in economic activity. The trajectories of legal development point to a form of revolution of the categories within which legal risk and liability have been allocated in the context of economic activity. Where private enterprises regulate and states operate like private entities in markets especially beyond their national borders, and where the operation of public law and private law increasingly differ only by reference to the scope of their applicability, then the old notions of treating states as a special form of shareholder and of state economic activity as a function of the form in which it occurs increasingly las lost meaning.[136] Emerging realities on the ground suggest that states as market actors might face the same sort of liability as other actors. Whether sovereign immunity ought to extend to the delegated regulatory activities of private actors (as well as to states and their SOEs) remains to be seen. For the moment, it seems likely that sovereign immunity for states in respect of their commercial (economic) activities will continue to face a challenge as a theory and that courts might start to nibble away at its edges. The likely drivers to that end will continue to emerge from the development of the legalisation of human rights due diligence from an international societally based soft law principle embedded first in the UN Guiding Principles for Business and Human Rights' Second (corporate responsibility to respect human rights) pillar,[137] as well as from the legalisation of its none state-based responsibilities through the emergence of international private law of human rights and sustainability tort. Whether these developments will give rise to remedial rights by individuals affected, or whether they instead will boomerang back to the state through the emergence of new forms of quasi-administrative civil

---

[135] The reference here is to the Chinese Marxist Leninist notion of economic capacity comprehensively understood. *See* Deng Xiaoping, "To Build Socialism We Must First Develop the Productive Forces" (Marxists.org, 5 May 1980) <https://www.marxists.org/reference/archive/deng-xiaoping/1980/101.htm> accessed 22 June 2021. The idea was to shift the focus from the strict division of public and private-of political-regulatory spheres and economic-productive spheres, in the interlinking of economic activity (in whatever form organized) and the political-regulatory authority of the state.

[136] "To stimulate the initiative of the enterprises, we have to separate ownership from management in various ways; that is a very important part of the reform... Actually, as means of developing the productive forces, different managerial forms can serve either capitalism or socialism. Whichever system uses them better will benefit most." Deng Xiaoping, "On the Reform of Enterprises and on the Banking System" (The Selected Works of Deng Xiaoping: Modern Day Contributions to Marxism–Leninism, 19 December 1980) <https://dengxiaopingworks.wordpress.com/2013/03/18/on-the-reform-of-enterprises-and-of-the-banking-system/>.

[137] Considered in Larry Catá Backer (n 64).

and administrative penalties and compulsions, remains to be seen. Until the realities of state immunity catch-up to the facts on the ground, the concept of state projection of economic power in markets remains little more than a beplumed donkey atop a bell tower as if on a throne.

Larry Catá Backer W. Richard and Mary Eshelman Faculty Scholar Professor of Law and International Affairs, Pennsylvania State University; member, Coalition for Peace & Ethics.

Corporate Social Responsibility with 'Chinese Characteristics' an Overview of the Obligations of Chinese State-Owned Enterprises

Flora Sapio

1 Introduction

This chapter explores the mechanisms used to monitor Chinese multinational corporations' (MCNs) compliance with corporate social responsibility (CSR) obligations. Despite the dynamism of China's private sector, state-owned MNCs play a pivotal role in the implementation of the 'One Belt One Road' strategy[1] and continue to account for roughly 30 per cent of domestic GDP.[2] SOEs' position within China's governance system and the ideological features of China's governance model make CSR obligations a binding regulatory duty of state-owned MNCs and of their domestic and foreign subsidiaries rather than a voluntary obligation.

In Western legal systems, CSR and its more recent evolution of business and human rights are understood as existing beyond state regulation. CSR is a form of regulation public and private enterprises may adopt on an entirely voluntary basis and integrate within their business model. Accordingly, from its very inception, scholarship on CSR has existed and moved beyond the limits of the state. Early CSR scholarship examined broader issues in corporate compliance. More recent scholarship is instead analysing emerging transnational structures of corporate governance outlined in the United Nations Principles on Business and Human Rights. Among these structures, non-state-based mechanisms of accountability occupy an essential place. While essential studies of CSR in China exist, they are primarily focused on the private

[1] Wu Gang, 'SOEs Lead Infrastructure Push in 1,700 'Belt and Road' Projects' *Caixin Global* (10 May 2017).

[2] University of Alberta China Institute, *State-owned Enterprises in the Chinese Economy Today: Role, Reform, and Evolution* (Edmonton: University of Alberta, 2018) 3.

F. Sapio (✉)
University of Naples "L'Orientale", Naples, Italy
e-mail: fsapio@unior.it

J. Chaisse et al. (eds.), *Regulation of State-Controlled Enterprises*, International Law and the Global South, https://doi.org/10.1007/978-981-19-1368-6_16

sector and on specific aspects of private corporations' responsibility.[3] Therefore, our knowledge of CSR mechanisms applicable to state-owned MNCs can still be augmented and enriched. This chapter does so by situating notions of CSR within the legal and political context of China and describing CSR norms and mechanisms grounded within the system of regulations of the Chinese Communist Party. State-owned MNCs are subject to leadership by the Chinese Communist Party. Therefore, their directors and management are bound to comply with relevant party regulations. Their non-compliance can be sanctioned through party discipline punishments (*dangde jilü chufen*).

The first part of this chapter places the notion of CSR (*gongsi shehui zeren*) against the backdrop of non-state-based compliance and monitoring mechanisms specific to state-owned MNCs. All of these mechanisms are grounded in the Statute of the Chinese Communist Party and the system of party regulations. These mechanisms are described in the second and third part of the article. They include party leadership over CSR exerted through party groups (*dangzu*); professional guidance by the State-owned Assets Supervision and Administration Commission (SASAC) Guidance Committee on Central Enterprises' Social Responsibility and monitoring through the 'inspection tour system' (*xunshi zhidu*). The fourth part of the chapter provides an overview of the methods used to assess CRS compliance. Beyond the generic duty of disclosure, compliance is mainly assessed through evaluation and ranking procedures, where 'social credit' and big data are beginning to play a pivotal role. In its concluding section, the chapter presents some reflections on the main features of CSR in China and their relevance to the One Belt One Road.

2 CSR with 'Chinese Characteristics'

CSR is a form of endogenous regulation all enterprises may adopt on an entirely voluntary basis and integrate within their business model. But what happens when an enterprise is owned or managed by the state and headquartered in China? In the CSR

---

[3] Karin Buhmann, 'Corporate social responsibility in China: current issues and their relevance for implementation of law' (2005) 22 (1) *The Copenhagen Journal of Asian Studies* 62; Karin Buhmann, 'Chinese human rights guidance on minerals sourcing: Building soft power' (2017) 46 (2) *Journal of Current Chinese Affairs* 135; Nadira Lamrad, 'Transnational Business, CSR, and Governance in China' (2012) 45 *UBCL Rev. 45* 691; Tian Zhilong, Rui Wang, and Wen Yang, 'Consumer responses to corporate social responsibility (CSR) in China' (2011) 101 (2) *Journal of Business Ethics* 197; Jeremy moon and Xi Shen, 'CSR in China research: Salience, focus and nature' (2010) 94 (4) *Journal of Business Ethics* 613; Yin, Juelin and Yuli Zhang, 'Institutional dynamics and corporate social responsibility (CSR) in an emerging country context: Evidence from China' (2012) 111 (2) *Journal of Business Ethics* 301; Kuo Lopin, Chin-Chen Yeh, and Hui-Cheng Yu, 'Disclosure of corporate social responsibility and environmental management: Evidence from China' (2012) 19 (5) *Corporate Social Responsibility and Environmental Management* 273; Tang, Zhi and Jintong Tang, 'Stakeholder–firm power difference, stakeholders' CSR orientation, and SMEs' environmental performance in China' (2012) 27 (4) *Journal of Business Venturing* 436.

literature, there is a consensus that CSR goes beyond 'that which is required by law'.[4] Therefore, the literature has inquired about the factors that can induce an enterprise to go beyond the duty to comply with state regulation.[5] In China, perhaps the most important factors to induce CSR compliance are notions of political responsibility (*zhengzhi zeren*) towards the Communist Party and the state, while discipline (*jilü*) is the most essential standard of conduct SOEs and their management ought to follow. Both political responsibility and discipline are mechanisms grounded outside of state regulation.

A defining feature of all Marxist–Leninist systems is the existence of a normative order based on laws promulgated by the state and a parallel regulatory system based on regulations enacted by ruling Communist Parties. These governance regimes were born through popular revolutions led by Communist Parties or by coalitions of revolutionary movements. Leading parties and revolutionary movements adopted their autonomous regulatory systems. Once those parties rose to power, their regulatory systems continued to exist side by side with the legal and administrative order of the state. After the fall of the Soviet Bloc, 'dual legal systems' exist in China, but also in Cuba, North Korea and Vietnam. In these systems, notions of 'all applicable laws' include at least: (1) state legislation and regulation, (2) political and administrative regulation by the ruling party, (3) binding international instruments, (4) non-binding instruments endorsed by the state, private, and public economic entities, and (5) private regulation. In Marxist–Leninist systems, these five regulatory orders are hierarchically arranged, according to political principles absent from Western liberal democracies.

The Communist Party's Statute occupies the topmost place in the hierarchy of legal norms of Marxist–Leninist systems. Next are party-based regulatory systems, binding international instruments, state legislation, and finally, non-binding international and domestic instruments. From this peculiar arrangement, it follows that the ruling party gives life to the state's administrative system and indirectly allows the state to ratify all

[4] Abagail McWilliams and Donald Siegel, 'Corporate social responsibility: A theory of the firm perspective' (2011) 26 (1) *Academy of Management Review* 117.

[5] Milton Friedman, 'The social responsibility of business is to increase its profits' in Walther C. Zimmerli, Klaus Richter, Markus Holzinger (eds.), Corporate ethics and corporate governance (Springer 2007), 173–178. Abagail McWilliams Donald S. Siegel, and Patrick M. Wright, 'Corporate social responsibility: Strategic implications' (2006) 43 (1) *Journal of Management Studies* 1; R. Edward Freeman and S. Ramakrishna Velamuri, 'A new approach to CSR: Company stakeholder responsibility' in José Allouche (ed.) Corporate Social Responsibility, (Palgrave Macmillan, 2006): 9–23. Lex Donaldson and James H. Davis, 'Stewardship theory or agency theory: CEO governance and shareholder returns' (1991) 1 *Australian Journal of Management* 49. Thomas Donaldson and Lee E. Preston, 'The stakeholder theory of the corporation: Concepts, evidence, and implications' (1995) 20 (1) *Academy of Management Review* 65. Thomas M. Jones, 'Instrumental stakeholder theory: A synthesis of ethics and economics' (1995) 20 (2) *Academy of Management Review* 404.Oliver Hart, 'Corporate governance: some theory and implications' (1995) 104 (430) *The Economic Journal* 678.

binding international instruments and endorse non-binding ones.[6] Moreover, state-owned entities are regulated first and foremost through political norms created by the ruling party. These norms may or may not be transposed to the Constitution of the state. They may or may not be aligned to state-based legislation and regulation. They may or may not be conveyed through a more technical language, making them actionable to legislative, executive, and administrative organs and intelligible to external observers. This complex dynamic, one where the hierarchies of law so familiar to us are turned upside down, also involves compliance with the UNGPs and, more generally, CSR obligations.

2.1 Notions of 'Social Responsibility' in Political Regulation

The Statute of the Chinese Communist Party does not contain principles or substantive provisions referencing the notion of CSR. Neither do such principles exist in the Constitution of the People's Republic of China. It is often observed that the Company Law of the PRC and the Partnership Enterprise Law make direct references to CSR. Article 5 of the Company Law reads:

> In their business activities, companies must (*bixu*) respect the law, and administrative regulations; respect social morality, and business ethics; be honest and trustworthy; accept the supervision of government and the public; fulfil social responsibility. (...)[7]

The notion of CSR exists in the Partnership Enterprises Law of the PRC, where article 7 reads:

> Partners in cooperative enterprises must (*bixu*) respect the law, and administrative regulations; respect social morality, and business ethics; be honest and trustworthy; accept the supervision of government and the public; fulfil social responsibility.[8]

Article 5 of the Company Law and article 7 of the Partnership Enterprises Law are interpreted as introducing declaratory provisions rather than creating a legal obligation to comply with CSR norms and codes of conduct.[9] The Company Law

---

[6] Larry Catá Backer and Keren Wang, 'The emerging structures of socialist constitutionalism with Chinese characteristics: extra-judicial detention and the Chinese constitutional order' (2014) 23 *Pacific Rim Law and Policy Journal*, 251.

[7] art 5, Company Law of the People's Republic of China (*Zhonghua Renmin Gongheguo Gongsifa*), issued on 29 December 1993, as amended on 26 October 2018, amendments effective from the same date, <http://www.npc.gov.cn/npc/xinwen/2018-11/05/content_2065671.htm>.

[8] art 7, Partnership Enterprises Law of the People's Republic of China (*Zhonghua Renmin Gongheguo Hehuo Qiyefa*), issued on 23 February 1997, as amended on 27 August 2006, amendments effective from 1 June 2007, <http://www.npc.gov.cn/wxzl/gongbao/2006-09/26/content_5354975.htm>.

[9] Zhang Hui, one of the most prominent scholars of CSR at the China Academy of Social Sciences, observes how: 'Given that the legalization of CSR is a form of legal responsibility, it should possess a legally binding force, particularly in terms of judicial remedies and enforcement. But the Company Law does not provide a precise definition of what CSR is, neither does it contain provisions on

and the Partnership Enterprises Law are the two only national-level laws containing a declaratory provision on CSR. While several documents on CSR exist in China, all of them belong to the category of normative documents (*guifangxing wenjian*).[10] Coherent with global CSR approaches, these documents merely provide guidance (*yindao*) to private enterprises without being a source of binding norms.

Once we move from the domain of state legislation to the realm of non-state-based mechanisms, the regulatory landscape changes substantially. An awareness of what the West conceptualised in the 1960s as 'corporate social responsibility'[11] emerges from the writings of Chinese revolutionaries produced as early as 1939.[12] Almost a century later, economic reform and the launch of the Belt and Road Initiative brought new actors to the table and caused changes in language and the core concept of 'social responsibility'. This change came about with the doctrine of 'Scientific Outlook on Development', which was included in the Statute of the Chinese Communist Party in 2007.[13] 'Scientific Outlook on Development' is a political doctrine that references each one of the features of the Western concepts of CSR and business and human rights. The political doctrine of 'Scientific Outlook on Development' is premised on the core notion of 'placing man as the foundation' (*yiren weiben*). As explained by Premier Wen Jiabao, 'placing man as the foundation' means balancing economic development with considerations about human health, quality of life, and man's rights, conducting economic activities that are 'comprehensive, coordinated, and sustainable', respectful of man and the natural environment.[14]

These meanings exceed legal obligations because they are premised on more abstract notions of ethics and morality. They include all the moral and ethical aspects

---

the legal responsibilities arising from non-compliance with CSR. Even as a declaratory provision of the Company Law, [CSR] must have a relatively clear connotation, to facilitate its explanation and enforcement. However, from the perspective of interpreting the Company Law, both of these circumstances are difficult to establish'. Zhang Hui, 'The Legal Status of Corporate Social Responsibility' (*Gongsi shehuizeren: falü weizhi*), (2009) 2 *China Annual Review of Business Law (Zhonguo Shangfa Niankan)* 56.

[10] On this category of documents, see Peter Howard Corne, 'Creation and Application of Law in the PRC' (2002) 50 (2) *The American Journal of Comparative Law* 369.

[11] Richard T. De George, *Business Ethics* (Pearson Education 2011).

[12] Liu Shaoqi, 'How to be a Good Communist' in *Selected Works of Liu Shaoqi Vol. 1* (1939), 107–168.

[13] The idea of a moral and ethical responsibility of businesses for the broader impact of economic processes was memorialised under the Preamble of the Statute of the Chinese Communist Party in 2007. Thus, the 'Scientific Outlook on Development' came to constitute a 'major guiding direction' (*zhongyao zhidao fangzheng*) of China's economic development, as well as a 'major strategic thought' (*zhongda zhanlüe sixiang*) to be followed in the development of China's economy, and to implement in all the realms of economic and social activity. 'Resolution of the 17th Congress of the Chinese Communist Party on the Amendments to the Statute of the Chinese Communist Party' (*Zhongguo Gongchandang dishiqi cu quanguo daibiao dahui guanyu Zhongguo Gongchandang Zhancheng (xiuzheng'an) de jueyi*), 21 October 2007. Paragraph 7, Preamble to the Statute of the Chinese Communist Party (*Zonggang, Zhongguo Gongchandang Zhancheng*), 21 October 2007.

[14] Wen Jiabao, 'Firmly Establish and Conscientiously Implement the Scientific Development Concept' (*Laogu shuli he renzhen luoshi kexue* fazhanguan), *Sina* (Beijing, 29 February 2004) <http://news.sina.com.cn/c/2004-02-29/11221926301s.shtml> accessed 18 November 2019.

of business processes. The doctrine of 'Scientific Outlook on Development' is not limited to 'apex enterprises'. It includes Chinese MNCs operating along China's New Silk Road and all their domestic and transnational suppliers. In 2007, the 'Scientific Outlook on Development' was made part of the four basic principles (*sixiang jiben yuanze*),[15] becoming an integral part of the political doctrine legitimising the leadership of the Chinese Communist Party. The Xi Jinping leadership endorsed the notion of 'Scientific Outlook on Development'. It also created a new ideological formulation, holding that the 'main contradiction' in China no longer is class warfare between the proletariat and the upper socio-economic strata. In the Xi Jinping period, such contradiction is the one between 'a development that is still unbalanced and inadequate, and the people's ever-growing needs for a better life'.[16] These political code words bear several meanings. The connotations most relevant to CSR are achieving economic development through means adequate to human needs, respectful of the natural environment,[17] transparent, inclusive,[18] and sustainable.[19]

The Statute of the Chinese Communist Party, however, only poses declaratory principles and programmatic norms. The Chinese Communist Party enjoys the power to discipline the directors and managers of state-owned MNCs who violate norms on CSR. But, neither the principle of 'Scientific Development' nor the 'Basic Line' or the 'main contradiction' can be directly invoked or interpreted by the Chinese Communist Party officials. These declaratory principles and norms have been given life through further specifications made by party regulatory documents.

2.2 *'Social Responsibility' (Shehui Zeren) as a Binding Duty in Party Regulations*

Party regulatory documents are binding on all members and organisations of the Chinese Communist Party. Most directors and managers of Chinese MNCs are party members, so they are obligated to respect notions of CSR articulated in party documents. The Statute of the Chinese Communist Party is extremely clear on this point. Prospective party members have to undergo a careful examination and a period of study and training before they are allowed to become full members of the party. A complex application procedure and a two-year training period involving intense work are necessary to make prospective members understand whether party membership is suitable to them. Once an individual has decided in favour of party membership, allegiance to the party is declared by uttering an oath. From that moment on, an individual

---

[15] Paragraphs 7, 23, Preamble to the Statute of the Chinese Communist Party (*Zonggang, Zhongguo Gongchandang Zhancheng*), 21 October 2007.

[16] Paragraph 10, Preamble to the Statute of the Chinese Communist Party (*Zonggang, Zhongguo Gongchandang Zhancheng*), 24 October 2017.

[17] Paragraph 19, *cit.*

[18] Paragraph 10, *cit.*

[19] Paragraph 13, *cit.*

is bound to observe all party regulations in their entirety, taking full responsibility for her conduct and the impact her conduct causes on society and the environment.

Party regulations use the notion of 'social responsibility' (*shehui zeren*) rather than the concept of CSR or the all-encompassing notion of 'business and human rights'. The absence of the adjective 'corporate' from this syntagm underscores how under party regulations, and the notion of 'social responsibility' includes a range of subjects and practices broader than the one referred to by the concept of 'corporate social responsibility (*gongsi shehui zeren*), or also by 'Western' notions of CSR. Chinese and Western notions of CSR focus exclusively on governance processes internal to enterprises. Under these notions, the responsibility belongs to corporate actors, and it excludes other stakeholders. The academic community and transnational fora have attempted to remedy this flaw in CSR notions either through the concept of 'business and human rights' or by designing accountability and remedial mechanisms, including diverse stakeholders. The notion of 'social responsibility' in party regulations is not limited to state-owned MNCs. Whether in their capacity as party members, government officials, or ordinary citizens, public institutions and physical persons are all accountable to organisations of the party. Responsibility exists for conduct that produces effects in China and conducts producing their effects in countries that have adhered to the Belt and Road Initiative.

In the hierarchy of party regulations, 'social responsibility' occupies the place immediately next to the Statute of the Chinese Communist Party. It is defined in 'decisions' and 'opinions' of the Central Committee. The 2003 *Decision on Some Major Issues in Comprehensively Deepening Reform* relates social responsibility to the conduct of state-owned MNCs and their cadres, using the formulation 'sense of social responsibility' (*zerengan*).[20] 'Social responsibility' is seen as an important part of the modernisation of SOEs, needed to enable Chinese MNCs to compete with MNCs headquartered in Western countries.[21] As it relates to individuals, the concept of social responsibility involves ideas about 'integrity', 'trustworthiness', or 'honesty' (*chengxin*). The notion of 'integrity' is, at the same time, one of the twelve core socialist values, a goal to be achieved by social responsibility, and a feature of the social credit system. In the 2013 *Opinion on Nurturing and Practicing Core Socialist Values*, the Central Committee stated that

[20] Decision of the Central Committee of the CPC on Some Major Issues in Deepening Reform (*Zhonggong Zhongyang guanyu quanmian shenhua gaige ruogan zhongda wentide jueding*) (12 November 2003), *cit.*: 97–116.

[21] Chapter II, Paragraph 7 of the Decision reads 'Push forward state-owned enterprises to improve modernization of the enterprise system. state-owned enterprises belong to the whole People and are major force in promoting the modernization of the State and in guaranteeing the common interest of the People. Overall, state-owned enterprises are already in harmony with the market, and they must conform to the new trends of marketization and internationalization, and the reform of state-owned enterprises must be further deepened by putting an emphasis on regulating business decisions, preserving capital value, fair competition, enhancing business efficiency, assuming social responsibility.' Translation mine.

> in determining the objectives of economic development and development plans, in enacting economic and social policies and major reform measures, in conducting any kind of productive and business activities the demands of the Core Socialist Values must be complied with, and [one must] achieve social responsibility, social effectiveness, business that comply with the law, fair competition, integrity/trustworthiness and respect for contracts, forming a good policy orientation, interest mechanisms and a social environment which will promote the worldview of the Core Socialist Values.[22]

Social responsibility occupies a central role in formulating economic policies and in their implementation by state-owned MNCs.[23] *Decisions* and *opinions* of the Central Committee are a source of general regulatory obligations applicable to all members of the party. Rights and duties specific to state-owned MNCs and their personnel are posed by regulations (*guiding*) and provisions (*tiaoli*). These documents primarily govern corporate social responsibility. Compliance with 'social responsibility' is always listed under headings and paragraphs on political goals, defined as a political task and a test of the political quality of cadres.

State-owned MNCs are characterised by a significant overlap between party systems and corporate governance structures. While these enterprises are owned or controlled by the state, they are ultimately led by the party. Responsibility towards the party, therefore, takes precedence over their duties to the state. Successful performance of 'social responsibility' in turn is proof of political quality and a prerequisite to be appointed to the posts of chairman, deputy chairman, director, general manager, chief accountant, and other leadership positions.[24] The duties of 'social responsibility' are limited to environmental compliance and anti-corruption compliance. Regulations of the Chinese Communist Party convey these duties using the vocabulary of political language. The same duties have been conveyed through a language closer to the Western vocabulary of CSR and business and human rights by SASAC. According to SASAC, CSR compliance as defined by party regulations involves[25] (1) legal compliance, (2) contractual compliance, (3) compliance with commercial credit (*shangye xinyong*), (4) achieving sustainable profits through improvements in corporate governance, an optimal resource allocation, and adequate risk

---

[22] Notice of the Central Office of the Central Committee Issuing the Opinions on Nurturing and Establishing the Core Socialist Values (*Zhonggong zhongyang Bangonting guanyu yinfa 'guanyu peiyu yu jianxing shehuizhuyi hexin jiazhede yijian' de tongzhi*) (11 December 2013), *cit.*: 171–177.

[23] Opinion of the Central Committee of the CPC and the General Office of the State Council on Further Integrating the Worldview of the Core Socialist Values in the Construction of the Rule of Law (*Zhonggong Zhongyang, Guowuyuan Bangonting guanyu jinyibu ba shehuizhuyi hexin jiazheguan ronru fazhi jianshede zhidao yijian*) (11 December 2016), cit.: 484.

[24] Article 4(1), 'Notice of the General Office of the Chinese Communist Party and the General Office of the State Council issuing the regulations on the management of leadership personnel in central state-owned enterprises' (*Zhonggong Zhongyang Bangongting, Guowuyuan Bangongtin guanyu yinfa 'Zhongyang qiye lingdao renyuan guanli zanxing guiding'de tongzhi*) (6 November 2009), *cit.*: 881–889.

[25] SASAC Notice issuing the Guiding Opinions on Central Enterprises' Social Responsibility (*Guowuyuan guoyou zichan jiandu guanli weiyuanhui guanyu yinfa guanyu zhongyang qiye lüxing shehui zerende zhidao yijian de tongzhi*) (29 December 2007), <http://wap.sasac.gov.cn/n2588030/n2588939/c4297490/content.html>.

prevention strategies, (5) improving the quality and safety of production, protecting the rights of consumers, and accepting their complaints and suggestions, (6) using resources efficiently, protecting the environment, and promoting technological innovation, (7) guaranteeing the safety of production, and (8) protecting the lawful rights and interests of labour and participating to public interest activities.

Monitoring compliance by state-owned MNCs is a task of organisations of the Chinese Communist Party. Party organisations are in part distinct from the leadership of state-owned MNCs. They belong to separate clusters within the architecture of the Chinese Communist Party and are subject to different incentive structures and lines of political and administrative authority. Also, the mechanisms of accountability that apply to party organisations are distinct from those applicable to state-owned MNCs.

3 Monitoring Compliance Through Party Organisations

In discussions of CSR in China, the SASAC Guidance Committee on Central Enterprises' Social Responsibility is cited as the most essential institution. The Guidance Committee this far has issued only one regulatory document on CSR: the Guidelines to the SOEs Directly Under the Central Government on Fulfilling Corporate Social Responsibility. The subjects mainly responsible for CSR, clean governance, and anti-corruption work are party groups.[26] Party groups are organisations of the Chinese Communist Party that can be formed in any public or private entity[27] where at least three party members are present.[28] State-owned MNCs are under an obligation to establish such organisations,[29] to oversee the conduct of party members. Party groups are responsible for (1) using corporate decision-making procedures to implement the party line on 'social responsibility' and (2) implementing party regulations on social responsibility and deciding on the punishment (*chufen*) of party members in MNCs who contravene such regulations. These powers place party groups above SASAC. SASAC is only responsible for the day-to-day management of party building within state-owned MNCs.[30] Thanks to their positioning in between party, state, and

[26] art 2.7 Opinions of the Office of the State Council on strengthening and improving supervision on state-owned assets and avoiding loss of assets (*Guowuyuan Bangongting guanyu jiaqiang he gaijin qiye guoyou zichan jiandu fangzhi guoyou zichan liushide yijian*) (31 October 2015) http://www.gov.cn/zhengce/content/2015-11/10/content_10282.htm.

[27] art 48, Preamble to the Statute of the Chinese Communist Party (*Zonggang, Zhongguo Gongchandang Zhancheng*), 24 October 2017. Party groups are not to be confused with basic organisations of the party, as party committees, general branches, or branches. Basic organisations of the party are responsible for the internal governance of the party, therefore their functions range from implementation of the party line to management and education of cadres; from the recruitment of new party members to their generic oversight.

[28] art 6, Rules on the Work of Party Groups of the Chinese Communist Party (*Zhongguo Gongchandang dangzu gongzuo tiaoli*) (15 April 2019), http://www.gov.cn/zhengce/2019-04/15/content_5383062.htm.

[29] art 7, *cit.*

[30] art 24, *cit.*

corporate governance structures, party groups have the power to manage state-owned MNCs compliance with their CSR obligations effectively.

3.1 *The Composition and Role of Party Groups in State-Owned MNCs*

The composition of party groups in state-owned MNCs mirrors the corporate governance structure. The secretary of the party group is usually the chairman of the board of directors. Other group members are discipline inspection personnel and party leaders chosen among members of the board of directors, the board of supervisors, or management.[31] Party groups enjoy the entire range of corporate governance powers belonging to the board, shareholders, and regulators.[32] Also, they enjoy broad supervisory duties[33] over the shareholders' meeting, the board of directors, the board of supervisors, and management.[34] Party groups participate in all governance and regulatory processes under party regulation, under the state law, and under corporate self-regulation. Their members have the right to participate in strategic decision-making processes taking place within SOEs.[35] These processes include decisions on outbound investments along with the Belt and Road, other major investment projects, and the use of a large amount of funds.[36]

Secretaries of party groups can be held vicariously liable for lack of compliance by MNCs. The liability of party group secretaries involves party legislation, state

[31] art 14, *cit.*

[32] par 4, Notice of the Central Committee of the Chinese Communist Party on further strengthening and improving Party building in state-owned enterprises (*Zhonggong Zhongyang guanyu jinyibu jiaqiang he gaijin guoyou qiye dangde jianshe gongzuode tongzhi*), (24 January 1997), in *Zhonggong Zhongyang Bangongting Faguisi, Zhongyang Dangnei fagui he guifangxin wenjian huibian (1949nian 10yue – 2016nian 12 yue), shangbian* (Beijing: Falü Chubanshe, 2017): 301.

[33] par 2, *cit.* See also Decision of the Central Committee on some major issues in the reform and development of State-owned enterprises (*Zhonggong Zhongyang guanyu guoyou qiye gaige he fazhan ruogan zhongda wentide jueding*) (22 September 1999) (Beijing: Renmin Chubanshe, 1999).

[34] art 33, Statute of the Chinese Communist Party, cit.; art 2.7, Opinions of the General Office of the State Council on strengthening and improving supervision over the state-owned assets of enterprises and avoiding the loss of state-owned assets (Guowuyuan Bangongting guanyu jiaqiang he gaijin qiye guoyou zichan jiandu fangzhi guoyou zichan liushide yijian) (31 October 2015), http://www.gov.cn/zhengce/content/2015-11/10/content_10282.htm.

[35] Cit.

[36] Opinions of the General Office of the Central Committee and of the General Office of the State Council on further promoting implementation of the decision-making system of the 'three important and one big' by state-owned enterprises (*Zhonggong Zhongyang Bangongting, Guowuyuan Bangonting guanyu jinyibu tuijin guoyou qiye guanche luoshi 'sanzhong yida' juece zhidude yijian*) (5 June 2010) http://www.gov.cn/jrzg/2010-07/15/content_1655395.htm Strategic decision-making processes are defined as all those matters which—according to the Company Law, the Law on state-owned Assets, the Law on Securities, etc.—shall be decided by the shareholders assembly or by the board of directors.

legislation, and enterprise self-regulation. This mechanism places a strong incentive on secretaries and members of party groups to ensure all party members within SOEs comply with the entire gamut of their obligations. Also, all members of party groups are to account for the conduct of their subordinates—which in some SOEs can constitute about 30% of human resources. Other accountability systems for party groups are based upon the value of 'integrity' (*chengxin*). They involve (1) performance evaluation, (2) clean governance,[37] (3) reporting to the Central Committee of the CPC,[38] (4) personal liability for all individual and corporate conducts that produce serious negative externalities,[39] and (5) all duties of compliance, publicity, disclosure, and transparency as based in party regulations and on state legislation. Accountability is also ensured by filing an annual report on professional activities and anti-corruption compliance within the party group.[40]

The single most significant limitation of party groups is their inability to reach beyond corporate headquarters. Party group in a SOE can monitor all party members and corporate governance structures as they exist at the very apex of value chains. But, they cannot be created in subsidiaries or branches of SOEs.[41] The performance indicators used to evaluate managers and directors of state-owned corporations include data and information about third-tier subsidiaries. But, the absence of party groups from corporate value chains places significant limitations on their power.

If the means to monitor corporate compliance with social responsibility obligations were limited to party groups and the existing societal complaint and remedial mechanisms, CSR compliance with 'Chinese characteristics' would display limitations similar to those of other CSR systems. The Party Central Committee, SASAC, and provincial committees have adopted the 'inspection tour' system to obviate this difficulty. After a relatively long period of experimentation, the inspection tour system (*xunshi zhidu*) was enshrined in the Party Statute in 2017.[42]

---

[37] art 8, Regulations on implementing the clean governance responsibility system (*Guanyu shixing dangfeng lianzheng jianshe zerenzhide guiding*) (10 October 2010) (Beijing: Zhongguo Fangzheng Chubanshe, 2010).

[38] *See* art 49, Statute of the Chinese Communist Party, cit.; arts 6, 15, 29, Rules on the Work of Party Groups of the Chinese Communist Party (*Zhongguo Gongchandang dangzu gongzuo tiaoli*) (15 April 2019), <http://www.gov.cn/zhengce/2019-04/15/content_5383062.htm>. Provincial party committees are not to be confused with enterprise party committees. Enterprise party committees are basic organisations established in government institutions, enterprises, etc., and having jurisdiction over the unit they exist in. Provincial party committees are organisations established in administrative jurisdictions as provinces, autonomous regions, municipalities, cities divided into districts, and counties.

[39] art 30(h), Rules on the Work of Party Groups of the Chinese Communist Party, also contain a non-exhaustive listing of all the duties of compliance, publicity, disclosure and transparency.

[40] The report is to be filed by board members, supervisors, and managers. art 2, Guising Opinions of the General Office of the State Council on further perfecting the governance structure of state-owned enterprises (*Guowuyuan bangongting guanyu jinyibu wanshan guoyou qiye faren zhili jiegoude zhidao yijian*) (24 April 2017) http://www.gov.cn/zhengce/content/2017-05/03/content_5190599.htm.

[41] art 9(6), Rules on the Work of Party Groups of the Chinese Communist Party, *cit.*

[42] art 14, Statute of the Chinese Communist Party, *cit.*

3.2 CSR and the Inspection Tour System

The inspection tour system is the most critical method of supervision within the party,[43] among the five oversight systems introduced in 1997.[44] The inspection tour system blends the investigative and enforcement powers of the Central Commission for Discipline Inspection to the managerial powers of the Central Organization Department. In 2009, these two party organisations established the Central Leading Group for Inspection Tour Work (the Central Leading Group). The Central Leading Group is hosted within the Central Commission for Discipline Inspection,[45] and it is directly answerable to the Central Committee of the CCP. Thus, it can override any other line of administrative authority within the party and directly monitor state-owned MNCs.

The Central Leading Group can dispatch an inspection team to any state-owned MNC. SASAC, too, can organise inspection tours of corporate headquarters and branches of central MNCs. From 2003, the Central Commission for Discipline Inspection and the Central Organization Department established three inspection teams with the specific goal to supervise state-owned MNCs,[46] their compliance with CSR,[47] and anti-corruption obligations.[48] State-owned MNCs controlled by provincial governments are monitored by inspection tours organised by provincial and county-level party committees and by the local chapters of SASAC.[49] Inspection teams are chaired by discipline inspection personnel posted at the central or

[43] Inspection tours were initially regulated by the Central Commission for Discipline Inspection Interim Measures on Establishing the Inspection Tour System (*Zhonggong Zhongyang Jilü Jiancha Weiyuanhui guanyu jianli xunshi zhidude shixing banfa*) (13 March 2016) in Yang Bo (ed.) *Professional Handbook of Discipline Inspection and Supervision, vol. 3* (*Jijian jiancha yewu sucha shouce*) (Zhongguo Zhishi Chubanshe 2005), 1209. Article 19, Interim provisions on supervision within the Chinese Communist Party (*Zhongguo Gongchandang dangnei jiandu tiaoli*) (27 October 2016), in *Zhonggong Zhongyang Bangongting Faguisi, Zhongyang Dangnei fagui he guifangxin wenjian huibian (1949nian 10yue – 2016nian 12 yue), shangbian* (Falü Chubanshe, 2017) 1270.

[44] art 1, Measures of the Central Commission for Discipline Inspection on reiterating and establishing the five systems of intra-party supervision (*Zhonggong Zhongyang Jilü Jiancha Weiyuanhui guanyu chongshen he jianli dangnei jiandu wuxian zhidude shishi banfade tongzhi*) (4 February 1997), in *Zhonggong Zhongyang Bangongting Faguisi, cit.*: 1233. article 11, Interim provisions on supervision within the Chinese Communist Party, cit. The inspection tour system was included in the 2007 Party Statute by the 17th Party Congress as one of the work systems of the Central Committee and of provincial-level Party committees.

[45] art 7, Interim Measures on Establishing the Inspection Tour System, cit.

[46] 'The inspection tour system, that should take place in each vertical system during its term in office has been written into the Party Statute' (*Xunshi zhidu danlie yitiao yijie renqi nei xunshi quan fugai xieru dangzhan*) Central Commission for Discipline Inspection, January 27, 2018, http://www.ccdi.gov.cn/toutiao/201801/t20180126_162643.html.

[47] art 15(1) Regulations of the Chinese Communist Party on inspection tour work (*Zhongguo Gongchandang xunshi gongzuo tiaoli*) (1 July 2017), in Zhonggong Zhongyang Bangongting Faguisi, *cit.*: 1263.

[48] art 15(2), *cit.*

[49] art 2, *cit.*

provincial level,[50] while the deputy chair is chosen among officials of the Organization Department. Inspections tours of state-owned MNCs can take place as often as deemed necessary. This is a significant exception to the general rule, mandating that inspections occur once or twice every five years. This exception testifies to the weight that has been placed on monitoring MNCs. To avoid interference by the corporate headquarters, inspection tours occur unannounced, and inspectors can conduct their investigations undercover. MNCs have a regulatory duty to receive inspection teams, allow them to set up a temporary office on their premises, and cooperate with inspectors to the maximum possible extent. Directors and members of the board and management have a duty to make truthful representations to inspectors.[51] Inspection tours last from 30 days to 4 months. During this period, inspectors (1) conduct a fact-finding mission by hearing reports from the CEO, board members, and the management, (2) participate in observing corporate meetings, and (3) hold confidential conversations with the staff, verifying reports filed by leading personnel of the MNC; consulting, reading, duplicating documents; conducting surveys, and investigations. At the end of inspections, party discipline officials outline CSR issues that need to be addressed. State-owned MNCs then draft an operational document outlining the steps to take to address relevant issues. The plan is submitted to the inspection team within 60 days after the inspection. All issues need to be solved within 12 months. A follow-up visit by the inspection team will ensure that the MNC has addressed all recommendations.

State-owned MNCs have been included in the inspection tour system since the very beginning of this mechanism.[52] The very first round of inspection tours was launched in 1996 and involved the then Ministry of Coal and state-owned MNCs in the coal industry.[53] From 2013 to the first half of 2018, inspection tours have taken place twice a year. Inspections have been conducted on seventy-two of the

[50] art 5, *cit.*

[51] art 4, Experimental regulations on local areas and units cooperating with the work of Central Inspection Tour Groups, (*Guanyu bei xunshi diwu, danwei peihe zhongyang xunshizu kaizhan xunzhi gongzuode zanxing guiding*) (1 April 2010), <https://baike.baidu.com/item/> 关于被巡视地区单位配合中央巡视组开展巡视工作的暂行规定.

[52] 'The Central Committee and Party Committees in Provinces, Autonomous Regions, Municipalities may, according to their needs, dispatch inspection work teams entrusted with necessary powers to all local organs and all departments, in order to conduct inspection, and report circumstances directly to the Central Committee or to Party Committees in Provinces, Autonomous Regions, Municipalities. Experienced and prestigious old comrades may participate to this work.' art 6(5) Decision of the Central Committee on strengthening the links between the Party and the Masses (*Zhonggong Zhongyang guanyu jiaqiang dang tong renmin qunzhong lianxide jueding*) (12 March 1990) <http://cpc.people.com.cn/GB/64162/71380/71387/71588/4854605.html>.

[53] Heilongjiang Province Commission for Discipline Inspection (Heilongjiangsheng Jiwei), 'An exploration of inspection tour work and its development' (*Xunshi zhidude tansuo he fazhan*), October 21, 2015, <http://www.hljjjc.gov.cn/gztl_show.php?id=454>.

existing ninety-seven state-owned MNC,[54] or 74 per cent of their total. All the state-owned MNCs inspected are involved in cooperation projects under the Belt and Road Initiative.[55] These enterprises are active in the most diverse sectors of the Chinese and the global economy. The majority of state-owned MNCs monitored through inspection tours belong to the financial sector (23.6 per cent). Next are MNCs in the energy sector (20.8 per cent), followed by conglomerates conducting investment projects in various sectors (11.11 per cent), in the fields of aviation (9.7 per cent), telecommunications (5.5 per cent), logistics (6.9 per cent), iron and metals (6.9 per cent), food (4.1 per cent), defence (2.7 per cent), and finally MNCs in the construction, philanthropy, postal, press, travel, and vehicle manufacture sectors, which together constitute 8.3 per cent of the enterprise monitored. The results of CSR inspections and are sometimes, even though not always, disclosed by state-owned MNCs. Information about the measures adopted by inspection teams on directors and managers of state-owned MNCs is more challenging to collect. Under party discipline, violations of CSR obligations can be punished as violations of political discipline, given that CSR is conceptualised as a political responsibility of directors and managers of MNCs. Individuating the precise response to violations of CSR by state-owned multinationals is therefore not always possible.

4 Assessing Compliance Through Social Credit Mechanisms

Compliance of state-owned MNCs with their social responsibility obligations is assessed through interlocking publicity, evaluation, and ranking mechanisms. These mechanisms provide the basis to reward compliant enterprises and punish those who do not fulfil their CSR obligations. Some of these mechanisms have already become components of the 'social credit system' (*shehui xinyong zhidu*).[56]

4.1 The Limits of Conventional Reporting Mechanisms

Almost all state-owned MNCs have been publishing annual or multi-year reports on their CSR, environmental, and philanthropic performance at least since 2009.

---

[54] This is the official figure for central state-owned MNCs, last published by SASAC in 2017. See SASAC, 'List of Central Enterprises' (*Yangqi minglu*), December 29, 2017, <http://www.sasac.gov.cn/n2588035/n2641579/n2641645/c4451749/content.html>.

[55] Data compiled by the author through the official website of the Central Commission for Discipline Inspection and the official website of the Belt and Road Initiative.

[56] On the social credit system see Larry Catá Backer, 'Measurement, Assessment and Reward: The Challenges of Building Institutionalized Social Credit and Rating Systems in China and in the West' (September 21, 2017), Proceedings of the Chinese Social Credit System, Shanghai Jaotong University, 23 September 2017. Available at SSRN: <https://ssrn.com/abstract=3040624>.

CSR reports published in English tend to focus on issues of marginal importance to CSR. In fact, from a standpoint internal to China's political–legal system, these reporting practices are less important than reporting to party organisations, the National People's Congress Standing Committee, and the public. In reality, state-owned MNCs must comply with reporting mechanisms far more stringent than Western-style CSR reporting. These mechanisms are internal, and they involve four different types of reports.

MNCs file the first type of report. Board members, supervisors, and managers of state-owned MNCs are obligated to file an annual report on CSR compliance, anti-corruption, and professional activities to the party group they are members of and inspection teams.[57] In turn, the party group reports on the activities of the directors and managers of state-owned MNCs to the Central Committee or Provincial Party Committees. The second type of report on MNCs social responsibility is filed by the State Council to the Standing Committee of the National People's Congress and accounts for the status of state-owned assets. This report is divided into two parts. The first part focuses on all categories of state-owned assets, while the second part of the report examines state-owned assets belonging to MNCs.[58] Reports filed to party groups, and those submitted to the National People's Congress include information on assets used by state-owned MNCs involved in Belt and Road cooperation projects.

These reporting practices and systems involve state-owned MNCs, party organisations, and the state. While useful, they do not provide stakeholders with opportunities to make their grievances to non-state-based, non-judicial actors coherent with the Third Pillar of the United Nations Principles on Business and Human Rights. However, the third type of reporting mechanism allows affected citizens and communities a limited space for grievances. Whenever an inspection tour is announced in advance, rather than conducted undercover, MNCs must publicise the contact information of inspectors. Publicity often takes place through the websites of state-owned MNCs or the Central Commission for Discipline Inspection website. This form of disclosure allows all stakeholders, such as MNC contractors, subcontractors, or employees, to discreetly contact inspectors and raise their grievances outside of state-based, judicial mechanisms. A fourth and last form of disclosure occurs through the public database maintained by the National Enterprise Credit Information Publicity System.[59] This type of disclosure involves breaches of CSR compliance by MNCs and breaches of contract, administrative violations, or even criminal offences. The information available through the National Enterprise Credit Information Publicity

[57] art 2, State Council General Office guiding opinions on further perfecting the corporate governance of state-owned enterprises (*Guowuyuan bangongting guanyu jinyibu wanshan guoyou qiye faren zhili jiegoude zhidao yijian*) (24 April 2017), <http://www.gov.cn/zhengce/content/2017-05/03/content_5190599.htm>.

[58] Central Committee Opinions on the establishing the system of the State Council Reporting on the Status of state-owned Assets Management to the NPC Standing Committee (*Zhonggong Zhongyang guanyu jianli Guowuyuan xian Quangguo Renda Changweihui baogao guoyou zichan guanli qingkuang zhidude yijian*), (15 January 2018), <http://www.npc.gov.cn/npc/xinwen/syxw/2018-01/15/content_2036526.htm>.

[59] Accessible at <gsxt.gdgs.gov.cn/>.

System consists of the name of the MNCs and their board members or management, its social credit registration number, and information about the kind of administrative violation or criminal offence.

4.2 Evaluation and Rating Through Big Data

CSR compliance is further assessed through social credit indicators and standards specific to CSR. These indicators are part of the broader social credit system. At the moment of writing, the evaluation and rating mechanisms that rely on big data are (1) party-based responsibility systems (*kaohe pingjia*), CSR technical standards (*biaozhun*), and responsibility systems tailored explicitly to state-owned MNCs. Responsibility systems internal to the party play a paramount role in evaluating CSR compliance. As this article has explained, the leadership role of the Chinese Communist Party takes place through appointing party members to the position of leadership within SOEs. In their capacity as party members, directors, board members, and managers must fulfil several tasks. Some of these are merely administrative. Other tasks are directly related to social responsibility. The most critical party responsibility systems related to social responsibility are the 'clean governance responsibility system' (*dangfeng lianzheng zerenzhi*) and the system of individual responsibility of secretaries of party groups (or committees) (*dangwei fuze zhuti zeren*).[60] Under both systems, directors and managers of MNCs are held responsible for their subordinates' lack of compliance with CSR. Responsibility systems were introduced in the mid-to-late 1990s and gradually improved. The data they generate is produced by party members and committees through self-reporting or by party groups, organisation departments, commissions for discipline inspection, and other party organisations. This data is not yet integrated within the social credit system.

Social responsibility standards and non-binding guidelines give a second mechanism of rating and evaluation. Social responsibility guidelines such as the OECD Guidelines for Multinational Enterprises and the Guiding Principles for Business and Human Rights are global and endorsed by the Chinese government. However, China has developed its own autonomous standards on corporate social responsibility, CSR reporting, CSR evaluation—among others. These standards are drafted under the guidance of the Standardization Administration of China. Their drafting involves the Administration, a panel of external experts, government officials, and Chinese MNCs. In most cases, these standards build upon relevant ISO standards and soft law documents and adapt them to the Chinese context by drawing on principles in party ideology, Chinese state legislation, existing management and risk control systems

[60] *Cit.*, at footnote 33.

and mechanisms, and customs and practices followed by MNCs.[61] They are one of the three pillars of the social credit system, together with regulation and contracts.[62]

A third component is given by responsibility systems specific to state-owned MNCs. Systems of evaluation and appraisal (*kaohe pingjia*) of leading personnel of Central SOEs were posed in 2009 have been designed to pursue the liability of leading personnel of Central SOEs for breaches of social responsibility, but also violations of the company charter, and norms and standards on safety, quality, environmental protection, etc.[63] These responsibility systems have gradually evolved to include not only directors and managers but also the personnel of MNCs as a whole. Evaluation is conducted annually and at the end of the term of appointment of directors, board members, and managers. Social responsibility is an autonomous item of assessment. Coherent with Chinese approaches to CSR, this item is included under the broader label of political quality (*zhengzhi suzhi*). Clean governance, anti-corruption self-regulation, trustworthiness/integrity, and close links with the masses are assessed under the variable of 'work style'.

Social responsibility weights significantly on evaluation. Evaluation of social responsibility performance weighs for up to twenty-five per cent of the assessment of political quality. Political quality, in turn, weighs fifty per cent on the final evaluation score of directors, board members, and managers of MNCs. The remaining fifty per cent of the score is calculated based on their business results. The ranking obtained by leading personnel of state-owned MNCs can be outstanding (*youxiu*), good (*lianghao*), ordinary (*yiban*), or insufficient (*jiaocha*). This ranking plays an

---

[61] State Administration of Quality Supervision, Inspection and Quarantine, National Standardisation Administration Committee (*Guojia Zhiliang Jiandu Jianyan Jianyu Zongju, Guojia Biaozhunhua Guanli Weiyuanhui*), *Guide to Social Responsibility GB/T 36000-2015* (*Shehui zeren zhinan*), (Beijing 2015); State Administration of Quality Supervision, Inspection and Quarantine, National Standardisation Administration Committee (*Guojia Zhiliang Jiandu Jianyan Jianyu Zongju, Guojia Biaozhunhua Guanli Weiyuanhui*), *Guide to Social Responsibility Reporting GB/T 36001-2015* (*Shehui zeren baogao bianzie zhinan*), (Beijing 2015); State Administration of Quality Supervision, Inspection and Quarantine, National Standardisation Administration Committee (*Guojia Zhiliang Jiandu Jianyan Jianyu Zongju, Guojia Biaozhunhua Guanli Weiyuanhui*), *Social Responsibility Performance Classification Guidelines GB/T 36002-2015* (*Shehui zeren fenxiao fenlei zhiying*), (Beijing 2015).

[62] According to the Planning outline for the construction of a social credit sytem (2014–2020), 'A social credit system is an important component part of the Socialist market economy system and the social governance system. It is founded on laws, regulations, standards and charters'. 'State Council Notice concerning Issuance of the Planning Outline for the Construction of a Social Credit System (2014–2020)', Rogier Creemers transl., <https://chinacopyrightandmedia.wordpress.com/2014/06/14/planning-outline-for-the-construction-of-a-social-credit-system-2014-2020/>.

[63] art 4 Experimental measures on the comprehensive evaluation and appraisal of leadership groups and leading personnel of central enterprises (*Zhongyang qiye lingdao banzi he lingdao renyuan zonghe kaohe pingjia banfa (shixing)*) (January 3, 2009), document on file with author. art 44, General Office of the Central Committee, General Office of the State Council Notice issuing the temporary regulations on managing leading personnel of central enterprises (*Zhonggong zhongyang bangongting, Guowuyuan Bangongting guanyu yinfa zhongyang qiye lingdao renyuan guanli zanxing guidingde tongzhi*) (6 November 2009), <https://www.pkulaw.com/chl/e1288602d4ba8198bdfb.html>.

important part in decisions about their appointment and removal. Performance indicators are highly adaptable. Regulations by the Central Committee and SASAC set only the broader categories and benchmarks of performance evaluation. As long as central and provincial MNCs respect those categories and benchmarks, they can adapt evaluation and rating items to their own industry. Evaluation is performed following the vertical lines of authority linking corporate headquarters to their subsidiaries, and it reaches the persons legally responsible for third-tier subsidiaries.[64] Differently from other evaluation systems, performance evaluation is not subject to geographical limitations. It can also be performed by MCNs contracting or carrying out projects in Belt and Road countries.

Internal performance evaluation is the direct antecedent of social credit. It is based on mechanisms to incentivise compliance, punish non-compliance, compiling and maintaining records of individual and corporate conduct,[65] and on sharing information across party organisations and administrative agencies of the state. Accordingly, the results of cadre evaluation by inspection tours[66] and the opinions expressed by inspection teams are among the factors considered in cadre appointment and recommendation.[67] Information gathered by inspection groups is also combined with information gathered through other assessment methods and used to compile records on supervision.[68]

---

[64] *See* SASAC notice issuing the measures on verification and scoring methods for the performance evaluation of all employees of central enterprises (*Guoziwei guanyu yinfa zhongyang qiye quanyuan yeji kaoke qingkuang hecha jifen banfade tongzhi*) (9 August 2010), <http://www.sasac.gov.cn/n2588035/n2588320/n2588335/c4260460/content.html>.

[65] art 3(4) SASAC Guiding Opinion on Further Strengthening the Work of Performance Evaluation of Employees of Central SOEs (*Guoziwei guanyu jinyibu jiaqiang zhongyang qiye quanyuan yeji kaoje gongzuode zhidao yijian*) (16 October 2009), <http://www.gov.cn/zwgk/2010-01/27/content_1520456.htm>.

[66] art 3(7), Notice of the General Office of the Central Committee on establishing and promoting leadership groups on scientific development and a clean government and a mechanisms of performance evaluation of leadership groups, (*Zhonggong Zhongyang Bangongting guanyu jianli cujin kexue fazhande dangzheng lingdao banzi he lingdao ganbu kaohe pingjia jizhide yijiande tongzhi*) (20 July 2009), in Zhonggong Zhongyang Bangongting Faguisi, *Zhongyang Dangnei fagui he guifangxin wenjian huibian (1949nian 10yue – 2016nian 12 yue), shangbian* (Beijing: Falü Chubanshe, 2017): 871.

[67] art 9, Experimental regulations on recommending leading cadres with a high career mobility (*Tuijin lingdao ganbu nengshang nengxiade ruogan guiding (shixing)* (18 July 2015), in Zhonggong Zhongyang Bangongting Faguisi, *Zhongyang Dangnei fagui he guifangxin wenjian huibian (1949nian 10yue – 2016nian 12 yue), shangbian* (Beijing: Falü Chubanshe, 2017): 973.

[68] art 2, Opinions on avoiding the promotion of problematic cadres (Guanyu fanzheng ganbu 'daibing tib' de yijian), *in Zhonggong Zhongyang Bangongting Faguisi, Zhongyang Dangnei fagui he guifangxin wenjian huibian (1949nian 10yue – 2016nian 12 yue), shangbian* (Beijing: Falü Chubanshe, 2017): 998.

5 Conclusion

CSR in China has taken roots and developed in ways consistent with the principles that shape the governance of the world's second economic power. Western conceptions of CSR highlight its entirely voluntary, non-binding nature. CSR with 'Chinese characteristics' is consistent with this approach. But, as limited to state-owned MNCs, it also displays entirely autonomous features.

CSR exists beyond the scope of state regulation. In China, an important regulatory domain beyond the state is given by the regulations of the Chinese Communist Party. According to these regulations, 'social responsibility' is a binding duty of the directors and managers of state-owned MNCs. Notions of political responsibility and discipline cross the conceptual divide between CSR and the more recent business and human rights concept. They are compatible with both regulatory frameworks. All codified, binding, and non-binding transnational instruments of corporate governance partly draw on practices that have been put into place by MNCs. These instruments do not create new obligations. They consolidate existing obligations. The consolidation of norms created by civil society, enterprises, and governments is premised on an implicit consensus that there are many different paths and ways to monitor and assess CSR compliance. This consensus also entails that an enterprise's actual respect for human rights in its business activity is inherently more important than its adherence to the mere forms of a single, across-the-board abstract model. Hence, there is no single model or 'appropriate form' of non-state-based compliance and monitoring mechanisms that Chinese MNCs should adopt.

These features of CSR with 'Chinese characteristics' are also crucial in the light of the ongoing debate on the drafting of an international Legally Binding Instrument on business and human rights. The UNGPs have received widespread support from Western MNCs and governments. China has endorsed them. Yet, global NGOs as Human Rights Watch have decried their lack of enforcement mechanisms, advocating for a greater degree of government engagement.[69] In July 2014, the UN Human Rights Council created an Open-Ended Intergovernmental Working Group on Transnational Corporations and Other Business Enterprises. The Working Group has the goal to elaborate a binding instrument on business and human rights. A Zero Draft of a Legally Binding Instrument on Transnational Corporations and Other Business Enterprises was released for public comment in July 2018. The Legally Binding Instrument may pave the way for a substantial change in global CSR regimes. Ecuador supported the Legally Binding Instrument. But, as described in this chapter, China has been at the forefront in creating and refining binding CSR mechanisms targeted to the state-owned sector. The creation of these binding mechanisms took place independently from the drafting of the Legally Binding Instrument as a response to domestic needs. Some of the CSR mechanisms created by China still display certain limitations. Monitoring mechanisms based in party regulation are most effective within the country and do not easily allow to monitor the outbound activities of state-owned MNCs. To do so, party groups would have to be allowed formal existence under

[69] Chris Albin-Lackey, *Without Rules. A Failed Approach to Corporate Accountability* (2013).

the legislation of Western countries. This arrangement, however, is not compatible with the governance principles of most of the countries adhering to the Belt and Road Initiative. In the meantime, the social credit system and big data seem may provide a viable alternative. These mechanisms are playing an increasingly important role in monitoring CSR compliance by state-owned MNCs. The social credit system is slowly broadening the scope of supervision, leading to greater data integration and initial attempts to more closely involve groups of the Chinese Communist Party to monitor compliance of state-owned MNCs in OBOR countries and beyond. Under the social credit system, subjects to be monitored and assessed include listed companies, their directors, supervisors, senior managers, controlling shareholders, and shareholders controlling more than 5% of the shares. The highly flexible nature of social credit and big data may allow for an unprecedented reach of CSR monitoring within all the recesses of value and supply chains existing in China and in the countries that joined the Belt and Road Initiatives.

At the moment of writing, the social credit system is not complete yet, and CSR mechanisms based in party regulation are undergoing a continuous process of fine-tuning. The Legally Binding Instrument is still at its drafting stage. While it is still too early to reach a definite conclusion as to the future shape of CSR, CSR mechanisms with Chinese characteristics already deserve a more significant consideration than they have thus far received.

Flora Sapio PhD (La Sapienza). Researcher at the University of Naples "L'Orientale.

National Security Review for Foreign Investment in China: A Transnational Evolution

Ji Ma

1 The Evolution of China's Security Review Mechanism for Foreign Investment: Toward a Unified Approach

The national security review mechanisms for foreign investments in China are influenced strongly by cross-border factors. Since China's reform and opening-up, the national security review mechanisms for foreign investment have gone through four phases. Facing peculiar economic and political situations in different phases, China had adopted distinct security review measures for foreign investments. The beginning phase is from 1979 to 1994, focusing on administrative licensing procedures of establishing enterprises; the second phase is from 1995 to 2002, strengthening the approvals of foreign companies' access to certain industries or sectors; the third phase is from 2003 to 2014, emphasizing to establish a national security review mechanism for foreign mergers and acquisitions; and the fourth phase is from 2014 to the present, striving to build a uniform national security review mechanism for foreign investments.

The original version of chapter was inadvertently published prematurely, before incorporation of the final corrections, which has now been updated. The correction to this chapter can be found at https://doi.org/10.1007/978-981-19-1368-6_31

J. Ma (✉)
Research Associate, The University of Oxford "China, Law and Development" Project, Shenzhen, China
e-mail: ji.ma@law.ox.ac.uk

J. Chaisse et al. (eds.), *Regulation of State-Controlled Enterprises*, International Law and the Global South, https://doi.org/10.1007/978-981-19-1368-6_17

1.1 The Embryonic Era: The Administrative Licensing Approach

From 1979 to 1994, the security review regime for foreign investment in China was embryonic. Beginning in the 1980s, the first wave of foreign direct investment in China mostly took the form of joint ventures.[1] To expand economic cooperation and technical exchange with foreign countries, China enacted Law of the PRC on Foreign-Capital Enterprises,[2] Law of the PRC on Chinese-Foreign Equity Joint Ventures,[3] Law of the PRC on Chinese-Foreign Contractual Joint Ventures[4] to permit foreign investors to set up enterprises in China and to establish equity joint ventures and contractual joint ventures with Chinese partners. Establishing such enterprises or joint ventures would be examined and approved by the State Council department in charge of foreign economic relations and trade, or to another agency authorized by the State Council.[5]

Later, China enacted detailed rules to implement these aforementioned basic laws on foreign investment.[6] These detailed rules pointed out that national sovereign or security will be considered when establishing such enterprises or joint ventures. The approval of such enterprises or joint ventures would be denied if such enterprises or

[1] See Harry G Broadman and Xiaolun Sun, *The Distribution of Foreign Direct Investment in China* (World Bank Publications 1997).

[2] Law of the People's Republic of China on Foreign-Capital Enterprises [中华人民共和国外资企业法] (issued on 04-12-1986, effective on 04-12-1986, issued by National People's Congress, invalidated by Foreign Investment Law of the People's Republic of China, which was issued on 03-15-2019 and was effective on 01-01-2020).

[3] The Law of the People Republic of China on Chinese-Foreign Equity Joint Ventures [中华人民共和国中外合资经营企业法] (Issued on 07-08-1979, effective on 07-08-1979, issued by National People's Congress, invalidated by Foreign Investment Law of the People's Republic of China (Issued on 03-15-2019 Effective on 01-01-2020).

[4] The Law of the People's Republic of China on Chinese-Foreign Contractual Joint Ventures [中华人民共和国中外合作经营企业法] (effective Date on 04-13-1988, issued by National People's Congress, invalidated by Foreign Investment Law of the People's Republic of China (Issued on 03-15-2019, effective on 01-01-2020).

[5] Law of the People's Republic of China on Foreign-Capital Enterprises Art. 6; Law of the People's Republic of China on Chinese-Foreign Equity Joint Ventures Art. 3; Law of the People's Republic of China on Chinese-Foreign Contractual Joint Ventures Art. 5.

[6] Regulations for the Implementation of the Law of PRC on Joint Ventures Using Chinese and Foreign Investment [中华人民共和国中外合资经营企业法实施条例] (issued on 09-20-1983, effective on 09-20-1983); Detailed Rules for the Implementation of the Law of the PRC on Wholly Foreign-Owned Enterprises in China [中华人民共和国外资企业法实施细则] (issued on 12-12-1990, effective on 12-12-1990, issued by Ministry of Foreign Trade & Economic Cooperation); Detailed Rules for the Implementation of the Law of PRC on Sino-Foreign Joint Cooperative Ventures [中华人民共和国中外合作经营企业法实施细则] (issued on 09-04-1995, effective on 09-04-1995); All these three regulations are invalidated by Foreign Investment Law of the People's Republic of China (issued on 03-15-2019, effective on 01-01-2020).

joint ventures are detrimental to China's sovereignty or public interest[7] or endangered to China's security.[8]

In this embryonic era, the two concepts—security and sovereignty—were closely linked when China permitted establishing foreign investment. China tried to address national security concern by approval of the establishment of foreign-funded enterprises or joint ventures. One possible explanation could be that China just moved to the period of reforming and opening-up, and China still considered security is part of national sovereignty.

1.2 The Trial Era: Approvals of Foreign Companies' Access to Certain Industries or Sectors

From 1995 to 2002, China tried to conduct security review by adopting the approval regime for foreign investments in limited sectors. In order to guide the orientation of foreign investment, to keep the orientation of foreign investment in line with the national economy and social development planning of China and to protect of the lawful rights and interests of investors, China had formulated Provisional Regulations on Direction Guide to Foreign Investment in 1995,[9] Catalog of Foreign-funded Industry Guidance in 1995[10] and Provisions on Guiding the Orientation of Foreign Investment 2002.[11]

In accordance with these provisions, foreign-funded projects fell into four categories: encouraged, permitted, restricted and prohibited projects. Foreign-funded projects that are encouraged, restricted and prohibited shall be listed in the Catalog of Foreign-funded Industry Guidance. Foreign-funded projects that do not fall into the categories of encouraged, restricted or prohibited projects shall be the permitted foreign-funded projects. Permitted foreign-funded projects will not be listed in

[7] Regulations for the Implementation of the Law of the People's Republic of China on Joint Ventures Using Chinese and Foreign Investment Art. 5 (1); Detailed Rules for the Implementation of the Law of the People's Republic of China on Wholly Foreign-Owned Enterprises in China Art. 6 (1); Detailed Rules for the Implementation of the Law of People's Republic of China on Sino-Foreign Joint Cooperative Ventures Art. 9(1).

[8] Detailed Rules for the Implementation of the Law of the People's Republic of China on Wholly Foreign-Owned Enterprises in China Art. 6 (2); Detailed Rules for the Implementation of the Law of People's Republic of China on Sino-Foreign Joint Cooperative Ventures Art. 9 (2).

[9] Provisional Regulations on Direction Guide to Foreign Investment [指导外商投资方向暂行规定] (issued on 06-20-1995, effective on 06-20-1995, invalidated by Notice of the State Administration for Industry and Commerce on Issues concerning the Implementation of New Policies on the Industries Open to the Foreign Investment, which was issued on 04-30-2002, effective on 04-30-2002).

[10] Catalogue for the Guidance of Foreign Investment Industries [外商投资产业指导目录] (amended in 2002, 2004, 2007 and 2011).

[11] Provisions on Guiding the Orientation of Foreign Investment [指导外商投资方向规定] (issued on 02-11-2002, effective on 04-01-2002, issued by State Council).

the Catalog.[12] As for the approval, foreign-funded projects shall be examined and approved and put on record, respectively, by the Departments of Development Planning and the Economic and Trade Departments according to the limit of authority for examination and approval; the contracts and articles of association of foreign-funded enterprises shall be examined and approved and put on record by the Department of Foreign Trade and Economic Cooperation.[13]

In this trial era, the national security concerns are addressed by categorizing foreign-funded projects into different natures—encouraged, permitted, restricted and prohibited ones. Depending on such categorization, national security risks would be reviewed and addressed to varied extent. First, the restricted projects imply the contents of national security. For example, a project engaged in the prospecting and exploitation of the specific type of mineral resources to which the State applies protective exploitation belongs to the restricted projects.[14] In addition, prohibited projects clearly pointed out that a project harming the state safety or impairing the public interests is a prohibited foreign-funded project.[15] Furthermore, a project harming the safety and usage of military facilities is prohibited.[16]

1.3 The Rapid Development Era: Establishing a National Security Review Mechanism for Foreign Mergers and Acquisitions

From 2003 to 2014, China's security review mechanism for foreign investments entered into the rapid development era. Since China entering into the World Trade Organization (WTO) in 2001, foreign merger and acquisition activities in China had increasingly raised as compared to foreign direct investment. Foreign investors increasingly used merger and acquisition transactions to establish or expand their business operations in China. In return, these increased foreign merger and acquisition activities had pushed China government to restructure the foreign merger and acquisition regime.

Amid the changing legal regime of merger and acquisition, economic security caused China government's great attention. The 2002 Notice on the Relevant Issues concerning the Transfer of State-Owned Shares and Corporate Shares of Listed Companies to Foreign Investors[17] regulates that the transfer of state-owned shares

[12] ibid Art. 4.

[13] ibid Art. 12.

[14] ibid Art. 6.

[15] ibid Art. 7 (1).

[16] ibid Art. 7 (4); See also ibid. Art. 7 (3) (Projects that have to occupy large tracts of farm land, are harmful to environment protection and development of land resources and/or endanger the security of military facilities and their effective use).

[17] Notice of China Securities Regulatory Commission, the Ministry of Finance and the State Economic and Trade Commission on the Relevant Issues concerning the Transfer of State-Owned

or corporate shares of a listed company to a foreign investor shall abide by the laws and regulations of the state, protect the *safety* of state economy and the public good, prevent the loss of state-owned assets and maintain social stability.[18] In the same year, the Interim Provisions on Restructuring State-owned Enterprises with Foreign Investment[19] states that restructuring state-owned enterprises with foreign investment shall abide by the statutory provisions of the state and safeguard the *economic security* of the state.[20] One year later, China enacted Interim Provisions for Foreign Investors to Merge Domestic Enterprises, within which the concept of 'economic security' appeared twice.[21] First, Article 1 clearly states that one aim is to maintain fair competition and national *economic security*.[22] Second, upon request by a domestic enterprise that is in a competitive relationship, a relevant functional department, or an industrial association, and if relevant department considers that the merger by the foreign investor involves huge market share, or other factors seriously impact market competition, national economy and public livelihood, or state *economic security*, the relevant department may demand the foreign investor to make a report.[23]

To ensure national economic security, the security on the increased foreign M&A became a focus. The procedure of national economic security review is first regulated in the Interim Provisions on the Takeover of Domestic Enterprises by Foreign Investors (2006 Revision).[24] Later, the State Council and Chinese Ministry of Commerce (MOFCOM) issued regulations in 2011 fleshing out a national security review procedure already referred to in general terms in the Foreign M&A Regulations. In the end, the State Council unified the approach to national security review of mergers and acquisitions in the Notice on the Establishment of the Security Review System for Mergers and Acquisitions of Domestic Enterprises by Foreign Investors.[25]

Shares and Corporate Shares of Listed Companies to Foreign Investors [中国证监会、财政部、国家经济贸易委员会关于向外商转让上市公司国有股和法人股有关问题的通知] (issued on 11-01-2002, effective on 11-01-2002, issued by China Securities Regulatory Commission, expired).

[18] ibid. Art. 1.

[19] The Interim Provisions on Restructuring State-owned Enterprises with Foreign Investment (issued on 11-08-2002, effective on 01-01-2003, issued by State Economic & Trade Commission).

[20] The Interim Provisions on Restructuring State-owned Enterprises with Foreign Investment Article 6.

[21] The Interim Provisions for Foreign Investors to Merge Domestic Enterprises [外国投资者并购境内企业暂行规定] (adopted at the first ministerial affairs meeting of the Ministry of Foreign Trade and Economic Cooperation of the People's Republic of China on January 2, 2003, effective on April 12, 2003).

[22] ibid Art. 1.

[23] ibid Art. 19.

[24] The Interim Provisions on the Takeover of Domestic Enterprises by Foreign Investors (amended and adopted at the 7th executive meeting of the Ministry of Commerce of the People's Republic of China, effective on September 8, 2006) Art. 12.

[25] Notice of the General Office of the State Council on the Establishment of the Security Review System for Mergers and Acquisitions of Domestic Enterprises by Foreign Investors [国务院办公厅关于建立外国投资者并购境内企业安全审查制度的通知] (issued on 02-03-2011, effective on 03-03-2011, issued by General Office of the State Council).

This notice, in detail, lays out the scope of security review of mergers and acquisitions,[26] the factors to be considered in the review,[27] the security review mechanism for mergers and acquisitions,[28] and the procedures for the security review of mergers and acquisitions.[29]

Moreover, the following Administrative Measures for the Confirmation and Recordation of Foreign-Funded Projects (2014 Amendment)[30] states that 'foreign-funded projects involving national security shall undergo security review according to the relevant provisions of the state.'[31]

1.4 The Systematic Era: Toward a Unified National Security Review Mechanism for Foreign Investment

Since 2014, China gradually unified its approach to national security review for foreign investments by absorbing lessons from the Pilot Free Trade Zones (FTZs) and adopting a holistic approach to national security.

1.4.1 The Experiment of Pilot Free Trade Zones in China

In 2013, to enhance the level and quality of reform and opening-up and to be highly involved in the development of international rules, China decided to accelerate implementing free trade zones (FTZ).[32] By the end of 2021, China has set up 21 FTZs.[33] With increasing foreign investment in the FTZ, the security concerns become apparent. The 2015 Notice of the General Office of the State Council on Issuing the Measures for the Pilot Program of National Security Review of Foreign Investment in Pilot Free Trade Zones[34] stipulates the mechanism of security review

---

[26] ibid Sec. I.

[27] ibid Sec. II.

[28] ibid Sec. III.

[29] ibid Sec. IV.

[30] Administrative Measures for the Confirmation and Recordation of Foreign-Funded Projects (2014 Amendment) (issued on 12-27-2014, effective on 12-27-2014, issued by State Development & Reform Commission).

[31] ibid Article 7.

[32] Several Opinions of the State Council on Accelerating the Implementation of the Strategies for Free Trade Area [国务院关于加快实施自由贸易区战略的若干意见] (issued on 12-06-2015, effective on 12-06-2015, issued by State Council) Part II Basic Principles.

[33] See Zhihua Liu, 'Pilot free trade zones inspire nation's higher level opening-up' *China Daily* (20 December 2021) <https://english.www.gov.cn/news/topnews/202112/20/content_WS61bfba9ac6d09c94e48a2749.html> accessed February 1, 2022.

[34] Notice of the General Office of the State Council on Issuing the Measures for the Pilot Program of National Security Review of Foreign Investment in Pilot Free Trade Zones [国务院办公厅关于

for foreign investment, including the scope of national security review,[35] the factors to be considered in the review,[36] and security review procedures.[37] In particular, the State Council would like to amend the foreign investment related laws, to research and develop new basic laws on foreign capital, to reform the foreign investment management system, to improve the system of national security review of foreign investment and to maintain the stability, transparency and predictability of foreign investment policies.[38]

Building upon the practice of the FTZ, China is willing to enhance its regulations on foreign investments. In 2021, the State Council issued Several Measures for Promoting the Reform and Innovation of Trade and Investment Facilitation in Pilot Free Trade Zones.[39] It upholds the holistic approach to national security; moreover, it safeguards the core national interests and political security, establish and improve the institutional arrangements for risk prevention and control.

1.4.2 Calling for Laws of National Security Review on Foreign Investment

Since the concept of 'national security review' first appeared in the Anti-Monopoly Law of the People's Republic of China in 2007,[40] China has strived to establish a holistic national security review for foreign investment. In 2015, the RPC National Security Law[41] clearly states that the state will establish the rules and mechanisms for national security review. In particular, China would conduct national security review of foreign investment, particular materials and key technologies and network information technology products and services that affect or may affect national security,

印发自由贸易试验区外商投资国家安全审查试行办法的通知] (issued on 04-08-2015, effective on 05-08-2015, issued by General Office of the State Council).

35 ibid Sec. I.

36 ibid Sec. II.

37 The national security review mechanism and procedures are governed by the Notice of the General Office of the State Council on the Establishment of the Security Review System for Mergers and Acquisitions of Domestic Enterprises by Foreign Investors.

38 Several Opinions of the State Council on Accelerating the Implementation of the Strategies for Free Trade Area [国务院关于加快实施自由贸易区战略的若干意见] (issued on 12-06-2015, effective on 12-06-2015, issued by State Council) Part IV 16.

39 Notice by the State Council of Issuing Several Measures for Promoting the Reform and Innovation of Trade and Investment Facilitation in Pilot Free Trade Zones [国务院印发关于推进自由贸易试验区贸易投资便利化改革创新若干措施的通知] (issued on August 2, 2021, effective on August 2, 2021, issued by State Council).

40 The Anti-Monopoly Law of the People's Republic of China [中华人民共和国反垄断法] (adopted at the 29th meeting of the Standing Committee of the Tenth National People's Congress of the People's Republic of China on August 30, 2007, effective as of August 1, 2008).

41 The National Security Law of the PRC [中华人民共和国国家安全法] (adopted at the 15th session of the Standing Committee of the Twelfth National People's Congress on July 1, 2015, effective on 07-01-2015, issued by Standing Committee of the National People's Congress).

construction projects that involve national security matters and other major matters and activities to effectively prevent and resolve national security risks.

In 2019, the PRC Foreign Investment Law[42] states that foreign investors and foreign-funded enterprises conducting investing activities within China shall abide by the laws and regulations of China; and they can neither compromise China's national security nor cause damage to the public interest.[43] In particular, China shall establish a foreign investment security review system to conduct a security review of foreign investment that impacts or may impact the national security.[44] A decision legally made upon a security review shall be final. The Regulation on the Implementation of the PRC Foreign Investment Law reaffirms that China shall establish a foreign investment security review system to conduct a security review of foreign investment.[45]

2 Reasons for the Transition

2.1 The Internal Perspective

Although China opened to foreign investment in 1980s, foreign investment had to go through many layers and procedures of approvals, which were inefficient. In addition, China's guidance on the foreign investment was nontransparent, uncertain and complicated, causing great inconvenience for foreign investors. Actually, most of foreign investments originated from Hong Kong, Macao or Taiwan; and rarely foreign investment were from other states.[46]

Furthermore, negative comments on the functions of foreign investments always appear, such as foreign capitals' potential intrusion of states' sovereignty and security. In the early 1980s, to attract foreign investments, China established special economic zones; however, such establishment was opposed due to the historical lesson of China leasing.[47]

[42] Foreign Investment Law of the People's Republic of China [中华人民共和国外商投资法] (issued on 03-15-2019, effective on 01-01-2020, issued by National People's Congress).

[43] ibid Art. 6.

[44] ibid Art. 35.

[45] Regulation on the Implementation of the Foreign Investment Law of the People's Republic of China [中华人民共和国外商投资法实施条例] (issued on 12-26-2019, effective on 01-01-2020, issued by State Council) Art. 40.

[46] Foreign companies, unfamiliar with Chinese culture, were unwilling to enter into Mainland China because China lacked proper regulations. Hong Kong based companies would risk investing in Mainland due to cultural connections as well as a better understanding business practice in mainland.

[47] One example is the Yangpu Port event in 1989. See Sheryl Wudunn, 'A Mini-Hong Kong, From Scratch' *The New York Times* (March 23, 1993) <https://www.nytimes.com/1993/03/23/business/a-mini-hong-kong-from-scratch.html> accessed February 1.

Due to the complicated procedures for foreign investment and the hostile environment for foreign investment, the pace of reform and opening-up in China was slow. Frustrated at the slowing pace of reform, Mr. Deng Xiaoping publicly encouraged the government to be bolder in carrying out reform and opening and to speed up economic development. Deng Xiaoping's 1992 south tour provided new impetus for the reform and opening-up that led a golden period for development. Moreover, in 1993, China formally put forward the goal of establishing a socialist market economy system to change from export-oriented economic development to market-oriented economic development, to further clarity foreign investment policy and to expand the area to allow foreign investment.

Since Deng Xiaoping's south tour, foreign investments soared. In 1992, the amount of foreign direct investment exceeded the sum of the thirteen years from 1979 to 1991, and in 1993, China became the second largest importer of foreign direct investment in the world.[48] The flux of foreign investment would inevitably impact national security. To guide the flux of foreign investment to be align with China particular situations, China enacted regulations to approve foreign companies' access to certain industries or sectors in the second phase.

2.2 *The External Perspective*

2.2.1 Transition from the Trial Era to the Rapid Development Era

With foreign investment deeply involving into the reform of state-owned enterprises and green investment, foreign investment's increasingly influenced China's economic structure. In 1989, China allowed foreign investment to reform small state-owned enterprises.[49] Then, China permitted foreign investment to participate the reform of state-owned enterprises deeply.[50]

The Japan Isuzu Corporation and Itochu Corporations' takeover 25% stake in Beijing Travel Bus Co. Ltd and the Ford Motor Company's takeover a stake in a Chinese light-truck maker Jiangling Motors Corporation started the era of foreign

---

[48] China External Economic Statistical Yearbook [1994] 527.

[49] Interim Measures of the State Economic Reform Commission, the Ministry of Finance and the State Administration of State-owned Assets on the Sale of Property Rights of State-owned Small Enterprises [国家经济体制改革委员会、财政部、国家国有资产管理局关于出售国有小型企业产权的暂行办法] (issued on Feb. 19, 1989, effective on Feb. 19, 1989). The purchaser of property rights of state-owned small enterprises may be domestic enterprises owned by the whole people, collectively owned enterprises, township enterprises, 'three-capital' enterprises, private enterprises, partnership groups and individuals.

[50] In 1994, the State Council issued the Regulations on the Supervision and Administration of Property of State-owned Enterprises [国有企业财产监督管理条例], in 1998 the State Economic and Trade Commission issued the Interim Provisions on the Use of Foreign Investment by State-owned Enterprises for Asset Reorganization [关于国有企业利用外商投资进行资产重组的暂行规定].

M&A in China.[51] However, such two takeovers caused great concerns over China's state-owned enterprises, and the state council suspended the takeover of China's state-owned enterprises until August 1999.[52]

However, China's joining the WTO in 2001 reopened its door to foreign investment; China needed to improve its socialist market economy, to create suitable conditions for fair competition between domestic and foreign enterprises and to adapt its laws and regulations to conform to the WTO's fundamental rules. In order to conform to the WTO's fundamental requirements, several regulations had been enacted to allow foreign M&A.[53] In 2003, China enacted the Interim Provisions for Foreign Investors to Merge Domestic Enterprises (2003).[54] Since then, China's M&A market was completely open to foreign investors.

With rules encouraging foreign M&A, foreign corporations had taken over Chinese corporations greatly. Furthermore, China's WTO obligations provided more market opportunities, greater stability and a larger scope of economic and trade cooperation for foreign investment. For instance, by 2009, foreign direct investment in services increased three times from that in 2000, while manufacturing foreign direct investment in China increased 81 percent.[55] In this phase, the significant takeovers included the French Food Company Danone Group's takeover a Chinese beverage

---

[51] 'Ford to Lift Stake In Chinese Truck Maker' *The New York Times* (23 January 1997) <https://www.nytimes.com/1997/01/23/business/ford-to-lift-stake-in-chinese-truck-maker.html> accessed February 1, 2022.

[52] See Regulations on Suspending the Transfer of State-Owned Shares and Corporate Shares of Listed Companies to Foreign Investor.

[53] The Interim Provisions on Drawing Foreign Capital into the Asset Restructuring and Disposal by Financial Asset Management Companies [金融资产管理公司吸收外资参与资产重组与处置的暂行规定] (issued on 10-26-2001, effective on 10-26-2001, issued by Ministry of Foreign Trade & Economic Cooperation); Some Opinions Relevant to Foreign Investment in Listed Companies [对外贸易经济合作部、中国证券监督管理委员会关于印发《关于上市公司涉及外商投资有关问题的若干意见》的通知] (issued on 10-08-2001, effective on 10-08-2001, issued by Ministry of Foreign Trade & Economic Cooperation); Rules for the Establishment of Foreign-shared Securities Company [外资参股证券公司设立规则] (issued on 06-01-2002, effective on 07-01-2002, issued by China Securities Regulatory Commission); Rules on the Establishment of Foreign-shared Fund Management Companies [外资参股基金管理公司设立规则] (issued on 06-01-2002, effective on 07-01-2002, Issued by China Securities Regulatory Commission); Notice on the Relevant Issues concerning the Transfer of State-Owned Shares and Corporate Shares of Listed Companies to Foreign Investors [中国证监会、财政部、国家经济贸易委员会关于向外商转让上市公司国有股和法人股有关问题的通知] (issued on 11-01-2002, effective on 11-01-2002, Issued by China Securities Regulatory Commission, invalidated by Announcement No. 36 [2010] of China Securities Regulatory Commission-Decision on Abolishing Some Administrative Rules on Securities and Futures (the 10th Batch) (Issued on 12-16-2010 Effective on 12-16-2010).

[54] The Interim Provisions on Restructuring State-owned Enterprises with Foreign Investment apply to the restructuring of state-owned enterprises and the enterprises in the form of companies which involve state-owned shares with foreign investment and to the establishment of foreign-funded enterprises in the form of companies. [利用外资改组国有企业暂行规定] (issued on 11-08-2002, effective on 01-01-2003, issued by State Economic & Trade Commission).

[55] *China Statistical Yearbook 2010* (China Statistics Press 2010) 254.

company Wahaha Group,[56] Anheuser-Busch's takeover Harbin Brewery,[57] Veolia Water's takeover Shenzhen Water Group,[58] Goldman Sachs' acquiring Shuanghui.[59] These acquisitions had caused great concerns over security among Chinese governments and the public.[60] Foreign investment's increasing control Chinese economic sectors intensified China's concerns over its own economy. The public begun to discuss the possible loss of national property. Within these concerns, the Coco-Cola Corporations' proposed acquisition of Huiyuan caused huge attention. MOFCOM, the authority responsible for merger control review under the China Anti-Monopoly Law (AML), decided to prohibit the Coca-Cola Company's proposed acquisition of a famous Chinese juice manufacturer China Huiyuan Juice Group Limited due to the transaction would have an adverse effect on competition.[61]

Besides foreign investment's increasing control over Chinese economic sectors, the increasing foreign states' reviewing Chinese investments further pressed China to establish its own national security regime upon foreign investment. For instance, in 2008, the CFIUS blocked Huawei Huawei's proposed acquisition of a communications networking equipment manufacturer 3Com Corp because of the possible effects the merger could have on the national security of the USA. Other similar cases also stimulated China to develop its own national security review regime for foreign M&A.[62]

[56] See Patti Waldmeir and Sundeep Tucker, 'Danone to quit joint venture with Wahaha' *Financial Times* (30 September 2009) <https://www.ft.com/content/849e7eda-ad87-11de-bb8a-00144feabdc0> accessed February 1.

[57] See Kimberly Song, 'Anheuser-Busch Completes Purchase of Harbin Stake' *The Wall Street Journal* (May 19, 2004) <https://www.wsj.com/articles/SB108498059089315795> accessed 1 February.

[58] See 'Veolia buys into Shenzhen water group' *China Daily* (December 23, 2003) <http://www.chinadaily.com.cn/en/doc/2003-12/23/content_292563.htm> accessed 1 February.

[59] See David Barboza, 'Chinese Bid for U.S. Pork Had Links to Wall Street' *The New York Times* (2 June 2013) <https://www.nytimes.com/2013/06/03/business/global/behind-the-chinese-bid-for-smithfield-foods.html> accessed February 1, 2022.

[60] In 1995, due to foreign M&A can cause economic problems and loss of national property, China suspended the Transfer of State-Owned Shares and Corporate Shares of Listed Companies to Foreign Investors.

[61] See 'China's Statement Blocking Coca-Cola Huiyuan Deal' *The Wall Street Journal* (18 March 2009) <https://www.wsj.com/articles/BL-CJB-1527> accessed February 1.

[62] In 2005, China National Offshore Oil Corporation withdrew its bid to acquire the U.S. energy company Unocal among concerns of foreign ownership of U.S. energy companies; in 2009, CFIUS blocked a Chinese corporation's purchase of a mining company Firstgold Corp. due to its location near sensitive military assets; in February 2011, CFIUS determined that Huawei should unwind its purchase of 3Leaf Systems after a post-closing review; in September 2012, President Obama required a Delaware corporation Ralls, owned by two Chinese nationals, to divest the acquired four wind farm companies due to national security.

2.2.2 Transition from the Rapid Development Era to the Systematic Era

Another significant stimulating factor to push China to improve its national security review regime is the increased outbound M&A. Since 2015, China outbound M&A increased greatly. For example, in 2016, China accounted for $92 billion of net purchases in cross-border acquisitions, over 10% of the worldwide total and more than the USA, with $78 billion.[63] However, China outbound M&A met significant obstacles due to foreign states' security concerns.[64] Out of security concerns, foreign states barred many China outbound investments.[65] Compared to the year of 2016, in 2017, the number of foreign M&As decreased by 55%; and the amount of foreign M&As decreased by 45%.[66] Foreign states' security review over Chinese investment motivated China to establish its own national security regime upon foreign investment and provided a template from which China can learn.

Another significant stimulating factor to push China to enact Foreign Investment Law was the China–US trade war. In 2018, former President Donald Trump began setting tariffs and other trade barriers on China to force China to make changes to 'unfair trade practices,' including the growing trade deficit, the theft of intellectual property and the forced transfer of US technology to China. To satisfy the US demand, the enactment of Foreign Investment Law and the Regulation on the Implementation of the Foreign Investment Law of the PRC clearly lay out the principle of equal

63 U.N. Conference on Trade and Development, *World Investment Report 2017* (2017) 230–231.

64 Some scholars called China's acquirers as national strategic buyers to further the interests of a nation state in the pursuit of national industrial policy or perhaps national security concerns. *See* Jeffrey N Gordon and Curtis J Milhaupt, 'China as a National Strategic Buyer: Toward a Multilateral Regime for Cross-Border M&A' Colum Bus L Rev 192.

65 For instance, in 2015 December, President Obama barred Fujian Grand Chip's takeover of Aixtron's US business; in August 2016, due to security concerns, Australia barred Chinese state-owned company State Grid and Hong Kong-based Cheung Kong Infrastructure Holdings from buying stake in Ausgrid; in September 2016, the city of Antwerp (Belgium) blocked the sale of a 14% stake in Belgian electricity and gas distributor Eandis to Chinese State Grid International Development Limited; in September 2017, President Trump blocked the proposed $1.3 billion acquisition of Lattice Semiconductor Corporation, a US chipmaker, by Canyon Bridge Capital Partners, a US-headquartered private equity firm reportedly funded by the Chinese government; in January 2018, CIFUS blocked the $1.2 billion sale of money-transfer service Moneygram to Ant Financial, an affiliate of Chinese e-commerce giant Alibaba; in July 2018, concerning public order and national security, Germany blocked Chinese state-owned company State Grid acquiring of a 20 percent minority stake in 50 Hz, one of Germany's four providers of high-voltage transmission systems; in August 2018, due to public order and national security, a consortium of France's Manoir Group and Chinass Yantai Taihai Group abandoned the acquisition of German company Leifeld Metal Spinning.

66 Yang Daoling 杨道玲, 'The Status, Problems and Countermeasures of China's Enterprises' Overseas Investment and Mergers and Acquisitions' [我国企业海外投资并购的现状、问题及对策研究] [2008] 29 China Economic and Trade Guide [中国经贸导刊(中)] 4–6.

treatment of foreign-funded enterprises,[67] the opening of financial service, investor protection,[68] and the prohibition of forced transfer to intellectual property.[69]

Because of foreign states security screening mechanisms for Chinese outward investment and the pressure from the China–US trade war, China has called for improving its own mechanisms of national security for foreign investment.[70] China's new national security review mechanism will be, to a great extent, based on its security review tryouts in FTZs, its learning experience from other countries and its own characteristics.

3 Conclusion

Globally, the national security review mechanisms share two characteristics: a broad definition of national security and a self-judgment nature of security.[71] With such characteristics, the new national security has brought significant challenges to the international economic order.[72] The security review mechanisms in the USA and in the EU can be two examples.

In the USA, the 2018 Foreign Investment Risk Review Modernization Act (FIRRMA) substantially expanded CFIUS's competence to address national security concerns over certain foreign investments.[73] Under the FIRRMA, the CFIUS has expanded the scope of covered transactions by adding new types of covered transactions. These new transactions involve certain real estate transactions, investments locating near sensitive government facilities, investments involving material technical information such as critical technology. Moreover, FIRRMA formalizes the requirements of material agreements related to the transaction and lengthens the review period.

In the EU, the EU enacted its Regulation Establishing a Framework for the Screening of Foreign Direct Investments into the European Union in 2020 to address foreign direct investments likely to affect security or public order.[74] This regulation allows the European Commission and other EU member states to intervene in EU member states' screening proceedings and to express their opinions. Although EU

---

[67] Regulation on the Implementation of the Foreign Investment Law of the PRC Art. 6.

[68] ibid Chapter 3.

[69] ibid Art. 24.

[70] Yongfu Huang 黄永富, 'the Influence and Countermeasure of the Western Strengthening the National Security Review of Foreign Investment on Chinese Enterprises' [西方加强外资国家安全审查对中国企业的影响及对策] [2019] 9 China Development Observation (中国发展观察) 44–48.

[71] Ji Ma, 'International Investment and National Security Review' (2019) 52 VanJTransnatlL 899.

[72] See J Benton Heath, 'The New National Security Challenge to the Economic Order' 129 Yale LJ 1020.

[73] Foreign Investment Risk Review Modernization Act of 2018 H.R.5841.

[74] Regulation (EU) 2019/452 of the European Parliament and of the Council of March 19, 2019, Establishing a Framework for the Screening of Foreign Direct Investments into the Union.

member states themselves can decide whether they should opt for any screening mechanism and can determine its thresholds triggering the screening, member states give due consideration to EU Commission and other states' opinions.[75]

Today, China has unified the approach to the governance of foreign investments by enacting Foreign Investment Law. In addition, China has created a uniform national security regime by enacting National Security Law and related security regulations.[76] Following the gradually clear framework of national security and the unified approach to foreign investments and learning from the USA and the EU, the next step would be establishing a uniform and consistent mechanism of national security review for foreign investments.

[75] ibid Art. 6.

[76] For instance, Data Security Law of the People's Republic of China [中华人民共和国数据安全法] (Issued on June 10, 2021, effective on September 1, 2021, issued by Standing Committee of the National People's Congress).

Dispute Settlement Mechanisms in Foreign Investment Contracts with Central American State-Owned Enterprises

Jorge Arturo González

1 Introduction

When doing business in developing countries, foreign investors typically evaluate the political stability of the host State, its adherence to the rule of law and the suitability of the local court systems to settle disputes and uphold private property rights. The host States usually addresses these concerns through international treaties, investment laws, arbitration laws and contracts providing arbitration as a dispute resolution mechanism.

The situation in Central America is no different, and the existence of instruments designed to attract and protect foreign investment is prevalent. Nonetheless, foreign investment contracts entered between foreign investors (or their local subsidiaries) and State-owned entities (SOEs) deserve particular attention. Although these contracts can be a profitable source of business, their unique characteristics may exacerbate the concerns mentioned above, and even domestic arbitration in the host State could ultimately prove to be an unreliable conflict resolution forum. This chapter explores this situation within the Central American context and draws conclusions from the Costa Rican experience.

As a starting point, the author provides an overview of the SOE sector in Central America (Sect. 2). The next section analyses a case in Costa Rica, where domestic arbitration was ultimately unfavourable for the foreign investor (Sect. 3). The following section examines similar risks in the rest of Central America (Sect. 4). The last section provides a conclusion (Sect. 5).

J. A. González (✉)
Utrecht University, Utrecht, Netherlands
e-mail: jgc@aguilarcastillolove.com

J. Chaisse et al. (eds.), *Regulation of State-Controlled Enterprises*, International Law and the Global South, https://doi.org/10.1007/978-981-19-1368-6_18

2 The SOE Sector in Central America

Central America is a democratic, Spanish-speaking region located between North and South America that refers, for the purposes of this chapter, to Costa Rica, El Salvador, Guatemala, Honduras, Nicaragua and Panama. The combined GDP of all Central American nations would rank as the fifth-largest economy in Latin America.[1] This region traditionally relies on economic activities such as tourism and agriculture, although more sophisticated services have experienced constant growth in recent decades.

Despite the wave of privatizations in the 1990s, SOEs are significant economic actors in Central America.[2] SOEs are entities separated from the public administration, having an independent legal personality under either public or private law, and undertaking commercial activities, e.g. sale of goods/services.[3]

The SOE sector is large relative to the size of each of these economies. The IDB estimates that there are 68 SOEs in total in Central America, with the following distribution: Costa Rica (25), El Salvador (7), Guatemala (10), Honduras (8), Nicaragua (11) and Panama (7).[4] The author considers that this data is likely to underestimate the actual number of SOEs per country, as it relies on a definition of SOE that is too narrow.[5] However, this only strengthens the finding that the SOE sector is large relative to each country's economy. The countries with the smallest SOE sector are El Salvador, Guatemala and Nicaragua.[6]

---

[1] Author's own calculation based on IMF, *Report for Selected Countries and Subjects' World Economic Outlook Database* (October 2020) <https://www.imf.org/en/Publications/SePROLLs/world-economic-outlook-databases> accessed 14 October 2020.

[2] World Bank, 'Corporate Governance of State-Owned Enterprises in Latin America: Current Trends and Country Cases', 28.

[3] OECD, *OECD Guidelines on Corporate Governance of State-Owned Enterprises* [2015] (2015 edn) <https://www.oecd-ilibrary.org/governance/oecd-guidelines-on-corporate-governance-of-state-owned-enterprises-2015_9789264244160-en;jsessionid=TM3IEle0Dn3HTRfOM1yNPBps.ip-10-240-5-59> accessed 9 October 2020; Daniel M Shapiro and Steven Globerman, 'The International Activities and Impacts of State-Owned Enterprises' in Karl Sauvant, Lisa E Sachs and Wouter PF Schmit Jongbloed (eds), *Sovereign Investment: Concerns and Policy Reactions* (OUP 2012), 102; World Bank, *Corporate Governance of State-Owned Enterprises in Latin America: Current Trends and Country Cases* (Governance Global Practice Latin America and the Caribbean Region, WB 2014), 15-16.

[4] Aldo Musacchio and Emilio I. Pineda Ayerbe (eds), *Fixing State-Owned Enterprises: New Policy Solutions to Old Problems* (IDB 2019), xxii.

[5] For instance, BCR, BNCR (the two largest commercial banks in Costa Rica) and ICE (the largest electric utility in Costa Rica) are legally categorized as *autonomous institutions*, rather than companies/enterprises, which excludes them from the data collected by the IDB. However, their incorporation under public law rather than commercial law should not affect their status as an SOE.

[6] In these countries, SOE revenue accounts for less than 1 billion US dollars per year, according to Aldo Musacchio and Emilio I. Pineda Ayerbe (eds), *Fixing State-Owned Enterprises: New Policy Solutions to Old Problems* (IDB 2019), 11.

SOEs in the electrical sector are crucial for the Central American governments. Over 80% of total SOE revenue in Honduras comes from the National Electrical Energy Company (*Empresa Nacional de Energía Eléctrica*). In contrast, two electrical SOEs in Nicaragua (*Empresa Nicaragüense de Electricidad* and *Empresa Nacional de Transmisión Eléctrica*) jointly represent nearly 30% of total SOE revenue.[7] SOEs involved in managing trade infrastructure (ports, airports and railroads) are also an essential source of revenue for governments. Ninety percentage of SOE revenue in Panama comes from the Panama Canal Authority (*Autoridad del Canal de Panamá*), whereas airport/port operators in Guatemala (e.g. *Empresa Portuaria Nacional Santo Tomás de Castilla* and *Empresa Portuaria Quetzal*) jointly represent over 20% of total SOE revenue.[8]

However, the size of SOEs in the region is not an indicator of their financial health. A large percentage of SOEs in Central America report annual losses. According to the IDB Database of State-Owned Enterprises in Latin America and the Caribbean, the following percentage of SOEs reported losses, on average, from 2010 to 2016: Costa Rica (42.06%), El Salvador (71.43%), Guatemala (57.14%), Honduras (76.19%), Nicaragua (95.24%) and Panama (8.57%).[9] For this reason, SOEs frequently require fiscal transfers to cover losses, representing a significant cash flow risk for their governments.[10]

The size of this contingency is significant, as SOE liabilities represent a large percentage of each of their government's budgets.[11] Therefore, a shock to the SOE sector could translate into the need for a large injection of fiscal resources for a bailout.[12] This is precisely what happened in El Salvador in 2019 when the water and sanitation public utility (*Administración Nacional de Acueductos y Alcantarillados*) could not repay its creditors after charging tariff prices 50% below cost.[13]

---

[7] Aldo Musacchio and Emilio I. Pineda Ayerbe (eds), *Fixing State-Owned Enterprises: New Policy Solutions to Old Problems* (IDB 2019), 10.

[8] Aldo Musacchio and Emilio I. Pineda Ayerbe (eds), *Fixing State-Owned Enterprises: New Policy Solutions to Old Problems* (IDB 2019), 10.

[9] Aldo Musacchio and Emilio I. Pineda Ayerbe (eds), *Fixing State-Owned Enterprises: New Policy Solutions to Old Problems* (IDB 2019), xxiii.

[10] World Bank, *Corporate Governance of State-Owned Enterprises in Latin America: Current Trends and Country Cases* (Governance Global Practice Latin America and the Caribbean Region, WB 2014), 63; Beatriz Calderón, 'ANDA debe más de $100 millones a CEL y tiene deuda de dos meses con distribuidores de energía' *La Prensa Gráfica* (El Salvador, 20 August 2019) <https://www.laprensagrafica.com/elsalvador/ANDA-debe-mas-de-100-millones-a-CEL-y-tiene-deuda-de-dos-meses-con-distribuidoras-de-energia-20190820-0364.html> accessed 10 October 2020.

[11] According to the IDB Database of State-Owned Enterprises in Latin America and the Caribbean, the ratio of SOE liabilities to total government budget from 2010 to 2016 was, on average: 51.92% in Costa Rica, 12.75% in El Salvador, 5.66% in Guatemala, 28.15% in Honduras, 21.88% in Nicaragua and 30.54% Panama.

[12] Aldo Musacchio and Emilio I. Pineda Ayerbe (eds), *Fixing State-Owned Enterprises: New Policy Solutions to Old Problems* (IDB 2019), xxviii.

[13] World Bank, *Corporate Governance of State-Owned Enterprises in Latin America: Current Trends and Country Cases* (Governance Global Practice Latin America and the Caribbean

SOEs not only provide goods and services to the public, but they also frequently act as buyers through public procurement mechanisms and as parties to foreign investment contracts.[14] In Central America, SOEs participate in some of the largest business operations as clients, partners, or co-ventures, attracting foreign investors across the region. In Nicaragua, Norwegian company Equinor and London-listed company Cairn Energy currently have a partnership with SOE Petronic (*Empresa Nicaragüense del Petróleo*) for an oil exploration concession along the Nicaraguan Pacific.[15] The expansion of the Panama Canal from 2009 to 2016 involved foreign investors from Spain, Italy and Belgium.[16] In 2018, a 1.4 billion US dollars contract for constructing a bridge over the Panama Canal was awarded to a Chinese consortium.[17] In this case, the investor itself represents a group of Chinese SOEs, a situation that might raise some concerns indirectly addressed by another chapter of this book (*Chinese State-Owned Enterprises in Africa: Always a Black-and-White Role?*).

In the region, foreign investment contracts entered by SOEs and foreign investors (or their local subsidiaries) are generally settled through domestic litigation,[18]

Region, WB 2014), 63; Beatriz Calderón, 'ANDA debe más de $100 millones a CEL y tiene deuda de dos meses con distribuidores de energía' *La Prensa Gráfica* (El Salvador, 20 August 2019) <https://www.laprensagrafica.com/elsalvador/ANDA-debe-mas-de-100-millones-a-CEL-y-tiene-deuda-de-dos-meses-con-distribuidoras-de-energia-20190820-0364.html> accessed 10 October 2020.

[14] OECD, 'Public procurement' <http://www.oecd.org/gov/public-procurement/> accessed 10 October 2020, 20 ("Public procurement refers to the purchase by governments and state-owned enterprises of goods, services and works").

[15] Equinor, 'In May 2015, Equinor was awarded four licences offshore the Nicaraguan Pacific, together with partner Petronic' <https://www.equinor.com/en/where-we-are/nicaragua.html> accessed 12 October 2020.

[16] Augusto Garcia Sanjur, 'The Panama Canal Expansion: Adaptation of Contracts' (2019) 11(1) Arbitration Law Review <https://elibrary.law.psu.edu/cgi/viewcontent.cgi?article=1254&context=arbitrationlawreview> accessed 10 September 2020, 90–92 ["Grupo Unidos por el Canal (GUPC or the Contractor) won the bid. This consortium was composed of the following companies: Sacyr (Spain), Salini Impregilo (Italy), Jan de Nul (Belgium), and Constructora Urbana (Panama)"].

[17] AFP, 'Panama awards $1.4 bn bride project to Chinese group' *France 24* (Panama City, 5 December 2018) <https://www.france24.com/en/20181205-panama-awards-14-bn-bridge-project-chinese-group> accessed 12 October 2020.

[18] ZV, 'Millonarias demandas y proyectos de Coalianza comprometen 15% del PIB > *La Tribuna* (Honduras, 9 December 2019) <https://www.latribuna.hn/2019/12/09/millonarias-demandas-y-proyectos-de-coalianza-comprometen-15-del-pib/> accessed 2 October 2020; Public Deed [Notary Public Enrique Villagra] between Instituto Nacional de Electricidad and Distribuidora de Electricidad del Norte [12 January 2002], *Escritura 14: Contrato de Concesión de Distribución* <https://www.disnorte-dissur.com.ni/images/quienes-somos/info-acceso-publico/Concesion-DISNORTE.pdf> accessed 25 October 2020; Public Deed [Notary Public Enrique Villagra] between Instituto Nacional de Electricidad and Distribuidora de Electricidad del Sur [27 June 2000], *Escritura 16: Contrato de Concesión de Distribución* <https://www.disnorte-dissur.com.ni/images/quienes-somos/info-acceso-publico/Concesion-DISSUR.pdf> accessed 25 October 2020.

domestic arbitration[19] or international arbitration.[20] Some contracts, such as the agreement for the design and construction for the third set of locks of the Panama Canal, based on the FIDIC Yellow Book template, have additionally provided mechanisms such as dispute adjudication boards.[21]

Domestic litigation could be perceived as the forum where SOEs have the most substantial standing and a 'home-court advantage'. Foreign investors could be concerned that the governmental ties of these entities could somehow influence the outcome of any dispute. Considerable delays in the court systems across the region likely discourage most foreign companies from relying on litigation.[22] Furthermore, cases of corruption by judges in Central America are sporadic but not completely unheard of.[23]

Domestic arbitration provides greater neutrality and allows the investors to bypass the State courts to a certain extent. Foreign investment contracts in Central America frequently provide for institutional arbitration administered by an arbitration centre within the host State, where most of the listed neutrals are also nationals of that State.[24] Nonetheless, in such cases, the State courts can still play a role in appeal, setting aside proceedings and/or applications for interim relief.

Alternatively, the SOE and the contractor could agree on international arbitration in a neutral third country. The choice of this forum would detach the dispute from the sphere of national influence of the SOE, consequently guaranteeing the greatest neutrality. Some arbitration cases involving Central American SOEs have been settled

---

19 *Instituto Costarricense de Electricidad v. P.H. Chucás S.A.* [27 June 2019] Supreme Court, First Chamber 989-2020; *Laurent Jean-Marc Parienti v. Autoridad de Tránsito y Transporte Terrestre* [27 January 2005] Centro de Solución de Conflictos de Panamá.

20 'Arbitraje Internacional resuelve disolver y liquidar SORESCO' (*RECOPE*, 31 October 2019) <https://www.recope.go.cr/arbitraje-internacional-resuelve-disolver-liquidar-soresco/> accessed 25 October 2020; Cosmo Sanderson, 'Panel dissolves Chinese-Costa Rican refinery project' (*GAR*, 1 November 2019) <https://www.arblit.com/wp-content/uploads/2019/11/Panel-dissolves-Chinese-Costa-Rican-refinery-project.pdf> accessed 25 October 2020; *Enel Green Power S.p.A. v. El Salvador* [2014] ICSID ARB/13/18 (throughout the proceedings, the parties referred to an ICC award rendered against a Salvadorian SOE in Paris prior to the ICSID claim).

21 Augusto Garcia Sanjur, 'The Panama Canal Expansion: Adaptation of Contracts' (2019) 11(1) Arbitration Law Review <https://elibrary.law.psu.edu/cgi/viewcontent.cgi?article=1254&context=arbitrationlawreview> accessed 10 September 2020, 99.

22 Fernando Maldonado, 'Crisis sanitaria tiene paralizados los juicios en el Poder Judicial' *El Heraldo* (Tegucigalpa, 15 August 2020) <https://www.elheraldo.hn/pais/1401379-466/crisis-sanitaria-tiene-paralizados-los-juicios-en-el-poder-judicial> accessed 12 October 2020.

23 Edwin Pitán and Irving Escobar, 'CSJ tramita antejuicio contra seis jueces y magistrados implicados en caso Comisiones Paralelas 2020' *Prensa Libre* (Guatemala, 12 August 2020) <https://www.prensalibre.com/guatemala/justicia/csj-tramita-antejuicio-contra-seis-jueces-y-magistrados-implicados-en-caso-comisiones-paralelas-2020-breaking/> accessed 15 October 2020.

24 CECAP, 'Listado de Árbitros por Especialidad' (Centro de Conciliación y Arbitraje de Panamá, 2018–2020 Period) <https://www.cecap.com.pa/wp-content/uploads/2020/02/Listado_Arbitros_por_Especialidad_2018_2020.pdf> accessed 15 October 2020; CICA, 'Árbitros y Conciliadores' <https://cicacr.org/arbitros-y-conciliadores/> accessed 15 October 2020; CENAC, 'Listado de Arbitrios' <http://www.cenac.com.gt/new-page-3> accessed 15 October 2020.

by international tribunals seated in arbitration hubs such as London,[25] Paris[26] and Miami.[27]

In addition to, or in the absence of, a contractual arbitration agreement, the investor may, in some cases, rely on investment instruments (e.g. an international treaty to which both its home State and the host State are contracting parties) to trigger the jurisdiction of an international arbitration tribunal. The tribunal may be ad hoc, or more frequently, appointed under the institutional auspices of *ICSID* (The International Center for the Settlement of Investment Disputes) or another dispute resolution institution. Usually, at this stage, the respondent is not the SOE but rather the State itself.[28] Furthermore, the claimant need not necessarily be a foreign investor but could be a foreign-controlled local entity. In some cases, the investor's own shareholders, parent companies and/or indirect owners may have legal standing to pursue the claim on their own.[29] According to the above paragraphs, both contract-based and treaty-based arbitration may be considered at an international level.[30] The latter is also known as international *investment* arbitration, as opposed to international *commercial* arbitration. Both of these systems are discussed, sometimes interchangeably, throughout this chapter although they have significant differences.

The author submits that opting for domestic arbitration in the host State may expose the foreign investor to some of the risks that the 'private' arbitration system is supposed to circumvent, e.g. inefficiency, delays and lack of independence from the court systems. The following section provides a case study from Costa Rica concerning some of these issues.

---

[25] 'Arbitraje Internacional resuelve disolver y liquidar SORESCO' (*RECOPE*, 31 October 2019) <https://www.recope.go.cr/arbitraje-internacional-resuelve-disolver-liquidar-soresco/> accessed 25 October 2020; Cosmo Sanderson, 'Panel dissolves Chinese-Costa Rican refinery project' (*GAR*, 1 November 2019) <https://www.arblit.com/wp-content/uploads/2019/11/Panel-dissolves-Chinese-Costa-Rican-refinery-project.pdf> accessed 25 October 2020.

[26] *Enel Green Power S.p.A. v. El Salvador* [2014] ICSID ARB/13/18 (throughout the proceedings, the parties referred to an ICC award rendered against a Salvadorian SOE in Paris prior to the ICSID claim).

[27] Augusto Garcia Sanjur, 'The Panama Canal Expansion: Adaptation of Contracts' (2019) 11(1) Arbitration Law Review <https://elibrary.law.psu.edu/cgi/viewcontent.cgi?article=1254&context=arbitrationlawreview> accessed 10 September 2020, 107.

[28] Article 25(1), ICSID Convention.

[29] *See Eskosol S.p.A. in liquidazione v. Italian Republic* [4 September 2020] ICSID ARB/15/50; *Also see* Vera Korzun, 'Shareholder Claims for Reflective Loss: How International Investment Law Changes Corporate Law and Governance' [2019] 40:1 U. Pa. J. Int'l L. <https://scholarship.law.upenn.edu/cgi/viewcontent.cgi?article=1975&context=jil> accessed 3 November 2020.

[30] Queen Mary University of London '2020 QMUL-CCIAG Survey: Investors' Perceptions of ISDS' (May 2020) <http://www.arbitration.qmul.ac.uk/media/arbitration/docs/QM-CCIAG-Survey-ISDS-2020.pdf> accessed 1 November 2020, 7.

3 *ICE v. Chucás*: The Case of Costa Rica

In 2017, an arbitration award rendered against one of the largest SOEs in Costa Rica made national headlines. The dispute had arisen out of an investment contract between the SOE and the subsidiary of a foreign investor. The award first made headlines due to its possible financial impact on the SOE (see reference below) and later due to allegations from the SOE that one of the arbitrators had failed to disclose a conflict of interest during the proceedings. Ultimately, the award was set aside, leaving the contractor empty-handed. The following paragraphs explain this case known as *Chucás* and the controversial circumstances surrounding the decision on annulment.

In 2011, the Costa Rican Electricity Institute ("ICE" for its acronym in Spanish), the largest electrical and telecom utility in Costa Rica entered a BOT[31] contract with P.H. Chucás, a subsidiary of Italian company Enel Green Power.[32] The price of the agreement, which included the construction and operation of a hydropower plant and the sale of the energy generated by the plant, was approximately 108 million US dollars.

After a series of delays, penalty fees,[33] and disagreements between the parties, P.H. Chucás filed for domestic arbitration administered by CICA[34] in Costa Rica. In November 2017, the arbitral tribunal issued its award, unanimously ordering ICE to pay an additional 112.5 million US dollars to P.H. Chucás to restore the contract's economic equilibrium. By comparison, the current liabilities of ICE as of 2018 were approximately 676 million US dollars.[35]

Once the arbitral award became public, it drew attention from politicians, media and even trade unions[36] due to concerns over the declining financial condition of

---

[31] In a Build-Operate-Transfer ("BOT") project, the SOE grants the right to develop and operate a facility or system for a certain period to a private company. The private company finances, owns and constructs the facility or system, and operates it commercially for the project period, after which the facility is transferred to the authority. Pursuant to PPPLRC, 'Concessions, Build-Operate-Transfer (BOT) and Design-Build-Operate (DBO) Projects' (*World Bank Group*, 2018-02-08) <https://ppp.worldbank.org/public-private-partnership/agreements/concessions-bots-dbos> accessed 30 October 2020.

[32] *Instituto Costarricense de Electricidad v. P.H. Chucás S.A.* [27 June 2019] Supreme Court, First Chamber 989-2020; 'Costa Rica' (*ENEL Green Power*) <https://www.enelgreenpower.com/es/paises/centroamerica/costa-rica> accessed 27 October 2020.

[33] *P.H. Chucás S.A. v. Instituto Costarricense de Electricidad* [15 September 2020] Administrative-Disputes Tribunal 00469-2020 (medida cautelar).

[34] International Center for Conciliation and Arbitration (*see* http://cica.co.cr/).

[35] Instituto Costarricense de Electricidad, *Estados Financieros Consolidados* (Finance Division, September 2019) <https://www.grupoice.com/wps/wcm/connect/9c9e0a41-b03f-46a1-a234-dacb98737904/III+Trimestre+2019+en+espa%C3%B1ol.pdf?MOD=AJPERES&CONVERT_TO=url&CACHEID=ROOTWORKSPACE-9c9e0a41-b03f-46a1-a234-dacb98737904-mWPUxfG> accessed 12 October 2020, 3.

[36] José Quirós Gallegos, 'Diputados aprueban moción para interpelar a Carlos Obregón y directora jurídica del ICE' *El Mundo* (San José, 8 December 2017) <https://www.elmundo.cr/costa-rica/diputados-aprueban-mocion-interpelar-carlos-obregon-directora-juridica-del-ice/> accessed 28

ICE.[37] The Congress of the Republic of Costa Rica called ICE officers to testify before the Public Expenditure Committee.[38] The legislators voiced concerns over the possibility that the award cost is transferred to Costa Rican consumers in their utility bills and the impact on ICE's finance.[39] During the legislative hearing, the Congress representatives demanded an explanation for the arbitration result and the potential use of public resources in paying for the award.[40] ICE officers took the opportunity to attack the merits of the award and claim that they were forced to go to arbitration.[41]

By the time of the legislative hearing, ICE had already filed for the judicial annulment of the award before the First Chamber of the Supreme Court of Costa Rica, claiming that at least one of the arbitrators had failed to disclose a conflict of interest and calling into question his impartiality and independence.[42] In a five-page judgement dated 27 June 2019, the Supreme Court ruled in favour of ICE and set the arbitration award aside, on the basis of the undisclosed conflict and its effects on due

September 2020; Juan Lara Salas, 'ICE deberá pagar al menos $112 millones al perder arbitraje con firma de hidroeléctrica Chucás' *La Nación* (San José, 27 November 2017) <https://www.nacion.com/el-pais/servicios/ice-debera-pagar-al-menos-112-millones-a-firma-de/IGATT2EVYZF6PB45UEUSL5BTVI/story/> accessed 28 September 2020 ("Por su parte, el Frente Interno de Trabajadores del ICE… dijo que 'son más de $150 millones' los que se pagarán con los recibos eléctricos y de telefonía. 'Este es un llamado a la transparencia, den la cara, respondan, ¿cómo y porqué perdieron este arbitraje con la hidroeléctrica Chucás?'"); Michael M. Soto, 'Condenan al ICE a pagar más de ¢75 mil millones a proyecto hidroeléctrico Chucás' *CR Hoy* (San José, 24 November 2017) <https://www.crhoy.com/nacionales/condenan-al-ice-a-pagar-mas-de-%C2%A275-mil-millones-a-proyecto-hidroelectrico-chucas/> accessed 28 September 2020;

37 Juan Fernando Lara, 'ICE admite tener números en rojo' *La Nación* (San José, 3 November 2018) <https://www.nacion.com/el-pais/servicios/ice-admite-tener-numeros-en-rojo/5TDFIBYZY5BNTN2DQJ3HE3Y52Q/story/> accessed 28 September 2020; Carlos Mora, 'La situación financiera del ICE es muy seria' *CR Hoy* (San José, 6 June 2019) <https://www.crhoy.com/nacionales/la-situacion-financiera-del-ice-es-muy-seria/> accessed 28 September 2020.

38 José Quirós Gallegos, 'Diputados aprueban moción para interpelar a Carlos Obregón y directora jurídica del ICE' *El Mundo* (San José, 8 December 2017) <https://www.elmundo.cr/costa-rica/diputados-aprueban-mocion-interpelar-carlos-obregon-directora-juridica-del-ice/> accessed 28 September 2020.

39 José Quirós Gallegos, 'Diputados aprueban moción para interpelar a Carlos Obregón y directora jurídica del ICE' *El Mundo* (San José, 8 December 2017) <https://www.elmundo.cr/costa-rica/diputados-aprueban-mocion-interpelar-carlos-obregon-directora-juridica-del-ice/> accessed 28 September 2020 ("los congresistas indagarán sobre el impacto que tendrá esta sentencia en la salud financiera del instituto y la posibilidad de trasladar dicho gasto a tarifas y a los consumidores").

40 Asamblea Legislativa de Costa Rica, 'Piden explicaciones al ICE por arbitraje que lo obligó a pagar 112 millones de dólares' (*YouTube*, 22 February 2018) <https://www.youtube.com/watch?v=b_RvcLdNA9A> accessed 3 November 2020.

41 Juan Lara Salas, 'ICE alega que fue obligado a enfrentar arbitraje en que resultó perdedor' *La Nación* (San José, 22 February 2018) <https://www.nacion.com/el-pais/servicios/ice-alega-que-fue-obligado-a-enfrentar-arbitraje/LMNVSFK5XFHTJLQRH7WMAUXCVI/story/> accessed 28 September 2020.

42 ICE, 'Pide nulidad de Laudo: ICE denuncia conflicto de interés en proceso de arbitraje de P.H. Chucás' *ICE Press Release* (1 February 2018) <https://perma.cc/TT3N-2HLL> accessed 2 October 2020.

process.[43] Some of the circumstances that persuaded the Supreme Court to find the existence of this conflict were that one of the arbitrator's business partners acted as a notary public in the claimant's deed of incorporation, that the arbitrator himself acted as a notary public for the claimant once in 2011 and that the arbitrator's son was once a member of the claimant's board of directors.[44]

Although the decision on annulment appears to be correct for upholding the principle of due process and the arbitrator's duty to disclose, a more in-depth analysis reveals that the legal bases that it relied on could be criticised.[45] The judgement had four main weaknesses. First, it overlooked the possibility that ICE was aware of the alleged conflict of interest during the entire arbitration proceedings and hid it as a 'smoking gun' for a later challenge in case of not prevailing.[46] Regarding this point, it is essential to note that some of the documents provided as evidence of the conflict were part of the administrative case file that adjudicated the public tender to the contractor.[47] Second, the judgement relied on certain instruments of questionable legal relevance to the matter (e.g. human rights instruments).[48] Third, the Court took a liberal approach towards annulling the award, going beyond the restrictive list of grounds provided by the Alternative Dispute Resolution Law, which governs domestic arbitration in Costa Rica.[49] Finally, it failed to substantiate the selection of a given ground for annulment under the Alternative Dispute Resolution Law.[50]

---

[43] *Instituto Costarricense de Electricidad v. P.H. Chucás S.A.* [27 June 2019] Supreme Court, First Chamber 989-2020.

[44] For an overview of the judgement, *see* Felipe Volio, 'Disclosing the Elephant in the Case File? Costa Rican Court Sets Aside Award' (*Kluwer Arbitration Blog*, 21 May 2020) <http://arbitrationblog.kluwerarbitration.com/2020/05/21/disclosing-the-elephant-in-the-case-file-costa-rican-court-sets-aside-award/> accessed 15 September 2020; The author notes that, unlike in many jurisdictions, in Costa Rica individuals are allowed to act simultaneously as lawyers and notaries.

[45] *See* Jorge Arturo González, 'Rules for thee, not for me? A commentary on the Supreme Court of Costa Rica judgement setting aside the *ICE v. Chucás* award' [2022] The Arbitration Brief (American University Washington College of Law) (forthcoming).

[46] Felipe Volio, 'Disclosing the Elephant in the Case File? Costa Rican Court Sets Aside Award' (*Kluwer Arbitration Blog*, 21 May 2020) <http://arbitrationblog.kluwerarbitration.com/2020/05/21/disclosing-the-elephant-in-the-case-file-costa-rican-court-sets-aside-award/> accessed 15 September 2020.

[47] The Court did not outright ignore this fact, but it considered that it was feasible that ICE had failed to notice this information.

[48] Jorge Arturo González, 'Rules for thee, not for me? A commentary on the Supreme Court of Costa Rica judgement setting aside the *ICE v. Chucás* award' [2022] The Arbitration Brief (American University Washington College of Law) (forthcoming).

[49] Jorge Arturo González, 'Rules for thee, not for me? A commentary on the Supreme Court of Costa Rica judgement setting aside the *ICE v. Chucás* award' [2022] The Arbitration Brief (American University Washington College of Law) (forthcoming).

[50] Jorge Arturo González, 'Rules for thee, not for me? A commentary on the Supreme Court of Costa Rica judgement setting aside the *ICE v. Chucás* award' [2021] The Arbitration Brief (American University Washington College of Law) (forthcoming).

Even if the aforementioned legal arguments against the correctness of the judgement were disputed, the concerns about the role of the Supreme Court in this case go beyond its legal reasoning. An additional conclusion to be drawn from this case refers to the independence of the Supreme Court judges in their role as the authority for setting aside domestic awards in Costa Rica. In this sense, judicial independence refers to both the judicial system's independence as an institution from external political influence and the ability of individual judges to make independent decisions in particular cases.[51] This requires that the judiciary is free from direct and indirect pressure from any source.[52] The author submits that the independence of the Supreme Court judges can be compromised when they are confronted with high-profile awards where the non-prevailing party is an SOE. As explained below, this is due to the constitutional system for the appointment of the judiciary in Costa Rica and not due to the judges themselves.

According to the Costa Rican Constitution, the judges of the Supreme Court are appointed for an eight-year term by Congress.[53] Their term is considered to be automatically renewed unless the members of Congress agree otherwise.[54] Therefore, the judges face the possibility that their appointment is revoked every eight years. This process has been criticized for undermining the independence of the Supreme Court judges, as their stability depends on the Congress, which is composed of representatives that could use the leverage to advance their own political agendas.[55] The potential effects of this system have been discussed in other fields.[56] However, the circumstances surrounding the *Chucás* case indicate that the system could also be a concern for foreign investors entering contracts with SOEs in Costa Rica in the context of the judicial annulment of arbitration awards.

[51] Joseph L. Staats and Jonathan T. Hiskey, 'Measuring judicial performance in Latin America' [2005] 4 Latin American Politics and Society, 79.

[52] Basic Principles on the Independence of the Judiciary, United Nations General Assembly resolutions 40/32 of 29 November 1985, and 40/146 of 13 December 1985.

[53] Articles 121(3) and 158, Costa Rican Constitution.

[54] Article 158, Costa Rican Constitution.

[55] Rosaura Chinchilla Calderón, 'Legitimación democrática e independencia judicial en Costa Rica' [2012] 127 Revista de Ciencias Jurídicas, 179–180; Manuel Fernando Jiménez Aguilar, *Estructura y funcionamiento del Poder Judicial* (Investigaciones Jurídicas 1997), 26; Carlos José Gutiérrez, *El funcionamiento del sistema jurídico* (Ediciones Juricentro 1979), 94.

[56] Rosaura Chinchilla Calderón, 'Legitimación democrática e independencia judicial en Costa Rica' [2012] 127 Revista de Ciencias Jurídicas, 179–180; Manuel Fernando Jiménez Aguilar, *Estructura y funcionamiento del Poder Judicial* (Investigaciones Jurídicas 1997), 26; Carlos José Gutiérrez, *El funcionamiento del sistema jurídico* (Ediciones Juricentro 1979), 94.

Out of the five judges who signed the *Chucás* annulment, two were re-elected,[57] and one was appointed for the first time during the 2014-2018 Congress period.[58] During this same period, Congress summoned ICE officers to testify before the Public Expenditure Committee, demanding an explanation for the arbitration result. In this context, the independence of the judges could have been endangered. As the only forum with the ability to stop the award, the Supreme Court represented the final opportunity to save ICE from a significant political defeat. Although the First Chamber of the Supreme Court regularly settles other cases involving SOEs (as it is also one of the two highest judicial authorities in administrative law[59]), there have been few occasions where a case has reached the high-profile that *Chucás* did, even drawing attention from the same politicians that could kick the judges off the bench. Unfortunately, this issue is not entirely hypothetical, as members of Congress publicly attempted to vote another Supreme Court judge off the bench for political reasons in 2012.[60]

Another interesting fact that could be considered in this context can be found on ICE's financial statements for 2019. It appears that ICE was so confident in the result of its request for annulment of the award that it failed to make an accounting provision for any losses derived from the dispute.[61] This was the case even though, according to the Alternative Dispute Resolution Law (which governs domestic arbitration in Costa Rica), the application for annulment does not suspend the effects of an award,[62] and the award in question ordered ICE to pay a large sum in favour of the contractor.

---

[57] Judge Román Solís was re-elected in 2017, and Judge Luis Guillermo Rivas was re-elected in 2015 [Esteban Oviedo, 'Magistrado Román Solís reelecto por ocho años' *La Nación* (San José, 7 April 2018) <https://www.nacion.com/el-pais/politica/magistrado-roman-solis-reelecto-por-ocho-anos/DGQN7EKPLRDOLJ6ZQRISJ3IJPA/story/> accessed 10 October 2020; María José Delgado Loría, 'Luis Guillermo Rivas asume nuevo período en la Sala Primera' *El País* (San José, 28 April 2015) <https://www.elpais.cr/2015/04/28/luis-guillermo-rivas-asume-nuevo-periodo-en-la-sala-primera/> accessed 10 October 2020].

[58] Judge William Molinari was appointed in 2015 [Luis Manuel Madrigal, 'William Molinari Vílchez es electo magistrado de la Sala I' *El Mundo* (San José, 3 August 2015) <https://www.elmundo.cr/costa-rica/william-molinari-vilchez-es-electo-magistrado-de-la-sala-i/> accessed 10 October 2020].

[59] Article 134, Code of Procedure for Administrative Disputes.

[60] Gerardo M. Ruiz, 'Futuro de magistrado Fernando Cruz quedó en manos de la Sala IV' *El Financiero* (San José, 20 November 2012) <https://www.elfinancierocr.com/economia-y-politica/futuro-de-magistrado-fernando-cruz-quedo-en-manos-de-la-sala-iv/543IF56XLZHPTHU623N7FVPFZI/story/> accessed 10 October 2020.

[61] Instituto Costarricense de Electricidad, *Estados Financieros Consolidados* (Finance Division, September 2019) <https://www.grupoice.com/wps/wcm/connect/9c9e0a41-b03f-46a1-a234-dacb98737904/III+Trimestre+2019+en+espa%C3%B1ol.pdf?MOD=AJPERES&CONVERT_TO=url&CACHEID=ROOTWORKSPACE-9c9e0a41-b03f-46a1-a234-dacb98737904-mWPUxfG> accessed 12 October 2020, 93 ("Es criterio de la administración del ICE y de sus asesores legales que debido a los argumentos del recurso de Nulidad interpuesto ante la Sala Primera de la Corte Suprema de Justicia… existe una expectativa positiva de que el caso finalmente se resuelva a favour del ICE, razón por la cual no se consideró necesario registrar provisión alguna, para cubrir pérdidas que se pudiesen derivar de la resolución de ese caso").

[62] Article 66.

Although it could be held that the outcome of the *Chucás* judgement on annulment was correct, the impression created by the members of Congress, the media and the ICE representatives could be that an award rendered against ICE or another high-profile SOE is extremely difficult to enforce due to political turmoil in Costa Rica. The Supreme Court's reasoning in the judgement ordering the award's annulment does not help make the opposite case.

For the sake of clarification, the author is by no means implying that the judges were involved in bribery, corruption or any of the like or even that they displayed actual bias in favour of the Costa Rican SOE. Instead, this is a comment on the constitutional system in Costa Rica and how its design does not insulate the judiciary from political pressure.

A recent development that may further speak of the negative impact of this judicial independence deficit for foreign investors is a new dispute faced by Kölbi, a subsidiary of ICE operating in the telecom market.[63] Although this dispute appears to have arisen from a contractual relationship between Kölbi and V-NET Comunicaciones (a private contractor), the contractor decided to avoid both arbitration and litigation in Costa Rica. Instead, its controlling shareholder, a Venezuelan national, structured the dispute as an international investment arbitration claim administered by ICSID. Although neither V-NET Comunicaciones nor its shareholders have stated that the *Chucás* case was an element influencing the decision to opt for ICSID arbitration, it is possible that this was no coincidence.

These events show that, in some cases, domestic arbitration may not be an entirely satisfactory dispute settlement mechanism for foreign investors. To manage this risk, foreign investors could either take a step forward or take a step back. 'A step forward' refers to taking the dispute to an international forum, such as an international arbitration tribunal. Both commercial and investment arbitration may be considered, depending on the nationality and standing of the investor, as well as the contractually agreed provisions and the available treaties. An international investment suit was the choice of the foreign investor in the ongoing ICE/Kölbi dispute.

In the case of opting for international commercial arbitration with a seat in a third country, the annulment of the award would not be possible in Costa Rica but rather only in the jurisdiction where the arbitration had its seat. In this case, the Costa Rican courts could only potentially intervene in the recognition and enforcement of the award, which would occur under the Convention on the Recognition and Enforcement of Foreign Arbitral Awards ("NY Convention") as the State is a Contracting Party. It could be argued that the Supreme Court could interpret the grounds for refusal of recognition/enforcement of a foreign award liberally, to the detriment of the foreign investor, in the same way, that it arguably misapplied the grounds for annulment in the *Chucás* case. However, the existing evidence shows that this possibility is narrow. There is a single reported decision where a foreign award was recognized in Costa

[63] *José Alejandro Hernández Contreras v. Costa Ric*a [18 August 2020] ICSID ARB(AF)/20/2; Johel Solano, 'Empresa demanda al país por $45 millones respaldada en convenio con Venezuela', *CRHoy.com* (San José, 20 August 2020) <https://www.crhoy.com/nacionales/empresa-demanda-al-pais-por-45-millones-respaldada-en-convenio-con-venezuela/> accessed 20 October 2020.

Rica, and the Supreme Court rejected all the arguments presented by the Costa Rican company attempting to avoid recognition.[64]

An investment arbitration claim would be the way forward if the investor wanted to, above all, insulate the dispute from any influence from the Costa Rican courts. Even if the investor had to enforce the award in Costa Rica, the latter is a Contracting State to the Convention on the Settlement of Investment Disputes Between States and Nationals of Other States ("ICSID Convention"), which essentially does not provide the courts with any grounds for refusing recognition/enforcement of an ICSID award.[65] Additionally, in an investment arbitration claim, the respondent is usually not the SOE but rather the State of Costa Rica,[66] which has a record of voluntary compliance with unfavourable awards. Moreover, under the ICSID Convention, none of the arbitrators may be nationals of the State party to the dispute.[67]

However, on the downside, the investor would have to meet a different and usually much higher threshold to prove that the State incurred international responsibility, compared to proving a simple breach of contract from the SOE. At the same time, investment arbitration is typically more expensive and takes a longer time than commercial arbitration.[68] This factor is also detrimental to the public resources of Costa Rica because investment treaty cases usually involve complex matters of international investment law that require the government to hire foreign law firms, which are typically more expensive. Although Costa Rica has been a respondent in 12 ICSID claims (two of which are ongoing),[69] it has been mostly successful.[70] As an attractive investment destination, Costa Rica ranks second only to Panama in net FDI inflows within Central America.[71]

---

[64] *Del Monte Internacional GmbH v. Inversiones y Procesadora Tropical Sociedad Anónima (INPROTSA)* [2019] First Chamber of the Supreme Court of Costa Rica 04655-2019, 16-000152-0004-AR.

[65] Article 54(1), ICSID Convention ("Each Contracting State shall recognize an award rendered pursuant to this Convention as binding and enforce the pecuniary obligations imposed by that award within its territories as if it were a final judgment of a court in that State").

[66] Article 25(1), ICSID Convention.

[67] Article 52(3).

[68] Matthew Hodgson, 'Investment Treaty Arbitration: cost, duration and size of claims all show steady increase' (*Allen & Overy*, 14 December 2017) <https://www.allenovery.com/en-gb/global/news-and-insights/publications/investment-treaty-arbitration-cost-duration-and-size-of-claims-all-show-steady-increase> accessed 28 October 2020.

[69] ICSID, 'Cases' (*World Bank*) <https://icsid.worldbank.org/cases/case-database> accessed 14 July 2021.

[70] Dyalá Jiménez-Figueres and Patricio Grané Labat, 'Costa Rica' [2018] The Arbitration Review of the Americas 2018 <http://www.djarbitraje.com/pdf/325CostaRica.pdf> accessed 25 October 2020; Dyalá Jiménez-Figueres and Karina Cherro, 'Investment arbitration in Costa Rica' [2012] 29(4) Journal of International Arbitration <http://www.djarbitraje.com/pdf/222JOIA_294_%20Dyala769%20Jime769nezFigueres%20%20Karina%20Cherro.pdf> accessed 25 October 2020.

[71] CEPAL, *Balance Preliminar de las Economías de América Latina y el Caribe* (United Nations, 2019) <https://repositorio.cepal.org/bitstream/handle/11362/45000/125/S1901097_es.pdf> accessed 20 October 2020, 129.

Returning to the author's proposals, 'a step back' refers to exhausting the available amicable dispute settlement mechanisms before ever considering arbitration. In this sense, the investor could first explore negotiation, conciliation and/or mediation. The ICSID Convention itself provides for the option of conciliation,[72] and the main regional Free Trade Agreements ("FTAs")—which contain investment provisions—prioritize consultations and negotiation over arbitration.[73] The 'cooling-off period' found in many investment instruments could be used to pursue such nonconfrontational methods.[74]

Furthermore, using mediation to settle foreign investment disputes is being increasingly discussed in academic literature.[75] One of the reasons for this is that amicable dispute settlement mechanisms facilitate the possibility of reaching a middle ground, where the investor can still receive compensation without compromising the financial resources of the SOE and/or the State. Finally, reaching a settlement reduces the length and uncertainty of the dispute and allows investors to preserve their relationship with the host State.[76]

Admittedly, there are some potential problems undermining the widespread use of amicable dispute settlement methods for these investment disputes. First, on a cultural level, decision-makers within SOEs (as public officials) may fear that agreeing to settle a disagreement through negotiation or conciliation could be perceived as a sign of collusion with the private contractor, even when that is not the case, and when arbitration is not always the most cost-efficient alternative.[77] For example, in a recent arbitration case against the Costa Rican water and sanitation public utility (*Instituto Costarricense de Acueductos y Alcantarillados*), the SOE refused to participate in conciliation hearings and ultimately was ordered to pay 6.7 million US dollars to the contractor by the arbitration tribunal.[78]

---

[72] Chapter III, ICSID Convention.

[73] Article 10.15, DR-CAFTA; Article 11.19 Central America-Mexico FTA.

[74] Siddharth S. Aatreya, 'Cooling-Off Periods' (*Jus Mundi*, 19 May 2020) <https://jusmundi.com/en/document/wiki/en-cooling-off-periods> accessed 3 November 2020.

[75] Catherine Kessedjian, Anne van Aken, Runar Lie, Loukas Mistelis, 'Mediation in Future Investor-State Dispute Settlement' [5 March 2020] Academic Forum on ISDS Concept Paper 2020/16 <https://www.jus.uio.no/pluricourts/english/projects/leginvest/academic-forum/papers/2020/isds-af-mediation-paper-16-march-2020.pdf> accessed 3 November 2020; Kun Fan, 'Mediation of Investor-State Disputes: A Treaty Survey' [6 April 2020, rev. 22 July 2020] Journal of Dispute Resolution (forthcoming) <https://papers.ssrn.com/sol3/papers.cfm?abstract_id=3549661> accessed 3 November 2020.

[76] Queen Mary University of London '2020 QMUL-CCIAG Survey: Investors' Perceptions of ISDS' (May 2020) <http://www.arbitration.qmul.ac.uk/media/arbitration/docs/QM-CCIAG-Survey-ISDS-2020.pdf> accessed 1 November 2020, 7.

[77] Luis Enrique Ames, '¿Conciliar o arbitrar? Análisis del Costo-Beneficio en las entidades públicas' *CIAR Global* (6 October 2020) <https://ciarglobal.com/conciliar-o-arbitrar-analisis-del-costo-beneficio-en-las-entidades-publicas/> accessed 25 October 2020.

[78] Josué Alvarado, 'AyA pierde demanda contra empresa española y tendrá que pagar millonaria multa' *CRHoy.com* (29 July 2020) <https://www.crhoy.com/nacionales/aya-pierde-demanda-contra-empresa-espanola-y-tendra-que-pagar-millonaria-multa/> accessed 25 October 2020.

Second, the potential enforcement of a settlement agreement arising out of conciliation or mediation is not always straightforward. Avoiding arbitration or litigation is likely to reduce the confrontation in a dispute, leading to voluntary compliance in most cases. However, if required, the enforcement of domestic settlement agreements is possible in Costa Rica.[79] The Singapore Mediation Convention[80] aims to enable the cross-border enforcement of settlement agreements resulting from mediation, which means that this method could be relied upon internationally in the future. For the moment, Honduras is the only State in the region to have signed but not ratified this Convention.[81] The author also notes that, unfortunately, the Singapore Mediation Convention contains a reservation allowing the Contracting States to exclude its scope of application from settlement agreements to which the State itself (or its governmental agencies) is a party.[82]

From investors' point of view, treaty-based and contract-based arbitration are the most highly rated dispute resolution mechanisms, according to a 2020 survey on investor-State dispute settlement conducted by the Queen Mary University of London.[83] However, notwithstanding their positive views on arbitration, most respondents to this survey stated that this is rarely their preferred course of action, as they would rather opt for 'amicable solutions that preserve their relationships with states'.[84] These findings should be seen as an opportunity for SOEs and/or States to pursue such nonconfrontational alternatives more frequently.

4 The Rest of Central America

When entering contracts with SOEs in Central America, foreign investors may note that all six countries in the region have ratified the NY Convention and the ICSID Convention. Moreover, all countries except for Panama are parties to the Dominican Republic-Central America FTA with the USA and the Dominican Republic ("DR-CAFTA") and the Mexico-Central America FTA with Mexico. Both of these instruments contain investment provisions and provide for ICSID arbitration as a dispute

[79] Article 9, Alternative Dispute Resolution Law; Article 51, Code of Civil Procedure.

[80] UN Convention on International Settlement Agreements Resulting from Mediation.

[81] Status as at: 03-11-2020, United Nations Convention on International Settlement Agreements Resulting from Mediation [New York, 20 December 2018] <https://treaties.un.org/pages/ViewDetails.aspx?src=TREATY&mtdsg_no=XXII-4&chapter=22&clang=_en> accessed 3 November 2020.

[82] Article 8.

[83] Queen Mary University of London '2020 QMUL-CCIAG Survey: Investors' Perceptions of ISDS' (May 2020) <http://www.arbitration.qmul.ac.uk/media/arbitration/docs/QM-CCIAG-Survey-ISDS-2020.pdf> accessed 1 November 2020, 7.

[84] Queen Mary University of London '2020 QMUL-CCIAG Survey: Investors' Perceptions of ISDS' (May 2020) <http://www.arbitration.qmul.ac.uk/media/arbitration/docs/QM-CCIAG-Survey-ISDS-2020.pdf> accessed 1 November 2020, 7.

settlement mechanism.[85] Similarly, each of these States has signed numerous Bilateral Investment Treaties ("BITs") and FTAs containing investment provisions.[86] However, as seen in Costa Rica, foreign investors may face certain risks when opting for domestic arbitration. This situation is analysed for the rest of the region below.

4.1 El Salvador

In El Salvador, domestic arbitration is not likely to be the most suitable alternative for foreign investors. Under the applicable domestic arbitration statute, an arbitration-in-law award is subject to appeal before the State courts,[87] rendering the desired benefits of neutrality and finality seemingly worthless.[88] At the same time, the Salvadorian courts are, as of recently, burdened by allegations of weakened judicial independence.[89] As seen above, this can also affect arbitration at various stages (e.g. annulment or enforcement of the award).

In this context, two factors provide assurances for foreign investors in El Salvador. First, parties can waive the right to appeal an award in advance, according to the Constitutional Court.[90] Second, El Salvador is not only a Contracting State of the

85 Article 10.16, CAFTA-DR; Article 11.20, Mexico-Central America FTA.

86 UNCTAD, 'International Investment Agreements Navigator: Honduras' (*United Nations*) <https://investmentpolicy.unctad.org/international-investment-agreements/countries/92/honduras> accessed 20 October 2020; UNCTAD, 'International Investment Agreements Navigator: Costa Rica' (*United Nations*) <https://investmentpolicy.unctad.org/international-investment-agreements/countries/49/costa-rica> accessed 20 October 2020; UNCTAD, 'International Investment Agreements Navigator: Guatemala' (*United Nations*) <https://investmentpolicy.unctad.org/international-investment-agreements/countries/86/guatemala> accessed 20 October 2020; UNCTAD, 'International Investment Agreements Navigator: El Salvador' (*United Nations*) <https://investmentpolicy.unctad.org/international-investment-agreements/countries/63/el-salvador> accessed 20 October 2020; UNCTAD, 'International Investment Agreements Navigator: Panama' (*United Nations*) <https://investmentpolicy.unctad.org/international-investment-agreements/countries/162/panama> accessed 20 October 2020; UNCTAD, 'International Investment Agreements Navigator: Nicaragua' (*United Nations*) <https://investmentpolicy.unctad.org/international-investment-agreements/countries/151/nicaragua> accessed 25 October 2020.

87 Article 66-A, Mediation, Conciliation and Arbitration Law.

88 Queen Mary University of London '2020 QMUL-CCIAG Survey: Investors' Perceptions of ISDS' (May 2020) <http://www.arbitration.qmul.ac.uk/media/arbitration/docs/QM-CCIAG-Survey-ISDS-2020.pdf> accessed 1 November 2020, 8 ("Other strengths of arbitration cited include the speed and efficiency of the process, and the neutrality and impartiality of the arbitrators").

89 Newsroom Infobae, 'Jueces salvadorenos denuncian violaciones a la independencia judicial por Bukele' *Infobae* (San Salvador, 22 September 2020) <https://www.infobae.com/america/agencias/2020/09/23/jueces-salvadorenos-denuncian-violaciones-a-la-independencia-judicial-por-bukele/> accessed 13 October 2020; 'Informe sobre la situación de la independencia judicial en El Salvador' Due Process and Law Foundation.

90 *Guillermo Alexander Parada Gámez, claimant* [30 November 2011] Salvadorian Constitutional Chamber, Supreme Court of Justice 11-2020.

ICSID Convention, but it also provides advance consent to ICSID arbitration under its domestic Investment Law, in the following terms:

> In case of disputes arising between foreign investors and the State, regarding their investments made in El Salvador, the investors may submit the controversy to: (a) The International Centre for Settlement of Investment Disputes (ICSID), in order to settle the dispute by conciliation and arbitration, in accordance with the Convention on the Settlement of Investment Disputes between States and Nationals of Other States (the ICSID Convention)…[91]

Therefore, El Salvador provides foreign investors of any nationality with access to ICSID arbitration pursuant to the terms of the Investment Law. However, El Salvador has only been a respondent in four ICSID claims, far less than countries such as Spain, Panama, Peru, Colombia, Argentina and Mexico.[92] Furthermore, El Salvador has never been found to be liable by an ICSID tribunal.[93]

The threat of ICSID arbitration may act as an incentive for Salvadorian authorities to uphold substantive investment standards and/or settle disputes before they escalate. Therefore, foreign investors could better reach a satisfactory solution if they try their luck with the author's proposal of 'taking a step back' before considering arbitration. For example, an investment dispute between Italian company Enel Green Power and a Salvadorian hydropower SOE over a partnership and shareholders' agreement was successfully conciliated after an ICSID claim had already been filed.[94]

4.2 Honduras

The situation in neighbouring Honduras is similar in that the State provides advance consent to ICSID arbitration for foreign investors through its Law for the Promotion and Protection of Investment.[95] However, during an ICSID arbitration proceeding, the State unsuccessfully argued that its advance consent was subject to the investor's compulsory registration as a foreign investor.[96] Simultaneously, under this statute, Honduras prioritizes negotiation, mediation and conciliation as means for settling investment disputes, which should leave arbitration as a last resource.[97] An example of the above can be illustrated through the case of a road improvement agreement entered between the government of Honduras and Italian company Astaldi in 2005.[98] The parties first submitted a disagreement arising from the contract to a 'conciliator'.

---

[91] Article 15.

[92] ICSID, 'Cases' (*World Bank*) <https://icsid.worldbank.org/cases/case-database> accessed 14 July 2021.

[93] ICSID, 'Cases' (*World Bank*) <https://icsid.worldbank.org/cases/case-database> accessed 14 July 2021.

[94] *Enel Green Power S.p.A. v. El Salvador* [2014] ICSID ARB/13/18.

[95] Article 25.

[96] *Elsamex S.A. v. República de Honduras* [16 November 2012] ICSID ARB/09/4.

[97] Article 25.

[98] *Astaldi S.p.A. v. República de Honduras* [17 September 2010] ICSID ARB/07/32.

Unsatisfied with the conciliator's recommendations, Astaldi filed an ICSID claim, which was resolved in its favour. Honduras requested the annulment of the award but eventually agreed to withdraw its request and settle the matter directly with Astaldi through negotiation.[99]

In Honduras, domestic arbitration legislation does not allow for appeal of the arbitration award,[100] unlike in El Salvador. Furthermore, foreign investment contracts may fall within the scope of the Law for the Promotion of Public-Private Partnerships, which states that an arbitration agreement must be included in any such partnerships.[101] Nonetheless, dispute settlement within Honduras may be disincentivized by several issues affecting the judicial system, such as the excessive duration of court proceedings and difficulties in preserving judicial independence.[102] A more recent problem is that during the ongoing COVID-19 crisis, the Honduran courts could not transition online and reportedly did not hold virtual hearings.[103] Admittedly, these are the kind of problems that usually justify bypassing the State courts by recurring to arbitration. However, as seen with the case of Costa Rica, they may very well affect arbitration itself. Additionally, in the absence of a provision empowering arbitration tribunals in Honduras to order interim relief themselves, parties may frequently have to go to court in connection with arbitration proceedings.[104]

Notwithstanding the latter issues and the advance consent provided for investment arbitration, Honduras has only been a respondent in four ICSID cases, the same amount as El Salvador.[105]

---

[99] *Astaldi S.p.A. v. República de Honduras* [15 June 2011] ICSID ARB/07/32.

[100] Article 73, Law on Arbitration and Conciliation; José María Díaz Castellanos, 'Arbitraje en Honduras' in Juan Enrique Vargas Viancos and Francisco Javier Gorjón Gómez (coords.), *Arbitraje y Mediación en las Américas* (Centro de Estudios de Justicia de las Américas) <biblioteca.cejamericas.org/bitstream/handle/2015/738/arbitrajeymediacionenlasamericas.pdf> accessed 3 November 2020, 300.

[101] Article 8(13).

[102] Asociación de Jueces por la Democracia, *Afectaciones a la independencia judicial en Honduras en el marco de la depuración judicial y la práctica de las pruebas de confianza* (AJD 2014) <https://www.icj.org/wp-content/uploads/2015/02/Honduras-AJD-report.pdf> accessed 12 October 2020.

[103] Ana Karen de la Torre, 'El camino hacia el Estado digital en Latinoamérica' *LexLatin* (27 May 2020) <https://lexlatin.com/entrevistas/el-camino-hacia-el-estado-digital-en-latinoamerica> accessed 12 October 2020; Fernando Maldonado, 'Crisis sanitaria tiene paralizados los juicios en el Poder Judicial' *El Heraldo* (Tegucigalpa, 15 August 2020) <https://www.elheraldo.hn/pais/1401379-466/crisis-sanitaria-tiene-paralizados-los-juicios-en-el-poder-judicial> accessed 12 October 2020.

[104] Article 36, Law on Arbitration and Conciliation; Marcela Rodríguez Mejía, *Medidas cautelares en el proceso arbitral* (Bogotá: Universidad externado de Colombia, 2013) <https://books.openedition.org/uec/287?lang=es#ftn2> accessed 3 November 2020, para. 6.

[105] ICSID, 'Cases' (*World Bank*) <https://icsid.worldbank.org/cases/case-database> accessed 14 July 2021.

4.3 Guatemala

Guatemala's Foreign Investment Law is more restrictive regarding investment arbitration and does not provide advance consent to ICSID on its own. Instead, it states that it is *possible* to submit investment disputes to international arbitration and other alternative dispute settlement mechanisms, but only according to the international treaties ratified by Guatemala.[106] Therefore, it cannot be interpreted as an offer to arbitrate, breaking with the Salvadorian and Honduran approaches. The foreign investors interested in pursuing this avenue must find the basis of consent in one of the many BITs[107] or FTAs[108] entered by this State.

A precedent where such an option was not explored is the contract for constructing the 'Northern Road', connecting Guatemala and Mexico. The contractor, Israeli company Solel Boneh FTN reportedly abandoned the project after part of its machinery, was burned down by locals.[109] The company did not file an ICSID claim, which it could have possibly been entitled to, according to the Israel-Guatemala BIT.[110] Despite the large number of BITs signed by Guatemala, it has only been a respondent in five ICSID proceedings[111] and two further investment claims administered by the PCA.[112] It was found to be liable in two of those cases.[113]

On the other hand, domestic arbitration in Guatemala has its own downsides. First, according to the Guatemalan Constitutional Court, in some instances, an award is susceptible to the action of *amparo* (which is a constitutional mechanism used across Latin American jurisdictions to protect human rights against a public authority or private acts).[114] Second, under the Arbitration Law, the non-prevailing party can in theory request a State court to not only set aside but also *modify* the content of the

---

106 Article 11.

107 *See* France-Guatemala BIT (1998); Argentina-Guatemala BIT (1998); Italy-Guatemala BIT (2003).

108 Article 10.16, CAFTA-DR; Article 11.20, Mexico-Central America FTA.

109 Sergio Morales, 'Conflictos frenan la construcción de la Franja Transversal del Norte' *Prensa Libre* (Guatemala, 9 August 2018) <https://www.prensalibre.com/guatemala/comunitario/conflictos-frenan-construccion-de-la-franja-transversal-del-norte/> accessed 10 October 2020.

110 Article 8.2.

111 ICSID, 'Cases' (*World Bank*) <https://icsid.worldbank.org/cases/case-database> accessed 14 July 2021.

112 *IC Power Asia Development Ltd. (Israel) v. Republic of Guatemala* [2019] PCA 2019-43; *Iberdrola Energía, S.A. (Spain) v. The Republic of Guatemala* [2017] PCA 2017-41.

113 *Teco Guatemala Holdings v. Republic of Guatemala* [19 December 2013] ICSID ARB/10/17; *Railroad Development Corporation v. Republic of Guatemala* [29 June 2012] ICSID ARB/07/23.

114 *Chevron Inc. v. Transportes Reyes* [5 July 2012] Guatemalan Constitutional Court 1076-2012; Iosif Alexander Sosa, 'Arbitration in Guatemala: The Admissibility of the Amparo Action Regarding Judicial Assistance on Jurisdictional Matters' (*Kluwer Arbitration Blog*, 12 April 2019) <http://arbitrationblog.kluwerarbitration.com/2019/04/12/arbitration-in-guatemala-the-admissibility-of-the-amparo-action-regarding-judicial-assistance-on-jurisdictional-matters/> accessed 20 October 2020; María José Asturias Santamarina, 'La procedencia del Amparo dentro de un Proceso Arbitral' (Bachelor's Degree thesis, Universidad Francisco Marroquín 2017) <http://www.tesis.ufm.edu/pdf/527646.pdf> , 93.

arbitration award through the mechanism of 'review' (*revisión*),[115] which undermines the principles of finality and neutrality that supposedly characterize arbitration.[116]

Under such circumstances, a foreign company might find itself in a position where a domestic award rendered against a Guatemalan SOE is ultimately modified by a Guatemalan court. The judicial system in Guatemala has been described, as of October 2020, as facing a crisis, starting with the fact that judges of the Supreme Court and the appeal courts have overstayed their constitutionally mandated terms on the bench.[117] Against this background, arbitration in Guatemala is possibly not the most convincing choice for foreign investors entering contracts with local SOEs.

In the case of Guatemala, it is currently unclear whether relying on amicable dispute settlement mechanisms is feasible, as shown by the recent *Grupo Energía Bogotá* dispute.[118] In 2010, local energy transport company TRECSA[119] (a local company controlled by Colombian Grupo Energía Bogotá) entered an agreement with the government to build energy transmission lines. During the fulfilment of the contract, TRECSA reported that certain measures taken by Guatemala (e.g. its unwillingness to recognize force majeure events as such) negatively affected the viability of its business. On 11 October 2019, TRECSA and Grupo Energía Bogota sent a notice letter requesting the government to enter a period of consultations and negotiations, according to the FTA in force between Colombia and Guatemala.[120] Although TRECSA publicly manifested its intent to continue its long-term operation in the country and honour its commitment to the government and the Guatemalan people during 2020, both TRECSA and Grupo Energía Bogota filed an ICSID claim against the State of Guatemala on 3 November 2020.[121]

---

[115] Article 43(1) Arbitration Law.

[116] 'Guatemala, ¿una sede efectiva para el arbitraje comercial internacional?, por Enrique Martínez Guzmán' CIAR Global (19 July 2018) <https://ciarglobal.com/guatemala-una-sede-efectiva-para-el-arbitraje-comercial-internacional-por-enrique-martinez-guzman/2/> accessed 1 November 2020; *Asesoría Diseño y Construcción v. Sala Segunda de la Corte de Apelaciones del ramo Civil y Mercantil.* [14 May 2015] Guatemalan Constitutional Court 252-2015; Queen Mary University of London '2020 QMUL-CCIAG Survey: Investors' Perceptions of ISDS' (May 2020) <http://www.arbitration.qmul.ac.uk/media/arbitration/docs/QM-CCIAG-Survey-ISDS-2020.pdf> accessed 1 November 2020, 8 ("Other strengths of arbitration cited include the speed and efficiency of the process, and the neutrality and impartiality of the arbitrators").

[117] José Domingo Paredes, 'Crisis en el poder judicial' *República* (1 October 2020) <https://republica.gt/2020/10/01/crisis-en-el-poder-judicial/> accessed 20 October 2020; Álvaro Montenegro, 'La crisis del Estado de derecho en Guatemala' *Univision Noticias* (Guatemala, 13 October 2020) <https://www.univision.com/noticias/opinion/la-crisis-del-estado-de-derecho-en-guatemala> accessed 20 October 2020.

[118] Grupo Energía Bogotá and TRECSA v. Republic of Guatemala [3 November 2020] ICSID ARB/20/48).

[119] Transportadora de Energía de Centroamérica, S.A.

[120] FTA between Colombia, Guatemala, El Salvador and Honduras.

[121] *Grupo Energía Bogotá and TRECSA v. Republic of Guatemala* [3 November 2020] ICSID ARB/20/48); However, the proceeding is currently suspended pursuant to the parties' agreement.

4.4 Nicaragua

Nicaragua is a unique country for analysis because, unfortunately, it has seen its democratic status ruptured by the government of President Daniel Ortega (in office since 2007). Even though Ortega is currently known for his authoritarianism[122] and the repression with which he tackled nationwide protests in 2018,[123] his economic policy was once more free-market oriented, notwithstanding his socialist narrative.[124] During the early years of his tenure, Nicaragua entered many FTAs and BITs, opening the country to foreign investment and private business.[125] His stance on the ICSID Convention was similarly inconsistent. In 2008, the government considered denouncing the Convention, following the steps of Bolivia.[126] However, this never materialized.

As could be expected, the massive protests in 2018 and the international downfall of the Ortega regime have negatively impacted economic growth and foreign investment.[127] FDI inflows in 2018 more than halved with regard to the year before.[128] Furthermore, Ortega is reportedly transforming his family-owned businesses to SOEs

[122] Yurany Arciniegas Salamanca, 'EE.UU. impone nuevas sanciones contra Gobierno de Nicaragua' *France24* (10 October 2020) <https://www.france24.com/es/20201009-eeuu-sanciones-nicaragua-guido-oquist-gobierno-daniel-ortega> accessed 1 November 2020; 'Downward spiral: Nicaragua's worsening crisis' *BBC News* (16 July 2018) <https://www.bbc.com/news/world-latin-america-44398673> accessed 1 November 2020.

[123] Toby Stirling Hill, 'Nicaragua: one year after protests erupt, Ortega clings to power' *The Guardian* (16 April 2019) <https://www.theguardian.com/world/2019/apr/16/nicaragua-protest-ortega-government-one-year> accessed 1 November 2020; 'Nicaragua unrest: what you should know' *Aljazeera* (17 July 2018) <https://www.aljazeera.com/news/2018/7/17/nicaragua-unrest-what-you-should-know> accessed 1 November 2020.

[124] "Ortega seduce en Nicaragua con su socialismo capitalista" *La Nación* (San José, 26 September 2011) <https://www.nacion.com/el-mundo/ortega-seduce-en-nicaragua-con-su-socialismo-capitalista/QJAHCJ2TAFEU7JMBFRTEX2TDPE/story/> accessed 15 October 2020.

[125] UNCTAD, 'International Investment Agreements Navigator: Nicaragua' (United Nations). <https://investmentpolicy.unctad.org/international-investment-agreements/countries/151/nicaragua> accessed 25 October 2020.

[126] "Posible salida de Nicaragua del Ciadi" *La Prensa* (Nicaragua, 14 April 2008) <https://www.laprensa.com.ni/2008/04/14/economia/1326742-posible-salida-de-nicaragua-de-ciadi>

[127] Jude Webber, 'Nicaragua's $13bn economy sinks as uprising persists' *Financial Times* (1 August 2018) <https://www.ft.com/content/f72e3086-947c-11e8-b67b-b8205561c3fe> accessed 25 October 2020.

[128] CEPAL, *Balance Preliminar de las Economías de América Latina y el Caribe* (United Nations, 2019) <https://repositorio.cepal.org/bitstream/handle/11362/45000/125/S1901097_es.pdf> accessed 20 October 2020, 129.

in order to avoid the effects of international sanctions[129] on his personal assets.[130] Nonetheless, some new foreign investment contracts with SOEs have been concluded in recent years, notably including a partnership between Nicaraguan SOE Petronic, Norwegian company Equinor and London-listed company Cairn Energy for an oil exploration concession along the Nicaraguan Pacific.[131]

As previously stated, the electrical SOE sector is crucial for Nicaragua. Two electrical SOEs (*Empresa Nicaragüense de Electricidad* and *Empresa Nacional de Transmisión Eléctrica*) reportedly make up for 30% of total SOE revenue in Nicaragua.[132] The latter entered a partnership agreement with Costa Rican SOE ICE to venture into the telecom market in Nicaragua.[133] Furthermore, electrical distribution SOE giants Disnorte and Dissur are vital players. According to rumours, these two sister companies are wholly owned by the Nicaraguan government after Spanish consortium TSK Melfosur divested its minority stake in 2020.[134] At the same time, the two companies are reportedly financed by Albanisa, a company under full ownership of Nicaraguan SOE Petronic, and Venezuelan SOE PDV Caribe.[135]

In any case, both Disnorte and Dissur have entered distribution, energy-purchase and energy-supply agreements with other SOEs from the electrical sector and private companies. As recently as September 2020, Disnorte and Dissur entered an energy-purchase agreement with Nasdaq-listed company New Fortress Energy, whereby the latter is building a natural gas plant in Nicaragua.[136] In some of these agreements,

---

[129] Maya Lester QC and Michael O'Kane, 'Sanctions Profile: Nicaragua' (*EU Sanctions*) <https://www.europeansanctions.com/region/nicaragua-2/> accessed 30 October 2020; 'Nicaragua-related Sanctions' (*U.S. Department of the Treasury*) <https://perma.cc/343M-89QY> accessed 30 October 2020.

[130] 'Dictadura Ortega Murillo manda a crear cuatro empresas para controlar hidrocarburos en Nicaragua' *100% Noticias* (Managua, 11 February 2020) <https://100noticias.com.ni/nacionales/98589-dictadura-ortega-murillo-manda-a-crear-cuatro-empr/> accessed 30 October 2020.

[131] Equinor, 'In May 2015, Equinor was awarded four licences offshore the Nicaraguan Pacific, together with partner Petronic' <https://www.equinor.com/en/where-we-are/nicaragua.html> accessed 12 October 2020.

[132] Aldo Musacchio and Emilio I. Pineda Ayerbe (eds), *Fixing State-Owned Enterprises: New Policy Solutions to Old Problems* (IDB 2019), 10.

[133] Mabel Calero, 'Te-Comunica, la nueva empresa de telecomunicaciones con beneficios estatales' *La Prensa* (20 July 2017) <https://www.laprensa.com.ni/2017/07/20/nacionales/2266168-te-comunica-la-nueva-empresa-de-telecomunicaciones-con-beneficios-estatales> accessed 25 October 2020.

[134] Juan Carlos Bow, 'Spanish Consortium TSK-Melfosur withdraws from Disnorte-Dissur' *Confidencial* (12 February 2020) <https://confidencial.com.ni/spanish-consortium-tsk-melfosur-withdraws-from-disnorte-dissur-nicaragua/> accessed 24 October 2020.

[135] "Constituida empresa mixta Venezuela-Nicaragua" *PDVSA* (Caracas, 17 July 2007) <http://www.pdvsa.com/index.php?option=com_content&view=article&id=2220:4158&catid=10&Itemid=589&lang=es> accessed 24 October 2020;

[136] "Nicaragua la nueva estrella naciente del gas natural con inversión New Fortress Energy" *Energia Limpia XXI* (19 September 2020) <https://energialimpiaparatodos.com/2020/09/19/nicaragua-la-nueva-estrella-naciente-del-gas-natural-con-inversion-new-fortress-energy/> ; NewFortress Energy, 'Operaciones' <https://www.newfortressenergy.com/es/operaciones> accessed 27 October 2020.

the dispute settlement forum of choice is court litigation,[137] whereas others refer to ad hoc or institutional arbitration in Nicaragua,[138] and others refer to ICC arbitration in the third country, such as Mexico.[139]

Litigation or arbitration in Nicaragua are most likely unsuitable alternatives for foreign investors. The influence of the Ortega regime in the judicial branch of government is likely to discourage any reliance on litigation.[140] As this chapter has repeatedly stressed, this situation can also affect arbitration, as the latter frequently requires the cooperation of the State courts. In the case of Nicaragua, reliance on the court system during arbitration may be significant, as the Law on Arbitration and Mediation states that the arbitral tribunal's decision on its own jurisdiction, when settled as a preliminary matter, is subject to a judicial appeal.[141] A similar appeal before the State courts is available in those instances where the challenge made against one of the arbitrators is rejected by the arbitral tribunal.[142] However, one advantage of Nicaragua's law, when compared to others in the region, is that it provides for the arbitral tribunal's express powers to order interim relief.[143]

---

[137] Public Deed [Notary Public Enrique Villagra] between Instituto Nacional de Electricidad and Distribuidora de Electricidad del Norte [12 January 2002], *Escritura 14: Contrato de Concesión de Distribución* <https://www.disnorte-dissur.com.ni/images/quienes-somos/info-acceso-publico/Concesion-DISNORTE.pdf> accessed 25 October 2020; Public Deed [Notary Public Enrique Villagra] between Instituto Nacional de Electricidad and Distribuidora de Electricidad del Sur [27 June 2000], *Escritura 16: Contrato de Concesión de Distribución* <https://www.disnorte-dissur.com.ni/images/quienes-somos/info-acceso-publico/Concesion-DISSUR.pdf> accessed 25 October 2020.

[138] 'Energy Sales Contract between El Wawule and DISNORTE' (*INE*, 20 September 2008) <https://www.ine.gob.ni/DGE/contratos/wawule/Contrato_Wawule_Disnorte.pdf> accessed 25 October 2020; 'Contrato de Generación entre GEOSA y DISNORTE' (*INE*, 7 January 2008) <https://www.ine.gob.ni/DGE/contratos/GEOSA/CONTRATO_GEOSA-DN.pdf> accessed 25 October 2020.

[139] Empresa Nicaragüense de Electricidad, *Energy Sales Contract between ENEL and CENSA* PPA-05-99 (July 1999) <https://www.ine.gob.ni/DGE/contratos/CENSA/CONTRATO_ENEL-CENSA.pdf> accessed 25 October 2020; Empresa Nicaragüense de Electricidad, *Energy Sales Contract between DISNORTE-DISSUR and CENSA* PPA-05-99 Addendum 2 <https://www.ine.gob.ni/DGE/contratos/CENSA/Adenda2_Censa_DN-DS.pdf> (ENEL assigned the contract to DISNORTE-DISSUR); Empresa Nicaragüense de Electricidad, *Energy Sales Contract between ENEL and Coastal Power* PPA-01-97 (December 1997) <https://www.ine.gob.ni/DGE/contratos/tipitapa_power_company/contrato_enel_coastal_power.pdf> accessed 25 October 2020 (this contract provides for ICAC arbitration with hearings to be held in Nicaragua, but the award to be issued in a third country); Empresa Nicaragüense de Electricidad, Energy Sales Contract between Tipitapa and DISNORTE & DISSUR PPA-01-97 Addendum 5 <https://www.ine.gob.ni/DGE/contratos/tipitapa_power_company/adenda_5_TPC-Disnorte-Dissur.pdf> accessed 25 October 2020.

[140] 'La justicia amañada de Ortega en Nicaragua' *El País* (media profiles) <https://elpais.com/especiales/2019/nicaragua-manipulacion-judicial/> accessed 25 October 2020; 'Senadores EE.UU. demandan sanciones para magistrados de la CSJ y la Fiscalía' *Confidencial* (28 May 2020) <https://confidencial.com.ni/senadores-ee-uu-demandan-sanciones-para-magistrados-de-la-corte-suprema-de-justicia/> accessed 25 October 2020.

[141] Article 42.

[142] Article 35.

[143] Article 43.

In this context, international arbitration may be a better choice for a foreign investor entering an agreement with an SOE in Nicaragua. Not many international arbitration awards involving Nicaraguan SOEs are known, whereas Nicaragua has only faced three ICSID claims, one of which it successfully settled[144] and two of which are ongoing.[145] The ongoing claim concerns the alleged expropriation of an oil exploration concession along the Nicaraguan Pacific formerly granted to local company Oklahoma Nicaragua (although it seems from the ICSID file that US investors owned the company).[146] A seemingly similar concession has now been granted to Equinor and Cairn Energy, as mentioned above.

Therefore, the author insists once more on the usefulness of amicable dispute settlement mechanisms, some of which may be more technical than legal. Many of the contracts referred to the above provisions, as a first option, for mechanisms such as expert determination,[147] consultations,[148] and even an 'operative committee',[149] which should leave arbitration or litigation as *ultima ratio.* Managing risks arising out of foreign investment agreements with Nicaraguan SOEs is currently difficult, given the political circumstances. In addition to negotiating adequate dispute settlement

[144] *Shell Brands International AG and Shell Nicaragua S.A. v. Republic of Nicaragua* [11 August 2006] ICSID ARB/06/14.

[145] *The Lopez-Goyne Family Trust and others v. Republic of Nicaragua* [19 December 2017] ICSID ARB/17/44; 'Tribunal de arbitraje Lopez-Goyne y otros-Nicaragua en CIADI' *CIAR Global* (28 June 2019).

<https://ciarglobal.com/tribunal-de-arbitraje-lopez-goyne-y-otros-nicaragua-en-ciadi/> ; UNCTAD, 'The Lopez-Goyne Family Trust and others v. Nicaragua' (*Investment Dispute Settlement Navigator*) <https://investmentpolicy.unctad.org/investment-dispute-settlement/cases/857/the-lopez-goyne-family-trust-and-others-v-nicaragua> accessed 28 October 2020; ICSID, 'Cases' (*World Bank*) <https://icsid.worldbank.org/cases/case-database> accessed 14 July 2021.

[146] "Nicaragua autoriza la exploración petrolera a británicos y noruegos" *El Mundo* (Managua, 4 September 2014) <https://www.elmundo.es/internacional/2014/09/04/5408a83c268e3ecb388b456c.html> accessed 20 October 2020.

[147] ENEL-Coastal Power; 'Contrato de Generación entre GEOSA y DISNORTE' (*INE*, 7 January 2008) <https://www.ine.gob.ni/DGE/contratos/GEOSA/CONTRATO_GEOSA-DN.pdf> accessed 25 October 2020.

[148] 'Contrato de Generación entre GEOSA y DISNORTE' (*INE*, 7 January 2008) <https://www.ine.gob.ni/DGE/contratos/GEOSA/CONTRATO_GEOSA-DN.pdf> accessed 25 October 2020; Empresa Nicaragüense de Electricidad, *Energy Sales Contract between ENEL and CENSA* PPA-05-99 (July 1999) <https://www.ine.gob.ni/DGE/contratos/CENSA/CONTRATO_ENEL-CENSA.pdf> accessed 25 October 2020; Empresa Nicaragüense de Electricidad, *Energy Sales Contract between DISNORTE-DISSUR and CENSA* PPA-05-99 Addendum 2 <https://www.ine.gob.ni/DGE/contratos/CENSA/Adenda2_Censa_DN-DS.pdf> (ENEL assigned the contract to DISNORTE-DISSUR).

[149] Empresa Nicaragüense de Electricidad, *Energy Sales Contract between ENEL and Coastal Power* PPA-01-97 (December 1997) <https://www.ine.gob.ni/DGE/contratos/tipitapa_power_company/contrato_enel_coastal_power.pdf> accessed 25 October 2020; 'Contrato de Generación entre GEOSA y DISNORTE' (*INE*, 7 January 2008) <https://www.ine.gob.ni/DGE/contratos/GEOSA/CONTRATO_GEOSA-DN.pdf> accessed 25 October 2020.

clauses, the author suggests that foreign investors may consider acquiring political risk insurance for their ventures in Nicaragua, to the extent that it is available.[150]

4.5 Panama

The importance of the Panama Canal within the Panamanian SOEs is difficult to overstate, with 90% of the revenue from this sector reportedly stemming from the Panama Canal Authority.[151] Panama leads net FDI inflows in the region, roughly doubling second-ranked Costa Rica as of recent years.[152] As a host State for foreign investment, Panama has faced several investment claims, including 13 ICSID proceedings (more than half of which are pending)[153] and an ongoing dispute administered by the PCA.[154] Some of these investment claims relate to contracts entered between foreign investors and SOEs,[155] including at least one arising out of the project to expand the Canal.[156]

Except for *Jean-Marc Parienti v. Autoridad de Transito y Transporte Terrestre*, which was settled substantively based on the Panama-France BIT but decided in Panama under the CESCON[157] dispute settlement rules, most arbitration cases arising out of foreign investment agreements in Panama have been referred to international tribunals.[158] The contracts for the expansion of the Panama Canal provided for ICC

[150] ‘Political Risk’ (*AIG*) <https://www.aig.com/business/insurance/political-risk> accessed 30 October 2020; Kausar Hamdani, Elise Liebers, and George Zanjani, ‘An Overview of Political Risk Insurance’ (Federal Reserve Bank of New York, May 2005) <https://www.bis.org/publ/cgfs22fedny3.pdf> accessed 30 October 2020.

[151] Aldo Musacchio and Emilio I. Pineda Ayerbe (eds), *Fixing State-Owned Enterprises: New Policy Solutions to Old Problems* (IDB 2019), 10.

[152] CEPAL, *Balance Preliminar de las Economías de América Latina y el Caribe* (United Nations, 2019) <https://repositorio.cepal.org/bitstream/handle/11362/45000/125/S1901097_es.pdf> accessed 20 October 2020, 129.

[153] ICSID, ‘Cases’ (*World Bank*) <https://icsid.worldbank.org/cases/case-database> accessed 14 July 2021.

[154] *Leopoldo Castillo Bozo v. Republic of Panama* [2019] PCA 2019-40.

[155] *Omega Engineering LLC and Oscar Rivera v. Republic of Panama* [20 November 2016] ICSID ARB/16/42; *Laurent Jean-Marc Parienti v. Autoridad de Tránsito y Transporte Terrestre* [27 January 2005] Centro de Solución de Conflictos de Panamá; *Transglobal Green Energy and other v. Republic of Panama* [2 June 2016] ICSID ARB/13/28.

[156] *Webuild S.p.A. v. Republic of Panama* [1 April 2020] ICSID ARB/20/10; Cosmo Sanderson, ‘Panama hit with second treaty claim over canal project’ (*Latin Lawyer*, 7 April 2020) <https://latinlawyer.com/article/1225157/panama-hit-with-second-treaty-claim-over-canal-project> accessed 24 October 2020.

[157] *Centro de Soluciones de Conflictos.*

[158] *IBT Group LLC and other v. Republic of Panama* [26 August 2020] ICSID ARB/20/31; https://www.prensa.com/impresa/economia/IBT-Group-Camara-Comercio-Internacional_0_4033096724.html; *Webuild S.p.A. v. Republic of Panama* [1 April 2020] ICSID ARB/20/10; *Omega Engineering LLC and Oscar Rivera v. Republic of Panama* [20 November 2016] ICSID

arbitration in Miami.[159] At least five *commercial* arbitration proceedings were initiated based on this contract, with one still ongoing.[160] As mentioned above, this project also resulted in at least one *investment* arbitration claim.[161]

The government's perspective on international arbitration may be summarized by the following statement from the Ministry of Health in 2014: 'Arbitration is not favourable for the State. Not only because of the risk to lose the case but also because these proceedings can lead to a negative impression of Panama internationally'.[162] If this is any indication of the government's current views, the window for pursuing amicable settlement mechanisms may be open.

In line with the above, another element to highlight from the contract for the expansion of the Canal is the use of dispute adjudication boards during the project. Dispute adjudication boards are expert panels set up to help parties avoid or overcome any disagreements that arise during the implementation of the contract, and they are particularly used in the construction sector.[163] Under some model contracts, the panel members are appointed ad hoc for each disagreement between the parties.[164] However, in the case of the contract in question, the parties agreed to appoint permanent members to ensure they had a more active and present role.[165] In the case of this contract, the dispute board allowed the parties to continue the works while the dispute was being settled expeditiously and efficiently.[166] This was following article 20.4 of the Contract, which stated that: 'at all times unless the Contract has already been abandoned, repudiated or the Contract has been terminated or the Contractor's right to complete the Contract has been terminated, the Contractor shall continue

ARB/16/42; *Transglobal Green Energy and other v. Republic of Panama* [2 June 2016] ICSID ARB/13/28.

159 Article 20.6 of the Contract.

160 'Issued an arbitration award (basalt) as part of the extensive litigation related to the Panama Canal. Accepted some of the Claims of the GUPC constructors consortium' (*WeBuild*, 26 September 2020) <https://www.webuildgroup.com/en/media/press-releases/issued-an-arbitration-award-basalt-as-part-of-the-extensive-litigation-related-to-the-panama-canal-accepted-some-of-the-claims-of-the-gupc-constructors-consortium> accessed 30 October 2020; Augusto Garcia Sanjur, 'The Panama Canal Expansion: Adaptation of Contracts' (2019) 11(1) Arbitration Law Review <https://elibrary.law.psu.edu/cgi/viewcontent.cgi?article=1254&context=arbitrationlawreview> accessed 10 September 2020, 104.

161 *Webuild S.p.A. v. Republic of Panama* [1 April 2020] ICSID ARB/20/10.

162 Author's own translation from 'IBT Group suspende arbitraje ante la Cámara de Comercio Internacional' *Prensa.com* (14 October 2014) <https://www.prensa.com/impresa/economia/IBT-Group-Camara-Comercio-Internacional_0_4033096724.html> accessed 4 November 2020.

163 'Dispute Boards' (*ICC*) <https://iccwbo.org/dispute-resolution-services/dispute-boards/> accessed 20 October 2020.

164 Yellow Book.

165 Augusto Garcia Sanjur, 'The Panama Canal Expansion: Adaptation of Contracts' (2019) 11(1) Arbitration Law Review <https://elibrary.law.psu.edu/cgi/viewcontent.cgi?article=1254&context=arbitrationlawreview> accessed 10 September 2020, 101.

166 Augusto Garcia Sanjur, 'The Panama Canal Expansion: Adaptation of Contracts' (2019) 11(1) Arbitration Law Review <https://elibrary.law.psu.edu/cgi/viewcontent.cgi?article=1254&context = arbitrationlawreview> accessed 10 September 2020, 100.

to proceed with the Works in accordance with the Contract". However, the dispute board was only one step in a multi-tiered dispute settlement clause, allowing the decisions to be eventually reviewed by an arbitration tribunal.[167]

With regard to domestic arbitration, there are two unique characteristics shared by the legal system of Panama and that of neighbouring Costa Rica. First, the Supreme Court in Panama is the authority in charge of setting aside arbitration awards.[168] This task is entrusted to the Fourth Chamber of the Court.[169] Second, the Supreme Court judges are confirmed by the members of Congress (however, in this case, they are first nominated by the Executive Branch).[170] As outlined above, this system is not optimal for judicial independence, which in some cases can potentially affect arbitration proceedings. For foreign investors entering agreements with SOEs, this could possibly tip the balance in favour of international arbitration in a third country rather than arbitration in Panama.

On a related matter, a recent ICSID claim filed against Panama by Bridgestone Licensing Services Inc. and Bridgestone Americas Inc. put in question the competence and the integrity of the Supreme Court. However, as the ICSID tribunal stated, the claimants were 'unable to produce a scintilla of evidence' to support their claim.[171]

5 Conclusion

Investing in Central America, and in particular, entering contracts with local SOEs can be a very profitable business. However, these ventures entail unique risks that foreign investors must manage. Regarding disputes, the author proposes that investors should attempt to rely on amicable dispute settlement mechanisms and/or international arbitration in a third country rather than attempting to solve the conflicts through domestic arbitration or litigation.

Although domestic arbitration in the host State provides some advantages over litigation (and furthermore, could justifiably be regarded by the SOE as more cost-efficient in comparison to arbitration in a third country), the local arbitration laws and systems in Central America have some not-so-attractive features. Because some of these statutes were adopted many years ago, they provide for mechanisms that are untenable by the standards of international arbitration today (e.g. a judicial appeal of the arbitration award). Furthermore, concerns over the independence of the judiciary to decide free from direct and/or indirect political influence are present in the region,

[167] Article 20.6 of the Contract.

[168] Article 67, Law no. 131 regulating domestic and international arbitration.

[169] Article 67, Law no. 131 regulating domestic and international arbitration.

[170] Articles 161 and 203, Constitution of Panama; Another difference is that in this system, unlike in Costa Rica, the judges are chosen for a ten-year term with no possibility of extension.

[171] *Bridgestone Licensing Services Inc. and Bridgestone Americas Inc. v. Republic of Panama* [14 August 2020] ICSID ARB/16/34.

as is usually the case in developing countries. This could be relevant in the light of two factors: first, the large size of SOEs relative to each of the Central American economies and government budgets; and, second, the financial status of many SOEs, which may require bailouts and fiscal transfers from the authorities. Under these circumstances, the Central American governments themselves may be incentivized to go to great lengths to avoid increasing the liabilities of a given SOE during a dispute with foreign investors. The fiscal situation of these governments, presumably affected by the COVID-19 pandemic, should also be considered in this context.

Although all of the factors mentioned above should be taken into account, the author also wishes to highlight the importance of other criteria for the attraction of foreign investment. Tax incentives, a qualified labour force and/or the presence of natural resources in the host State—all available across the Central American region—are usually more decisive elements in this context.

Acknowledgements The author wishes to thank Camila Herrera for her valuable research assistance, as well as Valeria Garro, Augusto García Sanjur, Ignacio Grazioso, Christopher Glasscock, Lorena Madrid and Thelma Carrión for their comments and feedback.

Jorge Arturo Gonzalez The author is an associate attorney at Aguilar Castillo Love in Costa Rica. This chapter does not represent the views of the organization.

From State-Controlled Enterprises to Investment Screening: Paving the Way for Stricter Rules on Foreign Investment

Andrés Eduardo Alvarado Garzón

1 Introduction

State-controlled enterprises (SCEs) have had an increasing role in global economy over the last two decades. Especially by means of foreign direct investment (FDI), states are keener to diversify their sovereign funds across borders.[1] However, either as state-owned enterprises (SOEs) or as sovereign wealth funds (SWFs), the role of SCEs as foreign investors remains controversial.[2]

Traditionally, SWFs have been identified as vehicles of investment, whereas SOEs are deemed to engage in trading or supplying of goods and services.[3] Similarly, SOEs are often considered to have closer ties with their national governments than SWFs but

[1] Mathias Audit, 'Is the erecting of Barriers against Foreign Sovereign Wealth Funds compatible with International Investment Law?' (2008) 5 (6) US-China Law Review 1, 2; Wouter PF Schmit Jongbloed, Lisa E Sachs and Karl Sauvant, 'Sovereign Investment: An introduction' in Karl Sauvant, Lisa E Sachs and Wouter PF Schmit Jongbloed (eds), *Sovereign Investment: Concerns and Policy Reactions* (OUP 2012) 3.

[2] Carlos Esplugues, *Foreign Investment, Strategic Assets and National Security* (Intersentia Ltd 2018) 189.

[3] Locknie Hsu, 'Sovereign Wealth Funds: Investors in Search of an Identity in the Twenty-First Century' [2015] (2) International Review of Law, 2015:swf.6, 1, 4 <http://www.qscience.com/doi/pdf/10.5339/irl.2015.swf.6> accessed 18 February 2019.

[4] Esplugues (n 2) 212.

This chapter draws upon the author's original publication also available at https://www.transnational-dispute-management.com/journal-advance-publication-article.asp?key=1836. Reprinted by permission from Maris BV: Maris BV, *Transnational Dispute Management* (TDM, ISSN 1875-4120), "From State-Controlled Enterprises to Investment Screening: Paving the Way for Stricter Rules on Foreign Investment", Andrés Eduardo Alvarado Garzón, Copyright (2000). Please cite accordingly. The views expressed in this article are solely those of the author.

A. E. Alvarado Garzón (✉)
Saarland University, Saarbrücken, Germany
e-mail: alvarado@europainstitut.de

J. Chaisse et al. (eds.), *Regulation of State-Controlled Enterprises*, International Law and the Global South, https://doi.org/10.1007/978-981-19-1368-6_19

such differences have become blurred in recent years.[4] Precisely due to the possible close connection with their governments, states are reluctant to treat SCEs as regular foreign investors. For instance, the possible hidden political objectives, geostrategic agenda or their ability to create market distortions are some of the concerns towards SCEs.[5] Therefore, states try to be more cautious with inward FDI, particularly made by SCEs, considering that it might present certain risks to their national security interests.[6]

Consequently, two approaches have been undertaken. On the one hand, the promotion of international instruments addressing the activities of SCEs, on the other hand, the introduction of investment screening laws. Since 2006, several states have either adopted or reformed their investment screening mechanisms in order to impose further restrictions on FDI.[7] States avail themselves of concepts such as 'national security' or 'essential security' as a way to preserve the utmost autonomy and discretion in designing those laws. Despite the effort to avoid discrimination between third countries and to provide those screening systems with transparency, the risk of economic protectionism is always present.[8]

Against this background, this contribution strives to draw the connection between investments of SCEs and the development of investment screening laws. The first part deals with SCEs and their role in FDI, highlighting the differences between the SWFs and SOEs. The second part presents the potential risks to host states by means of investments of SCEs. The third part provides an overview on the international instruments addressing SCEs. The fourth part looks over different types of screening mechanisms enacted around the globe, including the recent Regulation establishing a framework for screening FDI into the European Union (EU) of 2019. Finally, some conclusions are presented.

2 State-Controlled Enterprises and Their Role in International Investment Law

Host states may perceive foreign investors differently depending on their nationality or the sector they operate therein.[9] Similarly, if the foreign investor is an enterprise

[5] Daniel M Shapiro and Steven Globerman, 'The International Activities and Impacts of State-Owned Enterprises' in Karl Sauvant, Lisa E Sachs and Wouter PF Schmit Jongbloed (eds), *Sovereign Investment: Concerns and Policy Reactions* (OUP 2012) 132.

[6] A famous example can be tracked down in the US, where Saudi Arabian Dubai Ports World was blocked to assume management of six major seaports in the US. David Collins, *An Introduction to International Investment Law* (CUP 2017) 286. *See* also, Joongi Kim, 'Fears of Foreign Ownership: The Old Face of Economic Nationalism' (2007) 27 (2) SAIS Review of International Affairs 167, 168; Mark A Clodfelter and Francesca MS Guerrero, 'National Security and Foreign Government Ownership Restrictions on Foreign Investment: Predictability for Investors at the National Level' in Karl Sauvant, Lisa E Sachs and Wouter PF Schmit Jongbloed (eds), *Sovereign Investment: Concerns and Policy Reactions* (OUP 2012) 174.

[7] UNCTAD, *World Investment Report 2016, Investor Nationality: Policy Challenges* (United Nations Publication 2016) 95.

[8] Collins (n 6) 291.

[9] Esplugues (n 2) 165.

controlled by a third state, there might be certain reluctance of the prospective host state to accept its investment.

Considering that the involvement of SCEs confronts the idea of little state intervention in the economy,[10] such attitude of host states is at least understandable. The traditional *laissez-faire et laissez-passer* seems to yield some ground to states keener to diversify their resources, leading to a rising trend of 'state-led investment capitalism'.[11] Nevertheless, from a legal perspective, it is not clear whether the existing regulatory framework of economic law can deal with sovereign investments in markets created for predominantly private investors.[12]

When compared to other investors, SCEs have significant advantages such as possible influence on home state policies, preferential access to resources (either natural or financial) or they might simply receive direct support from their home state.[13]

2.1 *Investments by Sovereign Wealth Funds*

The particular characteristics of SWFs prevent to designate them neither as state organ nor as private company, but rather a mixture between those two.[14] The first SWF was the Kuwait Investment Authority (today Kuwait Investment Corporation) established in 1953, but currently, the number of SWFs has exponentially increased.[15] Their resources have risen in recent years as well, particularly during the financial crisis of 2008, with an estimated of over USD 14 trillion on assets as of March 2011.[16] The funding of SWFs derives mostly from oil and gas revenues, but also from export earnings and financial holdings.[17]

---

[10] ibid 182.

[11] George Gilligan, Megan Bowman and Justin O'Brien, 'The Global Impact of State Capital' (2013) University of New South Wales Faculty of Law Research Series 2013. Research Paper 55, 10ff <http://law.bepress.com/cgi/viewcontent.cgi?article=1054&context=unswwps-flrps13> accessed 18 February 2019.

[12] Paul Rose, 'Sovereigns as Shareholders' (2008) 87 North Carolina Law Review 83, 95.

[13] Esplugues (n 2) 187.

[14] Hsu (n 3) 3.

[15] Audit (n 1) 1; Brendan J Reed, 'Sovereign Wealth Funds: The New Barbarians at the Gate - An Analysis of the Legal and Business Implications of Their Ascendancy' (2009) 4 (1) Virginia Law & Business Review 97, 100; Greg Golding, 'Australia's Experience with Foreign Direct Investment by State Controlled Entities: A Move towards Xenophobia or Greater Openness?' (2014) 37 Seattle University Law Review 533, 537.

[16] Schmit Jongbloed, Sachs and Sauvant (n 1) 4.

[17] ibid 4: 'About sixty percent of total funding for sovereign wealth funds comes from oil and gas revenues; the remaining forty percent are more diffuse and include export earnings (mostly from raw materials and commodity trade) and financial holdings.'

A comprehensive definition of SWFs remains elusive due to the different structures, management, objectives or sources of funds they may have.[18] Nonetheless, under the auspices of the International Monetary Fund (IMF), three key elements were elaborated, which allow to identify SWFs: Ownership by the government, investments covering foreign financial assets and with macroeconomic purposes.[19]

The specific objectives pursued by home states through SWFs may vary from state to state. However, they can be broadly categorised in three groups: First, SWFs as a source of capital for future generations, second, SWFs providing stabilisation by reducing the volatility of government revenues and third, SWFs acting as holding companies wherein states have their strategic investments (diversification).[20] Additionally, SWFs may be used for securing strategic economic positions, enhancing regional development, funding socio-economic projects or guaranteeing voluntary pensions of its citizens.[21]

The possible advantages for the economy of the host state are also recognised, for instance, providing a steady cash flow from long-term investments, injecting liquidity to the financial market or stabilising companies when in need of investment.[22] In fact, SWFs were highly praised during the financial crisis of 2008 due to their investments in American and European financial companies verging on default.[23] Surprisingly, the more visible the role of SWFs in the international market became, the more world's attention was captured, which led to several reforms in investment screening laws in different states.[24]

---

[18] Jackie VanDerMeulen and Michael J Trebilcock, 'Canada's Policy Response to Foreign Sovereign Investment: Operationalizing National Security Exceptions' (2009) 47 Canada Business Law Journal 392, 396; Victoria Barbary and Bernardo Bortolotti, 'Sovereign Wealth Funds and Political Risk: New Challenges in the Regulation of Foreign Investment' in Zdenek Drabek and Petros C Mavroidis (eds), *Regulation of Foreign Investment: Challenges to International Harmonization* (World Scientific Publishing Company 2013) 311.

[19] IWG International Working Group of Sovereign Wealth Funds, *Sovereign Wealth Funds Generally Accepted Principles and Practice: GAPP (Santiago Principles)* [2008] <https://www.ifswf.org/sites/default/files/santiagoprinciples_0_0.pdf> accessed 18 February 2019.

[20] Julien Chaisse, Debashis Chakraborty and Jaydeep Mukherjee, 'Emerging Sovereign Wealth Funds in the Making: Assessing the Economic Feasibility and Regulatory Strategies' (2011) 45 (4) Journal of World Trade 837, 841; Mark Gordon and Sabastian V Niles, 'Sovereign Wealth Funds: An Overview' in Karl Sauvant, Lisa E Sachs and Wouter PF Schmit Jongbloed (eds), *Sovereign Investment: Concerns and Policy Reactions* (OUP 2012) 29; Shai Bernstein, Josh Lerner and Antoinette Schoar, 'The Investment Strategies of Sovereign Wealth Funds' (2013) 27 (2) Journal of Economic Perspectives 219, 222; Gilligan, Bowman and O'Brien (n 11) 6.

[21] Gordon and Niles (n 20) 31.

[22] Esplugues (n 2) 192.

[23] Audit (n 1) 2; Barbary and Bortolotti (n 18) 309.

[24] *See* further, sec 5.

2.2 *Investments by State-Owned Enterprises*

SOEs differ from SWFs in the source of their funding (by commercial activities, although they may receive state subsidies) as well as in their mandate (to generate revenues in the respective industry).[25] Therefore, SOEs can be defined as 'government-owned or government-controlled entities whose assets are held in a corporate form and which generate the bulk of their revenues from the sale of goods and services'.[26] In a broader sense, any enterprise established under national law, where the state exercises ownership and which undertakes economic activities.[27] Moreover, it is considered that SOEs report directly to the central government and have access to capital at below market rates.[28]

Initially, SOEs were introduced to overcome market failures, but in practice, nationalisations were used to foster national economic development.[29] SOEs are significantly important in various countries, especially in developing economies as China, India, Brazil and Russia, where their SOEs have expanded beyond their borders.[30] Despite the increasing role of SWFs in the international sphere, SOEs still have a main role to play in industries such as energy, banking or transport.[31] For instance, it was assessed that SOEs control around 90% of the world's oil reserves.[32] The outward FDI projects by SOEs increased from 88,810 in 2003 to 145,691 in 2010[33] and by 2014 more than two-thirds of Chinese FDI into the EU was undertaken by Chinese SOEs.[34]

3 Potential Risks to Host States by Means of Investments of SCEs

Every foreign investment might present risks to national security interests of the host state.[35] However, major concerns have arisen as regards the investments of

[25] Schmit Jongbloed, Sachs and Sauvant (n 1) 9.

[26] Shapiro and Globerman (n 5) 102.

[27] OECD, *Guidelines on Corporate Governance of State-Owned Enterprises* (OECD Publishing, 2015 Edition) 14.

[28] Reed (n 15) 110.

[29] Shapiro and Globerman (n 5) 101.

[30] ibid 98.

[31] Ilya Okhmatovskiy, 'Performance Implications of Ties to the Government and SOEs: a Political Embeddedness Perspective' (2010) 47 Journal of Management Studies 1020, 1024.

[32] Shapiro and Globerman (n 5) 113.

[33] ibid 99.

[34] Sophie Meunier, 'A Faustian Bargain or just a good Bargain? Chinese Foreign Direct Investment and Politics in Europe' [2014] Asia Europe Journal 1, 6.

[35] Christopher T Vrountas, 'The Necessity and Effectiveness of Barriers to Foreign Direct Investment' (1990) 13 (1) Boston College International & Comparative Law Review 167, 168.

SCEs, particularly from the way they operate and the difficulty to determine whether they have political objectives disguised as commercial activities.[36] This lack of transparency on their management is precisely the cause of growing suspicions.[37] Although not all private enterprises act with full transparency, e.g. hedge funds, the fact of being private companies presupposes that they are driven by commercial rather than political objectives.[38]

Investments of SWFs had been deemed more reliable in comparison with investments of SOEs,[39] but this perception has changed over the last years. By 2010, around 71% of the SWFs were owned by authoritarian governments or hybrid regimes, whereas only 27% were owned by democracies.[40] Nowadays, the reluctance to receive foreign investment made by SWFs and SOEs is echoed by the political leaders of developed countries.[41]

In this context, concerns regarding investments of SCEs can be divided in two groups: On the one hand, relating to the economic impact of SCEs investments; on the other hand, relating to the political issues stemming from the ties of SCEs with their home state government.[42]

First, with respect to the economic impact the investments of SCEs may have, it is advanced that having connections with their home states might entail certain benefits for SCEs, which, in contrast, private companies do not have.[43] Thus, SCEs can create market distortions, for instance, by gaining access to state funding at a lower rate than private competitors could obtain.[44] The case of SOEs is particularly suggestive, since market pressures do not play a significant role on them[45] and SOEs are not susceptible of going bankrupt given the financial support of their home states, which grants them a considerable advantage *vis-à-vis* private companies.[46] Furthermore, should SCEs operate in a strategic sector of the host state, the possibility of crippling that state's economy, by disrupting its operation, will always be feared.[47]

Second, with respect to the political issues stemming from the ties of SCEs with their home state governments, concerns are raised for the possibility of espionage

---

[36] Schmit Jongbloed, Sachs and Sauvant (n 1) 11; Golding (n 15) 538.

[37] Reed (n 15) 106; Schmit Jongbloed, Sachs and Sauvant (n 1) 14; Bernstein, Lerner and Schoar (n 20) 234.

[38] Julian Chaisse, 'The Regulation of Sovereign Wealth Funds in the European Union: Can the Supranational Level Limit the Rise of National Protectionism?' in Karl Sauvant, Lisa E Sachs and Wouter PF Schmit Jongbloed (eds), *Sovereign Investment: Concerns and Policy Reactions* (OUP 2012) 467; Gordon and Niles (n 20) 31.

[39] Esplugues (n 2) 186.

[40] Barbary and Bortolotti (n 18) 313.

[41] VanDerMeulen and Trebilcock (n 18) 393.

[42] ibid 401.

[43] Okhmatovskiy (n 31) 1022; Golding (n 15) 538.

[44] Esplugues (n 2) 183.

[45] Okhmatovskiy (n 31) 1025.

[46] Shapiro and Globerman (n 5) 99.

[47] Shapiro and Globerman (n 5) 132; Esplugues (n 2) 201.

and the promotion of political or geostrategic agendas.[48] Equally problematic is the potential unauthorised transfer of technology, which could have military applications.[49] In this sense, a looming threat to the national security interests appears to be the possibility of using investments of SCEs as leverage over host states even to prevent the enactment of certain public policy measures.[50] A recent example is the fear that while seeking to keep the influx of Chinese FDI, the EU could soften its public policy towards China.[51]

Those concerns are exacerbated by the lack of transparency of SCEs functioning, for instance, in their internal structure, management and level of involvement of the home state government on the particular SCE.[52] In contrast, when SCEs come from developed countries e.g. Government Pension Fund from Norway or Temasek Holdings from Singapore, which are considered the 'high watermark' of transparency, less opposition to their investment is perceived.[53]

At least in the case of SWFs, it may be argued that concerns are overstated since only few and very limited examples exist of SWFs abusing their power by means of foreign investment.[54] It seems that SWFs are reluctant to invest in politically sensitive sectors.[55] In fact, when political leaders are involved in the management of SWFs, their investments tend to be domestic, whereas SWFs with external management tend to invest internationally.[56] The same cannot be told for SOEs,[57] where examples of abuse of their market position are more common, for instance, the Russian Gazprom which in several occasions has threatened to cut off the gas supply of Ukraine.[58]

In response to the potential threats of SCEs portrayed above, measures on two fronts have been undertaken: at an international level, with focus on transparency and accountability of SCEs, and at a national level, by introducing or strengthening their screening mechanisms availing themselves of national security grounds.[59] The following sections will deal with those two reactions.

---

[48] Audit (n 1) 2; VanDerMeulen and Trebilcock (n 18) 399; Okhmatovskiy (n 31) 1026; Esplugues (n 2) 186-99.

[49] VanDerMeulen and Trebilcock (n 18) 402; Golding (n 15) 538.

[50] Vrountas (n 35) 182ff; Gordon and Niles (n 20) 25.

[51] Controversial issues such as human rights in China, its status of market economy at the WTO or Tibet could be handled differently by EU politicians in order to attract Chinese investments. *See* Meunier (n 34) 6.

[52] Esplugues (n 2) 218.

[53] VanDerMeulen and Trebilcock (n 18) 402.

[54] Reed (n 15) 105; Gordon and Niles (n 20) 25.

[55] Barbary and Bortolotti (n 18) 318.

[56] Bernstein, Lerner and Schoar (n 20) 231.

[57] For a different opinion considering that SOEs may have different political objectives that their home states e.g. compliance with CSR, *see* Mette Morsing, 'State-Owned Enterprises: A Corporatization of Governments?' (2011) 25 (4) Management Communication Quarterly 710, 712.

[58] Reed (n 15) 111. Nevertheless, for examples where SOEs behave in clear contradiction to the political objectives of their home states, *see* Morsing (n 57) 712.

[59] Schmit Jongbloed, Sachs and Sauvant (n 1) 16.

4 International Instruments Addressing State-Controlled Enterprises

Several international instruments were put in place as a coordinated response to some of the concerns raised by SCEs investments,[60] the most significant ones being the Sovereign Wealth Funds Generally Accepted Principles and Practice (Santiago Principles) of 2008, the Organisation for Economic Co-operation and Development (OECD) Guidelines on Corporate Governance of State-Owned Enterprises of 2005, reviewed in 2015 and the OECD Declaration on Sovereign Wealth Funds and Recipient Country Policies of 2008.

4.1 Sovereign Wealth Funds Generally Accepted Principles and Practice or 'Santiago Principles' of 2008

The Santiago Principles were developed by the IMF members in coordination with the World Bank, the OECD, the EU and some SWFs,[61] with the purpose of identifying 'a framework of generally accepted principles and practices that properly reflect appropriate governance and accountability arrangements as well as the conduct of investment practices by SWFs on a prudent and sound basis'.[62]

There are 24 principles and 11 sub-principles covering different issues of the governance of SWFs. For instance, SWFs should have a defined and publicly disclosed policy[63] and a clear and effective division of roles and responsibilities with independent operational management.[64] Moreover, activities of SWFs should comply with the regulatory framework of host states,[65] they should not seek or take advantage of privileged information or inappropriate influence by their home state's government[66] and the exercise of ownership should be consistent with investment policies.[67]

In a broader perspective, the Santiago Principles strive to ensure that SWFs are properly organised,[68] by setting up a framework for their operation, promoting transparency, predictability and accountability in their management.[69] Furthermore, the

[60] A Edward Safarian, 'The Canadian Policy Response to Sovereign Direct Investment' in Karl Sauvant, Lisa E Sachs and Wouter PF Schmit Jongbloed (eds), *Sovereign Investment: Concerns and Policy Reactions* (OUP 2012) 446.

[61] Rose (n 12) 134; VanDerMeulen and Trebilcock (n 18) 401.

[62] Santiago Principles of 2008 (n 19) Generally Accepted Principles and Practices (GAPP) Purpose.

[63] ibid GAPP 4. Principle.

[64] ibid GAPP 6. Principle.

[65] ibid GAPP 15. Principle.

[66] ibid GAPP 20. Principle.

[67] ibid GAPP 21. Principle.

[68] Gordon and Niles (n 20) 40.

[69] Audit (n 1) 3.

Santiago Principles seek to prevent possible conflict of interests between SWFs and their home state's government.[70] Although the application of the Santiago Principles does not seem widespread, states are complying with them gradually.[71] Arguably, host states would refrain from imposing obstacles to investments of SWFs insofar they follow those principles.[72]

Nevertheless, the Santiago Principles present some shortcomings. For example, there is no standard for regular disclosure nor recommendation of SWFs being separate from the international reserves of the home state.[73] No standards to measure compliance with the principles are set out either[74] and seeking political goals through investment decisions seems to be allowed.[75] It is understandable that due to the diverse structures of SWFs, broad formulations of independency and transparency were taken in order to cover as much SWFs as possible.[76] However, such 'one-size-fits-all' approach appears counterproductive since the scope of application of each principle turned out to be rather elusive.[77]

Finally, as a soft law instrument, there is no legal redress if SWFs do not follow the Santiago Principles.[78] Besides, most of the owners of large SWFs are states that are not borrowers of the IMF. Hence, they cannot be compelled in any manner to follow the standards set up under the auspices of the IMF such as the Santiago Principles.[79]

4.2 *OECD Guidelines on Corporate Governance of State-Owned Enterprises*

The possible interference of home states in their SOEs for political reasons may derive in less efficiency and unclear accountability for their business operations.[80] Hence, the OECD Guidelines on Corporate Governance of State-Owned Enterprises address government officials in charge of SOEs providing recommendations for the

---

[70] Chaisse, Chakraborty and Mukherjee (n 20) 866.

[71] Schmit Jongbloed, Sachs and Sauvant (n 1) 22.

[72] Chaisse, Chakraborty and Mukherjee (n 20) 869.

[73] Rose (n 12) 144; Edwin M Truman, 'Do the Rules Need to be Changed for State-Controlled Entities? The Case of Sovereign Wealth Funds' in Karl Sauvant, Lisa E Sachs and Wouter PF Schmit Jongbloed (eds), *Sovereign Investment: Concerns and Policy Reactions* (OUP 2012) 406.

[74] Chaisse, Chakraborty and Mukherjee (n 20) 867.

[75] *cf* Santiago Principles of 2008 (n 19) GAPP 19.1. Principle. *See* also, Chaisse, Chakraborty and Mukherjee (n 20) 866.

[76] VanDerMeulen and Trebilcock (n 18) 401.

[77] Rose (n 12) 138.

[78] Reed (n 15) 121; Chaisse, Chakraborty and Mukherjee (n 20) 867; Gordon and Niles (n 20) 40; Barbary and Bortolotti (n 18) 333.

[79] Reed (n 15) 121.

[80] OECD, *Guidelines on Corporate Governance of State-Owned Enterprises* (n 27) 12.

management.[81] These guidelines were published initially in 2005, but they were reviewed in 2015 based on the gathered experience of their implementation.[82]

In this sense, by addressing some of the concerns regarding the governance of SOEs, a benchmark for best practices can be established under these guidelines.[83] Some of the recommendations set forth are the disclosure of the objectives that justify state ownership,[84] governance in a transparent and accountable manner,[85] ensuring fair competition in the market place wherein SOEs operate,[86] accounting, disclosure, compliance and auditing standards as listed companies,[87] accountability of SOEs' boards for their actions.[88]

In a broader perspective, these guidelines provide 'recommendations to governments on how to ensure that SOEs operate efficiently, transparently and in an accountable manner'.[89] It must be highlighted that there is no differentiation between SOEs operating domestically and internationally.[90]

4.3 *OECD Declaration on Sovereign Wealth Funds and Recipient Country Policies of 2008*

Recognising the potential threats sovereign investment in the form of SWFs may pose, the OECD Declaration on Sovereign Wealth Funds and Recipient Country Policies maintains that national security clauses should be applied only exceptionally and not as a bypath for escaping investment commitments.[91]

Having market liberalisation in mind, host states and their rules on inward FDI are addressed, for instance, promoting non-discrimination between foreign and domestic investors.[92] In broader terms, the core principles of transparency, predictability, proportionality and accountability should be taken into consideration when drafting restrictions on investments made by SWFs.[93]

---

[81] ibid 14.

[82] ibid 13.

[83] VanDerMeulen and Trebilcock (n 18) 401.

[84] OECD, *Guidelines on Corporate Governance of State-Owned Enterprises* (n 27) I. Rationales for state ownership.

[85] ibid II. The state's role as an owner.

[86] ibid III. State-owned enterprises in the market place.

[87] ibid VI. Disclosure and transparency.

[88] ibid VII. The responsibilities of the boards of state-owned enterprises.

[89] ibid 7.

[90] ibid 14.

[91] OECD, 'Sovereign Wealth Funds and Recipient Countries Policies: Investment Committee Report, 4 April 2008 (2008) 4 <https://www.oecd.org/daf/inv/investment-policy/40408735.pdf> accessed 18 February 2019.

[92] ibid 5.

[93] ibid 4.

This OECD Declaration has a different approach when compared with the Santiago Principles, the former addressing host states policies towards investments of SWFs and the latter addressing management of SWFs. Thus, they complement each other covering both aspects of investments of SWFs.

The Santiago Principles and both OECD initiatives above-mentioned present the same problem of any soft law instrument, i.e. enforceability.[94] Conversely, the clear advantage of these instruments is the flexibility on adaptation in contrast to national legislation or international treaties, without discouraging investments of SCEs.[95]

5 Investment Screening Mechanisms: Tackling Investments of SCEs

Should the behaviour of SCEs be completely transparent at the beginning of the investment, the risk of future actions guided by political or market distortive goals is too big to take according to the majority of states. Thus, investment screening mechanisms became popular.[96] Moreover, domestic laws are indeed enforceable, in contrast to the international instruments of soft law.[97]

5.1 Why Choosing Investment Screening?

States have several options to control inward FDI such as market access restrictions, state monopolies, limits on shares owned by foreign investors, investment screening and mandatory registration and check and balances.[98] The specific FDI regime of each state is influenced by political ideologies and economic policies;[99] thus, it can be different from state to state or even from government to government within the same country.

The most popular response to the possible threats of sovereign foreign investment has been the enactment of screening laws, allowing government authorities to block foreign investments due to national security concerns.[100] Ironically, states promote free flow of FDI but at the same time engage on investment screening mechanisms.[101]

[94] Reed (n 15) 121; Barbary and Bortolotti (n 18) 333.

[95] Audit (n 1) 4.

[96] VanDerMeulen and Trebilcock (n 18) 410; Esplugues (n 2) 211.

[97] Audit (n 1) 4.

[98] Esplugues (n 2) 230-36.

[99] Syed Tariq Anwar, 'FDI Regimes, Investment Screening Process and Institutional Frameworks: China versus Others in Global Business' (2012) 46 (2) Journal of World Trade 213, 216.

[100] VanDerMeulen and Trebilcock (n 18) 393.

[101] This is the heavily criticised 'globalisation *à la carte*' or 'selective protectionism' whereby states pick-and-choose only those aspects they prefer from globalization. Kim (n 6) 170.

Investment screening is conducted by the host state either directly by its government or by a specialised entity, whereby the FDI project is analysed having in mind the sector of the economy, possible thresholds on ownership, the nature of the investors, among others.[102] Therefore, investment screening laws may be seen as a protectionist response to the activities of SCEs.[103]

The overall development of investment screening laws in the recent years is telling, since a handful of states have introduced stricter rules on FDI.[104] Alongside, concerns about national security by means of FDI keep rising nowadays.[105] This tendency responds to a desire of states to keep control over strategic firms, critical infrastructure and key technologies, specially, when related to competitiveness of domestic economy.[106]

Investment screening laws target foreign investments mainly in their pre-establishment stage where usually states have unlimited power of control over FDI. Hence, choosing investment screening seems understandable.[107] However, even if international obligations for the pre-establishment stage of FDI were in place, decisions on investment screening are likely to be unreviewable by international tribunals if a 'national security' exception is argued, which is considered to be self-judging.[108]

With respect to the investment screening mechanisms as such, different issues may vary from state to state, including the scope of 'national security', information required in the screening process or the possible consequences after the screening is

---

[102] Esplugues (n 2) 235.

[103] Audit (n 1) 5.

[104] UNCTAD, *World Investment Report 2016* (n 7) 95: 'Since 2006, at least eight developed, developing and transition economies have enacted legislation on foreign investment reviews on national security grounds (i.e. Canada (2009), China (2011 and 2015), Finland (2012), Germany (2009), Italy (2012), the Republic of Korea (2006), Poland (2015), and the Russian Federation (2008)). During the same period, various countries have revised their mechanisms for the national security-related review of foreign investment through the addition of new sectors, guidelines or thresholds (…) The majority of these amendments tended towards adding further restrictions on investment, while some countries also clarified procedural requirements, thereby improving the overall transparency of their national security-related review mechanisms.'

[105] UNCTAD, *World Investment Report 2018, Investment and New Industrial Policies* (United Nations Publication 2018) xiii: 'Recently, an increasing number of countries have taken a more critical stance towards foreign investment. New investment restrictions or regulations in 2017 mainly reflected concerns about national security and foreign ownership of land and natural resources. Some countries have heightened scrutiny of foreign takeovers, in particular of strategic assets and technology firms. Several countries are considering tightening investment screening procedures.'

[106] ibid 162.

[107] Audit (n 1) 6; Esplugues (n 2) 229.

[108] For example, US has included a self-judging 'national security' exception in all its investment agreements, which could turn an investment claim inadmissible, thus, preventing an arbitral tribunal from deciding. Jose E Alvarez, 'Sovereign Concerns and the International Investment Regime' in Karl Sauvant, Lisa E Sachs and Wouter PF Schmit Jongbloed (eds), *Sovereign Investment: Concerns and Policy Reactions* (OUP 2012) 273. *See* also, Andreas Heinemann, 'Government Control of Cross-Border M&A: Legitimate Regulation or Protectionism?' (2012) 15 (3) Journal of International Economic Law 843, 853.

carried out.[109] In fact, most of the states having investment screening mechanisms in place avail themselves of broad definitions of 'national security' in order to keep an ample room for manoeuvre when conducting the review.[110]

Naturally, all states have the sovereign right to design laws, procedures, mechanisms, *inter alia*, in order to protect their national security interests. Nevertheless, as recommended by the OECD, this should be done following the principles of non-discrimination, transparency of policies, predictability of outcomes, proportionality of measures and accountability of implementing authorities.[111] In this sense, five points are suggested relating to the design of investment screening laws: First, separating national security screening from other FDI screening purposes. Second, setting clear and transparent screening criteria. Third, providing for investor-host state dialogue. Fourth, building in procedural safeguards, like the possibility of review of decisions. Fifth, allowing for pre-screening FDI clearance.[112] These points would provide screening mechanisms with predictability and transparency.

5.2 *Domestic Legislations: Open Restrictions to Investments of SCEs?*

Existing investment screening mechanisms can be divided in three groups: First, cross-sectoral approach based on concepts of national security or public interest. Second, specific-sector approach where the sectors under which foreign investment must undergo screening procedures are listed. Third, investments on key technologies of high economic value, regardless of the economic sector.[113] The following examples will show the approach different states have taken for the design of their investment screening laws, pinpointing specific provisions targeting investments of SCEs.

5.2.1 Australia: Enforcing Investment Policy on SCEs

In Australia, under the Foreign Acquisitions and Takeovers Act of 1975, investments can be prohibited if a foreign person would be exercising effective control and that could be contrary to national interests.[114] The Federal Treasurer takes the final

[109] UNCTAD, *World Investment Report 2016* (n 7) 94.

[110] UNCTAD, *World Investment Report 2018* (n 105) 160.

[111] OECD, 'Guidelines for Recipient country Investment Policies relating to national security: Recommendation adopted by the OECD Council on 25 May 2009' (2009) <https://www.oecd.org/daf/inv/investment-policy/43384486.pdf> accessed 18 February 2019. *See* also, Golding (n 15) 536.

[112] UNCTAD, *World Investment Report 2018* (n 105) 171-72.

[113] ibid 161ff.

[114] Foreign Acquisitions and Takeovers Act of 1975, pt 2, s 67(2). *See* also, Clodfelter and Guerrero (n 6) 179; Anwar (n 99) 240.

decision relating to foreign investment in Australia, after the analysis and recommendations made by the Foreign Investment Review Board.[115] However, there is no definition of national interest in the Foreign Acquisitions and Takeovers Act, which is analysed case-by-case.[116]

The Foreign Investment Review Board focuses on 'sensitive businesses', which includes media, telecommunications, transport, defence and military-related industries and activities, operation of nuclear facilities, among others.[117] Additionally, the Federal Treasurer may impose certain conditions on the foreign investment if deemed necessary to protect national security.[118] The reasons for decisions taken under the Foreign Acquisitions and Takeovers Act are not published.[119] There is no administrative or judicial review of the decisions taken under the Australian screening mechanism.[120]

With respect to investments of SCEs, the Australian Government's Foreign Investment Policy imposes additional restrictions in some sensitive sectors and in investments made by a foreign government and their agencies (SWFs and SOEs included).[121] For example, SCEs acquiring direct interest in an Australian company '(at least 10% or the ability to influence, participate in or control), starting a new business or acquiring an interest in Australian land regardless of the value' must get prior approval.[122] Although Foreign Investment Policy has no legal force, its application is achieved by other means, for instance, when it is taken into consideration by the Federal Treasurer for deciding approvals or prohibitions of FDI.[123]

5.2.2 Canada: SCEs and the Net-Benefit Test

The Investment Canada Act of 1985 contains a screening mechanism for foreign investment that could be 'injurious to national security',[124] however, without defining

[115] Gilligan, Bowman and O'Brien (n 11) 19; Golding (n 15) 544.

[116] Gilligan, Bowman and O'Brien (n 11) 20; Golding (n 15) 544.

[117] Foreign Acquisitions and Takeovers Act of 1975, pt 1, s 26 *in conjunction with* Treasurer, 'Australian Government's Foreign Investment Policy' (1 January 2019) <https://cdn.tspace.gov.au/uploads/sites/82/2018/12/1-January-2019-Policy_.pdf> accessed 18 February 2019. *See* also, Collins (n 6) 291.

[118] Foreign Acquisitions and Takeovers Act of 1975, pt 2, s 67(2).

[119] Golding (n 15) 544.

[120] Administrative Decisions (Judicial Review) Act 1977 (No 59 of 1977) sch 1, para h.

[121] Treasurer, 'Australian Government's Foreign Investment Policy' (n 117).

[122] Treasurer, 'Australian Government's Foreign Investment Policy' (n 117) 5.

[123] Golding (n 15) 551.

[124] Investment Canada Act 1985, pt IV.1

this concept. Acquisitions of Canadian companies by foreign investors must be notified if exceeding certain thresholds.[125] This allowed Canada to block the sale of BlackBerry technology to the Chinese company Lenovo in 2013.[126]

Initially, the central factor of the Investment Canada Act for screening foreign investments was assessing the benefit to the state. Nevertheless, as from 2009, an amendment was introduced and a national security test was put in place.[127] This amendment was the result of the heating political debates over the increasing number of foreign investment made by SCEs in Canada.[128] In this sense, foreign investors may be required to disclose any information deemed relevant to assess whether the proposed investment is injurious to national security.[129] Finally, there is no appeal or review for the decisions taken during the investment screening and judicial redress is limited to errors of law.[130]

With respect to investments of SCEs, further regulations in the framework of the Investment Canada Act specifically included investment review for investments made by SOEs, conferring greater attention on corporate governance and reporting practices.[131] Although at first sight SWFs are not targeted, the broad definition of SOEs might encompass investments of SWFs as well.[132] Furthermore, special attention must be given to investments of SOEs by analysing whether they are of net-benefit to Canada and how susceptible are to state influence.[133]

5.2.3 China: A Great Wall Against all Foreign Investment?

In China, the substantive rules for investment screening are spread over different laws, namely, the Anti-Monopoly Law of 2008, Regulations Issued on Restructuring of State-Owned Enterprises with Foreign Funds of 2002, Law of the People's Republic of China on Wholly Foreign-Owned Enterprises of 2000, Law of the People's Republic of Chinese Contractual Joint Ventures of 2000, Provisions on

---

[125] ibid pt II, s 11.

[126] Collins (n 6) 291.

[127] Clodfelter and Guerrero (n 6) 179; Anwar (n 99) 241.

[128] VanDerMeulen and Trebilcock (n 18) 392-94.

[129] Investment Canada Act 1985, pt IV.1, sub-s 25(3).

[130] VanDerMeulen and Trebilcock (n 18) 406.

[131] Investment Canada Regulations SOR/85-611 (Investment Canada Act), s 3, modified by SOR/2015-64. *See* also Heinemann (n 108) 848.

[132] *cf* Investment Canada Act 1985, s 3: **'state-owned enterprise means**: **(a)** the government of a foreign state, whether federal, state or local, or an agency of such a government; **(b)** an entity that is controlled or influenced, directly or indirectly, by a government or agency referred to in paragraph (a); or **(c)** an individual who is acting under the direction of a government or agency referred to in paragraph (a) or who is acting under the influence, directly or indirectly, of such a government or agency; (*entreprise d'État*).'

[133] Guidelines – Investments by state-owned enterprises – Net Benefit Assessment <https://www.ic.gc.ca/eic/site/ica-lic.nsf/eng/lk00064.html#p2> accessed 18 February 2019.

Mergers and Acquisitions of Domestic Enterprises by Foreign Investors of 2006 and Regulations for Takeovers of Listed Companies of 2006.[134]

Additionally, China promulgated the Catalogue of Industries for Guiding Foreign Investment shedding some light on the restrictions on FDI. Originally, the Catalogue contained four categories of industries: Encouraged, permitted, restricted and prohibited.[135] However, this was modified by the Decree No 4 of the National Development and Reform Commission and the Ministry of Commerce of the People's Republic of China in 2017. Currently, there are only two categories: Catalogue of Encouraged Industries for Foreign Investment and Negative List for Foreign Investment Access, the latter is composed of the previous restricted and prohibited industries.[136] Before this reform, the Ministry of Commerce and the National Development and Reform Commission had to approve all FDI.[137] After the reform, only investments in the restricted list require prior approval, investment in the prohibited list are closed to foreign investment and any other investment requires only an online registration.[138]

Investments of SCEs are not specifically targeted, nevertheless, this does not mean SCEs escape from being screened but rather that they have to undergo the same process as private investors. The complexity of the Chinese FDI regime lies not only on the different domestic laws that must be taken into consideration,[139] but also on the bureaucratic burden since foreign companies face countless requirements and delays before obtaining approval to invest in China.[140] This comes along with lack of transparency and the perceived lack of rule of law given the discriminatory practices, selective enforcement of regulations, poor protection of intellectual property rights and forced transfer of technology.[141]

Recently, China has enacted a new Foreign Investment Law on 15 March 2019, entering into force on 1 January 2020, which prompts the state to establish a review system for foreign investment affecting or having the possibility to affect national security.[142] Although the new law retains the system of negative list for excluding

---

[134] Anwar (n 99) 234.

[135] Kevin B Goldstein, 'Reviewing Cross-Border Mergers and Acquisitions for Competition and National Security: A Comparative Look at How the United States, Europe, and China Separate Security Concerns from Competition Concerns in Reviewing Acquisitions by Foreign Entities' (2011) 3 Tsinghua China Law Review 215, 237.

[136] Catalogue of Industries for Guiding Foreign Investment (Revision 2017) <http://www.fdi.gov.cn/1800000121_39_4851_0_7.html> accessed 10 February 2019.

[137] Clodfelter and Guerrero (n 6) 179.

[138] Esplugues (n 2) 309.

[139] Anwar (n 99) 238.

[140] For instance, Carlyle Group was forced to reduce its acquisition of Xugong and a fund owned by Goldman Sachs encountered delays on the approval to buy Shineway. *See* Kim (n 6) 171.

[141] For instance, assessment made by the US Department of State: Bureau of Economic and Business Affairs, 'Investment Climate Statements 2018: China' (2018) <http://www.state.gov/e/eb/rls/othr/ics/investmentclimatestatements/index.htm?year=2018&dlid=281490> accessed 18 February 2019.

[142] Foreign Investment Law of the People's Republic of China enacted on 15 March 2019, entering into force on 1 January 2020, art 35.

certain foreign investment, it sets forth expressly that foreign investment outside the negative list should be treated uniformly with domestic investment.[143] In any case, whether the review of foreign investment under this new law would be more transparent remains to be seen.

5.2.4 France: Upholding the 'Economic Patriotism'

In France, investment screening is established in the *Code Monétaire et Financier* (Monetary and Financial Code), whereby, under certain circumstances, FDI requires the approval from the Minister for the Economy.[144] These circumstances pertain to investments that participate in the exercise of public authority, those that can jeopardise public order, or related with arms, munitions and explosives.[145] In this sense, investments of foreign SCEs fall into the scope of exercise of public authority,[146] thus, requiring prior approval of the Minister for the Economy.

The introduction of investment screening in France followed the fears for the takeover of the French company Danone by the American company PepsiCo, leading to the Decree 2005-1739 which granted the power to restrict FDI.[147] Going further, the French government openly defended the protection of French companies from the influence of sovereign funds.[148] This has been called *patriotisme économique* (economic patriotism) whereby the French government protects French companies from mergers and acquisitions (M&A) transactions with foreign investors when a French alternative is possible.[149]

5.2.5 Germany: Critical Infrastructure v Investments of SCEs?

Although Germany has experienced investments by foreign SCEs since the 1970s with positive results, only in 2009 widespread fears of the possible drawbacks of such investments arose, which led to stricter rules for foreign investment in Germany.[150] Nowadays, the framework for investment screening is set forth in the *Außenwirtschaftsgesetz—AWG* (Foreign Trade and Payments Act) together with the

143 Foreign Investment Law of the People's Republic of China enacted on 15 March 2019, entering into force on 1 January 2020, art 28.

144 Monetary and Financial Code, art L 151-3.

145 ibid.

146 Esplugues (n 2) 414.

147 Chaisse (n 38) 489.

148 Rose (n 12) 128; Heinemann (n 108) 848-49.

149 Heinemann (n 108) 848-49; Esplugues (n 2) 410-11.

150 Thomas Jost, 'Sovereign Wealth Funds and the German Policy Reaction' in Karl Sauvant, Lisa E Sachs and Wouter PF Schmit Jongbloed (eds), *Sovereign Investment: Concerns and Policy Reactions* (OUP 2012) 453-56.

Außenwirtschaftsverordnung—AWV (Foreign Trade and Payments Ordinance) especially for reasons of essential security. Nonetheless, that does not apply to foreign enterprises from the EU or from the European Free Trade Association states.[151]

The Federal Ministry of Economics and Technology is entitled to review *ex officio* FDI proposals and to suspend them or prohibit them if they are deemed to threaten national security.[152]

Germany has a cross-sectoral approach, with emphasis and stricter rules on investments in critical infrastructure, regardless whether the foreign investors are SCEs or not. In this sense, the Foreign Trade and Payments Ordinance sets forth the following thresholds: In critical infrastructure, acquisitions of 10% or more of voting rights are subject to investment screening,[153] whereas in other sectors, acquisitions of 25% or more of voting rights must undergo investment screening.[154]

5.2.6 United States: The Archetype of Investment Screening

The Committee on Foreign Investment in the United States (CFIUS) is a government board in charge of reviewing covered transactions, including M&A by or with a foreign investor, leading to the control of the company by that foreign investor, which might have an impact on the national security of the US.[155] Nevertheless, the concept of national security is undefined.[156]

The CFIUS was created in 1975, originally designed to monitor the impact of inward foreign investment and to coordinate US investment policy.[157] Only in 1988 by the Exon-Florio Amendment to the Defence Production Act of 1950, the US President was given the possibility to suspend or prohibit acquisitions that might threaten national security pursuant to recommendations of CFIUS.[158] Before this amendment, foreign acquisitions could not be blocked unless the US President would have declared national emergency.[159]

---

[151] Foreign Trade and Payments Act, § 5.

[152] Chaisse, Chakraborty and Mukherjee (n 20) 860; Esplugues (n 2) 425-26.

[153] Foreign Trade and Payments Ordinance, § 56(1)(1).

[154] ibid § 56(1)(2).

[155] Rose (n 12) 108; Anwar (n 99) 239.

[156] Chaisse, Chakraborty and Mukherjee (n 20) 856; Collins (n 6) 290.

[157] George Stephanov Georgiev, 'The reformed CFIUS Regulatory Framework: Mediating between continued Openness to Foreign Investment and National Security' (2008) 25 Yale Journal on Regulation 125, 126-27.

[158] Defense Production Act of 1950, 50 USC App 2170, s 721(d)(1).

[159] Jose E Alvarez, 'Political Protectionism and United States International Investment Obligations in Conflict: The Hazards of Exon-Florio' (1989) 30 Virginia Journal of International Law 2, 89; Jason Cox, 'Regulation of Foreign Direct Investment after Dubai Ports Controversy: Has the US Government finally figured out how to balance Foreign Threats to National Security without Alienating Foreign Companies?' (2008) 34 (1) The Journal of Corporation Law 293, 297; Barbary and Bortolotti (n 18) 329.

The most important change regarding SCEs was implemented in 1992, whereby CFIUS was entrusted with mandatory investigations of transactions when the potential acquirer is 'controlled by or acting on behalf of a foreign government' and 'seeks to engage in an acquisition that could affect the national security of US'.[160] Afterwards, the Foreign Investment and National Security Act or 'FINSA' of 2007 extended the scope of review on national security reasons.[161] There is a non-exhaustive list of factors that may be considered to pose a threat to national security.[162]

Critics to CFIUS wield that the system is not sufficiently transparent, however, it must be highlighted that between 1988 and 2011, only one transaction was blocked.[163] This has changed in recent years, since CFIUS is deemed more proactive by blocking and discouraging foreign investment into the US.[164] This should be added to the transactions withdrawn after informal consultations with CFIUS whose number is unknown.[165]

With respect to investments of SCEs, US legislation specifically takes into account 'foreign government-controlled transactions'.[166] These kind of transactions must undergo a national security investigation which may last up to 45 days.[167] Furthermore, when the US President is deciding to suspend or prohibit a covered transaction that may impair national security, one of the factors to consider is whether it is related to a foreign government-controlled transaction.[168]

Recently, the US has promulgated the Foreign Investment Risk Review Modernisation Act of 2018 (FIRRMA) entering in force on 13 August 2018, which, in broader terms, expands the scope of covered transactions subject to CFIUS review and prolongs the time for the review. FIRRMA targets particularly Chinese investments but it is deemed to cover also Iran, North Korea, Russia, Sudan, Syria and Venezuela.[169]

---

[160] Defense Production Act of 1950, 50 USC App 2170, s 721. *See* also Georgiev (n 157) 127.

[161] Rose (n 12) 128.

[162] Defense Production Act of 1950, 50 USC App 2170, as amended by the Foreign Investment and National Security Act of 2007, s 721.

[163] Georgiev (n 157) 129; Cox (n 159) 303; Chaisse, Chakraborty and Mukherjee (n 20) 857;

[164] UNCTAD, *World Investment Report 2018* (n 105) 16.

[165] Chaisse, Chakraborty and Mukherjee (n 20) 857.

[166] Defense Production Act of 1950, 50 USC App 2170, s 721(a)(4): '*Foreign government-controlled transaction.*—The term 'foreign government-controlled transaction' means any covered transaction that could result in the control of any person engaged in interstate commerce in the United States by a foreign government or an entity controlled by or acting on behalf of a foreign government.'

[167] ibid s 721(b)(2)(C).

[168] ibid s 721(f)(8).

[169] Paul Rose, 'FIRRMA and National Insecurity' (2018) Ohio State Public Law Working Paper No 452, 12-16 <https://papers.ssrn.com/sol3/papers.cfm?abstract_id=3235564> accessed 18 February 2019.

5.3 *EU Framework for Investment Screening: How Would it Work?*

The open environment for foreign investment in the EU seems to be overshadowed by the increasing acquisitions made by foreign SCEs over sensitive sectors for strategic reasons.[170] This may be the consequence of a perceived lenient regulation of FDI, in comparison, for example, with the US.[171] Therefore, strong reactions in the EU have surfaced and concerns about possible reshaping of politics in Europe by foreign investors, especially by Chinese SCEs, are on display.[172] A clear example is the acquisition of the port of Piraeus in Greece raising heated discussions in the EU.[173]

As a preliminary note, it must be highlighted that an intra-EU investment screening mechanism might seem unwarranted given the comprehensive level of integration of the EU. Restrictions on the freedom of establishment as well as on the free movement of capital are prohibited pursuant to Article 49 Treaty on the Functioning of the European Union (TFEU) and Article 63 TFEU respectively. Concerning the freedom of establishment, EU Member States may impose certain restrictions for 'public security' according to Article 52 TFEU.[174] However, the Court of Justice of the European Union (CJEU) have set a high threshold to justify restrictions based on public security reasons.[175] With regards to the free movement of capital, Article 65(1)(b) TFEU

---

[170] Commission, 'Reflection Paper on Harnessing Globalisation' (Reflection Paper) COM (2017) 240.

[171] Meunier (n 34) 3.

[172] Meunier (n 34) 4. *See* also, Leonie Reins, 'The European Union's Framework for FDI screening: Towards an ever more growing competence over energy policy?' (2019) 128 Energy Policy 665, 665; Marc Bungenberg and Angshuman Hazarika, 'Chinese Foreign Investments in the European Union Energy Sector: The Regulation of Security Concerns' (2019) 20 Journal of World Investment & Trade 375.

[173] To see public reactions in the EU to the Chinese acquisitions: Angeliki Koutantou, 'Workers protest as Greece sells Piraeus Port to China COSCO' (Reuters, 8 April 2016) <https://www.reuters.com/article/us-eurozone-greece-privatisation-china-c-idUSKCN0X50ZE> accessed 18 February 2019; Helena Smith, 'Greece blocks EU's criticism at UN of China's human rights record' (The Guardian, 18 June 2017) <https://www.theguardian.com/world/2017/jun/18/greece-eu-criticism-un-china-human-rights-record> accessed 18 February 2019; Keith Johnson, 'Why Is China Buying Up Europe's Ports?' (Foreign Policy, 2 February 2018) <https://foreignpolicy.com/2018/02/02/why-is-china-buying-up-europes-ports/> accessed 18 February 2019; Philip Blenkinsop, 'With eyes on China, EU agrees investment screening rules' (Reuters, 20 November 2018) <https://uk.reuters.com/article/us-eu-china-investment/with-eyes-on-china-eu-agrees-investment-screening-rules-idUKKCN1NP1IJ> accessed 18 February 2019.

[174] Paul Craig and Gráinne de Búrca, *EU Law: Text, Cases, and Materials* (5th edn, OUP 2011) 770; Robert Schütze, *European Union Law* (2nd edn, CUP 2018) 646.

[175] In this regard, the CJEU has explained that a measure restricting the freedom of establishment 'may be justified where it serves overriding requirements relating to the public interest, is suitable for securing the attainment of the objective it pursues and does not go beyond what is necessary in order to attain it' Case C-442/02 *Caixa-Bank France v Ministère d l'Économie, des Finances et de l'Industrie* [2004] ECR-I 8984, para 17. *See* also, Case C-439/99 *Commission v Italy* [2002] ECR-I 351, para 23.

allows to impose restrictions based on 'public security' as well.[176] Similar to the freedom of establishment, restrictions to the free movement of capital based on 'public security' must comply with strict requirements.[177] Consequently, investment screening mechanisms of an EU Member State for investors from another EU Member State seem difficult to envisage.

In spite of the abovementioned, the EU have certain mechanisms in place which allow EU Member States to review economic operations based on legitimate interests, for instance, the EU Merger Regulation.[178] Furthermore, in the energy sector,[179] obligations regarding the certification in relation to third countries and the unbundling requirement, also known as the Gazprom clause, can be considered as a screening mechanism as well.[180] Indeed, the Gazprom clause responds to the dominant position of Gazprom (largest oil and gas company in Russia), which might be used as a tool for exercising political pressure.[181] Although instruments such as the EU Merger Regulation and the Gazprom clause may imply screening of foreign investment, they are limited to specific sectors, i.e. competition law and energy law respectively.

In this context, the EU is mindful of the necessity of an EU cross-sectoral common approach to address sovereign investments since 2008,[182] without creating a CFIUS-like mechanism, but rather through the coordination with the Member States.[183] Hence, the EU Commission presented a Proposal for a Regulation 'Establishing a Framework for Screening of Foreign Direct Investment into the European Union'[184]

[176] Paul Craig and Gráinne de Búrca, *EU Law: Text, Cases, and Materials* (5th edn, OUP 2011) 697; Robert Schütze, *European Union Law* (2nd edn, CUP 2018) 699ff.

[177] Following the jurisprudence of the CJEU, 'measures which restrict the free movement of capital may be justified on public-policy and public-security grounds only if they are necessary for the protection of the interests which they are intended to guarantee and only in so far as those objectives cannot be attained by less restrictive measures' Case C-54/99 *Association Église de Scientologie de Paris v The Prime Minister*, Reference for a Preliminary Ruling: *Conseil d'Etat* – France [2000] ECR-I 1335, para 18.

[178] Council Regulation (EC) 139/2004 of 20 January 2004 on the Control of Concentrations between undertakings [2004] OJ L24/1.

[179] Directive (EC) 2009/73/EC of the European Parliament and of the Council of 13 July 2009 concerning Common Rules for the Internal Market in Natural Gas and Repealing Directive 2003/55/EC [2009] OJ L211/94; Directive (EC) 2009/72/EC of the European Parliament and of the Council of 13 July 2009 concerning Common Rules for the Internal Market in Electricity and Repealing Directive 2003/54/EC [2009] OJ L211/55.

[180] Thomas Cottier, Sofya Matteotti-Berkutova and Olga Nartova, 'Third Country Relations in EU Unbundling of Natural Gas Markets: The "Gazprom Clause" of Directive 2009/73 EC and WTO Law' (2010) Working Paper No 2010/06; Bungenberg and Hazarika (n 172) 384.

[181] Andreas Goldthau and Nick Sitter, 'A Liberal Actor in a Realist World? The Commission and the External Dimension of the Single Market for Energy' (2014) 21 (10) Journal of European Public Policy 1452; Ole Gunnar Austvik, 'The Energy Union and Security-of-Gas Supply' (2016) 96 Energy Policy 372.

[182] Chaisse (n 38) 469-75.

[183] ibid 474.

[184] Commission, 'Proposal for a Regulation of the European Parliament and of the Council establishing a framework for screening of foreign direct investments into the European Union' COM (2017) 487 final.

in September 2017, which, with some modifications, was finally enacted on 19 March 2019 (hereinafter Investment Screening Regulation).[185] The main goal of the Investment Screening Regulation is to set up a framework for the Member States to screen FDI that raises concerns for security or public order, as well as for the cooperation between Member States and the Commission.[186] However, Member States are not obliged to adopt, modify or maintain screening mechanisms.[187]

The Investment Screening Regulation strives to ensure that any screening law in the EU complies with three minimum requirements, namely, the possibility of judicial redress of the decisions, non-discrimination between third states and transparency.[188] Furthermore, there is an obligation to notify other Member States and the Commission of FDI undergoing screening.[189]

Two scenarios of cooperation with other Member States and with the Commission are set forth in the Investment Screening Regulation: first, FDI undergoing screening; second, FDI not undergoing screening. In both scenarios, other Member States can raise concerns and provide comments and the Commission may issue a non-binding opinion, nevertheless, the final decision is left to the Member State where the FDI is planned or was completed.[190] The main difference lies on the timeframes to provide comments and the opinion.[191] The Member State where FDI is planned or has been completed shall give 'due consideration' to the comments of the other Member States and to the opinion of the Commission.[192] However, the scope of this obligation or even the consequences if not followed are not clear.

In cases of FDI touching upon projects of Union interest,[193] Article 8(2)(c) Investment Screening Regulation states that the Member State were the FDI is planned or was completed 'shall take utmost account of the Commission's opinion' and provide explanations if the opinion is not followed. Once again, the lack of clarity of this obligation might raise some problems in its application. Perhaps, this provision grants the Commission great influence over Member States, since it could withhold EU funding if its opinion is not followed.[194]

---

[185] Regulation (EU) 2019/452 of the European Parliament and the Council of 19 March 2019 establishing a framework for the screening of direct investments into the Union [2019] OJ L79 I/1.

[186] Reg (EU) 2019/452 OJ L79 I/1, art 1(1).

[187] Reg (EU) 2019/452 OJ L79 I/1, art 3(1).

[188] Reg (EU) 2019/452 OJ L79 I/1, art 3(2-5).

[189] Reg (EU) 2019/452 OJ L79 I/1, art 6(1).

[190] Reg (EU) 2019/452 OJ L79 I/1, art 6-7.

[191] The timeframes for providing comments and the opinion are, regarding FDI undergoing screening, other Member States and the Commission have up to 35 calendar days since they were notified, whereas regarding FDI not undergoing screening other Member States and the Commission have up to 15 months after the FDI was completed. *See* Reg (EU) 2019/452 OJ L79 I/1, art 6(7) and art 7(8).

[192] Reg (EU) 2019/452 OJ L79 I/1, art 6(9) and art 7(7).

[193] For instance, projects with substantial EU funding or established by EU law regarding critical infrastructure, critical technology or critical inputs, which are essential for security or public order. *See* Reg (EU) 2019/452 OJ L79 I/1, art 8(3).

[194] *cf* Reins (n 172) 667.

Article 8(3) Investment Screening Regulation mentions a list of projects or programmes of Union interest embedded in the Annex thereof. Although that list may be modified, it seems that only those projects listed in the Annex are of Union interest (exhaustive list). This approach provides legal certainty in the application of the regulation and at the same time, it provides the Commission with certain room of manoeuvre to modify that list.

With respect to SCEs, pursuant to Article 9(2)(a) Investment Screening Regulation, the ownership structure up to the controlling investor must be disclosed. Moreover, as set forth in Article 4(2)(a) thereof, in determining the effects on security and public order, one of the factors to consider is 'whether a foreign investor is controlled directly or indirectly by the government (…) of a third country (…)'. There is no clear guidance on this aspect, which may create some problems, for instance, if a Member State and the Commission were to interpret it differently in a particular case. Would the acquisition on the port of Piraeus have been different if the Investment Screening Regulation would have been in place? In this context, it remains to be seen how the Investment Screening Regulation will be applied with regard to investments of foreign SCEs into the EU.

6 Conclusion

SCEs have an increasing role in global economy and the possible threats to host states by means of their investments cannot be ignored. The possibility of SCEs to create market distortions or the political issues stemming from SCEs and their ties with their home state governments should be tackled from the outset.

At an international level, instruments such as the Santiago Principles, the OECD Guidelines on Corporate Governance of State-Owned Enterprises and the OECD Declaration on Sovereign Wealth Funds and Recipient Country Policies are a good example of international efforts in this regard. These instruments embody standards for the management of SCEs as well as for the design of national laws regulating inward FDI. Although they present the advantage of being flexible to adaption for SCEs and host states, their lack of enforceability remains as an obstacle for their successful implementation.

In contrast, at a national level, the enactment of investment screening laws seems to be preferred. States base themselves on undefined concepts of 'national security' or 'essential security' to design those laws. Certainly, setting investment screening procedures does not necessary mean that the state is taking a stance on economic protectionism,[195] but even if not formally blocking of foreign investment, screening mechanisms may have a cooling effect, discouraging prospective foreign investments.[196]

[195] For a different view, Anwar (n 99) 224.

[196] UNCTAD, *World Investment Report 2018* (n 105) 163.

As evidenced from the examples of domestic legislation, many states enact investment screening mechanisms with specific provisions on SCEs. This appears redundant because screening laws are conceived to address exactly all concerns provoked by investments of SCEs. In other words, risks such as crippling host state's economy or using SCEs for political purposes may fall under the umbrella of 'national security' or 'essential security' concepts, which are the basis of investment screening laws. Despite the ample room of manoeuvre states already have by means of screening mechanisms, signalising SCEs might be the result of the historical reluctance to investments controlled by states.

Be that as it may, investment screening systems can be subject of political or even private pressures,[197] or even being misused as an excuse to impose hidden limitations on foreign investment.[198] Thus, transparency and clear rules must govern those procedures. Following the suggestions of the OECD, restrictions on inward FDI, including those investments made by SCEs, should be used as a last resource when other policies such as competition law or financial regulations are not equipped to address national security concerns.[199]

Andrés Eduardo Alvarado Garzón (LL.M.) (PhD Candidate) works as research associate at the Chair for Public Law, Public International Law and European Law of Prof. Dr. Marc Bungenberg, LL.M., at Saarland University, Germany.

[197] For example, controversy on British Tire and Rubber (UK investor) and Saint-Gobain (French investor) pursuing the acquisition of Norton Company (US company). Rose, 'Sovereigns as Shareholders' (n 12) 113.

[198] Georgiev (n 157) 129-30; Esplugues (n 2) 242.

[199] OECD, 'Guidelines for Recipient country Investment Policies' (n 111).

Investment Screening Mechanism (ISM) in Central and Eastern Europe (CEE): Case Study of Poland

Jędrzej Górski

1 Introduction

The Polish government joined the frenzy of counteracting hostile takeover of domestic companies across the West by investors from unallied countries in December 2020 when it expanded the scope of investment screening mechanism (ISM) from less than twenty companies at a given time under the 2015 Act on Some Investment's Control ('2015 ISM') to whole sectors of the economy, among others including all publicly-listed companies, some software producers, and all producers of chemicals, meat milk, grain, fruits and vegetables (on top of energy and utilities sectors usually subjected to some scrutiny).[1] Companies generating less than EUR 10 million in annual revenue have been exempted. The 2020 amendment of the 2015 ISM ('2020 ISM') came into being as part of the fourth legislative package of COVID-related stimulus measures commonly known as the 'fourth anti-crisis shield,' which somewhat explains the extraordinary, almost war-like, scope of its application.

Indeed, the 2020 ISM's bill justified the ISM expansion and counteracting all takeovers by enterprises originating from outside of the European Union (EU) or the

[1] *Ustawa z dnia 24 lipca 2015 r. o kontroli niektórych inwestycji,* Polish Official Journal (2015) item 1272 (the '2015 ISM') as amended by *Ustawa z dnia 19 czerwca 2020 r. o dopłatach do oprocentowania kredytów bankowych udzielanych przedsiębiorcom dotkniętym skutkami COVID-19 oraz o uproszczonym postępowaniu o zatwierdzenie układu w związku z wystąpieniem COVID-19,* Polish Official Journal (2020) item 1086 (the '2020 ISM').

The original version of chapter was inadvertently published prematurely, before incorporation of the final corrections, which has now been updated. The correction to this chapter can be found at https://doi.org/10.1007/978-981-19-1368-6_31

J. Górski (✉)
Department of Asian and International Studies (AIS), City University of Hong, Kowloon Tong, Hong Kong, China
e-mail: sclavius@gmail.com

J. Chaisse et al. (eds.), *Regulation of State-Controlled Enterprises*, International Law and the Global South, https://doi.org/10.1007/978-981-19-1368-6_20

European Economic Area (EEA) with the need to protect public security, order and health in the context of the generally deteriorating economic situation and collapsing financial liquidity of many enterprises exposed to such takeovers.[2] According to the bill, the choice of protected sectors has been meant to include strategic companies in the field of energy and communications, contributing to the country's GDP significantly, essential for the fight against the epidemic like the medical equipment and pharmaceuticals. Concerning food production, the bill argued that even this sector is 'gaining importance' in epidemics.[3] In essence, pretty much any kind of large scale economic activity merited governmental interference in case of purported mergers (M&A) or acquisitions involving third countries investors. To give some justice to the Polish government, though, this extensive ISM scope has so far been designed as temporary measures valid for two years and expiring at the end of 2020.[4]

Nonetheless, despite such COVID-related rhetoric and temporary nature of adopted measures, the Polish government fit perfectly into a general pan-European, if not a pan-Western statist trend to subject M&A landscape to government controls, which predated the outbreak of COVID, and the high-point of which was the adoption of the Regulation 2019/452 establishing a framework for the screening of foreign direct investments into the Union.[5] The regulation's preamble noted the concerns of several Member States about impacts of specific foreign direct investment (FDI) that had led to the adoption of pretty diverging measures derogating from the free flow of capital principle.[6] However, the recognition that "[i]t should be possible for Member States to assess risks to security or public order arising from significant changes to the ownership structure or key characteristics of a foreign Investor"[7] accompanied with the will to coordinate Member State's ISMs at the EU level merely followed individual Member State's prior legislative initiatives and analogical developments elsewhere. Indeed, the OECD mapped in 2018 that the inward FDI share subjected to cross-sector security-related ISM across fifty-eight countries participating in the 'OECD-hosted dialogue on international investment policies,' increased from about twenty per cent in the early 2000s to about fifty per cent in the late 2010s.[8]

[2] *Rządowy Projekt ustawy o dopłatach do oprocentowania kredytów bankowych udzielanych na zapewnienie płynności finansowej przedsiębiorcom dotkniętym skutkami COVID-19 oraz o zmianie niektórych innych ustaw*, (22 May 2020) parliamentary printed matter 382, 38.

[3] *Rządowy* (n 2) 39–40 (22 May 2020) parliamentary printed matter 382, 38.

[4] 2020 ISM (n 1) art. 89.2.

[5] Regulation (EU) 2019/452 of the European Parliament and of the Council of 19 March 2019 establishing a framework for the screening of foreign direct investments into the Union PE/72/2018/REV/1 (21 March 2019).

OJ L 79I, pp 1–14 ('Regulation 2019/452').

[6] Regulation 2019/452 (n 5) preamble, point 4.

[7] ibid preamble, point 11.

[8] OECD, 'Current trends in investment policies related tonational security and public order (OECD, November 2018) <https://www.oecd.org/daf/inv/investment-policy/Current-trends-in-OECD-NatSec-policies.pdf>, 2nd table at p 3. *See* also generally, CD, "Acquisition-and ownership-related policies to safeguard essential security interests: New policies to manage new threats: Research

As OECD's other study mapped in detail in 2020, the general trend across analysed jurisdictions has been to cure that the landscape of ISM-like instruments has been an amalgamation of some sector-specific restrictions bans on foreign especially in defence sectors, restrictions imposed on specific assets like real estate or critical energy and telecommunication infrastructures, golden shares or golden vetoes in mostly privatised formerly wholly state-owned enterprises.[9] It could have also been mere state ownership and participation in some economies that have allowed treasuries to control foreign investment under private-law instruments rather than public-law or administrative instruments. The answer to ISM instruments disorderly scattered across the particular legal system has been to adopt more universal cross-sector laws, sometimes aligned with particular jurisdiction's competition law procedures. One could also wonder where to draw the line between sector-specific and cross-sector ISM solutions, given that cross-sector ISM solutions would apply typically to a significant portion of a particular economy, as defined by positive enumerative lists sectors but some sensitive sectors would always remain subjected to sector-specific *leges speciales*.

In Western Europe, for example, Germany set some trend in 2009 by adding a cross-sector mechanism to its Foreign Trade and Payments Ordinance (*Außenwirtschaftsverordnung*—AWV),[10] as secondary legislation to subsequent incarnations of the Foreign Trade and Payments Act (*Außenwirtschaftsgesetz*—AWG),[11] both being consolidated in 2013.[12] However, Germany arguably failed to design a universal mechanism unequivocally applicable to all economy sectors that would have left no *leges speciales* in the legal system. Specifically, the cross-sector ISM of 2009 complemented two sector-specific regimes, including (1) AWV's provisions on enterprises' acquisitions in sectors such as, among others, weaponry and tank engines manufacturing, or security and encryption software production first introduced in 2004, and (2) a separate law introducing ISM for the acquisitions of

note on current and emerging trends' (OECD, 12 March 2019) <https://www.oecd.org/investment/Current-and-emerging-trends-2019.pdf>.

[9] *See* generally, OECD, 'Acquisition-and ownership-related policies to safeguard essential security interests Current and emerging trends, observed designs, and policy practice in 62 economies: Research note by the OECD Secretariat' (OECD May 2020) <https://www.oecd.org/investment/OECD-Acquisition-ownership-policies-security-May2020.pdf>.

[10] Foreign Trade and Payments of 2 August 2013 (Federal Law Gazette I S. 2865), as last amended by art 7 seco 19 of the Act of 12 May 2021 (Federal Law Gazette I S. 990) (*Außenwirtschaftsverordnung* – AWV).

[11] Foreign Trade and Payments Act of 6 June 2013 (Federal Law Gazette I p. 1482), as last amended by art 4 of the Act of 20 July 2017 (Federal Law Gazette I p. 2789) (*Außenwirtschaftsgesetz* - AWG).

[12] As a matter of fact, the original AWG entered into force in 1961 and the AWV in 1987, and mostly regulated arms and other sensitive technology exports controls. *See* Tamotsu Aoi, 'Historical Background of Export Control Development in Selected Countries and Regions' (Mitsui & Co Ltd, April 2016) <https://www.cistec.or.jp/english/service/report/1605historical_background_export_control_development.pdf>.

enterprises with access to high-quality earth data generated in space.[13] The cross-sector mechanism has evolved since its inception, splitting into a two-tier system in July 2017 with differing rules for security-related and ordinary sectors and differing application thresholds since April 2019 with the review process kicking in investment over twenty-five per cent of equity in less sensitive sectors, and over ten per cent in more sensitive sectors.[14]

Likewise, the Austrian cross-sector mechanism first adopted in the 2011 Foreign Trade Act (*Außenwirtschaftsgesetz*)[15] was significantly scaled-down under the pressure of the European Commission in 2012, and the original application threshold of twenty-five per cent of target enterprises' equity was proposed to be reduced to ten per cent in May 2019.[16] In turn, Italy detached its controls mechanism from treasury ownership in 2012 by replacing golden share rights (previously adopted in 1994 and questioned under the EU law[17]) with two 'golden powers' mechanisms differentiating between national-security-related and other strategic sectors.[18] Portugal introduced controls of transactions covering specific critical infrastructure assets in 2014.[19] And finally, Norway adopted its modern ISM only in January 2019 to trigger in the case transactions leading to the acquisition of control or more than one-third of equity in enterprises operating in specific sectors or possessing specific strategic infrastructure assets.[20] In several Western European countries, the ISM design has been a work in progress, among others, including Sweden since October 2020[21] and Ireland since December 2019.[22] Finally, a handful of countries Western European

---

[13] The weaponry-related and IT-related ISM is regulated in AWV art 60 while the satellite imagery is regulated in *Gesetz zum Schutz vor Gefährdung der Sicherheit der Bundesrepublik Deutschlanddurch das Verbreiten von hochwertigen Erdfernerkundungsdaten (Satellitendatensicherheitsgesetz—SatDSiG)* (adopted 23 November 2007, Federal Law Gazette I 58 of 28. November 2007.

[14] OECD (n 9) paras 439–445 at 127–129.

[15] Außenwirtschaftsgesetz 2011 (AußWG 2011) StF: BGBl. I Nr. 26/2011 DAF/INV/RD(2013)3. See DAF/INV/RD(2012)6 for the notification of the initial legislation. For the unofficial translation of the AußWG 2011, *see* OECD, 'Investment Measure Relating to National Security: Notification by Austria' (3 October 2013) DAF/INV/RD(2013)3. *See* also, Frédéric Wehrlé, Joachim Pohl, 'Investment Policies Related to National Security: A Survey of Country Practices' (OECD 2016) Working Papers on International Investment 2016/02 <https://dx.doi.org/10.1787/5jlwrrf038nx-en>, 46.

[16] OECD (n 9) paras 393–396 at 115–116.

[17] Case C-326/07, *Commission of the European Communities v Italian Republic* (26 March 2009, Judgment of the Court, Third Chamber: Failure of a Member State to fulfil obligations -Articles 43 EC and 56 EC - Articles of association of privatised undertakings - Criteria for the exercise of certain special powers held by the State) [2009] ECR I-02291.

[18] *Decreto-Legge 15 marzo 2012, n. 21: Norme in materia di poteri speciali sugli assetti societari nei settori della difesa e della sicurezza nazionale, nonche' per le attivita' di rilevanza strategica nei settori dell'energia, dei trasporti e delle comunicazioni.* (12G0040); OECD (n 9) paras 458–463 at 133–135.

[19] OECD (n 9) paras 506–508 at 145–146.

[20] ibid paras 495–496 at 143.

[21] ibid paras 536–539 at 152.

[22] paras 536–539 at 152.

Countries that have so far resisted the ISM frenzy have, among others included (1) Switzerland, which has only kept very narrow sector-specific restrictions like in the banking industry,[23] (2) the Netherlands has only kept some sectoral screening mechanism in the field mining, electricity, natural, and drinking water supply, and has only planned to add communications to that list,[24] (3) Luxemburg,[25] (4) Belgium at the federal level subject to several golden share arrangements,[26]

France, Spain and Finland have had sector-specific restrictions in place for decades yet did not move towards morphing such limited ISM mechanisms into more universal all-sector solutions. France has had an ISM limited to several sectors in place since at least 1966, which it had to modify many times to patch up gaps which only became apparent on occasions of particular controversial takeovers.[27] The general trend has been to expand the protected sectors list and lower equity thresholds, which happened first from thirty-three to twenty-five per cent in January 2020, and second from twenty-five to ten per cent in April 2020 tentatively until the end of 2020 in the COVID context.[28] Finland has had ISM in place since at least 1939 as a combination of enterprises' and real estate's acquisitions screening, though real estate purchases were liberalised in 2000 to be again subjected to scrutiny in 2020.[29] Spain seems to have by far the most complicated ISM system composed of (1) real estate restrictions first introduced in 1975, (2) defence-specific screening first introduced in 1981, (3) mining permitting restrictions first introduced in 1986, (4) restrictions on acquisitions of specific assets or enterprises operating in specific sectors imposed in particular persons deemed threatening Spain's national security, (5) possible intervention of the government in mergers controls under competition law based on national defence grounds, and (6) energy-specific screening adopted in 2013.[30]

Compared with Western Europe, the EU members located in the Central and Eastern Europe (CEE) region have found themselves in a pretty schizophrenic situation in the 2010s. For three at least three decades since the fall of the Berlin Wall and Iron Curtain, have the CEE countries aspiring to participate in the European economic integration project been coerced into giving broad leeway to foreign, primarily Western European and North American investors, to start with the association agreement concluded by the EU since the early 1990s. The CEE countries were expected and ushered to open their markets to Western investment widely and on a national treatment standard. As foreign investment flowing to the CEE region mainly was Western with no Chinese or Russian investment on the horizon,

[23] ibid paras 539–542 at 153.

[24] ibid paras 487–489 at 141–142.

[25] ibid paras 454–455 at 131–132.

[26] ibid paras 397–399 at 131–132.

[27] *See* further Sect. 5.1.4 on France's problems with the EU-law compliance of some of such measures.

[28] ibid paras 435–438 at 126–128.

[29] ibid paras 431–434 at 124–125.

[30] ibid paras 533–535 at 151–152.

such attitude has usually meant scrapping initial ISM-like instruments adopted in the event of economic transformation all along, without differentiating between investors originating in allied and unallied countries. Japanese and South Korean investors, which intensified the CEE investment since the early 2000s, have also been deemed unproblematic. The problem of lax or the lack of ISM-like regulation aimed at non-EU, non-EEA, or non-US-allied countries did not emerge before the wave of Chinese takeovers, subject to that some earlier restriction might have been driven by prospects of extensive Russian investment in CEE's hydrocarbons, energy or chemical sectors. In addition, the uncompleted privatisation process across the region has allowed CEE governments to control strategic enterprises with private-law instruments. Being strategic enterprises' full or partial owners, the CEE governments could simply keep that equity and not put it for sale.

For those reasons, as the OECD mapped as of May 2020, the CEE countries which still did not have ISM-like mechanism in place included (1) Slovakia, which, however, commenced works on its ISM in late 2019,[31] (2) Slovenia, which, nonetheless, compensated it very high levels of treasury ownership,[32] (3) Bulgaria whose treasury also maintained high stakes in strategic companies and did not plan to implement the Regulation 2019/452 beyond the absolute required minimum,[33] (4) Croatia which only had restrictions on sensitive areas real estate acquisition,[34] (5) Czekia which only commenced working on its ISM in March 2019,[35] (6) Estonia which only maintained real estate acquisition restrictions on the Russian border on top of significant state ownership,[36] By May 2020, in reverse order, Hungary adopted its first cross-sector ISM only in force in January 2019, differentiating between sectors subjected to screening above ten or twenty-five per cent equity thresholds.[37] Latvia adopted its ISM in March 2017, confining it two enumeratively listed enterprises in critical sectors, in practice within the range from twenty to thirty enterprises.[38] Romania adopted its ISM-like instrument initially in 2011 by allowing national-defence-related bodies to intervene in merger controls carried out under competition law, and only added a more conventional self-standing ISM in strategic sectors in February 2020.[39] Finally, Lithuania had adopted sector-specific ISM confined to the security and defences fields as early as 1995 and added an additional asset-based screening regime in 2009, which is also ahead of the CEE region.[40]

[31] ibid para 525 at 150.

[32] ibid paras 527–528 at 150.

[33] ibid paras 402–403 at 117.

[34] ibid paras 417–419 at 121–122.

[35] ibid paras 420–421 at 122.

[36] ibid paras 428–430 at 122–123.

[37] ibid paras 447–448 at 130.

[38] ibid paras 472–473 at 139–139.

[39] ibid paras 509–512 at 145.

[40] ibid paras 474–477 at 139–140.

COVID only exacerbated the factors behind the Regulation 2019/452. The actual necessity to fend off an easy takeover in the moment of economic downturn seemed to require measures going much beyond what Regulation 2019/452 has required initially.[41] The Regulation 2019/452 had initially provided a skeleton ISM framework, in essence, aiming to secure some civility of Member State's ISMs, including their transparency, non-discrimination between third countries, protection of enterprises' trade secrets or the right to challenge Member State's ISM-related decisions before courts.[42] It has also offered some loose guidelines of what to consider while assessing threats to public security or public order. Concerning the characteristics of the companies or assets targeted by acquisitions, scrutinised shall be the acquisitions' impact on critical infrastructure,[43] critical technologies and dual-use items,[44] supply of critical inputs in the ambit of energy, raw materials, and food security, access to sensitive information including personal data, and media's freedom and pluralism.[45] Concerning the characteristics of the foreign enterprises intending acquisitions, scrutinised shall be investor's ties to thirds countries' governments and militaries or to criminal organisations and investor's past record in this regard.[46] While such provisions were pretty superfluous given the organic ISM-related developments all across Europe, the actual value of the Regulation 2019/452 has lain in the new coordination procedures. Specifically, the Regulation 2019/452 has required the Members States in control of specific acquisitions to notify other potentially affected member states via the European Commission on specific transactions while also empowering potentially affected the Member States to seek information on transactions which the Members States in control of specific acquisitions do not subject to any screening procedures.[47] Ergo, Regulation 2019/452 did not mandate screening under any circumstances and left the decisions to greenlight specific transactions within Member States' discretion. However, in the wake of the COVID outbreak, the European Commission also followed up on the Regulation 2019/452 passage with soft-law guidelines, calling the Member States with ISMs in place to make full use of those, and the Member States still lacking ISMs to pass necessary legislation as soon as possible.[48]

---

[41] *See* generally, OECD, 'Inventory of investment measures taken between 16 September 2019 and 15 October 2020' (OECD, December 2020) <https://www.oecd.org/daf/inv/investment-policy/FOI-investment-measure-monitoring-October-2020.pdf>.

[42] Regulation 2019/452 (n 5) art 3.

[43] Regulation 2019/452 (n 5) art 4.1.a *See* further, Sect. 3.3.2 on Poland's ISM-like instruments aiming to protect takeover of critical infrastructure adopted in 2010.

[44] Including artificial intelligence, robotics, semiconductors, cybersecurity, aerospace, defence, energy storage, quantum and nuclear technologies as well as nanotechnologies and biotechnologies as defined in article 2 of Council Regulation 428/2009. *See* Regulation 2019/452 (n 5) art 4.1.b; Council Regulation 428/2009 setting up a Community regime for the control of exports, transfer, brokering and transit of dual-use items (29 May 2009) OJ L 13, pp 1–26.

[45] Regulation 2019/452 (n 5) art 4.1.c-e.

[46] Regulation 2019/452 (n 5) arts 5–6.

[47] Regulation 2019/452 (n 5) art 4.2.

[48] European Commission, 'Guidance to the Member States concerning foreign direct investment and free movement of capital from third countries, and the protection of Europe's strategic assets,

The ISM-related developments in Poland have aligned both with Europe-wide and CEE-specific trends. Concerning Europe-wide trends, the 2015 ISM's bill hinted that the passage of ISM 2015 would essentially parrot the above-discussed developments in Germany and Austria.[49] Even if that was not the case in the details of the adopted solutions, directionally, Poland did not go against the tide. The subsequent passage of ISM 2020 as a response to COVID followed European Commission's recommendations strictly. Concerning CEE-specific trends, Poland had its early designs for strict ISMs dismantled throughout the 1990s by the EU-integration requirements similar to other countries of the region. Any attempts in the 2010s to restore any limited ISM in Poland under the single market regime were torpedoed by the European Commission. Leading Western European economies had to send some legislative trends first, which the CEE countries could only follow. Meanwhile, inward FDI onto the Polish economy should have been at the forefront of the EU-wide ISM-related debate. Being Europe's third-largest industrial powerhouse after Germany and Italy and excluding Russia,[50] Poland has long surpassed France and United Kingdom in terms of the aggregate manufacturing workforce, benefitting from the pivotal geoeconomic situation in Europe and gradually moving up the production and value chains. Assembly plants opened by mostly Western investors since the early 1990s have gradually been assigned with increasingly tech-intensive production tasks and even research and development works. The landscape of the investors has gradually turned towards greater diversity in terms of their origins, including grassroots domestic high-tech start-ups up for grabs. Out of the world's most preferred destinations for greenfield investment or utmost brownfield transactions involving inefficient post-communist plants requiring substantial modernisation and expenditures, Poland has gradually turn into a jurisdiction hosting existing enterprises attracting acquisitions. Moreover, geopolitically, out of Germany industrial hinterland realising the Mitteleuropa agenda, Poland—sitting on the crossing of new landmass trade routes—has turned into a playground of several competing geoeconomic projects, including Intermarium as Poland's homegrown geoeconomic agenda, Three Seas Initiative (Trimarium) backed up Anglo-Saxons and Group 16 + 1 backed up by China.[51]

---

ahead of the application of Regulation (EU) 2019/452 (FDI Screening Regulation)' (25 March 2020) C(2020) 1981 final, at 2.

[49] *Poselski Projekt Ustawy o kontroli niektórych inwestycji* (19 March 2015) parliamentary printed matter no 3454, 17–18.

[50] Excluding Russia whose magnitude of actual industrial base has, perhaps except for the short period of the 1990s' economic downturn, outsized even the German economy – which many often miss because of the Russian assets' and economic activity's underappreciation in international statistics cause by Russia's and Eurasian Economic Union's strong insulation from the world trade and price-discovery mechanism.

[51] *See* generally, Jędrzej Górski, 'Central and Eastern Europe, Group 16 + 1 and One Belt One Road: The Case of 2016 Sino-Polish Comprehensive Strategic Partnership' in Julien Chaisse, Jędrzej Górski (eds), The Belt and Road Initiative Law, Economics, and Politics 557–604, Jędrzej Górski, 'China's Strategy Toward Central and Eastern Europe Within the Framework of 16 + 1 Group: The Case of Poland' in Wenxian Zhang, Alon Ilan,, Christoph Lattemann (eds) China's Belt and Road Initiative Changing the Rules of Globalization (Palgrave MacMillan 2018) 115–134.

This chapter aims to present the evolution of Poland's various ISM or ISM-like cross-sector and sector-specific instruments over the last four decades. The historical background offered in Sect. 2 starts with a discussion of the first attempts to regulate FDI adopted yet before a political decision on Poland's economic transformation (Sect. 2.1), including the first fragmentary regulation of small-scale FDI of 1982 (Sect. 2.1.1), and more complex Foreign Companies Act (Sect. 2.1.1). Section 2.2 continues this historical overview by revealing behind the scenes of reaching an agreement between the Polish socialist government and American industrialists in on letting foreign investors in. And Sect. 2.3 closes the historical part by discussing ISMs crafted randomly liberalised economy, including the 1988 Foreign Companies Act (Sect. 2.3.1), 1991 Foreign Companies Act (Sect. 2.3.2) and the impact of the 1991 Europe Agreement between Poland and European Communities (Sect. 2.3.3). Section 3 moves from a historical perspective onto elaborating on special or sector-specific ISM-like instruments, including restrictions imposed on purchases of real estate by foreigners (Sect. 3.1), permitting process in special economic zones as foreign investors' preferred solution for greenfield industrial projects (Sect. 3.2), and a shift from treasury's golden share approach first adopted in 2005 (Sect. 3.3.1) to treasury's golden veto in companies controlling critical infrastructure assets adopted superseding the golden share instruments in 2010 under the pressure of the European Commission (Sect. 3.3.2).

Subsequently, Sects. 4 and 5 explain more recent ISM-related developments since 2015, which have been aligned with global and European trends briefly mentioned above. Section 4 presents an ISM-like prequalification procedure under mining law screening third countries investors interested in hydrocarbon's prospection or exploration. Section 5.1 sheds light on the return to the list of several protected enterprises in the 2015 ISM akin to 2005 golden share instruments but detached from treasury's equity in such enterprises, while Sect. 5.2 discusses COVID-driven dramatic expansion of that mechanism to multiple sectors of the economy. Section 6 concludes.

The analysis of the Polish regulatory environment offered in this chapter leaves other sectors that slip some ISM-like mechanism by directly or indirectly differentiating between domestic and foreign investors, including banking, aviation, transportation, gambling, pension funds, insurance, and investment funds. Neither does this chapter seek to compare and address intersections between Poland's various ISM-like mechanisms with mergers controls under the EU's competition law, which would per se be suitable for a stand-alone paper.

2 Historical Regulation 1982–2000

Poland had experienced over a decade of strict foreign investment regulation and centralised control akin to modern ISM solutions during the most turbulent phase of its transition from planned to the market economy throughout the late 1980s and whole 1990s. Concerning micro, and small and medium enterprises (SMEs) particularly, Poland's domestic economy experienced a rather radical transformation overnight. However, all cross-border economic activity remained regulated heavily for much longer, including permitting of all exports, imports and inward FDI. Such new regulations were officially necessitated by public policies to stabilise the balance of trade and payments and shield domestic industries from excessive international competition. Nonetheless, this category of economic activities had traditionally fallen in the grip of special government forces, including both military and civil intelligence units. Therefore such regulations have always been associated in public perception with *Nomenklatura's* attempts to grab previously state-owned assets in the obscure process of deregulation, restructuring and foremost privatisation. In essence, economic activities involving cross-border trade and interactions with western investors flooding Poland's gates were deemed most lucrative.

2.1 First Provisions on Foreign Entrepreneurs

2.1.1 1982 Act

The first imperfect and minimal provisions recognising and regulating economic activity with some foreign element were passed yet when the 1981 Polish Martial Law was in force. The stated purpose of the 1982 Act on small-scale economy activity by foreign natural persons and entities (the '1982 Act')[52] was to support foreign entities and natural persons, especially of Polish descent, in supplying goods and services both to the country's domestic market and for exports.[53] To this end, the 1982 Act's subjective coverage included 'foreign economic subjects' defined as legal entities and natural persons residing or registered abroad plus foreign citizens with permanent residency in Poland.[54] Such foreign economic subjects could operate in two legal forms. Firstly, they could establish 'foreign enterprises' covered in a special newly established register gathering natural persons and legal entities.[55] Secondly, together with domestic economic subjects, they could establish 'enterprises with foreign participation' in the form of private-law law companies registered under the 1934 Company Code,[56] which remained in force in post-WW2 socialist Poland.[57] The authorisations for such joint ventures could be conditional

---

[52] *Ustawa z dnia 6 lipca 1982 r. o zasadach prowadzenia na terytorium Polskiej Rzeczypospolitej Ludowej działalności gospodarczej w zakresie drobnej wytwórczości przez zagraniczne osoby prawne i fizyczne,* Polish Official Journal (1982) no 19 item 146 ('1982 Act').

[53] 1982 Act (n 51) Preamble.

[54] ibid art 1.1.

[55] ibid art 1.1, art 5.2.

[56] *Rozporządzenie Prezydenta Rzeczypospolitej z dnia 27 czerwca 1934 r. – Kodeks handlowy,* Polish Official Journal (1934) no 57 item 502.

[57] 1982 Act (n 51) art 1.2, art 5.3.

upon domestic economic subjects controlling the majority stakes.[58] The incoherence of that framework laid in that 'enterprises with foreign participation' gained full and separate legal capacity under company law while 'foreign enterprises' did not. The latter could perhaps be best described in modern terms as local branches of foreign enterprises. Regardless of which option was chosen, both types of enterprises could only engage in a 'small-scale' supply of goods and services either for the domestic market or exports. However, they could only engage in imports of goods and services as their inputs rather than for resale in the domestic market.[59]

Procedurally, the authorisations were granted either by regional administration at the regional level or by the foreign trade minister—the latter in case of enterprises engaging in any export–import activities.[60] Any administrative decisions issued under the 1982 Act (authorisations, refusals, amendments, cancellations, etc.) could be challenged before administrative courts.[61] Ergo, foreign economic subjects could only appeal against breaches of the law rather than ask to have the discretionary elements of those decisions reviewed by some other administrative body. And the discretion of either regional administration or foreign trade minister was, indeed, unlimited given that the 1982 Act did not offer any indicative conditions in favour or against authorisations' grants.

The 1985 amendment of the 1982 Act cured several of its flaws. The definition of foreign economic subjects was fine-tuned to include, more precisely, legal entities registered abroad, foreign citizens regardless of residence, Polish citizens residing abroad, as well as companies registered in Poland and owned exclusively by such persons. In line with that, the definition of 'foreign enterprises' was also expanded to include such domestically registered and wholly foreign-owned companies. As a result, foreign economic subjects did not have to enter into joint ventures with domestic economic subjects to establish entities with full and separate legal capacity. Moreover, some negative conditions of authorisations' grants missing in the original 1982 Act entirely were added, including public and national economy's interests, state's security and state secrets protection. Also, the right of appeal to administrative courts was excluded in the case of refusal based on state security and secrets considerations, and any pending appeals were dismissed by virtue of law.[62]

Strikingly, the 1982 Act was not formally repealed until 2018, even though it overlapped with several subsequent acts and became superfluous in the Polish legal system. Being a kind of *lex specialis* for the small-scale economic activity, it formally remained in force but did not have practical application after the enactment of a series of better-thought-out statutes adopted in late the 1980s to accommodate foreign economic activity of any scale.

---

[58] ibid art 14.

[59] ibid art 2.

[60] ibid art 7.

[61] ibid art 18.

[62] Polish Official Journal (1985) no 3 item 12.

2.1.2 1986 FCA

Similar to the 1982 Act, the first *lex generalis* addressing foreign investment controls in Poland was also imperfect and lacked sufficiently detailed provisions. The 1986 Foreign Companies Act (the '1986 FCA')[63] left out foreign natural persons interested in operating in Poland as sole proprietorships or partnerships. It only covered investment in Poland-registered joint-stock companies and private limited liability companies[64]—a limitation that has lingered on in the Polish legal system ever since. Foreign subjects defined as companies registered abroad, foreign citizens, Polish citizens residing abroad or their partnerships registered abroad[65] could not establish partnerships or local branches without separate legal capacity in Poland.

The 1986 FCA was very restrictive and vested discretionary solid powers with the foreign trade ministry in charge of all authorisation under this act. Namely, the 1986 FCA set forth by default that the Polish shareholders (i.e. excluding non-resident Polish citizens) ought to have at least fifty-one per cent of equity in such companies, but the foreign trade minister could waive such requirement.[66] The same applied to the default stator ban of foreign participation in companies engaged in the defence industry, railway and air transport, communications, insurance, publishing except for printing and cross-border merchandising. The ban could be waived discretionally.[67]

2.2 *New Opening*

The framework of Poland's economic transformation in the early 1990s is usually associated with so-called shock therapy administered by Leszek Balcerowicz, the former finance minister, vice prime minister, and central bank president, who was ushered by Geoffrey Sachs accompanied by cohorts of Western economists and advisors. However, the understanding between Polish leadership and collective West on embarking upon the transformation process had arguably been reached at the level yet in 1985 on the sidelines of the United Nations (UN) general assembly. As *New York Times* reported succinctly, Zbigniew Brzeziński and Lawrence S. Eagleburger arranged a meeting between David Rockefeller and General Wojciech Jaruzelski, who stopped over for several days in New York on his way back to Poland from a state visit to Cuba.[68] Active US government officials were bypassed arguably because of tense diplomatic relations between two countries in the wake of the 1981

[63] *Ustawa z dnia 23 kwietnia 1986 r. o spółkach z udziałem zagranicznym,* Polish Official Journal (1986) no 17 item 88 ('1986 FCA').

[64] 1986 FCA (n 62) art 2.1.

[65] ibid art 3.1.

[66] ibid art 8.

[67] ibid art 7.

[68] Elaine Sciolino, 'Polish Chief is Caught up in the Whirl' *The New York Times* (26 September 1985) retrieved from Factiva.

Polish Martial Law and resulting US economic sanctions imposed on Poland. The lunch at the Rockefeller Centre allegedly primarily covered Poland's prospective agriculture industry reform and 'agricultural exports' which is congruent with *New York Times*'s mentioning of Jaruzelski's meetings with Seagram's Edgar Bronfman and some 'distillers.'[69] Brzezinski's notes published in *Polityka* in 2009 offered more insights into the nature of those negotiations that also involved on the Polish side, among others the foreign Stefan Olszewski, and the former foreign minister Józef Czyrek.[70] Brzeziński revealed the details of discussions on imports of western farming machinery and establishing a Poland-based agriculture-related foundation to be funded by the Rockefeller Foundation and Rockefeller Brothers Fund, which materialised in 1988.[71] However, he omitted and did not release text which clearly must have covered the discussions about concessions made by the Polish government in exchange for waiving US economic sanctions.[72]

With political reform looming on the horizon, the 1988 Act on Economic Activity, effective 1 January 1989[73] and commonly known as the 'Wilczek Act' (after Mieczysław Wilczek, the then minister of industry in the cabinet of prime minister Mieczycław Rakowski),[74] marked the end of the centrally planned economy, changing Polish entrepreneurs' life.[75] The Wilczek Act on Economic Activity generally deregulated economic activities which could be conducted without authorisation, except for mining (prospection, exploration and exploitation), tooling and sales of gemstones and precious metals, production and sales of munitions, production and sales of pharmaceuticals and sanitary equipment, production of spirits or tobacco, sea transport, air transport, running pharmacies, and security services.[76] *Wall Street Journal* from 19 July 1989 noted on Mr Wilczek that "[a]s a Communist, it soon became clear, Mr Wilczek has something in common with many of Poland's Roman Catholics: He may belong, but he doesn't believe. "There haven't been Communists in Poland for a long time," he says. "Nobody wants to hear about Marx and Lenin anymore." Mr Wilczek comes out foursquare for private ownership and dead set

---

[69] ibid.

[70] Zbigniew Brzeziński, 'Osobiste i poufne' *Polityka* (2 May 2009) <https://www.polityka.pl/archiwumpolityki/1911540,1,osobiste-i-poufne.read>.

[71] This entity (*Fundacja na rzecz Rozwoju Polskiego Rolnictwa*) exists until today and is registered under KRS number 000014383.

[72] Brzeziński (n 69).

[73] *Ustawa z dnia 23 grudnia 1988 r. o działalności gospodarczej*, Polish Official Journal (1988) no. 41 item 324 (Wilczek Act).

[74] "Chosen to head the Industry Ministry was Mieczyslaw Wilczek, a 56-year-old Communist Party member who left a lucrative job in state industry to found a successful animal-feeds company that employs 60 people. He is also part owner of an enterprise that buys rabbit skins for use in apparel." *See* John Tagliabue, 'Poland Names New Officials to Bolster Economy' *New York Times* (14 October 1988) 7.

[75] Oskar Kowalewski, and Krzysztof Rybiński, 'The hidden transformation: the changing role of the state after the collapse of communism in Central and Eastern Europe' (2011) 27(4) Oxford Review of Economic Policy 634, 637.

[76] Wilczek Act (n 72), art 11.

against unions. Among 19th-century thinkers, he would seem to lean more toward Carnegie and Gould."[77]

As mentioned, such liberalisation proved elusive for those involved and planning to get involved in cross-border business activities. The Wilczek Act failed to liberalise cross-border trade, allowed to introduce a secondary-legislation obligation to receive permits for foreign trade in virtually all goods,[78] which was introduced indeed. The original executive regulation required authorisations for trading, among others, explosives various types of meat, grain, corn, grain of leguminous vegetables, rice, cattle, flock, other slaughter animals (sheep, goat, horses, donkeys), coal, briquettes, fuels, energy, steel products, nonferrous-metal-products, lumber, timber prefabricates, stationery, fabrics and clothes (with some exceptions), meat cans, cold cuts, furs, slaughtered and slaughter poultry, frozen fruits, eggs, butter, powdered milk, cheese, spirits, strawberry raspberry jams etc.[79] This list was gradually reduced throughout the 1990s. The last list from January 2000 included only explosives, detonation fuses, arms (sports, hunting, non-lethal/neutralising along with accessories), cigars, fuels, natural gas and some parts of farming/forestry tractors.[80]

2.3 *Inward FDIs Controls 1988–2000*

2.3.1 1988 Foreign Companies Act

The gradual liberalisation of imports and exports controls came in tandem with gradual liberalisation of inward FDIs controls first passed in 1988 in a package with the Wilczek Act. Similar to the 1986 FCA, the 1988 Act on Economic Activity with the participation of foreigners (the '1988 Foreign Companies Act or '1988 FCA'[81]) laid down the conditions of investing in Poland by 'foreign persons,' defined as (1) natural persons residing abroad, (2) companies headquartered abroad, and (3) partnerships of such natural persons and companies.[82] The first oddity of such FCA's subjective coverage consisted in that Polish citizens residing abroad still could be subjected to inward FDI restrictions in Poland, just like under the 1982 Act and the 1986 FCA. The second lacuna consisted in that the FCA failed to address the notion of companies' control, implying that foreign-registered companies could have been subjected to inward FDI restrictions in Poland even if wholly owned by Polish

[77] Barry Newman, 'The Privatizer: Polish Entrepreneur, Now Industry Minister, Takes a Capitalist Line -- Mieczyslaw Wilczek, Known As the 'Polish Iacocca,' Thrives in Era of Reform -- Giving Shares to Apparatchiks' *Wall Street Journal* (19 July 1989) 1.

[78] Wilczek Act (n 72), art 11.9.

[79] Polish Official Journal (1988) no 44 item 355.

[80] Polish Official Journal (2000) no.8 item 109.

[81] *Ustawa z dnia 23 grudnia 1988 r. o działalności gospodarczej z udziałem podmiotów zagranicznych,* Polish Official Journal (1988) no. 41 item. 325 (1988 FCA).

[82] 1998 FCA (n 80) art 3.2.

citizens, whether residing outside of the country or not. The third peculiarity consisted in that the foreigners operating abroad in the form of partnerships could invest in Poland. Still, the legal form of Polish subsidiaries must have always been a joint-stock company or a private limited liability company.[83] Finally, the FCA remained tacit to classify various configurations involving partnerships involving both foreign and non-foreign persons as defined in the FCA.

Nonetheless, the most striking requirement was the requirement, not included in the 1986 Act, that foreign persons could hold a share of not less than twenty per cent of capital in such companies.[84] On the other hand, authorisations could also be conditional upon a specific maximum share in equity owned by foreign persons,[85] meaning that such persons' ownership could range from twenty to one hundred per cent depending on the pretty discretionary administrative decision. Still, the most significant liberalising factor compared with the 1986 Act laid in that the default requirement of fifty-one per cent in equity for domestic shareholders was not included in the 1988 FCA.

The twenty per cent threshold *prima facie* also indicated that the 1988 FCA was intended to cover privately negotiated transactions and could barely be applied to publicly traded companies, diluted ownership and dispersed foreign investment in small packages of securities. After all, no equities were traded at the Warsaw Stock Exchange until April 1991. However, the detailed provisions of the 1998 FCA act allowed for special authorisation for foreign subscriptions to in Polish public offerings and determining a maximum share of specific publicly trade joint-stock company capital's that can be subscribed to by foreign persons.[86] Moreover, in the case of privately held companies, additional authorisations were required for any subsequent amendments to articles of association (AoA) and companies' objects, as well as subsequent equity transfers.[87] In contrast, in the case of publicly offered companies, changes to AoA and objects still required authorisations but subsequent equity transfers within the total cap for foreign ownership did not.[88]

Procedurally, the authorisations under the 1988 FCA were granted by the newly established Foreign Investment Agency (*Agencja do Spraw Inwestycji Zagranicznych*) instead of the foreign trade minister under the 1986 FCA. The 1998 FCA offered very vague criteria of when to grant investment authorisation, such as that foreign investments ought to contribute to (1) the implementation of innovative technological or organisational solutions to the national economy, (2) exports of goods and services, (3) improvement of the supply of domestic market in modern and high-quality goods and services, and (4) environment protection.[89] Should specific

[83] ibid art 2.1.

[84] ibid.

[85] ibid article 8.1.

[86] ibid art 8.2.

[87] ibid art 5.3.

[88] ibid art 8.2.

[89] ibid art 5.2.

economic activity by foreign persons also require industry/sector-specific authorisations, the authorities responsible for those ought to coordinate their proceeding with the Foreign Investment Agency.[90] On the other hand, the agency had to refuse an authorisation in the case of foreign investment endangering the country's economic interests, environments, or state's security, defence and secrets. Refusals did not have to be reasoned and could not be challenged in any appeal procedure.[91]

2.3.2 1991 Foreign Companies Act 1991

Strict 1988 FCA was soon replaced with a much more liberal 1991 Act on Companies with Foreign Participation (the '1991 Foreign Companies Act' or '1991 FCA'),[92] which still covered the same group of ill-defined 'foreign persons.'[93] The only improvement in 1991 FCA's subjective coverage consisted of clarifying that investment in other companies by Poland-based companies controlled by foreign persons should also require authorisations.[94] While a minimum twenty-per cent-equity-stake requirement was dropped, the choice between joint-stock and limited liability companies remained in place.[95]

The substantial liberalisation consisted in limiting 1991 FCA's objective coverage to expressly listed sectors compared to 1991 FCA, which covered any activity by foreign persons. Namely, foreign persons were obliged to obtain authorisations to establish or equity purchase in companies involved in (1) management of seaports or airports, (2) real estate brokerage, (3) non-licenced military-related industry, and (4) providing legal advice.[96] In addition, they also needed double authorisations for activities requiring authorisation for all persons regardless of their citizenship or place of registration.[97] It would have been reasonable for two proceedings, like under the 1988 FCA, to be coordinated by authorities in charge of foreign investment on the one side and in charge of a specific regulated sector on the other side. However, the 1991 FCA mandated foreign persons to obtain specific regulated-sector approvals before applying for consent under the FCA.[98]

---

[90] ibid art 8.7.

[91] ibid art 8.5.

[92] *Ustawa z dnia 14 czerwca 1991 r. o spółkach z udziałem zagranicznym* Polish Official Journal (1991) no. item 253 (1991 FCA).

[93] 1991 FCA (n 91) art 3.

[94] ibid art 7.

[95] ibid art 1.2.

[96] ibid art 4.1.

[97] ibid art 6.1.

[98] ibid art 5.

The 1991 FC Act expired on 1 January 2001. After, foreign investors could set up business in Poland pretty much unconstrained and without having to apply for authorisations. The complex 1999 Act on the Freedom of Economic Activity ('SDG')[99] fixed several flaws of previous legislation discussed above. Regarding foreign citizens with permanent residency in Poland, the SDG fully equated the right of such persons to carry out economic activity with citizens.[100] Regarding the participation of foreign persons in business organisations, the SGG differentiated between foreign persons originating from countries that offer full freedom of economic activity on a reciprocal basis and countries which do not. In the latter case, the available forms of business organisations were limited not only to joint-stock and limited liability companies but also to limited partnerships.[101] In the former case, foreigners could, on a reciprocal basis, organise their business as other available vehicles such as registered and non-registered partnerships, sole proprietorships, or invest in assets directly[102] (like by purchasing lettable estates and outsourcing management to local sub-contractors without establishing any entity in Poland). Tied with that was SDG's specific provision for foreign enterprises' branches, which could be only established in Poland on condition of reciprocity.[103]

The repeal of the 1991 FCA by the FCA ended the era of the old transitional ISM and authorisations system, as the SGD did not vest an authority to block foreign investment in any public agency. Naturally, numerous industry-specific authorisations systems in the sensitive and highly regulated sectors or competition law could be employed profusely to achieve similar results, prevent specific foreign investments, and indirectly put foreign investors at some disadvantage.[104] However, all directly discriminatory provisions restricting foreign capital were removed at the time.

2.3.3 1991 Europe Agreement

It must also be mentioned that even pretty limited ISM under 1991 FCA could de facto have gradually dismantled under the 1991 Association Agreement between the European Communities and their Member States, of the one part, and the Republic of Poland, of the other part (the '1991 Europe Agreement') effective I January 1992.[105] The Europe Agreement laid down the foundation for prospective full integration of

---

[99] *Ustawa z dnia 19 listopada 1999 r. Prawo działalności gospodarczej,* Polish Official Journal (1999) no 101 item 1178 ('SDG').

[100] SDG (n 98) art 6.1.

[101] ibid 6.3.

[102] ibid 6.2.

[103] ibid 35.

[104] *See* generally e.g., Alexandr Svetlicinii, *Chinese state owned enterprises and EU merger control* (Routledge 2021).

[105] Europe Agreement establishing an association between the European Communities and their Member States, of the one part, and the Republic of Poland, of the other part (done 16 October 1991) (the '1991 Europe Agreement').

Poland's economy into European Communities' single market within a total transition period of ten years.[106] The repeal of the 1991 FCA on 1 January 2001 happened just a year ahead of the expiry of the transitional period under the 1991 Europe Agreement on 1 February 2002.

Concerning inward FDIs, the 1991 Europe Agreement has required that the Polish side shall—subject to transitional periods—grant (1) "for the establishment of Community companies and nationals as defined in Article 48 [[107]] a treatment no less favourable than that accorded to its own nationals and companies,"[108] and (2) "from entry into force of this Agreement, in the operation of Community companies and nationals established in Poland a treatment no less favourable than that accorded to its own companies and nationals."[109] No transitional period applied to 'processing industry' and construction services.[110] National treatment was to gradually granted by the end of the transitional period in (1) "mining, processing of metals and precious stones, production of explosives, ammunition and weapons, pharmaceutical industry, production of toxic substances, production of distilled alcohols,"[111] (2) services, "except for [...] real estate and natural resources transaction services and brokerage;—legal services, not including legal advice on commercial matters and international law,"[112] 3) financial services,[113] (4) acquisition of state property in the privatisation process,[114] (5) ownership, use, sale and rental of real estate,[115] (6) transaction operations and brokerage in real estate and natural resources trading, (7) high-voltage transmission lines,[116] and (8) pipeline transport.[117] The liberalisation

[106] 1991 Europe Agreement (n 104) art. 6.

[107] Treaty Establishing the European Community (Consolidated Version): "Article 48 (ex Article 58) Companies or firms formed in accordance with the law of a Member State and having their registered office, central administration or principal place of business within the Community shall, for the purposes of this Chapter, be treated in the same way as natural persons who are nationals of Member States". "Companies or firms' means companies or firms constituted under civil or commercial law, including cooperative societies, and other legal persons governed by public or private law, save for those which are non profit making".

[108] Europe Agreement (n 104) art. 44.1.i.

[109] ibid art 44.1.ii.

[110] Processing industry "including fuel and energy industry, metallurgical industry, electromechanical industry, transport means industry, chemical industry, building materials industry, wood and paper industry, textile, leather and clothing industry, food processing industry; excluding mining, processing metals and precious stones, production of explosives, ammunition and armaments, pharmaceutical industry, production of toxic substances, production of distilled alcohol, high voltage transmission lines, pipeline transport." *See* Europe Agreement (n 104) art. 44.1.i first *tiret*, Annex XIIa.

[111] Europe Agreement (n 104) art. 44.1.i second *tiret*, Annex XII b.

[112] ibid.

[113] ibid art. 44.1.i third *tiret*, Annex XIIc.

[114] ibid art. 44.1.i third *tiret*, Annex XIId.

[115] ibid.

[116] ibid.

[117] ibid.

under the Europe Agreement covered neither (1) the acquisition and sale of natural resources nor (2) the acquisition and sale of agricultural land and forests.[118]

A detailed comparison of sectors covered by the 1991 FCA with the permissible transitional periods under the 1991 Europe Agreement would go much beyond the scope of this chapter. However, it is safe to say that the ISM scope under the 1991 FCA was narrower than what was permitted under the 1991 Europe Agreement. Furthermore, at no point did Poland violate the latter's provisions regarding national treatment for foreign investors originating in the EU.[119]

3 Special Regimes

Despite significant liberalisation of FDI and virtually relinquishing the old transitional ISM system, foreign enterprises could also be screened and de facto blocked from making investments under other mechanisms. Needless to say, all permitting procedures, concessions, and other governmental approvals might, in theory, encumber domestic and foreign enterprises equally. However, in practice, all such discretionary administrative proceedings involving foreigners could always attract much more scrutiny from public officials, which could have amounted to a kind of indirect discrimination against foreigners. Much more straightforward ISM-like rules directly targeting foreigners have been embodied in the provisions on (1) the purchases of real property by foreigners, (2) SEZs, and (3) the treasury's golden shares or vetoes in the strategic companies.

Firstly, real property purchases screening and controls used to discriminate directly against all foreigners, to gradually discriminate directly only against foreigners from outside of the European Economic Area (EEA) and Switzerland (*see* Sect. 3.1). Those rules have kicked in the case of pretty much any greenfield or brownfield industrial investment seeing that freehold (and post-communist perpetual usufruct gradually converted to freehold all over the country) has been the most common and preferred title to the property in Poland, whether that be commercial or residential property. Land and building leases for industrial sites, other than leases by banks for tax purposes, have been uncommon. Secondly, nearly all greenfield foreign industrial investments were situated in SEZs to benefit from very generous fiscal breaks, meaning that nearly all such investments were subjected to the SEZ-specific ISM (*see* Sect. 3.2). Thirdly, treasury's golden share in strategic companies introduced in 2005 and revamped as special veto detached from treasury's equity in 2010 could prevent foreign takeovers of specific companies, with a lot of initial

[118] ibid art. 44.6, Annex XIIe.

[119] All the more that the Polish legislators have always very meticulously implemented EU acquis, and that the 1991 FCA did not contain any Europe-Agreement safety clause (stipulating just in case that the EU Agreement supersedes the 1991 FCA) - hinting that in Polish legislators' view, there been no discrepancies between two acts.

controversies concerning the extent to which golden shares could be exercised against non-EEA investors and against non-Polish EEA investors (*see* Sect. 3.3).

3.1 Real Estate Purchases

Foreign investment in real Polish real estate, either directly or indirectly via Poland-registered companies, has constantly been subjected to a separate strict regulation, especially in the case of agricultural land and forests. And it has always been left to the discretionary dictions of the central agencies—most often of the Ministry of the Interior consulting ministries in charge of defence, agriculture and environment. The repeal of the 1991 FCA by the SDG did not imply any loosening of real-estate-specific rules. Those were significantly tempered only after Poland acceded to the EU in 2004, granting national treatment in this regard to about half a billion people from the EEA and Switzerland—at which point remaining restrictions for third countries ceased to make much sense. The 1920 Act on Acquiring Real Easter by Foreigners ('AREFA')[120] is Poland's longest primary legislation remaining in force. The AREFA has been amended twenty-five times since its inception, and going over all subsequent changes would go beyond the scope of this chapter. It is, nonetheless, worth looking at several consolidated versions of the AREFA to grasp how a kind of real-estate-specific ISM has evolved in Poland.

For example, AREFA's consolidated version of 1996[121] defined foreigners as non-citizens, legal entities registered abroad, and domestic legal entities controlled directly or indirectly by non-citizens or legal entities registered abroad (at least fifty per cent of equity).[122] This implies that, unlike in the case of the 1982 Act, the 1986 FCA, the 1988 FCA and the 1991 FCA, Polish citizens permanently residing abroad were not subjected to the real-estate-specific permitting regime. Non-citizens or business entities controlled by non-citizens had to obtain permits for the purchases of freehold titles or perpetual usufruct of virtually all kinds of real estate (or equity in entities owning such real estate) except for apartments in condominiums, non-citizens with at least five years of permanent residency, spouse of citizens with at least two years of permanent residency, statutory heirs entitled to a specific property, legal entities purchasing up to 0.4 hectare of undeveloped land in cities to carry out their statutory activities.[123]

The release of the AREFA's consolidated version of 2004[124] coincided with Poland's accession to the EU. Minor non-EU-related changes consisted that small ancillary premises like garages and foreign-controlled bank foreclosures were added

---

[120] *Ustawa z dnia 24 marca 1920 r. o nabywaniu nieruchomości przez cudzoziemców*, Polish Official Journal (1920) no 31 item 178 ('AREFA').

[121] Polish Official Journal (1996) no 54 item 245 ('1996 AREFA').

[122] 1996 AREFA (n 119) art 2.

[123] ibid art 8.

[124] Polish Official Journal (2004) no 167 item 1758 ('2004 AREFA').

to the exemption list, while the area of land deemed sufficient for one foreigners' private needs (i.e. not applicable to commercial or agricultural activities) was capped at 0.5 hectares.[125] The transitional periods agreed with the EU delayed the national treatment for EEA citizens in case of agricultural land and so-called second homes. Regarding agricultural land, transitional periods lasted three, seven or twelve years from the accession, depending on the region.[126] Regarding second homes, the transitional period lasted for five years. Still, it did not apply to persons living in Poland for at least four years or purchasing second homes as a commercial lettable property in the tourism industry.[127] Thus, the AREFA has not changed significantly since 2004, except that all transitional periods have expired by now.

It is noteworthy that, just like establishing foreign companies controls under the 1991 FCA, the real estate purchases liberalisation was also propelled by the 1991 Europe Agreement. The 1991 Europe agreement differentiated between (1) 'Community companies established in the territory of Poland,' (2) 'agencies established in Poland of Community companies,' and (3) 'Community nationals established as self-employed persons in Poland.' Community companies were to, "from entry into force of this Agreement, the right to acquire, use, rent and sell real property, and as regards natural resources, agricultural and forestry, [and] the right to lease, where these are directly necessary for the conduct of the economic activities for which they are established."[128] Branches of community companies were to acquire analogical rights five years later (at the end of the transitional period's stage one, expiring on 1 January 1997) while community self-employed natural persons were to acquire analogical rights ten years later (at the end of the transitional period's stage two, expiring on 1 January 2002).[129]

One could get an impression from such a brief screening of the AREFA's evolution that this statute—unlike the 1991 Europe Agreement—has been addressed to natural persons primary, instead of large foreign investors needing commercial property for manufacturing, logistics, wholesale, office spaces or hospitality—in which case, why to discuss permitting under the AREFA in the ISM context at all. However, the AREFA has indeed covered all commercial property, and foreign investors had to undergo the permitting process even if the authorisations were rubber-stamped, seeing that FDIs were generally welcome—subject to investment gradually liberated under the 1991 Europe Agreement, which did not even need rubber-stamping. AREFA's apparent focus on natural persons investing in apartments, second homes, and foremost agricultural land was simply the more sensitive politically, to the extent that transitional periods of the purchases of agricultural land became one of the central points of the public debate preceding Poland's accession referendum. Large-scale investment in most lucrative commercial properties by, e.g. foreign investment funds, has always fallen under public opinion's radar.

[125] 2004 AREFA (n 122) art 1a.5, art 8.1a and 8.7.

[126] ibid art 8.2a.1.

[127] ibid art 8.2a.2.

[128] Europe Agreement (n 104) art 44.7.

[129] ibid.

Moreover, while real estate permitting in principle has added to the investment-approval complexity in Poland, several *lacunas* have allowed foreign investors to get around this regime. Firstly, registered partnerships and limited partnerships with at least one Polish partner could be used. However, such entities, on the whole, could not be classified as foreigners under AREFA in the lack of any clear rules on how to establish the notion of control in partnerships. Secondly, Poland's accession to the EU de facto liberalised real estate purchases for investors not only from the EEA but also from all third countries. Specifically, all EEA companies have enjoyed national treatment in this regard regardless of whether their controlling shareholders originated in the EEA or third countries. In other words, it has sufficed for non-EEA persons to register a commercial company in any EEA country to be exempt from the AREFA. Moreover, in order to avoid reverse-discrimination of companies registered by non-EEA persons in Poland compared with companies registered by non-EEA persons in other EEA member states, the AREFA has been construed to exempt real estate purchases by such companies.

3.2 Special Economic Zones (SEZ)

A parallel system involving some ISM elements has existed in Polish SEZs ever since their inception in 1994.[130] The general idea was to zone land for industrial parks, in which economic activity by both foreign and domestic investors would enjoy some preferences. For each new SEZ, the Councils of the Ministers' had to (1) secure local governments' consents, (2) determine a particular SEZ's boundaries, lifetime, industrial profile, scope of preferences, among other things, and (3) establish an SEZ authority in the form of either joint-stock company or limited liability company.[131] Land plots zoned for SEZ, in principle, had to be owned by a particular SEZ's authority, state treasury, local councils or their associations, and private land could only be included in SEZ upon their owners' consent.[132]

As such, SEZs were meant to host mostly new greenfield investment, seeing that SEZs authorities, coordinating with central government and local councils, in principle designated 'sub-zones' of contiguous undeveloped investment plots in medium-sized town's suburbs, hoping to attract new investment in underdeveloped areas. Unlike outside of the SEZs, where the repeal of the 1991 FCA in 2001 ended the old ISM, the SEZ-specific kind of ISM will continue to exist until the final closure of SEZs at the end of 2026. SEZ's closure has been looming on the horizon for long as the original SEZ model characterised by powerful fiscal incentives went flat

[130] *Ustawa z dnia 20 października 1994 r. o specjalnych strefach ekonomicznych*, Polish Official Journal (1994) no 123 item 600 (the 1994 'SEZA').

[131] 1994 SEZA (n 128) art 5–6.

[132] ibid art 5.3.

upon Poland's accession to the EU when EU's state aid rules kicked in.[133] Ever since the accession, the advantage of locating FDIs in the SEZ over regular areas had diminished year on year.

The original fiscal breaks in SEZs consisted in (1) the total exemption from the Corporate Income Tax (CIT) or Personal Income Tax (PIT) lasting for the half of the period for which specific SEZ was established,[134] (2) the exemption of half of the income from the CIT or PIT for the remaining period of a particular SEZ's existence,[135] (3) the deductibility of investment expenditures for items other than fixed assets from income subjected to CIT or PIT if a particular investor did not enjoy exemption from those taxes,[136] and (4) accelerated depreciation of fixed assets.[137] Out of seventeen SEZs established in the 1990s, fifteen were established initially for twenty years and two SEZs for twelve years.[138] That meant that the original total exemption from CIT or PIT was meant to last for either ten or six years.[139] Still, the details of breaks could vary from one SEZ to another depending on specific SEZ's founding documents.

The permitting process, to some extent, depended on the specific SEZ in the sense that the proposed investment had to be in sync with an SEZ's profile determined by the Council of the Ministers as well as local economic and natural conditions. Namely, the ministry responsible for industry and commerce (later, the ministry responsible for 'economy' after some changes to naming of central government departments), while reviewing investors' applications, ought to take into consideration: (1) the compliance of investors' purported activity with the scope of SEZ-specific permitted activities predetermined by the Council of Ministers, (2) the physical conditions in place, allowing to carry out purported activity, such as availability of undeveloped land or existing building or other infrastructures that the SEZ authority could allot for such purported activity, (3) the conduciveness of the purported activity to achieved specific SEZ's goals predetermined by the Council of the Ministers.[140] The minister responsible for the economy was vested with broad discretion concerning the permitting process, to the extent that he was also empowered to determine further the details of how to carry out negotiations with prospective investors or how to organise tenders for slots in the SEZs.[141] The minister could also delegate the power to grant permits to specific SEZs' authorities.[142] In practice, the Minister released the

---

[133] *See generally* Adam A Ambroziak,'Funkcjonowanie specjalnych stref ekonomicznych po akcesji Polski do UE' (2004) 4/5 (150) Wspólnoty Europejskie 43.

[134] 1994 SEZA (n 128) art 12.1.

[135] ibid art 12.2.

[136] ibid art 12.3.

[137] ibid art 12.4.

[138] Ambroziak (n 131) Table 1 at 44.

[139] The total number of industrial parks was, of course, much higher because, as mentioned, SEZs could and each one did established several sub-zones.

[140] 1994 SEZA (n 128) art 16.7.

[141] ibid art 17.1.

[142] ibid art 20.

SEZ-specific negotiations, tendering and permitting rules separately and delegated permitting powers to SEZs' authorities profusely. Finally, the permitting process for the activities in the SEZ did not relieve investors of the duty to obtain general sector-specific permits for regulated activities. Neither did it loosen requirements under the AREFA for investors wanting to purchase rather than lease land plots in the SEZ, subject to that AREFA at some point required the Ministry of the Interior to prioritise applications concerning land included in the SEZ and decided those within thirty days.

Following dozens of amendments dictated by the EU competition law, the chronological review of which would go beyond the scope of this chapter, the elements of the ISM under the consolidated text of SEZA from 2020[143] were not substantially altered compared with the original 1994 SEZA text. Instead, as mentioned, the fiscal breaks had to be aligned with the EU's public-aid, regional, and cohesion policies.[144] Also, the originally unlimited total area of SEZ at the national level was capped at twelve thousand hectares in 2000,[145] and later increased to twenty thousand hectares in 2008[146] and finally twenty-five hectares in 2015.[147] As of 31 December 2012, the total SEZs' area stood at 15,829 hectares with an average land utilisation rate of sixty per cent. One thousand five hundred forty-five permits were in force. The cumulative investment value stood at PLN 85.8 billion. The total employment stood at 247.5 thousand. Three-fourths of the total investment portfolio had come from investors originating in Poland, Germany, the USA, the Netherlands, Italy and Japan.[148] For comparison, the total SEZs' area stood at 22,949.5 hectares with an average land utilisation rate of sixty-five per cent. Two thousand three hundred ninety-two permits were in force. The cumulative investment value stood at PLN 132.8 billion. The total employment stood at two 388 thousand. Two-thirds of the total investment portfolio had come from investors originating in Poland, Germany, the Netherlands, Luxemburg and the USA.[149]

143 Polish Official Journal (2020) item 1670 (the '2020 SEZA').

144 *See* generally, Ambroziak (n 131).

145 SEZA art 5.a added in December 2000 by Polish Official Journal (2000) no 117 item 1228, art 1.3.

146 SEZA art 5.a amended in May 2008 by Polish Official Journal (2008) no 118 item 746, art 1.2.

147 SEZA art 5.a amended in January 2015 by Polish Official Journal (2015) item 143, art 2.2.

148 *Informacja o realizacji ustawy o specjalnych strefach ekonomicznych. Stan na 31 grudnia 2012 r.* (31 May 2012) parliamentary printed matter no 1412.

149 *Informacja o realizacji ustawy o specjalnych strefach ekonomicznych. Stan na 31 grudnia 2019 r.* (29 May 2020) parliamentary printed matter no 397.

3.3 Golden Share and Special Veto Acts

While subsequent incarnations of the AREFA and the SEZA affected hundreds of transactions each year, the subsequent golden share acts could potentially prevent foreign takeovers of the largest companies and existing strategic assets. The Golden Share Act of 2005 (the '2005 GSA')[150] and the subsequent Critical Infrastructure Act of 2010 (the '2010 CIA')[151] differed in their objective and subject coverage. The former had applied expressly listed enterprises deemed essential for public order and safety, in which treasury had to keep at least some minimum equity stake. In contrast, the latter has applied to unknown enterprises holding critical assets in the energy and petrochemical sectors designated as such in secrecy, regardless of whether treasury has kept any equity stake in such companies or not. In other words, the 2005 GSA's focus used to be subjective (on specific enterprises) while the 2010 CIA has been objective (on specific assets).

3.3.1 2005 GSA

The 2005 GSA was a very succinct, concise and straightforward piece of legislation. It stated that, so long as the treasury remains a shareholder or partner in a specific enterprise, the ministry for the treasury may object to a management board resolution or any other deed in law resulting in the disposal of its essential assets—a condition that such a deed law was inconsistent with public order or security requirements. In particular, the ministry could object to deeds in law that would (1) wind down such enterprises (2), relocate their registered office, (3) alter such enterprises' objects clauses, and (4) sale, lease or pledge such enterprises organised parts.[152]

The Council of Ministers was empowered to list strategic companies within the boundaries delineated under the 2005 GSA that clearly targeted formerly wholly state-owned companies in which the treasury's stake gradually diminished and the government risked losing control over. Specifically, the Council of Ministers was authorised to designate as strategic the enterprises involved in (1) electricity generation if the enterprise share's in the country's total generation exceeds fifteen per cent; (2) the operation or ownership of a gas or electricity transmission system, if the enterprises owns or uses more than fifty per cent of the country's gas or electricity transmission network capacity (3) gasolines or diesel oil production, if the enterprise's share in the country's total production exceeds twenty per cent, (4)

---

150 *Ustawa z dnia 3 czerwca 2005 r. o szczególnych uprawnieniach Skarbu Państwa oraz ich wykonywaniu w spółkach kapitałowych o istotnym znaczeniu dla porządku publicznego lub bezpieczeństwa publicznego,* Polish Official Journal (2005) no 2005 item 1108 (the '2005 GSA').

151 *Ustawa z dnia 18 marca 2010 r. o szczególnych uprawnieniach ministra właściwego do spraw skarbu Państwa oraz ich wykonywaniu w niektórych spółkach kapitałowych lub grupach kapitałowych prowadzących działalność w sektorach energii elektrycznej, ropy naftowej oraz paliw gazowych,* Polish Official Journal (2020) no 65 item 404 (the '2010 CIA').

152 2005 GSA (n 148) art. 2.1.

pipeline transportation of crude oil, gasoline or diesel fuel, if the enterprise's share in the country's total transmission capacity exceeds fifty per cent, (5) gasoline, diesel fuel, natural gas storage or underground crude oil storage, if the enterprise's storage capacity exceeds thirty days of the country consumption, 6) crude oil and crude oil derivatives transshipments in seaports, if the enterprise's share in the country's cargo-handling capacity exceeds fitty per cent, (7) hard coal or natural gas extraction, if the enterprise's share in the country's total extraction exceeds fifty per cent, (8) copper ore extraction and processing, if the enterprise's share in the country's total extraction and processing seventy per cent, (9) ownership of telecommunications infrastructure transmitting public radio and television signals in the area covering at least country's the territory, and (10) ownership of railway infrastructure making up at least fifty per cent of such infrastructure.[153]

Based on such criteria targeting specific strategic companies, the Council of Ministers composed the list three times in December 2005 covering fifteen entities,[154] September 2007 covering seventeen entities,[155] and September 2008 covering thirteen entities.[156] At its peak of 2017, the list covered (1) *PGNiG SA*, Poland's leading oil and gas mining company, (2) *LOTOS SA*, Poland second-largest oil refiner, (3) *Operator Logistyczny Paliw Płynnych* SP zoo, Poland's largest oil storage provider until 2017 when it was merged into *PERN SA* operating in the same sector, (4) ORLEN S.A, Poland largest oil refiner, (5) *BOT-Górnictwo i Energetyka SA,* a holding of state-owned electricity producers dissolved in 2007, (6) *Polskie Sieci Elektroenergetyczne (PSE) SA,* the owner of high voltage grid, (7) *PSE-Operator SA,* (8) *Gaz-System SA,* Poland's natural gas transmission system operator, (9) *Przyjaźń SA,* the operations of the Druzhba Pipeline's Polish section soon renamed as *PERN SA* (with *przyjaźń* in Polish and *druzba* in Russian both standing for 'friendship'), (10) *Naftoport Sp zoo,* an oil transhipment based in the port of Gdańsk, (11) PKP SA, Poland's state railway, (12) *Emitel Sp zoo,* a leading terrestrial TV and radio broadcast infrastructure operator in Poland, (13) *KGHM SA* one of the world's largest copper and silver producers, (14) *Solino SA,* a salt mine, (15) *Telekomunikacja Polska SA (TPSA,* an ex-state monopoly for landline phone communications purchased by *France Telekom,* and later renamed as Orange Poland, (16) *Exatel SA,* an owner of the fibre-optic grid, and (17) Polkomtel SA, a mobile operator.[157]

Procedurally, the ministry for the treasury was authorised to appoint one or two observers for each designated enterprise from among the civil servants and paid by the treasury to oversee the 2005 GSA's enforcement and sure that the ministry was could keep track of all deeds in law that could be inconsistent with public order or security requirements potentially.[158]

---

[153] ibid ar 8.

[154] Polish Official Journal (2005) no 260 item 2174.

[155] Polish Official Journal (2007) no 178 item 1251.

[156] Polish Official Journal (2008) no 192 item 1184.

[157] *See* n 153.

[158] 2005 GSA (n 148) art. 5.

The observers were obliged to notify the ministry of a particular deed in law falling within the scope of the 2005 GSA within three days, while the ministry was obliged to decide on the possible objection to such deeds within fourteen days of the notification but no later than twenty-one days of the deed. The ministry's decisions could be challenged first by a motion of a reconsideration by the ministry and subsequently by a petition to the administrative court, both of which ought to be decided within further fourteen days by either the ministry of the court.[159]

The 2005 GSA's Black letter did mention or differentiate between EU/EEA and non-EU/non-EEA foreign enterprises, meaning that this statute had been designed to also apply to and discriminate against EU/EEA enterprises protected under the freedoms of the single market and the non-discrimination principles proclaimed in the founding treaties of the community. Indeed, the 2005 GSA's bill's official rationale discussed in depth how such an approach could be justified under community law in line with the European Court of Justice's (ECJ) case law.[160] The 2005 GSA's bill discussed C-503/99 *Commission v Belgium*[161] primarily. It also referred to C-463/00 *Commission v Spain*[162] and C-367/98 *Commission v Portugal*[163] to further its argumentation. Specifically, the 2005 GSA's focus on public utility enterprises stemmed from that the ECJ reminded in *Commission v Portugal* based on its ubiquitous case law and repeated n *Commission v Spain* using the same language that "it is undeniable that, depending on the circumstances, certain concerns may justify the retention by the Member States of a degree of influence within undertakings that were initially public and subsequently privatised, where those undertakings are active in fields involving the provision of services in the public interest or strategic services."[164]

Despite such a general principle, the case-specific facts and details of the treasury's golden shares design under Spanish and Portuguese domestic laws and regulations could not be justified on the grounds of public security in ECJ's view. Therefore, the 2005 GSA's bill focused on aligning its golden share design with instruments scrutinised in *Commission v Belgium,* which the ECJ found compliant with the treaties.

---

[159] ibid 2.3–8.

[160] *Rządowy projekt ustawy o szczególnych uprawnieniach Skarbu Państwa oraz ich wykonywaniu w spółkach kapitałowych o istotnym znaczeniu dla porządku publicznego lub bezpieczeństwa publicznego* (28 December 2004) parliamentary printed matter no 3635.

[161] Case C-503/99, *Commission of the European Communities v Kingdom of Belgium* [2002] ECR I-04809 (Failure by a Member State to fulfil its obligations - Articles 52 of the EC Treaty (now, after amendment, Article 43 EC) and 73b of the EC Treaty (now Article 56 EC) - Rights attaching to the 'golden shares held by the Kingdom of Belgium in Société nationale de transport par canalisations SA and in Société de distribution du gaz SA).

[162] Case C-463/00, *Commission of the European Communities v Kingdom of Spain* [2003] ECR I-04581 (Failure by a Member State to fulfil its obligations - Articles 43 EC and 56 EC - System of administrative approval relating to privatised undertakings.

[163] Case C-367/98, *Commission of the European Communities v Portuguese Republic* [2002] ECR I-04731 (Failure by a Member State to fulfil its obligations - Articles 52 of the EC Treaty (now, after amendment, Article 43 EC) and 73b of the EC Treaty (now Article 56 EC) - System of administrative authorisation relating to privatised undertakings).

[164] *Commission v Portugal* (n 161) para 66.

To this end, apart from the focus on specific utility enterprises, while drafting the 2005 GSA's bill, the government focused specifically on assuring that (1) the actions within designated enterprises be only controlled ex-post, (2) the time window for the objection be very short, and (3) the mechanism is subjected to judicial oversight.[165]

However, the 2010 CIA's bill, proposing to replace the 2005 GSA, admitted that the 2005 GSA had significant flaws, including (1) very vaguely defined scope of enterprises' deeds subjected to the control by the ministry for treasury, (2) vague legal status of deeds which were not yet should have been notified to the ministry for the treasury, (3) excessive number of sectors, in which controlled enterprises could be designated, and (4) excessive costs of observers to be borne by the treasury.[166] Such a self-reflection within the Polish government did not occur, though, until one month after the Commission had decided to refer Poland to the ECJ in October 2009.[167]

3.3.2 2010 CIA

To be more compliant with the community law, the entire mechanism under the GSA 2010 drew upon a list of 'critical infrastructure' determined by the Government Security Centre's director as required under the 2007 Crisis Management Act,[168] implementing the 2008 Directive 2008/114/EC.[169] While the entire breakdown of those assets has remained classified, the owners and actual holders of such infrastructure have been notified about being covered by this list and encumbered with resulting obligations. Out of all critical infrastructures listed according to the 2007 Crisis Management Act, the GSA has only applied to assets in the sector of (1) electricity, including generation and transmission (2) oil, including extraction, refining, processing, storage, pipeline transportation and port terminals, and (3) gaseous fuels, including production, extraction, refining, processing, storage, and transportation via pipelines and liquefied natural gas (LNG) terminals.[170]

---

[165] *Rządowy*...(n 158) para at 16.

[166] *Rządowy projekt ustawy o szczególnych uprawnieniach ministra właściwego do spraw Skarbu Państwa oraz ich wykonywaniu w niektórych spółkach kapitałowych lub grupach kapitałowych prowadzących działalność w sektorach energii elektrycznej, ropy naftowej oraz paliw gazowych* (27 November 2009) parliamentary printed matter no 2548, para 1.

[167] European Commission, 'Free movement of capital: Commission refers Poland to Court of Justice over special rights granted to the State in certain companies' (29 October 2009) IP/09/1634 <https://ec.europa.eu/commission/presscorner/detail/en/IP_09_1634>.

[168] *Ustawa z dnia 26 kwietnia 2007 r. o zarządzaniu kryzysowym*, Polish Official Journal (2007) no 89 item 590, consolidated version Polish Official Journal (2020) item 1856, art. 5b.7.1.

[169] Directive Council Directive 2008/114/EC of 8 December 2008 on the identification and designation of European critical infrastructures and the assessment of the need to improve their protection (23 December 2008).

OJ L345 pp 75–82.

[170] 2010 CIA (n 149) art 1.2.

The essence of so-called golden share under the 2010 CIA laid in that the ministry for the treasury could block management board resolutions or any other legal deed affecting enterprise holding critical assets if their execution would pose a threat to the critical infrastructures' functioning, business continuity or integrity, including (1) winding down such enterprises (2) changes to or discontinuation of critical asset's use, (3) alteration of such enterprises' objects clauses, (4) sales, lease of or pledge over such enterprises or their organised parts (5) adoption of such enterprises' financial, investment or strategic plans, (6) registered office relocation abroad.[171] Procedurally, all enterprises holding critical assets were obliged to appoint an agent responsible for communications with the treasury ministry (instead of hosting an observer appointed by the ministry),[172] and the ministry was allowed fourteen days from the notification to object to a specific deed in law.[173] The ministry's decisions could be challenged first by a motion of a reconsideration by the ministry and subsequently by a petition to the administrative court, both of which ought to be decided within further fourteen days by either the ministry or the court.[174] Any claims that enterprises holding critical infrastructure could have for the losses incurred from the GSA's application were governed by a compensation regime applicable in principle in the constitutional state of emergency.[175]

Altogether, the 2010 CIA mechanism had fulfilled a role similar to an ISM, though with significant differences. Unlike under a typical ISM, a foreign investor potentially interested in a specific takeover could not clearly map the regulatory environment, let alone participate in the permitting process. The secrecy of the critical infrastructure list has implied that foreign investors could not know upfront which enterprises and assets could be subjected to the GSA mechanism and which not. The dealings with the ministry for the treasure was left exclusively to the enterprises targeted by prospective takeovers with no rules under the GSA clarifying to which extent prospective purchasers could be familiarised with the process.

4 Hydrocarbons Production Restrictions 2014

The ISM-like mechanism designed exclusively for hydrocarbons production predated by one year the new general ISM of 2015 (see further Sect. 5.1). The legislative

---

[171] ibid art 2.1.

[172] ibid art 5.1.

[173] However, not in excess of thirty days from the deed (ibid art 2.3). The reason for such thirty days limitation stems from that, under Polish company law, resolutions of commercial companies' bodies' resolutions are pretty much irrebuttable after thirty days from their adoption.

[174] 2010 CIA (n 149) art 2.5–6.

[175] ibid art 2.3; *Ustawa z dnia 22 listopada 2002 r. o wyrównywaniu strat majątkowych wynikających z ograniczenia w czasie stanu nadzwyczajnego wolności i praw człowieka i obywatela,* Polish Official Journal (2002) no 233 item 1955.

works on an extensive revamp 2011 Mining Law[176] throughout 2014 were dictated by several factors, including the need to (1) increase the domestic natural gas supply and thereby improving Poland's energy security, (2) introduce a more efficient oversight system conducive to the hydrocarbons prospection and production safety, (3) secure treasury's and local governments' fair share in hydrocarbons-derived revenue, (4) create new jobs in the mining sector, (5) adjust domestic mining regulations to the Hydrocarbons Directive 94/22/EC[177] in the wake of ECJ's decision declaring Poland's mining law's non-compliance with that directive,[178] and (6) most importantly for the SIM, secure of state interests such as energy security when granting mining concessions.[179]

The concerns about shortcoming of the 2011 Mining Law were exacerbated by the prospects for unconventional hydrocarbons production (e.g. shale, tight gas and oil) in which three and state-controlled oil and gas enterprises with established presence in the domestic and regional market (*Orlen*, *Lotos* and *PGNiG*) could not lead the charge. Rather, those three had to compete with over a dozen of mostly North American companies, equipped with shale-related technology and knowhow, know-how, including *Canadian Oil International Ltd*, *Chevron Corporation*, *Total SA*, *Marathon Oil Company*, *San Leon Energy Plc*, *Conoco Philips BV*, *or BNK Petroleum* late renamed as *Kolibri Global Energy Inc*.[180] As a result, the gaps in the existing regulatory framework concerning the oversight of mining concessions performance or mergers and acquisitions of concessionaires could not be made up for with exercise of treasury's ownerships rights anymore.[181] In particular, the lack of any prequalification mechanism screening entities potentially controlled by the government of third countries gave rise to the Polish government's grave concerns.[182] The bill proposed to focus on the control by third countries which are neither EEA nor NATO members and involve several intelligence agencies in such prequalification process.[183]

[176] *Ustawa z dnia 9 czerwca 2011 r. - Prawo geologiczne i górnicze*, Polish Official Journal (2011) no 163 item 981 as amended (the '2011 Mining Law'). For the amending statute of 2014 *see Ustawa z dnia 11 lipca 2014 r. o zmianie ustawy - Prawo geologiczne i górnicze oraz niektórych innych ustaw*, Polish Official Journal (2014) item 1133.

[177] Directive of the European Parliament and of the Council of 30 May 1994 on the conditions for granting and using authorizations for the prospection, exploration and production of hydrocarbons (30 June 1994) OJ L 164 pp 3–8.

[178] Case C-569/10, *European Commission v Republic of Poland* (27 June 2013, Judgment of the Court, Fourth Chamber: Failure of a Member State to fulfil obligations - Directive 94/22/EC - Conditions for granting and using authorisations for the prospection, exploration and extraction of hydrocarbons - Non-discriminatory access). For the discussion of C-569/10 *see* Sławomir Raszewski, Jędrzej Górski, 'Energy security or energy governance? Legal and political aspects of sustainable exploration of shale gas in Poland' (2014) (3) OGEL 1–51, 31–32.

[179] *Rządowy projekt ustawy o zmianie ustawy - Prawo geologiczne i górnicze oraz niektórych innych ustaw.*

(23 April 201) druk nr parliamentary printed matter 2352, 12–13.

[180] *Rządowy*... (n 175) 13.

[181] ibid 14.

[182] ibid 14, 15.

[183] ibid 15, 18.

To address all those issues, the 2014 statute amending the 2011 Mining Law added an entirely new chapter regulating hydrocarbons concessioning separately and differently from the previous concession regime, whose application was now confined to non-hydrocarbons deposits. The prequalification procedure was entrusted with the ministry for the environment as the coordinator.[184] The ministry for the environment, among other things, should analyse whether an enterprise applying for a hydrocarbon concession is under a 'corporate control' of a 'third country,' or third country's enterprises or citizen and whether such control may pose a threat to state security.[185] The third country has been oddly defined as a non-member of either EU, EFTA or NATO, implying that, under no circumstance should the ministry of the environment be in a position to declare enterprises under the corporate control of these blocks a threat to national security.[186] In turn, the notion of 'corporate control' has been defined very widely, all forms of direct or indirect rights which, separately or jointly, enable to exert a decisive influence on another entity or entities, considering all legal or factual circumstances.[187]

Procedurally, the ministry for the environment was designated to de facto merely coordinate the prequalification procedure. Specifically, the opinions of other authorities consulted by the ministry in the process are conclusive and could block positive decisions, thereby hindering the ministry's discretionary powers as to whether prequalify a specific enterprise or not. All of (1) the General Inspectorate of Financial Information, (2) the Polish Financial Supervision Authority, (3) the Internal Security Agency, and (4) the Foreign Intelligence Agency have to opine on the prequalification motion. Any single negative opinion blocks the prequalification, and the ministry for the environment cannot overturn such "opinions" of those authorities.[188]

5 New ISM Regime

The new era of a complex Polish ISM commenced a few years ahead of the EU-wide discussion about the need to screen takeovers of the EU critical enterprises by non-EU investors, emphasising Chinese investors. The set of initial solutions adopted in 2015 did not seem to live up to their premises put forth by their promoters. According to the bill, the new ISM regime has been, in theory, meant to cure the existing fragmentation by offering a uniform solution across selected critical sectors following similar developments in Germany and Austria (*see* Sect. 1).[189] However, the 2015 ISM did not repeal the 2010 CIA listing critical infrastructure assets, which has remained in force. Neither did the 2015 ISM repeal or somehow integrate ISM

[184] 2011 Mining Law (n 172) art 49a.1.

[185] ibid art 49a.2.1.

[186] ibid art 49a.5.

[187] ibid art 49a.4.

[188] ibid art 49a.10.

[189] *Poselski...* (n 48) point 1 at 17.

elements crafted for hydrocarbon concessions discussed in Sect. 4 above. In fact, the 2015 ISM's bill mapped a whole list of minor sectoral ISM-like mechanisms, including those discussed in this chapter (the AREFA discussed in Sect. 3.1 and the 2010 CIA discussed in Sect. 3.3.2) and those left out from the analysis deliberately (in the field of banking, aviation, transportation, gambling, pension funds, insurance and investment funds). All such scattered sector-specific provisions remained untouched. Instead of cross-sector consolidation, the 2015 ISM restored the list of designated enterprises akin to GSA 2005, which the Council of the Ministers was authorised to compose (*see* further Sect. 5.1). The subsequent consolidation impact of the 2020 ISM was at best mixed. On a positive note, the 2020 ISM has not only offered a multi-sector procedure but also aimed to align this procedure with procedures under competition law. On the negative note, the set of rules provided in the 2020 ISM did not supersede any of the pre-existing sector-specific, asset-specific or entity-specific measures (*see* further Sect. 5.2).

5.1 2015 ISM Regime

The 2015 ISM was an improvement over the 2005 GSA in several respects. Firstly, concerning its objective coverage, i.e., determining specific critical sectors and specific enterprises targeted by foreign takeovers, the 2015 ISM got detached from the golden share logics and treasury's equity state in the targeted enterprises compared with the 2005 GSA. In other words, it became irrelevant under the 2015 ISM whether a targeted enterprise was a partly privatised formerly wholly state-owned enterprise or entirely private enterprises from its inceptions, similar to the detachment from treasury's equity under the 2010 CIA and the 2011 Mining Law as amended in 2014 (*see* further Sect. 5.1.1). Secondly, concerning its subjective coverage, i.e. the determination of foreign enterprises, the acquisitions by which ought to be subject to scrutiny, the 2015 ISM expanded and detailed the notions of control, dominance, acquisitions, etc., greatly (*see* further Sect. 5.1.2). Thirdly, at least as its bill's authors intended, the 2015 ISM was meant to comply with EU law and case law fully (*see* further Sect. 5.1.3).

5.1.1 Objective Coverage

Apart from relinquishing the golden share logics and detachment from treasury's equity, the 2015 ISM's objective coverage has copied the 2005 GSA, in the primary legislation has indicated specific sectors of interest where governmental executive agencies have been meant to take further actions and designate specific protected enterprises in secondary legislation. Sector-wise, 2015 ISM specifically covered (1) electricity production, (2) gasoline and petrol fuel production, (3) pipeline transport of crude oil, gasoline or diesel fuel, (4) gasoline, diesel fuel and natural gas storage (5) underground crude oil or natural gas storage, (6) production of chemicals, fertilisers and chemical products, (7) production and trade in explosives, weapons and ammunition as well as products and technology for military or police purposes, (8) natural gas regasification or liquefaction, (9) reloading of crude oil and oil-derived products in seaports, (10) natural gas or electricity distribution, (11) telecommunications activities or (12) transmission of gaseous fuels.[190]

The Council of the Ministers, which was vested with the right to list specific domestic enterprises subjected to protection under the 2015 ISM Act,[191] first released such list in June 2016 to cover just two enterprises, including (1) *Azoty SA*, Poland's largest chemical company and Europe's major producer of fertilisers, plastics, chemicals, oxo alcohols and pigments, and (2) *KGHM Polska Miedź SA,* one of the world's largest copper and silver producers.[192] The list was soon expanded. In August 2016, the Council of Ministers added to it: (1) *EDF Polska SA,* a former branch of EDF (*Électricité de France*) which had owned several municipal cogeneration plants, all sold to *PGE SA* in May 2017, (2) *ENGIE Energia Polska SA* which had owned several power plants all sold to *ENEA SA* in March 2017, (3) *ORLEN SA,* Poland's largest and Central Europe's major oil refiner, (4) *PKP Energetyka SA* being a subsidiary of Polish State Railways ('*PKP*') in charge of electric traction, and (5) *TAURON SA*, Poland's second-largest electricity generator after *PGE*.[193]

The changes to the protected enterprises' list of December 2017 consisted, firstly, in deleting *ENGIE's* and *EDF's* Polish branches taken over by state-controlled *PGE* and *ENEA*. And, secondly, in adding telecommunications enterprises, including (1) *EmiTel Sp zoo,* a leading terrestrial TV and radio broadcast infrastructure operator in Poland, and (2) *TK Telekom Sp zoo,* another *PKP's* subsidiary.[194] *Innogy Stoen Operator Sp zoo,* Warsaw's grid operator, was added in December 2018.[195] *HAWE Telekom Sp zoo*, an owner of the fibre-optic grid, was added in December 2019.[196] *Telesystem-Mesko Sp zoo,* an R&D firm in the defence sector, was added in October 2020.[197] Finally, *Orange Polska SA* and *Polkomtel Sp zoo,* two major mobile network operators, plus *Europol Gaz SA,* a gas pipeline operator, were added in December 2020,[198] at which point the total number of controlled enterprises stood at thirteen.

5.1.2 Subjective Coverage

Interestingly, the 2015 ISM forewent references individuals' and their business' national origin or citizenship. At no point did it differentiate between enterprises

[190] 2015 ISM Act (n 1) art 4.1.
[191] ibid art 4.2.
[192] Polish Official Journal (2016) item 977.
[193] Polish Official Journal (2016) item 1316.
[194] Polish Official Journal (2017) item 2387.
[195] Polish Official Journal (2018) item 2523.
[196] Polish Official Journal (2019) item 2501.
[197] Polish Official Journal (2020) item 1765.
[198] Polish Official Journal (2020) item 2349.

under the control of Poles and foreigners. And, perforce, among the latter, it did not differentiate between foreigners originating in the EEA or outside it. The reasonable premise has been that all transactions targeting designated protected enterprises ought to be subjected to screening,[199] only in the course of which a governmental executive agency would assess transaction-specific risks to state security (*see* further Sect. 5.1.3). To this end, the ISM 2015 classified covered transactions as acquisitions of either 'substantial participation,' or 'dominance' in one of the designated protected enterprises.

The notion of substantial participation has been entirely novel and unknown to the 2005 GSA. The 2015 ISM defined this concept as the ability to exert influence on an enterprise's activities and detailed it for corporations and partnerships separately. For corporations, substantial participation has meant holding more than twenty per cent of all shares or shares entitled to at least twenty per cent of votes over the period of the last two years, calculated as the weighted average within that period.[200] For partnerships, substantial participation has meant holding capital contributions worth at least twenty per cent of the total capital contributions paid up to the partnership.[201] In addition, the 2015 ISM also defined 'acquisition of substantial influence' as (1) surpassing equity levels respectively of twenty, twenty-five, and thirty-five per cent of all shares or equity levels entitling to respectively twenty, twenty-five, and thirty-five per cent of total votes (calculated as the weighted average within the mentioned period of two years), and (2) purchasing enterprises spun-off from designated protected enterprises.[202] Ergo, each transaction resulting in surpassing one of these voting-rights thresholds has implied an obligation to go through the ISM, and the entire construct has somewhat resembled regulation encumbering publicly listed corporations.

In turn, the 'acquisition of dominance' was defined as surpassing equity entitling to over fifty per cent of shares or share entitling to over fifty per cent of total votes in the designated protected company.[203] Altogether, the apparent distinction between acquisitions of substantial influence and dominance has been distinction without differentiation in the sense that surpassing twenty, twenty-five, thirty-three, and fifty per cent thresholds in designated protected enterprise's equity or voting rights has resulted in precisely the same ISM obligations.

The 2015 ISM has avoided *lacunas* and made it very hard to circumvent the ISM by listing broad classes of transactions leading to the indirect acquisitions of either substantial influence or dominance. The catalogue of indirect acquisitions has included, among others transactions carried out by an entity (1) which is a subsidiary of a dominant/parent[204] entity including on a contractual basis with the parent entity

---

[199] 2015 ISM Act (n 1) art 5.1.

[200] ibid art 3.1.4.a.

[201] ibid art 3.1.4.b.

[202] ibid art 3.4.

[203] ibid art 3.3.

[204] The 'dominant entity' has been defined as an entity 1) which, directly or indirectly through other entities, holds a majority of the total number of votes in the bodies of another entity, also on

or parent entity's other subsidiaries, (2) whose articles of association or other bylaws regulating its operation contains provisions regarding the right to its property upon its dissolution or other form of its cessation, including the right to dispose of this property without purchasing it, (3) which acts on own behalf, but on commission of another entity, including under a portfolio management agreement, (4) with which another entity has concluded an agreement regulating the transfer of voting rights or other rights to shares or rights from shares in a designated protected company, (5) a group of two or more entities, whereby at least one of them is an entity with which another entity has concluded an agreement for the purchase of shares in a designated protected company, and (6) by an entity acting based on a written or oral agreement regarding the acquisition of shares in a designated protected by the parties of such an agreement.[205]

5.1.3 ISM Procedure

Procedurally, the intended transactions targeting designated protected enterprises ought to be notified to the ministry for the treasury in principle before conclusions of any agreement, shareholder meetings, public tender offers or any other acts in law leading to the changes to significant participation or dominance on protected enterprises.[206] However, such acts in law could also be concluded conditionally and become effective only after a green light from the ministry for the treasury.[207] The transactions concluded without a required notification or despite a negative decision shall be null and void, and right stemming from shares acquired as a result of such transactions shall not be exercised.[208] Time-wise, the procedure should not last more than ninety days,[209] within which the ministry for the treasury could consult in essence all other ministries, all intelligence agencies, and several sub-ministerial central agencies such as the Energy Regulator Office or the Electronic Telecommunications Office.[210] Appeal procedures have been incorporated into the 2015 ISM by

---

the basis of agreements with other persons, 2) which is entitled to appoint or dismiss the majority of members of the management or supervisory bodies of another entity, or 3) if more than half of the members of the management board of another entity are at the same time members of the management board, commercial proxy or persons holding managerial positions of the first entity or other entity remaining with the first relationship of dependence, 4) which has a share capital of at least fifty per cent the value of all contributions made to this company, or 5) which has the ability to otherwise decide on the directions of the activities of another entity, in particular on the basis of an agreement providing for the management of this entity or the transfer of profit by this entity. *See* 2015 ISM Act (n 1) art 3.1.1.

[205] 2015 ISM (n 1) art 3.5.

[206] ibid arts 3.6, 5.

[207] ibid art 9.9.

[208] ibid art 12.1-3. In addition, the shareholders' resolution in the protected companies shall be null and void if their adoption depended on voting right which should not have been exercised. *See* ibid art 12.4.

[209] 2015 ISM art 9.7.

[210] ibid art 13.

a simple reference to the general administrative procedure without any deviations.[211] Ergo, the interested party had the right to first ask the ministry for the treasury to review its decision and subsequently challenge such decision before administrative courts.

5.1.4 Community and International Law Compliance

Apart from adding to the disorderly mosaic of ISM-like sector-specific solutions instead of consolidating them all, the 2015 ISM also brought the questions of community law compliance that had made the European Commission question the 2005 GSA and forced Poland to replace it with the 2010 CIA.[212] Anticipating such renewed community law compliance hassles, the 2015 ISM's bill elaborated on those concerns. The bill started the discussion on this subject with the bold claim that the 2015 ISM would violate neither the Treaty on the Functioning of the European Union (TFUE)[213] art 49 (Freedom of Establishment)[214] nor TFUE art 63 (Capital and Payments).[215] Pretty predictably, the bill recalled permissible exceptions to the freedoms of establishment and capital flows, including:

(1) TFUE art 52.1 stating that "[t]he provisions of this Chapter [Freedom of Establishment] and measures taken in pursuance thereof shall not prejudice the applicability of provisions laid down by law, regulation or administrative action providing for special treatment for foreign nationals on the grounds of public policy, public security or public health," and
(2) TFUE art 65.1 stating that "[t]he provisions of Article 63 [freedom of capital flows] shall be without prejudice to the right of Member States [...] to take all requisite measures to prevent infringements of national law and regulations, in particular in the field of taxation and the prudential supervision of financial institutions, or to lay down procedures for the declaration of capital movements

[211] ibid art 11.5.

[212] *See* European Commission (n 163).

[213] Consolidated versions of the Treaty on European Union and the Treaty on the Functioning of the European Union (26 October 2012) OJ C 326, pp 1–390 (TFUE).

[214] TFUE (n 209) art 49 (ex art 43 TEC): "Within the framework of the provisions set out below, restrictions on the freedom of establishment of nationals of a Member State in the territory of another Member State shall be prohibited. Such prohibition shall also apply to restrictions on the setting-up of agencies, branches or subsidiaries by nationals of any Member State established in the territory of any Member State. Freedom of establishment shall include the right to take up and pursue activities as self-employed persons and to set up and manage undertakings, in particular companies or firms within the meaning of the second paragraph of Article 54, under the conditions laid down for its own nationals by the law of the country where such establishment is effected, subject to the provisions of the Chapter relating to capital".

[215] TFUE (n 209) art 63 (ex art 56 TEC): "1. Within the framework of the provisions set out in this Chapter, all restrictions on the movement of capital between Member States and between Member States and third countries shall be prohibited. 2. Within the framework of the provisions set out in this Chapter, all restrictions on payments between Member States and between Member States and third countries shall be prohibited".

for purposes of administrative or statistical information, or to take measures which are justified on the grounds of public policy or public security."

The authors of the bill argued that the measures provided for in the 2015 ISM met the proportionality test encumbering all Member States' measures exploiting various exceptions to the single market allowed by the Treaties by point to the minimal objective coverage as defined by the short enumerative list of protected companies (*see* Sect. 5.1.1) as opposed to restrictive measures covering whole sectors which might have been deemed disproportionate.[216] In addition, the lack of differentiation between acquisition between domestic and foreign persons (*see* Sect. 5.1.2) arguably implied that the TFEU art 18's ban on discrimination on the grounds of nationality was not violated.[217]

Interestingly, the 2015 ISM was passed even though the Parliamentary Research Office disagreed with the bill authors and found it in violation of the EU law.[218] Specifically, the Office likened the mechanism proposed under the bill to the facts of C-54/99 *Eglise de Scientologie*[219] in which similar French measures were scrutinised. The French measures in question required investors to seek prior acquisition approvals in the case "a foreign investment […] made in activities which are connected, even on an occasional basis, with the exercise of public authority in France, or that a foreign investment is such as to represent a threat to public policy, public health or public security, or if that investment has been made in activities involving research into, production of or trade in arms, munitions, explosive powders or substances intended for military purposes, or materials designed for warfare."[220] While analysing such provisions, the ECJ yet again conceded that, in principle, "measures which restrict the free movement of capital may be justified on public-policy and public-security grounds […] if they are necessary for the protection of the interests which they are intended to guarantee and only in so far as those objectives cannot be attained by less restrictive measures."[221] However, in those particular circumstances, the ECJ found the French measures noncompliant with the free movement of capital freedom because:

---

[216] *Poselski…* (n 48) point 2 at 20.

[217] ibid.

[218] *See* generally, Biuro Analiz Sejmowych (Parlamentary Research Office). 'Opinia w sprawie zgodności z prawem Unii Europejskiej poselskiego projektu ustawy o kontroli niektórych inwestycji Opinia w sprawie zgodności z prawem Unii Europejskiej poselskiego projektu ustawy o kontroli niektórych inwestycji' (8 April 2015) BAS-WAPEiM-628/15 <https://orka.sejm.gov.pl/Druki7ka.nsf/0/EDA006ADCEF12769C1257E52002F08D2/%24File/3454.pdf>.

[219] Case C-54/99, *Association Eglise de scientologie de Paris and Scientology International Reserves Trust v The Prime Minister* [2000] ECR I-01335 (Reference for a preliminary ruling: Conseil d'Etat – France, Free movement of capital - Direct foreign investments - Prior authorisation - Public policy and public security).

[220] Case C-54/99 (n 218) para 7, citing Article 5-1(I)(1) of Law No 66-1008, introduced by Law No 96-109 of 14 February 1996 on financial relations with foreign countries in regard to foreign investments in France.

[221] Case C-54/99 (n 218) para 18.

(1) "the essence of the system in question is that prior authorisation is required for every direct foreign investment which is 'such as to represent a threat to public policy [and] public security', without any more detailed definition [whereby] the investors concerned are given no indication whatever as to the specific circumstances in which prior authorisation is required,"[222]
(2) "[s]uch lack of precision does not enable individuals to be apprised of the extent of their rights and obligations deriving from [...] the Treaty [and] t]hat being so, the system established is contrary to the principle of legal certainty,"[223] and
(3) "the Treaty must be interpreted as precluding a system of prior authorisation for direct foreign investments which confines itself to defining in general terms the affected investments as being investments that are such as to represent a threat to public policy and public security, with the result that the persons concerned are unable to ascertain the specific circumstances in which prior authorisation is required."[224]

The Parliamentary Research Office argued that the 2015 ISM similarly lacked legal certainty, failing to provide a more elaborate definition of threats to national security or national interest.[225] However, their concerns were arguably overblown in that they did not consider at all the bill's authors argument mentioned above about ISM's minimal objective coverage limited to a shortlist of specifically designated protected enterprises as opposed to French measures loosely defining not only the decision criteria (what constitutes a threat and what does not) but also covered sectors. After all, one could argue that the very precise objective coverage delimitation, like under the 2015 ISM, is much conducive to legal certainty than more elaborate decision criteria. In other words, a concrete listing of protected enterprises, with regard to which threats to public security and interest out to be scrutinised, is much more conducive to understanding which such threats are than any attempt to offer their abstract definitions. Unlike the 2005 GSA, the 2015 ISM was not challenged by the commissions, implying that the 2015 ISM bill's authors were right and the parliamentary experts were wrong.

5.2 2020 ISM

While the 2015 ISM could still be found controversial upon its adoption given that the Europe-wide ISM-related trends were still shaped a few years ago, the 2020 ISM expanding the 2015 ISM followed the line drawn by the European crowd and the European Commission as discussed in the introduction of this chapter. Ergo, the ISM 2020's EU-law compliance has been no issue. Technically, the 2020 ISM offered a complex parallel system provided for in a set of new arts added to the ISM 2015

[222] ibid, para 21.

[223] ibid, para 22.

[224] ibid, para 22.

[225] Biuro (n 217) point 2.F at 7–8.

Table 1 Sectors covered by ISM 2020

– All publicly traded companies. *See* 2020 ISM (n 1) art 12.d.1
All entities in possession of critical infrastructure assets. *See* 2020 ISM (n 1) art 12.d.4; *see* also, Sect. 3.3.2 on the 2010 CIA)
– Software producers: • for the control of power plants, networks or the operation of facilities or systems for the supply of electricity, gas, fuel, heating oil or district heat, • for the management, control and automation of drinking water supply or sewage treatment installations, • for the operation of devices or systems used for voice and data transmission or for the storage and processing of data, • for the operation of devices or systems used for the supply of cash, card payments, conventional transactions, for the settlement or management of securities and derivative transactions or for the provision of insurance services, • to operate hospital information systems, to operate devices and systems used to sell prescription drugs, and to operate a laboratory information system or tests laboratories, • for the operation of equipment or systems used in the transport of passengers or goods by air, rail, sea or inland waterway, road, public transport or logistics, or • for the operation of equipment or systems used in the supply of food
– All providers of data collection or processing services in the cloud. *See* 2020 ISM (n 1) art 12.d.2
– SECTORS: • electricity generation, or • gasoline or diesel production, • pipeline transport of crude oil, gasoline or diesel, • storage of gasoline, diesel, natural gas, • underground storage of crude oil or natural gas, • chemicals production, fertilizers and chemical products, • production and trade in explosives, weapons and ammunition as well as products and technology for military or police purposes, • regasification or liquefaction of natural gas, • reloading of crude oil at sea ports, or • distribution of natural gas or of electricity, • telecommunications activities, • transmission of gaseous fuels, • rhenium production, • mining and processing of metal ores used for the production of explosives, weapons, ammunition and products and technology for military or police purposes, • medical instruments and devices production, • drugs and other pharmaceutical products production, • trade in gaseous fuels and gas with foreign countries, • production or transmission or distribution of heat, • transhipment in inland ports, and 20) processing of meat, milk, cereals, fruit and vegetables. *See* 2020 ISM (n 1) art 12.d.4

without integrating them with the existing system.[226] The logic of such a legislative technique might have been driven by the tentatively temporary nature of the 2020 ISM. Namely, should the ISM 2020 expire after two years without any extension, the temporary provisions could be deleted easily, leaving only the original 2015 ISM system in place without having to further modify it. The overlap between two systems has been resolved by designating the 2020 ISM provisions, for the time when they remain in force as *leges generals* applicable to a considerable part of the economy (*see* Table 1) and the 2015 ISM provisions as *leges specials* covering a shortlist of designated protected enterprises. In other words, the 2020 ISM hot not altered the ISM shape for designated protected enterprises subjected to stricter rules.[227]

[226] 2020 ISM (n 1) arts 12a–12k.

[227] 2020 ISM (n 1) art 12a.1.2.

The 2020 ISM have been less strict in several regards (*see* Table 2). Concerning the subjective coverage, i.e. the qualities of the investors, the 2020 ISM has only covered acquisitions by natural persons without EU/EEA/OECD citizenship or entities which has not had their seat in the EU/EEA/OECD for at least two years[228]—in contrast to 2015 which triggers in for the designated protected enterprises regardless of investment origin. Also, the number of equity thresholds triggering screening has been reduced from four to three, i.e. from twenty, twenty-five, thirty-three and fifty per cent to twenty, forty and fifty per cent.[229] Procedurally and institutionally, the lesser strictness of the 2020 ISM compared with the 2015 ISM could be seen in that the decision-making process was shifted from the political level of the ministry for the treasury to the civil-service level of the antimonopoly office, which, under EU law, enjoys a great deal of autonomy from politicians.[230] The extension of the maximum screening timeline from ninety days under the 2015 ISM to one hundred fifty days in total under the 2020 ISM might be seen as more burdensome for the entrepreneurs. However, the idea has been to align the screening procedure to the control-of-concentration procedure as prescribed by Regulation 139/2004, which allows differentiating between less and more complicated cases.[231] Like the Regulation 139/2004, the antimonopoly office should first decide within a short period set at thirty days whether a particular case is not controversial and greenlight the acquisition or refer the case to a full investigation which could last up to further one hundred twenty days.[232]

6 Conclusion

The assessment of the developments in the Polish ISM system has to consist, first, of remarks on the efficiency and legislative quality of the adopted solutions as measured by their rationales shaped by global ISM trends, which constitutes the domestic aspect of the case. And, second, on the impact of these global trends on the freedom capital flows and openness of the global economy, which constitutes the universal aspect

[228] ibid art 14a.1.1.

[229] ibid art. 12.c 4.2.

[230] ibid art 12h 8.

[231] Council Regulation (EC) No 139/2004 of 20 January 2004 on the control of concentrations between undertakings (the EC Merger Regulation) [2004] OJ L 24, pp 1–22: "Article 6 (..) 1. The Commission shall examine the notification as soon as it is received. (a) Where it concludes that the concentration notified does not fall within the scope of this Regulation, it shall record that finding by means of a decision. (b) Where it finds that the concentration notified, although falling within the scope of this Regulation, does not raise serious doubts as to its compatibility with the common market, it shall decide not to oppose it and shall declare that it is compatible with the common market. (…). (c) (…) where the Commission finds that the concentration notified falls within the scope of this Regulation and raises serious doubts as to its compatibility with the common market, it shall decide to initiate proceedings. (…)".

[232] 2020 ISM (n 1) arts 12.h.5 and arts 12.h.8; *Rządowy* (n 2) 38.

Table 2 Key differences between 2015 ISM versus 2020 ISM

	2015 ISM	2020 ISM
Objective coverage/targeted enterprises	Short list of designated strategic enterprises	Huge part of the Polish economy defined by the long list of covered sectors
Subjective coverage/origin of investors	ISM regardless of nationality, origin or seat	ISM for persons and companies without either EU/EEA/OECD citizenship or seat
Subjective coverage/investors; participation thresholds	20, 25, 33 and 50% of votes, equity or profits	20, 40, and 50% of votes, equity or profits
Government agency	Ministry for the treasury	Antimonopoly office
Responsible authority	Ministry for the treasury	Antimonopoly office

of the case. Concerning the domestics angle, Polish lawmakers have achieved their objectives only if these were to put significant obstacles in the way of private business with even minor participation of international capital. They have piled numerous often overlapping sector-specific, asset-specific or enterprise-specific ISM rules up over the course of a few decades. Keeping sectors-specific ISM *leges specialies* in heavily regulated sectors left out by this chapter (like banking, aviation, transportation, insurance and other financial and investment services) might still be justified by the unique nature of those sectors or EU-wide requirements to limit access to such sectors for non-EU investors. However, barely anything could justify the developments since 2010 when the 2010 CIA was joined by the 2014 amendment to the 2011 Mining Law, the 2015 ISM and eventually the 2020 ISM. Each of those defined covered targeted enterprises differently by referring divergently to possessed assets (critical infrastructure), granted licences (hydrocarbons), being individually designated (energy sectors), and, finally, operating in listed sectors covering a huge part of the economy. Moreover, each of those provided for varying procedures, ranging from having insider intelligence-services-approved snitches reporting to the ministry for the energy to having to apply to various authorities such as the ministry for the environment (hydrocarbons mining), the ministry for the treasury (energy sectors) and the antimonopoly office (the default cross-sector procedure). And this is on top of the real estate permitting procedure under the AREPA handled by the ministry for the interior. Out of the European ISM systems mapped by the OECD, one could perhaps see only that of Spain with six parallel ISM instruments as uniquely haywire.

Concerning the global and universal angle, the expanding scope of ISM worldwide only adds to the deglobalisation processes. The fragmentation and multipolarisation of the global economy, trade, multilateral rules-based order or international economic law imply the end of unlimited global freedom of strategic flows such as raw material, fuels, merchandise, technology and capital, which the world has enjoyed within the framework of the unipolar moment since the early 1990s. The ever-expanding ISMs' coverage is consistent with the high tide turn of protectionism conducive to forming new autarchic trading blocks trapped in a kind of siege mentality whereby interactions with other blocks pose a risk to the place of a specific block in the global value and production chains. Particularly the Western block centred around the North Atlantic seems to be running out of runway as far as remaining in control to high-tech industries and innovation cycles within a multilateral trading system that the West created. On the one hand, Western policymakers have for decades pushed for trade and investment liberalisation within the framework of WTO, regional trade agreements or in exchange for development aid. On the other hand, they have also bent over backwards to make up for the lack of competitiveness against emerging regions cause by overpriced production inputs in the West, including not only labour but also, e.g. energy costs. Various product–process-related requirements have gradually shifted from moderately controversial product-related standards to more indirectly discriminatory process-related requirements interfering with their competitors' social and environmental standards. Likewise, in the field of investment, they have attempted to resists the inversion of the FDI flaws cause by their chronic negative payment balances with indirectly discriminatory forms of inward FDI controls, mainly via concentration controls under antimonopoly laws. By doing so, they could save the face of openness' champions while picturing emerging markets with their directly discriminatory restrictions of inward FDI as protectionists and backward. Yet when concentration controls did not suffice, as the takeover by more competitive enterprises from the competing politico-economic blocks only intensified, the West resorted to public security and similar notions usually embodied in ISM instruments. As a result, whether they like it or not, many countries linked to specific trading blocs tightly dig in against freedom of strategic flows third countries. By adopting wide coordinated cross-sector peripheral ISMs, peripheral countries of such blocs—like Poland and the whole CEE region—most often defend economic interests of their metropoles than of their own.

Jędrzej Górski MJur (Warsaw), PhD in laws (CUHK), Research Fellow and PhD cand. in political Science, The Department of Asian and International Studies (AIS), City University of Hong.

Political Support, Competitive Advantage, and the Regulation of State-Owned Enterprises (SOEs)

Peter Enderwick

1 Introduction

Despite the recent protectionist sentiment, global trade and investment continue at high levels. Such exchanges are widely seen positively, offering greater competition, specialisation, consumer choice and lower prices. However, one aspect of globalisation that has created significant host country concern is the growing international involvement of state-owned enterprises, particularly those originating in emerging economies. State-owned enterprises, defined as state-owned legal entities that undertake commercial activities for a government, while long-established in many economies, are increasingly engaging in cross-border business activities.

In a domestic context, there may be solid arguments for the creation of SOEs—they may be used to provide public goods, increase access to public services, protect strategic industries or encourage economic development—however, when they operate internationally, competitive distortions resulting from state resource dependence, limited transparency, governance weaknesses, and pursuit of non-commercial goals, can spill over into other economies, creating challenges for local firms and host country regulators.[1] These concerns are magnified in emerging markets such as China where SOEs are used strategically to secure needed resources, access frontier technologies, or act as 'national champions' in strategic industries.[2]

[1] A. Cuervo-Cazurra, 'Thanks but no thanks: state-owned multinationals from emerging markets and host-country policies '(2018) *Journal of International Business Policy* 1(3–4) 128.

[2] S. Liao and Y. Zhang, 'A new context for managing overseas direct investment by Chinese state-owned enterprises' (2014) *China Economic Journal* 7(1) 126.

P. Enderwick (✉)
Department of International Business, Strategy and Entrepreneurship, Auckland University of Technology, Auckland, New Zealand
e-mail: peter.enderwick@aut.ac.nz

J. Chaisse et al. (eds.), *Regulation of State-Controlled Enterprises*, International Law and the Global South, https://doi.org/10.1007/978-981-19-1368-6_21

Host country screening and regulation of state-owned multinational enterprises (SOEMNEs) recognises the possible distortions that could arise, with several countries,[3,4,5] as well as international organisations[6] offering specific tests and proposals to counteract competitive distortions. Such tests are based on structural and behavioural differences between state-owned and privately owned firms and the possible distortions these can introduce in international business.

However, while such distortions are costly, what is not usually acknowledged is the considerable assistance that many SOEMNEs, particularly those from emerging markets, receive from home country governments in terms of learning and competitive upgrading. In their earlier stages of growth and development, state-supported firms may benefit from access to resources, information, potential partners, and a favoured domestic position to build globally competitive firms. The creation of infant industries and global champions as part of strategic industrialisation policy means that market incentives are replaced by state reliance, reflected in subsequent corporate decisions. For example, SOEs are likely to internationalise at an earlier stage or a faster pace when the home country has an explicit goal of increased internationalisation, such as China's 'Go Global' policy. The advantages enjoyed by state-owned enterprises are unlikely to be fully reflected in the structural distortions attributed to SOEMNEs and thus may not be incorporated in host country screening and regulation.

This chapter aims to identify four critical dynamic areas that impact effective evaluation—two of which—competitive upgrading and accelerated internationalisation—are likely to add to competitive distortions and two—economic transition and hybrid SOE ownership—that could have the opposite effect. The chapter argues the need to incorporate these dynamic aspects of SOE behaviour into investment evaluation processes.

The effective assessment of SOEs and their impacts is a complex issue. Such complexity results from several considerations. First, SOEs assume a wide range of forms varying, for example, in terms of the degree of government ownership, the level of ownership (central, regional, local), whether the enterprise has a stock market listing, and whether it is state-controlled rather than being state-owned.[7] While various SOE forms provide advantages of flexibility to a home country, it complicates ownership policy, transparency concerns, and legal applicability of

[3] R. Mendelsohn and A. Fels, 'Australia's foreign investment review board and the regulation of Chinese investment' (2014) *China Economic Journal* 7(1) 59.

[4] T.H. Moran, 'Towards a multilateral framework for identifying national security threats posed by foreign acquisitions: with special reference to Chinese acquisitions in the United States, Canada and Australia' (2014) *China Economic Journal* 7(1) 39.

[5] Y.P. Woo, 'Chinese lessons: state-owned enterprises and the regulation of foreign investment in Canada' (2014) *China Economic Journal* 7(1) 21.

[6] OECD '*Ownership and governance of state-owned enterprises: A compendium of national practices' (OECD 2018).*

[7] G.D. Bruton, M.W. Peng, D. Ahlstrom, C. Stan, and K. Xu 'State-owned firms around the world as hybrid organizations' (2015) *Academy of Management Perspectives* 29(1) 92.

national laws and provisions of international agreements.[8] A recent trend has been the growth of marketised SOEs listed on stock exchanges that have reconfigured ownership, competitive strategies, and governance practices to more closely align with the demands of market-based economies.[9] Such hybrid forms question traditional assumptions applied to SOEs.

Second, SOEs vary in terms of the heterogeneity and strength of their political connections. One study[10] draws a distinction between SOEs with ascribed and those with acquired political connections. Ascribed connections are stronger, more robust and likely to lead to a more dominant domestic market position, possibly discouraging firm internationalisation. In contrast, SOEs with acquired political connections carry a heavier obligation (in return for resources) to pursue state goals, including internationalisation. In addition, the acquisition of political connections provides learning opportunities to create political skills that might be used in overseas markets. The SOEs of countries such as Russia are perhaps best described as 'state-influenced' while in private hands.[11] These distinctions suggest the need to explore firm history when considering their likely impacts in overseas markets.

Third, theoretical reasoning offers few precise predictions on SOEs' likely behaviour and success as they internationalise. On the one hand, state-provided resources may augment the competitive advantages of SOEs, facilitating internationalisation. On the other hand, such advantages may inhibit risk-taking and entry to overseas markets.[12] Equally, government ownership may diminish market orientation, operational flexibility and foreign legitimacy, all critical to overseas market success.[13] Such ambiguity argues against the adoption of predetermined rules in the evaluation of SOMNEs[14] and for the benefits of more flexible guidelines.

For all these reasons, a nuanced approach to evaluating the likely impacts of SOMNEs is required. This chapter emphasises the strategy of emerging market SOEs, focusing mainly on China, and develops implications for effective screening and regulation of such firms to minimise distortions and maximise welfare benefits. Such a review is useful given the growth of SOEs, particularly those from emerging economies, and their increased international reach.

---

[8] PWC, '*State-owned enterprises: Catalysts for public value creation?*' (PWC 2015).

[9] Li, M.H., L. Cui and J. Lu 'Marketized state ownership and foreign expansion of emerging market multinationals: leveraging institutional competitive advantages' (2017) *Asia Pacific Journal of Management* 34(1) 19, 23.

[10] Z. Deng, Z., J. Yan and M. van Essen, 'Heterogeneity of political connections and outward foreign direct investment' (2018) *International Business Review* 27(4) 893.

[11] D.M. Shapiro, and S. Globerman, 'The international activities and impacts of state-owned enterprises' in K. Sauvant, L.E. Sachs and W.P.F. Schmit Jongbloed (eds) *Sovereign Investment: Concerns and Policy Reactions* (OUP 2012) 98–144.

[12] N. Boubakri, J.C. Cossett, and W. Saffar, 'The role of the state and foreign owners in corporate risk-taking: evidence from privatization' (2013) *Journal of Financial Economics* 108(3) 641.

[13] J. Song, J., R. Wang, R. and S.T. Cavusgil, 'State ownership and market orientation in China's public firms: an agency theory perspective' (2015) *International Business Review* 24(4) 690.

[14] A. Cuervo-Cazurra (n 1).

SOEs are found in every economy.[15] While privatisation has meant a contraction in the public enterprise sector within developed economies, an offsetting increase has occurred with both re-nationalisations following the global financial crisis,[16] as well as the rise of emerging markets that have strong SOE representation. Data suggests that in 2010 amongst the largest 2000 public enterprises, more than ten per cent of sales were accounted for by SOEs, an amount comparable to almost six per cent of world GDP.[17] The proportion of SOEs within the Global Fortune 500 increased from nine per cent in 2004 to 23 per cent in 2014, with most of the increase accounted for by Chinese SOEs.[18]

It is not only through FDI that SOEs can transfer competitive distortions: many of the leading home countries of SOEs are also significant traders. China, for example, accounted for almost 13 percent of world trade in 2017. Indeed, the eight economies with the most significant SOE shares domestically accounted in total for more than 23 percent of world exports in 2017. The links between domestic production, exports and overseas investment are increasingly complex due to the growth of fragmented production systems characterised by global value chains, outsourcing, and trade in intermediates.[19] While the operations of SOEs within their home markets may be acceptable and ably regulated, difficulties can arise when these firms internationalise.[20] For example, a dominant domestic market position might be used to subsidise operations in overseas markets or to help capture host market share.

The discussion is organised around five principal sections. Following this introduction, an overview of the competitive distortions traditionally attributed to SOMNEs is presented. This highlights the influence of state goals and policies, resource dependence and governance weaknesses within SOEs. Section 3 introduces four dynamic aspects of SOE development and strategy reflecting state assistance in competitive upgrading and accelerated internationalisation, economic transition and hybrid SOE ownership forms. In the light of these factors, we discuss critical implications for investment evaluation and screening. The final section offers concluding thoughts.

---

[15] K.P. Sauvant, K.P. and J. Strauss '*State-controlled entities control nearly US$2 trillion in foreign assets*' (2012) Perspectives on foreign direct investment issues, Vale Columbia Center on Sustainable International Investment No. 64, April.

[16] A. Musacchio, A. and F. Flores-Macias, 'The return of state-owned enterprises: should we be afraid?' (2009) *Harvard International Review* April.

[17] P. Kowalski, M. Buge, M. Sztajerowska, and M. Egeland, '*State-owned enterprises: trade effects and policy implications*' OECD Trade Policy Papers No 147, (OECD 2013), 6.

[18] PWC (n 8), 9.

[19] OECD, '*State-owned enterprises as global competitors: a challenge or an opportunity?*' (OECD 2016).

[20] P. Kowalski, M. Buge, M. Sztajerowska, and M. Egeland (n 17), 13.

2 The Competitive Distortions of SOEs

While SOEs may be used to address market failures in the home market, their internationalisation does not extend this role into other markets. The specific interests of SOMNEs mean that they are not suited to tackling foreign market or institutional failures that would be better addressed by overseas government action, nor in providing global public goods, the domain of cross-border government cooperation.[21] The role that SOEs play in the home country, and the supports they receive to enable this, may be perceived as distortionary by host governments when such firms internationalise. Because SOEs do not face the market discipline that applies to privately owned firms, their impact within overseas markets may be competitively distortive. The literature highlights four principal sources of competitive distortions.

2.1 State Policies

The first results from home country policies supportive of SOEs. Policies that contribute to competitive deviations include concessions (subsidised loans, acceptance of lower rates of return or dividends), compensation for social obligations (protection against corporate failure, acceptance of overcapacity, preferential public procurement or the provision of strategic overseas market information or diplomatic support), and the toleration of home market domination or protection. While perhaps designed to meet domestic goals, such policies create asymmetric contestability, a condition that can be transferred to overseas markets.

In overseas markets, home country policies can create several observable distortions. A lower cost of capital may enable SOMNEs to offer higher prices for overseas assets, and they may also place greater reliance on cash as opposed to debt or equity when financing acquisitions.[22] The existence of protected revenue sources and a significantly reduced likelihood of takeover in the home country can encourage higher levels of risk-taking by SOEs and possible cross-subsidisation of fledging overseas operations. Risk-taking may not just be commercial: SOEs may be willing to assume higher levels of political risk when they can draw on home-based political capital.

[21] A. Cuervo-Cazurra (n 1), 142.

[22] OECD (n 19), 55.

2.2 SOE Goals

A second distortionary effect results from the non-commercial goals that are an expectation of SOMNEs. Indeed, it is such obligations that distinguish state-owned from privately-owned businesses. When the pursuit of home country interests is detrimental to the host country economy, concerns arise. The pursuit of multiple goals may result in lower productivity levels detrimental to economic welfare. Several studies show that productivity is positively related to international involvement.[23] Detrimental impacts on productivity are not simply the result of state ownership per se. A significant presence of SOEs in a sector may also impede private-sector productivity.[24]

A refinement of this argument is that SOMNEs may be 'repurposed' by the home-country government when they venture overseas, obliged to pursue government interests in the absence of institutional linkages.[25] In effect, SOMNEs become an instrument of state foreign policy, substituting for lack of political capital.

2.3 Resource Dependence

A third mechanism contributing to competitive distortions is the result of resource dependency on the state. Where the state is the primary supplier of essential resources, there is a noticeable weakening of market processes in the asset augmentation activities of SOEs. SOEs can attract resources on more favourable terms than privately owned firms and avoid the discipline of market transactions (meeting obligations to repay, pressures to perform efficiently, and managerial incentives). Such dependence strengthens obligations to pursue state goals.[26]

SOEs benefit from privileged access to a range of resources. The benefits stem from the quantity, cost, or exclusivity of such resources. Government resources may be provided directly or indirectly. Financial resources may be offered through concessionary funding, direct subsidies, or state-provided guarantees. Such considerations may provide additional funding or lower the costs at which funds are supplied. State provision of exclusive information can enable an early move into attractive business opportunities or reduce risk levels. Other resources include preferential regulatory action, perhaps offering exemptions from anti-monopoly rules, bankruptcy, or

[23] E. Helpmann, M. Melitz, and S. Yeaple, 'Exports versus FDI with heterogenous firms' (2004) *American Economic Review* 94 (1), 300.

[24] P. Kowalski, M. Buge, M. Sztajerowska, and M. Egeland (n 17).

[25] L.J. Clegg, H. Voss, and J.A. Tardios, 'The autocratic advantage: internationalization of state-owned multinationals' (2018) *Journal of World Business* 53(5) 668.

[26] K.E Meyer, 'Catch-up and leapfrogging: emerging economy multinational enterprises on the global stage' (2018) *International Journal of the Economics of Business* 25(1) 19, 24.

import competition. In such cases, a protected domestic market position may facilitate earnings and scale advantages as SOEs benefit from lower fixed or variable costs.[27]

Where the state regulates outward investment, political connections are useful in obtaining permission for overseas investment, providing both additional resources (where investment is asset-seeking) and experience (for both market- and asset-seeking motives). State connections in overseas markets may be useful in assuring entry, accessing seemingly closed markets, and identifying preferred partners.

Additional resources may be provided to SOEs directly, from the state, or indirectly, where SOEs form part of business groups. SOEs can pool resources and work collectively to overcome market or institutional weaknesses or tap into social capital in the latter case. In some cases, larger central SOEs have used groups to assist smaller local SOEs seeking to internationalise.[28]

It is essential to note that not all such concessions are a 'net' advantage to SOEs. In many cases, they are designed to compensate for the acceptance of non-commercial or strategic obligations that constrain profit-seeking behaviour. However, while this may be justified in the domestic context, with home-country taxpayers carrying the costs, such costs become distortionary with SOE internationalisation.

2.4 *Governance Issues*

Much of the distortionary concerns over SOMNE behaviour relate to their weak governance structures. SOEs face several governance challenges. One is the result of their multiple levels of delegation, from owners (voters) to politicians (agents), to bureaucrats and, ultimately, SOE managers. This means that while ownership (and cash flow) rights are widely dispersed, substantial control rights are enjoyed by politicians.

Their pursuit of multiple goals means that SOEs must accommodate social goals. They face government officials playing multiple and conflicting roles as regulators, regulation enforcers, and owners of assets, opening up the possibility of discriminatory favourable treatment. In terms of agency theory, compared with privately-owned businesses, SOEs face decreased monitoring by their delegated principals, may experience less financial accountability to state banks and investors, are managed by internal and politically appointed boards, exhibit limited transparency, and generally avoid takeover or bankruptcy threats.[29]

---

[27] A. Capobianco and H. Christiansen *Competitive neutrality and state-owned enterprises: challenges and policy options* (OECD 2011).

[28] Li, M.H., L. Cui and J. Lu (n 9), 29.

[29] D.M. Shapiro, and S. Globerman (n 11).

If, as a result, SOEs enjoy a 'soft budget constraint', there is a danger that they may overextend themselves in foreign markets, investing in large-scale projects,[30] assume excessive levels of risk,[31] over-pay for acquired assets[32] or 'crowd-out' private-sector competitors. A lack of transparency also increases the risk for host country stakeholders such as employees or suppliers who may struggle to evaluate the likelihood of foreign SOEs meeting contractual obligations.

3 Dynamic Considerations in the Evaluation of SOMNEs

Host country concerns with state-owned enterprises generally result from a perception that compared with privately owned firms, SOEs benefit from government-provided advantages that weaken their proclivity to adhere to market logic and competitive behaviour. Deviations from market principles create competitive distortions that impose costs on competitors and consumers. While there is considerable merit in this traditional view of the distortionary impacts of SOEs, such a view is incomplete. In particular, it fails to consider other important benefits that SOEs may enjoy, and it suffers from its adoption of a static view of SOEs as the archetypical antithesis of privately owned firms.

We highlight four areas that offer ambiguous predictions of the possible competitive distortions attributable to SOMNEs, but that should be incorporated into screening and regulation decisions. Two effects—enhanced competitive upgrading through learning opportunities and accelerated internationalisation—can add to distortionary effects. Conversely, economic transition and the increasing hybridisation of SOEs can have the opposite effect, bringing closer alignment with the incentives faced by privately owned firms. We consider each of these issues below.

3.1 Competitive Upgrading and Learning

In the face of rapid economic growth, emerging market firms cannot expect to maintain their cost advantages indefinitely. They need to plan to upgrade their competitiveness in areas such as innovation, production technology, and quality. Research has identified three generic upgrading paths: (1) path-following catch-up, (2) compressed

---

[30] A. Cuervo-Cazurra, A., Inkpen, A., Musacchio, and K. Ramaswamy, 'Governments as owners: state-owned multinational companies' (2014) *Journal of International Business Studies* 45(8) 919.

[31] H.W. Hu and L. Cui, 'Outward foreign direct investment of publicly listed firms from China: a corporate governance perspective' (2014) *International Business Review* 23(4) 750.

[32] K.E. Meyer, Y. Ding, L. Ji and H. Zhang, 'Overcoming distrust: How state-owned enterprises adapt their foreign entries to institutional pressures abroad' (2014) *Journal of International Business Studies* 45(8)1005.

catch-up, and (3) path-creating.[33] The first two are based on replicating the success of more advanced competitor firms; the latter on creating new business models founded on home market conditions and opportunities.[34] Given the relative knowledge isolation of most emerging economies,[35] government support in fostering competitive upgrading is not unexpected.

The type and degree of support vary with the upgrading path pursued. For conventional catch-up, home country governments have several options for facilitating knowledge acquisition. Where foreign investors see a large or rapidly growing market, they may be willing to form partnerships with local firms with technology sharing as the price for market access. SOEs have profited from technology transfer from joint venture partners.[36] More generally, the presence of foreign competitors can be a source of positive spillovers benefiting a wide range of local firms. Important production locations such as China can facilitate insertion into regional and global value chains when the state invests in specialist clusters, facilities, and skills, in conjunction with an open trading regime.

These same benefits apply to firms pursuing a compressed catch-up strategy where strategic asset-seeking overseas acquisitions further enhance competitiveness. In such cases, it is the state that provides permission to undertake such ventures, may offer financial and other support, and facilitates the transfer of acquired capabilities back to the home market. More general policies that benefit such firms include policies on skilled returnees and implementing strategies such as the 2002 Going Global policy under which the Chinese authorities committed to creating up to 50 'national champions', often SOEs, capable of competing globally in several nascent industries. These firms have enjoyed significant assistance in both their domestic development and early internationalisation.[37]

Path creating firms benefit indirectly from policies applicable to all types of businesses and from economic transition. Government investment in domestic R&D programmes, educational upgrading, the creation of business clusters, and lax policies on intellectual property protection all provide benefits to path creating firms. In many cases, the tolerance of dominant market positions and restrictions on foreign competitors enables local firms to learn through knowledge integration (in the absence of local specialists), through trial and error (where the absence of foreign competitors means solutions are still to be found) and repetition (favoured by large

---

[33] K. Lee, 'Making a technological catch-up: barriers and opportunities' (2005) *Asian Journal of Technology Innovation* 13(2): 97, 101.

[34] P. Enderwick and P.J. Buckley, 'Catch-up, spring boarding and path-creating emerging market firms: the case of China's mobile payments industry' (2020) unpublished paper.

[35] H. Rui, A. Cuervo-Cazurra and C. A. Un, 'Learning-by-doing in emerging market multinationals: integration, trial and error, repetition, and extension' (2016) *Journal of World Business* 51(5) 686, 695.

[36] S. Girma and Y. Gong, 'FDI, linkages and the efficiency of state-owned enterprises in China' (2008) *Journal of Development Studies* 44(5) 728.

[37] J. Lu, X. Liu and H. Wang, 'Motives for outward FDI of Chinese private firms: firm resources, industry dynamics, and government policies' (2011) *Management and Organization Review* 7(2) 223.

and rapidly growing markets).[38] More positively, emerging markets such as China are now taking the initiative to set or influence global industry standards that can provide their firms with solid early mover advantages.

3.2 Accelerated Internationalisation

As a second source of advantage, both the provision of additional resources and assistance in competitive upgrading has enabled emerging market, and particularly Chinese, SOEs, to compress their internationalisation processes. There is debate on the motives for SOE internationalisation. One view is that emerging market SOEs internationalise to acquire additional resources, particularly technological and marketing assets difficult to source in the home market.[39] The need for such strategic assets may prompt early, aggressive and recurrent internationalisation.[40] Similarly, as instruments of state policy, SOEs may be expected to internationalise to ensure the supply of needed resources.[41]

An alternative view is that SOEs leave the home country in the face of institutional constraints. Such escape may be prompted by excessive competition, discriminatory action favouring competitors, a desire to reduce dependence on state providers, or an inability to meet domestic market demands in terms of quality or safety[42].[43] Early internationalisation is encouraged by the risk reduction that comes from government financial and regulatory support as well as access to established networks in host countries.[44] However, pressures for escape are likely lower for SOEs than for privately owned firms.[45]

Several emerging markets, most notably China, adopt policies designed to encourage outward foreign direct investment. Such policies favour particular industries and activities that contribute to national development. Outward FDI offers two primary benefits for the domestic economy: access to critical resources that may

---

[38] H. Rui, A. Cuervo-Cazurra and C. A. Un (n 36) 696.

[39] J.A. Mathews, 'Dragon multinationals: new players in 21st century globalization' (2006) *Asia Pacific Journal of Management* 23(1) 5.

[40] Y. Luo and R.L. Tung, 'A general theory of springboard MNEs' (2018) *Journal of International Business Studies* 49(2) 129.

[41] I. Alon, H. Wang, J. Shen, and W. Zhang, 'Chinese state-owned enterprises go global' (2014) *Journal of Business Strategy* 35(6) 3, 4.

[42] P. Enderwick, 'Viewpoint: escape FDI From emerging markets: clarifying and extending the concept' (2017) *International Journal of Emerging Markets* 12(3) 418.

[43] M.A. Witt and A.Y. Lewin, 'Outward foreign direct investment as escape response to home country institutional constraints' (2007) *Journal of International Business Studies* 38(4) 579.

[44] T. Wei, J. Clegg J. and L. Ma, 'The conscious and unconscious facilitating role of the Chinese government in shaping the internationalization of Chinese MNEs' (2015) *International Business Review* 24(2) 331.

[45] Li, M.H., L. Cui and J. Lu (n 9).

be lacking at home, including raw materials, technology, brand names and management skills; and entry to economic processes that contribute to home market growth such as global value chains, new market segments and opportunities for upgrading.[46] Such policies are exacerbated in cases where market access reciprocity is lacking and asymmetries entrench unfair competition.[47]

An explanation for accelerated internationalisation is offered by springboard theory that suggests emerging market multinationals may engage in a systematic strategy of accelerated catch-up through asset-seeking internationalisation[48,49]. As a deliberate strategy, Springboarding facilitates firm growth and competitive capability through recurrent and revolving international activities. Aggressive spring boarding means that a firm is likely to undertake a series of overseas investments or acquisitions to overcome competitive weaknesses,[50,51] to compensate for latecomer disadvantages[52] and to address domestic institutional and market failures.[53] Such behaviour is revolving in that acquired assets may also be used to augment competitiveness in the firm's home market.

The ability to undertake aggressive internationalisation at an early stage of firm development, and often with limited resources and experience, carries a high level of risk, particularly when overseas entry involves dissimilar markets and high control modes such as greenfield investments or mergers and acquisitions. Such risks may be offset by home government support for internationalisation and the willingness of competitors to share knowledge or resources that might be contingent on their access to a large and rapidly developing market such as China or India. The Chinese state is well placed to assist the largest central SOEs as a restructuring process has reduced the number of central SOEs from 196 in 2003 to 97 at the end of 2017.

A preference for international mergers and acquisitions (M&As) is another characteristic of outward FDI from emerging economies. The share of cross-border M&As undertaken by SOEs increased markedly from the late 1990s, accounting for around

[46] K.P. Sauvant and V.Z. Chen, 'China's regulatory framework for outward direct foreign investment' (2014) *China Economic Journal* 7(1) 141.

[47] D.H. Rosen and T. Hanemann, 'The changing US-China investment relationship' (2014) *China Economic Journal* 7(1) 84.

[48] Y. Luo and R.L. Tung, 'International expansion of emerging market enterprises: a springboard perspective' (2007) *Journal of International Business Studies* 38(4): 481–498.

[49] Y. Luo and R.L. Tung (n 41).

[50] F. De Beule, S. Elia and L. Piscitello, 'Entry and access to competences abroad: emerging market firms versus advanced market firms' (2014) *Journal of International Management* 20(2) 137.

[51] R. Ramamurti and P.J. Williamson, 'Rivalry between emerging-market MNEs and developed-country MNEs: capability holes and the race to the future' (2019) *Business Horizons* 62(2) 157.

[52] G.S. Carpenter and K. Nakamoto, 'Consumer preference formation and pioneering advantage' (1989) *Journal of Marketing Research* 26(3) 285.

[53] D. Rottig, 'Institutions and emerging markets: effects and implications for multinational corporations' (2016) *International Journal of Emerging Markets* 11(1) 2.

one-third of all transactions in the decade, peaking during the 2008–10 global financial crisis.[54] During this challenging period, SOEs appeared to be relatively less adversely affected in cash-flow terms and could take advantage of the weakened position of private-sector competitors. In 2016, China became the largest source of cross-border M&As, exceeding the United States in terms of both the number and value of acquisitions.[55]

Research on the motivations for M&As reveals a desire to acquire strategic assets such as leading technologies and international market knowledge. The attraction of M&As is that they give direct access to tacit knowledge that is difficult to transact through markets.[56] Not surprisingly, developed economies such as the United States and Germany have become the primary targets for Chinese acquisitions.

While there appears to be a perception amongst competitors that government preferences provide advantages to SOEs,[57] it is essential to acknowledge that government connections can also imply disadvantages. The first of these might be termed the 'liabilities of stateness,' describing the negative connotations of having strong political connections. These include greater incompatibility with host country institutions, particularly in market economies, the pursuit of non-commercial goals, the danger of transfer of home-country values, and concerns about decision-making independence. Second, a primary constraint on the internationalisation of Chinese SOEs is likely to be the lack of experienced senior staff, particularly those with international experience.[58] This may help explain the higher failure rates of SOE cross-border mergers and acquisitions.[59]

3.3 Economic Transition

A defining characteristic of emerging markets is their dynamism, expressed as a transition towards greater reliance on market processes.[60] For many emerging economies, the primary transition is from a centrally planned regime governed by bureaucratic controls towards a rules-based market economy. The speed and degree of transition

[54] A. Baroncelli and M. Landoni, 'Chinese state-owned enterprises in the market for corporate control. Evidences and rationales of acquisitions in western countries' in A. Vecchi (ed) *Chinese Acquisitions in Developed Countries* (Springer 2019) 17–37.

[55] Y. Yang, L. Chen, and Z. Tang, '*Chinese M&As in Germany*' (Springer 2019).

[56] M. Florio, M. Ferraris and D. Vandone, '*State-owned enterprises: rationales for mergers and acquisitions*' (2018) CIRIEC Working Paper 1801 Universite de Liege.

[57] OECD (n 19).

[58] K.E. Meyer and K. Xin, 'Managing talent in emerging economy multinationals: integrating strategic management and human resource management' *International Journal of Human Resource Management* 29(11) 1827.

[59] J. Zhang, C. Zhou and H. Ebbers, 'Completion of Chinese overseas acquisitions: institutional perspectives and evidence' (2011) *International Business Review* 20(2) 226.

[60] P. Enderwick, '*The competitive challenge of emerging markets: China and India*' (Cambridge Scholars Publishing 2020).

Table 1 Changing nature of economic characteristics under transition

Economic characteristics	Under a centrally planned economy	Changes within a transition economy
Resource allocation	Determined by central planning	Increasing reliance on market allocation
Resource allocation processes	Central plan, devolution of targets	Forces of demand and supply, adjustment through relative price changes
Controls on economic activity	Bureaucratic, State apparatus	Rules-based competition
Ownership of resources	State, e.g. SOEs	Private, possible privatisation of SOEs
Controls on economic activity	Bureaucratic	Rules-based competition
Property rights	Held collectively (the State)	Move towards private property rights
Strategic factor markets	Under State control (plans)	Developed increasingly independently
Values	Collectivism	Individualism
Markets	Narrow, static, determined by State priorities	Wider, dynamic and driven by rising consumer sovereignty
Role of competition	Limited, focus on cooperation	Increasingly driven by commercial considerations
Contractual enforcement	State determined	Network relations with the growth of an independent legal framework
Scale, scope and complexity of transactions	Modest, subsumed within plans	Growing meaning increased reliance on a rules-based contractual system
Political structures	Stable	Increasingly unstable during a transition period
Firm strategy	State-driven	Increasingly a determinant of firm success
Firm growth	Bureaucratic priorities	Network-based growth with independent decision-making

vary considerably: some Eastern European economies such as Russia have experienced 'shock' transitions; in contrast, China has adopted a more gradualist approach. Regardless of the pace of transition, an underlying determinant of a successful transition is an appropriate alignment of institutional frameworks and firm strategy.[61]

Table 1 provides an overview of the critical economic changes associated with the transition in emerging economies, particularly those with a socialist legacy. They highlight the overall move from dependence on state planning and bureaucratic control to a greater reliance on market forces to determine supply and prices.

[61] D.C. North, *'Institutions, institutional change, and economic performance'* (CUP 1990).

This occurs through the growing importance of competition in determining economic outcomes.

As the state's role is reduced, greater independence is assumed by firms, particularly SOEs and their managers. Unfortunately, this is also a time of growing uncertainty as an effective market economy does not entirely displace socialist planning. Instead, economic activities occur within a hybrid system incorporating a legacy of state direction and the growing challenge of increasingly independent consumers and producers.[62] The institutions that underpin an effective market economy are missing or nascent. The process of transition is neither smooth nor linear: it is characterised by progress and setbacks. As a result, SOEs still rely on the networks of personal relationships that steered them under collective planning. However, economic growth, the widening of markets, increased international engagement and the complexity of transition highlight the limitations of a relationship-based economy. While relationships may be useful in managing uncertainty or in the pooling of resources in a transition period, greater economic scale and complexity imply rising transaction costs under such a system.

Firms, including SOEs, require new proprietary advantages, particularly in the areas of product innovation, marketing and quality management, to succeed. But it is just such competitive advantages that contribute to accelerated internationalisation, as discussed above. Accelerated internationalisation can occur either because SOEs can better develop the capabilities needed to succeed in world markets or are pressured to internationalise to acquire such skills. If the transition is accompanied by an opening up of the domestic market to allow inward FDI or greater import competition, the pressures to internationalise (from competition), or the capabilities to internationalise (from spillovers), are that much greater. As a result of these changes in institutions, operating environment and competition, SOEs will shift to become more closely aligned with private sector firms in terms of strategy. However, given the well-established relationship between strategy and structure,[63] changes in SOEs' ownership and organisational structure are also likely to be observed through hybridisation.

3.4 SOE Hybridisation

The economic transition has been accompanied by changes in the ownership structures of SOEs. The archetypical centralised, wholly state-owned and directed SOE is declining in importance. The listing of SOEs on stock markets has created hybrid organisations with a mix of private and public ownership traits.[64] Changes in ownership structures have brought corresponding changes in governance. Hybridisation

---

[62] M.W. Peng, 'Institutional transitions and strategic choices' (2003) *Academy of Management Review* 28(2) 275.

[63] A.D. Chandler, '*Strategy and structure*' (MIT Press 1982).

[64] G.D. Bruton, M.W. Peng, D. Ahlstrom, C. Stan, and K. Xu (n 7).

introduces to the state sector mechanisms for scrutinising managerial behaviour that is commonplace for listed private firms, including shareholder monitoring, the threat of takeover (where state ownership is minor), and bankruptcy. Listed SOEs are subject to both state and private sector governance mechanisms. In particular, minority private shareholders can observe the behaviour of state officials.[65] However, their ability to do so is tied to economic transition and the development of effective market-supporting institutions. Developed capital markets impose regular reporting requirements, enabling more effective monitoring. Benchmarking with comparable peers can reveal shortcomings and provide incentives for improvement. The incentive for managers is that accountability for their performance is an indicator of their prospects in managerial labour markets. In countries such as China, the move to mixed ownership of SOEs has been significant, By 2013, more than half of all central SOEs had transitioned to mixed ownership.[66] Worldwide, hybrid SOEs account for around ten per cent of global GDP and are the preferred organisational form for some of the world's leading MNEs.[67]

Marketised SOEs experience reconfigured governance systems, management practices and competitive strategies designed to increase their effectiveness in a market economy. This occurs in several ways. One is the increased degree of managerial autonomy enjoyed within hybrid SOEs. This encourages the pursuit of improved efficiency and responses to market demand through innovation and brand investment.[68] Second, greater state independence offers strategic flexibility and the opportunity to pursue profitable new opportunities, particularly in recently liberalised sectors of the economy. Third, in many cases, central SOEs that have been restructured have also been consolidated, increasing their financial, informational and reputational resources, all of which can contribute to international strategy.[69]

It is worth noting that the considerations discussed here are not necessarily independent. It is clear that both transition and marketisation of SOEs bring closer alignment with market incentives and may reduce the 'liabilities of stateness' that SOEs face in overseas markets. For example, the finding that legitimisation of SOMNEs is lower in overseas markets that advocate market principles supports this expectation.[70] Second, the quality of government is likely to impact all these areas. Higher government quality is positively correlated with both transition and attempts to restructure SOEs. More generally, higher government quality reduces the likelihood that SOEs

---

[65] R. Dharwadkar, G. George and P. Brandes, 'Privatisation in emerging economies: an agency theory perspective' (2000) *Academy of Management Review* 25(3) 650.

[66] Li, M.H., L. Cui and J. Lu (n 9), 22.

[67] G.D. Bruton, M.W. Peng, D. Ahlstrom, C. Stan, and K. Xu (n 7).

[68] G. Jefferson and J. Su, 'Privatisation and restructuring in China: Evidence from shareholding ownership, 1995–2001 (2006) *Journal of Comparative Economics* 34(1) 146.

[69] J. Child and S.B. Rodriguez, 'The internationalization of Chinese firms: a case for theoretical extension?' (2005) *Management and Organization Review* 1(3) 381.

[70] J. Li, J. Xia, D. Shapiro and Z. Lin, 'Institutional compatibility and the internationalization of Chinese SOEs: the moderating role of home subnational institutions' (2018) *Journal of World Business* 53(5) 641, 642.

will be forced to pursue non-commercial goals, the existence of independent institutions can help mitigate such behaviour, while the moral hazard issue of soft budget constraints is reduced where a higher level of effective governance evolves.[71]

The interaction of transition and hybridisation has brought three principal changes: in the level of state ownership (majority, minority), the geographical focus of SOEs (central, regional, local),[72] and in the implementation of new formal and informal institutions in the monitoring of SOEs.[73] Empirical research confirms behavioural differences along these dimensions. The consolidation of central SOEs as 'national champions' magnifies the influence of both home and host country institutions on their international behaviour, reinforcing their access to home country advantages, and simultaneously, exposure to host country animosity. Local SOEs, with less home country market power, enjoy higher levels of both managerial discretion and market orientation.[74] Benito et al.[75] present evidence that Norwegian listed SOEs may benefit more from internationalisation than non-listed firms, as while the former enjoy government support, they also assume fewer non-economic obligations. Similarly, Estrin et al.[76] and Clo et al.[77] find that constraints on listed SOE behaviour, particularly from capital markets and formal governance mechanisms, propel such firms to emulate comparable private sector firms.

4 Implications for Screening and Regulation of SOEs

Beliefs about the likely behaviour of SOMNEs have led to concerns by host countries over both screening (whether such investment is permitted or not) and regulation (the monitoring and control of acceptable foreign investments) of SOEs.

Screening of foreign investment by SOEs has increased in recent years, mirroring the growth of SOEs from emerging economies. The OECD reports that around a third of their investment policy dialogue country members now operate screening

[71] B. Grogaard, A. Rygh and G.R. G. Benito, 'Bringing corporate governance into internalization theory: state ownership and foreign entry strategies (2019) *Journal of International Business Studies* 50(8): 1310, 1316.

[72] M.H. Li, L. Cui and J. Lu, 'Varieties in state capitalism: outward FDI strategies of central and local state-owned enterprises from emerging economy countries' (2014) *Journal of International Business Studies* 45(8) 980.

[73] S. Estrin, K.E. Meyer, B.B. Nielsen and S.T. Nielsen, 'Home country institutions and the internationalization of state-owned enterprises: a cross-country analysis' (2016) *Journal of World Business* 51(2) 294.

[74] M.H. Li, L. Cui and J. Lu (n 74).

[75] G.R.G. Benito, A. Rygh and R. Lunnan, 'The benefits of internationalization for state-owned enterprises' (2016) *Global Strategy Journal* 6(4) 269.

[76] S. Estrin, K.E. Meyer, B.B. Nielsen and S.T. Nielsen (n 75).

[77] S. Clo, C.V. Fiorio and M. Florio,'The targets of state capitalism: evidence from M&A deals' (2017) *European Journal of Political Economy* 47(C): 61.

mechanisms.[78] Existing regimes in countries including the United States, Australia, and Canada have strengthened processes applicable to SOEs, and several countries now separate SOE investments from those of private-sector firms.[79] The regulation of SOMNEs occurs at several levels with provisions included in WTO agreements, at the regional level with OECD stipulations,[80] in bilateral trade and investment agreements and nationally, such as the US-based CFIUS.[81]

Perhaps the distinguishing trait of SOMNE screening and regulation is its subjective nature. In many cases, the criteria adopted are narrow: often based on national security issues. For example, in the United States, CFIUS, the Committee on Foreign Investment in the United States, is charged with evaluating only national security threats and not the more general case of 'national economic benefit'. In almost all cases, the evaluation criteria are outdated, failing to consider the changing nature of SOEs as discussed above. Evaluation is typically based on a simple binary approach—state versus privately owned businesses. SOEs are assumed to be wholly state-owned and controlled. They are also assumed to reflect home-country interests and hence may be excluded from critical sectors of the economy. In several cases, particularly regarding proposed critical infrastructure investments, it is unclear if the host country objections are based on public ownership, foreign ownership, or a combination of the two.[82] Some commentators even suggest that screening by ownership is unnecessary: all that is required is a simple net economic benefits test. If the investment passes such a test, the nature of ownership is irrelevant and simply increases the likelihood that a host country will forego valuable investment projects.[83] It is perhaps not surprising that screening in these ways results in frustration and misunderstanding for potential investors.[84]

The uncertainty created by diverse subjective screening regimes has led some to call for a more rules-based approach to the evaluation of SOEMNEs. Cuervo-Cazurra[85] has suggested separating the concerns with SOEs into three groups: economic, political, and psychological, categorised according to ownership and home country development status (emerging economies). He proposes an ex-ante rule of exclusion of SOE investment when security or technological superiority is threatened,

[78] F. Wehrle, F. and H. Christiansen, '*State-owned enterprises, international investment and national security: the way forward*' (OECD 2017), 1.

[79] K.P. Sauvant and J. Strauss, '*State-controlled entities control nearly US$2 trillion in foreign assets*' Vale Columbia Center on Sustainable International Investment (2012).

[80] OECD, '*Guidelines on corporate governance of state-owned enterprises*' (OECD 2015).

[81] T. H. Moran, 'Towards a multilateral framework for identifying national security threats posed by foreign acquisitions: with special reference to Chinese acquisitions in the United States, Canada and Australia' (2014) *China Economic Journal* 7(1) 39.

[82] OECD (n 19), 60.

[83] Y.P. Woo, 'Chinese lessons: state-owned enterprises and the regulation of foreign investment in Canada' (2014) *China Economic Journal* 7(1) 21, 34.

[84] D.H. Rosen and T. Hanemann, 'The changing US-China investment relationship' (2014) *China Economic Journal* 7(1) 84, 97.

[85] A. Cuervo-Cazurra (n 1), 140.

monitoring when governance distortions are suspected, and controls when psychological concerns such as loss of relative economic status occur. While such rules may appear to offer greater certainty, the effect of the latter two is unclear. When does monitoring trigger action, and what types of action? What forms of controls will be employed, and how will they be implemented? This approach does little to overcome the uncertainty that currently prevails. It is also unlikely that any host government would be willing to relinquish control over international investment decisions for reasons of political survival.

What is paramount is the need to minimise unnecessary uncertainty and safeguard consistency. If not, worthwhile investments will be deterred with resultant welfare losses. For many host countries, screening fulfils the dual role of both ensuring that potentially worthwhile investments are not unnecessarily excluded and that the public interest is paramount in such decision-making. This may involve a trade-off between public confidence and investor uncertainty when final approval is the responsibility of publicly elected officials (government ministers), guided by evaluations produced by advisory bodies.[86]

Host country discretion is also necessary to reflect the dynamics of SOMNEs, particularly as the transition occurs and new hybrid organisational and ownership forms develop. SOEs are not passive in the face of screening and regulation. They may, for example, invest in legitimacy building when entering hostile host countries through greater local sourcing, appointing nationals to senior positions, or engaging in socially beneficial activities. Also relevant is the nature of the home-country government, with recent evidence[87] suggesting that more autocratic governments demand more from their SOEs, implying a likely greater deviation from host-country interests.

It could also be argued that an effective way to improve SOE governance is to allow them to invest in economies with more sophisticated institutions and governance structures so that they might learn and upgrade their processes. The same argument could be applied to opportunities for SOEs to achieve greater market orientation and responsiveness to levels of competition that they may not face at home. In effect, this enables the creation, rather than the acquisition, of firm-specific advantages critical to success in the global economy. Such arguments are reinforced in a period of rising protectionism.

Home-country governments also have a significant role to play in facilitating the acceptance of SOMNEs. While transition as a development path positively affects SOE behaviour, more specific domestic reforms could be used to accelerate acceptance. Key reforms include increasing transparency, improving governance, and ensuring competitive neutrality between state-owned and private-sector firms. In addition, emerging economies such as China could improve access to foreign investors tackling the widely held concern over investment reciprocity. Opening up

86 R. Mendelsohn and A. Fels, 'Australia's foreign investment review board and the regulation of Chinese investment' (2014) *China Economic Journal* 7(1) 59.

87 L.J. Clegg, H. Voss, and J.A. Tardios (n 25).

to inward FDI may help to erode the home market advantage that some SOEs enjoy, and that offers them a continuing source of funding.[88]

5 Conclusion

This chapter argues that host country perceptions of SOMNEs provide, at best, a partial and largely static portrait of their likely impacts. Much of the current policy analysis is based on structural differences (size, ownership patterns, assumption of social obligations, dominant market positions) that SOEs display and the competitive distortions that could arise when such firms' cross national borders. The analysis is generally based on a simplistic model of SOEs: wholly state owned and directed and diverging significantly from market-determined economic outcomes.

Acknowledging the dynamism of home country economies, particularly emerging economies, provides a more comprehensive picture of SOEs' issues and challenges. The discussion offered here highlights two often neglected areas that can exacerbate competitive distortions—supported competitive upgrading and accelerated internationalisation. Offsetting these are moves towards transition and the hybridisation of SOEs, both of which may help to reduce competitive distortions. The thrust of such policies is to ensure the inducements experienced by SOEs more closely resemble the market incentives that drive private firms. The expectation is that SOE behaviour will then mirror that anticipated of the private sector.

Our discussion in highlighting the dynamics of SOMNEs suggests that host countries should strive to achieve investment policies that are non-discriminatory and transparent towards SOEs. National security concerns need to be separated from economic benefit tests. Combining the two simply adds to uncertainty and claims of discrimination.

Reductions in the competitive distortions attributed to SOEs are possible when host countries move towards competitive neutrality and implement policies designed to offset the taxation, financing and regulatory advantages enjoyed by SOEs in their home countries. Of course, the transparency problems with many SOEs make the design of such policies challenging as they require detailed information on market position, the extent of social obligations, financing arrangements, public procurement policies, direct state support and dividend expectations.[89] Given the design challenges of such policies, they should perhaps be seen as complementary to investment screening and not an alternative, that is, liberalised investment approval with host market monitoring and enforcement.

The central argument remains: the competitive strengths of SOEs do not reflect just the distortions they may bring; in addition, they have benefited from policies that have enhanced their competitiveness and in ways that might be perceived as unfair

[88] OECD (n 19).

[89] OECD, *'Competitive neutrality: Maintaining a level playing field between public and private business'* (OECD 2012).

in many developed host economies. While difficult to quantify and to incorporate objectively into approval decisions, these are relevant and important considerations for host country policy.

The arguments presented here do suggest that over time some of the challenges presented by SOMNEs might be mitigated as they move closer to market incentives. However, this remains a complex area that requires further analysis. For example, there are likely to be marked differences in the behaviour of central when compared to local SOEs. Similarly, market competition, and not just simply market orientation, appears important in driving SOE behaviour.[90]

It is also worth noting that we have assumed that declining levels of state ownership mean declining state control, but this may not be the case. Control can be exercised in other ways. Similarly, we have not considered the broader international political economy question that opposition to SOEs, particularly those from China, might be interpreted in terms of realism theory, with such firms acting as flagships for future home country dominance[91] and likely to trigger discriminatory protectionist measures. All of these issues are worthy of further investigation.

[90] Y. Huang, E. Xie, Y. Li and K.S. Reddy, 'Does state ownership facilitate outward FDI of Chinese SOEs? Institutional development, market competition, and the logic of interdependence between governments and SOEs' (2017) *International Business Review* 26(1) 176.

[91] S. Krasner, 'State power and the structure of international trade' (1976) *World Politics* 28(3) 317.

The End of European Naivety: Difficult Times Ahead for SCEs/SOEs Investing in the European Union?

Ondřej Svoboda

1 Introduction

At present, we are witnessing growing concerns about investment originating in less transparent economies and about investment by foreign State-controlled entities (SCEs), especially State-owned enterprises (SOEs). Although they are not a new phenomenon, the rise of state capitalism generates a new reality which "in the area of foreign direct investment (FDI) supposes the coexistence, or even the displacement, of purely commercial motives with political ones in certain operations and activities."[1] Responding to these changes of investment flows, a number of countries are adapting their foreign investment screening mechanisms as a part of risk-management strategies.[2] This global development has affected also the EU and resulted in the new

[1] Carlos Esplugues, *Foreign Investment, Strategic Assets and National Security* (Intersentia 2018) 181.

[2] For a general overview of the current state of play, *see* e.g., Laura Fraedrich, Chase Kaniecki and Sara Rafferty, 'Foreign Investment Control Heats Up: A Global Survey of Existing Regimes and Potential Significant Changes on the Horizon' (2018) 13 Global Trade and Customs Journal 141.

[3] Regulation (EU) 2019/452 of the European Parliament and of the Council of 19 March 2019 establishing a framework for the screening of foreign direct investments into the Union, OJ L 79I, 21.3.2019 ('EU Regulation').

This chapter draws upon the author's original publication also available at https://www.transnational-dispute-management.com/journal-advance-publication-article.asp?key=1836. Reprinted by permission from Maris BV: Maris BV, *Transnational Dispute Management* (TDM, ISSN 1875-4120), "The End of European Naivety: Difficult Times Ahead for SCEs/SOEs Investing in the European Union?", Ondřej Svoboda, Copyright (2000). Please cite accordingly.

O. Svoboda (✉)
Faculty of Law, Charles University, Prague, Czech Republic
e-mail: ondrej.svobod@gmail.com

Embassy of the Czech Republic in Tokyo, Ministry of Foreign Affairs of the Czech Republic, Tokyo, Japan

J. Chaisse et al. (eds.), *Regulation of State-Controlled Enterprises*, International Law and the Global South, https://doi.org/10.1007/978-981-19-1368-6_22

EU framework for the screening of foreign direct investments created by Regulation 2019/452 establishing a framework for the screening of foreign direct investments into the Union ("EU Regulation"). The EU Regulation officially entered into force in April 2019 and has applied since 11 October 2020.[3] Notably, the legislative process was extremely fast given that the European Commission tabled its proposal for this regulation in September 2017.

Currently, only half of the EU Member States have national legislation in place that establishes a multi-sectoral instrument to review FDI.[4] In principle, their policies are designed to safeguard national security and public order. Considering this relatively limited number of screening mechanisms in the EU and the lack of a EU-wide mechanism comparable with other developed states such the US, Japan, Canada or Australia, and an increasing inflow of foreign investment into sensitive assets in the EU, the calls for the EU to take a more active role in scrutinising foreign investment finally received prominent political support. According to a leading European parliamentarian in the process of adopting the EU Regulation, Franck Proust, the EU's persisting openness to foreign investment was "naïve" and "it [was] about to end very soon now."[5]

Specifically, this rapid development was triggered by a letter jointly signed by ministers from Germany, France and Italy and addressed to the European Commission in February 2017. In the letter, the ministers called for "an additional protection" from investments by foreign buyers in areas sensitive to security and industrial policy.[6] The European Commission, in response, proposed a mechanism for the screening of foreign direct investments as part of the trade package announced in September 2017. The response raised many important questions but the European Parliament, the European Commission and the Council reached the final political agreement on the framework of the mechanism a year later, in November 2018.

The establishment of the EU screening mechanism was an important milestone in two main aspects. Firstly, it represented a big change to the EU's very open attitude towards FDI. Secondly, there is a risk that screening mechanisms may be abused as a protectionist instrument. The second aspect has triggered debates over the legitimacy and use of the screening policies in the EU. The two aspects also mark further consolidation of the EU investment policy. On top of the already covered investment liberalisation and investment protection policy tools, EU investment policy will soon cover policies designed to safeguard national security and public order.

Although the recent steps taken by the EU are not openly directed towards any specific state or enterprise, it is presumed that the EU targets the risks associated with operations of SCEs/SOEs. In practice, certain companies are directly or indirectly

---

[4] Austria, Finland, France, Germany, Hungary, Italy, Latvia, Lithuania, Poland, Portugal, Spain, United Kingdom.

[5] EurActiv, 'With eyes on China, EU agrees investment screening rules' (21 November 2018) <https://www.euractiv.com/section/economy-jobs/news/with-eyes-on-china-eu-agrees-investment-screening-rules/> accessed 2 April 2019.

[6] 'Proposals for ensuring an improved level playing field in trade and investment' (February 2017) <https://www.bmwi.de/Redaktion/DE/Downloads/E/eckpunktepapier-proposals-for-ensuring-an-improved-level-playing-field-in-trade-and-investment.pdf?__blob=publicationFile&v=2> accessed 5 March 2019.

influenced by their home states through various means, or where foreign government facilitate foreign take-overs by national companies, notably through facilitating access to financing or other means of control.[7] Cross-border investment in general and cross-border investment from Chinese entities specifically has accelerated in recent years and this has received large attention in the media coverage. The rise in Chinese acquisitions is sometimes described as a "splurge," or a "shopping spree," or "scramble for Europe" with negative implications for the acquired EU unity.[8] Often, the suspicion is that the enterprises are tasked by a home state government following non-commercial policy objectives. Certain controversies surrounding Chinese economic influence have been experienced in several EU Members States, most frequently in Germany, where Chinese efforts to take over local high-tech companies continue to raise serious concerns.[9]

SCEs and SOEs entering in the EU Single Market thus invite further investigations into the actual track record of SCEs/SOEs, predominantly from China and Russia, investing in the EU. This contribution explores the newly established European approach towards foreign direct investments and focuses particularly on investment made by SCEs/SOEs. To address this emerging issue, the chapter reviews the relevant primary data as well as the EU internal debates and sources in other jurisdictions. The focus is devoted to the regulation itself and above all its part dealing with SCEs/SOEs. Hence, the contribution puts the approach of the EU into a broader context as an increasing number of countries have recently started re-evaluating their investment policies and new trends in this field continue to emerge.

2 Increasing Role of SCEs/SOEs as Foreign Investors in the EU

It is generally recognised that SOEs play a growing role in the global economy and in some instances they represent a significant share of outward foreign direct investment or even their creation and operation is a part of a declared government strategy.[10] Data on FDI flows in the EU confirm this general view.[11]

According the European Commission, over the period 2007–2017, foreign states, usually through companies that have the foreign state as their ultimate owner, acquired almost 400 EU companies. The most active SOEs have been from EFTA

[7] OECD, *State-Owned Enterprises as Global Competitors: A Challenge or an Opportunity?* (OECD Publishing, Paris 2016).

[8] Sophie Meunier, 'Divide and conquer? China and the cacophony of foreign investment rules in the EU' (2014) 21 Journal of European Public Policy 996.

[9] The Economist, 'How China has pushed Germany to rethink industrial policy' (21 February 2019) <https://www.economist.com/europe/2019/02/21/how-china-has-pushed-germany-to-rethink-industrial-policy> accessed 14 April 2019.

[10] UNCTAD, *World Investment Report 2017: Investment and the Digital Economy* (2017).

[11] Copenhagen Economics, 'Screening of FDI towards the EU' (January 2018) 16.

countries, Norway and Switzerland, which have made almost one-third of the acquisitions, followed by Russia with 93 acquisitions and Gulf Cooperation Countries with 80. China and Hong Kong, although latecomers, have made 60 acquisitions, 34 of which mostly in the last four years.[12] SOEs are in general a significant driver of Chinese investment in the EU:

> More than 60 percent of total investment since 2000 originated from firms with 20 percent or more government ownership. In 2016, the share of [Chinese] state-owned investors slightly went down to 40 percent of the total – mostly as a result of soaring private sector investment – but it has since then come back up to over half of the total investment in 2017 and the first three quarters of 2018.[13]

State-owned investors continue to account for the majority of China's EU FDI in the past years as the share of SOEs in total Chinese investment increased from 62% in 2014 to 70% in 2015. Sectors that recently received the most state-owned capital by value include transportation services and logistics, automotive equipment and components, utilities and real estate. SOEs made in these sectors several large-value deals: the acquisition of Logicor by a sovereign wealth fund China Investment Corporation (CIC) in transportation services and logistics, the acquisition of Pirelli by ChemChina in automotive equipment and components, China Three Gorges' investment in EDP and State Grid's investment in CDP Reti in utilities.[14] Sovereign and state-related investment from China in combination with China's new policy-driven financing push has according to some observers the potential to undermine the integrity of the EU[15] and geo-economic interests in its neighbourhood.[16]

These trends are a part of China's broader new strategic "One Belt One Road" initiative, which enables financing for large-scale projects in Europe by using SOEs, sovereign wealth funds or state banks. For many Europeans, the actual targets of the SOEs' activities are concerning. For instance, in transport, five of the most important ports for European trade logistics (by volume) have been the subject of Chinese investment: Rotterdam, Antwerp, Valencia, Piraeus and Le Havre. Overall, the Chinese government has through SCEs/SOEs a majority share in 6 of the European 14 ports in which it has invested.[17] Regarding airports, a strong role for Chinese

[12] European Commission, 'Staff Working Document on Foreign Direct Investment in the EU," following up on the Commission Communication "Welcoming Foreign Direct Investment while Protecting Essential Interests" of 13 September 2017' (2019) 56.

[13] ibid, 60.

[14] ibid.

[15] Such may be the 16 + 1 initiative which covers China, 11 EU Member States and 5 Balkan countries.

[16] Thilo Hanemann and Mikko Huotari, 'A New Record Year for Chinese Outbound Investment in Europe' (2017) 5.

[17] E.g. the SOE China Ocean Shipping Company (COSCO) has minority stakes in the ports of Rotterdam and Antwerp, and majority stakes in Bilbao, Valencia, Piraeus and Zeebrugge. Partly state-owned China Merchants Port Holding has minority stakes in container terminals in Dunkirk, Le Havre, Nantes, Marseille and Malta.

SOEs is behind investment into Heathrow and Toulouse airports.[18] In 2018, the OECD's International Transport Forum published a study stating that Chinese control of European container capacity had expanded from less than 1 to 10% between 2007 and 2017.[19] But even private companies may serve as agents for suspicious investments with state influence. For example, the former sixth largest Chinese private company CEFC China Energy became the dominant vehicle of Chinese investment in the Czech Republic. It invested mainly in real estate, as well as in already operating companies in tourism businesses and the banking and financial sector. According to the media, CEFC China Energy even planned an acquisition of the most popular Czech TV station Nova. However, that acquisition did not materialise due to discovered serious financial problems and corruption accusations. In May 2019, the Chinese state-controlled financial company CITIC paid CEFC's debt and took control over it.[20]

Strong Chinese influence may be soon arising in the 5G networks as Huawei is one of the world's leading network technology suppliers. Although the position of respective Member State differs on question, the EU recently issued a serious warning regarding 5G networks stressing that "threats posed by states or state-backed actors are perceived to be of highest relevance"[21] In addition, among the various potential actors in the role of mobile network operators or suppliers, non-EU states or state-backed are considered by the EU as the most serious ones and the most likely to target 5G networks.[22]

Another important aspect of the discussion is that both SCEs/SOEs are more able to secure funding from the state for their acquisitions. In practice, that means subsidised financing. Such behaviour is regarded as highly problematic from the perspective of fair competition and a level playing field. Under the EU law, state support could give companies investing in the EU an unfair competitive advantage causing a risk of distorting the market and a violation of rules. Under such circumstances, the EU merger control regime may in certain situations allow for reviews of FDI. Those reviews happen in cases of mergers, acquisitions or joint ventures where they take form of concentrations falling within the scope of the EU Merger Regulation,[23] but such control is exclusively based on the effect on competition in the

---

[18] Elvire Fabry and Jacopo Maria d'Adria, 'The Challenges of Chinese Investment Control in Europe' (11 February 2019) 3.

[19] OECD/ITF, 'Container Shipping in Europe: Data for the Evaluation of the EU Consortia Block Exemption Regulation' (19 March 2019) <https://www.itf-oecd.org/sites/default/files/docs/container-shipping-europe-eu-consortia_3.pdf> accessed 28 April 2019.

[20] Krzysztof Dębiec, Jakub Jakóbowski, 'Chinese investments in the Czech Republic: changing the expansion model (6 June 2018)' <https://www.osw.waw.pl/en/publikacje/analyses/2018-06-06/chinese-investments-czech-republic-changing-expansion-model-0> accessed 2 November 2019.

[21] European Commission, 'EU coordinated risk assessment of the cybersecurity of 5G networks, Report' (9 October 2019) para 2.10.

[22] European Commission, 'Press release by the European Commission and the Finnish Presidency of the Council of the EU' (9 October 2019).

[23] Council Regulation (EC) No 139/2004 of 20 January 2004 on the control of concentrations between undertakings, OJ L 24, 29.1.2004.

Single Market, not security-related concerns. Despite the limitations, the European Commission subjects foreign SCEs/SOEs attempting to acquire assets in the EU to strict examination.

For instance, there is a precedential case from March 2016, in which the European Commission's Directorate-General (DG) Competition decided on a proposed joint venture between China General Nuclear Power Group (CGN) and France's EDF. DG Competition concluded that state-owned CGN should not be viewed as separate from the Chinese State-owned Assets Supervision and Administration Commission of the State Council (SASAC). Accordingly, CGN's turnover into account should have been calculated as the combined revenue of all Chinese SOEs in the energy sector which subsequently led to overreaching the EUR 250 million threshold for merger clearance: "In view of the fact that Central SASAC can interfere with strategic investment decisions and can impose or facilitate coordination between SOEs at least with regard to SOEs active in the energy industry, the DG Competition concludes in the case at hand that CGN and other Chinese SOEs in that industry should not be deemed to have an independent power of decision from the central SASAC. The turnover of all companies controlled by the central SASAC that are active in the energy industry should therefore be aggregated."[24] The case was the first instance when the European Commission stated that all Chinese SOEs should be treated as one single entity[25] and it is expected to have wide-ranging consequences for SOEs active in the energy sector in the EU.[26] The monitoring of SCEs/SOEs investment on grounds of competition policy nevertheless remains rather a complementary avenue as it cannot address national security implications properly.

Another rather complementary measure aims at energy security. The EU law in the field of energy markets provides for the identification of critical infrastructure and resources in the energy, raw materials and electronic communications sectors and, in some cases such as gas and electricity transmission systems, requires an assessment of the implications of foreign ownership. Under the third energy package adopted in 2009,[27] the EU introduced an energy security review mechanism in order to assess possible risks related to non-EU investors in the EU energy sector. Among other implications, Member States had to unbundle the ownership/control over network and supply assets, in practice to separate gas production operations from gas transmission operations. The regulations had likely the most serious impact for Russian company Gazprom, a state-owned energy group. In Lithuania, implementation of the EU rules

---

[24] Case M.7850 – EDF/CGN/NNB Group of Companies, Commission decision pursuant to Article 6(1) of Council Regulation No 139/2001 and Article 57 of the Agreement on the European Economic Area (10 March 2016) 49.

[25] For an analyse of previous practice *see* Tanisha A. James and Howard M. Morse, 'Regulatory hurdles Facing Mergers With Chinese State-Owned Enterprises in the United States and the European Union' (2017) 1 China Antitrust Law Journal 20.

[26] Marc Bungenberg and Angshuman Hazarika, Chinese Foreign Investments in the European Union Energy Sector: The Regulation of Security Concerns (2019) 20 Journal of Trade & Investment 395.

[27] *See* summary in European Commission, 'Third energy package' (20 August 2019) <https://ec.europa.eu/energy/en/topics/markets-and-consumers/market-legislation/third-energy-package#content-heading-0> accessed 10 November 2019.

even led to commencement of an investment arbitration against the government under the Lithuania-Russian Federation bilateral investment treaty (BIT) due to the alleged forced sale of Gazprom's stake in Lietuvos Dujos, Lithuania's gas distribution company.[28] At that time, there were fears that the dispute could be replicated in other Eastern European EU member states where similar issues could arise.[29] However, the case was discontinued in 2015.[30] Given the investment made by Chinese SOEs in energy and gas companies such Eni Spa and Enel or Energias de Portugal, their increasing acquisition activity in the future can be limited by the same regulation.[31]

At the Member States' level, there has recently been an increasing trend of cases underlying the need to protect the state's national security and public order in relation to foreign investments by SCE/SOEs. Germany, in particular, seems increasingly worried about the number of acquisitions of domestic companies. The German Government continuously pursues a stricter regime for foreign investors. Particularly, the growing unease with Chinese SOEs was lately highlighted by two proposed acquisitions in Germany.[32] One of the latest changes was introduced in December 2018 by lowering the threshold for screening FDI in the area of the defence sector, IT security products relevant for state security, critical infrastructure, related software development, telecommunications, cloud computing services, telematics infrastructure and the media industry from 25 to 10%.

France, Italy and the United Kingdom have followed a similar path. In France, after a parliamentary report by an investigative committee on this subject targeting some potential improvements, important reforms were passed in late 2018 and further changes are pending.[33] The Italian Government updated its mechanism in May 2019 in order to include components and contracts related to 5G telecommunications within the scope of the special powers to impose conditions on, or veto, certain transactions.[34] The UK prepared for significant overhaul of its regime as envisaged in the National Security and Investment White Paper of July 2018.[35] It is worth

---

[28] Jarrod Hepburn, 'Lithuania claims round-up: Lesser-known arbitrations move forward alongside high-profile gas unbundling battles', IAReporter (2 September 2012).

[29] Aleks Vickovich, 'The Gazprom enigma, Commercial Dispute Resolution' (7 March 2012) <https://www.cdr-news.com/categories/arbitration/gazprom-turns-up-gas-on-lithuania-with-uncitral-arbitration-threat> accessed 10 November 2019.

[30] OAO Gazprom v. The Republic of Lithuania (PCA Case No. 2011-16), Award on costs and order for the termination of the proceedings (31 March 2015).

[31] Bungenberg, Hazarika (n 26) 380,387.

[32] In July 2018, the German state bank acquired a 20% stake in high-voltage grid operator 50 Hz just before the acquisition by China's state company, officially admitting security reasons for the purchase. In August 2018, the German Government approved to veto n national security grounds a proposed acquisition of Leifeld Metal Spinning, a local maker of machines for producing high-specification metals for nuclear and other applications, by a Chinese private company, although with ties to the Chinese Government.

[33] The so-called "Pacte Law" (Loi portant Plan d'Action pour la Croissance et la Transformation des Entreprises).

[34] Law No. 41 of 20 May 2019 (amending Law No. 56 dated 11 May 2012).

[35] Department for Business, Energy and Industrial Strategy, 'National security and investment: proposed legislative reforms' (24 July 2018).

highlighting that hostile actors for the purpose of this contemplated mechanism are defined in the accompanying draft statutory statement as "individuals or entities acting on behalf of hostile states or affiliated to the hostile state".[36]

3 The EU Screening Framework for FDI

Under the Lisbon Treaty, the European Union has extended its exclusive competence to cover FDI. That competence was until now mostly visible in the external EU policy in negotiating investment treaties and investment protection chapters in comprehensive free-trade agreements, such as the Comprehensive Economic and Trade Agreement (CETA) on 30 November 2016. The EU investment policy has now developed a new dimension.

As described above, the EU has not been equipped with any mechanism to assess the impact of FDI on security and public order. The limited assessment which would go beyond the borders of an individual Member State has been provided only by a merger control regime. However, such state of affairs was seen increasingly as a gap in the EU trade and investment policy's toolkit. The importance of having one framework is in addition underlined by the distinctive feature of the EU where an investment in one EU Member State serves as an entry point to the whole EU given the level of integration of the Single Market.

Accordingly, it did not come as a surprise when on 13 September 2017 the European Commission published its own legislative proposal for establishing a supranational framework for screening of FDI flowing into the EU.[37] A year after, the proposal passed the stage of the trialogue between the Council, the European Parliament and the European Commission with a transition period of 18 months to fully implement the Regulation. As such, in 2020, the EU will have in place an established framework for cooperation and information exchange that providing legal certainty for Member States which maintain their own screening mechanisms.

Currently, half of the twenty-eight Member States have already their own national FDI screening mechanisms in place. Other Member States may have different arrangements in place to control or restrict the acquisition and ownership of certain assets that are essential their essential security interests. Or they simply want to signal the high degree of openness to FDI as much possible by not imposing sometimes

[36] Department for Business, Energy and Industrial Strategy, 'National Security and Investment, Draft Statutory Statement of Policy Intent' (24 July 2018) para 4.19.

[37] European Commission, 'Proposal for a Regulation of the European Parliament and of the Council establishing a framework for screening of foreign direct investments into the European Union' (2017).

burdensome administrative screening processes.[38] Such a decentralised and fragmented system could not adequately respond to new trends in international investment flows. Under the new EU Regulation, there is still no requirement for the rest of Member States, which do not have one, to adopt a screening mechanism. However, given the context of the EU Regulation and other developments in security environment, it is likely that most Member States will consider seriously the option of introducing such mechanism.[39]

3.1 SOEs Investors Under Spotlight

Several governments modified their approaches to protect national security by putting screening mechanisms in place in order to have adequate mechanisms in place for dealing with potential sources of concern arising from the internationalisation of the SOEs. For example, in Australia, SOE investors are subjected to stricter reviews and filters. In the US, the Committee on Foreign Investment in the United States (CFIUS) requires mandatory filings for transactions in which a foreign government holds a "substantial interest" in the foreign investor. In 2017, Congress's US-China Economic and Security Review Commission even recommended considering expanding the scope of CFIUS review to reject all Chinese SOEs acquisitions of US firms.[40] In the Russian Federation, equity caps for foreign investment in certain enterprises are lower for this kind of investors than for private investors.[41]

---

[38] In February 2019, the Swiss Government concluded that investment controls "would currently bring no additional benefits to Switzerland. On the contrary, restricting capital flows into Switzerland would increase red tape, generate uncertainty and make Switzerland a less attractive place to invest." Even though Switzerland is not an EU Member State, this publicly declared position can provide an explanation for a position of some EU Member States such Luxembourg, Malta, Cyprus or Ireland. See State Secretariat for Economic Affairs SECO, 'Federal Council decides against investment controls for time being, but supports monitoring procedure' (13 February 2019) <https://www.seco.admin.ch/seco/en/home/seco/nsb-news.msg-id-73973.html> accessed 11 November 2019.

[39] For instance, very recently, two Member States traditionally open towards foreign investments, the Czech Republic and Denmark, initiated steps towards the establishment of their national screening mechanisms. The Czech Government discussed this question at its meeting in March 2019 and the Czech Ministry of Industry and Trade published regular reports on deliberations of the working group, which prepares the draft bill. In February 2019, the Danish Government announced the setting up of an inter-ministerial group to explore the possibility of a national mechanism for foreign investment screening and the public consultation on this issue with expectations of putting forward a proposal for relevant legislation during 2019.

[40] U.S.-China Economic and Security Review Commission, 'Report to Congress of the U.S.-China Economic and Security Review Commission' (2017) 25, 72.

[41] Federal Law No. 57-FZ On the Procedure of Making Foreign Investments in Companies of Strategic Importance.

for National Defence and State Security of 29 April 2008; Frédéric Wehrlé and Joachim Pohl, 'Investment Policies Related to National Security – A Survey of Country Practices' (2016) 2 OECD Working Papers on International Investment 25-26.

The EU's concerns over SOEs as foreign investors in the EU have been recently singled out by the European Commission's "Reflection Paper on Harnessing Globalisation", published in May 2017. The Commission emphasised that "[o]penness to foreign investment remains a key principle for the EU and a major source of growth. However, concerns have recently been voiced about foreign investors, notably state-owned enterprises, taking over European companies with key technologies for strategic reasons. Often, EU investors do not enjoy the same rights to invest in the country from which the foreign investment originates. These concerns need careful analysis and appropriate action."[42] In a similar vein, the European Commission later warned of such acquisitions, which may allow foreign governments to use critical assets not only to the detriment of the EU's technological edge but also those threatening security and public order of the EU and its Member States.[43]

The EU Regulation has several objectives. Principal objectives include safeguarding security and public order, but arguably the central objective is strengthening the convergence of Member States' FDI assessment criteria. The criteria that the legislators have laid down under Art. 4 of the EU Regulation show perceptions of where and under which conditions risk relating to FDI is concentrated. The provision makes clear that, when assessing an FDI, Member States and the European Commission must take into account, among other factors, whether a foreign investor is controlled directly or indirectly by the government of a third country, including state bodies or armed forces of a third country, whether through ownership structure, significant funding or otherwise.

The EU Regulation also supports review of investments that form part of "state-led outward projects or programs,"[44] for example whether the state-owned or controlled investor's acquisition aims to develop a project or programme led by the Government of a third country. SCEs/SOEs, through their close links to government in the home country, are generally thought to have preferential treatment and access to capital. Such benefits may be provided if the industry concerned is one targeted by the government's strategy. This vague formulation of the EU Regulation in this regard could encourage Member States to review a large portion of Chinese investment in the EU, especially in the light of the investment financed by state-owned banks under the strategy Made in China 2025.[45] According to that strategy, investments are preferred in high-tech industries like artificial intelligence, robotics and space travel, in order to help China's technological advance. In this way, Chinese FDI to European enterprises are an organic part of the Chinese industrial policy to stimulate growth of national champions facilitating access to technology and management know-how.

---

[42] European Commission, 'Reflection Paper on Harnessing Globalisation' (2017) 15.

[43] European Commission, 'Communication from the Commission to the European Parliament, the European Council, the Council, the European Economic and Social Committee and the Committee of the Regions – Welcoming Foreign Direct Investment while Protecting Essential Interests' (2017) 5.

[44] EU Regulation (n 3), Recital 13.

[45] Thilo Hanemann, Mikko Huotari and Agatha Kratz, 'Chinese FDI in Europe: 2018 Trends and Impact of New Screening Policies, A report by Rhodium Group and the Mercator Institute for China Studies' (2019) 18.

In some countries, the nationality of the investor can affect the assessment, or the state-owned foreign investor triggers additional criteria. In case of the EU, private/state ownership is the most important one. Due consideration thus may be given to four elements: (1) the extent to which the investment decision of the non-EU investor has directly or indirectly been influenced by Government regulation; (2) the extent to which the investment is directly or indirectly subsidised by government agencies; (3) the extent to which the actual acquisition is funded or co-financed by government-influenced agencies, the extent to which the acquisition is part of a state-led industrial policy strategy geared towards making targeted FDI in companies in certain economic sectors in a bid to pursue overriding national interests; and (4) the extent to which the investor's bid for the target company clearly exceeds the market price. The EU thus devotes increased effort towards addressing policy concerns regarding internationalisation of SOEs considering the increased volume of this kind of investment.[46]

Art. 4 is the key part of the EU Regulation because it provides guidance when assessing the effects on security and public order of a Member State arising out of FDI coming from third countries. Accordingly, Member States should be able to follow a comprehensive approach in their different screening procedures, which should consequently improve the protection of the EU's essential interests. At the same time, the non-exhaustive list of factors in the EU Regulation provides flexibility because there could be unforeseen risks related to extra-EU investment, and therefore, unanticipated factors may be considered when screening such FDI.

Despite the focus of the EU Regulation on investment from third countries, it may also affect intra-EU investments involving non-EU ultimate owners through an anti-circumvention clause.[47] Under this provision, the Member States' screening mechanisms will have the possibility of scrutinising a broad range of EU investors and considering risks emerging from changes to their ownership structure. This approach should not treat SCEs/SOEs less favourably. However, it will mean in practice a higher likelihood that SCEs/SOEs may be subject to review or their investments may be more thoroughly scrutinised.

Still, the EU Regulation does not limit the Member States' ultimate decision-making power over the approval of investments. In spite of the new role of the European Commission in the process, its assessments should rather be advisory. Unavoidably, some of the Commission's opinions issued under the Regulation will not be in favour of certain potential investors. More scrutiny is to be expected, particularly with regard to SOEs as the European Commission has already devoted considerable attention to those investors. It is likely that the Member States will be pressured and at the end quasi-obliged to follow such "non-binding" opinions.[48]

---

[46] *See* also OECD Guidelines on Corporate Governance of State-Owned Enterprises and other work of the OECD Working Party on State Ownership and Privatisation Practices.

[47] EU Regulation (n 3) art. 3(6).

[48] Giani Pandey, Davide Rovetta and Agnieszka Smiatacz, 'How Many Barriers Should a Steeple Chase Have? Will the EU's Proposed Regulation on Screening of Foreign Direct Investments Add yet More Delaying Barriers When Getting a Merger Deal through the Clearance Gate, and Other

The EU Regulation also includes an obligation on the part of the European Commission to publish an in-depth analysis of FDIs into the EU, highlighting past FDI concerns from the perspective of security or public interest and reducing the current lack of transparency.[49] And in its first report, published in March 2019, the European Commission has raised concerns with regard to links of foreign investors and their home states: "State influence may lead them to acquire an EU company for strategic, rather than purely commercial, reasons, while state support may result, for instance, in their ability to pay more than other potential domestic or third-country acquirers might."[50] The report identifies SOEs as one of the types of investors that are more active in merger activities as compared to industrial companies, the traditional type of investor. This trend, according to the European Commission, is a validation of the ongoing policy reflection around investment screening within the EU as well as on international level.[51]

3.2 Broader Implications of the EU Regulation

The EU's screening mechanism should be able to increase awareness and enhanced scrutiny of FDI into the EU. But it should be also considered in the broader context. It clearly marks a shift from a free-trade policy and shows growing impatience with certain unfair practices in international trade as well as a worsening security environment, including using economic tools for geopolitical purposes.[52]

While non-discrimination as one of the core principles of the EU is encompassed in the EU Regulation, some of its provisions overlap with core characteristics of Chinese investment in Europe to date.[53] The EU Regulation does not mention China explicitly, but it is clear that Chinese companies and their investments are the main source of concern with respect to the EU's security and public order. For instance, other European Parliament's documents mention China in this context frequently.[54]

Considerations' (2019) 14 Global Trade and Customs Journal. 58; but for opposite view and a need for mandatory opinions *see* Carlos Esplugues, 'A future European FDI screening system: solution or problem?' (2019) 245 Columbia FDI Perspectives 1.

[49] EU Regulation (n 3), art. 5.

[50] European Commission, 'Staff Working Document on Foreign Direct Investment in the EU," following up on the Commission Communication "Welcoming Foreign Direct Investment while Protecting Essential Interests".

of 13 September 2017' (2019) 61.

[51] ibid, 67.

[52] On the rise of 'geoeconomics' *see* Robert D. Blackwill and Jennifer M. Harris, *War By Other Means* (Harvard University Press 2016).

[53] Thilo Hanemann, Mikko Huotari and Agatha Kratz, 'Chinese FDI in Europe: 2018 Trends and Impact of New Screening Policies, A report by Rhodium Group and the Mercator Institute for China Studies' (March 2019) 18.

[54] European Parliamentary Research Service, 'Foreign direct investment screening. A debate in light of China-EU FDI flows' (2017).

Indeed, the preferential treatment of Chinese SOEs by the government or their non-commercial objectives are regular topics for meeting between both sides at the highest level and have become one the most contentious topics of the ongoing negotiations on the EU-China bilateral investment agreement.[55] The investment negotiations have been so far essentially asymmetrical given the EU openness to foreign investment across the majority of economic sectors.[56] Russia is another important country of origin for SCEs/SOEs investing in the EU.[57] In addition, the current mutual relations are in strain due to many factors, predominantly the conflict involving the East Ukraine and activities of Russian intelligence agencies in the EU Member States. Together, Chinese and Russian SOEs between 2003 and 2016 covered 27.6% of all SOEs transactions across the EU.[58]

On other hand, the EU Regulation explicitly calls for international cooperation and encourages Member States and the European Commission to collaborate with like-minded third countries.[59] Considering possible venues, the European Commission explicitly admits pursuing cooperation in bilateral or plurilateral format, such as the G7 or the OECD, covering sharing experiences, best practices and information regarding investment trends.[60] Such activities may help align the EU mechanism with those of like-minded countries.[61] For instance, the US military uses technology developed by European firms and their acquisition by SOEs from certain states could be considered dangerous. FDI in the EU thus can have serious ramifications for US

[55] Some IIAs contain specific provisions relating to SOEs as they play increasingly important role in international investment. *See* more Yuri Shima, 'The Policy Landscape for International Investment by Government-controlled Investors: A Fact Finding Survey' (2015) 1 OECD Working Papers on International Investment; Anran Zhang, 'The Standing of Chinese State-Owned Enterprises in Investor-State Arbitration: The First Two Cases' (2018) 17 Chinese Journal of International Law 1 147; Alicia García-Herrero and Jianwei Xu, 'How to handle state-owned enterprises in EU-China investment talks' (2017) 8 Bruegel Policy Contribution 12.

[56] Jeremy Clegg and Hinrich Voss, 'The new two-way street of Chinese direct investment in the European Union' (2016) 5 China-EU Law Journal 85.

[57] Although the motives behind Russian SOEs can be very complex. *See* Sanja Tepavcevic, 'The motives of Russian state-owned companies for outward foreign direct investment and its impact on state company cooperation: observations concerning the energy sector' (2015) 23 Transnational Corporations 29.

[58] Copenhagen Economics, 'Screening of FDI towards the EU' (2018) 18.

[59] EU Regulation, Recital 29, Art. 13. The like-minded countries are understood to be the US, Canada, Australia or Japan.

[60] European Commission, 'MEMO - Frequently asked questions on Regulation (EU) 2019/452 establishing a framework for the screening of foreign direct investments into the Union' (24 June 2019) 5.

[61] However, some authors are rather sceptical about prospects in this area, for instance *see* Jason Jacobs, 'Tiptoeing the Line Between National Security and Protectionism: A Comparative Approach to Foreign Direct Investment Screening in the United States and European Union' (2019) 47 International Journal of Legal Information 117.

national security,[62] as it has already happened recently in case of German robot maker Kuka recently acquired by a Chinese investor.[63]

Moreover, if the EU intends to be involved at the global level, it had to take appropriate steps at home. Also, thanks to the new EU Regulation on investment review for national security purposes it seems now that the EU is regarded as a serious partner by the US and Japan.[64] Given this development and possibilities opened by expressed willingness in respective countries,[65] closer cooperation, e.g. in sharing of information on the ownership structure of the foreign investor and the financing of the planned or completed investment or about subsidies granted by third countries, may be expected.[66]

4 Conclusion

While being open to foreign investment, the EU has witnessed some new investment trends that have recently raised important concerns and attracted political and public attention. The influx of Chinese FDI by SCEs/SOEs particularly has triggered a strong call for an EU foreign investments screening mechanism in the so far decentralised and fragmented EU's environment. Since the first eye-catching acquisition of part of the Piraeus Port by a Chinese SOE in 2009, the situation has changed dramatically with rising SCEs/SOEs investment. While all major economic powers have had the capacity to screen FDI, the EU has been rather keen on signalling openness to foreign

[62] Sophie Meunier, 'A Faustian bargain or just a good bargain? Chinese foreign direct investment and politics in Europe' (2014) 12 Asia Europe Journal 155.

[63] Reuters, 'Robot maker Kuka sells U.S. unit to get approval for deal with Chinese buyer' (15 December 2016) <https://www.reuters.com/article/us-kuka-m-a-midea-usa-idUSKBN1441S4> accessed 15 March 2019.

[64] E.g. Joint Statement of the Trilateral Meeting of the Trade Ministers of the European Union, Japan and the United States (9 January 2019); Joint Statement on Trilateral Meeting of the Trade Ministers of the United States, Japan, and the European Union (25 September 2018).

[65] EU Regulation, Art. 13, which states: "Members States and the Commission may cooperate with the responsible authorities of third countries on issues related to screening of foreign direct investment on grounds of security and public order". *See* also Foreign Investment Risk Review Modernization Act of 2017 (FIRRMA), Section 1713, which allows CFIUS to establish "a formal process for the exchange of information with governments of countries that are allies or partners of the United States that facilitates the harmonization of action with respect to trends in investment and technology that could pose risks to the national security of the United States and countries that are allies or partners of the United States; provide for the sharing of information with respect to specific technologies and entities acquiring such technologies as appropriate to ensure national security; and include consultations and meetings with representatives of the governments of such countries on a recurring basis".

[66] The multilateral framework has been already contemplated on the basis of OECD Guidelines for Recipient Country Investment Policies Relating to National Security. *See* Theodore H. Moran, 'Towards a multilateral framework for identifying national security threats posed by foreign acquisitions: with special reference to Chinese acquisitions in the United States, Canada, and Australia' (2014) 7 China Economic Journal 39–58.

capital. This chapter argues that the situation has changed now, and the EU has only recently adopted a framework to coordinate and to assess risks to national security and public order related to FDI.

One of the risk identification features according to the new EU Regulation is ownership and other links to a home State, which closely relates to the emergence in the last few years of newcomers from emerging markets. The concerns are predominantly associated with the increasing role of some non-traditional sources of FDI, targeting strategic European assets, such as critical technologies and critical infrastructure. Sensitivities expressed over some acquisitions tend to be highlighted in cases where one of the bidders is an SCE/SOE. The other concerning issue is often the lack of transparency on the part of foreign investors. In some cases, it may be difficult or even impossible to determine the ownership or the control of a certain investing company.[67] Still, despite the fact that particularly Chinese investments are dominated by SCEs/SOEs, the role of the State in their commercial activities should not be exaggerated.[68] And it seems that the EU has adopted a balanced approach when it did not establish special rules for the review and admission of investments by SOEs as some countries did.

There is a difference between protecting one's legitimate interests in national security and adopting measures motived by hidden protectionist motives. Investment screening should not become a tool that is used for unfair discrimination of certain type of foreign investors, not even SCEs/SOEs. On the other hand, it must be recognised that many foreign investors have too close ties to their governments, and thus represent not only concerns for EU's trade and Single Market policies, but political and security risks as well. It remains to be seen what implications the new mechanism will have for SCE/SOE investment activities in the EU. Moreover, the EU is now possibly a more attractive destination due to the ongoing trade and tech war between the US and China, especially when many technology-intensive firms operating in the EU Single Market constitute an alternative to the US market.

In the wake of increasing internalisation of SCEs/SOEs from emerging economies, the EU has equipped itself with a new investment policy mechanism in order to be able to react to cross-border investment of those entities. But this policy shift does not necessarily mean the imposition of outright or unqualified restrictions on SCE/SOE-investments foreign and these types of companies should not automatically expect a less favourable legal and political business climate in the EU. In any case, the new

[67] For instance, the transaction of the Chinese private company CEFC Europe was blocked by the Czech National Bank because of ambiguities concerning company's ownership structure. A few months later, the company was taken over by the China's state-owned conglomerate CITIC. This problem is not limited only to investment screening or licencing. The determination of ultimate beneficial owners or controllers has become increasingly important. It plays an essential role in transparency, the integrity of the financial sector, anti-corruption and law enforcement efforts. *See* Secretariat of the Global Forum on Transparency and Exchange of Information for Tax Purposes and Inter-American Development Bank, 'A Beneficial Ownership Implementation Toolkit' (March 2019).

[68] Francoise Nicolas, 'China's direct investment in the European Union: challenges and policy responses' (2014) 7 China Economic Journal 112.

EU rules demonstrate heightened attention to investment by foreign SCEs/SOEs on the part of recipient countries confirming thus a trend when state-owned or otherwise state-related actors appear more prominently in application of screening mechanisms.

Acknowledgements This contribution was supported by the Charles University, project Progress Q04. The views and opinions expressed in this article are those of the author and do not reflect the official policy or position of the Ministry of Foreign Affairs of the Czech Republic. The author acknowledges gratefully valuable comments from Jan Kunstýř, Nicolás Rosselot and the editors of this volume.

Ondřej Svoboda serves as a Deputy Head of Political and Economic Section of the Embassy of the Czech Republic in Tokyo. Before his posting he was a Deputy Head of the Unit of International Law of the Ministry of Industry and Trade of the Czech Republic where he provided legal expertise in investment and trade law issues and led the Czech delegation at the OECD Investment Committee and the UNCITRAL Working Group III on the reform of ISDS. Furthermore, he acted as a Deputy Head of the Secretariat of the Czech National Contact Point for the OECD Guidelines for Multinational Enterprises and lectured public international law and international economic law at the Faculty of Law of the Charles University in Prague where he also received his Ph.D. degree in 2020.

Regional and Country Perspectives

Vietnam's Reform of State-Owned Entities: Domestic and External Drivers

Dini Sejko and Viet Hoang

1 Introduction

Vietnam initiated a process of market-oriented reforms in 1986 when the Sixth Party Congress formally endorsed the Đổi Mới (renovation) policy. Since then, the country has transformed radically and become one of Southeast Asia's most resilient and dynamic economies.[1] The Đổi Mới process triggered policy changes for the modernisation of the domestic economy and transformed the role of Vietnam at the international level. From the domestic perspective, the new policy marked the beginning of significant structural reforms that affected all economic sectors, including a transformation of part of the state-owned enterprises (SOEs). The process of reforms of SOEs has continued in various stages in which domestic drivers interact with international forces. In recent years there have been changes in the objectives of SOEs' transformation and governance improvement. Current ongoing reforms aim to overcome challenges that Vietnam's economic structure will face in becoming an upper-middle-income economy by 2035.

From the international perspective, the Đổi Mới has resulted in a proactive pursuit of regional and global economic integration to sustain and boost domestic economic growth. One of the significant achievements has been the integration of Vietnam in the World Trade Organisation (WTO) in 2007. In several economies (notably China's)

[1] See Albert Park, Angela Tritto and Dini Sejko, 'The Belt and Road Initiative in ASEAN – Overview' (HKUST December 2020) IEMS Reports No. 2021–03 <https://cutt.ly/KEEBQnD> accessed 25 October 2021.

D. Sejko (✉)
Faculty of Law, Chinese University of Hong Kong, Shatin, Hong Kong SAR
e-mail: dinisejko@cuhk.edu.hk

V. Hoang
Ho Chi Minh City University of Law, Thành phố Hồ Chí Minh, Vietnam

J. Chaisse et al. (eds.), *Regulation of State-Controlled Enterprises*, International Law and the Global South, https://doi.org/10.1007/978-981-19-1368-6_23

WTO accession has triggered significant domestic reforms. Similarly, WTO accession stimulated a partial transformation of the Vietnamese SOEs system.[2] Vietnam has continued the reform process to address SOEs inefficiencies.

As a result, Vietnam is now at a new stage of reforms of its SOEs that aims to reframe the State's role in the economy, improve their governance, further integrate with global markets, and improve their attractiveness to foreign investors. To enhance investors attractiveness, in the last decade, Vietnam has pursued a proactive trade and investment strategy and currently has more than ninety bilateral investment agreements and free trade agreements.[3] Recently, the Vietnamese authorities ratified two FTAs that contain comprehensive and specific rules that regulate the activities of SOEs.

The chapter initially provides an overview of the domestic reform process, focussing on recent legislative changes that aim to rationalise SOEs and examines improvements in their governance that aim at a more decisive role of Vietnamese SOEs in domestic and international markets. Then we explore the trade and investment strategy and analyse the impact of the European Union Vietnam Free Trade Agreement (EVFTA) and the Comprehensive and Progressive Agreement for Trans-Pacific Partnership (CPTPP) to assess the impact of international commitments on domestic legislation. We examine how the new treaty language of the CPTPP and the EVFTA and the new specific obligations that target the operations of SOEs, and affect domestic legislation.

2 Domestic Reforms

The Đổi Mới began in 1986 and brought significant changes in the structure of the Vietnamese economy. However, the transformation of the pervasive system of Vietnamese SOEs only started in June 1992 when the government approved a pilot project for the conversion of some SOEs into joint-stock companies through a process called 'equitisation.[4] The term "equitisation" is used to describe the privatisation through which state enterprises are turned into joint-stock companies in which the State, workers, and private investors hold shares. Even though the Doi Moi started in 1986, the first equitisation occurred only six years later. The process of reform of the Vietnamese SOEs is a continuum, but it is generally divided by scholars and specialists into three main periods: the first was from 1992 to mid-1998, the second was from 1998 to 2011, and the third period of reform started in 2012.[5] In

[2] Tu-Anh Vu-Thanh, 'Does WTO Accession Help Domestic Reform? The Political Economy of SOE Reform Backsliding in Vietnam' (2017) 16(1) World Trade Review 85–109.

[3] UNCTAD, 'Investment Policy Hub' <https://cutt.ly/aEWwqvB> accessed 25 October 2021.

[4] Kunmin Kim and Nguyen Anh Tru, 'Reform Of State-Owned Enterprises In Viet Nam To Increase Performance And Profit' <https://www.adb.org/sites/default/files/publication/524106/adbi-wp999.pdf> accessed 25 October 2021.

[5] ibid, *cfr* Mai Fujita, Vietnamese State-owned Enterprises under International Economic Integration, RIETI Discussion Paper Series 17-E-121.

addition to equitisation, the SOEs' reform includes two other significant changes. The government has decided to divest from SOEs, resulting in a smaller state involvement. At the same time, an increasing number of the privatised SOEs are listing on the stock exchange, which requires them to comply with transparency and governance regulations, and pursue economic objectives to attract foreign and local investors.

2.1 Gradual Transformation

The equitisation process has so far consisted of three main periods. The first reform period began on 8 June 1992, following Decision 202 with a pilot transformation of some SOEs into joint-stock companies. Only a limited number of SOEs were involved in the reform process. The government expanded the scope of the reform and accelerated with the transformation of SOEs into joint-stock companies in May 1996 when Decision 202 was replaced with Decree 28/C but the first stage of reforms had a minor practical impact, with only 17 enterprises equitised by 1997.[6]

The Second Period of reforms has significant domestic and international implications because it coincides with Vietnam's WTO accession.[7] Government Decree 44, on 29 June 1998, further expanded the scope of the transformation of SOEs into joint-stock enterprises. The reform though did not affect how the Vietnamese Communist Party and the government projected the state's role in the economy. In fact, the 9th Party Central Committee 2001 confirmed that "*the state sector plays the decisive role in holding fast the socialist orientation'*... and SOEs must be '*the core force, main contributor for the state economic sector to perform the leading role in the socialist-oriented market economy, and the main force in international economic integration.*[8] The government, however, gradually expanded the scope of the transformation of state enterprises into joint-stock companies with other decrees,[9] and in 2005, in a political objective and attempt to follow the model of Korean Chaebols and Japanese Keiretsu, the government established state economic groups (SEGs).[10]

On 26 June 2007, the government also decided the conversion of other enterprises with 100% state-owned capital into shareholding companies and paved the way for

---

[6] Alexander Ewart, 'State-Owned Enterprises in Viet Nam' in Edimon Ginting and Kaukab Naqvi (eds), *Reforms, Opportunities, and Challenges for State-Owned Enterprises*, (ADB 2020).

[7] Viet Nam has been a member of the WTO since 11 January 2007. Viet Nam and the WTO, Member information, World Trade Organisation, <https://www.wto.org/english/thewto_e/countries_e/vietnam_e.htm> accessed 28 October 2021.

[8] Tu-Anh Vu-Thanh at n 2.

[9] Decree 64 (19 June 2002) and Decree 187 (16 November 2004) on transforming SOEs into joint-stock companies.

[10] OECD, 'Multi-dimensional Review of Viet Nam: Towards an Integrated, Transparent and Sustainable Economy' <https://www.oecd-ilibrary.org/sites/c8ba4a5e-en/index.html?itemId=/content/component/c8ba4a5e-en> accessed 25 October 2021.

the listing of SOEs through initial public offerings.[11] The objective of the legislation was to mobilise capital from both domestic and foreign investors to increase financial capacity, improve management and governance and raise the efficiency and competitiveness of the economy, and improve transparency based on market principles, to overcome the situation of equitisation taking place in secret within enterprises; and to ensure that equitisation runs parallel with the development of the capital market and the securities market.[12]

During the second phase of SOEs' reform, the Prime Minister established the State Capital Investment Corporation (SCIC),[13] also known as the sovereign wealth fund of Vietnam.[14] SCIC aimed to enhance efficiency in using state capital, to separate the functions of management from state ownership of SOEs by line ministries and provincial-level People's Committees. Its primary objectives were to represent the interest of state capital in enterprises and invest in critical sectors and essential industries to strengthen the state sector's role while respecting market rules.[15] As such, SCIC has been an active shareholder in equitised and partly privatised SOEs, and as of December 2018, it managed an extensive portfolio of 142 enterprises that are operating in various sectors, including finance, energy, manufacturing, telecommunications, transportation, consumer products, health care and information technology.[16] SCIC has continued to divest from some of its portfolio enterprises.

The SCIC is an active investor and has co-investment agreements with other SWFs. Still, differently from some of the most successful peers, SCIC does not formally comply with the Santiago Principles. Similarly, SCIC is not a member of the International Forum of Sovereign Wealth Funds. This international body works to improve the governance, transparency, and perception of SWFs, and at the same time, provides a platform for collaboration in positive initiatives such as the One Planet Sovereign Wealth Fund Framework.[17]

The National Assembly approved the Law of Enterprises on 26 November 2014,[18] an essential legal document because it regulates enterprises' foundation, operation, and dissolution. In addition to the Law of Enterprises, different authorities have

[11] Decree No. 109/2007/ND-CP of June 26, 2007, on conversion of enterprises with 100% state owned capital into shareholding companies.

[12] ibid.

[13] Prime Minister's Decision No. 151/2005/QD-TTg.

[14] Sovereign Wealth Funds 2020 Fighting the Pandemic, Embracing Change, IE Business School 2020.

[15] OECD, 'Corporate Governance Frameworks in Cambodia, Lao PDR, Myanmar and Viet Nam' (OECD 2019, <https://www.oecd.org/daf/ca/Corporate-Governance-Frameworks-Cambodia-Lao-PDR-Myanmar-Viet-Nam.pdf> .

[16] See n 10.

[17] SWFs that are members of the IFSWF and comply with the Santiago Principles generally have better governance, higher degree of transparency regarding their organizational structure, and better economic performance. See International Forum of Sovereign Wealth Funds, https://www.ifswf.org/general-news/international-forum-sovereign-wealth-funds-welcomes-expansion-one-planet-sovereign and *cfr* n 14.

[18] Law on Enterprise No. 68/2014/QH13 ("Law on Enterprise 2014").

issued laws, regulations, and communications that further promote restructuring and equitisation of SOEs and state divestment in enterprises. In addition, Decree 69/2014/ND-CP improved transparency with new disclosure requirements. SEGs and SOEs need to publish on websites of state-owned economic groups, corporations or websites of enterprises of the Ministry of Planning and Investment (MPI) additional ownership and governance information.[19] In addition, SEGs and parent corporations operating in joint-stock companies must also comply with the provisions on information disclosure on the stock market.[20]

2.2 *A New Era for Vietnamese State Capitalism?*

The 12th Party Congress in 2016 is a pathbreaker regarding the role of the state in the economy:

> The socialist-oriented market economy of Viet Nam includes many forms of ownership, many economic sectors, with the private sector as an important driving force of the economy; *the market plays the major role in mobilising and effectively allocating resources for development, the State plays the role in orientation, building and perfecting the economic institutions for fair, transparent and healthy competition.*[21]

SOE reforms are part of a sizeable political-economic change and challenges in Vietnam, but the state's role remains still significant. At the end of 2019, Viet Nam had 487 SOEs, of which 54 were centrally managed, and 433 were managed by Provincial People's Committee. Data provided by the authorities indicate that the number of 100% SOEs fell from 1309 at the end of 2011 to 487 at the end of 2019. The government continues to hold a controlling stake, i.e. more than 51% of the charter capital, in 185 enterprises.[22] Businesses that will remain 100% state-owned include enterprises considered essential for national security and the maintenance of public order, socio-economic development, or guaranteeing the supply of critical services.[23]

---

[19] Decree on State Economic Groups and State Corporation, No. 69/2014/Nd-Cp, Hanoi, 15 July 2014. transparent, from the tasks assigned by the state owner; information on ownership structures and assets; list of investment projects, investment forms, total investment budget, and schedule for implementation of current investment projects; transactions, loans, large-scale loans. Process of using capital, land, natural resources and other resources; the process of implementation and results of the implementation of long-term strategies and plans of the parent company; decide on the annual plan of the parent company that the owner has approved; to decide on strategies, long-term plans and business lines of subsidiaries which the parent company wholly owns; The use of profits or the handling of losses are required to be reported periodically.

[20] ibid.

[21] World Bank and Ministry of Planning and Investment of Vietnam "Vietnam 2035: Toward Prosperity, Creativity, Equity, and Democracy" Washington, DC: World Bank 2016. https://doi.org/10.1596/978-1-4648-0824-1.

[22] Trade Policy Review Report Viet Nam, WT/TPR/S/410.

[23] ibid These enterprises are involved in electricity distribution, grid management, multipurpose hydropower, railroad infrastructure, air traffic services and related safety services, maritime safety, public postal services, lottery businesses, and publishing.

The government also intends to maintain majority ownership in equitised companies in large and "sensitive" sectors of the economy.[24] However, the government has continued its divestment process, and listing of SOEs. In both cases there has been great attention from foreign investors, from ASEAN, but also from the European Union. In addition, since the Vietnamese government has been collaborating with China within the framework of the Belt and Road Initiative, that process has been attractive also for Chinese investors that are trying to acquire Vietnamese SOEs. A Chinese fund manager investing in Southeast Asia has pointed out that it is very competitive to acquire shares in the Vietnamese SOEs due to the great interest by other foreign investors.[25]

Vietnam faces significant challenges in becoming an upper-middle-income economy by 2035.[26] For this reason deeper integration in the global economy and agreements provide additional opportunities for Vietnam to deepen its commitment to reform.[27]

Three central governmental agencies with separate functions overview the operations of Vietnamese SOEs, including the Enterprise Development Agency (Ministry of Planning and Investment), Corporate Finance Department (Ministry of Finance), and Department of Enterprise Reform (Office of the Government). The Enterprise Development Agency coordinates with relevant units in setting up strategies, programs and plans of state-owned enterprise arrangement, innovation and development to submit to the government by the Minister; to give instructions on orders, procedures of state-owned enterprise arrangement, innovation and development; ii) to participate with relevant units in appraising, contributing ideas on projects of state-owned enterprise establishment, arrangement and reorganisation as assigned; to consolidate the situation of state-owned enterprise arrangement, innovation reform development.[28] The Corporate Finance Department (CFD) provides that the CFD has the mandates to advise and assist the Ministry of Finance on the corporate finance, cooperative finance, and collective economy; financial mechanisms and policies to serve ownership change, SOE restructuring, transformation, equalisation of state-owned economic units/ institutions into enterprises; to act as the focal point to assist the Minister and the financial administration on FDI; and implement rights and obligations of the representative of the state fund owner at enterprises as assigned by the

---

[24] ibid food (rice wholesale), energy (large-scale mineral mining, gas, manufacture of basic metals, petrol and oil importation, electricity retail), telecommunications services with a network infrastructure, aviation (airport management, air navigation systems, air transport services), and financial and banking services.

[25] Dini Sejko and Albert Park, The Belt and Road Initiative in ASEAN – Vietnam HKUST IEMS Reports No. 2021–07.

[26] World Bank and Ministry of Planning and Investment of Vietnam (n 21).

[27] ibid (n 21) 78.

[28] Clause 3, Art 2 of Decision No. 1908/QD-BKH dated 8 November 2010 by the Minister of Planning and Investment on Functions, Responsibilities and Structural Organization of the Enterprise Development Agency.

MOF Minister.[29] The Department of Enterprise Reform assists the Prime Minister in developing programs and plans for SOEs reform within the country. It also provides support to the Prime Minister to guide, instruct and follow the implementation of these programs and plans once they have been approved. The Department of Enterprise Reform (DEP) coordinates its activities with relevant authorities. According to the Law on Enterprises, the DEP conducts research on models of organisation, mechanism, and policy to serve SOEs reform. Simultaneously, it carries out the regular and ad hoc sum-up, collection, consolidation and reporting to the Prime Minister on the state-of-play of the SOEs reform as provided by the Law on Enterprise.

The Ministry of Planning and Investment was assigned to build a project on "Developing large-scale state enterprises, especially state-owned multi-ownership economic groups, to promote the role of SOEs under the Party's guidelines and policies in the new era."

2.2.1 Establishment of the Committee for State Capital Management

The Committee for State Capital Management, established by the government, has one Chairman and four Vice-Chairmen appointed or dismissed by the Prime Minister. The SCIC is now one of 19 state economic groups and corporations that are overseen by the newly established CMSC. It has nine departments, including the Department of Agriculture, Department of Industry, Department of Energy, Department of Technology and Infrastructure, Department of General Affairs, Department of Legislation and Internal Control, Department of Staff Organization, Administration Office, and the Information Centre. The Committee is responsible for managing capital worth VND 820 trillion (nearly US$ 36 billion) and a total value of assets at over VND 1.5 quadrillion invested at 19 State corporations and groups,[30] proposing an overall strategy for investment development of these enterprises and submitting it to the government and the Prime Minister for approval.[31] The Prime Minister has the power to include other enterprises under the CMSC umbrella.

---

[29] Art 1 of Decision No. 2123/QD-BTC dated 26 August 2014 by the Minister Finance on Functions, Responsibilities and Structural Organization of the Corporate Finance Department.

[30] State Capital Investment Corporation (SCIC), Viet Nam Oil and Gas Group (PVN), Electricity of Viet Nam (EVN), Viet Nam National Petroleum Group (Petrolimex), Viet Nam National Chemical Group (VINACHEM), Nam Rubber Group (VRG), Viet Nam National Coal-Mineral Industries Holding Corporation Limited (VINACOMIN), Viet Nam Post and Telecommunications Group (VNPT), Viet Nam Mobile Telecom Services One Member Limited Liability (MobiFone), Viet Nam National Tobacco Corporation (VINATAB), Viet Nam Airlines; Viet Nam National Shipping Lines (VINALINES), Viet Nam Railways (VNR), Viet Nam Expressway Corporation (VEC), Airports Corporation of Viet Nam (ACV), Viet Nam National Coffee Corporation (VINACAFE), Viet Nam Southern Food Corporation (VINAFOOD 2), Viet Nam Northern Food Corporation (VINAFOOD 1), Viet Nam Forest Corporation (VINAFOR).

[31] The Socialist Republic of Vietnam, Online Newspaper of the Government, 'Committee for State Capital Management to make debut' (*Chinhphu.vn*, 30 September 2018, <http://news.chinhphu.vn/Home/Committee-for-State-Capital-Management-to-make-debut/20189/34783.vgp> accessed 25 October 2021.

3 Vietnam's FTAs Strategy and State Capitalism

Vietnam's integration in global value chains has been one of the main drivers of the Vietnamese governments that have actively promoted economic relationships through the negotiation and ratification of bilateral and multilateral free trade and investment agreements. Vietnam ratified the CPTPP in November 2018, and it is now in force. It is expected to promote trade with better-developed markets that are part of the agreement. As a member state of the ASEAN, Vietnam also has comprehensive free trade agreements with mainland China and Hong Kong SAR as a member of ASEAN.

Vietnam also signed the Regional Comprehensive Economic Partnership (RCEP) on 15 November 2020. RCEP is a megaregional FTA driven by ASEAN, including Australia, mainland China, Japan, New Zealand, and South Korea. While some critics have complained about the missed opportunities of the treaty *vis-a-vis* its potential, RCEP indicates the role of ASEAN in treaty drafting. In addition, RCEP highlights the regional engagement of China as a significant economic actor in treatymaking under the framework of the Belt and Road Initiative[32] when some of the RCEP signatories were facing a series of issues in their bilateral relations. Vietnam has also pursued an independent trade and investment agenda, signing bilateral agreements with Chile, South Korea, Japan, Israel, and the Eurasian Economic Union (Armenia, Belarus, Kazakhstan, Kyrgyzstan, and Russia). Vietnam is also one of very few countries to have an FTA with the European Union. These agreements give foreign companies established in Vietnam access to quite a few markets, which creates an essential competitive advantage in an environment of increasing protectionism and trade tensions.

The CPTPP and the EVFTA represent a new trend in FTA negotiations as they introduce new norms for the regulation of SOEs. With few exceptions, the CPTPP and the EVFTA are the first free trade agreements to provide unique and comprehensive rules on state-owned enterprises.[33] In addition to the new specific Chapters on SOEs, both treaties have specific chapters on competition, dumping, subsidies, and safeguards that mimic the WTO approach and directly affect the operations of SCEs.[34] Even though RCEP was drafted after the conclusion of the CPTPP and the EVFTA, the ASEAN lead agreement does not contain a specific chapter on the transnational activities of SOEs, especially concerning SOEs activities in foreign markets.

---

[32] The Chinese support of RCEP as part of their engagement under the BRI framework has led to the inappropriate identification of the treaty as a Chinese agreement.

[33] J. S. Fleury and J.-M. Marcoux, 'The US Shaping of State-Owned Enterprise Disciplines in the Trans-Pacific Partnership', 19 Journal of International Economic Law (2016).

[34] Julien Chaisse and Dini Sejko, 'The Latest on the Best? Reflections on Trade Defence Regulation in EU-Vietnam FTA' in Marc Bungenberg, Michael Hahn, Christoph Herrmann and Till Müller-Ibold (eds), *The Future of Trade Defence Instruments: Global Policy Trends and Legal Challenges* (European Yearbook of International Economic Law. Springer 2018) 295–313.

3.1 CPTPP and EVFTA Influence on SOEs' Regulation

The EVFTA and the CPTPP regulate SOEs respectively in Chaps. 11 and 17. Both chapters share similar objectives in drafting new regulations on SOEs. They aim to address market distortions that transnational activities of SOEs create in global markets through regulations that contracting parties are obligated to comply with. At the same time, the new set of rules can serve as a model in other bilateral and regional negotiations to govern the activities of SOEs. SOEs assisted and subsidised by the government do not unduly exercise their powers and impede activities of enterprises of other contracting parties in trade and investment in the market of the contracting party or other contracting parties.[35] Both chapters covering provisions on State-owned enterprises, enterprises granted special rights or privileges and monopolies includes 7 Arts: (i) Definitions, (ii) Scope of application, (iii) General provisions, (iv) Non-discrimination and commercial considerations, (v) Neutral regulation, (vi) Transparency, and (vii) Technical Cooperation. The text of the TPP Chap. 17 remained substantially unchanged in the CPTTP, except for some additional carveouts added by Malaysia.[36]

These chapters regulate trading activities by state-owned enterprises, enterprises granted special rights or privileges and monopolies who have scale large commercial operations (namely annual revenue derived from the commercial activities of that enterprise is more than 200 million Special Drawing Rights—equivalent to 6500 billion VND). The new rules do not apply to Vietnamese SOEs providing services as the state-agency mandate, operating in the sectors/ areas that Vietnam does not commit the market open, operating in national defence, public order or public security, operating in some other sectors like oil & gas, electricity, coal, financial development which the State needs to regulate in terms of macroeconomic policy.

Commitments and obligations to SOEs are consistent with Vietnam SOEs laws and regulations. For SOEs, their primary duties include: (i) operating under the market mechanism, i.e. the SOEs are entitled to have their own decision in business activities without the state intervention, except for the cases of realising the public policy goals, (ii) there is no discrimination in the purchase of goods and services in sectors that Vietnam commits to open the market, (iii) transparency of basic information about relevant in line with provisions of the law on business.

The definition of an SOE varies in different countries. The rise of state-owned investment funds determining the distinction between entities became a significant challenge because its implications on the regulatory framework. The OECD, in the guidelines, defines an SOE as any corporate entity recognised by national law as an enterprise, and in which the state exercises ownership, should be considered

---

[35] Mitsuo Matsushita 'State-Owned Enterprises in the TPP Agreement' in: Julien Chaisse, Henry Gao, and Chang-fa Lo (eds), *Paradigm Shift in International Economic Law Rule-Making. Economics, Law, and Institutions in Asia Pacific* (Springer 2017).

[36] *cfr* Mitsuo Matsushita and C L Lim. 'Taming Leviathan as Merchant: Lingering Questions about the Practical Application of Trans-Pacific Partnership's State-owned Enterprises Rules' (2020) 19(3) World Trade Review 402–423, 403.

Table 1 Comparing SOE's definition EVFTA v CPTPP

EVFTA SOEs definition[41]*	CPTPP SOEs definition[42]**
"State-owned enterprise" means an enterprise, *including any subsidiary*, in which a party, *directly or indirectly:*	state-owned enterprise means an enterprise that is principally engaged in commercial activities in which a Party:
(a) owns more than 50% of the enterprise's subscribed capital or the votes attached to the shares issued by the enterprise;	(a) directly owns more than 50 per cent of the share capital;
(b) can appoint more than half of the members of the enterprise's board of directors or an equivalent body; or	(c) holds the power to appoint a majority of members of the board of directors or any other equivalent management body.; or
(c) can exercise *control over the strategic decisions* of the enterprise.	(b) controls, through ownership interests, the exercise of more than 50 per cent of the voting rights.

an SOE.[37] The OECD definition includes joint-stock companies, limited liability companies and partnerships limited by shares independently for the underpinning legislation. Moreover, with their legal personality established through specific laws, statutory corporations should be considered SOEs if their purpose, activities, or parts of their activities have a primarily economic nature. In the language of the OECD Guidelines, the term 'ownership' is understood to imply control.[38] This definition is broad and can include SWFs. This definition is part of the OECD Guidelines on SOEs and is a soft law definition. As a non-binding definition, it provides valuable guidance for the identification of SOEs.

3.2 Defining SOEs in FTAs

The need to address with enforceable regulations some of the issues related to state capitalism and to circumvent the stalemate of multilateral negotiations, a large number of states have decided to negotiate FTAs at a regional scale. The CPTPP, EVFTA, and other FTAs under negotiation include specific chapters on state-owned enterprises that define and regulate SOEs. A comparative analysis of the definitions of SOE applied in the EVFTA, and the CPTPP exemplifies the EU approach[39] and the US approach[40]clarifying at the same time similarities and distinctions in features that the two regulatory approaches select (Table 1).

The EVFTA represents the benchmark for EU FTA negotiations, while the CPTPP maintains the text drafted during the TPP negotiations. Both definitions have many commonalities concerning the criteria used to determine the existence of an SOE and the language used. The three common standards are a) ownership, b) appointment of board members, and c) control over decision-making. The ownership threshold alone might exclude many SOEs from the scope of the definition, which might be deemed so by the country's domestic law. The two approaches improve the clarity and add precision to the definition of SOEs going beyond the WTO approach in GATT Article XVII that defines state trading enterprises.[43]

Unlike the CPTPP, the EVFTA definition includes the subsidiaries into the scope of the definition. Concerning control over SOE's decision-making, the EVFTA language creates a higher threshold as it requires the ability of the State to interfere over strategic decisions, which can happen indirectly and without the need to control the majority of the voting rights as is in the case of the CPTPP. The same negotiators from some signatory countries were involved in parallel negotiations, and prior versions of the texts were made available.[44]

The definition could also include SWFs, but the EVFTA and the CPTPP used the language of the Santiago Principles to determine the differences between the two types of sovereign investors.[45] The EVFTA and other treaties negotiated by the EU and the CPTPP show a general convergence on the meaning of state-owned enterprise that can serve as a basis for multilateral negotiations once there is a sufficient political will. The distinctions between SOEs and SWFs remain blurred. The two entities can be juxtaposed, primarily when SOEs operate as holdings or conglomerates.[46] SWFs

---

[37] OECD, 'OECD Guidelines on Corporate Governance of State-Owned Enterprises, 2015 Edition) (OECD Publishing 2015), 14. The 2005 edition used to define SOEs as "enterprises in which the state has significant control, through full, majority, or significant minority ownership.".

[38] OECD (n 38) 15.

[39] *See* generally, Chaisse and Sejko (n 34).

[40] Julien Sylvestre Fleury and Jean-Michel Marcoux, 'The US Shaping of State-Owned Enterprise Disciplines in the Trans-Pacific Partnership' (2016) 19 Journal of International Economic Law 445.

[41] European Union – Vietnam Free Trade Agreement, Chapter 11, Art 11.1 (g).

[42] Comprehensive and Progressive Agreement for Trans-Pacific Partnership (CPTPP) was released on 21 February 2018, Chapter 17, Art 17.1 The CPTPP was signed by Australia, Brunei, Canada, Chile, Japan, Malaysia, Mexico, New Zealand, Peru, Singapore, and Vietnam, and by 7 August 2018 has already been ratified by Mexico, Japan, and Singapore.

[43] GATT Article XVII.

[44] The TPP text was agreed in November 2015 and released in January 2016, like the first version of the EVFTA text.

[45] *See* Chap 3.5 for an analysis of the influence of Santiago Principles on the treaty-drafting and their incorporation in the language of new treaties.

[46] *See,* for example, Temasek that does not identify itself as an SWF, but is often classified as one and is comparable to Khazanah Nasional (Malaysia), or Qatar Investment Authority and Mubadala (UAE) that identify as SWFs. *See* Khalid A Alsweilem, Angela Cummine, Malan Rietveld and Katherine Tweedie, 'A Comparative Study of Sovereign Investor Models: Sovereign Fund

might have a corporate structure and specialise in limited economic sectors or have a branch or subsidiary that invests in a specific manner. The relationship between SWFs and SOEs is becoming more complicated in the case of a new approach in managing the assets of SOEs as they are used to finance the creation of new SWFs.[47]

The ownership threshold indicated in the definitions on the SOE in the two FTA is broader than the one in the Law on Enterprises 2014 that defines a SOEs as an enterprise in which the State holds one hundred per cent of the charter capital.[48] The provisions in Law on Enterprises 2014 and commitments in the EVFTA aim at different activities. The definition of the SOE in the EVFTA and the CPTPP does not create any obligation for Vietnam to reform domestic legislation. The sole objective of the definition is to determine the scope of application, namely, providing that the SOEs meeting the conditions mentioned in the definition shall comply with the commitments in the Agreement. The definition of SOEs only applies to legal relations established under the EVFTA. As a result, there is no need to change the definition of SOEs in the Law 2014, but in the legal documents relating to SOEs, it is necessary to refer to the target groups that must comply with the obligations as committed in the EVFTA.

Paragraph Art 1 of the EVFTA defines 'commercial activities' means activities, the result of which is the production of a good or supply of a service, which will be sold in the relevant market in quantities and at prices determined by the enterprise and are undertaken with an orientation towards profit-making. In more detail, any activities conducted by enterprises based on non-profit or only cost recovery are not considered to be undertaken and oriented towards profit-making.

The Vietnam Commercial Law provides that "*Commercial activity means an activity for profit-making purposes, comprising purchase and sale of goods, provision of services, investment, commercial enhancement, and other activities for profit-making purposes*".[49] This definition provides for a certain degree of independence in the decision-making processes of the enterprise from the state administrative agencies. This provision is consistent (a little bit narrower) with the one on commercial activities in the EVFTA. However, this definition only applies to activities of the SOEs under the EVFTA coverage. Thus Vietnam current legislation has wholly met the Agreement requirement. According to Paragraph b Art 1, "commercial considerations" means price, quality, availability, marketability, transportation and other terms and conditions of purchase or sale; or other factors that would generally be taken into account in the commercial decisions of an enterprise operating according to market economy principles in the relevant business or industry. Vietnam legislation does not have a specific provision on this terminology. Since 2007, only the definition of "commercial considerations" in the WTO Agreement on Subsidies is applicable. This terminology in the EVFTA is hence entirely appropriate to the WTO

Profiles' The Belfer Center for Science and International Affairs, and The Center for International Development, Harvard Kennedy School (2015).

[47] *See* secs 2.3.1.3 and 3.2.1.2.

[48] Clause 9 Art 4 of the Law on Enterprises 2014.

[49] Clause 1, Art 3 of Vietnam Commercial Law 2005.

practical regulation on Subsidies. Art 2 of the SOEs Section in the EVFTA provides for the scope of application. Accordingly, the Parties confirm their rights and obligations under Art XVII, paragraphs 1 through 3, of GATT 1994, the Understanding on the Interpretation of Art XVII of GATT 1994, as well as under Art VIII of GATS, paragraphs 1, 2 and 5. The SOEs chapters shall not apply to enterprises defined in Art 1 for which a Party has taken measures temporarily in response to a national or global economic emergency.[50] It shall not apply to covered procurement by a Party or its procuring entities within the meaning of Art II of (Chapter XX—Public procurement).[51]

State-owned enterprises, enterprises granted special rights or privileges and designated monopolies if in any one of the three previous consecutive years the annual revenue derived from the commercial activities of that enterprise was less than 200 million Special Drawing Rights are excluded from the application of the two treaties. This threshold shall apply to state-owned enterprises, enterprises granted special rights or privileges and designated monopolies at sub-central levels of government after five years from the entry into force of this Agreement. This Section shall not apply to state-owned enterprises, enterprises granted special rights or privileges, and designated monopolies owned or controlled by a governmental authority of a Party in charge of national defence, public order or public security, except if these are engaged exclusively in commercial activities unrelated to national defence, public order or public security.

The provisions are consistent with the objective of Vietnam and EU public policies. In addition, Vietnam has a separate Annex of exemption for the obligations mentioned in the SOEs Chapter in the EVFTA. This article provides that Each Party shall ensure that its state-owned enterprises, designated monopolies and enterprises granted special rights or privileges when engaging in commercial activities: (a) act in accordance with commercial considerations in their purchases or sales of goods or services, except to fulfil any terms of their public mandate that are not inconsistent with paragraph 1(b); and (b) accord to enterprises of the other Party, enterprises that

[50] This Section shall not apply to the adoption, enforcement or implementation of the privatization, equalization, restructuring or divestment of assets owned or controlled by the Government of Viet Nam. This Section shall not apply to measures by the Government of Viet Nam related to the ensuring of economic stability in the territory of Viet Nam. In achieving this policy objective, the government may require or direct a state-owned enterprise or a designated monopoly to sell or purchase at a regulated price, quantity or other terms and conditions than that enterprise could decide on commercial consideration basis, subject to its laws, regulations, or a governmental measure. This Section shall not apply to measures by the Government of Viet Nam aiming at development issues in the territory of Viet Nam, such as income security and insurance, social security, social welfare, social development, social housing, poverty reduction, public education, public training, public health, and childcare, promoting the welfare and employment of ethnic minorities and people living in disadvantaged areas, provided that the activities to implement such measures do not circumvent the application of Article 4 to the commercial activities of the enterprises.

[51] On the procurement rules in the CPTPP, *see* generally Jędrzej Górski, 'The Impact of the TPP on Opening Government Procurement to International Competition in the Asia-Pacific Region' (2016) 8(2) Trade, Law & Development 65–150; Jędrzej Górski, 'TPP and Government Procurement' (2019) 16 (5) TDM 1–44.

are investments of investors of the other Party, goods of the other Party, and services of the other Party, treatment no less favourable than they accord to, respectively, enterprises of the Party which are in like situations, like goods of the Party, and like services of the Party, concerning their purchases or sales of goods or services in the relevant market.

The concept of 'commercial considerations' was introduced in the Vietnamese legislation through the terminology used in the WTO Agreement on Subsidies. Nevertheless, the provision on non-discrimination at Art 5.1 of the Law on Enterprises 2014 recognises the principle of non-discrimination among enterprises from different economic sectors, as detailed in the following: "*The State recognises the long-term existence and the development of the types of enterprise prescribed in this Law, ensures the equality of enterprises before the law irrespective of their form of ownership and economic sector; and recognises the lawful profit-making nature of business activities.*"[52]

The Commercial Law 2005 stipulates the principle of traders' equality before the law in commercial activities, in which traders of all economic sectors are equal before the law in commercial activities. Art 7 of the Law on Enterprises 2014 defines the rights of enterprises (including SOEs) to freely and independently conduct business (in line with the provision on commercial considerations). When the State requests enterprises to consider other factors than commercial considerations, it shall be achieved through a specific legal document. This is not inconsistent with the obligations in the EVFTA. In the case of companies operating in the oil & gas, electricity, publication, broadcasting and television, etc., when there is discrimination or preferential treatment, they shall be in line with the current legislation. Preferential treatment and discrimination in the trade relations of SOEs since the Agreement take effect shall be applied within the scope of commitments in the EVFTA.

3.3 Competitive Neutrality

Article 17.11 5 in the CPTPP provides for policies related to competitive neutrality. Particularly the rules require Parties to ensure that enterprises from the target group shall comply with internationally recognised standards of corporate governance.

In the context of competition between SOEs and non-SOEs, a level playing field means 'competitive neutrality', defined as government business activities that do not enjoy net competitive advantages over their private-sector competitors simply by virtue of their public ownership.[53] Both EVFTA and the CPTPP referred to the concept of competitive neutrality without creating specific treaty commitments on

[52] Art 5.1 of the Law on Enterprises 2014.

[53] "Competitive neutrality implies that no business entity is advantaged (or disadvantaged) solely because of its ownership." *See* Antonio Capobianco and Hans Christiansen, 'Competitive Neutrality and State-Owned Enterprises: Challenges and Policy Options' (May 2011) OECD Corporate Governance Working Papers No. 1, https://doi.org/10.1787/22230939.

how states should regulate it in detail. The OECD has provided guidelines on competitive neutrality, referring to many conditions that should be pursued to create a level playing field:

(1) Streamlining the organisational form of government businesses—in regulated sectors, particularly public utilities and network industries and banking, regulatory functions should be separated into entities distinct from those engaged in commercial operations.
(2) Identifying the direct costs of any given function—cost identification is essential to identifying where the public sector bears additional costs or where the SOE benefits from its ownership. In the absence of this, implicit subsidisation is a very likely prospect.
(3) Achieving commercial rates of return—SOEs should be operated on the basis that they should earn a profit and pay a commercial level of return (e.g. in the form of a dividend) to the government on the equity capital allocated to the commercial operations.
(4) Tax neutrality—SOEs should ideally be subject to the same tax obligations as any other corporate entity or, where this is not feasible, should be required to make other compensatory payments to maintain a level playing field.
(5) Regulatory neutrality—SOEs should be required to meet the same regulatory requirements as private sector entities and should not enjoy any immunities or exceptions from laws.
(6) Debt neutrality and outright subsidies—SOEs should not receive concessionary financing from state-owned financial entities or through trade credits from other SOEs. Nor should they be allowed to benefit from lower market interest rates arising from a perceived government guarantee for their debts.
(7) Public procurement—SOEs should not be required to provide goods and services to the government at below-market prices. Conversely, the government should exhibit no preference to buy from its own SOEs. Public procurement should be the same regardless of ownership.[54]

Both treaties refer to international standards of governance without however providing details or specifications as in the works drafted by the OECD. The Commercial Law 2005 stipulates the principle of traders' equality before the law in commercial activities, in which traders of all economic sectors are equal before the law in commercial activities. The Commercial Law also defines the rights of enterprises (including SOEs) to freely and independently conduct business (in line with the provision on commercial considerations).[55] When the State requests enterprises to consider other factors than commercial considerations, it shall be conducted through a specific legal document.[56]

[54] Capobianco and Christiansen (59), OECD Corporate Governance Working Papers No. 1 Competitive Neutrality and State-Owned Enterprises: Challenges and Policy Options.

[55] Art 10 of the Commercial Law 2005.

[56] Art 7 of the Law on Enterprises 2014.

In the case of companies operating in sensitive sectors such as oil and gas, electricity, publication, broadcasting, and television, etc., when there is discrimination or preferential treatment, they shall be in line with the current legislation. It is noted that the preferential treatment and discrimination in the trade relations of SOEs since the Agreement takes effect shall be applied within the scope of commitments in the EVFTA.

The Parties shall endeavour to ensure that state-owned enterprises, enterprises granted special rights or privileges, and designated monopolies observe internationally recognised standards of corporate governance.[57] In addition, and differently from the CPTPP and other modern FTA, the EVFTA requires that within five years after the entry into force of this Agreement, SCIC shall endeavour to become a member of the International Forum of Sovereign Wealth Funds or endorse the Generally Accepted Principles and Practices ("Santiago Principles") issued by the International Working Group of Sovereign Wealth Funds in October 2008, which will improve compliance with international standards, including competitive neutrality, disclosure, and transparency.[58]

3.4 *Transparency*

EVFTA and the CPTPP have specific provisions on transparency. Specifically, a Party which has reasonable reason to believe that its interests under this Section are adversely affected by the commercial activities of an enterprise or enterprises defined in Art 1 of the other Party and subject to the scope of this Section as defined in Art 2 may request in written form that Party supply information about the operations of that enterprise related to the carrying out of the provisions of this Section. Requests for such information shall indicate the enterprise, the products/services and markets concerned and include indications that the enterprise is engaging in practices that hinder trade or investment between the Parties. For the EU, Paragraph 1(a) to (e) do not apply to enterprises that qualify as small or medium-sized enterprises as defined in the European Union law.[59] The transparency requirements in the new treaties are

---

[57] EVFTA Article 11.5 Regulatory Framework.

[58] EVFTA Annex 11-A: Specific Rules for Vietnam on State-Owned Enterprises, Enterprises Granted Special Rights or Privileges, and Designated Monopolies.

[59] This information includes the following: (a) the ownership and the voting structure of the enterprise, indicating the percentage of shares and the percentage of voting rights that a Party and/or an enterprise defined in Art 1 cumulatively own, (b) a description of any special shares or special voting or other rights that a Party and/or an enterprise defined in Art 1 hold, where such rights differ from the rights attached to the general common shares of such entity, (c) the organisational structure of the enterprise, the composition of its board of directors or of an equivalent body exercising direct or indirect control in such an enterprise; and cross-holdings and other links with different enterprises or groups of enterprises, as defined in Art 1, (d) a description of which government departments or public bodies regulate and/or monitor the enterprise, a description of the reporting lines, and the rights and practices of the government or any public bodies in the appointment, dismissal or remuneration of managers, (e) annual revenue or total assets, or both, (f) exemptions, non-conforming

consistent with the provisions on information disclosure stipulated in the Law on Enterprises 2014, Securities Law and Decree No. 87/2015/ND-CP on supervision of State capital investment in enterprises; financial supervision, performance assessment and disclosure of information of state-owned and state-invested enterprises, and Decree No. 81/2015/ND-CP on disclosure of information of state enterprises, and do not create additional obligations for the Vietnamese government to amend the legislation.

3.5 *Technical Assistance*

Article 7 of the SOEs Chapter in the EVFTA creates a framework for technical cooperation between the Parties. In detail, recognising the importance of promoting effective legal and regulatory frameworks for state-owned enterprises, the Parties shall engage in mutually agreed technical cooperation activities to boost efficiency and transparency of state-owned enterprises, subject to the availability of funding under the Party's cooperation instruments and programming. In the same fashion, the CPTPP drafters included in the meaning of technical cooperation the organisation of international seminars, workshops or any other appropriate forum for sharing technical information and expertise related to the governance and operations of state-owned enterprises.

The Parties shall conduct further talks within five years of the date of entry into force of this Agreement, on extending the application of (a) the disciplines in this chapter to the activities of state-owned enterprises that are owned or controlled by a sub-central level of government, and designated monopolies designated by a sub-central level of government, where such activities have been listed in Annex 17-D (Application to Sub-Central State-Owned Enterprises and Designated Monopolies); and (b) the disciplines in Art 17.6 (Non-commercial Assistance) and Art 17.7 (Adverse Effects) to address effects caused, in a market of a non-Party, by the supply of services by a state-owned enterprise.[60] Seen the treaty commitment and the framework that the Vietnamese government has created for the administration of the SOEs, it is possible to expect that the government will continue the reforms for greater efficiency, transparency of the SOEs despite the implications of the COVID-19.[61]

measures, immunities and any other measures, including more favourable treatment, applicable in the territory of the requested Party to any enterprise defined in Art 1.

[60] CPTPP Chap 17 Annex 17-C.

[61] cfr n 22.

4 Conclusion

After almost thirty years of reforms in the SOEs' sector, the Vietnamese governments have transformed the economic system. The state has significantly reduced its involvement in the economic system, firstly through the equitisation, and eventually through the divestment programmes, both from the state and the SCIC. The governmental drive to improve the legal framework for SOEs have produced positive results in improving the governance and efficiency of Vietnamese SOEs, making them also very attractive for foreign investors. Greater openness will further pressure Vietnamese SOEs to become more competitive.

The CPTPP Chap. 17 and EVFTA Chap. 11 are both ambitious agreements that require incremental regulatory efforts to regulate SOEs' transnational trade and investment activities. The two chapters are innovative and aim to fill a regulatory void in international economic law by creating new norms for SOEs. The two agreements establish some general obligations for the State to the relationship with SOEs: (i) SOEs should not be used to evade the obligations already committed in the Agreement; (ii) State administrative agencies should behave impartially and equally to all enterprises and not give more favourable treatment to SOEs when enforcing regulations and policies, than enterprises of different economic sectors under similar conditions. Thanks to the agreements, Vietnam has established platforms for cooperation with the states that have ratified the CPTPP, and with the EU, that commits to cooperate and provide technical assistance to Vietnam during the reform of the SOEs sector. While the new agreements, with some differences, provides high-level rules, at the same time, both agreements contain a large number of annexes, carveouts and clauses that limit the application of the norms. In this way, it became possible for the country to agree to the commitments. The gap analysis does not suggest amendment or revision of domestic law implement EVFTA Chap. 11.[62] Vietnam's progress with the reform of the system of SOEs is significant, and the fundamental drivers to create a more efficient public sector remain within the domain of the local legislators.

The Chapters on SOE's regulations in the CPTTP and the EVFTA have at the current stage limited impact in triggering significant changes in the domestic legislation of the member states that already have signed the agreements due to the number of exceptions, carveouts, and annexes. The language used in the CPTPP and the EVFTA will acquire a more significant systemic value especially in light of China's application to become a member of the CPTPP, the interest shown by other economies

[62] World Bank, 'Vietnam: Deepening International Integration and Implementing the EVFTA' (World Bank, May 2020) <https://openknowledge.worldbank.org/bitstream/handle/10986/33787/Vietnam-Deepening-International-Integration-and-Implementing-the-EVFTA.pdf?sequence=1&isAllowed=y> accessed 26 October 2021.

such as South Korea[63] and the Philippines[64] to join the CPTPP, and the potential relevance of the provisions in the negotiations between EU and China as part of the negotiations for the Comprehensive Agreement of Investment.

Acknowledgements Dr. Sejko would like to acknowledge generous support from the Institute for Emerging Market Studies at the Hong Kong University of Science and Technology under the 'Green and Smart or Black and Clumsy? Examining the Role of Chinese Investors in ASEAN's Sustainable Development' Research Grant. This study has greatly benefited from the fieldwork that Dr Sejko conducted as a Postdoctoral Fellow at the IEMS-HKUST.

---

[63] Bryce Baschuk and Jiyeun Lee, South Korea 'Seriously' Looking to Join CPTPP Following China Bid, Bloomberg, 8 October 2021, <https://www.bloomberg.com/news/articles/2021-10-08/korea-seriously-looking-to-join-cptpp-following-china-bid?sref=RW26lVU0> accessed 28 October 2021.

[64] Yuichi Shiga, Philippines explores joining TPP to expand free trade network, Nikkei Asia, 2 April 2021, <https://asia.nikkei.com/Economy/Trade/Philippines-explores-joining-TPP-to-expand-free-trade-network> accessed 28 October 2021.

How to Handle State-Owned Enterprises in EU-China Investment Talks

Alicia García-Herrero and Jianwei Xu

1 Introduction

Although trade between the European Union and China has been soaring, bilateral investment has remained moderate. Only relatively recently has Chinese outward foreign direct investment (FDI) in the EU started to rise substantially, but there is increasing uncertainty about whether this can continue. At the same time, European FDI in China has remained stagnant as European companies increasingly struggle on the Chinese market.

Aware of the potential benefits of FDI, the EU and China has been negotiating a bilateral investment treaty (BIT) for more than six years, with the objectives of unifying and further relaxing restrictions on FDI and of putting on an equal footing Chinese and EU investors and EU member states, most of which already have BITs with China. In the same vein, the USA has also been negotiating a BIT with China, and bilateral investment has been at the centre of the trade war as well.

This article draws upon the report: Alicia García-Herrero and Jianwei Xu, 'How to handle state-owned enterprises in EU-China investment talks' (June 2017) Bruegel Policy Contribution Issue n °18.

Both authors are affiliated with Bruegel and have written this paper in 2017.

A. García-Herrero (✉) · J. Xu
Department of Economics, Hong Kong University of Science and Technology, Kowloon, Hong Kong
e-mail: alicia@ust.hk

J. Xu
e-mail: jianwei.xu@bruegel.org

A. García-Herrero
Senior Research Fellow, Bruegel, Brussels, Belgium

J. Xu
Non-visiting research fellow, Bruegel, Brussels, Belgium

J. Chaisse et al. (eds.), *Regulation of State-Controlled Enterprises*, International Law and the Global South, https://doi.org/10.1007/978-981-19-1368-6_24

While the content of the negotiations is not fully disclosed, either for the USA or the EU BIT with China, there are enough official statements and even official updates on the negotiations from the European Commission to argue that the dominance of state-owned enterprises (SOEs) in China is clearly a complex issue. More specifically, the EU argues that SOEs do not follow market principles fully, partly because of the explicit or implicit government support they receive, undermining market efficiency. In addition, there is also a disagreement over how to settle disputes between investors, particularly those that involve SOEs. The treatment of SOEs seems to have become one of the most contentious aspects of the ongoing negotiations on an EU-China BIT.

We suggest ways in which the EU and China can enhance their bilateral investments while protecting their interests and understanding the differences in their economic structures. In other words, China, with an economy that continues to be state-driven to a considerable extent, will need to make changes to allow for equal treatment in market access, while the EU will need to acknowledge the role that SOEs play in China's economic model.

We start with a comparison between the roles played by Chinese SOEs and by their European counterparts, finding striking differences in their sectoral coverage. We then look at two significant concerns about Chinese SOEs: preferential treatment by the government and their non-commercial objectives. Though these concerns might be justified, there could be similar concerns about private companies, especially if they are large enough and operate in strategic sectors in which natural security could potentially be at stake. On this basis, we offer guidelines on the treatment of SOEs in a potential EU-China BIT. The key issue is market access in China to guide Chinese SOE behaviour in Europe and to ensure European companies in China can operate on an equal footing. We argue that focusing on market access—rather than on the type of ownership—is more relevant for the EU-China BIT negotiations. Finally, we consider the SOE chapter of the EU-Vietnam free trade agreement (FTA) as a potential benchmark for the ongoing negotiations between China and the EU.

2 The EU-China Investment Relationship

Economic cooperation between China and the EU has increased over the past thirty years to the point where the EU is now China's largest trading partner, and China is the EU's second-largest trading partner after the USA. Nevertheless, bilateral FDI has until quite recently remained relatively subdued, especially China's outward FDI. In 2011, China's outward FDI (including that from Hong Kong) accounted for only 1% of EU total inward FDI, whereas China took 3.5% of the EU's outward FDI. Given the size of the Chinese economy in the world already in 2011, this can be considered relatively modest.

More recently, Chinese entrepreneurs have started to head abroad for direct investment, and Chinese FDI in the EU has scaled up. The push factor for Chinese investors has been decreasing returns on domestic investment; the pull factor has been more availability of potential investments since the global financial crisis and their relatively lower cost. Against this backdrop, Chinese FDI in the EU soared to about €17.3 billion in 2018. The EU has become one of China's key destinations, accounting for around 20% of China's total direct investment (excluding Hong Kong, Cayman Islands and the British Virgin Islands). Meanwhile, the EU's FDI inflow into China was 7.17 billion in 2017, three times as large as that from the USA. The closer investment relationship between China and the EU is more apparent in their relative shares compared to other partners, with China's share leaping significantly during the past decade (Table 1, Figs. 1 and 2).

In terms of Chinese FDI in Europe, there has also been a sea change in terms of destination. A decade ago, Chinese FDI was concentrated in the European 'big three' economies (Germany, the UK and France). As of 2018, their share in total

Table 1 Partners' shares of EU outward and inward FDI

	2011 (%)	2012 (%)	2013 (%)	2014 (%)	2011 (%)	2012 (%)	2013 (%)	2014 (%)
Europe (non- EU, including EFTA)	13.28	21.76	4.25	41.13	21.06	23.25	−10.49	2.71
The USA	60.98	38.61	69.85	−17.07	34.48	39.45	−47.47	−72.63
Japan	2.43	0.58	0.93	5.80	−0.91	0.32	−1.14	0.42
China	1.04	2.71	0.76	6.48	3.55	5.14	3.22	9.57

Source Bruegel based on Eurostat

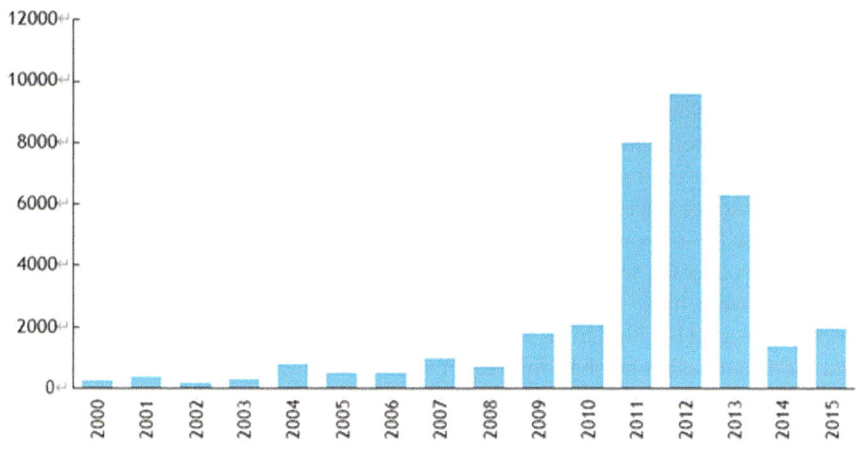

Fig. 1 Chines FDI transaction in the EU (€ millions). *Source* Bruegel based on Thilo Hanemen and Mikko Huotaro, 'A New Record year for Chinese Outbound Investment Europe' (2016) MERICS and Rhdium Group <https://www.merics.org/en/media-contact/press-release/a-new-record-year-for-chinese-outbound-investment-in-europe/>

Fig. 2 EU FDI transactions in China (€ millions). *Source* Bruegel based on Eurostat

Chinese FDI declined significantly, while Sweden and Luxembourg were making it into the top five list and more southern European countries attracting Chinese investors' attention.

The rapid increase in FDI has triggered more frequent high-level exchanges between EU countries and China and has occasionally led also to frictions and disputes. To further eliminate obstacles to bilateral FDI, China and the EU started to negotiate a BIT in November 2013.

This has not happened in a vacuum as nearly all EU countries (except Ireland) already have a BIT in place with China; most of these treaties were agreed between the 1980s and early 1990s. However, the objectives of those treaties were to bring FDI into China while protecting the legitimate operations of foreign businesses. The role of China in the global economy has changed, and these old treaties clearly need to be updated. Some EU countries have upgraded their BITs with China (Table 2). The other very relevant reason to revisit the existing treaties between China and EU countries is that the responsibility for agreeing on BITs is no longer in the hands of member states since the agreement of the Lisbon Treaty in 2009. Negotiation of BITs is now the responsibility of the European Commission, and a new EU-China BIT would cover the whole of the EU.

At the same time, there are two main reasons for the European Commission to push for a BIT with China. First, since the Lisbon Treaty was signed in 2009, and the Commission has had full responsibility for investment issues. Second, the Commission wants to avoid unfair competition between EU countries for Chinese investment.

In this context, the EU and China have agreed to pursue a deal that would protect investment, increase market access and address key challenges related to the regulatory environment, including those related to transparency, licensing and authorisation. Although most of these issues are covered by existing bilateral agreements, an

Table 2 China's existing BITs with EU member states

	Signature date	Valid date	Remarks
Sweden	29/03/1982	29/03/1982	
	27/09/2004	27/09/2004	Valid since signature
Germany	10/7/1983	18/03/1985	
	1/12/2003	11/11/2005	Re-signed
France	30/05/1984	19/03/1985	
	26/11/2007	20/08/2010	Re-signed
Belgium and Luxembourg	4/6/1984	5/10/1986	
	6/6/2005	1/12/2009	Re-signed
Finland	9/4/1984	26/01/1986	
	15/11/2004	15/11/2006	Re-signed
Norway	21/11/1984	10/7/1985	
Italy	28/01/1985	28/08/1987	
Denmark	29/041985	29/04/1985	
Netherlands	17/06/1985	1/2/1987	
	26/11/2001	1/8/2004	Re-signed
Austria	12/9/1985	11/10/1986	
UK	15/05/1986	15/05/1986	
Switzerland	12/11/1986	18/03/1987	
	27/01/2009	13/04/2010	Re-signed
Poland	7/6/1988	8/1/1989	
Bulgaria	27/06/1989	21/08/1994	
	26/06/2007	10/11/2007	Re-signed
Russia	9/11/2006	1/5/2009	
Hungary	29/05/1991	1/4/1993	
Czech and Slovak	12/4/1991	1/12/1992	
Slovak	7/12/2005	25/05/2007	New revision
Portugal	3/2/1992	1/12/1992	
	9/12/2005	26/07/2008	Re-signed
Spain	6/2/1992	1/5/1993	
	24/11/2005	1/7/2008	Re-signed
Greece	25/06/1992	21/12/1993	
Ukraine	31/10/1992	29/05/1993	
Moldova	6/11/1992	1/3/1995	
Belarus	11/1/1993	14/01/1995	

(continued)

Table 2 (continued)

	Signature date	Valid date	Remarks
Albania	13/02/1993	1/9/1995	
Croatia	7/6/1993	1/7/1994	
Estonia	2/9/1993	1/6/1994	
Slovenia	13/09/1993	1/1/1995	
Lithuania	8/11/1993	1/6/1994	
Iceland	31/03/1994	1/3/1997	
Romania	12/7/1994	1/9/1995	
	16/04/2007	1/9/2008	Revised
Yugoslavia	18/121995	12/9/1996	
Macedonia	9/6/1997	1/11/1997	
Malta	22/02/2009	1/4/2009	
Cyprus	17/01/2001	29/04/2002	

Source Chinese Ministry of Commerce

EU-level BIT with China provides a new opportunity to reduce barriers to investment further and boost bilateral FDI. The BIT also offers excellent benefits to China, given the rapid increase in Chinese investment in European Union countries in the last few years. Furthermore, a successful EU-China BIT could pave the way to a potential free trade agreement (FTA).

The twenty-sixth round of EU-China BIT negotiations was wrapped up in January 2020 in Brussels. On several issues, however, there is no apparent convergence between the two negotiating parties. A key point of difference appears to be market access. Market access for EU investors in China is restricted. According to an index of restrictiveness in market access compiled by the OECD, China is one of the most restrictive countries in terms of market access for foreign investors. Beyond market access, EU authorities are concerned about potential discrimination against EU investors operating in China, including explicit or implicit preferential subsidies for specific enterprises. Such discrimination may also be a factor for Chinese companies operating in Europe.

While market access is a more general issue, potential discrimination employing implicit or explicit subsidies has linkages to the role played by Chinese SOEs. Specially, the EU argues that SOEs do not follow market principles fully, partly because of the explicit or implicit government support they receive, and this undermines market efficiency. In addition, there is also a disagreement over how to settle disputes between investors, particularly those that involve SOEs. The discriminative consequence is not only true for the Chinese market but also Chinese investment in Europe because a good part of it (most of it until very recently) originates from SOEs.

As such, understanding the behaviour of Chinese SOEs, including how they differ from their European counterparts, is crucial for any further negotiations on the EU-China BIT.

3 What Is Special About SOEs? A Comparison Between the EU and China

Theoretically, the most convincing justification for the existence of SOEs is achieving social objectives and/or correcting market failures. As such, most SOEs do not need to pursue a profit maximisation objective and are often strictly regulated and assessed by the government. In China, SOEs have a much broader scope as they originate from the planned economy era when they dominated all sectors (either SOEs or collectively owned companies). Most Chinese SOEs, even now, are not established based on correcting market failure but more to carry out government objectives.

3.1 Chinese SOEs: Bigger, More Pervasive and More Dominant than Their EU Counterparts

Although China started on its path of market reform and openness in the 1980s, it was only in the 1990s that reform started to impact SOEs—a movement that happened under the slogan 'Grasping the large, letting go of the small'. As a result, the number of SOEs declined more rapidly than SOEs' share of employees. Another important consequence was that a good part of the private firms in China today were SOEs until the late 1990s, meaning their current owners still have connections, directly or indirectly, with the Chinese government (Fig. 3).

Since the late 1990s reforms, the Chinese government has pursued several initiatives to reform SOEs, but the logic has switched away from privatisation to improving efficiency while maintaining the state's role in the production of goods and services. The ultimate objective of the ongoing reform has shifted to creating corporate giants that can compete globally. Those giants remain state-controlled, especially in strategic sectors. Nearly, 70% of the Chinese firms in the Forbes Global 2000 list of the world's largest public companies are SOEs. However, in terms of the share of SOEs in the market value of its most prominent companies, China ranks third globally after Qatar and the UAE.

State-owned enterprises in the EU are very different. They are generally smaller than Chinese SOEs. They are typically found in sectors affected by potential market failure and externalities, such as utilities (Fig. 4).

Though relatively large, Chinese SOEs tend to perform worse than their private peers. Another important characteristic of Chinese SOEs is their industry coverage. Chinese SOEs seem to be much more engaged in manufacturing than European SOEs.

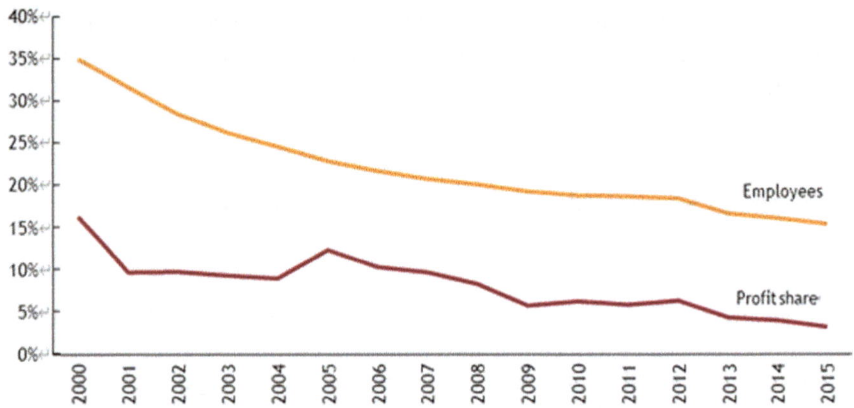

Fig. 3 Chinese SOEs, shares of employees and profits. *Source* Bruegel based on China statistics Yearbook. Note: Data for number of SOEs is missing from 2003–05, so the plots are smoothed over the *three year* period

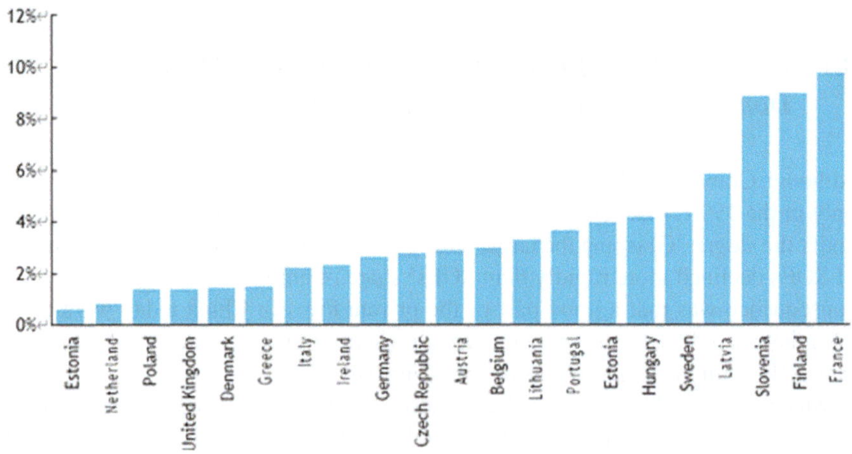

Fig. 4 Employment in SOEs, % of total employment. *Source* Brugel based on: European Commission, 'State-Owned Enterprises in the EU: Lessons Learnt and Ways Forward in a Post-Crisis Context' (July 2016) Institutional Paper 031 ISSN 2443–801; World Bank, Eurostat

This is not surprising if we consider that the manufacturing sector is larger in China, but this is not the whole story. The figures also highlight the Chinese government's industrial policy to develop what has long been a key strategic sector (Fig. 5).

Another important characteristic of Chinese SOEs is their industry coverage. Chinese SOEs seem to be much more engaged in manufacturing than European SOEs. A quarter of Chinese SOEs are in the manufacturing sector, and 34% of Chinese manufacturing employees work for SOEs. The equivalent EU figures are 2.8 and 4.8% (Table 3). This is not so surprising if we consider that the manufacturing

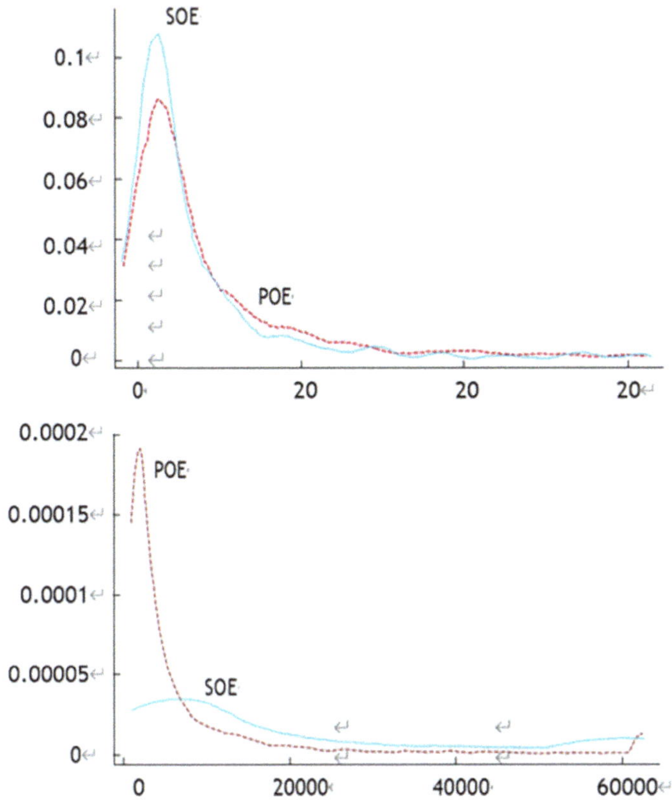

Fig. 5 State-owned enterprises (SOEs) versus private-owned enterprises (POEs) in asset and profit performance. *Source* Bruegel. Note: we calculated the probability distribution of the listed companies' assets (left) and profits (right) for Chinese SOEs and POEs separately. To make sure our results are not sensitive to extreme values, data is truncated with firms above and below 5 percentiles for both variables

Table 3 Sectoral distribution of SOEs in China and the EU: number of firms and employments

	% of firms that are SOEs		% of workers employed by SOEs*	
	China (%)	EU (%)	China (%)	EU (%)
Agriculture, forest, fishing	2.21	0.70	1.69	2.48
Manufacturing	24.92	2.81	33.66	4 81
Services	66 47	96 49	42.83	92.71

Source Bruegel based on (1) Chinese national Bureau of Statistics: (2) BvD Amadeus/Orbis dataset. Note: Kalemli-Ozcan et al. (2015) present a comprehensive introduction to the dataset

Table 4 Sectorial sales distribution of SOEs, POEs and FOEs in China in 2008

	SOE (%)	POE (%)	FOE (%)
Health	58 92	41.06	0.02
Wholesale and retail	2.20	97.73	0.08
Construction	24 43	75.26	0.30
Culture	54.71	44.36	0 94
Education	34 06	64.85	1 09
Finance	21.74	76 78	1 48
Accommodation	25.96	71.60	2.44
Real estate	7.32	90 11	2.57
Environment	43.65	53.51	2.83
Research	33.94	62.28	3.78
Lease and business	26 94	64 65	8 41
Restaurant	4.00	86.96	9.04
Manufacturing	15.11	75.26	9.63

Source Bruegel based on China's Economic Census Data. Note: FOE = foreign-owned enterprise

sector is larger in China, but this is not the whole story. The figures also highlight the Chinese government's industrial policy to develop what has long been a key strategic sector.

To further highlight the extensive presence of SOEs in China, even among large firms, Table 4 shows the sectoral breakdown of the revenues of Chinese firms for state-owned, private-owned and foreign-owned firms. Chinese SOEs lead in many strategically essential sectors beyond manufacturing, while foreign ownership is minimal even in sectors that are officially open to foreign competition.

3.2 The Special Environment for Chinese SOEs

The fact that Chinese SOEs are generally larger and more pervasive than their global peers but are also less profitable than private companies has its roots in the special corporate governance of SOEs. The appointment of SOEs' managers is still political, at least to some extent. Before 1992, SOEs' managers were government officials. After China's deepening market economy reform, the method of selecting SOE leaders was changed to a combination of official recommendation and market recruitment. Nevertheless, given that most SOE executives still retain an administrative rank, prospects for promotion in SOEs are significantly influenced by political decisions. A second reason for the relatively lower profitability of Chinese SOEs is their compliance with non-economic administrative orders. This is very hard to quantify but can be illustrated by several examples. A well-known issue is the treatment of overcapacity in SOEs. Bankruptcy is not an option for fear of its social

Table 5 Types of preferential treatment for SOE investments

Type of preferential treatment	Level of concern		
	Strong (%)	Somewhat	Low
Preferential financing	15	62%	23%
Explicit/implicit guarantee	15	31%	54%
Outright subsidies	38	23%	39%
Regulatory exemptions	25	33 K	42 K
Position in domestic marketplace	38	39%	23%
Access to state information	46	36%	18%

Source OECD. 'State-Owned Enterprises as Global Competitors A Challenge or an Opporturnity' (OECD Publishing 2015)

impact through increased unemployment. Therefore, many steel companies have had no choice but to turn into unprofitable 'zombie enterprises'. Such non-economic orders can come from local, as well as central, government. A good example is the Beijing government's political objective to reduce the population density in Beijing. To do this, the Beijing government requires some SOEs in Beijing's urban region to move to suburban areas, regardless of the potentially negative impacts on profits and employees.

However, also because of SOEs' connections to the political hierarchy, they have access to benefits from the government, such as cheaper and easier access to financing than is available to private enterprises. According to an OECD survey, other sources of preferential treatment for SOEs seem to raise even greater levels of concern (Table 5).

3.3 *Will Global Consumers Benefit from Chinese SOEs? Not Necessarily*

One could make a case that Chinese SOEs might not foster competition but could still be good for global consumers because they drive prices down even in tradable sectors, such as manufacturing. More specifically, given the intrinsic advantages that SOEs have coupled with their relatively lower profitability and managerial efficiency, the key question is whether such undue advantages can enable SOEs to set lower than equilibrium prices, which could undercut competitors. Even if Chinese SOEs are capable of setting prices lower than their marginal costs because of subsidies (i.e. conduct dumping policies) and could thus weaken the EU's competitive environment, the final impact on welfare for the EU is ambiguous because the consumer can benefit from lower prices and increased product variety. In that regard, market access seems to be the key factor for tilting the balance from a positive to a negative impact, according to Brander and Krugman.[1] In other words, market access helps maintain consumer welfare when dumping happens. The problem is that market access is indeed an issue in China, not only for foreign companies but even for private Chinese companies. This is why it is hard to argue that consumer welfare might be increased as a consequence of lower prices being set by Chinese SOEs.

3.4 Should the Focus Be on SOEs When Looking at Market Dominance and Its Consequences?

Chinese private firms, including many in the manufacturing sector, were partially privatised in the late 1990s and early 2000s but still retain strong connections to the Chinese government. More specifically, five per cent of Chinese private firms are under the direct control of Communist Party of China (CPC) members,[2] and even non-party entrepreneurs are also likely to pursue political resources and sometimes recruit CPC members or those people with relationships with government, in order to improve their chances of accessing scarce resources. A striking example is that more than 150 Chinese billionaires belong to a group of lawmakers in the National People's Congress, China's top legislature or to the Chinese People's Political Consultative Conference, the leading political advisory board. More generally, Milhaupt and Zheng[3] show striking similarities between SOEs and some special private companies, leading them to argue that 'drawing a stark distinction between SOEs and privately owned firms (POEs) misperceives the reality of China's institutional environment'. In the same vein, a number of surveys conducted by Chinese officials show that private firms directly owned by Party members and those related to political elites obtained significantly more bank loans than others. This result is also verified by Kung and Ma, who find that China's poor environment in terms of property rights has not affected private enterprises much because, in such an environment, many private business owners devote time and money to developing political connections with the government in exchange for looser regulation and easier access to finance, which is similar to the general environment for SOEs.[4]

[1] James A. Brander and Paul Krugman, 'A Reciprocal Dumping Model of International Trade' (1983) NBER Working Paper No.1194, National Bureau of Economic Research.

[2] Curtis J. Milhaupt and Wentong Zheng, 'Beyond ownership: state capitalism and the Chinese firm' (2015) 103(3) Georgetown Law Journal 665–722.

[3] ibid.

[4] James Kai-Sing Kung and Chicheng Ma, 'Friends with Benefits: How Political Connections Help Sustain Private Enterprise Growth in China' (2018) 85(337) Economica 41–74.

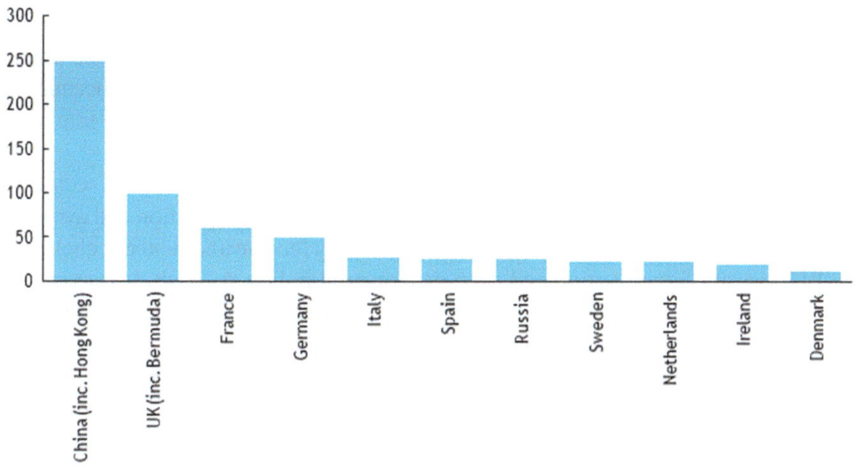

Fig. 6 Forbes 2000 companies foe China and selected European countries. *Source* Bruegel based on Forbes

4 The EU's Concerns About Chinese SOEs: Is It Seeing the Whole Picture?

The increasing economic magnitude of China's SOEs, and their eagerness to acquire foreign assets, has come as a shock for many European corporates. Some examples of recent European acquisitions by Chinese corporates are Pirelli by ChemChina and Louvre Hotels by Shanghai Jinjiang.

While Chinese corporates expand abroad, EU corporates seem to have increasing difficulty in accessing China's market. In this context, China has introduced a massive plan to support its own manufacturing industrial, the China Manufacturing 2025 Initiative. The ultimate goal of this initiative is to further enhance competitiveness in ten critical sectors, including new energy and rail transport equipment. Because targets have been set for the amount of local content, it seems clear that this plan will make it even more difficult for foreign investors to access China's market. According to a business confidence survey conducted in 2019, 40 per cent of European firms see increased discrimination against foreign companies compared to Chinese companies under China Manufacturing 2025.[5]

Chinese SOEs, aided by government industrial policy support schemes, have become major competitors for European firms. Figure 6 shows the number of companies included in the Forbes Global 2000 from China and ten major European countries. Excluding the UK, the number of Chinese Forbes Global 2000 firms has already reached the sum of the number of firms from all the other nine countries (France,

[5] European Union Chamber of Commerce in China, 'European Business in China: Business Confidence Survey 2019' (2019). <https://static.europeanchamber.com.cn/upload/documents/documents/Business_Confidence_Survey_2019_updated[663].pdf>.

Germany, Italy, Spain, Russia, Sweden, Netherlands, Ireland and Denmark). Competitive concerns are especially pressing for European manufacturers, because manufacturing is where China traditionally has a comparative advantage, and because of China's ambitious Manufacturing 2025 Initiative, which seeks to further strengthen the competitiveness of Chinese firms.

Against this backdrop, the EU is also taking steps to revive its industrial sector but within a very different framework, which aims to preserve competition and avoiding distortions.[6] China's rising SOEs and the support they receive undoubtedly challenge the EU's spirit of competition and even its industrial policy. As such, correcting the apparently undue advantages that Chinese SOEs enjoy is an obvious policy target for the EU in the ongoing negotiations with China on a BIT.

However, from a practical point of view, targeting SOEs in the BIT negotiation might not be the best strategy for the EU to tackle this concern. As we have noted, several Chinese private companies also benefit from political access, similarly to the SOEs. Suppose, the EU were to set particularly rigorous rules for Chinese SOEs. In that case, it could leave more room for politically connected Chinese private firms to gain government support for mergers and acquisitions in the European market. It is also hard to argue that all Chinese SOEs behave in the same way. Zhao finds evidence of a competitive environment for several Chinese SOEs insofar as they make investment decisions without government influence.[7]

On this basis, the EU should not impose specific conditions on SOEs within the EU-China BIT but should instead push for general policies that apply to both SOEs and private companies. In other words, instead of focusing on ownership, the EU should look into the state-centred institutional framework in which firms operate in China and how that might give them an advantage over European companies. The most important advantage Chinese companies enjoy is the difficult access to the Chinese market that their foreign competitors face. Therefore, liberalising market access is the most urgent step to be taken to create a level playing field so that European firms can compete with Chinese SOEs. This relates to the second aspect of the EU-China BIT: European investment in China.

5 European Companies Investing in China

European companies have long been present in China and have accumulated a stock of FDI of €333 billion as of 2017 if Hong Kong is included. Though the flow of FDI has stagnated since 2011, China remains an important market for many European corporations.

---

[6] Reinhilde Veugelers (ed), 'Manufacturing Europe's Future' (2013) Bruegel Blueprint Series 21.

[7] Hongtu Zhao, 'The Myth of China's Overseas Energy Investment' (East Asia Forum, 4 March 2015) <https://www.eastasiaforum.org/2015/03/04/the-myth-of-chinas-overseas-energy-investment/> .

From the perspective of European companies investing in China, the first and foremost issue is market access. The EU Chamber of Commerce in Beijing has reported increasingly unfair treatment of foreign companies,[8] and the OECD ranks China the second most restrictive country for FDI in the world, with only the Philippines more restrictive. The question is whether this is related to the pervasive role of SOEs in the Chinese economy.

The answer, from our perspective, is that even Chinese private companies are denied access to some critical sectors in the Chinese market on the grounds of security (including economic security) and based on a web of different laws and regulations, the most important being the anti-monopoly law. As we have shown (Table 4), the sectoral distribution of Chinese SOEs confirms that they are particularly favoured in the sectors considered strategically important by the government, including energy, infrastructure, utilities and finance. The EU Chamber of Commerce in China finds these sectors to be the most difficult for European firms to access.[9]

6 Policy Suggestions for the European Union

Our analysis shows that Chinese SOEs differ from European SOEs in many ways and represent a risk of unfair competition for EU companies in both China and Europe. However, the EU should not over-focus on SOEs in the EU-China BIT negotiations because some large Chinese private companies also benefit from preferential market access in China, giving them a comparative advantage when operating abroad.

The first priority issue that an EU-China BIT should pursue is market liberalisation, so that any market access granted through the BIT puts European companies on an equal footing to their Chinese competitors (even with SOEs). This obviously requires, at least, reciprocity. In fact, market liberalisation is essential not only for foreign companies but also for Chinese private companies so that gains are also shared with China.[10]

Within the negotiation of the EU-China BIT, it seems essential for the EU to continue to pursue reciprocity in terms of the treatment of corporate governance and, more generally, market access. Many concerns about the behaviour of SOEs are rooted in their complex corporate structures, which result in limited disclosure of their financial information. Beyond the EU's bilateral negotiations with China, one could think of other—multilateral—venues through which to pursue more market-driven corporate governance for Chinese SOEs. The most apparent route would be for

[8] European Union Chamber of Commerce in China, 'Annual Report 2016' <http://www.europeanchamber.com.cn/en/publications-archive/514/Annual_Report_2016> .

[9] European Union Chamber of Commerce in China, 'European Business in China Position Paper 2016/2017' (2016) Nanjing Position Paper <http://www.europeanchamber.com.cn/en/publications-position-paper> .

[10] Gisela Grieger, 'State-owned Enterprise (SOE) Reforms in China: A Decisive Role for the Market at Last?' (May 2016) EPRS Briefing PE 583.796 <http://www.europarl.europa.eu/RegData/etudes/BRIE/2016/583796/EPRS_BRI(2016)583796_EN.pdf> .

China to become a member of OECD or, at least, to comply voluntarily with global principles of corporate governance. Such measures would be in the EU's interests and in the interests of China, which has repeatedly declared its determination to continue with its economic liberalisation. Pressure from the EU can only help Chinese authorities push for further liberalisation.

Regarding the EU-China BIT, the first priority, clearly based on the principle of reciprocity, should be that China's 'negative list' for market access should be narrowed considerably and extended beyond China's special economic zones to the whole Chinese territory. This goal remains distant as China's negative list continues to get longer, underpinned by a law that can limit investment for national security—or even economic—reasons. FDI is highly restricted in China outside the special economic zones, with foreign investment permitted in very few sectors (positive list) and requirements to comply with as many as three foreign company laws. A shorter negative list with broader coverage would significantly lift market access restrictions in the currently prohibited industries for EU companies. Opening up more sectors would be mutually beneficial, as it would help China further liberalise.

The second issue for the EU-China BIT relates to market access beyond the treatment of foreign companies. As we have noted, a key advantage for Chinese SOEs is their favourable access to specific industries. The Chinese government sometimes even uses anti-monopoly laws to protect the interests of some specific companies—and not only SOEs.[11] Revising the anti-monopoly law and other legal protections that benefit SOEs relative to other corporations is also essential and beneficial for China. More generally, EU negotiators would do well in pushing the concept of competitive neutrality as a way to demonstrate the lack of a level playing field and also for Chinese authorities to take action.

Third, the EU should build a firewall against potential problems related to Chinese investment in Europe. In this respect, the two key instruments are the EU's competition policy and dispute resolution framework to regulate the operations of Chinese SOEs in the EU. Identifying unfair behaviour by a firm can be more manageable after a firm reveals its status by operating in the EU market. An appropriate dispute settlement mechanism can protect both European and Chinese corporates. Among the different options, an investor-state dispute settlement system (ISDS) seems to be favoured internationally but would need to be revised so that governments (either China or EU governments) do not fall prey to corporates suing them without clear justification. Furthermore, in the Chinese case, the very close links between corporates and the Chinese government (especially when operating abroad) could make ISDS a double-edged sword for the EU, because in some instances, China could, for its own purposes, support its enterprises in suing EU companies. In addition, the implementation of the ISDS might be difficult in China, where experience with investor-state arbitration is somewhat limited, and there is a very low probability that

[11] Epstein, Richard A. 'Curbing the Abuses of China's Anti-Monopoly Law: An Indictment and Reform Agenda' (December 2014) George Mason University School of Law Center for the Protection of Intellectual Property <https://sls.gmu.edu/cpip/wp-content/uploads/sites/31/2014/04/Curbing-the-Abuses-of-Chinas-Anti-Monopoly-Law.pdf> .

the Chinese government will enforce foreign court decisions (US-China Economic and Security Review Commission, 2016).[12] A revision of the ISDS is thus warranted to balance the parties' interests in the BIT negotiation.

---

12 US-China Economic and Security Review Commission, 'Policy Considerations for Negotiating a US-China Bilateral Investment Treaty' (August 2016) Staff Research Report <https://www.uscc.gov/sites/default/files/Research/Staff%20Report_Policy%20Considerations%20for%20Negotiating%20a%20U.S.-China%20Bilateral%20Investment%20Treaty080116.pdf> .

[illegible] Chinese government will enhance foreign court [illegible] of US SOEs [illegible] Commission, 2019.[33] A [illegible] of the SOEs [illegible] tests in the BIT negotiation.

State-Owned and Influenced Enterprises and the Evolution of Canada's Foreign Direct Investment Regime

Geoffrey Hale

1 Introduction

Canada's foreign direct investment (FDI) regime might best be described as having multiple personalities. Its combined outward and inward stock of foreign direct investment (FDI) has been the largest among G-20 counties for some years. At 98.9% in 2019, its outward FDI was the largest, relative to GDP, among major advanced industrial economies. Inward FDI accounted for 61.0% of GDP, second after the UK among G-20 nations, although well below the levels of smaller entrepot economies in Europe and Southeast Asia.[1]

Canada liberalised its FDI regime significantly during the 1980s, intending to open all but a handful of strategic sectors to foreign investors based on market governance norms and, subsequently, national treatment of foreign investors under domestic laws of "host" countries. These measures were institutionalised through a series of bilateral, regional and multilateral trade agreements in the 1990s and after that. Subsequent reforms to Canadian financial and capital markets policies have enabled a large-scale international expansion of its financial institutions and extensive external investments by major pension and related investment management funds operating at arms-length from governments. However, the growing global profiles of state-owned, controlled, or influenced enterprises (SCEs), particularly from regimes with state-dominated legal systems, have led to regulatory and legislative changes since 2009, increasing the opacity and unpredictability of processes affecting such firms, particularly when influenced by national security factors.

[1] OECD, 'FDI stocks' 2021. https://doi.org/10.1787/80eca1f9-en. <https://data.oecd.org/fdi/fdi-stocks.htm> accessed 26 June 2021.

G. Hale (✉)
Political Science at the University of Lethbridge, Lethbridge, AB, Canada
e-mail: geoffrey.hale@uleth.ca

J. Chaisse et al. (eds.), *Regulation of State-Controlled Enterprises*, International Law and the Global South, https://doi.org/10.1007/978-981-19-1368-6_25

Most investment flows are subject to a combination of WTO rules, those of Canada's regional and bilateral trade agreements, with provisions for domestic screening regimes. The *Investment Canada Act*,[2] amended periodically in recent years, provides for review of inward FDI over specified thresholds for their "net benefit" to Canada, with significantly lower thresholds applicable to SCEs.[3] Other domestic legislation restricts foreign ownership over specified thresholds for firms in financial, transportation, telecommunications, and cultural industries, among others.[4] Since 2009, paralleling actions by most other industrial countries,[5] Canada has introduced and intensified national security screening of FDI—with significant implications for SCEs.

This chapter explores the evolution of Canadian foreign investment review policies with particular attention to SCEs and distinguishes between market-based and politically influenced models of governance in both inward and outward foreign investment. It notes the persistence of "net benefit" principles in screening FDI under the *Investment Canada Act* (ICA), along with principles that have come to shape their application to investment and takeover proposals by state-controlled and influenced enterprises. It also notes the evolving design and implementation of national security provisions to proposed transactions since policy and legislative changes introduced since 2013, changes in concepts of "strategic" or "critical" sectors, and their application to several contested transactions in recent years.

2 Historical Evolution of Canada's Foreign Investment Regime

Canada's inward foreign investment regime has been reshaped by its prolonged transition from neo-mercantilist economic development strategies, which heavily influenced its economic structure between the late nineteenth and late twentieth centuries, through a period of intense resource nationalism during the 1970s and early 1980s, to a post-1985 emphasis on market-driven integration in the North American and global economies.[6]

The *Investment Canada Act,* which replaced the more restrictive *Foreign Investment Review Act* (FIRA) in that year, recognised benefits from "increased capital

[2] *Investment Canada Act,* R.S.C., 1985, c. 28 (1st Supp.).

[3] Investment Canada, 'Thresholds for Review' (Innovation, Science and Economic Development Canada, February 2019). <https://www.ic.gc.ca/eic/site/ica-lic.nsf/eng/h_lk00050.html> accessed 17 January 2020.

[4] Andrea Mandel-Campbell, 'Foreign Investment Review Regimes: How Canada Stacks Up' Conference Board of Canada, April 2008.

[5] Farhad Jalinous (ed), 'Foreign Investment Reviews 2019: A Global Perspective' (White & Case, December 2019). <https://www.whitecase.com/sites/default/files/2019-12/foreign-direct-investment-reviews-2019.pdf> accessed January 17, 2020.

[6] Geoffrey Hale, *Uneasy Partnership: The Politics of Business and Government in Canada*, 2nd ed. (University of Toronto Press 2018), 76–108.

and technology in Canada" subject to its "promotion of growth and economic opportunities" (s. 2). It provided for review of FDI transactions over specified financial thresholds to promote "net benefit to Canada"[7] rather than the "significant benefit test" of the previous regime.[8] It also eliminated reviews for "greenfield investments" (i.e. newly established firms) outside the cultural industries sector, although maintaining legal notification requirements and setting formal timelines for reviews. The net benefit test is one of three main processes affecting FDI—as distinct from broader regulation of merger and acquisition (M&A) activities—the others being notification requirements and, since 2009, national security screening.

Section 20 of the ICA lists six criteria considered in the net benefit test:

(a) the effect of the investment on the level and nature of economic activity in Canada, including, without limiting the generality of the foregoing, the effect on employment, on resource processing, on the utilisation of parts, components and services produced in Canada and on exports from Canada;
(b) the degree and significance of participation by Canadians in the Canadian business or new Canadian business and in any industry or industries in Canada of which the Canadian business or new Canadian business forms or would form a part;
(c) the effect of the investment on productivity, industrial efficiency, technological development, product innovation and product variety in Canada;
(d) the effect of the investment on competition within any industry or industries in Canada;
(e) the compatibility of the investment with national industrial, economic and cultural policies, taking into consideration industrial, economic and cultural policy objectives enunciated by the government or legislature of any province likely to be significantly affected by the investment;
(f) the contribution of the investment to Canada's ability to compete in world markets.[9]

Screening thresholds were entrenched in the Canada-U.S. Free Trade Agreement of 1988, and later extended through Uruguay Round negotiations leading to the formation of the World Trade Organisation (WTO). Progressive increases in threshold levels have removed most transactions from requirements for review, notwithstanding continuing requirements for notification. WTO provisions eliminated review of "indirect" acquisitions: takeovers of existing Canadian subsidiaries of foreign firms by investors from other WTO member countries.

However, "negative list" measures continued to restrict FDI, either in absolute terms or by capping shares of equity ownership in "cultural industries" (e.g. broadcasting, newspapers, magazines), telecommunications, transportation sectors (e.g. railways, trucking, airlines, ports, airports), and selected financial industries, among

---

[7] *Investment Canada Act* (n 2).

[8] Canada. Competition Policy Review Panel. *Compete to Win: Final Report*. Industry Canada, June 2008, 28.

[9] *Investment Canada Act* (n 2) s 20.

others. In some cases, as in banks, railways, and some privatised state corporations, requirements for firm ownership to be widely held have replaced formal FDI restrictions.[10] A 2014 federal report notes that between 1985 and 2013, only 1,687 acquisitions (average 58 per year) have been subject to investment review out of 13,728 notifications—an average of 12.2%.[11]

Of these investments, the federal government formally rejected only two: the first by an American company of Macdonald Dettwiler Associates (MDA) in 2008, involving satellite technologies with significant national security implications,[12] the second by an Egyptian telecommunications firm, Accelero, of Manitoba Telecom's Allstream division in 2013, also on national security grounds. A third application—Anglo-Australian mining giant BHP Billiton's proposed takeover of Potash Corporation of Saskatchewan—was formally withdrawn in 2010 in response to Ottawa's change of outlook following intense opposition from the Saskatchewan government for the proposed deal's perceived risks to its resource management policies.[13] Canadian provinces are sovereign actors in many social and economic development policies, particularly involving natural resource development, which often motivates and enables them to act independently of the federal government.

Foreign investment reviews may also occur in parallel with merger reviews carried out by Canada's Competition Bureau. Although the Competition Bureau routinely coordinates its review of transactions with broader international implications with counterparts in the USA and the European Union, there is little evidence of coordination with Investment Canada or related national security reviews.[14]

Inward FDI stocks in Canada increased rapidly during the late-1990s and mid-2000s, generally paralleling stock market expansions and broader cycles of merger and acquisition (M&A) activity.[15] Figure 1 tracks the annual value of Canadian businesses acquired by foreign investors between 1985 and 2013. Although these trends aroused concerns in nationalist circles, including some business leaders, about the "hollowing-out" of major Canadian firms resulting from foreign takeovers, takeover activity by Canadian firms expanding abroad was comparable to that of foreign-based

[10] Mandel-Campbell (n 4), 10–17.

[11] Mathieu Frigon, 'The Foreign Investment Review Process in Canada' Library of Parliament, rev. 21 July 2014 <https://lop.parl.ca/sites/PublicWebsite/default/en_CA/ResearchPublications/201142E#a3> accessed 18 January 2020.

[12] Ironically, MDA used a foreign acquisition to shift its head office to the United States as Maxar Technologies in 2016 before selling its Canadian assets back to Canadian investors in early 2020. Sean Silcoff and David Milstead, 'Canadarm maker to be repatriated from U.S. in $1 billion deal' *The Globe and Mail*, (Toronto: 31 Dec. 2019) A1.

[13] Frigon (n 9) 5; Shawn McCarthy and Brenda Bouw, 'Premier puts heat on Harper over Potash deal' *The Globe and Mail* (Toronto: 26 October 2010) A7.

[14] Calvin S. Goldman and Michael S. Koch, 'Competition Law' Goodmans LLP, *2016 Lexpert Directory*, B150. <https://www.goodmans.ca/files/file/docs/Goodmans%20Competition%20Law%20June%202016.pdf> accessed 17 January 2020.

[15] Frigon (n 9) 6; Geoffrey Hale. 'The Dog that Hasn't Barked: The political economy of contemporary debates on Canada's foreign investment policies' (2008) 41 (3) *Canadian Journal of Political Science*, 720–725.

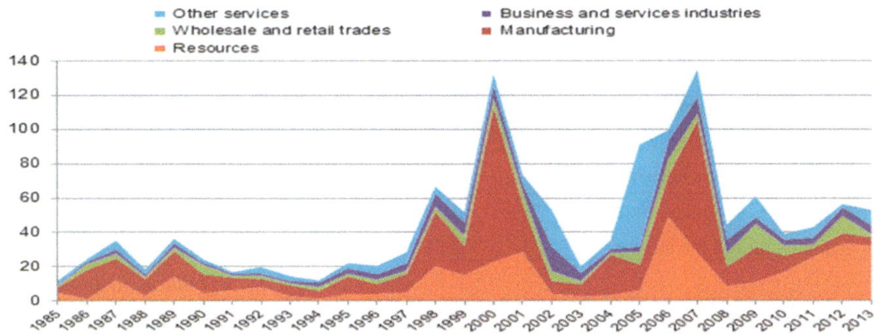

Fig. 1 Acquisition of Canadian Businesses by Foreign Investors: 1985–2013 ($C 2013 constant dollars). *Source* Mathieu Frigon. 'The Foreign Investment Review Process in Canada' Library of Parliament, 21 July 2014, 6

firms in Canada during both market cycles.[16] A panel of business leaders appointed by the Harper government in 2007 to study the issue recommended increases in the FDI review threshold to $1 billion (a level surpassed in subsequent trade agreements) and substitution of an enterprise value threshold for one based on asset value to acknowledge the growing role of service and knowledge-based industries.[17] It also recognised the potential relevance of reciprocity in liberalising sectoral restrictions on foreign investment to ensure the comparable ability of Canadian firms to expand their operations in foreign countries.[18]

Its major proposals on raising "net benefit" review thresholds, discussed below, were ultimately implemented in 2015–17 and extended the following conclusion of the Comprehensive Economic and Trade Agreement (CETA) with the European Union in 2017. Table 1 notes current FDI review thresholds under the *Investment Canada Act*. These measures have significantly reduced the relative restrictiveness of Canada's FDI screening requirements as measured by the OECD and noted in Table 2—although the latter does not appear to consider the general tightening of national security screening in most Western countries. Thresholds are adjusted annually based on changes in nominal GDP.

Investment Canada reviews of proposed investments remain exceptional—averaging 14 or 1.9% of notifications annually of foreign acquisitions of Canadian-based firms under the Act's "net benefit" provisions annually between 2014–15 and 2018–19, and 5 reviews annually (0.55% of notifications) under the Act's national security provisions, as noted in Table 5. No application has been rejected under "net benefit" rules since 2010. However, only 11 of the 25 proposed acquisitions (44%) subject to national

[16] Yvan Guillemette and Jack M. Mintz, 'A Capital Story: Exploding the myths around foreign investment in Canada' *Commentary 201*. C.D. Howe Institute, 2004; Geoffrey Hale, 'CNOOC-Nexen, State-Controlled Enterprises and Canadian Foreign Investment Policies: Adapting to divergent modernization' (2014) 47(3) *Canadian Journal of Political Science* 359–63.

[17] Canada. Competition Policy Review Panel (n 8) 31.

[18] ibid (n 8) 39.

Table 1 Screening thresholds for foreign direct investment (Enterprise value)

	Category	Value
"Net benefit" provisions	Introduced	2020
"Trade agreement investors"*	2016	$C 1565 million*
WTO private sector investors	1995, rev. 2014	$C 1043 million
State-owned/influenced Enterprises**	2014	$C 415 million
Canadian cultural businesses	1985	$C 5 million (direct)
		$C 50 million (indirect)
National security issues	2009	no threshold

* NAFTA/USMCA, CETA, CPTPP, FTAs with Korea, UK, 5 Latin American countries
** Broad definition in s. 3 of *Investment Canada Act.*
† $1 Cdn. = $0.759 US in January 2020.
Source Innovation, Science and Economic Development Canada. '*Investment Canada Act*' 30 March 2021. <https://www.ic.gc.ca/eic/site/ica-lic.nsf/eng/home> accessed 26 June 2021; Mathieu Frigon. 'The Foreign Investment Review Process in Canada' Library of Parliament, 21 July 2014.

Table 2 Relative restrictiveness (OECD FDI restrictiveness index)

	Canada	USA	OECD	China
1997	0.267	0.089	0.127	0.613
2003	0.263	0.089	0.098	0.567
2010	0.175	0.089	0.067	0.427
2015	0.166	0.089	0.067	0.384
2020	0.161	0.089	0.065	0.251

Source OECD, 'FDI restrictiveness (indicator)' 2021. https://doi.org/10.1787/c176b7fa-en; accessed 26 June 2021

security review since 2014 have been allowed to proceed, often with conditions. Nine (36%) have been blocked (or divestiture required), and five others (20%) have withdrawn their proposed transactions.[19] These figures suggest that national security issues have become the principal barrier to foreign investment outside traditionally protected economic sectors for reasons discussed below (Table 3).

Some observers, including the Competition Policy Review Panel (2007–08), have suggested that the burden of proof in "net benefit" cases should be shifted from proponents of individual transactions to governments, using a "national interest" test to reduce investor uncertainty.[20] However, the exemption of 98% of inward investments

---

[19] Investment Canada Act. 'Annual Report: 2018–19' Innovation, Science and Innovation Canada, 2019. <https://www.ic.gc.ca/eic/site/ica-lic.nsf/eng/h_lk81126.html#Toc528931162> accessed 17 January 2020.

[20] Competition Policy Review Panel (n 6) 32–33; Michael Grant, 'Fear the Dragon? Chinese Foreign Direct Investment in Canada' Conference Board of Canada, May 2012, iii. <https://www.conferenceboard.ca/temp/cdb14a41-943f-4ef6-bcee-9c768a0f396f/13-018_FeartheDragon-RPT.pdf> accessed 21 January 2020.

Table 3 Foreign investment review statistics—investment Canada—2014–15 to 2018–19

	2014–15	2015–16	2016–17	2017–18	2018–19	Average
Notifications of acquisitions (#)	704	659	715	742	953	754.6
Net benefit reviews: Per cent of notifications	2.1	2.3	3.1	1.2	0.9	1.9
Approvals	15	15	22	9	9	14
Total enterprise value ($C billion)	na	9	30	35	21	23.75
National security reviews*	8	0	4	4	9	5.0
Investment proceeds following review	4	0	4	0	3	2.8
New businesses (#)	180	137	185	197	255	190.8
Total enterprise value (Total Enterprise value ($C billion)$C billion)	na	19	20	29	63	32.75

* Reviews under ICA Sections 25.2, 25.3
Source Investment Canada, 'Annual Report: 2018–2019' Fig. 2, Table 4.
<https://www.ic.gc/eic/site//ica-lic.nsf/eng/lk81226.html> accessed 18 April 2022.

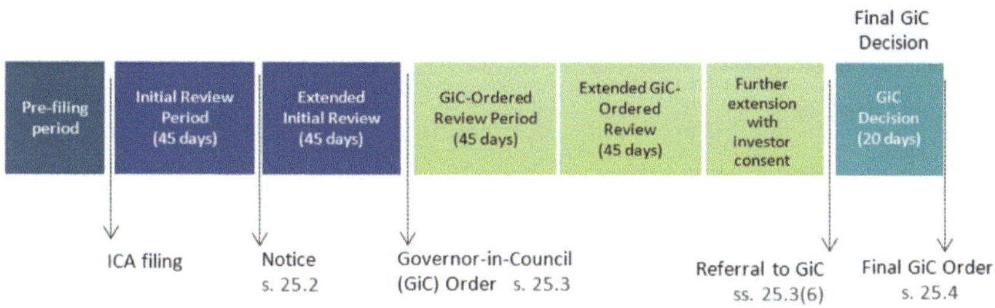

Fig. 2 *Investment Canada Act* National security review process. *Notes* The initial period of review may begin during the pre-filing period, but the statutory clock begins with a certified filing (or implementation, where a filing is not required). Time periods are prescribed in the N*ational Security Review of Investments Regulations* and reflect maximums. *Source* Investment Canada, 'Annual Report 2018–2019' (Ottawa: Innovation, Science and Economic Development, 2019), 15

from such reviews in recent years and the extreme rarity of rejections suggest that this concern is overblown for any firm with market-based governance structures and competent professional advice, notwithstanding the application of net benefit criteria to state-owned and influenced firms active in international markets. For this reason, it is worth examining the evolution of Canadian state and broader public sector enterprises and their activities in international markets to identify opportunities for and barriers to national treatment in investment rules.

Table 4 National security reviews under ICA Section 25(3)—2014–15 to 2018–19

Country of origin	Allowed to proceed	Approved with conditions	Withdrawn	Blocked/Divestment ordered	Total
China	2	4	2	5	13
Cyprus	–	–	–	1	1
Russia	–	–	–	1	1
Singapore	–	–	1	–	1
Switzerland	1	–	–	1	2
UK	–	–	–	1	1
Total	3	4	3	9	19
Industry sector					
Manufacturing	1	2	3	1	7
Telecommunications (Mfg/other)	–	1	–	2	3
Heavy/civil engineering and construction	–	–	–	1	1
Credit intermediation	1	–	–	–	1
Business services					
Computer services	–	1	–	1	2
Electronic shopping	1	–	–	–	1
Oil and gas	–	–	–	1	1
Rail transportation	–	–	–	1	1
Ship/boat building	–	–	–	1	1
Urban transit systems	–	–	–	1	1
Total	3	4		9	19

Source Investment Canada, 'Annual Report: 2018–2019' Table 5.

3 Canadian State Enterprise in Transition

The Canadian state enterprise sector also experienced a significant transformation between the mid-1980s and late-2000s. Federal and provincial governments commercialised and/or privatised numerous state-owned firms, especially in the transportation, resource, and telecommunications sectors, to pursue greater efficiency and market competitiveness.[21] Canada formalised sectoral ownership restrictions in 2016, extending them in 2021, along with other national security measures discussed

[21] Hale (n 6) 236–54; Anthony Boardman and Aidan Vining, 'A Review and Assessment of Privatization in Canada' (12) 2012 5 *SPP Research Paper*, School of Public Policy, University of Calgary.

later in this chapter.[22] Major Crown Corporations, as state-owned firms are known in Canada, were privatised in energy and other resource sectors, including commercial or quasi-commercial firms such as Petro-Canada and Alberta Energy Company, leading uranium miner Cameco, and Nova Scotia Power (now Emera Inc.), usually with requirements for widely held ownership. Others, such as Ontario's transmission utility, Hydro One, later became mixed enterprises with substantial private ownership. Concentrations of state enterprises shifted sharply towards the financial sector and provincial liquor and gambling monopolies, with residual strength among public utilities in most provinces.[23] However, the international operations of the first group are by far the most extensive.

Facing significant fiscal challenges and rising costs of demographic ageing, Canadian governments introduced major reforms to public and public sector (employee) pension and related investment regimes during and after the 1990s. Critically, the major investment funds emerging from these reforms were mandated to operate at arms-length from governments in their commercial operations and governance structures.[24] Over time, senior management of these organisations has come to report to independent boards of directors with institutionalised, competence-based appointment processes insulated from political interference.[25]

Regulatory caps on offshore investments by pension and retirement savings funds were removed in 2003 to enable them to pursue greater diversification and returns while reducing risks of abuse of market power in Canada's relatively concentrated equity markets. For example, the Canada Pension Plan Investment Board reports that 85% of its $C 392 billion portfolio was invested outside Canada in 2018–19.[26] By 2017, the ten largest Canadian pension funds were among the world's 100 largest private equity investors.[27]

Maintaining strategic and operational independence is widely viewed as essential to the effectiveness and reputation of such firms in pursuing their commercial mandates—and in distinguishing themselves from SCEs. Most such firms invest heavily in various forms of critical infrastructure, including port terminals, airports, pipelines and other energy transmission, generation and distribution systems which

[22] Canada, 'Guidelines on the National Security Review of Investments, Investment Canada, 24 March 2021. Accessed June 25, 2021.

[23] Daria Crisan and Kenneth J. McKenzie, 'Government-Owned Enterprises in Canada' 2013 6 SPP Research Paper 8, School of Public Policy, University of Calgary, 19–23.

[24] Guillaume Bédard-Pagé, Annick Demers, Eric Tuer, and Miville Tremblay, 'Large Canadian Public Pension Funds: A financial system perspective' *Financial System Review*, Bank of Canada, June 2016, 33–38; Hale (n 6) 331–33.

[25] CommonWealth. 'The Evolution of the Canadian Pension Model' World Bank Group, November 2017; Canada Pension Plan Investment Board, 'Governance' 2019. <http://www.cppib.com/en/who-we-are/governance-overview/> accessed January 20, 2020; Alberta Investment Management Corp., 'Governance and Business Standards' 2019. <https://www.aimco.alberta.ca/Who-We-Are/Governance> accessed January 20, 2020.

[26] Canada Pension Plan Investment Board. 'Investing for Generations: 2019 Annual Report' 5.

[27] Jennifer Patterson. '10 major Canadian pension funds listed among top global equity investors: report' *Benefits Canada*, 10 February 2017.

are generally subject to the public interest and/or natural security regulations. Investors seen to be subject to actual or prospective control of foreign governments in their operational and/or investment decisions are likely to be subject to far more restrictive regulation—including regulatory vetoes of major investments by host country governments or regulators. Several advanced industrial countries, including the USA, Germany, France, and Australia, have intensified national security regulations associated with foreign acquisitions of public infrastructure in recent years.[28] This lesson was driven home for Canadian governments in 2018–19 by the rejection by two state regulators of Ontario-based Hydro One's proposed acquisition of Avista, a public utility in the US Pacific Northwest, following Ontario Premier Doug Ford's forcing out the former's President and Board of Directors over a political dispute—despite the former's partial privatisation by a previous government.[29]

4 Concerns Over State-Owned and Influenced Investors

The growing international activities of state-owned enterprises and Sovereign Wealth Funds (SWFs) attracted significant political attention in Canada during the mid-2000s. Growing resource nationalism associated with the rapid escalation of global commodity prices after 2000 led to the "crowding out" of private Canadian firms in several developing countries, although Canadian governments generally welcomed the rapid growth of SCE investments in Canada's energy sector. However, Canada was not immune to this resource nationalism, as illustrated by the public backlash to China Minmetals' friendly takeover bid for Noranda Inc. in 2004 and the proposed BHP Billiton-Potash Corp. takeover discussed above.[30]

However, SCEs from numerous countries made growing investments in Canada's oil and gas industry during the 2000s and early 2010s, frequently in partnership with other foreign and domestic investor-owned firms. Dobson notes that all Chinese investments in oil and gas firms in 2009–12 and about 78% of mining sector investments during the same period were made by state firms—with the former typically characterised by majority ownership and the latter by minority investments.[31] These developments were consistent with the Chinese government's post-2002 "Go Global" policy to promote outward investments, initially by SCEs, to obtain resources or raw materials needed by the Chinese economy, along with enhancing China's technological research and development (R&D) capacity and facilitating macro-economic stabilisation during periods of sizeable trade surpluses.[32] Other SCEs with significant

[28] Jalinous (n 5).

[29] David Ebner, 'Idaho state regulator rejects Hydro One's proposed $4.4 billion acquisition of Avista' *The Globe and Mail* (Toronto: 4 January 2019) B1.

[30] Wendy Dobson, 'China's State-Owned Enterprises and Canada's Foreign Direct Investment Policy' (2017) 43 (S2) *Canadian Public Policy* S37.

[31] Dobson (n 28) S38.

[32] Grant (n 20) ii.

investments in the Canadian oil and gas sector during this period were from Norway, Korea, Japan, and Abu Dhabi.

The first FDI guidelines for state-owned enterprises were published by the Conservative federal government of Stephen Harper in December 2007, towards the end of that decade's takeover boom in global equity markets. They applied the net benefit test, noted above, to the acquisition of Canadian-based firms valued over the WTO FDI threshold, emphasising the "governance and commercial orientation of SOEs" including "transparency and disclosure, independent directors, audit committees, the equitable treatment of shareholders, and compliance with Canadian laws and practices".[33] Such practices were widely seen to encourage market-based rather than politicised decision-making and promote greater economic efficiency in competition with domestic and foreign investors.

However, there is little evidence that transactions involving foreign SCEs were subject to closer governmental scrutiny until the coincidence of two significant transactions in mid-2012: CNOOC's $15.1 billion acquisition of Nexen Inc., Canada's eighth-largest oil company, with sizeable investments in Alberta's oil sands region, and the $5.2 million acquisition of natural gas producer Progress Energy by Malaysia's Petronas with a view to the eventual development of a Liquid Natural Gas export terminal. The Nexen takeover, in particular, prompted a heated domestic debate. Proponents supported closer economic ties with China along with increased investment to promote economic development and maximisation of shareholder value in takeover markets. Others emphasised the risks of "nationalisation" of Canadian resources by foreign SCEs, the potential for lower economic efficiency, unfair competitive advantages due to state subsidies (especially access to credit) and regulatory preferences, and reduced competitiveness due to possible political constraints on their management.[34]

Although the Harper government ultimately approved both transactions,[35] it also announced policy changes that would tighten the burden of proof for SCE takeovers of Canadian firms, including:

> freedom from political influence; adherence to Canadian laws, standards and practices that promote sound corporate governance and transparency; and positive contributions to the productivity and industrial efficiency of the Canadian business . . . the degree of control or influence an SOE would likely exert on the industry in which the Canadian business operates;

---

[33] 'New guidelines for foreign investments by Canadian state enterprises' Stikeman Elliott LLP, December 2007. <https://www.stikeman.com/en-ca/kh/canadian-ma-law/new-guidelines-for-canadian-investments-by-foreign-state-owned-enterprises> accessed 21 January 2020.

[34] Jack M. Mintz, 'Limit state takeovers' *Financial Post* (Toronto, 25 July 2012), FP15; Hale (n 15).

[35] Initial rejection of Petronas' bid was reportedly linked to its reluctance to defer closing until the federal government had completed its review of policies governing foreign SCE investments. Stikeman Elliott LLP, 'Investment Canada Act FAQ' 31 October 2016, 5. <https://www.stikeman.com/en-ca/kh/guides/FAQ-Investment-Canada-Act> accessed 22 January 2020.

> and, the extent to which a foreign state is likely to exercise control or influence over the SOE acquiring the Canadian business.[36]

Subsequently published guidelines emphasise SCEs' "susceptib(ility) to state influence" and "the extent to which … its conduct or operations are influenced by a state" as key criteria for determining "net benefit" to Canada.[37] However, while members of the legal profession have expressed concerns over the relative opacity with which these guidelines have been administered,[38] national security reviews appear to have taken priority over traditional "net benefit" review as Ottawa's screening tool of choice in recent years. The 2021 revisions to the guidelines have provided "greater clarity" to these measures while extending them.[39]

Section 3 of the revised ICA utilises a broad definition of "state-owned enterprise," which encompasses:

(a) the government of a foreign state, whether federal, state or local, or an agency of such a government;
(b) an entity that is controlled or influenced, directly or indirectly, by a government or agency referred to in paragraph (a); or
(c) an individual who is acting under the direction of a government or agency referred to in paragraph (a) or who is acting under the influence, directly or indirectly, of such a government or agency; (*entreprise d'État*).[40]

The Canadian government has reportedly intervened in several prospective transactions to discourage the sale of technologically significant Canadian companies to potential purchasers seen as instruments of foreign state agencies, including Blackberry (Lenovo, 2013), wireless telecom provider Wind Mobile (to Russian-controlled VimpelCom, 2013), and MTS fibre-optic network subsidiary Allstream (by Egyptian-controlled Accelero, 2013). Chinese firm Baida Jade Bird was reportedly blocked from building a fire-alarm manufacturing facility near Montreal in 2015 due to its proximity to a Canadian Space Agency facility, raising concerns for possible surveillance.[41] What is known of some of these transactions suggests that sizeable investments in acquiring companies by wealthy "oligarchs" known to have close connections to the governments of certain authoritarian states are likely to attract the attention of Canadian security agencies, increasing the potential for government intervention.

---

[36] Rt. Hon. Stephen Harper, 'Statement regarding investment by foreign state-owned enterprises, Government of Canada' 7 December 2012. <https://www.ic.gc.ca/eic/site/ica-lic.nsf/eng/lk81147.html> accessed 21 January 2020.

[37] Innovation, Science and Economic Development Canada. 'Guidelines – Investment by State-Owned Enterprises – Net Benefit Assessment' revised 12 December 2016 <https://www.ic.gc.ca/eic/site/ica-lic.nsf/eng/lk00064.html#p2> accessed 21 January 2020.

[38] Goodman and Koch (n 14) B146-B150.

[39] Canada 2021 (n 22); Elizabeth Raymer, 'Updated guidelines on Canada's national security review bring clarity' *Canadian Lawyer,* 6 April 2021; <https://www.ic.gc.ca/eic/site/ica-lic.nsf/eng/lk81190.html> .

[40] *Investment Canada Act* (n 2) s. 3.

[41] Goldman and Koch (n 14) B148-B149.

More recently, the well-documented Chinese government practices of requiring the creation of functioning Communist Party committees in private businesses and enabling party officials to take active roles in the management of both state and private businesses have tended to blur distinctions between the party-state and corporate governance, even in notionally privately controlled businesses.[42] Canadian and other western security agencies perceive clear risks to national security, particularly in technology-related industries, in Article 7 of China's 2017 National Intelligence Law which requires Chinese companies to respond to requests from state agencies to "support, co-operate with and collaborate in national intelligence work".[43]

The national security review process, under Section 25 of the ICA, applies to new business applications and proposed takeovers of any size, whether of existing foreign subsidiaries or Canadian-owned firms. Key criteria involved in national security reviews include potential effects or impact on:

- Canada's defence capabilities, interests, or the "research, manufacture or sale of goods/technology" restricted under Section 35 of the Defence Production Act;
- transfer of sensitive technology or "know-how" outside Canada;
- critical infrastructure, broadly defined;
- supply of critical goods and services to Canadians or the government of Canada;
- enabling foreign surveillance, espionage, or hindering current or future intelligence or law enforcement;
- international interests, including foreign relationships;
- involving or facilitating the interests of terrorists, organised crime, and (other) illicit actors.[44]

The 2021 guidelines extend these criteria to include:

- the potential impact of the investment on critical minerals and critical mineral supply chains;
- the potential of the investment to enable access to sensitive personal data that could be leveraged to harm Canadian national security through its exploitation, including, personally identifiable health or genetic … biometric (e.g. fingerprints) … financial … communications … geolocation, or personal data concerning government officials;

[42] Jennifer Hughes, 'China's Communist Party writes itself into company law' *Financial Times* (London, 14 August 2017); <https://www.ft.com/content/a4b28218-80db-11e7-94e2-c5b903247afd> accessed 21 January 2020; Ashley Feng, 'We can't tell if Chinese firms work for the party' *Foreign Policy*, 7 February 2019; <https://foreignpolicy.com/2019/02/07/we-cant-tell-if-chinese-firms-work-for-the-party/> accessed 21 January 2020; Richard McGregor, 'How the state runs business in China' *The Guardian* (London: 25 July 2019). <https://www.theguardian.com/world/2019/jul/25/china-business-xi-jinping-communist-party-state-private-enterprise-huawei> , accessed 21 January 2020.

[43] Daniel Leblanc and Steven Chase, 'Ottawa says geopolitical considerations a factor in Huawei 5G decision' *The Globe and Mail* (Toronto: 22 January 2020) A1.

[44] Innovation, Science, and Economic Development Canada. 'Guidelines on the National Security Review of Investments' Updated 12 December 2016. <https://www.ic.gc.ca/eic/site/ica-lic.nsf/eng/lk81190.html> accessed 21 January 2020.

- Expanded definitions of “sensitive technologies” and “critical infrastructure”.[45]

National security reviews may arise from informal discussions between investors and the Investment Canada Division of Innovation, Science and Economic Development Canada, the filing of “net benefit” notices under the ICA, or government initiatives, possibly on the advice of federal security and intelligence officials. Professional advisors recommend notifying Industry Canada before closing transactions, even on deals not requiring “net benefit” review, to identify potential security issues requiring resolution.[46] Initial reviews may take 45 days, with the potential for further extension of 45 days under Section 25(2) of the ICA indicating the potential for national security review, as noted in Fig. 2. Investors may withdraw their application at this stage, or the Minister may certify that no further action will be taken. A formal national security review requires an application to the federal cabinet (Governor-in-Council) following consultation with Public Safety and Emergency Preparedness Canada, which oversees national police and intelligence agencies. Security review may take up to 45 days, with the potential for a further 45-day extension. Cumulative review periods may thus take up to 200 days. The final decision is made by the federal cabinet, headed by the Prime Minister. The proposed investment may be approved with or without conditions or blocked—with the potential for divestiture orders for transactions “finalised” before completion of the review process. Such actions are possible as the Minister has the authority to initiate national security reviews of completed transactions that would not otherwise require foreign investment reviews. SCE shareholdings of at least 33% are subject to review. However, security officials are at liberty to “look behind” related party transactions, which may trigger concerns about relations with foreign state agencies.

Much public commentary on these issues has focused on investments by Chinese SCEs, which have declined sharply in recent years, reflecting a combination of lower global resource prices, domestic policy shifts in China, and increasing geopolitical tensions. Chinese firms have attracted the largest share—13 of 19 (69%)—of formal national security reviews since 2014, as noted in Table 4. Other firms subject to national security reviews have come from Switzerland (2), Cyprus, Russia, Singapore, and the UK. Manufacturers (7), telecommunications (3), other technology (3) and transportation-related (4) firms have accounted for most national security reviews.

In 2016, the Trudeau government reversed the decision of its predecessor to block the takeover of ITF Technologies, a telecommunications equipment manufacturer, by O-Net Communications, a public company listed on the Hong Kong Stock Exchange, surprising many observers.[47] However, current and former federal security officials have sometimes commented publicly on their concerns with particular transactions—most notably state-owned China Construction Communications Co. (CCCC)’s a friendly takeover in 2017–18 of Aecon Group, a major civil engineering

[45] Canada 2021 (n 22).

[46] Stikeman Elliott (n 34) 7.

[47] Oliver Borgers, ‘Canada’ in Farhad Jalinous, ed. Foreign Direct Investment Reviews 2019: A Global Perspective, White & Case, December 2019, 11–12.

and construction firm with significant involvement in building and maintaining critical infrastructure, and more recently, Huawei Inc.'s efforts to expand its Canadian research activities and supply the building out of its 5G wireless network.[48]

The latter's implications for telecommunications security has raised significant alarm given Canada's extensive intelligence sharing with the USA, which has banned Huawei from its networks as part of widening geopolitical competition with China. It has also raised extensive concerns over institutionalised linkages between Chinese security services (and the Chinese party-state apparatus) and major Chinese companies and the latter's cultivation of close relations with Canadian political and economic elites.[49] These issues have been further embroiled in geopolitical conflicts following Canada's arrest and possible extradition of a senior Huawei executive to face charges of violating US financial regulations related to alleged evasion of sanctions against Iran. This incident is widely seen to be related to retaliatory arrests and prolonged detention of Canadians travelling in China, and extensive Chinese sanctions against imports from Canada, although the latter were partially relaxed during the 2020–21 COVID pandemic. These disputes appear to have had second and third-order effects on international merger and acquisition activity. After a friendly takeover bid by privately owned China Oceanwide Holdings Group for US financial services firm Genworth Inc. faced lengthy regulatory delays in Canada, Genworth sold its Canadian subsidiary, Genworth MI, Canada's second-largest mortgage insurer, to Brookfield Business Holdings in 2019 to facilitate the transaction's completion.[50]

As noted above, the federal government has identified the critical minerals sector as increasingly sensitive to national security. Its critical minerals list, released in 2021, identifies 31 minerals whose supply, processing and distribution are "considered critical" for Canada's "sustainable economic success" and that of allied nations, particularly for communications technology, aerospace, defence, and "clear technology" sectors.[51] However, the Trudeau government's 2020 veto of Shandong Gold Mining's friendly bid for TMAC Resources, a medium-sized firm with operations in

---

[48] Robert Fife and Steven Chase, 'Ottawa blocks Chinese takeover of Aecon after security review' *The Globe and Mail* (Toronto, 24 May 2018) A1; Richard Fadden and Brian Lee Crowley, 'On Huawei and 5G, Canada must unapologetically pursue our national interest,' *The Globe and Mail* (Toronto, 7 December 2018); Robert Fife and Steven Chase, 'Five Eyes spy chiefs warned Trudeau twice on Huawei risk' *The Globe and Mail* (Toronto, 17 December 2018) A1; Richard Fadden and J. Berkshire Miller, 'Why Canada must protect its 5G Networks from Huawei' *The National Interest*, 13 July 2019. <https://nationalinterest.org/feature/why-canada-must-protect-its-5g-networks-huawei-66932> accessed 8 August 2019.

[49] Jonathan Manthorpe, *Claws of the Panda: Beijing's campaign of influence and intimidation in Canada.* Cormorant Books, 2019, 207–26, 247–67.

[50] Tim Kiladze, 'Chinese takeover of mortgage insurer Genworth held up by Canada's national security concerns' *The Globe and Mail* (Toronto, 3 May 2019); James Bradshaw, 'Brookfield acquires mortgage insurer Genworth Canada in $2.4 billion deal' *The Globe and Mail* (Toronto, 13 August 2019), B1.

[51] Natural Resources Canada, 'Critical Minerals,' 29 March 2021; <https://www.nrcan.gc.ca/our-natural-resources/minerals-mining/critical-minerals/23414> accessed 26 June 2021; Natural Resources Canada, 'U.S., Canada finalize joint action plan on critical minerals cooperation,' News release, 9 January 2020. <https://www.canada.ca/en/natural-resources-canada/news/2020/01/canada-and-us-finalize-joint-action-plan-on-critical-minerals-collaboration.html> accessed 26 June 2021.

the Canadian Arctic,[52] suggests that future national security reviews may be applied more widely to resource sector investments.

5 Conclusion

The sharp reduction in foreign investment reviews and success of the "overwhelming majority of reviews"[53] indicates that Canada is open to foreign investment by private sector investors and by state-controlled enterprises with transparently independent governance structures and commercial mandates. Minority investments by state-owned enterprises and sovereign wealth funds are unlikely to attract regulatory attention if part of larger consortia functioning on commercial terms unless in designated sectors identified as national security priorities.

However, growing geopolitical tensions, the blurring of distinctions between publicly and investor-owned firms in state-capitalist regimes, and the projection of their interests through global investment networks have increased uncertainties related to national security reviews in Canada, as in other industrial countries. The history of national security reviews since 2009 suggests that those sectors in which SCE investments are most likely to face political sensitivities include telecommunications, advanced technology sectors, construction or maintenance of critical infrastructure, and locations in close proximity to major government facilities. The 2021 guideline expansion promises tighter screening for firms involved in producing and processing critical minerals and those with extensive resources or access to personal and/or commercial data.

Other factors may contribute to the blurring of distinctions between privately owned and state-controlled enterprises, raising potential questions of organisational independence. The presence of mixed enterprise structures with less than transparent governance may create opportunities for excessive political influence in such firms' strategy or operations. Principal or significant shareholders perceived to be dependent on political or regulatory favouritism or discretionary access to credit, particularly in countries whose regulatory and financial systems are subject to extensive government influence, are more likely to be viewed as security risks. Such provisions may be mitigated by creating Canadian subsidiaries employing best practices in corporate governance, including protection for minority shareholder interests.

Traditional concerns of smaller countries over "net benefit" of foreign takeovers may be addressed through robust trade agreements providing for reciprocal access and national treatment of investors in mergers and acquisitions, the negotiation of disciplines on Trade-Related Aspects on Intellectual Property (TRIPs), and of robust dispute resolution mechanisms with reasonable provisions for enforcement. The latter have greater credibility when associated with plurilateral agreements in

---

[52] John Bowden, 'Canada blocks Chinese takeover of Arctic gold mine citing national security' *The Hill*, 22 December 2020.

[53] Goodman and Koch (n 14) B146.

which spillover effects may induce cooperative intergovernmental actions to sanction non-compliance.[54] However, such measures are less likely to be effective in bilateral agreements between countries with systemic incompatibilities,[55] particularly the absence of independent judicial and regulatory systems or effective protections for intellectual property rights.

Combined with Canada's pursuit of reciprocal market access provisions (with selective exemptions of sensitive industries) in trade negotiations, these developments suggest that Canadian foreign investment policies will continue to have multiple personalities. Existing trends suggest continued openness towards market-based transactions among firms from countries with robust systems of property rights and independent legal systems, but with increased national security screening at the margins, reflecting evolving geopolitical considerations.

Geoffrey Hale is Professor Emeritus of Political Science at the University of Lethbridge, and author of Uneasy Partnership: The Politics of Business and Government in Canada (University of Toronto Press), and varied articles on Canadian trade, investment and other economic policies

[54] Geraldo Vidigal, 'Why is there so little litigation under Free Trade Agreements? Retaliation and adjudication in international dispute settlement' (20) 2017 (4) *Journal of International Economic Law*, 927–950.

[55] Charles Burton, 'The dynamic of relations between Canada and China' in Duane Bratt and Christopher Kukucha (eds), *Readings in Canadian Foreign Policy: Classic Debates and New Ideas.* OUP, 2015, 177–182.

FinTech Regulation and Its Impact on State-Owned Companies in Europe

Gianni Lo Schiavo

1 Introduction

FinTech represents a new trend in financial regulation and standards that have developed in the last few years.[1] FinTech consists of the use of IT technologies to provide services by companies in everyday work and provide more efficient and fast services to clients. As part of the development of FinTech rules, it is important to ensure that an appropriate level of regulation exists. Specific companies can provide their services to their clients, but at the same time they shall respect rules on transparency, consumer/investor protection and public authorities should appropriately supervise some FinTech services.

The question of the involvement of FinTech for State-owned companies (SOEs)[2] raises a debate on the topic as there are unclear rules and approaches to FinTech treatment in the field nowadays. This is for a number of reasons. First, the term FinTech is vague and refers to the broad use of IT technologies for the provision of (financial) services. Second, there have been many international, regional and national

[1] On FinTech *see generally* Douglas W Arner and Janos Barberis and Ross P Buckley, 'The Evolution of FinTech: A New Post-Crisis Paradigm' (2016) 47 Geo J Int'l L 1271.

[2] On SOEs in general there is already abundant literature. *See* A. Cuervo-Cazurra, A. Inkpen, A. Musacchio and K. Ramaswamy, 'Governments as Owners: State-Owned Multinational Companies' (2014) 45 Journal of International Business Studies 919; I. Willemyns, 'Disciplines on State-Owned Enterprises in International Economic Law: Are We Moving in the Right Direction?' (2016) 19 Journal of International Economic Law 657.

Dr, LLM. European Central Bank. The views expressed in this commentary are purely personal and they are in no way intended to represent those of the ECB. The paper was last updated in December 2020.

G. L. Schiavo (✉)
European Central Bank, Frankfurt, Germany
e-mail: gianni.loschiavo@kcl.ac.uk

J. Chaisse et al. (eds.), *Regulation of State-Controlled Enterprises*, International Law and the Global South, https://doi.org/10.1007/978-981-19-1368-6_26

responses to address the increase of FinTech. However, there fails to be a comprehensive regulatory approach to the question of the interaction with SOEs. Third, FinTech treatments considerably vary from sector to sector, where much depends on public authorities' level of regulation and supervision.

This chapter intends to analyse the interaction between FinTech and SOEs by looking at the European rules for the regulation and supervision of FinTech services. The main research question is whether there is an appropriate level of EU FinTech regulation to address the opportunities and risks of FinTech services applied to SOEs. The paper will argue whether a general or a specific treatment should be afforded to SOEs aiming to provide FinTech services in Europe. The perspective is focused on the European level.

This chapter is structured as follows. The first part introduces FinTech and its importance for the economy. The second part examines the European rules on FinTech services in more detail by focusing strictly on the rules regarding capital markets integration and investor protection. The third part elaborates on the interaction between FinTech and State-owned enterprises from a European regulatory perspective.

2 FinTech: Definition and Importance for the International Economy

2.1 General Overview

FinTech can be broadly defined as the use of IT applications for the provision of services. To date, different definitions have been provided in literature, and there seems not to be a unanimous understanding of the definition, scope and role of FinTech in everyday society.[3] Some argue that the use of IT technologies has brought a (r)evolution in the provision of services.[4] Already in 2016, one author collected around 200 definitions on use of the term FinTech and discussed possible ways to define it. The proposal generally defined FinTech as a 'new financial industry that applies technology to improve financial activities.'[5] The Financial Stability Board (FSB) defines FinTech 'as technologically enabled innovation in financial services that could result in new business models, applications, processes or products with an associated material effect on financial markets and institutions and the provision

[3] Patrick Schueffel, 'Taming the Beast: A Scientific Definition of Fintech' (2016) 4 Journal of Innovation Management 32–54.

[4] Peter Gomber, Robert J. Kauffman, Chris Parker and Bruce W. Weber, 'On the Fintech Revolution: Interpreting the Forces of Innovation, Disruption, and Transformation' (2018) 35 Financial Services, Journal of Management Information Systems 220–265.

[5] Schueffel (n 3) 45. Italics in original text.

of financial services.'[6] Undoubtedly, FinTech represents a new trend in the provision of (financial) services that is subject to increased interest in practice, literature, and regulation. FinTech has prompted access, use and regulation of technologies in financial services. FinTech technologies leverage innovative IT software and other IT instruments to increase efficiency in the provision of services such as banking, investment services, cryptocurrencies.[7]

The objectives of the increased use of FinTech are marked in the 'increased efficiency in providing (financial) services'. While the simplicity of this expression goes at the core of FinTech, it requires further explanations, which can be summarised in at least four advantages. Firstly, FinTech can reduce costs (e.g. reduce cost intermediation, increased automatisation). Secondly, it can develop a broader range of products and services, thereby widening consumers' and businesses' choices and potentially providing them with better financing opportunities to finance activities (e.g. more and better products such as crypto-assets, P2P/B2B lending). Thirdly, it may open certain products or services to consumers or businesses that were previously excluded due to a higher degree of personalisation, broader product offerings, better pricing through lower marginal cost and improved accuracy of credit scoring (e.g. increase wealth management or alternative funds opportunities). Fourthly, it can be used for more effective regulation, supervision and compliance of market operators (e.g. data analysis, automated reporting, transactions monitoring). Overall, FinTech can be considered as a versatile use of IT for various purposes and objectives intended to increase financial instruments, opportunities and processes.

The scope of activity in FinTech started from mobile payments, money transfers, peer-to-peer loans, and crowdfunding and has moved to blockchain, cryptocurrencies, and robo-investing. The purpose of FinTech technologies is not only the use of innovative technologies for the efficient provision of services but also the development of new business models and even businesses.[8] The main providers of FinTech services are active in financial markets and are banks, investment firms, but also technology companies and start-ups.

Overall, this brief analysis suggests that Fintech has raised the debate on using IT technologies and innovative ways to provide financial services.

2.2 *FinTech and International Bodies*

This subsection explores the international standard setter bodies in more detail to the evolving FinTech innovation in the last five years. As of 2016, the development of

[6] *See* FSB, 'Monitoring of FinTech' <https://www.fsb.org/work-of-the-fsb/policy-development/additional-policy-areas/monitoring-of-FinTech>.

[7] *See* Dirk Zetzsche, Douglas Arner, Ross Buckley and Rolf Weber, 'The Evolution and future of data-driven finance in the EU' (2020) 57 Common Market Law Review 333–334.

[8] *See* Kelvin Leong, Anna Sung, 'FinTech (Financial Technology): What is It and How to Use Technologies to Create Business Value in FinTech Way?' (2018) 9(2) International Journal of Innovation, Management and Technology 74–78.

FinTech has raised attention of international bodies on the regulatory and supervisory treatment of FinTech. In 2017, the G20 raised the issue of the regulatory treatment of FinTech.[9] This G20 initiative was followed by the FSB, which established a FinTech Issues Group.[10] This body has evaluated potential financial stability implications of emerging FinTech innovations and regulatory and supervisory issues. It takes a two-sided approach, considering the potential of FinTech innovations to support financial stability and limit new systemic risks. In June 2017, the FSB published a report on FinTech that was presented to the G20.[11] The report focused on the potential financial stability implications of FinTech. Ten areas of attention were identified, of which three were seen as priorities for international collaboration: (1) the need to manage operational risk from third-party service providers, (2) mitigating cyber risks, and (3) monitoring macrofinancial risks that could emerge as FinTech activities increase.[12] Subsequently, the FSB produced other policy papers intended to address FinTech from a financial stability perspective, notably on FinTech and market structures, crypto-assets, BigTech in finance.[13]

Also, the World Bank has promoted the assessment of FinTech developments in recent years. Together with the IMF, the World Bank has launched a FinTech agenda paper and has promoted a framework on high-level FinTech issues that countries should consider for national policy discussions.[14]

The examination in detail of the international policy response to the FinTech evolution would go beyond the purpose of this paper. Suffice here is to make some general comments on the international response to this phenomenon. First, these policy positions at the international level show the increasing importance of appropriate regulation and supervision of FinTech worldwide. Second, the attention of international bodies is concentrated though on systemic risk and the possible disruption of the economy or financial market infrastructures by the evolution of FinTech services worldwide. Less attention is devoted to other issues, such as risks of market fragmentation and national regulatory responses, risks related to small and non-systemic FinTech entities, as well as risks to competition and consumers. Third, the limits of an international binding regulatory response to FinTech have been compensated by developments in various areas that have pushed intervention on how to deal

---

[9] G20, 'Hamburg Action Plan (2017)' <https://www.g20germany.de/Content/DE/_Anlagen/G7_G20/2017-g20-hamburg-action-plan-en___blob=publicationFile&v=4.pdf>. *See also* Mark Carney, 'The Promise of FinTech – Something New Under the Sun?' (2017 FSB Speech) <https://www.fsb.org/wp-content/uploads/The-Promise-of-FinTech-%E2%80%93-Something-New-Under-the-Sun.pdf>.

[10] *See* <https://www.fsb.org/work-of-the-fsb/policy-development/additional-policy-areas/monitoring-of-fintech/>.

[11] FSB, 'Financial Stability Implications from FinTech. Supervisory and Regulatory Issues that Merit Authorities' Attention' (2017) <https://www.fsb.org/wp-content/uploads/R270617.pdf>.

[12] ibid.

[13] All the FSB papers are available at <https://www.fsb.org/work-of-the-fsb/policy-development/additional-policy-areas/monitoring-of-FinTech/>.

[14] World Bank, 'The Bali Fintech Agenda: Chapeau Paper' (2018) <http://documents.worldbank.org/curated/en/390701539097118625/The-Bali-Fintech-Agenda-Chapeau-Paper>.

with this phenomenon. In particular, regional and national regulatory and supervisory interventions have developed in the last five years to address the broad expansion of FinTech services, cyber risks, system opacity, new market entrants and market fragmentation. Given the focus of attention of this paper on the European dimension for SOEs, the following section examines regulatory and supervisory initiatives at the European level.

3 FinTech Regulation in Europe: An Overview

This part of the chapter aims to explore the level of regulation of FinTech from a European perspective in more detail. The purpose is to look for the current approaches on FinTech in European regulation with specific attention to activities in financial markets.

FinTech has only recently been the object of attention in some soft law communications and papers by the EU Commission (Commission) to clarify its position on the evolution of FinTech. In 2015, the Commission launched the Capital Markets Union (CMU) as a major project to increase the use, transparency and regulation of European capital markets.[15] The 2015 action plan was not much concerned with FinTech providers or beneficiaries. In 2017, a Mid-Term Review of the CMU allowed the Commission to expand its scope on FinTech policy and regulation.[16] Also, the European Parliament has promoted an institutional analysis on the FinTech developments and addressed opportunities and challenges in 2017.[17] Given technology developments in financial services, in 2018, the Commission elaborated a more detailed strategy on the impact of FinTech in an action plan.[18] This action plan intends to promote the following aspects:

> - host an EU FinTech Laboratory where European and national authorities will engage with tech providers in a neutral, non-commercial space; - consult on how best to promote the digitisation of information published by listed companies in Europe, including by using innovative technologies to interconnect national databases; - run workshops to improve information-sharing when it comes to cybersecurity; - present a best practice guide on regulatory sandboxes based on guidance from European Supervisory Authorities (…); - report on the challenges and opportunities of crypto assets later in 2018 in the framework of its

[15] Commission, Communication, 'Action Plan on Building a Capital Markets Union' (30 September 2015) COM/2015/0468 final.

[16] Commission, Communication, 'Mid-Term Review of the Capital Markets Union Action Plan' (8 June 2017) COM(2017) 292 final.

[17] European Parliament, 'Report on FinTech: the influence of technology on the future of the financial sector' 2016/2243(INI) <https://www.europarl.europa.eu/doceo/document/A-8-2017-0176_EN.html>.

[18] Commission, Communication, 'FinTech Action plan: For a more competitive and innovative European financial sector' COM/2018/0109 final. See also the European Parliament briefing on FinTech: 'Financial technology (FinTech): Prospects and challenges for the EU' (March 2017) <https://www.europarl.europa.eu/RegData/etudes/BRIE/2017/599348/EPRS_BRI(2017)599348_EN.pdf>.

> EU Blockchain Observatory and Forum. The Commission is also working on a comprehensive strategy on distributed ledger technology and blockchain addressing all sectors of the economy. (…)[19]

All of these initiatives have been framed in line with other EU Commission policies, such as the efforts to build the CMU, the Digital Single Market agenda[20] and developments in the protection of consumers in financial services.[21]

Subsequent to the 2018 Action Plan, the Commission has followed up on these initiatives to improve the understanding and use of FinTech across Europe. Following endorsement by the Commission, at the end of 2019, an Expert Group on Regulatory Obstacles to Financial Innovation (ROFIEG) has published a long list of 30 recommendations on regulation, innovation and finance.[22] Without going into the details of this report, the recommendations of this expert group suggest ways to boost financial services via FinTech, taking into account the risks and challenges of the expansive use of digital technology for the provision of financial services, while being mindful of the increased need for a regulatory framework in the sector.

An overall assessment shows that the development of FinTech requires adequate supranational regulation to ensure the level playing field in Europe and end regulatory fragmentation in some areas while not impeding the potential use of technology-driven innovations and maintaining customers' choices. This suggests moving to the main argument of the paper, i.e. the impact of EU FinTech regulation on SOEs.

4 The Application of FinTech Regulation to State-Owned Entities: Some Reflections

After examining FinTech, this part of the chapter aims to reflect on the interaction of FinTech regulation with SOEs in Europe. This is not an easy task in the absence of a European framework for the regulation of SOEs and the lack of studies or reports on the impact of FinTech on SOEs. Firstly, EU law and policy is not concerned with the system of the property ownership at the national level. Secondly, there is no 'special' treatment for FinTech used on SOEs. Thirdly, both regulation and literature are not (yet) concerned with this relationship. Nonetheless, this section aims to examine existing European FinTech initiatives and question whether this body of regulation can be applied to SOEs from a European perspective. Therefore,

[19] Commission, 'Frequently asked questions: Financial Technology (FinTech) Action Plan' (8 March 2018) <https://ec.europa.eu/commission/presscorner/detail/en/MEMO_18_1406>.

[20] *See* Commission, Communication 'A Digital Single Market Strategy for Europe' (6 May 2015) COM/2015/0192 final.

[21] *See* Commission, 'Communication: Consumer Financial Services Action Plan: Better Products, More Choice' (23 March 2017) COM/2017/0139 final.

[22] Expert Group on Regulatory Obstacles to Financial Innovation (ROFIEG), '30 Recommendations on Regulation, Innovation and Finance: Final Report to the European Commission' (December 2019) <https://ec.europa.eu/info/sites/info/files/business_economy_euro/banking_and_finance/documents/191113-report-expert-group-regulatory-obstacles-financial-innovation_en.pdf>.

this section reflects on the following topics: whether SOEs are afforded a specific recognition or protection in European rules; whether FinTech regulation applies as such to SOEs; the pros and cons of the interaction between FinTech regulation and SOEs; finally, if the level of European regulation on FinTech is adequate to protect activities carried out by SOEs.

4.1 SOEs and EU Law

In general terms, SOEs are companies that the State or other public authority wholly own or where it exercises control. SOEs are also companies where the State or other public authority own a significant minority share, with the granting of special rights connected to the shareholding. An important distinction should be made between SOEs in the financial sector and the non-financial sector. The former are usually banks or other financial institutions that are fully or partially controlled or where the State or other public authority hold a significant minority shareholding. Financial SOEs can be divided into two groups: those subject to special regimes given their importance for the State and those subject to standard competition rules as other financial companies. The latter is a group of entities, mainly in liberalised sectors such as energy, post, telecommunications, that the State or other public authority fully or partially controls or has a significant minority holding.

SOEs do not have a special status in EU law and policy. This is because the EU Treaties in Article 345 TFEU clearly states that '[they] shall in no way prejudice the rules in Member States governing the system of property ownership.'[23] Without going into the details of this provision,[24] Article 345 TFEU excludes that EU law and policy affect in any ways the provisions in national law on how property ownership is regulated. There are no specific rules on the treatment of State-owned entities in EU law and how financial services provided by these entities are treated. However, this does not mean that EU law and policy are not involved at all in the measures taken at the national level to regulate and supervise State-owned companies. In particular, EU rules on State aid control,[25] free movement rules,[26] and competition,[27] especially

[23] Art 345 of the Treaty on the Functioning of the European Union (TFEU).

[24] *See* Kristín Haraldsdóttir, 'The nature of neutrality in EU law: article 345 TFEU' (2020) 45(1) EL Rev 3–24.

[25] *See* Amaryllis Verhoeven 'Privatisation and EC Law: Is the European Commission "Neutral" with Respect to Public Versus Private Ownership of Companies?' (1996) 45 International Comparative Law Quarterly 861–887.

[26] In particular, this is the case of the CJEU case law on golden shares, i.e. the existence of State powers on shares in privatised companies is a clear example of the involvement of EU law on SOEs. *See* Daniele Gallo 'On the Content and Scope of National and European Solidarity Under Free Movement Rules: The Case of Golden Shares and Sovereign Investments' in E Dagilyte, A Biondi, E Kucuk (eds) *Solidarity in EU Law: Legal Principle in the Making* (Edward Elgar 2018) 191–218.

[27] Mathew Heim, 'How can European competition law address market distortions caused by state-owned enterprises?' (December 2019) Breugel Policy Contribution no 18 <https://www.bruegel.org/wp-content/uploads/2019/12/PC-18_2019-181219.pdf>.

on merger control,[28] may impact how the State, local authorities or SOEs operate in the market. Nevertheless, there is no general regulatory treatment of SOEs at the EU law and policy level.

At the same time, the Commission has published a recent report on State-owned enterprises where some considerations on the level of efficiency of these companies are assessed in detail.[29] While acknowledging that there is no common definition of SOEs, the Commission provides interesting data on the economic impact of SOEs from a macroeconomic perspective and fiscal position. However, this study is concerned with non-financial SOEs. So it does not give specific insights on how SOEs may use FinTech as financial services under the EU regulatory framework.

4.2 FinTech and State-Owned Entities: Advantages

This subsection aims to explore further the relationship between FinTech as currently regulated in EU law and policy and SOEs by looking in particular at the opportunities offered by FinTech for SOEs. Bearing in mind that FinTech is primarily a phenomenon affecting financial services, it essential to look at how FinTech can impact the exercise of activities by SOEs.

As stated above, FinTech comprises four dimensions on the way it affects the provision of financial services.

Firstly, FinTech benefits reduction of costs. It is clear that the primary purpose of FinTech is to reduce costs through the digitalisation of the activity of a corporation. Such development could serve SOEs through reduction of costs and algorithm automation in the various activities SOEs perform. Financial SOEs conduct various types of operations in financial markets. In the case of SOE banks or other financial institutions, FinTech activities in mobile banking, home banking, wealth management or investment service online access, and other online services can benefit the revenues and performances of financial SOEs and serve to improve the relationship with customers. Similarly, in the case of SOE non-financial companies, the use of online systems to monitor the activities and the contractual relationships with customers or related parties gives the advantage to reduce costs connected to the physical presence in branches or offices and to save time and resources for the provision of services to customers. Furthermore, SOEs' governance and internal structures can benefit a lot from automated services and functions developed as part of FinTech technologies. These developments allow reduction of costs, straightforward structures and easier ways of communications and relations within SOEs.

---

[28] *See* Geneviève Lallemand-Kirche, Caroline Tixier, and Henri Piffaut, 'The Treatment of State-owned Enterprises in EU Competition Law: New Developments and Future Challenges' (2017) 8 Journal of European Competition Law & Practice 295–308.

[29] *See e.g.* Commission, 'State-Owned Enterprises in the EU: Lessons Learnt and Ways Forward in a Post-Crisis Context' (July 2016) European Economy Institutional Paper no. 031 <https://ec.europa.eu/info/sites/info/files/file_import/ip031_en_2.pdf>.

Secondly, offering a broader range of products and services represents an area where FinTech can offer new perspectives for SOEs. The different opportunities of FinTech span from new securities, exchange-traded instruments to cryptocurrencies. Investments focus, in particular, is on digitalising securities and other financial assets and increasing interest in digital comparison platforms for banking and other forms of financial services. In this area, there are indeed developments regarding the forms of the offering of financial products and services. At the same time, there should also be limits and requirements for such developments.

Thirdly, FinTech allows the opening of products or services to consumers or businesses that were previously excluded. FinTech opens up markets that were previously unreachable for small and medium-range market operators. In this sense, SOEs may look for other products or services in start-ups, emerging markets and alternative forms of finance.

Fourthly, the use of FinTech requires more effective regulation, supervision and compliance of market operators. EU FinTech regulation[30] aims to ensure that some new products or services are subject to forms of regulation and authorisations related to their provision in the market. SOEs will have to take into account also this dimension and make sure that their compliance functions are well equipped to address challenges from new regulatory or supervisory regimes in the field.

4.3 FinTech and State-Owned Entities: Risks

The interaction between FinTech and SOEs opens up reflections also on the risks that the (massive) use of FinTech could have on SOEs at present and in future. Risks in general on FinTech can be summarised as follows: systemic risks, shadow banking and other opaque activity risks, lack of transparency, reputational risks. These are analysed.

Systemic risks are the risk of disruption of the system and the economy's performance due to shocks.[31] The FinTech industry can influence the SOEs both internally and externally. From an internal dimension, extensive use of FinTech services, such as automated algorithms for financial transactions, contracts, and smart activities by SOEs, may impair SOEs' revenues and income should there be disruption of the IT framework. This requires robust IT frameworks, efficient business continuity plans and operational risk management that ensure continuity of the activity also in case of sudden lack of the IT infrastructure. From an external dimension, investments in FinTech companies or the use of external FinTech resources such as blockchains or outsourced IT services can also raise systemic risk in case of severe disruptions to the economy that impact primarily small and disaggregated counterparties or investees.

[30] *See* Gomber, Kauffman, Parker Weber (n 4).

[31] *See* 'Douglas W. Arner, Ross P. Buckley and Dirk Zetzsche, FinTech, RegTech and systemic risk: the rise of global technology risk' in L. Schwarcz, E. Avgouleas, D. Busch, and D.W. Arner (eds) *Systemic risk in the financial sector: ten years after the global financial crisis* (CIGI Press 2019).

SOEs may have to diversify their portfolios or limit the use of blockchains to ensure that wrong investments or disruptions to blockchain systems in FinTech companies can risk SOEs' financial soundness.

Shadow banking and other opaque activity risks relate to the use of FinTech in leveraged activities or investments that do not have an adequate level of transparency and risk management. Firstly, the increased use of FinTech may impact regulatory frameworks and regimes. The entry in the financial service market of new financial providers, such as BigTechs (social networks or online marketplaces), and small or new entrants concentrated on tech-enabled financial services may also risk jeopardising existing regulated entities' activities including SOEs. These entities may be established under a different regulatory regime, which has a different supervisory framework or even has no supervisory framework for the entities in question. Similarly, the activities performed may not be under the EU regulatory perimeter. Therefore, there may divergences creating significant regulatory obstacles or regulatory gaps. These may impact the level playing field for providers of the same services and imposing additional costs for compliance with multiple regimes by SOEs.

A general lack of transparency is the risk that the use of FinTech may complicate and reduce the level of openness to the public and/or supervisory authorities on the activities of SOEs. Transparency is expressed in various forms such as additional disclosure requirements for large companies, periodic stress tests to assess the riskiness of companies' behaviours, and additional forms of monitors tasked with identifying systemic risks posed by large companies. Transparency is a key aspect for companies having public ownership, especially because of the special mandates from a state or the special forms of accountability towards public bodies that SOEs might have. Insufficient public information on investments or activities carried out via FinTech or overreliance on non-transparent FinTech external companies might jeopardise the level of transparency of SOEs.

Reputational risk is the risk that some events might impact a company's image and public perception. The use of automated technologies or riskier products or services might impact companies, including SOEs, if one day, some events raise criticisms or issues related to some FinTech services. Therefore, it is essential that companies, including SOEs, run appropriate impact analyses on the reputational risks related to the new use of FinTech services. Otherwise, there is a real risk that the image of the SOE is negatively affected and also indirectly, the State's or public entity's role is put into question.

Overall, the level of risks needs to be present when SOEs use FinTech services or new technologies. This requires that appropriate forms of impact assessments are conducted internally. Risk management frameworks should be robustly developed to ensure that FinTech does not jeopardise SOEs' activities with their customers and clients. Such a conclusion then justifies looking at the interaction between recent EU FinTech regulation and SOEs in the next paragraph.

4.4 EU FinTech Regulation and State-Owned Entities

This subsection intends to discuss the impact of existing EU FinTech regulation on SOEs briefly. Additional requirements for new FinTech companies do not impact SOEs directly as they are already established, or they are afforded specific forms of protection in national laws. Nevertheless, it is worth looking at some of the recent EU regulatory initiatives that may directly or indirectly impact SOEs. Furthermore, there are several complex EU rules regarding how (financial) companies make use of FinTech in the conduct of their activities. These are also part of the body of regulation that is currently part of the EU Commission action plan on FinTech. Therefore, it is important to examine existing EU financial regulations related to FinTech that can affect the activities of SOEs.

Firstly, the Commission has recently proposed important developments in Artificial Intelligence (AI) for companies and the public sector to support 'a regulatory and investment-oriented approach with the twin objective of promoting AI uptake and addressing the risks associated with certain uses of this new technology.'[32] As part of relevant proposals for SOEs, the Commission highlighted the need that operators deploy products and services that rely on AI in their activities. This requires the promotion of public procurement for AI systems. The promotion of an EU AI general regulatory system, also applicable to SOEs, might considerably change companies' provision of goods and services. At the same time, such developments require some safeguards against significant risks that may materialise, such as safety, data protection or fundamental rights. These need to be considered in developing a regime for the progressive use of AI in the provision of goods or services also by SOEs.

Secondly, as regards financial markets and the development of the EU Capital Markets Union,[33] FinTech may boost financial services performed by SOEs and can offer solutions in several capital market areas, such as equity issuance, corporate governance, asset management, investment intermediation, product distribution, and post-trade market infrastructure including securities custody services. In 2019 the Commission acknowledged the progress made.[34] In particular, the new EU Prospectus Regulation recognises 'incorporation by reference' as a technique to refer to the information contained electronically in the file submitted to the supervisor and intended to avoid duplication. Furthermore, EU regulation on specific products, such

[32] Commission, 'White Paper on Artificial Intelligence - A European approach to excellence and trust' (19 February 2020) COM(2020) 65 final, 1.

[33] *See* Maria Demertzis, Gerardo Mombelli, and Guntram Wolff, 'Capital Markets Union and the fintech opportunity' (September 2017) Bruegel Policy Contribution 22 <https://www.bruegel.org/2017/09/capital-markets-union-and-the-fintech-opportunity/>.

[34] Commission, 'Communication: Capital Markets Union: progress on building a single market for capital for a strong Economic and Monetary Union' (15 March 2019) COM(2019) 136 final.

as covered bonds[35] or securitisation[36] or crowdfunding,[37] shows important developments on FinTech services that may also affect the market activities performed by SOEs.

Thirdly, the new EU payments directive of 2015[38] (PSD2) aims to improve the forms of payments through FinTech services and sectors typically where SOEs are active benefit from the new payments directive provisions. In particular, new ways of initiating and processing payments are subject to the rules of the PSD2. PSD2 covers new services and players, extends the scope of existing services (payment instruments issued by payment service providers that do not manage the account of the payment service user) and enable easier ways to access to the payment accounts. PSD2 also updates the telecom exemption by limiting it mainly to micro-payments for digital services. Furthermore, to make electronic payments safer and more secure, the PSD2 enhances security measures to be implemented by all payment service providers, including banks. In particular, PSD2 requires payment service providers to apply strong customer authentication (SCA) for electronic payment transactions as a general rule. Overall, the PSD2 is an essential instrument to strengthen the provision of payment services by companies in Europe. It also affects SOEs in how their payment services are carried out, particularly with clients and creditors. PSDII aims to establish a system that makes identification of customers easier, enables the customers to make more use of financial services.[39] At the same time, there is a clear push to reinforce financial integrity with better customer identification and tracking. The PSDII framework is particularly relevant to boost client identification while offering mobile or alternative forms of payments for services provided by SOEs.

Fourthly, the area of Anti-Money Laundering and Counter-Terrorism Finance has been subject to reinforced EU regulation that can also affect SOEs. The latest piece of EU legislation is the 5th EU Directive on AML.[40] Its main developments refer to increase transparency rules on the real owners of companies, which intends to

---

[35] Directive (EU) 2019/2162 of the European Parliament and of the Council of 27 November 2019 on the issue of covered bonds and covered bond public supervision and amending Directives 2009/65/EC and 2014/59/EU (Text with EEA relevance) PE/86/2019/REV/1, OJ L 328 [2019].

[36] Regulation (EU) 2017/2402 of the European Parliament and of the Council of 12 December 2017 laying down a general framework for securitisation and creating a specific framework for simple, transparent and standardised securitisation, and amending Directives 2009/65/EC, 2009/138/EC and 2011/61/EU and Regulations (EC) No 1060/2009 and (EU) No 648/2012, OJ L 347 [2017].

[37] Proposal for a REGULATION OF THE EUROPEAN PARLIAMENT AND OF THE COUNCIL on European Crowdfunding Service Providers (ECSP) for Business, COM/2018/0113 final. At the end of 2019 the EU Commission proposal has been agreed by the EU legislators.

[38] Directive (EU) 2015/2366 of the European Parliament and of the Council of 25 November 2015 on payment services in the internal market, amending Directives 2002/65/EC, 2009/110/EC and 2013/36/EU and Regulation (EU) No 1093/2010, and repealing Directive 2007/64/EC, OJ L 337, 23.12.2015.

[39] *See* Zetzsche, Arner, Buckley and Weber (n 7) 349.

[40] Directive (EU) 2018/843 of the European Parliament and of the Council of 30 May 2018 amending Directive (EU) 2015/849 on the prevention of the use of the financial system for the purposes of money laundering or terrorist financing, and amending Directives 2009/138/EC and 2013/36/EU, PE/72/2017/REV/1, OJ L 156 [2018].

enhance public scrutiny and contribute to preventing the misuse of legal entities for money laundering and terrorist financing purposes. Further, the Directive reinforces the criteria to assess high-risk third countries, including transparency of beneficial ownership. This requires that enhanced controls are performed for third country countries having strategic deficiencies in their AML/CTF regimes and apply systematic enhanced controls on the financial transactions from and to these countries. Moreover, the Directive requires centralised bank account registers and retrieval systems to identify bank and payment accounts holders. Overall, these rules on AML/CTF affect also the activities of both financial and non-financial SOEs as they create rules that impact the online and electronic transactions SOEs make as part of their activities. These rules are also connected to FinTech developments in Europe as they aim to enhance control of financial services performed with advanced electronic systems.

In sum, the broad analysis of the above recent developments related to FinTech in Europe suggests that SOEs should also carefully consider the above regulatory efforts to ensure the use of FinTech services. At the same time, SOEs need to be wary at all times of controls, integrity and risks, which can have multiple dimensions.

5 Conclusion

This paper has shown that FinTech is a new frontier in the provision of financial services in Europe. The European approach to Fintech shows that opportunities arising from more efficient and technologically driven services are welcome while maintaining appropriate forms of controls on risks and challenges. The FinTech developments reveal that SOEs have to consider such technological changes and that they need to be aware of changes in the field.

While the provision of FinTech services is currently under more and more scrutiny in Europe, SOEs can undoubtedly benefit from the provision of automated and technological services. This is, in particular, the case of the use of artificial intelligence, automated counselling and servicing, new products and services and blockchain technologies. SOEs are indeed part of this new development and can greatly benefit from it.

At the same time, SOEs need to be aware of risks and challenges coming from the uncontrolled and progressive use of FinTech services in Europe. In particular, reputation and operational risks might undermine the use of efficient technologies and services by SOEs. Furthermore, the level of regulation and supervision requires appropriate attention by compliance and risks functions in SOEs.

In future, it is expected a more prominent use of FinTech services and products. These will also be available to SOEs. It remains to be seen whether European stakeholders appropriately address the future challenges that will exist in a FinTech world and SOEs make a good assessment of FinTech risks and opportunities.

Chinese State-Owned Enterprises in Africa: Always a Black-and-White Role?

Wei Yin and Anran Zhang

1 Introduction

The 2018 Forum for China-African Cooperation (FOCAC), with an aim to enhance the Sino-Africa bilateral relation, highlighted China's increasing interest in the African continent and the desire of both sides for further cooperation. China's growing engagement in Africa has triggered heated debates, particularly from the Western world, concerning the real benefits of China's strategy and policy for Africa's development. It was argued that China's cooperative approaches with African countries, representing a new form of 'colonialism', are undermining the sustainable development and good governance of Africa that Western countries and/or interna-

This chapter draws upon the author's original publication also available at https://www.transnational-dispute-management.com/journal-advance-publication-article.asp?key=1836. Reprinted by permission from Maris BV: Maris BV, *Transnational Dispute Management* (TDM, ISSN 1875-4120), "Chinese State-Owned Enterprises in Africa: Always a Black-and-White Role?", Wei Yin, Anran Zhang, Copyright (2000). Please cite accordingly.

W. Yin (✉)
School of International Law, Southwest University of Political Science and Law and Research Fellow, China-ASEAN Legal Research Centre, Chongqing, China
e-mail: weiyin77@gmail.com

A. Zhang
Erasmus School of Law, Erasmus University Rotterdam, Rotterdam, Netherlands
e-mail: ryanzhanganran@outlook.com

J. Chaisse et al. (eds.), *Regulation of State-Controlled Enterprises*, International Law and the Global South, https://doi.org/10.1007/978-981-19-1368-6_27

tional efforts intend to achieve.[1] The activities and behaviours of Chinese investors, both private-owned enterprises (POEs) and SOEs, are being criticised or suspected.[2] A majority of Chinese investors in Africa are individuals or small and medium enterprises (SMEs), while large projects are usually conducted by Chinese SOEs in critical industries of the African economy, in particular infrastructure and energy sectors.[3]

The operation of these Chinese SOEs in Africa and their alleged 'bad behaviours' are arguably posing an impact on the long-term development of Africa.[4] One of the main reasons behind the criticism can be owed to the different governance structure of Chinese SOEs, different approaches to commercial activities compared with Western firms and different development models. However, although Chinese SOEs, by definition, have some connection with the Chinese government and are usually embedded in China's national policy, they act with their own capacity and preferences. It is therefore that the focus of this chapter is put on the role of Chinese SOEs as investors rather than overall China's interests in Africa.

This chapter aims to build a closer understanding of the role that Chinese SOEs played in overseas investment and the impact of their investment on local development of Africa, as well as the barriers to further engagement.[5] This chapter first reviews the status quo of Chinese investment in Africa, followed by an illustration of the role that Chinese SOEs played in Africa. It then discussed the controversy of Chinese SOEs. The problems posed by the investment of Chinese SOEs to local development and stakeholders as well as benefits brought by Chinese SOEs are analysed. This chapter further explores the regulatory challenges to China and African countries. Lastly, it questions further efforts and actions that need to be done for sustainable investment and development, taking account of current China's domestic

[1] Noah Smith, 'The Future Is in Africa, and China Knows It' (*Bloomberg*, 20 September 2018) <https://www.google.com/amp/s/www.bloomberg.com/amp/opinion/articles/2018-09-21/africa-economy-west-should-try-to-match-chinese-investment> accessed 15 February 2019.

[2] The investment model adopted by Chinese investors also takes various forms. In addition to sole proprietorship and joint venture, there are equity participation and merger and acquisition. Both SOEs and POEs are involved in Chinese investment in Africa. A study provided that in recent years the involvement of central and local SOEs maintains its stable status or even experienced a slow rise while the proportion of POEs has grown rapidly. See Ming Li et al., 'Spatio - Temporal Evolution of China's OFDI in Africa Countries and Its Influence Factors' [中国对非直接投资时空演化及其影响因素] (2017) 11 Economic Geography 19, 21.

[3] See Lucy Corkin et al., 'China's Role in the Development of Africa's Infrastructure' (2008) SAIS Working Papers in African Studies <https://sais.jhu.edu/sites/default/files/China%27s-Role-in-the-Development-of-Africa%27s-Infrastructure.pdf> accessed 27 December 2020; see Luka Powanga, 'China's Contribution to the African Power Sector: Policy Implications for African Countries' (2019) Journal of Energy <https://downloads.hindawi.com/journals/jen/2019/7013594.pdf> accessed 27 December 2020.

[4] Yi-Chong Xu, 'Chinese State-owned Enterprises in Africa: Ambassadors or Freebooters' (2014) 23 Journal of Contemporary China 822, 823.

[5] Some portions of this chapter have been reproduced and published on the AfronomicsLaw blog. Please see Anran Zhang and Wei Yin, 'Chinese State-Owned Enterprises' Investment in Africa: An Unequivocal Role?' (*AfronomicsLaw*, 7 January 2021) <https://www.afronomicslaw.org/2021/01/07/chinese-state-owned-enterprises-investment-in-africa-an-unequivocal-role> accessed 15 February 2022.

reforms (i.e. the regulatory reform and the SOE reform) and the implication of the Belt and Road Initiative (BRI) on Chinese SOEs.

2 Status Quo of Investment by Chinese SOEs in Africa

China's engagement overseas is an essential part of the 'Going Out' strategy incorporated in the Tenth Five-Year Plan for National Economic and Social Development.[6] It aims partly to promote the internationalism of Chinese companies. Currently, enlarged Chinese overseas involvement is encouraged under the BRI since 2013.[7] It provides opportunities for further investment and trade deals among countries along the BRI.[8] The BRI consists primarily of State and/or private-financed infrastructure projects in developing countries, especially in those countries that have the 'infrastructure gap'. This initiative has been met with both praise and scepticism.

Previously, China was mainly a significant capital importer while it is now a critical capital importer and exporter. Chinese companies are increasingly becoming active in overseas markets and rapidly expanding their business footprints in Africa. Since 2016, China's direct investment in Africa has exceeded $8 billion, making Africa an important emerging destination for China's outbound investment.[9] According to the latest statistics of the Ministry of Commerce of China (MOFCOM), from January to October of 2018, China's non-financial direct investment in Africa reached $2.463 billion, and East African countries were still China's main investment destinations.[10] About one-quarter of Chinese investment in Africa is concentrated in Nigeria and Angola, and Nigeria is one of China's largest partners on the African continent.[11]

[6] Rongji Zhu, 'Report on the Outline of the Tenth Five-Year Plan for National Economic and Social Development' (5 March 2001) <http://www.gov.cn/english/official/2005-07/29/content_18334.htm> accessed 15 February 2019.

[7] BRI aims to promote a trans-continental trade and infrastructure network, covering the Eurasian continent, Latin America, Africa and the Caribbean and the South Pacific region. It includes the Silk Road Economic Belt and the 21st Century Maritime Silk Road.

[8] To facilitate and guarantee the implication of BRI, the National Development and Reform Commission (NDRC) issued an action plan on the Belt and Road Initiative with State Council's authorisation, on 28 March 2015. For more information of the action plan, please see 'Action plan on the Belt and Road Initiative' (30 March 2015) <http://english.gov.cn/archive/publications/2015/03/30/content_281475080249035.htm> accessed 15 February 2019.

[9] MOFCOM, 'Africa has become an important destination for China's outbound investment' [非洲成为中国对外投资重要目的地] (13 September 2018) <http://www.mofcom.gov.cn/article/difang/201809/20180902786189.shtml> accessed 15 February 2019.

[10] MOFCOM, 'Yearly Overview VI for Commerce Work in 2018) Beijing Summit Injected New Energy for China-African Economic and Trade Cooperation' (29 December 2018) <http://english.mofcom.gov.cn/article/newsrelease/significantnews/201901/20190102824046.shtml> accessed 15 February 2019.

[11] Mariama Sow, 'Figures of the week: Chinese investment in Africa' (*Brookings*, 6 September 2018) <https://www.brookings.edu/blog/africa-in-focus/2018/09/06/figures-of-the-week-chinese-investment-in-africa/amp/> accessed 15 February 2019.

The Sino-Africa relation has been closer owing to not only the emerging role of Chinese investment in Africa, but also China's being an important trade partner with African countries.[12]

China's involvement in Africa is usually arguably attributed to China's desire to exploit the natural resources of Africa while supporting Chinese business. Nevertheless, this is not the whole picture. Western firms are still the leading group of investors in the African continent.[13] It is important to note that more than 65% of international oil companies operating in Africa are Western-based firms so that Chinese oil companies have less impact than Western companies in this region.[14] It is true that the abundant natural resources in Africa can meet the increasing demand of the Chinese manufacturing sector to satisfy the need of its rapid growth. Meanwhile, China's 'outward-facing orientation' can also be attributed to economic reform and newly liberalised markets in many African countries and the requirement of Chinese SOEs to complete their reforms and transition, such as privatisation.[15]

In the past decades, China has significantly enhanced its engagement in Africa, covering a wide range of sectors. The initial focus of Chinese investment in Africa is put on securing its access to energy and natural resources. However, it has expanded the distribution of its investment to cover infrastructure construction, followed by its footprints in other areas, e.g. trade, telecommunication, science and technology, real estate, finance and agriculture.[16] The distribution of Chinese investment in Africa is increasingly diversified with a decrease in the proportion of investment in resource-rich countries and an increase in non-resource-oriented countries. It was suggested that China's investment in Africa before 2007 was mainly concentrated in resource-rich countries, e.g. Sudan Algeria, Zambia and Nigeria. Since then, the investment in oil and mineral countries has gradually declined, falling to 41.6% in 2016 while the investment in non-oil and mineral countries increased from 38.6% in 2006 to

[12] Although the amount of Chinese investment in Africa is relatively low, the Sino-Africa two-way trade has grown 40 time over the last 20 years and now exceeds $ 200 billion. *See* Witney Scheidman and Joel Wiegert, 'Competing in Africa: China, the European Union, and the United States' (*Brookings*, 16 April 2018) <https://www.brookings.edu/blog/africa-in-focus/2018/04/16/competing-in-africa-china-the-european-union-and-the-united-states/amp/> accessed 15 February 2019.

[13] According to the World Investment Report 2018, multinational enterprises (MNEs) from developed economies, e.g. the US, UK ad France still hold the largest FDI stock in Africa. At the same time, investors from developing economies, i.e. China and South Africa, followed by Singapore, India and Hong Kong (China), are among the top 10 investors in Africa. *See* UNCTAD, 'World Investment Report 2018' (6 June 2018) <https://unctad.org/en/PublicationsLibrary/wir2018_overview_en.pdf> accessed 15 February 2019.

[14] Thompson Ayodele, 'Misconceptions about China's Interest in Africa' (20 October 2015) Georgetown Journal of International Affairs <https://www.georgetownjournalofinternationalaffairs.org/online-edition/misconceptions-about-chinas-interest-in-africa> accessed 15 February 2019.

[15] ibid.

[16] MOFCOM, 'Africa has become an important destination for China's outbound investment' [非洲成为中国对外投资重要目的地] (13 September 2018) <http://www.mofcom.gov.cn/article/difang/201809/20180902786189.shtml> accessed 15 February 2019.

58.4% in 2016.[17] Thus, non-oil and mineral countries become the major host States for Chinese investors.[18]

The disproportionate attention on China's presence in Africa is partially due to the players involved, among which the group of central-government-level SOEs is the critical player. It was reported that in 2014 there were 620 central-government-level SOEs, 371 local-government-level SOEs and 1762 non-SOEs investing in Africa.[19] The forms of support, especially financial support, have continuously been improved. The China-Africa Development Fund, the China-Africa Fund for Production Capacity Cooperation and particular loan for African SMEs provide concessional loans for investment projects in Africa. The investment is concentrated in energy and infrastructure, both of which are capital-intensive sectors. A large proportion of investment, economic cooperation and assistance to Africa went to infrastructure projects.[20] These projects are mostly undertaken by national level (central-government-level) SOEs governed by the State-owned Assets Supervision and Administration Commission (SASAC) while the engagement of municipal or provincial-level (local-government-level) SOEs is still limited. National-level SOEs tend to undertake various types of larger projects in different countries. They are more likely affected or guided by the national policy, while local government level SOEs are less constrained. However, the blame for their conducts and problems raised in China has also been extended to their operations in Africa. A major concern is that the development in the regulatory governance of investment and improvement in environmental protection and labour conditions cannot match the rapid economic development. Every country may face such problems at its stage of development, so the effective solution focuses on how to improve the legal environment and provide an appropriate way to achieve sustainable development. In this regard, joint efforts taken by stakeholders may be required, in particular, the efforts made by host States, home States and investors. In the context of this chapter, the stakeholders are African countries, China and Chinese SOEs.

3 The Controversial Role of Chinese SOEs in Africa

The debate concerning whether Chinese SOEs play a negative or positive role in Africa can be usually found in media and literature. There is usually a misunderstanding on SOEs due to their state ownership. State ownership can provide Chinese

[17] Chen Liu and Shunqi Ge, 'Chinese enterprises investing in Africa: Economic Growth and Structural Transformation' [中国企业对非洲投资: 经济增长与结构变革] (2018) 5 International Economic Review 9, 12.

[18] ibid.

[19] ibid.

[20] Hannah Edinger and Jean-Pierre Labuschagne, 'If you want to prosper, consider building roads: China's role in African infrastructure and capital projects' (22 March 2019) <https://www2.deloitte.com/insights/us/en/industry/public-sector/china-investment-africa-infrastructure-development.html> accessed 20 February 2019.

SOEs initial advantages in accessing cheap capital and assets easily. However, the reality is that SOEs have not acted so differently from POEs and many Chinese SOEs have achieved success in their operation and business. SOE reforms, like the privatisation and mix-ownership reform, are efforts to ensure the commercial operation and modern corporate governance of SOEs.

It is therefore necessary to clarify and even correct the common perception and the reality of SOEs before assessing the balance of benefits and concerns of Chinese SOEs in Africa. This chapter will make this clarification by analysing the behaviours of Chinese SOEs in Africa. Chinese SOEs are usually criticised for violating human rights and/or labour rights, polluting the environment, spreading corruption and lack of transparency in projects.[21] Investment made by SOEs is also regarded as a form to spread 'state capitalism' to the African continent.[22] However, Chinese SOEs also provide benefits for local development, helping African countries create jobs, increasing exports and taxes, as well as improving the economic structure of Africa countries. The Special Economic Zones (SEZs) established by Chinese SOEs have facilitated the establishment of complementary local activities that can support relevant projects.[23] It is important to note that the role of Chinese SOEs in Africa is complicated. It is not appropriate to only emphasise the benefits provided or overstress concerns raised or even merely blame the state ownership of Chinese SOEs.

3.1 Concerns of Investments by Chinese SOEs

3.1.1 Close Tie with Chinese Government

The puzzling role of Chinese SOEs in Africa, first of all, can be attributed to its close tie with Chinese government due to the state ownership. As some have claimed, SOEs are questioned as agents of the Chinese government to pursue political rather than purely commercial goals, either by controlling natural resources and inserting its influence in Africa or by undermining values and practices exerted by Western countries in Africa.[24]

[21] For more discussion and information of Chinese SOEs, *see* Qingxiu Bu, 'Chinese Multinational Companies in Africa: The Human Rights Discourse' (2015) 8 African Journal of Legal Studies 33; David H. Shinn, 'The Environmental Impact of China's Investment in Africa' (2016) 49 Cornell International Law Journal 25; Barry Sautman, Yan Hairong, 'Trade, Investment, Power and the China-in-Africa Discourse' (2009) 7 The Asia–Pacific Journal: Japan Focus 1.

[22] Martyn Davies, 'How China is Influencing Africa's Development' (2010) OECD 9 <https://www.oecd.org/development/pgd/45068325.pdf> accessed on 29 April 2019.

[23] Deborah Bräutigam and Tang Xiaoyang, 'African Shenzhen: China's special economic zones in Africa' (2011) 49 (1) The Journal of Modern African Studies 27, 36.

[24] Elizabeth J. Drake, 'Chinese State-Owned and State-Controlled Enterprises: Policy Options for Addressing Chinese State-Owned Enterprises' (15 February 2012) <https://www.uscc.gov/sites/default/files/2.15.12drake_testimony.pdf> accessed 5 March 2019; Ming Du, 'The Regulation of

The issue concerning 'political versus commercial objectives' of these state-owned investors has been widely debated in international investment.[25] It can be admitted that although the initial plan of large projects (e.g. the BRI projects) is announced by the Chinese government in line with Chinese national policy, it is Chinese SOEs that decide their own overseas operation. Some of the rules governing SOEs may not be designed on the basis of economic principles, while their operations are constrained by accountability, which requires them to invest in areas or projects that are economically feasible and profitable.

National policy is not always incompatible with commercial interests. Intergovernmental cooperation (e.g. FOCAC) and Chinese national policy (e.g. 'Going Out' and the BRI) can provide advantages for those who intend to follow the direction to invest. For example, during the 2018 FOCAC, President Xi announced that China would extend a total of $60 billion of financing in the form of government assistance, investment and finance by financial institutions and companies.[26] In addition, China's investment in infrastructural development in Africa comes 'with no political strings attached'.[27] Chinese Premier Minister Li Keqiang stated during his visit to Africa, 'China will not follow the beaten track of colonialism of other countries or allow the re-emergence of colonialism in Africa. For Africa and China, collaboration means opportunities and mutual gain'.[28] Chinese SOEs may invest in Africa to fulfil these promises, and they may enjoy a range of subsidies and privileges, such as loans with lower than market rates, special government funds or direct capital contribution.[29]

There is also fierce competition between SOEs and POEs, between different Chinese SOEs and even with their international counterparts to obtain specific bid or project.[30] In this regard, SOEs often act no differently from other market players. They prefer to invest in projects that are guaranteed with funding from the Chinese government in the form of foreign assistance or cooperation and aid or even projects

Chinese State-Owned Enterprises in National Foreign Investment Laws: A Comparative Analysis' (2016) 5 Global Journal of Comparative Law 118, 122.

25 OECD, 'Foreign Government-Controlled Investors and Recipient Country Investment Policies: A Scoping Pape' (January 2009) <https://www.oecd.org/daf/inv/investment-policy/42022469.pdf> accessed 5 March 2019.

26 Xinhua, 'Xi announces 60 billion USD of financing to Africa' (03 September 2018) <http://xinhuanet.com/english/2018-09/03/c_137441596.htm> accessed 5 March 2019.

27 Catherine Wong and Laura Zhou, 'No political strings attached: China doubles financial pledges to Africa and vows to waive debt for poorest nations' (South China Morning Post, 4 September 2018) <https://www.google.com/amp/s/amp.scmp.com/news/china/diplomacy/article/2162590/no-political-strings-attached-china-doubles-financial-pledges> accessed 5 March 2019.

28 Yabin Wu and Xiao Bai, 'China's Infrastructure Development Strategy in Africa: Mutual Gain?' (21 March 2017) <https://www.ictsd.org/bridges-news/bridges-africa/news/china's-infrastructure-development-strategy-in-africa-mutual-gain> accessed 5 March 2019.

29 Ming Du, 'The Regulation of Chinese State-Owned Enterprises in National Foreign Investment Laws: A Comparative Analysis' (2016) 5 Global Journal of Comparative Law 118, 123.

30 POEs in Africa often face less constrains by state regulation, national policy and they do not necessarily receive subsidies. Tak-Wing Ngo, 'Chinese State-owned Enterprises in China's Africa Policy' (2008) Expert Meeting Report-Chinese State-owned Enterprises and Stability in Africa <http://www.bibalex.org/Search4Dev/files/345107/178469.pdf> accessed 5 March 2019.

funded by multinational institutions. Chinese SOEs undoubtedly have to take some social responsibilities.[31] Chinese SOEs can seek government support to carry out these responsibilities, but they rarely do so at the expense of their financial interests. In the cases where the financial interests of Chinese SOEs and China's strategic goals come into conflicts, the SOEs have to strike a balance.[32] Moreover, since many Chinese SOEs have already conducted overseas investment for several years, for their international image and reputation, it is wise for these actors to follow commercial standards and practice for the purpose of maintaining long-term operation rather than short-term benefits.

3.1.2 Lack of Transparency and Alleged 'Debt Trap'

Lack of transparency is another problem that is usually criticised in the process of bidding for projects. The Western approach usually comes in the form of direct transfers of material and cash with conditions while China's approach is mainly via the means of providing low-interest commercial loans and exporting credits to African countries for large infrastructure projects that are more flexible, faster and without additional condition.[33] According to statistics, as of 2015, nearly two-thirds of new debts of African countries were from loans provided by China.[34] It was argued that these loans were used to purchase Chinese goods, services and labour in exchange for natural resources.[35] For example, there are a variety of banks financing infrastructure projects, including Chinese commercial banks, Chinese government-linked banks (e.g. the China Export–Import Bank-Exim Bank and China Development Bank) and multilateral institutions, e.g. the African Development Bank and World Bank.[36] Since both Chinese SOEs and financial institutions are most related to the Chinese government, the question may arise concerning the less transparency of the bidding process. For example, the Parliament of Uganda initiated an investigation of the procurement process of the railroad where Chinese investors were involved, and it was reported

[31] Qinghua Zhu et al., 'Corporate Social Responsibility Practices and Performance Improvement among Chinese National State-Owned Enterprises' (2016) 171 (3) International Journal of Production Economics 417.

[32] Yi-Chong Xu, 'Chinese State-owned Enterprises in Africa: ambassadors or freebooters' (2014) 23 Journal of Contemporary China 822, 836.

[33] J. Peter Pham et al., 'Chinese Aid and Investment Are Good for Africa' (*Foreign Policy*, 31 August 2018) <https://foreignpolicy.com/2018/08/31/chinese-aid-and-investment-are-good-for-africa/> accessed 5 March 2019.

[34] Heather Brown, 'Chinese investment in Africa: New Model for Economic Development or Business as Usual?' (13 September 2018) <https://doc-research.org/2018/09/chinas-approach-to-africa/> accessed 5 March 2019.

[35] Witney Schneidman, 'Are Chinese Companies Retooling in Africa?' (Brookings, 18 December 2018) <https://www.brookings.edu/blog/africa-in-focus/2014/12/18/are-chinese-companies-retooling-in-africa-2/amp/> accessed 5 March 2019.

[36] Lorenzo Cotula, Xiaoxue Weng, Qianru Ma & Peng Re, *China- Africa Investment Treaties: Do They Work?* (International Institute for Environment and Development 2016) 20.

that the Kenya portion of rail was awarded to the China Road and Bridge Corporation (CRBC) without a competitive bidding process.[37]

Furthermore, the claim of 'debt trap' is nowadays frequently labelled on Chinese overseas projects, in particular, those projects under the BRI.[38] However, despite using debt as leverage, there is no evidence to support that China is intentionally creating 'debt trap' via the BRI projects and the main thing to consider is how to deal with issues that have happened.[39] The $60 billion mentioned by President Xi as financial support to Africa, which will come in the form of government assistance and investment, has drawn criticism stating that it could burden developing countries with unsustainable levels of debt.[40] Taking power projects building as an example, although Chinese-built power projects can help to support electricity access and increase power generation, these projects may pose challenges for African countries, particularly those countries with higher constraints on their budgets.[41] Power projects have relied heavily on sovereign debt while some African countries are reaching their external debt limits or facing severe financial situations. Given that, the lower construction and equipment costs and the benefit are provided by Chinese financing for the development of the power system, but this adds to a burden of the public debt of African countries.

It should be noted that the loan provided by China is neither inherently bad nor good but the impact it can have depends on how African countries utilise it. The success of these projects also depends on the ability of African governments (as host States) to negotiate and implement them.[42] It also depends on whether the projects only focus on deals providing short-term gains rather than long-term costs.[43] It means that if the African countries use Chinese aid to offset poor governance and irresponsible policies, then Chinese SOE's investment may lead to further problems. If the African countries use Chinese finance in a wise and responsible manner, then

---

[37] Witney Schneidman, 'Are Chinese Companies Retooling in Africa?' (Brookings, 18 December 2018) <https://www.brookings.edu/blog/africa-in-focus/2014/12/18/are-chinese-companies-retooling-in-africa-2/amp/> accessed 5 March 2019.

[38] Nyshka Chandran, 'Fears of excessive debt drive more countries to cut down their Belt and Road investments' (CNBC, 17 January 2019) <https://www.cnbc.com/amp/2019/01/18/countries-are-reducing-belt-and-road-investments-over-financing-fears.html> accessed 5 March 2019; The ASEAN Post, 'Is the BRI debt trap real' (The ASEAN Post, 11 December 2018) <https://theaseanpost.com/article/bri-debt-trap-real?amp> accessed 5 March 2019.

[39] Laurie Chen, 'China defends belt and road strategy against debt trap claims' (SCMP, 5 March 2019) <https://amp.scmp.com/news/china/diplomacy/article/2188577/china-defends-belt-and-road-strategy-against-debt-trap-claims> accessed 20 March 2019.

[40] Mariama Sow, 'Figures of the week: Chinese investment in Africa' (Brookings, 6 September 2018) <https://www.brookings.edu/blog/africa-in-focus/2018/09/06/figures-of-the-week-chinese-investment-in-africa/amp/> accessed 2 March 2019.

[41] International Energy Agency, *Boosting the Power Sector in Sub-Saharan Africa: China's Involvement* (OECD/IEA, 2016) 8.

[42] ibid.

[43] J. Peter Pham et al., 'Chinese Aid and Investment Are Good for Africa' (*Foreign Policy*, 31 August 2018) <https://foreignpolicy.com/2018/08/31/chinese-aid-and-investment-are-good-for-africa/> accessed 2 March 2019.

the loan may help to improve the necessary infrastructure, thus spurring economic development.

On the side of Chinese SOEs, investment projects conducted by them are usually funded by a variety of stakeholders, ranging from development aid to equity financing.[44] To diversify sources of financing and find a more sustainable approach, Chinese SOEs have begun to seek alternative and market-based solutions for their projects. These solutions may include private equity from Western countries and other sources, e.g. co-financing fund established by the People's Bank of China and the African Development Bank (AfDB), thus creating new opportunities for trilateral cooperation in infrastructure investment.[45]

3.1.3 Environmental and Labour Concerns

The challenge to environmental protection has been in the spotlight. It is usually claimed that since the enforcement of environmental standards in China is usually lax, and many Chinese SOEs are the source of serious pollution incidents, critics have grounds to believe that Chinese SOEs may generate concerns regarding weak environmental standards, unrestored land and pollution.[46] Likewise, there are concerns that infrastructure construction may affect the life of the local people. Chinese SOEs often adopt a fast or even different approach compared to those accepted by many Western countries in responding to these issues. However, a different path does not necessarily mean there is a problem. Instead, actions adopted by many Chinese SOEs have shown their increasing significant interests in protecting the environment.[47] For example, in order to eliminate the discharge of effluents, the world's largest biodegradable wastewater treatment facility was built by China National Petroleum Corporation (CNPC) in Sudan.[48] As one of Chinese SOEs engaged in

[44] Development aid or development assistance refers to financial aid provided by governments and other agencies or multilateral to support the economic development and social welfare of development countries.

[45] Witney Schneidman, 'Are Chinese Companies Retooling in Africa?' (Brookings, 18 December 2018) <https://www.brookings.edu/blog/africa-in-focus/2014/12/18/are-chinese-companies-retooling-in-africa-2/amp/> accessed 5 March 2019.

[46] Sarah Eaton and Genia Kostka, 'Central Protectionism in China: The 'Central SOE Problem' in Environmental Governance' (2017) 231 The China Quarterly 685; Mehran Idris Khan and Yen-Chiang Chang, 'Environmental Challenges and Current Practices in China – A Thorough Analysis' (2018) 10 Sustainability 1.

[47] David H. Shinn, 'The Environmental Impact of China's Investment in Africa' (2016) 49 Cornell International Law Journal 25, 32.

[48] May Tan-Mullins, 'China: Gradual Change – Increasing Transparency and Accountability in the Extractive Industries' (2012) Revenue Watch Institute & the Transparency and Accountability Initiative Working Paper Series <http://www.transparency-initiative.org/archive/wp-content/uploads/2012/12/TAIChinaEng1.pdf> accessed 5 March 2019; Namukale Chintu et al., 'Chinese State-Owned Enterprises in Africa: Myths and Realities' (2013) IVEY Business Journal <https://iveybusinessjournal.com/publication/chinese-state-owned-enterprises-in-africa-myths-and-realities/> accessed 5 March 2019.

Africa, the China Petroleum and Chemical Corporation (SINOPEC) was committed to the United Nation Global Compact[49] and released its white paper on environmental protection.[50] On the other hand, China Development Bank and China Exim Bank also have their own policies concerning their social and environmental responsibilities, but these are different, to a certain extent, from the environmental impact assessments required by global financial institutions.

In addition, the employment practices by Chinese SOEs in Africa are usually criticised. For instance, critics argue that Chinese companies often bring their workers from China instead of hiring local workers. It is true that there are many Chinese workers who come to Africa after Chinese SOEs have made an investment there. In particular, at the beginning stage of an investment project, many Chinese workers come to Africa because they are familiar with the operation and working process of these companies.[51] However, the available database from the local governments shows different results.[52] In 2013, a report provided by the Chinese Academy of International Trade and Economic Cooperation (CAITEC) stated that 82% or 17,600 employees of the CNPC staff in Africa are local people and Chinese National Minerals Corporation (CNMC) had 12,500 local hires in Zambia.[53]

Chinese SOEs are usually accused of paying lower wages, providing poor working conditions or less work training programme, etc., to the worker to cover their basic needs. However, a report provided by the World Bank demonstrated that in Ethiopia, employees' monthly salary provided by Chinese companies were more than the average salary and Chinese companies also provided formal training programmes to these hires.[54] Apart from that, Chinese SOEs need to pay attention to cultural difference in working place. Workers from China and local hires may not have strong ties or relationship with each other due to different living habits, languages and ways of working.[55] This difference will cause mistrust, conflicts and potentially bring a negative effect on ongoing projects if not adequately managed.

---

[49] United Nation Global Compact is a non-binding and voluntary initiative to encourage businesses to implement socially responsible and sustainable policies and to provide reports concerning their implementation. It includes ten principles in the areas of labour, environment, human rights and anti-corruption.

[50] David H. Shinn, 'The Environmental Impact of China's Investment in Africa' (2016) 49 Cornell International Law Journal 25, 33.

[51] Tang Xiaoyang, 'Does Chinese Employment Benefit Africans? Investigating Chinese Enterprises and their Operations in Africa' (2016) 16 African Studies Quarterly 107, 110.

[52] ibid 109.

[53] Witney Schneidman, 'Here's how Chinese investors are rebooting their approach to Africa' (30 December 2019) <https://www.google.com/amp/s/qz.com/318985/heres-how-chinese-investors-are-rebooting-their-approach-to-africa/amp/> accessed 5 March 2019.

[54] World Bank, *Chinese FDI in Ethiopia, A World Bank Survey* (World Bank 2012) 12.

[55] Tang Xiaoyang, 'Does Chinese Employment Benefit Africans? Investigating Chinese Enterprises and their Operations in Africa' (2016) 16 African Studies Quarterly 107, 120.

3.2 Benefits Provided by Chinese SOEs

It is crucial to notice that compared to Western firms in Africa, Chinese SOEs are still newcomers. Problems associated with their conducts can be partly attributed to their less experience in internationalism and overseas operation. Although the Chinese model is different from the Western approach, many studies and reports have illustrated the benefits provided by Chinese SOEs for local development.

First, as discussed above, the state ownership of Chinese SOEs is not always a bad thing or counter-productive to their operation overseas, and this background may help Chinese SOEs get support from the FOCAC. Chinese SOEs can incorporate their investment strategies within the broad framework of Sino-African cooperation, thus reducing political risks and improving the compatibility with the development policies of African countries. Given that, they can contribute to a wide range of investment projects that are important in Sino-Africa cooperation and for Africa's development. During the 2018 FOCAC, the President of African Development Bank Group addressed that Chinese financing to Africa primarily focused on energy and agricultural sectors.[56] To promote investment in these sectors, infrastructure is essential for substantial investment. Even though the infrastructure gap in many developing and less-developed countries has been recognised by the international community, the West does not really address this issue, which requires further engagement and various supports.[57] Under this circumstance, as Africa is a key part in the geographical coverage of the BRI, the notion of the BRI is to address these issues by investing hugely in infrastructure with the Chinese SOEs playing essential roles.

Infrastructure, such as transportation, is a critical asset for the sustainable growth of the economic and inclusive development of Africa,[58] China has provided funding for a variety of infrastructure projects in Africa and China's infrastructure commitments to Africa vary from 16.1% of total funds in 2013 to 4.1% in 2014, 26.5% in 2015 and 10.2% in 2016.[59] China funded the railway projects in at least five African countries, including Kenya, Ethiopia, Angola, Djibouti and Nigeria.[60] China funded Kenya's largest infrastructure project, the Mombasa-Nairobi Standard Gauge

---

[56] 'Chinese financing to Africa focused in energy and agricultural sectors: African Development Bank' (*People's Daily*, 5 September 2018) <http://en.people.cn/n3/2018/0905/c90000-9497827.html> (accessed 20 March 2019).

[57] Rene Vollgraaff and Ntando Thukwana, 'AfDB Seeks to Plug Africa $ 170 Billion Infrastructure Needs' (*Bloomberg*, 8 May 2018) <https://www.google.com/amp/s/www.bloomberg.com/amp/news/articles/2018-05-08/afdb-seeks-funds-to-plug-africa-170-billion-infrastructure-gap> (accessed 20 March 2019).

[58] African Development Bank, 'African Economic Outlook 2018' (2018) <https://www.afdb.org/fileadmin/uploads/afdb/Documents/Publications/African_Economic_Outlook_2018_-_EN.pdf> accessed 20 March 2019.

[59] ibid.

[60] George Tubel, '10 massive projects the Chinese are funding in Africa - including railways and a brand-new city' (*Business Insider*, 25 September 2018) <https://www.businessinsider.co.za/here-are-150-million-rand-projects-in-africa-funded-by-china-2018-9> accessed 20 March 2019.

Railway, since the independence of Kenya at an estimated cost of R57.2 billion.[61] Other highlighted projects include the African Union Headquarters, the Headquarters of the Economic Community of West African States (ECOWAS), the new city of Egypt and the new parliament of Zimbabwe, etc. These projects are somewhat the symbols of their countries.

The energy sector as the foundation of industrialisation and development is another priority of Africa.[62] Many other infrastructure projects are for the purpose of facilitating the development of the energy sector. China is the most significant partner with Africa in the energy sector.[63] Africa is also the largest overseas market for the energy infrastructure that Chinese SOEs provide services.[64] Despite being driven by the need for overseas markets, projects conducted by Chinese SOEs contribute to the development of the power sector through the construction of new generation capacity and new grids. This kind of investment projects can be divided into two main categories: upstream activities such as oil and gas, and power projects, such as power generation, transmission and distribution.[65]

Energy access is one of the critical missions for African countries. For instance, in 2015, there were still over 635 million people in sub-Saharan living without access to electricity.[66] A reliable supply of power is critical for economic growth, which also has a positive impact on productivity: for individuals to improve health care, increase educational opportunities and for businesses to improve their commercial ability and decreases costs.[67] Chinese SOEs also play a growing role in developing cross-border energy infrastructure. These projects provide reliable and affordable energy access to people in Africa.[68]

The merits of investment by Chinese SOEs that are attractive to African countries may be various. First, compared to Western companies, Chinese SOEs focus primarily on tangible outcomes of projects while they may put less attention or spend less time in project designing, capacity building and environmental assessment. Second, Chinese SOEs are less risk-averse while other countries' financing institutions may be not keen to support large power plants or hydropower projects. The costs of Chinese-built projects are lower than other Western countries, supported by loans with lower interests or rates issued by policy banks. Chinese SOEs' access to preferential loans for social development and infrastructure has been facilitated

---

[61] ibid.

[62] 'Chinese financing to Africa focused in energy and agricultural sectors: African Development Bank' (*People's Daily*, 05 September 2018) <http://en.people.cn/n3/2018/0905/c90000-9497827.html> (accessed 20 March 2019).

[63] Giorgio Gualberti, 'Energy Investments in Africa by the US, Europe, and China' (20 August 2014) <https://www.aiddata.org/blog/energy-investments-in-africa-by-the-us-europe-and-china> accessed 20 March 2019.

[64] International Energy Agency, *Boosting the Power Sector in Sub-Saharan Africa: China's Investment* (OECD/IEA 2016) 7.

[65] ibid 10.

[66] ibid.

[67] ibid.

[68] ibid 27.

through support from China Exim Bank and China-African Development Fund.[69] Thirdly, grids and power plants built by Chinese SOEs can have direct impacts on social, economic and environmental development. For example, renewable power plant or low-carbon projects built by Chinese companies may help African countries' transition to lower CO_2 emitting electricity system.[70] However, although a combination of loans, government-driven investment and equity investment was provided, power sector development and large infrastructure projects building require massive support and greater access to capital funds, technologies and capacity building.

Another good example of Chinese SOEs that can benefit their projects and Africa's society and economy as well as many other Western investors are not interested in, is the establishment of SEZs in Africa.[71] SEZs can be found in Zambia, Mauritius, Egypt, Ethiopia, Algeria and Nigeria.[72] These SEZs were designed by MOFCOM but executed by Chinese SOEs. These SEZs not only support Chinese SOE's projects by facilitating the establishment of complementary local activities (e.g. construction materials, logistics, manufacture of equipment), but also contribute to the economic development of African countries by supporting other industries, e.g. production of medicines, textiles, furniture. Moreover, compared to Chinese SOEs' involvement in large-scale infrastructure projects, Western investors prefer engaging in public–private partnerships (PPPs) in infrastructure projects. However, they usually engage in projects that are directly linked to their major business operation as their shareholders may pressure them to focus on their activities and assess each investment projects. Investors from other Western countries and Asian countries (e.g. India) may prefer engaging in smaller projects.[73] In this regard, Chinese SOEs have played a significant role in helping African countries meet their infrastructure needs, thus further promoting economic growth.

It is wise to recognise that Chinese SOEs in Africa have neither wholly black nor wholly white roles. They bring both challenges and benefits. On the positive side, SOEs' links with the Chinese government and constraints by China's policy initiative

---

[69] A study provided that China has become the world's largest development bank and China Development Bank and China Exim Bank provides as much financing as the World Bank. *See* Kevin P. Gallagher, 'Opinion: China's Roles as the World's Development Cannot Be ignored' (11 October 2018) <https://www.npr.org/2018/10/11/646421776/opinion-chinas-role-as-the-world-s-development-bank-cannot-be-ignored> accessed 20 March 2019.

[70] David Bénazéraf and Yilun Yan, 'Commentary: Another Look at China's Involvement in the Power Sector in Sub-Saharan Africa' (1 April 2019) <https://www.iea.org/newsroom/news/2019/april/another-look-at-chinas-involvement-in-the-power-sector-in-sub-saharan-africa.html> accessed 10 April 2019.

[71] Deborah Bräutigam and Tang Xiaoyang, 'African Shenzhen: China's Special Economic Zones in Africa' (2011) 49 The Journal of Modern African Studies 27.

[72] For more discussion of SEZs in Africa, please see Thomas Farole and Lotta Moberg, 'Special Economic Zones in Africa: Political Economy Challenges and Solutions' in John Page and Finn Tarp (eds), *The Practice of Industrial Policy Government – Business Coordination in Africa and East Asia* (OUP 2017) 234.

[73] Anusree Paul, 'Indian Foreign Direct Investment: A Way to Africa' (2014) 157 Procedia – Social and Behavioral Sciences 183, 189; see Saif Mohd. Khan and Karan Arora, 'Scope of India's and China's Investment in African Continent' (2017) 122 Procedia Computer Science 691, 695–969.

in Africa have allowed them to engage more deeply in the development of Africa than many other Western investors. Chinese SOEs have played an important role in building hard infrastructure and soft institutions like SEZs. On the negative side, given their lack of enough and sufficient practice in internationalisation and less experience in ensuring transparency and delivering governance notions, the flexibility of Chinese approach sometimes is regarded as imposing harmful and unethical influence on the African continent.

4 Regulatory Challenges of Investing in Africa by Chinese SOEs

Given the size of projects Chinese SOEs involved and their lack of enough practices, they have raised regulatory challenges to both African countries and China. The regulatory challenge on the side of African countries is the way to address investment risks and disputes, i.e. the accountability of Chinese SOEs as foreign investors and responsibility of African governments as host States. In many African countries, the supervision mechanism of several kinds of projects is not sufficient, and governments do not provide appropriate requirements to ensure the sound and sustainable operation of projects with significant social, economic and environmental impacts.

Greater political proximity between China and African governments has led to higher investment inflows.[74] However, political risks arising from uncertainty around elections and successions increase sharply in several African countries, such as the Democratic Republic of the Congo, Kenya, Zimbabwe, Ivory Coast and Gabon.[75] The political risks might threaten foreign investors' desire to invest in Africa. In particular, whether there are political risks is a prominent consideration in the long-term incentives of large SOEs.[76] In stark contrast to Western investors, Chinese SOEs may prefer investing in less politically stable countries since those countries host fewer competitors from Western countries, thus leading to easy access to these markets.[77] Chinese foreign investments are attractive to countries that have political risks along with valuable natural resources.[78] Although the 'Five No' approach of China to deal with Sino-Africa relation aims to build mutual trust between Africa and

[74] Dhruv Gandhi, 'Figures of the week: Trends and Determinants in Chinese FDI in Africa' (Brookings, 25 July 2018) <https://www.brookings.edu/blog/africa-in-focus/2018/07/25/figures-of-the-week-trends-and-determinants-in-chinese-fdi-in-africa/amp/> accessed 20 March 2019.

[75] Marsh, 'Political Risk Map 2018: Tensions and Turbulence Ahead'. <https://www.marsh.com/in/campaigns/political-risk-map-2018.html> accessed 20 March 2018.

[76] Lorenzo Cotula et al., 'China-Africa Investment Treaties: Do They Work?' (2016) International Institute for Environment and Development (IIED) 43.

[77] Wenjie Chen et al., 'Why is China Investing in Africa? Evidence from the Firm Level' (2018) 32 The World Bank Economic Review 610.

[78] Bala Ramasamy, Matthew Yeung and Sylvie Laforet, 'China's Outward Foreign Direct Investment: Location Choice and Firm Ownership' (2012) 47 Journal of World Business 17, 20.

China, political risks within some African countries remain the top issues in Africa.[79] The dispute is inevitable while under this circumstance. Therefore, an appropriate dispute resolution mechanism is necessary for the interests of investors and host States.

Apart from the business strategy and tradition of Chinese investors to maintain a good relationship with African government, bilateral investment treaties (BITs) signed between China and African countries also restrict investors from pursuing investor-State arbitration. China has signed BITs with most of the sub-Saharan African countries since it signed the BIT with Ghana in 1989.[80] Albeit the BITs with most African countries, there is no publicly available investor-State arbitration case that Chinese investors would bring against African countries as respondents. On the one hand, some BITs, like the China-Ghana BIT, signed in the earlier time only limit the investor-State dispute concerning the amount of compensation for expropriation to be submitted to the arbitral tribunal. On the other hand, some BITs may impose a mandatory negotiation between parties in dispute before an investor-State arbitration claim can be raised. For instance, the China-Tanzania BIT, the latest BIT signed between China and an African country, requests that any investor-State dispute shall, 'as far as possible, be settled amicably through negotiations between the parties to the dispute, including conciliation procedures'.[81] In consequence, when Chinese SOEs undertake projects in Africa, they are more likely to choose other alternative ways to claim damages or losses, e.g. guarantees under commercial insurance.[82]

In practice, African countries have frequently appeared as respondents before international arbitration tribunals due to their violation of investment treaty obligations and most of these are based on expropriation relevant provisions. For instance, African countries have been involved in about 20% of arbitral disputes administered by International Centre for Investment Dispute Settlement (ICSID).[83] In recent times,

[79] The 'Five No' approach was proposed by President Xi at the FOCAC. It includes 'no interference in African countries' pursuit of development paths that fit their national conditions; no interference in African countries' internal affairs; no imposition of our will on African countries; no attachment of political strings to assistance to Africa; and no seeking of selfish political gains in investment and financing cooperation with Africa'. Xinhua, 'Full text of Chinese President Xi Jinping's speech at opening ceremony of 2018 FOCAC Beijing Summit (1)' (3 September 2018) <http://www.xinhuanet.com/english/2018-09/03/c_137441987.htm> accessed 20 March 2019.APO, 'Political risk remains the key consideration for dealmaking in Africa' (9 April 2018) <https://www.cnbcafrica.com/apo/2018/04/09/political-risk-remains-the-key-consideration-for-dealmaking-in-africa/> accessed 20 March 2019; Pauline Bax et al., 'Crisis and Hope: A Country Guide to Africa's Top Political Risks', (Bloomberg, 10 January 2019) <https://www.bloomberg.com/news/articles/2019-01-10/crisis-and-hope-a-country-guide-to-africa-s-top-political-risks> accessed 20 March 2019.

[80] The China-Ghana BIT, signed on 12 October 1989, entered into force on 22 November 1990.

[81] Article 13 of the China-Tanzania BIT, signed on 24 March 2013, entered into force on 17 April 2014.

[82] Lorenzo Cotula et al., 'China-Africa Investment Treaties: Do They Work?' (2016) (International Institute for Environment and Development) 44 <https://pubs.iied.org/pdfs/17588IIED.pdf> accessed 20 March 2019.

[83] ISDS Platform, 'Africa' (February 2017) <https://isds.bilaterals.org/?-africa-263-&lang=en> accessed 20 March 2019.

African countries have raised concerns about the investor-State dispute settlement (ISDS) provisions since they claimed that these provisions focus on the interests of investors from developed countries and do not address concerns of developing countries. The lack of legitimacy, transparency, high costs of arbitration proceedings and inconsistent decision are criticised.[84] Host States concerned that the ISDS system undermines state sovereignty and the 'right to regulate', thus resulting in so-called regulatory chill.[85] Given that, countries have adopted measures and/or national investment regulations limiting or even omitting ISDS provisions. For example, in 2014, the Namibian government raised its doubts about the correlation between BITs including ISDS and FDI and argued that ISDS would bring developing countries risks rather than benefits.[86] Protection of Investment Act 22 of 2015 was enacted by South African to limit ISDS to mediation or arbitration via domestic authorities or tribunals.[87] The 2016 amendments to the Southern African Development Community (SADC) Finance and Investment Protocol limited ISDS provision and narrowed the scope of investors' rights.[88] Only state-to-state arbitration has been preserved and it requires the use of domestic remedies.[89] For instance, Tanzania excludes international arbitration.[90] The Public–Private Partnership Act No. 9 of 2018 (Amendment) prohibits international arbitration as a means to resolve investor-state disputes.[91]

On the other hand, African regional economic communities have adopted diverse ISDS approaches, which may lead to the confusion or an overlap of approaches that a country may use. For example, the Investment Agreement for the Common Market for Eastern and Southern Africa (COMESA) Common Investment Area (CCIA) provides ISDS arbitration via African arbitration tribunals, the COMESA Court of Justice and also ICSID and arbitral tribunals based on United Nations Commission on International Trade Law (UNCITRAL) arbitration rules. But the Economic Community of West African States (ECOWAS) Supplementary Act on Investment and the SADC Finance and Investment Protocol exclude ISDS but rather provide

[84] Talkmore Chidede, 'Investors-State Dispute Settlement in Africa and the AfCFTA Investment Protocol' (11 December 2018) <https://www.tralac.org/blog/article/13787-investor-state-dispute-settlement-in-africa-and-the-afcfta-investment-protocol.html> accessed 20 March 2019.

[85] ibid.

[86] ibid.

[87] ibid.

[88] ibid.

[89] ISDS Platform, 'Africa' (February 2017) <https://isds.bilaterals.org/?-africa-263-&lang=en> accessed 20 March 2019.

[90] At present, international arbitration is prohibited in disputes related to Tanzania's natural resource sector and Public Private Partnership agreements. Tanzania also terminated the Tanzania-Netherlands BIT. See Ibrahim Amir, 'A Wind of Change! Tanzania's Attitude towards Foreign Investors and International Arbitration' (28 December 2018) <http://arbitrationblog.kluwerarbitration.com/2018/12/28/a-wind-of-change-tanzanias-attitude-towards-foreign-investors-and-international-arbitration/> accessed 20 March 2019.

[91] Aisha Ally Sinda, 'Investor-State Dispute Settlement in Tanzania' (11 February 2019) <https://isds.bilaterals.org/?investor-state-dispute-settlement-38352&lang=en> accessed 20 March 2019.

local remedies.[92] The Pan-African Investment Code provides arbitration via African arbitration institutions, which are governed by UNCITRAL arbitration rules and subject to exhaustion of local remedies and the applicable law of host States. It seems that different approaches to ISDS adopted by African countries may depend on the partners they are dealing with. It may leave a question, i.e. which approach they may choose and will be adopted in the African Continental Free Trade Agreement (AfCFTA) Investment Protocol if one country belongs to more than one of these regional communities.

Under this circumstance, if there is no unified Pan-African approach to investment dispute resolution, Chinese SOEs undertaking projects in different African countries may resort to different or even confrontational ways to claim damages or losses. Since infrastructure project often takes a long time to complete, maintaining a sustainable business relationship is important for investors. As many African countries have expressed the concerns that international arbitration for investor-state dispute resolution and existing BITs between China and African countries are outdated or only limited to specific disputes, it is crucial for China to ensure the interests of its overseas investment. To promote the development of Africa and to maintain a healthy business environment for foreign investment, it is necessary for China and Africa to find an appropriate way to address investment disputes.

The regulatory challenges on the side of China are how to regulate overseas investment of Chinese SOEs, in particular, the issues concerning competition and corporate social responsibility (CSR). Since the behaviour of foreign investors is usually governed by the local law of host States, the home State of foreign investors cannot supervise and regulate the behaviour of these investors in the territory of the host State. It should be noted that although many central-government-level Chinese SOEs may be constrained by national policy or have to comply with goals, small companies or municipal SOEs may not operate in the same way. Large Chinese SOEs may dominate Chinese investment in Africa, especially in large-scale projects, but their activities often are a small part of their global activities. Private enterprises and a large group of small SOEs have brought unregulated competition into Africa.[93] Many SOEs have to compete among themselves and with others in the fields of operation, strategies and policies.[94]

In terms of accountability of Chinese SOEs in labour rights and environmental protection, some Chinese investors may not comply with soft CSR requirements and they may even be not constrained by CSR policies set by the Chinese government. However, although Chinese SOEs are not the members of global initiatives that aim to improve corporate governance to the extent they might be expected to, China has developed a number of internal policies followed by SOEs and POEs. The SASAC

---

[92] Talkmore Chidede, 'Investors-State Dispute Settlement in Africa and the AfCFTA Investment Protocol' (11 December 2018) <https://www.tralac.org/blog/article/13787-investor-state-dispute-settlement-in-africa-and-the-afcfta-investment-protocol.html> accessed 20 March 2019.

[93] Yi-Chong Xu, 'Chinese State-owned Enterprises in Africa: ambassadors or freebooters' (2014) 23 (89) Journal of Contemporary China 822, 824.

[94] Zhangming Jin, 'Corporate Strategies of Chinese Multinationals' in Jean-Paul Larcon (ed) *Chinese Multinationals* (World Scientific Publishing Co, 2008) 11–49.

has issued specific Guidelines for SOEs to fulfil CSR, so as to realise the sustainable development of enterprises, society and environment in all respects.[95] It includes an obligation for all SOEs under the Central Government to release CSR reports. An increase in CSR management, training and skills development programmes have been organised.[96] In 2016, SASAC published the *Guiding Opinions on Better Fulfilling Social Responsibilities of State-Owned Enterprises*, which emphasises the 'CSR performance plays its part in deepening SOE reform'.[97] The reality, however, is that the complex and uncertain politics and poor governance of many African countries inevitably pose challenges for Chinese SOEs. This may require Chinese SOEs to be more cautious about their conducts and pay much attention to their CSR performance.

5 Way Forward: Implication of China's Internal and External Actions

Sustainable investment and sustainable development are the common interests of China and Africa. To maximise the benefits of Chinese SOEs and to reduce the issues or threats to local development, further efforts should be made by China, and the enhanced cooperation between African countries is indispensable. In reality, China has adopted many measures to improve the operation of SOEs and to regulate Chinese outbound investment. Domestic reforms are ongoing. To improve the current operation and governance of SOEs, a new round of SOE reform is undertaking on the central government level and the local government level. The 19th National Congress of the Community Party of China reinforced the notion that China was determined to make SOEs leaner and healthier. It was stated that 'overcapacity, poor corporate governance, and low labour productivity had dragged down profits of China's SOEs, which deteriorated in 2015'.[98] By realising the significant role of SOEs to the country's sustainable growth, China has launched a series of reforms to promote the modern corporate governance of SOEs, improve share-holding structure. Since 2015, 50 SOEs have been selected to conduct pilot reform, and in 2019, more than 100 SOEs are included in the fourth round of mixed ownership reform.[99]

---

[95] State-owned Assets Supervision and Administration Commission of the State Council, 'Guidelines to the State-Owned Enterprises Directly under the Central Government' (6 December 2011) <http://en.sasac.gov.cn/2011/12/06/c_313.htm> accessed 20 March 2019.

[96] MOFCOM, 'Research Bureau of the SASAC held a CSR Management Training in Beijing' (2 July 2014) <http://csr2.mofcom.gov.cn/article/policies/national/sasacnews/201407/20140700648755.shtml> accessed 20 March 2019.

[97] MOFCOM, 'Guiding Opinion on Better Fulfilling Social Responsibilities of State-Owned Enterprises' (30 September 2017) <http://csr2.mofcom.gov.cn/article/policies/national/sasac/201709/20170902653924.shtml> accessed 20 March 2019.

[98] Xinhua, 'Economic Watch: China SOE Reform Set to Accelerate' (*Xinhua*, 26 October 2017) <http://www.xinhuanet.com//english/2017-10/26/c_136707498.htm> accessed 20 March 2019.

[99] Xinhua, 'China to expand SOE mixed ownership reform: spokesperson' (*Xinhua*, 18 April 2019) <http://www.xinhuanet.com/english/2019-04/18/c_137988405.htm> accessed 20 April 2019.

To regulate overseas investment and to ensure the legitimate investment activities, on 4 August 2017, a guiding opinion for overseas investment was released jointly by MOFCOM, People's Bank of China and the Ministry of Foreign Affairs. It classifies overseas investment into three categories, i.e. encouraged investment, limited investment and prohibited investment. The Opinion provides that overseas investment that does not meet the environmental, security and energy consumption standards should be limited. On 26 December 2017, the National Development and Reform Commission (NDRC) released the Measures for the Administration of Overseas Investments of Enterprises (hereafter the 'Measures'). Article 41 of the Measures requires that investors are encouraged to innovate in the modes of overseas investment, adhere to the principles of operation in good faith, abstain from acts of unfair competition, protect the lawful rights and interests of their employees, respect local public order and good morals, fulfil necessary social responsibilities, pay attention to environmental protection and build a good image of Chinese investors. The sufficient and necessary regulation of overseas investment, as well as CSR relevant requirement, are necessary to promote sustainable and green investment, environmental assessment based on global standard. At the same time, the enforcement and implementation of these requirements should be guaranteed.

In addition, China's current environmental regulations and practice are necessary, as its domestic performance or policies eventually tend to be reflected in approach overseas. China has tightened its environmental regulation and governance.[100] It even reinforced the enforcement of environmental rules.[101] Apart from the actions of the government, financial institutions can also influence the behaviour of Chinese SOEs. Relevant standards can be adopted by the government to decide whether to grant loans and whether to control the credit of SOEs and projects with environmental violations. Financial institutions can set environmental protection of Chinese SOEs as one of the necessary requirements for approval of loans and veto projects that are below acceptable environmental protection facilities. Alternatively, they can even veto financing projects that do not pass environmental impact assessment.

Foreign direct investment and financial assistance bring important capitals to support the development of Africa. Infrastructure is critical to inclusive and sustainable development. The BRI, proposed by China, aims to enhance and promote international cooperation. It also features the UN Sustainable Development Goals and the African Union's Agenda 2063. These initiatives require partners to work together on joint market development. On the side of China, in order to accelerate interconnection and intercommunication in the field of infrastructure at the global level, at the

[100] Jonathan Kaiman, 'China strengthens environmental laws' (*The Guardian*, 25 April 2014) <https://www.google.com/amp/s/amp.theguardian.com/environment/2014/apr/25/china-strengthens-environmental-laws-polluting-factories> accessed 20 April 2019; Genia Kostka and Chunman Zhang, 'Tightening the grip: environmental governance under Xi Jinping' (2018) 27 Environmental Politics 769, 769.

[101] Rob Schmitz, 'China Shuts Down Tens of Thousands of Factories in Unprecedented Pollution Crackdown' (23 October 2017) <https://www.npr.org/sections/parallels/2017/10/23/559009961/china-shuts-down-tens-of-thousands-of-factories-in-unprecedented-pollution-crack> accessed 20 April 2019.

G20 Hangzhou Summit, Chinese President Xi Jinping proposed the establishment of the Global Infrastructure Connectivity Alliance to support connectivity through cooperation and knowledge exchange.[102] Promoted by China, the Asian Infrastructure Investment Bank (AIIB) was established in 2013 that aims to use infrastructure to improve economic development in the region. These initiatives demonstrate China's interests and determination in promoting infrastructure development as a global public good.

On the side of Africa, the 2063 Agenda emphasises the need for Africa to build world-class infrastructure across the continent, thus further enhancing the connectivity of African countries through plans to develop the interconnection of roads, railways, civil aviation and shipping and also regional and pan-African communication technologies and power grids.[103] It can be found that China has the capacity and desire to tackle the infrastructure deficit of Africa, in particular in power and transport. Africa can provide the markets and natural resources that can fuel China's growth. Deepening Sino-African cooperation serves the interests of both sides, while this requires that investments made by Chinese SOEs are commercial sound, well-managed and socially responsible.

Furthermore, although the FOCAC provides business opportunities for investors from both sides, it mainly focuses on political partnership. To attract need-based investment, the sound regulatory governance and politically stable and business-friendly environment are the guarantees of successful Sino-African collaboration in infrastructure investment and sustainable development. At the initial stage, preferential investment policies need to be in place while regulations are necessary to manage relevant risks (e.g. security concerns, environmental pollution and corruption). On the other hand, legal protection for foreign investors should be safeguarded.

---

[102] World Bank, 'Global Infrastructure Connectivity Alliance' (12 April 2017) <http://www.worldbank.org/en/topic/transport/brief/global-infrastructure-connectivity-alliance> accessed 20 April 2019.

[103] African Union, 'Goals & Priority Areas of Agenda 2063' <https://au.int/en/agenda2063/goals> accessed 20 April 2019.

Policy Framework on Procurement of SOEs in China

Xinquan Tu and Dingsha Shi

1 Introduction

The capital of state-owned enterprises (SOEs) is wholly (or mainly) invested by the state. The enterprise's profits are all (or partly) owned by the state, which is an important part of China's economic development. The procurement activities of SOEs distinct themselves with numerous projects, large amounts of funds and long cycles. They are also related to technological innovation and product development. They occupy an important position in the public procurement market and contribute to the socio-economic development of the area where the enterprise is located, as well as the establishment of fair competition and a trustworthy market. The trading system has a significant impact. The procurement of SOEs is not only related to the economic benefits and development prospects of enterprises but also related to the preservation and appreciation of state-owned assets. It is also a hot issue concerned by the public. With the continuous reform of the market economic system, the scale of SOEs' procurement is becoming more prominent. At the same time, many problems, such as the loss of state-owned assets and the accountability of relevant supervisors, have been exposed due to the incomplete system. Research on the procurement system of SOEs has become increasingly important.

X. Tu (✉)
China Institute for WTO Studies, University of International Business and Economics, Beijing, China
e-mail: tuxinquan@126.com

D. Shi
Research Center of General Administration of Customs of China, Beijing, China
e-mail: shidingsha@163.com

J. Chaisse et al. (eds.), *Regulation of State-Controlled Enterprises*, International Law and the Global South, https://doi.org/10.1007/978-981-19-1368-6_28

2 Historical Development of the Procurement of SOEs

With the continuous changes in the production and management of SOEs, the management model of the procurement of SOEs has mainly experienced the development stages of decentralised procurement, centralised procurement and refined procurement management in China.

2.1 *Phase I: Decentralised Procurement*

Since the reform and opening up to the promulgation of the Tendering Law in 1999, multi-level decentralised procurement was the traditional procurement model of SOEs in China.

To ensure production, supply and convenient use, the enterprise implements procurement activities that meet the needs of its own production and operation by relevant departments of the enterprise or subordinate units (such as subsidiaries, branches, workshops or branches). This procurement model not only leads to vast and cumbersome organisational structure and increases labour costs, but also shows deficiencies in procurement implementation: (1) multi-department procurement standards are not uniform, prices are confusing, and after-sales costs are high, (2) different departments have different procurement methods for the same supplier, and management is not uniform, which is not conducive to corporate image, (3) lack of a unified supplier management mechanism. Although decentralised procurement may result in wasted corporate manpower and material resources, increase enterprise inventory and occupy liquidity, many companies still use decentralised procurement at this stage. It still has some advantages such as convenience, speed and flexibility. Decentralised enterprises, or those that mainly purchase small quantities, have low value and low total expenditures. Comprehensive SOE groups are more representative. The annual purchase batches of comprehensive SOE groups are usually tens of thousands. In the continuous operation process, the same category of procurement repeats, such as simply purchasing according to the frequency of demand, without planning and integrating procurement needs. It not only causes inefficiency due to frequently repeated procurement but also fails to exert the scale effect of a comprehensive SOE group.

2.2 *Phase II: Focus on Centralised Procurement*

The Tendering Law in 1999 established the legal system for bidding and tendering, based on which procurement of SOEs was gradually standardised. SOEs entered the stage at which centralised procurement is the main procurement method.

With the rapid development of economic globalisation and information network technology, market competition has gradually become an international competition.

The proportion of centralised purchases by group companies in China continues to increase. The scale of centralised procurement rises year by year. And, the portion of decentralised procurement continues to decrease. Centralised procurement is an important part of enterprise development. It is not only a comprehensive cost reduction for enterprises but also a powerful guarantee for gaining a competitive advantage. It is also an important method for enterprises to strengthen group management and control in the enterprise system of construction and management. The centralised procurement model is generally applicable to the following situations: (1) the enterprise group has a relatively large production and operation scale, and the departments and subordinate units are relatively concentrated, (2) the product types are similar, but the purchase volume is large, which can form a batch advantage, (3) the enterprise group has strong internal control capabilities and member units relatively high degree of control, (4) the management quality of enterprise groups is high, with a complete procurement management system and a high-quality procurement team.[1]

The SOE adopts a centralised procurement management model. Subordinate units of the SOE prepare the procurement plan for the enterprise's production material demand based on the unit's actual material needs in production and operation. To a certain extent, this model is conducive to control procurement costs and prevent subordinate units to avoid irregularities in procurement.

The state-owned group enterprise's centralised procurement model adopted the "management and procurement integration" model at the beginning of its construction. The model is the only way to implement the centralised procurement system of the group company. As the implementation of centralised procurement involves the redistribution of multiple interests and rights within the group, it will inevitably be hindered. Therefore, it is necessary to have senior management functions in the early stage of implementation. However, "management and procurement integration" is a working mechanism that combines "referees and athletes", and it may cause concentrated corruption. "[M]anagement and procurement integration" should only be an initial stage in the establishment of the initial model of the centralised procurement department in the state-owned group enterprises. The state-owned group enterprise's centralised procurement gradually entered the "management and procurement separation" model after maturity.[2]

2.3 Phase III: Refined Management of Procurement

"*Regulations for the implementation of the Tendering Law*" issued in 2011 marked the beginning of a period of refined procurement management for SOEs. The promulgation of the "*Electronic Tendering and Bidding Measures*" in 2013 laid the foundation

[1] Fan He. Analysis of problems and countermeasures for centralized procurement of state-owned enterprises [J]. Commercial News, 2020 (13): 98–99.

[2] Quanyou Li. Procurement management problems of state-owned enterprises and their countermeasures [J]. Enterprise Reform and Management, 2018 (21): 22–23.

for using information technology to promote the refined development of procurement management.

With the development of the market, the centralised procurement model of state-owned group enterprises gradually develops in the "separation-of-management-and-procurement" mode. After the normal operation of the centralised procurement department of the state-owned group enterprises, the "management-and-procurement-separation" mode should be implemented. "Separation" can fully reflect the service awareness of the procurement department. It is conducive to preventing corruption and exerting the best benefits of centralised procurement. It is also conducive to full competition between suppliers. A large state-owned group enterprise adopts the centralised procurement model by establishing platform companies that are responsible for the specific implementation of centralised material procurement within the group. The group enterprise formulates procurement regulations and implements unified management of centralised procurement, effectively reducing costs and improving effectiveness.

The management of enterprises is changing from extensive management to refined management. No matter what type of enterprise, they all have the goals of low-cost, high-efficiency, the same is SOEs. Procurement is an important part of production which is directly related to the cost and benefit of the enterprise. Therefore, refined procurement management will inevitably become a development trend. SOEs conform to this trend, adopt refined procurement management concepts and implement corresponding measures within the enterprise management to grasp the implementation, thereby effectively improving market competition for the SOEs force.

3 Legal System of the Procurement of SOEs

3.1 Procurement of SOEs Under National Laws Adopted by the NPC

3.1.1 Tendering Law

The first public procurement legislation drafted by the National Development and Reform Commission (NDRC, then State Planning Commission) and enacted by the NPC in 1999 was titled Tendering Law (TL). It applies to tendering activities of both the public and private sectors. It lacks many modern public procurement legislation features such as a clear definition of public procurement, procurement methods other than open and selective tendering procedures and supplier review mechanism. The TL covers the procurement of works and works-related goods and services by SOEs. The national law applies to all tendering activities, public or private, due to the involvement of tendering procedure and the nature of the procurement project (works and related goods/services) but not to SOEs' special characteristics. In other words, such procurement is not regarded as "government procurement" under Chinese law but remains to a large extent subject to tendering rules established by the procurement law.

The TL defines the coverage by a combination of general and specific coverage. It can be argued that the scope provided in Art.3 indicates the real scope of coverage of TL. All procurement by SOEs will arguably fall under the TL's (Art.2) general coverage if the tendering procedure is employed in such a process. However, the extent to which procurement of works or related goods/services by SOEs will also fall under the narrower compulsory requirements for tendering (Art.3) is unclear. This is because it is not clear what constitutes "public interests". Although two examples were given (large infrastructure or utilities), they are seemingly not exclusive, it is not clear either whether "state-owned fund" refers to only further investment from the government account or it also includes funds owned by an SOE itself. It is unclear whether "state-borrowed fund" refers only to money borrowed by the government, such as treasury bonds, or it also includes money borrowed by SOEs from commercial banks.

3.1.2 Government Procurement Law

Government Procurement Law (GPL) was enacted in 2002. Procurement by SOEs falls arguably outside of the narrow term of "government procurement" defined in the GPL. Art.2 of GPL defines government procurement as "the purchasing activities conducted with fiscal funds by government departments, institutions and public organisations at all levels, where the goods, construction and services concerned are in the centralised procurement catalogue compiled under the law or the value of goods, construction or services exceeds the respective prescribed procurement thresholds". The procurement by the state government agencies, institutions and organisations at all levels, using financial funds to purchase within the centralised procurement catalogue established by law or the purchase limit standard for the above goods, projects and services. The main body of procurement did not include SOEs. The regulations on the implementation of the GPL, which came into effect on 1 March 2015, did not include SOEs in the scope of government procurement.

Whether the procurement of SOEs should be included in the scope of government procurement, there are three points of view in theory and practice: (1) all the SOEs that use financial funds should be included in the scope of government procurement, (2) the autonomy of operation should not be included in the scope of government procurement, (3) SOEs such as aerospace, military, and urban transportation need to assume public government functions. Their operations cannot be carried out entirely under the market mechanism. Their procurement should be included in the scope of GPL.

SOEs are arguably not procuring with fiscal funds and normally not classified as "government departments", "institutions" or "public organisations". The term "government procurement" is narrow in its scope under Chinese law and does not cover SOEs' procurement in theory or practice. However, procurement of works and works-related goods and services by SOEs is covered by TL. In other words, such procurement is not regarded as "government procurement" under Chinese law but remains to a large extent subject to tendering rules established by the procurement law. With the public nature of state-owned enterprise procurement funds, many localities have issued local regulatory documents to incorporate procurement of SOEs into the scope of government procurement and regulate the procurement behaviour of SOEs in accordance with the relevant provisions of the GPL.

It is worth noting that there has been a tension between the GPL and the TL, which is manifested, in particular, in the issue of coverage.[3] The TL in principle applies to "all tendering proceedings [open and selective tendering] within the territory of the People's Republic of China". The TL also requires that procurement of certain works/construction projects and procurement of related services (such as ground exploration, design and monitoring) and related goods (important materials and equipment) incidental to such construction projects must be conducted through tendering proceedings.

3.1.3 Other Laws

In addition to the above two laws, other legal adjustments should be applied to SOEs' procurement projects. State-owned enterprise procurement activities are a kind of market economic activity. SOEs and suppliers, procurement agencies and other related parties have a civil relationship of equal subjects. SOE-procurement activities should be mainly regulated and constrained by "*General Provisions of the Civil Law*" and "*Contract Law*". "*General Provisions of the Civil Law*" stipulates the basic economic and civil activities of citizens and social/economic organisations: "the principle of equality and voluntariness, the principle of fairness and integrity, the principle of not violating the law, the principle of public order and good customs and the principle of conserving resources and protecting the environment". It also stipulates that the application of "not violating legal principles" in procurement practice is to set up the supply of projects (or products) that needs to obtain national approval or pre-licence before listed on the market or engaged in production or operation. Relevant qualifications standards must be set to evaluate the supplier and bidding product qualifications. The preparation of procurement documents, contract signing and resolution of procurement disputes in the procurement activities of SOEs should be subject to the terms of the initiation of offers and the signing of contracts in "*Contract Law*".

Besides, the capital of an SOE is wholly (or mainly) invested by the state, and the company's profits or profits are all (or part) owned by the state. Therefore, state-owned enterprise procurement is subject to "*Enterprise State-owned Assets Law*" to standardise the procurement behaviour of state-owned enterprises, strengthen

[3] Xiaopin Ding. Defects and Improvements in Government Procurement Bidding Work [J]. Enterprise Reform and Management, 2017 (05):211 + 214.

the supervision and management of SOE assets, save state-owned enterprise funds, prevent the loss of state-owned assets and prevent corruption.

3.2 Procurement of SOEs Under Ministerial Regulations

As the national laws' provisions are often abstract in nature, the departmental rules are more important in practice. There are a few departmental rules that have regulated the procurement of SOEs to varying degrees. However, concerning procurement by Chinese SOEs operating in the utility sector, domestic and foreign suppliers have to follow the internal procurement rules adopted by such SOEs, concerning a significant proportion of their procurement, which do not have a place in the legal hierarchy and, in many aspects, deviate away from the legislation.

3.2.1 Ministerial Regulations of NDRC

To deepen the reform of delegating power and optimising service in the field of bidding and tendering, standardise the bidding and procurement activities and better play the role of the bidding and procurement system, the NDRC has successively issued the "*Provisions on Engineering Projects Which Must Be Subject to Bidding*", "*Provisions on The Scope of Infrastructure and Public Utility Projects Subject to Tender*" and "*Measures on Tender Announcement and Public Information Release*". They have further narrowed the scope of projects that must be tendered, leaving more room for enterprises to choose their procurement methods flexibly. The procurement of SOEs has the dual attributes of corporate and public procurement. How to deal with the issues of fairness and efficiency, achieve compliance, reduce costs and increase the coordination of efficiency is one of the main problems facing the procurement of SOEs.

SOEs implement bidding activities under the TL. Art.3 of the TL does contain a built-in mechanism for further clarifications, i.e. that detailed scope and threshold of those projects subject to the compulsory tendering requirement shall be promulgated by NDRC with the approval of the State Council. "*Provisions on Engineering Projects Which Must Be Subject to Bidding*" were approved by the State Council on 8 March 2018 and enacted by the NDRC on 1 June 2018. It provides that (1) infrastructure projects that concern public interests or security include projects concerning energy, transportation, post, telecommunication, water (dams, flood control facilities), refuse, road and bridges, parking, environmental protection and so on, (2) public utility projects that concern public interests or security include projects concerning supply of water, electricity, gas and heat to the public, technology, education, culture, sport, tourism, hygiene, social welfare, housing, etc., (3) projects funded by state-owned capital include projects funded by state budget of various level, specialised governmental construction funds run by financial departments, or fund of state-owned enterprises and institutions provided that the investor has control of the project, (4) projects funded by state-borrowed capital include projects funded by national bond, loans borrowed or guaranteed by the state, loans of policy from the state, loans borrowed by the investor but authorised by the state. On thresholds, it provides that the mandatory tendering requirement shall apply to any construction contract the estimated value of which is above 4 million Yuan; any goods (materials and equipment) or contracts the estimated value of which is above 2 million Yuan; any relevant services contract the estimated value of which is above 1 million Yuan. The procurement of the above-mentioned engineering projects by SOEs, whether they are operational or non-operational projects, shall be implemented according to TL and the implementation regulations.

3.2.2 Ministerial Regulations of MOF

MOF is the guardian of GPL. In terms of departmental administrative regulations, MOF early issued "*Interim Measures for the Administration of State-owned Capital and Financial Management of Enterprises*" in 2001, but the regulations on enterprise procurement are more general and not operable. The measures of procurement for various non-financial enterprises holding state-owned capital include (1) enterprises should formulate quotas for the consumption of various labour and materials, prepare budgets for various operating and management expenses, improve various original records and related auditing systems and establish effective internal control systems, (2) the purchase of bulk raw and auxiliary materials or commodities of enterprises, the purchase and construction of fixed assets and engineering construction should generally be conducted in accordance with the principles of openness and fairness through tendering and (3) if commodity materials procurement and fixed asset construction, etc., cause losses to the enterprise, or bulk commodity materials procurement and fixed asset construction, etc., cause losses, and the enterprise should be ordered to correct within a time limit, recover losses and confiscate illegal income.

To improve the efficiency of centralised procurement of state-owned financial enterprises, standardise the centralised procurement behaviour of state-owned financial enterprises and better implement the reform of delegating power and optimising service, MOF issued the "*Interim Provisions on the Management of Centralised Procurement of State-owned Financial Enterprises*" on 5 February 2018, which entered into force on 1 March 2018. Provisions implement the requirements of "simplification of government and decentralisation" based on clear principles of centralised procurement and management framework, cancel the relevant reporting, reporting and auditing to the competent financial department. State-owned financial enterprises should do an excellent job in the organisation and system construction related to centralised procurement and give enterprises the flexibility to make independent decisions. Based on abolishing the pre-reporting requirements, new information disclosure requirements for centralised procurement have been added, and the supervision and inspection responsibilities of the financial department have been clarified. Through market-oriented means and strengthening of post-event supervision and inspection, relevant state-owned financial enterprises are urged to establish rules and regulations.

3.3 Local Policies in Procurement of SOEs

The annual operating income of local SOEs is about 26 trillion yuan in 2019, and the amount of bidding and procurement exceeds 10 trillion yuan. Because TL is mainly applicable to the bidding of engineering construction projects, GPL is only applicable to government procurement projects that administrative agencies, institutions and groups use fiscal funds for local SOEs do not have the advantage of setting up electronic bidding and procurement platforms for central enterprises, resulting in a large number of local SOEs' bidding and procurement activities in the "grey zone" of legal supervision. Therefore, some local governments have promulgated management measures of state-owned enterprise procurement, such as Wenzhou, Huzhou, Leshan and Dongyang, which systematically regulate the centralised procurement of bulk materials in SOEs in the aspects of system construction, trading platform, procurement procedures, supervision and management, etc.

To strengthen the management of material procurement of municipal SOEs, reduce costs and improve efficiency, Ningbo issued "guidance on regulating the management of bulk materials procurement of municipal state-owned enterprises". The guidance requires that municipal SASAC-funded enterprises and single-asset supervision enterprises,[4] as well as sub-enterprises at all levels with actual control rights, should establish and improve bulk material procurement management systems and strengthen procurement management. With many bulk material procurement projects and conditions, an enterprise group should establish a small tender procurement platform. It also formulates the procurement catalogue and determines the limit standards for implementing relevant procedures and regulations on bidding and procurement strictly.

Yinchuan issued "*Measures for the Supervision and Administration of Material Procurement and Engineering Construction Bidding of State-owned Enterprises in Yinchuan*" to regulate the procurement of materials and bidding and procurement activities of municipal state-owned and other SOEs, strengthen the supervision of state-owned assets of enterprises, effectively prevent the loss of state-owned assets and corruption.

[4] SASAC: State Assets Administration Committee Capital Administration.

3.4 *Standards Issued by Social Organisations*

3.4.1 Operation Specification for Procurement of SOEs

With the continuous deepening of the construction of party style and clean government in SOEs, the fight against corruption and the comprehensive promotion of inspections, the discipline inspection and supervision departments and audit institutions have become more and more strict about the "compliance" of procurement of SOEs. To standardise the procurement behaviours of SOEs, improve procurement efficiency, reduce enterprise costs and solve the confusion in procurement execution, the China Federation of Logistics and Purchasing (CFLP) issued an "*Operation specification for Procurement of SOEs*".[5] Operation specification is the first recommended industry standard in the procurement by SOEs in China, which was implemented on 1 May 2019. It has refined the two general procurement organisation forms of "centralised procurement" and "framework-agreement-procurement". It has summarised nine different procurement methods in four categories commonly used by SOEs and internationally accepted. The effective procurement experience of enterprises has been refined and finalised, which will promote the standardisation, specialisation and internationalisation of the procurement of SOEs.

3.4.2 Service Specification for Non-bidding Procurement Agency

In the procurement practice of SOEs, the procurement methods include open bidding, invitation bidding, competitive negotiation, single-source procurement and inquiry procurement. For procurement in the form of bidding, SOEs apply the TL; for non-bidding procurement, SOEs do not have a system of laws and regulations and are more constrained by the internal system of the group.

To standardise the production materials and small-scale engineering projects with short procurement cycles and flexible procurement forms, as well as the projects, goods and services that must be tendered according to laws, the procurement of projects that do not tender or fail to tender after the tender fails under the legal conditions, China Tendering and Bidding Association (CTBA) issued "*Service Specification for Non-bidding Procurement Agency*" on 1 June 2018.[6] The specification applies to not only non-bidding procurement services provided by legally established bidding and procurement agency service intermediaries but also all types of market purchasers (mainly referring to corporate purchasers) who set up full-time organisations (departments) to organise their implementation. At the same time, the specification sets forth the professional service capability requirements of procurement practitioners. Pursuant to the requirements of professional procurement services, technical expertise, economics, management, legal policies and other procurement expertise, the specification have comprehensive analysis and resolution of actual

[5] Social Organization Standard: T/CFLP 0016-2019.

[6] Social Organization Standard: T/CTBA001-2019.

procurement issues. A professional level of procurement services is also required in the specification.

4 Problems in the Procurement of SOEs

4.1 Inconsistencies in the Application of the Laws

As the evolution of the legal framework demonstrated, there are numerous industry sectors and local governments involved in regulating the procurement by SOEs. The NDRC is in charge of the TL. At the same time, the MOF is the guardian of the GPL. The MOFCOM regulates international tendering of electronic and mechanic equipment and controls the procurement of imported electronic and mechanical products by government agencies and SOEs. Due to the fragmented institutional framework, there is a legal framework with the TL and the GPL in which the two laws is operating in parallel and sometimes in conflicts. On one side, it can be argued that the conflicts of procurement regulations at various levels are inevitable because of this fragmented institutional framework, in which the MOF as the "bookkeeper", the NDRC as the "investor" and "planner" and the MOFCOM as the "trader". SOEs must comply with the regulations of all sectors on procurement. Other line ministries such as the Ministry of Housing and Urban–Rural Construction, the MIIT, the Ministry of Transportation, the Ministry of Water Resources and the General Administration of Civil Aviation are in charge of supervising tendering activities within their respective fields. On the other side, other ministries such as the Ministry of Housing and Urban–Rural Development (MOHURD), the Ministry of Transport (MOT), the Ministry of Water Resources (MWR) and the General Administration of Civil Aviation (CAAC) are in charge of supervising tendering activities within their respective fields.

4.2 Main Body of SOEs is not Clearly Defined

Public procurement emerged in the early 1990s, and the tendering system was introduced. Since then, SOEs often used public funds for certain public procurement, especially procurement of construction works, mechanical and electrical equipment. The tendering rules were finally codified in the TL in 1999. At present, some advanced management concepts in the world are gradually being absorbed and used by China. The concept of public service has been increasingly recognised and applied, but no law has clearly defined public procurement until now. It is important to note that the terms of government procurement and tendering are often used disjunctively due to the parallel existence of the GPL and the TL. The GPL in 2002 adopted a narrow definition of "government procurement", which excludes the procurement of SOEs. Therefore, official statistics on "government procurement" arguably do not reflect the actual size of China's public procurement market. In 2018, the size of goods, works and services procurement was, respectively, 806.53 billion Yuan, 1571.42 billion Yuan and 1208.19 billion Yuan; account for, respectively, 22.5%, 43.8% and 33.7% of annual government procurement expenditure. It is noteworthy that large infrastructure projects involving billions of investment, such as the Beijing-Shanghai High-Speed Railway system and Three-Gorges Dam, are procured by SOEs specially set up for such projects, and their procurement of works, while subject to tendering rules contained in TL, is outside of GPL and not incorporated into official government procurement data. Procurement of SOEs is outside of both TL (unless works) and GPL, therefore, also not reflected in the official data for government procurement. It is not clearly defined whether SOEs are the main body of public procurement. In the negotiations on China's accession to GPA, SOEs were excluded from the submission of the government procurement market open list. How to gradually develop China's government procurement into public procurement is a new topic that urgently needs to be studied and considered at this stage. It is also a new change in government management concepts and methods.

4.3 Open Bidding is Abused

Bidding is a common task in the procurement, operation and management of SOEs. Open bidding can reduce project costs, introduce excellent project construction teams, improve project construction quality, shorten the construction period, save procurement cost, etc. and play an irreplaceable role in constructing a clean government. Non-bidding procurement accounts for nearly half of the total procurement. Some SOEs exposed many outstanding problems in procurement and bidding.[7] SOEs use open bidding regardless of the amount of purchases and the attributes of the procurement targets to avoid responsibility, resulting in severe damage to procurement efficiency.

5 Development of SOEs Procurement

5.1 Procurement of SOEs Accelerates Docking with International Rules

As President Xi Jinping clearly stated at the Boao Forum for Asia in April 2018, China will accelerate the process of joining the "Government Procurement Agreement" (GPA). It is the first time to show the political will to join the GPA as the head

[7] Wen Yao, Limin Yuan, Dongguo Liu. Discussion on the construction of large-scale state-owned enterprises specialized bidding organization system [J]. China Tendering, 2013 (15):20–23.

of state, showing China's determination to join the GPA and its sincerity in opening up. To join the GPA, it is necessary to not only clarify the public and commercial boundaries of SOEs, but also improve the procurement efficiency of SOEs under the premise of ensuring fairness is an urgent problem to be solved.[8] Under the background of opening to the outside world, procurement of SOEs is changing to supply chain management, from the pursuit of the lowest price in the past to the focus on quality and service and the pursuit of supply stability. To further enhance vitality, control, influence and global competitiveness, SOEs must strengthen supply chain management.

In China's accession to GPA negotiations, SOEs in the public sector that are indeed controlled or affected by the government may be included in the scope of government procurement. Based on the "*Report of the working party on the accession of China to the WTO*", it is necessary to ensure the commercialisation orientation of the purchase behaviour of SOEs. It also means that the SOEs must be based solely on commercial considerations to ensure that the procurement of SOEs is not subject to GPA.[9] However, in practice, some SOEs in China have undertaken social public service functions. Their procurement activities are not entirely based on commercial considerations but based on the needs of government management and social services, which are subject to government control and influence to a certain extent. In the concept of competition neutrality, the separation of commercial functions and public service functions of SOEs is the key to ensuring fair competition between state-owned and private enterprises.[10] In the context of the further expansion of government procurement market opening to the outside world, it has become an international practice to use public service functions to judge the main body of government procurement in the international government procurement. Therefore, it may become a trend to gradually include SOEs that undertake public service functions into the scope of GPA-covered subjects.[11]

5.2 Procurement of SOEs Accelerates Electronic Development

Due to the openness, universality and interactivity of the network, electronic procurement can better reflect the principles of openness, fairness and justice than other media. It also can increase the openness and transparency of bidding and tendering

---

[8] Lu Wang. Thinking of the procurement problems and countermeasures of state-owned enterprises in the new period [J]. China Management Informationization, 2017, 20 (2):107.

[9] Liangmei Liao, Wei Gu. Classification and selection of state-owned enterprises under the framework of GPA [J]. Journal of Hubei University of Economics (Humanities and Social Sciences Edition), 2014,11 (07): 42–43.

[10] Yanzhen Weng, Nan Niu, Chenguang Liu. The reference of GPA participating state-owned enterprise bids to China [J]. International Economic Cooperation, 2014 (03): 52–57.

[11] Wen Hai, Jin Li, Mi Dai. Research on the bidding strategy of state-owned enterprises after China joined the "Government Procurement Agreement" [J]. International Trade Issues, 2012 (09): 3–15.

and is conducive to fair competition. On one side, it is possible to avoid the black box operation in the tendering and bidding activities based on strengthening the reliability and safety guarantee of the electronic procurement system. An electronic procurement platform, which publishes the bidding announcement results and answers questions, can help to avoid rent-seeking behaviour due to asymmetric information. Information can be disclosed in time so that the tenderer, bidder and procurement supervision department can effectively monitor and master the timeliness and legality of the entire procurement process and improve the participation and competitiveness of the procurement of SOEs. On the other side, electronic procurement raises the possibility of incorporating procurement of SOEs from non-regulated into regulated. The "*Interim Measures for the Management of Public Resource Trading Platform*" consists of three systems: an electronic trading system, an electronic service system and an electronic supervision system. According to different functions, the electronic bidding system in the "*Electronic Tendering and Bidding Measures*" is divided into the trading platform, public service platform and administrative supervision platform. The architectural design ideas of the platform show that the administrative supervision function will be one of the important functions of the electronic bidding platform, which will also be reflected in the electronic procurement of SOEs.

5.3 Non-bidding Procurement of SOEs Will Be More Standardised

There are currently two trends. One is that the state is gradually narrowing the scope of bidding required by law through a revision of the TL. The other is that the content of bidding in projects that SOEs must tender has also been reduced. The procurement of profit-oriented projects for market entities should be based on the principle of "self-management, independent decision-making and efficiency first", with the goal of "value for money, lower costs and higher profits", refocusing on procurement results rather than procurement programmes. Therefore, for the procurement of such projects, private enterprises generally do not purchase through the methods stipulated in the TL or GPL, and any procurement method that maximises profits will be effectively adopted, such as direct purchase, ordering, negotiation and other modes of procurement. For SOEs, to standardise procurement activities and prevent profit-seeking or corruption, it is necessary to implement open, transparent and standardised procurement methods and procedures. The procurement will not be completely restricted by the provisions of the TL or the GPL.[12] SOEs may explore the procurement methods suitable for the characteristics of the projects of the enterprise and make the procurement methods institutionalised, standardised and internalised to guide the procurement activities of the enterprise. Relevant government departments and industry organisations will put forward more unified standards and requirements

[12] Rui Liu. Discussion on the state-owned enterprises' bidding and procurement activities for non-legally required tender projects [J]. Tendering and Procurement Management, 2015 (10):28–30.

for procurement procedures, procurement documents, service standards for negotiated procurement, inquiry procurement, bidding procurement, direct procurement and framework-agreement procurement, making non-bidding procurement without unified procedures in the past in a consistent procurement procedure, which will lay the foundation for the SOEs to carry out non-bidding procurement business.

5.4 Introducing e-Commerce in Procurement of SOEs

The transaction scale of China's e-commerce market reached 36.8 trillion yuan in 2019, an increase of 16.3%. In addition to the growth of local life O2O and online shopping, the enterprise-level e-commerce market in China is also expanding rapidly. In 2019, firm-level e-commerce accounted for more than 85% of the overall market. However, the e-commerce platform has not completely exploded in the field of corporate procurement. Compared with the 75% penetration rate in the USA, the penetration rate of e-commerce purchases by Chinese companies is only 20%. Due to SOEs' own regulations and business development requirements, the introduction of e-commerce in procurement of SOEs has become an important way to solve many problems. Mature e-commerce platforms can effectively achieve anti-corruption goals, prevent the loss of state-owned assets, reduce costs, improve quality and efficiency and information disclosure.[13] The positioning of a procurement department in a group company should not be a cost centre but a profit centre. E-commerce platforms should complement existing procurement methods. Although e-commerce procurement is not omnipotent which cannot be fully applied to some special situations, it should be boldly tried in the non-hazardous field of civilian grade and bulk raw materials. The current situation of SOEs procurement is like an information island, unable to make full use of social resources. The social e-commerce platform has the advantages of fastness, convenience and abundant goods. In future, enterprises will purchase more through an e-commerce platform. SOEs are no exception.

[13] Yin Li. Practice and consideration of electronic procurement of state-owned enterprises that must bid for projects that are not required by law [J]. Housing and Real Estate, 2020 (03):15 + 23.

Port and Rail Investments: Reform of Chinese Regulations, Paradigm Shift of Chinese State-Controlled Entities and Global Freedom of Investments

Carlos K. L. Li

1 Introduction

Subsequent to the global financial crisis, China has adopted a wide variety of measures in order to recover its economy and explore further room for economic growth other than its conventional reliance on the monotonous export-led economic model. Belt and Road Initiative (BRI), among others, is one of the strategic ways whereby China attempts to build up closer economic ties with the BRI states in a bid to counteract the risk of dwindling economic growth rate as well as excess production capacity.[1]

Invariably, state-controlled entities (SCEs) including sovereign wealth funds (SWFs) and state-owned enterprises (SOEs) are the main vehicles for foreign direct investments (FDIs). Under the BRI, it is the fact that connectivity is a prerequisite

[1] Ziqiang Wan and Shanmin Li, 'National Economic Security and The "Belt and Road" Initiative', in Lutz-Christian Wolff and Chao Xi (eds) *Legal Dimensions of China's Belt and Road Initiative* (Wolters Kluwer 2016).

[2] ibid.

[3] Reuters, 'After Piraeus Port, China's COSCO eyes Greek trains to build Europe hub – sources' (*Reuters*, 5 February 2016) <https://www.reuters.com/article/greece-china-port/after-piraeus-port-chinas-cosco-eyes-greek-trains-to-build-europe-hub-sources-idUSL8N14X17R>.

This chapter draws upon the author's original publication also available at https://www.transnational-dispute-management.com/journal-advance-publication-article.asp?key=1836. Reprinted by permission from Maris BV: Maris BV, *Transnational Dispute Management* (TDM, ISSN 1875-4120), "Port and Rail Investments: Reform of Chinese Regulations, Paradigm Shift of Chinese State-Controlled Entities and Global Freedom of Investments", Carlos K.L. Li, Copyright (2000). Please cite accordingly.

C. K. L. Li (✉)
Chinese University of Hong Kong, Shatin, NT, Hong Kong SAR, The People's Republic of China
e-mail: klcarlos@hotmail.com

Law Society of Hong Kong, Hong Kong, The People's Republic of China

J. Chaisse et al. (eds.), *Regulation of State-Controlled Enterprises*, International Law and the Global South, https://doi.org/10.1007/978-981-19-1368-6_29

component to bolster and sustain the investment and trade flows.[2] SCEs strategically direct substantial portion of their capitals to invest in port and rail infrastructures such as the port acquisition in Greece. With the inception of the railway infrastructure in Piraeus port, the transport network of Greece can now be extended from Piraeus to the Balkans and Central Europe.[3] In the circumstances, China will continue to put considerable amount of resources in port construction facilitation, land–water transportation channels and port cooperation in these BRI regions.[4]

In order to facilitate FDIs in port and rail infrastructures in BRI countries that are regarded as the key areas of future economic growth, China has been continually striving for changing its paradigms in the SCEs and their related regulations. That said, albeit the sheer benefits of freedom of investment brought to local economies, some host states, especially those developed states such as the US, do not necessarily welcome all foreign infrastructure investments in their territories for the reason of their great concern over national security and public interest. In the circumstances, this paper will look into three key issues, i.e., (1) what the reform of Chinese regulations on port and rail FDIs would be, (2) to what extent the paradigm shift of Chinese SCEs is made toward international standards and (3) how is the interaction of SCEs with the host states such as the US, EU and five selected BRI states including Turkey, Djibouti, Nigeria, Pakistan and Sri Lanka in terms of the World Trade Organization's (WTO) GATS Mode 3, International Monetary Fund's (IMF) Santiago Principles and various OECD Guidelines and national security measures?

2 Reform of Chinese Regulations on Port and Rail FDIs

By and large, the reform of Chinese regulations relating to outbound port and rail FDIs is manifested in several aspects.

2.1 Toward a More Simplified and Efficient Outbound FDIs Regime

Inefficient administrative procedures are the chronic hurdles to Chinese outbound FDIs in the sense that SCEs consume a lot of time to obtain the necessary approvals from the corresponding authorities that could be likely otherwise saved if an efficient mechanism was in place. In China, four main administrative and regulatory authorities are designated to take charge of outbound FDIs. They are the National Development and Reform commission (NDRC), the Ministry of Commerce (MOFCOM), the State Administration of Foreign Exchange (SAFE) and the State-owned Assets

[4] National Development and Reform Commission, Ministry of Foreign Affairs, and Ministry of Commerce of the People's Republic of China, with State Council authorization, 'Vision and Actions on Jointly Building Silk Road Economic Belt and 21st Century Maritime Silk Road' (March 2015).

Supervision and Administration Commission (SASAC).[5] In the event that SCEs find the suitable target companies in foreign jurisdictions, they are required to undergo four steps for regulatory verification, specifically (1) NDRC pre-approval, (2) NDRC approval, (3) MOFCOM approval and (4) SAFE registration.[6]

Under the rapidly changing business environment, such a slow approval mechanism is attributed to make Chinese bids on FDIs less competitive than those tendered by other bidders. In the circumstances, in Shanghai Free Trade Zone (FTZ), a specialized record-filing procedure subject to Shanghai municipal-level regulatory approval has been adopted on an experimental basis.[7] In 2014, other nationwide regulatory procedures such as the MOFCOM Administrative Measures on Overseas Investments,[8] the NDRC Measures for the Administration of Approval and Filing of Outbound Investment Projects[9] and the Catalogue of Investment Projects Subject to Governmental Approval (2014 Version) were also established for the sake of simplifying the application procedures.[10] To further deepen the reform in outbound FDIs regimes, the pre-signing of investment agreements has been set up. In other words, SCEs are allowed to sign investment agreements in advance so far as the agreements stipulate that the agreements will become effective only after the approval documents have been obtained or the notice of filing has been issued by the NDRC.[11]

In the BRI context, apart from enhancing the efficiency of the approval procedures, collaboration with other states in the region also plays a critical role in fostering the atmosphere of freedom of investments for which one of the measures is to set up BRI-based free trade areas (FTAs). In brief, the advantages of FTAs over WTO mechanism include, but are not limited to, (1) the regional free trades among trading partners such as ASEAN members,[12] (2) quicker negotiation process among trading members in FTAs than the multilateral process in WTO,[13] (3) more trade and investment activities in developing countries[14] and (4) the discussion of specific issues that cannot be tabled on the multilateral level of WTO.[15]

---

[5] Interim Measures on the Administration of Overseas State-owned Properties of Central Enterprises, (effective on 1 July 2011).

[6] Henry Ningning Huang and Terri Cheyue Tian, '"One Belt, One Road" And China's Outbound Investment Regime' in Wolff and Xi (n 2).

[7] Arts 4–7, Administrative Measures on Record Filing of Outbound Investment Projects of China (Shanghai) Pilot Free Trade Zone (effective on 1 October 2013).

[8] The Administrative Measures on Overseas Investments (effective since 6 October 2014).

[9] The Measures for the Administration of Approval and Filing of Outbound Investment Projects (effective since 27 December 2014).

[10] The Catalogue of Investment Projects Subject to Government Approval (2014 Version) (effective since 31 October 2014).

[11] Art 25, New NDRC Measures.

[12] Simon Lester, Bryan Mercurio and Arwel Davies, 'World Trade Law: Text, Materials and Commentary' (2nd end, Hart Publishing 2012), 332.

[13] ibid.

[14] ibid.

[15] ibid.

In the BRI-based FTAs, China can take an initiative to position itself as the founding and key member with its advantages over other members in terms of its tremendous imports from the FTAs and the huge exports to other member countries from its manufacturing center.[16] With a greater policy coordination, China can even have further collaborations with other member states on other value-added sectors such as opening FDIs and financial integration.[17] Indeed, the BRI-based FTAs may cover Association of Southeast Asian Nations (ASEAN), Gulf Cooperation Council (GCC), Eurasian Economic Union (EAEU), Economic Community of West African States (ECOWAS) and European Union (EU). In the premises, China can leverage the synergy brought about by the FTAs to achieve further deregulation, red-tape reduction and liberalization of prices for goods and services.[18]

2.2 *Toward a More Open Inbound FDIs Regime Enhancing Reciprocal Market Access*

At the international level, Table 1 shows the horizontal commitments of China in the hard law of WTO's GATS Mode 3, stating that foreign invested enterprises include foreign capital enterprises and joint venture enterprises for which the latter also comprises equity joint ventures and contractual joint ventures. Foreign investors should not invest less than 25% of the registered capital in the joint venture. However, China has made no commitment to the establishment of branches but permitted to set up representative offices that cannot engage in any profit-making activities. Further, the conditions of ownership, operation and scope of activities as set forth in the contractual or shareholder agreement or license establishing or authorizing the operation or supply of services should not be made more restrictive than they exist at the time of China 's accession to the WTO. Furthermore, in transport sector, there is no specific commitments made to both port services and rail transport services.

In relation to such soft laws as various Organization for Economic Cooperation and Development (OECD) guidelines, China is not yet a country member of OECD Declaration and Decision on International Investment and Multinational Enterprises (OECD Declaration) but a key partner member playing an essential role in the review programs.

At the national level, it has been seen that China has pursued further liberalization by means of setting up FTZs. Traditionally, Chinese government provided subsidies to protect their SOEs in the course of opening-up part of the domestic

[16] The Economist, 'Trade, at what price?' (The Economist, 2 April 2016) <https://www.economist.com/news/united-states/21695855-americas-economy-benefits-hugely-trade-its-costs-have-been-amplied-policy> accessed 5 September 2017.

[17] Carolyn Dong, 'One belt one road – China's new outbound trade initiative. Regulatory Update' (*DLA Paper*, 18 January 2016) <https://www.dlapiper.com/en/singapore/insights/publications/2016/01/chinas-new-outbound-trade-initiative/>.

[18] Sridhar Kanthadai, "Why China needs to champion free trade" (Chinadaily USA, 17 March 2016) <http://www.chinadaily.com.cn/opinion/2016-03/17/content_23903327.htm>.

industries.[19] However, such a protection measure led to corruption and inequitable income distribution. To rectify the side effect, the Chinese government has further deepened the reform in the administrative mechanism and set up the first FTZs in Shanghai to reach a fully liberalized market except those sensitive markets pertaining to national defense and security. Subsequently, the FTZs in Fujian, Guangdong and Fujian followed.

Apart from FTZs, China announced to further open up its financial industry in April 2018, and the related measures include the relaxation of foreign share ownership restriction in the banking, insurance and securities sectors.[20] In March 2019, the Chinese government promulgated a new foreign investment law to "*further expand opening-up, vigorously promote foreign investment, protect the legitimate rights and interests of foreign investors, standardize the management of foreign investment, impel the formation of a new pattern of all-round opening-up and boost the sound development of the socialist market economy*".[21] In the premises, the new laws and measures of China not only liberalize the local market to attract inbound FDIs but also facilitate fair and reciprocal market access of outbound FDIs to foreign jurisdictions.

2.3 *Toward a More Decentralized and Flexible Chinese Port Governance*

To keep pace with the outbound port and rail FDIs, there are three phrases in Chinese port governance reforms.[22] The first phrase started in 1979 and ended in 1984 during which all the functions of port governance were centralized in the hands of the Chinese government. From 1984 to 2004, the second phrase shifted from centralization to decentralization where the local port authorities acted as both a regulator and a SOE. It came to the third phrase in 2004 when the 2004 Port Law and the "Rules on Port Operation and Management" were promulgated by which the port authority was split into Port Administration Bureau and port business enterprises.[23] Under

---

[19] Justin Yifu Lin, 'One Belt and One Road" and Free Trade Zones – China's New Opening-up Initiatives' (the speech at the Free Trade Zones and New Openness in China Summit Forum organized by the School of International Business Administration, Shanghai University of Finance and Economics on 15 May 2015).

[20] Deloitte, 'Chinese Financial Industry Updates: Opportunities and Challenges to Foreign Institutions as Chinese Financial Industry Opens Further' (2018) <https://www2.deloitte.com/content/dam/Deloitte/cn/Documents/risk/deloitte-cn-ra-china-financial-industry-opening-en-180924.pdf>.

[21] Art 1 of Foreign Investment Law of the People's Republic of China adopted at the Second Session of the 13th National People's Congress (15 March 2019) <http://www.fdi.gov.cn/1800000121_39_4872_0_7.html>.

[22] Kevin Cullinane, Teng-Fei Wang, 'Port governance in China' (2006) 17 Research in Transportation Economics 331–356.

[23] Mary R. Brooks & Kevin Cullinane, 'Devolution, Port Governance and Port Performance' (2007) 17 Research in Transportation Economics 237.

such a port governance reform, port business enterprises as a kind of SOEs are said to be corporations or vehicles investing in ports and rail infrastructures literally for commercial purposes only.

In the third phrase, China has undertaken an incremental port governance evolution so that local or provincial port administrative bureaus can flexibly adjust their rules and regulations, and in the meanwhile, port business entities are able to incorporate those new rules and regulations in their FDIs strategies.[24] Indeed, under the 13th Five-Year Plan (2016–2020), both port administrative bureaus and port business entities are ordered to reinforce port integration and cooperation and strengthen multi-modal transport system linking ports to hinterland via railway system.

3 Paradigm Shift of SCEs Toward Higher Transparency and Greater Accountability

Three core features of a SCE encompass that (1) it is wholly owned and controlled directly or indirectly by the foreign sovereign, (2) it is organized under the laws of the foreign sovereign by which it is owned and (3) it has its net earnings credited to its own account or to the accounts of the foreign sovereign, with no portion inuring to the benefit of any private person.[25] In response to port and rail FDIs by SCEs allegedly with various degree of political elements, different host states carry out various mechanisms subject to their evaluation on where the balance point between freedom of investment and national security would be. From the perspectives of China, as it is well known that port and rail infrastructures are regarded as sensitive and strategic FDIs, Chinese SCEs should keep reforming themselves to the extent that their corporate paradigm shifts can be proven to ease the concern of the host states over their national security. In the premises, both Chinese SWFs and SOEs may procedurally comply with the relevant international regulations such as IMF's Santiago Principles and OECD's Guidelines on Corporate Governance of SOEs, whereas they may also substantively reform their corporate structures and governance such as privatization and collaboration with private sectors like public–private partnership (PPP) so as to convince the host states to believe that the intent of their infrastructure investments is solely for commercial purpose rather than political purpose.

[24] Theo Notteboom and Zhongzhen Yang, 'Port governance in China since 2004: Institutional layering and the growing impact of broader policies' (2017) 22 Research in Transportation Business & Management 184–200.

[25] Li and Chaisse (n 1).

3.1 *Sovereign Wealth Funds (SWFs)*

In China, China Investment Corporation (CIC) is the Chinese SWF, and its portfolio of investments also extend to cover port and rail investments in other jurisdictions. For instance, CIC purchased a 20% share in the Port of Melbourne in 2016[26] and, in collaboration with Cosco and China Merchants, acquired Kumport Terminal in Turkey.[27] Nevertheless, owing to the fact that infrastructures are regarded as sensitive investments, CIC's investment decisions are always criticized for political purposes.[28]

In theory, the perceived risks of SWFs comprise national security, systemic stability affecting consumer confidence and market imperfections, abuse of voting power, political interference and political leveraging.[29] Considering both Chinese SWFs and SOEs, Backer[30] suggested they have three critical features such as (1) corporate autonomy is not applicable to Chinese SWFs and SOEs with their close relationship with the Chinese Communist Party (CCP), (2) SWFs and SOEs may be functionally autonomous but subject to overall direction of the CCP and (3) SWFs and SOEs are the extension of power of CCP with the sole direction to attain the same set of objectives. In respect of its organizational structure, CIC is found under SASAC and directly reports to the State Council. As a result, CIC's investment planning and decisions are in effect subject to the overall direction of the CCP and state policy.

To ease the concern of host states over CIC's FDIs, CIC has complied with various international regulations and one of which is the IMF's Santiago Principles (or the 24 Generally Accepted Principles and Practices (GAAP)) to ensure that all SWFs are properly established and their investments are made on an objective economic and financial basis.[31] Indeed, the Santiago Principles have four guiding objectives including to (1) help maintain a stable global financial system and free flow of capital and investment, (2) comply with all applicable regulatory and disclosure requirements in the countries in which they invest, (3) invest on the basis of economic and financial risk and return-related consideration and (4) have in place a transparent

---

[26] Xinhua, 'Chinese investment fund secures 20 percent of Australia's busiest port' (20 September 2016) <http://en.chinagate.cn/2016-09/20/content_39332606.htm>.

[27] LAW360, 'Chinese Investor Group Pays $920M For Turkish Port Terminal' (27 September 2015) <https://www.law360.com/articles/703950/chinese-investor-group-pays-920m-for-turkish-port-terminal>.

[28] Nancy Brune, 'SWFs: Passive Investors or National Security threat?' in Al Mehaiza Myrna (ed), *The Impact of the Growth of Sovereign Wealth Funds* (Arab Financial Forum 2009) 73.

[29] David Llewellyn, 'The Economic Rationale for Financial Regulation' FSA Occasional Paper Series 1 (April 1999), 9–10.

[30] Larry Cata Backer, 'Sovereign Investing in Times of Crisis: Global Regulation of Sovereign Wealth Funds, State Owned Enterprises and the Chinese Experience' (2009) 19 (1), 'Transnational Law & Contemporary Problems' 101–293.

[31] International Working Group of Sovereign Wealth Funds, 'SWFs Generally Accepted Principles and Practices "Santiago Principles"' (October 2008).

and sound governance structure that provides for adequate operational controls, risk management and accountability.[32]

To achieve these objectives, firstly, CIC becomes a charter member of the International Forum of Sovereign Wealth Funds (Forum), implementing the Santiago Principles in good faith.[33] Secondly, CIC actively participates in the Forum such as by taking part in deliberation on the Forum's governance and development and the drafting of the Santiago principles.[34] Thirdly, the CIC cooperates with other SWFs to engage in foreign investment, and it has always sustained a high degree of transparency by disclosing key operational and management information on corporate governance, investment strategies and philosophies, major investment activities, executive personal changes and investment performance in various channels.[35] In 2015, the result of self-assessment showed that CIC features its adherence to the Santiago Principles to assure its investment management and policy in openness and transparency.

Nonetheless, despite the fact that GAPP 19 emphasizes on commercial motives by stating that "*the SWF's investment decisions should aim to maximize risk-adjusted financial returns in a manner consistent with its investment policy, and based on economic and financial grounds*", it does not explicitly stipulate a pledge not to invest for political purposes. To address this concern, CIC should show more pragmatic evidence to prove that their investment decisions are aligned with GAPP 19. In the circumstances, CIC has undertaken some substantive moves, which include the recent appointment of chairman who is an ex-chairman of state-owned Bank of Communication with the minimal political connection comparing to both of his predecessors[36] and the collaboration with private financial institutions such as HSBC and the British private equity firm to set up a fund investing in potential UK companies with close ties with China.[37] In spite of piecemeal changes, the potential synergy generated could more or less be able to mitigate the perceived risk of political purposes and lead CIC toward more commercial nature.

---

[32] ibid.

[33] <www.china-inv.cn/en/>.

[34] ibid.

[35] IFSWF, 'Implementing the Santiago Principles: 12 Case Studies from demonstrating commitment to creating value'.

[36] Laura He and William Zheng, "Who is the new boss of China's US$941 billion sovereign wealth fund?" (South China Morning Post, 2 April 2019): <https://www.scmp.com/business/china-business/article/3004356/who-new-boss-chinas-us941-billion-sovereign-wealth-fund>.

[37] Chad Bray, "HSBC and Chinese sovereign wealth fund prepare to make 1 billion pound bet on British companies" (*South China Morning Post*, 16 November 2018): <https://www.scmp.com/business/banking-finance/article/2173544/hsbc-and-chinese-sovereign-wealth-fund-prepare-make-ps1>.

3.2 State-owned Enterprises (SOEs)

A SOE refers to a company over which the state has significant control, through full, majority or significant minority ownership.[38] In the context of China, Chinese SOEs are the main vehicles for overseas transport infrastructure projects whereby, for instance, Cosco signed an equity transfer agreement with Greece to buy the stakes in Piraeus port in 2016.[39] However, Chinese SOEs are regarded as investment vehicles substantially controlled by the Chinese government. To rectify this perception, SOEs have undertaken various measures such as the compliance with the OECD Guidelines on Corporate Governance.

The OECD Guidelines on Corporate Governance aim to (1) professionalize the state as an owner, (2) make SOEs operate with similar efficiency, transparency and accountability as good practice private enterprises and (3) ensure that competition between SOEs and private enterprises, where such occurs, is conducted on a level playing field.[40] To attain these aims, Chinese SOEs should always act in the best interest of the general public and should disclose the objectives and rationales for state ownership subject to a periodical review.[41] Also, they should act as an informed and active owners to ensure the overall corporate governance executed in a transparent and accountable manner.[42] A legal and regulatory framework should be established where SOEs can carry out economic activities in a level playing field with other private companies.[43] Further, Chinese SOEs should also retain high transparency subject to the same accounting, disclosure, compliance and auditing standard as listed companies.[44]

Similar to other Chinese SOEs, Cosco, China Merchants and COPHC are also thought to have undertaken the process of SOEs reform in a gradualist and staged approach. Despite this, politics is still a key ingredient in the corporate governance of OECD.[45] The SASAC has all along been retaining direct or indirect control over Chinese SOEs like a shadow director and regulator even after the modernization and reforms. The Law on State-owned Assets of Enterprises (SOAE) confers on SASAC wide discretionary power to control the board, make policies and nominate

---

38 Robert M. Kimmitt, 'Public Footprints in Private Markets: Sovereign Wealth Funds and the World Economy (*Foreign* Affairs, Jan/Feb, 2008) <https://www.foreignaffairs.com/articles/2008-01-01/public-footprints-private-markets>.

39 Xinhua, 'China Cosco Shipping acquires majority stake in Greek port to boost economy' (*Xinhua*, 11 August 2016) <http://www.chinadaily.com.cn/business/2016-08/11/content_26431003.htm>.

40 OECD, 'OECD Guidelines on Corporate Governance of State-owned Enterprises' (2015 edn).

41 ibid.

42 ibid.

43 ibid.

44 ibid.

45 Daniel Ho and Angus Young, 'China's Experience in Reforming its State-owned Enterprises: something new, something old and something Chinese?' (April 2013) 2(4) International Journal of Economy, Management and Social Sciences 84–90.

the appointment of the board of directors that appear to go against the direction of the OECD Guidelines.[46]

To further reform SOEs, China is undertaking the process of privatizing SOEs to reduce their dependence on the government and achieve a greater efficiency with their decision-making procedures based on market and economic considerations.[47] Even though some critics argue that the privatized SOEs can still enjoy more favorable subsidies and cheap financing than private entities, at least it can be seen that the reform on Chinese SOEs is on the right direction with a gradual process.

4 Interaction of Chinese SCEs with the US, EU and BRI States

Although home states are concerned about their national security, they recognize the great contributions of FDIs made to local economies. In the premises, the states receiving FDIs should comply with both WTO's GATS Mode 3 as a hard law and the related OECD guidelines as soft laws in order to show their commitments to achieving the goal of maintaining freedom of investment that has taken account into national security and public interest.

For WTO's GATS Mode 3, the positive list approach is used in the sense that countries put their horizontal commitments and/or sector-specific commitments to the schedule of commitment. In other words, no commitments are made if they do not insert any commitments into the schedule. Concerning maritime transport sector, it has four pillars where port services belong to the third pillar "*Access to and use of port facilities, such as pilotage, towing and tug assistance, provisioning, garbage collection, port captain's services and anchorage. Negotiations deal with rights of foreign ships to gain access to these services without discrimination*".[48] In the schedule of commitment, the W120 and UNCPC of port service are 11-A-F Supporting services for maritime transport and 74,510, respectively.[49]

[46] ibid.

[47] Ann Harrison, Marshall W. Meyer, Will Wang, Linda Zhao and Minyuan Zhao, "Changing the tiger's stripes: Refrom of Chinese state-owned enterprises in the penumbra of the state" (17 June 2019) CEPR Policy Portal <https://voxeu.org/>.

[48] 'Press Brief: Maritime Transport', <https://www.wto.org/english/thewto_e/minist_e/min96_e/maritime.htm> accessed 5 September 2017.

[49] NCPC Descriptions of The GATS Sectoral Classification List Entries: <http://db2.wtocenter.org.tw/W120_Detail.aspx?ID=147>/74,510 Port and waterway operation services (excl. cargo handling): "Port operation services such as wharves, docks, piers, quays and other marine terminal facilities related services, including passenger terminal services in connection with marine transportation, on a fee or contract basis, and operating and maintenance services of boat, barge and ship canals, of canalized rivers and of other artificial inland waterways. Also included here are services of locks, boat lifts, weirs, sluices and towing services on canals other than by tugboat, e.g. by tractors or locomotives on the towpath. Exclusions: (1) Stevedoring services are classified in

OECD Declaration and Decisions on International Investment and Multinational Enterprises ("OECD Declaration") was adopted in 1976, consisting of the Guidelines for Multinational Enterprises, national treatment, conflicting requirements and international investment incentives and disincentives. It is a policy commitment made by adhering states to provide a transparent and open environment for international investment that can positively contribute to the local economic and social progress.

Considering the concern over excess national security that may suppress the freedom of investment, OECD issued the Guidelines for Recipient Country Investment Policies Relating to National Security in 2009, recommending that recipient countries should adhere to the principles of non-discrimination, transparency of policies and predictability of outcomes, proportionality of measures and accountability of implementing authorities for their investment policies introduced to safeguard national security. Further, OECD formulates general investment policy principles for countries receiving SWF investment[50] whereby recipient countries should not disguise national security to deter foreign investment and discriminate investors in like situations. Where national security is a real concern to recipient countries, investment safeguards imposed must be transparent, predictable, proportional to national security risks and subject to accountability in the application.

4.1 The United States

4.1.1 WTO's GATS Mode 3

Table 1 shows that the US provides neither horizontal commitment nor specific commitment relating to port services at all, but no restriction is made at the same time. Regarding rail transport including both passenger and freight transportation except high-speed rail, commerce presence only stipulates that foreign investors are required to incorporate in Vermont or other adjacent state in order to directly or indirectly own the stock of any railroad company incorporated in Vermont. In other words, no specific commitment is made to rail transport sector save as an investment is undertaken in Vermont.

---

subclass 74,110 (Container handling services), if for containerized freight, and in 74,190 (Other cargo handling services), if for non-containerized freight. (2) Port storage and warehousing services are classified in group 742 (Storage and warehousing services) and (3) Tugboat-assisted docking and towing services are classified in subclass/74,520 (Pilotage and berthing services)".

[50] OECD, 'Sovereign Wealth Funds and Recipient Countries – Working together to maintain and expand freedom of investment' (11 October 2008) <http://www.oecd.org/daf/inv/investment-policy/41456730.pdf>.

4.1.2 OECD Guidelines

The US is a member country of OECD Declaration, and it is recommended to abide by various OECD Guidelines in order to provide a transparent and open environment for international investment.

4.1.3 Freedom of Investment/National Security

The United States is very anxious about the hostile acquisitions especially some iconic national undertakings acquired by foreign SOEs such as the Dubai Ports World (DP World) controversy in 2006.[51] Concerning the Dubai port deal, DP World, a state-owned enterprise in the United Arab Emirates (UAE) successfully acquired the London-based Peninsular and Oriental (P&O) Steam Navigation Company, and as part of the deal, DP World attained the right to operate six major US ports such as the terminals in Philadelphia and New Orleans. Although the Committee on Foreign Investment in the United States (CFIUS) approved the acquisition, many lawmakers argued that the takeover by the UAE's SOE would compromise the national security since two of the 911 hijackers came from the UAE that was one of the three nations to recognize the Taliban's regime in Afghanistan.[52] Eventually, DP World dropped out of the deal, bowing to the unrelenting political pressure.[53] For such national protectionism against port purchases by foreign SOEs, there are four main concerns, namely (1) non-commercial investment motives such as fear of state capitalism and economic espionage, (2) transparency concerns, (3) financial stability implications and (4) governance concern such as distortion of market disciplines and political interference.[54]

In the United States, CFIUS is responsible to review all foreign investments.[55] Following the saga of DP World, the Foreign Investment and National Security Act (FINSA) was enacted to codify the preexisting administrative procedures and add the new process therein. Furthermore, FINSA restructured CFIUS in the form of multi-agency including the Secretaries of the Treasury, Homeland Security, Commerce and so on. Under FINSA, CFIUS bears the legal duty to launch an investigation on any SWFs' transactions that may threaten the US national security or take full control of any iconic US infrastructures. In any transactions of foreign investment, CFIUS is vested with a power to negotiate and insert appropriate terms and conditions and

---

[51] Wan and Li (n 2).

[52] CNN, 'Key questions about the Dubai port deal' (*CNN*, 7 March 2006) <http://edition.cnn.com/2006/POLITICS/03/06/dubai.ports.qa/>.

[53] David E. Sanger, 'Under pressure, Dubai Company Drops Port Deal' (*New York Times*, 10 March 2016) <https://www.nytimes.com/2006/03/10/politics/under-pressure-dubai-company-drops-port-deal.html>.

[54] Julien Chaisse, *Legal Problems of Economic Globalisation – A Commentary on the Law and Practice* (Wolters Kluwer 2015).

[55] Cata Backer (n 31).

enforce them for the purpose of minimizing the potential threat to the US national security. Other acts such as Defense Production Act and Bank Holding Company are also examined to see whether any amendments are needed to counteract the risk brought about by the continued growth of SWFs.

In the wake of the stringent US national security review, although the robust growth in the global M&A market with the transaction value up to USD3.5tn worth of activity was recorded in 2018, Chinese investment in the US dramatically plummeted appropriately 95% from a record USD55.3bn in 2016 to only USD3bn.[56] Such an abrupt slump of the Chinese FDIs attributed to the change in the US regulations. In August 2018, the Foreign Investment Risk Review Modernization Act (FIRRMA) was promulgated to further extend the scope of the CFIUS's jurisdiction including the review on non-controlling investments by Chinese FDIs to US in high tech technology. Further, Bureau of Industry and Security (BIS) intended to make a negative list restricting Chinese investments that may include biotechnology, artificial intelligence (AI), robotics and even some critical infrastructures such as telecommunications, power generation, transport.[57] In addition to the recent US-China Trade War, it is likely that the US national security policy would continue to hamper Chinese SCIs investing in port and rail infrastructures in its territory.

4.2 The European Union

4.2.1 WTO's GATS Mode 3

According to Table 1, all member states except Cyprus, Spain, France, Hungary, Finland, Italy, Malta, Portugal, Poland and Slovenia have made full horizontal commitments to FDIs. As no member expresses any specific commitments to port services, foreign investors literally can invest in port services with no limitations on market access in the EU save as otherwise expressly provided by Cyprus, Spain, France, Hungary, Finland, Italy, Malta, Portugal, Poland and Slovenia in their horizontal commitments. For instances, Cyprus stipulates that foreign investors are required to obtain the permission of the Central Bank and their equity participation in all sectors/subsectors is normally limited up to 49% (30% in public companies; 40% in mutual funds). Corporate bodies have to be registered pursuant to the local company law. For Spain, prior authorization is required for investments made by foreign government, foreign public entities and/or companies controlled directly or indirectly by foreign governments.

Considering rail transport services, all member states except Hungary do not make any specific commitments to both passenger and freight rail transportation. Hungary stipulates that, in the event of commercial presence, services may be provided through a contract of concession granted by the state or the local authority.

[56] Mergermarket, '2018 Global M&A Report' (3 January 2019) <https://www.mergermarket.com/info/mergermarket-releases-2018-global-ma-report>.

[57] ibid.

4.2.2 OECD Guidelines

Twenty-three member states of the European Union are declaring countries of OECD Declaration, which are committed to providing an open and transparent environment for international investments and encouraging positive contribution to economic and social progress. They include Austria, Belgium, The Czech Republic, Denmark, Estonia, Finland, France, Germany, Greece, Hungary, Ireland, Italy, Latvia, Lithuania, Luxembourg, Netherlands, Poland, Portugal, Slovak Republic, Slovenia, Spain, Sweden, and the United Kingdom.

4.2.3 Freedom of Investment/National Security

Among others, Germany and France follow the US approach to regulate SWFs including CIC investing in their territories. In Germany, the German government takes on case-by-case approach to review and, if necessary, block any 25% or more acquisitions of German enterprises by foreign investors that may endanger the public order or national security.[58] In contrast, the French government enacted a new FDI law to require any investment subject to government review if foreign investors gain control of a firm, exceed 33% of total company's shares or establish the headquarters of their firms or branches thereof in France.[59]

Considering Chinese SOEs, the EU merger regulation is the maturely developed as to Chinese FDI transactions.[60] One of the jurisdictional issues of the EU Competition Law is how to characterize Chinese SOEs for which the EU would evaluate "*to what extent a Chinese SOE·is independent of other nation-level SOEs supervised or controlled by the SASAC or its regional equivalents. SASAC acts not only as a state shareholder but also exercises a significant degree of managerial control of the strategic corporate planning and evaluation process, as well as having a decisive say in major investment decision*".[61] In effect, as Chinese SOEs are concurrently controlled by SASAC and CCP, such an organizational structure always make them susceptible to Article 1(2) and (3) of the European Merger Regulation (EUMR).[62] In addition, even though a single SOE does not exceed the threshold for notification, if it is deemed as part of a group, the turnover should be calculated on the basis of a group rather than an individual. A SOE belongs to part of a group or links with other SOEs if, by reference to Article 5(4) of the EUMR, it directly or indirectly owns

[58] Nermina Biberovic, 'SWFs: Common European Approach Need of the Hour' (*Arab News*, 25 April 2008).

[59] American Chamber of Commerce in France, 'The French Investment Climate' <http://www.amchamfrance.org/theme1.php?idcontenu=107&idpage=15>.

[60] ibid.

[61] Richard Mcgregor, The Party: The Secret World of China's Communist Rulers (Great Britain: Allen Lane 2010).

[62] Mark Williams, 'Merger and Acquisition Control of China's Outward Investments' in Wolff and Xi (n 2).

more than half of the capital or business assets of other SOEs, or has more than half of the voting rights of other SOEs or has the power to appoint more than half of the member of boards or has the right to manage the internal affair of the undertaking.[63] In the light of this interpretation, it is anticipated that it is easy to see a single Chinese SOE's turnover hitting the threshold for notification. In Hinkley Point, the court held that SASAC controlled China General Nuclear Power Corporation (CGN), and this Chinese SOE did not act autonomously and independently but belonged to a group.[64] Therefore, it is likely to foresee that such national regulations would significantly hinder Chinese port and rail FDIs.

In fact, a recent survey reveals that the completed Chinese FDI transactions valued at only 17.3bn euros in 2018, representing more than 50% fall from the peak of 37bn euros in 2016.[65] Such a drastic drop attributes to the concern of the EU over national security relating to infrastructures, strategic assets, defense technology, the lack of reciprocity and fair competition, fear of being overtaken by China in term of technological leadership, etc.[66] In September 2018, a new legislation was even proposed to set up a Common European Framework for Screening FDIs. The European Commission aims to resort to the proposed legislation to protect strategic assets such as critical technologies, infrastructure or sensitive information that are essential to European security and public order.[67]

4.3 BRI: Turkey

4.3.1 WTO's GATS Mode 3

From Table 1, according to the Turkish GATS horizontal commitments, if foreign investment is made between $50,000 and $150 m by a foreign investment company, it is generally authorized by the General Directorate of Foreign Capital as long as the investment is conducive to the local economy. However, if foreign investment is over $150 m, it requires the approval of the Council of Ministers. Besides, if a new line of business is involved and participation or takeover of existing enterprises is undertaken, authorization is also required. In contrast, proposals of the same line of business are generally accepted and approved. Furthermore, administration of

[63] ibid.

[64] Case COMP/M.7850 EDF/CGN/NNB Group of Companies.

[65] The survey conducted by Germany's Mercator Institute for China Studies and the New York's Rhodium Group (RHG). *See* Reuters, 'Chinese FDI in Europe drops, investment screening will cut it more – Survey' (*Reu*ters Business News, 6 March 2019) <https://www.reuters.com/article/us-eu-china-fdi/chinese-fdi-in-europe-drops-investment-screening-will-cut-it-more-survey-idUSKCN1QN1T6>.

[66] Valbona Zeneli, 'Mapping China's Investments in Europe' (*The Diplomat*, 14 March 2019) <https://www.reuters.com/article/us-eu-china-fdi/chinese-fdi-in-europe-drops-investment-screening-will-cut-it-more-survey-idUSKCN1QN1T6>.

[67] ibid.

harbor, quay and railways is closed to private investment due to public monopolies. In relation to transport services, no specific commitment is made to port services, while commercial presence only states internal rail transportation is a public monopoly in rail transport services.

With regard to Chinese port and rail investments in Turkey, the General Directorate of Foreign Capital generally authorizes them if the value involved is between $50,000 and $150 m. If a foreign investment is over $150 m, the approval of the Council of Ministers is required. Port and rail investments in Turkey are of public monopolies, and no other specific commitments are made regarding them. Therefore, despite no specific commitments, no restrictions are imposed on the admission of Chinese SCEs investing in Turkey's local port and rail investments.

4.3.2 OECD Guidelines

Turkey is a declaring country committed to providing an open and transparent environment for international investments and encouraging positive contribution to economic and social progress through various OECD guidelines.

4.3.3 Freedom of Investment/National Security

Regarding the terminal Kumport in Turkey, CIC, China Merchant and Cosco formed a joint venture company called Euro-Asia Oceangate to invest $940.2 M to buy 64.5% stake in Fina Liman, which was the holding company for Kumport in Turkey.[68] In the light of this transaction, as the value of this port purchase is over $150 M, it is likely that the approval of the Council of Ministers was required at that time. Also, such an acquisition merely engaged in the same line of business; therefore, its proposal was generally approved.

4.4 BRI: Nigeria

4.4.1 WTO's GATS Mode 3

From Table 1, Nigeria's GATS horizontal commitments state that commercial presence requires that foreign service providers are required to incorporate or establish the business locally in accordance with the relevant provisions of Nigerian Laws. Nevertheless, no specific commitments are made regarding port and rail sectors.

[68] Seatrade Maritime News, 'Cosco Pacific in jv to buy into Turkey's Kumport Terminal' (17 September 2015) <http://www.seatrade-maritime.com/news/asia/cosco-pacific-in-jv-to-buy-into-turkeys-kumport-terminal.html>.

If Chinese SCEs invest in port and rail infrastructures in Nigeria, they are required to incorporate or establish the local business in accordance with the relevant provisions of Nigerian Laws. Despite no specific commitments, no restrictions are imposed to the admission of Chinese SCEs investing in Nigeria's local port and rail investments.

4.4.2 OECD Guidelines

Nigeria is not a declaring member of OECD Declaration.

4.4.3 Freedom of Investment/National Security

In 2010, China Merchants and the China-Africa Development Fund bought 47.5% stake in Tin-Can Container Terminal in Nigeria (TICT) in Lagos of Nigeria.[69] In the light of this transaction, the Chinese SOEs should comply with Nigerian laws to establish their port and rail businesses in Lagos.

4.5 BRI: Djibouti

4.5.1 WTO's GATS Mode 3

From Table 1, neither horizontal nor specific commitment as to port and rail sectors is found in Djibouti's GATS schedule of commitments. Despite no commitments made by Djibouti, no restrictions are imposed to the admission of Chinese SCEs investing in Djibouti's local port and rail investments.

4.5.2 OECD Guidelines

Djibouti is not a declaring member of OECD Declaration.

[69] World Cargo News, 'Chinese firms buy Zim's Lagos terminal stake' (8 November 2010) <http://www.seatrade-maritime.com/news/asia/China-Merchants-buys-into-Lagos-container-terminal.html>.

4.5.3 Freedom of Investment/National Security

In 2013, China Merchants paid US185m to acquire 23.5% share in Port de Djibouti in Djibouti.[70]

4.6 *BRI: Pakistan*

4.6.1 WTO's GATS Mode 3

From Table 1, pursuant to Pakistani GATS commitments under commercial presence, except representative offices, the commitments are subject to incorporation in Pakistan with maximum 51% foreign equity participation unless a different percentage is inscribed against a particular sector or subsector. For representative offices, all their expenses shall be met by remittances from aboard and their activities are restricted to liaison work or representing the interest of the parent company aboard. Nevertheless, no specific commitments are made to port and rail sectors.

Chinese SCEs investing in port and rail infrastructures in Pakistan are required to incorporate an undertaking in Pakistan with maximum 51% shares. Despite this, no other restrictions are imposed to the admission of Chinese SCEs in Pakistani local port and rail investments.

4.6.2 OECD Guidelines

Pakistan is not a declaring member of OECD Declaration.

4.6.3 Freedom of Investment/National Security

Chinese Overseas Port Holdings Company (COPHCL), a Chinese SOE, has been granted to take control of and operate Gwadar Port in Pakistan for 40 years, marking a milestone in the implementation phase of the China-Pakistan Economic Corridor (CPEC) under the BRI.[71] COPHCL sets up a branch company of COPHC Pakistan and has registered its regional office in Pakistan.[72]

---

[70] Port Technology, 'China Merchants invest in African Port of Djibouti' (4 January 2013) <https://www.porttechnology.org/news/china_merchants_invests_in_african_port_of_djibouti>.

[71] Ankit Panda, 'Chinese State Firm Takes Control of Strategically Vital Gwadar Port: A Chinese state-owned firm officially signed a multi-decade lease for control of the Gwadar Port free-trade zone' (*The Diplomat*, 13 November 2015) <https://thediplomat.com/2015/11/chinese-state-firm-takes-control-of-strategically-vital-gwadar-port/>.

[72] China Overseas Ports Holding Company Pakistan (Pvt.) Ltd.

4.7 *BRI: Sri Lanka*

4.7.1 WTO's GATS Mode 3

From Table 1, Sri Lanka's GATS's commitments under commercial presence prescribe that foreign investors may invest in any sector of the economy except money lending, pawn brokering, retail trade with a capital less than US$1 m, personal services business other than export of tourism and coasting fishing. The applicable foreign investment law is the Greater Colombo Economic Commission Law. The Board of Investment of Sri Lanka (BOISL) is responsible for the approval and facilitation of foreign investment throughout the country except banking, financial institutions, insurance, trading services on the Colombo Stock Exchange, air transportation, coastal shipping, branch or liaison office of companies incorporated outside Sri Lanka and Lotteries. If foreign investment acquires up to 40% of equity of a business including construction and residential building, mass transportation, telecommunications, mass communications, education, professional services, freight forwarding, travel agencies and shipping agencies, it will be automatically approved by the BOISL. Otherwise, foreign investment in excess of 40% up to 100% will be approved by the BOISL on a case-by-case basis in consultation with the relevant state agencies. For joint venture, if it involves a public sector enterprise or a government undertaking, preference will be given to foreign entities that offer the best terms for transfer of technology.

Chinese SCEs can invest in port and rail infrastructures in Sri Lanka, which are not under the list of exceptions. Unlike mass transportation, freight forwarding or shipping agencies that may get the automatic approval from BOISL under 40% acquisition of shares, port and rail investments still must get the approval, either automatic or case-by-case, from BOISL. For any transactions, the applicable foreign investment law is the Greater Colombo Economic Commission Law. If a public sector companies engage in joint venture, foreign entities that can offer the best terms for transfer of technology will be preferred. Overall, no restrictions are imposed to the admission of Chinese SCEs investing in local port and rail infrastructures.

4.7.2 OECD Guidelines

Sri Lanka is not a declaring member of OECD Declaration.

4.7.3 Freedom of Investment/National Security

In 2001, China Merchants, Aitken Spence Plc and Sri Lanka Ports Authority (SLPA) formed a joint venture, China International Container Terminal (CICT), to operate the Colombo South Terminal in Sri Lanka.[73] The value of total investment exceeded US500m for which China Merchant holds 55% of CICT, Aitken Spence Plc holds 30%, and SLPA holds 15%. In this transaction, the Chinese SOE should get the approval from BOISL for its investment in CICT, and the governing law is the Greater Colombo Economic Commission Law.

5 Conclusion

In the light of the global market access for Chinese port and rail FDIs, the new phenomenon is likely that the developed states such as the US and EU generally adopt protectionism to ward off foreign infrastructure investments from China, whereas the less developed states such as the five selected BRI states including Turkey, Nigeria, Djibouti, Pakistan and Sri Lanka are more poised to freedom of investments even though they may neither specify their commitments on WTO's GATS nor be a member country of OECD Declaration. In response to this new phenomenon, China has carried out reforms on its regulations to ease the administrative process of FDIs. These reforms include (1) a more simplified and efficient outbound FDIs regime, (2) a more open inbound FDIs regime enhancing reciprocal market access and (3) a more decentralized and flexible Chinese port governance. Apart from FDIs regulations, Chinese SCEs also abide by IMF's Santiago Principles, OECD Guidelines on Corporate Governance of SOEs and some private practices to approach toward higher transparency and greater accountability.

Given that the attitude toward Chinese port and rail FDIs is subject to the national policies and regulations of host states, what China may do is to keep reforming its regulations and shifting its paradigms of SCEs in a bid to attain the fair reciprocal market access to other jurisdictions such as the US and EU. In the circumstances, on one hand, China should maintain the preexisting freedom of investment in the BRI states that are receiving Chinese FDIs and take the relevant measures in an attempt to foster such freedom of investment in other BRI states which have yet to allow port and rail FDIs from China. On the other hand, China should continuously reform its relevant regulations and SCEs so as to prove to other developed states adopting protectionism that it has procedurally and substantively complied with international standards which, however, may take time.

[73] Ministry of Foreign Affairs Sir Lanka, 'Sri Lanka enters into a US$500 million BOT agreement with China Merchants Holdings to upgrade Colombo South Container Terminal' <https://www.mfa.gov.lk/si/2964-sri-lanka-enters-in-to-a-us500-million-bot-agreement-with-china-merchants-holdings-to-upgrade-colombo-south-container-terminal/>.

Appendix

See Table 1.

Table 1 GATS: Sector/subsector-specific commitments (Maritime transport services (port services are included), rail transport services) and limitation on market access (Mode 3: commercial presence)

Country	Sector or subsector	Limitations on market access
China	Horizontal commitments	• (3) In China, foreign invested enterprises include foreign capital enterprises (also referred to as wholly foreign-owned enterprises) and joint venture enterprises, and there are two types of joint venture enterprises: equity joint ventures and contractual joint ventures • The proportion of foreign investment in an equity joint venture shall be no less than 25% of the registered capital of the joint venture • The establishment of branches by foreign enterprises is unbound, unless otherwise indicated in specific subsectors, as the laws and regulations on branches of foreign enterprises are under formulation • Representative offices of foreign enterprises are permitted to be established in China, but they shall not engage in any profit-making activities except for the representative offices under CPC 861, 862, 863, 865 in the sectoral specific commitments • The conditions of ownership, operation and scope of activities, as set out in the respective contractual or shareholder agreement or in a license establishing or authorizing the operation or supply of services by an existing foreign service supplier, will not be made more restrictive than they exist as of the date of China's accession to the WTO
	11. Transport services A. Maritime transport services • International transport (freight and passengers) (CPC 7211 and 7212 less cabotage transport services) E. Rail transport service	• (3) (a) Establishment of registered companies for the purpose of operating a fleet under the national flag of the People's Republic of China: – Foreign service suppliers are permitted to establish joint venture shipping companies – Foreign investment shall not exceed 49% of the total registered capital of the joint venture – The chairman of board of directors and the general manager of the joint venture shall be appointed by the Chinese side • (3) (b) Other forms of commercial presence for the supply of international maritime transport services: Unbound • NIL

(continued)

Table 1 (continued)

Country	Sector or subsector	Limitations on market access
Djibouti	None	None
Nigeria	Horizontal commitments	• (3) Commercial presence requires that foreign service providers incorporate or establish the business locally in accordance with the relevant provisions of Nigerian Laws and, where applicable, regulations particularly with respect to land and building acquisition, lease rental, etc. This requirement operates on a non-discriminatory basis • Foreign enterprises with investment in Nigeria have the same rights and responsibilities as domestic enterprises and could transfer abroad their profits in accordance with the existing regulations
	11. Transport services • A. Maritime transport services – (b) Foreign transportation (cabotage is excluded) (CPC 7212) – (c) Rental vessels with crew (CPC 7213) – (d) Maintenance and repair of vessels (CPC 8868) • E. Rail transport services – (D) Maintenance and repair of rail transport equipment	• (3) None • (3) Unbound • (3) None • (3) None
Pakistan	Horizontal commitments	• (3) (i): Except in the case of representative offices where specifically provided for in this schedule, commitments under "commercial presence" are subject to incorporation in Pakistan with maximum foreign equity participation of 51% unless a different percentage is inscribed against a particular sector or subsector • (ii) All expenses of representative offices where specifically provided for in this schedule shall be met by remittances from abroad. Such offices shall restrict their activities to the undertaking of liaison work or of representing the interest of the parent company abroad
Sri Lanka	Horizontal commitments	• (3) Foreign Investment: Certain limitations, conditions and qualifications pertain specifically to some forms of commercial presence by foreign enterprises, as indicated below: – (a) Foreign investors may invest in any sector of the economy other than the following activities, which are reserved for citizens of Sri Lanka: (i) money-lending; (ii) pawn brokering; (iii) retail trade with a capital of less than US$1 million; (iv) businesses providing personal services other than for export of tourism; and (v) coastal fishing

(continued)

Table 1 (continued)

Country	Sector or subsector	Limitations on market access
		– (b) The foreign investment law applicable to foreign investors is the Greater Colombo Economic Commission (GCEC) Law No. 4 of 1978, as amended to date, presently known as the Board of Investment of Sri Lanka (BOISL) Act by G.C.E.C. (Amendment) Act No. 49 of 1992 (referred to as "the Law"), supplemented by: (i) BOISL Regulation No. 1 of 1978, as amended to date; and ii) BOISL Regulation No. 1 of 1991 – (c) The BOISL is responsible for the approval and facilitation of foreign investment throughout the country, other than for investments made by purchasing shares in the Colombo Stock Exchange, or for investments in a number of activities, which are regulated by other Statutory Agencies, including the following: (i) banking; (ii) financial institutions; (iii) insurance; (iv) trading services on the Colombo Stock Exchange; (v) air transportation; (vi) coastal shipping; (vii) branch or Liaison Office of companies incorporated outside Sri Lanka; (viii) lotteries – (d) Foreign investment of up to 40% of equity in a company proposing to carry on a business activity listed below other than those listed above will be automatically approved by the BOISL. Foreign investment in excess of 40% (and up to 100%) in a company proposing to carry on a business activity listed below other than those listed above will be approved by the BOISL on a case-by-case basis in consultation with the relevant State Agencies. This situation will be reviewed every two years with the aim of further simplification. The relevant sectors are the following: (i) construction and residential buildings; (ii) mass transportation; (iii) telecommunications; (iv) mass communications; (v) education; (vi) professional services; (vii) freight forwarding; (viii) travel agencies; (ix) shipping agencies – (e) ……….. Joint venture. In relevant sectors when a joint venture partner is a public sector enterprise or a government undertaking, while granting access, preference will be given to foreign service suppliers/entities, which offer the best terms for transfer of technology

(continued)

Table 1 (continued)

Country	Sector or subsector	Limitations on market access
The European Communities	Horizontal commitment	• Investments • (3) All member states except CY, ES, FR, HU, FI, IT, MT, PT, PL, SI: None • CY: The permission of the Central Bank is required for the participation of any non-resident in a corporate body or partnership in Cyprus. Foreign participation in all sectors/subsectors included in the Schedule of Commitments is normally limited up to 49%. The decision of the authorities to grant permission for foreign participation is based on an economic needs test, for which the following criteria are used in general (a) Provision of services which are new to Cyprus (b) Promotion of the export orientation of the economy with development of existing and new markets (c) Transfer of modern technology, know-how and new management techniques (d) Improvement either of the productive structure of the economy or of the quality of existing products and services (e) Complementary impact on existing units or activities (f) Viability of proposed project (g) Creation of new job opportunities for scientists, qualitative improvement and training of local staff In exceptional cases, in which a proposed investment satisfies most of the economic needs test criteria to a large extent, permission for foreign participation exceeding 49% may be granted In the case of public companies, foreign equity participation is normally allowed to the extent of up to 30%. In Mutual Funds, the extent of allowable foreign ownership is 40% Corporate bodies have to be registered under the Companies Law. Same law requires that a foreign company wishing to establish a place of business or an office in Cyprus must register it as a foreign branch. For the registration, the prior approval of the Central Bank is required under the Exchange Control Law. Such approval is subject to the foreign investment policy applicable at the time with regard to the Corporate Body's proposed activities in Cyprus and the general investment criteria stipulated above • ES: Investment in Spain by foreign government and foreign public entities (which tends to imply, besides economic, also non-economic interests to entity's part), directly or through companies or other entities controlled directly or indirectly by foreign governments, need prior authorization by the government

(continued)

Table 1 (continued)

Country	Sector or subsector	Limitations on market access
		• FR: Foreign purchases exceeding 33,33% of the shares of capital or voting rights in existing French enterprise, or 20% in publicly quoted French companies, are subject to the following regulations – Investments 7 of less than 50 million FF in French enterprises with a turnover not exceeding 500 million FF are free, after a delay of 15 days following prior notification and verification that these amounts are met – After a period of one month following prior notification, authorization is tacitly granted for other investments unless the Minister of Economic Affairs has, in exceptional circumstances, exercised its right to postpone the investment Foreign participation in newly privatized companies may be limited to a variable amount, determined by the government of France on a case-by-case basis, of the equity offered to the public For establishing in certain8 commercial, industrial or artisanal activities, a specific authorization is needed if the managing director is not holder of a permanent residence permit • HU: Unbound for the acquisition of state-owned properties • FI: Acquisition of shares by foreign owners giving more than one third of the voting rights of a major Finnish company or a major business undertaking (with more than 1000 employees or with a turnover exceeding 1000 million Finnish markka or with a balance sheet total exceeding 1000 million Finnish markka) is subject to confirmation by the Finnish authorities; the confirmation may be denied only if an important national interest would be jeopardized. These limitations do not apply to telecommunications services • IT: Exclusive rights may be granted or maintained to newly privatized companies. Voting rights in newly privatized companies may be restricted in some cases. For a period of five years, the acquisition of large equity stakes of companies operating in the fields of defense, transport services, telecommunications and energy may be subject to the approval of the Ministry of Treasury • MT: In terms of Section 17 of the Exchange Control Act, non-residents of Malta, wishing to supply any service through Commercial Presence in Malta, may do so only by registering a local company with the prior permission of the Central Bank of Malta

(continued)

Table 1 (continued)

Country	Sector or subsector	Limitations on market access
		• PT: Authorization9 is required for investments by non-EC companies, when exceeding 20% of the capital of the company or when the investments result in effective control or in strengthening of the decision-making power. Foreign participation in newly privatized companies may be limited to a variable amount, determined by the Government of Portugal on a case-by-case basis, of the equity offered to the public • PL: Authorization of the establishment of a company with foreign equity is required in the case of: – Establishment of company, purchase or acquiring of shares or stocks in an existing company; extending of the activity of the company when the scope of activity embraces at least one of the following areas Management of seaports and airports Dealing in real estate or acting as intermediary in real estate transactions Supply to defense industry that is not covered by other licensing requirements Wholesale trade in imported consumer goods Provision of legal advisory services – Establishment of a joint venture company with a foreign equity in which the Polish party is a state legal person and is contributing non-pecuniary assets as initial capital – Arranging a contract that includes right to use of state property for more than 6 months or decides on acquiring of such property • SI: For financial services, authorization is issued by the authorities indicated in sector-specific commitments and according to conditions indicated in sector-specific commitments There are no limitations on establishment of a new business establishment ("greenfield" investments)
	11. Transport services A. Maritime transport services MT: Excluding cabotage transport (a) Passenger transportation (CPC 7211); (b) Freight transportation (CPC 7212) E. Rail transport services (a) Passenger transportation (b) Freight transportation (d) Maintenance and repair of rail transport equipment (part of CPC 8868) (e) Supporting services for rail transport services Rail freight agency and forwarding services (CPC part of 7480)	• (3) All member states except LV, MT: Unbound LV, MT: none • (3) All member states except HU: Unbound HU: Services may be provided through a Contract of Concession granted by the state or the local authority • (3) All member states except HU: Unbound HU: Services may be provided through a Contract of Concession granted by the state or the local authority • (3) All member states except AT, CY, CZ, LV, MT, PL, SE, SK: None AT, CY, CZ, LV, MT, PL, SK: Unbound SE: Operators allowed to establish and maintain their own terminal infrastructure facilities, subject to space and capacity constraints • (3) All member states except LT: Unbound LT: None

(continued)

Table 1 (continued)

Country	Sector or subsector	Limitations on market access
The United States of America	Horizontal	• NIL
	11. Transport services A. Maritime transport services E. Rail transport (a) Passenger transportation, excluding high-speed rail, and (b) freight transportation (d) Maintenance and repair of rail transport equipment	• NIL • (3) Foreign railroads must incorporate in Vermont or in an adjacent state in order to own directly or indirectly the stock of a railroad company incorporated in Vermont • (3) None
Turkey	Horizontal commitments	• (3) All investment to be made within the range of $50,000 and $150,000,000 by non-residents (natural or juridical persons) through – The establishment of incorporated or limited liability companies – The purchase of shares including the portfolio investment registered under the Foreign Investment Encouragement Law No. 6224 (portfolio investment, according to the Article No. 15-F of the Decree No. 32 is subject to the registration within the framework of the Law No. 6224, if the investor desires to participate in the board of directors or general assembly of the company, as well as to interfere in the management of it in any other way) – The opening of branches; and – The creation of liaison offices • Will be authorized by the General Directorate of Foreign Capital provided that such activities are beneficial to the economic development of Turkey, are in the areas open to the Turkish private sector and do not entail a monopoly or special privilege. Foreign investment above $ 150 million requires the approval of the Council of Ministers. A new Decree removing this limitation is under preparation. The capital must be brought in as foreign exchange • Authorization is required for the investments by established foreign-owned enterprises or joint ventures in a new line of business and for participation or takeover of existing enterprises. For the investments in the same line of business, proposals are generally approved as a matter of course • Monopolies – The following sectors are closed to private investments because of the public monopolies: postal services and telecommunications, railways; administration of harbor and quay; lotteries in cash, football pools and public utilities

(continued)

Table 1 (continued)

Country	Sector or subsector	Limitations on market access
	11. Transport services • A. Maritime transport services – (a) Passenger transportation (CPC 7211) – (b) Freight transportation (CPC 7212) – (c) Rental of vessels with crew (CPC 7213) – (d) Maintenance and repair of vessels (CPC 8868) • E. Rail transport services (CPC 7111, 7112)	• (3) In order to fly the Turkish flag, the shipping companies must have the majority of 51% Turkish shareholders............ • (3) In order to fly the Turkish flag, the shipping companies must have the majority of 51% Turkish shareholders............ • (3) None • (3) None • (3) Internal rail transportation is a public monopoly

Carlos K. L. Li Solicitor, PhD in Laws candidate (2018-2021), PCLL and Juris Doctor (CUHK); M.A. in Transport Policy and Planning (HKU); M.Sc. in International Shipping and Transport Logistics and B.A. (Hons) in Tourism Management (PolyU HK).

Chinese Enterprises and Investments in the Arctic: Implications for the Development of the Polar Silk Road

Vasilii Erokhin and Gao Tianming

1 Introduction

From long ago, the natural wealth and resources of the Arctic have been attracting the interest of many countries. The region holds about one-quarter of the world's untapped deposits of oil and gas, rare earth and precious metals, coal, and diamonds.[1] However, since only recently, the state of technology along with the progressing climate change have allowed the development and exploration of circumpolar territories, while Arctic regional issues have received global ramifications.[2]

The opportunities for accessing huge reserves and shortening shipping routes have turned the Arctic into one of the most promising destinations for investors from all over the world. The increasing accessibility of new shorter transport routes previously closed by ice has stimulated the aspirations of many countries to secure their positions in the Arctic.[3] Since the early 2000s, China has been particularly emerging among the non-Arctic actors as a prominent investor, stakeholder, and contributor to the region's development. The country has been attempting to take an active role in establishing

[1] Vasilii Erokhin and others (eds), *Handbook of Research on International Collaboration, Economic Development, and Sustainability in the Arctic* (IGI Global 2019).

[2] Kathrin Keil and Sebastian Knecht (eds), *Governing Arctic Change* (Springer 2017).

[3] Vasilii Erokhin, 'Arctic Connectivity for Sustainable Development: Major Actors, Policies, and Approaches' in Vasilii Erokhin and others (eds), *Handbook of Research on International Collaboration, Economic Development, and Sustainability in the Arctic* (IGI Global 2019).

V. Erokhin (✉) · G. Tianming
School of Economics and Management, Harbin Engineering University, 145, Nantong Street, Harbin 150001, China
e-mail: basilic@list.ru

G. Tianming
e-mail: gaotianming@hrbeu.edu.cn

J. Chaisse et al. (eds.), *Regulation of State-Controlled Enterprises*, International Law and the Global South, https://doi.org/10.1007/978-981-19-1368-6_30

feasible and secure transport routes in the Arctic Ocean and developing bilateral and multilateral collaboration networks in the sphere of investment and business.[4]

As China consolidates its involvement in the Arctic agenda in various political, research, and business formats, the theme of Chinese investment activity in the Arctic countries is attracting increasing attention in both academic studies and professional readings. In the comprehensive studies of Chinese investment projects, Seaman and others[5] and Katainen[6] brought together the cases from the EU countries, including Norway and Denmark (Greenland), to reveal the trends and their implications for policymaking and EU-China relations. At a country-specific level, Pezard,[7] Morozov,[8] and Pilyasov[9] addressed China–Russia economic and investment collaboration in the Arctic, Koivurova, and others[10] examined China's evolving Arctic policy with particular attention to the ramifications that China's interests in the Arctic may have on Finland, Mortensen, and others[11] analysed Chinese investments in the mining industry in Greenland and investigated the hurdles faced by the investors.

Even though China's approach to the Arctic policy is increasingly driven by the convergence between the international obligations undertaken in the framework of the Arctic Council and other multilateral formats, from one side, and the governing principles of the Belt and Road initiative (BRI), from the other, there have been few studies which correctly linked that agenda with investment activity of Chinese enterprises in the region. The majority of the studies, for instance, Yang and Zhao,[12] Li

[4] Vasilii Erokhin and others, 'Arctic Blue Economic Corridor: China's Role in the Development of a New Connectivity Paradigm in the North' in Lassi Heininen and Heather Exner-Pirot (eds), *Arctic Yearbook 2018* (Northern Research Forum 2018).

[5] John Seaman and others, *Chinese Investment in Europe: A Country-Level Approach* (French Institute of International Relations (Ifri), Elcano Royal Institute, Mercator Institute for China Studies 2017).

[6] Jyrki Katainen, 'Chinese Investments in the EU' in Tim Wenniges and Walter Lohman (eds), *Chinese FDI in the EU and the US* (Springer 2019).

[7] Stephanie Pezard, *The New Geopolitics of the Arctic: Russia's and China's Evolving Role in the Region* (RAND Corporation 2018).

[8] Yury Morozov, 'China in the Arctic Region: Targets and Risks for Russian-Chinese Relations' [2016] FEA 21.

[9] Alexander Pilyasov, 'The Magnet of Globalization – China's Arctic Policy' [2018] AEE 112.

[10] Timo Koivurova and others, *China in the Arctic and the Opportunities and Challenges for Chinese-Finnish Arctic Co-operation* (Prime Minister's Office 2019).

[11] Bent Ole Gram Mortensen and others, 'Chinese Investment in Greenland' [2016] APS 192.

[12] Jian Yang and Long Zhao, 'Opportunities and Challenges of Jointly Building of the Polar Silk Road: China's Perspective' [2019] OGT 130.

and others,[13] Moscato,[14] Hossain,[15] and Kobzeva,[16] concentrate on the geopolitical shifts in the Arctic policy and international relations in the region caused by the inclusion of the Polar Silk Road in the BRI network. Tillman and others[17] focused on analysing economic opportunities and challenges brought by the Polar Silk Road initiative to Chinese enterprises and other stakeholders in Russia and Nordic countries but did not specifically studied the collaboration in the sphere of investment. In an attempt to bridge the existing gap in investment-related issues in the China-Arctic agenda, this chapter provides an overview of Chinese foreign direct investments in the countries which may be potentially involved in the Polar Silk Road initiative, including Russia and the countries of North Europe (Finland, Norway, Iceland, and Greenland as an autonomous territory within Denmark). The authors analyse the existing opportunities as well as major challenges for Chinese enterprises in the Arctic and propose solutions for the effective investment collaboration between China and its counterparts in the light of the development of economic and transport corridors in the High North.

2 China's Approaches to the Development of Polar Silk Road

In its approach to developing and exploring the Arctic, China is driven by various rationales, including strategic geopolitical, business, and research interests.[18] China is willing to work with all parties in conducting scientific surveys of navigational routes, setting up land-based monitoring stations, carrying out research on climatic and environmental changes in the Arctic, as well as providing navigational forecasting services. China supports the efforts of the countries bordering the Arctic in improving marine transportation conditions and encourages Chinese enterprises to take part in the commercial use of the maritime routes.[19]

China officially articulated its concernment in the Arctic issues by joining the Arctic Council as an observer state in 2013. Four years later, China incorporated

[13] Zhenfu Li and others, 'Research on the Construction of 'Polar Silk Road' and Arctic Destiny Community' [2019] ASS 1417.

[14] Derek Moscato, 'The Polar Silk Road in the Popular Press: Global Media Framing of China's 2018 Arctic Policy White Paper' in Lassi Heininen and Heather Exner-Pirot (eds), *Arctic Yearbook 2018* (Northern Research Forum 2018).

[15] Kamrul Hossain, 'China's BRI Expansion and Great Power Ambition: The Silk Road on the Ice Connecting the Arctic' [2019] CJES 3.

[16] Mariia Kobzeva, 'China's Arctic Policy: Present and Future' [2019] PJ 94.

[17] Henry Tillman and others, 'The Polar Silk Road: China's New Frontier of International Cooperation' [2018] CQISS 345.

[18] Jingchao Peng and Njord Wegge, 'China's Bilateral Diplomacy in the Arctic' [2015] PG 233.

[19] Mia Bennett, 'China's Belt and Road Initiative Moves into the Arctic' (*Cryopolitics*, 27 June 2017) <https://cryopolitics.com/2017/06/27/CHINAS-BELT-AND-ROAD-INITIATIVE-MOVES-INTO-THE-ARCTIC/> accessed 19 January 2020.

the Arctic into the BRI network of corridors, articulated the economic and trade corridor initiative in the High North, and outlined its interest in working with Arctic countries to improve sea transit conditions and survey for new resources.[20] In 2018, in the national Arctic Policy,[21] China outlined the development and participation in the governance of the Arctic, safeguarding the common interests of all countries in the region, and promotion of sustainable development among its core goals in the High North as well as formalised the inclusion of northern maritime routes into a network of blue maritime passages of the BRI[22] as a Polar or Ice Silk Road (in various interpretations).[23,24,25]

According to Lanteigne[26] and Górski,[27] the Arctic Policy stressed China's support for the peaceful use of the Arctic and cooperation in various non-military areas, but also noted that China as a non-Arctic state still had the rights to economic, trade, shipping, and investment activities in the High North following international law including the United Nations Convention on the Law of the Sea (UNCLOS). China's perspective vision of its role in the Arctic is not only about opening and securing new trade routes but about facilitating Asia-Europe connectivity and bridging the existing gap between traditional industries in the Arctic and China's market.[28] The polar Silk Road initiative demonstrates China's intention to collaborate with all concerned countries to establish a workable BRI corridor in the High North. Notably, China expects its involvement in cargo transportation in polar waters (import of mineral and other resources from Russia and Europe, Asia-Europe and Asia-America transit shipping and cabotage), as well as in marine and ice engineering and navigation security, to pave the way for Chinese commercial, exploration, transport, and logistics operations in the Arctic Ocean.[29]

---

[20] Xinhua, 'Vision for Maritime Cooperation under the Belt and Road Initiative' <http://news.xinhuanet.com/english/2017-06/20/c_136380414.htm> accessed 13 January 2020.

[21] China's Arctic Policy 2018.

[22] Xiuhua Zhang, 'Regional Aspects of the Arctic Ice Silk Road: Case of Heilongjiang Province, China' in Vasilii Erokhin and others (eds), *Handbook of Research on International Collaboration, Economic Development, and Sustainability in the Arctic* (IGI Global 2019).

[23] Kobzeva (n 16).

[24] Tianming Gao, 'Going North: China's Role in the Arctic Blue Economic Corridor' in Vasilii Erokhin and others (eds), *Handbook of Research on International Collaboration, Economic Development, and Sustainability in the Arctic* (IGI Global 2019).

[25] Kong Soon Lim, 'China's Arctic Policy and the Polar Silk Road Vision' in Lassi Heininen and Heather Exner-Pirot (eds), *Arctic Yearbook 2018* (Northern Research Forum 2018).

[26] Marc Lanteigne, 'China's Emerging Strategies in the Arctic' (*High North News*, 19 April 2019) <https://www.highnorthnews.com/en/chinas-emerging-strategies-arctic> accessed 15 January 2020.

[27] Jędrzej Górski, 'Northern Sea Route: International Law Perspectives' in Vasilii Erokhin and others (eds), *Handbook of Research on International Collaboration, Economic Development, and Sustainability in the Arctic* (IGI Global 2019).

[28] Tianming Gao and Vasilii Erokhin, 'China-Russia Collaboration in Shipping and Marine Engineering as One of the Key Factors of Secure Navigation along the NSR' in Lassi Heininen and others (eds), *Redefining Arctic Security: Arctic Yearbook 2019* (Arctic Portal 2019).

[29] ibid.

Chinese enterprises have been entering joint investment projects in the Arctic since the 2000s. Currently, the strengthened investment collaboration with the Arctic region is predominantly based on the development of relations with Russia. Chinese enterprises and investment funds have been particularly active in the Arctic zone of Russia, where at least two megaprojects with Chinese financial and technological contribution have been launched so far: Yamal (three out of four production trains have been launched already) and Arctic 2 (under construction) facilities for the production of liquefied natural gas (LNG) in Yamal and Gydan peninsulas, respectively. Chinese enterprises also increase their investment in infrastructural development to facilitate cargo shipment and trade further.

In parallel with the so-far successful significant investments in Russia, China has promoted the less visible benefits of the northern BRI's corridor, such as sharing development experience and expertise, promoting regional cooperation, and delivering more global public goods. In addition to their activities in Russia, Chinese enterprises have been increasingly engaged with other key partners along the Polar Silk Road, such as Finland, Norway, Iceland, and autonomous territory of Greenland to further a broader investment and trade cooperation. The economies along the potential Polar Silk Road may provide the benefits in many sectors which Chinese investors seek, i.e. hydrocarbons and maritime transport in Norway, shipbuilding and transport in Finland, research and development and renewable energy in Iceland, and mining in Greenland, among others.

3 Chinese Investments in the Arctic

3.1 An Overview

Being a non-Arctic state, China is now one of the most valuable partners for many countries that regard the Arctic as a traditional zone of their interests and governance. China contributes to the development of the Arctic in many ways, including science and research, development and use of maritime routes, infrastructure improvement, economic evaluation and exploration of mineral, biological, and other resources, tourism, ecology and protection of ecosystems.[30] Among various types of contribution, strategic investment has been particularly emerging in recent years as a form of China's anchoring in the region.[31]

Major investment projects with the involvement of Chinese enterprises include Yamal LNG and Arctic LNG 2 in Russia; Boreal Bioref Ltd. (bio-refinery), Kaidi (biofuels), and Arctic tourism in Finland; ChemChina (energy sector and chemical industry), CNOOC (energy), and Grand China Logistics (transportation) in Norway;

[30] Guangmiao Xu, 'China's Arctic Interests and Policy: History, Legal Ground and Implementation' [2016] WEIR 52.

[31] Sherri Goodman, 'China's Growing Arctic Presence' (*Wilson Center*, 19 November 2018) <https://www.wilsoncenter.org/article/chinas-growing-arctic-presence> accessed 12 January 2020.

Geely (methane production), Huawei (5G networks), and China-Iceland Joint Arctic Science Observatory in Iceland; exploration of uranium and rare earth metals in Kvanefjeld site, Greenland.

As Chinese enterprises have been entering many investment projects in the Arctic and participating in what some countries consider critical infrastructure, there have been concerns raised from the Arctic countries regarding China's ambitions in the region.[32] In May 2019, US Secretary of State Michael Pompeo criticised China for increasing its role in the High North and investing over $90 billion in the Arctic.[33] The figure was most likely based on the recent report on the Arctic investment released by CNA[34] in which, however, the USA-based think-tank acknowledged the fact that the scope of China's investment in the region was underreported. It is estimated that in 2005–2017, China invested over $1.4 trillion in the development of infrastructure, assets, various agreements, and other projects located north of the 60 latitude.[35]

There are alternative estimations according to which China's investments in the Arctic are massively smaller. Herberg[36] assesses China's combined investment in the region on the order of $25–30 billion, the most significant portion being the participation in the Yamal LNG project in Russia, as well as smaller investments in Iceland and Greenland. Lanteigne[37] also reports LNG and oil projects in Russia as the biggest beneficiaries of China's Arctic investment, including a combined 29.9% share by CNPC and the Silk Road Fund in Yamal LNG[38] and credit agreement for an additional $12 billion with China Development Bank and China's Export–Import Bank. Despite these numbers, in Russia, Chinese investments still represent a negligible percentage of the country's annual GDP, while those in some Nordic countries are rather substantial (for instance, 11.6% in Greenland and 5.7% in Iceland in 2012–2017).[39]

---

[32] Simone McCarthy, 'Trade, Tech... and Now the Arctic? The Next Frontier in the China-US Struggle for Global Control' (*South China Morning Post*, 14 January 2020) <https://www.scmp.com/news/china/diplomacy/article/3046072/trade-tech-and-now-arctic-next-frontier-china-us-struggle> accessed 15 January 2020.

[33] Michael Lelyveld, 'China's Arctic Investments Generate Heat' (*Radio Free Asia*, 24 May 2019) <https://www.rfa.org/english/commentaries/energy_watch/chinas-arctic-investments-generate-heat-05242019113856.html> accessed 15 January 2020.

[34] Mark Rosen and Cara Thuringer, *Unconstrained Foreign Direct Investment: An Emerging Challenge to Arctic Security* (CNA 2017).

[35] ibid.

[36] Lelyveld (n 33).

[37] Lanteigne (n 26).

[38] Finbarr Bermingham, 'China Funds Mega Yamal LNG Project' (*Global Trade Review*, 4 May 2016) <https://www.gtreview.com/news/europe/china-funds-mega-russian-lng-project/> accessed 11 January 2020.

[39] David Auerswald, 'China's Multifaceted Arctic Strategy' (*War on the Rocks*, 24 May 2019) <https://warontherocks.com/2019/05/chinas-multifaceted-arctic-strategy/> accessed 20 January 2020.

3.2 *Russia*

In terms of developing economic and transport corridors in the High North, Russia is a crucial partner for China.[40] Bilateral agreements concluded between the countries articulate the intensions to collaborate in the development and use of maritime routes, infrastructure improvement, economic evaluation and exploration of mineral, biological, and other resources of the Arctic, tourism, ecology and protection of ecosystems, polar research and joint Arctic expeditions and research projects.[41] All these activities require substantial investment support.

As mentioned earlier, Russia is so far the biggest recipient of Chinese investment in the Arctic projects. The $27 billion Yamal LNG project (CNPC—20% equity stake, Silk Road Fund—9.9%) was followed by the $25.5 billion Arctic LNG 2, where CNPC and CNOOC took 10% shares each.[42] Yamal LNG is based on the feedstock resources of the South-Tambeyskoye field with proved and probable reserves estimated at 926 billion cubic metres of natural gas and 30 million metric tonnes of liquid hydrocarbons. The field's production potential amounts to approximately 27 billion cubic metres of natural gas per annum, with a plateau duration of at least twenty years.[43] Arctic LNG 2 will be built in the Gydan Peninsula (Utrenneye field) and include three LNG trains with a capacity of 6.6 million tonnes per annum. The total projected capacity of Arctic LNG 2 is 19.8 million tonnes per annum.[44] The two projects are estimated to have an aggregated capacity of over 37 million tonnes of LNG per year,[45] moving both Russia and China to the top positions in the global LNG market. In 2020, Novatek, Russian operator of both Yamal LNG and Arctic LNG 2, will announce the search for investors for its Arctic LNG 3 project. Most probably, Chinese investors will join it.

Apart from a skyrocketing development of the LNG industry in the Russian Arctic, other investment projects where Chinese enterprises were expected to participate have not been that successful. There were plans to attract Chinese investment in the exploration of the continental shelf in the Barents and Pechora seas, as well as to exploit the Shtokman gas field and Prirazlomnoe offshore oilfield, but as global oil prices went down, Rosneft, a Russian state-backed oil company, suspended the

---

[40] Juntao Wang, 'Russian-Chinese Relations in the Arctic: Problems and Prospects' [2016] SPSPUJ 92.

[41] Tianming Gao, 'Collaboration between Russia and China in the Arctic in the Format of Development Zones' [2018] VU 43.

[42] Tim Daiss, 'China Invests in Game-Changing Arctic LNG Project' (*Oilprice*, 4 May 2019) <https://oilprice.com/Energy/Natural-Gas/China-Invests-In-Game-Changing-Arctic-LNG-Project.html#> accessed 14 January 2020.

[43] Novatek, 'Yamal LNG Infrastructure' <http://www.novatek.ru/en/business/yamal-lng/yamal_infrastructure/> accessed 13 January 2020.

[44] Novatek, 'Arctic LNG 2' <http://www.novatek.ru/en/business/arctic-lng/> accessed 13 January 2020.

[45] Malte Humpert, 'China Acquires 20 Percent Stake in Novatek's Latest Arctic LNG Project' (*High North News*, 29 April 2019) <https://www.highnorthnews.com/en/china-acquires-20-percent-stake-novateks-latest-arctic-lng-project> accessed 19 January 2020.

implementation of those projects. Most of the infrastructure development projects in which China initially declared its interest (Belkomur railroad, Arkhangelsk seaport, among others[46]) have not been launched yet due to the delays and concerns from the Russian side.

One of the approaches to attract investments to infrastructure development and other non-resource industries is to refocus the development efforts from particular territories (administrative divisions) to the networks of interrelated investment projects (economic clusters). According to the National Program on Social and Economic Development of the Arctic Zone of the Russian Federation,[47] eight development zones (major industrial sites and transport hubs) were defined,[48] including Kola, Arkhangelsk, Nenets, Vorkuta, Yamal-Nenets, Taimyr-Turukhan, North Yakut, and Chukotka.[49] The idea was to establish favourable conditions for implementing large-scale infrastructure projects in the Russian Arctic, modernise the existing infrastructure, and create the centres of attraction for foreign investments.[50] Over 140 potential projects were attributed to the development zones, including those in the spheres of mining and processing of mineral resources, transport, extraction and processing of diamonds, geological survey and exploration, power generation, fishing and agriculture, environmental protection, and tourism. For Chinese enterprises, the initiative looks attractive to participate in as it fits the concept of economic and trade corridor in the North. The zones located along the Arctic Ocean coast will allow creating a cargo base for the NSR and improving the Polar Silk Road infrastructure connectivity.[51]

In October 2019, the Russian government announced a raft of measures to encourage investment in Arctic projects.[52] New investment projects above RUB 10 million each (nearly $160,000) will be granted tax reductions and other preferences. For offshore oil production projects, the mineral extraction tax (MET) rate will be reduced down to 5% within fifteen years, depending on the level of oil field depletion. For selected oil fields explored by Rosneft and Neftegazholding, a 0% MET rate will be applied until the depletion reaches 1%. After that, the MET rate will be increased gradually. In addition to lower tax rates, investment projects in the Arctic will be

[46] Vasilii Erokhin and Tianming Gao, 'Northern Sea Route: An Alternative Transport Corridor within China's Belt and Road Initiative' in Julien Chaisse and Jedrzej Gorski (eds), *The Belt and Road Initiative: Law, Economics, and Politics* (Brill Nijhoff 2018).

[47] National Program on Social and Economic Development of the Arctic zone of the Russian Federation 2017.

[48] Olga Smirnova and others, 'Creation of Development Zones in the Arctic: Methodology and Practice' [2016] AN 148.

[49] Gao (n 24).

[50] Gao and Erokhin (n 28).

[51] Vasilii Erokhin, 'Northern Sea Route and Arctic Transport Corridors: Problems of Utilization and Forecasts of Cargo Traffic Commercialization' [2018] ML 22.

[52] Vitaly Petlevoy and others, 'The Government Approved the Preferences for Rosneft Project in the Arctic' (*Vedomosti*, 24 October 2019) <https://www.vedomosti.ru/business/articles/2019/10/24/814648-pravitelstvo-soglasovalo-lgoti> accessed 20 January 2020.

granted other preferences, including non-regression of tax environment and protection in the court, as well as the possibility to attract foreign labour above quotas, conclude concessional agreements without tendering, and receive federal subsidies for the construction of external infrastructure. LNG projects that Chinese enterprises are particularly interested in participating in will also receive preferences, including the MET exemption for twelve years after the start of production. Regional governments may add by introducing zero rates of profit tax, property tax, and land tax. Specifically, the regime will be applied to Novatek's projects, including Arctic LNG 3.

3.3 Finland

Unlike Russia, Finland does have direct access to the Arctic Ocean. However, the country is still one of the key actors in the Polar Silk Road due to its unique expertise in shipbuilding and shipping, offshore and maritime industries, construction and infrastructure, and other industries. Chinese enterprises started to enter Finland several years ago and became particularly active against the backdrop of the flourishing China-Finland political dialogue.[53]

Chinese enterprises invest in various sectors in Finland, including transport, bioenergy, tourism, information, and telecommunication. There are two investment projects in the sphere of bio-refinery and production of biofuels in Kemijärvi (Boreal Bioref Ltd.) and Kemi (Kaidi company, €900 million), respectively. In Lapland, Chinese investors participate in two projects in the sphere of tourism and amusement. There is a potential for the joint establishment of data centres and cloud technologies in Oulu and northern parts of the country (preliminary, €400 million). There is a discussion of a possibility of China's participation in the constriction of the railways to connect Finland with the seaports in the Arctic (Kirkenes in Norway), as well as fibre optic cable stretching from Finland to China via the Arctic Ocean.[54] The railroad is one of the critical infrastructure projects for the future success of the Polar Silk Road as it will allow to shorten the distance from Chinese ports to Europe by nearly 30% compared to the Strait of Malacca or the Suez Canal and make transarctic shipping more viable. The cable will improve the connectivity between the continents and enhance navigation support and data exchange along the NSR.

3.4 Norway

The establishment of a transport corridor between Finnish Oulu and Norwegian Kirkenes will have a significant role in the success of the Polar Silk Road. That is why

[53] Koivurova and others (n 10).

[54] Lanteigne (n 26).

Chinese enterprises are particularly interested in participation in the infrastructure and construction projects in Nordic countries. In Norway, Chinese investments are now total around $7 billion. Like Russian oil and gas projects, China primarily invests in the energy sector (Sinochem, $105 million; COSL Norwegian and CNOOC, $2.5 billion; ChemChina, $640 million). There are joint projects in transportation (Grand China Logistics and HNA, nearly $380 million), chemical industry (China Bluestar and ChemChina, $2.0 billion), information technologies (Golden Brick, Qihoo, and Beijing Kunlun, $575 million), and retail (Reignwood, $105 million).

According to Gåsemyr and Sverdrup-Thygeson,[55] there are several distinct trends in Chinese investments in Norway. In the 2000s, Chinese enterprises focused on energy sectors and natural resources. For China, these two sectors became the entrance points to the Norwegian market and actually conditioned the penetration of Chinese firms to other industries (information technologies, retail) in the 2010s. However, the amount of investment is still relatively low compared to some other Nordic countries and Russia. Despite the particular degree of diversification among Chinese investors, the main actors in the Norwegian market are still state-owned enterprises. It is expected that an anticipated conclusion of the Norway–China free trade agreement will boost and diversify not only trade but also investment linkages between the two countries.[56]

3.5 *Iceland*

In Iceland, Chinese enterprises became particularly active after the global economic crisis of 2008. At that hard time for Iceland's economy, the government came out for closer economic, trade, and investment collaboration with China. In 2012, the two countries signed a bilateral energy accord, in 2013—free trade agreement. As a result of such rapprochement, over the course of just five years, Chinese investment in Iceland amounted to nearly 6% of the country's average annual GDP. The major sectors Chinese enterprises invest in are geothermal energy, telecommunication, and environmental research. One of the first investment projects was that of Geely in methane production in 2015.[57] One year later, China established a research facility (currently, the China-Iceland Joint Arctic Science Observatory) in Northern Iceland to monitor the northern lights.[58] In 2018, China and Iceland concluded a $250 million agreement to start a joint project in the sphere of power generation from geothermal springs and hot water fields. One of the most recent investment deals is that between

[55] Hans Jørgen Gåsemyr and Bjørnar Sverdrup-Thygeson, 'Chinese Investments in Norway: A Typical Case despite Special Circumstances' in John Seaman and others (eds), *Chinese Investment in Europe: A Country-Level Approach* (French Institute of International Relations (Ifri), Elcano Royal Institute, Mercator Institute for China Studies 2017).

[56] Lanteigne (n 26).

[57] Auerswald (n 39).

[58] Daniel Molenaars, 'Chinese Activity in the Arctic' (*Global Risk Insights*, 3 June 2019) <https://globalriskinsights.com/2019/06/chinese-us-arctic/> accessed 18 January 2020.

Chinese Huawei and a pool of telecommunication companies in Iceland to set up and test 5G networks.

For Iceland, the attraction of Chinese investments is a way to diversify economic and trade linkages. Own resources of the country are somewhat fragile (primarily fishing, tourism, and geothermal energy). Due to the scarcity of resources, Iceland embeds its activities in and approaches to developing and exploring the Arctic to the context of the EU's policy.[59] In this respect, the Icelandic government may view an alternative source of financial support as a kind of leverage with both the EU and the USA[60] in pursuing particular Iceland's interests in the region. Among the founding principles of Iceland's contemporary policy in the Arctic are the development of trade and economic relations with Nordic countries and other states[61] and the promotion of the country into a hub for Arctic-related enterprises and research facilities,[62] which well fits China's vision of how partner countries may contribute to the development of the Polar Silk Road initiative and the establishment of economic and transport corridors in the High North.

3.6 *Greenland*

In contrast to the resource-scarce Iceland, Greenland is rich in rare earth metals, iron, copper, uranium, and other natural resources. Progressing melting of the glaciers due to climate change provides a massive opportunity for the development of the mining industry on the island.[63] It appears reasonable that China is now focusing on mineral extraction in Greenland. According to Auerswald,[64] in the past several years, Chinese firms have invested a good deal of money in the country, contributing nearly 12% of Greenland's annual average GDP. Currently, Chinese enterprises in Greenland are primarily involved in extracting minerals in growing demand in China, including uranium and rare earth metals. The most significant venture is the exploration of the Kvanefjeld site in the form of the China–Greenland–Australia partnership. Chinese energy firms are now assessing the potential benefits and risks of the investment in the onshore oil and gas exploration projects.[65]

Greenland also remains interesting for China as a potential hub on the Arctic shipping route.[66] In terms of the involvement of Greenland in the Polar Silk Road

---

[59] Erokhin (n 3).

[60] Auerswald (n 39).

[61] A Parliamentary Resolution on Iceland's Arctic Policy 2011.

[62] Vincent-Gregor Schulze, *Arctic Strategy Round-Up 2017* (Helmholtz Centre for Polar and Marine Research 2017).

[63] Molenaars (n 59).

[64] Auerswald (n 39).

[65] Lanteigne (n 26).

[66] Jiang Yang, 'Chinese Investments in Denmark: An Open Economy and Rare Political Questions' in John Seaman and others (eds), *Chinese Investment in Europe: A Country-Level Approach* (French

corridors, a problem of a significant shortage of infrastructure (production, power supply, transport, logistics, and other sectors) must be solved first. However, this shortcoming may make the island even more attractive for Chinese enterprises to invest in.

4 Chinese Enterprises in the Arctic: Challenges and Solutions

Generally speaking, Chinese enterprises and their investments are welcomed in the Arctic, but some countries, notably Russia in the NSR, claim to control their resources and navigation in their waters. China's Arctic policy actually supports persevering with the existing rules of the Law of the Sea.[67] Specifically, China stipulates that (1) the management of the Arctic shipping routes should be conducted following treaties including the UNCLOS and general international law and that the freedom of navigation enjoyed by all countries following the law and their rights to use the Arctic shipping routes should be ensured; (2) China hopes to work with all parties to build the Polar Silk Road through developing the Arctic shipping routes; (3) China respects the sovereign rights of Arctic States over oil, gas, and mineral resources in the areas subject to their jurisdiction following international law, and respects the interests and concerns of residents in the region.[68] However, while the increase of the volume of Chinese investments in the Arctic and cargo traffic along the NSR both require greater involvement of Chinese enterprises in Arctic affairs,[69] Nordic countries and Russia have been expressing a hostile and suspicious attitude towards China's activities in the region[70] which has for ages been considered as a territory critical for the economic and military security of the Arctic states. For instance, despite the fact of flourishing Russia–China relations, starting from the early 2010s, Russia has been continually warning foreign states, including China, that in every possible way, it observes the 'penetration' of non-Arctic countries which intensively advance their interests in the region and that Russia would defend its national interests, including in a military way.[71]

Along with the changing attitude to China's growing presence in the region, the diversification of the sectors to invest in is an emerging challenge for Chinese companies. The northern corridor will hardly become economically feasible and

Institute of International Relations (Ifri), Elcano Royal Institute, Mercator Institute for China Studies 2017).

[67] Górski (n 27).

[68] China's Arctic Policy (n 21).

[69] Yun Sun, *The Northern Sea Route: The Myth of Sino-Russian Cooperation* (Stimson 2019).

[70] ibid.

[71] Guy Faulconbridge, 'Russian Navy Boss Warns of China's Race for Arctic' (*Reuters*, 4 October 2010) <https://www.reuters.com/article/russia-arctic-idAFLDE6931GL20101004> accessed 18 January 2020.

sustainable based on LNG supplies only. Indeed, Yamal LNG and future Arctic LNG 2 are the cases of successful Chinese investments that come up among the projects in the Arctic. However, according to Guo,[72] these projects cannot be seen as models for the sustainable development of the Polar Silk Road corridor for China. Being the flagship of Russia's successes in exploring the Arctic resources, the projects are directly supported and promoted by the Russian government and subsidised from the federal budget. The reduction or abolishment of fiscal, investment, infrastructure, logistics, and other preferences may adversely affect the performance of all Novatek's facilities in the High North and radically decrease the return on Chinese investments.

Sustainable shipping in the NSR without state support is also questionable. COSCO vessels had ventured into the Arctic before the release of the Arctic Policy by the Chinese government. Since 2013, COSCO has conducted over thirty commercial voyages along the NSR, most of which were destined for the Port of Sabetta and included the delivery of construction materials and modules for Yamal LNG. Nevertheless, compared to the total number of vessels on the NSR and total cargo turnover, the share of China's transit is still meagre. In 2018, international transit accounted for only 2.4% of total cargo tonnage. Aside from state-backed COSCO, most Chinese shipping companies baulk at the risks of navigation in polar waters and the high investment costs required to construct or purchase ice-strengthened ships.[73] Cost-sharing mechanisms of collaboration would appear commercially advantageous for Chinese companies to be increasingly involved in more intense shipping in the North. One of the mechanisms was actually established in 2018 with a $9.5 billion credit line from China, aimed at joint integration processes on the area of the Eurasian Economic Union and the BRI, with the NSR mentioned as a priority.[74]

The success of the Polar Silk Road initiative depends on the volume but also the efficiency of the Chinese investments in Russia and Nordic countries in the spheres of development of infrastructure for cargo shipping, icebreaking assistance, safer navigation, and rescue, as well as the creation of new materials and technologies to construct enforced vessels able to operate in the polar waters. Most of the territories along the prospective Polar Silk Road, particularly in the eastern part of the Russian Arctic and the NSR, lack an adequate infrastructure to support the growing shipping volume by China. The establishment of economically viable, technologically feasible, and stable cargo shipping in the High North requires extensive investment in the construction and modernisation of the infrastructure along the entire route of the future Polar Silk corridor from Russian Chukotka in the east to Iceland and Greenland in the west, including deep-water seaports able to receive large-capacity vessels, transport hubs with appropriate logistics and capacities for loading and reloading of

---

[72] Wenwen Xie, 'For Chinese Companies, Investment in the Arctic Infrastructure Offers both Opportunities and Challenges' (*Arctic Today*, 17 June 2019) <https://www.arctictoday.com/for-chinese-companies-investment-in-arctic-infrastructure-offers-both-opportunities-and-challenges/> accessed 20 January 2020.

[73] Linyan Huang and others, 'Is China's Interest for the Arctic Driven by Arctic Shipping Potential?' [2015] AG 59.

[74] Arild Moe and Olav Schram Stokke, 'Asian Countries and Arctic Shipping Policies, Interests and Footprints on Governance' [2019] ARLP 24.

various types of cargo, support and rescue points for safe and stable navigation in the severe and fast-changing weather, wave, and ice conditions, and refuelling points for Chinese transit vessels. The significant challenges are the capacity of seaports and port facilities required for the acceptance of various types of vessels, specifically, large-tonnage LNG tankers used in Yamal LNG and, potentially, Arctic LNG 2, the accuracy and availability of information required for safe navigation, as well as the availability of search and rescue assets. It is necessary to develop infrastructure for berthing, loading, and discharging of vessels at various points of the route throughout the year. Communication systems are generally adequate for the lower parts of the Arctic, but data transmission becomes problematic when the vessels move to high-latitude routes. The provision of transport and logistics infrastructure sites with reliable sources of power is also a problem. The perspective solution is a fleet of floating nuclear power plants that can be used as a mobile and flexible power source for seaports and production sites in remote territories.

5 Conclusions

The Arctic has strategic importance for China in many aspects, from fundamental science to business. The volume of Chinese investment in the Arctic countries is increasing and will most probably continue to increase in the years to come as China is committed to the improvement of connectivity and the development of economic and trade corridor in the High North with the involvement of Russia, Northern Europe, and, potentially, the USA and Canada. Investing in the Arctic, however, is radically different from that in China or elsewhere. Along with the opportunities (exploration of mineral resources, shorter transportation distances, etc.), there are specific setbacks to the establishment of the Polar Silk Road and connecting the NSR and other maritime routes in the Arctic Ocean into a network of economically feasible, stable, and safe trade corridors: lack of icebreakers and transport vessels of appropriate deadweight and ice-class, scarcity of port facilities and coastal infrastructure for sustainable all-year-round cargo shipping, underdeveloped systems of navigation aids and ice monitoring, and many more of them apart from still heavy climate conditions and fast-changing ice situation. Considering the bulk of varying economic, technical, environmental, and even climate controversies Chinese investors encounter when investing in the projects in the Russian or European Arctic, there should be conducted thorough research of all existing and potential threats to the success of a particular project. Before investing, there should be elaborated responses with targeted strategies, including risk assessment, as well as the understanding of the demand of Arctic countries in Chinese contribution and the background of the attitude to the forms of Chinese presence in particular territories.

Acknowledgements This study is supported by the National Key R&D Program of China (project no. 2020YFE0202600).

Correction to: Regulation of State-Controlled Enterprises

Julien Chaisse, Jędrzej Górski, and Dini Sejko

Correction to:
J. Chaisse et al. (eds.), *Regulation of State-Controlled Enterprises*, International Law and the Global South, https://doi.org/10.1007/978-981-19-1368-6

The original version of book was inadvertently published prematurely, before incorporation of the final corrections, which has now been updated as in below:

In Chapter 3, the Single quotes has been updated for introduction of short often idiomatic expressions

In Chapter 12, missed out author corrections has been updated

In Chapter 17, chapter author's affiliation and email ID has been updated

In Chapter 20, section citations has been changed from "5.2.1, 5.2.2, 5.2.3" to "5.1.1, 5.1.2, 5.1.3" respectively

The book and the chapters have been updated with the changes.

The updated original version of these chapters can be found at
https://doi.org/10.1007/978-981-19-1368-6_3
https://doi.org/10.1007/978-981-19-1368-6_12
https://doi.org/10.1007/978-981-19-1368-6_17
https://doi.org/10.1007/978-981-19-1368-6_20

J. Chaisse et al. (eds.), *Regulation of State-Controlled Enterprises*, International Law and the Global South, https://doi.org/10.1007/978-981-19-1368-6_31

MIX
Papier aus verantwortungsvollen Quellen
Paper from responsible sources
FSC® C105338

If you have any concerns about our products,
you can contact us on
ProductSafety@springernature.com

In case Publisher is established outside the EU,
the EU authorized representative is:
Springer Nature Customer Service Center GmbH
Europaplatz 3, 69115 Heidelberg, Germany

Printed by Libri Plureos GmbH
in Hamburg, Germany